S0-BRP-288

GREEK LANDS IN HISTORY

MACEDONIA

4000 YEARS OF GREEK HISTORY
AND CIVILIZATION

DONATED BY

PAN-MACEDONIAN ASSOCIATION OF
THE UNITED STATES AND CANADA
246 Eighth Avenue
New York, NY 10011

GREEK LANDS IN HISTORY

MACEDONIA

4000 YEARS OF GREEK HISTORY AND CIVILIZATION

General Editor
M.B. SAKELLARIOU
Member of the Academy of Athens

EKDOTIKE ATHENON S.A.
1983

Copyright © 1982 by EKDOTIKE ATHENON S.A.
I, Vissarionos Street, Athens 135, Greece
First published in Greek under the title
"ΜΑΚΕΔΟΝΙΑ 4000 χρόνια ἑλληνικῆς ἱστορίας καί πολιτισμοῦ"

This edition
Copyright © 1983 by EKDOTIKE ATHENON S.A.
Printed and bound in Greece by EKDOTIKE ELLADOS S.A.
An affiliated company - 8, Philadelphias Street, Athens

Publishers: George A. Christopoulos, John C. Bastias
Editors:
ANCIENT MACEDONIA: Miltiades B. Hatzopoulos, Louisa D. Loukopoulos
BYZANTINE MACEDONIA: Kyriaki Mamoni
MODERN MACEDONIA: Joanna Diamantourou
Editorial Supervision and Illustrations: Iris Tzachili-Douskou
English edition supervised by H.L. Turner
Art Director: Angela Simou
Bibliography: Litsa Katsa
Byzantine maps: Barbara Delivoria
Maps and diagrams drawn by Tonia Kotsoni

All rights reserved
Reproduction of this book, in whole or in part, without
written permission of the publisher, is prohibited

CONTRIBUTORS

Manolis Andronikos
Professor of Archaeology, University of Thessalonike

Robert Browning
Emeritus Professor, Birkbeck College, University of London

Manolis Chatzidakis
Historian of Byzantine Art, Member of the Academy of Athens

Aikaterini Christophilopoulou
Professor of Byzantine History, University of Athens

Joanna Diamantourou
Historian

Constantine Dimaras
Emeritus Professor, University of Paris, Sorbonne

Jack R. Ellis
Senior Lecturer, Department of Classical Studies, Monash University, Australia

Helen Glykatzi-Ahrweiler
Professor of Byzantine History, University of Paris, I.

N. G. L. Hammond
Emeritus Professor of Greek, University of Bristol, Honorary Fellow of Clare College, Cambridge

John Karayannopulos
Professor of Byzantine History, University of Thessalonike

Constantine Kephalas
Honorary President of the Museum of Folklore and Ethnology, Thessalonike

Evangelos Kofos
Historian, Ph. D. in History, London University.

John Koliopoulos
Associate Professor, Department of Medieval and Modern History, University of Thessalonike

Nicholas Moutsopoulos
Professor of Architecture at the Thessalonike Polytechnic School, Corresponding Member, Academy of Athens

Dimitrios Pandermalis
Professor of Archaeology, University of Thessalonike

Charalambos Papastathis
Associate Professor, Department of History, Philosophy and Sociology of Law, University of Thessalonike

Fanoula Papazoglou
Professor of Ancient History, University of Belgrade

Michael B. Sakellariou
Member of the Academy of Athens. Emeritus Professor, University of Thessalonike, Director of the Institute for Ancient Greek and Roman Studies, National Hellenic Research Foundation

Michel Sivignon
Professor of Geography, University Paris-Nord

Nicholas Svoronos
Emeritus Professor, Ecole Pratique des Hautes Etudes, Paris

Stavros Theophanides
Professor of Applied Economics, Panteios Graduate School of Political Sciences, Athens

John Touratsoglou
Inspector of Antiquities, Ph. D. Saarland University, West Germany

Anna Tsitouridou
Assistant Lecturer, Department of Byzantine History, University of Thessalonike

Apostolos Vacalopoulos
Emeritus Professor, University of Thessalonike

F.W. Walbank
Emeritus Professor, University of Liverpool

Kenneth A. Wardle
Lecturer in Aegean Prehistory, Department of Ancient History and Archaeology, University of Birmingham, England

CONTENTS

TRANSLATORS

P. Athanassiadi-Fowden: pp. 192-263
J. Binder: pp. 266-271; 292-305; 338-351
D.A. Hardy: pp. 44-63; 172-191; 314-318; 354-361; 426-484; 502-527
P. Ramp: pp. 371-394; 490-501
S. Reinert: pp. 272-291; 306-314; 318-332; 361-371; 394-409
H. L. Turner: pp. 12-27; 92-109; 410-425; 484-490

PUBLISHER'S PROLOGUE

Macedonia, 4000 Years of Greek History and Civilization *constitutes the first volume of a new series,* Greek Lands in History, *which will include another five volumes devoted to Epirus, Thrace, Asia Minor, the Aegean and Cyprus. This series is unique in international historiography as it presents in an impressive continuity the history of Hellenism from antiquity to our times. Each of these regions has provided its own contribution to Greek history throughout the ages.*

Each volume begins with a geographical description of the region. An account of the prehistoric evidence is followed by sections devoted to antiquity, the Byzantine era and modern times. These works have two original aspects; firstly, they delineate the history of these regions from antiquity to the present day; secondly, they record not only the historical events, but also the institutions, the social, economic and intellectual life and the culture of each specific period. A survey of the region as it is today rounds out the historical picture. The text is accompanied by maps, diagrams and lavish photographs of landscape, buildings and works of art.

Macedonia *unfolds before the reader's eye a region whose Hellenic character in ancient times has been confirmed by recent archaeological discoveries at Pella, Dion and, particularly, Vergina. In the Byzantine era, Christian tradition developed its own distinct presence in Macedonia in both art and literature. Its supreme expression was the monastic state of Mount Athos. In modern times, the story of Macedonian Hellenism for survival and national emancipation during the five centuries of Ottoman rule is unveiled on the basis of new findings of scholarly research. The book concludes with the attainment of national liberation within the unified independent Greek state.*

It is our belief that this volume, written by a team of leading experts in the history and civilization of Macedonia, will be appreciated by both the specialist and the general public.

GEORGE A. CHRISTOPOULOS

INTRODUCTION

The object of historical action and the subject of historical knowledge are neither countries nor cities, but people. Countries and cities are but the framework within which these people act; on the one hand they unleash some of the factors which influence human groups, on the other hand they are the result of some of that action. However, when we chronicle the history of the various people who lived either simultaneously or successively in the same area or city, it is more suitable to mention the area in the title of the work than to ennumerate the peoples, even though these are its real subject. This book is concerned with those who lived in Macedonia from earliest antiquity until today.

Macedonia, understood as the name of a geographical area, is derived from the ethnic name of one unit of its inhabitants, the ancient Greek tribe, the Macedonians. Macedonia means the land or state of the Macedonians; the name spread over every territory they occupied. Before the accession of Philip II the southern boundaries of Macedonia were the lower Olympos and Kambounia mountains, the western boundary the Pindos range. To the north, its border was close to that of present day Greece and Yugoslavia, stretching as far as lake Kerkine and Mounts Bertiskos and Kerdyllion. Philip II added Pelagonia, Chalkidike and the belt beyond Kerkine, Bertiskos and Kerdyllion as far as the mountains west of the river Nestos. Of the other territories he controlled, some were his personal possessions, others became his allies on terms which did not cost them their independence. Under the Antigonid kings upper Paionia was annexed to the Macedonian state, except for Dardania (the upper part of the Axios basin) in which lay the ancient town of Scupi, modern Skopje. The Romans used Macedonia in its geographical sense to describe a province established in 148 B.C., though this included many areas which were never Macedonian — parts of Illyria, all Epirus and, until 27 B.C., southern Greece. Towards the end of the third century A.D. the province of Macedonia lost the lands which had not belonged to the Macedonian kingdom as well as certain areas in the south-west which devolved into a new province, Thessaly. Later, other northern parts were split off, which, together with non-Macedonian territory, became a province with the name Macedonia Salutaris, subsequently replaced by Macedonia Secunda, an area whose boundaries were slightly different. Administrative changes in 535 abolished this unit and Macedonia reverted to her ancient northern boundary. The Byzantine administrative unit, the theme 'of Macedonia', in existence from the end of the ninth century, corresponded to territory in Thrace, and bore no relation to historic Macedonia. The Ottoman empire parcelled ancient Macedonia out into *sanjaks;* the boundaries of several extended beyond Macedonia and no use was made of the name. However, it was not forgotten by educated Greeks or foreigners through the centuries. It was through them that it crept back into the diplomatic vocabulary of the nineteenth century. When the ancient Macedonian territories were freed from the Ottoman yoke and were divided between Yugoslavia, Bulgaria and Greece, it once again came into use as a term of administrative convenience.

Today there is agreement only on the southern and western boundaries of Macedonia which are the same as the ancient borders and are clearly marked on the ground and on maps. As for the northern and eastern boundaries, some identify these with the frontiers of the Macedonian state under the Antigonids — that is during the last phase of its existence — which continued to be the limits of the Roman province for many centuries. Some exclude Chalkidike and the region between the mountain ranges Dysoron - Bertiskos - Kerdyllion - Falakron - Lekane; others exclude Chalkidike and the river Nestos, though they include the upper reaches of the Axios valley. Still others combine the two views. The arguments used are sometimes purely historical, sometimes purely geographical and sometimes a combination.

In our opinion the problem should not be resolved from a single viewpoint; for even a combination of historical and geographical arguments is inadequate if it is static; we must search for the real dynamics of geographical factors as expressed through historical phenomena. We therefore need to take into account the following considerations:
1) the geographical category of Macedonia was formed by the Makedones. It is not therefore possible to ignore, in general terms, either its historical origins or, more specifically, the extent of the original area inhabited by them. 2) The northern and eastern borders of Macedonia as the state of the Macedonians survived for some time; they were also retained in the province of Macedonia established by the Romans. 3) The geographical unity of the Axios valley played no historical role at any time. During the prehistoric period it was divided between a variety of peoples and populations. The Macedonians only annexed Paionia at a late date, and never annexed the region around Scupi (Skopje) which belonged to Dardania. Later, the borders of Paionia and Dardania marked the dividing line between the use of the Latin language to the north and the Greek language to the south. From the seventh century A.D. until the Ottoman conquest, the shifting boundaries of the Byzantine empire, on occasion expanding northwards and at other times contracting southwards, invariably cut across the valleys of the Axios and the Strymon rivers. The upper Axios, together with Skopje, was in the possession of the Byzantines only from 1004 to 1282, and the Bulgarians repeatedly invaded the lower parts of the valleys. During the Ottoman period the valleys in question were no longer divided by political boundaries, and Greeks peacefully penetrated the middle and upper Axios, while Slav-speakers infiltrated the lower parts and settled the length of the river Strymon; despite this, the

10

area stretching from one end of these river valleys to the other never came to be inhabited by people of a single ethnic origin. Quite the reverse: the lower Axios and Strymon valleys repeatedly came within the ambit of the same economic, political and cultural systems and were occupied by a variety of linguistic groups in roughly the same proportions. One obstacle preventing these two river valleys from evolving into historical units was clearly the restricted nature of the upper reaches. The fact that the lower valleys have shared a common history continuously from the fifth century B.C. to the present day is precisely because they acquired a national entity at this date that was not shaken either by the Slav invasions or by Ottoman interference, and also to the easy communication between these areas by land and by sea. There were equally easy land and sea communications between Chalkidike and the lower Axios (and the Haliakmon delta) to the west and the lower Strymon to the east.

Macedonia has revolved within the sphere of Greek history for more than four millenia. Around 2300 B.C. groups of people who spoke a very early form of the Greek language entered Macedonia, Epirus and the north-west corner of Thessaly. Some groups from Epirus and Macedonia moved further south around 1900 B.C. and later. On the borders of these two areas the Greek tribe of the Macedonians took shape. Part then became a founding element of the Dorians and the other part spread over southern Macedonia. From the eighth century Chalkidike and the coast of the rest of Macedonia saw the establishment of colonies sent out by cities of Euboia and the Cyclades.

The Macedonians, like the peoples beyond the Pindos and on its southern fringes, were less culturally advanced than other Greeks, especially the Athenians. But they were never cut off from the mainstream of Greek life or from its history. From 490 B.C. rulers of the Macedonians were successful in narrowing the gap, and from time to time even played an important role in events in the Greek world. Of greater importance was the fact that the Macedonian state grew in strength as its political institutions became more robust. In this way, certain disadvantages became advantages, of increasing value as, for other reasons, the balance of power within the Greek world tilted in favour of Macedonia. Within a very short space of time Macedonia became the leading Greek power; in 337 B.C. its king, Philip II, was recognized as the head of a Greek confederation. Alexander set out on his Asian campaign to revenge the Greeks for the damage they had suffered from the Persians. Without the Macedonians this huge undertaking would scarcely have been possible; its success would undoubtedly have been less. Had it been carried out by the Greeks of the city states, they would have established in the East only a few states of the same type, which because of their nature, would have been closed to the indigenous population. The successors of Alexander established multinational states, through which Hellenism could be disseminated to non-Greeks.

After the death of Alexander, the old kingdom of the Macedonians was reborn. This differed from the kingdoms like it in the East in so far as it maintained many of the elements of the political organization of the Macedonians and, because of its geographical position, it had much greater contact with the Greek states of the south. This position, together with its interests in the direction of the Adriatic sea, combined to make Macedonia the first Greek state to clash with the rising power of Rome and then to bow to her sovereignty.

From the end of the sixth century A.D. the earliest migrations of the Slavs into the Balkan peninsula began, affecting some parts of Macedonia. Groups of Slavs who settled in Macedonia were undoubtedly aggressive, but they were met by the sustained opposition of the local Greek forces. When the central power intervened, it succeeded in bringing these groups under control and later transported them to Asia Minor, bringing Greeks from other areas to replace them. At the same time, it prepared to convert the Slavs, but neither then, nor later, was there any concerted effort to spread the Greek way of life.

Later, the Bulgarians attacked Macedonia from the strong kingdom they had established in the north-east part of the Balkan peninsula. Bloody wars ensued to save Macedonia, which eventually succeeded, so that Byzantine supremacy over the greater part of the region continued and its Greek character was preserved.

During the period of the Ottoman occupation the Greeks of Macedonia were one of the most vulnerable sections of the Greek people, but at the same time they were one of the most determined in any stand against the consequences of subservience. There were severe losses of population due to people being displaced, taken prisoner-of-war, slaughtered or converted to Islam. However, from the ranks of the survivors there emerged the most active figures in the economic and intellectual regeneration of the Greek nation. With them cooperated the Latin-speaking Vlachs who came to think of themselves as Greeks during this process. Nevertheless, the Greek economic revival had some negative consequences, in that Greeks who were cultivating Ottoman *timars* and *chiftliks* abandoned them to settle in townships and towns of Macedonia or to move away from it; the Ottoman landowners replaced them with Slavs who came down from the north looking for work.

In the first half of the twentieth century Greek blood was freely shed to secure, and then preserve, the unification with Greece of that part of Macedonia which had an overwhelmingly Greek population. Subsequently, many Greeks from the northern areas which were divided up amongst neighbouring powers settled in this section of Macedonia. Most important of all, however, hundreds of thousands of the one and a half million refugees from Asia Minor and eastern Thrace found new homes here. Thanks to the industry and determination to succeed displayed by both natives and newcomers, helped by the inauguration of an extensive programme of public works, Greek Macedonia swiftly advanced from being an underdeveloped area into a dynamically developing region of the greatest importance to the modern Greek state.

THE GEOGRAPHICAL SETTING
OF MACEDONIA

The description of the natural environment set out in the following pages does not aim to give the most recent information in any academic field concerned with Macedonia, whether geomorphology, climatology or biogeography. It has been designed to further the reader's acquaintance with the physical framework against which Macedonian history has unfolded.

On the historical time scale, the natural environment is a factor which hardly changes. But no predestined pattern of political combinations is to be deduced from this stability. Present frontiers are very recent, most of them dating only from the end of the Balkan War of 1912-13; they have been disputed twice, during both World Wars. None follows a natural line; rather, they reflect the relative balance of power between states. As might be expected, during the negotiations which preceded their establishment, physical barriers, such as mountain ranges, watersheds and, more rarely, rivers, were taken into account, and the states concerned tried to use the principle of natural boundaries to justify their territorial designs. These designs do not, of course, belong to the sphere of physical geography, but to that of political history.

Notwithstanding the above reservations, we must roughly delimit the area which concerns us, namely the countries which during antiquity made up the kingdom of Macedonia. It should not be forgotten that frontiers then were not so precisely demarcated as they are today.

Though political formations are not to be inferred from natural surroundings, the latter would, at first sight, seem to exercise a definite influence on the cultivation of the land and the exploitation of the soil and sub-soil; the role played by the presence of the gold-bearing veins of Mt. Pangaion in the political fortunes of Macedonia is well known. But the influence exercised by the natural environment is related to the level of technology reached by the people who exploit it.

Civilizations can undoubtedly be characterized as much by their techniques of production as by their techniques for controlling the environment. Lines of communication, for example, benefit from natural features. But their existence and their maintenance assume that the political circumstances and the economy of the countryside through which they pass will be favourable to change. It is not Nature that alters, but the distribution of political power within an area.

It is true, and it is the basic tenet of this chapter, that 'the history of a people is inseparable from the region it inhabits.'

SITUATION AND GENERAL CHARACTERISTICS

In the context of the Mediterranean basin as a whole, Macedonia appears favoured: the two connecting valleys of the Morava and the Axios (Vardar) rivers allow a relatively easy passage from central Europe towards the Mediterranean. At the southern end of the Axios valley the Thermaic Gulf forms a remarkable complement to the land route, its shelter being of great assistance to sea-borne traffic. But on a smaller scale and looking at the landscape in detail, Macedonia does not appear to be so well favoured. The route along the Morava and the Axios (Vardar) valleys is frequently no more than a narrow corridor, and not a broad river valley, but a succession of basins and gorges.

The jagged relief of the countryside of the Morava and the Axios valleys is typical of all Macedonia, divided into very 'fragmented relief in which certain characteristics constantly repeat' — the characteristics being the mountains and basins. The mountains are not very high, never reaching 3000 m. though the summits are always almost consistently above 2000 m.; the basins are at altitudes ranging from sea level to close on 1000 m. Always surrounded by mountains, these basins have never easily served as lines of communication.

There are only two littoral plains not so enclosed: that of Katerini, the more southerly, is also the smaller, while the larger, that of central Macedonia, borders the western coast of the Thermaic Gulf.

APPROACHES TO MACEDONIA

From Thessaly. It is not easy to cross from Thessaly to Macedonia. The most convenient route follows the coast. But to reach the delta of the Peneios river it is necessary to thread one's way past the Ossa range and lower Olympos by following the river through the Vale of Tempe with its giant plane trees nourished by the many springs gushing from the limestone cliffs, a passage which was always a problem for armies. Thereafter the route follows the base of Mt. Olympos whose high peak emerges out of the wooded slopes scored by deep ravines. Further north, the plain of Katerini represents the area of ancient Pieria. The low hills at Pydna separate it from the plain of central Macedonia.

The formidable Vale of Tempe was frequently by-passed. The first possibility was the route commanded by Gonnoi in Thessaly, to the west of lower Olympos. But this alternative crossing is difficult and much less valuable than others which skirted Olympos on the west.

The most important of these is that now called Sarandaporos where, by a col at 950 m., one passes from the Thessalian basin of Elassona to the Macedonian town of Servia. This pass was the only route linking Thessaly and Macedonia suitable for wheeled traffic until the opening of the National Route 1 through Tempe. Starting from Elassona another route enters Macedonia forcing its way between Olympos and the Pierian Mts. But this route is still indifferent, and the Pass of Petra arduous and toilsome to negotiate.

One has to go much further west to find another important route into Macedonia — that which from the vicinity of Kalambaka, Thessaly, climbs out of the upper valley of the Peneios, crosses the endless and sparsely inhabited hills of the Chassia Mts. covered with small stunted oaks to descend at Grevena into the depression in which the waters of the Haliakmon flow, called by geologists the Meso-Hellenic Furrow.

From Epirus and Albania: the western approaches. To the south-west the Pindos range forms a formidable barrier: precipitous slopes, several hundred metres high, difficult to scale and obscured by forest, rise above the Haliakmon valley. For a long time the only easy pass was that of Zygos (1700 m.) above Metsovo. But this route has little relevance to Macedonia and is of interest to communications between Thessaly and Epirus.

Further north there is no route between Epirus and Macedonia apart from the shepherds' tracks across the saddles of the Pindos range. The modern Greek-Albanian border crosses the Pindos range at Mt. Grammos. Here, in the area of the Prespa Lakes (Great and Little) the mountain barrier lies further to the west. Mt. Grammos lengthens into the Morava chain (1779 m.) which dominates the town of Korytsa (Korcë) on the east. This range extends northwards between Great Prespa and lake Ochrid (ancient Lychnitis), to the Livaniskos (Xerovouni or Mali i Thatë, the white mountain of the Albanians). Between the two mountains the Devoli (ancient Eordaikos) valley provides a broad and easy thoroughfare towards central Albania. But though today lake Maliq which occupies this valley has receded, its marshy shore for a long time was an important obstacle to communication with the areas round Berat and Elbasan.

Throughout this entire frontier region of Macedonia the relief has the form of successive corridors amongst which the roads must dodge about in order to gain any ground. Thus the course of the Devoli between Mt. Morava and Livaniskos is in a way screened from the east by the Vernon range, whose highest point is Mt. Vitsi (2128 m.). This range extends north into Yugoslavia and includes Mt. Peristeri (2000 m.). During antiquity this constituted a sort of frontier march of Macedonia towards the west.

The Via Egnatia, which we shall discuss later, skirts Mt. Peristeri to the north, passing between it and Mt. Planenska (1933 m.).

From the North: the northern passes. From Skopje (on the site of ancient Scupi, capital of Dardania, and some 40 km. north of the frontier of ancient Macedonia) there are two easy routes to the north — the westernmost is drained by a tributary of the Axios, the Lepenac, which rises in the Kossovo valley. However, the main route opens up further east, that of Preševo-Kumanovo. The watershed of Preševo, less than 400 m. high, makes for an easy connection between the Danube basin and the Aegean. It is thus from the Serbian side that access to Macedonia is easiest.

To the east: the Bulgarian stronghold. To the east the mountains are particularly rugged. The present Bulgarian-Yugoslav frontier runs along the mountain tops, the highest of which is Osogovo (2252 m.). The road from Skopje to Sofia via Kyustendil passes north of Osogovo by a pass at 1192 m., following the line of a Roman road.

The most savage obstacles, however, lie further east, the Rhodope Mts. which are divided into two main massifs, the Rila and the Pirin, both of which are sufficiently high (more than 2900 m.) to have the Alpine type landscape, with lakes of glacial origin and corries where the snow lies for a long time even at the beginning of summer. The Pirin range is the lower of these mountains, despite the fact that

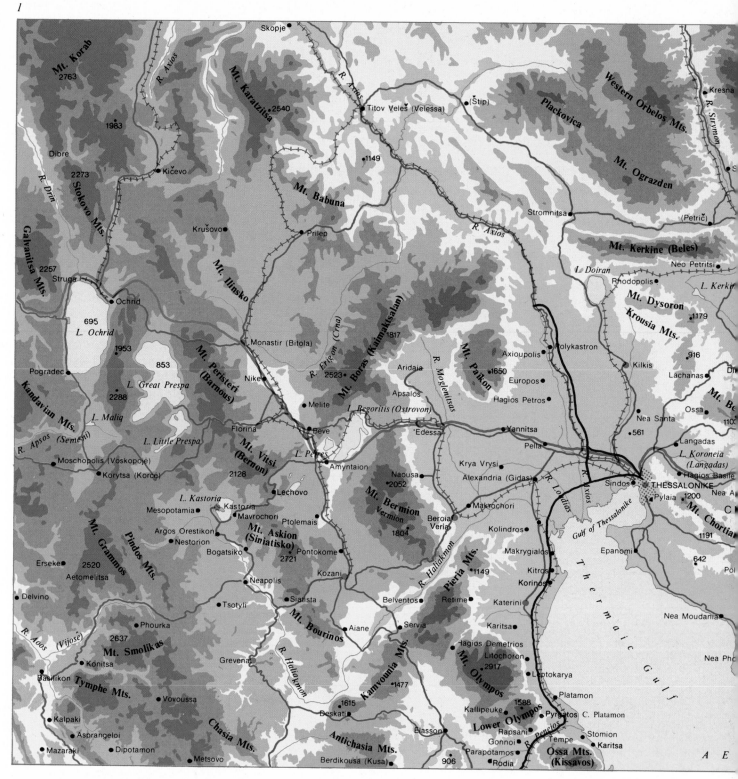

1. The heart of Macedonia is the littoral plain of Thessalonike stretching inland from the Thermaic Gulf, across which flow the rivers Haliakmon, Loudias and Gallikos. Alluvium deposited by these rivers has considerably altered the coastline in historic times. The hinterland, especially to the north-west, is parcelled out into mountain ranges separated by plains. Access to

its peak, Mt. Vichren, reaches 2915 m. The Rila range boasts the highest summit of the Balkan peninsula, Mt. Musala (2925 m.). Both Rila and Pirin block advance eastwards. The two rivers, Strymon (Strouma) and Nestos (Mesta) force communication southward so effectively that the main route to the east passes close to the Aegean shore.

INTERNAL COMMUNICATION

The general structure of the relief does not make internal communication within Macedonia easy. Except for short distances, the valleys are never very wide; gorges are frequently encountered, which the road must avoid at the cost

east-west, owing to the river system: the Axios (Vardar) like the Strymon (Strouma) and the Nestos (Mesta) follow a roughly north-south direction.

From Skopje the Axios flows across the plain of Tikveš, passing Titov Veles (the ancient Bylazora). On the plain stands the modern town of Gradsko. In antiquity the town of Stoboi was an important staging point on the Roman road which descended the valley. At this point the Axios is fed from the west bank by its tributary, the Crna Reka (ancient Erigon) which drains the vast basin of Pelagonia. Its valley does not form a line of communication, because it is divided by gorges which are today utilized as near natural dams for the production of hydro-electric power. Downstream, another gorge opens up, Demir Kapu, which stretches some 20 kms. The Turkish words mean Iron Gates. Beyond Gevgelija and the 'gorge of the gypsies' over which passes the modern Greek-Yugoslav frontier, the Axios valley becomes progressively wider and wider.

Until about 1925 there was still much marshland and several lakes, such as that of Amatovo. The Axios flows into the Thermaic Gulf along a straight course, virtually due south, which in its lowest part is entirely man-made; for a long time the Axios flowed south-east and at its delta merged with the waters of the Gallikos (ancient Echedoros). The quantity of alluvium brought down by the Axios threatened to choke the port of Thessalonike and for this reason its mouth was artificially diverted southwards. The entire lower plain is formed from the combined alluvial deposits of the Gallikos, the Axios and the Haliakmon. The coast line, marshy and shifting, extends southwards year by year. Inland, lagoons and lakes have been steadily drained by long and costly works. Heavy sodden soils have never favoured communication: the ancient routes traversed the plain on its northern side.

The Strymon valley is far from having the same importance for communications as that of the Axios. Nevertheless, from the north it ensures the link with the lateral connection leading from Niš (Roman Naissus) to Sofia (Roman Sardica) and on to Byzantium.

Moving downstream, the connection with the Aegean Sea presents difficulties. Below the Blagoevgrad basin the river enters the Kresna gorge (Kresnenska Klissoura), famous because of the battles between Greeks and Bulgars in 1913. At Petrič the Strymon (Strouma) is joined by the Stroumitsa whose lower reaches only have belonged to Bulgaria from 1918.

Further south, the Strymon negotiates another obstacle, the Belacica massif (Kerkine in Greek), whose peak reaches 2029 m., via the Roupel gorge. This marks the Bulgarian-Greek frontier, and was the scene of fierce fighting between Greeks and Germans in the Second World War. Unlike the Axios which, from its entry to Greece until it reaches the sea, meets no physical obstacle, the Strymon before joining the sea at the site of the ancient city of Amphipolis, has to flow through one last gorge. It is scarcely surprising that in these conditions its waters become obstructed in the Serres (ancient Serrhai) basin, and even at the beginning of this century formed a very ex-

Macedonia is difficult from both the south (Thessaly) and west (Epirus), but relatively easy from the north, Yugoslavia and Bulgaria via the Axios and Strymon valleys.

of long detours. Moreover, the mountain massifs, notwithstanding the limited area they cover, frequently terminate in steep escarpments, so much so that it is necessary to skirt them, because it is impossible to go over them easily.

In general, north-south communication is easier than

15

tensive lake, lake Achinos, surrounded by marshes for over 50 kms. The outlet to the Gulf of Orphanos (Strymonic Gulf) has been enlarged and the flood water channelled into lake Kerkine in the north-west of the basin.

LATERAL COMMUNICATIONS

The Via Egnatia

The orientation of the relief does not favour west-east communication; nevertheless this traffic was of vital importance for centuries and yet, even at the beginning of the twentieth century, the only route even remotely possible for wheeled traffic out of European Turkey followed the line of the ancient Via Egnatia. Today, however, the importance of this line of communication has considerably diminished, largely for political reasons.

The Via Egnatia originated at Dyrrachion; in its first stage it negotiated the Shkumbin valley and skirted lake Ochrid to the north. Its line is now preserved in one of the only two roads which link Albania to the outside world. At Struga, the Via Egnatia crosses the river Black Drin. Via the pass of Bukovo (1190 m.), the small town of Resen and the pass of Diavato (1169 m.), it descends to Bitola (Monastir) which lies at the foot of Mt. Peristeri, close to the site of ancient Herakleia, another ancient town on the Via Egnatia and thence to the plain of Pelagonia, the largest of the inland basins, covering more than 1000 sq. kms.

Thereafter the Via Egnatia is forced to play leap-frog to make any progress eastwards across inhospitable terrain — punch-bowls, denuded mountains and basins, partly occupied by lakes without outflows.

The Via Egnatia winds alongside lake Vegoritis (ancient Bokeritis) leaving Mt. Vermion (ancient Bermion) (2052 m.) to the south. Through the pass of Edessa it reaches the central Macedonian plain.

Until Thessalonike there is no obstacle in the relief, because flat, open and level countryside stretches all the way to the common delta of the rivers Gallikos, Axios and Haliakmon. But until recently, this beautiful plain was marshland, and before that there was a lake, lake Loudias. The Via Egnatia was forced to skirt this lake on its northern side in the lee of the gentle slopes of the hills which flank the southern edge of the Païkon massif. The draining of lake Loudias took place in the twentieth century.

Having reached Thessalonike, the Via Egnatia crosses the hills which stretch north-west of Mt. Chortiatis (ancient

2. Aerial photograph of Mt. Olympos, the traditional boundary between Thessaly and Macedonia. The only routes past lay through the Vale of Tempe or over the Pass of Petra and Voloustana.

3. The river Peneios as it flows across the plain between lower Olympos and Mt. Ossa, before it enters the sea. ▶

Kissos, 1200 m.). It then descends to the valley occupied by the vast lakes of Langada (ancient Koroneia) and Volvi (ancient Bolbe) with their ill-defined marshy edges. It runs south of these, but to the north of the steep hills which define the northern edge of the Chalkidike plateau.

Here in antiquity was the town of Apollonia. The frontier of Macedonia must have run along the line of the Rentina gorge, shaded by plane trees, through which the outflow from lake Volvi makes its way to the Strymonic Gulf. In antiquity the mouth of the Strymon marked the site of Amphipolis: it was a remarkable site, for on three sides the town was protected by the Strymon whose gorge it commanded. A few kilometres away are the ruins of the port of Eion, a town which played an important role in the exploitation of the Mt. Pangaion gold mines. It is surprising that there is no modern town here.

Leaving the Gulf, the Via Egnatia climbed through the successive valleys of two short coastal water courses which drained a valley between Mt. Pangaion to the north and Mt. Symbolon to the south. It then descended into the Drama basin. It had to avoid the extensive marshes on the edge of which stood the town of Philippi, another ancient town with no modern successor. The marsh extended to a narrow but steep mountain ridge on the coast. The road traverses it to descend to the ancient town of Neapolis on the site of which is now the modern port of Kavala in the shelter of a rocky promontory.

From there eastwards the route follows the coast, soon to arrive at the vast delta of the Nestos which for a long time was marshy, forested and fringed with lagoons. To avoid these difficulties the road kept its distance from the lower part of the plain, passing instead over the hills which flank it, to cross the Nestos at the head of the delta into Thrace.

A LAND APART:

THE CHALKIDIKE PENINSULA

Chalkidike is an area unique for Macedonia. The peninsula, though hilly, is nowhere very high except for the magnificent pyramid of Mt. Athos (2033 m.) on the easternmost of its three prongs. Otherwise the average height is below 1000 m. except at two points, Mt. Chortiatis, east of Thessalonike and Mt. Cholomon (1165 m.) at the centre of the peninsula.

Until the reign of Philip II, this area remained outside the mainstream of Macedonian life, its interests always tending towards southern Greece.

RELIEF AND FRONTIERS

One factor remains constant in the siting of the frontiers of Macedonia — the particularly important role played by gorges (klissoura as both the Greeks and the neighbouring Slav people call them).

In antiquity, for long centuries, Macedonian domination

did not extend further east than the gorge of Rentina which closes the entry to the Strymonic Gulf. On the north, in the Axios valley, the frontier between Dardania and Paionia, which Philip II subjected to Macedonia, ran along the gorge now called Veleska Klissoura, slightly to the north of the modern town of Titov Veles.

In the twentieth century the southern frontier of Bulgaria, determined in 1878, runs along the Kresnenska Klissoura; it was here that Greeks and Bulgars confronted each other in 1913 during the second Balkan War. After the end of hostilities, another gorge, the Roupel, was adopted as the frontier.

On the Axios, the Greek-Yugoslav frontier runs across the Gevgelija gorge. The case of the Pelagonia basin alone is exceptional; now divided between Yugoslavia and Greece, the border runs across the plain.

Basing a frontier on the line of a gorge offers advantages; it facilitates the control of crossings while troop movements to its rear may be concealed. Conversely, frontiers in mountainous territory are usually both less well-defined and more restrictive. Such territory is often inhabited by people whose livelihood depends on pastoral activity, for whom freedom of movement, both for themselves and for their flocks is essential. For them, both sides of the mountain are the same and the real distinction lies between the higher land where the summer pastures are to be found and the lower, winter, pastures. Thus the strict political frontiers of the twentieth century act in mountainous regions as a source of irritation for populations whose way of life is not related to limited territory

CLIMATIC DISPOSITIONS

A region on the fringes of the Mediterranean world

The Mediterranean world is often defined in terms of the culture of the olive. Though specialists may have objections to the choice of a cultivated plant to determine frontiers of physical geography, nevertheless the areas in which the olive grows have the advantage of being immediately definable, however approximately.

In Thessaly the olive grows on the Aegean coast though not above the 100 m. contour on the western slope of Mt. Ossa. Over the Macedonian border, the olive is rare on the lower slopes of Mt. Olympos, and absent from the plain of Katerini; it reappears near the site of ancient Pydna.

It grows along the Chalkidike littoral, especially on the Kassandra peninsula, and it covers large areas on the island of Thasos.

In the hinterland the olive is almost non-existent, the only place where trees have been planted being the Prodromos monastery sited in a very sheltered valley north-east of Serres where the groves have given their name to the settlement, Elaion (the olive grove).

Thus the Mediterranean climate in the strict sense of the term is limited to the peninsula and the islands. Everywhere else continental influences predominate.

Continental influences

The inhabitants of Macedonia are well acquainted with the 'Vardaris', the cold wind which blows down the Axios valley or from the Šar mountains which in a few hours can bring about a drop in temperature of as much as ten degrees, producing rain and snow showers in spring, and sometimes severe frosts.

The effects of the relationship of mountain chains and basins are to be observed in climatological conditions, particularly rainfall. Everywhere the basins are sheltered from atmospheric disturbances which pass over the Aegean Sea and hurl themselves against the mountains creating north-easterly winds. The Morava-Axios valley has less than 600 mm. annual rainfall. Similar figures are found for the Thessalonike basin. No meteorological station in any basin, even at considerable altitudes, records more than 700 mm. — (Kastoria 562 mm., Ptolemaïs 575 mm., Kozani 630 mm.).

In contrast, high ground receives much more rain. In the Šar Planina and the mountains above the Prespa lakes and lake Ochrid annual precipitation exceeds 1500 mm. while in the mountains of central and eastern Macedonia annual rainfall averages 100 mm., and less than that the along mountains of its Bulgarian frontier.

The effects of the continental climate prevailing in Macedonia are felt in the seasonal distribution of precipitation. Continental zones are characterized by plentiful summer rain. Thus it is surprising to observe that the percentage of summer rain in the year's total does not differ noticeably between Belgrade, Sofia and Thessalonike.

Belgrade	Sofia	Skopje	Thessalonike	Kozani	Larisa	Athens
22%	23%	18%	17%	20%	14%	5.6%

Percentage of summer rainfall in the annual rainfall total

But a continental climate is more than the pattern of precipitation; it is also a matter of temperature. The inland basins of Macedonia, often at high altitudes and always mountain-rimmed have the characteristic cold and snowy winters. Kozani and Kastoria have a January mean of 1.6° and Florina only 0.4° C.

On the other hand, summer temperatures are very high, especially in the basins: 23.5° in July at Skopje; 22.6° at Bitola; 23.1° at Kozani and 23.6° at Kastoria, even though the last three towns are at altitudes between 600 and 670m.

This produces the high annual averages typical of continental climates.

Belgrade	Sofia	Skopje	Bitola	Thessalonike	Athens
21.8°	20.6°	23.2°	22.2°	20.8°	18.3°

Mean annual average temperatures: (the difference between the lowest and the highest mean temperatures).

It is noticeable that Thessalonike, though coastal, also has a high average; it is as though central Europe stretched right to the Aegean Sea.

Maritime influences

Influences from the south make themselves felt and clash with those from the north on the Macedonian littoral. They prevail over Chalkidike and further east over a coastal strip only a few kilometres wide as far as the Nestos, and over the isle of Thasos. Moving inland, maritime influences temper the winter: the proximity of the Mediterranean produces the mild rainy winter climate of the Serres and Drama basins and of the plain of Thessalonike. It is this mildness which permits the growth of grass in the cooler months, and thus invites the descent of flocks from the upland pastures. The Mediterranean influence is also at work in the brevity of the transition from season to season (spring and autumn); winter gives way abruptly to summer.

This is why, if to the Greeks Macedonia appears as a northern region with a harsh climate, the valley of the Axios for Yugoslavs and that of the Strymon for the Bulgarians are vested with the magic of the south linked to a warmth and a luminosity unknown in the regions further north.

Two Macedonian rivers: the Axios and the Haliakmon

The character of Macedonian rivers is formed jointly by the lie of the land and by climatic patterns. From source to mouth Macedonian rivers pass from basin to basin switching from sections with a slow rate of flow and easy descent to sections with a rapid rate in the gorges.

Such is the Axios, whose total length is three hundred and seventy-six kms., three hundred in Yugoslavia and seventy-six in Greece. The river passes through four major gorges and its principal tributary, the Crna which drains Pelagonia also flows through deep gorges before its confluence with the Axios. The flow of water over the year in the rivers reflects the rainfall pattern. But although rainfall shows an autumn high, the river maximum occurs in spring, in other words at the time when heavy rainfall and melting snows coincide. The summer low is very marked, for summer rain, not inconsiderable as we have seen above, evaporates rapidly because of the high air temperature and low humidity. It thus does not enter the drainage network.

In addition to this, the irregularity from year to year is great, so much so that the average annual flow of the Axios, estimated 164m³ per sec. at Gevgelija presents enormous peaks (1851 m³ per sec.) and extreme lows (16m³ per sec. in 1925).

The Haliakmon, two hundred and ninety-seven kms., is the longest Greek river. It has an average flow rather less high (54 m³ per sec.). The pattern follows that of the Axios, but snowfalls on the mountains surrounding its valley are less heavy and so their thaw plays less part. On the other hand, karst springs with a constant volume, help to boost the summer drops.

The existence of a relatively well supplied hydrographic network is not without interest to man. But few dams have been built across Macedonian rivers: seven in Yugoslavia

in the Axios valley (of which two are on the Crna); two in Greece, one on the Haliakmon at Imera and the other, much smaller, on the Edessaios above Edessa. The current of Macedonian rivers is slow and irregular. To overcome such irregularities it would be necessary to construct reservoir dams of huge capacity. But, on a river like the Axios, such a dam would require the submerging of a large acreage as well as the loss of even more arable land on which the barrage would be built. Schemes have therefore been abandoned. On the other hand the rivers can be easily used for irrigation whether by pumping in the phreatic zones or by direct diversion of water to agricultural use.

THE TAMED ENVIRONMENT

From the geological disposition to mineral exploitation

Macedonia lies on the Aegean side of the Dinaric Alps, here known by geologists as 'Hellenids'. It has long been established that the Hellenids are arranged in a parallel series with a north-west/south-east orientation.

Between the Pindos and the Rhodope, Macedonia is a complex zone where the present relief forms have resulted mainly from the rifts and fractures which occurred in the Tertiary and Quaternary eras. The massifs are raised zones, the basins collapsed zones, while the slopes which bound them are situated on the very line of the fracture. There is still considerable seismic activity: the earthquakes which hit Thessalonike in 1978 bear witness to the persistence of the instability which is not a characteristic only of Macedonia but one which spreads over the whole of Greece.

The geological formation of Macedonia has determined the apportionment of its mineral wealth and of its arable land. Of precious metals, gold is to be found in the Gallikos valley and of course, at Mt. Pangaion from which it has been mined since antiquity. There is also gold at Stratoniki in Chalkidike and at Servia, south-east of Kozani. But the quantities extracted today are negligible, and without economic significance, though this was not so in antiquity. Iron is present on the isle of Thasos. It was discovered after 1945 and mining is intermittent. Iron pyrites are found at Madem Lakkos in Chalkidike, where there is also lead, mined since the Middle Ages. The word *Madem* is Turkish and means both mine and metal.

Macedonia also possesses manganese beds in the Drama region. Extensive magnesium deposits are exploited in the Chalkidike peninsula, particularly at Baudos. At Mt. Bourinos, south-east of Kozani, there are appreciable quantities of chromite. Numerous small mines and deposits which are not worked could be added to this list.

Naturally, before the twentieth century, interest was centred on precious metals, iron, lead, zinc and tin. The other minerals (chrome, nickel) used nowadays as alloys of iron were not sought after until very recently.

4. The central Macedonian plain, close to the ruins of ancient Pella. Until recently this plain was virtually marshland.

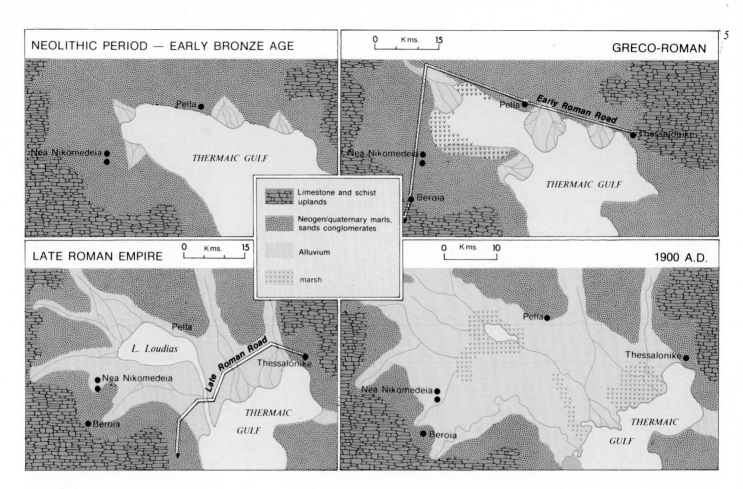

NEOLITHIC PERIOD — EARLY BRONZE AGE

GRECO-ROMAN

THERMAIC GULF

Pella

Nea Nikomedeia

Early Roman Road

Thessaloniki

Beroia

Limestone and schist uplands

Neogen/quaternary marls, sands conglomerates

Alluvium

marsh

LATE ROMAN EMPIRE

1900 A.D.

Pella

L. Loudias

Late Roman Road

Thessaloniki

Nea Nikomedeia

THERMAIC GULF

Beroia

Pella

Thessaloniki

Nea Nikomedeia

Beroia

THERMAIC GULF

5. *Over the centuries the alluvial deposits of the rivers Haliakmon, Loudias and Gallikos have brought about great changes in the coastline at the head of the Thermaic Gulf. The maps above show four successive phases in the silting up, from Prehistoric times through antiquity to the beginning of the 20th century.*

Mineral fuel sources should also be included, though the deposits of natural gas and oil petroleum located off Thasos have only recently been exploited. By contrast lignite, one of the main sources of energy in Greece, is present in deposits in the inland basins.

Geology and Arable Land

Arable land represents approximately 30% of the entire surface area of Greek Macedonia, a proportion which covers wide local variations (62% of the eparchy of Yannitsa and only 14% of Grevena).

There is a close link between the composition of the soil and its cultivation — those most heavily tilled are the most recently deposited alluvial soils of the plains at sea level (the plains of central Macedonia and Katerini), beginning with the highest alluviums, i.e those furthest removed from recurring floods. The same is true in the inland basins (Serres, Drama) close to the sea, and in the upland plains of the hinterland — the Florina basin, the Ptolemaïs-Kozani corridor.

In contrast, in these plains and basins, the marshy soils have been far slower to be brought under cultivation because they were heavy and were subject to seasonal flooding — such is the case in the Philippi marshes in the Drama basin, those surrounding lake Achinos in the Serres basin, of the 'valtos' (=marsh) at the outflow of the Yannitsa lake in the central Macedonian plain. Marshes are also to be found in the upland basins: for example at Sarigöl south of Ptolemaïs and those near Florina which extend beyond the frontier into Yugoslav Pelagonia.

These marshy soils have the excellent property of not drying out in summer as long as they are properly drained.

The soils on the hills are very unevenly exploited, though they have the advantage of being relatively sandy and light. For long given over to grazing flocks, they have often been brought under cultivation and provide good land for the growing of cereal crops: such is the case, for example on the Pydna hills dividing the Katerini plain from that of central Macedonia. It holds good also for the hills round Goumenissa which bound the Axios valley below the gorge of Gevgelija. These rich soils, though dry, today carry cereal crops.

Vegetation Zones

The present distribution of the vegetation in part results from natural conditions, in part from the activity of man.

The only area of Macedonia where in its natural state vegetation of a Mediterranean type is to be found is on the three prongs of the Chalkidike peninsula and the linking coastal strip. Only there is the lentisc found and of course the olive fairly thickly distributed.

The natural covering of the holm-oak *(Quercus ilex)* and the Kermes oak *(Quercus coccifera)* is much more commonly found. It covers much of the shore with the exception of the delta areas.

The Mediterranean forest covering is not in fact found except on relatively steep slopes. Overall Chalkidike is forested, apart from the south-west coast of the Kassandra peninsula.

Most of the rest of Macedonia is the domain of deciduous oaks, most noticeably the White or Downy Oak *(Quercus pubescens)*. About the 1000 m. contour the oak gives way to tracts of mountain forestation.

Above this level and making allowance for a multitude of local variations, one finds three successive stages of vegetation. The first zone extends from the 1000 m. contour to the 2000 m. contour. It consists of trees which have spread from central Europe. In this belt one finds the sweet chestnut, sometimes in magnificent groves (like that of Skotina on the lower Olympos) or on the range of mountains situated west of Florina. But there are other trees besides the chestnut — conifers, also of northern origin like the spruce on the borders of Thrace or the Austrian black pine *(Pinus nigra)* on the Pindos, on Mt. Olympos and in the Pierian mountains, on Mts. Paikon and Kaimakchalan and even in Chalkidike and on Mt. Pangaion.

Above that the sweet chestnut and, locally, the black pine are replaced, if the height of the mountain is sufficient, by one of the most beautiful trees in Greece, the Bosnian pine *(Pinus leucodermis)* with a white translucent bark. It grows only at considerable altitudes for example on Mt. Olympos and elsewhere between 1600-1700 m. and 2100-2200 m.

Higher up, the trees thin out, become less tall and gradually give way to dwarf junipers and then to alpine pastures.

Denudation of vegetation

The layering of vegetation just described may leave the impression that Macedonia is tree-covered. However, the traveller passing through the region is struck by the absence of forest and by the prominence of bare slopes. We have already stressed that both plains and basins are almost entirely under tillage and have been for a very long time. It is thus useless to search for evidence of the original vegetation.

But the stripping of the vegetal cover is not limited to the areas under cultivation: Macedonia also has large areas of denuded mountain slopes.

The coastal region is far from being the barest, despite the fact that the Mediterranean forestation is considered to have only a tenuous hold. Chalkidike remains very wooded, with dense pine forests on the Sithonian peninsula; thick sweet chestnut groves continue to be an important asset of the Mount Athos monasteries. In the hinterland, woodland has very often given ground to maquis and then to garrigue. Moreover, the highest tree level is almost never a natural limit, but the result of over-grazing.

THE CHANGING LANDSCAPE IN HISTORICAL TIMES

Deforestation

In the Classical era vast forests clothed the Macedonian mountains. The most heavily exploited were the forests of Chalkidike and the Rhodope Mts. because of their proximity to ports from which timber could be shipped elsewhere. There is considerable evidence for this.

The historian Hammond indicates the extent of woodland, particularly in Pieria which even today is amongst the most heavily wooded areas of Macedonia. He also summarizes the diversity of sources which indicate the forest-dwelling fauna — the bear, the deer, the wild ox and the wild boar, — which not only encourage hunting, but also the survival of predatory animals, for example lions and lynx. Herodotos records their presence on Mt. Dysoron (east of Kilkis) and Xenophon in the Pindos. Hunting scenes are repeatedly depicted in mosaics, in particular of lions hunted with the javelin.

Dense forest land corresponded to a period when Macedonia had only thinly spaced human settlement; the Hellenistic and Roman periods were an age when the density of settlement increased.

The silting of the Thermaic Gulf

Struck's theory that the Thermaic Gulf silted up and its coastline formed as a result of concentrated alluvial deposition which took place in the later centuries of the Roman period has never really been questioned. On it Hammond bases his account of the road network.

In the Neolithic period and at the beginning of the Bronze Age the Thermaic Gulf must be imagined as a very deep inlet, stretching almost to the sites of Pella and Nea Nikomedeia, viz. to the limit of the alluvial deposits and the conglomerate clays and sands of the Neogenous period. From the fifth to the first centuries B.C. the deltas of the Haliakmon, Axios and Gallikos advanced further and further into the Gulf as marshland spread over its head. Towards the end of the Roman period (second-third centuries A.D.), an intense period of alluviation imprisoned lake Loudias.

After the Roman period

Macedonia did not again know the stability she had enjoyed under the kingdom of Macedonia and under Roman rule. The misfortunes which struck certainly led to a decrease in population. The advent of the Turks in the fourteenth century introduced new stock into the Macedonian villages and countryside which led to the redistribution which appears on the ethnographic map of 1912, the date at which southern Macedonia was incorporated into Greece.

Studies in progress show that river beds started to deepen from the end of the sixteenth century, whereas there had been a long period of stability from the end of the Roman period. At the beginning of the twentieth century lake Loudias, known then as the lake of Yannitsa, was no more than an extensive shallow swamp, bound to be filled up soon as the cones of the Haliakmon and Axios deltas increased in size, swollen by erosion in their basins.

At the same time there was erosion on a wide scale. Thus it came about that the Haliakmon sank ten metres below its alluvial deposits, and then below these to bedrock.

Possible explanations: tectonic movements, climatic changes and cultivation

Three factors can be used to explain ecological evolution: tectonic movements, climatic changes and the cultivation of the land by man. It is not easy to know to which of these factors the spectacular phenomenon of the silting up of the Thermaic Gulf should be attributed. Is it perhaps a slowing-down of a movement of subsidence which made itself felt progressively through the plain of central Macedonia and the Axios and Haliakmon deltas? Is it connected to a more arid climatic phase during which the vegetation, more readily laid bare, could not protect the soil to the same extent and thus permitted large-scale erosion? Or, lastly, is it connected to an appreciable increase in population expressed in an increase in the cultivated area of the steep slopes, again resulting in erosion? In the absence of cores from the alluvial deposits on the plain, it is impossible to answer this question, but it is not impossible that all three factors worked together.

THE EXTENT OF STAGNANT WATER AND MALARIA

Swamps

At the beginning of the twentieth century stagnant water covered a large area. In Yugoslavia vast swamps covered Pelagonia, their southern edge bordering the Greek frontier. The situation was no better in Greek Macedonia; the banks of both Great and Little Prespa were marshy, as were parts of the Kozani-Ptolemaïs corridor, where there are several deep lakes (for example Vegoritis), and the fens of the Sarigöl. Further west, lake Kastoria was also marsh-fringed. To the east the waters of the Drama basin fed the immense swamps round Philippi and those of the Serres basin supplied lakes Achinos and Butkovo (ancient Prasias). The valley which runs from the Thermaic to the Strymonic Gulf shelters lakes with ill-defined shores, Langada and Volvi.

The greatest area of marshland lay in central Macedonia. Parallel to the left bank of the river Axios are the elongated lakes of Amatovo and Ardjane which served to catch the flood waters. Downstream from Aridaia the surrounding region was marshy in winter because the river which drains the area, the Moglenitsa, had difficulty in flowing through the gorges to reach the central plain where water really came into its own. The swamp (or lake) of Yannitsa formed a vast depression, 5 m. above sea-level. Its ever-changing muddy edges were scored by artificial channels at right-angles to the shore, serving as drainage channels, into which the boats of fishermen penetrated in the cooler months. In effect, from June onwards, the fishermen could not spend the night there because of the mosquitoes.

Mosquitoes and Malaria

Not all species of mosquito are carriers of malaria. But amongst them the anophele was both common and redoubtable. The lack of maintenance of ditches, the total absence of any thought-out drainage policy and the socio-economic system of *chiftlik* have all contributed to worsen the sanitary conditions over the later centuries of Turkish domination, so that the anophele found an ideal habitat.

At the beginning of this century, malaria was not confined to the low-lying coastal regions. The entire population of the areas round the Haliakmon and the Axios estuaries was afflicted, certainly, but the disease was also found round lake Kastoria, lakes Prespa and even in the mountains of Yugoslav Macedonia.

MAN AND THE NATURAL ENVIRONMENT

It is easy to see that in Macedonia Nature has not conferred her blessings without also bestowing drawbacks.

The basins frequently have heavy soils, and are malaria infested — facts which recent prosperity should not be allowed to obscure: they did not lend themselves to easy exploitation by people with only limited technical means at their disposal. The realization of their maximum potential demanded more than just the mastery of tools. It required a political power sufficiently solidly based to be able to plan and to implement drainage works and to enforce their maintenance. Macedonia has rarely enjoyed such direction.

The mountains were for a long time regarded as an inexhaustible source of timber and pasture. Abusive assarting has resulted in the bare slopes so characteristic of inland Macedonia. However, the natural conditions are propitious: it is to be noted that in the very beautiful sweet chestnut groves round Florina, most of the trees are less than twenty years old and regeneration is speedy. Reconstruction of a balanced natural environment could therefore be achieved by placing limits on grazing rights and by good forest management. Errors to be seen with hindsight can yet be remedied with foresight.

6. The mouth of the river Axios. The cones slowly forming from the alluvial deposits appear clearly.

ANCIENT
MACEDONIA

EARLY YEARS

THE CULTURES

During the past century chance finds and systematic excavation have revealed the rich variety of prehistoric cultures in Macedonia and demonstrated that this region has had its own identity in almost every period despite plentiful evidence of contact and exchange with neighbouring areas to the north and south. As a bridge between the Aegean and southern Greece on the one hand and the Balkans and the Danube valley on the other, Macedonia has provided specialists working in every region of southeast Europe with valuable cultural and chronological links which help to establish the pattern of civilization and its spread.

Nevertheless, before any attempt is made to reconstruct a 'historical' account from the archaeological evidence or to deduce movements of population within the area or into it from outside, it should be clearly recognized that as yet none of the districts of Macedonia shows a continuous sequence of settlement, nor is it likely that generalizations drawn from a single area can necessarily be applied to all the different landscapes and climatic regimes of this large province. Considerable local variation can be expected between the Haliakmon valley in the south and the Axios in the north, from the upland basin of Korytsa (Korcë) and the Crna valley in the west to the landlocked Drama plain in the east, or from the Balkan climate of the hills and valleys to the Mediterranean coast of Chalkidike. It is clear from the early history of Macedon that separate clans or tribes controlled each district until the monarchs of the Argead dynasty imposed their hegemony by force. There is no reason to suppose that there was greater unity in the prehistoric period.

Until the scale of research increases, whether by study of existing finds, by topographical and environmental survey or by excavation, any account which summarizes the early history of the settlement of Macedonia, as indeed that which follows, should be regarded as provisional. Macedonia is probably as well explored as her neighbours, but a single excavation within or near her borders could bring to light evidence which would radically change our understanding of her past. The facts will remain the same, but the inferences from them may have to be discarded.

THE PALAEOLITHIC AND NEOLITHIC PERIODS

The earliest periods of man's settlement of Greece are still poorly known. Two fine flaked stone hand-axes found to the south of Siatista near Palaiokastron, in western Macedonia,[1] and human and animal skeletal remains found in association with chipped stone tools in a cave near Petralona in Chalkidike,[2] indicate human activity in Macedonia in the Palaeolithic period, perhaps fifty thousand years ago (figs. 7,8). The bones of bear and deer found in the Petralona cave suggest the kind of animals which provided such early groups of hunters with part of their diet.

Agriculture, stockraising and permanent settlements appear to have been introduced to Greece as part of the spread of the neolithic economy which was probably developed in western Iran and northern Syria and had reached Anatolia by c. 8000 B.C. The routes by which these innovations reached Knossos in central Crete, Franchthi in the Argolid, Argissa in central Thessaly and Nea Nikomedeia in western Macedonia are uncertain, but radio-carbon dates indicate a similar period at each site, *c.* 6000 B.C. These settlements have produced evidence for a mixed subsistence economy. The inhabitants kept sheep and goats, which were not native to the Greek landscape, and a smaller number of cattle and pigs; they cultivated the primitive wheats einkorn and emmer, different varieties of barley, and legumes such as vetch, peas and lentils. The presence of other forms of wheat developed by the selective practices of harvesting, threshing and sowing, is a further indication that cereal agriculture was brought to Greece after a lengthy period of use in another area, rather than locally evolved. Hunting does not seem to play a very important role in the economy though wild fruits such as pistachio, almonds and berries were collected in season.

Unlike the earliest excavated settlements in southern Greece where aceramic strata have been discovered, the first occupants of Nea Nikomedeia[3] and of Anza,[4] one hundred and twenty-five km. to the north near Štip, were already making simple forms of pottery vessels. The ware was well-prepared, hand-shaped (as indeed was the great majority of prehistoric pottery from Macedonia), burnished and then evenly fired to produce a red or buff coloured surface. The shapes include hemispherical bowls with flat bases or low feet and small jars with slightly constricted necks. Pierced suspension lugs or rudimentary lug-handles enabled the pots to be hung or grasped more readily. Some of the pottery was simply decorated with rectilinear patterns before firing: at Anza these were predominantly in white on red in the same manner as the Early Neolithic Starčevo culture of the middle Danube region, while red paint on a cream or buff ground was preferred at Nea Nikomedeia, as at Argissa and other sites in Thessaly. Incised decoration occurs more rarely. Other vessels at Nea Nikomedeia have a human face modelled in relief on one side. Fragments of storage jars in coarser clay have also been found, but the same function was also served, perhaps more frequently, by containers of unbaked clay or of wickerwork, of which traces have been found at Nea Nikomedeia.

Other artefacts in use at this period include knife and sickle blades of chipped quartz or chert, polished axes in a variety of hard stones and tools of bone, such as awls, needles, burnishers and spatulae. The craft of weaving is indicated by impressions of material and by conical clay spindle whorls. Some spoons were made of clay, or simply of shells, particularly at Nea Nikomedeia where molluscs were clearly an important additional food resource. Ornaments are relatively rare at any settlement site; they include beads and pendants of clay, stone, bone or shell. At Anza there were fragments of bracelets of Aegean *spondylus* shell and of clay.

8

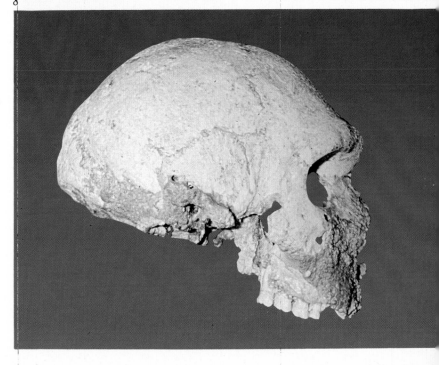

7. *The Petralona Cave where the fossilized skull of a Neanderthal man and skeletal remains of animals were found.*

8. *The Petralona skull is the oldest evidence for the presence of man in Greece in Paleolithic times. It is probably that of a woman, who lived 50,000 years ago.*

Figurines of clay or stone are a further indication of the sophisticated culture and art of these early communities. Nea Nikomedeia was particularly rich in examples of both human and animal types. Some are schematic, while others show careful attention to detail. Among the human forms, those with elongated necks and, at best, rudimentary heads and features are the most distinctive and belong to a class found spread over northern Greece and the southern Balkans from Thessaly to the Danube (fig. 10). Animals include a clay calf's head and a frog in steatite.

At Nea Nikomedeia the settlers built separate square or rectangular houses about 7 m. wide: they used large timber uprights at intervals to provide a frame and to support a pitched roof covered with mud-plastered thatch. The walls were set in clay-packed foundation trenches and formed of vertical reeds or rushes, covered in and out with mud. The floors were laid with rushes and covered with trodden clay. One large building about 12 m. square was divided into three parts and has been identified as a shrine by the excavator because of the figurines and other unusual objects found there. At Anza the first settlers were using plano-convex mud-bricks, similar to those found in the aceramic levels at Knossos, but soon changed to building in timber, perhaps in response to local conditions.

Nea Nikomedeia provides a little evidence for Neolithic burial practices, although from the scarcity of skeletal finds in settlements it can be presumed that burial normally took place outside the settlement. Bones of a woman and two children were found in a disused storage pit without any offerings, while those of a man were found with a smooth stone placed between the jaws.

At Anza the Early Neolithic is represented by three phases of occupation strata and shows a continuous development parallel to that of the Starčevo culture. Links can be seen between this material and that from Vršnik twenty-five km. to east,[5] and also that from the earlier levels at Porodin in the Crna valley to the west.[6] At Servia in the Haliakmon valley traces of a small settlement of similar date show stronger links with the Proto-Sesklo sites in Thessaly than with Nea Nikomedeia.[7] Recently, the first Early Neolithic settlement in eastern Macedonia has been located at Toumba near Serrhai,[8] covering an enormous area, c. 60,000 square metres.

In common with most eastern Mediterranean prehistoric groups, pottery with its many variations of ware, shape and decoration, is the principal indicator of chronology, contact and divergent development. Throughout Greece and south-east Europe the Middle Neolithic period shows both continuity from the preceding phase and considerable variation, locally and regionally.

In the south the inhabitants of Servia used a form of the elaborate red-on-cream Sesklo pottery of Thessaly, with linear patterns, blurred stripes or flame-like designs. Favourite shapes included wide bowls with flat bases or pedestal feet, 'mugs' with vertical ribbon handles, and globular jars with flaring or funnel necks. Decoration is richly applied to a majority of the finer wares, and on the interior surfaces of open shapes. Even the larger storage

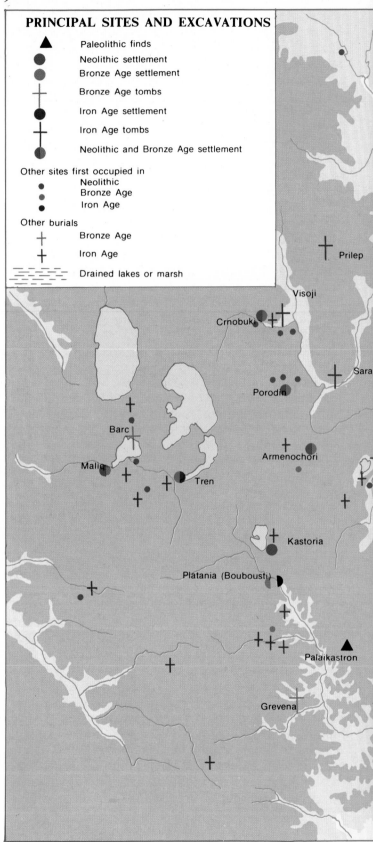

9. Map of the principal sites in prehistoric Macedonia. Excavations, old and new, have augmented our knowledge of the general development of particular settlements and illuminated

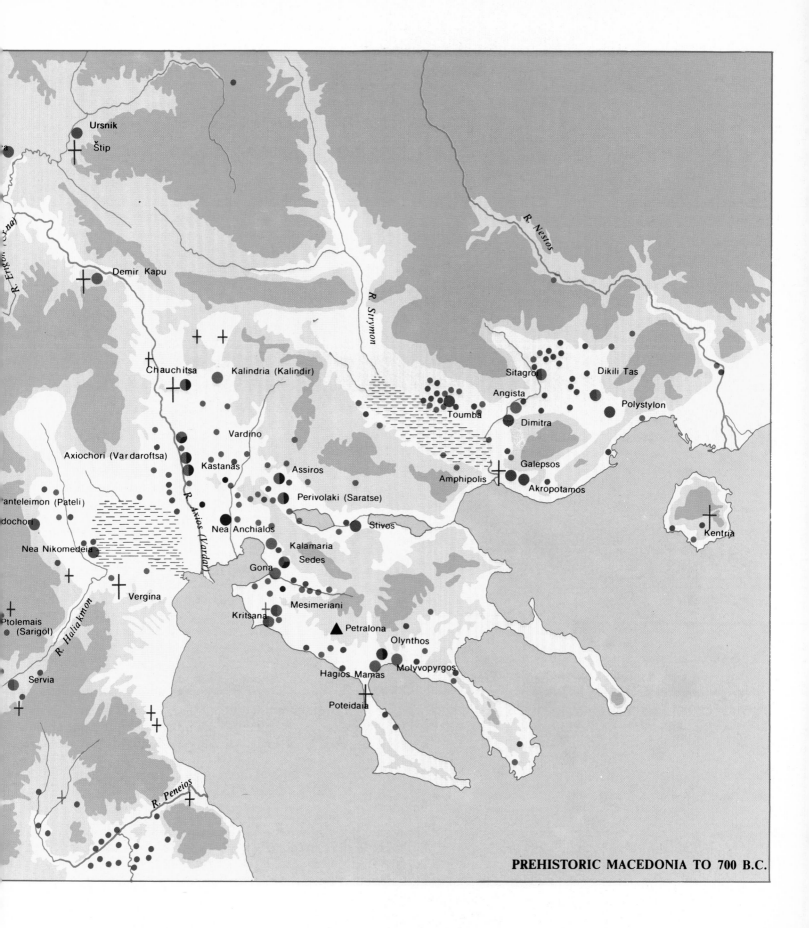

Ursnik

Štip

R. Erigón (Crna)

Demir Kapu

R. Nestos

R. Strymon

Chauchitsa

Kalindria (Kalindir)

Sitagro

Dikili Tas

Angista

Polystylon

Vardino

Toumba

Dimitra

Axiochori (Vardaroftsa)

Kastanas

Assiros

R. Axios (Vardar)

Perivolaki (Saratse)

Galepsos

Amphipolis

Akropotamos

Panteleimon (Pateli)

dochori

Stivos

Nea Anchialos

Kentria

Nea Nikomedeia

Kalamaria

Sedes

Gona

Mesimeriani

Vergina

R. Haliakmon

Kritsana

Ptolemais
(Sarigöl)

Petralona

Olynthos

Molyvopyrgos

Servia

Hagios Mamas

Poteidaia

R. Peneios

PREHISTORIC MACEDONIA TO 700 B.C.

more specialized studies (architecture, pottery, economy, burial customs, contacts etc.). The prehistoric cultures of Macedonia are markedly individual though the contacts and relations with *the surrounding regions testify to archaeological links which influenced cultural developments to a different degree in every period.*

33

jars are made of fine clay and often decorated.

Recent excavation at this site has disclosed a long-lived settlement of considerable size with remains of timber buildings, which contrast with the stone and mud-brick tradition of Thessaly. The earliest houses were separate structures *c.* 5×5 m. square with large central posts to support the roof, mud-packed stakes for the walls and split planks on some floors. Circular hearths with packed river pebbles in the base to help retain the heat were placed in the courtyards. In a later phase half metre deep cuttings were made for houses about 7 m. square, with a 'basement' storeroom and an upper storey. This was demonstrated by the massive posts along the walls and within the houses and by the presence of fallen objects in the upper fill of a house destroyed by fire.

These finds included a fine selection of ornaments, flat pendants of stone, and bracelets of shell or polished stone. Elsewhere in the Middle Neolithic strata were abundant flint and bone tools similar to those from earlier periods, together with large numbers of 'waisted' river pebbles which could have served as weights. Arrow-heads are new, as are the drilled stone cores from shaft-hole axes. Figurines of different types were present, although the earlier long-necked type has gone out of favour. Amongst other things which suggest contact with southern Greece are the clay figurines made in two parts, left and right, and joined after firing by small wooden pegs.

Economically, at Servia as at other contemporary sites, cattle and pigs became a more important food resource, in preference to sheep or goats, which may not have been so successful in the still largely wooded landscape. Hunting increased in importance.

Further to the north and north-west are a series of sites in the Sarigöl,[9] on the edge of lake Kastoria,[10] and at Porodin in the Crna valley, where remains of Middle Neolithic culture have been found which differ in several respects from the Thessalian form or from the early stages of the Vinča culture of central Yugoslavia.

There is little trace of this period in the central part of Macedonia, although Thessalian red-on-cream wares are reported from Mesimeriani.[11] At Anza, the final phase of settlement shows contact with eastern Macedonia where several sites, particularly in the Drama plain, such as Dikili Tas[12] and Sitagroi,[13] were first occupied in the Middle Neolithic period. These sites show strong links with contemporary levels at Karanovo, Azmak, and Veselinovo in the Maritsa (Hebros) basin in south-east Bulgaria. Similar

10. *Early Neolithic clay figurine from Nea Nikomedeia, c. 6000 B.C. Female figurines were typical of the Neolithic cultures of Macedonia and adjacent areas. The thighs and buttocks were often exaggerated to emphasize fertility while facial details were only schematically indicated. Beroia, Archaeological Museum.*

11-12. *Clay heads of Neolithic figurines from the settlement of Sitagroi near Drama. They date to c. 4000 B.C. Philippi, Archaeological Museum.*

material has also been found in Thrace at Paradimi. Characteristic pottery includes tall biconical jars and flat plates, often on four tall legs; firing is controlled to produce a bi-coloured effect with the upper part of the vase black and the lower red or buff. Small horns or knobs on the handles are typical, as is channelled, grooved and incised decoration. So far excavation has not exposed sufficient areas of these settlements to permit any assessment of the architecture.

The chronological relationship of each of these groups is difficult to determine from the pottery, but radio-carbon dates from Servia and Sitagroi indicate that this phase lasted from *c.* 5000-4000 B.C.

In the past it has been suggested that the Late Neolithic of Thessaly was the product of a new population group arriving to disturb the existing pattern, but in Macedonia continuity was at least as marked in each region as change. The geographical groupings established in the Middle Neolithic persist, but there is also more evidence for occasional contact between the different areas of Macedonia, perhaps in the form of trade.

Southern Macedonia is again closely linked with Thessaly, both in the distribution of the characteristic polychrome wares with curvilinear patterns, of which the Dimini type is the best known, and of the fine black-burnished 'Larisa' pottery with ripple decoration or simple designs in white paint. Even in Thessaly the relative date of these two wares is not clear, while at Servia it seems probable that black-burnished forms and the distinctive grey-on-grey pottery develop directly from Middle Neolithic wares. Wide bowls, rounded or biconical, are common in both painted and burnished wares.

Three phases of activity could be distinguished at Servia, again using simple timber-framed houses, although the two-storey form seems to have gone out of use. In one case a floor had been prepared with closely set logs covered with clay. These logs were all straight and of even size, suggesting that the inhabitants of this settlement were managing the neighbouring woodlands to encourage the growth of similar sized saplings. Deep bottle-shaped pits were also a feature of this period.

Black-burnished wares are also frequent in central Macedonia where on present evidence extensive settlement starts in this period. At Olynthos on the coast of Chalkidike traces of a Late Neolithic village were found below the remains of the classical town.[14] Three successive phases of occupation were detected, but buildings were only preserved in the two lower levels. Groups of rectangular or trapezoidal rooms were built with walls of rough river stones set in mud and perhaps completed above with mud brick. No timbers were detected in the construction of the walls or to support the roof. Nearby were the remains of a kiln, elaborately constructed with a clay floor raised above the fire-pit beneath and traces of ventilation passages which allowed the draught to be controlled. Fine quality black-burnished pottery occurred in small quantities and was decorated, as at Servia, with white paint or with the ripple technique. The lowest level also

contained a few sherds of a fine red ware decorated with paint in curvilinear patterns: this has similarities with both the Dimini wares of Late Neolithic Thessaly and with wares found in eastern Macedonia. Incised decoration was also used, again with curvilinear patterns similar to those normal further east. Other finds included stone bracelets and a clay object which could have served as a sling bullet.

Other excavated sites include Vardina (modern Limnotopos) beside the Axios,[15] Stivos in the Langadas basin,[16] and Kritsana in Chalkidike.[17] Nea Nikomedia was reoccupied at this period and protected by a ditch.

Several sites in the north-west, including Porodin and Crnobuki in the Crna valley[18] and Maliq in the Korytsa basin,[19] provide long sequences of occupation in the Late Neolithic period. At Maliq the first phase is represented by timber structures and by floors of logs with a clay covering as at Servia. The pottery of this period includes many examples of painted wares with curvilinear patterns of the same general type as those in Thessaly, but with a distinct local character. In a later phase there are traces of a palisade enclosing part of the site. Figurines continue in use while clay stamps and cylinders with incised decoration are common. Rectangular 'altars' with legs are a feature of this period. At Porodin, especially fine house models in clay help complete the picture of the architecture of the period.

In the east the Middle Neolithic sites of the Drama plain were still occupied and maintained their cultural links with the Hebros district.[20] Here the pottery was frequently elaborately decorated in black on a red ground, or with a graphite-based slip on a lustrous black surface (fig. 15). The control of kiln conditions and the high temperature required to fix this medium indicate that the potters of this area had attained skills similar to those necessary for metallurgy. At Sitagroi, indeed, a few copper pins were found, but also, and of greater significance, fragments of clay crucibles with traces of copper slags adhering to them. To the north in the closely related Gumelnitsa culture group, copper finds are more frequent. At the same time, nearer to the probable sources of copper ore in the Carpathian mountains, copper objects such as the heavy axes in the Karbuna hoard were common in the Cucuteni culture. In the Hebros valley, at least, the houses of this period were substantial two or three room dwellings with hearths and ovens whose position inside was probably dictated by climatic factors. Other features common to the whole region from eastern Macedonia to the Danube are rectangular altar stands and numerous elaborate figurines, both human and animal.

Eastern Macedonian black-on-red wares have been found as occasional imports in Thessaly, at Servia and in central Macedonia. Straw-impressed sherds, relatively common at Čakran in southern Albania,[21] are found in Late Neolithic levels at Servia and at Stavroupolis near Thessalonike. Obsidian from the island of Melos reached both Servia and Nea Nikomedeia, while even more striking evidence for the extent of trade in this period can be seen in the wide distribution in the eastern Balkans and Danube area of pieces and ornaments of *spondylus* shell. Technical analysis has demonstrated that this shell came from the Aegean, perhaps by means of trade routes through central or eastern Macedonia.

The subsistence economy of the Late Neolithic continued that established two thousand years earlier, though there was a tendency to make more use of cattle and pigs at the expense of goats or sheep. The preference for barley in place of wheat and the dependence on legumes may well indicate the different climate of Dikili Tas and Sitagroi. Soft fruit such as figs and grapes occur for the first time although these were probably still wild rather than cultivated. Millet appears for the first time at Olynthos in the vicinity of the kiln mentioned above.

Earlier chronological reconstructions have tended to place the Late Neolithic of northern Greece, and more especially of the Danube area, in the third millenium B.C., partly contemporary with the metal-using cultures of southern Greece and Anatolia. In this way it appears that metal technology spread from south to north. More recent indications, both from internal evidence such as pottery 'exports' and from radio-carbon techniques, indicate an earlier date for this phase, between 4000 and 3000 B.C. and, very probably, an independent origin of metallurgy in the lower Danube area.

THE BRONZE AGE

For the next two millenia Macedonia seems a cultural backwater in contrast to the rapidly developing civilization of Crete, the Cyclades or the Peloponnese. Even so there are many points of contact with those areas as well as with the Bronze Age groups of the Balkans. Trade, especially along the shores of the Aegean, was one of the most marked features of the new period. Climatically, most of Macedonia is unsuited to the cultivation of the olive — a vital food resource in the Bronze Age subsistence economy of the south — and this may be part of the reason why the level of life and society in this region did not, for a long time, advance beyond the level achieved in the Neolithic.

The nature of the change from the Neolithic to the Early Bronze Age is as little understood in Macedonia as it is in southern Greece and resulted in a broad cultural continuum stretching from Cernavoda and Ezero on the Black Sea littoral, to Troy and Therme in the north-east Aegean and to Thessaly and central Greece in the west. The pottery of all regions is characterized by a return to plain wares and relatively simple shapes while the rich decorative schemes of much of the Late Neolithic period have largely disappeared. Although copper alloys gradually came into use in the southern Aegean, in the north metals were as rare as in the final Neolithic, and in Bulgaria and Roumania there was a marked decline in the amount of copper in use.

Servia was reoccupied after a long interval by settlers

13. Clay head of a figurine of the Late Neolithic period from the settlement of Dikili Tas. Kavala, Archaeological Museum.

who defended their homesteads with a multiplicity of ditches. These features, as well as the simple repertoire of burnished wares, link them to Thessalian groups as at Argissa. In a following phase where traces of clay floors and timber-framed buildings were recognized, the pottery showed links with both Thessaly and central Macedonia. A well-fired black-burnished ware was used for shapes such as bowls with incurved rims, tall jugs like those from Orchomenos in central Greece, and features such as tubular and ledge lugs or the horizontal handles more typical of sites such as Kritsana in Chalkidike. Coarser ware was used for storage vessels and small vases. These were often decorated with the typical Macedonian and Thessalian technique of wiping the surface of the wet clay with a bunch of grasses or reeds. The same fabric was used for so-called 'baking-plates' with a low rim, spout and thin, slightly convex, base. The function of these is uncertain, but they have been linked with processes for making cheese or yogourt. Similar dishes occur, though more rarely, in many southern Greek contexts.

Other frequent finds which connect Macedonia and southern Greece are curious clay 'anchors'. Figurines dropped out of use. Flint and chert blades and polished stone axes remained the basic wood-cutting tools, despite the knowledge of the use of metal. Loom weights and spindle whorls indicate that spinning and weaving were still important crafts.

Similar material has been found elsewhere in south-west and central Macedonia where excavated sites include Demir Kapu[22] and Vardaroftsa (modern Axiochori) in the Axios valley.[23] Repeated rebuilding of timber-framed houses on these sites shows the long duration of the Early Bronze Age.

In the western part of Macedonia at Maliq much of the pottery resembles that from the earlier phase at Servia but also includes handled cups and mugs not found there. Similar mugs were common at Armenochori in the Crna valley[24] and imply that these two sites were more closely linked to northerly sites such as Bubanj and Velika

14. Middle Neolithic vase from Servia, c. 4500 B.C. The local potters made fine red-on-cream ware in a wide variety of shapes. The style of decoration is closely related to that of the Sesklo culture of Thessaly. Florina, Archaeological Museum.

15. Clay pot of the Late Neolithic period from Dikili Tas. The graphite-based slip applied before firing required exceptional skill to achieve success. Philippi, Archaeological Museum.

16. Anthropomorphic bust incised on a pot of the Late Neolithic period from Dikili Tas. The pottery of the period is characterized by curvilinear incised patterns sometimes emphasized by white inlaid paste. Philippi, Archaeological Museum.

17-18-19. Pottery from Assiros, Chauchitsa and Kalindria of the Late Bronze Age (1500-1050 B.C.). By this time shapes have become more elaborate while decoration frequently consists of incised meanders. Thessalonike, Archaeological Museum

Humska Čuka in the Morava valley near Niš. Clay anchors found at Maliq and Armenochori suggest that part, at least, of this phase of occupation was contemporary with Early Bronze Age sites in central Macedonia.

At Sitagroi, also, the two-handled mug is a common shape, though here the links were perhaps greater with Trojan pottery. In the upper level at this site were discovered the remains of an apsidal house *c.* 8 m. long. A partition across the curved end divided the main room from the kitchen area which contained two ovens, some storage bins and corn-grinding equipment. The walls themselves were of clay plastered over stakes or saplings. Similar houses are known at Balkan sites such as Ezero and Vučedol and are characteristic of the Early Helladic III and Middle Helladic periods in southern Greece.

The date of Macedonian Early Bronze Age finds in comparison with the Early Helladic sequence is in dispute. Imports of Peloponnesian pottery, including Early Helladic II 'sauceboats' have been found at Servia, while a fragment of Early Helladic III dark-on-light 'Hagia Marina' ware was noted in the upper Early Bronze Age levels at Kritsana. In contrast, 'sauceboat' fragments have recently been found in the final Neolithic levels at Pevkakia in Thessaly. It is therefore not clear whether a high date of *c.* 3000 B.C. should be accepted for the start of the Bronze Age in Macedonia, or a lower one, nearer to 2500 B.C.

The Middle Bronze Age is probably the most poorly represented in Macedonian prehistory, though it seems likely that the Middle and Late Bronze Age in this area were very similar. Only at Molyvopyrgos in Chalkidike does the import of Grey Minyan ware allow any levels to be assigned with certainty to this period and here the character of the local pottery is not very well defined.[25] Grooved decoration found at this site and at Hagios Mamas may derive from the type used on Grey Minyan,[26] while examples of neat incision at Saratse (modern Perivolaki) may belong to the same period.[27] Jugs with cutaway necks and bowls with wishbone handles probably came into fashion at the beginning of this phase. At Maliq wishbone-handled bowls were used alongside the two-handled mugs of the Early Bronze Age and may indicate that here and at Armenochori Early Bronze Age forms continued in use.

In the Late Bronze Age there is the same dearth of information for much of Macedonia, with the exception of the region between the Axios and the Strymon including Chalkidike. Here settlement was surprisingly dense and the steep-sided mounds, formed chiefly by accumulation of building debris during this period, are often no more than five kilometres apart.[28] Several of these have been excavated and permit a fairly accurate picture of the settlement plan, construction techniques, artifacts and subsistence economy to be created.

Recent excavation at Assiros in the Langadas basin has shown the inhabitants to have been conservative both in the construction of their buildings and in the pottery they used.[29] The earliest levels at this site, perhaps to be dated soon after 2000 B.C., in the Middle Bronze Age period,

17

18

19

were protected by a substantial wall of packed clay which was renewed at intervals as the height of the mound grew. The structures on the summit of the mound were supported by a massive terrace bank of mud-brick and clay which was also continually raised. The buildings themselves had a timber frame to support the roof and walls of regular mud bricks (fig. 20). Interiors were kept clean and debris from the settlement accumulated in yard areas. Storage jars were found in many rooms and the overall character of the settlement seems to be complex: no separate houses have yet been identified. It is possible that these mounds formed the focal point of a more scattered community, the seat of a petty chieftain and his retinue, and the defended point to which the settlers could retreat in times of difficulty.

The normal pottery of these phases is a fine brown-burnished ware with the typical cut-away neck jugs and wishbone-handled bowls or the tall-necked storage jar with four vertical handles. Decorated ware at this site, as at most of the sites to the east of the Axios, is achieved by roughly incising spiral meander patterns on the surface of the vase which formed the keying for a chalky paste applied after firing to give the effect of solid bands of white, red or pinkish colour. This technique was used principally on globular jars with two vertical handles and both shape and decoration have close parallels in southern Bulgaria and in the Danube valley (figs. 17,18). A further link with the Danube area can be seen in cooking pots combining a perforated stand with a globular jar.

Another type of fine ware is decorated with a purple-red paint with simple geometric patterns, such as triangles and zigzags. This is most common in the Axios valley at Vardaroftsa, Kilindir (modern Kalindria[30]) and Chauchitsa,[31] and at sites further to the west (fig. 19). Its origins are obscure, but it could relate to earlier Middle Helladic matt-painted pottery and it is almost certainly the ancestor of the painted wares which are widespread in western Macedonia in the Early Iron Age.

Imported Mycenaean pottery was introduced to many coastal settlements from 1350 B.C. onwards during the Late Helladic III A and B periods, and a limited number of vases reached inland sites, particularly along the Axios. Soon after, local imitations came into use, which were wheel-made unlike the local burnished wares. Spectrographic comparison of these imitations with local fabrics has confirmed their Macedonian origin. The existence of two very different fabrics at the same time suggests that different workshops were engaged in producing each type. The decoration of the Mycenaean imitations follows that of the imported pieces but is generally restricted to simple bands and wavy lines.

Metal objects are still rare, but include curved bronze knives, nearer to Danubian than Mycenaean types, pins and simple beads. The regular use of metal, however, is demonstrated by the marks of butchers' knives on animal bones and by the presence of small whetstones, often designed to be worn as pendants or perhaps at the belt. At Assiros the latest Bronze Age levels included fragments of stone moulds for casting chisels, awls and perhaps a spear-head. Stone axes and chert sickle-inserts remained the commonest tools for agricultural purposes. Bone was widely used for awls and needles, but pins with elaborate heads and ornamental objects were also made from this material. Mycenaean imports other than pottery are rare in the settlements, though a marble sword pommel of southern type was found at Assiros.

Subsistence was still based on a mixed farming economy though millet was now an important element in the diet at Kastanas[32] and at Assiros, the two sites where detailed information is becoming available. Grape pips are common suggesting widespread viticulture and possibly the knowledge of wine. Even though Assiros is some twenty-five km. from the sea, marine molluscs were also a popular food.

At Maliq occupation seems to have continued throughout the Bronze Age, while the rest of Macedonia provides a little information from burials. In the south-west, tombs near Kozani contained late Mycenaean pottery,[33] while Mycenaean swords and a spearhead have been found near Grevena.[34] Late in the Mycenaean period, tumulus burial, extensively practised in Albania since the end of the Middle Bronze Age, reached the Korytsa basin where early examples of matt-painted decoration on pottery were found at Barc in association with a Mycenaean stirrup-jar.[35]

These are isolated examples, however, and in the absence of better evidence for burial practices in the Bronze Age it is difficult to explain the changes which resulted in the Early Iron Age, best represented in such cemeteries as Hagios Panteleimon (Pateli),[36] or Vergina in western Macedonia,[37] or in such central Macedonian settlements as Assiros, Kastanas, Saratse or Vardaroftsa where occupation continued. Although destruction levels have been noted at Vardaroftsa and Assiros, these can not be placed in a single horizon at the end of the Bronze Age, and similar destructions, probably as a result of domestic accidents, occur in earlier levels at the same sites.

THE EARLY IRON AGE

The relationship between the artifacts of archaeological study and the identity of their users is always a vexed question and it is no easier in Macedonia than it is in southern Greece to establish whether any major change of population took place at this time. Although it has frequently been asserted that invasion of Macedonia by peoples from the north took place at the end of the Bronze Age, there are many clear elements of continuity with that period. Small groups may have arrived bringing the distinctive innovations which link the Iron Age culture of Macedonia to the broader spectrum of cultural groups spread across southeast Europe at this time, from the Axios to the Troad and north to the Danube and beyond. There is no identical cultural assemblage further to the north from which alone that of Macedonia could have derived and the individual elements of comparison are found separately over a wide area rather than together. The links between the inhabitants of Macedonia and their neighbours to the north and east were as strong but no stronger in the Iron Age than they had been in the Bronze Age, while the individuality of the region was strongly marked.

Many of the mound settlements continued to be occupied, though the habitable area on the summit was becoming more and more restricted. The result was that buildings spread for the first time around the base of the mound, as at Vardaroftsa, or sites were abandoned quite soon in favour of more spacious locations, as at Assiros. After a while these Iron Age sites took on the form of wide plateaux with steep edges suggesting that a defensive perimeter was maintained. This form was characteristic of Macedonian settlements for the next five hundred years.

At Assiros and Kastanas the earliest Iron Age levels had rather flimsy buildings with stone footings or with timber uprights. Soon after, mud-brick returned as the normal walling material, though the bricks are narrower and shorter than those used in the Bronze Age. At Assiros, a series of five adjacent rooms of similar size, 7×5 m., may have been individual dwellings.

The pottery shows both the strongest contact with Bronze Age forms and the clearest examples of innovation. Fabric and basic shapes such as cut-away neck jugs, wishbone-handle bowls and jars with knobbed handles all continue the earlier tradition. Channelled and grooved decoration, which entirely replace the earlier incised and paste-filled styles, is new and links Macedonian pottery with developments further north and east. Twisted handles, 'turban' rims and the increasing angularity of details such as necks and handles are the marks of this period. At Kastanas new discoveries show clearly that these innovations occurred after the introduction of the first early Proto-Geometric imports from southern Greece and demonstrate that the Macedonian Iron Age commenced no earlier than that in the south. Its start should probably be set between 1050 and 1000 B.C. Wheel-made pottery with simple decoration deriving from Mycenaean types may have persisted in the Axios valley until the regular adoption of Proto-Geometric forms at a late date, *c.* 900 B.C., when the style was already passing out of fashion in the south.

This second phase is characterized by increasing angularity and exaggeration of shapes and details and by the preference for incised forms of decoration. This change in preference can also be seen in Bulgaria and Roumania at

20. Buildings from the settlement of Assiros in the Langada basin (phase 7). Small rectangular rooms (c. 4×2 m.) are *separated by a street from the yard areas of buildings beyond. c. 1200 B.C.*

20

the same period. Proto-Geometric imports and especially local imitations were common. A local wheel-made grey ware appears at this time. Its shapes are angular and it is decorated with regular horizontal grooves. With the passage of time, hand-made wares became rarer while wheel-made forms, particularly those with simple linear decoration in purplish paint, predominated. This decoration is especially common at Olynthos and other sites on the coast of Chalkidike. At Nea Anchialos this stage is dated to the Late Geometric period by occasional imports,[38] but in general the ceramic tradition remained isolated from that of southern Greece. Exaggerated local forms, such as the knobbed handles from the 'Pre-Persian' levels at Olynthos, persisted well into the seventh century, even while Greek colonies were being established from about 730 B.C. onwards on the coasts of Macedonia.

Settlements outside the area of central Macedonia are not well known and the majority of the evidence for these areas derives from burials and cemeteries. These show many varieties of grave type, although inhumation is practised almost without exception. In the large cemetery of Vergina, close to the point where the Haliakmon river emerges from a deep gorge and reaches the coastal plain, several hundred small tumuli have been recorded and over a hundred of these have been excavated. These take the form of low mounds, generally between 15 and 20 m. in diameter, covering a dozen or so irregularly placed graves. The burials themselves were in simple earth graves, in rectangular stone-lined graves or in pithoi. The whole was sometimes encircled by a rough stone wall and then covered over with earth. In some cases, the tumulus was used for a long period and graves were cut through the existing mound to reach the original surface, and often disturbed earlier burials. The majority were provided with offerings of pottery, weapons and jewellery.

The use of tumuli for burial at that time was usual in southern Albania and extended to the Crna valley where at Visoji a tumulus covered regularly spaced slab-lined graves.[39] At Saraj, in the same district, cist and boulder graves were grouped together in a small cemetery.[40] Not far to the south at Pateli (modern Hagios Panteleimon) two or three separate cemetery areas contained large numbers of pit and cist burials as well as pithoi, but no tumuli were reported. In one case graves were enclosed within a circular perimeter some 22 m. across. Cist and pit graves are also found isolated or in small groups near Prilep,[41] Gevgelija, Demir Kapu, Štip,[42] and Chauchitsa in the north and at Kozani and Aiane in the south,[43] to name but a few examples. A cemetery has also been found at Kentria on Thasos.[44]

21-22. From the cemetery of the tumuli at Vergina, rich in iron weapons and bronze ornaments, come less common objects such as this diadem with its punched decoration (21), or the triple double axe (22). Both probably belonged to the burials of chief-

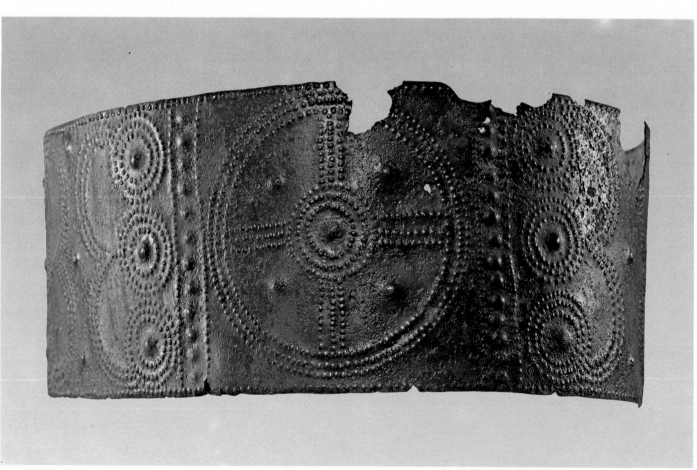

The dating of individual graves or grave groups at these sites is often difficult since each area has a local style of pottery which does not change greatly during the life of the cemetery. Wide bowls with discs on the handles are characteristic of Vergina, while cut-away neck jugs were still popular in central and northern Macedonia. Matt-painted decoration, particularly on *kantharoi* and jars with tall necks, is very common at Pateli and Aiane, in south-east Albania and indeed the region to the west as at Vitsa in Epirus. Incised decoration is more popular in the Axios valley and to the east, while at Vergina local imitations of Proto-geometric occur frequently, especially *skyphoi* with compass-drawn circles and semicircles.

A few graves may date to the transition from the Bronze Age, as at Prilep where a bronze sword with iron rivets was found, while at Vergina stray finds, such as a similar sword and small vessels imitating Mycenaean prototypes, indicate early graves which were later disturbed. The majority of the burials, even at Vergina, cannot be dated earlier than *c.* 900 B.C.

Ornaments are, relatively, far more common in Macedonian graves of this period than in southern Greece and often enable rough dates to be established by comparison with similar finds in southern contexts. Early forms include long pins with a swelling near the head and arched fibulae

tains of families, perhaps ancestors of Philip II and Alexander the Great. c. 900 B.C. Thessalonike, Archaeological Museum.

22

with twisted bows. Neck rings of twisted bronze with rolled ends, fibulae with large dot-ornamented catch-plates, fibulae with knobs on the bow, 'spectacle' fibulae, spiral arm bands of sheet or wire, rings with spiral terminals, and *phalerae* (used here as belt ornaments) all belong to a later phase, at Vergina and elsewhere. Further developments include ring and wheel pendants, heavy bracelets, diadems of sheet metal and pins with conical heads, among many other forms (figs. 21,22).

By the middle of the eighth century more advanced bronze-casting techniques permitted the production of a wide variety of pendants and other ornaments. Although this period is not well represented at Vergina, many examples are found at Chauchitsa and Pateli as well as at the new cemeteries connected with Greek settlers at Poteidaia,[45] Olynthos and Amphipolis.[46] The same basic forms and elaborations of these, such as solid or openwork globes, miniature cut-away neck jugs and pyxides, sticks with knobs sometimes with a monkey-like figure on top, birds, horses, cylindrical and cruciform beads, continued in use in Macedonia until the early part of the sixth century. These objects are typically Macedonian, but examples can be found in the sanctuary sites of southern Greece, and even in Greek settlements in southern Italy (figs. 23-27). In the other direction, many Macedonian forms as well as local variants are to be found in Hallstatt C contexts as far away as the Illyrian coast, northern Yugoslavia and the Carpathians. The distribution of all these objects amply demonstrates the close relationship between Macedonia, southern Greece and the whole of south-east Europe, in the period immediately before and after the Greek colonization movement. Trade may well have attracted Greeks to Macedonia regularly before they settled permanently, but the settlements themselves help to intensify this trade and exchange.

Although traces of iron slag have been reported from Late Bronze Age levels at Vardaroftsa, in general the use of iron came later to Macedonia than to southern Greece. Bronze was still available and iron was rarely used for ornaments. Iron weapons from Vergina are probably no older than the beginning of the ninth century B.C. These include swords derived from the European type introduced to the Mycenaean world in the twelfth century, spearheads with flat or ribbed blades, and long single-edged weapons with a slight curve. These 'cutlasses' have been found at Vergina, Hagios Panteleimon (Pateli) and Vitsa in Epirus but do not appear to be used further south. Small curved knives of iron are also common.

During the six millenia since settled communities of farmers first appeared in Macedonia, a wide variety of material remains represents the differing cultures of different periods and regions. Some elements demonstrate continuity of culture from earlier periods and suggest that part, at least, of the population could trace its ancestry to indigenous stock. Others are new and cannot yet be adequately explained. As Professor Sakellariou will show in the following chapter, Macedonia had its share of legendary and traditional accounts of early peoples and their

23. Macedonian bronze pendant of the type known as 'bird in a cage'. Athens, Benaki Museum.

movements from place to place. The marked changes which occur at the end of the Neolithic and at the end of the Bronze Age may reflect some of these movements. Scholars such as N.G.L. Hammond go further and equate every change with the influx of new tribes from different directions. Only time and further research will provide sufficient information to allow the archaeological and historical sources to be correlated with complete confidence. At present this early part of the rich history of Macedonia permits us an enigmatic, though fascinating, picture of human development and gives some idea of the different strands of culture which may have combined to produce Macedonian civilization.

THE INHABITANTS

BEFORE THE ARRIVAL OF THE PROTO-GREEKS

For certain areas of the Greek mainland and many of the islands the names of some fifteen pre-Greek peoples are preserved in ancient traditions, together with a number of other references; information of this quantity or importance is wanting in the case of the inhabitants of Macedonia, however, not only for the period prior to the advent of the Proto-Greeks, but even before the end of the Bronze Age. This deficiency can be remedied to some extent by recourse to indirect evidence.

Firstly, it is a safe assumption that during the Stone and Bronze Ages, Macedonia was not settled by people very different from the population of southern Greece and the rest of the Balkan peninsula (or of Asia Minor, Italy and the Iberian peninsula). These regions are known to have been inhabited at an early date by pre-Indo-European (or Mediterranean) peoples and subsequently by Indo-Europeans. South of Olympos, the first Indo-Europeans made their appearance towards the end of the Neolithic and the beginning of the Chalcolithic periods (about 3000 B.C.)[1].

Archaeological evidence may be used to add details to this broad picture; there is, however, no agreement amongst the experts as to its interpretation.[2]

In southern Greece, the traditions concerning the pre-Greek Pelasgians coincide to a remarkable degree with certain innovations in the pottery that had made their appearance slightly earlier in western Macedonia, central Macedonia, Chalkidike, eastern Macedonia and further to the east and north.[3] This suggests that Macedonia was inhabited by Pelasgians at the end of the Neolithic period.[4] The Pelasgians were one of the pre-Greek Indo-European peoples,[5] as were the Dryopes,[6] a section of whom remained in the valley of the Erigon (Crna) and survived into the historical period, when they were known by the name Derriopes, or Deuriopes or Douriopes: *Dry-, Derr-, Deur-* and *Dour-* are all the evolved form or rendering of the same root, the original meaning of which was 'tree' and which later came to mean oak tree.[7]

The features of the 'Tumulus Culture' that appeared in southern Macedonia towards the end of the Neolithic period and somewhat later in the Chalkidike and eastern Macedonia, suggest the arrival of a number of Indo-European groups that cannot be identified.[8]

THE PROTO-GREEKS IN MACEDONIA (2300/2200-1900 B.C.)

The language and religion of the ancient Greeks contain features derived from a variety of different sources. They are predominantly Indo-European, but the non - Indo-European, or 'Mediterranean' features are by no means insignificant. The Indo-European elements may in turn be divided into a main and a secondary group; the latter are connected with a variety of Indo-European peoples that had been absorbed by the dominant group, which had also absorbed the remnants of 'Mediterranean' peoples. The

24
25

26

27

24-27. Macedonian jewellery from graves of the 8th-7th centuries B.C. Pendants and other bronze items are frequently found in tombs after 750. The presence of identical objects in many shrines of southern Greece, central Europe, southern Italy and Sicily reveals the wide-ranging contacts established by Macedonians during the period of Greek expansion. Athens, Benaki Museum; Kilkis, Archaeological Museum.

main ancestors of the ancient Greeks are usually also described as Greeks. This term, however, obscures the fact that the ancient Greeks also had other forebears, both Indo-European and 'Mediterranean'. In order to distinguish the historical Greeks from the main group of their prehistoric ancestors, the term Proto-Greeks has recently come to be applied to the latter.[9]

Study of the interrelations between the various Indo-European languages has shown that the Proto-Greek tongue had its closest and longest contact with Proto-Aryan (the forerunner of Indian and Iranian languages); that these two languages took shape in the centre of the area occupied by the Indo-European peoples (from the Ukraine to east of the Caspian); and that they separated out after the dispersal of the Indo-European peoples surrounding the Proto-Greeks and Proto-Aryans.[10] A variety of archaeological evidence has demonstrated that the fragmentation of the main mass of the Indo-Europeans was already completed by the beginning of the fourth phase of the 'Tumulus Culture' of the Eurasian steppes (c. 2500 B.C.). Some features of this culture make their appearance on the Greek mainland and on adjacent islands, under conditions that suggest they were brought by immigrants, at the beginning of Early Helladic III (c. 2100 B.C.), though the main immigration dates to the beginning of the Middle Helladic period (1900 B.C.).[11] From that time to the end of the Late Helladic period (c. 1125 B.C.) there is no trace of any migration to Greece. These considerations, combined with the circumstance that the Greek mainland and adjacent islands were undoubtedly occupied by Greeks during the Late Helladic period, clearly indicate that the immigrants of Early Helladic III and the Middle Helladic period were Proto-Greeks.[12]

The Proto-Greek settlements on the mainland during the Early Helladic period were few in number and were either on coastal sites or a short distance inland. It seems, therefore, that their founders arrived by sea, setting out either from Chalkidike or from the coast of eastern Macedonia. By contrast, the Proto-Greek settlements of the Middle Helladic period were much greater in number and extended over the area from north-east Thessaly to the southern Peloponnese. This suggests that the immigrants of the second wave were significantly more numerous and travelled overland. Their point of departure may be located in north-east Thessaly and western Macedonia.[13] Other evidence indicates that between 2100 (and possibly as early as 2300) and 1900 B.C. the main body of the Proto-Greeks was concentrated in these two areas, and also further west.[14]

FROM THE DEPARTURE OF THE PROTO-AIOLIANS AND PROTO-ARKADIANS TO THE MIGRATIONS AT THE END OF THE BRONZE AGE (1900-1200/1100 B.C.)

The Proto-Greeks who migrated from Macedonia to the south at the beginning of the Middle Helladic period (1900 B.C.) belonged for the most part to the Proto-Arkadian and Proto-Aiolian groups.[15] If these migrations were not caused by the pressure of hostile peoples but were motivated by a search for new *lebensraum,* then a section

of these Proto-Greek peoples will have remained in Macedonia. Even so, the result will have been to dilute the Proto-Greek population in the area in such a way as to invite, or at least to permit, other peoples to move into it. The following facts are clear from the archaeological record: a people belonging to the Budanj-Hum II culture came down from the Morava valley to Pelagonia: a number of groups of an inferior culture came from the east and penetrated into Pieria, Eordaia, Lynkestis and Pelagonia. Cultural changes can also be detected at Axiochori (Vardaroftsa) in central Macedonia. Saratse (Perivolaki) and Kilindir, (Kalindria) in this same area, were destroyed, presumably by invaders.[16] The Greek tribes who inhabited the Pindos, especially the Boiotoi (Boiotians and the Makednoi (see below), did not move from their homes.

The archaeological evidence for migrations to and from Macedonia after 1900 B.C. dates from the end of the Bronze Age and the beginning of the Iron Age, or about 1200-1100 B.C. in absolute dates. It follows that during the intervening period there were no changes of population in Macedonia significant enough to leave any archaeological traces. This conclusion leads to a second: that, unless there is specific evidence to the contrary, the peoples that will be discussed below must have established themselves in Macedonia either before 1900 B.C. or after 1200 B.C.

As we descend the chronological scale, our knowledge of the inhabitants of Macedonia is enriched from other sources. Many of the peoples on the archaeological horizon about 1200 B.C. survived into later periods and a number of observations or traditions about them were recorded, some of which have survived to the present day.

A number of other traditions, though fewer in number and less convincing, refer also to tribes that either vanished or departed from Macedonia at an earlier date, during the course of the first centuries of the first millennium B.C. A critical analysis of this evidence makes it possible to draw a number of conclusions that are probably close enough to the historical reality. Some of these ancient traditions are in any event verified by other evidence drawn from linguistics, mythology and archaeology.

The earliest surviving memory of the Macedonians locates them in the Pindos. Herodotos refers to it twice: on the first occasion he informs us that the Dorians once dwelt about Pindos and were then called Makednoi;[17] on the second he describes the Lacedaemonians, the Corinthians, the Sikyonians, the Epidaurians and the Troizenians as of Dorian and Makednian stock, and traces their early origins to the Pindos.[18] Other authors knew that the Dorians originally came from the Pindos, and specifically from that part of it known in antiquity as Lakmos (its modern name in the vernacular is Zygos). These authors refer neither to the Makednoi nor to the Makedones, but their statements accord perfectly with the tradition preserved by Herodotos. However, critical analysis of the sources, together with a variety of other evidence, leads to a slight correction of the tradition in the form in which it is preserved: the Dorian peoples seem to have been formed about the middle of the thirteenth century B.C. in central Greece from a number of different tribes, one of which was a section of the Makednoi or Makedones that had come from Lakmos at least as early as 1400 B.C. The ancestors of the Makednoi had entered the wider area of Macedonia and Epirus at an earlier date, about 2100 B.C., along with other Proto-Greek tribes.[19] The surviving tradition appears to be mistaken on a second point, too: the home of the Makednoi could not have been limited to Lakmos; they will undoubtedly also have occupied territory lying at a lower altitude. Lakmos, like the entire Pindos range, is only suitable for the summer grazing of sheep and goats and as a source of wood. From October to April shepherds are obliged to graze their flocks in the plains. It is a reasonable hypothesis that the Makednoi had winter grazing grounds not only in Epirus, but also in south-west Macedonia since it was from here that they later expanded to the east and north. They very probably succeeded in occupying all the territory abandoned by the Proto-Arkadians when they migrated to the Peloponnese about 1900 B.C. (see page 46). One branch of the Makednoi, known later by the name Magnetes (see page 47), spread into Pieria, from where they migrated to the region around Ossa and Pelion during the century of the great population movements between 1200 and 1100 B.C. To the north of the Makednoi lived the Boiotoi. The name points to Mt. Boion in the northern Pindos, but this tribe too will have also occupied some territory in the plains. Towards the end of the Bronze Age the Boiotoi migrated to south-west Thessaly, from where they moved shortly afterwards to the land that was named after them.

The vacuum created by the departure of the Boiotoi facilitated the expansion of Greek tribes from Epirus into those areas of western Macedonia known in the first millennium B.C. as Orestis, Lynkestis and Pelagonia.[20] These tribes were later absorbed by the Makedones (see page 47). The remaining areas of Macedonia were occupied towards the end of the Bronze Age by the Paiones, the Bottiaioi, the Eordoi, the Almopes, the Derriopes or Deuriopes and the Pelagones. Towards the end of the period, and a little later, Macedonia was penetrated by Phryges, Mygdones, Thrakes and Pelasgoi, who destroyed, displaced or subjugated the Paiones. During the following centuries all the peoples mentioned above suffered a similar fate as a result of the expansion of the Makedones from the sites they had originally occupied to the south-western extremity of Macedonia, to the east, and to the north.

The Derriopes, or Deuriopes, and the Pelagones continued to dwell in the valley of the Erigon throughout the whole of the Bronze Age and afterwards, until they were absorbed by the Macedonians. The Eordoi entered Macedonia during the Bronze Age. The area that became known as Eordaia, north-west of Mt. Bermion, perhaps corresponds to that occupied by this people at the time they were conquered by the Macedonians. Traces of the extent to which they had expanded earlier are preserved in the place-name Ordaia, near Naousa, and the name of the river Eordaikos south and south-west of Prespa.[21] When the Makedones took Eordaia, some of the Eordoi fled to Physka in Mygdonia,[22] part of which was called Eordaia as a result.[23] The Almopes dwelt to the north of the Eordoi. The Bottiaioi, who were located at Pella and along the coast between the Haliakmon and the Echedoros (Gallikos), are described as colonists from Crete.[24] This tradition is confirmed by the existence of Cretan toponyms in the area[25] and also by the survival of representations of the double axe, in the form of bronze sacred emblems, at various sites in Macedonia and neighbouring territories; the double axe will have been disseminated from Bottia by the movements of semi-nomadic shepherds.[26] It has been suggested that the Cretans who settled in the inner bays of the Thermaic Gulf abandoned their homes about 1400 B.C. when Crete was captured by the Achaians.[27] The Bottiaioi who were displaced by the Macedonians fled to Chalkidike, more specifically to that section of it that was called Bottike after them.

Homeric geography locates the homeland of the Paiones at Amydon, near the east bank of the Axios, and states that their eastern neighbours were the Kikones, whose territory seems to have extended from the Nestos to the Hebros.[28] According to traditions preserved in later writers, however, the Paiones once also extended to the west of the Axios, as far as Emathia, Almopia, Pelagonia, Eordaia and Pieria. These traditions cannot refer to a period later than the end of the Bronze Age, for at that time Mygdonia, Emathia and Pieria were conquered by Phrygian and Thracian tribes (see below). It is unlikely, however, that they go back to a period before the establishment of the Pelagones, Almopes and Eordoi in the regions that bear the names of these peoples.

On the other hand, we have seen that on the eve of their subjugation by the Macedonians, the Pelagones, the Almopes and the Eordoi were distinct peoples. The explanation must be either that the Paiones conquered Almopia, Pelagonia and Eordaia without extirpating the local population; or that these peoples were kinsfolk of the Paiones and were covered by the same name.[29]

About 1200 B.C. Mygdonia, Emathia and Pieria were conquered by Thracians, Pelasgians and Phrygians. The Thracians and the Pelasgians came from the east. In fact, according to the evidence of the Iliad, the Thracians occupied an area in eastern Thrace before their expansion (the area west of the Hebros was the territory of the Kikones, whom Homer distinguishes from the Thracians), while the Pelasgians dwelt to the north of the Thracians.[30] Tradition and survivals of names demonstrate that bands of Thracians and Pelasgians penetrated much further south than Macedonia to the eastern mainland and the eastern Peloponnese. The evidence of tradition, myths and archaeology points to the conclusion that Thracians settled in Pieria.[31] The name 'Pieria' however, is Greek, demonstrating that the area was earlier inhabited by Greeks, who were probably none other than the Magnetes, for it is precisely in Pieria that the latter are located by Hesiod. The Thracians of Pieria were displaced by the Macedonians, at which time they settled east of the Strymon.

The Phrygians entered Macedonia from the north. Hammond attributes the dissemination of the Lausitz culture southwards to them.[32] There was an ancient tradition preserving the memory that Macedonia had been inhabited by Phrygians.[33] The plain to the east of Bermion was called the 'gardens of Midas':[34] Midas was, of course, the king of Phrygia in Asia Minor. Moreover, the name Edessa is connected with the Phrygian word *vedu,* which means water. At the beginning of the fifth century, the inhabitants of Mygdonia were still called Brygoi,[35] i.e. Phrygians (as we shall see below, page 57, the substitution of 'b' for 'ph' is a phenomenon attested in Macedonia). The name *Mygdones* (from which is derived the geographical term *Mygdonia*) is also Phrygian, however: in the Iliad, Mygdon is the name of a king of the Phrygians to the east of Troy.[36] The region of Phrygia called Mygdonia (Stephanos of Byzantium, s.v. *Mygdonia*) almost certainly had received its name from Mygdonian immigrants. Further, the Macedonian proper names Halys and Marsyas seem to be survivals from the Phrygian population of Macedonia.[37] Brygoi, or Briges, are also attested in traditions connected with Epirus and the area around Dyrrachion.[38]

Krestonia, to the north of Mygdonia, was inhabited in the fifth century B.C. by Pelasgians.[39] Central and eastern Macedonia have yielded archaeological remains dating from the end of the Neolithic period that can be attributed to the Pelasgians, and the hypothesis therefore suggests itself that the Pelasgians dwelt here without disturbance from that time until the fifth century. When we reflect, however, that the intervening centuries saw many population movements, and in particular that about 1200 B.C. Pelasgians came to Greece from the eastern Balkans, it seems not impossible that the Pelasgians of Krestonia in the fifth century were descended from a group who settled there at the end of the Bronze Age.[40] In the fifth century B.C., a number of pre-Greek tribes also survived on the Athos peninsula.[41]

The ancient Greeks knew the rest of the inhabitants of Chalkidike, central and eastern Macedonia with whom they came into contact by a variety of names, such as Sithonoi, Bisaltai, Edonoi, Saioi, Sinties and Odomantes; they also used the general designation Thracians *(Thrakes),* thereby identifying them with the peoples who dwelt to the east and north of the Nestos. Until very recently, modern scholarship followed the ancient Greek example, without concerning itself in detail with the matter; it was then noted, however, that there are significant differences between the non-Greek names of central and eastern Macedonia and typically Thracian names, and that the former resemble names that occur to the north of Macedonia (in Paionia and Dardania); the thesis was thus propounded that the Bisaltai, the Edonoi and other tribes of central and eastern Macedonia should no longer be considered Thracian.[42] This new approach to the question of the nationality of the tribes mentioned above is interesting.

The Bisaltai lived to the west of the Strymon, and the Edonoi, or Edones, to the east of this river. Strabo was of the opinion that the Sithonoi, who inhabited Chalkidike, and the Mygdones, discussed above, were sub-groups of the Edonoi.[43] As we have seen, however, the Mygdones were connected with the Phrygians: either Strabo is reflecting some confusion in his sources, therefore, or the Edonoi were a branch of the Phrygians that included the Sithonoi and the Mygdones. The Mygdones, the Pelasgians of Krestonia, the Bisaltai, the Edonoi, the Saioi, the Sinties

and the Odomantes expanded to territories that had earlier been occupied by the Paionians (see page 47). These last were confined to a region outside the final boundaries of Macedonia.

THE NATIONALITY OF THE MACEDONIANS

There has been much discussion in the nineteenth and twentieth centuries of the nationality of the Macedonians. The views expressed are basically three: the first recognizes the Macedonians as Greeks; the second denies that they were Greeks; and the third adopts an intermediate position. The same views have been propounded with reference to a more specific subject: the Macedonian tongue. This depends upon the more general question, however. The first view has met with the support or the acceptance of the majority of historians and philologists.[44] Those who differ from them and are opposed to the idea that the Macedonians and their tongue were Greek in origin are not agreed as to who the Macedonians were or what language they spoke. Some are of the opinion that the Macedonians were Illyrians and Macedonian an Illyrian dialect;[45] others regard them as Thracians;[46] others see them as a distinct people, with a separate language,[47] and lastly others have declined to express any definite opinion.[48] The third view also has its variations. Some, for example, have asserted that the Macedonians separated from the Greeks at a very early point in time,[49] while others suggest that the Macedonians were a product of intercourse between Greeks and non-Greeks.[50] Reference should also be made at this point to those who feel that the available evidence does not permit the drawing of conclusions as to the nationality of the Macedonians or the nature of their speech.[51]

These differences of opinion are due (1) to some extent to the nature of the evidence and (2) to non-academic reasons. The truth is:

1) The information handed down from antiquity concerning the nationality of the Macedonians is contradictory, and very few examples of their language remain; 2) the conclusions reached have frequently been influenced by the views of various modern powers (and not only Balkan states) on Macedonia.

The arguments used by all sides have remained within the pages of monographs or articles in academic journals. Outside this context, the various views have been presented only in a very brief and dogmatic fashion (frequently in a single phrase). In the belief that the readers to whom this volume is addressed will wish to acquire a rounded, comprehensive picture of the issues involved in the question of the nationality of the Macedonians, I shall attempt to set the evidence before them as briefly as is consistent with completeness, to enable them to check the conclusions I draw from it.

I ANCIENT TRADITIONS, TESTIMONIA AND OPINIONS

Many passages in ancient authors record echoes of the traditions, testimonia and opinions regarding the nationality of the Macedonians, or, more narrowly, of the

Macedonian royal family. We shall first examine what these passages have to say. After completing this review, we shall proceed to an assessment of their content and arrive at definitive conclusions derived from this kind of evidence.

a) Concerning the Macedonian people

It is convenient to refer separately to the passages (1) that support the idea that the Macedonians were Greeks; (2) that are opposed to this idea; and (3) that can be used to argue either case, or that are inconclusive. We shall also (4) deal with the hypotheses put forward by modern historians on the view held by Philip and Alexander as to the nationality of their subjects.

1) Reference has been made above (see page 46) to an ancient tradition, according to which the Dorians were descended from a section of the Makednoi or Makedones. This tradition came down to Herodotos either through information he himself gathered in some Doric city,[52] or through a very ancient epic poem, the *Aigimios*.[53] The surviving fragments of this poem, together with other sources, reveal more precisely that the Dorians were formed by the union of some Macedonians with other tribes. The Dorians were pure Greeks. Various attempts to derive one section of them from Illyrian origins have been unsuccessful. In any case, these attempts were concerned with the Doric tribe the Hylleis, which was certainly not identical with the Makednoi.[54] The fact that the Dorians were Greek naturally presupposes that the tribes of which they were composed were also Greek, and these include the Makednoi or Makedones, at a date earlier than the fourteenth century (see page 46).

A Persian inscription dating from 513 B.C. records the European peoples who were at that date subject to the Great King. One of these is described as Yauna Takabara — 'Ionians whose head-dress is like a shield'. The Persians, like the other eastern peoples of antiquity, are known to have applied the term 'Ionians' to all the Greeks; on the other hand the head-dress resembling a shield has been rightly recognized as that depicted on Macedonian coins. The people called by the Persians 'Greeks whose head-dress is like a shield' are therefore identified with the Macedonians. The identification is supported by the fact that, in another Persian inscription, of 479 or 478, also listing the peoples of Europe subject to the Great King, this name is missing; at this date, it is known that the Macedonians were fighting the Persians. This Persian name for the Macedonians is the earliest piece of direct evidence available so far for the nationality of the Macedonians.[55]

In a fragment of Hellanikos (fifth century B.C.), Makedon, the mythical founder of the Macedonians, appears as the son of Aiolos.[56] This genealogical relationship reflects the idea that the Macedonians were a section of the Aiolians, a sub-division of the Greek race.

After the battle of Issos, Alexander the Great sent a letter to Darius that began as follows: 'Your ancestors came to Macedonia and the rest of Greece and did us much harm though we had done them no prior injury; I have been appointed commander-in-chief of the Greeks and in-

vaded Asia in the desire to take vengeance on Persia for your aggressions.'[57] From this extract it emerges clearly that Alexander regarded Macedonia as a Greek country, identified the sufferings of Macedonia at the hands of the Persians with the destruction they had wrought in southern Greece, and represented himself as the avenger of all these wrongs.

The formulation 'Macedonia and the rest of Greece' also occurs in the treaty of alliance between Philip V of Macedonia and Hannibal.[58] In the same text the phrase 'the Macedonians and the rest of the Greeks' occurs twice. The ambassador of this same king, in his address to the Aitolians in 200 B.C., ranged the Macedonians with the Greeks and not with the 'foreigners' (ἀλλοεθνεῖς) and 'barbarians' (βάρβαροι).[59]

Other passages demonstrate that non-Macedonian Greeks also thought of the Macedonians as their kindred, and of Macedonia as a Greek country. In 217 B.C. Agelaos of Naupaktos, speaking to a gathering at which Philip V and representatives of his allies were present, prayed that internecine wars between the Greeks would cease.[60] In 211 B.C., Lykiskos, representative of the Akarnanians, described the Macedonians as kinsfolk of the Achaeans.[61] Macedonia is accounted part of Greece by various authors.[62] As late as the second century A.D., the Ephesians referred in a decree to 'the Macedonians and the other Greek peoples'.[63]

2) The general sense of a passage in Thucydides gives the impression that the historian considered the Macedonians barbarians.[64] The Macedonians are also distinguished from the Greeks and classified with the barbarians in the *Peri Politeias,* an anonymous work written about the end of the fifth or the beginning of the fourth century B.C.[65] Various ancient geographers and historians of the classical and post-classical periods, such as Ephoros, Pseudo-Skylax, Dionysios son of Kalliphon and Dionysios Periegetes, put the northern borders of Greece at the line from the Ambrakian Gulf to the Peneios.[66] Isokrates places Macedonia outside the boundaries of Greece and describes the Macedonians as οὐχ ὁμόφυλον γένος ('an unrelated race').[67] Medeios of Larisa, who accompanied Alexander on his campaign in Asia, calls the Thessalians 'the most northerly of the Greeks'.[68]

3) In contrast with the genealogy of the mythical founder of the Macedonians to be found in Hellanikos (see above), there are three other genealogies of Makedon in which he is not included in the stemma of Hellen. About 700 B.C., Hesiod refers to Makedon as the son of Zeus and Thyia.[69] Pseudo-Skymnos calls him γηγενής, that is, born from the earth.[70] Pseudo-Apollodoros and Aelian reflect a tradition according to which Makedon was the son of Lykaon.[71] However, the lack of any genealogical connection between Makedon and Hellen does not imply that the Macedonians were not Greeks. These three genealogies were not concerned with the question of the nationality of the Macedonians, as was that preserved by Hellanikos, but had different sources and different concerns. This also happens with many other genealogies of the mythical founders of Greek tribes. I shall refer here to only two examples: in the same fragment of Hesiod, Zeus

and Thyia are said to be the parents not only of Makedon, but also of Magnes, the eponymous hero of the Greek tribe the Magnetes. Arkas, founder of another Greek tribe, is usually said to be the offspring of Zeus and the nymph Kallisto. Although the three genealogies of Makedon referred to above do not indicate that the Macedonians were distinct from the Greeks, we cannot deduce from this negative conclusion its opposite — that they support the view that the Macedonians were Greeks. The fragment of Hesiod, on the other hand, does reflect a knowledge of Magnetes, who were Greeks. It also portrays the mother of Makedon as the sister of Hellen.

When Alexander I, king of the Macedonians, wanted to compete at Olympia (possibly in 496 B.C.),[71] his prospective opponents attempted to exclude him by arguing that only Greeks, and not barbarians, could take part in the Olympic games. Alexander proved that he was a Greek and was therefore allowed to compete.[72] We may safely conclude from this episode that the Greeks who attended the Olympic games had no reason, at the beginning of the fifth century B.C., to know the nationality of the Macedonians. It is also certain that when Alexander I submitted to the *Hellanodikai* proofs of his own, but not of his subjects' Greek descent, he left the question open. But this was not the question that had been posed. Thus it cannot be argued that Alexander I considered the Macedonians to be Greeks; but neither can the reverse. These same considerations hold good in a number of other cases: when, for example, Alexander I, speaking only of himself, says 'for I am a Greek by race'[73] or when other kings, or the Macedonian royal family in general, are described as Greek.[74] One further point should be added: the application of the term 'philhellene' to Alexander I does not imply that the king was not a Greek. Jason of Pherai was also so called,[75] and a number of other passages demonstrate that this epithet was also applied to Greeks in antiquity, in which cases it was equivalent to 'patriotic'.[76]

The distinction is made in a passage of Isokrates between Greeks, Macedonians and barbarians.[77] Those who believe that the Macedonians were not Greeks concentrate on the distinction between Greeks and Macedonians rather than that between Macedonians and barbarians. From the context, it emerges clearly that the basis used by the author to distinguish between the Greeks and the Macedonians was the difference in their political relationship to Philip.

4) Those who believe that the Macedonians were not Greek have used the argument that the term *Makedones* is never employed in negotiations, treaties and other political actions in which the Macedonian state was involved, as was the Greek custom (cf. the use of *Athenaioi, Lakedaimonioi, Korinthioi*),[78] but that it was always

28. *The palace at Vergina, discovered at the end of the nineteenth century. The site is identified as that of Aigai, the original capital of the Macedonian kingdom, sacred thereafter as the burial place of their kings. Sited in the lower Haliakmon valley, it marks an important staging point in the progress of the Argead Macedonians from the Pindos mountains and the area round lake Kastoria eastwards towards the coastal plain of Pieria.*

represented by its king. Even Philip did not admit his subjects to the Delphic Amphiktyony in 346 B.C. nor to the confederation 'of the Greeks' in 338/337 B.C. This argument, however, does not take account of the fact that those ancient Greek states that were ruled by monarchs entered into agreements and negotiated alliances through the agency and in the name of their rulers. It was thus perfectly normal practice for Philip, but not the Macedonians, to become a member of the Delphic Amphiktyony. As for the confederation 'of the Greeks', even Philip himself did not become a member, but rather assumed the titles and responsibilities of its 'leader' and of commander-in-chief of its military forces.

The same scholars argue that Alexander the Great did not believe that the Macedonians were Greeks, supporting their case by reference to the fact that when he sent spoils to Athens, he accompanied them with the inscription 'Alexander and the Greeks with the exception of the Lacedaemonians....' and that in many passages of Arrian he addresses his soldiers as 'Macedonians and Greeks'. In both cases, however, the term 'Greeks' is used to indicate the soldiers of the confederation of the 'Greeks' of 338/337, which was renewed after the death of Philip and which bestowed upon Alexander the same powers and offices it had given to his father. Thus, in the inscription, Alexander uses his own name to include his subjects and the term 'Greeks' to cover the soldiers of the allied cities. In his speeches, 'Macedonians and Greeks' is addressed to the two component parts of his army with each of which he had a different relationship: to the Macedonians he was king, to the 'Greeks' commander-in-chief. In any event, Alexander's letter to Darius, referred to above (see page 49) leaves no doubt that Alexander considered his Macedonians to be Greeks.

5) Lastly, on the following grounds, it has been maintained that Macedonians no more felt like Greeks than Greeks recognized them as compatriots: a) many thousands of Greek mercenaries served the Persians during Alexander's campaigns; b) others who eventually enlisted in Alexander's army revolted after his death, and seventeen thousand were butchered by Macedonians; c) as soon as the news of Alexander's death reached Greece, the main cities tried to throw off the Macedonian yoke.

These arguments are unconvincing. Let us consider how many Greek states should be discounted as Greek because they encountered Greek mercenaries on the field of battle; or because they revolted against Greek domination; or because they shed the blood of those who had revolted. In the particular connection of the Greeks of the city-states and Alexander, and indeed with Philip, it should not be ignored that these were determined, to a large extent, by fear of the popular classes, that the domination of the Macedonians would reinforce the oligarchic parties and limit the autonomy of the city states. Because the mercenaries came from the poorer classes they probably harboured deeper resentment of the Macedonians. Finally, it should be noted that the revolt of the Greek mercenaries in 323 B.C. was motivated by a desire to return home after long years of absence, first in the service of the Great King and then of Alexander.

b) Concerning the royal family

1) From the time that Alexander I asserted at Olympia that he was Greek, and the tradition that the Macedonian dynasty was descended from the Temenids of Argos became generally known, it was commonly accepted by the Greeks that the Macedonian royal family was part of the Greek race (see above).

2) There were exceptions, however: in a fragment of the speech 'for the people of Larisa' by the orator Thrasymachus of Chalkedon (second half of the fifth century), Archelaos, king of the Macedonians, is described as a barbarian,[79] and similar descriptions of Philip were formulated by Demosthenes[80] and even by Aischines at the beginning of his political career.[81]

Evaluation of the categorical evidence

Thus far we have set out the evidence to be derived from ancient traditions, testimonia and opinions concerning the nationality of the Macedonians or, more specifically, of the Macedonian royal family, distinguishing between that which expresses a definite view, whether for or against the idea that they were Greeks, and that which is inconclusive or inconsistent (see page 49). We shall now attempt to evaluate the former, with a view to seeing which of it is credible and which is not.

1) *Traditions.* Amongst the categorical evidence, we have met one ancient tradition that connects the Macedonians with the Dorians and another which traces the royal family to Argos in the Peloponnese. The former contains a kernel of truth that is a synopsis of events earlier than the middle of the thirteenth century. From this it can be deduced indirectly, but with certainty, that the Macedonians, like the Dorians, were Greeks (see page 49). The opinions of historians are divided on the second tradition: some accept that it reflects a historical memory, while others believe that it arose from the circumstance that the Temenids who ruled in Macedonia had the same name as the royal house of the Argives, and explain this fact in terms of the presence of a Macedonian element amongst the Dorians. The first view founders on the phenomenon to be observed in early societies whereby the royal family emerged from within the ranks of the tribe. The second view, on the contrary, is consistent with the thesis that the Dorians were in part descended from Macedonians. The Temenids of Macedonia will have been part of that branch of the original tribe that did not move southwards, while the Temenids of Argos will have been descended from a

29. Herakles, direct descendant of Temenos, was the mythical progenitor of the Temenid dynasty which ruled the Argead Macedonians, and was adopted as their national hero. Several inscriptions, as well as other evidence, provide information about the extent and nature of his cult. The picture shows a detail from a silver alabastron found in the Great Tomb of Vergina bearing a representation of the head of Herakles. 350-325 B.C. Thessalonike, Archaeological Museum.

branch that migrated from the Pindos to central Greece where, with other groups, it helped to form the Dorian people.

2) *The official Macedonian view.* In official documents of Alexander the Great and Philip V, Macedonia is described as a Greek country; in the first of them, moreover, Alexander represents himself as the avenger of the evils wrought by the Persians both in Macedonia and in the rest of Greece; and an ambassador of Philip V classifies the Macedonians with the Greeks in contradistinction with 'foreigners' (ἀλλοεθνεῖς) and 'barbarians' (βάρβαροι) (see page 49). The Macedonian kings, therefore, although they believed that they had a different ancestry from their subjects, did not consider themselves to be ruling outside Greece, or over a people foreign to the Greeks.

3) *External Testimonia.* The rest of the evidence cited above consists of testimonia about the Macedonians deriving from external observers. By their very nature, these are less valuable as evidence than a genuine tradition recalling that a branch of the Macedonians had made its contribution to the formation of the Greek tribe of the Dorians, or the official Macedonian view. Let us examine them in their own right, however, as though we did not have more reliable evidence at our disposal.

The external testimonia fall into two conflicting groups. A Persian inscription of 513 B.C., the representation of Makedon as son of Aiolos in a fragment of Hellanikos, the speeches of Agelaos and Lykiskos, and a number of passages in other authors and a decree of the Ephesians afford evidence in support of the thesis that the Macedonians were Greeks (see page 49). In contrast, Thucydides, the unknown author of the *Peri Politeias,* Isokrates, Medeios, Ephoros, Pseudo-Skylax, Dionysios son of Kalliphon and Dionysios Periegetes, all depict the Macedonians as non-Greeks, or Macedonia as a non-Greek country (see page 49). The passages in the orators that portray Archelaos and Philip II as barbarians point in the same direction (see page 52). In which of the two groups should we place our trust? The Persian inscription is an early and direct piece of evidence. The earliest of the authors of the first group is the sole writer who knew the Macedonians at first hand: he resided at the court of Amyntas I, some time before the middle of the fifth century B.C.[82] He himself, as a native of Mytilene, spoke Aiolic, and recognized in the Macedonian language a dialect resembling his own: it was for this reason that he made Makedon son of Aiolos. On the other hand, it is interesting that one of the authors in the second group, Ephoros, refers to the Pamphylians as barbarians[83] though they were in fact Greeks. This demonstrates that some Greeks came close to being thought barbarians by their fellow Greeks. The backward institutions and coarseness of the Macedonians will have been among the reasons why they seemed to other Greeks to be barbarians. The rhetorical apostrophes of Thrasymachos and Demosthenes should, *a fortiori,* be considered unreliable: the former was attempting to arouse the people of Larisa, the latter the Athenians, to resist the Macedonian kings, and they described them as barbarians in spite of the fact that they had officially and widely been recognized as Greeks.[84] The

rhetorical accusations that they were 'barbarians' made not against the Macedonians but against their kings, refer in any case to court scandals, or to the incontinence and violence of the rulers (cf. Plato on Archelaos and Theopompos[85] and other authors on Philip.).

4) *Conclusion.* The hypothesis that the Macedonians were Greeks is supported by all the reliable evidence: the ancient tradition that the Dorians were descended from a section of the Macedonians; the view the Macedonian kings held about themselves; and the testimony of Hellanikos, who lived at the Macedonian court. All the testimonia that contradict this view are external and derive either from observers who might have been mistaken, or from enemies of the Macedonians.

2. THE MACEDONIAN TONGUE

The eaiest Macedonian written documents contain only names. When more extensive Macedonian texts begin to appear, they are expressed in the Attic dialect. This fact furnishes one of the arguments used by those who deny that the Macedonians were Greeks and claim that the Macedonians were a people who spoke a different tongue and who became hellenized. Those who support the view that the Macedonians were Greeks counter that their kings introduced the Attic dialect into the court and the administration because the local dialect was undeveloped; Attic thus became widespread amongst the Macedonians as a means of expressing themselves in writing. Both these explanations are hypotheses that require proof. And the proof of either depends on other factors that will be examined below.

Despite the lack of Macedonian texts written in the local language, the nature of Macedonian may be discerned from certain testimonia; from about one hundred surviving Macedonian words; and from several hundred Macedonian names.

1) *Testimonia.* There are three ancient pieces of indirect evidence of a conclusive nature: a) In a scene from the Attic comedy *Macedonians,* by the fifth-century writer Strattis, an Athenian asks ἡ σφύραινα δ' ἔστι τίς; ('sledfish, what do you mean?'), and a Macedonian replies κέστραν μὲν ὕμμες ὠττικοὶ κικλήσκετε ('wha ye Attics ca' a hammer-fush, ma freen').[86] In order to appreciate the value of the Macedonian's reply for the problem under discussion, we must not forget that, as is clear from many passages in Aristophanes, the Attic comedians made their non-Greeks speak broken Greek with an admixture of barbarian words (some of them imaginary), while Lacedaemonians, Megarians, Boiotians and other Greeks spoke in their own dialects (albeit with a number of inaccuracies). The Macedonian's reply is in good Greek with dialect (ὕμμες, σφύραινα) and archaizing (κικλήσκετε) elements. b) Alexander the Great, having selected thirty thousand Persian youths, gave an order that they were 'to learn Greek letters and be trained in the use of Macedonian weapons'.[87] From this it may be deduced that the Macedonian soldiers spoke Greek: it would be pointless to teach the young Per-

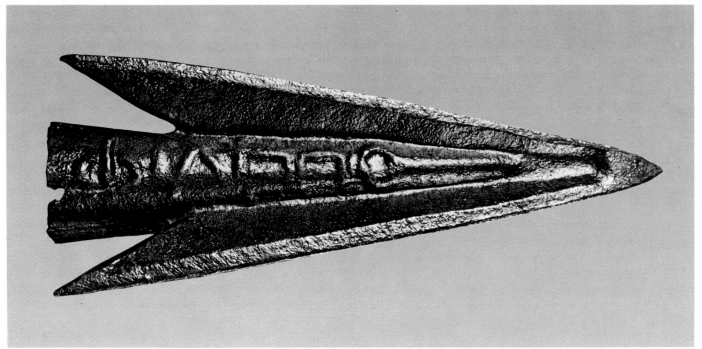

30. One characteristic of the Macedonian tongue which differentiates it from the Greek is the conversion of the Indo-European voiced aspirates (bh, dh, gh) into muted aspirates (b (β), d (δ), g (γ); in Greek these became φ, θ, χ. On the other hand it is to be noted that on coins, tiles and arrowheads the Macedonian name Philip is written with Φ. This fact leads to the conclusion that the pronunciation β for the ancient bh was not universal in the Macedonian tongue, but occurred alongside the pronunciation φ. The arrowhead above comes from Olynthos. Mid-4th century B.C. Thessalonike, Archaeological Museum.

sians who were to fight alongside the Macedonians a language that the Macedonians did not understand. c) An ambassador from Macedonia, speaking to the Aitolians in 200 B.C. says of the Macedonians, the Aitolians, and the Akarnanians that they spoke the same language.[88]

The expressions «ἀνεβόα μακεδονιστί»,[89] «μακεδονιστί τῇ φωνῇ»,[90] «μακεδονίζειν,[91] «μακεδονίζοντα τῇ φωνῇ»,[92] «ἐκ τῆς φωνῆς Μακεδόνας καὶ Δημήτριον τὸν Φιλίππου γνωρίζουσιν ὄντας»,[93] *patrio sermone, sermonis patrii*,[94] μακεδονίζοντας τ᾽ οἶδα πολλοὺς τῶν Ἀττικῶν,[95] have been taken by opponents of the thesis that the Macedonians were Greeks as indicating that their language differed from Greek; the supporters of the thesis declare that these formulations indicate a Greek dialect (cf. αἰολίζειν, αἰολιστί, αἰοληΐδι μολπᾷ, ἀττικίζειν, ἀττικιστί, βοιωτιάζειν, δωρίζειν, δωριστί, πελοποννασαστί etc.) The expressions are in fact susceptible of either interpretation,[96] and cannot therefore be used to form part of the argumentation with which either is supported. Their sense will become clear after Macedonian has been shown to be Greek, or not, from other data.

2) *W o r d s.* Today, over a hundred Macedonian words and a few hundred Macedonian names are known from a variety of sources. Although the names presuppose words, they will be examined separately for a number of methodological reasons.

A total of one hundred and twelve words, with ninety-nine different stems, are attested directly. Of these, sixty-five words, or sixty-three stems, have been preserved in lexica, while forty-seven words, with thirty-six stems, survive in various ancient texts, none of which is Macedonian.[97] All the words in the second group are Greek. The opponents of the view that the Macedonians were Greeks refuse to take them into consideration, arguing that they were all words borrowed by the Macedonians from Greek at the time they began to use the Attic dialect as the official language — which they ascribe to the reign of Philip II. However: a) the word σφύραινα and the form ὕμμες are not Attic in origin, and are attributed to the Macedonians half a century before the accession of Philip (see above); b) the majority of these words are military and, as has already been observed, it would be illogical to suppose that Philip would impose a foreign military terminology on the Macedonians; moreover, twelve of these same words are not attested as common to all dialects and fourteen more, while being common words, have a different meaning in Macedonian.[98] In dealing with the Macedonian material in the lexica, the opponents of the view that the Macedonians were Greeks have made use to varying extents of the following method: they select from amongst these words the ones that cannot be shown to have a Greek derivation; they do not always inquire whether the form of some of these has changed as a result of copying errors; they suggest derivations for these words from Indo-European roots without always demonstrating adequately that their derivations are well-grounded; using this kind of etymology as their point of departure they draw up rules for the conversion of Indo-European vowels or consonants to 'Macedonian'; finally, since the same rules can be detected in words that are not attested as Macedonian in the sources, they declare that these words, notwithstanding, should be considered Macedonian.[99]

The latest, and most complete, monograph on the nationality of the Macedonians, devotes hundreds of pages to the study of Macedonian words, and contains some perceptive critical observations and original views. It concludes that fifty-two of the sixty-five words in the lexica are Greek, while the remaining thirteen include not only genuinely non-Greek words but also ambiguous forms, copyists' errors and words used by children.[100]

Let us assume, however, that *all* the Macedonian words handed down by the lexica are demonstrably non-Greek (which is not claimed even by the most extreme opponents of the theory that the Macedonians were Greeks). Even in this eventuality, it would not necessarily follow that the Macedonians did not speak Greek. The reason is that these words are not a representative sample of the Macedonian tongue. This would require that they had been preserved at random and from a variety of sources. Quite the reverse is true: they have all been catalogued in lexica whose purpose is the interpretation of rare words only. It follows that the Alexandrian scholars who were the first to compose lexica of this sort (the forerunners of the surviving lexica in which the words in question are preserved) found only a few dozen Macedonian words that required interpretation. However, there is no language or dialect that does not have a number of words of foreign origin.

3) *N a m e s*. In addition to the Macedonian ethnic name, we today know the ethnic names of some of the Macedonian tribes, scores of place names in Macedonia and dozens of names of gods and heroes, the names of six festivals and twelve months, and hundreds of personal names, covering thousands of men and women.

The ethnic names of the *Elimiotai, Lynkestai* and *Orestai* derive from place names. The first has an undoubtedly Greek termination. Some scholars believe that the στ of the second and third are an affix that is found in Illyrian names. In the name of the Orestai at least, the σ belongs to the root (Ορεσ-) and the τ to the termination (-ται), which is Greek. Furthermore, both the Orestai and the Lynkestai were undoubtedly Greeks (see page 59).

Alexander I, other Macedonian kings, Philip II, Alexander the Great and his successors all gave Greek names to the cities they founded; Alexander the Great and some of his officers went further and translated some of the local names into Greek. Those opposed to the view that the Macedonians were Greeks are not prepared to take this evidence into consideration, justifying their stance with the argument that it all post-dates the introduction of Attic into the court and the state administration. There is no proof of this argument, however, other than the claim that the Macedonians did not speak Greek, and it is this claim that the argument is designed to support. The introduction of this argument into the chain of reasoning designed to demonstrate the above view thus leads to a vicious circle. In order to avoid the accusation that we are using these same toponyms as proof that the Macedonians were Greek, while the evidence for and against this view is still being discussed, we shall restrict ourselves to toponyms in areas where the expansion of the Macedonians ante-dates

Philip, and to those names attested before his reign. Some of these names were Greek and some non-Greek. The latter do not prove that the Macedonians were not Greeks, for the areas in question were inhabited for many millennia (from the beginning of human habitation until *c.* 2300/2200, and from 1900 until the eighth, seventh, sixth and even the fifth centuries B.C.) by non-Greek peoples. We also know that place-names survive even after the disappearance of the ethnic groups from which they derive. Further, if the non-Greek toponyms of western and central Macedonia are attributed to the Macedonians, this has two consequences. Firstly, we have to concede that the Pelasgians, the Paiones, the Bottiaioi, the Eordoi, the Almopes, the Phrygians, the Thracians and other races left no mark on the toponyms of Macedonia, which is improbable. Secondly, the following problem arises: if we exclude the possibility that the Macedonians were responsible for the Greek toponyms in western and central Macedonia before Philip, to which Greeks are they to be attributed? It is possible that only the names *Haliakmon* and *Pieria* are earlier than the Macedonian expansion. There are many more toponyms that are connected by our sources with the Macedonian expansion, or that cannot be dated to the period when the Proto-Greeks occupied Macedonia, for in this case they would exhibit a more archaic form which would have been fossilized or corrupted through the intervention of a non-Greek language.

Of seventy-two names and epithets of gods and heroes, fifty-six are panhellenic or Greek from a linguistic point of view, at least one is Greek with non-Greek phonetics, eleven are foreign (nine of these came from areas where non-Macedonian populations survived), and two derive from foreign toponyms, with a Greek termination; the rest are doubtful (see page 60). The proportion of non-Greek names of gods is very small, especially in view of the fact that they are attested at very late periods, when the entire Greek world was feeling the influence of foreign religions.

All the names of festivals are Greek (see page 60). All the names of the months have Greek terminations, and only two of them have roots that are possibly non-Greek (see page 60).

No comprehensive collection of the personal names has yet been made. The few collections that have been made for prosopographical purposes have not inspired any exhaustive linguistic studies or statistical evaluations. A review of the names borne by members of the royal family of the Temenids, of the dynasties of upper Macedonia, and other Macedonians,[101] before the rule of Philip, reveals only very small percentages for each of the three groups. The recent discovery of large numbers of grave stelai at Vergina has increased our knowledge of Macedonian personal names by adding dozens of examples. With one or two exceptions, these are Greek, and a number of them date from before the accession of Philip. They are all names of members of the middle classes.

Those who deny that the Macedonians were Greeks assert that they took the Greek names for gods, heroes, festivals, months and people from the Greeks. In the first place, however, there is no other example of a people neighbouring on the Greeks whose names were 95% Greek before the middle of the fourth century; many centuries later than this, a large percentage of Paionians, Thracians, Mysians, Lydians, Karians and Lycians had local names, even though they had begun to feel Greek cultural influences much earlier. Furthermore, a number of the Greek-sounding names given by the Macedonians to gods, heroes, festivals, months and persons do not occur outside Macedonia or areas in which Macedonians had settled.

The majority of Macedonian names in all categories are either nouns as such, or adjectives, or their derivatives, or a variety of compounds; they also include a number of verb-stems, prepositions and affixes. As a result, the names help us to form a picture of the vocabulary, phonetics and rules of derivation and synthesis of the Macedonian tongue which is quantitatively richer and qualitatively superior to that derived from the hundred or so roots of words that have been handed down directly. Consequently, in attempting to trace the features of Macedonian, it is necessary to go beyond the words and make use of all the data to be gleaned from the Macedonian names.

Synthesis

a) The nature of the Macedonian tongue

From the above evidence — testimonia, words and names — it is clear that Macedonian was not a separate language but a Greek dialect.

b) The relationship of Macedonian to other Greek dialects

The fact that there are no texts written in Macedonian prevents us from forming as good an idea of this dialect and its relationship to other Greek dialects as we can for those in which even a few written documents survive. Nonetheless, the material at our disposal enables us to make a number of observations that demonstrate a relationship between Macedonian and the West Greek dialect (to which Doric and north-west Greek belong), and the Aiolic and Thessalian dialects.[102]

1) Macedonian and West Greek: a) -δδ- in place of -ζζ- b) nominative singular of certain compounds in -ας instead of -ος c) a number of words (to those already recorded[103] should be added the word κᾶλον, the existence of which in Macedonian was recently demonstrated by the name Δρύκαλος, read on one of the stelai from Vergina (fig.31); this name will have meant 'He who is of the wood of the oak' — cf. the Macedonian name Πευκέστας: 'He who is of the wood of the pine').

2) Macedonian and Aeolic:[104] a) -νν- from -σν- (consequently, also -λλ- from -σλ- etc); this phonetic rule is attested in Macedonian by the toponym Κράννα (Doric: Κράνα; Ionic-Attic: Κρήνη); b) nominative plural of the second person of the personal pronoun ὔμμες (Ionic-Attic: ὑμεῖς; Doric: ὑμές); for the Macedonian example, see page 55.

3) Macedonian and Thessalian: ω instead of ου attested in both Macedonian and Thessalian.

4) Macedonian and Arcadian: conversion of εν to ιν

5) Macedonian, Thessalian and Arcadian: conversion of α into ε under certain conditions; Macedonian σε- (in Σέλευκος) from διέ- which is attested in Thessalian (διά- in the other Greek dialects)· Macedonian ζέρεθρον=Arcadian ζέρεθρον, Thessalian βέρεθρον, for βάραθρον.

c) Non-Greek features of Macedonian

A number of features may be observed in the surviving Macedonian linguistic material that are not Greek. All those who have asserted that Macedonian was a distinct language and not a dialect of Greek have represented these features as having universal application. In fact, they have relied on selected evidence, which they have put forward as being the only genuine examples of Macedonian. This evidence consists of: a) those of the Macedonian words in the ancient lexica (see page 56) which cannot be assigned a Greek derivation; b) the very few Macedonian names for gods, heroes, festivals, months, places and people, that are not Greek, at least phonetically; c) words known from ancient lexica or other sources which are not stated to be Macedonian but which have features either identical with or similar to those of the first two groups. The evidence is selected on the bases of the following arguments: all the examples that are stated to be Macedonian but have Greek characteristics are not genuinely Macedonian, but will have passed into the Macedonian language as loan-words; all the examples that are not stated to be Macedonian but display the same characteristics as Macedonian are concealed examples of the Macedonian language. These arguments, however, fall into the logical trap of taking as assumed that which has to be proven, namely, that Macedonian was a separate language which was gradually influenced to a considerable degree by Greek; and that the examples in the third group are Macedonian.

The following characteristics have been suggested as features distinguishing Macedonian from Greek, though most of them in fact suggest an affinity with Thracian and Illyrian: 1) the retention of the Indo-European *s* before an initial vowel (in Greek, the *s* became *h*, the *daseia*); 2) the conversion of the Indo-European voiced aspirates *bh, dh, gh* into voiced stops, b (β), d (δ), g (γ) (in Greek these became (φ, θ, χ), the dissimilation of the first aspirate in cases where two of these sounds occur in successive syllables; 4) the conversion of b (β), g (γ), d (δ) into p (π), k (κ), t (τ); 5) the conversion of the vowel group αι into α; 6) the conversion of the vowel group au (αυ) into α; 7) the dropping of final r (ρ); 8) the formation of feminines in -ισσα; 9) the formation of ethnic names by the affix -στ . Let us examine matters more closely.

1) Only three Macedonian words have σ- before a vowel in their first syllable: σάρισσα, Σαυάδαι/Σαῦδοι and σιγύνη/σιβύνη. However: a) none of these has been convincingly derived from an Indo-European root; b) the third is also attested in the Greek dialect of Cyprus from as early as the third century, and the second corresponds to the god's name Σαβάζιος, which spread through southern Greece at an early date; c) Greek has many examples of the retention of Indo-European -*s*- before a vowel in the

first syllable, occurring in words borrowed by Greek from the languages spoken by populations subjected to Greek tribes. Thus: either the Macedonian examples do not prove the existence of the phenomenon in question or, if they prove it, they do not constitute criteria for distinguishing the Macedonian tongue from Greek; in the latter eventuality, they will have derived from Pelasgians or Thracians who were subjugated by the Macedonians. The fact that Macedonian has examples in which initial s- is converted into an aspiration cannot be ignored, however. This phenomenon cannot be interpreted in terms of Greek influence, for it occurs in the names Ὑπερβερέτας and Ὑπερβερεταῖος amongst others; these are not only unknown outside Macedonia, but exhibit β in the place of φ. It is illogical to cite these names amongst the examples in which β appears in place of the Greek φ and simultaneously to ignore the fact that they represent examples of the change of the initial s into h- in accordance with a Greek phonetic law.

2) The second phenomenon is attested in Plutarch,[105] Eustathios of Thessalonike,[106] and a number of lemmata in Byzantine lexica. One of the passages in Plutarch gives the impression that the phenomenon was widespread in Macedonia. Examples are the names Βίλιππος, Βερενίκη, Βάλακρος, Βέροια, Κεβαλῖνος, Βρύγες (for: Φίλιππος, Φερενίκη, Φάλακρος, Φέροια, Κεφαλῖνος, Φρύγες), Ὑπερβερεταῖος (=-φερ.), *Ξάνδος (=Ξανθος), Μάγας (=Μάχας), and words such as ἀββροῦτες (=ὀφρῦς), ἀδραία (αἰθρία), δάνος (=θάνατος), δανῶν (=θαν-). On the other hand, it is to be noted that the name Φίλιππος, and Macedonian names in general in which the first component is φιλ, are written more frequently with φ from the beginning of the written tradition; also, that φ and not β occurs in: ἀμφοτερός, ἀρφύς, Βουκεφάλας, φάλαγξ, Φόβος, Φυλακαί and φύλαξ; χ and not γ in: ἄγχαρμος, διμάχαι, λόχος,-οχος, Πολυπέρχων, Χαρικλῆς and Χάρων; θ and not δ in ζέρεθρον, Θαῦλος Θούριδες and Πείθων. Those who oppose the view that elements of Macedonian were Greek argue, of course, that the versions with φ, θ, χ, represent Macedonian names transmitted in Greek texts, and also names and words borrowed by the Macedonians from the Greeks. If the evidence of the Greek texts is excluded, on the grounds that it is untrustworthy, then exception cannot be made for those passages which attest to β, δ, γ in place of φ, θ, χ. If these latter are not excluded, and it is thus conceded that the Greek authors rendered the Macedonian pronunciation correctly by writing Βίλιππος etc., then it is illegitimate to assert that the versions with φ, θ, χ are errors. Furthermore, the spelling Φίλιππος is not attested solely in non-Macedonian texts; it also occurs on coins of Philip II, and on Macedonian arrows, and tiles of the same period. It would be curious if the coins issued by the Macedonian state did not accurately reflect the national pronunciation. Let us concede, however, that Philip insisted that his name be written with Φ, since he had established the Attic dialect as the official language of the state: this explanation might account for the phonetic form of the royal name on the coinage, but not also on arrows and tiles. The hypothesis that Macedonian names and words having φ, θ, χ in place of β, δ, γ are borrowed

from Greek has properly been countered with the hypothesis that this is unacceptable in the case of words like ἀρφύς, which is otherwise unknown; ἄγχαρμον, which had fallen into disuse in the rest of Greece; ζέρεθρον, which was used in the isolated region of Arcadia; χάρων, which in Macedonia was not used to mean 'Charon' but 'lion'. Two conclusions emerge: 1) the pronunciation of the ancient *bh, gh, dh* as β, γ, δ, was not universal throughout Macedonia, but occurred alongside the pronunciation φ, χ, θ; 2) the pronunciation φ, χ, θ appears in some words which could not have been borrowed by the Macedonians from a Greek people. In the light of these conclusions, we must look for some other explanation of the appearance of β, γ, δ in Macedonia. This demand can be satisfied by the following observations: 1) the same phenomenon also occurs sporadically in words and names transmitted in indisputably Greek sources; 2) these words and names are thought to be loan-words borrowed by the Greeks from other Indo-European peoples that they first conquered and then absorbed; 3) the Macedonians too conquered the Pelasgians (see page 47) and after them the Thracians (see page 47) and Illyrians who, like the Pelasgians, had converted Indo-European *bh, gh, dh* into β, γ, δ. Since, on the one hand, the appearance in Macedonian of φ, χ, θ deriving from Indo-European *bh, gh, dh* cannot be attributed to external influences and since, on the other, the conversion of the same sounds to β, γ, δ, occurred in Macedonian under conditions similar to those that account for it in an indisputably Greek linguistic area, we are obliged to give the same interpretation to the Macedonian data.

3 and 4) These two phenomena also occur in words and names found in the Greek world in general, where they are regarded as vestiges of Pelasgian, or of pre-Greek languages generally, that have been preserved in Greek. Their occurrence in Macedonian can therefore also be attributed to pre-Macedonian substrata (both Pelasgian and Thracian).

5) That the group *au* was converted to *a* is a conjecture based on a very small number of names and words. Since there are also reliable indications that the group was also preserved, we may reasonably assume that this is another case in which we have to deal with two different kinds of development;[107] that one of these (the preservation of the group) does not distinguish Macedonian from Greek; and that the other (the conversion of the group to *a*), since it was sporadic, is not an ancient hallmark of Macedonian but is due to the influence of populations conquered by the Macedonians.[108]

6) The hypothesis that the group *au* became *a* in Macedonian is based entirely on a dubious derivation. By contrast, the preservation of the group *au* in this tongue is well attested.[109]

7) The dropping of final *r* is similarly supported by unlikely etymologies.[110]

8) The formation of feminines in -ισσα is attested in Macedonian by: βασίλισσα, Μακεδόνισσα and σάρισσα. The view that the -ισσα in these examples corresponds to -izza in Illyrian remains undecided. On the other hand, the Greek Κίλισσα and Φοίνισσα cannot be ignored. Admittedly, the -ισσα of the Macedonian examples cannot be in-

terpreted phonetically in the same way as the -ισσα in the two Greek words (from Κίλικ-j-α and Φοίνικ-j-α); but it is not impossible that *Μακεδόνισσα, βασίλισσα* and *σάρισσα* were formed by analogy with Κίλισσα and Φοίνισσα, in accordance with a phenomenon familiar in linguistics.[111] Furthermore, the most likely derivation of *σάρισσα* relates it to a common noun indicating a type of oak-tree, which is attested in Greek.[112]

9) The names of the nations of upper Macedonia, Ὀρέσται and Λυγκῆσται, the ethnics found in various parts of Macedonia derived from the names of cities, such as *Ἀργεσταῖοι (from Ἄργος), Διέσται/Διάσται (from Δῖον), Ἐορδισταί (from Ἐορδαία), Εὐϊέσται (from Εὐΐα), Κραννέσται (from *Κράννα), Κυρρέσται/Κυρρησταί (from Κύρρος), and personal names like Πευκέστας have been thought to be Illyrian, since an affix does in fact appear in ethnic names in Illyria and in regions inhabited by Illyrian tribes. However: a) the names *Ἀργεσταῖοι, Ὀρέσται, Πευκέστας have stems in -εσ- (Ἀργεσ- Ὀρεσ-, Πευκεσ-) and a termination -τας (-της), like the familiar Greek words and names Θυέστης, ὀρέστης, Ὀρέστης, ὀρχηστής, τελεστάς -ής, etc. They do not, therefore, belong to the category of names that have an affix -στ-.[113] Moreover, the Λυγκῆσται and the Ὀρέσται were Greek tribes, and Argos, whose inhabitants were called *Ἀργεσταῖοι, was a city of the second of these two tribes. The Ἐορδισταί derived their name from the verb ἐορδίζω. b) The toponyms Δῖον and Κράννα were Greek. In these, and all the others that were also Greek, the -στ- may best be attributed to the influence of the Greek Ὀρέσται. For the others, we have to assume a double influence both from the Greek and from the Illyrian names.

3. RELIGIOUS AND ETHNOLOGICAL EVIDENCE

From the point of view of the question of the nationality of the Macedonians, the surviving religious and ethnological evidence may be divided into Greek, non-Greek, doubtful and irrelevant; the Greek evidence may in turn be subdivided into (a) that found throughout Greece, (b) that which is attested in various parts of Greece, and (c) local Macedonian. This subdivision is rendered necessary by the fact that opinion is divided as to the value as evidence of the first group, and also of some of the items in the second. Some scholars agree that this evidence demonstrates that the Macedonians were Greeks, while others claim that it does not prove this, since the relevant information dates mainly from the period of Alexander and his successors and only rarely from the time of Philip and earlier. If this argument holds good, however, then *a fortiori*, we must reject as irrelevant all the non-Greek evidence, since the passages concerning them are of much later date.

31. The recent discovery of many grave stelai at Vergina enriched Macedonian anthroponymic material with a series of Greek personal names of members of the middle classes. A notable example is the name Drykalos to be read on the stele in the picture. It means 'he who is of the wood of the oak.'

A. Greek elements

a) Panhellenic elements

From the data at our disposal at present, we know that the Macedonians worshipped the twelve Olympian gods (fig. 32), both collectively and individually, and also Pluto, Persephone, Dionysos, Pan, Hestia, Herakles (fig. 29), Asklepios, Okeanos, Amphitrite, the Nereids, Tethys, Orpheus, the Dioskouroi, Amphilochos, the Nymphs, the Graces, the Fates, Hygieia, Lethe, Nemesis and Eros. They also gave them the familiar Greek epithets, such as Agoraios, Basileus, Olympios, Hypsistos of Zeus, Basileia of Hera, Soter of Apollo, Hagemona (Attic-Ionic Hegemone) and Soteira of Artemis, Boulaia of Hestia, etc. Some of the evidence for the worship of Ge, Helios, Dionysos, Pan, Asklepios and Herakles is earlier than the period of Philip, while the earliest evidence for the twelve gods comes from this period.[114] The large number of these gods' names and the early date of the evidence militates against the familiar false argument advanced by those opposed to the idea that the Macedonians were Greeks — namely, that the Greek cultural features that appear in Macedonia were imposed by kings who admired things Greek, especially Philip. Moreover, Philip or one of his immediate predecessors introduced the Attic dialect as the official language of the state, and if the Greek names of gods used by the Macedonians were imported, they ought to be Attic in form. The name Ἀγεμόνα[115] however, has retained the original long *a* in both the first syllable of the stem and the termination. If this word did not have its roots in Macedonia but had been imported as a result of royal initiative, we would know it in the form Ἡγεμόνη.

b) Elements limited to particular areas

In Macedonia, the name Θαῦλ(λ)ος was used of a god who was identified with Ares. The hypothesis that this god was Thraco-Phrygian is groundless. On the contrary, he has been convincingly related to Zeus Thaulios of Thessaly, the clan of the Thaulonidai of Attica, and the Doric festival, the Thaulia.[116] The god Thaulos was probably originally a separate god who had qualities which later led to his identification with Ares in some regions and with Zeus in others.

Pasikrata is attested as a goddess in Macedonia and at Demetrias in Thessaly; we also find an Artemis *Pasikrata* in Ambrakia and a *Pasikrateia* (Persephone?) at Selinous.[117]

Phobos was worshipped by the Macedonians and the Dorians.[118]

It has been conjectured that the Macedonians had a festival called the *Apellaia,* both from the name of the month *Apellaios* and from an independent reference to a special bread called δράμις; this was similar in both form and etymology to the δαράτα, an offering made by the inhabitants of Delphi during the Apellaia. This same festival was widespread amongst the Dorians. The bread δράμις or δράμιξ or δαράτα or δάρατος is also attested amongst the Thessalians and the Athamanes.[119] The Hetaireidia were celebrated by the Macedonians and the Magnesians.[120]

The months *Artemisios* and *Apellaios* connect the Macedonians with the Dorians. *Panamos* or *Panemos* was also known in mainland Greece and some of the cities in Ionia. *Loos,* or *Homoloos* appears to have come from pre-Thessalian, or Aiolian Thessaly, whence he spread to mainland Greece and Lesbos. Δαίσιος or Θεοδαίσιος is attested to a certain extent in Doric regions, and also appears in Aiolic territory. *Dios* is attested in the Mycenaean calendar and in areas inhabited by Aiolians.

In addition to the above religious evidence, reference should also be made to the dance *karpaia* since it too is attested outside Macedonia, in regions to the south of Olympos, notably in Magnesia and Ainis.[121]

c) Elements limited to Macedonia

The following Greek names are cited or occur as exclusively Macedonian: *Alkidemos* (as an epithet of Athena), *Aidonaios, Aid(u)naios* (name of a month, from the name *Aidoneus*=Hades),[122] *Aretos* (epithet of Herakles),[123] Arantides (Macedonian name for the Erinyes),[124] *Thourides* epithet of the Nymphs or the Muses),[125] *Hippalkmos* (epithet of a hero),[126] *Klodones* (Macedonian name for the maenads),[127] *Kynagidas* (epithet of Herakles),[128] *Mimallones* (another Macedonian name for the maenads),[129] *Xanthika* (name of a festival) and *Xandikos* (name of a month),[130] *Peritia* (name of a festival) and *Peritios* (name of a month),[131] *telesias* (name of a dance),[132] *Hyperairetas, Hyperberetas, Hyperpheretes* (epithets of Zeus); *Hyperberetaios* (name of a month),[133] *Pseudanor* (epithet of Dionysos).[134] The names *Xandikos* and *Hyperberetaios (Hyperberetas)* have δ and β in place of the Greek θ and φ, but are Greek in all other respects.

B. Thracian elements

The names of the gods *Asdoules, Bendis, Daimones Antanoi, Dyalos, Eteudoniskos* or *Oteudanos* or *Oteudonikos, Pyrmerylas* and the epithet *Derronaios* (of Herakles) are indigenous to Pelagonia, Derriopos and Paionia[135] — all areas in which the pre-Macedonian populations survived. Moreover, they are attested at late dates, chiefly from the Christian centuries when Thracian and other foreign religions were to be found throughout the Greek world. The names *Zeirene* (a goddess identified with Aphrodite) and *Sauadai* (the name of demons identified with the Satyrs) are each attested once. The reference to each, in an article in the lexicon of Hesychios, contains the statement that they were local to Macedonia. Bearing in mind that the gods' names mentioned above occurred in very restricted areas, it seems at least possible that these latter names too were restricted to regions in which the pre-Macedonian populations survived, and were disseminated throughout Macedonia in the Hellenistic period.

C. Doubtful elements

The names of two Macedonian months, *Gorpiaios*[136]

32. Zeus was perhaps the most important divinity in Macedonia. The head of Zeus, with an oak wreath, was depicted on silver coins minted by Philip. Athens, Numismatic Museum.

33. *Evidence shows that the Dionysiac cult with local variations was well-established in Macedonia. Dionysos and his attendants, Silenus and the maenads, were frequently depicted on metal objects. The Silenus above is the centrepiece on the base of a silver kylix found in the Great Tomb of Vergina. The beard, hair and crown are gilded. The facial characteristics and the pleasing shape are skilfully rendered. 350-325 B.C. Thessalonike, Archaeological Museum.*

and *Dystros*[137] have given rise to inadequately supported etymologies.

D. Evidence without value

The passage stating that the Macedonians worshipped the air under the name *Bedu* has been disputed, with very convincing arguments.[138] It has also been shown that *Totoes,* the god of sleep, who was thought to be Thracian or 'Macedonian', was imported from Egypt.[139]

Some of the other names of deities and nymphs are of no value, since they are derived from place-names: cf. *Bloureitis* and *Gazoreitis* (epithets of Artemis), *Echedorides* (epithet of the nymphs of the river Echedoros), *Pierides* and *Pimpleiai* (epithet of the Muses who were worshipped in Pieria and were connected with the spring Pimpleia).[140] The suggestion that these names indicate distinct deities is erroneous, as is the attribution of the first two to Thracian deities identified with Artemis.

E. Conclusions from a comparison of the Greek and non-Greek religious and ethnological elements

Elements that are unquestionably Greek are much more numerous than those which are not Greek. The great majority of the Greek elements is earlier in date than the non-Greek and the doubtful elements.

Some fifteen Greek elements had a limited dissemination which did not coincide with a particular geographical area; some of them were local to areas a considerable distance from Macedonia. Furthermore, none of them had any particular influence. A further fifteen Greek elements do not occur outside Macedonia.

Nine of the eleven items of non-Greek evidence were local to areas that had pre-Macedonian populations.

When taken as a whole, these observations show that the Macedonians were not Thracians, or Illyrians, or any other race that became hellenized, but Greeks whose culture was slightly influenced by non-Greek features.

4. RELATIONS BETWEEN THE MACEDONIANS AND OTHER GREEK TRIBES

We have already met various indications of the relations between the Macedonians and some of the Greek tribes. These relations demonstrate that the Macedonians were a Greek tribe from as early as the Bronze Age.

The Macedonians were bound to the Dorians and the Magnesians by very close ties of kinship. Their ties with the former are attested by a tradition preserved in Herodotos, corrected by other evidence (see page 46). They are also implicit in a number of dialect features common to both Doric and Macedonian (see page 57); the fact that the kings of Sparta and of the Macedonians offered sacrifices to the Dioskouroi; the cult of Pasikrata in Macedonia and in the Doric world (at Selinous, a colony of the Dorian Megarians); and the division of the Temenids into two branches, one of which stayed in Macedonia, while the other appears at Dorian Argos (see page 52).

The relationship between the Macedonians and the Magnesians was familiar to the ancients, for Hesiod portrays Makedon and Magnes as brothers (see page 49). It is confirmed by the fact that the name of both peoples is derived from the root *mak* —'high, tall'— and by the circumstance that the Macedonians and the Magnesians celebrated a festival called the *Hetaireidia,* unknown elsewhere (see page 60).

A number of cultural features common to the Macedonians and the Dorians are also shared by other Greek tribes that were formerly neighbours of the Macedonians. The festival of the *Apellaia* and the names of three months, *Apellaios, Artemisios* and *Panamos* or *Panemos* occur in the calendars of the Macedonians, various Doric cities (see page 60), the Lokrians, the Phokians and the Aiolians (see p. 60). The names of three more months, *Dios, Daisios* or *Theodaisios* and *Loos* or *Homoloos* link the Macedonians, the Dorians and the Aiolians. The Macedonians and the Dorians worshipped the god *Phobos* (see page 60). The Macedonians sacrificed to this god on the eve of battle, and legend has it that Theseus did the same before he fought with the Amazons. Theseus himself did not originally belong to the Ionians of Attica, but to sections of other Greek tribes (the Lapithae and Molossoi) that neighboured on the Macedonians. The *Thaulia* of the Dorians implies the existence amongst them of the Macedonian god Thaul(i)os, with whom the Thessalian Zeus Thaulios and the Athenian clan of the Thaulonidai are connected.

The dance *karpaia* is one of the cultural features uniting the Macedonians and the Magnesians; the same dance was performed by the Aenianai, who were once neighbours of both tribes.

When the Macedonians lived at Lakmos and in the surrounding area, the Athamanians were bounded by the Athamanian mountains to the south of Lakmos. This explains the connection between the name of the mountain *Laphystion,* the epithet *Laphystios* used of Zeus, and *Laphystiai,* one of the names given to the Bacchae by the Macedonians (see page 46). The same explanation accounts for the use of the word *dramis* by the Macedonians and the word *dramix* by the Athamanians to mean a kind of bread (see page 60).

The fact that the Macedonians were once neighbours of the Aiolians also accounts for the features common to these two dialects.

CROSS-CHECK OF CONCLUSIONS DRAWN FROM THE DIFFERENT CATEGORIES OF EVIDENCE

We have examined in turn (1) the surviving traditions and testimonia concerning the Macedonians; (2) the available evidence for the Macedonian tongue; (3) what is known today of their religion and ethnology; (4) the relations between the Macedonians and various Greek tribes. The valid data under all these headings leads naturally and definitively to the same conclusion: the Macedonians were a Greek tribe. Some of the evidence, indeed, points to a more specific conclusion: that the Macedonians constituted a distinct tribe from as early as the Bronze Age.

THE ESTABLISHMENT AND CONSOLIDATION OF THE KINGDOM OF MACEDONIA

POLITICAL HISTORY

7th century — 360/59 B.C.

STRUGGLES FOR THE CONTROL OF LOWER MACEDONIA (750-650 B.C.)

The coastal plain, which formed the heart of what Thucydides called 'lower Macedonia', was rich in agricultural potential and provided winter pastures for transhumant herds; the products of the interior, especially timber, passed through it to reach the Aegean Sea. Thus it was always the ambition of the strongest power in the southern Balkans to possess this plain. Entries into it were from upper Macedonia by Beroia and by Edessa; from the middle Axios valley via Valandovo (not via Demir Kapu, then impassable); and from the east via Lete. The Axios, a formidable barrier for primitive people, divided the plain into unequal parts, the greater being to the west of the river.

The descendants of Makedon, the Makedones, lived, in the opinion of Hesiod,[1] in the Pierian mountains from the earliest times. We find them there in the history of Herodotos. They dwelt with or alongside the Bryges who held the plain by Vergina in the Early Iron Age until c. 800 B.C. Their homeland, 'the Macedonian land' proper,[2] lay south of the Haliakmon, and the road which Perseus built on the north side of Olympos (via the Petra pass) went over the 'Macedonian mountain.'[3] This is where they lived for the period we are considering, c. 800-650 B.C., an area

famous for its summer pastures and its timber. No doubt the Makedones practised transhumant pastoralism in these early times and developed their own particular dialect, one which they may have shared with the Magnesians. For, in historic times the Makedones and the Magnesians both had cults of Zeus Hetaireios and engaged in the same war dance.

The first Greeks from the south to colonize the coast of the Thermaic Gulf were Eretrians, driven out of Korkyra by the Corinthians, rejected by their mother-country and sent on to colonize Methone, which lay just south of the navigable river, the Haliakmon. At the time c. 733 B.C., Methone was near the territories of four peoples who were probably at variance with one another: Thracians, Makedones, Bottiaioi and Illyrioi, both around Vergina. Eretrians also founded a colony called Dikaia at the head of the Gulf on the east coast, probably near Mikro Karabournou. What attracted the colonists was ship-timber, floated down the Haliakmon and the Axios, or cut on the Pierian mountains and on Mt. Kissos, perhaps gold from the river Gallikos and foodstuffs, as well as good arable land in the vicinity of the colony. The next waves of colonists went to the prongs of Chalkidike, where they found timber, land, fisheries and mines of silver and iron inland near Stageiros. They were interested not primarily in Macedonia but in the main trade route from south Greece to the Hellespont along the Aegean coast and in the exports of the Strymon basin. But the Greeks were unable to establish any colony in that desirable basin. The local tribes were too strong: Illyrian warrior-groups as we see from typically Illyrian objects found in graves in the Kumli valley and at Nine Ways (later Amphipolis), and Thracians about whom we know more after 650 B.C.

THE MAKEDONES WIN LOWER MACEDONIA WEST OF THE AXIOS, 650-513 B.C.

The Illyrian recession gave the Makedones an opportunity of which the founder of the Temenid dynasty took advantage. The king, Perdikkas, brought his people down from the Pierian mountains and occupied the edge of the western plain, making his new capital at Vergina. This decisive event was blessed by Delphi in a *vaticinium post eventum,* which attributed to Zeus the gift of the Macedonian crown to the Temenids and instructed the king to found a city where goats were sunk in sleep.[4] This place proved to be called Edessa (a Phrygian name, meaning water-place (the Greek Ὑδροῦς) and was renamed as Aigai (Bleaters) in memory of the goats (in Greek αἶγες). Herodotos recorded the next step, the conquest of the so-called gardens of Midas below Mt. Bermion, of which the modern Beroia, Naousa and Edessa are the ruling towns. For a long time thereafter the border between the Makedones and the Bottiaioi was formed by the Loudias and the Haliakmon, into which the Loudias flowed,[5] and a great part of the Makedones adopted a settled agricultural life.

That Perdikkas and his successors were Temenidai from Argos in the Peloponnese was officially confirmed when the right of Alexander I to compete in the Olympic Games at the turn of the sixth to the fifth century B.C. was upheld by the Judges at Olympia. Herodotos,[6] Thucydides[7] and others described the kings as Temenidai and it is their statement of the generations from father to son that enables us to date their arrival in Macedonia to sometime around 650 B.C. The Temenid family, being descended from Zeus and his son Herakles, was a branch of the Herakleidai, a clan to which the kings of Sparta and Aleuadai of Thessaly belonged. The ancestor of this branch, Temenos, had led the Dorians into the Argolid and fallen in battle during the conquest of the land; and his descendants were the rulers of Argos until shortly before Perdikkas came to Macedonia and became king. How did Perdikkas win the throne? Herodotos evidently asked that question of Alexander I, and the reply was in the form of a story based on an Iranian folktale, which Herodotos retold with relish.[8] The truth is not known. But the tribe over which the first kings ruled was the Argeadai; for they were sometimes known as the Argead kings, and it was the Argeadai tribe which led the expansion in the sixth century B.C. Undoubtedly their rule extended rapidly over the other 'Makedones.'

The countries which we know as Epirus, Albania and Macedonia were occupied in the seventh century B.C. by a very large number of small tribes, whose origins lay in the practice of transhumant pastoralism. Sometimes a tribe may have been no larger than a group of families which formed a single shepherd company, a *parea* as it is called by the nomadic Sarakatsani today. These tribes banded themselves together into regional groups under a common name such as Thesprotoi, Molossoi, Chaones, Taulantioi, Orestai, Pelagones, Paiones and Makedones. Fourth century inscriptions in Epirus have revealed the substructure of small tribes and the way in which one tribe might move from one regional group to another; elsewhere we know only from occasional literary references or inscriptions that a sub-tribe of the Orestai was called the Triklaroi, of the Perrhaiboi the Imphees, of the Pelagones the Geneatai and of the Paiones the Doberes. The Makedones were no exception. The individual tribes and the regional groups alike were governed normally by 'kings', but the consolidation of power in a regional group caused the elimination or absorption of the lesser kings. This stage had already been reached when the Molossoi and the Makedones, for instance, emerged into the light of history; and this is equally true of the Taulantioi or the Paiones or the Odrysai. Indeed the Balkan tribes at this time were indistinguishable from one another in their socio-political system.

The self-conscious city-states of the Greek peninsula regarded all the Balkan tribes as barbaric *ethne* from the fifth century onwards, because the Balkan institutions were not based on the city-state. Thus Thucydides, for instance, referred to Molossoi, Makedones, Taulantioi and Edonoi alike as barbarians. This did not mean that they all spoke non-Greek languages. Hesiod, as we have seen, regarded Makedon and Magnes as sons of Thyia by Zeus. As Thyia was the sister of Hellen, the father of Doros, Xouthos and Aiolos, who were the eponyms of three branches of the Greek-speaking race, Hesiod considered Makedon and Magnes — and the Makedones and Magnesians for whom they were eponyms — to be a collateral branch of the Greek-speaking race. The distinction, in fact, was one of dialect, not of language. This is made abundantly clear by Hellanikos, a contemporary of Thucydides, who made Makedon a son of Aiolos, i.e. not only Greek-speaking but using the Aiolic dialect of Greek. In Classical times the Magnesians spoke a form of the Aiolic dialect, and it is correct to infer from Hellanikos that the Makedones also spoke a form of the Aiolic dialect, one which may well have been at a primitive stage of development and pronunciation, because the Makedones had been isolated for centuries from other speakers of that dialect (see chapter, The Inhabitants).

The Molossoi provide a relevant analogy. That they were Greek-speaking might have been deduced from Herodotos' inclusion of them among those who participated in Greek colonization; but it was only the discovery of inscriptions which showed that in 370-68 B.C. their speech, nomenclature and political terms were entirely Greek and had been in the time of Thucydides, since the patronymics too and the tribal names were Greek. In the seventh century B.C. the Molossoi probably spoke a north-west dialect of Greek.[9] So too the Thesprotoi and the Chaones, for whom similar later fourth century inscriptions have come to light. Further, the tribes which Strabo termed 'Epirotic'[10] — Orestai, Tymphaioi, Elimiotai, Lynkestai and Pelagones — are likely to have spoken the same dialect as the Molossians, to whom they were in some sense related. In any case the tribes on both sides of the broad Pindos range were associated with the western groups of tribes and not with the Makedones by Hekataios in the sixth century B.C.; for he defined the Dexaroi (later called Dassaretai) as a constituent tribe of the Chaones, and the Orestai as a constituent tribe of the Molossoi.[11] The Dexaroi were then adjacent to the Illyrian Encheleai, so that their lands stretched as far north as the ridge between Maliq and Pogradec.

The Makedones were less interested in the hinterland than in the coastal plain. By force of arms they acquired southern Pieria, Almopia (north of Edessa) and Bottiaia, which was the richest part of the western plain. In this last exploit they were led by the Argeadai. It was perhaps in the decade 520-10 B.C. that they turned inland and conquered Eordaia, thereby blocking the routes from upper Macedonia which led into lower Macedonia near Beroia and Edessa. These conquests were to be permanent. For whereas Illyrians, Thracians and city-state Greeks tended to reduce those they conquered to serfdom, slavery or tributory status, the Makedones exterminated or expelled every native and peopled the land with their own race, in which the birthrate must have been high. One consequence was that all Makedones were free men and they had no dissident population which had to be held down by force. Another advantage was an inner unity which served them well against their many enemies.

The survivors escaped to the east: the Pieres to settle among other Thracian tribes on the south side of Mt. Pangaion, the Bottiaioi to settle in the base of the Chalkidike peninsula, and the Eordoi at Physka in Thracian Mygdonia. After the collapse of the Illyrians, the most powerful people east of the Axios were the Thracian tribes, headed by the Edonoi, after whom the Gallikos river was called the Edonos. While they held Krestonia, one of their constituent tribes, the Mygdones, held the head of the Thermaic Gulf east of the Axios and the rich area of lake Koroneia and lake Bolbe. Another tribe, the Sithones, held parts of Chalkidike, including the central prong which was called Sithonia. To the north another people, the Paiones, expanded into the areas east of the upper Axios as the Illyrians withdrew. They were a large group of tribes, which included the Agrianes at the head of the Strymon and the Laiaioi lower down the Strymon by Kyustendil. Soon after 550 B.C. the Paiones became the leading power. They acquired Amphaxitis from the Edonoi and came down to the mouth of the Axios, then close to Pella and Ichnai; they occupied Mygdonia and the Kumli valley, which link Amphaxitis to the Strymon basin; one tribe, the Siriopaiones, established themselves at Siris (now Serrhai) and ruled the Strymon basin. So strong and aggressive were they that they marched through southern Thrace and attacked the Greek city of Perinthos on the coast of the Propontis.

The archaeological evidence for this period is relatively slight. Vergina provides no burials in its great cemetery; but some of the two hundred unexcavated tumuli may hold remains of the leading Makedones. Burials of leading Thracians are notable for the mouthpieces of gold leaf with strings which were tied over the mouth of the corpse; they have been found at Chauchitsa, Zeitenlik and Kalamaria near Thessalonike, Hagios Basileios in Mygdonia and as far afield as Kuci Zi near Korytsa. Inland, the cantons of upper Macedonia were a backwater except that some trade from Thessaly reached the middle Haliakmon valley and its influence was apparent in some rich graves at Kozani. In Pelagonia Illyrian burials lasted into the early sixth century in tumuli near Prilep (e.g. at Visoï II); but at Saraj near the border between Pelagonia and Lynkos the cemetery of what was probably a local dynasty was in use until the end of the sixth century, and a number of agricultural settlements appeared, each with its own cemetery nearby, on the edge of the fertile plain by the Erigon. These were to develop into 'the cities of the Derrhiopes all by the Erigon'.[12] Pottery and bronze objects exported from Ionia, Chalkidike and Corinth reached Pelagonia in the sixth century, and there was evidently a trade route westwards to the Ochrid basin, where the graves of a royal family at Trebenište contained many objects which had come from southern Greece. Another trade route went from Pelagonia to the Korytsa plain, where Illyrian burials ceased early in the seventh century B.C. and a second tumulus at Kuci Zi had eighteen burials with some imported Greek pottery and bronze objects which showed close connections with the tumulus-burying peoples of northern Epirus, namely the group known as the Chaones.

To the east of the Axios the withdrawal of Illyrian bands seems to have occurred c. 600 B.C., e.g. at Orlova Čuka near Štip. A remarkable cemetery came into use in the latter part of the sixth century B.C. at Karaorman near Štip; for there was clear evidence of sacrifice both at the time of burial and for some decades afterwards. It is possible that the cemetery was that of the Paionian dynasty which had its capital at Astibos (Štip) and controlled the Bregalnitsa valley. This area, like Pelagonia, was devoted to agriculture and famous for its oxen. To the south of the Thracian tribes in Mygdonia, the Bottiaioi found a refuge in inland Chalkidike but with an outlet to the coast at Olynthos. Excavation there has shown that they brought the emblem of the three double-axes from Emathia, and that in the sixth century they were influenced less by their Greek neighbours than by Balkan taste in pottery and in bronze ornaments, such as the collared bronze beads and reels, which were in vogue inland in the Axios and Strymon valleys.

The number of southern Greek colonies grew during the seventh and sixth centuries B.C. Another Greek city appeared near Methone, Pydna; and on the east side of the Thermaic Gulf, Therme near Dikaia and an older city Aineia, reputedly founded by Aeneas. The people of Krousis began to live in cities near their coast. And the prongs of Chalkidike were thickly studded with colonial cities, the most important being a Corinthian colony,

34. A royal cemetery was discovered at Trebenište north of lake Ochrid, whose graves were mainly of warriors. The dead wore gold face masks, gold sandals and gloves; like the Mycenaean rulers they were buried in full armour. The finds include other gold and silver objects and beautiful bronze vessels which were most probably imported from Greek settlements on the shores of the Thermaic Gulf and of the Adriatic coast. The photograph shows a mask from Trebenište decorated with meanders and braided ornament. Sofia, Archaeological Museum

Poteidaia, which was well placed on the eastern approach to the Thermaic Gulf. By the middle of the sixth century B.C. Greek trade was penetrating far inland, especially on the eastern side of the Axios valley into Paionia and thence into southern Serbia and also westwards into central Albania. Greek traders and adventurers, such as Peisistratos who settled at Rhaikalos near Aineia, were attracted not only by timber, foodstuffs and animal products but also by the mineral wealth which was already being exploited by the native peoples.

THE PERIOD OF THE PERSIAN WARS, 513-477 B.C.

The conquest of Asia Minor by Persia created an important market for the Balkan peoples. In particular Balkan silver was highly prized in Asia and Egypt for its purity, and silver bullion, in the form of ingots and coins of large denomination, was provided by a considerable number of tribes: the Tyntenoi (later Atintanoi) who mined silver on the east side of lake Ochrid; the Derrones near Štip mining at Kratovo; the Laiaioi near Kyustendil; the Orreskioi and other Thracian tribes by Mt. Pangaion. During their period of power the Paionians issued coinage also from Ichnai and from Lete, and in the Strymon basin from Siris, the capital of the Siriopaeones. As the Greek cities in the East were the intermediaries in this traffic, the coins were inscribed in Greek letters. This became unnecessary when Darius invaded Europe and established his authority in Thrace *c.* 513 B.C., and the large coins of the ensuing period down to 498 B.C. were mostly not inscribed. The Thracian tribes seem to have made little or no resistance to

Persia, but the Paionians mustered their forces in defence of the Strymon. They were outmanoeuvred and then defeated piecemeal; their leading families were deported to Asia. The tribes of western Thrace were the gainers: they took control of the Strymon basin, Mygdonia and Krestonia as loyal subjects of Persia. The Edonoi were the most powerful tribe in this area, but later another Thracian tribe, the Bisaltai, based on Mt. Dysoron, gained ground at their expense and captured an important mine near lake Prasias (Butkovo). The Bisaltai began to issue large coins soon after 500 B.C.[13]

The weakening of Paionian power in general gave the Makedones their chance. They seized Amphaxitis and the Argeadai tribe led the way across the Axios and destroyed a strongpoint on the left bank at Amydon (Vardaroftsa). When the Persian commander, Megabazos, sent his envoys through the territory of the Bisaltai into Amphaxitis c. 510 B.C., the Macedonian king, Amyntas I, submitted and was left as a subject-king. He curried favour with Persia by marrying his daughter to a Persian grandee, Boubares, and he was entrusted with the control of the Axios crossing by Persia. To this end he received from Persia the lands east of the Axios mouth and Anthemous. Here and in Amphaxitis the Makedones did not exterminate the native peoples but incorporated them into the kingdom. It was a radical and important change of policy.

During the Ionian Revolt, Macedonia and Thrace remained loyal to Persia. The successor of Amyntas, Alexander I, a skilful diplomat, found favour with Darius and Xerxes as the guardian of the Axios ford between Amydon and Ichnai. When Xerxes planned the invasion of Greece, he wished to deepen the defences of the Axios crossing by controlling the hinterland, and for this purpose he enabled Alexander to extend his rule over the region between Mt. Olympos and Mt. Haimos,[14] a grandiose expression for the high country from Pieria to the Šar Planina. It was at this time that Alexander claimed that the tribes of this region — Elimiotai, Tymphaioi, Orestai, Lynkestai and Pelagones — were 'Makedones' and not 'Molossoi' (as hitherto), and that their territory was 'upper Macedonia'. Here too there was no policy of expulsion. Alexander wished to incorporate these Greek-speaking tribes into his kingdom.

Thirty years of Persian presence in Macedonia indirectly favoured the economy of the country. Large military and naval forces needed provisions, clothing and equipment which the native peoples were ready to supply at a price, and there was now an immediate market for precious and useful metals. Alexander's kingdom could supply everything except the gold and silver, and in particular it had ship-timber which was needed for construction and repair. The extent to which trade in the Balkans was invigorated is seen most markedly at Trebeniŝte north of lake Ochrid, where members of a royal family were buried with gold death masks, gloves, sandals, gold and silver objects, iron armour and iron weapons, fine bronzes of Corinthian style, and rich ornaments (fig. 34). The burials covered the period c. 540-c. 475 B.C., and the richer were in its second half. Imports reached Trebeniŝte from Greek colonies on

the Adriatic coast and from the ports of the Thermaic Gulf, and traffic in silver to the west is revealed by a hoard of silver coins of Lete, Poteidaia, Akanthos and Mende at Taras in southern Italy. The gold and silver in the burials came probably from Metohija and Kossovo in the north, and there were contacts with Dodona in the south.[15] This wealthy dynasty at Trebeniŝte was probably that mentioned in a corrupt passage in Strabo[16] as closely associated with the Encheleai (who held the Ochrid basin) and the name of the dynasty may be accepted tentatively as 'Peresadyes', which suggests a Thracian connection, Berisades being a royal name later among the Odrysians. The silver mine at Damasteion lay within the territory of the Peresadyes-Encheleai, and large coins inscribed TYNTENON (the later Atintanoi) were exported from there to Macedonia and Thrace. The bulk of the trade in silver in 510-480 B.C. was in the hands of the Greek cities of Chalkidike and the Thracian coast, Thasos, and the Thracian tribes of Krestonia, Mygdonia, the Strymon basin and the Pangaion area. The Bisaltai exploited their mine and issued large coins c. 498-c. 480 B.C.

Alexander I was elected king c. 495 B.C. He was already known in southern Greece as a sprinter and in the pentathlon in the Olympic Games, where his Greek descent (i.e. from Temenos) had been upheld by the Judges of the Games, Pindar composed an ode in his honour, addressing him as 'bold-scheming son of Amyntas', and the poet was said to have been entertained lavishly at his court. Thus Alexander had a place both in the Balkan-Persian world and in the Greek world. Our knowledge of him is due mainly to the Greek historian of the Persian Wars, Herodotos, who seems to have visited Thasos, Eïon and lake Prasias but not the plain of lower Macedonia. It is evident that Herodotos met the king and put the king's stories into his history. One at least can hardly be true: that Alexander as prince arranged the assassination of the first set of Persian envoys at the Macedonian court and then thwarted Persian enquiries by systematic bribery.[17] Alexander was portrayed by Herodotos as an engaging personality, honest, shrewd, foresighted, a benefactor of Athens, and eager for the liberation both of Macedonia and Greece from Persia. His real feelings will never be known. What is certain is that before 480 B.C. the survival of Macedonia depended on cultivating the favour of the Persians, and this, it seems, was achieved with the help of Boubares, Alexander's brother-in-law.

As representative of the Great King, Boubares had a military force at his headquarters somewhere in Macedonia, probably west of the Axios river from c. 510 B.C. until his departure to Persia in the early 490s.[18] We do not know the name of Boubares' successor, but Macedonia certainly remained within the satrapy, 'Skudra'. In 492 B.C. a large army and navy under the command of Mardonios moved along the Thracian coast in order to reduce any Greek cities which had aided the Ionians in their revolt, and perhaps to prepare the way for invading the Greek peninsula. The fleet suffered severe losses in a storm off Mt. Athos, but the residue probably came to

37

35. *Possession of the mines of eastern Macedonia and their subsequent exploitation was sought by Thracians, Macedonians and by colonists from southern Greece. The coins which they minted were high denominations and circulated widely in the East. Stater of Lete depicting a satyr and nymph 500-480 B.C. Athens, Numismatic Museum.*

36. *Octodrachm of the Edones. 590-580 B.C. London, British Museum.*

37. *Octodrachm of Alexander I Philhellene, depicting a mounted warrior holding two spears (495-445 B.C. Paris, Bibliothèque Nationale.*

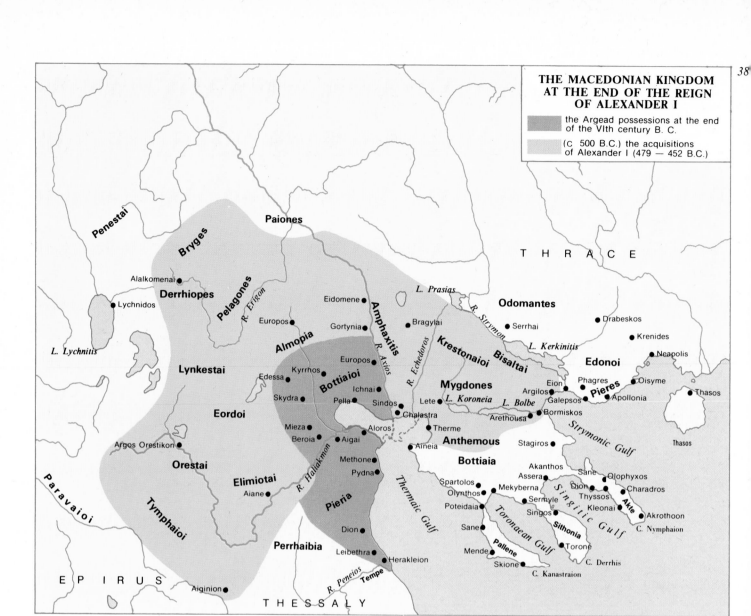

**THE MACEDONIAN KINGDOM
AT THE END OF THE REIGN
OF ALEXANDER I**

the Argead possessions at the end
of the VIth century B. C.

(C 500 B.C.) the acquisitions
of Alexander I (479 — 452 B.C.)

38. *After the withdrawal of the Persians from Greece the in-*
fluence of the Macedonian kingdom, till then confined to Pieria
and Bottiaia, greatly increased. King Alexander I succeeded in
pushing his frontier eastwards to the river Strymon at the ex-
pense of the barbarian tribes and in imposing his authority over
the related Macedonian peoples of upper Macedonia.

the head of the Thermaic Gulf to keep contact with the
army which advanced into Amphaxitis and encamped
there in the realm of Alexander. A night attack by 'Thracian Brygoi' (probably from the region of Valandovo) inflicted losses on the Persian army, but they and no doubt
other inland tribes were subjugated to Persian rule. In the
event the Persian attack on Eretria and Athens in 490 B.C.
was delivered by sea. Its failure meant that the next invasion would be by land. It was in preparation for this that
Boubares, the patron of Alexander, took charge of the
building of a canal through the neck of the Athos peninsula
in 483-81 B.C., and that Alexander was enabled to extend
his rule over upper Macedonia. At the same time Alexander rendered some service to Themistocles, who was
building a fleet at Athens to resist Persia; this may have
been the sending to Athens of ship-timber, which was a
royal monopoly.

The Persian army and navy of Xerxes used lower
Macedonia as its chief base while preparations were made
for the invasion of Thessaly in 480 B.C. These included the
building of a mountain road over the Petra pass into the
high plateau of Perrhaibia, a canton which neighboured
Alexander's kingdom, and a naval reconnaissance of the
mouth of the Peneios river. A Greek force had encamped
in the Vale of Tempe, close to the mouth of the river.
Herodotos states that Alexander sent secret warning of
Xerxes' forces and plans to the Greeks, and that this was a
cause of the Greek withdrawal from Tempe. This could be
represented later as a service to Persia or to Greece,
whichever suited Alexander's book.

The Persian forces included levies from their subjects in
Europe, and among them were Makedones, commanded
by their king Alexander. They served as light-armed skir-
mishers. According to Herodotos, Alexander continued to

play a double game, warning and advising the Greeks, acting as a Persian emissary and arranging for Macedonian troops to garrison cities of Boiotia. When Xerxes withdrew late in 480 B.C., he was not attacked by the Macedonians, and again Artabazos marched unopposed through Thessaly and Macedonia into Thrace where he was attacked, probably by the dissident Bisaltai among others, in 479 B.C. But in the wake of the retreating Persians Alexander annexed by force of arms Mygdonia, Krestonia, Bisaltia and the western side of the Strymon basin; he even held Nine Ways, the site of the later Amphipolis, for a short time. While enlarging his kingdom in this way, Alexander attacked some Persian forces, and from the spoils he dedicated gold statues of himself at Delphi and Olympia. By then he was exploiting the mine he had won from the Bisaltai; his first coins had the Bisaltic types — the kneeling goat and the man with a walking horse — but the inscription 'of Alexander' instead of 'of the Bisaltai'.[19] By intelligent opportunism and 'bold scheming' Alexander enlarged and strengthened his kingdom in the latter part of the Persian period. In his new territories east of the Axios he left most of the tribes in possession of their lands; but others were driven out and took refuge in the Athos peninsula, where their presence was mentioned by Thucydides.[20]

ATTEMPTS TO HOLD THE GREATER KINGDOM AGAINST ATHENS AND OTHER ENEMIES, 476-399 B.C.

Escaping from the grip of Persia, Alexander fell into conflicts with Athens and with the Edonoi over possession of the Strymon basin. Having created the Alliance which had its centre at Delos in 477 B.C., Athens led its forces first to the capture of Eion at the mouth of the Strymon in 476 or 475 B.C. and to an attack on the Thracian tribes inland which had supported the Persian garrison of Eion. The aim of Athens and her Allies was not liberation but possession; for they put all adult males to death and enslaved the women and children of Eion and occupied as much territory as they could hold. The Macedonians, the Thracians led by the Edonoi and the Athenians and their Allies then engaged in a three-sided struggle, which became a major war when Thasos defied Athens in 465 B.C. Late that year Athens landed troops and ten thousand would-be settlers on the banks of the Strymon, captured Nine Ways from the Edonoi and advanced into Edonian territory in order to cover the establishment of a fortified colony at Nine Ways. But they were heavily defeated near Drama and had to abandon the project of founding the colony. Meanwhile they operated against Thasos with success, used her as a naval base against the Thracians and took possession of Thasian mines and territory on Thracian soil in 462 B.C. As Kimon, the commander of the forces, was prosecuted for failing to invade Macedonia and cut off a large part of its territory,[21] it is probable that Athenian forces had clashed with Alexander already on the western

side of the Strymon basin. Then in 460 B.C. Athens turned her attention elsewhere. The only thing we know about Alexander at this time is that he held Pydna, a Greek city on his coast, gave Themistocles asylum there and defied Athens by helping him to cross by sea to Asia.

With Athens absent from the scene, the Macedonians and the Edonoi fought one another for several years, and Alexander lost the Bisaltic mines for a period. Both sides were weakened as result, and c. 452 B.C. Alexander died a violent death. Nothing is known of his activities in upper Macedonia and the hinterland. At Trebenište the graves of the dynasty were much poorer after c. 455 B.C. and this was probably characteristic of a general decline in prosperity after the withdrawal of Persia from western Thrace.

The vicissitudes of Alexander's fortunes were reflected in his coinage. Although the interpretation is controversial, it seems that he issued large denominations as bullion for as long as he owned the Bisaltic mines from which he drew a talent of silver a day, and that these issues were intended for exchange in the Balkans and in Asia. From c. 467 to c. 460 B.C. he issued tetradrachms and tetrobols on a standard which facilitated trade with Athens and her Allies in the Aegean; for large forces were then present on the Thracian coast and in Thasos. Then in c. 459-52 B.C. the output of coins declined considerably, and he used a different standard which was suitable for trade in the Balkans and with Greek states outside the Athenian orbit. He probably provided export facilities for the inland Paionian tribes, Derrones in the upper Axios valley and Laiaioi in the upper Strymon valley. In general, his coinage was only one of several coinages issued by Balkan tribal states, and there were many Greek city-states with equally strong, or stronger, currencies on the coasts of Chalkidike and Thrace.

The death of Alexander was followed by a period of dissension between his sons and some division of the kingdom between three of them until 435 B.C., when Perdikkas II became sole king and reigned until c. 413 B.C. During this period Athens assessed for tribute three cities on the east coast of the inner part of the Thermaic Gulf: Strepsa near the mouth then of the Gallikos (it is now some thirteen kms. inland), Dikaia and Aineia; the cities of Krousis and of most of Chalkidike; and on the west side of the Strymon, then navigable far inland, Berge in Bisaltia and Argilos. She also planted a colony shared with some Bisaltai at Berge. Thus Athens had no footing west of the Axios but controlled the best part of the Thermaic coast for purposes of export, the coast from there to the mouth of the Strymon, and then upstream to Berge, which evidently had some access to the Bisaltic mines. Bisaltia itself was independent of Macedon, and its king, Mosses, issued his own coinage. Thus Macedonian territory east of the Axios had shrunk considerably. In 436 B.C. Athens greatly strengthened her position by driving the Edonoi out of Nine Ways and founded a colony there, named Amphipolis; it contained people from Argilos as well as from overseas. During this period there were no Macedonian coins above a tetrobol although from c. 445 to 435 B.C. the Bisaltic mines may have been in Macedonian hands and in the latter part of it Perdikkas was perforce an 'ally and friend' of Athens.[22]

From 434 B.C. until his death c. 413 B.C. Perdikkas was involved in the war between Athens and Sparta. While Athens supported Philip, a brother of Perdikkas, as pretender to the throne, and also Derdas, king of Elimiotis in upper Macedonia, Perdikkas retaliated by urging the Peloponnesians to instigate risings against Athens in Chalkidike. In 432 B.C. an Athenian expeditionary force found that Perdikkas had already raised the Chalkidians and Bottiaians in revolt and given them part of his territory in Mygdonia to farm for the duration of the war. So the Athenians collaborated with the forces of Philip and Derdas against Perdikkas. They captured Therme at the head of the Thermaic Gulf and then laid siege to Pydna; but the news that a Peloponnesian force had reached Poteidaia compelled them to make an agreement and even an alliance with Perdikkas: 'they departed from Macedonia (i.e. the original Macedonia of Herodotos),[23] came to Beroia and thence towards Strepsa which they tried but failed to take, and then proceeded overland to Poteidaia'. There they found Perdikkas in support of the Poteidaians — in breach of his agreement — and in the ensuing battle neither group of Macedonian cavalry went into action (Perdikkas' two hundred and the other of six hundred 'with Philip and Pausanias', probably a brother of Derdas).[24] In 431 B.C. Perdikkas and Athens made a deal; Perdikkas was given Therme and in exchange helped Athens against Poteidaia. Nominally they became allies, but neither party trusted the other.

The pressure of Derdas and his own brother Philip made Perdikkas look for allies in his hinterland. There, the Orestai were independent; but Perdikkas acted in sympathy with their king, Antiochos, in summer 429 B.C. when he sent one thousand Macedonians to support a Spartan commander in Akarnania. This was done 'without the knowledge of Athens'.[25] In fact, both Perdikkas and Athens were intriguing secretly with Sitalkes in the hope of damaging one another. A bone of contention between them was the Greek city, Methone, which had become an ally of Athens; as it lay so close to his capital at Aigai, Perdikkas proceeded to boycott it, and Athens told him to desist in a decree which has survived.[26] Shortly after this decree was passed, the intrigue with Sitalkes resulted in action.

The father of Sitalkes, Teres, had created a powerful state as king of the Odrysians, a tribe which held a strategic part of the lower Hebros; and Sitalkes had gained control of the great plain of the upper Hebros. Sitalkes called himself 'king of the Thracians' with some justification, since his rule extended from the Getai of the Danube to Abdera near the mouth of the Nestos and from the coast of the Black Sea to the Paionian tribes on both sides of the upper valley of the Strymon, especially the Agrianes and the Laiaioi, and to the tribes east of the upper Isker, a tributary of the Danube. The Thracians who were still independent were those west of the lower Nestos, the moun-

tain tribes of Rhodope and Orbelos being particularly warlike. For his campaign in autumn 429 B.C. Sitalkes was said to have taken one hundred thousand infantry and fifty thousand cavalry, which included both his subjects and volunteers or mercenaries from the independent Thracians. His purpose was to punish Perdikkas for bad faith and to replace him with Amyntas, a son of the pretender Philip, and to join an Athenian naval force and make the Chalkidians return to their membership of the Athenian empire. So he brought with him Amyntas and an Athenian mission, headed by Hagnon, the founder of Amphipolis. No doubt Sitalkes intended to increase his own kingdom by annexing the lands between the Nestos and the Axios and by having a puppet king in Macedonia west of the Axios. This constituted the greatest threat yet to the existence of Macedon.

Leaving the Odrysian kingdom at the upper Strymon valley, Sitalkes avoided the Kresna defile of the middle Strymon by marching through Mt. Kerkine (Ograzden) with the independent Maedoi and Sintoi on his left and then descended into Paionian Doberos,[27] i.e. the upper Stroumiča valley, where the full force mustered. He then crossed (via Valandovo) into upper Amphaxitis, the old realm of Philip, where he won over most of the towns, took Eidomene by storm and failed to capture Europos. His huge forces then ravaged and looted Emathia (but kept clear of Bottiaia and Pieria, the main centres of Macedonian manpower), Mygdonia, Krestonia and Anthemous. While the rest of the population fled to hills and strongholds, the Macedonian cavalry — 'brave cuirassiers' as Thucydides called them[28] — both of lower and of upper Macedonia succeeded wherever they attacked the enemy, but had to desist in case they were surrounded and cut down. If the Athenian fleet had arrived with an army, the Athenians and Sitalkes could have overrun Pieria and installed Amyntas as king. But the fleet did not appear either there or off Chalkidike, where a part of Sitalkes' army was ravaging the lands of the Bottiaians and the Chalkidians, and Sitalkes had to withdraw for lack of supplies, which the fleet might well have been able to provide. So after a campaign of thirty days he went away, persuaded by his nephew Seuthes, to whom Perdikkas had made a secret offer of his sister in marriage and a sum of money as a dowry. This was a promise which Perdikkas kept, no doubt with a sigh of relief. Sitalkes died on campaign against the Triballoi in 424 B.C.; Seuthes succeeded and stayed on friendly terms with Perdikkas.

Perdikkas had other enemies in his hinterland. One was a dynasty founded c. 450 B.C. by Arrhabaios, a member of the Bacchiadai, a clan which claimed descent from Herakles and had ruled over Corinth in the distant past. Arrhabaios became king of the Lynkestai — it is not known how — and maintained his independence. In 424 B.C. Perdikkas and the Chalkidians persuaded Sparta to send a force of one thousand seven hundred infantry under Brasidas, and they undertook to support it. Although its avowed purpose was to extend the area of revolt from Athens, Perdikkas led Brasidas at once to the frontier of

Lynkos. But Brasidas refused to invade and offered to arbitrate, much to Perdikkas' annoyance.[29]

But in 423 B.C. Perdikkas got his way. He, Brasidas and the Chalkidians invaded Lynkos with a force of three thousand Greek hoplites (of whom a part were from Perdikkas' kingdom), almost one thousand cavalry from Macedonia and Chalkidike, and a great crowd of barbarians, as Thucydides scornfully called the Macedonian infantry.[30] Perdikkas had also hired some Illyrian mercenaries who were said to be on the way. Arrhabaios had a comparable force of cavalry, Lynkestian hoplites and other infantry, drawn probably from Pelagonia as well as Lynkos. He chose a position in north Lynkos near the exit of the Diavat Pass from Illyris.

When the cavalry fought in the plain, the Lynkestian hoplites came down from a hill to support their side, and a general battle ensued, in which Arrhabaios suffered heavy losses. However, he regained a position higher up. Neither Perdikkas nor Brasidas was prepared to assault his position. Perdikkas proposed, pending the arrival of his Illyrians, to advance against the villages of Arrhabaios[31] (presumably the small towns of Derrhiopos), but Brasidas wanted to withdraw altogether.[32] While they disputed, news arrived of the Illyrian mercenaries. They had joined Arrhabaios. It was already evening when Brasidas went off to his camp, which was separate from that of Perdikkas. In their fear of the dreaded Illyrians the Macedonians panicked. They fled under cover of darkness without a word to Brasidas (the lame excuses which Thucydides reported were probably given to him by Perdikkas). The Peloponnesians and the Chalkidians were saved by the brilliance of Brasidas, and they took their revenge by killing any draught-oxen and seizing any baggage of the Macedonians *en route*. Perdikkas with more anger than sense concluded an agreement with Athens and prevented the arrival of any reinforcements for Brasidas. In 422 B.C. he was ordered by Athens to send troops in accordance with his alliance, but he had not acted when the Athenians made a premature march on Amphipolis and were defeated. But Brasidas was killed, and in 421 B.C. the great powers made an uneasy peace.

Perdikkas now paid for his mistaken policy. Having alienated the Chalkidians, he was at the mercy of Athens which exacted its price. Herakleion, controlling the route from Thessaly into Pieria, Bormiskos controlling the route from Mygdonia into the Strymon plain, and Trailos, which had access to a Bisaltic mine, appeared on the tribute lists of Athens, and Perdikkas had to supply troops at Athens'

39. *The heirs of Alexander Philhellene, Perdikkas II and Archelaos, had to face vigorous military opposition from the southern Greek powers who plagued the Macedonian kingdoms. Battles and campaigns on Macedonian territory were a regular occurrence at the time of the Peloponnesian War. The picture shows a grave stele of a Macedonian warrior who carries a spear and sword and wears a helmet. It was found at Pella. Late 5th century B.C. Istanbul, Archaeological Museum.*

call. To all intents and purposes a subject of Athens, Perdikkas could sell timber only at Athens' price, and he ceased to issue coinage altogether. He escaped for a time by making an alliance with Sparta and Argos, and he advertized his connection with Argos by issuing tetrobols with Herakles' head and club and the boar Herakles had slain; but it was a false move, since Argos soon joined Athens, and Sparta sent no help. He faked his coinage, putting silver on copper, and then submitted to Athens. In 414 B.C. he was serving, like some Thracian tribes, on the side of Athens against Amphipolis,[33] and he must have been a disappointed man when he died a natural death in 413 B.C.

His successor, Archelaos, reaped the benefit of the defeat of Athens at Syracuse late in 413 B.C. He could now call the tune, as Athens had hardly any ships and needed huge amounts of timber at his price. In 410 B.C. an Athenian general was helping him to capture and keep Pydna, and in 407/6 the Athenian people hailed Archelaos and his sons as state benefactors for supplying ship timber and special facilities.[34] His kingdom prospered. He issued a fine coinage, ranging from didrachms to obols, and he evidently held the Bisaltic mines. Inland he was hard pressed for a time by the rulers of Lynkos (Arrhabaios II and Sirras), but he gained the support of the independent ruler of Elimeia[35] to whom he gave his daughter in marriage. Athens presumably let him recover Herakleion, Bormiskos and Trailos, and he planted an important colony at the northern end of the Demir Kapu defile, which has become known through excavation.[36] Thucydides said that Archelaos did more than his eight predecessors to strengthen his kingdom. He built some strongpoints (one stood above his colony), cut straight roads (i.e. through forested areas for military purposes), and made military improvements particularly in the matters of cavalry and hoplite infantry.[37] In these ways he became more of a match for Athens, Chalkidike or Lynkos; but at the same time he must have trained some infantry as peltasts to contend with his enemies in the Balkans.

The Aleuadai, a Heraklid clan of nobles at Larisa, invited him to intervene on their side in Thessaly c. 400 B.C. It was a tribute to his power, and his army did succeed in storming the important city of Larisa. The Aleuadai made him a citizen of Larisa and gave him some territory, probably in Perrhaibia. In 399 B.C. he was killed during a hunt by one of the Royal Pages. Some thought the killing

40. *Tetradrachm of Akanthos, 530-480 B.C., showing a lion tearing a bull apart. London, British Museum.*

41. *Stater of Neapolis (modern Kavala), depicting a gorgon. 500-480 B.C. Athens, Numismatic Museum.*

42. *Tetradrachm of Mende with the well-known representation of Dionysos on an ass. 460-420 B.C. Athens, Numismatic Museum.*

deliberate and suspected a conspiracy; but nothing was proven.

A PERIOD OF WEAKNESS 399-359 B.C.

The consequences of Archelaos' death were disastrous. Between 399 B.C. and 393 B.C. no fewer than six kings held office. They derived from three branches of the royal house: Orestes, Aëropos and Pausanias, descendants of Perdikkas; Amyntas 'the Little', descended from Menelaos; and Amyntas, descended from Amyntas (Perdikkas, Menelaos and this last Amyntas being three of Alexander I's five sons). During this troubled period Aëropos was forced to make a treaty with Sparta, then the leading power. Amyntas III became king in 393 B.C. only to be expelled by an Illyrian dynast, who was almost as dangerous as Sitalkes had been.

Bardylis created a powerful kingdom, of which the centre was formed by the Dardanians, themselves a group of tribes, and he controlled the rich mineral and agricultural resources of Kosovo and Metohija. From there he overran the impoverished dynasty of Trebenište — the 'poor graves' ending at this time — and occupied the lakeland, so that he became a threat to both Molossia and Macedonia. In 393 B.C., his huge forces occupied both western and lower Macedonia and he placed on the Macedonian throne his puppet, Argaios, a son probably of Archelaos, who reigned from 393/2 to 392/1. Then in 385/4 he invaded Molossia, killed fifteen thousand Molossians in battle and would have set up a puppet king, Alketas, if Sparta had not intervened. In 383/2 he invaded Macedonia again, defeated Amyntas in battle and occupied lower Macedonia. These hammer-blows were accompanied by the massacre and the looting which were characteristic of warfare among the Balkan tribes. In her weakness Macedonia had to turn to her Greek neighbours. In 393/2 Amyntas entrusted a district, probably Mygdonia, to the Chalkidian League, and he took refuge himself with the Aleuadai. They expelled the Illyrians and reinstated Amyntas in 391 B.C. No doubt he received his territory back from the Chalkidians; for he entered into a defensive alliance with the Chalkidian League, of which a record survives.[38] It contained provision for joint action and gave the Chalkidians some concessions in the matter of Macedonian timber.

In 383/2 Amyntas deposited even more of his territory with the Chalkidian League, which was now extremely strong. This time he did not leave the country. He fought on from some small base, and within three months he freed his country. This amazing achievement won him the devotion of his people. But his troubles were not ended. The Chalkidian League not only refused to return his territory but even invaded lower Macedonia and captured Pella, the capital since the end of the fifth century and now the largest city. In desperation he turned to Kotys, king of the Odrysians, and became a close friend of Kotys' general, an Athenian called Iphikrates; but it is unlikely that Kotys

sent any troops. What saved Amyntas was the intervention of Sparta, which was determined to break up the Chalkidian League and entered into an agreement with Amyntas. He was told to hire mercenaries (Sparta evidently rated Macedonian infantry low) and to obtain the alliance of kings inland. In the ensuing campaigns the most distinguished cavalry was that of Derdas, ruler of Elimeia. In 379 B.C. the Chalkidian League was disbanded, the Spartan force went home and Amyntas resumed his territories.

In 377 B.C. Athens needed ship-timber in large quantities. Amyntas provided it on his own terms, and was made an ally of Athens.[39] But soon the situation was reversed; for Athens became the leading sea power in a few years and in 371 B.C. Amyntas was represented at a general peace conference, probably as a stooge of Athens, and voted in favour of Amphipolis being restored to Athens. In the 370s Bardylis abstained from invading lower Macedonia only because Amyntas paid him money. By 371 B.C. Amyntas did not possess the Bisaltic mines; indeed he may have been coining only in bronze, as his successor had to do. His reign had been one of remarkable ups and downs. But his people thought the world of him and showed it by worshipping him as a god after his death, which occurred naturally in 370 B.C.[40]

Amyntas was the founder of that branch of the Temenid house which was destined to make Macedonia a world power. He set the example for some of his son Philip's methods in diplomacy, and he stressed, as his successors did, his family's descent from Herakles. He placed on his coins the head of Herakles, the club of Herakles and the boar which Herakles slew; and also the eagle (probably of Zeus) striking a snake. His successor, Alexander II, continued to buy off the Illyrians but engaged in an adventure in Thessaly, where the Aleuadai invited him to intervene. He gained control of Larisa and won over some other cities; but contrary to a promise he had given he placed Macedonian garrisons in them. This brought onto the scene an army from Boiotia, now the leading military power in Greece, and its commander Pelopidas freed the cities, invaded Macedonia and compelled Alexander to become the ally of Boiotia and hand over hostages. One was his youngest brother, Philip, who had already been a hostage in Illyria; he had to live in the house of a leading Theban general, called Pammenes, from 368 to 365 B.C.

Alexander was assassinated during a festival in 368/7. His brother was elected king, Perdikkas III, but as he was under age a regent was appointed, Ptolemy Alorites (i.e. a resident of Aloros), probably a son of Amyntas 'the Little'. But there was another candidate, Pausanias, probably a son of Archelaos, who had been exiled by Amyntas III. He enjoyed much support in Macedonia, and he invaded at the head of a Greek force, recruited perhaps in Chalkidike, since he won Anthemous and the area of Therme and Strepsa. Ptolemy was saved by Iphikrates, serving Athens now and anxious to obtain Macedonian help against Amphipolis. But the intervention of Athens alarmed Thebes, which sent Pelopidas and a mercenary force into Macedonia. Ptolemy was forced to make an alliance with

43. The cheek-piece of a bronze helmet found near Grevena. It bears a representation of a winged Victory bearing a spear and shield. 4th century B.C. Thessalonike, Archaeological Museum.

the Boiotian League and to send to Thebes his son and fifty Companions as hostages. During this period of weakness the Orestai became a member of the Molossian group of tribes, which was expanding in Epirus.[41]

Perdikkas came of age in 365 B.C. Ptolemy disappeared from the scene, perhaps being assassinated. Perdikkas honoured his alliance by supplying timber to the Boiotian League which was building a fleet to challenge Athens, and in return he obtained the release of his brother Philip. Athens retaliated by capturing Pydna, Methone and Poteidaia, which were valuable bases for a naval blockade, and by instigating the inland kings to make attacks; and this forced Perdikkas to come to terms with Athens. He may have paid tribute.[42] In 364/3 he was helping Athenian troops against Chalkidike. He broke away in 363 B.C., but was attacked by an Athenian expedition and had to sue for an armistice in 362 B.C. Philip, coming of age at eighteen at this time, was given part of the kingdom to defend. An inscription which lists the hosts of a sacred mission from Epidauros in these years shows that Pydna, Methone, Dikaia, Aineia and Poteidaia were independent states ringing the Thermaic Gulf; that Kalindoia north of Chalkidike was represented by Pausanias, probably the pretender to the throne; and that Apollonia in Mygdonia, Arethusa (near Bormiskos), Berge, Argilos and Trailos were independent states. Amphipolis was maintaining its independence with the help of a Macedonian garrison.

A greater danger still was Bardylis. With superior forces he invaded and looted Molossia c. 360 B.C. but suffered some losses through ambushes. In 360/59 B.C. he invaded Macedonia. Perdikkas, unlike the Molossian king, Arybbas, challenged Bardylis in a set battle. He was killed with four thousand of his men; the Illyrians raided and looted and occupied western Macedonia. The other enemies of Macedon — Athens, Paionians, Thracians supporting Pausanias, and the Chalkidian League — stood ready to invade the enfeebled and demoralized kingdom.[43]

THE ECONOMIC AND SOCIAL DEVELOPMENT OF MACEDONIA TO 359 B.C.

Before and during the period 750-650 B.C. the economy of Macedonia was based on transhumant pastoralism. In this respect it was like its neighbours Epirus, Illyria and much of western Thrace, but unlike Thessaly, where agriculture had developed. One characteristic of such an economy is that it is almost self-sufficient in food and clothing, and needs only fruit, pulses and vegetables and salt which was obtained from coastal salt-pans. Then and throughout Classical times the shepherds needed spears, javelins and knives to contend with the beasts of prey — from lions and bears to wolves and jackals — which roamed the forests and meadows of the mountain ranges. Moreover, they fought one another for the best pastures; and had to obtain winter pastures and protect their flocks

from the settled population in the lowlands. They preferred, like migrating birds, to return to the same pastures summer and winter, but they could do so only if strong enough to master any opposition.

The basic unit in transhumant pastoralism was until recently a company (parea) or encampment (stani), which moved with its flocks, horses and dogs from summer to winter pastures, each autumn and spring. The size of the unit was determined by geographical conditions and organizational requirements. Thus such a unit among the Sarakatsani, who had access only to the poorer pastures and those rented, was of the order of fifty adults; but among the Vlachs, who owned the best summer pastures and rented only winter pastures, it was about fifty families. The tribal system of the Vlachs was based on these units. Each unit was a tribe originally, but the units tended to coalesce in the summer into a group, which became itself a tribe but not of more than two hundred families (so G. Weigand in the 1890s). Such groups of tribes, practising endogamy within the tribe or the cluster, developed their own character, dialect and habitats; for example, five hundred families used pastures on Mt. Grammos and in the plain south of Bouthroton in the 1920s, and were known as the Grammosteanoi.[44]

We see here the origins of the Tymphaioi (named after Mt. Tymphe) Orestai, Lynkestai and Pelagones, who practised this way of life and were each a cluster of tribes. In medieval times Kantakouzenos wrote with alarm of the marauding tribesmen who descended into Thessaly and were known as Malakasioi, Bouioi and Mesaritai. They too were evidently well armed.

In a period of fully migratory pastoralism, men live in the open or in thatched huts, but the summer encampments sometimes coalesce into a synoikismos or 'living together'. Out of such a combination of three to five encampments there developed the high villages of Pindos, e.g. Samarina, Avdhella and Perivoli according to their own traditions; but in the winter each encampment went its own way. There are no such villages by the winter pastures. When the migratory life was abandoned by some Vlachs, they settled in the lowlands or the plains and practised mixed farming or crafts, for instance round Grevena, Almiros and Stratos, without losing their identity at least for some centuries. The ancient Makedones seem to have gone through these stages: fully migratory with a centre at Lebaia in the Pierian mountains (like Vlakho-livadhi for the Vlachs of Olympos), then in part settled at Vergina (Aigai) in the plain, and then mainly in the towns which grew up in the whole of the coastal plain. In upper Macedonia the old way of life persisted until the reign of Philip II, as we read in Alexander's speech to his soldiers reported by Arrian.[45]

In peaceful times transhumant pastoralism is more than self-sufficient. It produces a surplus of meat, cheese (sheep being milked), wool and hides, and this surplus was readily exported to markets in the Aegean basin and southern Greece. Indications of this trade are the fine bronze vessels and the Greek pottery found at centres of summer pasture such as Votonosi, Vitsa and Kuci Zi. An important asset which was developed primarily by pastoral peoples was the timber of Macedonia, logged in the mountains and floated down the great rivers, Axios and Haliakmon, to where the settled people of Amphaxitis and the Emathian plain worked it for export. Demand was unlimited, especially for ship-timber, which Athens, Corinth and other naval states needed desperately; and so was the supply since agriculture was comparatively recent even in the lowlands and most of upper Macedonia was pastoral. There were stands of fine timber even on Mt. Kissos (Chortiatis east of Thessalonike) and in Pieria which were in the possession of the Makedones proper.

What is called Macedonia today is particularly rich in minerals. But it is important to note that the area west of the Axios held by the Makedones proper had no gold or silver. There were deposits of iron and iron pyrites (by Beroia, in Pieria, Almopia and Amphaxitis); molybdenum (used in alloying steel) in Eordaia; and some copper in Amphaxitis. But the rich deposits were elsewhere: silver in quantity at Damasteion east and north of lake Ochrid, near Tetovo in Pelagia north of Pelagonia, in the Pecinj and Bregalnitsa valleys of Paionia and in the Kumli valley of Bisaltia. Gold was washed in the Echedoros (Gallikos); it is found near Kilkis in Krestonia, near Lete in Mygdonia, in Paionia and at Nigrita (near Trailos) in Bisaltia. Copper ores are found in Tymphaia, Orestis and Dassaretis; in Krestonia and Paionia. Outside Macedonia Chalkidike had its own gold, silver, copper and iron north of Akanthos.

The working of gold, copper, lead, bronze and iron was practised in Bronze Age Macedonia, and the art was not lost in the Early Iron Age. The hammered iron of spearheads, knives and swords in tumulus burials at Vergina from the tenth century onwards was some form of mild steel. The first datable slag of this kind was in the post-seventh century layer at Vardaroftsa. In 359-8 B.C., when Philip equipped his army with the long-bladed *sarissa,* he must have used local metal. Macedonian metalworkers were probably adept too in the making of gold and bronze vessels and jewellery.

When Alexander I acquired territories beyond the Axios, he was the first Macedonian king to obtain gold and silver ores and his wealth seemed vast to contemporary Greeks. His mine in Bisaltia alone produced a talent of silver a day.[46] But his successors were frequently without these territories, and then they either coined only in tetrobols, or plated coins, or ceased to coin at all.

Anyone who has seen the harvesting of grain in the coastal plain realizes the great agricultural potential of lower Macedonia. It has been developed mainly by flood-control and irrigation, methods first introduced by Philip II. Until then the area famous for agriculture was Paionia with its magnificent draught-oxen, but even so lower Macedonia probably provided a surplus of grain in most years. And as a whole, upper and lower Macedonia together did not depend at all on imports for subsistence. Export was often in the hands of others — Chalkidians, Greek cities of the Thermaic Gulf, Athenians and others.

The harbour dues of Macedonian (as opposed to Greek) harbours on the Thermaic Gulf were only twenty talents a year until an Athenian emigre, Kallistratos, pushed them up to forty talents. It was Philip II who captured all the ports and developed direct Macedonian trade on a large scale.[47]

The economic development of the Makedones may be summarized in stages. At first migratory transhumant pastoralists in several small tribes, they began to develop also a settled life of farming in the western part of the Emathian plain from 650 B.C. onwards. An expansion of farming came with the conquest up to the Axios and beyond into Anthemous by 500 B.C. But pastoralism was still on a large scale in Pieria and Eordaia. Alexander I gained further experience of good agriculture in the Strymon basin, where the Paionians had worked the soil and built towns, and he brought much mineral wealth into his kingdom after 479 B.C. The state seemed capable of attaining great economic strength. But after 475 B.C. it was an almost constant struggle for survival. Archelaos did most to modernize the state by building roads and planting at least one colony. He showed that Macedonia could become very prosperous, if it was left in peace to develop its own coast and hinterland.

SOCIAL AND POLITICAL INSTITUTIONS *c.* 750-359 B.C.

In the pastoral unit which we have described, men, women and children, living mainly in the open, lead a communal life and each have their own tasks and contribute to the well-being of the company *(parea).* Land, herds and timber are owned in common. It is a strongly-knit society with an inbuilt sense of obligation and honour. There is neither individualism nor serfdom. On the other hand, there is a strong patriarchal authority. The elected head of a group or tribe has full powers which are exercised to hold the company together and negotiate on its behalf; he is called the *tshelniku* among Vlachs, the *tselingas* among Sarakatsani and the *phylarchos* by Kantakouzenos in the Middle Ages. The same system obtains where units coalesce into a larger tribal unit; the title in antiquity was then often *basileus,* king. The leader or king commanded in hunting and in war, conducted the religious ceremonies of the group and disciplined its members, but his authority

44-46. Silver staters minted by Archelaos, showing a mounted warrior and a goat; of Amyntas III and of Perdikkas III both depicting the head of Herakles on one side; the other side is engraved with the name of the king and a horse. London, British Museum.

44

45

46

was founded on the consent of the members of a group with which he was in daily contact.

The concept of self-government within each pastoral unit or tribe persisted even when larger groups were formed, such as the Grammosteanoi. This is most apparent in the fourth century inscriptions of Molossia, where many small tribes had each their own assembly and state, but yet combined together to form the Molossian state under a hereditary monarchy. Thus in the 330s τὸ κοινὸν τῶν Ἀμύμνων recorded a manumission and in the third century. B.C. τὸ κοινὸν τῶν Ἀτεράργων renewed friendship with the Pergamioi, a tribal state outside the Molossian group. The decisions of the Molossian state in the same way were those of τὸ κοινὸν τῶν Μολοσσῶν. Similar systems existed also in the Thesprotian state and in the Chaonian state. The evidence for the related tribal groups of upper Macedonia is later but points in the same direction. Some of the constituent tribes are known from inscriptions or literary texts: Triklaroi and Battynaioi among the Orestai; Dostoneis, Geneatai and Argestaioi among the Pelagones; and Malei (? atai) among the Elimiotai. Resolutions by some of these tribes have survived: by the Malei (? atai), the Argestaioi and among the Derrhiopes the Styberraioi. The inscriptions are indeed much later; but the institutions are likely to have existed from early times. The tribal groups to which they belonged were themselves independent self-governing entities, *ethne* as Thucydides called them, with a hereditary monarchy at the head of their government.[48]

The Makedones were not related to the Molossian group, to which the tribes of upper Macedonia had belonged in the sixth century. They were *sui generis*. That they too had consisted of individual tribes is shown by the mention of the Argeadai in a passage which referred to the sixth century B.C. and was derived probably from Hekataios as a tribe or people.[49] This tribe led the way in the advance across the Axios to destroy Amydon; and we may infer from this that it was itself headed by the king as commander in war and so may be called 'the royal tribe', like the Edones among the Edonoi. The members of this tribe in the local tradition were the descendants of Argeas, a son of Makedon,[50] who had other sons: Pieros, Amathos and Brousis;[51] the Argeadai had come from Argos in Orestis to their later habitat, i.e. in Pieria. Their full title was Ἀργεάδαι Μακεδόνες.[52] When Perdikkas I gained the throne *c.* 650 B.C., he became king both of the Argeadai and of the Makedones.

In the course of the sixth century B.C. some of the constituent tribes adopted a settled life in the Emathian plain and created their own towns. For some time the tribal names may have persisted, as with the Vlachs; but certainly by the end of the fifth century B.C. the towns were of considerable size and formed the centre after which the citizens were named. Each town had its own territory, e.g. ἡ Πελλαία sc. γῆ,[53] and its own finances,[54] and a citizen called himself Pellaios or Alorites etc. Only in Eordaia, where pastoral life probably continued, were men called not by a town but by the territory Eordaia 'Eordaioi', as

the 'Tymphaioi' were so named from the mountain Tymphe. When the Makedones conquered Amphaxitis and the territories east of the Axios, they found well-established cities which the Paionians and the Thracians had developed, such as Ichnai and Lete. These cities kept their name and identity within the Macedonian kingdom, and their citizens were Ichnaioi and Letaioi. All these centres were evidently self-governing in their municipal affairs; that is how they maintained their identity. In upper Macedonia towns were rare; but already in 423 B.C. the towns of Arrhabaios were such centres under the name *komai.*[55]

Within Macedonia in the modern geographical sense two forms of local citizenship evolved: tribal citizenships such as Eordaioi, Elimiotai, Lynkestai, and town citizenships such as Aloritai, Pellaioi and Letaioi. The same phenomenon is attested in fourth century Molossia, where Arctanes and Tripolitai occur in inscriptions alongside Dodonaioi and Eurymenaioi; and there the further complication arises that a man may have both a tribal and a town citizenship, e.g. Ἀρκτὰν Εὐρυμεναίων. An analogous case in upper Macedonia is a township-state, ἡ πόλις τῶν Στυβερραίων inside a tribal state, ἡ πόλις τῶν Δερριόπων so that a man might have been called Δερρίοψ Στυβερραίων. Similarly a double tribal citizenship occurred in purely tribal areas, such as Ἀργεάδης Μακεδών, Τρίκλαρος Ὀρέστης and Ἀργεσταῖος Πελαγών; and likewise in Epirus Ἀρκτάν Μολοσσός and Ἰκαδωτός Θεσπρωτός.

The Temenid house claimed suzerainty over all these self-governing bodies. The suzerainty was expressed in our literary sources by the addition of 'Makedones' after the tribal ethnic in upper Macedonia. Thus in Thucydides,[56] although Arrhabaios was at war with Perdikkas, his people are described as Λυγκησταὶ Μακεδόνες. And the Orestai, having been Ὀρέσται Μολοσσοί in the sixth century B.C., became Ὀρέσται Μακεδόνες in the fifth century. This extended use of the term Μακεδόνες is not to be confused by us with the original use of Μακεδόνες as the conquerors of lower Macedonia, οἱ Μακεδόνες οὗτοι in Thucydides,[57] and with the specific use of Μακεδών for an inner citizenship, to which we shall now turn.

It is clear from literary sources that a man might be either a Πελλαῖος or a Πελλαῖος Μακεδών, e.g. Μαρσύας Μακεδὼν Πελλαῖος[58] and inscriptions provide examples of both appellations, e.g. Ἄρχων Φιλίσκου Ληταῖος,[59] Μακεδόσι ἐκ Πέλλης[60] and Εὐρωπαῖος Μακεδών.[61]

This inner citizenship was conferred by the king on anyone he chose, in the lifetime of Philip II and probably earlier, so that even Greeks from southern Greece were made not only 'Makedones' but also 'Companions'. In the literary tradition,[62] 'the Companionship of Archelaos' paid honours to Euripides who was buried at Arethousa in Macedonia, not as a resident alien, we may be sure, but as a member of the King's Companionship with Macedonian citizenship. As such, Euripides had attended royal banquets,[63] and had been in the company of Royal Pages;[64] and the Macedonians refused to let the Athenians exhume his corpse and remove his remains to Attica, presumably on the grounds that he was a Macedonian citizen.[65] The holders of the citizenship in general were certainly those who served as soldiers under the king's command, since Macedonia was constantly on a war footing, if not actually at war. They met in the Assembly under arms; for on electing a king they clashed their spears on their shields to indicate their readiness to serve him, and they used their spears (or stones) to execute anyone they found guilty of high treason. Some ceremonials of state were carried out by the Makedones under arms,[66] such as the purification after the death of a king. Those who had served their time and were above military age presumably remained 'Makedones' and attended the Assembly. It was these who constituted the Macedonian Assembly (Diodoros' τὸ κοινὸν τῶν Μακεδόνων πλῆθος[67]) and the Macedonian state (τὸ κοινὸν τῶν Μακεδόνων as Arrian referred to it,[68] like τὸ κοινὸν τῶν Μολοσσῶν) and in this narrow sense Perdikkas was βασιλεὺς Μακεδόνων.[69]

Mentions of the 'Makedones' in inscriptions are rare, but important. The contracting parties of an inscription[70] (probably *c.* 415 B.C.) are the Athenians and the Macedonians on behalf of whom Perdikkas and others took the oath, Μακεδ[ον]ον Περδίκκας. Similarly in 346 B.C. if Pausanias was drawing on inscribed records of the Delphic Amphiktyony,[71] the votes of the Phokians were given to the 'Makedones', correctly so stated, because the Amphiktyony was one of tribes, not individuals. In an alliance recorded between Amyntas and Chalkidike *c.* 393 B.C.,[72] there are regulations governing the transit and export of goods which are subject to dues payable by the Makedones to the Chalkidians and vice versa (τελέουσιν τέλεα... Μακεδόσιν). In 325 B.C. a payment of five talents to the Delphic Amphiktyony was made by Μακεδόνες, i.e. by the Macedonian state, whereas the *hieromnemones* were appointed by Alexander.[73] These instances show that Diodoros[74] and Arrian,[75] were accurate in saying that tribute was payable to τοῖς Μακεδόσιν. The Macedonian Assembly, no less than the Athenian Assembly, was competent to receive and expend monies. In general our literary sources were interested only in the king and attributed all actions to him alone, e.g. in the remission of taxes which were payable probably to the state and not to the king.[76] Only occasionally in the context of Alexander the Great does a literary source distinguish between the king and the Macedonian state. Thus in Plutarch's life of Alexander[77] an exemption from enslavement at Thebes was made for τοὺς

47. The stele from Nea Kallikrateia is an outstanding work, influenced by Cycladic workshops. It depicts a young girl with a dove. Artists from various places, mainly Ionia, established themselves in northern Greece and created local artistic traditions. As the Macedonians abandoned the nomadic life following the expansion of their kingdom eastwards, they came into contact with the products of southern Greek civilization which in many instances they admired and assimilated. c. 440 B.C. Thessalonike, Archaeological Museum.

48. *The stele of Aiane (near Kozani) belongs to a series of Macedonian grave stelai of the 4th century B.C. executed by local craftsmen influenced by Attic originals. Though marked by provincial clumsiness, they nevertheless possess a certain* novelty. *Here we see a Macedonian family; the dead man, wearing a chlamys and a hat is seated; two women and a child stand in front of him. Behind stands another man. 4th century B.C. Paris, Louvre.*

ξένους τῶν Μακεδόνων ἅπαντας, i.e. all diplomatic representatives of the Macedonian people; and in the corresponding passage in Arrian we find that the king had *xenoi* or personal guest-friends and that the Macedonian people also had its diplomatic representatives or *proxenoi*.[78] We infer, then, that the Macedonian Assembly appointed its representatives in foreign states. Where there was no possibility of conflating king and people, the distinction was clear in the literary sources: the people elected a king or deposed a king (of Amyntas III, ὑπὸ Μακεδόνων ἐξεβλήθη;[79] were addressed by a king[80] (τοὺς Μακεδόνας ἐν.. ἐκκλησίαις), and tried cases of treason (ἐν

Μακεδόσι),[81] even as the Athenian Assembly did.

Was there anything analogous to a Council, as in a Greek state? In upper Macedonia we can only conjecture that the kings may well have consulted the heads of the individual tribes and convened them for that purpose. Their name may have survived in the word πελιγᾶνες[82] or πελιγόνες (meaning 'elders').[83] The former of these, being attested in the inscription, is more likely to be correct; and as it is a west Greek form, it originated among the tribes of upper Macedonia. In lower Macedonia, however, the tribal system was replaced by the town system sometime before the fourth century, and we have only slight evidence for the period before that change occurred. In the story which Herodotos recounts of the arrival of Perdikkas and his brothers in Macedonia, the reigning king was advised what to do by one of his councillors,[84] and he sent horsemen in pursuit. Whoever told Herodotos this story, whether Alexander I or one of his courtiers, was reflecting conditions of his own day, when a king did have councillors and his chief aides were cavalrymen. They were no doubt already called Companions of the king (ἑταῖροι). For the worship of Zeus Hetaireios in Macedonia and the existence of a festival the Hetaireidia, which was common to the Macedonians and the Magnetes, testify to the importance of the Companions in even earlier times than those of Alexander I. Later and certainly in the fourth century the Companions were chosen by the king to accompany him in the hunt and in battle and they earned the praise of Thucydides as 'brave cuirassiers' in 429 B.C.[85] As we see in the reign of Alexander III and may assume was the case earlier, the king invited some of his Companions to counsel and advise him; but there was no official membership, no regular meeting or procedure, and no obligation on the king to follow their advice. Those who stood highest in his confidence were called his 'Friends', whether they acted as advisers or as his entourage on ceremonial occasions;[86] and it was from them that he chose his subordinate commanders, the *Hegemones*, and his personal Bodyguards, seven in number, the *Somatophylakes*. Thus the initial selection and the subsequent career of a Companion depended entirely on the pleasure of the king.

Boys of the royal family and sons of 'the Companionship of Archelaos', for instance, were educated at the court of the king as Royal Pages (βασιλικοί παῖδες). This is apparent from the circumstances of Archelaos' death, known to us from Aristotle, whose father was a doctor at the Macedonian court. In 399 B.C. Archelaos was killed during a hunt by a boy Krateuas, who had been his 'beloved'; and suspicion attached also to another 'beloved', Hellanokrates of Larisa, a boy probably of the Aleuad house, and to a boy Decamnichos, who had been delivered to Euripides for a flogging.[87] They belonged then to the group of Royal Pages who waited on the king, guarded him at night, joined him in the hunt and at war, and sometimes shared his bed. Greeks from southern Greece regarded such boys as slaves attendant upon their owner, especially as flogging was the punishment of Greek slaves. But they were in fact the élite of Macedonian society, likely to become Companions in due course and to be promoted to the positions of Friend, *Hegemon* or *Somatophylax*.

There was no nobility, that is no aristocracy of birth, in Macedonian society in the latter part of our period. The tribal system had lapsed long since in lower Macedonia. On the other hand, a number of leading families emerged. They earned the king's favour by their services in the first place, and thereafter, as in most meritocracies, they obtained for their sons the training at court which was likely to bring them promotion in later life. After the royal house itself they were 'the most distinguished' Macedonians (οἱ ἐνδοξότατοι).

The extension of the Companionship to infantrymen was attributed to 'Alexander' by Anaximenes, a contemporary of Philip II and Alexander III. Since the infantry was a rabble in 424 B.C.,[88] but formidable from the early years of Philip II, this Alexander is most reasonably identified with Alexander II. The shortness of his reign, 370-68/7 B.C., does not debar him; for Philip II reformed the army in a year. Alexander II, then, created 'Infantry-Companions', called *pezhetairoi*, who were an élite group close to the king and some of whom acted as a Royal Guard, if they were analogous to the Companions proper, the Cavalrymen. The purpose was to increase the prestige of the infantry and to promote zeal in the king's service. The details of Alexander's reform of the Macedonian infantry are lost; for the brief account given by the lexicographer Harpokration is confused.[89] But we may be confident that he intended to create some sort of phalanx infantry, capable of fighting against Greek hoplites, because his most dangerous enemy was the Boiotian army. To some extent his intention was fulfilled in the years 360-59 B.C.; the Molossians did not dare to engage the army of Bardylis, but the Macedonians fought a pitched battle. True, they were defeated; but Philip inherited an infantry force which had had more training than any previous one in Macedonia.

Finally we come to the apex of the Macedonian state, the monarchy. It was in origin a tribal institution in a pastoral society. At first it was particular to one tribe, the Argeadai; then it came to dominate the Makedones, a group of tribes which included the Argeadai; and in the reign of Alexander I it claimed suzerainty over the tribes of upper Macedonia, to which the same title, 'Makedones', was added. The first stage left its legacy in the forms of traditional sacrifices and nomenclature. In a letter of Olympias to Alexander III she wrote of special knowledge of 'the ancestral sacrifices, both the Ἀργαδιστικά (which is usually emended to Ἀργεαδικά) and the Bacchic ones'.[90] Next, a papyrus fragment which relates to the 'Will of Alexander the Great'[91] has the following lines with probable restorations: καὶ συντελείσθωσ[αν; 17 letters] Μακεδόνες Ἀργεάδ[αι, 17 letters]τ]ὰ νομιζόμενα [μετα, 16 letters] Βασιλέως· ἐξέστω δ[έ, 16 letters]. 'And let Makedones Argeadai celebrate the customary rites with (the) king'. The performing of 'customary rites' was recorded in the Royal Diaries of Alexander.[92] When Perdikkas became king of the Argeadai and so of the Makedones *c.* 650 B.C. it seems that he took the title 'Argeades' in addition to his own proud title 'Temenides'. For this title was twice used of later kings. In Plutarch[93] 'being a king' is expanded into 'being wealthy and (an) Argeades', à propos of Alexander III meeting Diogenes. In a Sibylline oracle[94] the phrase 'O Makedones who take pride in Argeadai kings, the rule of Philip is for you a boon and a disaster', the title was used to cover Philip II, the boon, who was a Temenid, and Philip V, the disaster, who was an Antigonid. In order to bridge the two dynasties the Sibylline oracle used the traditional title which they had in common, 'Argeades'.

These passages (of which the interpretation is controver-

49. *Stele from Poteidaia depicting a young lyre-player. The dead man is shown frontally, a stance not often found in carvings of that time. The skilled and experienced craftsman was influenced by Ionic originals. c. 380-370 B.C. Thessalonike, Archaeological Museum.*

50. *Relief stele from Pella, one of the oldest and most beautiful made in Macedonia. The inscription tells us that the name of the dead woman was Philopatra. She is seated; the bearded man on the right is probably her husband, Pausanias, son of Andriskos. The other figures, one male and two female, are perhaps her children and grandchild. Two smaller female figures, in front of Philopatra, are probably slaves. Second half of the 4th century B.C. London, British Museum.*

sial) serve anyhow to show that the king had an inherited duty, to represent his people in relation to the gods. The king began every day with sacrifice, whatever his circumstances or state of health. He awaited favourable omens, revealing the approval of a god, before he took any decisive step in peace and war. He conducted numerous festivals of state in honour of the gods. As head of the royal family he sacrificed to its founder, Herakles Patroos, at Aigai; and probably at Pella, where worship of Herakles and Herakles Phylakos (guardian) is attested. On visiting Pella the king was met by a cup-bearer, probably a priest of Herakles Propylaios (protector of the gates), and he poured a libation before entering the precincts. The chief god of the state was Zeus the Highest, the ruler of Olympos, father of Makedon and of Herakles and god of the Hetairoi; and special festivals were held by the king at Aigai and Dion in thanksgiving to Zeus. Special honour was paid to the protectress of the state in war, Athena Alkidemos, and to the war-spirit, Xanthos. A festival called *Xanthika* was held every spring and attended by the Makedones under arms; the weapons of past kings were carried in the procession, the army passed between the severed parts of a dog, and there was a mock fight. Second to war came hunting. Herakles Kynagidas was worshipped throughout Macedonia, and the king was always Master of the Royal Hunt, as on the fresco of the large tomb at Vergina.

The royal family was unique among the Makedones and had no rival. In origin it was Greek, not Macedonian; descended from Herakles; and above any local or family rivalries of the Macedonians. It was natural for the Temenid kings to treat all their subjects alike, whether Greek, Macedonian or Thracian in blood, and they were repaid by an extraordinary devotion and respect.[95]

To the Makedones it was unthinkable that anyone except a Temenid should be king or regent, and on the death of Alexander III they insisted on electing Philip Arrhidaios, half-witted though he was, because 'he was the dead king's brother; closest in kinship and associated with him in sacrifices and ceremonies'.[96] The procedure for election was traditional. The Makedones met under arms, indicated their choice by acclamation and hailed the new king. He put on the diadem, and royal dress and received the royal signet-ring. The Royal Guard moved to his side, some of the most distinguished Macedonians put on their cuirasses and the Assembly clashed their spears against their shields. The king was then escorted to the palace. It was a military affair; for he was chosen to lead them in war, and even if he was a minor he had to be present during a battle in order to win divine support.[97] He was a warrior-king in a warrior-state. A reign of peace was unthinkable if you lived in lower Macedonia.

The body of the king who had died lay in state. His Friends sat by the body, and those objects which were to accompany it to the grave were laid beside the head. The nature of the state funeral and the form of burial will be described in later chapters. If the king had been assassinated, the first duty of his successor was to apprehend any suspects, bring them before the Assembly for trial and himself conduct the prosecution. The decision lay with the Assembly, and the king acted only as the Assembly's executive agent if further inquiries had to be made. The king chose his own Friends and Bodyguards, and if at war his *Hegemones* (he did not inherit his predecessor's choices). The royal patronage was personal and immediate. One of his first duties was to beget male heirs, sufficiently numerous to offset the hazards of war, hunting and disease, and several (probably all) kings were polygamous. Their wives were all royal consorts and their sons were all royal princes, as Justin remarks of Philip II.[98] His marriages and those of the royal house were arranged with a view to strengthening the kingdom by a web of matrimonial alliances.

The male members of the royal house took precedence after the king and before the commoners in all ceremonies. Thus in the treaty between Macedonia and Athens the oaths for the Makedones were taken by the following: Perdikkas son of Alexander, Alketas son of Alexander, Archelaos son of P[erdikkas, two other members of the house], Menelaos son of Alexander, Agelaos son of A[ketas, ---]yros son of Alketas, Byrginos son of Kraston. The last is the first commoner in the list, i.e. the leading Friend of Perdikkas outside the royal family.[99]

The king used them if he could as *Hegemones* and as envoys. On the other hand, if a member of the royal family acted against the king, the law of high treason operated against him as against any commoner: he and his relations by blood were executed.[100] Every step had to be taken to protect the life of the king; for the safety of the state resided in him. The women of the royal house made clothes, ground corn and baked bread at home, as all Macedonian housewives did. They were not present at royal banquets or royal ceremonies. The king was waited upon by his Friends and by the Royal Pages, and there is no record of any slaves at this period. When a commoner addressed the king, he removed his hat or helmet; but otherwise he spoke as man to man. 'The king's subjects were accustomed to royal rule and lived with a greater sense of freedom than any other people subject to a monarchy', as Curtius observed.[101] Etiquette was traditional and accepted. It is seen most clearly in stories of the Royal Hunt, in which lions and bears as well as deer were attacked with spears. The Macedonian Assembly laid down the general rule that the king should hunt only on horseback and be accompanied by his leading Friends.[102]

The king did not have a bureaucracy. The units of the Macedonian state — the towns, the tribes and the tribal groups — administered their own affairs. His task was to deal with the Makedones proper, the élite armed forces of the kingdom. Here he relied to some extent on his Friends and *Hegemones* who were equally available for military and administrative and diplomatic duties; there were no strictly professional services, just as there were no professional priests. He was extremely wealthy, in that he owned the mineral resources, the quarries and the timber of the realm. He issued and owned his currency which was in-

51. *The chief companions of the Macedonian kings were the* Hetairoi *from whom he chose his officers and generals. Mounted, they escorted him hunting and into battle. The picture shows* a young Macedonian on horseback wearing a chlamys. It was found at Pella. Mid-4th century B.C. Pella, Archaeological Museum.

scribed with his name. He owned large tracts of land, mainly, it seems, east of the Axios. Some were kept as hunting parks; some were given to his Friends as rewards; and some were entrusted to his allies in time of war.[103] He demanded unpaid services at need, and he was entitled to raise money by levy *(eisphora)*. In a successful war he took for himself the arms and property of the enemy king. In the conduct of a war his powers of command were total. He made all decisions, issued all orders and enforced strict discipline, even to the extent of flogging and execution. And he led the attack in person.

Thus the Macedonian monarchy was monarchy in the literal sense, one-man in command. But it was constitutional monarchy, established by the people and operating within the law; and it was hereditary monarchy, so that heirs were trained by example and by precept for the practice of one-man rule. The cohesion of the state depended on the monarchy, the Companionship and the Assembly of the Makedones proper. When they were one in their purpose, the state took its direction from the monarch entirely, and if he was dynamic and capable the state had a potential for power. In the Greek world there was no such monarchy; for the only form of one-man rule, tyranny or as we should say dictatorship, was totally different in its illegality and repression. There were analogies in the Balkan world, where there were warrior-states and monarchs such as Sitalkes and Bardylis. But there was one all-important difference between the Balkan states and Macedonia. The Macedonian kings were Greek, not merely in descent but in outlook, religion and culture. They understood the mentality of the city-state Greeks; indeed they even outwitted them in diplomacy. They worshipped the Twelve Olympian gods with a simpler faith perhaps, but with a deeper conviction. They welcomed into their kingdom Greek communities which had been driven out by their rivals, the people of Mycenae and the people of Hestia. They invited to their court many leaders of Greek culture — poets, tragedians, historians, philosophers, doctors, actors, painters, craftsmen of all kinds, and even financiers and statesmen. Thus Macedonia was attached through the court of the king to the Greek world. But it was not a part of it, and in 359 B.C. no one thought that it would even play a part in it, except perhaps Philip.

INTELLECTUAL LIFE

We have relatively little information about the cultural life of Macedonia during this period. The Greek colonies on the coast of the Thermaic Gulf and on the Chalkidike peninsula shared fully in the political and cultural development which radiated from Athens and other centres of the Greek mainland. Thus there was nothing surprising in the fact that the most innovating and scientific philosopher of antiquity, Aristotle, was a native of Stageira in eastern Chalkidike. However, the tribal groups of the interior — Makedones, Paiones, Bottiaiai, Bisaltai and Edonoi — were to some extent separated from the main stream of Greek civilization and it was only incidentally that they were exposed to the influence of Greek ideas emanating from the colonies on their coasts. From this point of view the Makedones were the most favoured. For they had immediate contact with the colonies of Pydna, Methone, Dikaia, Aineia and Poteidaia; their own mother tongue was Greek, even if they spoke a dialect which was originally very marked; and their royal house was recognized by the Greeks as being an offshoot of the Herakleidai, the most prestigious clan in the entire Greek world.

The Macedonian kings attracted leading writers to their court. In the first decade of the fifth century B.C. Pindar composed an ode in honour of Alexander I, who competed at Olympia in the stadion and the pentathlon and was victorious in one of them. There is no doubt that Pindar's ode in his honour was performed with music and dance at the Macedonian court and that Pindar himself was present as the guest of the king. The relations of guest-friendship between Pindar and Alexander I led Alexander the Great to make an exception of the house and the descendants of Pindar during the destruction of Thebes in 335 B.C. In the decade 470-60 BC. or shortly thereafter Herodotos travelled through parts of Macedonia and he certainly met Alexander I, to whom he attributed an important role in the promotion of the Greek cause in the Persian Wars. Quite apart from the eulogies of Herodotos, Alexander impressed the Greek world with his brilliant diplomacy, his victory over the Persians and his dedication from the spoils of golden statues of himself at Delphi and Olympia — a unique and unparalleled dedication which no ordinary citizen of a Greek state had the ability to make.

Alexander's successor, Perdikkas II, entertained at his court Melanippides, a dithyrambic poet, and Hippokrates of Kos, the originator of scientific medicine. Archelaos, famous in Greece for his victories in the chariot-race at the Pythian games and the Olympic games, secured the services of the outstanding painter Zeuxis, the leading musician Timotheos, and the fine epic poet Choirilos. It is apparent that the royal court — a term which comprises not only the royal family but also the families of the king's Companions — was imbued with Greek ideas and showed a lively interest in literature and the arts. Consequently it is not a matter of surprise that two of the most distinguished Attic tragedians lived and worked in Macedonia over a period of years: Agathon c. 407-01 B.C. and Euripides in 408-06 B.C., because they found there not only a more acceptable centre than wartime Athens but also, although archaeological evidence is lacking, some tradition of theatrical performance. During his stay in Macedonia Euripides became a Companion of the king and composed two tragedies, *Archelaos,* in the course of which he endowed the royal line with a new ancestor, the mythical Archelaos, and *Bacchae,* a play which was inspired by his own experience of Dionysiac worship as he found it in Macedonia.

Greek religion was the starting-point of many forms of Greek literature and exerted a decisive influence on the development of ideas. We do not know whether Macedonia had developed any native forms of literature in an oral rather than written form, but there were certainly native traditions of music and local forms of dance. Macedonian religious festivals had a long tradition, and there are other indications of deep-rooted religious beliefs. The king and his close relations represented the state on the religious plane and they played the leading role in ritual services. The objects of worship were not confined to the Olympian gods of the Greek pantheon. For the Macedonians, earlier than the Greek world, came to know some forms of worship practised by their neighbours the Phrygians, the Paiones, the Krestones and the Thracians, and they adopted the Orphic mysteries, the Dionysiac ecstasy and the worship of the Kabeiroi of Samothrace. The earliest Orphic hymn was found during the excavation of a tomb of the fourth century B.C. at Derveni in central Macedonia. We should think of the Macedonians as more deeply religious and more inclined towards the syncretism of religious beliefs than the city-state Greeks of the fifth century B.C.

We know less about the fourth century B.C. Amyntas

52. Detail from the krater of Derveni showing a man who wears one sandal and carries a sword and spear while executing dance steps. He has been interpreted as Pentheus or Lykourgos, king of the Thracians, with two members of the Dionysiac retinue. The presentation of the Bacchae *of Euripides at Pella is perhaps not without relevance to the spread, significance and singularity of the Dionysiac cult in Macedonia. c. 330 B.C. Thessalonike, Archaeological Museum.*

III employed the father of Aristotle as his court doctor, and Perdikkas III used as his political adviser a pupil of Plato, Euphraios of Oreos. When Philip rose to power, he attracted a large number of southern Greeks into his service as soldiers, sailors, economic advisers, technicians, geographers, scientists, writers and among them Aristotle and Theophrastos. Still others who did not visit him as friends or as emissaries wrote letters of advice on political matters to him, such as Speusippos and Isokrates. At this time Philip and his court were fully integrated into the main body of Greek cultural development. It was characteristic of the respect in which Philip held the Greek spirit that he entrusted the education of his own heir and of the circle which was to provide the leaders of the future to Aristotle. Native literature developed with Antipater's *History of the Wars of Perdikkas with the Illyrians,* while two young contemporaries of Alexander called Marsyas and Ptolemy were acquiring the education which enabled them later to write works of exceptional value on the history of Macedonia and the achievements of Alexander. Philip himself, if not his predecessors, established the keeping at the Macedonian court of a record of the king's acts and orders day by day, the so-called *Ephemerides* or *King's Journal.* The fact that Philip and then Alexander entrusted the keeping of the *Journal* to Greeks of other areas was due to the need to engage capable, educated Macedonians in military and administrative duties.

The cultural and religious development of the Macedonians thus has two aspects. On the one hand the Macedonians were receptive of the influences of the city-state Greeks and admired their cultural and artistic gifts. On the other hand they did not accept them uncritically but they preserved their own cultural and religious identity; and it was from this source that the kings and people drew that special contribution in culture which brought to birth and enriched the so-called 'Hellenistic civilization' which might with more accuracy be called the 'Greco-Macedonian civilization' of the world of Alexander and his successors.

53-54. During Euripides' stay in Macedonia from 408-406 B.C. he wrote two tragedies, the Archelaos *and the* Bacchae. *He seems to have impressed the Macedonians greatly, if we are to judge by their refusal to return to the Athenians the bones of the great poet. In the middle of the second century B.C. an entire series of Macedonian relief vases were decorated with scenes from his works. Left: details from a relief skyphos with scenes from* Iphigenia in Aulis. *Athens, National Archaeological Museum.*

ART DURING THE ARCHAIC
AND CLASSICAL PERIODS

INTRODUCTION

In the present state of our knowledge, it is neither easy, nor perhaps permissible, to write a definitive account of art in Macedonia. The chief impediment is that archaeological investigation in Macedonia is still in its preliminary stages, and the objects which we have at our disposal are exceptionally few, covering only some aspects of its recorded history, and even these intermittently. A second reason, however, is the very different level of civilization reached in the cities established in this area by colonists from southern Greece and that of the indigenous settlements, at least in the earliest period, which lasts until the end of the fifth century B.C. Having made these observations, we shall attempt to provide a framework within which we shall describe the monuments known up to now in chronological and geographical sequence, so that the reader may form as coherent a picture as possible of the cultural level in this region of northern Greece.

GEOMETRIC PERIOD

In the first centuries of the first millenium B.C. artistic expression found outlet only on pottery and in small objects. A long tradition of ceramics shows us craftsmen fashioning hand-made vessels distinguished both for their functional shape and for their technical standard. Jugs with cut-away necks are one of the commonest and best-loved forms. Many types, including two-handled vases, small amphorae (*amphoriskoi*), kantharos-shaped vessels, bear witness to the survival of old forms and the imitation of vessels made in other materials (for example wood). Most of these are undecorated.

Quite quickly, however, we find the first examples of pottery styles which, more ambitious artistically, must be the product of direct contact with southern Greece and the result of the new tendencies at work there. The Proto-geometric style created in Attica before 1000 B.C., which spread over almost all Greece in the following centuries, reached Macedonia about 900 B.C. We may take it as certain that during the ninth century B.C., Proto-geometric vases were made in Macedonia which, despite provincial characteristics, reveal their independent existence.[1]

ARCHAIC PERIOD

Contact with southern Greece was uninterrupted over the subsequent centuries. This is shown both by the few Geometric sherds which have been found in various places (Kavala, Nea Peramos, Karabournaki near Thessalonike, Chalkidike, Nea Anchialos near Thessalonike) and also by the Corinthian and black figure Attic sherds which are found on all sites known to have been inhabited during that period. From the relatively scant information available at the moment, much of it derived from chance finds, we may deduce that while the native production of metal and pottery continued throughout the seventh and sixth centuries, imports of Corinthian and Attic vases multiplied at an

55-56. The remains of an impressive archaic Ionic temple have been found at the centre of modern Thessalonike, within the area occupied by the original settlement of ancient Therme.

ever-increasing rate, reaching not only coastal sites, but also penetrating the hinterland. Strikingly rich are the recent finds (not yet published) from the tombs of Sindos (not far from Thessalonike) where, in addition to quantities of gold and silver jewellery and bronze vessels, scores of Corinthian and Attic vases of the sixth century B.C. were found.

But, apart from the presence of such vases throughout Macedonia even at its most northerly point, Pelagonia, it would be difficult to trace other forms of artistic creativity in the Archaic period without other examples which, though few, are representative. Thus three *kouroi,* albeit from three widely separated places and of disparate merits, are of great importance. The first, only half-finished and now worn away by the sea, was found in the harbour of ancient Stagiros on the eastern shore of Chalkidike. The second (a small bronze statuette) comes from Retine, Pieria; as far as the corroded surface allows us to judge, it is probably earlier than the last phases of the Archaic period. The third, preserved in good condition, was found at Europos near Kilkis, (fig. 57). It is nearly life-size and may be dated to the last years of the sixth century B.C. It is difficult to attribute it to any particular workshop since the statue has not yet been fully studied, but it is evident that the lithe *kouros* does not belong to workshops which we call eastern Ionic. The chances are that we should probably also exclude workshops of mainland Greece (whether Attic or Peloponnesian) so that we end by ascrib-

ing it to some Cycladic workshop, perhaps to one of those whose influence we may discern in northern Greece in the next period.[2]

Some few but outstanding examples of architectural activity of the later Archaic period have survived both in eastern and in central Macedonia. The Ionic column capitals, the bases and fragments of columns and kymatia which come from the shrine of the Parthenos at ancient Neapolis (modern Kavala) testify that at the beginning of the fifth century B.C. a splendid Ionic temple stood here. The craftsmen who designed and executed it must have drawn both their inspiration and their expertise from the large Ionic temples of Asia Minor or the Aegean islands. The sensitivity of the design and the wealth of decoration are equalled by the dexterous execution of the full-bodied architectural members.

Contemporary, if not a little earlier, is the Ionic temple which existed at ancient Therme. Its abundant architectural remains (Ionic column capitals, bases, fragments of columns and rich decorative elements — kymatia — of a stately doorway) found within the city of Thessalonike make it certain that the influence of the brilliant creativity of Ionic territories in Archaic times had spread across all northern Greece (fig. 56). The temple from which all these examples come must have been quite exceptionally imposing, not only because of its size but also because of its decoration. The only part of the sculptured frieze to have survived is a small relief head (fig. 55). The plump cheeks

Below: left a small relief head from the sculptured frieze of the temple; right: a column capital from the same temple. The style both of the architectural members and of their finish lead us to *conclude that the influence of the brilliant archaic Ionic activity had spread far into northern Greece. Thessalonike, Archaeological Museum.*

56

are bordered by the waves of soft hair arranged on the forehead in locks of well-dressed curls. Even more than the architectonic forms, the dimensional rendering of the flesh and the hair brings across to us the message of 'fertile' Ionia.[3]

CLASSICAL PERIOD

If the meagre remains of the sixth century do no more than indicate the artistic creativity of Macedonia without being sufficient to supply a coherent picture or indicate its full range, the finds made up to now which date from the fifth century B.C. offer somewhat richer material for study and permit us to estimate more correctly the characteristics of northern Greek art. The ultimate triumph of the Greeks in 479 B.C., which brought the Persian War to an end, caused the disappeareance of the Persian presence from the Aegean coast and forged closer links between the Ionian world and mainland Greece, establishing the Aegean as a Greek lake linking all the Greek cities. Macedonia, cultivating closer relationships with the rest of Greece under the leadership of Alexander I, was naturally also more open to cultural influences from that area. Before the close of the century, in which Greek creativity reached one of its peaks, Macedonia had opened her doors to some of the best known artists. Her new capital, Pella, became the home of some of the most distinguished artists and poets. It was there that Euripides wrote four of his tragedies, amongst them the *Bacchae* and *Iphigenia in Aulis;* when he died he was buried there. Zeuxis executed the murals of the palace of Archelaos in the same city and hospitality was also given to the poet Agathon amongst others. It is premature to discuss the Pella of Archelaos and his immediate successors, since only now are we beginning to learn something about it from recent excavations. Nevertheless the picture presented by the finds is impressive and testifies not only to prosperity, but also to a high standard of living. Similarly, it is still premature to of-

57. *The Kouros of Kilkis. Recently the target of the vandalism of antique-smugglers, the lithe figure of the youth should perhaps be attributed to a Cycladic workshop. It dates to the last years of the 6th century B.C. Kilkis, Archaeological Museum.*

58. *This stele from Dion depicts a young girl. The details of the hair style and of the folds of the drapery are conscientiously rendered by the craftsman who was certainly influenced by Ionian artistic centres. Mid-5th century B.C. Thessalonike, Archaeological Museum.*

59. *The fragments of the stele portray the head of a young man (?athlete or hunter). It comes from Kassandra, Chalkidike. It has links with both island and Attic influences. c. 420 B.C. Thessalonike, Archaeological Museum.*

fer comment on another Macedonian city, Dion, the sacred
city of the Macedonians. The earliest discoveries there,
dating to the fifth century B.C., permit us to hope that at
last some light may be shed on the obscure and little
known state of Macedonia before Alexander. The earliest
indications for the existence of a shrine of Demeter in the
first years of the fifth century B.C. and the deposits of offerings found there reveal their panhellenic character and
bear out the identification of the Macedonian goddess with
the southern Greek worship of the Eleusinian divinity.

One of the oldest pieces of sculpture found to date is the
stele of Nea Kallikrateia in Chalkidike (fig. 47). Dated with
certainty to around 440 B.C., it offers us not only the
oldest, but also the most notable sculpture to have been un-
earthed so far in northern Greece. Because of the nobility
of its plastic rendering and its human tenderness, this grave
stele depicting the figure of a young girl holding her
beloved dove, bears close comparison with the similar
figure in the Metropolitan Museum, New York. Mrs
Despini has shown beyond doubt that it is a product of a
brilliant Parian workshop.[4] But one has to ask if the
craftsman worked here in Chalkidike; for if he did, then
this is perhaps not the sole example of his work; he may
have set up his studio here, thus training pupils whose influence spread over all northern Greece. This reflection is
based on the fact that in the second half of the fifth century
B.C. every sculptured piece found in Macedonia manifests
the Ionic physiognomy without the identification of any
particular Ionic workshop being possible. The most
probable interpretation of this phenomenon — beyond the
general observation that all northern Greece, from Boiotia
to Macedonia, felt the effect of Ionic influences — seems to
be that workshops in this area were established at an early
point in time and had a fairly long established tradition.
Contact with their original roots of creativity preserved
their artistic integrity and the plastic idiom of their modelling, while parallel to this the new environment in which
they worked sapped their expressive intensity and led to a
novel elaboration of forms which, steadily enriched by the
absorption of foreign elements, changed decisively in the
course of the fourth century B.C. and acquired its own
special character.

The few pieces of sculpture found to date allow us to
sketch this progress. Almost contemporary with the stele
of Nea Kallikrateia is that from Dion (fig. 58) portraying
the figure of a young girl. Though the standard reached by
the plasticity is not the equal of the first, it is a notable
work and must be attributed to a craftsman still in direct
contact with the Ionian artistic centres of his age, a practised eye and a sure hand. The waves of the hair and the set
of the curls balance the folds of the drapery. It is worth
noting that this stele comes from a truly Macedonian city
close to the coast where the colony of Methone is known to
have existed.[5]

Two other grave stelai transport us to a different atmosphere both visual and technical. Their significance for
our acquaintance with artistic currents in Macedonia is especially noteworthy, because they come from the two cen-

tres of the Macedonian kingdom. One was found at Vergina which recent excavations have shown is to be identified with the first capital of the Macedonians, Aigai, and the second comes from Pella. Both depict men, warriors. On the first the warrior wears a broad-brimmed *petasos* and a chiton. In his left hand he holds a bird, in his right two spears, upright. The bottom part of the figure is missing, so we do not know if an inscription gave the name of the dead man. The male figure brings to mind many similar figures from other Thessalian stelai, but the plastic elaboration is more studied and bears witness to the skill of the sculptor. A date somewhere around 425 B.C. seems likely, for we must also take into account the fact that we are dealing with a provincial work. It is difficult to discover its artistic roots because the craftsman was obliged to portray a figure not familiar to the repertoire of southern or island Greece.[6]

The stele from Pella, dated a little later, shows the warrior in heroic nudity (fig. 39). The tunic is thrown back over his left shoulder, thus barely covering the left side of his body. His head alone is covered by a conical hat (or helmet); in his left hand he grasps his spear while in the other he holds his shield upright, so that the perspective presents us with its inner face. His stance — the weight on the right leg, the left bent and very slightly behind — anticipates the Polycleitan spear-holder, while the relaxed rendering of the figure in three-quarter pose recalls the almost contemporary reliefs. However, the fleshy fullness of the cheeks and the naked body reveal a tradition which does not have its roots in Athens.[7]

This mingling of Ionic traditions with markedly Attic elements spreading throughout northern Greece is to be observed again in another stele, also shattered, found at Kassandra, Chalkidike, dating to *c.* 420 B.C. Only the head of a young man has survived; he may have been depicted as an athlete or as a hunter. Its similarity to island stelai is beyond doubt, but equally obvious is the influence of Attic sculpture whose refulgence throughout the entire Greek world after the execution of the Parthenon sculptures became steadily more marked.[8]

All these examples are of very high standard and show that in the towns of Macedonia there were both competent craftsmen and a clientele capable of appreciating objects of high quality. However, all these works are grave stelai; they belong, therefore, to the sphere of personal choice and subjective judgement. One exception to this is a metope found at Aedonochori, Serrhai. Although it is much damaged, it is still possible to discern a duel between two hoplites. Of far greater importance than the subject is the quality of the modelled expression; from the very few points at which the original surface survives we may deduce that it was a splendid work of the last years of the fifth century B.C. This minute example from a building now lost, probably a temple, permits us to draw the conclusion that the two splendid temples whose existence we know of — at Therme (Thessalonike) and Neapolis (Kavala) were not without successors and this within the regions of the Macedonian hinterland.[9]

A larger quantity of monuments in closer chronological sequence have come to light in the course of excavations at two renowned cities of northern Greece, Olynthos and Amphipolis. As is well known, Olynthos is one of the few examples of ancient Greek cities laid out as an entity at a specific point in time with an identifiable plan. The date of its foundation is known — 432 B.C. Its historic destiny ordained a special fate: it was totally destroyed by Philip II in 348 B.C. Finally, one more rare example: systematic excavations have recovered the remains of the town almost *in toto*. Of even greater significance for research, the results and the finds from the excavations have been published in full detail in fourteen massive volumes.[10]

The first important gain from these excavations is the very complete and detailed knowledge of the entire town plan that we call 'Hippodameian'; squares, avenues and the narrower streets which bisect them at right angles define the blocks, each of which consists of two groups of five dwellings separated by a very narrow runnel for drainage. Perfectly designed water supply and drainage systems complete the town plan. The rooms of each dwelling opened off a central court providing ample space for all the needs of the family. Particularly worth mentioning are the terracotta baths, basins and lavatories whose practical shapes, paralleled still today, make an immediate impact.

As is natural, countless vessels, tools and of course red figure vases have been found in houses, together with a large number of pottery figurines. There was no significant quantity of sculpture, an unexpected lack. A marble head, beautifully executed, and two decorative reliefs, all belonging to the last years of the fifth century B.C. are the only examples of sculpture to have been recovered. Counterbalancing this lacuna and of exceptional importance in their own right are the numerous mosaic floors found in many houses at Olynthos, the oldest mosaics on Greek soil. In addition to the superb decorative motifs (stars, wheels, meanders, bounding animals, griffins, spirals and plant decoration) there are some striking mythological compositions such as the two figures of Pan facing each other, Bellerophon, Achilles, and Thetis and Dionysos riding in a chariot drawn by panthers and surrounded by Maenads. The technically simple arrangement of the natural pebbles, together with their limited colour range, matches the severity of vase painting before the latter embarked on the adventurous perspective renderings which led to the destruction of the decorated surface. Totally unlooked-for, and quite unique, is the mosaic floor with clear-cut geometric themes scattered across its surface leaving the viewer with the same impression as a modern avant-gard creation.[11]

At Amphipolis excavations are still in progress at

60. *The rape of Persephone by Pluto is depicted in the small rectangular tomb of the Great Tomb of Vergina. The god, with one foot on the chariot, holds the reins and sceptre in his right hand while the left grasps Persephone who stretches out her arms in an attempt to escape.*

96

various points. In addition to red figure vases and jewellery of considerable value, there are many typical clay busts and figurines as well as a selection of marble grave stelai. It may be taken as virtually certain that both pottery and sculpture are the products of local workshops. Each terracotta protome depicts a female figure, probably a goddess; the painted surface is relatively well preserved; they date to the middle of the fourth century B.C. The grave stelai start from the end of the fifth century B.C. and continue into the first half of the fourth. If amongst the oldest, one may discern a far-distant memory of Ionian workshops, in later ones the common Attic idiom has triumphed; but neither the first nor the second category includes works of more than average craftsmanship — presentable grave monuments matched to the commemorative tastes of the not specially wealthy inhabitants of this important city. Perhaps the most notable monument is that depicting a Siren with considerable pathos and strength, which reflects the anti-classical tendencies of the mid-fourth century B.C.[12]

It is even more difficult to present a clear - cut picture of artistic activity in other areas, where of necessity it is based on finds known to us by chance rather than by systematic search. If we had to base our comments only on the stele from Makrygialos,[13] a grave monument of the first half of the fourth century B.C., we would have to believe that there was no artistic tradition in the area in which it was found, and we could never imagine that the stele already described above could have existed in neighbouring Dion. The stele is the work of a somewhat mediocre craftsman who may have drawn his inspiration from Attic works, but was not capable of transmitting in marble more than the fact that he had a moving subject: a dead mother with her baby in her arms. His aspirations foundered on the outline and rendering of the figures, which do not rise above the level of inept provincial craftsmanship.[14] From the same region (Kitros, ancient Pydna) comes a second grave stele which shows a young hunter seated on a rock fondling the muzzle of his hunting dog, whose head is turned towards his master. Chronologically it must be slightly later (around the middle of the fourth century B.C.) and the craftsman was endowed with better developed talents as a draughtsman and sculptor than the former. Both the subject and its treatment hark back to the Ionian school which, as we have seen, influenced all northern Greece.[15]

Four typical examples of sculpture are to be found from Chalkidike in the fourth century B.C. One of the earliest and best turned turned up by chance at Kassandra. It is a relief grave stele dated to the beginning of the fourth cen-

tury (380-370 B.C.) which portrays a young man full front, holding a lyre in his left hand (fig. 49). This rarely found pose and the sculptural rendering of the volume suggest that this is a work stemming from Ionic traditions, with rather less Attic influence than might have been expected. It is most certainly the work of a skilled and dexterous craftsman who did not confine himself to showing the human figure from the side as it was repeatedly portrayed in contemporary reliefs, grave monuments and votive offerings, but sought to try his skill on this unusual stance for the young man. Without reserve, we may say that he succeeded in producing an interesting result.[16]

From nearby Poteidaia comes a votive relief, of the funeral banquet type, which belongs to the same period. A set piece, with no outstanding claim to artistic merit, it nevertheless testifies to the capabilities of the sculptor, well-versed in his craft and able to render his subject with uncomplicated masses and correct design. Here the Attic plastic idiom is more apparent, and one has difficulty in tracing the Ionic elements although they continue to exist and influence the art of this region.[17]

With these four examples — two from Chalkidike, two from Pieria — we may judge the confusion which reigned in northern Greece, both in modes of expression and in quality. Within the same region, craftsmen manifesting obvious Ionian antecedents worked side by side with others who display more definitely the influence of Attic creativity, and, irrespective of school, were of very different artistic aptitude.

It is impossible to base a reliable and authoritative historical survey of artistic development in Macedonia on these occasional and unrelated finds which luck alone has brought into our hands. In any case it was not possible for large workshops to exist in Macedonia before the fourth century B.C., as indeed they did not exist in many other Greek regions with an agricultural economy and a more archaic social structure (Arkadia and Akarnania). Nevertheless we know from written sources that at the end of the fifth century B.C. Archelaos not only transferred the capital of his kingdom from Aigai to Pella, so that he came into direct contact with the shipping lanes of the Aegean, but also nursed the ambition to turn his court into an intellectual centre, inviting and giving a home to some of the most famous poets and artists of Athens. As yet the excavation of Pella has not uncovered Archelaos' city, and only a few tombs, with abundant grave goods, bear witness to its flourishing condition at the end of the fifth century B.C. But from the fourth century the artistic energy of the Macedonian capital is evidenced by a few random finds. (The very important mosaics belong to the Hellenistic period, to the years around 300 B.C.) Despite the fact that they have not yet been studied or published, so that we have no authoritative opinion on the date, I nevertheless think that they belong in this chapter since my own view is that they are not later than 330 B.C. We would single out for mention the marvellous marble dog, the small mutilated horseman and another small rider, also defaced, which perhaps belonged to the architectural adornment of some

61. Painted stele from the cemetery of Vergina. More than fifty such painted or relief stelai have been recovered from the graves of ordinary citizens. As the inscription tells us, members of the same family are depicted. The clearly Greek names of Macedonians between 400-350 B.C. decisively reinforce the view that they were a Greek tribe without Illyrian or Thracian admixtures.

building unless it comes from an imposing funerary monument. The exceptional modelling of the dog, with its severe quality, originally led to the belief that it was a work of the fifth century. But a more careful examination permits us, or so I believe, to admit that a date around the middle of the fourth century B.C. is nearer the mark. It is certainly a work of a skilled and sensitive craftsman, lacking the slightest trace of provincial bashfulness.[18]

The same standard is achieved by the small, headless equestrian figure which has been considered to be a late Hellenistic work (fig. 51). My own opinion is that its entire structure, the shaping of the surfaces of both the horse and the rider, and the composition of the plastic elements still belong to the classical tradition, so that a date close to the middle of the fourth century B.C. is justifiable. The nobility of man and beast, the exceptionally sensitive movements and the lyricism which emanate from the two bodies class this small piece amongst the marvels of Greek sculpture.[19]

The other horseman is so badly damaged and mutilated that the amateur viewer is scarcely able to appreciate the modelling of the surface for what it is worth; however, the experienced eye immediately detects the hand of a practised craftsman and the sculptural adroitness which declare his apprenticeship in an atelier alongside men of very high calibre.[20]

All three sculptures clearly show the influence of Attic *koine* which throughout the fourth century was spreading across the Greek world, paving the way for the eruption of Hellenistic pathos which was to be the expression of the new world shaped by the oecumenic expansion of Hellenism, spread by the Macedonian campaigns penetrating far into the East.

As we have said, the excavations at Pella up to now have uncovered buildings dateable to the last years of the fourth century apparently laid out on the Hippodameian system, with well planned and strictly observed co-ordinates. We may regard as very probable, almost certain, that these plots follow the same lines as their predecessors. We may also say that Archelaos' city, built a few years later than Olynthos, was carefully planned from the beginning, taking the most modern principles of town planning as its base, those which the great fifth century architect Hippodamos, had first worked out in theory and then carried out in practice. Thus to Piraeus, Thourion and Rhodes, all of which are said to have been laid out by Hippodamos, we must add Olynthos and Pella which so exactly follow his principles of spatial arrangement.

From the sixth century onwards throughout northern Greece from Kavala to Kozani, Attic vases are both abundant and characteristic. Their presence denotes the hardheaded commercial activities of the Athenians and the acceptance of their products by the inhabitants of Macedonia. Although it has not yet been convincingly demonstrated, it seems highly likely that in some areas of Macedonia (Chalkidike, for example) pottery workshops had been established which copied Attic originals — sometimes with considerable success.

Nevertheless the historical factors operating thoughout the entire northern Greek region, in the kingdom of the Macedonians and in the autonomous cities did not favour the development of a unified artistic style nor did they spur the systematic production of works of art. Only after the Macedonian state had acquired strength and organization sufficient to guarantee its economic progress and its social stability were the necessary pre-conditions generated for its artistic and intellectual activity. And this only occurred when Philip removed any external threat to the safety of his kingdom and was thus in a position to pursue his energetic longer term policies. This culminating moment in Macedonian history has not always been easy for us to understand on the basis of information derived from written sources alone, for these most frequently originate amongst hostile political powers, such as Athens. However, recent archaeological discoveries offer tangible and irrefutable tokens of the incredible cultural blossoming which must have burgeoned in Macedonia around the middle of the fourth century B.C. The finds from two sites are sufficiently representative for us to be able to outline a clear picture of this world which contrived to prolong in creative terms, and in the most brilliant fashion, the already long established cultural heritage of southern Greece, assimilating its prolific traditions and injecting them with new dynamism. I refer to the finds from Derveni and Vergina. By sheer coincidence, both groups belong to the same period, the years immediately following the middle of the fourth century B.C., and, again by chance, they were found in tombs which belonged to dead men of different social rank; the tombs of Vergina are royal, those of Derveni, rich though their contents are, are graves of men who were not noble, but very well-to-do bourgeois or landowners. It is noteworthy that in one of the tombs of Derveni there survived a charred papyrus with an Orphic text, perhaps the oldest Greek papyrus to have come down to us. The text is the most eloquent and direct testimony to the intellectual tradition to which Macedonia owes its cultural life during Philip's years, a fact corroborated by the finds from the tombs, in particular the superb bronze krater with its unique sculptured ornament. The chief subject — Dionysos with Ariadne — and his divinely inspired companions, the Satyrs and Maenads, cover the entire surface of the krater's body. The relief projection of the figures is sufficient to render their volume convincingly, but at the same time it is calculated so as not to destroy the solid nature of the surface. All around the calm, almost languorous and

62. The gilded silver diadem from the Great Tomb of Vergina, probably the dead man's crown. Its diameter was adjustable. The cylindrical screw at the back is embossed with the knot of Herakles. Thessalonike, Archaeological Museum.

63. The gold larnax from the chamber of the Great Tomb of Vergina. All four sides bear plant decoration and rosettes inlaid with blue glass paste. On its lid is the star, emblem of the Macedonian dynasty. Thessalonike, Archaeological Museum.

64

65

66

67

64-67. Magnificent pieces of Macedonian metalwork have recently been found either by excavation or by chance. The krater-situla from Stavroupolis (64), the hydria from Torone and the vessels from Derveni (65, 67) testify to the high level of artistic productivity of Macedonian workshops. Thessalonike, Archaeological Museum.

68. Silver oinochoe from the Great Tomb at Vergina. The relief head of Silenus which decorates the base of a handle is a splendid example of 4th century casting. Thessalonike, Archaeological Museum.

68

sensual portrayal of the youthful god with his 'divine consort' stand Satyrs with the Maenads cavorting in orgiastic frenzy and bacchic abandon. Amongst them the solitary figure of a mature bearded man, his sword sheathed and a javelin in his right hand, moves like a dancer on his toes, his left hand raised. His identity is enigmatic; he wears only one sandal, but even this clue failed to help archaeologists identify him, serving rather to increase their difficulties. Some have suggested that he is Pentheus, others Lykourgos. Whatever his identity, he has to be a figure connected with Dionysiac worship, although within the scene he remains an isolated and withdrawn figure. The decoration of the krater is completed by two groups of animals which cover the bottom part of the vase. Around the neck a row of wild animals surrounds its upper part. But the most notable sculptural touch consists of four small figurines, seated in pairs on either shoulder of the krater; Dionysos and a sleeping Maenad, and the slumbering Dionysos and a Maenad in ecstasy. The fluid lines of the body vie with the perfect finish of the faces and the unrivalled expression of their feelings. In these works the composition of the previous solid world created by the lengthy tradition of Greek sculpture was permeated by the rising tide of the new tendencies which would express the creative phase of Greek art in its headlong rush towards the univeral dimensions of the Hellenistic epoch. This harbinger of things to come is clearly declared in the shape of this monumental krater as a whole: the weight of decoration and the profuse plasticity have laid down the lines for the Hellenistic baroque and the anti-classical principles which were to impose their own artistic rules corresponding to the new social and political conditions obtaining in the extensive post-Alexandrine kingdoms. The dating of this work to the third quarter of the fourth century B.C. seems plausible, and is re-inforced by the discovery of a gold triobol of Philip II in the same tomb. The recent opinion of K. Schefeld, proposing a date around the middle of the century (*c.* 350 B.C.) rather than at the end of the third quarter (325 B.C.), seems very likely to me and more in accord with what we are in a position to say about sculpture in the fourth century B.C.[21]

If this krater is a spectacular work of art, the other metal vessels, whether found in the same tomb or others at Derveni, allow us to state with confidence that this masterpiece was not created to indulge the whim of a rich man, but that other such works were far from uncommon in Macedonia. We may go so far as to assert that the workshop which produced both the krater and the other dishes must have been sited in Macedonia. It would not even be too rash to claim that such workshops existed from at least the fifth century B.C. in northern Greece, as the sporadic finds which date from the fifth century from various regions would suggest, for example at Thessalonike or from Chalkidike. This view receives support from the recent finds made at Sindos whose quantity testifies to flourishing production from the sixth and fifth centuries. Moreover, there are certain characteristic patterns; while they are oft-repeated on Macedonian objects, they are either unknown

or uncommon in southern Greece where discoveries of metal vessels are less frequent.

Jewellery is another sphere in which Macedonian metalwork is outstanding. The lavish use of precious metals, both silver and gold, linked with exceptionally skilful and delicate craftsmanship places these ornaments in the front rank of Greek jewellery. Nevertheless, a true evaluation, classification and presentation of conclusions is still difficult because most of these finds remain unstudied and only the basic facts about their discovery have as yet been set out. Of particular importance is the group of finds made at Derveni in 1962, amongst which was the krater published first in 1978. All the other objects — silver, gold and bronze — await publication and are thus not available for study.

But an initial comparison of the finds from Derveni with those from the royal tombs of Vergina reveal the difference in quality and leads to the useful conclusion that their production depended on demand, on the artistic taste of the customer and, of course, his purse. The comparison of (a) the two lanterns and (b) of the 'frying-pan' vessels from Derveni and Vergina provide immediate confirmation of this judgement. It might even be justifiable to advance the theory that certain works, created for the royal court by great masters, formed the models which other workshops then attempted to copy for a wider market. The information of Plutarch is revealing, that at the battle of Gaugamela Alexander wore an iron helmet made by the craftsman Theophilos.

Vergina, which the latest excavations show must be identified with the first capital, Aigai, has so far offered us such a quantity of high quality finds that we are able to sketch a picture of the art of Macedonia in the fourth century B.C. not only brilliant, but, far more, certain and complete. We discussed earlier a stele of the fifth century B.C. which came from the cemetery in this area. From this same cemetery more than fifty funeral stelai have been recovered, all of which date from 350 to the beginning of the third century B.C. A number of these carry relief themes, while most are painted and come from tombs of ordinary citizens (fig. 61). Their quantity leaves no doubt that nearby there must have been one or more workshops employing skilled men, sometimes of very considerable ability, as we may deduce from the standard of a large relief stele depicting a young man, from a painted stele with three figures or from yet another where one female figure

69. Macedonian jewellery has already given us outstanding examples of the workmanship of precious metals linked to delicate and skilful techniques. The magic amma — knot of Herakles — *above is a detail from a gold thigh ornament. A six-petalled rose and lion-headed dragons at the four corners decorated the surface. 4th century B.C. Thessalonike, Archaeological Museum.*

70. The gold oak wreath found inside the larnax from the Great Tomb of Vergina above the bones of the dead man. Thessalonike, Archaeological Museum.

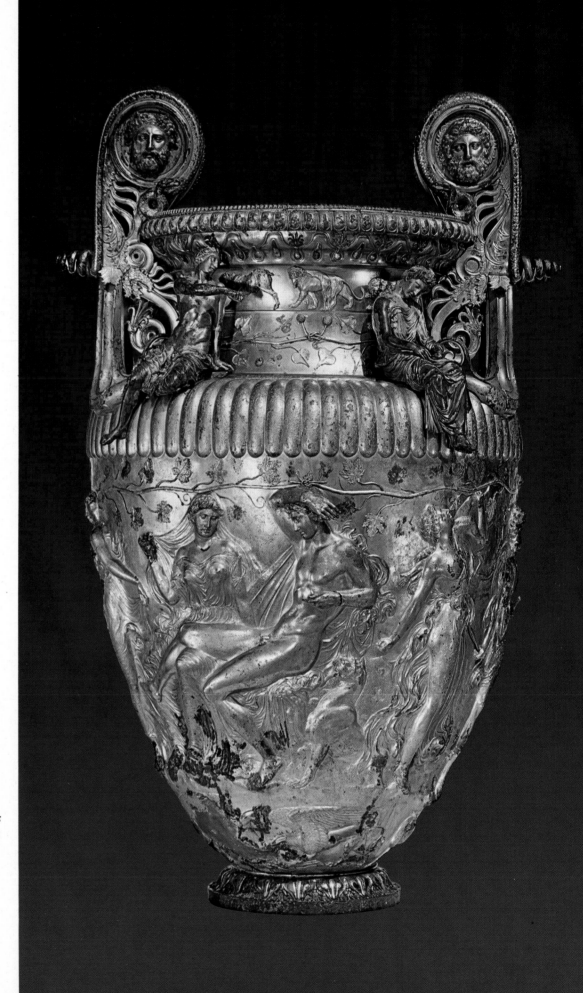

71-72. The wonderful bronze krater of Derveni. Its relief decoration depicts the sacred marriage of Dionysos and Ariadne, and their companions the Satyrs and Maenads. The fluid modelling of the bodies rivals the perfect finish of the faces with their clear cut lines and unmatched expression of their inner feelings. c. 330 B.C. Thessalonike, Archaeological Museum.

73. *The sleeping Satyr. One of the marvellous figurines from the shoulder of the krater of Derveni. c. 330 B.C. Thessalonike, Archaeological Museum.*

at least is sufficiently well preserved to reveal the talent of the painter. The relief stelai from Vergina serve also to confirm our earlier comments on Ionic and Attic influences in northern Greece, since next to the stele of the young man which we mentioned and in which the Ionic traditions are clear, we find others, for example the fragments of a horseman, where both the subject and the sculptural rendering find parallels only on Attic soil. Over and above this confirmation, the grave monuments of Vergina provide a collection which permits us to assess the cultural standards of a Macedonian city, as well as unfolding before our eyes a cemetery with well-cared for graves, relief figures of the dead strikingly decorated in colour or with painted depiction of the quick and the dead. These humble monuments alone would suffice to recreate this world and allow us to perceive its identity with that of the southern Greeks as we know it from the corresponding grave monuments, even if the names of the dead were not cut in letters filled in with colour: Alkinous, Peukolaos, Laandros, Xenokrates, Pierion, Philotas, Kleio, Berenno and others.

The long term excavation of Vergina has yielded other choice finds. Up to the moment of writing six impressive tombs and a splendid palace have been discovered in this area, while the uncovering of the walls of the city and of some dwellings has only just begun. Four of the tombs belong to the period under discussion, while the palace must be dated rather later, to the last years of the fourth century B.C. Beyond all doubt the tombs are royal; the excavator believes that the biggest and richest must be that of Philip II and is thus dateable to 336 B.C., the year in which Philip was murdered at Aigai, to be laid to rest there in accordance with the ancient Macedonian custom of burying their kings in the original capital.

The first imporant factor about the tombs is the construction itself: two of them preserved the Doric facade intact, the coloured decoration of the architectural members and the imposing marble doors *in situ*. Another tomb was found, not only totally destroyed, but also entirely robbed of stone, probably by the ancients. Nevertheless the four free-standing Doric columns which survived from its facade provide us with a unique form of Macedonian tomb with the free prostasis in front of its facade. Theoretically we should probably regard it as the fore-runner of the type of facade with pilasters against the wall, the type known from all tombs discovered to date.

But the most significant contribution made by the royal tombs is indisputably their unique wall paintings. For the very first time we find ourselves confronted by masterpieces of a great Greek painter of the classical period. A tradition of painting in Macedonia can be substantiated, as we noted above, from the years of Archelaos who invited Zeuxis to decorate his palace at Pella. Written evidence provides fuller details about well known painters of the fourth century B.C. employed at the royal court of Macedonia, amongst whom Apelles is perhaps the most famous of all.

Surviving at Vergina we find: 1) a narrow frieze with the depiction of a chariot race, on the walls of the antechamber of the smaller domed tomb. The painting of the frieze was indeed decorative, though its painter was not in the least uneducated nor lacking imagination but was endowed with notable artistic capabilities, imagination and originality. The extensive surface of the frieze is covered by lively moving figures.

2) In the 'small' rectangular tomb the painted ornamentation of the three walls surpasses the capabilities of an ordinary craftsman. There can be no doubt that the paintings of this tomb are the work of one of the most gifted painters of the age. There is every reason to believe that these compositions are entirely original; the innumerable rough outlines which can be distinguished next to the final result suggests that his inspiration was transferred directly onto the fresh plaster of the walls.

The main composition is to be found on the north wall, 3.50 m. long; it depicts the rape of Persephone by Pluto. With one foot on the four-wheeled chariot, the god holds his sceptre and the reins in his right hand while his left grasps Persephone, who stretches out her hands in a despairing attempt to escape from her captor. The drawing is endowed with an unmatched strength of expression, executed with deftness and mastery. Hermes runs in front of the chariot while behind it, on her knees and obviously aghast, the young godess' friend flings her arms upwards. The suggestion that this wall painting could be the work of the great painter of the mid-fourth century B.C., Nikomachos, can be upheld by Pliny's testimony and can be considered highly probable (fig. 60).

On the adjoining narrow east wall a seated female figure is depicted. The rock on which she is seated, the morose expression and the proximity to the rape of Persephone points to the interpretation of the figure as Demeter.

On the south wall, opposite the rape, three seated female figures are portrayed; they are not as well preserved. Perhaps the most plausible interpretation is that they are the Three Fates, Klotho, Lachesis and Atropos.

3) On the facade of the Great Macedonian Tomb, above the Doric entablature, a frieze runs the entire width of the tomb (5.60 m.) The whole surface is covered by a wall painting depicting a hunt in a forest. Seven huntsmen on foot, three on horseback, a deer, two boar, a lion and a pack of hunting dogs move within the space bounded by four trees, a stele and rocks. The composition of the painting, the drawing of the figures and the harmonization of the colours reveal that this is a work of a very talented artist which, though still based on the principles of the classical tradition, yet dares to invest the movement of the figures within the space available with unaccustomed strength. Despite the difference in subject, one may distinguish a close artistic affinity between the Vergina frieze and the original of the Naples mosaic which shows Alexander against Darius. The possibility that the hunting scene of the tomb is an earlier work of the same artist, or of the same workshop, cannot be excluded.

These paintings, especially the two big compositions, constitute an unexpected discovery for the historian of Greek art. Comparing them with the paintings of Pompei and other Italian cities, until now the only examples through which to see this kind of painting, we may observe the vast difference which exists between the creation and inspiration of the originals and their far-removed derivatives. But we should not forget that these works were intended to be covered over for ever and to remain unseen by the living: they belonged to the dead buried within the tombs.

Two of the tombs were found unrobbed, so that their entire contents remained untouched. Time, however, has destroyed some of the most valuable objects inside. According to Macedonian custom, wooden beds were placed in the tombs which naturally have rotted and disintegrated. Over and above the very slight traces of wood which remained, totally disconnected, sufficient of their decoration survived made of ivory, gold and glass. Though the work of conservation is still in progress, we may say with certainty that these beds were furniture of a very high quality and their decoration, from which many ivory figures have survived, was a masterpiece. A number of these were portraits, amongst them a distinguished portrait of Philip and another of Alexander (figs. 79, 78). Another group depicts mythological figures (Dionysos, Muses, Silenus etc.). To this category belonged a group of three figures, Pan and a Dionysiac couple, which, without exaggeration, may be considered to be the most beautiful ivories to have survived from the ancient world. It is certainly a unique masterpiece which sheds new light on our knowledge not only of a craft, but also of all sculpture in the fourth century B.C. which opened new approaches to the big adventure of Hellenistic art.

One further unexpected find which in splendid fashion completes the picture given by the ivories of the beds is a ceremonial shield which was found in a state of total disintegration, alongside the other weapons of the dead man. Onto the wood and leather frame the craftsman fastened ivory decoration to the surface over which he let his skill run riot, ornamenting it with gilt and glass. In addition to the decorative meanders and spirals which curl about the outer edge he placed at the centre, against a gold background, an ivory carved in high relief; two figures, one male, the other female. Although the deterioration of the figures is considerable we are still able to make out not only their marvellous stance, but also several well preserved details, sufficient for a correct evaluation of this work. The unique nature of this item does not lie only in the use of precious material (on the inner surface there are gold strips), but more especially in the very high standard of the work which suggests that we should attribute it to a notable craftsman 'skilled' and 'not unknowledgeable' as the ancient Greeks would have phrased it.

Other objects include vessels, vases, weapons, the two unique gold larnakes (ossuaries), the gold wreaths, a gold diadem for a woman and a gold and purple textile (figs. 62, 63, 70). The wealth is royal indeed: but of far greater significance than the opulence is the artistic level achieved by each individual object. It is beyond question that they were fashioned not by merely skilled and capable craftsmen, but by great artists, so that they may be taken to represent the very best in contemporary art. The iron spear heads, for example, each one of which carries its own pattern, are in themselves distinguished works of art and, of course, splendid examples of a very advanced technology. Another matchless example of the same technique is the iron cuirass, in any case a rarely found object (fig. 84).

Of particular significance is the large collection of silver vases which delight the viewer not only with the perfection of their artistry, but also with their elegant if severe shapes. Most of them bear decorative relief heads, of Herakles, Pan and Silenus which serve to demonstrate the triumph of Greek casting in the fourth century B.C. and enable us to appreciate fully the sculpture of this period in its proper perspective, before its subsequent maltreatment in later Roman copies. The grace and nobility of the figures do not destroy the compact consistency of the forms and their inner expressional power; nor do they turn into sickly-sweet theatrical contortions as one might imagine from looking at the innumerable copies of fourth century B.C. sculpture that have survived while almost all the originals have been lost (figs. 29, 68).[22]

The finds of the tombs of Vergina open up a new approach to the study of fourth century art. It is clear that many of the most active workshops functioned outside Attica and had gone beyond the traditional forms of sculpture. The conventions of Greek art which had spread through every branch of production catering for man's daily needs, succeeded in transforming even essential vessels into works of art and in applying its principles to the simplest and commonest objects of daily life. This cultural penetration of regions which up to now we have regarded as backward, if not indeed even as uncivilized, marks a happy archaeological discovery and confirms that the roots of Greek art were very deep and extensive and its branches strong enough to spread over the entire Hellenistic world.

ZENITH AND END
OF THE MACEDONIAN KINGDOM

POLITICAL HISTORY
360/59-148 B.C.

MACEDONIA AT PHILIP'S ACCESSION

To measure in broad terms the effect of Philip's reign on the kingdom one needs only to contrast its first with its last days. After their crushing defeat at the hands of Bardylis and his Dardanian Illyrian tribesmen in late 360 B.C. in north-western Macedonia, no fewer than four thousand Macedonians and their king lay dead. While the victors rejoiced, the surviving defeated made their way back in disorder toward their homes, seeking escape from the new Illyrian thrust they feared would follow. Discipline and morale collapsed. While Macedonia trembled, news of the disaster spread beyond the frontiers, where it was welcomed.

A large Paionian tribe, under its overlord Agis, began pressing southwards down the valley of the Axios towards the settlements and grainfields of central Macedonia. King Kotys, ruler of all Thrace, saw advantage for himself and looked for some means of realizing it. Athenian hopes of recovering Amphipolis rose. Once, briefly, her prized colony, it had grown independent and stalwart enough over six decades to resist all her attempts at its recovery. At this moment it accommodated a garrison of Macedonian troops lent by Perdikkas to stiffen its defences. A weakened and dispirited Macedonia might now be compelled to serve Athenian interests there instead of thwarting them.

Even over so beleaguered a throne there was rivalry.

Perdikkas III had met his death young, at barely more than twenty-five years. His son was no more, and perhaps much less, than eight. The only other surviving member of the direct royal line was the child's uncle, Philip, then twenty-two. Others too had plans for their own advancement.

Ambitions and interests coalesced. Kotys, in Thrace, gave his support to Pausanias who eight years before had obtained Chalkidian assistance in an abortive attempt to capture the throne. Athens despatched troops to see what might be gained from supporting Argaios, another pretender who in the past had actually held the throne with foreign backing; no doubt he now gave Athens assurances over Amphipolis. There were other claimants, though whether they declared themselves openly at this time or a few years later is not certain. In such circumstances, with — it hardly exaggerates to say — the kingdom on the point of dismemberment, the reign of Philip began.

MACEDONIA AT PHILIP'S DEATH

Some twenty-four years later, in mid-336 B.C., it ended. The occasion was the marriage of one of Philip's daughters, Cleopatra, to Alexander, the young Molossian king of Epirus. Games and festivities were held in the old Macedonian capital, Aigai. But these arrangements marked more than a wedding. Rather, they were in effect a celebration of Macedonian achievements under Philip, and it was he who was the centre of all attention (even, ironically and tragically, at the moment of his death, for it was here that he was assassinated). Mostly they signalized two things: the settlement of mainland Greece under his leadership in the recently established Hellenic League (338/7 B.C.) and the beginnings of his panhellenic campaign in Asia Minor, launched by the despatch of an advance-party a few months earlier in spring 336 B.C.

A great many visitors from all over Hellas flocked to Aigai for the entertainment. Individuals and the representatives of governments brought with them honours to confer upon Philip; the herald from Athens proclaimed the award of a gold crown to the king and added his fellow-citizens' declaration that their city would harbour no refugee who had plotted against him.

Some, though by no means all of these accolades were hollow and grudging. But that does not alter the truth which they represented. Philip's plans for the settlement of Greece and the eastern crusade had now become realities. The mainland was at peace and from coastal Asia Minor the news was beginning to arrive of Greek cities there welcoming the advance-force as their liberator from bondage to the Persian king. The basis of the main campaign, shortly to be launched, seemed secure. To such an extent Macedonia's position had changed during the reign of Philip. From an insignificant fringe-dweller she had become the leading power of the Aegean. Our task is to discover why and how this transformation occurred.

UNIFICATION

The potential in resources — manpower, foodstuffs and minerals — was already there. Philip continued and increased their exploitation. But Macedonia, although created by the expansion of a single tribe, was a badly disunited kingdom and this had previously stood in the way of its effectiveness as a state. The main cause of division was the failure of the ruling houses in the past to assert its power more than temporarily over the tribes of mountainous western (upper) Macedonia, different in economy, in social and political organization and in temperament from their kinsmen of the central plain. Other divisions no doubt existed, for this was a kingdom wrested from earlier inhabitants of a variety of stocks. Disunity had been, it is clear, the fundamental reason for Macedonian weakness in the past, making her vulnerable to exploitation by her enemies, internal and external. It must have been particularly acute at the time of Philip's accession on account both of the general disarray and of the occupation of parts of upper Macedonia by the victorious Illyrians.

Philip responded to this persistent problem in several ways. Firstly, after decisively defeating the Illyrians in 358 B.C., he brought the western highlands firmly under central control. But battlefield solutions are unlikely to last and the more important instruments of unification were more far-reaching.

A means of social manipulation related in principle to colonization and practised by this time in several parts of the Hellenic world, especially Sicily, involved the transfer of population-groups from their own land to new locations. This might be to break up hostile groups or, conversely, to inject reliable elements into unstable areas, especially along borders ill defined by natural features. There is evidence that for both reasons Philip engineered such population-transplants not only in his newly won territories in Thrace and Paionia and perhaps the Chalkidian peninsula but also in upper Macedonia, where they also assisted in defining the frontier against the Illyrian tribes. Here it formed part of a general policy of amalgamating smaller, scattered communities into larger, more defensible settlements on the plains of the region.

It was in the ranks of the old Macedonian nobility, especially that of upper Macedonia, that divisiveness had often been particularly evident, and it is no doubt with this in mind that Philip greatly increased the size of the noble *hetairos*-class by adding to it large numbers of his own appointees from among both native Macedonians of lesser status and capable immigrants from Thessaly and elsewhere in Greece, so diluting the influence of the traditional members. The institution of the Royal Pages, boys whose function was to serve the king during their teenage while gaining experience towards the responsibilities they would hold in adulthood, not only helped him foster a sense of national unity among the young but gave him through them a direct hold over their parents, those of the *hetairos*-class.

But, useful as these devices were, none by itself was likely to be wholly successful in fostering unity where it was absent before. In this regard the most important instrument of all was the army. Its expansion, reorganization and refinement were of course needed for pressing military reasons, which was in part why so much energy was expended on it from the first days of the reign onwards. The effect — the creation of a well-knit, efficient and confident fighting-unit — also had its implications on the wider, social level. Through a system of promotions, rewards and bonuses, through lengthy and effective training and, above all, through the success of this revitalized body there was instilled in its members a new degree of loyalty to the military organization, to its king-commander and to the state he and it stood for.

PHILIP'S EARLY POLICIES

Prior to Philip's reign, for most of her history, the kingdom had been prey to the interests of the major Hellenic powers, Athens, Thebes, Sparta and Olynthos, as well as to the periodic movements of Thracian, Illyrian and Paionian tribes to her east, west and north. In her weakened and demoralized condition at his accession there was little chance of survival except under the umbrella of alliance with a greater power. In the first months, therefore, Philip carefully aligned the state with Athenian interests and secured an agreement with her. This allowed him to concentrate on the more immediate threats to the throne and frontiers, the authority of Athens, enjoying at this time her last resurgence of imperial power, giving him some protection.

74. A Roman gold medallion portraying Philip II. His reign saw the emergence of Macedonia as the foremost Greek power, due to his exceptional diplomatic and military abilities, the strong, effective army he created and the economic and cultural development of the country. His many efforts succeeded in achieving first the unification of Macedonia and then panhellenic unity. Paris, Bibliothèque Nationale.

75. A Roman gold medallion portraying Olympias, wife of Philip II. Her iron will and ambition were influences on her son Alexander, and played an important role in the political events in the years before and after the death of Philip. Thessalonike, Archaeological Museum.

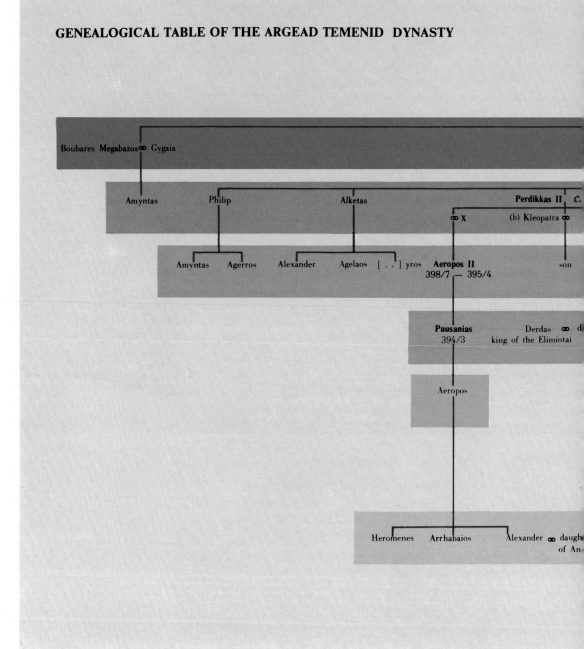

GENEALOGICAL TABLE OF THE ARGEAD TEMENID DYNASTY

Boubares Megabazos ∞ Gygaia

Amyntas   Philip   Alketas   Perdikkas II   C.

∞ X   (b) Kleopatra ∞

Amyntas Agerros   Alexander Agelaos [. .] yros **Aeropos II**   son
398/7 — 395/4

Pausanias   Derdas ∞ d
394/3   king of the Elimiotai

Aeropos

Heromenes Arrhabaios   Alexander ∞ daught
of An

76. The history of the Macedonian kingdom during the Archaic and Classical periods was closely bound up with the illustrious Temenid dynasty who traced their descent back to Herakles. The genealogical tree shows all the members of the dynasty from Amyntas I to Philip II and Alexander the Great.

As it happened, Athenian power soon came under challenge. In 357 B.C. a massive revolt of her allies broke out with the connivance of Persia. The result could not be predicted with certainty, but Philip's judgement, that Athens could no longer be relied upon, proved correct. Soon after the revolt's outbreak he abandoned his major alignment, provoking Athens' enmity but winning the alliance of the neighbouring Chalkidian League, headed by powerful Olynthos. Then, with sufficient protection on the Aegean side, he was able to begin eradicating Athenian and other influences from the Macedonian and nearby coastal areas. Amphipolis, Pydna, Krenides (which he renamed Philippi), Apollonia, Galepsos, Oisyme (renamed Emathia), Methone, Abdera, Maroneia and Neapolis came under Macedonian control in the next three or four years,

securing the coastline from the Thessalian frontier to the river Hebros, and Philip's influence increased markedly in the Thracian and, especially, the Thessalian areas. The price of this newly won security and stability had to be paid, however, in the growing disquiet felt by Olynthos, and by about 350 B.C. Philip had to give serious attention to the future, for the Chalkidian alliance clearly would not hold much longer.

MACEDONIA'S NEIGHBOURS

It is with his problems concerning the major Greek centres that our sources are mostly concerned, and we shall return to the policies that evolved towards them. But

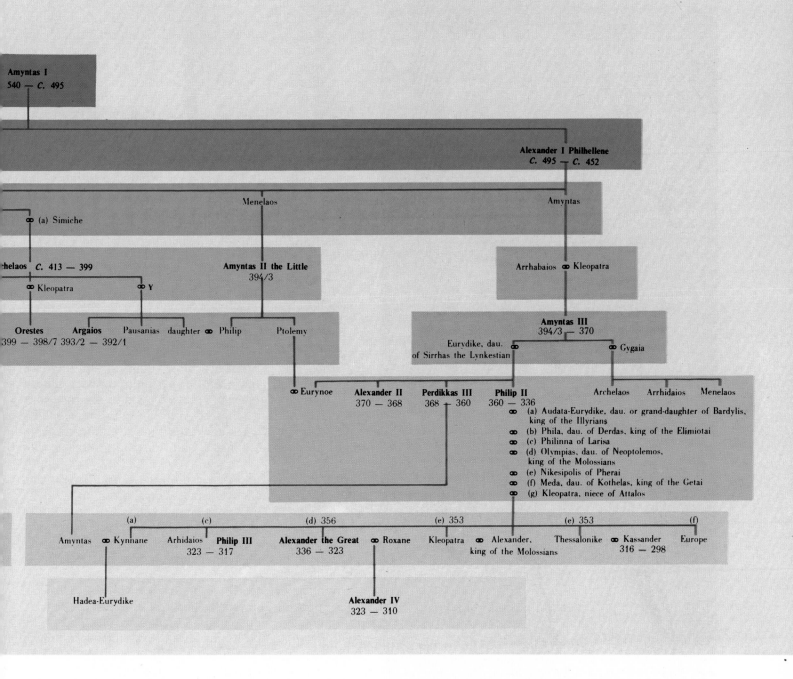

equally important were Macedonia's relationships with her more immediate neighbours.

In general terms, it may be seen, Philip's strategy was to build a ring of client-territories around the kingdom. By the consolidation of upper Macedonia in 358 B.C. and the annexation of western Thrace in the late 350s Macedonian frontiers were advanced, along much of their length, to more easily defensible natural features: broadly speaking, the Pindos range in the west, the river Nestos in the east and a series of mountains some two hundred kilometres north of the Thermaic Gulf. In the south-west the Pierian range and Mt. Olympos divided the kingdom from Thessaly. Only one problematical frontier remained, that with the Chalkidian peninsula, dotted with over thirty towns dominated by Olynthos. When his alliance with this area began to collapse, Philip's response was direct. His campaign of 349-8 B.C. led to the annexation of the whole area, thus giving him control over the entire Macedonian coastline.

So far as those beyond the borders were concerned, the Illyrian and Paionian areas and the far north of Thrace were significant mainly in that, while dangerous if uncontrolled, they might ideally be made to form buffers cushioning the kingdom against tribal movements from further north and north-west. Their populations were relatively loosely organized and unstable, posing no very serious threat to a good army. Philip's approach towards them, therefore, was almost exclusively to make periodic demonstrations of military strength, especially in answer to local upheavals.

Considerably more difficult were the areas of Epirus, Thessaly and Thrace, all of which occupied vital positions between Macedonia and either the Greek peninsula or the Hellespont and Asia Minor. Towards these areas, with their more settled populations and more stable governments, Philip's policies were calculated and effected with much more care. In Epirus the Molossian tribe was dominant and he early formed alliance with its ruling family; his marriage in 357 B.C. with Olympias was one result. But in the long term, dynastic tensions made the alignment unreliable and eventually in 342 B.C. he installed Olympias' young brother, Alexander, on the Molossian throne as his virtual client. In 336 B.C. Alexander was given Cleopatra, daughter of Philip and Olympias, for his wife.

Similarly, following patterns set in previous reigns, Philip from an early date (while his Athenian and then Chalkidian alliances gave him protection from the sea) pursued a close relationship with his Thessalian neighbours. Thessaly was at this time rent by opposition from a tyrant house at Pherai to the ruling organization of the Thessalian League. Macedonian assistance led, in the late 350s, to Philip's appointment as Archon of the League, a position he used not only to suppress the Pheraian regime but also to foster an extremely close relationship between Macedonia and Thessaly in the person of the Macedonian king. In spite of difficulties caused by local dissensions in the mid-340s, demanding the Archon's intervention and his reorganization of Thessaly's governing structure, this continued throughout Philip's and Alexander's reigns and later.

Thrace proved more of a problem. Unlike Epirus and Thessaly it was no longer, since Kotys' death in 359 B.C., under the control of a single government, so that a stable settlement was more difficult to effect. In fact, more years of campaigning and rearrangement were devoted to this area than to any other, an indication of its fractiousness as well as its importance.

From the very early years western Thrace was of obvious concern. The establishment of a colony at Philippi, an internally autonomous foundation intended as a Macedonian outpost, made Philip's intentions clear, though it was not until after 352 B.C., when Athenian influence in the region had been cleared, that the territory as far east as the Nestos was annexed to Macedonia. With central and eastern Thrace Philip attempted to apply a policy similar to that which he was evolving in Thessaly and Epirus. But his reorganization of governments and installation of rulers of his own choice, at least at local level, were not successful and his great Thracian campaign of 342-0 B.C. saw the final overthrow of the two recalcitrant Thracian kings and the appointment of a military governor

77-79. These small ivory portrait heads of Philip (79), Alexander the Great (78) and probably Olympias (77) decorated the wooden bed from the Great Tomb of the tumulus at Vergina. Thessalonike, Archaeological Museum.

Pannonians

Dacians

Getai

Scythians

R. Istros

Istros

Tomis

Kallatis

Triballians

Odessos

E
U
X
I
N
E

Autariatai

Dardanoi

Agrianes

Mesembria
Anchialos
Apollonia

Kabyle

Beroe

Philippoupolis

THRACE

Salmydessos

Lissos

Illyrians

R. Drilon

Bylazora
Astibos

Stoboi

Paiones

R. Axios

R. Strymon

R. Nestos

R. Hebros

R. R. Agrianes

Selymbria
Perinthos
Bisanthe

Byzantion

Kalchedon

Propontis

Parthinoi

Epidamnos

Idomenai

Odomantike

Serrhai

Dikaia
Stryme

Doriskos
Kypsela
Ornoi
Ganos

Philippi

Lychnidos

Alkomenai
Eidomene

Styberra

Krestonia

Edonis

Neapolis

Abdera

Sale

Ainos

Prokonnesos

Kios

Taulantioi

L. Lychnitis

Lynkos
Tyrissa

Bragylai
Kyrrhos

Herakleia
Amphipolis

Oisyme
Apollonia
Maroneia

Kardia
Kallipolis

Panion

Priapos
Kyzikos

Apollonia

Dimale

Edessa

Bottiaia
Pella

Lete
Therme

Arethousa
Stagiros
Akanthos

Thasos

Samothrace

Alopekonnesos
Imbros

Lampsakos
Sestos
Madytos
Abydos

Dardanos

Sigeion

Skepsis

Amantia

Byllis

Eordaia

Methone
Beroia

Aineia
Pydna

Olynthos
Poteidaia
Sane
Sermyle
Singos
Torone

Olophyxos
Charadros
Akrothoon

Elaious

Skione
Mende

Hephaistia

Tenedos

Antandros

Orikos

Argos

Orestis

Aigai
Dion

Pieria

Python
Herakleion

Skione

Myrina

Lemnos

Larisa

Adramyttion

Phoinike

Chaones

Aianeae

Doliche
Azoros

Tymphaia

Aiginion

Oloosson

Homolion

Thermaic Gulf

A
E
G
E
A
N

Assos

Korkyra

Bouthrotos

Passaron

Hestiaiotis

Trikke

Larisa
Meliboia

PERSIAN
EMPIRE

Dodone

Molossos

Perrhaibia

Skotoussa

Pherai
Pagasai

Antisa
Eresos

Atarneus
Pitane

MOLOSSIAN
KINGDOM

Ephyra

THESSALY

Pharsalos

Skiathos

Ikos

Lesbos

Mytilene

Kyme

Gryneion

Korkyra

Pandosia

Kassope

Athamanes

Dolopia

Phthiotis

Peparethos

Skyros

Phokaia

Ambrakia

Argos

Ainis

Malis

Oreos

Magnesia

Thyrreion

Herakleia

Nikaia

Leukas

Stratos

Aitolia

Amphissa

Doris

Elateia

Boiotia

Euboia

Chios

Erythrai

Smyrna

Ithake

Thermos

Delphi

Phokis

Chalkis

Eretria

Klazomenai

Oiniadai

Lokris

Naupaktos

Thebes

Oropos

Teos

Kolophon

Kalydon

Patrai

Aigion

Attica

Notion

Magnesia

Same

Dyme

Achaia

Sikyon

Megara

Athens

Karystos

Andros

Samos

Ephesos

Priene

Kephallenia

Elis

Corinthia

Corinth

Salamis

Piraeus

Samos

Elis

Argos

Argolis

Epidauros

Aigina

Keos

Tenos

Ikaros

Miletos

Zakynthos

Olympia

Arkadia

Tegea

Troizen

Hermione

Mykonos

Megalopolis

Thyrea

Kythnos

Delos

Naxos

Patmos

Leros

Halikarnassos

Messene

Sparta

Seriphos

Paros

Sikinos

Amorgos

Kos

Knidos

Messenia

Lakonia

Gytheion

Epidauros Limera

Melos

Ios

Astypalaia

Nisyros

Telos

Rhodes

Boiai

Anaphe

Lindos

Kythera

Rhodes

Karpathos

THE MACEDONIAN KINGDOM
AND THE OTHER GREEK STATES
AT THE DEATH OF PHILIP II, 336 B.C.

Macedonian kingdom and dependent states

Thessaly, personally attached to Philip

Molossian kingdom, Philip's ally

Greek states, members of the League of Corinth

neutral Greek states

Kydonia

Knossos

Crete

Itanos

Gortys

ADRIATIC GULF

R. Aoos

over Thrace, which was thereafter required to render tribute and military service to the Macedonian throne.

HELLENIC AND EASTERN POLICIES

Around 350 B.C., as his alliance with Olynthos and the Chalkidian League approached breakdown, Philip and his advisers again needed to reorder Macedonian perspectives. The state and its frontiers were secure, or relatively so, owing in large measure to the kingdom's growing military supremacy in the region. The army was now a formidable weapon, capable of devastating use in Macedonia's interests. Over the whole of the reign its numbers were to treble and more, its elements to become differentiated efficiently and drilled in their respective special functions and its members to develop an unsurpassable level of devotion and confidence. But its very size and importance, it must already have been recognized, created their own imperatives, for a highly trained and ambitious militia without goals is a danger to itself and its society. Its officers and men, attracted by the rewards of service, were likely to cohere only so long as the opportunities and successes continued. Suitable outlets were therefore necessary for these dynamic energies. But which way to turn? There were two main possibilities.

By about this time, although the date may be disputed, Philip began to look eastwards. He was well informed about Asia Minor by refugees from Persian rule and he could no doubt see there immense potential in military objectives and tribute as well as in the achievement of ends dear to many Greek states, who had suffered Persian interference, and worse, over nearly two centuries. By contrast, Greece itself was poor, difficult to control and could be defended against him by heavy-armed hoplite armies, which, though less trained and versatile than his more lightly armed infantry and cavalry, could inflict heavy damage on his Macedonians. Moreover, he seems, as he often demonstrated, to have been loth to throw his military forces against the communities of his fellow Hellenes, numbers of whose citizens had by now joined the flow of immigrants into Macedonia. Eastern ambitions seemed altogether more attractive.

But Greece could not be ignored. Some reliable arrangement would be needed to assure his country's security with its king and many troops absent. By this time, growing in-

fluence was bringing Philip into increasing contact with the central and southern Greek states and he well knew where the difficulties would lie. Two states, Athens and Thebes, especially should they, with their allies, ever combine against him, posed the weightiest threat to continued Macedonian prosperity and prestige. The two states were not natural allies, but common dangers had united them before and would again. So, even as he began in 349 B.C. his campaign against the defecting Chalkidian League, Philip set in motion negotiations that he hoped would divide Athenian interests from those of Thebes and bring Athens into alliance with him. Such an arrangement would allow him to contain Hellenic ambitions while exploiting, to the allies' mutual benefit (for the Athenian fleet would once more gain access to the ports of the eastern Aegean and perhaps beyond), the opportunities offered by Asia Minor.

Initially he failed. At this time central Greece was torn by a destructive war, now several years old, between the forces of Phokis and those of Thebes and Thessaly, both sides with their respective allies acting in the name of the primarily religious grouping known as the Amphiktyonic League — the Phokians with some moral justification but their opponents with the weight of legality. Following an invitation by the official Amphiktyons to intervene, Philip in 346 B.C. laid his plans to use the settlement of this war to achieve the ends his interests demanded. His peace with Athens was to be central to the necessary reversal of expectations.

But the past decade of Athenian suspicion and hatred could not so easily be eradicated. The Athenian assembly, while accepting his formal terms, declined, when the moment came to crush Theban power, to accede to his military requirements and he was obliged to leave Thebes untouched. The peace with Athens (the Peace of Philokrates) however gave him what might at least form the basis of an improved relationship with her, and for another three years he strove, through one concession after another, to dispel her mistrust. Equally assiduously his critics in Athens disparaged and nullified his efforts. Finally he abandoned the attempt, turning to much needed action in Epirus and Thrace, though he was well aware that this would bring relations with Athens to a head, for eastern Thrace bordered on her vital interests in the Hellespontine area. Tensions quickly escalated and Athens declared war late in 340 B.C.

Although his hopes had not been realized in 346 B.C., the settlement of the Sacred War had still brought gains, the most important of which was that now Macedonia, in his name, occupied an official position among the Amphiktyons (literally and originally 'neighbours'). When in 339 B.C. a similar war broke out, Philip again entered central Greece on the League's behalf. On this occasion Athens determined to resist him, as did Thebes. On the battlefield, at Chaironeia, he faced this most redoubtable alliance. The discipline and mobility of the Macedonian forces however, triumphed and the king now found himself in the position to dictate to the Greek states the kind of settlement he required.

80. The formation of the Hellenic League, crowning achievement of many years of fighting and diplomatic manoeuvring, marked the realization of the ambitious plans of Philip II. Having brought the greater part of the peninsula under Macedonian rule, he had also succeeded on the eve of his untimely death in uniting most of the Greek states under the aegis of the Macedonian throne into an alliance whose aim was the mounting of a panhellenic campaign against the Persians. The map shows the spectrum of political relationships which linked the Macedonian kingdom to the other Greek states of the Balkan peninsula just before Alexander the Great ascended the Macedonian throne.

It proved to be, other than for Thebes and Sparta, whose power was severely reduced, a moderate one, a vehicle for general peace and security guaranteed by relatively inconspicuous but real Macedonian authority. Athens, despite her record over the past years, was treated generously — although perhaps too much damage had now been done for most Athenians ever to become happy with a role that, however honoured and however profitable, was in cold reality subordinate to the Macedonian. A general peace and alliance (the Hellenic League, or 'League of Corinth') formalized the individual settlements and, although Alexander and his deputy were at times to ignore its provisions, the form became a model for the future. At its first convention Philip, as its elected Hegemon, put before the delegates of the Greek states his plans for an eastern crusade.

The most visible aim would be the punishment of the Persians for the despoliation of Hellenic sanctuaries in the invasion of 481-80 B.C. and for that reason all members of the League would be expected to contribute. There would certainly be more tangible rewards for some participants, especially Athens, whose naval and commercial interests could only be served by any success. The Hellenic cities of Anatolia might be freed from Persian overlordship and large numbers of refugees and unemployed mercenaries, a serious problem after decades of war in Greece, might be settled in the hinterland of Asia Minor as buffers against Persian reclamation.

It was the beginning of this campaign after the completion of the Hellenic settlement that gave special significance to the festivities in Aigai at which, as we have seen, Philip met his death.

What should be clear from this brief survey of foreign policy during Philip's reign is the steep increase in Macedonian importance in the Hellenic world. This was in part the consequence of Macedonia's newfound strength in unity. It was made possible by the effectiveness of the revitalized army. It was aided by the final dismemberment in 355 B.C. of Athens' resurgent empire and the growing exhaustion of Thebes in the Third Sacred War of 355-46 B.C. But it was also the result of adroit and constructive diplomacy on the part of Philip and his advisers. It was certainly no record of uninterrupted triumph; even the final settlement after Chaironeia, unavoidably the outcome of military compulsion, was for that reason less conducive to genuine cooperation than Philip had hoped in 346 B.C., at the time of the Peace of Philokrates. Nevertheless, what had been achieved was tangible and effective and gave promise at least of stability on the mainland while Philip directed Macedonian energies eastwards in conjunction with his panhellenic allies. There was, in short, good reason to celebrate at Aigai in 336... until the assassin struck.

81. Aerial photograph of the Great Tumulus of Vergina in which three royal graves have been found. The largest and richest is thought to be that of Philip II. In the background can be seen small earth mounds, the cemetery of the tumuli, which date to the Late Iron Age and the Geometric period.

82-84. Weapons found in the Great Tomb of the tumulus of Vergina, which evidence shows belonged to Philip II. Amongst the best preserved are the Macedonian helmet (82) a unique example with a crest, cheekpieces and the head of Athena in the centre of the forehead; a pair of gilt greaves (83) and the iron cuirass of the dead man, a skilfully made work decorated with gold bands and discs bearing lion's heads. Thessalonike, Archaeological Museum.

ALEXANDER'S ACCESSION

In a moment the murder swept away the spirit of the festivities and threw into jeopardy all they represented. Presumed accessories were quickly identified and punished, but there could be no certainty as the killer himself, one Pausanias, had died silent seconds after his act. Rumours of unpunished guilt began to spread, blending in later years with the varying propaganda of different seasons and circumstances. At the time there were matters of more urgent importance. Alexander, twenty years old, had been swiftly acclaimed king at Aigai, his task to save for Macedonia a situation deteriorating by the minute. Philip's body was cremated and entombed with ceremony and honour but without delay, for the king was needed elsewhere. (If Tomb II at Vergina is indeed Philip's the incompleteness of the interior of the main chamber may be explained by this need for haste.)

In Thrace, Illyria and Thessaly revolt immediately broke out. Further south, the Thebans and Ambrakiots expelled their garrisons and other cities prepared to take up arms. In Athens the assembly, which had so lately sworn to deny refuge to any who plotted against Philip, now passed a decree lauding his murderer. The Hellenic settlement had been prudently constructed and gave promise of peace and stability, but general confidence in its purpose and efficacy had had little time to take root; meanwhile some were deeply offended by it, especially those for whom autonomy had always given promise of licence. Not surprisingly now opportunism flourished. Macedonia itself was exposed, as one writer has it, to 'great jealousies, dreadful hatreds and dangers on every hand'. The kingdom was in ferment, not over Alexander's title to the throne, for that was unquestioned, but over his untried capacity to salvage what Philip's genius had laboured to achieve and his death thrown into doubt. Some, pessimistic, advised him to abandon Hellas altogether to save the kingdom from its barbarian neighbours. Others turned to treason and he would have to deal with them when there was time. But that, like the eastern campaign, must be postponed for the moment. In Asia Minor the advance force before long lost its impetus and a determined Persian counter-offensive began to push it back towards the Hellespont.

The king's response was as prompt and positive as could be wished and set the tone for thirteen years of military and

85. The possession and exploitation of the mineral deposits of eastern Macedonia formed part of the material basis of the achievement both of the unifying policy of Philip II and of the panhellenic campaign of Alexander the Great. The picture shows the two sides of a gold stater of Philip II, with the head of Apollo on one side and a two-horsed chariot on the other. Athens, Numismatic Museum.

86. Silver tetradrachm of Alexander with the head of Herakles on the obverse. On the reverse is Zeus, seated on a throne with a sceptre in one hand and an eagle in the other. Athens, Numismatic Museum.

diplomatic success. He quickly forced Thessaly to confer on him the life-archonship held by his father before him; the Amphiktyonic states were given no option but to grant him Philip's hegemony of the league; Thebes, confronted by *force majeure,* capitulated without a blow; Athens apologetically followed suit. But the early fears over his capacity, the strains on personal loyalties and on the commander's confidence in his senior officers, all of whom were Philip's men, would exacerbate the crucial difficulties of decision-making and command in the years ahead.

THE LEGACY OF PHILIP

Alexander began his reign with a number of strengths, first among which was a large, increasingly populous kingdom now growing in the unity Philip had given it. Its inhabitants were hardy, accustomed to a sometimes harsh climate and, in some places, the most rugged of terrain, open to discipline and well able, as the growing prosperity showed, to exploit their land's rich resources in food, timber and minerals. The king, with mining now on a firm footing, had access to large reserves of copper and iron, silver and gold, as well as to the wealth that came of their sale and export. The royal coinage was plentiful and well respected for its quality and its penetration abroad. His army, the best in the world of the time, was by usual standards large and its elements extremely well trained, mobile and versatile, imbued with confidence born of success and capable of remarkable fortitude in difficult conditions.

To cynical Athenians the Macedonians may have seemed unsophisticated, but, to judge from the quality of the commanders and administrators on which Alexander was able to draw with such success in the East, Philip had surrounded the throne with a pool of immense talent, native and immigrant, especially in the King's Companions *(hetairoi).* From an inner group Alexander might seek advice on all matters, though he was not constitutionally bound to accept any of it. From a wider number he could draw men experienced in responsibility. From the younger members, some of them his friends and contemporaries, he would eventually create a new command structure.

ALEXANDER'S AIMS

The question of Alexander's initial aims is difficult to answer, for no doubt they expanded with the possibilities. All of those who wrote later of his exploits found it impossible to credit him with aspirations inferior to his triumphs, simply assuming that what he won was what he had always had in view. In one sense his future had been moulded for him from the beginning: as soon as it became practicable to put them into operation, Philip's eastern plans unavoidably became his. He could do no less than men expected of the son and chosen heir of his father.

His earliest territorial ambitions are undiscoverable and

may indeed have been flexible. But probably Asia Minor, defensible if the passes of the Tauros range and the coastal landing-places were secure and if Athens cooperated in defending the Aegean islands, was considered at once a credible and a profitable addition to the Macedonian empire. Its loss would be seen as lawful retribution for Persia; the Greek cities of the coastal zone would become allies of the liberator instead of subjects of the Persian king; and the bulk of Anatolia would become tributory to the kingdom and open to commercial exploitation by traders friendly to Macedonia. Whether or not Alexander from the beginning hoped for more (and he could not yet know that his main adversary would prove a poor strategist and leader), there are signs that at least some of those about him considered it enough.

At any rate the aims of the expedition soon began to expand. Hints that Alexander, at least, was more ambitious appear in the sources for the first year of campaigning (334 B.C.) and are confirmed by his flat rejection late in 333 B.C. and again in the next year of Persian concessions amounting to the whole of Asia Minor (and more in the latter case). He would go on, with Zeus on his side. He would become king of Asia.

Details of the conquests are outside the scope of this work. But their nature and consequences were affected by and themselves helped to shape Macedonian history fundamentally and we shall have to examine them briefly, together with their implications.

THE CONQUESTS

Before turning to the East, Alexander took his army to the far north, as far as the Danube, to secure his frontiers as firmly as possible. In the autumn of 335 B.C. as he was campaigning north-west of Macedonia, word came that Thebes was again in revolt. Breaking off he marched at high speed to the south, captured the city and turned it over to the Hellenic League for judgement. It was razed to the ground, a harsh action which has been harshly judged. The revolutionary movement in Greece collapsed and in the following spring the great expedition could begin.

During the first eighteeen months the west and south of Asia Minor were taken. In the process Alexander removed from office the Persian-backed regimes in the Greek cities (in many cases this happened without his intervention), usually installing democracies in their place — the operative feature being not the form of government but the change of personnel. Disbanding the Hellenic fleet he pushed through the Cilician Gates, defeated the Grand Army of Darius at Issos (late 333 B.C.) and moved down the Phoenician coast, aiming to cut Persia off from the sea. The capture of Tyre in mid-332 B.C. after a six-month siege, was probably his greatest military achievement, a tribute to the extraordinary level of engineering technology attained in Macedonia during Philip's and his reigns. In Egypt, which willingly came over to him, he was crowned pharaoh.

Hence he advanced towards Mesopotamia and Babylonia, with the Persian strongholds now under maximum pressure. At the Battle of Gaugamela (1 October 331 B.C.) he again outclassed and decisively defeated the Persian monarch. The years 330-27 B.C. saw the conquest of the centre and north-east of the empire, followed in 327-26 B.C. by the extension of his frontiers to the river Hyphasis, a tributary of the Indus. Here, although the disunity of the Indian tribes and his conviction that the great Ocean lay not far beyond lured him further, his Macedonians united in refusing to follow. Reluctantly turning back he subdued the south-eastern satrapies and made his way back to Babylon, while a fleet sailed a parallel course to explore the important route from the Indus to the head of the Persian Gulf.

Successful as he had been, Alexander's path had been narrow, and in 324 B.C. revolts and corruption, together with dissatisfaction among his own men, showed how thinly his power was spread. Had he lived longer (he died in June 323 B.C.) he would doubtless have given more time to consolidation, as well as to further exploration. Whether he would also have attempted to continue expanding his empire is difficult to tell, since the surviving evidence for it is of dubious value.

ALEXANDER AND THE EAST

The nature and permanence of Alexander's plans for the organization of the East, a much debated subject, have a complementary relevance to our particular interest here, the role Macedonia came to play in his thinking. His adoption of some local customs in his court, including his wearing of Asian dress (though not that of the Persian monarchy) and an ill-fated attempt to extend to his Macedonians the Persian ritual of *proskynesis* (prostration and kissing) by those entering the royal presence, represents an element in his thought on the subject of affiliating the western and the eastern in his organization. It caused great resentment among his own men, his elevation of Asian military units to a level of equality with the Macedonians even more so. The Macedonians naturally saw this as a diminution of their proper status as conquerors.

His problem was shortage of manpower, given the size and diversity of his empire, which meant that he could afford to do little to interfere with existing structures of government. He did not impose Hellenic forms but made use of native administrators of proven worth, usually plac-

87. *The different aspects of the personality and career of Alexander the Great have generated a wealth of comment and supposition amongst both ancient and modern historians. His unique military capabilities, his daring political concepts and the extremes of his character have all been emphasized. Perhaps, however, his most lasting achievement was the spread of Greek civilization and language across central Asia. The picture shows the well-known stele of Azara, copy of the celebrated portrait of Alexander by Lysippos. Paris, Louvre.*

ΚΥΝΗΓΙΟΝ ΛΕΟΝ
LION HUNTING SC

88. Hunting was the favourite sport of the royal family of Macedonia, of the Hetairoi and naturally of Alexander. Two youths are shown in this well-known mosaic at Pella which depicts a lion hunt; one, hatted, has a spear, the other is about to strike the animal. They are usually identified as Alexander and Krateros.

89. Alexander's military victories in the East were to a large extent due to the excellently trained army of Philip. His tactics were based on the well-drilled cavalry which usually determined the issue of the battle into which Alexander himself frequently led his troops. The picture shows Alexander on horseback and wearing a lion's head as he strikes down a Persian infantryman. Detail from the so-called Alexander Sarcophagus. End of the 4th century B.C. Istanbul, Archaeological Museum

ing financial and military officials from among his own men alongside them. All were responsible to him and could be tried and punished without mercy when charges of corruption, maladministration or insubordination were brought against them. It was, for its time, a creative and unusual solution to the problems of imperial government, but had not really begun to settle into a reliable network of command when his death brought it to ruin.

Whether or not a postponement of his death would have conferred greater permanence on his arrangements — for when it occurred his empire still depended much too heavily on the personal drive of one man — it is at least clear that Alexander regarded himself as much more than a mere conqueror. His adoption of the all-encompassing title 'king of Asia', his retention in his own person of the Egyptian pharaonic succession, his interest in extending his territories over the whole of what he took to be the Asian continent suggest too that he did not see himself just as the Persian king's successor.

ALEXANDER AND MACEDONIA

It is also clear that in his last years his kingdom of Macedonia came to play a subsidiary role in his thinking, at least in the judgement of his fellow countrymen. But here again the denial of more time probably limited the effects of such a shift. And, although the removal for so long of so many men in their prime must have slowed the increase in the birthrate, Macedonia itself, so far as we can tell, continued to prosper during the reign. But the king's absence created other problems.

On setting out for the East Alexander appointed Antipater as his deputy with certain powers of command over Macedonia and Greece (the latter through the Hellenic League) and over some of the kingdom's neighbours. In that position the old general must have been authorized to administer the king's justice and presumably to carry out in his stead the royal religious duties; he was certainly empowered to levy troops, raise taxes and to deal, as the Hegemon's deputy, with the Hellenic League, and, as Alexander's representative, with the Delphic Amphiktyony and the Thessalian League. But at all times he was, when the king chose to intervene or to override him, under Alexander's orders. And when it suited Alexander he himself dealt directly with these bodies, bypassing his deputy.

Since what we think of as 'the Macedonian state' meant to its members 'the king and the Macedonians' ('the Macedonians' meaning in practice those in the company of the king), it followed that 'the state', in any technical sense, travelled to the East in 334 B.C. Thus, for instance, decisions taken by the army after Alexander's death were assumed to be as binding on the homeland as on the conquered territories. Strains eventuated. (Perhaps we see them reflected in the complaints about Antipater sent to Alexander by his mother Olympias; they are evident too in the ambiguous roles of Antipater, Alexander and even Olympias in their dealing with foreign states.)

The structures of Macedonian society had begun their evolution in the homeland of the Makedones and had adapted to the expansion of the kingdom over three centuries. Now something quite unprecedented, the extended absence of the king, was beginning to impose strains upon their basis and operation. Yet, while the king's personal authority and his military reputation remained high and while Antipater's reliability and loyalty remained firm, the practical difficulties were minimal.

Thus Macedonia continued throughout the reign to supply its portion of the reinforcements bidden to headquarters to replace casualties and retirements. At the same time Antipater was able to keep sufficient men under arms to maintain order in the Hellenic and Balkan areas and, on the few occasions when serious revolts threatened or occurred, to settle matters adequately.

But as Alexander's Asian plans matured it is likely that they provoked at least as much resentment at home as in the army itself. Unfortunately, our sources' interest is almost wholly in the conquests, so that we are starved of information. But if those on the spot found it impossible to endorse his policy towards Asiatics wholeheartedly, although they must have been aware of the practical difficulties that inspired it, it is hardly likely that those whose information often can have been no better than exaggerated rumours will have been more sympathetic. It is known that Antipater himself was opposed to the deification of Alexander. And it may perhaps be inferred from the apparent smoothness of the deputy's relations with the Macedonians at home and the ease with which he maintained and increased his power over the kingdom after Alexander's death that some transference of loyalty was occurring — in short that a breakdown of the traditional equation of king and state was approaching. However, the establishment of a new dynasty a few years after Alexander's reign resolved the practical problem by returning the kingship to its direct relationship with Macedonian soil.

THE SPREAD OF HELLENISM

If Alexander's conception of the significance of his conquests created difficulties for his subjects, the influence of Macedonia and the Macedonians was certainly spread far and wide. The court had long been associated with the culture of the major Hellenic centres, itself encouraging a lively blend of traditional Macedonian customs and contemporary ideas and techniques from the most advanced cities of Greece. Like his father Alexander began and ended his reign as an enthusiastic devotee of the best in Greek culture, and, particularly when he reached lands little known to his countrymen, his zeal for discovery expressed the best traditions of Greek science.

His strongest influence in this respect, however, was indirect. As the conquered territory expanded, many cities were founded in which Macedonian and other Greek veterans were settled alongside native Asiatics. These settlements were probably intended first of all as military outposts to inhibit revolt. But they were more than that. In Philip's reign such colonization within the kingdom had seen the gradual spread of a more uniform culture, as Alexander must have known. In his reign the effects were vastly wider, for some seventy-odd foundations were made in a variety of areas, but the purposes may have remained much the same. Then, as Hellenic traders followed in the army's wake, such influences grew and spread.

To this kind of Hellenization must be added Alexander's actions, in the more backward parts of his domains, in encouraging the growth of agriculture and urbanization, again following his father's example. For instance, in the fertile and populous but far distant regions of Baktria and Sogdiana alone eight new cities were founded, fostering a settled life among the hill tribes of the area and assisting in holding back the Skythians to the north. The effects were long-lasting.

ACHIEVEMENTS

Alexander's achievements as a general go practically without saying. His was a breathtaking record of success. Likewise, as a leader of men, despite the strains imposed by some of his policies on the loyalties of his Macedonians, he attracted in almost all circumstances a remarkable level of devotion in his soldiers. Although he was better able

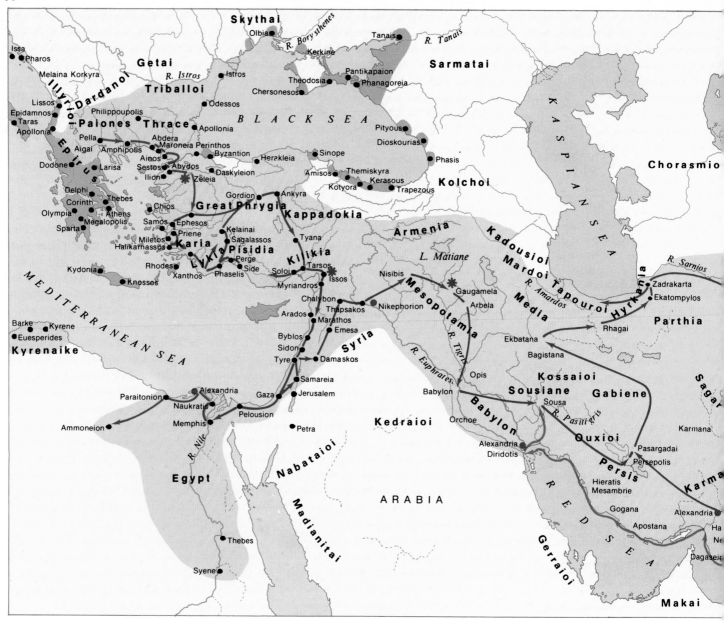

90. The campaigns of Alexander to the heart of central Asia were both a great military achievement and no mean political *and cultural feat. The toppling of the Achaimenides dynasty and the advance of the Greek army to India brought about the crea-*

than most Hellenes to appreciate the virtues of the Asians he conquered, he was a Hellene and a Macedonian to the end. By comparison with other forms of kingship, the access of his countrymen to their king remained as easy and informal as it had been traditionally. In the customary way he shared their toils and dangers throughout his reign.

Yet this was not the whole truth. The grandiosity of his eastern arrangements and his attempts to foster some degree of uniformity in court ritual and military organization put pressure on the relationship because his men feared that they were being demoted to something less than the status of conquerors. That there was not more trouble is a tribute partly to the strength of Alexander's personality and his unqualified conviction that the gods supported him and even more to his imaginative brilliance as a soldier. As

in all things success begets success and it took much to drive his followers to revolt.

While his role in the spread of Hellenism was vital, his influence on the history of the homeland was not all positive. The prestige of Macedonia was enhanced for all time, but, as we have noticed, in some respects Philip had contributed more.

Towards the end of his brief life, already the greatest of conquerors, in his exploits the rival of Achilles, even Herakles and Dionysos, acknowledged as 'son of Zeus' (or Ra or Ammon) in Egypt and parts of Ionia, already the recipient of divine honours on Thasos and Rhodes and in some of the liberated cities of Anatolia, Alexander made it known that he would be pleased to receive similar honours in mainland Greece. (Such a tribute would be neither un-

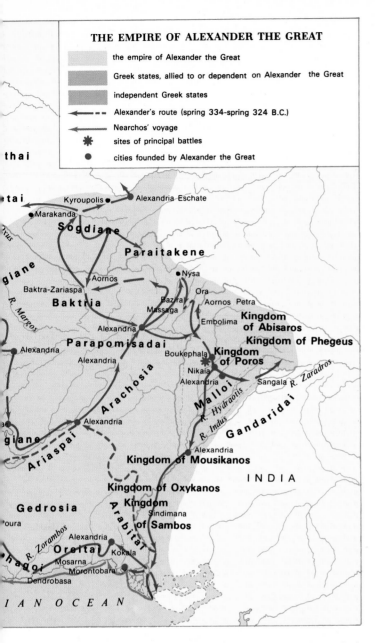

THE EMPIRE OF ALEXANDER THE GREAT

the empire of Alexander the Great

Greek states, allied to or dependent on Alexander the Great

independent Greek states

Alexander's route (spring 334–spring 324 B.C.)

Nearchos' voyage

sites of principal battles

cities founded by Alexander the Great

tion of a universal Greek state. The map shows Alexander's progress, the chief battle sites and the new cities he founded.

precedented nor necessarily outrageous, signifying recognition as a benefactor of outstanding worth.) Some, perhaps many, Greek states acceded. But in Macedonia itself, where cults of his father and grandfather already existed, and in the Macedonian army in the East Alexander remained a man. And this sums up the difference between father and son: Alexander's achievements, in international breadth and effect, surpassed all others; but the greatest king of Macedonia and the Macedonians was Philip, son of Amyntas.

DEATH AND SUCCESSION

Alexander's death fell on the 10 June 323 B.C. The accounts of it are laden with propaganda. On the one hand,

some could not believe that a mere illness (probably malaria) had carried off such a giant, and suspected poison. On the other, those around him, with no appeal to post-mortem or pathology defended themselves by an account that over-emphasized his own responsibility, in extended drinking and self-neglect.

He had died too young. At 33, barely into his prime, he had plans for more conquests, but his rule, especially as regards the relationship between new territories and old, had had no time to evolve beyond the personal dynamism of Alexander the man. There was no one to continue that. There was no suitable successor and no established bureaucratic framework of government to carry a diverse empire over an uneasy transition. When asked, as he was dying, to whom he left his empire, he is said to have replied, 'to the strongest'. The words, if not apocryphal, reflect realism rather than megalomania: however he might have wanted it, that is how it must be. The coming years of turbulence and bloodshed were well foreshadowed.

For the moment there could only be tension and compromise. As kings the army in Babylon acclaimed both Philip's mentally defective son, Arridaios (Philip III), and Alexander's unborn child (Alexander IV), should it be male, by his Iranian wife Roxane. Krateros was appointed their guardian. Senior generals took control of the empire's provinces: Perdikkas, to whom the king at the last had handed his signet ring, Babylon and the east; Ptolemy Egypt and Antigonos Greater Phrygia; Antipater was confirmed in Macedonia and Greece, but with Thrace detached and under Lysimachos. The neatness of the dispositions camouflaged the reality, which soon began to emerge.

ANTIPATER AND CASSANDER

News of Alexander's death provoked a fresh rising in Greece (known as the Lamian War), led this time by Athens, where Hyperides and the democrats bitterly resented the decree recalling exiles, and supported by an army of discontented mercenaries under Leosthenes. Aitolia, Thessaly and most of central Greece joined in, as did Sikyon, Elis, Messenia and Argos. Outnumbered, Antipater asked help from Krateros who was on his way from Asia with ten thousand veterans, and from Leonnatos, the satrap of Hellespontine Phrygia. After a defeat by Leosthenes he was blockaded in Lamia throughout the winter of 323-2. B.C. Leosthenes' death and the Aitolians' departure home brought a respite; and though on his arrival with over twenty thousand men Leonnatos was soon killed, his coming enabled Antipater to slip out of Lamia and return to Macedonia. In spring 222 B.C. the defeat of her fleet off Amorgos marked the effective end of Athens' naval power and made the Aegean a Macedonian sea. Krateros, having accepted Antipater's continued command, fought an indecisive battle at Krannon and the allies were forced to treat separately. Athens lost Oropos and had to receive a Macedonian garrison in Mounchyia and pay an indemnity. The democratic leaders, including Hyperides and Demosthenes, perished in the reprisals which followed and an oligarchic government bound lightly to Macedonia was set up under Phokion and Demades. The League of Corinth now no longer existed.

The settlement at Babylon was soon followed by fresh manoeuvres which inevitably involved Antipater. While Krateros was away in Europe Perdikkas, who had been appointed chiliarch (or grand vezier), himself assumed the guardianship of the kings, and though betrothed to Antipter's daughter he threw her over in order to marry Alexander's sister Cleopatra. Suspicion of Perdikkas' ambitions led to the formation of a coalition of generals against him — Antipater, Krateros, Antigonos Monophthalmos, the One-Eyed, Lysimachos and Ptolemy (governor of Egypt). But in 321 B.C. Perdikkas was assassinated by his own officers while invading Egypt; and Krateros' death soon afterwards in a campaign against Perdikkas' ally, Eumenes of Kardia, further reduced the ranks of the contestants. The same year (or early in 320 B.C.) these met at Triparadeisos in north Syria and Antipater was appointed guardian of the kings, Philip III and Alexander IV; this post carried a general regency over the empire. Leaving the ambitious Antigonos as general of Asia to hound down Eumenes, Antipater returned with the kings to Macedonia.

From Perdikkas' death in 321 B.C. until his own death in 301 B.C. Antigonos was the main contender for the imperial crown; and though he failed to secure this, he founded a dynasty which, beginning with his grandson Antigonos, ruled over Macedonia for over a century. Antigonos spent the years 321 to 319 B.C. pursuing Eumenes, whom he eventually penned up in Nora in Kappadokia. But a new situation then arose. Antipater died (319 B.C.) having arbitrarily appointed Polyperchon, one of Philip II's officers, regent in preference to his own son Cassander. Cassander, who was capable and ambitious, crossed to Asia to organize a coalition of Lysimachos, Ptolemy and Antigonos against Polyperchon. Attracted by the new possibilities Antigonos offered Eumenes his satrapy back in return for his collaboration; but Eumenes soon found a way out of this alliance and at Polyperchon's instigation prepared for further war against Antigonos.

With Macedonia Polyperchon inherited the secular problems of the kingdom and in particular relations with Greece. To win support there he made several belated and half-hearted concessions, promising Athens the return of Oropos and Samos, the formal annulment in the name of king Philip of the penalties imposed after the Lamian War and the restoration of those then exiled. Athenian democracy was briefly restored; but as soon as Polyperchon was seen to be losing ground negotiations were opened with Cassander, his troops were introduced into Piraeus, and a moderate government was set up under Demetrios of Phaleron, who remained in power for ten years. Meanwhile Antigonos had made great gains in Asia Minor and besides sending Cassander with a fleet into Greece was himself preparing to cross into Thrace. Polyperchon sent his admiral Kleitos against him but he,

after a victory over the combined fleets of Antigonos and Cassander, let himself be trapped on land and lost all his ships. The Aegean was now at the mercy of Polyperchon's enemies; and soon he lost Macedonia too, for while he was absent in Epirus, hoping to bring back Olympias to Macedonia, Philip III's wife Eurydike joined Cassander and attempted a coup. When Polyperchon and Olympias approached, her troops deserted and soon afterwards Olympias executed both her and Philip and carried out a massacre of her enemies. Cassander now forced his way into Macedonia from Greece, and in 316 B.C. Olympias, who had taken refuge in Pydna, surrendered on promise of her life; but once Cassander held all Macedonia, he had her condemned by a Macedonian assembly and executed. To improve his own claims he now married Thessalonike, a daughter of Philip II (and later named the city which he founded at the head of the Thermaic Gulf after her). About the same time Eumenes, who had fought impressively against the united generals, was betrayed by his own troops and executed by Antigonos, who was now well on the way to controlling the whole empire. The next years saw the first phase in the struggle of the rest against him. In that struggle Cassander, now master of Macedonia, was deeply committed.

Following Eumenes' defeat and death Antigonos controlled the whole area from Asia Minor to Iran and he now expelled Seleukos from Babylonia, which had been assigned to him at Triparadeisos; Seleukos took refuge with Ptolemy. In a joint ultimatum Ptolemy, Lysimachos and Cassander now called on Antigonos to restore Babylonia to Seleukos and to surrender Syria to Ptolemy, Hellespontine Phrygia to Lysimachos, and Kappadokia and Lykia to Cassander; he was also to share with the rest the treasure captured from Eumenes. Ignoring this, Antigonos continued to make territorial gains; very soon he held all southern Syria (except Tyre), Karia and Bithynia. Polyperchon he appointed general of the Peloponnese and as a gesture had Cassander condemned to death by *his* army-assembly for the 'murder' of Olympias and the seizure of Alexander IV and Roxane. In a manifesto announcing this he declared himself guardian of the surviving king and proclaimed all Greek cities to be free, autonomous and without garrisons, a claim clearly directed against Cassander's policy in Greece, and promptly echoed in a counter-manifesto by Ptolemy, despite his alliance with Cassander. It was partly in support of this programme and partly in response to military considerations that Antigonos now (315-14 B.C.) created a Confederation of the Aegean Islanders (the Nesiotai), encouraging Imbros and Delos to secede from Athens; he also sent agents with money to intrigue against Cassander in the Peloponnese.

But Macedonia was not Antigonos' first target. Leaving Syria under his son Demetrios he planned to deal with Lysimachos in Thrace before attacking Cassander; Ptolemy was to be left to the last. This plan was thwarted by Ptolemy who, by his defeat of Demetrios at Gaza in 312 B.C., enabled Seleukos to occupy Mesopotamia and impelled Antigonos to make peace. The result was a compromise settlement based on the *status quo* and the *de facto* recognition of at least four independent states, though the pretence of Alexander IV's kingship was still maintained. Cassander was to remain general of Europe during his minority, Antigonos was to be general of all Asia, Lysimachos and Ptolemy were confirmed in their possession of Thrace and Egypt. Neither Seleukos nor Polyperchon was mentioned; but a clause guaranteeing Greek freedom provided a useful *casus belli* for the future. In a letter to the people of Skepsis, Antigonos boldly represents the peace as a triumphant vindication of Greek liberty. It certainly won him popularity and support in the Greek states.

The peace of 311 B.C. merely put off the struggle against Antigonos; and in Macedonia shortly afterwards, Cassander strengthened his position by murdering Alexander IV and Roxane. He was now threatened by Polyperchon, who invaded Tymphaia via Aitolia and Epirus, nominally on behalf of Herakles, an alleged bastard of Alexander the Great. Fearing that the pretender might win support, Cassander made peace with Polyperchon, confirming him as general in the Peloponnese, and Herakles was quietly assassinated. In reaction to this Ptolemy made a compact with Antigonos' son Demetrios, later known as the Besieger of Cities (Poliorketes). Antigonos had perhaps noted that the cities of Greece, fearing Cassander's compact with Polyperchon, were appealing to Ptolemy and hoped to share in any gains. Ptolemy's motives are less clear. In 308 B.C. Ptolemy sent an expedition to the Peloponnese; but when this failed to win support he made it up with Cassander on terms advantageous to the latter and returned home leaving Ptolemaic garrisons in several cities.

In 307 B.C. Cassander, his position thus strengthened, was campaigning in Epirus when Demetrios sailed with a large fleet and army and substantial funds from Ephesos to Athens in the role of liberator. Seizing Athens he expelled Demetrios of Phaleron and restored the democracy — a considerable blow to Macedonia. In 306 B.C. Antigonos took the title of king for both himself and Demetrios, a gesture implying rule over the whole empire. A year later Ptolemy followed suit, and after him Cassander, Lysimachos and Seleukos, who thereby rejected the Antigonid claim and asserted the existence of separate kingdoms. But these were words; only by crushing Antigonos in battle could the rest dispose of his claim.

Demetrios now extended his influence in the Isthmus region at the expense of Ptolemy and Cassander. In 302 B.C. he revived the League of Corinth with Antigonos and himself as presidents. Its constitution is known from an inscription found at Epidauros, which shows it to have been the work of Adeimantos of Lampsakos. Like Philip II's league it was meant to control Greece; but it was also to furnish a political base for the conquest of Macedonia — for this was bound to play a key role in Antigonid ambitions. It was thus an alliance first, a common Peace only second. In these manoeuvres we hear nothing of Polyperchon; evidently he had died since 303 B.C.

Demetrios' successes stimulated the Antigonids' opponents to form a new coalition. Cassander, Lysimachos, Ptolemy and Seleukos (who had by now returned to the west with a troop of war elephants given him by Candragupta in exchange for India) made plans to confront Antigonos in Asia Minor, so forcing him to withdraw Demetrios from Europe. While Lysimachos crossed into Asia (302 B.C.) Cassander took up position in Thessaly. Demetrios marched north and, evading a full battle against Cassander, captured and liberated several towns. But Seleukos' approach forced Antigonos to recall Demetrios as the allies had foreseen. Demetrios made a truce with Cassander based on the *status quo* and a promise that the Greeks in Asia and Europe should be free. But once he had gone, Cassander retook Thessaly. In Asia Demetrios had some successes; but in spring 301 B.C. the combined armies of Lysimachos and Seleukos met Antigonos and his son at Ipsos in Phrygia; it was a decisive victory for the allies and the aged Antigonos perished in the battle.

The victors shared the spoils. But Cassander, who had been absent from Ipsos, merely kept his possessions in Europe and the prospect of challenging Demetrios, who still held some Greek strong-points. With the battle of Ipsos the dream of uniting Alexander's empire in one man's hands was over; and though for a time Lysimachos' realm bestrode the Straits, Europe and Asia — and Egypt — were henceforth to go different ways.

THE STRUGGLE FOR MACEDONIA (297-276 B.C.)

Cassander took Antigonos' fall as an invitation to try once again to conquer Greece; but the Athenians allied with Aitolia expelled him from Attica, and an Athenian general drove him off when he besieged Elateia in Phokis. Though he managed to establish Macedonian power in Epirus he was forced from Korkyra by Agathokles, the tyrant of Syracuse. These desultory and ineffective attempts to extend Macedonian power ceased in 298 or 297 B.C. with Cassander's death; and for the next two decades Macedonia lacked stable government as Macedonian generals fought for her possession. Not all were equally interested — Seleukos for instance less than Lysimachos, Demetrios and a new contestant, the young Molossian king, Pyrrhos. As a kinsman of Alexander and a supporter of Ptolemy, Pyrrhos was a useful watchdog on the western frontier of Macedonia and a counter-weight to Demetrios.

After Ipsos the Athenians, outraged by his excesses, had expelled Demetrios, and Lachares, a tool of Cassander, had assumed control (though Athens was nominally free). But Demetrios made a good recovery. Following a marriage alliance between Lysimachos and Ptolemy, Seleukos met Demetrios at Rhosos in Syria, where it was agreed that he should marry Demetrios' daughter Stratonike and Demetrios should receive Kilikia. But on Cassander's death Demetrios quickly dropped this connection, returned to Greece and retook Athens (294 B.C.). His goal was Macedonia, where Cassander had been suc-

91. *Wherever he marched, Alexander's campaign in the East left ineradicable traces in folk memory. His proverbial personal courage called forth the undivided love of his soldiers and formed the core of mythical adventures, even after the passing of*

91

many centuries. The magnificent mosaic from Pompeii, copy of a painting by Philoxenos of Eretria, shows a vital moment in the battle of Issos. Mounted, Alexander rides impetuously towards Darius on his decorated chariot. Naples, Museo Nazionale.

ceeded briefly by an ailing son Philip and then, upon his death, by two other sons, Antipater and Alexander; both were young and power was exercised by their forceful mother Thessalonike. Demetrios was fighting against Sparta, however, when he learnt that Lysimachos, Ptolemy and Seleukos had stripped him of his Asian possessions. With little left he now saw the conquest of Macedonia as urgent. There war had broken out between the brothers. Antipater had murdered his mother and expelled Alexander, who appealed to both Pyrrhos and Demetrios. Pyrrhos was nearer and in exchange for Tymphaia, Paravaia, Ambrakia, Amphilochia and Akarnania he set Alexander on the throne and patched up peace between the brothers. On arriving in Macedonia Demetrios was met by Alexander at Dion; he quickly had the young king murdered, won over the Macedonian army — that his wife was the regent Antipater's daughter counted in his favour — and was hailed king (293 B.C.); he then seized the areas held by the young Antipater and Lysimachos, and Thessaly, where he founded a new capital at Demetrias. Since he already held Athens, Megara, Euboia and most of the Peloponnese, and exercised general control over the Aegean islands, the addition of Macedonia, Thessaly and, very soon, Boiotia, looked like establishing him firmly in the position previously held by Cassander. But his volatile temperament and the hostility of Pyrrhos and Lysimachos were both against him.

In 292/1 B.C., hearing that Lysimachos had been made prisoner by the king of the Getai, Dromichaites, (he was in fact soon released), Demetrios invaded Thrace; but he was soon recalled by a rising in Boiotia and an attack from Pyrrhos' allies, the Aitolians. Pyrrhos too invaded Thessaly. After some resistance Thebes fell to Demetrios who, as a move against Pyrrhos and Aitolia, then sailed to Korkyra and, by marrying Lanassa who had left Pyrrhos and so regained the island as her dowry, took possession of his important western base (291/0 B.C.). The marriage also created a useful relationship with Lanassa's father Agathokles of Syracuse. In 289 B.C. Demetrios invaded Aitolia, now Pyrrhos' ally, but after ravaging the country was soundly defeated in Epirus — an event which shook his popularity in Macedonia, where his wars seemed purposeless and his licentious character unattractive. When Pyrrhos advanced to Edessa he won much support, and Demetrios made peace, probably on the *status quo,* and prepared to invade Asia. He had lost the Island League, which Ptolemy had taken over unopposed while Demetrios was occupied against Pyrrhos and Aitolia.

In 288 B.C. Pyrrhos broke his word and invaded Macedonia a second time, while Lysimachos came in from Thrace. Abandoned by his troops Demetrios fled to Asia, where in 286 B.C. he finally surrendered to Seleukos, who held him in luxurious captivity until his death in 283 B.C. Pyrrhos and Lysimachos partitioned Macedonia, Pyrrhos taking the greater part and some of the royal elephants. In Greece Athens was liberated and after some fighting Demetrios' son Antigonos, who was holding the remnant of the Antigonid possession there, was forced to make

peace. An Athenian inscription celebrates the services of one Strombichos, a soldier in Demetrios' garrison, who joined the Athenians. For a time Pyrrhos also fought Antigonos but then, distrusting Lysimachos, made an agreement with him. The chief beneficiary of Demetrios' fall was Lysimachos who, outwitting Pyrrhos, got himself accepted as king of all Macedonia. Cassander's son Antipater was put to death and for a time his possession of so large a realm — Thessaly (except Demetrias), Macedonia, Thrace, and most of Asia Minor north and west of Tauros (except Bithynia and Pontos) — seemed to mark him out as a possible ruler of the whole. Lysimacheia, his new city on the Thracian Chersonese, looked both to Europe and to Asia.

A domestic drama precipitated Lysimachos' downfall. His third wife Arsinoe, Ptolemy's daughter, in her own children's interests persuaded him to execute his son Agathokles as a traitor. Agathokles' widow Lysandra and her brother Ptolemy Keraunos (the Thunderbolt) (also Ptolemy's children by a former marriage) therefore invited Seleukos to seize Macedonia. In 282 B.C. he entered western Asia Minor, where Lysimachos' governor in Pergamon promptly made over to him the citadel and nine thousand talents, and Zipoites of Bithynia joined him. In 281 B.C. the two armies met at Kouroupedion in Lykia, where Lysimachos was defeated and killed. Seleukos, Alexander's last surviving general (since Ptolemy's death in 283 B.C.), now crossed over into Europe but was promptly murdered by Ptolemy Keraunos (August/September 281 B.C.) outside Lysimacheia. Keraunos was then himself hailed as king. These events encouraged Antigonos to invade Macedonia from Greece, hoping to anticipate Keraunos; but with the combined fleets of Lysimachos and Herakleia Keraunos inflicted a devastating naval defeat which encouraged a movement against him in Greece, led by Areus of Sparta. By 279 B.C. Antigonos held only a few places in Achaia and the Argolid along with Demetrias, Corinth and Piraeus. Keraunos was thus able to establish himself on the Macedonian throne. His early downfall was due to his neglect of a prime consideration for any Macedonian king, the defence of the northern frontiers. Encouraged by the collapse of Lysimachos' realm in Thrace, an army of Gauls migrating from central Europe poured into Macedonia (January 279 B.C.) Keraunos fell in battle and chaos ensued. First his brother Meleager was hailed king, but then dismissed after two months in favour of Cassander's nephew Antipater. His reign lasted only forty-five days and brought him the nickname Etesias, 'the Dogday King'. The subsequent penetration of central Greece and the saving of Delphi by the Aitolians falls outside this survey; but the setting up of a Gaulish kingdom of Tylis in Thrace changed the political situation there for several decades.

For two years after Antipater's fall Macedonia lacked a king; but the royal power (without the title) was exercised by the general Sosthenes, who averted complete disruption. Antigonos was still bent on winning the kingdom. In 278 B.C. his attack from Thrace was repelled by Sosthenes; but in 277 B.C., he decisively defeated a body of Gauls near Lysimacheia — Pan was said to have assisted his victory — and with enhanced prestige he again entered Macedonia and was accepted as king. Somehow or other he crushed three pretenders — Antipater 'Etesias', Ptolemy the son of Lysimachos, and one Arrhidaios — and he used pirates to expel its tyrant Apollodoros from Kassandreia. Detailed information on these events is slight; but by the end of 277 B.C. he was seated on the throne of the Argeads. A king since 283 B.C. — he subsequently counted his regnal years from that date — he had now acquired a kingdom; and with his accession was associated an important event, the reconciliation of the Antigonid and Seleucid houses. It was probably in 278 B.C. that Antiochos I and Antigonos II

made an alliance by which they renounced all claim, the former to Macedonia and the latter to Asia. Antigonos married his own niece Phila, Antiochos' half-sister, and the wedding-hymns, written by Aratos of Soli, celebrated the treaty and the help given by Pan in the victory over the Gauls.

ANTIGONOS II GONATAS (276-239 B.C.)

Antigonos Gonatas possessed a striking and in many ways sympathetic personality. Himself a pupil of Zeno, the founder of Stoicism, he encouraged philosophers and writers to frequent his court in the hope of transforming Pella into a centre of Greek culture (see page 167).

92. Detail from the 'Alexander Sarcophagus'. Some scholars identify the warrior on the right with Antigonos Monophthalmos. Of the diadochoi, he was the one who came closest to reviving the empire of Alexander under his own centralized command. End of the 4th century B.C. Istanbul, Archaeological Museum.

Plutarch said that he possessed moderation, and his kindliness and generosity are quoted by many writers. Tradition credits him with little patience for flattery and pretentiousness. Thus to the poet who hailed him a god he replied that 'the slave who brings me my chamber-pot does not think so!'; and reproving his son for some excess he told him that 'our kingship is a noble servitude (ἔνδοξος δουλεία).' But there is little or nothing in Antigonos' public career that can be directly related to any philosophical tenets. He inherited a kingdom with its practical problems and he spent his life trying to solve these as best he could and to devise and maintain a realistic policy towards Greece.

Macedonia was an exhausted country and this counselled a prudent and conservative policy for some years; there could be no question of pursuing the ambitions entertained by Antigonos' father and grandfather. The Seleucid treaty freed him from anxiety about the north-east frontier — though like all Macedonian kings he had to watch the barbarians. The status of eastern Thrace at this time is uncertain. It evaded direct Macedonian control until Philip V's reign, perhaps as a no-man's land in which the Greek cities maintained an uneasy independence. To the south the growth in prestige and influence of the Aitolian League forced Antigonos to consolidate his hold on Thessaly and maintain his bases in southern Greece. From Corinth, which he put under his brother Krateros, he could prevent any hostile army like that of Sparta from crossing the Isthmus, and his garrisons in Chalkis, Demetrias and (until 272 B.C.) Piraeus, besides holding down the areas around, guaranteed safe communications along the coast between Thessaly and Corinth. Thessaly was vital to the safety of southern Macedonia and was very soon in Antigonos' hands, as the records of the peoples sitting on the Amphiktyonic Council at Delphi show. The Aitolians first appear there in 277 B.C., but the Thessalians, after occupying the presidency in that year, subsequently vanish from the lists. Throughout the century of Antigonid rule it was normal practice for Macedonia and any voting states within her sphere of influence to boycott Amphiktyonic meetings dominated by the Aitolians. The disappearance of the Thessalians from the list of 276 B.C. indicates that they were now once more under Macedonia.

For the moment the main danger to Gonatas lay in the west. The recent chaotic conditions had brought a loss of territory in two areas. Paionia had regained its independence after Cassander's death and coins show it organized as a *koinon* of the Paionians under one Dropion; Antigonos made no attempt to recover it for many years. On the Epeirote frontier Pyrrhos, still Antigonos' most serious rival, held Tymphaia and Paravaia. Though tempted to make a bid for the Macedonian throne in 281 B.C., Pyrrhos finally preferred to accept a Tarentine invitation to cross into Italy, and from 281 to 275 B.C. had operated first against the Romans, then — despite the new opportunity which Keraunos' death seemed to afford for intervention in Macedonia — against the Carthaginians in Sicily, and finally once more in Italy, where the Romans

defeated him at Beneventum. In 275 B.C. he returned to Epirus and invaded Macedonia from the west. He may have been in search of plunder to pay his army; or perhaps he suspected — as indeed proved true — that he could still command support in Macedonia. The suggestion that he was acting for Ptolemy II is unlikely.

Pyrrhos' attack met with unforeseen success. In a battle, fought perhaps in the Aoos valley, where there was a *castra Pyrrhi*, he completely routed Antigonos, who fled to Thessalonike; the Macedonian army went over, giving Pyrrhos most of Macedonia and Thessaly, but the pillaging of the royal tombs at Aigai by his Galatian mercenaries was resented in Macedonia. Soon afterwards Pyrrhos left for Epirus. Kleonymos of Sparta had asked for help against the Spartan king Areus, his nephew, and Pyrrhos saw in this alignment a chance to expel Antigonos from his strongholds in Greece. He left his son Ptolemaios behind in charge of Macedonia but within a few months Antigonos had recovered the country and was confident enough to follow Pyrrhos into Greece. In autumn 272 B.C. Pyrrhos perished in a mêlée inside Argos and Antigonos was free of his most dangerous rival and in a position to reshape his relations with Greece and Epirus.

Meanwhile Sparta had joined Antigonos, who now consolidated the Macedonian enclave round Corinth with pro-Macedonian tyrannies in Elis and Megalopolis. On Argos there is no firm information; but Athens probably expelled the Macedonian garrison from Piraeus in 272 B.C. and made with the Aitolian League the treaty recorded on an inscription found at Delphi. There were other Aitolian diplomatic successes at this time; the annexation of Ainiania and the Boiotian absorption of Opuntian Lokris strengthened the anti-Macedonian *bloc* in central Greece. In Epirus, however, Pyrrhos was succeeded by Alexander, his son by Lanassa, and for several years relations with Macedonia were peaceful. All in all the situation was quiet but unstable, with Antigonos concentrating his efforts on winning support and loyalty in Macedonia.

The detailed history of Macedonia during the next few years is obscure, partly because the main source on Alexander's successors, the lost work of Hieronymos of Kardia, ended with Pyrrhos' death. But one new factor is Ptolemy II's growing interest in Greece. Between 274 and 271 B.C. he was busy fighting to ward Antiochos I off from Koile-Syria (Palestine); his success in this war left him free to intrigue against Antigonos in Greece. What he hoped for there is far from certain; but the likelihood is that Antigonos needed a navy for communications with Corinth and Ptolemy saw this as a threat to the maritime

93. The most eminent of the diadochoi, *Demetrios Poliorketes was the son of Antigonos and the chief executor of his policies. A brilliant general, he demonstrated astonishing vigour and ability to recover from sudden reversals of policy. The picture shows a detail of the 'Alexander sarcophagus' depicting Demetrios on horseback. End of the 4th century B.C. Istanbul, Archaeological Museum.*

supremacy which enabled him to control the Anatolian coastline and the Island League. Ptolemy's intrigues bore fruit in the Chremonidean War (268/7 B.C.). This war took its name from the Athenian Chremonides, who initiated an alliance between Athens and Sparta and her allies, viz. Elis (where the tyrant had been murdered), the newly reorganized Achaian League, Tegea, Mantineia, Orchomenos, Phigaleia, Kaphyai and some Cretan cities. This coalition was directed against Macedonia, now once more at loggerheads with Sparta. Of the war few details are known and their dates mostly uncertain. Antigonos quickly reached and blockaded Athens before Patroklos, the Ptolemaic admiral, appeared off Attica; and though the latter may have landed some troops, Antigonos prevented Sparta from breaking the blockade. Other events in the war were Antigonos' successful defeat of a body of Gauls — probably mercenaries in revolt — near Megara, and the death of Areus of Sparta near Corinth. Eventually Athens had to surrender, probably in 261 B.C., for Ptolemy's support was inadequate — perhaps owing to Macedonian naval action off the Ptolemaic coast of Asia Minor. The Macedonian naval victory off Kos, which Antigonos celebrated by dedicating his flagship to Apollo, was perhaps also in 261 B.C.

During the war, while Antigonos was besieging Athens, Alexander of Epirus tried to invade Macedonia but was defeated by an army nominally under Antigonos' young son, the future Demetrios II, and driven out of his own kingdom. In 261 B.C. Antigonos made peace with Ptolemy and with the Greek allies. At sea, even if Kos belongs to this war, there had been no decisive change in the balance of power. A handful of inscriptions from Kos, Amorgos, Keos, Ios and Skyros (if indeed they all concern Antigonos II) show some growth in Macedonian naval influence; but substantially Alexandria still dominated the Aegean. On land however Macedonia was much strengthened. To the garrisons in Corinth and Chalkis was now added the military occupation of Piraeus and Athens. Five years later Antigonos nominally restored Athenian freedom, but this gesture did not diminish Macedonian control or the presence of the garrisons. In the Peloponnese friendly tyrants in Megalopolis and Sikyon contributed to the stability of Macedonian power.

Towards the middle of the century that power was shattered. In 251 B.C. Nikokles, the tyrant of Sikyon and a friend of Gonatas, was expelled by Aratos, the young son of an earlier ruler; soon afterwards Aratos brought the liberated city into the Achaian League. An attempt by Antigonos to win him over with a gift of twenty-five talents failed; instead Aratos obtained a large subsidy from Ptolemy II. Soon afterwards, perhaps in 249 B.C., Gonatas sustained a further blow when his nephew Alexander, who had inherited his father Krateros' command in Corinth, revolted and declared himself king. In reply Gonatas succeeded in installing Aristomachos as tyrant in Argos and in setting up a pro-Macedonian tyranny in Megalopolis, which had been temporarily liberated. But Alexander made an alliance with Achaia and forced both Argos and Athens to suspend their attacks on Corinth. In central Greece the Aitolians used their neutrality to expand their territory and their authority; victory over Boiotia in 245 B.C. gave them Opuntian Lokris and control of the land route southwards. Thus, as a result of these events, the whole edifice of Macedonian power south of Thessaly was shaken; and Antigonos' failure to prevent or counter these events suggests that he was becoming lethargic from old age or had troubles on his northern frontiers. None are recorded; but the *Paneia* and *Soteria* festivals which he founded on Delos in 245 B.C. may celebrate victories achieved there.

Alexander died in *c.* 247 B.C. and in 245 B.C. Antigonos regained Corinth (and Euboia) from his widow by a pretended marriage alliance with the crown prince Demetrios. The consequent threat to Achaia was accentuated in 244 B.C., when the Aitolians established relations with Elis, Messenia and several cities in Arkadia, where a new tyranny arose at Megalopolis. Suspicions that Antigonos was behind this initiative may have encouraged Aratos' next move. In 243 B.C. by a clever coup he seized Acrocorinth and with it the ports of Corinth; soon afterwards Epidauros, Troezen and Megara all joined the League. Antigonos' reaction was muted; he was nearly eighty. According to a tradition going back to Aratos, he made a compact with the Aitolians to dismember Achaia; but throughout 242 B.C. neither Aitolia nor Macedonia acted, although Aretos launched attacks on Attica and Athens itself. He also made an alliance with Agis IV of Sparta and successfully solicited an annual subsidy from Ptolemy III. In 241 B.C. the Aitolians penetrated the Peloponnese but were defeated near Pellene and shortly afterwards made peace with Achaia. The plan to divide Achaia — if it was ever more than Aratos' propaganda — had collapsed. The Achaian alliance with Sparta also came to nothing through Aratos' suspicion of Agis (who was soon afterwards overthrown); and when in 240 B.C. the Aetolians again invaded the Peloponnese it was Lakonia that they ravaged. In 240/39 B.C. Antigonos died.

In his thirty-seven year reign he had restored stability and set his dynasty firmly on the throne. Details of much that he did, especially in the north, are lost. In the south for most of his reign he maintained a loose military system, inherited from Demetrios, but designed no longer for expansion but to deny Greece to any rival power. It was planned as a whole, and each of the so-called 'fetters of Greece' — except perhaps Demetrias — was closely related to the maintenance of the rest. Antigonos' moves to set up centres of support in the Aegean were slight and tentative and a reaction to Ptolemy's interference in Greece; in this his aims and methods were a contrast to those of his father and grandfather. From 278 B.C. onwards he was on good terms with the Seleucids; and despite underlying opposition his relations with Egypt were mostly peaceful, though not cordial. The Chremonidean War, which the Greeks saw as a crusade, was forced on Antigonos because his minimum requirements for Macedonian security were incompatible with freedom for the Greek cities. The battle of Kos, whatever its date, was clearly a setback for Egypt, but hardly a catastrophe; it caused little change in the balance of naval power.

Antigonos' military system in Greece was shattered by Aratos' capture of Corinth. It had served as a bulwark as much against the growing power of Aitolia as against Achaia. Aitolia was nearer Macedonia and Thessaly and through Delphi it could use leverage against Antigonos. It is evidence of his diplomatic skill that he remained at peace with this expanding and ebullient neighbour throughout his whole reign. At home he spared the Macedonian people, using Greek, Celtic and Anatolian mercenaries to garrison his strongpoints in Greece and so allowing the population to recover from the losses of the previous reigns. He gave Macedonia a breathing-space and passed on the throne to his son without hitch or crisis.

DEMETRIOS II (239-229 B.C.)

Antigonos' successor, Demetrios II, was in his late thirties and an experienced general; he had probably carried much of the government during his father's last years. His reign brought new political alignments closely linked with events in Epirus. Alexander II had died about the same time as Antigonos, and his widow Olympias, left as regent during the minority of his two sons Pyrrhos and Ptolemy, was soon the object of Aitolian aggression. In 243 B.C. Alexander and the Aitolians had partitioned Akarnania, the eastern part going to the latter and the western to Epirus. Encouraged by Alexander's death the Aitolians now attacked the western half and Olympias looked for foreign aid. Demetrios was persuaded to marry Phthia, Olympias' daughter; but whether Epirus gained much from this is doubtful for no Macedonian expedition to Epirus or Akarnania is attested. To marry Phthia Demetrios divorced his former wife, the Seleucid princess Stratonike (the marriage with Alexander's widow had probably been annulled). The new marriage marked a new political alignment in Greece; it seems not to have caused a breach with Seleukos, but it probably led Achaia and Aitolia to convert their peace into a military alliance against Macedonia. The result of all this was the so-called Demetrian War.

Demetrios must have foreseen this result of his new Epirote alliance, so evidently a war with Aitolia suited his purpose. Given that his ultimate aim was to recover Corinth he perhaps welcomed the chance to strike at the expanding power of Aitolia, which increasingly threatened his route to the south. Only the general outlines of the war can be established. From Achaia Aratos opened hostilities with a fresh attack on Attica where Athens and Piraeus were still Macedonian; an Athenian inscription dates the outbreak of the war to an archon year which is probably 239/8 B.C. But when this attack failed Aratos began to harass the Peloponnesian tyrants, whose position was much weakened since Antigonos lost Corinth though the Argives remained loyal to the tyrant Aristippos. At some stage (the date is uncertain) Demetrios sent his general Bithys into the Peloponnese, where he defeated Aratos at a place called Phylakia; and somewhat later Demetrios himself entered Boiotia and detached it from Aitolia.

In the Peloponnese the Achaians were joined by Lydiades, who resigned his tyranny at Megalopolis in 235 B.C. and brought this city into the League. The Aitolians meanwhile made no headway against Epirus and Akarnania; but internal disaster overtook the Epirote royal house. Pyrrhos soon died and his brother Ptolemy perished on a campaign; soon Olympias also died and a surviving princess, Deidamia, Olympias' great-niece, was murdered in sanctuary at Ambrakia (c. 233 B.C.). The monarchy was thus completely wiped out and a diminished Epirus bereft of Akarnania, Ambrakia and Amphilochia, was organized on federal lines like Aitolia. The fall of the monarchy ended the Macedonian alignment. Whatever Demetrios' ambitions in Epirus they remained unrealized for reasons beyond his control.

Soon, however, events in the west took a new turn. In 231 B.C. the Aitolians, encouraged by the collapse of Epirus, tried to force Medeon in central Akarnania to join their League. Medeon asked Demetrios for help and he, unable to respond for reasons to be considered shortly, hired Agron, the king of the powerful Illyrian Ardiaioi, to relieve the city and attack the Aitolians — which he effectively did. Agron's success and subsequent death unleashed a general plundering expedition. Illyrians under the loose control of his widow Teuta raided Elis and Messenia and in 230 B.C. took the new Epirote capital Phoenike by a trick, while another Illyrian leader, Skerdilaidas, seized Antigoneia. The Epirote League appealed to the Aitolians and Achaians, who sent help; but soon after its arrival the Illyrians retired to meet a Dardanian attack, making a truce with the Epirotes, who promptly reversed their policy and, by a treaty with Teuta, linked themselves once more with Macedonia; and Akarnania joined in.

Demetrios, however, was too busy elsewhere to exploit this change in his fortunes. Like the Illyrians he was facing an attack by the Dardanians, who may themselves have been under pressure from tribes further north, and in 229 B.C. after a defeat at their hands he died. Demetrios remains a shadowy figure who scarcely emerges as a person from the meagre sources of his reign. His death threw Macedonia into disarray; and his heir was an eight-year old boy, Philip, his son by Phthia, known also as Chryseis.

ANTIGONOS III DOSON (229-221 B.C.)

The crisis demanded a capable regent; and the choice of the Macedonians fell on Antigonos, the son of Demetrios the Fair, half-brother of Antigonos II, and so cousin of Demetrios II. He was made regent, perhaps with the title of *strategos,* but very soon assumed the full kingship. Antigonos seems to have regarded himself as holding the throne as if in trust for Philip, for though he married Phthia he refrained from raising any of their children, lest Philip's claims should be endangered.

Antigonos' first task was to expel the Dardanians from the lower Axios valley, where he left them in control of Bylazora in Paionia. He then attacked the Aitolians who, after a rising in Thessaly, had annexed Phthiotic Achaia, Phthiotis, Thessaliotis and Hestiaiotis. After a victory Antigonos made an agreement with them by which they kept Phthiotic Achaia. These campaigns were followed by a mutiny in the Macedonian army; perhaps morale was low after ten years of exhausting campaigning. Antigonos soon quelled the rising by appealing to his victories. Whether he also made popular concessions is not clear. But it is perhaps significant that we hear more of the Macedonians as a separate element in the state under Doson than in earlier reigns (see page 159). But if so, it was a concession without substance, for the mutiny left Antigonos stronger than before. In southern Greece, however, the Macedonian position had worsened. Boiotia wavered in allegiance (though the friends of Macedonia still had some power), Athens bought its independence from the Macedonian garrison (229/8 B.C.) becoming prudently neutral with Ptolemy as patron, and Achaia besides recovering Megara acquired Argos, Hermione and Phlious, where the tyrants saw the red light in the recession of Macedonian power; Aegina too joined the League. Only Euboia remained in Macedonian hands.

For Antigonos there were however grounds for consolation and hope. The Achaian and Aitolian Leagues were still collaborating in spring 229 B.C. when Korkyra, attacked by Teuta's Illyrians, called in their joint help; but the ships lost in the defeat of Paxos were Achaian and this proved to be the two Leagues' last joint enterprise. The same year the Aitolians made over to Kleomenes III of Sparta four cities in eastern Arkadia which were in their confederacy; they were Tegea, Mantineia, Orchomenos and Kaphyai, and they furnished Sparta with a hostile salient extending into the heart of the Achaian League and separating Argos from Megalopolis.

Kleomenes III had become king at Sparta in 235 B.C. Later events were soon to reveal him as heir to the revolutionary ideas of Agis IV, Aratos' ally, whose idealistic attempt to recall Sparta to its traditional communal institutions and social organization had provoked his death. Kleomenes now sought to harness social revolution to a programme of Spartan expansion. When he conceived this plan is not recorded. But the accession of Megalopolis in 235 B.C. had introduced into the Achaian League an anti-Spartan policy hitherto absent, and almost at once Lydiades had tried to involve Achaia in invading Laconia. In 229 B.C. Kleomenes seized the Athenaion, a frontier fortress in Belbinatis. The Achaians retaliated by declaring war (end of 229 B.C.). These events gave Antigonos reason to hope that with Achaia cool towards Aitolia and openly hostile to Sparta sooner or later an opportunity would arise for Macedonian intervention. He still had friends in several cities and even without Athens

Euboia gave him an approach to the Isthmus.

At this juncture Antigonos undertook an expedition which still puzzles historians. In spring 227 B.C., after crushing the mutiny, he set sail for Karia in south-west Asia Minor and though he made no acquisitions there he established relations with several cities including Priene and in particular with a local ruler, Olympichos of Alinda, who was still a Macedonian agent under Philip V. This expedition has been interpreted as anti-Ptolemaic; but Antigonos had probably other aims. Karia had been a recent object of contention between Antiochos Hierax, Seleukos II's younger son, who ruled virtually as an independent king in Asia Minor, and Attalos I of Pergamon. Seeing Hierax expelled and a refugee in Thrace, Antigonos may have hoped to make acquisitions for himself either in collaboration with Attalos or at his expense. Such a policy of expansion into Asia would represent a return to the ambitions of his great-grandfather Antigonos I and his grandfather Poliorketes, of which there is no trace under Gonatas and Demetrios II. In that way Doson would underline the legitimacy of his role as an Antigonid. But he may also have had his eyes on the Cyclades where Egypt still predominated.

There is, however, no reason to relate this expedition to events in the Adriatic. There, shortly after the Achaian and Aitolian defeat off Paxos and the consequent annexation of Korkyra by Teuta's lieutenant, Demetrios of Pharos, the Romans had undertaken a short, decisive campaign against Teuta in Illyrian waters (229 B.C.). This First Illyrian War left Rome with a loose hold on Korkyra, the Greek mainland cities of Apollonia and Dyrrachion and the territories of the Parthinoi and the Atintanoi which the territories of the Parthinoi and the Atintanoi, which extended to the watershed between Illyria and western Macedonia. This gave Rome a military capability in the Balkan peninsula and so altered the balance of power. This is not to say that the Romans were already envisaging expansion further east. Their motives in the war had been defensive, to check Illyrian piracy; but with a skill that was by now second nature they settled matters in such a way as to leave them poised to deal expeditiously with whatever situation the future might bring. How this was seen at Pella we cannot tell. Antigonos' Karian expedition might seem to indicate lack of concern with Illyria and the west; or, like the later Asian policy of Philip V, it could mean that the king was tentatively looking in new directions well away from his new and powerful neighbour. Which — if either — deduction is correct cannot easily be answered since the Karian expedition was brief and has been scantily reported. A Macedonian naval victory by an 'Antigonos'

94. The well-known wall painting from the villa of Fannius Sinistor at Boscoreale. The figures have been interpreted as the royal family of Macedonia — Antigonos Gonatas and his mother Phila — listening to the teaching of the philosopher Menedemos (not shown in the picture). Naples, Museo Nazionale.

could be an episode in this expedition; but this battle and the identity of 'Antigonos' in fact remain a mystery.

By autumn 227 B.C. Doson was back in Macedonia, where events in Greece soon claimed his attention. Following the Achaian declaration of war on Sparta (229 B.C.) fighting was at first on a small scale; on the one side Aratos and on the other Kleomenes' opponents, grouped around the ephors, tried to damp down hostilities. But in 227 B.C. Aratos was defeated with heavy losses at Mt. Lykeion and then went on to recover Mantineia and besiege Orchomenos; soon afterwards in a skirmish at Laodikeia near Megalopolis the ex-tyrant Lydiades was killed. At this point the whole situation was transformed by Kleomenes, who, in a carefully planned coup d'état, assassinated the ephors and exiled twenty-four political opponents. What purported to be the Lykourgan constitution was restored. Lydiades' death had raised an outcry against Aratos, who was accused of withholding support. But he weathered the storm and in winter 227/6 B.C. took the bold step of making a clandestine approach to Antigonos through a Megalopolitan embassy acting nominally on behalf of that city, which stood to lose most from Kleomenes' aggression and was well placed, because of personal ties going back to Philip II, to negotiate at Pella. Whether Aratos already envisaged a full-scale Macedonian alliance or merely sought to forestall any compact with Kleomenes is uncertain. Antigonos' reply was favourable; but discussion of the conditions on which any later and more far-reaching arrangements might be based was left to future negotiations. Meanwhile Antigonos promised Megapolis limited help and the League consented to this. The indication of Doson's attitude greatly encouraged Aratos, who now had a promise of support on which to fall back in the last resort. For the king the Achaian approach opened up the possibility of recovering Corinth, the main aim of Macedonian policy in Greece since 243 B.C. Meanwhile sometime between 228 and winter 227/6 B.C. Achaia had made agreements with Boiotia and eastern Phokis (which was now independent of Aitolia).

During the next two years almost everything went in Kleomenes' favour. Soon much of the territory of the Achaian League was in his hands, and faced with the possibility that the League might completely disintegrate Aratos now approached Antigonos once more and this time detailed conditions were put forward: to Aratos' son who went as envoy the king indicated that he would require hostages and the ceding of Acrocorinth. These terms were accepted at an Achaian meeting held probably in spring 224 B.C., and Antigonos was invited to march south.

For the man who had seized Acrocorinth in 243 B.C. its surrender was a bitter pill to swallow and an obstacle at which the Achaians might well have jibbed. But Corinth held many supporters of Kleomenes who called him in, thus making it easier for the League to cede the citadel (which was still Achaian) to Antigonos. Aratos had already lost the support of Ptolemy, who had transferred his subsidies to Kleomenes and established friendly relations with Aitolia. Antigonos had been uncommonly for-tunate. The Achaian approach had given him his dearest wish, and that by a voluntary act of cession, which allowed him to recover Corinth while fighting alongside the Achaians against Kleomenes, whose social programme and ambition made him suspect. Antigonos was waiting at the ready and once the word was given he marched south, passing through Euboia to avoid any clash with Aitolia at Thermopylai. He was held up for a time at the Isthmus, but the timely return of Argos to the Achaian fold forced Kleomenes to abandon Corinth and the Isthmus line. Antigonos was now free to initiate a project which looked forward to the future.

In autumn 224 B.C. a new organization was set up at Aigion to unite various peoples of Greece under Macedonian leadership; the king was appointed president, *Hegemon*. The *Symmachia* clearly signified a return to the policy of Philip II and Antigonos I. But Doson's alliance, unlike theirs, was based, not on city-states, *poleis*, but on confederations, *ethne*, and so took account of the growth in importance of federal institutions. The original members were the Achaians, Macedonians, Thessalians, Epirotes, Akarnanians, Boiotians, Phokians, Euboians and possibly Opuntian Lokrians. The Council (or *synedrion*) of the Symmachy could be summoned by the president and had the responsibility for peace and war and matters of supplies and membership. There was no treasury however and all decisions had to be ratified by the member states. The Symmachy was thus a compromise between Greek ideas of autonomy and the Macedonian concept of a controlled Greece; it excluded any resumption by Doson of Gonatas' system of tyrants. That Rome featured in Doson's calculations is unlikely. It is true that about this time Antigonos was joined by Demetrios of Pharos, who was to fight alongside him at Sellasia (222 B.C.). In 229 B.C. the Romans had assigned to Demetrios a buffer state to the north of the Roman zone in Illyria, but his marriage to Triteuta, the mother of the infant heir Pinnes, after Teuta's death, and his expansion south of Lissos and into the territory of the Atintanoi, while the Romans were occupied with the Gauls in north Italy, had made havoc of the settlement after the First Illyrian War. To Antigonos, Demetrios was a useful ally against Aitolia. For though the Symmachy was originally directed against Kleomenes of Sparta, the list of members reveals its political threat to the Aitolian League, which it hemmed in on all sides. How far Aratos had a hand in the planning of the Symmachy, which could thus so well serve Achaian ends, is unknown.

To crush Kleomenes required two more campaigns. Late in the winter of 223/2 B.C. he destroyed Megalopolis and ravaged the Argolid; but Antigonos forced him back into Lakonia and placed Macedonian garrisons in Heraia and Orchomenos. In summer 222 B.C. the Macedonian army met and defeated Kleomenes at Sellasia in northern Lakonia and he fled to Egypt, leaving Sparta to receive a conqueror. Before the battle Antigonos had persuaded Ptolemy III to suspend his subsidies to Kleomenes. Shortly afterwards Antigonos was summoned north by the news of an Illyrian invasion of Macedonia, probably by Darda-

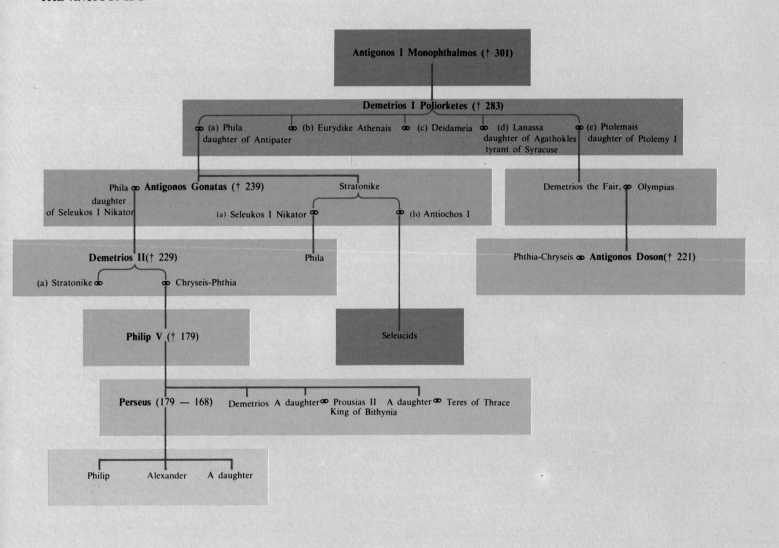

95. *The Antigonid dynasty is linked to the fortunes of the Macedonian kingdom during the Hellenistic period. Its members succeeded, thanks to their outstanding military and diplomatic talents and their shrewd policies, in maintaining the Macedonian throne as a first-rate power amongst the Hellenistic kingdoms, in dominating the political stage of the Balkan peninsula and also in constituting perhaps the most serious obstacle to Roman expansion in the eastern Mediterranean.*

nians or tribes akin to them. He defeated the invaders but his exertions brought on a haemorrhage; the following summer (221 B.C.) he died, leaving the throne to Philip V, the son of Demetrios II, who though only seventeen, succeeded unopposed. In his eight-year reign Antigonos III had shown remarkable skill, first in tiding over the disasters which faced him on his accession and then in seizing the opportunities afforded by Kleomenes' rise and the collapse of Achaia to restore the Macedonian position in southern Greece and set up a new political framework to guarantee this for the future. One of his last acts was to send Philip on a visit to the Peloponnese with instructions to attach himself particularly to Aratos.

PHILIP V (221-179 B.C.)

Philip's accession in 221 B.C. coincided with other changes in the major Hellenistic kingdoms. In late summer 223 B.C. Antiochos III succeeded Seleukos III, and in February 221 B.C. Ptolemy IV ascended the throne in Egypt. Also in 221 B.C. Hannibal took over the Carthaginian armies in Spain from his murdered predecessor Hasdrubal. Within the lifetime of these four men the affairs of the western and eastern halves of the Mediterranean world were to become inextricably involved, and that largely through the actions of Philip V. But more immediately Philip was implicated in a war with the Aitolians, foreshadowed in the creation of the Symmachy but precipitated by Aitolian aggression in the Peloponnese.

This conflict, known as the War of the Allies since it involved the members of the new Symmachy, began with Aitolian raids directed towards drawing Sparta, Elis and Messenia into a coalition against Achaia. In 220 B.C. an Aitolian force crossed the Corinthian Gulf, penetrated the Peloponnese and defeated Aratos at Kaphyai. Since Taurion, the Macedonian commissioner at Corinth, had given the Achaians help, the affair clearly concerned Macedonia; and though Philip sent mild warnings to Aitolia the rash seizure of a Macedonian ship by Aitolian pirates off Kythera compelled his intervention. A further factor was the disquieting news of an Aitolian alliance with Skerdilaidas, the Illyrian dynast. And so in summer 220 B.C. Philip summoned the Council of the Symmachy to Corinth and there a programme of war-aims was put forward; the allies pledged themselves to liberate all lands and cities annexed by Aitolia since Antigonos III's accession and to expel the Aitolians from Delphi.

The War of the Allies lasted three years. It was fought on several fronts, since the Aitolians joined Sparta and Elis in attacking the territories of the Achaian League, but also raided Thessaly and even southern Macedonia. Its savagery was partly due to its social aspects, Kleomenes being still remembered and the supporters of social revolution tending to align themselves with Aitolia and Sparta. For a time Philip was reluctant to go far from his own confines. The winning of Skerdilaidas and the agreement between Taurion and Demetrios of Pharos show his anxiety not to have hostile neighbours on his western frontiers. Also in winter 220/19 B.C. Philip took steps to secure his northern bounds against the Dardanians. In 219 B.C. he operated in north-west Greece, where after a long siege he took Ambrakos and gave it to the Epirotes, refusing to be diverted by an Aitolian raid into Macedonia. Then, advancing slowly south, he seized and fortified Oiniadai. Throughout this summer his eye was undoubtedly on Illyria where, after Demetrios had violated the terms imposed on Teuta by sailing south of Lissos, the Romans had sent a punitive expedition, which captured Dimale (east of Apollonia) and expelled Demetrios from his island home of Pharos. Demetrios, seeking refuge, joined Philip at Aktion on his way south to Oiniadai. He had fought at Sellasia and had collaborated with Taurion the previous year. His arrival at Philip's court was an event which was to prove of considerable importance later, but for the moment was of no great significance. A Roman request to Philip for his surrender was however ignored.

While Philip campaigned in the north-west, bent it would seem on opening up a western coast route through the friendly territories of Epirus, western Ambrakia and Akarnania, the Achaians had been reduced to desperation by attacks from Aitolia, Sparta and Elis. In winter 219/18 B.C Philip therefore carried out an unexpected campaign in the Peloponnese which in its disregard of the season and in its speed and planning recalled the methods of his namesake Philip II. Psophis in western Arkadia, southern Elis and Triphylia were all seized; and Philip followed up these gains with an expedition in northern Elis. The following spring he assembled a fleet consisting of old Macedonian and Achaian ships to attack Kephallenia and so interrupt communications between Aitolia and her allies in the Peloponnese. This, the first instance of Macedonian naval activity since the Karian expedition of 227 B.C. is important as a pointer to later events, and though explicable within the context of the Aitolian war it probably reflects Demetrios' growing influence.

The campaigns of 219 and winter 219/18 B.C. formed the background for a political struggle at Philip's court. Antigonos III on his death had left guardians for Philip and these, in particular Apelles, Leontios, the captain of the peltasts, and Megaleas, the secretary of state, were strongly opposed to Aratos who was seeking to bend Philip's policy to benefit Achaia; whereas they saw the Symmachy as an instrument for achieving the political and financial aggrandisement of Macedonia. Philip was young and impressionable, but as he matured he found the influence of these men oppressive and in the summer of 218 B.C. he exploited an incident at court involving Aratos to destroy the whole group on charges of treason; Apelles and Leontios were executed, Megaleas committed suicide, and the way was now open for new influences, in particular that of Demetrios.

The same summer (218 B.C.) was distinguished by two remarkable campaigns in which Philip penetrated to the heart of Aitolia and ravaged the religious centre at Thermon and then within a fortnight appeared at Sparta to pillage the Lakonian plain. These achievements brought plunder but did nothing substantial towards deciding the war. In 217 B.C., however, he made two gains of direct benefit to Macedonia. By his capture of Bylazora he consolidated his hold on Paionia, while that of Phthiotic Thebes was a step towards the recovery of Phthiotic Achaia, which Doson had left in Aitolian hands. Meanwhile the war dragged on, despite the attempts of various neutral powers — Rhodes, Chios and Ptolemy IV — to effect a settlement. By now Philip too was increasingly anxious to end it. The turning point came in summer 217 B.C. when Philip, who was evidently well informed about the war between Hannibal and Rome, learnt of the Roman disaster at lake Trasimene (June 217 B.C.). He showed the message to Demetrios and he, with the loss of his kingdom in mind, urged Philip to end the Aitolian war and turn his eyes west. According to Polybios Demetrios spoke of invading Italy and even of world dominion. This can be ignored as hyperbole or flattery: the solid reality behind it was a concern with the Illyrian coast, where Philip might well exploit the Roman catastrophe to his own (and Demetrios') advantage. At Naupaktos peace was made on the basis of the *status quo* (autumn 217 B.C.); the ambitious claims of the allies were conveniently forgotten. In the four years since his accession Philip had become the decisive force in the Balkan peninsula, master in his own house, in full control of the army and already a brilliant strategist. Outside Greece he was president of a confederacy which included most of the cities of Crete. He had extended his frontiers in Paionia and Thessaly and occupied Zakynthos; further south Macedonian garrisons under a Macedonian *epimeletes* held Triphylia. Yet his many benefactions at this time led Polybios to describe him as 'the darling of Greece'. This picture was bound to change, however, as his new ambitions involved him (and his allies) in the Mediterranean conflict between Rome and Carthage.

In 217 B.C. Philip successfully recovered parts of Pelagonia and Dassaretia from Skerdilaidas, who had deserted to Aitolia and annexed these frontier areas. That he also took steps to strengthen his southern borders is revealed in a letter which he wrote in September 217 B.C. to the authorities in Larisa in northern Thessaly, urging them to supplement the citizen body from resident aliens. In spring 216 B.C. he sailed with a newly built fleet of one hundred light galleys *(lemboi)* capable of transporting troops round Cape Malea into the Ionian Sea; but while off the mouth of the Aoos he learnt of the approach of a Roman squadron, panicked and returned full speed to Macedonia — unaware that Skerdilaidas had asked for help and that the arrival of the few ships involved was thus fortuitous. In the summer of 215 B.C. his emissary in Italy swore a treaty with Hannibal. The terms, preserved in Polybios, indicate clearly both that the initiative came from Phillip and that he merely sought to ensure that in any settlement with Rome Hannibal would include a clause to guarantee Macedonian immunity from attack. The Romans were also to relinquish control of Korkyra, Apollonia, Epidamnos, Pharos, Dimale, and the territory of the Parthinoi and the Atintanoi and to return to Demetrios those of his friends who were in the hands of the Romans. Philip in return was to give Hannibal such help as might subsequently be agreed. It is clear that whatever Philip's earlier dreams for action in Italy — and for these we have only Polybios' assertions — he had now no aims beyond the elimination of Roman influence from the Adriatic and its eastern shore. Without a Macedonian victory the treaty meant nothing; but meanwhile the Romans, who had captured Philip's first emissary and so knew the terms of the treaty, now regarded Philip as their enemy. The First Macedonian War had begun, and a Roman squadron was stationed at Taras and later at Brundisium, to keep an eye on Macedonia. Meanwhile in August 215 B.C. Philip sent a second letter to Larisa reinforcing his request that the citizen body be replenished and adding an exaggerated account of how the Romans had increased their numbers by manumissions and the sending out of colonies.

During the next three years (214-12 B.C.) Philip continued to campaign in Illyria. In 214 B.C. he attacked Apollonia and Orikos with a fleet of one hundred and twenty *lemboi*; the expedition was to coincide with an attack by Hannibal on Taras. But the Roman commander, M. Valerius Laevinus, sailed over from Brundisium, recovered Orikos and trapped Philip in the river Aoos. He was forced to burn his fleet and retreat overland. As a result he changed his strategy and in 213 and 212 B.C. he advanced by land, seizing towns in Dassaretis and among the Atintanoi and Parthinoi (including Dimale) until finally he reached the coast at Lissos, which he captured; he had now an Adriatic port on which to base his *lemboi*. These years saw a deterioration in Philip's relations with Achaia; in 215 B.C. he exacerbated social conflicts in Messene in the hope of seizing and garrisoning the city, and was only deterred by Aratos' strong opposition. Later, Demetrios of Pharos died in an unsuccessful attempt on the town and in 214 B.C. Philip again attacked Messenia, ravaging its territory and driving the country into the arms of Aitolia.

Upon Philip's seizing Lissos, Laevinus approached the Aitolians and in 211 B.C. an agreement was made, by which they undertook to attack Philip on land while the Romans gave naval help. All lands captured between Aitolia and Korkyra (and Akarnania) were to go to Aitolia, but the booty was to belong to the Romans. States taken by force were to join the Aitolian League. Any booty taken by both parties together was to be shared. Neither side was to make a separate peace and there was to be provision for Sparta, Elis, Pergamon, Skerdilaidas and his son Pleuratos, and perhaps Messenia to become allies. The effect of this treaty was to involve the whole of Greece in what was in effect a renewal of the War of the Allies. It compelled Philip to campaign on behalf of his allies in the Peloponnese to the detriment of his interests in Illyria.

In 211 B.C. the Aitolians opened hostilities with a raid on Thessaly before joining Laevinus in an attack on Zakynthos and Oiniadai in Akarnania. But Philip decided to close his own back door before going south — a traditional Macedonian policy — and so, after a blow against Orikos and Apollonia, he marched through Pelagonia, Lynkestis and Bottiaia to Tempe, which he garrisoned before swooping north again into Thrace to seize Iamphorynna. The next summer (210 B.C.) he pressed south down the coast road along the Pagasian Gulf from Phthiotic Thebes towards Thermopylai. His special aim was to open up the route to southern Greece. Meanwhile Laevinus and the Aitolians captured Antikyra in Phokis; the brutal enslavement of its population was a foretaste of Roman methods of warfare. The same summer Sparta joined the Roman alliance.

Throughout 209 and 208 B.C. Philip's unceasing and brilliant warfare on his allies' behalf did much to restore his good repute in Greece. We need not pursue the details. In the Peloponnese or from a base in central Greece he awaited and countered every move made by the enemy. Pressure grew with the arrival in Greek waters of Attalos of Pergamon, to whom the Aitolians had sold Aegina (made over to them by the Romans) as a naval base; but in summer 208 B.C. an attack by Prousias of Bithynia forced Attalos to return to home waters and Philip was once more free to take the offensive. It is noteworthy, however, that in both years he had to interrupt his fighting in Greece in order to deal with barbarian invasions of Macedonia, by Illyrians around lake Lychnitis in 209 B.C. and by Dardanians in 208 B.C.

96-97. The Tomb of Lyson and Kallikles between Beroia and Edessa contains notable wall paintings. The ashes of the dead were placed in two rows of niches. Their names were painted above the recesses, those of their wives or descendants below.

Already the Aitolians were tiring and willing to listen to approaches made by neutral powers, Egypt, Rhodes, Chios and Athens, to end the war. In 207 B.C. Philip bought the support of Amynander of Athamania and invaded Aitolia through his territory, once again ravaging Thermon. The Aitolians were also depressed by the decisive defeat at Mantineia the same summer of their Spartan ally at the hands of an Achaian army (reorganized by the young general Philopoemen); the Spartan king Machanidas was killed. An appeal to Rome brought no help and in 206 B.C. the Aitolians, despite the terms of their agreement with Laevinus, made a separate treaty with Philip, probably based on the *status quo*. They thus surrendered all claim to most of Thessaly; and if, as seems possible, Philip promised to make over to them Phthiotic Thebes, Echinos, Larisa Kremaste and Pharsalos, he never kept his word. The Romans, taken by surprise, tried to persuade the Aitolians to resume hostilities, but when this attempt failed they themselves responded to an Epirote appeal and at Phoinike in 205 B.C. they made peace. Philip agreed to surrender the Parthinoi with the towns of Dimale, Bargullum and Eugenium (the site of the two latter is unknown), but kept the Atintanoi and probably the area of the Ardiaioi to the north of Atintanis. Rome kept Dyrrachion, Apollonia and Orikos, which provided a bridgehead on the eastern shore of the Adriatic. The peace included all belligerents and left the Romans free from the eastern entanglement into which Philip's treaty with Hannibal had thrust them; they could now concentrate on defeating Hannibal. Macedonia emerged from the war with few gains but unexpectedly little damage; but although the Symmachy was still theoretically intact, its members had

The wall paintings depict Macedonian weapons; shields with typical Macedonian emblems, helmets, swords, greaves and two trophies. The tomb is usually dated to the last quarter of the 2nd century B.C.

suffered too much as allies of Macedonia for it to serve Philip any longer as a means of controlling Greece.

With the peace Philip did not lose interest in Illyria. There is some evidence that he made gains there, though where exactly these were is not known. His new ambitions, however, lay elsewhere. Late in 205 B.C. Antiochos III had returned from a triumphant expedition in the east with the title of Great King, and it seemed certain that he would seek to restore Seleucid power in Asia Minor and reverse the verdict of Raphia, where in 217 B.C. Ptolemy IV's decisive victory had thwarted his attack on Koile-Syria. Thrace was a likely object of Seleucid ambitions and there Philip's interests were involved. His next moves were therefore in part defensive; but he also had ancestral interests in Asia Minor where recently Antigonos III had been active. To advance in Thrace or the Aegean Philip

needed a fleet — not just *lemboi;* and for that he required money. So, not without Antigonid precedent, he turned to the pirates, supporting those of Crete, where piracy was endemic, against Rhodes, and using one Dikairchos to raid the Troad and Cyclades on his behalf. In all this Rhodes, the policing power, was an obstacle and Philip even sent a certain Herakleides to burn the Rhodian dockyards, while he himself was innocently campaigning against the Dardanians in Thrace.

In summer 204 B.C. Ptolemy IV died, leaving a six-year-old son as heir. Since Raphia, troubles in upper Egypt, consequent economic difficulties, and the growing power of the native population had weakened Egypt abroad; and in 203 B.C. Sosibios, as guardian of the boy-king, tried to arrange a marriage alliance for him with a daughter of Philip, so as to counter the power of Antiochos

151

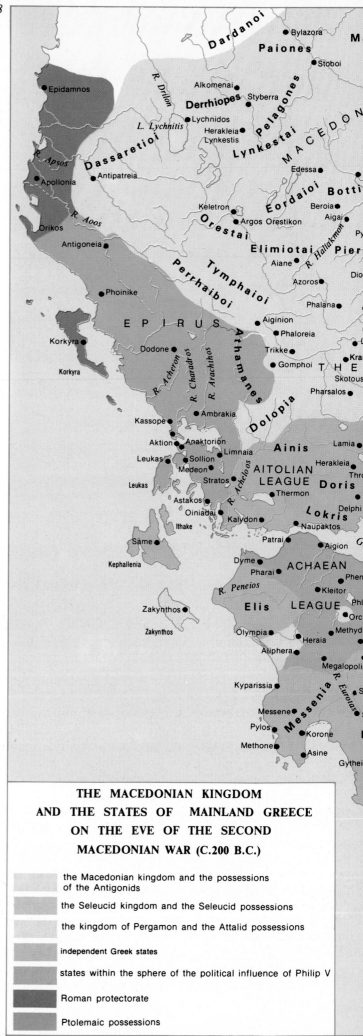

who was already advancing in Asia Minor. Philip however had other ideas. In winter 203 B.C. he approached Antiochos with a proposal to share out Ptolemy's possessions; Antiochos was to have Koile-Syria and Phoenicia, Philip Karia and Samos. Polybios' statement that Philip was also to have Egypt cannot however be correct.

In 202 B.C. Antiochos launched his attack on Koele-Syria and was master of it by 200 B.C. Philip at first held off Egyptian possessions. In 202 B.C. he seized Lysimacheia, Chalcedon and Kios, all Aitolian allies, and also Perinthos, ignoring neutral appeals; and in 201 B.C. he sailed with a fleet into the Aegean, seized the Cyclades and the Ptolemaic base at Samos and became involved in war with Attalos of Pergamon. After an indecisive sea-battle off Chios he invaded Pergamon and later, after a further sea-battle at Lade, he attacked Karia, with collaboration from Antiochos' governor Zeuxis and set up a Macedonian province there. A joint Rhodian and Pergamene fleet succeeded, however, in trapping him in the bay of Bargylia throughout the winter of 201/200 B.C. and he escaped only in spring 200 B.C.

Meanwhile information about the Syro-Macedonian pact had leaked out and had been reported at Rome by Rhodian and Pergamene envoys, probably in an exaggerated form. The Roman government welcomed the opportunity to act against Philip, though it rejected an Aitolian appeal for help — perhaps in order to distance itself from the former alliance, which had brought so much destruction to Greece. Roman motives in embarking on a fresh war with Philip have long been controversial. But recent discussion, in emphasizing Roman alarm at the revival of Macedonian naval power and the apparently sinister compact with Antiochos, has perhaps paid insufficient attention to the general character and organization of the Roman state, in which glory derived from military achievement was a mainspring of individual and senatorial political action, and where war, not peace, was the normal condition of life. Probably the Senate had taken it for granted that in due course they would deal with Philip. The situation in 201 B.C. provided the occasion and a plausible pretext — the wrongs done to friendly Greek states.

In 200 B.C. Philip's troops ravaged Attica in order to satisfy an Akarnanian grievance against the Athenians. Roman envoys and Attalos were both in Athens at the time and the former presented his general with an ul-

98. The rapid increase of Macedonian power during the two last decades of the third century B.C. under the rule of the ambitious Antigonid king Philip V could not but provoke disquiet in Rome at a time when her eastern policy was developing. In particular, the success of Philip in creating considerable naval strength, and his initiative in concluding a secret agreement with the Seleucid king Antiochos III aiming at the partition of the Ptolemaic possessions in the Aegean, Koile Syria and Palestine, was regarded by Rome and the rival Hellenistic states as a serious threat to the balance of power in the eastern Mediterranean. The map shows the area under Macedonian domination and influence on the eve of the Second Macedonian War.

THE MACEDONIAN KINGDOM AND THE STATES OF MAINLAND GREECE ON THE EVE OF THE SECOND MACEDONIAN WAR (C.200 B.C.)

the Macedonian kingdom and the possessions of the Antigonids

the Seleucid kingdom and the Seleucid possessions

the kingdom of Pergamon and the Attalid possessions

independent Greek states

states within the sphere of the political influence of Philip V

Roman protectorate

Ptolemaic possessions

timatum, while Athens declared war on Macedonia. Philip however resumed his advance towards the Hellespont and, while sending Philokles to ravage Attica yet again, he himself took Maroneia, Ainos and a number of other towns, many Egyptian, around the Straits. When the Roman envoys produced a further ultimatum, they found him besieging Abydos. Here M. Aemilius Lepidus delivered an official declaration of war after presenting the following demands: Philip was to make war on no Greek states; he was to refrain from touching Ptolemy's possessions and to submit the question of wrongs done to Attalos and Rhodes to an impartial tribunal. Rejecting these requirements Philip returned to winter in Macedonia, having first taken Abydos; by this time a Roman army had landed in Illyria. Whatever the motives behind the Roman action, Philip was clearly guilty of a serious miscalculation. His brutal and aggressive campaign had alienated Greek feeling; and his compact with Antiochos had gained him nothing and had played into the hands of those at Rome whose fear or ambition led them to seek a war against him. He had evidently been misled by the Roman inaction during the previous war, when Rome's main concern was Hannibal, to suppose that the Senate was not in earnest this time; it was a fatal error.

The Second Macedonian War was to last for three years. For Philip it was a defensive war fought not to gain new territory but to hold on to what he possessed. In it he showed the same ruthless vigour as in the former war. In autumn 200 B.C. the Romans campaigned west of Pindos and Philip again ravaged Athens. In 199 B.C. the Roman army invaded western Macedonia plundering Lynkestis, Eordaia and Orestis, while Roman and Rhodian ships operated in the Aegean against such islands as were held by the Macedonians. Meanwhile steps were taken by the Romans to secure new allies. Baton, the Dardanian leader, Pleuratos of Skodra and Amynander of Athamania all joined Rome, and Philip had to meet a Dardanian invasion. The Aitolians, perhaps chary since their recent rebuff, at first hesitated, but in autumn 199 B.C. they too joined the Romans and invaded Thessaly. In 198 B.C. Philip took the initiative by occupying the Aoos pass near modern Tepeleni, probably to deter the consul from invading Macedonia through the Tsangon Pass (thus exposing his communications). But the new Roman consul, T. Quinctius Flamininus, at a conference on the Aoos demanded a complete withdrawal from Greece. These

99. Tetradrachm of Philip V depicting the head of the king. During his long reign he frequently came into collision with Rome and her expansionist policy. Athens, Numismatic Museum.

100. Gold stater bearing the head of T. Quinctius Flamininus, victor against Philip at Kynoskephalai. The proclamation of the freedom of the Greek cities undermined the basis of the attempts of the Macedonian kingdom to withstand Roman expansion. Athens, Numismatic Museum.

terms proved unacceptable to Philip but shortly afterwards the consul forced the pass by a ruse, and Philip had to retreat into Thessaly, where many cities closed their gates against him, and thence to Macedonia. The Romans now entered Thessaly, anticipated by Aitolian and Athamanian raids. In autumn the Achaians, despite Argive opposition, voted to join Rome; and soon afterwards with the fall of Elateia, Flamininus gained control of the whole of central Greece.

In November 198 B.C. a peace conference was held in Lokris and Philip was granted a two months' truce to send envoys to Rome. This truce was largely a device of Flamininus to provide a possible basis for a settlement in the event of his being replaced as consul. When his command was renewed his supporters at Rome ensured that Philip's envoys were dismissed on the grounds that they were not empowered to make a firm statement about Philip's garrisons in Greece.

In June 197 B.C. the war was brought to an end with Philip's defeat at Kynoskephalai near Pharsalos in Thessaly. He was granted a truce and the following winter the Senate ratified peace on the terms proposed at the conference in Lokris. Philip was now limited to Macedonia; and a senatorial decree conveyed to Greece in 196 B.C. by ten Commissioners required him to surrender his navy but for five ships and one large warship and to pay an indemnity of one thousand talents, half at once and the rest in ten annual instalments. The Commissioners also communicated to the Greeks Roman decisions covering the general settlement; and the theatrical announcement of the policy of a free Greece at the Isthmian Games of 196 B.C. was designed to bring glory to Flamininus. For Philip the war had been disastrous. Thessaly was now divided among a group of independent and hostile leagues, he had lost all territory west of the Great Lakes and east of Abdera and also his possessions in Karia and the Aegean as well as his navy. But meanwhile his rival and recent ally Antiochos was advancing in the direction of Thrace; if he clashed with Rome a policy of collaboration with his late enemy might bring Philip some advantage.

The next eight years (196-88 B.C.) centred on such collaboration. They were to bring limited gains and leave Philip resentful and dissatisfied; but he had no effective alternative. The events of 195 B.C. gave him his first chance. In that year Flamininus carried out a campaign against Nabis of Sparta on behalf of Achaia and in order to prove that the declaration of freedom for the Greek cities meant something. Philip had a private grudge against Nabis. In winter 198/7 B.C. he had made over Argos to him, since he could no longer garrison it; Nabis had accepted the town and then promptly joined the Romans. Now in 195 B.C. Philip sent fifteen hundred men as a contribution to the allied cause. In 194 B.C. the Romans evacuated Greece; and the following winter Macedonian envoys at Rome were encouraged to entertain hopes of recovering Magnesia and Demetrias as well as the return of Philip's son Demetrios (who was a hostage at Rome since the peace) and the remission of his indemnity in return for

loyalty to Rome. For already the Romans had their eyes on Antiochos.

The recent war against Philip had left the Aitolians with a grievance; and between 196 and 192 B.C. they kept up a constant anti-Roman propaganda inside Greece which culminated in 192 B.C. in an invitation to Antiochos to come over and 'liberate Greece', an invitation which Antiochos with a folly comparable to that of Philip in 200 B.C. accepted. In October 192 B.C. he crossed to Pteleon at the entrance to the Pagasian Gulf and quickly occupied Demetrias, which the Aitolians had recently seized. They had hoped to form a coalition with Sparta and Macedonia; but when Nabis was murdered by an Aitolian the Spartans rejected the plan. In late winter 192/1 B.C. Philip met the Roman commander, M. Baebius, in Dassaretia to concert action; any hesitation had been dissipated by the Aitolian seizure of Demetrias and the action of a pretender, Philip of Megalopolis, who had attached himself to Antiochos and, in the misguided hope of currying favour in Macedonia, had tactlessly carried out the burial of the Macedonian dead at Kynoskephalai. Baebius agreed that Philip might keep any possessions he won from Aitolia and her allies.

The results, however, were disappointing. Defeated at Thermopylai by the Romans in April 191 B.C. Antiochos fled to Asia; and in July the Aitolians were granted a short armistice which limited Philip's acquisitions though he succeeded in annexing Athamania. Later in 191 B.C., he recovered the Pagasian coast road together with Dolopia, Aperantia, Perrhaibia and Demetrias, before a further Aitolian truce put an end to his advance. In winter 191 B.C. Philip sent further envoys to Rome and this time they brought back Demetrios and a promise to remit the balance of the indemnity: the Romans were anxious to ensure Philip's collaboration in their march through Macedonia and Thrace to the Hellespont. This was forthcoming; supplies of corn were laid in, rivers bridged, roads repaired and the advance went forward without a hitch. Philip now had his payments remitted. But his loyalty brought him little else, for early in 189 B.C. Amynandros got back Athamania and the Aitolians Amphilochia and Aperantia; and further east the Roman commander laid down boundaries which excluded Philip from Ainos and Maroneia. Complaints at Rome brought no response: with Antiochos and the Aitolians both defeated — the former at Magnesia in the winter of 190/89 B.C. the latter in the summer of 189 B.C. — the Romans had no more need of Philip; though when the proconsul Cn. Manlius Vulso took no steps to ensure Philip's help during his march back through Thrace in the autumn of 188 B.C. he lost many men and most of his plunder. This too did nothing to increase Philip's popularity at Rome. In fact the reward of his collaboration had been meagre: he now controlled Magnesia with Demetrias, part of the Mallian coast road and several towns in Perrhaibia and western Thessaly; but the Thessalian League now began to take the place of Aitolia as Philip's chief enemy in Greece.

Philip's last eight years (187-79 B.C.) were devoted to

consolidation. Roman tradition claimed that he was planning a war of revenge and that it was this war that his son Perseus was eventually to fight. It would be truer to say that his experiences during the war with Antiochos had taught Philip that the Romans gave only limited rewards for loyalty and that in the long run he could expect further trouble. Against that day he decided to build up as strong a kingdom as he could, with special care for his northern frontiers and for his relations with the peoples who lived beyond them.

In 187 B.C. he took the initiative by moving the road so as to establish a shaky title to Maroneia and he seized both that city and Ainos, where he was able to exploit internal differences between pro-Macedonian and pro-Pergamene factions; this move could be interpreted as a rounding-off of his eastern frontiers, but it no doubt took on a different complexion at Rome. Philip also went ahead with the internal consolidation of his kingdom (see page 164); this policy involved steps to increase revenue, new issues of coinage, the encouragement of large families and the importation of Thracian settlers. Further, an inscription from Amphipolis throws light on the discipline of Philip's army which may indicate that this too fell within the scope of his reorganization and consolidation at this time. In 185 B.C., following complaints from many of Philip's neighbours, the Romans sent out a commission, whose members sitting in Tempe, listened to the long and complicated charges brought against the king by the Thessalians, Perrhaibians and Athamanians and to his angry answers; their final decision was that Macedonia should be restricted to its 'ancient boundaries' — whatever they might be. In fact Philip continued to hold Demetrias, much of Magnesia and Dolopia and parts of Phthiotic Achaia. After a further conference held at Thessalonike on the Thracian towns, about which the Romans were especially concerned, Philip was ordered to evacuate both Ainos and Maroneia. His response to this decision was to massacre his political opponents in Maroneia and to leave his garrisons occupying both towns. In 184 B.C. a further Roman embassy gave instruction that those allegedly responsible for the massacre should be sent to Rome for questioning; Philip had one excused but then (his enemies alleged) had the other poisoned on the way to Rome.

Between 184 and 179 B.C. Philip directed his main attention to his northern frontiers, where he went ahead with plans to encourage the Bastarnai, a Germanic people, to move west and attack his old enemies, the Dardanians; in this way he probably hoped to substitute for the latter a friendly people which would also be a source of mercenaries. Polybios' assertion that he was planning an attack on Italy reflects Roman alarm and propaganda against Philip. At the same time the king began negotiating with the Skordiskoi, another people living north of the Danube, and offered a marriage-alliance to a Thracian king Teres, perhaps the successor of Amadokos, against whom Philip had campaigned in 184 B.C. on behalf of Byzantion. In 183 B.C. Philip led an expedition against the Odrysai, the Bessoi and the Dentheletai in Thrace, garrisoning Philippoupolis and founding a new city, Perseis, in the Axios valley near Stoboi. These operations were linked to the population exchange (see below) by which Philip sought to consolidate Macedonia. They aroused hostility in the more Hellenized cities and may connect with a conspiracy involving several eminent nobles, including Samos, the son of Chrysogonos. The hostile tradition emphasizes Philip's increasing use of terror.

In 181 B.C. Philip made an expedition into northern Thrace, in the course of which he led his army to the top of Mt. Haimos — perhaps in this case Mt. Vitosha near Sofia. The mountain was alleged (quite falsely) to furnish a view embracing the Adriatic, the Alps, the Black Sea and the Danube; but Philip's real purpose in ascending this mountain is obscure and certainly nothing was achieved. About the same time a conflict between his heir Perseus and his younger son Demetrios came to a head. By representing favours as concessions to Demetrios (who had spent some time as a hostage at Rome) the Romans created the impression that they were grooming him as Philip's successor. In 180 B.C., after a series of quarrels, Perseus persuaded Philip to execute Demetrios as a traitor. Subsequently Philip is said to have repented and to have turned against Perseus. In the winter of 180/79 B.C. he turned in his distress to a nephew of Antigonos Doson, named Antigonos the son of Echecratos, who encouraged the view that Demetrios was innocent and whom Philip now began commending to the leading citizens as his successor in Perseus' place. However in 179 B.C. Philip died, and Perseus succeeded without serious challenge; Antigonos the son of Echecratos was put to death. The same year the Bastarnai moved south following the arrangement with Philip; but on the news of his death the invasion degenerated into a pointless migration which soon came to nothing.

PERSEUS (179-168 B.C.)

Perseus opened his reign with the successful repulse of an invasion by a Thracian chieftain, from the tribe of the Sapaioi, named Abroupolis, who got as far as Amphipolis; he may have been encouraged in this attack by Eumenes of Pergamon. But Perseus' next move signified a return to a more Hellenic policy than that of Philip's last decade. He issued an amnesty recalling exiles, releasing prisoners and cancelling debts, and promulgated this with notices at the main panhellenic sanctuaries. In addition he recovered control in some way of the Amphiktyonic Council. Amphiktyonic decrees recorded on inscriptions dated to 184 and 182 B.C. speak of freedom and democracy and of 'bad kings who plot against the Greeks' — in a manner impossible had Philip been sitting as a member of the body which passed them. But in 178 B.C. another inscription records the presence of members from various Aitolian-controlled states, the king of Macedonia (Perseus) and the Magnesians (who were dominated by Macedonia); these three groups together control twelve votes and so form a majority on the Council of twenty-three.

Perseus also tried to improve relations with other Hellenistic states. Probably in 177 B.C. he married Laodike, the daughter of Seleukos IV, who sent her to Pella with a Rhodian escort (since he was forbidden to sail with his own ships into the Aegean by his treaty with Rome). This alliance renewed an old friendship with the Seleucid house and united two kings with a common enemy, Eumenes of Pergamon — who was also a danger to Rhodian ships passing through the Hellespont. But this alliance came to nothing when Seleukos was murdered in 175 B.C., perhaps with the connivance of Eumenes, who helped Seleukos' brother Antiochos IV, to succeed him.

Perseus' policy of renewing his links with the Seleucid dynasty in Asia and currying favour in the cities of Greece did not go unnoticed at Rome, but the Senate took no immediate steps to counter this. In 174 B.C. Perseus invaded Dolopia, which was in revolt, and reduced it; and following upon this campaign he proceeded to a demonstration of strength at Delphi followed by a disciplined march back to Macedonia through Phthiotic Achaia and Thessaly. It was later alleged by Eumenes that the purpose of this march was to win over the worst elements in the cities. It was also alleged that Perseus had intervened to exacerbate social conflicts in Aitolia. Furthermore he made an alliance with Boiotia; two Thebans sent to Rome to object seem never to have arrived. By the winter of 173/2 B.C. some Romans already favoured war; but the Senate took no action beyond sending an embassy to Macedonia, Pergamon, Kappadokia, Rhodes and the kings of Syria and Egypt; it seemed likely that the two latter states were on the verge of going to war. About the same time Perseus sent help to Byzantion against the Thracians. The situation was tense and in these circumstances the visit of Eumenes of Pergamon to Rome in the winter of 173/2 B.C. was perhaps decisive. Eumenes gave a full and comprehensive report, painting everything in the blackest colours. On his way home he decided to visit Delphi, and on the road between Kirrha and Delphi he was struck by rocks from above. Few doubted that Perseus was behind this attack. In autumn 172 B.C. a Roman embassy toured Greece and Q. Marcius Philippus, who led it, granted Perseus a truce (though there was as yet no war) in order that he might send envoys to Rome. But this was little more than a ruse to give the Romans the winter in which to complete their preparations. Early in 171 B.C. the Romans declared war on Perseus. The accusations that he had attacked Rome's allies and was preparing war on Rome herself were both false. Perseus' fault was to have attempted to pursue an independent policy and this the Romans would not tolerate.

The Third Macedonian War lasted four years — probably far longer than the Romans had envisaged. In 171 B.C. the king had some success against the Romans in north Thessaly, where he won a battle at Kallinikos; but his offer of peace terms was refused. In 170 B.C. one area in Epirus (chiefly the Molossis) threw in its lot with Perseus and it now became an urgent matter for the Romans to secure Greek support. The next year (169 B.C.) the consul Q. Marcius Philippus conducted an offensive through the

101. Restoration drawing of the monument of Lucius Aemilius Paullus erected at Delphi after the battle of Pydna. The Roman general made use of the same base prepared by his defeated rival to erect a gold statue of himself. The relief frieze depicts the battle between Macedonian and Roman cavalry. By Theodore Homolle.

massif of Mt. Olympos which compelled Perseus to withdraw his forces northwards from Tempe; but the problem of communications and the maintaining of supplies caused Marcius to fall back on Phila to the south of Herakleion. Meanwhile Perseus had been working hard to gain allies. In 170/69 B.C. he approached Genthios, the son of Pleuratos of Skodra, for an alliance but, according to the sources, he missed his opportunity of securing this through an avaricious reluctance to pay the Illyrian the sum he asked. Eventually Genthios did join Perseus but by then it was too late and he was crushed in 168 B.C. The Rhodians were unfortunate in adopting an attitude of neutrality; and, when their envoys sent to Rome with an offer to mediate were brought before the Senate at the very time that the news arrived of Perseus' final defeat, the position of the city became exceedingly delicate. Even Eumenes lost the goodwill of the Senate by his hesitations. Perhaps he now seemed too powerful and the Senate welcomed an opportunity to take him down. None of these various moves and hesitations had, however, a substantial effect on the outcome of the war.

In 168 B.C. the new consul, L. Aemilius Paullus, acted with decision. Soon after taking over the command he sent a detachment over Mt. Olympos, thus compelling Perseus to withdraw to a position near Pydna in southern

Macedonia. Here on June 22 he was decisively defeated by the Romans and his army annihilated. A single battle thus destroyed the kingdom of Macedonia. Perseus fled, first to Pella and then to Samothrace, where he was taken prisoner, and the Roman army occupied the country and Pella, the capital. Later Perseus was brought to Italy, where he died five years later in captivity at Alba Fucens.

The Antigonid monarchy had thus come to an end; but the Romans were not yet ready to create a province in its place. The Macedonian arrangements were experimental and showed little understanding of historic loyalties. Though they left the people better off materially, they failed to recognize the Macedonian attachment to the monarchy and the sense of belonging to a nation with a great past. The rising of Andriskos was to reveal the depth of this feeling and was to lead to a different and final settlement.

POLITICAL SOCIAL AND ECONOMIC INSTITUTIONS

POLITICAL INSTITUTIONS

We have now followed the political fortunes of Macedonia from its rise to dominance in Greece under Philip II to the extinguishing of the monarchy by the Romans after Pydna. The two intervening centuries saw great changes occur both in the social and economic conditions of the kingdom and in the cultural level of its people; but during the same period there were few institutional changes. The traditional monarchy continued to provide the stable nucleus of the state and there is no evidence that, as an institution, it was ever under any serious threat. Whereas in the neighbouring state of Epirus the death of Pyrrhos was soon followed by a swing to republicanism and the extinction of the royal house, the devotion of the Macedonians to their kings remained unshaken. For this there were two obvious reasons. In the first place Philip II and Alexander the Great had identified the monarchy with Macedonian success and greatness; henceforth to be a Macedonian was to wear a badge of superiority anywhere in Greece or the Middle East. Secondly, for at least a century after Alexander monarchy was the most prevalent form of political organization outside the city-states of Greece proper. After his son, Demetrios Poliorketes, had defeated Ptolemy's fleet off Cypriote Salamis in 306 Antigonos Monophtalmos styled himself king; and when Cassander, like Seleukos and Lysimachos, decided to follow his example, the ghost of Alexander's universal empire was finally laid to rest. In its place there now stood a group of major kingdoms, and monarchy was henceforth the appropriate and preferred political institution for any state with pretensions to importance and was to remain so until the Hellenistic kingdoms fell one by one before the legions of the Roman republic.

Within Macedonia under both the Argead and the An-

102. Tetradrachm depicting the head of Perseus. The last of the Macedonian kings tried to restore the kingdom both politically and economically. The inevitable clash with Rome led to the final subjugation of Macedonia. Athens, Numismatic Museum.

tigonid dynasties the people continued to exercise certain traditional, though limited powers, perhaps similar in scope to those attested for the neighbouring people of the Molossians who, like the Macedonians, are referred to as a *koinon,* or commonalty. Among their prerogatives may have been the right to appoint the king by acclamation and to act as judge in cases of high treason as indeed Curtius informs us. In practice, however, circumstances were such, especially during the fifty years following the death of Alexander, that the formal rights of the Macedonian people were more often exercised by the army, a part of the army, or such citizen body as was available on the spot where decisive events were taking place. It was moreover clearly expedient that in the arrangements following Alexander's death at Babylon the leading generals took the precaution of consulting the army and ensuring its support for what they proposed to do in relation to the succession. Similarly inside Macedonia itself, in the years following Cassander's death, various rival contestants for the throne depended for their success on the support of the troops, and this being so to obtain the acclamation of the army was an obvious act of realism quite apart from any constitutional right that the army or people may have possessed. According to Diodoros, Demetrios Poliorketes was hailed king by the people in 293 B.C.; but for kings who ruled outside these troubled times evidence is rather scanty. Philip II is recorded as having been urged to take over the throne by the people, which may be a reference to an assembly, but could equally well indicate a spontaneous and informal rising; and Alexander was already king when he harangued the people and won their enthusiastic support. A century later Antigonos Doson is reported by Plutarch to have been placed on the throne by the leading Macedonians; and there seems little doubt that in practice it was the support of these leading Macedonians that any new heir to the throne would make it his business to secure. That their choice was subsequently validated by the formal decision of an assembly or of the army is possible but nowhere clearly recorded; nor has any decree emanating from a national Macedonian assembly survived. It is known that the army took an oath of allegiance to the new king; whether the king responded with similar oath, as was the case among the Molossians, is not certain, though indeed it is possible.

The role of the Macedonians as an element in the state is however attested epigraphically. They figure in a treaty made by Antigonos III with the Cretan city of Eleutherna, and on a Delian dedication by 'king Antigonos, son of king Demetrios, and the Macedonians and the allies' to celebrate the defeat of Sparta at Sellasia (222 B.C.); they are also mentioned along with the Greek allies in the treaty of 215 B.C. between Philip V and Hannibal. Philip V is honoured on an inscription at Delos by the 'corporate body of the Macedonians', the κοινόν Μακεδόνων; a dedication to the Great Gods on Samothrace is made on his behalf by the Macedonians; and, as we shall see shortly, 'the Macedonians' as well as certain regional groupings issued coins towards the end of Philip V's reign. The

Macedonians seem also to have appointed representatives (*proxenoi*) in other cities (this is attested for Thebes in the time of Philip II) and to have made payments to the Delphic Amphiktyony. Nevertheless, in terms of power and capacity to restrict the actions of the king all this added up to very little. Once acclaimed, a king of Macedonia reigned autocratically with few limitations beyond the need to carry the people with him.

On this the evidence is unequivocal. Inscriptions show that Macedonian treaties — the one mentioned above is exceptional — were normally made in the name of the king alone. The contemporary historian Polybios nowhere even hints that the Antigonid kings felt themselves to be constrained by any rival authority within the state; and though Macedonians continued, as a matter of tradition, to address their kings with a frankness that was alien to the atmosphere of the other Hellenistic monarchies, and never (unlike the cities both inside and outside Macedonia) made them the object of ruler-cult, that did not alter the fact that throughout the period we are considering for all practical purposes the king was the state.

The acceptance of monarchy and powers exercised by the monarch did not in themselves guarantee stability. From the accession of Alexander in 336 B.C. down to 276 B.C., when Antigonos Gonatas established himself on the throne, Macedonia was ruled by an absent king, by regents, and by a rapid succession of rival dynasts; and at the end of those years there was virtual anarchy, stability returning only with the rule of the Antigonid dynasty, which was to last for rather more than a century. When eventually the Antigonids were dislodged by the Romans the Macedonian people still saw its monarchy as the force that knit them together, and two decades later the pretender Andriskos could command a following and a loyalty which evoked the amazement and incomprehension of the Greek Polybios.

Though its political power was small, nevertheless the Macedonian people, especially as represented through the army, furnished the basic support for the king's policy and the kingdom's strength. For Philip II, at the outset of this period, the army was all-important as an instrument of expansion and equally as a force binding together a realm hitherto liable to fall apart. From congeries of weak and ineffective *ad hoc* levies he converted it into a national citizen army, efficiently organized, raised regionally yet quickly learning to surmount regional prejudices and to act as a united force. The distinction between the cantons of upper Macedonia, which were mostly without the advantage of urban centres, and lower Macedonia with its Greek or Hellenized cities still persisted; but Philip's programme of almost unbroken military activity tended — and may have been in part designed — to reduce its significance.

It was mainly around the army that Philip assembled his court; and here too he employed a variety of methods to knit the country together and to reduce opposition. The *Hetairoi,* the Companions who made up his immediate entourage, included rich landowners drawn from all parts of the kingdom, including the cantons of the hill country, but

159

also new men who flocked to Macedonia from all over Greece. In either case they were the king's men, chosen by him and owing loyalty to him personally. Writing as a contemporary of Philip, Theopompos roundly abuses the *Hetairoi* as being a set of brutal and debauched adventurers; but Polybios, who was more sympathetic towards Philip, applauds them for their energy and daring. There can be no doubt that Philip profited greatly from attracting men of character and ability from outside Macedonia who by their influence could both contribute to the Greek element at court and serve as a counter-weight to the native nobility. Though potentially dangerous, the latter were held in check by being kept in close proximity to the king. Their sons were brought up at court as royal pages, themselves schooled in loyalty and, in a sense, acting as hostages for the loyalty of their fathers.

The king's Companions continued to be an important element in Alexander's mobile court and in the organization and structure of his empire. They did not survive its break-up under that name. But the Friends, Φίλοι, who form a Council of State in most of the Hellenistic kingdoms, including Antigonid Macedonia, are their counterpart. The Friends were personal to the king; his successor need not retain them. Apelles, Megaleas and Leontios, whom Antigonos III had left as his guardians, were all ruthlessly destroyed within a year or two by the young Philip V and that without any recourse to the traditional popular assembly. Others took their place, more obedient to the king's will; and Philip also made use of a succession of advisers drawn from various outside states — Aratos the Achaian, Demetrios the Illyrian, Herakleides of Tarentum — whose role recalls that of the Greek *Hetairoi* at the court of Philip II.

From among the Friends came the personnel to fill the major administrative posts. The most important of these were the Secretary of State (ὁ ἐπὶ τοῦ γραμματείου) and the Captain of the Bodyguard (ὁ ἐπὶ τῆς θεραπείας); another was the Captain of the Peltasts, a body of infantry perhaps the equivalent of Alexander's hypaspists. Other institutions which helped to make up the court are paralleled elsewhere and are derived from those of the court of Philip II and Alexander; they are the royal pages (βασιλικοὶ παῖδες), sons of nobles and other men of high family (as we saw above) and themselves future Friends and officers, and σύντροφοι, boys coming from the same social group who had been chosen to be brought up as the 'foster brothers' of the royal princes. There was also a Treasurer (θησαυροφύλαξ) and Bodyguards (σωματοφύλακες), a group of officers attached to the court and employed by the king on special, confidential duties; for example, when Perseus lost his nerve at the approach of the Roman army near Mt. Olympos he is said to have despatched a bodyguard to burn his dockyards.

During the two centuries which we are now considering Macedonia experienced a considerable growth in urbanization. Under Philip II virtually the only cities were those situated in lower Macedonia — and of course the coastal Greek cities such as Amphipolis and Pydna, which Philip gradually absorbed into his kingdom. The highlands of upper Macedonia were divided into cantons still governed by their own independent princes — Elimiotis, Orestis, Lynkestis, Eordaia and Pelagonia — and contained no cities except Alkomenai and Philip's new foundation at Herakleia in Lynkestis. A man coming from upper Macedonia was a citizen of his particular canton and called himself, for example, Μακεδὼν Ἐλιμιώτης; when, later on, a few cities sprang up in these areas, if he belonged to one of these he would add its name, e.g. ἐκ Πυθείου. At the time of Philip II most Macedonian cities were little more than market towns. Arrian, in his account of Alexander's Indian campaigns, gives a list of the ships' captains in Alexander's Indus fleet and this reveals the fact that by 326 B.C. and so probably under Philip II as well, since it is unlikely that Alexander carried out substantial changes in the organization of Macedonia — lower Macedonia was divided into communities consisting each of a city with its territory; and the Greek cities were integrated into that pattern, for several of the Macedonians mentioned in Arrian's list are described as coming from Amphipolis. A man whose home was in lower Macedonia identified himself by naming his city, e.g. Μακεδὼν ἐκ Πέλλης, a Macedonian from Pella. Several of Alexander's trierarchs from Amphipolis were in fact Greeks hailing from outside Macedonia, for instance the Cretan Nearchos and Androsthenes of Samos, and it is likely that they had acquired its citizenship by being granted land and taking up residence within the territory of Amphipolis.

Under Alexander's successors cities multiplied. Cassander was responsible for two important foundations, both probably in 316 B.C. Thessalonike, a synoecism of several small towns at the head of the Thermaic Gulf, he named after his wife, and Kassandreia, which incorporated the cities of Pallene, including Poteidaia, after himself. Though Macedonian foundations, these new cities had large Greek populations and at Kassandreia the Greek element probably predominated. Though the available evidence about these — and about other cities in lower Macedonia — comes from the Antigonid period, what it tells us concerning their organization was no doubt true from the time of their foundation. It is perhaps a sign of growing unity and national consciousness within Macedonia that men from all the cities, whatever their origins, call themselves Macedonians — with the one unexplained exception of Kassandreia; and the Kassandreians too clearly included themselves within the kingdom, since a decree of that city, dating from 242 B.C. and conferring freedom from plunder *(asylia)* on the Asklepeion at Kos, mentions the goodwill of Kos towards 'king Antigonos (sc. Gonatas), the city of Kassandreia and all the rest of the Macedonians'.

Outwardly the cities display the structure and institutions of a democratic Greek state. There is a council *(boule)* at Kassandreia and both a council and an assembly *(ekklesia)* at Thessalonike. Philippi and Amphipolis each had an assembly, and it is likely that all, including the older Macedonian cities proper, like Pella and Aigai, had both institutions. Like Greek cities elsewhere, those of

Macedonia were divided into tribes and demes, e.g. the tribes Antigonis, Dionysias and Asklepias and the demes Bukephaleia and Kekropis at Thessalonike. Much of our information on this subject derives from four decrees granting *asylia* to the Asklepeion at Kos in 242 B.C. from Philippi, Kassandreia, Pella and Amphipolis. These mention generals *(strategoi)*, guardians of the law *(nomophylakes)* and a treasurer *(tamias)* at Philippi, priests and archons at Amphipolis, and priests and *tamiai* at Pella.

The cities of Macedonia cultivated an active exchange of embassies and honorific grants of *proxenia* with other cities throughout the Greek world, voting honorary decrees and outwardly behaving like independent city-states. But the reality was different. In fact, they were wholly under the control of the king. Thus, a letter (διάγραμμα) written by Philip V to his representative in Thessalonike, Andronikos, guarantees the revenues of the temple of Serapis against sequestration by the municipal authorities, who may not touch them without the consent of the royal *epistates* and judges *(dikastai)*. *Epistatai* — Andronikos will be one — were royal officers stationed in the main cities of Macedonia and in other areas of the king's possessions. The names of several are known from Amphipolis and at Thessalonike Sopatros was a sub-*epistates* (ὑπεπιστάτης). The Archippos to whom Philip V wrote about a grant of land to a tetrarch Nicanor in an otherwise unknown city of Greia was probably also an *epistates*.

These officers — and others like Harpalos, the *dioiketes* at Beroia, to whom Demetrios II sent instructions about various moneys in 248/7 B.C. (this was before his accession) — ensured that no important decisions were taken without the royal consent. In the Koan inscriptions mentioned above Kassandreia, Philippi and Amphipolis specifically refer to the king's wishes, and it is clear that they could not have granted *asylia* without his consent. But within these limitations, which were common to most Greek cities controlled by Hellenistic kings, those of Macedonia enjoyed local autonomy. They had their own funds (hence the *tamiai)* and they could confer a local citizenship. This is clear from Philip V's letter to Archippos (see above), in which the previous owner of the land to be assigned to Nicanor — he has the good Macedonian name of Korrhagos, son of Perdikkas — is described as 'one of the metics in Greia'; evidently he was a Macedonian from some other city or canton exercising 'resident alien' rights in Greia, and in this respect enjoying a status similar to that of aliens from Ainos mentioned in an inscription of 187 B.C. as resident in Amphipolis. Towards the end of Philip V's reign some cities were granted a hithero unprecedented right to issue coinage. This need not imply any relaxation of royal control; it will be considered below when we come to examine the social and economic aspects of this period.

For their security all Macedonian kings from Philip II to Perseus felt obliged to control some areas outside Macedonia. In particular Greece was a region of constant concern. From the early fifth century onwards it represents both an object of cultural aspiration and a political and military threat. After the expansion under Philip II control of Greece was essential to Macedonian safety; and various methods were devised to achieve this. A strong, independent Thessaly was always a menace to Macedonia, and from 353 B.C. (or 352 B.C.), when he was elected archon of the Thessalian League, Philip II never relaxed his grip on this area (to which he soon added the outlying regions of Perrhaibia and Magnesia and later Phthiotic Achaia). In 344 B.C. he reorganized the League under four tetrarchs (an ancient title) with the strongly developed cities as basic units within each of the four tetrarchies. The details are controversial, but as archon Philip retained the main power in his hands. From then until the Roman victory in 197 B.C. Thessaly remained under the kings of Macedonia, theoretically as heads of the Thessalian League (which gave them the Thessalian vote in the Delphic Amphiktyony) though in fact they treated Thessaly as if it were part of Macedonia. Following his seizure of the throne in 249 B.C. Demetrios I set up a new capital, Demetrias, in Magnesia (in Thessaly) near the ancient city of Pagasai. Demetrias developed into an important cosmopolitan port, frequented and inhabited by men from as far afield as Asia Minor, Syria, Phoenicia and Sicily; its royal garrison kept it firmly under Macedonian control, and though Philip V lost it after Kynoskephalai (197 B.C.), he recovered it in 191 B.C. and it remained Macedonian until the end of the monarchy.

Further south Philip II was concerned to neutralize Greece and enlist its support for his projected war against Persia. The instrument he devised was the Hellenic League with a synod of representatives from the constituent cities and ethnic groups, to serve as a standing committee with himself as leader *(hegemon)*. This League guaranteed stability in the Greek cities and it underwrote a common peace. It was as *hegemon* of the League that Philip planned to invade Persia and Alexander did so. But once on the throne of Persia Alexander lost interest in the panhellenic aspect of his enterprise; consequently the Hellenic League lost its *raison d'être* and it did not outlast the Lamian War. Demetrios I and Antigonos I tried to revive it in 302 B.C as a means of winning Macedonia from Cassander. But both Demetrios and his father supplemented it with a garrison at Corinth, and this was to become a vital element in the scheme of control exercised by the Antigonid dynasty in Greece. Philip V described the three Macedonian garrisons in Demetrias, Chalkis and Corinth as the 'fetters of Greece'; and it was by the combination of this system of garrisons — supplemented for many years by similar garrisons in Athens and the Piraeus — and the support of a group of tyrants well-disposed towards Macedonia in the cities of the Peloponnese that Antigonos Gonatas maintained his control over southern Greece and denied it to any rival dynasty. As governor of Corinth his half-brother Krateros was virtually an independent viceroy, and the revolt of his son Alexander after his father's death dealt a severe blow to Macedonian power in the Peloponnese. In

245 B.C. Antigonos recovered Corinth, but lost it to Aratos of Sicyon in 243 B.C. and the Macedonian position was reestablished in southern Greece only when Antigonos Doson was called in by Aratos to save the Achaian League from Kleomenes III of Sparta, and once more garrisoned the Acrocorinth. Antigonos, as we saw above, also revived the Hellenic League with ethnic leagues as its units; and it was through this League that Philip involved many of the Greek states in war against Rome. Thus for over a century and a half the institutions employed by Macedonia in its relations with Greece were characterized by experiment and opportunism; the object throughout was to control and neutralize, not to annex.

The northern and western frontiers presented different problems. There Macedonia was under constant threat from Thracians, Dardanians and Illyrians from the wilder parts of the Balkans and poor defences could lead to complete disaster, as all but happened under Ptolemy Keraunos. These dangers were mainly dealt with as they arose or by the use of preemptive strikes, as under Philip II. He established a military governorship of Thrace, probably *c.* 341 B.C. following his colonization of the central Hebros valley, and under Philip V the post was reestablished, this time to administer the coastal areas east of the Nestos. To the north the Dardanians seized Paionia from Demetrios II and there too, after its recovery, Philip V set up a regular command, to which both he and his successor Perseus appointed a member of the Paionian princely family. This use of local princes recalls a similar practice in the Seleucid kingdom and their employment by the Romans to control small mountainous provinces. Subject to the king of Macedonia's overriding power these native commanders exercised a virtually independent authority over an area stretching from the Illyrian border to the Nestos, a vast buffer zone shielding Macedonia — and so incidentally Greece as well.

SOCIAL AND ECONOMIC DEVELOPMENTS

The consolidation of Macedonia under Philip II, its role as a base for Alexander's vast career of conquest, and its transformation into a Hellenistic state under his immediate successors and later under the direction of the Antigonid dynasty presupposes a solid background of wealth and man-power; the creation of this was largely the handiwork of Philip II. There are of course few if any reliable statistics available. Any estimate of the population of Macedonia during this period must depend on controlled guesswork. One, that of Beloch, based on the recorded size of Macedonian armies, puts the total population at the time of Alexander at about half a million (including Chalkidike, Amphipolis and Philippi). It has also been calculated that Philip II's economic policy led to a growth of over 25% in the number of men available for military duties between 334 B.C., when perhaps fifty thousand Macedonians were mobilized in Europe and Asia together, and 323, when a comparable figure reaches around fifty-five thousand,

allowing for estimated casualties of fourteen thousand, a figure perhaps double a normal death rate.

When every allowance has been made for the element of error in calculations such as these, it is clear that Philip II's reign saw a remarkable population explosion. This was made possible by his successful policy of military expansion. Although his armies were almost continually campaigning, Philip took care to protect Macedonian citizens from excessive burdens and demands. He kept his armies small and efficient and only once are they recorded as suffering heavy casualties. Individual Macedonians are unlikely to have been subject to an annual call-up. Furthermore, Philip enriched both his Companion Cavalry and his soldiers generally with grants of land taken from the conquered Greek coastal cities. The former are exemplified by the cavalry squadrons from the originally Greek cities of Anthemous and Apollonia in Chalkidike and by Macedonians who claim citizenship of Amphipolis and Pydna on the same grounds; and when Philip seized and razed Methone in 354 he divided the land among the Macedonians. Similarly the population of Philippi, his new foundation at the former mining centre of Krenides was swelled out with fresh, and presumably Macedonian, settlers. The conditions on which the king made these grants of land is not recorded; but lots seem to have been hereditary and alienable and to have been accompanied by an obligation to perform certain duties and pay taxes. Philip's services to the more outlying areas of the kingdom were perhaps even more striking. In a speech which Arrian puts into the mouth of Alexander — it is rhetorically elaborated, but not for that reason to be dismissed — Philip's transformation of the character of Macedonia is described in these words: 'Philip found you vagabonds and helpless, most of you clothed in sheepskins, pasturing a few sheep on the mountainsides and fighting for these, with ill success, against the Illyrians, Triballians and the Thracians on your borders, Philip gave you cloaks to wear in place of sheepskins, brought you down from the hills to the plains, made you doughty opponents of your neighbouring enemies, so that you trusted now not so much to the natural strength of your villages as to your own courage. Nay, he made you into dwellers of cities and civilized you with good laws and customs.' (*Anabasis*, vii. 9.2)

This harangue describes a fundamental change in the pattern of life for the highlanders. From shepherds clad in skins they have become civilized farmers and town-dwellers, wearing decent woven garments and enjoying the benefits of law and order. This picture receives some confirmation from the fact that Philip is known to have carried out other transfers of population on a large scale, and often ruthlessly, in order to further his military and political aims, especially in the years around 346/5 B.C. after the peace with Athens. Macedonians were drafted to the frontiers and the gaps thus created in the cities were partly filled by bringing in prisoners of war. Both in upper Macedonia and in the coastal plain measures were introduced to provide flood-control, drainage and deforestation. New agricultural land was thus opened up for development, and the native peasantry was reinforced by Skythians, Thracians and Illyrians. Stockbreeding was encouraged and we read of vineyards and orchards, and wheatfields, in the district between the Axios and the Strymon, all adding to the growing wealth of the country. But Philip's movements of population also served a further end. They increased security at threatened points along the frontier and, by breaking up potential opposition groups within Macedonia, helped to unify it under the central control of the king. These measures must have led to much turmoil and caused some distress; but by and large the people were richer and the land more secure, and this is reflected in the greater number of children born and surviving.

Both the economic and the military aspects of this programme depended very considerably on tapping the mineral wealth of Macedonia. The form and organization of the new army have been briefly described above (see page 112). Its maintenance was costly, especially since it was well supplied with the new artillery and assault machines devised by the Thessalian Polyidos (and later improved by his pupils Diades and Charias, who served under Alexander). In addition, partly to further his economic programme and partly for military ends Philip developed roads and bridged rivers and opened up a waterway to Pella, so as to convert it into a port. All this, though it no doubt brought returns in the form of trade, demanded a substantial outlay of wealth in the first instance. From 341 B.C. onwards Philip exacted a tithe from the Thracians in the Hebros valley, but for most of his revenue he was for-ced to depend on the mines under his control. Like Alexander I, Philip put great effort into developing these. The silver mines of Damasteion somewhere in the neighbourhood of lake Lychnitis (Ochrid), those of Mt. Pangaion near Amphipolis, and those of Philippi, were all intensively exploited; and according to Diodoros the gold-mines of Philippi were bringing in one thousand talents a year. The silver which Philip acquired from these operations was minted at Pella from 359 B.C. onwards and later, from 357 or 356 B.C., at Amphipolis; these issues were intended primarily to meet the cost of the army. Gold was perhaps less important. Philip did not coin gold before 346 B.C. and most of the famous 'philippi', to which the literary tradition attaches so much importance as the substance of Philip's bribery, are now thought to be posthumous. But besides the mines Macedonia also possessed vast potential wealth in the form of timber and the pitch which also came from the large forests. If Philip II made no attempt to develop a Macedonian navy and chose to depend primarily on the Greek cities for naval power, that was probably for want of skilled crews rather than of cash and raw materials. Additional wealth came, as we have seen, from the tithes which he imposed on the conquered Thracians from 341 B.C. onwards. The colonies which he founded in the Hebros valley, though their main object was military, may also have had a role in the collection of this tax.

Alexander's expedition laid a heavy strain on the resources of Macedonia and especially on its manpower.

103. Reconstruction drawing of the Macedonian phalanx, in whose success the sarissa played a large part. The sarissa was the long spear used by the Macedonian hoplites; those in the first rank held it out in front of them, while those behind held it upright. The phalanx was the basic factor in the triumphs of the Macedonian army in Greece as in Asia.

103

At a single stroke half the men of military age were removed from their native land, many to die and many others never to return. Once the army was in Asia Alexander was able to finance his campaign from the enemy. He did indeed receive one body of reinforcements from Macedonia, but in return he sent a large quantity of precious metal from Susa to help Antipater finance the Lamian war. After his death the link between the army — shortly to become the armies — and Macedonia grew more and more tenuous, as the empire fell apart. Of those who had left Macedonia some made their way home and of these a few were outstandingly rich. One such veteran was the Karanos, of whose wealth Athenaios gives a perhaps exaggerated account in his description of a banquet of fabulous dimensions, at which the gifts of gold and silver taken away by the guests were large enough to be invested in houses, land and slaves. But such men will have formed a minority; and in the wars of Alexander's successors the land of Macedonia was devastated by the warring of rival factions and by a series of barbarian inroads which culminated in the Gaulish invasion of 279 B.C. In addition, any advantages that accrued from soldiers returning home enriched will have been more than cancelled out by the emigration of younger men to the new kingdoms of Syria and Egypt and to the Far East, especially in the first half-century following Alexander's death. It has been suggested that Antigonos II's cautious policy in Greece may indeed have sprung from his desire to give Macedonia an opportunity to recuperate. Unfortunately detailed evidence concerning Macedonian manpower is lacking until the reign of Philip V; and some scholars, including Rostovtzeff, have interpreted the fact that Antigonos Gonatas issued an abundant, reliable, silver coinage as evidence that his reign was a time of Macedonian prosperity. There is however no firm proof nor is it very likely that these issues were made with commercial ends in view, nor may one safely draw general conclusions about the level of Macedonian trade from occasional records left by Macedonians on Delos. Antigonos II's adoption of a naval policy directed against Egypt is perhaps some indication of his increased resources. But Macedonia never achieved the scale of wealth found in Egypt and some other Hellenistic states. In 168 B.C. the land tax brought in only two hundred talents a year.

Under the last two kings the evidence is rather fuller. In addition to Polybios' *History* and a large part of Livy derived from it there are several inscriptions which throw light on Macedonian administration, on the economic conditions of the country and especially on Philip V's patronage of lesser shrines such as those of Lindian Athena on Rhodes or Karian Zeus at Panamara, as well as the more famous international religious centres like Delos, where he established a special festival, the *Philippeia,* and built a Doric portico. A crown presented by the Delians to Philip shortly before his death may have been in recognition of concessions made by him for the purchase of Macedonian pitch and timber. Such patronage was a way of underlining the Macedonian claim to parity of status

with richer neighbours such as Syria, Egypt and Pergamon. But it was costly to sustain, and a considerable burden when it had to be financed out of a treasury depleted by constant wars and, in particular, those against Rome.

After the Second Macedonian War (200-197 B.C.), which stripped Philip of all his domains except Macedonia and saddled him with an indemnity of one thousand talents (see page 155), he therefore embarked on a deliberate policy of expanding his revenues. He increased the taxes levelled on agricultural produce and harbour dues, he sank new mines and reopened old, and with the proceeds he

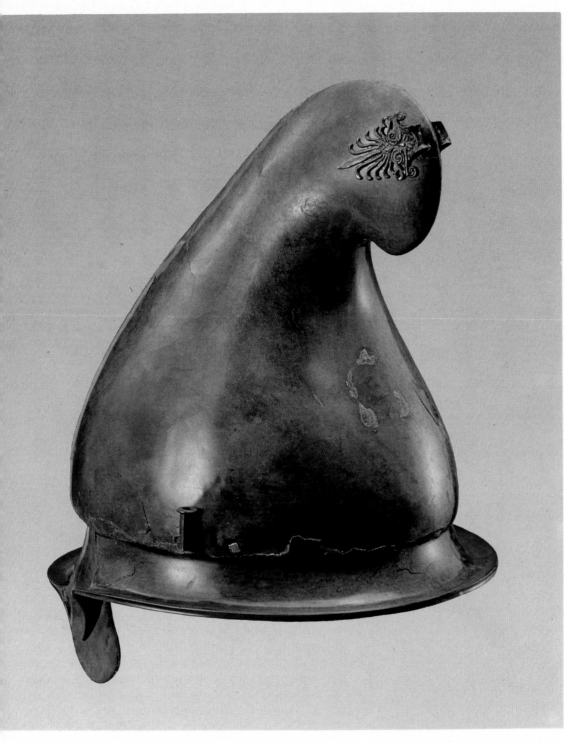

104. *The head and butt of the sarissa, a long wooden spear whose exact length has not yet been ascertained. The butt was used to thrust the sarissa into the ground. Thessalonike Archaeological Museum.*

105. *Iron sword from Beroia. Golden figures of Nike (winged Victory) adorn the hilt. 370-350 B.C. Beroia, Archaeological Museum.*

106. *Helmet of the Macedonian type worn chiefly by the infantry in the Macedonian army. On the upper part is an inlaid decorative anthemion. It comes from Vitsa in Epirus. 4th century B.C. Ioannina, Archaeological Museum.*

issued large quantities of coins. It is against this background that one has to assess the new privileges apparently accorded to the cities and regions of Macedonia under Philip V and Perseus.

For the first time in the history of the Antigonid dynasty coins were now issued by regional mints and by several Macedonian cities. If, as seems likely, the legend on a coin of Thessalonike is a reference to the thirty-fourth regnal year of Philip V, this coin was issued in 189/8 B.C., after the conclusion of the Roman war against Antiochos, in which Philip's expectations of Roman concessions had been so decisively disappointed. Livy indeed describes

Philip's new economic measures, including his development of the mines, under the year 185 B.C.; but his account implies that the policy had been initiated earlier. Whatever the precise date at which these measures began, it is clear that during the last decade of Philip V's reign, besides silver coinage from the royal mint, bronze was being issued in the name of the Macedonians (at Amphipolis), of the Amphaxians (at Thessalonike), of the Bottiaians (at Pella), and of two Paionian peoples, the Doberes and the Paroreians (the location of these mints is uncertain). In addition, the cities of Amphipolis, Thessalonike, Aphytis, Apollonia in Mygdonia, and Pella also issued coins in their own name. A plentiful coinage was a help to commerce and the districts and cities thus privileged may well have paid handsomely for these coining rights; but it is less easy to assess the political implications (if any) of this development, and the relationship (if any) between the regional groups represented on some of the coins, the 'Macedonians' who appear on others, and the Macedonian *koinon* which made a dedication to Philip V on Delos (see page 159). There is certainly no reason to believe that the concession to mint granted to local groups and cities implied any relaxation of royal supervision over local affairs of the centralized control exercised by the monarchy. Given time, these concessions might of course have led to others; but speculation along these lines is idle, since the Macedonian monarchy was only to last another twenty years.

Perseus also coined on a large scale and built up substantial financial reserves in his treasury. He continued to issue large quantities of silver coins, at first tetradrachms and later smaller denominations. The results were impressive. In an estimate of Perseus' economic and military situation made in 172 B.C. by his enemy Eumenes, the king of Pergamon, — it may be exaggerated — he is said to have possessed enough grain to feed an army of thirty thousand infantry and five thousand cavalry for ten years (without drawing on current harvests), enough money to hire ten thousand mercenaries for ten years (in addition to his Macedonian troops) together with the revenue from the royal mines, arms for three armies such as he already possessed, and Thrace as a recruiting ground, should Macedonia itself fail him. In view of their unfriendly origin these figures must clearly be taken with a pinch of salt; but it can be seen from the size of the armies which he actually put in the field that since 197 B.C. the national levy had grown by some nine thousand men and that he was in a position to pay at least eighteen thousand mercenaries. After his fall Aemilius Paullus found six thousand talents still in the treasury. So great was the potential strength and wealth of the kingdom when it fell to Rome.

How far this development of the resources of Macedonia under its later kings was connected with the growth of intensive commercial activity is not clear. Urbanization had undoubtedly gone further than was once supposed — indeed this was already true under Philip II; but a city need not derive its wealth from commerce, nor was the movement of commodities always effected through trade. The king owned outright many primary resources in Macedonia — the mines and the forests and much of the land — and he could and did use his autocratic power to dispose of their products as he thought fit. It has been shown that between 310 and 169 B.C. the price of pitch at Delos was entirely dependent on political factors in Macedonia. The king fixed prices to suit his own purposes, in which prestige and politics played a large part. They no doubt also included the acquisition of wealth; but for a king of Macedonia there were easier and more traditional ways than trade to acquire this.

Despite the growth of the cities many Macedonians still lived in the countryside as peasant-farmers or as tenants farming the estates of the king or the nobility. As we saw, their lot had been improved under Philip II, and figs, grapes and olives were now widely cultivated. How far there were also serfs in the countryside is not clear; but it is likely that the immigrant Skythians, Dardanians and Illyrians, and the indigenous Thracians in the eastern parts of the country, will have been of inferior status, certainly not citizens and perhaps in some sense unfree. Their number can only be guessed at, but may have amounted to as much as a quarter or even a half of the total population. Altogether the economic and social pattern in Macedonia was probably closer to that in north-west Greece than to that of the Peloponnese. Slave-owning seems not yet to have become widely established. Evidence is indeed scanty, even in the cities, where such slavery as we find was on a small scale. At Beroia there is some record of manumissions under the monarchy, and there were some home-reared slaves, a number of whom had wives, children and even property. But in general the features characteristic of a highly-developed system of chattel slavery are absent from Macedonia under the kings.

INTELLECTUAL LIFE

Between 359 and 168 B.C. Macedonia was increasingly integrated into the intellectual and cultural life of Greece. A distinction must of course be drawn between the cities and the countryside and perhaps even more between the court circle and the land as a whole. As we have seen, except for the fact that they were without the fundamental right to enjoy freedom and autonomy, the cities of Macedonia came in all other respects to resemble those of Greece proper. Life inside Thessalonike must have been very similar to life in any other large Greek maritime city such as Corinth or Demetrias. There was the same social and religious activity, revealed to us by inscriptions, and centering more and more around oriental cults such as those of Isis and Serapis, as well as more traditional objects of worship like Herakles. In the Hellenistic period ruler cult, the worship first of dead and later even of living kings or queens, came to play an important role in most monarchic states and in the Greek cities which came into close contact with their rulers. In Macedonia a cult of Amyntas, Philip II's father, existed at Pydna and one of Philip II himself at Amphipolis and Thasos. Kassandreia produces evidence of a cult of Lysimachos and (probably) of Cassander himself, its founder, and also one of Eurydike, the daughter of Antipater, who had freed the city. Later, Philip V is known to have been worshipped at Amphipolis. But in contrast to the other monarchies this institution was confined in Macedonia to the cities and was, as far as we know, never sponsored by the Macedonian state. This distinction no doubt reflects a traditionally freer attitude of the Macedonian people towards its king.

In the cities Hellenization was encouraged through contact with traders and immigrants from all over the Greek world; and at a higher level the Macedonian court provided a milieu for Greek culture through the attraction of its patronage. In the fifth century Archelaos had sought to make his new capital at Pella a focus for Greek artistic and intellectual life by inviting Greek writers, musicians and artists such as Zeuxis, Timotheos, Choirilos, Agathon and Euripides to his court and instituting a festival to Zeus and the Muses at Dion. Philip II continued this tradition. The claim to an Argive origin made by his family inclined him towards Greek culture, and like Archelaos he encouraged Greek celebrities to make their home at his court in Pella. Among these were Speusippos, Plato's nephew and his successor as Head of the Academy in Athens, Theophrastos of the Peripatetic school, who studied natural phenomena in Macedonia, and the historian Theopompos, who visited the Macedonian court towards 340 B.C. and who, as we saw above, though he expressed himself with virulence and contempt concerning Philip's *Hetairoi,* nevertheless broke off the composition of his *Hellenica* in order to write *Philippica* centring on the career of the Macedonian king. Europe, Theopompos asserted, had never produced such a man as Philip, the son of Amyntas. But the greatest and the most celebrated writer to take up residence in Macedonia at this time was Aristotle of Stageiros, whose father Nikomachos had been Amyntas' court physician. Rejecting the services of a certain Antipater, sponsored in a letter to him by Speusippos, Philip succeeded in persuading the great philosopher to come as tutor to his son Alexander in 343/2 B.C. and in the Nymphaion at Mieza — the probable site among the orchards below Mt. Bermion has recently been excavated — he set up a school in which he taught Philip's heir along with the royal pages and perhaps inspired him with that curiosity for new things which remained with him throughout his life.

Aristotle had been a member of the Academy and the links between that school and Pella continued to be close. Under Philip's predecessor, Perdikkas III, Plato's pupil Euphraios of Oreos had also run a school for the Macedonian court; and Philip himself was a close friend of another of Plato's pupils, Hermias, the ruler of Atarneus on the coast of Asia Minor opposite Lesbos. Aristotle had stayed with him there for some time and had married his niece, before accepting Philip's invitation to go to Pella. When later Hermias was trapped by the king of Persia and executed as an alleged accomplice in Philip's plans to invade the king's dominions, Aristotle expressed his grief in a commemorative poem; his nephew Kallisthenes, who was later to become court historian to Alexander's Persian expedition, wrote his encomium.

Other Greeks too were attracted to Pella by Philip's patronage — Isokrates' pupil Python, who was probably the real author of a letter sent to Athens by Philip in 346 B.C., and who as Macedonian envoy to Athens in 343 B.C. clashed with Demosthenes, Eumenes of Kardia, who became Philip's secretary and was eventually to play a significant part in the struggle between Alexander's successors and the Cretan Nearchos, who was to become Alexander's admiral in India and one of the historians of the expedition. Of other writers who accompanied the Per-

sian expedition and produced histories of it, the Greek engineer Aristobulos later acquired the citizenship of Kassandreia and so evidently returned to Macedonia; but Ptolemy, who was Arrian's main source for his history of Alexander, was to achieve fame of a different sort as founder of the Lagid dynasty in Egypt, and so hardly earns a place in the history of Macedonia.

Under the regency Macedonia lacked the lustre and attraction of a royal court. But Antipater did something to compensate for this. He had shared Philip's friendship with Aristotle, who eventually named him as his executor; and he supported him at Athens at a time when that great centre of Greek civilization was under direct Macedonian influence. Antipater was himself the author of letters and of a history of Perdikkas' Illyrian wars. Like Antipater, his son Cassander, who in due course followed him as governor and later became king of Macedonia, maintained links with the Peripatetic school. He established Demetrios of Phaleron, the Peripatetic philosopher, as lawgiver and governor at Athens, and was a good friend of Theophrastos, who dedicated a book *On Kingship* to him. Nicanor, the Macedonian commander in the Piraeus, was Aristotle's son-in-law and adopted son; and Cassander's friend, the orator Dinarchos, was a pupil of Theophrastos and of Demetrios of Phaleron. Though they made no direct contribution to the intellectual life of Pella, these many personal links are significant as an indication of the close relations maintained over several decades between the Macedonian court and the schools of Plato and Aristotle. Cassander also patronized the visual arts. We read of his association with the painter Philoxenos of Eretria and the sculptor Lysippos of Sikyon; but this aspect of the cultural life of Macedonia will be discussed below.

During the twenty years following Cassander's death Macedonia was unhappily subjected to constant invasion and fighting between rival dynasts and this was hardly conducive to cultural activities. Of the contestants for the throne Lysimachos gave some encouragement to literature. Onesikritos wrote his book on Alexander at Lysimachos' court and he may also have acted as patron to the famous Peripatetic philosopher, Dikaiarchos of Messana; but it was only after Antigonos Gonatas had established himself securely on the throne that Greek culture could again flourish in the Macedonian capital. Antigonos had himself been a pupil of Menedemos of Eretria and of Zeno, and as a result his sympathies were chiefly with the Stoics. Under him Greeks once more frequented the court, particularly those who shared his own interest in poetry, philosophy and history. The new political currents of the Hellenistic world and the foundation of new kingdoms had been accompanied by the growth of new cultural centres, of which Alexandria and, somewhat later, Pergamon were the most famous. Antigonid Macedonia lacked the wealth and the prestige necessary to create a comparable centre. But under Antigonos II Pella gave shelter to several writers of distinction, including Aratos of Soli, a fellow-pupil of Menedemos, who wrote a Stoic poem on astronomy based on the treatises of Eudoxos, the *Phainomena,* the *Ap-*

pearances, which dealt with the physical universe, the rising and setting of the stars and, in the second half, with the lore of weather-signs; this long and learned work somewhat strangely maintained its popularity throughout antiquity. Persaios of Kition also came to Pella in place of Zeno (who declined Antigonos' invitation); he became tutor to Antigonos' son Halkyoneus, and also a courtier and a political and military figure; he was indeed commander of the Acrocorinth in 243 B.C. when Aratos seized it, and following this failure he committed suicide. Persaios wrote many works including a treatise *On Kingship.* The popularity of this theme reflects a philosophical interest in the new monarchical regimes. The sceptic Timon of Phlious, author of lampoons, satyr-plays and various philosophical writings, spent some time at Pella; and Bion of Borysthenes, the wandering Cynic, was there fleetingly but, as usual, moved on.

Perhaps more important were the historians. In the Hellenistic world, as later on at Rome, the writing of history was actively cultivated by men of the highest rank. Marsyas of Pella, who wrote a history of Macedonia, was perhaps the first native writer of importance; he was the half-brother (or perhaps the nephew) of Antigonos Monophthalmos, and it was probably Antigonos II's half-brother Krateros who published a collection of Athenian decrees accompanied by a commentary. But the outstanding historian of Antigonos' court was Hieronymos of Kardia, the most reliable and substantial writer on the events from Alexander to the death of Pyrrhos in 272. Originally in the service of Eumenes of Kardia, he transferred his allegiance to Antigonus Monophthalmos after Eumenes' death and remained loyal to his dynasty until his own death around 250 B.C. His *History of the Successors* (i.e. of Alexander) has not survived, but indirectly, through its use by Arrian and Diodoros, and by Plutarch in his *Lives* of Eumenes, Pyrrhos and Demetrios, it provides the soundest account of the political history of the late fourth and early third centuries. Other branches of literature were also represented at Pella; we have for example the tragedian Alexander of Aitolia, and Antagoras of Rhodes who wrote a Theban epic, among the writers of Antigonos' court.

Antigonos Gonatas thus cultivated a literary circle of some distinction; but this practice was not maintained under the later Antigonids. After its sack by Kleomenes Antigonos Doson entrusted the reconstruction of Megalopolis to the Peripatetic philosopher Prytanis; but the only known literary figure at the court of Philip V was an epigrammatist, Samos, the son of Chrysogonos, one of Philip's Friends, and his foster-brother. Samos is known for some witticisms written in flattery of the king, but towards the end of Philip's reign he was executed for treason. Of Perseus we know only that he owned an impressive library, perhaps originally assembled by the Argeads or by Antigonos Gonatas, which Aemilius Paullus, the victor of Pydna, removed to Rome and gave to his sons, Q. Fabius Maximus and P. Cornelius Scipio Aemilianus. A valuable addition to the amenities of second century Rome, it may have been consulted by Polybios, who first became intimate with Aemilianus 'over some books'.

All this will have made little impact outside the court and certainly none on the peasantry and on country life. But that was true in varying degrees elsewhere. Hellenic and Hellenistic civilization depended basically on life in cities and it was the growth of urban development and court patronage that together brought Macedonia into the mainstream of Greek intellectual life. This Hellenism was however in many respects a veneer. The old national traditions and values were not submerged even in the upper ranks of society. The ancient Macedonian passion for hunting, fighting, feasting and drinking remained a characteristic of the Antigonid capital. Herakles, the ancestor of the royal house, was worshipped as a huntsman; and Philip V still carried out the traditional army-purification in which the host paraded between the two halves of a severed dog before the holding of a tournament in honour of the god Xanthos. In all these activities the royal house played by tradition a leading part. Its destruction in 168 B.C. brought a long chapter in the history of the country to an end, and a new one followed, in which, after a short interlude which saw the country divided into four separate republics, Macedonia was reunited and had gradually to come to terms with its new role as a province of the Roman empire.

07

107. *A silver-gilt 'medallion', the decoration of the Lid of a pyxis. Aphrodite Epitragia, riding on a goat, is a subject frequently encountered in Hellenistic iconography. Mid-2nd century B.C. Beroia, Archaeological Museum.*

169

ART IN THE HELLENISTIC PERIOD

In the new era, in which Hellenism stretched across three continents, the restless cosmopolitan spirit, thirsting for new ideas and conquests, escaped once more, and this time more boldly than ever before, from the narrow confines of the city-state and the limited borders of the Greek mainland. The centrifugal and centripetal forces of art quested for new horizons and gifted artists sought new modes of expression. The territorial expansion of Hellenism was accompanied and followed by a variety of currents and trends that adapted themselves to the artistic achievements of the immediate past, lending them a new dimension. At no other time, perhaps, was the old so new or the novel so familiar.

TOWN PLANNING

The urban design of the major cities is now based on certain fundamental principles of town planning that had been successfully tested as early as the fifth century B.C. It aimed at as rational a distribution as possible of the various focal points (temples, palaces, market places, etc.) within the urban complex with a view to securing the maximum convenience, the unimpeded movement of the population around the city, and the most effective protection of its safety and its health. The new cities were an expression of the desire of the central authority to execute grandiose schemes and proclaim the glory of the dynasty; built on sites of vital strategic and political importance and cultural and commercial significance, they bore the indelible stamp of their founder, whose name they perpetuated (Kassandreia, Thessalonike, Phila, Antigoneia). At the same time, the town plans of the older cities were improved and adapted to meet the new living conditions and the new demands of the age; Pella and Beroia, for example, were now extended to satisfy the demand for housing arising from the return of the veterans of the campaign in the East and from the more general trend towards urban life. The planned development of towns, initiated by Philip II (Dion, Pella, Philippi, Herakleia Lynkestis and Herakleia Sintike in Macedonia, and Philippoupolis in Thrace) was deployed methodically by Alexander, who founded dozens of cities named after himself; subsequently it formed part of the ambitious cultural policies of each of the *epigonoi,* of Cassander, of Antigonos, of Philip V, and of Demetrios Poliorketes, to mention at least those who founded towns in Macedonia.

The cities that were established after about the middle of the fourth century B.C. or that were extended, for the most part after the campaign in the East, were built according to the 'Hippodameian' system that had been tried so successfully at Olynthos,[1] during the second phase of settlement of the capital of the Chalkidian League (432-348 B.C.): large rectangular blocks of buildings measuring 110×50 m. (Pella[2]) or 100×50 m. (Thessalonike[3]) were separated by broad streets at right angles to each other. These blocks might include three contiguous houses arranged along the main axis (Pella) or two rows of four houses (Thessalonike); occasionally, side streets ran from one side of the block to the other, dividing it into two unequal parts and thereby facilitating movement about the city (Pella).

Pella, the 'greatest of the cities in Macedonia', which was enlarged in the time of Philip II and further expanded in accord with the new 'rules' of urban design during the period immediately after the death of Alexander; Beroia, the favourite city of the Antigonids; and Thessalonike (founded in 315, or 305 B.C. according to one view), described in the Palatine Anthology as 'mother of all Macedonia', all took maximum advantage of the configuration of the terrain on which they were built: Pella on the lower slopes of two hills, Beroia on a low, flat plateau, and Thessalonike spreading in a semicircle up the sides of a mountain. The buildings were arranged in such a way as to ensure that all the rooms were abundantly lit for most months of the year (the houses faced south, and the northern wings had two storeys), and that the main and ancillary rooms were disposed in a rational manner.

The water supply of the cities was secured by a system of ceramic pipes running beneath the streets that was at once complex yet simple in conception. It is attested by excavation at Pella.[4] Inspection jars (rather like modern manholes) were placed at the junctions between the streets to ensure that the drinking water was automatically purified of the various foreign substances that it contained. Under the new system of urban design, the administrative, commercial and religious centres were located in separate sectors of the city. At Pella, the commercial sector lay to the north of a series of residential *insulae* and occupied two entire blocks: pebble-paved courtyards were surrounded by a vast number of small shops, in many of which were discovered storage jars and pits. In this city, the shrines and sanctuaries, whether private or public, were sited at various points but were always incorporated within the block pat-

08

108. Theatrical
presentations in eastern
Macedonia were as
widely known and loved
as in the rest of Greece.
The typical comic
masks on a terracotta
plaque from Amphipolis
show that the
inhabitants were
familiar with the human
types of New Comedy.
Beginning of the 3rd
century B.C. Kavala,
Archaeological
Museum.

109. Detail of a relief
vase from Florina
showing a scene from
the fall of Troy. The
love of Macedonians for
the Homeric epics is
revealed by the
frequency with which
Homeric themes
occurred in the
decoration of
Macedonian vessels of
the 2nd century B.C.
Thessalonike,
Archaeological
Museum.

tern; the single exception is the large building on the acropolis resembling a temple,[5] in the precinct of which are a number of stone bases that once carried bronze, clearly votive, tripods. We know from literary and epigraphical evidence that the capital of the Macedonian kingdom had temples to Zeus, Asklepios, Athena Alkidemos, Herakles Phylakos, the Kabeiroi, the Muses and Poseidon.[6] Within the city of Beroia there were also a number of sanctuaries – of Herakles Kynagidas, Dionysos, Asklepios, Poseidon, Athena, Hermes, Aphrodite and Artemis – though the existence of these is known only from epigraphic evidence. This is also true of the sanctuary of the Egyptian deities Serapis and Isis which has been located within the city of Thessalonike.[7]

At Dion, in contrast, where recent discoveries have revealed the existence of an extensive, organized cult area on the pattern of the major sanctuaries in southern Greece (Olympia, Nemea, Isthmia), the *oikos* of Asklepios and Hygeia and that of Demeter was outside the defensive enceinte, as was the sanctuary of Olympian Zeus.[8]

Nothing survived of the various public buildings that, according to the tradition, adorned the Macedonian cities during the Hellenistic period – the baths and theatre at Pella, for example, the stoa at Beroia and the administrative centre-palace at Thessalonike.[9] The semicircular theatre at Dion, built of earth brought in from outside, is a clear indication of the attachment of the Macedonians to the immortal works of the Greek spirit,[10] as is the monumental theatre with stone seats at the lower levels recently discovered during archaeological excavations at Vergina.

There are only fragmentary remains of the fortifications of the cities: a few sections of ashlar masonry, and some of mud brick at one point of the enclosure near the acropolis at Thessalonike,[11] short stretches of the defence wall constructed of rectangular blocks of poros at the north gate and on the south-west side of the city at Beroia,[12] and a wall of similar construction, in which the mud bricks of the superstructure also survive, on the west side of Pella.[13] The square enceinte at Dion, which has rectangular towers spaced at intervals, is at present the best-preserved example of a Hellenistic defensive system in Macedonia: the wall consists of a levelling course on which stood two courses of large blocks, forming a base for the mud bricks that will have been used for the superstructure. Outside the south wall there was a ditch to collect the water from the winter torrent Baphyras, which gushed down from the peaks of Olympos.[14] The defence wall recently discovered at Vergina is undoubtedly impressive in its overall effect, despite its rather rough and ready construction of uncut stones.

ARCHITECTURE

Although the architectural styles in the main centres in the Greek world are fairly well known and have been ade-

quately studied, the achievements of the queen of sciences (in Aristotle's phrase) on the periphery of the Greek world have been slow to attract the attention of the historians of architecture. In Macedonia, in particular, archaeological exploration has lagged behind for historical reasons, and the questions of how far there was an identifiable Macedonian style, especially in the Hellenistic period, and how far this style was influenced by or exercised an influence on other areas, have received answers only very recently. A comparative study of the monumental tombs and of the buildings in urban centres has revealed the specific features of Macedonian architecture that distinguish it from that of other areas.

The most characteristic feature of Macedonian architecture, at least in the period under consideration, is the eclecticism with which it borrowed and combined elements from the major centres of architecture in Greece proper and Asia Minor, adapting them to local aesthetic demands. Not only are elements of a single order to be found disposed in a rather unorthodox fashion, but features borrowed from both the Doric and Ionic orders are to be found mixed together in one and the same building. (Strangely, Macedonian architecture never seems to have been influenced by the Corinthian order.) A second characteristic is the lavish use of plaster, to render a range of plastic features, and of painting, which is deployed not only to emphasize details or to substitute decoration of a two-dimensional nature for reliefs, but frequently to cover entire surfaces with narrative scenes. The close relationship between strictly decorative painting and architectural structure, the frequent replacement of the latter by the former, and the pronounced tendency to experiment (a good example of the quest for new modes of expression) give Macedonian architecture an illusionistic character and a strikingly unique individual quality. And the suggestion that the roots of the painting styles known as 'first' and 'second Pompeian' are to be sought in Macedonia is not entirely groundless.

The erection of imposing buildings at the great Panhellenic sanctuaries, such as the Philippeion at Olympia (built after 338 B.C.) and the two stoas on Delos, one built by Antigonos Gonatas (between 246 and 239 B.C.) and the other by Philip V (about the end of the third century B.C.) represent a deliberate attempt by the Macedonian kings to impose Macedonian models on the old Greek world. In all three, the proportions and architectural principles closely resemble those in Macedonian buildings, and it seems probable that Macedonian craftsmen were used in their design and construction.[15]

TEMPLES

The earliest temple so far known in northern Greece was discovered by the sea, near the settlement of Kallithea in Chalkidike. Thanks to a fragment of an inscribed marble cult bowl bearing the name of Zeus Ammon, and the head of a marble statuette of an eagle, it has been identified with

110. *Aerial photograph of the palace of Vergina. It shows the large square central court, the apartments which surround it and the second smaller palace to the west. The entrance to the palace and the cult areas lay on the eastern side. The official state rooms are probably those in the south wing, the right-hand side of the picture. The tholos, a circular room inscribed in a square, definitely intended for religious ceremonies, is also visible. End of the 4th century B.C.*

the sanctuary of this Egyptian god known to have existed at Aphytis, a Euboian colony dating from the eighth century B.C.

The building has six Doric columns along the short sides and eleven on the longer sides and is shown by some of the proportions and the forms of the architectural members to have been erected in the second half of the fourth century B.C. The material used in its construction was the local conglomerate, covered with white stucco. About the end of the third or the beginning of the second century B.C. the entablature was replaced in marble, clearly after the fourth century entablature had been destroyed. It is still too early to decide whether this was due to the subsidence of the original structure, or whether it is to be connected with the appearance of the Gauls and the plundering of the sanctuaries and cities of Macedonia. There was a narrow stone altar in front of the temple, which was covered with

soil and replaced by a smaller altar in the early Roman period.[16]

PALACES

The only palace so far discovered in Macedonia lies to the east of Vergina.[17] It is built on a superb site in the eastern foothills of Mt. Bermion, from which it dominates the plain of the Haliakmon (fig.110). There are remains of other buildings at the northern edge of the terrace on which the palace stands and also remains of a defence wall enclosing the wider area, suggesting that an ancient Macedonian city of considerable importance once stood on this site. The astounding discoveries yielded by the recent excavations in the area demonstrate with increasing certainty that the site is to be identified with the sacred Macedonian city of Aigai.

The palace is 104.50 m. long and 88.50 m. wide. The residential areas are arranged regularly around a central square courtyard with a side of 44.50 m., around which there was a Doric peristyle (sixteen columns on each side). On the northern, outer facade of the complex, facing the plain, a long, broad balcony was added, as part of the original plan, with a low parapet of poros in imitation of a wooden balustrade. The entire building was of poros, only the thresholds being of marble. The superstructure above the orthostats was of mud bricks, surfaced on both the inside and the outside with plaster in a variety of colours. The various architectural members were also plastered and painted. The roof-tiling was of Corinthian style and in addition to hip tiles and valley tiles, a number of fine relief, painted antefixes with palmettes have survived. The sima also had painted decoration.

The palace has been described variously as a complex designed exclusively for the holding of banquets[18] and as a large country villa. The most widely accepted view, however, seems to be that it was a royal residence — it may indeed not be too extravagant to combine the two theories referred to above and assume that the building served as the residence of the Macedonian kings and their families whenever they visited Aigai for cult banquets or for other rituals, connected with the remains of the important deceased interred in the royal cemetery near by. The complex used to be dated to the beginning of the third century B.C. at the opening of the long reign of Antigonos Gonatas, but this date will now have to be reviewed in the light of recent observations connected with the architecture both of the palace itself and of the buildings at Pella; all the evidence now suggests that the palace was probably erected during the last quarter of the fourth century B.C.[19]

The entrance to the palace was on the east side, which probably had two storeys (to judge from a number of rather small Ionic architectural members) with a Doric stoa on the outside of the ground-floor level. Three successive antechambers led to the eastern side of the peristyle around the inner courtyard, and the doorway between the second and third antechamber was divided into three sections by two imposing double columns with very fine Ionic capitals. The apartments in the eastern wing of the palace are thought to have served cult purposes, and to have been connected with the public appearances of the head of the state. The *tholos,* a circular, roofed room inscribed in a square, is of especial interest. The recent discovery inside it of part of a marble architectural member carved in relief with *boukrania* (oxheads) and garlands, and bearing the inscription ΗΡΑΚΛΗΙ ΠΑΤΡΩΙΩΙ, together with the finds reported there by Heuzey, suggest that the *tholos* had a religious character and was probably devoted to the cult of the ancestor of the Macedonian kings.

The disposition of the rooms in the south wing of the palace, which should probably be considered as the most important official wing, is of particular interest: in the middle of it three imposing double Ionic columns led from the south section of the peristyle to the *prostas* a large hall that served as an antechamber to the two most splendid rooms

in the palace complex. The floors of these rooms are decorated with mosaics; the composition in the eastern room has a superb plant motif in the centre, surrounded by four female figures with baskets (plant goddesses) while that in the west room portrays tritons or cupids on dolphins — indicating the importance of this room and confirming its identification with the *oikos* of the palace.

The southern part of the west wing consists of three rooms, a built conduit that may have been associated with toilets, wash-rooms and similar facilities and three contiguous halls that were the most spacious in the entire complex and had floors paved with marble with a raised border around the edge; the suggestion that these were banquet halls designed to cater for an appreciable number of guests seems quite probable.

From the north part of the palace nothing but foundations survive. Moreover, it is not clear whether the arrangement of these foundations reflects the actual arrangement of the rooms above ground level: more probably they belonged to walls designed to support the mass of earth forming the terrace on which the palace complex was built.

The excavations of recent years have brought to light a second palace, resembling an extension immediately to the west of the large complex; it is smaller and its construction is not as fine, but it has the same general plan;[20] here, too, there was a central square courtyard, (though in this case the columns of the stoas along each side seem, from the surviving bases, to have been of wood), around which were built the residential quarters, best preserved in the south-west corner. It has been suggested that this extension was probably built at the same time as the large palace, despite the fact that much of the material in it is reused and that it has a generally rather crude character. The original theory, that it was a temporary residence, erected immediately after the destruction of the large palace and certainly before the conquest of Macedonia by the Romans, is perhaps more probable.

PRIVATE HOUSES

For the plan of Macedonian houses during the Hellenistic period, or at least of the houses so far discovered, we turn again to Pella.[21] In general terms the type is that of the classical Greek house: the living quarters are arranged around a square peristyle courtyard, usually with Doric columns, in the centre of which there is often a fountain; the residential areas usually occupied only three sides of the courtyard — the north, east and west — leaving the south open (figs. 111,112). There is some indication that the north wings had a second storey. The importance attaching to this wing is further demonstrated by the fact

111. Aerial photograph of a house at Pella, typical of dwellings built at the end of the 4th century B.C. The living quarters flanked a central peristyle court. Some of the most important rooms were paved with sophisticated pebble mosaics.

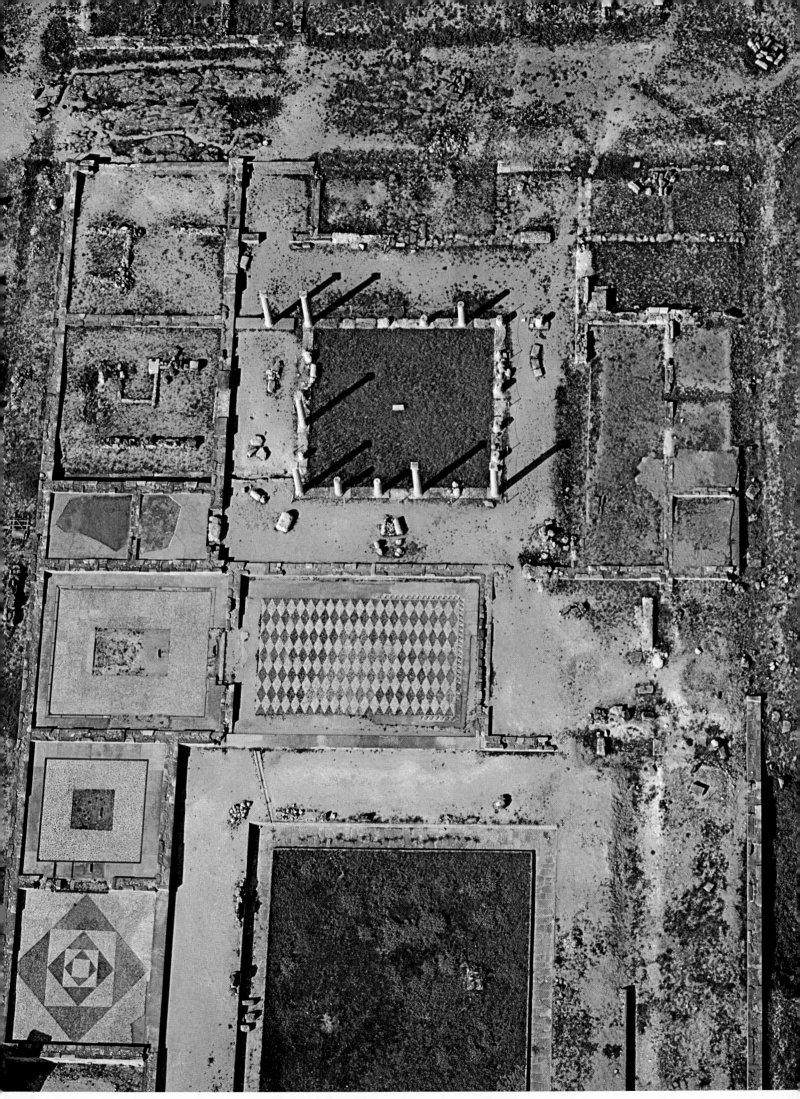

112. The peristyle court of the so-called house A at Pella, show-ing the magnificent mosaic composed of white and ash-blue *rhomboids which decorated the antechamber and the slender Ionic columns of the peristyle court.*

that, with very few exceptions, it was on the ground floor of the north wing that the finest, most formal rooms were located — those with mosaic floors, which were usually reception rooms and rooms in which the owners relaxed.

CEMETERIES AND TOMBS

The cemeteries were located a considerable distance out-side the defensive enceinte during the early Hellenistic period and somewhat closer to them later. They invariably stretched alongside the roads leading from the main gates of the cities and consisted of groups of rock-cut or built cist-graves, or sometimes of groups of rock-cut vaulted tombs.

Until about the end of the third century B.C. 'Macedo-nian' tombs were also built as the last resting place of a

small group of citizens, clearly belonging to the ruling class, which alone possessed the economic means to con-struct them.

Macedonian tombs

The term 'Macedonian tomb' is used to describe the sub-terranean built, vaulted funerary monuments that are found throughout the Greek world and the eastern Mediterranean more generally but which are particularly common in Macedonia, from which they derive their name.[22]

Depending on the wealth and status of the owner, some of the tombs have two chambers (those at Vergina and Langada, tomb I at Dion, etc.) and others a single chamber (the tombs at Toumba in Paionia, Olynthos, Larisa, Vatheia in Euboia, etc.). The facade is usually an imitation of the facade of a temple, with Doric or Ionic half-columns and the corresponding entablature and pediment. The tombs exhibit so many differences, however, that it is difficult to classify them, even though the number of known examples is fairly large.

Macedonian tombs, as we have noted, were subterranean: they were covered with earth, forming a tumulus, or *toumba,* around which trees were planted, in accordance with ancient custom. The deliberate burial of the monument in this fashion meant that the often very expensive structure, which frequently had an exceptionally fine facade, remained totally invisible to human eyes and was intended to be seen only by the gods of the underworld.

The material most used in the construction of these tombs was the soft poros that abounds in Macedonia; to transport marble from elsewhere would have been both difficult and expensive. This 'precious' material was used only for the leaves of the doors (where there were such leaves) and for the lintels. In order to soften the appearance of the rather rough surface of the stone, the facade and the interior wall surfaces were coated with a plaster designed to look like marble. One of the most impressive features of the tombs is the wealth of tones and shades of colours used to accentuate architectural details, to enliven scenes containing many figures, to add vigour to compositions of plant motifs, to give a chiaroscuro effect to isolated scenes, and to imitate the interiors of houses of the period.

The burial chamber normally contained a funerary bed — usually a large, dressed poros slab, more rarely a real marble bed — on which the body of the deceased was laid. Some tombs had rectangular hollows in the wall to receive the ashes after the body been cremated (the tomb of Lyson and Kallikles); lastly, others had a monolithic table with a hollow to hold an ossuary (the 'Haliakmon dam' tomb). The tomb at Vergina (Rhomaios' tomb), in which there was a marble throne as well as the bed, is a rare, perhaps unique, example and calls to mind the famous ornate palanquin built to carry the body of Alexander the Great from Persia to Alexandria. Some of the tombs (mainly in eastern Macedonia), have built, rock-cut or dug-out *dromoi* leading to their facades. The entrance to the monument is closed sometimes with a rather roughly constructed wall of poros, as in the Great Tomb at Lefkadia and (probably) Kinch's Tomb, and sometimes with superb double marble doors designed in imitation of wooden doors, as in the two Macedonian tombs near Palatitsa and Vergina (the Heuzey and Rhomaios tombs). In some cases the inner door leading to the burial chamber was also a two-leaf marble door (the Rhomaios tomb at Vergina, the tomb at Langada and Kinch's Tomb).

It is clear that these monuments normally served as family tombs from the great number of burials found in many of them, and from the repairs and additions to the facade and interior of some of them, taken in conjunction with the ancient literary evidence.

As far as we can tell at present, the 'Macedonian' tombs all belong to the period from about the middle of the fourth century B.C. up to the end of the first quarter of the second century B.C. — which coincides with the period at which the Macedonian kingdom was at its most flourishing.

One of the most important of the tombs is the 'Great Tomb of Lefakdia'[23] or the 'tomb of the Judgement', which is built entirely of the poros that is so plentiful in this area. It consists of two vaulted rooms — the main burial chamber and the antechamber. The grandiose facade is of striking dimensions (height 8.60 m., width 8.68 m.) and has two storeys. The intercolumnar spaces between the Doric half-columns of the lower storey are given over to four paintings which form the centre of attraction on account of their originality and the grandeur of their subject matter. The paintings form a four-figure scene, the subject of which is unique in monumental art and which is worthy of the building it adorns; the dead man is being taken by Hermes, the escorter of souls, to Hades, to face judgement by the judges of the underworld, Aiakos and Rhadamanthys; the few parallels for the scene known from vase painting do not compare with it either in size or quality.

The relief frieze is made of stucco, which was nailed to the wall in several places. Its subject is a battle between cavalry and infantry, Greeks and barbarians — and very probably between Macedonians and Persians. The latter can be distinguished by their colourful breeches and head dresses, the former by their *chlamydes* and breast-plates. The scene consists of a series of pairs of infantryman and horseman, of two infantrymen, and even of two horsemen, locked in a life or death struggle. The horseman at the left end of the frieze may perhaps not unreasonably be identified with the deceased for whom the tomb was built, portrayed here as a warrior in one of the many victorious battles fought by the Macedonian army in the heart of Asia.

The eleven metopes — three above the entrance and two above each of the spaces between the columns — have painted scenes from the legendary confrontation between the Centaurs and the Lapiths.

Only three pieces of the tympanum of the pediment survive, some of them still having traces of blue stucco and, more importantly, of the relief decoration with which they were adorned. The antechamber is a parallelogram of imposing dimension (6.50 m. ×2.12 m. and a maximum estimated height of 7.70 m.) with simple decoration, in which the dominating features are the two relief circular shields, 0.78 m. in diameter, to the right and left of the door to the burial chamber.

The burial chamber itself is almost square (4.80 m. ×4.72 m., with a maximum height of 5.26 m.) and is paved with poros. The upright slabs at the base of the walls stand on a toichobate 0.50 m. high, and form a podium of about 1.20 m. in height that serves as a stylobate to support a row of relief pilasters (*antae*). The front of each *anta* capital is decorated with Ionic kymatia and blue bands, while the intervals between the pilasters are painted a deep red colour. The whole is surmounted by an Ionic architrave and a relief cornice that marks the springing of the barrel vault forming the roof.

113-115. *One of the most important Macedonian tombs is the Great Tomb of Lefkadia near Naousa. It dates to the beginning of the 3rd century B.C. In the lower storey, four half-columns support a Doric frieze with triglyphs and metopes depicting incidents from the Centauromachy. Above that is a band with painted plant motifs and then a plaster frieze, moulded and painted with scenes from the War of the Macedonians and the Persians.*

The second storey is made up of Ionic half-columns separated by blind windows with imitation wooden shutters. A painted scene, which dominates the facade, occupies four panels between the half-columns of the first storey. It depicted the judgement of the Dead, where the dead man (114) is accompanied by Hermes to the two judges of the underworld, Aiakos and Rhadamanthys (115).

The Great Tomb at Lefkadia, or at least the first phase of its construction, dates from the beginning of the first half of the third century B.C. Its original owner will undoubtedly have been a member of the glorious generation of Alexander the Great — a veteran of the battles against the Persians who died at an advanced age and was buried with exceptional honours in the soil of Bottiaia, on the fringes of ancient Mieza.

The Rhomaios tomb at Vergina (so called after its discoverer, Professor K. Rhomaios) is another good example of a variation on the basic architectural type.[24] Built of poros (only the door leaves, the jambs and the lintels are of marble), it consists of a square chamber with a side measuring 4.66 m., and a smaller antechamber. One important architectural feature is the way the walls slope inwards.

The decoration of both the facade and the interior surfaces of the tomb is based on the use of painted plaster. The facade is emphasized by four unusually tall Ionic half-columns with nine flutings, whose bases have only a single moulding; both the half-columns and the wall between stand on a stylobate, 0.18 m. high. The half-columns follow the inward inclination of the walls and terminate in small, severe Ionic capitals that seem larger than they are thanks to their rich painted decoration; they recall similar examples from the Philippeion at Olympia. The elegant entablature is made up of a two-tiered architrave with an Ionic kymation, a frieze crowned by a relatively deep-stepped cornice and two Lesbian kymatia. The whole is crowned by a pediment with a sima that appears to have been richly decorated. The most imposing part of the front of the tomb, however, is the frieze above the architrave, adorned with pairs of decorative palmettes.

The tomb has an imposing entrance with marble door leaves, leading to the antechamber. The walls are covered with stucco, in which the artist has essayed a pictorial representation of masonry, indicating the joints between the stones by gilded incisions. A striking frieze with alternating multi-coloured flowers runs round the sides of the room. Compared with the exterior frieze, in which white is the predominating colour, the decoration here is more complex and its variety resides in its decorative details, rather than in the overall composition.

In contrast with the rich decoration of the antechamber, that of the burial chamber itself has a severe simplicity and austerity. A bright blue band bordered by an Ionic kymation above it and a Lesbian kymation below runs round all four walls of the room at a height of 2.22 m. above the floor; holes can be seen at intervals, made by nails on which the relatives of the deceased had hung his weapons and armour, his clothes, and some of his personal possessions. The body of the deceased was laid on the poros bed in the left corner of the burial chamber. In the right corner, facing the entrance to the chamber, was a striking marble throne, 1.98 m. in height, standing on a base, also of marble, 0.15 m. high. Elegant and unpretentious, with a footstool carved from a separate block of marble, it forms an instructive comparison with wooden models. The attachment of the seat to the legs, where the one appears to be supporting the other, is not uncharacteristic, whereas the legs are unusually high. They rise above the horizontal line of the seat itself to support a sphinx carved in the round on which the armrests are carried; about calf-level a carved anthemion breaks the vertical line. The delicate workmanship in the palmette, where the leaves are painted a deep red colour and give a three-dimensional effect, is most impressive. There is an equally impressive painted scene on the side of the throne: within a broad band, or panel, 0.61 m. long and 0.165 m. high two griffins are tearing a deer to pieces, the whole rendered very economically in the encaustic technique. This fascinating composition has a remarkable harmony of colour, clarity of decoration, and richness.

OTHER BURIAL BUILDINGS

The middle and lower social classes used simple pit graves (in the area around Naousa and elsewhere) or, at best, built cist-graves (Thessalonike, Beroia, Vergina, Derveni, Sedes,[25] Pella, Amphipolis, etc.) in which to bury their dead. Although these were not generally distinguished for their elaborate construction methods or the wealth of grave goods they contained (the tombs at Derveni and Nikisiani near Mt. Pangaion are exceptions, of course[26]), a good number of the cist-graves had plastered interiors with bands of decorative motifs or narrative scenes, or had paintings on the walls depicting the grave goods that accompanied the deceased (tombs at Amphipolis, Pella, Mikhaniona near Thessalonike).

The predominant type of tomb in Macedonia from the end of the third to the first centuries B.C. was undoubtedly the rock-cut vaulted tomb with either one or two chambers, which may or may not have had an architecturally modelled facade.[27] The origins of this type are possibly to be sought in Cyprus or Egypt, but the form in which it is known in Macedonia undoubtedly owes much to a variety of influences from other areas. The slightly earlier 'Macedonian' tombs in this region will certainly have had a decisive influence on the monumental form taken by their facades (at least for Bottiaia). Tombs of this type (Beroia, Edessa, Amphipolis etc) were usually family tombs. Most of them had beds hewn into the soft rock for the body of the deceased, and arcosolia and niches cut into the walls for offerings. The outer doorways sometimes took an architectural form and sometimes consisted of simple rectangular openings closed by courses of dressed blocks of poros.

MOSAIC FLOORS

The bedding for mosaics was prepared in a fairly simple manner in the Hellenistic period: a firm foundation was constructed of layers of soil flattened with a marble roller, on which the ancient mosaic-workers laid the substructure proper, which consisted of a thick layer of river pebbles dipped in liberal quantities of mortar and set in closely packed rows. This was followed by a fine intermediate layer, also of water resistant mortar with a small quantity of gravel, and finally by the mosaic itself, the tesserae being small natural pebbles. The care that went into the preparation of the substructure was designed to produce a water-proof layer that would prevent the delicate floor from being destroyed by the dampness in the soil.[28]

The main differences between the two major groups of mosaic floors in Macedonia — those at Olynthos and those of Pella and Vergina — may be summarized as follows: in the mosaics of Olynthos, which were early examples of the art (fifth-fourth centuries B.C.), the figures are rendered for the most part in light colours on a dark background, a technique that connects them with the red-figure vase-painting of the period. The decorative motifs — palmettes, meanders and spiral-meanders — form an organic part of the overall composition, their severely geometrical shapes recalling weaving patterns, by which they must have been influenced. At Pella and Vergina, by contrast, the use of different coloured pebbles for the details gives rise to chiaroscuro effects and foreshortening. In conjunction with the wide range of colour, use was made in places, particularly the outlines of figures, of applied strips of fired clay or lead, making it possible to achieve a three-dimensional treatment of the figures. As a result, the scene, which is usually of a monumental character, assumes a grandeur which is otherwise only associated with works of large-scale painting. This impression is confirmed most strongly by the suggestion, albeit on a limited scale, of the natural space in which the scene is set.

The mosaic floors uncovered by the excavations at ancient Pella are all dated,[29] like the houses in which they were found, to the last quarter of the fourth century B.C.; some have decorative geometric motifs while others depict scenes taken from mythology or from history. White and black river pebbles were used in the former, in which the main decorative motifs are rhombuses in alternating light and dark shades, or patterns of inscribed squares and triangles, also in light and dark.

The second group of mosaics (figs. 116, 117) are used either as the central motifs or panels in the decoration of the main hall (andron), or to adorn the threshold between the antechambers and the hall (the mosaic of Dionysos, the Lion-hunt, the Battle of the Amazons, the Deer-hunt, the Rape of Helen, a fragmentary mosaic with palmettes, the mosaic of the centaurs, and a griffin tearing apart a deer).

Of the mosaic floors with iconographic scenes, discovered at Vergina, that in room E, with a plant motif, is preserved in very good condition.[30] It has greater delicacy of detail and is technically more competent than the mosaic at Pella with a similar motif, and has a fluid linear rendering of the main motif that nonetheless has a suggestion of perspective. The central motif is rich in colour and design: in the centre is a whitish flower with eight petals

and eight sepals, from which spring lyre-shaped decorative motifs with slender, waving stalks, broad-leaved acanthus flowers and spiral tendrils curling round lotus flowers. In each corner of the square room, set as though in spandrels, there is a young female figure — half human and half flower — wearing a *polos* on her head and holding branches in her hands.

As yet, no mosaic floors dating from the third and second centuries B.C. are known from Macedonia. This may be due to the fact that they were very expensive to construct, or because the luxury and sumptuousness of the years immediately after Alexander's death did not continue into the succeeding centuries; it is certainly accounted for in part by the limited scale of archaeological discoveries.

PAINTING

From as early as the time of Archelaos, the Macedonian court had played host to some of the most famous painters of antiquity. After the accession to the throne of Philip II in the middle of the fourth century B.C., the multifarious royal interests attracted to Macedonia the flower of the Greek intelligentsia — philosophers, poets, historians and, along with them, the great painters of the period. From the moment at which the new military power deemed it to be an indispensable, indeed, self-evident, aspect of its political propaganda, to celebrate and immortalize the grandeur of its inspirer through painting, it was thought proper that wealth, too, should find expression through expensive wall-paintings — so much so, that even subterranean tombs were decorated with large-scale paintings. As Quintilian was to write epigrammatically in the first century A.D. 'It was, however, from about the period of the reign of Philip down to that of the successors of Alexander that painting flourished more especially...' At a time when Aristotle's vision of a philosopher king seemed to be acquiring flesh and bones, first in the form of the learned ruler and patron of the arts, Philip, then in the unique character of the 'philhellene' Alexander, after him in Cassander and finally in the person of Antigonos Gonatas, pupil of the Cynic philosopher Menedemos, it was inconceivable that painting, and all the fine arts, should remain without patrons, especially when they served the authority of those very patrons.[31]

It has been observed that whereas the classical moment in sculpture coincided with the classical moment of Greek thought and culture generally in the Athens of Perikles, painting reached its apogee when the city-state was facing dissolution and the monarchic states were rising in the firmament of political life. At the moment of its creative climax, painting was thus called upon to serve a non-classical patron, and an ideal that transcended the narrow boundaries of Greece to acquire a panhellenic and oecumenical character.

The great achievements and huge strides made, mostly

116. The mosaic floors at Pella display a more advanced technique than those of Olynthos. Their chief characteristics are the alternation of coloured tesserae and the use of thin strips of clay or lead to emphasize detail. In the picture, Dionysos rides a panther, grasping the neck of the animal in one hand and a thyrsos in the other. End of the 4th century B.C.

117. A deer hunt; detail from the well-known mosaic whose
maker, Gnosis, put his signature on it. By calculated sophistication, foreshortening and chiaroscuro he succeeds in conveying a
sense of space and three-dimensionality.

118. Detail from a beautiful painted stele from the filling of the Great Tumulus of Vergina. The woman's face is rendered with delicacy and grace, reminiscent of figures in Renaissance art. End of the 4th century B.C. Beroia, Archaeological Museum.

rigeur to give some indication of space — closed or open — to define the place in which the events are taking place (fresco on the facade of the Great Tomb at Vergina).

Apelles of Kolophon, or possibly Kos,[32] who was perhaps the greatest painter of antiquity, was Alexander the Great's personal painter. One of his many works depicting the Macedonian warrior, at Ephesos, portrayed Alexander on horseback; another, in the same city, showed him holding a thunderbolt, like a second Zeus. He was given permission to paint Pankaspe, Alexander's official concubine. Apelles was also said to have worked for Philip before Alexander, while after the latter's death we find him painting for Ptolemy I in Egypt. It was Apelles, too, who painted the portrait of Antigonos Monophthalmos, the father of Demetrios Poliorketes. Apelles was particularly interested in technique; he is even said to have invented a kind of black paint, the shade of burnt ivory, and to have used a thin polish that softened the effect of his colours, while at the same time protecting them. The most distinctive feature of his work, however, on which the ancient tradition lays great emphasis, was the grace of his facial expressions.

One of Apelles' great rivals was Protogenes of Kaunos, or Xanthos, though the various anecdotes surviving from antiquity portray the two as friends; Apelles is even said to have promoted Protogenes. Tradition has it that Aristotle urged him to paint the achievements of Alexander, on the grounds that a theme of that nature carried with it eternal glory. Protogenes, however, mockingly depicted Alexander as Dionysos accompanied by Pan. He was famous for his craftsmanship and his insistence on detail.

Nikomachos of Thebes, of the generation before Apelles, was the teacher of Philoxenos of Eretria, who painted the famous battle of Issos. Nikomachos owed his fame to the skill with which he combined power with grace and to the speed with which he executed his paintings. His works included a portrait of Antipater.

Lucian records that Aëtion,[33] who probably lived during the second half of the fourth century and served his apprenticeship in the Attic-Theban school, painted the wedding of Alexander and Roxane, giving it an erotic, playful tone. The painting must have received praise, for it was later carried off to Italy as booty.

Macedonia itself, however, also produced great painters. Pamphilos, the teacher of Apelles and head of the Sikyonian school, came from Amphipolis. Herakleides and Metrodoros of Stratonike, who were active just before the Roman conquest of Macedonia, were also Macedonians; the latter was a philosopher and is said to have followed Aemilius Paullus to Rome to act as tutor to his children and to paint his military successes. In the years that followed, if not before this date, painting was to adorn other houses, serve other masters and commemorate other achievements. For centuries, however, it would learn from and be inspired by its ancient glories.

In contrast with the wealth of information preserved in the written tradition, the surviving examples of large-scale painting in Macedonia are very few, and are restricted

in technique, in the period between roughly the middle of the fourth century B.C. and the Roman conquest were mainly in the attempt to render three-dimensionality. Typical of these achievements are the skilful deployment of chiaroscuro and foreshortening, the rendering of depth and three-dimensions by creating a series of planes of action, the interlocking of human figures and objects, and the disposition of details according to the rules of perspective. The scenes depicted now become multifigural, movement is frequently particularly pronounced, and it becomes *de* almost exclusively to wall paintings in 'Macedonian' tombs (executed in both the *a freso* and *a secco* techniques) and to the decorative painting on marble grave stelai (in the encaustic technique) (fig. 118). The samples of stucco from residential buildings are very few in number and are adorned with motifs of a purely decorative nature (Pella). In evaluating the artistic merit of the wall paintings (narrative scenes and decorative motifs) that adorned the last resting places of the powerful figures of the period, however, and in comparing them with the descriptions preserved in the literary tradition of works by the great artists, or with the surviving Roman copies, the limitations under which they were produced must be taken into consideration: the painted scenes in the Macedonian tombs have a specific character and frequently serve a particular purpose in an almost routine manner — the decoration of a monument which, by its very nature, was destined to be buried as soon as its painting was complete. These observations in no way detract from the quality and the originality of the funerary painting in Hellenistic Macedonia, which, more often than not, reflects the artistic currents and the technical achievements of the large-scale painting of the period.

The impressionistic tendency reflected in the rendering of three-dimensional volumes and of chiaroscuro through skilful use of colour stands in contrast with and represents a different conception of painting from the delineation of contours in an attempt to isolate the figures and make them stand out from the background against which they are portrayed; both techniques are represented in the wall paintings that fill the spaces between the columns on the facade of the Great Tomb at Lefkadia, where the deceased and Rhadamanthys are treated in a fundamentally different way from Hermes and Aiakos, the other judge. In the former pair, the linear values of drawing predominate, and the volumes are rendered by close-set, delicate lines, sometimes in a light and sometimes in a dark colour; in the latter, the three-dimensional volumes are given expression through the use of colour. The same impressionistic tendencies can be seen in a variety of objects drawn from everyday life painted on the surface of the walls in some of the tombs, which are treated in such a way as to give them a three-dimensional effect and make them quite lifelike. In the tomb of Lyson and Kallikles at Lefkadia (last quarter of the third century B.C.),[34] the appropriate use of a range of shades of green, from dark olive-green to the light shade of pistacchios, gives the leaves of the garland encircling the interior of the building a very lifelike appearance; and in the same tomb, the plain dark yellow used for the armour and trophies, the large 'Macedonian' shield and the greaves (this on the tympana of the short walls) convincingly reproduces the lustre of bronze, while the curved surfaces are rendered in warm red and orange (figs. 96, 97). The limpidity of the water in the *perirrhanterion* in the antechamber is suggested by the use of a sky-green colour, and the veins of the marble of the *toichobates* in the main chamber are rendered by oblique grey-brown lines. A similar aesthetic effect is achieved in the plant decoration on the ceiling of the antechamber of the Tomb of the

Anthemia at Lefkadia, though in this case the naturalism of the motif (anthemia, water plants, etc.) achieves a formalized sophistication.

Entire buildings, or sections of buildings are painted in this same illusionistic spirit, creating the impression of multi-dimensional space and a succession of planes with a depth of perspective (tomb of Lyson and Kallikles; painted stelai from Vergina and Demetrias).

Finally, the use of a monochrome technique to render scenes from the mythical battle of the Centaurs and Lapiths on the metopes of the Great Tomb at Lefkadia, where the figures are all painted in a yellow-grey colour, reveals yet another approach to the painting of a subject, which today would be called a 'study'.

POTTERY

The local pottery of Macedonia, at least from what is known of it from the fourth century B.C. onwards, is distinguished neither for its originality, nor for the quality of the materials used in it — far less for its technical excellence. The interests and imagination of the local potters were content to move within a repertoire composed of conservative shapes, many of them strongly reminiscent of similar types dating from the Early Iron Age, or even earlier, and rather clumsy imitations of Athenian black-glazed ware, with its characteristic ash-grey colour and usually without any burnishing. To date there has been no attempt to produce a typology of this pottery, and it can only be dated when samples of it are found together with imported Athenian pottery (for example, in cemeteries near Kozani and Naousa, at Pella and elsewhere). In Chalkidike, there was some production of local imitations of Attic red-figure vases alongside this monochrome ware, particularly in the fourth century B.C., due mainly to the proximity of the southern Greek colonies. The pottery in question consists of black-figure vases with palmette motifs that suggest parallels with pottery from Boiotia and southern Italy, and some frequently large vases in reddish clay with rich decoration (group from Pyrgadikia).[35]

In the years that followed, Macedonian pottery steadily lost its autonomy, and from the middle of the Hellenistic period was increasingly influenced by the art, the typology and the technique of the *koine* pottery, of which it was now a part.[36]

It has recently been suggested that one category of 'Megarian' bowls, consisting for the most part of pots with relief scenes from tragedies by famous poets or from the Homeric poems on their inner surfaces (dating from the mid-second century B.C.) are really local products and should be called 'Macedonian' bowls.[37]

METALWORK — MINIATURE ART

Until a few years ago, our knowledge of the achievements in the sphere of the goldsmith's art in the early

Hellenistic period was limited almost entirely to what could be learnt from the wealth of imported finds in tombs discovered in southern Russia last century. In the inter-war years, however, a number of chance finds in Macedonia and Thessaly brought to light a considerable quantity of jewellery of great significance artistically, and of precious vases dating from the fourth century B.C., some of them forming sets. And since the Second World War, intensive excavation activity throughout the length and breadth of Macedonia, mostly in the form of rescue digs, has resulted in the discovery and the study of groups of jewellery and vessels mostly found in tombs and dating from the late third and, in the main, from the early second centuries B.C.[38]

Gold was always scarce in Greece. The mines of Siphnos and Thasos had already been exhausted by the end of the classical period, and the new vein discovered by Philip II in the foothills of Mt. Pangaion about the middle of the fourth century B.C. seems to have run out very quickly. No one now doubts that the route followed by Alexander the Great in his campaign against the Persian empire was selected not only for political and strategic reasons, but also in an attempt to discover regions rich in gold and goldmines. After the defeat of Darius at the battle of Issos, and the capture of the Persian empire and, along with it, the royal treasury, unprecedented quantities of precious metals appear to have flooded into Greece. Even though the great warrior failed to unify the ancient world, he did succeed in creating a vast Greco-Persian state, a major contribution to its character being made by the fruitful interaction of the artistic and cultural achievements of each nation. Persian art and opulence were known to the Greeks earlier than this, of course, as a result of the frequent contacts between them since the fifth century B.C., most of them admittedly hostile rather than peaceful. It is certain, however, that after the conquest of the Persian empire, first the Macedonians and then the rest of the Greeks were greatly impressed by the exquisite Persian jewellery and precious vases which they copied and transformed, and into which they breathed new life. The influence on both motifs and typology is quite clear. The basic morphological features that had always been typical of Greek art and constituted its distinctive identity, however, continued to form the basic canvas whose threads, the Hellenistic *koine* of gold and metalwork, were to be interwoven with new experiences. In this world, graceful palmettes and delicate tendrils on exquisite diadems from tombs at Sedes and Thessalonike wave in the wind; here gold and silver brooches from tombs in the area of Derveni arch their bodies tensely; the breath of the new era ruffles the myrtle leaves on the gold crowns from Amphipolis, and Erotes spread their wings in flight on floral earrings. And a whole world of animals, both wild and domesticated, stand at the end of fine chains and heavy bracelets, unsleeping guardians and protectors on the clasp of the jewellery. The women of Macedonia and Thessaly beautified themselves with a new range of expensive jewellery: chariots, driven by Victories, that course wildly in mythical competitions;

dancing girls whirling in fantastic dances; chain-mesh hairnets surmounted by superb relief 'medallions'; diadems blossoming with frontlets of semi-precious stones or with figures worked in the round; and necklaces that are true masterpieces of 'weaving'. Archaeological finds have demonstrated that the privileged owners of treasures like these usually possessed an entire range of jewellery, which they will undoubtedly have worn on special occasions (figs. 122-126).

One particularly characteristic feature of the jewellery of this period is the great variety of colour: alongside the granulated and filigree decorative techniques, use was made of precious and, more commonly, semi-precious coloured stones (emeralds, sards, agate etc) to point up the details, giving these masterpieces of the goldsmith's art a superb aesthetic quality.

IVORIES

Under miniature art we should include a number of small ivory plaques[39] with elegant incised figures and relief decorative motifs, which are paralleled by finds in southern Russia thought to have been imports. They are mainly overlays from wooden chests found in tombs at Derveni, Sedes near Thessalonike, Lefkadia and also in Thessaly.

TABLEWARE

The custom of collecting expensive sets of tableware, usually made of precious metals, had its roots in this period. It was clearly intended as a display of wealth and affluence, and the custom continued to be practised until the end of the Hellenistic period, when it was imitated by the Romans and was later handed on to the Renaissance. In contrast with the Classical period, local centres of silver ware multiplied from about the middle of the fourth century, and provincial styles developed. At the same time, the free movement of artists and craftsmen working in this sphere resulted in the creation of a common art, inspired by a common tradition. The dynasts of the peripheral states and the new lords of the world took pleasure in the possession of these precious vessels, which usually accompanied them to their final resting place. New types of vases were invented and, in the quest for vessels with more

119. Bronze statuette of a young girl found at Beroia. It is considered to be one of the best examples of modelling of the post-Lysippian period, although this dating is often questioned. Munich, Staatliche Antikensammlungen und Glypotek.

120-121. Two pieces of metalwork from Pella, probably both decorative elements from the same wooden bed. The supports of the head-board (121) terminate in an ass's head between vine leaves and grapes, while the lower part is decorated with a bust of Dionysos. 2nd century B.C. Pella, Archaeological Museum.

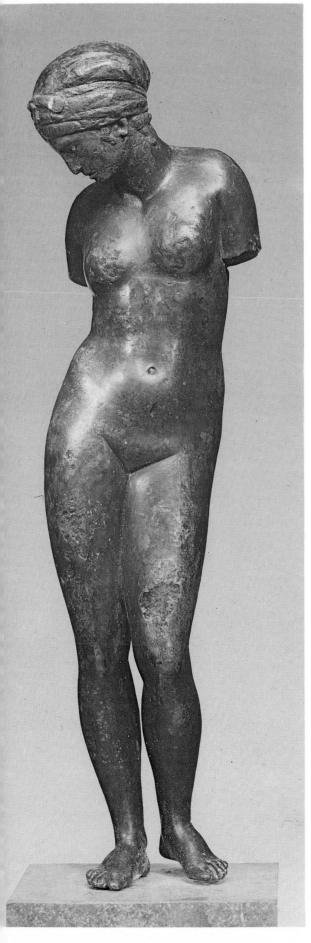

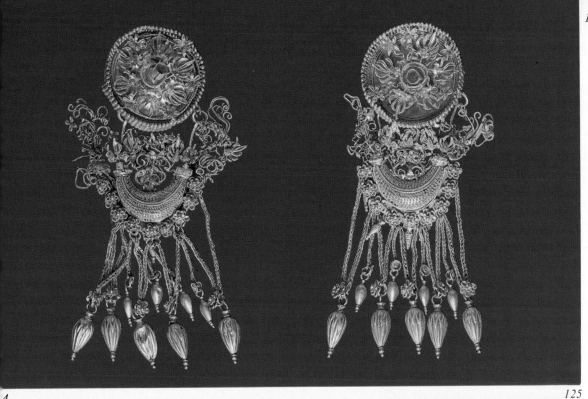

122. Gold wreath of olive leaves from Derveni. End of the 4th century B.C. Thessalonike, Archaeological Museum.

123. Gold earrings from Derveni with exquisite plant decoration of spirals, palmettes, small blossoms and fruit. End of the 4th century B.C. Thessalonike, Archaeological Museum.

124. Two arched fibulae of gold from Beroia. Second half of the 4th century B.C. Beroia, Archaeological Museum.

125. Gold earrings in pyramidal shape from Amphipolis with filigrane decoration. At the edges and corners are applied gold pellets. Second half of the 4th century B.C. Kavala, Archaeological Museum.

126. A gold ornament; acanthus leaves are worked into a heraldic composition of spirals, tendrils and flowers, terminating in palmettes on the outer edges. It was found at Stavroupolis, near Thessalonike in 1974. Second half of the 4th century B.C. Thessalonike, Archaeological Museum.

sophisticated shapes, earlier types were now adapted to the new demands of the buying public. The delicate shapes and, above all, the simple construction of the pottery at the beginning of the period gave way to elegant vases, with particularly contrived decoration, frequently involving the application of three-dimensional attachments. Here, too, many of the models are to be sought in the world of the East: some of the decorative solutions may be connected with motifs familiar in the earlier art of Persia and Egypt. The basis is still clearly Greek, however, and restraint never gives way to *hubris*. Ladles, strainers and plates, *kantharoi* and kylikes, skyphoi and bossed *phialai*, kadoi and elaborate amphorae formed the sets used at the Macedonian symposia, famous for their opulence, and accompanied the dead to the after-life. The range of toilet-articles included *pyxides*, mirrors with relief scenes and perfume bottles.[40]

The years from 221 to 168 B.C. which saw the long reign of Philip V and the troubled early years of his son Perseus, were the last period of Macedonian independence before the country was split up into four administrative areas by the new masters of the world, the Romans. The steady decline in the economic resources of the state, especially after the turn of the third century B.C. and the weakening of the country in terms of manpower as a result of the long and bloody wars fought in the attempt to execute the ambitious, not to say vainglorious, plans of Philip V and the imprudent policies of Perseus in the face of the impending danger, are reflected accurately in the finds revealed by the excavation of settlements and tombs of the period.[41]

The economic straits in which the inhabitants of Macedonia found themselves in the first half of the second century B.C. are attested by the translation into cheap materials (clay, lead) of the shapes of vessels originally made in precious metals; by the huge numbers of uniform, cheaply made, clay pots found in the tombs as funerary offerings — clearly reflecting a desire on the part of the relatives of the deceased to compensate through quantity for the lost quality and affluence; and by the way in which the faces of loved ones were adorned with imitations of real jewellery made of badly cut fine leaves of gold and silver with scenes, usually of a symbolic nature, chased lightly on them in low relief (tombs at Beroia and Amphipolis). There are a few cases, however, in which the deceased members of what seems to be a comparatively affluent class are accompanied by real jewellery, recalling happier times (tombs at Beroia, Thessalonike and Amphipolis).

It should be made clear at this point that the pillaging of Macedonian treasures by the Romans (for example, the three-day triumph of Aemilius Paullus in Rome[42]) mainly involved the plundering of the wealth stored in the royal treasuries and household; of various works of art, both contemporary and earlier; and of the family heirlooms belonging to the royal family. It did not involve looting of the personal valuable possessions of the middle classes, who had been devastated economically by repeated upheavals caused by population transplants and war.

127. *Statuette of Aphrodite from Beroia. The goddess is leaning against a column on top of which sits a Cupid. In her left hand she holds a cornucopia and in her right a mask of Silenos. 2nd century B.C. Beroia, Archaeological Museum.*

128. *Statuette of Athena. The goddess wears a peplos fastened with a brooch fashioned as a gorgon's head. On her head she wears a head-dress in the form of bull's horns. It is perhaps a copy of the cult statue of Athena Alkidemos whose worship is attested at Pella. Thessalonike, Archaeological Museum.*

MACEDONIA
UNDER THE ROMANS

POLITICAL AND ADMINISTRATIVE DEVELOPMENTS
148 B.C. — 3rd century A.D.

REPUBLICAN MACEDONIA

The Twenty Years of Nominal Independence

The defeat of Perseus at Pydna was fatal not only to the Antigonid monarchy, but also to the Macedonian state itself. There followed twenty years of partial freedom, after which the Macedonians were never again to enjoy an independent political life. Such was the tragic end to which the illustrious state of Philip and Alexander came, an end which must have painfully affected all Macedonians. The annihilation of the army in the terrible slaughter at Pydna, the deportation of the royal family and the exile of the Macedonian élite, the seizure of immense loot and the confiscation of the royal estates and mines, all left the country decapitated, as it were, humiliated and disoriented. Could anyone guess that the fatal year 168 B.C. marked the end of Macedonia?

Indeed Rome did not immediately proceed to annex conquered Macedonia, either because she lacked the means to keep so vast a country in subjection, or because she still preferred to dissimulate her expansionist aims behind the liberator's mask. According to the formula preserved by Livy, the Senate decided and Aemilius Paullus proclaimed at Amphipolis 'that the Macedonians should be free, in order to demonstrate to all the world that the arms of the Roman people did not bring slavery to the free but freedom to the slaves'. For the Romans, 'freedom' was incompatible with kingship, though not with Roman tutelage. Thus they proclaimed that, by suppressing kingship, they gave each race the chance to live according to its own laws. Nor was

'freedom' incompatible with the subjection of the Macedonians to an annual tribute. By declaring the Macedonians free, the Romans committed themselves to withdraw their troops from the country — which they actually did — but only after having taken all necessary precautions against any risk of insurrection on the part of so redoubtable an enemy.

Macedonia was stripped of all its foreign possessions, but the integrity of its territory was in no way impaired. However, in order to prevent a resurgence of its power, Rome had recourse to a measure that was felt by the Macedonians to be the cruellest blow their nation had suffered: Macedonia was divided into four districts *(merides)*, and neither buildings nor land could be sold across boundaries. Marriages between people of different districts were also prohibited. Except in the case of Paionia, the division took account of the historic regional frontiers. Every district was organized as an administrative unit with a capital of its own (Amphipolis, Pella, Thessalonike and Pelagonia respectively), where representatives of the towns gathered to choose their common magistrates, and tax money was collected. According to the annalistic tradition, Macedonia was so vast and so easily divided that each one of its regions could be self-sufficient.[1] It is, however, probable (though the sources are not clear on this point) that the Senate allowed the Macedonians to create a common *synedrion*, covering the entire territory of Macedonia, and that, by dividing Macedonia into four *merides*, Rome did not cease to regard it as an ethno-political unity.[2]

The armed troops that the Macedonians had the right to post on their frontier seem to have been sufficient to keep the barbarians at bay, for there is no mention of any attacks during the following years. On the other hand, internal troubles are often mentioned during the period between the catastrophe of Pydna and the creation of the province of Macedonia, though their exact nature and extent are not clear.[3] Were these troubles patriotic, anti-Roman movements? Or were they social conflicts between the privileged classes and the masses, who must have suffered particularly from the disruption caused by the war and the ensuing defeat? Or were they due to personal rivalries? In fact nothing is more apt to engender intestine discords than foreign tutelage. According to Polybios, the explanation of these troubles lies in the fact that the Macedonians were unaccustomed to republican and deliberative government. But the possibility of the existence of patriotic movements should not, though, be underestimated in a period in which the freedom proclaimed by Rome could still be taken seriously, and the hope that national independence might still be restored did not yet appear a vain dream.

The insurrection of Andriskos, an adventurer who proclaimed himself to be the son of Perseus and was crowned at Pella in 149 B.C. under the name Philip, provoked a new military intervention on the part of Rome, and gave her the opportunity to put an end to this false state of independence. Andriskos succeeded in becoming master of the country, even though he encountered some resistance. Apart from his obscure origins and personal ambitions, one point is crucial to the understanding of his revolt: Andriskos relied on the lower social classes, and proceeded to proscribe the rich. Evidently, the Roman protectorate had deepened the social divisions in Macedonia. The ruling class was pro-Roman, while the poor, to whom we must add the slaves, desired the restoration of the monarchy. The appearance of another two pretenders to the throne of the Antigonids during the next few years shows that slogans against Rome and in favour of the monarchy evoked a response among the Macedonian masses.

After the repression of Andriskos' revolt, the Roman domination of Macedonia became an irreversible reality. Macedonia was finally incorporated into the Roman Commonwealth.

The formal transformation of the country into a Roman province is not expressly attested in the sources, and it is not easy to establish either the precise moment when the decision was taken, or to establish the exact significance of this reorganization.[4] The impression one has is that there were no extensive constitutional changes. Certainly there was no new *lex provinciae*: the laws laid down by Aemilius Paullus remained valid, the division of the country into four parts was also maintained, while the federal *synedrion*, if indeed there was one, must have been transformed, perhaps as early as 146 B.C. into a Macedonian *koinon*. In brief, the creation of the province becomes apparent to us only through the presence of the Roman governor and his legions, permanent from now onwards.

It is generally agreed that the so-called 'provincial era', which starts in the autumn of 148 B.C., is connected with the organization of the province. The results of recent research, however, suggest that the new era coincides with an act of gratitude commemorating the liberation of the country from the usurper and the restoration of the republic, which would suggest that the formation of the province should be dated after the autumn of 148 B.C.[5]

The province of Macedonia extended beyond the frontier as it had been in 167 B.C. In the west it extended as far as the Ionian Sea, comprising southern Illyria, which probably formed a part of the province right from the beginning, as it ensured direct communication between Italy and the new Balkan possessions. Yet, although Macedonia and Illyria were united under a common government for a period of over four centuries, they remained two entirely distinct countries from the ethnic and cultural point of view; indeed there is no indication in the sources that the two parts of the province were in any particularly close contact. In addition to Illyria, the authority of the governor of Macedonia extended to all territories north and south of Macedonia which had been conquered and annexed to the Roman Commonwealth. At the core of this immense province, whose northern frontiers were constantly extended until they reached the Danube and the Black Sea, Macedonia proper formed a well-defined unity, with stable frontiers.

Macedonia as the centre of military operations and of Roman expansion in the Peninsula

The period which extends from 148 B.C. to the Augustan era is one of the most difficult Macedonia experienced. Integrated into the Roman world, the Macedonians no longer had a history of their own. The events which took place in their land were only episodes against the wider backdrop of Roman history. Now it was up to the Roman governors to defend the country against the recurrent barbarian invasions, or to lead Roman arms beyond the frontier in an attempt to submit and pacify the neighbouring lands.[6] Yet all the destruction and pillage involved in such operations, with the carrying off of men and cattle, was not without effect on Macedonia itself. The security of its towns and inhabitants depended on the governors sent from Rome; and in this way the 'Roman benefactors', to whom Macedonia owed her 'freedom', became also her 'saviours'.

The appearance of the Roman legions in Macedonia does not seem, however, to have intimidated the barbarian tribes north of her territory. The protection of the province from the barbarians was the primary preoccupation of its governors during the pre-Sullan period, when the greatest danger for the province was represented by the Gallic tribe of the Skordiskoi, who lived at the confluence of the Sava and the Danube.[7] The decree of Lete (119 B.C.) provides an eloquent testimony to the terror inspired in the inhabitants by the raids of these aggressive horsemen and of other barbarians who accompanied them in their attacks.[8] The inscription in question offers a detailed description of the invasion, dwelling on the merits of the quaestor M. Annius, who put the barbarians to flight and found no need to call on the Macedonians to raise new forces. This earned him, among other rewards, the institution of annual games to honour him as an *euergetes*. Two other honorific inscriptions, respectively from Europos on the lower Axios and from Delphi, commemorate the victories of the consul for 110 B.C., M. Minucius Rufus, over the Skordiskoi, the Bessoi and other Thracian tribes.[9] Minucius repelled the Skordiskoi beyond the frontier and reduced them, at least for a time, to impotence. His campaign against the Bessoi

in the Rhodope region meant the opening of a new channel of expansion for the Romans.

During the long governorship of C. Sentius Saturninus (93-87 B.C.), a general uprising of the barbarians occurred. Apparently bribed and urged on by Mithridates, the Maidoi, Dardanians, Sintoi and other tribes entered the province from all sides and devastated it thoroughly. The raids were repeated every year, and in 88 B.C. the barbarians advanced as far as Dodona and pillaged the sanctuary of Zeus. Towards the end of 87 B.C. Macedonia was invaded by the troops of Mithridates. A year later, after the victories of Sulla in Boiotia, it was reoccupied by the Romans. Sulla stayed in Macedonia for some time and led the campaigns against the barbarians in person. In 84 B.C. the Skordiskoi, the Maidoi and the Dardanians invaded Macedonia yet again and advanced as far as Delphi, where they burned down the temple. This time the Roman counter-attack was violent; Scipio Asiagenus repelled the Skordiskoi once and for all. In the ensuing period the military activity of the Macedonian governors was concentrated outside the province, in expansionist campaigns against the Thracian tribes.

The rule of L. Calpurnius Piso (57-55 B.C.), who became famous thanks to the invective of Cicero, provoked an irruption of the Dardanians, the Bessoi and the Dentheletai, who, if we are to believe Cicero, attacked Macedonia in order to avenge the evil done by the proconsul: 'They threw our revenues into confusion, they captured our cities, they laid waste our lands, they led away our allies into slavery, they carried off their households, they drove off their cattle, and they compelled the people of Thessalonike, who despaired of saving their town, to fortify the citadel'.[10] The 'allies', i.e. the Macedonians, must have found themselves in truly lamentable straits.

A decade later, during the civil wars which set first Caesar against Pompey, then the defenders of the Republic against the triumvirs, Macedonia was one of the main theatres of hostilities.[11] From the spring of 49 B.C. until the battle of Pharsalos in August 48 B.C., the province became the residence of the exile Republican government and the centre of Pompey's military strength. Accompanied by the two consuls and by two hundred senators, Pompey established himself in Thessalonike, the official seat of the Macedonian governor. Under his command he had nine legions, and he directed in person the training and

129-131. *After the battle of Pydna the Romans divided Macedonia into four administrative areas,* merides, *each with its own centre, a measure which bitterly wounded the national pride of the Macedonians. The picture shows above: the two sides of a coin of Amphipolis, the 'first' area. Certain traditional Macedonian motifs have been retained, such as Herakles' club and the Macedonian shield. Below: the head of Andriskos, according to one view. The brief success of his rising in 149 B.C. was due to the nationalistic and markedly anti-Roman feeling in Macedonia. His action, however, gave the Romans the opportunity to impose tighter control over the province and bring it finally into the framework of the Roman world. Athens, Numismatic Museum, London, British Museum.*

manoeuvres of his troops in camp near Beroia. The task of supplying the army with provisions must have weighed heavily on the country.

After the battle of Pharsalos, Macedonia came under the authority of Caesar; and, after the director's death, it changed masters again several times. In the autumn of 44 B.C., Brutus succeeded in rallying Macedonia, Illyria and Greece to the republican side, and remained the master of the country until the battle of Philippi (October/November 42 B.C.). Then, from November 42 to September 31 B.C. Macedonia came under the jurisdiction of Mark Antony. The campaigns led by the proconsul M. Licinius Crassus after Aktion (2 September 31 B.C.) resulted in the establishment of Roman control over the region that extends between the Balkans and the Danube. Thus, by the first years of the Principate, a huge province was created consisting of all the central part of the peninsula, extending from cape Taenaron in the south to the Danube in the north, and from the Adriatic to the Black Sea.

Administrative organization of Macedonia under the Republic

Having been Rome's most dangerous rival Macedonia remained for a century after its subjection Rome's only Balkan province. It was in this capacity, as much as by virtue of its crucial position in the peninsula between Italy and Asia Minor, that it played so important a role in the history of Roman expansionism and in the civil wars. Described by Cicero as 'a source and breeding ground of triumphs',[12] Macedonia was for a long period one of the provinces most sought after by ambitious generals and by those who wished to make their fortune.

Yet, on the evidence of archaeological data, the Republican era was for Macedonia a period of economic and demographic decline. Unlike Epirus and Illyria, Macedonia was not devastated; nevertheless its enormous wealth was carried off and its human resources were exhausted. After their subjection to the Romans, the Macedonians submitted to their lot with resignation. Yet some time had to pass until the memories of so humiliating a catastrophe were obliterated and all hope of revolt abandoned. During the troubled years of Sentius Saturninus' rule, a last attempt at a rebellion against the Romans and a restoration of the *patrios basileia* was undertaken by a young Macedonian called Euphanes. But, dismissed even by the pretender's own father as a lost cause, the revolt was stifled at birth.[13] Cicero, who in the summer of 58 B.C. spent six months of his exile in Thessalonike, described Macedonia as a province loyal in friendship with the Roman people.[14] By that time, three generations after the defeat, a new upper class, relying on the forces of occupation, had already come into being.

The regular levies imposed on Macedonia do not seem to have been very heavy. The land tax *(stipendium)* was apparently equal to the tribute fixed by Aemilius Paullus at one hundred talents, perhaps half the sum that had previously been paid to the kings.[15] The exploitation of the iron and copper mines was ceded to concessionaires whose royalties were again half of what had been paid to the kings. From 157 B.C. the prohibition on the exploitation of the gold and silver mines was lifted. In all likelihood the gold mines were exhausted, but the great number of silver coins minted by the *merides* (especially the first one) shows that the silver mines were efficiently exploited, and causes one to think that the local governments must also have drawn some profit from their working. A regular and important part of the revenues that the public treasury of the Roman people drew from Macedonia came from the renting of the *ager publicus,* made up of the confiscated royal domains.[16]

The arbitrary conduct of its governors weighed even more heavily on the inhabitants than the laws that had been imposed on the province. The authority of the governor, who exercised military command and wielded supreme administrative and judicial power, was immense in the Republican period, while his accountability was almost non-existent.[17] In fact, it was only very rarely that the provincials dared bring a case of concussion against their governors to the courts in Rome, which anyway served as instruments of the political rivalries of the powerful rather than as bodies existing for the protection of the provinces. In case of urgent need, the governor had the right to make requisitions and order extraordinary levies. He could abuse his power on all sorts of pretexts without really risking his position. The speeches of Cicero against Verres and Piso show the kind of speculations, transactions and exactions to which a dishonest and greedy governor could have recourse if he wanted to amass riches by exploiting his province.

Another sphere in which the governor's authority was unchecked was that of compulsory recruitment. Though the provincials were not obliged to do military service, the governor could use his *imperium* to order local recruiting drives whenever he judged it necessary. In Macedonia this must have happened more often than in other provinces because of the barbarian invasions. During the last decades of the Republic the powerful military leaders did not hesitate to demand all sorts of contributions from the provinces and to form auxiliary units. The Macedonians went to war as 'allies' *(auxilia)* for Sulla, Pompey and Brutus.[18] The last even formed two Macedonian legions, which he trained in the Roman manner.[19] When necessary, the provincials were enrolled forcibly. There is also a reference to Macedonian mercenaries, though by that period the military profession does not seem to have appealed any longer to the Macedonians.

The integration of the Macedonians into the Roman world, which was completed only with the inauguration of the Augustan peace, was facilitated by one fact of prime importance: even before the Roman conquest there were in Macedonia autonomous towns and regional communities, which were subsequently consecrated by the Romans as administrative units.[20] Though these units were taxed they nevertheless seem to have retained the right, proclaimed by Aemilius Paullus, to use their own laws and to govern themselves. In so far as municipal institutions are concerned, the Republican era seems to have produced no innovation. Even politarchy, whose origin has been the subject of much discussion, can now be proven to date back to the period of the monarchy.[21]

The economic, demographic and cultural development of Roman Macedonia was strongly influenced by the construction of the Via Egnatia, the establishment of Roman merchants in the Macedonian towns and the creation of Roman colonies. The great road, which bears the name of its builder, the proconsul Cnaeus Egnatius, was an extension of the Via Appia and the maritime route from Brundisium to Dyrrachion and Apollonia, it formed the most direct and convenient line of communication between Rome and the East.[22] Built as a military road to facilitate the control of Roman possessions in the Balkan peninsula, the Via Egnatia soon became an instrument of the expansionist policy of Rome in the East. Thanks to it, both troops engaged in campaigns in the Balkans and the East and agents of the administration could move quickly from one place to another. At the same time, however, the road served as the artery for the peaceful immigration of Italian settlers, for the transportation of goods and for cultural exchanges. The oldest dated evidence we have for Roman merchants living in Macedonia is an inscription dedicated by the city of Beroia and 'the Romans resident there' in honour of the proconsul Calpurnius Piso, the rival of Cicero.[23] Other texts confirm the presence of Roman and Italian business men in Amphipolis, Apollonia and Pella, while, during the first decades of the Empire, Roman communities are attested in Akanthos, Idomenai, Styberra, Edessa and Thessalonike.[24] This influx of Roman merchants is a sign of the resurgence of economic life in Macedonia during the last period of the Republic, to whose revival they provided an important stimulus.

The installation of veterans in the provinces where they had fought was practised by Roman generals before the time of Caesar. Apparently, this colonization was undertaken on an individual basis, and the role played by the State in the allotment of land to the veterans is not quite clear. But they must have been quite numerous, since in 49 B.C. Pompey was able to recruit a legion from those who had gone to live in Macedonia and Crete after their demobilization.[25] But organized colonization did not start in Macedonia before the time of Caesar's successors, who, whether consciously or not, followed the dictator's innovatory policy, which aimed at the consolidation and unification of the empire. The first colonies were created in 43 or 42 B.C. at Kassandreia and Dion, on the order of Brutus. Immediately after the victory at Philippi, Octavian and Antony in turn decided to establish on the spot a number of the soldiers they had disbanded. It is less clear whether Pella had received her first colonists before 30 B.C. But after Aktion, on the initiative of Octavian, the existent colonies were 'refounded' and new ones created.[26] Though there were some veterans amongst them, the majority of newcomers to the colonies just mentioned were Italians, dispossessed by Octavian for the benefit of his own veterans. Our sources are silent as to the manner of acquisition of the lands which were divided among the colonists. It is highly probable that in the first place the *ager publicus* was used to this end, so that not much of it was left in the imperial era, a hypothesis that would explain the lack of information about the imperial domains during that period.

MACEDONIA DURING THE EARLY EMPIRE

The Augustan Peace

For Macedonia, as for most of the provinces, the establishment of the Principate marks the beginning of a period of peace, order and prosperity which lasted for almost three centuries. After the upheavals of the age of Caesar, the empire found in Augustus a master capable of giving it a constitution which ensured permanent stability, economic prosperity and cultural flowering from which all the inhabitants of the empire benefited. The Macedonians were quick to honour Augustus by inaugurating an 'Augustan era' starting on 2 September 31 B.C., the day of the victory at Aktion.[27]

In 27 B.C., when Augustus and the Senate divided the control of the provinces between them, Macedonia came under the administration of the Senate as a peaceful province. Achaia together with Thessaly and Epirus constituted a separate province, also senatorial. After the reorganization of the army, which took place between 30 and 28 B.C., Macedonia proper was evacuated, though it was not until the beginning of the Christian era that Macedonia really became a *provincia inermis*. The exact date of this event is not known, but it coincides with the transfer of the command of the legions from the proconsul of Macedonia to an imperial legate based in what was to become the province of Moesia.[28] With the creation of the province of Moesia, attested for the first time in A.D. 15, the territory of the province of Macedonia returned to its earlier boundaries. Not a frontier province, and protected by the legions stationed on the Danube, Macedonia was to suffer only rarely from the results of Roman external policies.

The administration of Macedonia was in principle entrusted to a proconsul of praetorian rank, drawn by lot each year from amongst the ex-praetors. Yet under the new regime all the real authority belonged to the emperor and we know of more than one case when he actively interfered in the sphere of senatorial prerogative in Macedonia. Such interventions sometimes took the form of the appointment as governor of an imperial favourite, without the drawing of lots.[29] On other occasions they took a more spectacular form. For example, when, at the beginning of Tiberius' reign in A.D. 15, Macedonia and Achaia asked for an alleviation of their financial burdens, the emperor decided to transfer these two senatorial provinces to his own administration. By putting them under the command of the consular legate of Moesia, C. Poppaeus Sabinus, Tiberius brought together under his own authority the whole of the central part of the peninsula, extending from the Peloponnese to the Danube. This suggests that imperial administration was less onerous than senatorial; and it had the additional advantage of encouraging the implementation of a more definite administrative policy, since imperial legates held office for an unlimited period. Tiberius was not afraid

196

to let Poppaeus administer his vast province and command the Danubian legions for more than twenty years. His successor, P. Memmius Regulus, who took over A.D. 35, remained in office for an equally long period and under the reign of three emperors, until in A.D. 44 when Macedonia and Achaia were placed again under the authority of the Senate.[30] In this same year Thrace was also turned into a province as part of a larger administrative reorganization which marked the final consolidation of Roman power in the Balkans.

Another way of interfering in the affairs of senatorial provinces was by sending imperial legates on special missions.[31] In A.D. 101, Trajan appointed an arbiter to settle the differences between neighbouring communities and fix their boundaries.[32] Hadrian's intervention in A.D. 119, on the other hand, was of an entirely different nature. The emperor sent to Macedonia as supervisor of the assessment a former consul, L. Terentius Gentianus. As it is difficult to conceive that, given his consular rank, Terentius shared his office with a praetorian governor, it is to be assumed that for a period of one or two years he administered the province in his capacity of imperial legate; and this means that for some time Macedonia ceased to be under the authority of the Senate. The presence in Macedonia in A.D. 120 of a cohort under the orders of a certain Octavius Antoninus, whose duties and rank alike remain unknown to us, indicates that, during these first years of Hadrian's rule, the situation in Macedonia was complicated, though the specific facts elude us.[33]

From Septimius Severus onwards imperial encroachments on senatorial jurisdiction became more frequent and serious. As the principate evolved, greater power was concentrated in the hands of the emperor and senatorial governors were replaced by imperial officials. The first known case of a governor of Macedonia of equestrian rank entitled 'procurator Augusti agens vice proconsulis' dates from A.D. 217. Thus the post of procurator served as a legal pretext for the vicariate. The process resulted in the introduction of the 'independent vicariate' under Gallienus.[34]

As in republican times, so too in the imperial era, provincial administration in Macedonia was based on the cities, which enjoyed local autonomy to a greater or lesser extent. The most privileged statutes were those of the four Augustan colonies — Philippi, Kassandreia, Dion and Pella — the first three of which enjoyed the *ius italicum,* which rendered them equal to the communities of Italy and freed their lands and citizens alike from any kind of direct taxation The Paionian city of Stoboi became one of the few *municipia* in the Greek world, also endowed with the *ius italicum.*[35] What we do not know is what status the in-

132. The tombstone of Paterinos, son of Antigonos. It was made in Beroia by a local craftsman. In the centre the dead man stands upright; to his right is the young slave who leads his horse, to the left his daughter, Agathe, seated. The inspirational sources of this work spring from earlier sculptures of the Hellenistic world. Beginning of the 1st century B.C. Beroia, Archaeological Museum.

MACEDONIA AS A PROVINCE OF THE ROMAN EMPIRE

- non-Macedonian regions for a long time part of the province of Macedonia
- boundaries of the four *merides*
- capital town of the *meris*
- Roman colonies
- Via Egnatia

133. To prevent the resurgence of Macedonian power after the crushing defeat of Perseus at Pydna, Rome divided the kingdom into four administrative units, merides, *whose boundaries coincided to a large extent with the traditional frontiers of historic Macedonia. The province of Macedonia was only finally established in 148 B.C. It included the four* merides *and all the Roman possessions in the Balkan peninsula. Expanding Roman conquests necessitated the establishment of new provinces and a redrawing of the frontiers of the province of Macedonia, but it was only after the radical administrative measures of Diocletian that the boundaries really came to represent true Macedonian territory.*

digenous population had in these colonies. It has been assumed that the centres of the peregrine cities were integrated in the Roman communities, but the admission of all their citizens to Roman citizenship appears just as improbable as their reduction to the status of *incolae*, that is subordinate inhabitants deprived of all civic rights. An old theory (which has recently been revived), according to which peregrine communities continued to coexist next to Roman colonies, deserves the attention of future researchers in this important field.[36]

On the whole, the *civitates peregrinae* came under the category of tributary cities. These were *poleis*, which had retained their old institutions — their assembly, council and magistrates. Three towns enjoyed the status of free city (*civitas libera*): the metropolis of the province, Thessalonike, which gained her freedom in 42 B.C. by the

favour of the victorious triumvirs; the capital of the first *meris*, Amphipolis, which was probably proclaimed free when the province itself came into existence; and Skotoussa, a city of eastern Macedonia, about which we know almost nothing.[37]

In upper Macedonia, where economic and social development progressed more slowly than in the other regions, so that the urbanization and the disintegration of tribal structures were well behind compared to other regions, we find in the imperial period the typical institution of the regional *koina*, an institution which was favoured by the Romans as an intermediary body between the provincial administration and the local authorities. The koinon of *Orestai*, about which we know a lot thanks to the important inscription from Battynna, appears as a confederation of small autonomous communities either rural or urban in character. As regards internal affairs, the *koinon* was independent, but in its relations with the other regions of the province it was heavily dependent on the governor.[38] It is not easy to establish whether the other *koina* of upper Macedonia (Lynkestai, Elimiotai, Derrhiopes) were identical in structure and enjoyed a similar degree of independence.[39] In all likelihood free cities enjoyed judicial autonomy, whereas the other inhabitants of the province, whether Roman citizens or not, were subject to the judicial authority of the governor. An inscription from Beroia mentions the governor's tribunal *(agoraia)*, before which all cases were tried.[40]

Civic autonomy was often limited by the intervention of the emperor to whom, anyway, the cities frequently addressed themselves by sending embassies, and appealing for favours. Imperial letters which have survived testify to the interest of various emperors in the economic and social improvement of such and such a Macedonian city.[41] From the time of Trajan the imperial government started using higher imperial officials *(logistai)*, who were sent to the cities to supervise municipal finances. The subordination of the cities to the central government was fully accomplished when these imperial officials, who started by being extraordinary commissioners, acquired permanent status and arrogated to themselves the functions of the municipal magistrates.

In order to strengthen the bonds of loyalty which united the provincials with the emperor, and to promote the unity of each province, the Principate favoured the creation of provincial *koina*. The Macedonian *koinon* which was probably a direct descendant of the Hellenistic league was a confederation of all Macedonian communities united around the imperial cult.[42] The head of the *koinon* was a high-priest of the cult of the Augusti, and organized the games which were given in their honour on the occasion of the annual assembly of the delegates of the Macedonian cities. At the same time the very existence of a *koinon* served the illusion of provincial autonomy: the *koinon* as such could appeal directly to the emperor, without the intervention of the governor; it could lay complaints and charges against him and it could also bring a lawsuit against him for bad administration; its mints struck coins, on the obverse of which appeared the emperor and his name, while the reverse had the legend ΜΑΚΕΔΟΝΩΝ or ΚΟΙΝΟΝ ΜΑΚΕΔΟΝΩΝ;[43] its high officials were known as Macedoniarchs; and its *synedrion* awarded the honorary title of *protos tou ethnous*. In this way, the *koinon* helped to maintain national feeling, a last resurgence of which is to be seen in the renaissance of the memory of Alexander the Great, encouraged in particular by Caracalla and Alexander Severus.[44]

Few events of imperial history left their trace in Macedonia. Among those few were the visits of emperors on their way to, or returning from, some eastern campaign. Such visits were commemorated by inscriptions or coins of the type ADVENTUI AUG. MACED. The oddest visit was that of the eccentric Caracalla, the New Alexander, who recruited a genuine 'phalanx' in Macedonia.[45] There were also the wars against the barbarians, whose raids the legions and the *castella* of the *limes* were no longer in a position to check.[46] The invasion of the Costoboci in A.D. 170-71, during the war against the Marcomani, was an isolated event; but in the middle of the third century, under Philip the Arab, a spate of barbarian invasions necessitated the organization of defence in the interior of the country, the fortification of towns and the recruitment of armed forces on the spot. One of the repercussions of the invasion of the Carpi in A.D. 246-47 was the closing down of all mints in Macedonia, Thrace and Moesia Inferior.[47] In A.D. 254, under Valerian and Gallienus, the Goths raided Thessalonike, though they did not succeed in capturing the city. The gravest of all the third century invasions was that of the Herulians and the Goths who, on their way back from Greece in A.D. 268, devastated Epirus and Macedonia. The whole region was thrown into anarchy. Among other usurpers, a certain Valens was proclaimed emperor in Thessalonike.[48] An inscription from Lychnidos, dating from the reign of Gallienus, speaks of the presence of detached troop-formations *(vexillationes)*, under the orders of a *dux*, at that strategic point on the Via Egnatia.[49] The victory won over the Goths by Claudius II near Naissus put a temporary end to the barbarian danger.

ECONOMY AND SOCIETY

Macedonia occupied a rather modest place in the economic life of the empire. Despite its natural resources, it could not compete with the rich provinces of Asia Minor and the West in the scope of its international trade.

However, under the Principate, Macedonia enjoyed a period of prosperity. Peace and security, good roads and a more equitable system of exploitation than had prevailed in the Republican era brought an economic boom, which benefited not only the Roman state and the provincial ruling class, but the masses too. The widening of the economic base, namely the increase in the numbers of producers and consumers alike and the improvement in the living conditions of the producing classes, is the main feature of the economic progress made during this period.[50]

As in any ancient society, the Macedonian economy of the imperial period was largely based on slave labour. Unfortunately, the fragmentary character of our evidence means that anything we say about the slave class is bound to be partial and hypothetical. The great majority of workers, free or slave, vanished without leaving any trace of their existence other than the product of their work; and when this work consisted in the cultivation of the soil or cattle raising, then they left no trace whatever. The humbler the condition of these workers, the less money they had for cutting epitaphs and dedications on stone. Thus the extreme rarity of epigraphic evidence about slaves is in flagrant disproportion to their numbers.

The few epitaphs of slaves which have reached us belong to servants of private individuals who knew how to attract their master's affection. Moreover, these modest inscriptions hardly ever contain anything more than the name of the slave and of his master. It is touching to read on the epitaph of a young slave the compassionate word, *miser,*

134. One of the milestones which stood along the Via Egnatia the main line of communication from the Adriatic coast to Thrace, constructed around 130 B.C. It was found near the river Gallikos. The Greek and Latin inscription gives the name of the consul Gnaius Egnatius, after whom the road was named. Thessalonike, Archaeological Museum.

ploitation of servile labour must have become widespread in Macedonia from the second century A.D. onwards. The condition of the slave to whom his master had given a plot of land to exploit probably did not differ much from that of a farmer, though in this case both the slave and his land remained the property of the master. To this category of privileged servants there belonged also the *actores (pragmateutai, oikonomoi),* who had to supervise works and keep the accounts on part of the domain of their master, and about whom some epigraphic evidence survives.[54]

Two (unfortunately badly mutilated) documents shed some light on the trade in human beings as it was conducted in Macedonia. One is an unpublished inscription from Beroia containing rules for the sale of slaves in the Macedonian markets;[55] the other is the beginning of a letter by Antoninus Pius to the citizens of Parthikopolis, in which the emperor speaks about cattle, silverware and slaves, used apparently as productive capital; no doubt the slaves in question were primarily employed in agriculture.[56] Even more expressive is the funerary stele of a *somatemporos,* himself a freedman who, it seems, occupied himself with the export of slaves on the international market. His stele shows a file of slaves, bound together by chains round the neck, led by a supervisor and followed by women and children.[57]

The number of freedmen mentioned in inscriptions is, naturally, much greater. We know the names of dozens of them from dedications and epitaphs, and we also have lists of names which may be those of manumitted slaves (in one of them a group of people is explicitly referred to as *exeleutheroi).*[58] The whole series of acts of manumission (from Leukopetra alone there are more than a hundred), form a first class source of information, insufficiently studied so far, on the problem of slavery.[59] Freedmen played a significant role in the economic life of the community, occupying themselves, as they did in most cases, with trade. It is especially worth noting that the overwhelming majority of freedmen were former slaves of Roman citizens.

An important question on which insufficient light is shed by our sources concerns the character of landed property and the social condition of farmers. Macedonia has a lot of arable land and excellent pasture; it is, therefore, *a priori* likely that, even under the empire, when urban life had reached its peak of development, Macedonia was essentially a rural area. Yet our evidence does not allow us to establish either the extent to which small properties succeeded in avoiding absorption by large estates, or whether there were any really large estates of the *saltus* type. Small landowners, who personally cultivated their fields, vines, olive-trees, orchards and vegetable gardens, or raised their herds, did not bother to indicate their condition on their funerary stelai. How can we know how many among them had the means to rent a slave or two for their house or their labours in the fields? The single reference to a *chorikos apo chorarchion,* on an inscription from Thessalonike of the mid-third century A.D., is more perplexing than illuminating.[60] This 'peasant' must have been an important person, since, having held a post (of what sort is unknown)

and one wonders whether it comes from the master or the parents of the dead.[51] But this is an exception, just like that other funerary inscription of a slave 'born at home and regarded as a son'; despite his youth (he was but fifteen when he died), his master had entrusted him with the management of a tavern.[52] About the slaves who worked either in the mines or in the fields, and who occupied the lowest grade in the social hierarchy, there is no evidence at all. One had to rise above servile status in order to deserve to be remembered by posterity. Such is the case of a vine-dresser who consecrated to Zeus Hypsistos two rows of vines from his *peculium* 'for the sake of his master'.[53] This inscription constitutes the only piece of evidence we have from Macedonia for servile tenure, though this type of ex-in the administration of the *chora,* he was agonothete in the first Pythian games where his son (a former politarch and member of the council) was *eisagogeus.* Under the early empire, the important landowners normally resided in the towns, so that the adjective *chorikos* would not suit them at all. Could it be that in this document we have a first indication of that extension of seigneurial landholdings that was so characteristic of the socio-economic system in the late empire? It is noteworthy that we lack any testimony on the system of colonate in Macedonia.

We are equally ill-informed about the artisan work-force and about other metiers, (miners, smiths, goldsmiths, stonecutters, donkey drivers etc.). Nor is our evidence any more substantial as regards commerce. The epitaph of a wheat merchant from Rome who died in Amphipolis may allow us to conclude that there was enough wheat for export; but the modest funerary stele of a banker from Thessalonike tells us nothing.[61] How then is it possible to discover the economic basis of the enormous riches possessed by the great families of Beroia, Thessalonike or Philippi? Whence came the fortune of K. Popillios Python, the citizen of Beroia and high-priest of the emperors who, not content to mark the year of his priesthood by bestowing the customary largesses (such as organizing scenic and gymnic games, gladiatorial combats, hunts in the arena involving 'animals from home and from abroad', the sale of wheat at subsidized prices, the repair of roads at his own expense, and the giving of banquets for all the delegates at each reunion of the *koinon*), also paid the poll tax *epikephalaion* for 'the province'.[62] Leaving aside the ambiguity of the term *eparcheia* in this context, our uncertainty as to which categories of people had to pay the *tributum capitis,* and our ignorance of its exact amount, still one cannot help being impressed by such liberality.[63] Other such cases involve only one city, but in the case of Python we must think in terms of dozens of cities and, possibly, hundreds of thousands of inhabitants. If Python was a great landowner, how large must his estate have been to produce such wealth?

We must also leave open the question of imperial domains in Macedonia. One discovers with astonishment that there is no evidence whatsoever about imperial freedmen or anybody else engaged in the exploitation of imperial land. All we have, unless I am mistaken, is a single reference to a *Caesaris nostri serva* on the tombstone of uncertain provenance of a twelve-year-old girl which is now in Thessalonike.[64] Conclusions from silence are always risky, but it would be equally bold to conclude on the basis of such evidence as we have that there existed in Macedonia imperial agricultural estates. An inscription from Thessalonike referring to an *epitropos chorion despotikon* cannot be dated before the fourth century,[65] while the only mention of *procuratores metallorum intra Macedoniam* is dated A.D. 386.[66] If the lack of data concerning the mines, whose exploitation came under imperial jurisdiction, is fortuitous, we must admit that as regards imperial estates we have to do with a socio-economic development which must have started about the middle of the third century A.D.[67]

The socio-economic division between free and slave, workers and exploiters of other people's work, poor and

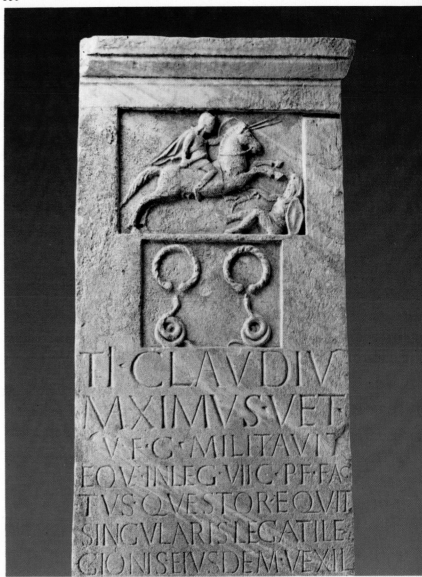

135. *The stele of Tiberius Claudius Maximus, a Roman veteran who settled in Macedonia. Its inscription tells us that he was the man who captured and killed Decebalus, king of the Dacians, in battle in A.D. 106 Maximus, mounted, is shown about to attack the fallen Decebalus with his sword. Kavala, Archaeological Museum.*

rich, which is so characteristic of a slave society, was complicated in the Roman provinces by the socio-political division between Romans and *peregrini* (non-Romans). The Romans belonged to the class of the rich, of the slave-owners. Those who came to live in Macedonia under the Republic or at the beginning of the imperial era were businessmen and colonists. In certain Macedonian cities one encounters Roman landowners *(enkektemenoi)* as well. We do not know whether the right of acquiring property was offered to the Romans as an exceptional privilege, or whether the Romans appropriated for themselves land which belonged to the public Roman domain, but happened to form part of a city territory. In any case the Romans led a privileged existence, and the non-Romans

must have felt it as such and seen the Romans as representatives of the ruling power. Yet Roman citizenship was not inaccessible to others. It is to the credit of Rome (and the foundation of its enduring power) that she did not exclude from her citizenship either conquered enemies or manumitted slaves. That the sons of freedmen could be treated as citizens with full rights is something that no other slave society has ever tolerated. Thus, through enfranchisement and manumission, the privileged class of Roman citizens was constantly being enlarged so that it embraced, under the name of Roman, elements of various ethnic and social origin, till the Antoninian Constitution abolished once and for all the difference between Romans and *peregrini*.

Political Romanization did not affect language and national conscience, which for the Macedonian was nurtured by the grandeur of a unique past. One became a Roman citizen without ceasing to speak Greek and feeling a Macedonian. But national feeling was now divorced from any aspiration towards independence. The paradox of this situation is illustrated by the case of a Thessalonian who simultaneously is described as 'Hellene and Philhellene', and bears the *tria nomina* of the Romans.[68] Moreover, Hadrian's *Panhellenion,* of which Thessalonike was a member, served also as the instrument of a policy that encouraged Greek feelings of loyalty towards Rome. The Roman occupation, which in Republican times was so painfully felt, was succeeded under the empire by the irreversible integration of Macedonia into the broader Roman community.

INTELLECTUAL LIFE

Education, literature, entertainments

Simple inscriptional references, anyway few and far between, to a pedagogue or a teacher or a foundling boy who was taught by his adopted father, himself a rhetor, or a little girl, who displayed uncommon zeal in her studies, tell us very little about the level and character of education in Roman Macedonia.[69] Yet we are indebted to epigraphic evidence at least for the realization that many more people were literate in Roman than in Hellenistic times: the number of inscriptions was never higher than in imperial times, when one finds material everywhere, even in the most remote places, and concerning people of all social conditions.

Going to school was clearly the privilege of those children whose parents could pay a master to teach them. If in the great cities basic and more advanced education was controlled by the municipal authorities, it is legitimate

136. Under Roman rule the coins issued by Macedonian cities retain certain traditional subjects, such as Zeus and Athena from the mint of Dion in the 3rd century A.D. Athens, Numismatic Museum.

137-138. Coins from Thessalonike (137), 3rd century A.D., and Pella (138), 2nd century B.C. Athens, Numismatic Museum.

to assume that rural communities were not in a position to maintain a school. No doubt the illiteracy-rate was high, though specific evidence for illiteracy is extremely uncommon. Among the rare items of evidence is a letter quoted in an act of manumission from Beroia, ending in the following words: 'We have written this letter... by the hand of Flavius..., because we cannot write ourselves'.[70] It is not without interest that the scribe and the three witnesses who have signed this document are, judging by their names, Roman citizens, whereas the illiterate authors of the letter, two brothers, bear a native patronymic.

Secondary and higher education was exclusively the privilege of urban youth. Consequently our evidence in this connection is more copious, though largely confined to honorific inscriptions for gymnasiarchs or lists of ephebes, which tell us nothing about the content and methods of education. Of course there is the gymnasiarchal law of Beroia,[71] which shows the care the Macedonian cities devoted to educational establishments, and contains very important and interesting details about the division into classes of those who frequented the gymnasium (children, ephebes, *neaniskoi* under the age of twenty-two, and young men under thirty; it also prohibits entry to the gymnasium 'to slaves, freedmen, sons of freedmen, to those who have not exercised themselves in the palaestra, to vulgar traders, pederasts, drunkards and madmen'; and it provides information about the responsibilities of the gymnasiarch, the punishments inflicted and the prizes awarded, the examinations and competitions at the end of each school year, and so on. But this precious document predates the creation of the province, and should be used with caution as a source of information about the gymnasia of the imperial era or as a basis for any other generalizations. All one can say is that the gymnasium, as the framework for the physical education of the young and their initiation into civic life, was maintained without break after the Roman conquest, and flourished with renewed vigour under the early empire.[72] In the remote town of Styberra the number of ephebes in A.D. 74/5 was over one hundred and thirty.[73] Their organization was similar to that of other Greek towns, and they profited from the help of rich citizens, who established endowments to ensure the regular distribution of oil. The boys and youths who frequented the gymnasium displayed their educational achievements in various processions, sacrifices, competitions and feasts, where their attendance was obligatory. The last reference to ephebes in Macedonia dates from the year A.D. 269/70.[74]

References to Macedonian artists, writers and men of learning that can be gleaned from inscriptions or from literary sources throw some sidelights on the cultural life of Macedonian cities. We know of a mime-artist from Beroia who won a number of crowns in lyric competitions; of a 'phorminx-player and an expert in lyric poetry' from Amastris who died at Beroia; of an artist of Attaleia admired at the theatre in Thessalonike; of a flautist from Kassandreia who won a victory in Akraiphia of Boiotia, and so on.[75] It was to Thessalonike, a cultural centre of international repute, that poets, philosophers and rhetors came to teach or to address a cultivated audience; we know of a Bithynian from Niceaea 'a learned rhetor'; of a

certain Dassarete, 'a man endowed with many talents', and of many others.[76] Thessalonike also produced her own poets. Antipater, a friend and favourite of Calpurnius Piso (c. 15 B.C.), was one of the most famous epigrammatists. About eighty of his epigrams were included in the *Garland*, compiled in the reign of Caligula by his compatriot, the poet Philippos.[77] Towards the end of the second century A.D. the victory in processional song at the Mousaia at Thespiae was won by Damaios, one of whose poems, dedicated to the Egyptian gods, is to be found on an inscription from Thessalonike.[78]

A Macedonian of great repute was Andronikos of Kyrrhos, who designed the famous clock known as the Tower of the Winds which adorned the Athenian Agora. His interest in astronomy and his interpretation of Aratos' *Phaenomena* earned him the surname of 'the Second Aratos' that we find in an epigram from Tenos inscribed on a clock built according to his plans.[79] The Macedonian Amerias occupied himself with foreign words as also with terms of culinary pharmacology. We owe to him almost all Macedonian glosses.[80] Theagenes was interested in ancient Macedonian institutions. In the age of the so-called Second Sophistic, three Macedonians enjoyed a certain celebrity: Nikostratos, a sophist and professor of rhetoric, whose full name (T. Aurelios Nikostratos Nikostratou) has been revealed to us by a newly found inscription, was a prolific writer who excelled in many genres; Philip of Amphipolis was the author of novels, and Polyainos is the only Macedonian writer from whose works a complete specimen has survived, namely the *Strategemata*. Despite the richness of information contained in this compilation, any historian of Macedonia would undoubtedly have preferred to have instead his lost orations *On the Synedrion* and *On the koinon of the Macedonians*.[81]

The gymnastic and musical competitions must have constituted in Macedonia, as in any othr part of Greece, the most attractive part of the public festivals. The interest of the man in the street in this type of entertainment is well illustrated by the epitaph of a baker from Beroia who travelled to Olympia twelve times just in order to see the games.[82] The towns organized games on the occasion of public festivals and in honour either of local benefactors or of members of the imperial family. At the end of the second and in the third century the youth of Thessalonike celebrated at the gymnasium games dedicated to the god Fulvus (probably the son of Marcus Aurelius, who died at the age of four and was deified).[83] As regards stage spectacles organized by municipalities, we know of the director of a company of comedians (*archimimus latinus*) at Philippi, who also held the function of contractor of spectacles (*promisthota*); we also know of a *choragiarius* obliged to supply theatrical sets.[84]

The most famous and, possibly, oldest oecumenical games in Macedonia were the *Olympia* at Dion, the last reference to which comes from the republican era.[85] Under the empire, a competitive and athletic spirit marked games held at Beroia by the Macedonian *koinon*. They are referred to from the end of the first century A.D. (the famous C. Popillius Python gave dramatic and gymnastic games 'equal to the *Aktia*', and at the cost of one talent, with participants from various parts of the Greek world).[86] Federal festivals enjoyed especial prestige during the third century, A.D. when they were granted the name *Alexandreia,* in memory of the national hero.[87] Then, probably on the occasion of the visit of Gordian III in A.D. 242, they were renamed *Olympia,* and classified among 'sacred and oecumenical games'.[88] In A.D. 240/41 the city of Thessalonike instituted quinquennial Pythian games, surnamed *Epinikia, Kabeireia* or *Kaisareia,* after the city's guardian deities.[89]

It was, however, another type of spectacle which, from the first century of the empire, attracted the biggest public, namely the gladiatorial fights and hunts staged in arenas. These particularly costly games were related to the imperial cult of the emperors, and served as propaganda for Roman power as well as buttressing the popularity of the highly placed personalities who footed the bill. An announcement, dating from June 229 A.D., informs us that the high-priest of the emperor and *agonothetes* of the 'Alexandrian games of the Macedonian *koinon*', and his wife, high-priestess of the empress, will give in the most illustrious metropolis of Macedonia games consisting of animal hunts and gladiatorial combats lasting for three days, 'for the health, salvation, victory and eternity of Alexander Severus, of his mother, of the imperial household, the imperial Senate, the illustrious praetorian prefects, the imperial army and the Roman people'.[90] A similar announcement of the year A.D. 240 adds that, thanks to the good will of the emperor, there will be not just the customary two pairs of gladiators, but three, who will fight each day 'to the death', that is to say to the point where one of the gladiators will be killed.[91] Sanguinary spectacles of this sort are attested in all the big Macedonian towns by epitaphs and also by references to, or representations of, gladiators, fighters of wild beasts *(munerarii)* and mention of associations of fighters of wild beasts. Indirect evidence is also provided by the rebuilding of the theatres which was done to ensure the security of spectators (as at Stoboi, Philippi and Herakleia).

Cults and customs

If *paideia* was the main factor that ensured the cultural unification of the Greco-Roman world, what more than anything else allowed its specific regional characteristics to survive was the religious mentality of the masses, which tend to remain attached to their cults and national traditions even when they are on the point of losing both their language and identity. Of all aspects of social life in Macedonia the one which displays most originality is religion.[92] This is due to the fact that since remote antiquity two different religious conceptions coexisted on its soil, and in the course of time were superimposed and eventually interpenetrated each other. On the one hand there was the Greek religion of the Macedonians, with its aloof and majestic gods, and on the other hand the more emotional religion of the indigenous population, with its mystic and orgiastic cults. The older population, which was more or less completely repressed by the Macedonians, consisted of the Paionians, Pelagonians of the middle Axios, the Bryges of central Macedonia, and the Edonoi/Mygdones, Bisaltai and Sintoi of eastern Macedonia.[93] The linguistic and cultural assimilation of this substratum varied from place to place. In Paionia and lower Macedonia it was almost complete, and yet even there one can detect traces of non-Macedonian beliefs which must have exerted a certain influence on the official religion. In the region of the Strymon and of Mt. Pangaion the indigenous population, which was more concentrated than elsewhere and annexed to Macedonia at a later date, maintained its national characteristics in a purer form. This ethnic element, which was racially akin to the Phrygians and Bithynians of Asia Minor (as also were the Bryges of lower Macedonia), played a significant role in the formation of he religion of the Aegean world. From this ethnic substratum, and not from the Thracians, with whom they are erroneously confused, emerged the cults of Dionysos, Bendis, Kotyto and the Kabeiroi, which were eventually adopted by the Thracians, the Greeks and the Macedonians. These cults should not, therefore, be regarded as foreign to Macedonia. They are just as indigenous as the Macedonian cults themselves.

The national Macedonian divinities continued to be worshipped with undiminished fervour in Roman times.[94] *Zeus Olympios, Kronides,* kept his place of honour. The coins of the Macedonian *koinon* bore his effigy, while the province's most prestigious games were consecrated to him. Associated with the goddess *Roma,* as *Eleutherios,* he became the protector of the new regime.[95] The cult of *Zeus Hypsistos,* which, without any connection with Judaism, was so widely diffused, originated in all probability in Macedonia.[96] Apollo too kept his Greek character. He appears either alone or in association with the Kabeiroi on coins from Thessalonike, while the quinquennial games, by which the capital of the province aspired to surpass those of the *koinon* at Beroia, were called *Pythia* in his honour.[97] Yet in a village sanctuary of Pelagonia, Apollo was worshipped as *Oteudanos, Eteudaniskos,* surnames (possibly of Illyrian or Paionian origin) which indicate the assimilation of a local divinity to the Greek god.[98]

The most widespread cult in Roman Macedonia was that of Artemis. There is no region where it is not attested. But we must distinguish the Greek Artemis venerated in Macedonia proper and in the area of ancient Paionia, as *Kynagogos, Agrotera, Ephesia, Lochia,* from *Artemis-Bendis* of eastern Macedonia.[99] Bendis was an Edonian goddess of the forests and of fertility, who was often assimilated to Hekate and Persephone. Under the name of Artemis she was represented as a hunter, holding in one hand a bow or a spear, and in the other the mystic bough which opens the way into the Underworld. The cult of Artemis-Bendis was dominant in the region of the middle Strymon.

The worship of a female divinity is also characteristic of central Macedonia. Usually the goddess is assimilated to Artemis, but often she has a special name, such as *Ennodia,* the goddess on horseback holding a torch, or 'the almighty' *Pasikrata,* who is akin either to Artemis or to Kore.[100] Even the goddess *Ma Aneiketos,* whom one finds on numerous dedications made by slaves at Edessa, and whose cult is regarded as an importation from Asia Minor, figures possibly as *Artemis Ma* in a dedication made by a certain Ma, daughter of Makedon.[101] The recent discovery of the sanctuary of the Autochthonous Mother of the Gods at Leukopetra raises the question of the roots of the cult of these female divinities, who seem to be connected with old Macedonian beliefs.[102]

Herakles, the national hero of the Macedonians, maintained his popularity and is attested on many votive monuments as *Kynagidas, Propylaios* or *Theos Megas*, as also on funerary stelai as *Psychopompos*. His cult was not known in eastern Macedonia. The same is true of the healing gods (Asklepios, Hygieia, Telesphoros), as also of the saving gods, the Dioskouroi.[103] Dedications to the Dioskouroi are not found at all outside the area of ancient Paionia (the coins of the fourth *meris*, struck in Pelagonia, bear their effigy) and the Aegean coast where their cult was fused with that of the Kabeiroi. The ties binding the Great Gods of Samothrace with Magna-Mater and Phrygia are well known; but it is worth mentioning here that at Lemnos, where the Kabeiroi were worshipped as sons of Hephaistos (the hammer is the symbol of Kabeiros on coins from Thessalonike), the ancient population consisted of Sintoi; while the names of the Kabeiroi *Axieros, Axiokersa* and *Axiokersos* must be connected with the name of the river Axios, whose lower course flowed in high antiquity through Paionian-Edonian territory. Thessalonike, founded in this region at a time when the pre-Macedonian stock must have still retained all its vitality, adopted Kabeiros, 'the very holy ancestral god', as her special god. It was he who saved the city from the great Gothic attack of A.D. 268, an event which was commemorated by an Antoninianus of Claudius II bearing the legend DEO CABIRO.[104]

The cult of Dionysos, deeply rooted in this country, had adherents in all social strata. As god of agriculture, fertility and wine Dionysos-Bacchos (who had been assimilated to the Roman Liber) attracted numerous devotees to his orgiastic cult involving belief in a future life. These devotees grouped themselves into brotherhoods (Dionysiac thiasoi, *baccheia*) in order to celebrate their mysteries and funerary ceremonies. From the many documents which attest the role payed by this cult in municipal and private life, we shall mention here only two: an inscription from Thessalonike, in which Dionysos is associated with Zeus and the unknown divinity *Gongylos*, and a remarkable relief from the region of the middle Strymon, on which Dionysos is represented on horseback, in the manner of the Thracian Horseman, but with all his characteristic attributes and symbols, and bearing the name *Asdoules*.[105]

Passing over all the other gods of the Greek pantheon, the personified abstractions and the minor divinities (abundant evidence for whose cults, dispersed all over Macedonia, attests to the vitality of the classical religion), as also the various local cults of heroes or river gods, we must deal at the end of this survey of the indigenous cults with the Thracian Horseman, who holds a special place in popular belief. As in Thrace, in eastern Macedonia the Thracian hunter god, known in Greek as *Heros* or *Heron*,

139. Bust of the river god Olganos, one of the three children of Beres, son of Makedon; the others, Mieza and Beroia, gave their names to those towns. The work is evidence for the survival of Macedonian legends for centuries after the Roman conquest. Mid-2nd century A.D. Beroia, Archaeological Museum.

was worshipped as a god, and his adherents or initiates were grouped in thiasoi in the Thracian manner.[106] On the other hand, in northern Macedonia he appears chiefly on funerary stelai: it is clear that there the cult of the Thracian Horseman was contaminated by local belief in an afterlife which represented the dead as heroes. The anthropomorphic stelai found in Pelagonia, on which the Thracian Horseman is a very common subject, can only be interpreted as representations of the dead as a hero.[107]

Conservatism is nowhere stronger than in the cult of the dead, and thus it is here that distinctive local customs are

140. *Relief grave stele, an example of Macedonian art. Seven members of the same family are depicted as relief busts of une-* *qual size. Some of their names are recorded in the Greek inscription. Mid-3rd century A.D. Florina, Archaeological Museum.*

best known to us. In the villages of the colony of Philippi there took place a special rite called *parakausis*, performed on the 'day of the roses' *(Rosalia).* This was a funerary ceremony that the colonists had brought with them from Italy. On that day the tombs were decorated with roses and offerings were burnt nearby.[108] A will from Alkomenai (in Derrhiopos), giving a donation for this purpose, shows that the sacrifices were followed by a funerary feast, a custom still practised in certain parts of the peninsula.[109] Under the empire, banqueting scenes were frequently depicted on funerary stelai.

Roman rule brought to Macedonia the cult of *Roma* and of Roman benefactors, a cult which owed its inspiration to the Greeks; then, from the time of Augustus onwards, the cult of the reigning emperor and of his deified predecessors was also introduced; this was an official cult required by the authorities as a guarantee of loyalism.[110] In this respect Macedonia did not differ from the other provinces of the Greek East. The imperial cult was the *raison d'être* of the Macedonian *koinon,* whose president was the high priest of the Augusti. At the same time each Macedonian city rendered its own imperial cult by erecting altars and temples to the dead emperors and by organizing ceremonies and sacrifices.[111] The right to erect a temple to the reigning emperor and to institute a cult became an object of rivalry between Beroia, the capital of the *koinon,* and Thessalonike, the capital of the province. Beroia succeeded in obtaining, for a period, the title of *tetrakis neokoros.*[112] As for the national Roman divinities which were introduced by the colonists, their popularity never extended beyond the local level and most of them were anyway assimilated to the main Greek divinities.

Of the oriental cults, the one that took firmest root in Macedonia was that of Serapis and Isis.[113] The fervour that the Egyptian religion must have inspired in its many devotees in this part of the world is well attested by the great Serapeion of Thessalonike, the complex of buildings at Philippi consecrated to the Egyptian gods, a small sanctuary recently excavated near the fortress on the Via Egnatia west of Herakleia as well as by the great number of statues, reliefs and dedications found all over the country and donated by people of all social categories. The Alexandrian gods were accepted as gods of healing and salvation. The mysteries, with their rites of purification and initiation, their incubations and mystical repasts, their daily ceremonies and special feasts, sustained in the heart of the initiate the hope of blissful immortality. Isis, the compassionate and merciful goddess with her thousand names, was raised to the rank of supreme female divinity, and Serapis tended to be associated with other divinities and to absorb them, thus progressively opening up the road to monotheism.

The cult of the *Dea Syria (Atargatis Soteira, Thea Syria Parthenos)* is attested only at Beroia in the second century B.C. and in the third century A.D.[114] Could it be entirely fortuitous that the picturesque description given by Pseudo-Lucian in his *Lucius* of a company of fancily-dressed charlatans parading the image of the *Dea Syria* on an ass and indulging in their exotic and sanguinary rites before the crowds for the sake of some food and money should be situated in the suburbs of Beroia?[115]

We have not so far mentioned Judaism and Christianity, two monotheistic religions which originated in the same country and were equally austere in their rejection of any kind of syncretism with other religions. We do not know when the first Jews were established in Macedonia; yet by the mid-first century A.D. there were at Philippi, Thessalonike and Beroia fairly numerous Jewish communities grouped around their synagogues.[116] The inscription mentioning the 'father of the synagogue' Klaudios Tiberios Polycharmos, found at Stoboi and dating from the end of the third century A.D., is a document of great importance for the history of the Diaspora because it contains the oldest reference to the patriarchate. The most recent excavations have yielded, underneath the fifth century basilica where the inscription in question was re-used, traces of a synagogue and painted ex-votos of the same Polycharmos.[117] In the Roman empire the Jews were permitted to practise their religion freely; but we do not know whether they were successful in proselytizing the Macedonians.

The introduction of Christianity to Macedonia, which was also its beginning in Europe, was the work of St. Paul, one of its founders and its most important propagator among the Gentiles. It is at Philippi, at the Jewish 'place of prayer' just outside the western gate of the city, that on a Sabbath towards the end of the year A.D. 49, Paul preached the Gospel for the first time on European soil, teaching faith in salvation by the grace of God and the love of one's fellow man. Jews and pagans were converted and founded the first Christian community on the continent. Paul also preached in Thessalonike (on three consecutive Sabbaths) and at Beroia, and converted many people, both Jews and pagans. Yet everywhere the majority of the Jews faced him with implacable hostility and provoked riots which obliged him to move on, successively, from Philippi, Thessalonike and Beroia.[118] Either from Athens or from Corinth, whither he went after he left Macedonia, he addressed two epistles to the Thessalonians, in which he praises their perseverance in the faith and regrets the fact that they have to suffer at the hands of his *symphyletai,* who prevented him from pursuing his mission in Macedonia.[119] Paul visited Beroia twice more: in A.D. 56, on his way from Asia Minor to Greece, and at the beginning of A.D. 57 on his return by the same route. A few years later, Paul addressed an epistle to the Philippians, in all likelihood from Rome. The church of Philippi, which remained to the last steadfastly faithful to him,[120] already appears to be a well organized body with a bishop and deacons.

After these glorious beginnings, an almost complete obscurity envelopes the evolution of Christianity in the cities of Macedonia. When, later on, churches once more appear in our sources in great numbers, they are without any rivals. Christianity had become the official ideology of the empire.

MONUMENTS AND ART
IN THE ROMAN PERIOD

Although the Macedonians' long struggle against the Romans ended in 148 B.C. with their final defeat and subjection, one cannot claim that there was any substantial corresponding change in the field of art. But the systematic stripping of Macedonian sculptures, paintings and metalwork, which were taken off to Rome by Aemilius Paullus and Caecilius Metellus,[1] together with the economic dislocation that followed on the Roman conquest, naturally were not without consequences. Pella no longer had anything of its former glory to show, the palace of Vergina slipped slowly into decay, and, in the course of the second half of the second century B.C., the Macedonians gradually stopped building the magnificent funerary monuments with sumptuous facades that had reflected the high point of their political fortunes in the fourth century B.C.

THE HELLENISTIC TRADITION

Insofar as there was still artistic activity, it continued to draw its inspiration from the creations of Hellenistic art.[2] Such specimens of the plastic arts from the years after the conquest as have been found to date are typically Hellenistic, and faithfully follow the artistic fashions of the period. Thus a group of small female statues from Dion and Thessalonike is characterized by familiar broken axes,[3] the tapering proportions and sensitive rendering of dress; while a male head from Beroia vividly recalls figures from the great frieze of the Altar of Pergamon.[4] On a ddicatory relief from Dion, dated by its inscription to the late Hellenistic period, the bust of Isis is shown, holding ears of grain in the one hand and a sceptre in the other.[5] The face of the goddess has been rendered in an evidently classicizing manner. In another dedicatory relief, also inscribed, from the Thessalonike Serapeion, a bearded man and a woman offer a sacrifice at an altar, while their son, leaning on a support, turns towards his father.[6] In this relief, which recalls parallels from Asia Minor, it is particularly worth noting how the artist has placed the youth in the middle of the composition and high up, thus imparting perspective depth to the whole.

We are much better informed about late Hellenistic funerary reliefs. Enough have been preserved to allow us to follow their development up to the time of Augustus. Among them, some particularly large works stand out. Two stelai from Beroia, for example, represent youths virtually identical both in general composition and in details, and holding a scroll.[7] A relief from Lete, showing men, women and servants, carries the signature of the artist: 'Evander, son of Evander, from Beroia, made this'.[8] From the same cemetery comes another relief (three re-used slabs) which, as becomes clear from the hair-styles of the men and the women, must date from the end of the first century B.C. (fig. 147).[9] What distinguishes this group of works is that, despite the stereotyped repetition of forms and neglect of details, there is a real dynamism in their structure, a vivid sense of plastic volume, and an increasing tendency towards greater care in the execution of the head, at the expense of the body. Thus, in these sculptures of the first century B.C., we see the emergence of the Roman conception of the portrait. The enthroned dead with his servant, the curtain hanging behind them, the tree and the serpent on a stele with crowning pediment, are derived typologically from the Hellenistic tradition.[10] But the head of the man, with its rounded contours, strongly recalls Roman portraits of the first century B.C. The dual character of this stone is clear from the bilingual inscription:

Γάιε Ποπίλλιε χαῖρε· καὶ σὺ πολλὰ τίς ποτε εἶ.

C. Popillii salve, et tu quisquis es.

But the finest specimen of a portrait from the later part of this period is the head, carved almost in the round, from a relief in Thessalonike.[11] Here, the individual features of the subject have been rendered with rare dynamism of expression.

Town planning

No new towns of any significance were built in Macedonia during the imperial period. But archaeological discoveries reveal that extensive building programmes were undertaken in the old urban centres, with the erection of civic buildings and the undertaking of public works; while at the same time new private dwellings were being built. From the evidence available about urban structures, it is difficult to judge what is completely new, and what is simply restoration and modernization of older buildings. A good deal of excavation and careful research is needed before we can claim any precise knowledge of Roman architecture in Macedonia. It should be emphasized here that the material we know best derives from the middle imperial period and from late antiquity.

Thessalonike was divided by a grid-system of streets into uniform *insulae*.[12] The public buildings were in the central section, constructed on stepped terraces. It seems that the stoa around the market place *(forum)*, the greater part of which has been excavated, bordered on its southern side a much larger market place, so that the two complexes together covered the whole space between the present-day St. Demetrios and Egnatia Streets.[13] North of the market place, and on terraces higher up, were in all probability to be found the stadium and a gymnasium. On the site of the basilica of St. Demetrios, and to the west of it, was a large bath-complex. On the western side of the city was the

141. Aerial view of Dion with the ancient agora in the centre. Behind it can be seen the small covered theatre and bath complex. The city was laid out on the grid-iron pattern in Hellenistic times and it remained unchanged thereafter.

142. *View of a large area of the* forum *of Philippi, a paved open space bordered by two Corinthian temples, two fountains, a plat-* *form for speakers and shops. In the photograph can be seen the columns of the stoa which enclosed it on three sides.*

Sanctuary of the Egyptian Gods, and to the north-west of the market place was to be found the temple that housed the imperial cult. In the north-east corner of the city walls, where the terrain becomes precipitous and rocky, was the acropolis. The walls followed a parallel course on their eastern and western sides, while on the north they followed the contours of the hill, rising in steps towards the acropolis.[14] To the south, the sea-wall turned inwards on the western side, slanting towards the south-east.[15]

The town plan of Philippi was not dissimilar.[16] The market place, divided into civic and commercial sections, lay between two parallel central streets. The sanctuaries stood on higher terraces; and the summit was crowned by the fortified acropolis.

Dion, even after the foundation of the Roman colony there, preserved the distinctive plan that it had possessed since at least the Hellenistic period (fig. 141). The sanctuary of Olympian Zeus, as well as others, the theatre, the stadium and the odeion, were grouped in a large complex outside the walls, covering much the same area as the city itself. From archaeological discoveries and inscriptions

we know that a number of important buildings, such as temples, stoas, an odeion and so forth, were constructed within the sanctuary during the Roman period.[17] The town itself had a carefully planned street system, with a grid of major and minor arteries. Access to the large *insulae* was by small streets that eased the circulation of traffic. According to the present state of knowledge, it seems that the centre of Dion's civic life was in the southern part of the city, closer, in other words, to the temples. An *insula,* having at its centre a paved square, probably the *forum,* contained a row of shops, a small roofed theatre, spacious baths, and on the axis of the square a well-constructed single-chambered building, perhaps the temple of a state cult. On the basis of some trial trenches that have been opened, it can be cautiously stated that the changes made in Dion's street plan during the Roman period must have been minor. The walls of the city, with only small modifications to the south, preserved their original line. On three sides they were absolutely straight, while the fourth (eastern) side followed the bank of the navigable river that flowed along its length.

Particular attention was given to the provision of an abundant water supply to the cities. Large aqueducts were built to bring the water from its source to be stored in cisterns; thence it was distributed to the baths, springs, fountains and so on by means of clay or lead pipes. Drainage was also carefully attended to. Ducts from each building debouched into a central sewer under the paved surface of the streets. This hydraulic system was also fitted out with filter jars, inspection shafts, retaining constructions and so forth.

The circulation of pedestrians and traffic within the cities was facilitated by a fairly closely-spaced network of streets, which were often paved with flattish stones. The width of the streets varied between 10 and 1.50-2.00 m. Typical examples of such streets can be seen at Dion, Philippi and Thessalonike.

Until the mid-third century A.D. Macedonia, like the rest of Greece, was not seriously threatened by barbarian invasion. Consequently, the fortifications of the cities were neglected, and the old walls began to fall into ruin. But the end of Gallienus' reign witnessed the beginning of serious disturbances caused by the inroads of the Heruls. To counter this immediate threat, hurried repairs were made to fortifications, using not just stone and brick, but whatever else came to hand, such as funerary altars, sarcophagi, tombstones, sculpture and all sorts of architectural elements, to be seen clearly on the walls of Thessalonike, Beroia and Dion. It is recorded that in A.D. 269 Kassandreia succeeded in resisting an onslaught by the Goths.

ARCHITECTURE

Public buildings

The market place in Thessalonike is constructed according to the well-known plan of a large, rectangular, open-air space surrounded by stoas; a theatre stands on one of the shorter sides.[18] Underneath the southern wing was a double subterranean stoa (cryptoporticus). It seems that the line of pillars, with its large relief figures — the famous 'idols', known as 'Las Incantadas':[19] Dionysos and Ariadne, Nike, Leda and the swan, Ganymede and the eagle, etc. — belonged to the larger market place, which has not yet been excavated. It is not clear whether this complex, in the form in which it has been preserved, should be dated, as has been suggested, to the second century A.D., or perhaps rather later.[20] Our knowledge of Thessalonike's other public buildings, the gymnasium, the baths, and the nymphaion, is extremely fragmentary.

The *forum* of Philippi was a relatively small (100×50 m.) paved open-air space.[21] Arranged around it were two Corinthian temples, distyle in antis, their stone walls sheathed in marble, and with carved acroteria; — in one of these temples was found the base for the statue of Faustina and the Genius of the colony; two large fountains; the rostrum for speakers; and the offices of the civic authorities (fig. 142). The commercial market place, situated immediately to the south, was later levelled to make way for the great Christian basilica. From the palaestra, with its internal portico, public toilets with forty-two stone seats have been preserved in good condition.[22] A

bit further to the south a sumptuous building was investigated, part of which was a bath.[23] The main hall, on the western side, contained a large rectangular basin surrounded by a Corinthian colonnade in the shape of the Greek letter Π, with a small fountain house on its short side. Adjacent to the north-eastern wall, the old Hellenistic theatre of Philippi was restored and extensively remodelled during the imperial period.[24] Statues of the Muses probably occupied the recesses on the stage front. In a later rearrangement the orchestra was converted into an arena suitable for fights staged with wild animals and gladiatorial combats.

The most imposing building of this sort to survive in the region of ancient Macedonia is the theatre at Stoboi, which appears to have been built in the second century A.D.[25] Its plan is essentially that of the Greek theatre, — that is to say, its *cavea* is built in an arc that is rather more than a semi-circle, and it is not joined to the stage as in Roman theatres. Names of tribes and of citizens are inscribed at various points in the tiers of stone seats, which accommodated seven to eight thousand spectators. The stage had a magnificent two storey facade, with Corinthian columns and niches containing statues, in one of which was the statue of an emperor. The central part of the *skene* took the form of a small temple of Nemesis, the protectress of dramatic competitions. Alterations to orchestra and seating arrangements that were necessary for the staging of combats with wild animals were executed in the third century A.D.

Among public buildings at Dion, where there was a great deal of building activity during the third century A.D., we know of two odeia and the public baths. The large odeion was situated on the southern end of the sanctuary and its *cavea*, here again more than a semi-circle, was supported on thirteen conical vaults, arranged radially.[26] The odeion was built with field stones, bound together at intervals with bands of brick, while certain parts, such as external arches and the corners of walls, were made of poros or conglomerate stone. Parts of a figure wearing a cuirass, a headless Hermes and other carved fragments have survived from the decoration of the stage. The *cavea* of the small odeion, which was located close to the baths, was inscribed within a thick rectangular external wall, whose main function was to bear the weight of the roof, with the help of Ionic columns arranged in an arc above and behind the tiers of seats. The building was probably covered by a double-pitched roof. Large numbers of roof tiles, of the Laconian type, together with the nails that held the wooden rafters in place, were found in the ruins — it was a real *theatrum tectum*. As for the odeion's purpose, it cannot be said with certainty whether it served the visitors to the baths, or whether perhaps it was mainly intended for public functions, since a large entrance on its northern side affords convenient access from the market place. The public baths were a large group of buildings with a facade on the east, opening onto a courtyard. On the side bordering the central street, and at a lower level, the complex ends in the public toilets and a row of shops. The interior of the baths was luxurious. The floors were covered by mosaics, among them one showing a marine

thiasos, which originally adorned the room which contained the large marble-clad hot baths. The north wing, which comprised three chambers, was of special importance. A series of statues representing the family of Asklepios was found in the ruins of one of these rooms. A building with a single chamber was excavated in the centre of the western side of the square. Parts of the mosaic floor and of the frescoes, painted to resemble polychrome marble cladding, have been preserved. In the rear part of the room, on a semi-circular plinth, stood statues, of which some fragments have been found.

Temples

Nothing is known about the architectural form of the Augustaeum in Thessalonike, where the statues of Augustus and (?) Claudius were presumably housed. We have only a small amount of information about the sanctuary of the Egyptian gods,[27] where, although excavations took place, the ruins have subsequently been covered over by modern buildings. In addition to a small temple and other minor buildings, there came to light a peculiar structure (11×8 m.) consisting of antechamber, cella, and subterranean crypt, which was approached by way of a long *dromos*. In a recess of the crypt a small herm, standing in its original position, was found. In the sanctuary were inscriptions and statues of the Egyptian gods and other divinities. There was also a sanctuary of the Egyptian gods at Philippi, on one of the terraces above the city.[28] Five small contiguous shrines were excavated here; one, with a recess in its rear wall, was dedicated to the worship of Isis. During the second and third centuries A.D. small sanctuaries with shrines were founded on the rocky slope; of these, the best-known are those of Artemis-Bendis and Silvanus.[29]

143. To the left, one of the four portrait statues discovered in a family heroon at Palatiano near Kilkis, dating to A.D. 100. The female figure is that of Ammia. She was depicted in the style known as the 'young Herakleiotissa'. It is probably the work of a Macedonian craftsman in a local atelier. Kilkis, Archaeological Museum

144. The statue of Augustus (28 B.C. - 14 A.D.), one of the best known imperial portraits from Macedonia. The head reproduces the Primaporta model, though the body is shown in the heroic stance, wearing a himation that leaves the greater part uncovered. Thessalonike, Archaeological Museum.

145. Bronze portrait head of Severus Alexander (A.D. 222-235). The artist made use of a well-known type, endowing it with some character and feeling in the expression of the face. Thessalonike, Archaeological Museum.

146. Some portraits of individuals imitate well known types of imperial portraits. Reproduced here is a woman's head, in marble, a work of exceptionally high standard, which has been given features closely resembling those of the empress Sabina. Thessalonike, Archaeological Museum.

The most recent excavations at Dion have revealed an important sanctuary of Isis, comprising (to date) three temples, in one of which the statue of the goddess still stood on its pedestal. The focal position is occupied by a tetrastyle prostyle Ionic temple with a monumental stairway on its eastern side. On the *prostasis* and the stairway stood dedications to Isis Lochia, Poseidon, Demeter and Artemis Eileithyia, who was apparently worshipped there before Isis. A small statue of Aphrodite was discovered next to the perfectly preserved altar. The small triconch temple where the cult statue was found had on its floor an oblong built basin with curved ends, evidently destined for ritual use. Two rooms with very simple masonry, situated in the northern part of the sanctuary, were probably intended for the use of the temple personnel. Inscriptions from the same site mention other buildings, which it is hoped future excavation will discover.

Private dwellings

We have only extremely fragmented information about private dwellings in Macedonia during this period. The excavations at Dion are just beginning to reveal the first houses. Mosaic floors are the best-known feature; some have geometrical decoration, others scenes from mythology or everyday life. Although it falls outside our chronological limits, it is worth mentioning an especially luxurious residence at Stoboi, of which we have a very full picture. This is the so-called 'Theodosian palace', located between two main streets in the centre of the town.[30] It had one main entrance, two secondary ones, and a courtyard bordered by colonnades in the shape of the Greek letter Γ. The nymphaion, with three reservoirs on its south-eastern side, was adorned by eight statues standing on pedestals. In the south-western part of the complex was a large apsidal room with a raised floor. A series of small, richly appointed rooms looked on to the courtyard. There was also a smaller house, with central court, belonging to the same complex.

SCULPTURE

The portrait

In Macedonia, as in all parts of the Roman empire, sculptural ateliers were mainly occupied with producing portraits of the ruler, of officials and of citizens. Never before in the ancient world had people been so eager to immortalize the human image. It was a major ambition of the wealthy to see erected an honorific statue in the market place or in some temple to commemorate some praiseworthy action of theirs on behalf of the community, while citizens of less privileged background contented themselves with a portrait on their funerary monument.

For the most part, these portraits are made of local marble, and in most cases, there can be no doubt that they were manufactured in the place where they were to be erected. The question of the workshop is more complicated in the case of imperial portraits, since they were modelled on the official portraits of the emperor in Rome.

Imperial portraits

At the beginning of the sequence stands the statue of Augustus in Thessalonike (fig. 144).[31] The head of the empire's founder follows the 'Primaporta' model; but Augustus does not wear a cuirass, as in the Vatican copy, but is portrayed in the heroic stance, wearing a *himation* that leaves the greater part of the body uncovered. A study of the details suggests that this work dates from after Augustus' death, in the reign of Tiberius or Caligula. The head of Vespasian, also in the Thessalonike Museum, is more than life-size, and possesses all the characteristic features of the official portrait, placing the identification beyond doubt.[32] It differs from the western models, not typologically, but only stylistically, being characterized by a more lively rendering of details, and a marked inclination and turning of the head reflecting the Hellenistic tradition that lies behind the portrait.

The cuirass-clad bust of Septimius Severus in Thessalonike, with its severe frontalism and neutral expression, is more strongly infused with the spirit of the official portrait.[33] Another portrait type of the same emperor, that with 'the curls of Serapis', is represented by a head from Dion.[34]

Other portraits of members of the Severan dynasty have also been preserved. A colossal head of Caracalla from Drama, now in the Louvre, with the severe frontalism of the 'autocrat' type;[35] and a portrait of high quality, retrieved in fragments from the ruins of Dion, depicts the emperor according to the same type, but with his head turned sharply towards the left.[36] Finally, the bronze head of Severus Alexander from Riakia in Pieria, though based on a familiar model, is the only portrait that shows the young emperor with full beard (fig. 145).[37] The finishing touches to the work, after the casting of the metal, were confined to such incisions as were necessary for the definition of details. Even so, the artist managed to convey some character and feeling to the expression of the face.

Private portraits

Private portraits were of several types: busts with their own bases, full-length portraits and herms. Busts in relief are also to be found, on tomb-stones, funerary altars, *imagines clipeatae* and some sarcophagi. As elsewhere in the Roman world, so too in Macedonia, the private portrait often imitates and adopts the changing styles of imperial portraiture. This is true of external features, such as the size and shape of the bust or the type of hairstyle; but the dependence can also be detected even in matters of fundamental artistic development, which constitute the distinctive style of each period. The degree of this dependence varies with time and circumstances, because, apart from the artistic currents that flowed from Rome, there were also local traditions that still flourished and which, especially in Macedonia, were fertilized by influences from Asia Minor and, even more so, from Attica.

The hairstyles of many portraits from the middle imperial period follow the latest fashion; a good example is provided by a sarcophagus from Thessalonike with four busts, where one woman has the hairstyle of the elder

147. *Detail of a funerary relief from Lete, one of a series of grave reliefs characterized by the careful finish of the head in* *contrast to the body which is rendered more summarily. Late 1st century B.C. Thessalonike, Archaeological Museum.*

Faustina, while the young man with curly hair next to her vividly recalls the portrait of the young Marcus Aurelius.[38] Sometimes the resemblance goes even further, to the point of reproducing the emperor's personal features. Thus a superb private portrait from Thessalonike (fig. 146) is almost identical with the empress Sabina,[39] while the face of the deceased on a stele from Beroia presents a more than striking resemblance to the physiognomy of Hadrian.[40] On the other hand, a small group of male portraits, probably of philosophers, in Thessalonike, makes clear references to Classical and Hellenistic prototypes. The rich long locks of hair crowning a magnificent bust of Olganos (perhaps a river god), now in the Beroia Museum, clearly reflects its creation in the classicizing milieu (fig. 139).[41]

The problem of the workshop provenance of Macedonian portraits has been touched on only occasionally by scholarly research. Nonetheless, we can recognize with certainty some of the products of local workshops, for example the busts, often of superb quality, on the funerary altars of Beroia or the portraits on the stelai and sarcophagi of Thessalonike.

Funerary reliefs

The portraits on funerary reliefs are often of a simplified form, giving the impression that they constantly repeat the same models. But a careful observation of our material persuades us that the craftsmen, even in the humblest reliefs, did attempt to differentiate faces by bestowing some personal features on them.

Not all those represented on the funerary reliefs, which often portray a number of different individuals, are necessarily dead. Inscriptions on the monuments themselves make a clear distinction by attaching the formula 'in memory' after the name or the names of the dead, and by

215

qualifying as 'living' the names of relatives and of the person responsible for erecting the monument.

Sometimes funerary inscriptions call the monument on which they are inscribed a 'heroon' or the deceased a 'hero'. This heroization of the dead, a widely disseminated custom in the imperial period, is in many instances made even clearer by the visual representation. Certain stelai have two representations.[42] In the first the deceased and his relatives are shown in bust, arrayed in sequence according to the traditional order, and wearing the dress of the period. In the second, the setting and costume change. Here the same persons are represented, but in heroic roles, participating in a banquet of the dead or in the shape of the 'Thracian horseman' or even of Hermes or Aphrodite. It is worth noting that no change in physiognomy occurs in the course of the transition from one world to another; the viewer could recognize the figures represented in the heroic context.[43]

Stelai of Roman officers

Among the funerary reliefs of Roman officers and veterans in Macedonia, that of Picenus (at Dion) stands out.[44] Picenus served as standard-bearer *(signifer)* and as aedile and reached the highest office in the colony, that of *duumvir quinquennalis*. On the relief, alongside the inscription that recounts his offices, Picenus' weapons and decorations are represented. Also noteworthy is the large stele found in 1965 outside the village of Grammeni near Drama, now in the Kavala Museum (fig. 135).[45] The long text of the inscription refers to the successful career of the veteran Tiberius Claudius Maximus, the Roman soldier who captured and killed Decebalus, the famous king of the Dacians, during the war of A.D. 105-06. Maximus is represented astride his horse; with his sword in his right hand he attacks Decebalus, who has fallen on his back. Decebalus is the typical barbarian in both appearance and dress. He wears breeches and a sharp-pointed head-dress, he has a long beard and prominent nose, holds a hexagonal shield and lets his curious curved sword fall from his right hand. The capture of Decebalus is also shown in one of the scenes on Trajan's column in Rome. It is extremely illuminating to compare the two representations, the one on a public monument in the capital, the other on a private memorial in Macedonia.

Attic sarcophagi

Looking at Macedonian statues (whether idealistic or realistic), certain relationships emerge, of greater or lesser significance, to works from the so-called neo-Attic workshops, whose activity did not come to an end with the relief plaques of the time of Hadrian and Antoninus Pius, but continued at least until the reign of Gallienus, with the production of the well-known Attic sarcophagi.[46] The most representative group of these monuments is to be seen in the Thessalonike Museum, while important fragments have been found at Dion, in the Pieria area and in ancient Paionia. Today it can be regarded as certain that these sarcophagi, with mythological scenes on all four sides, were not only prepared, up to a certain point, in Athens, and

thereafter completed in the place for which they were destined by either Athenian or local artists (as has been maintained), but might also be exported *after* the whole of their decoration had been completed. Thus the Attic sarcophagi provide a stable criterion for comparison with works from local workshops.

Two masterpieces of this genre may be mentioned here: firstly, the sarcophagus depicting the Dionysiac thiasos from the western necropolis of Thessalonike (fig. 148).[47] On three of its sides are carved satyrs and maenads, Cupids and little children amidst panthers and a goat. They gather grapes with graceful gestures and play music. On the back we see two griffins attacking Centaurs. The figures, rendered in high relief, are densely packed. The lid of the sarcophagus is in the form of a richly decorated mattress on which a man and a woman repose.

The main face of another sarcophagus from the same cemetery depicts an epic struggle close to some ships.[48] One of the short sides shows a battle between infantry and cavalry, while the other portrays Orpheus among the beasts. On the back is the Calydonian boar hunt. The anatomical details of the bodies are carved with meticulous attention.

Copies of Classical works

As well as contemporary idealistic sculptures and honorific statues, a number of copies of Classical masterpieces stood in temples and public places. Although some of them are merely simplified and banal repetitions of their prototypes, the average quality of such copies in Macedonia was commendably high. The best known are a group of copies of works by Pheidias; for example the colossal acrolithic copy of the Medici Athena,[49] now in the Thessalonike Museum, altered under the Severi into a portrait of Julia Domna, and the variation on the well-known type of Artemis Ariccia.[50] The Thessalonike copy more clearly conveys the character of a genuine work of Pheidias. From the early Classical period we have a copy of the so-called 'head of Aspasia',[51] the work of a Peloponnesian artist, which probably represents Demeter. Of particularly fine quality is the copy of the 'Fréjus' Aphrodite,[52] of which we also have the black stone base. This statue, probably made in the first half of the second century A.D., is a copy of a Classical masterpiece of the post-Pheidian period. This was one of the most popular statues in the imperial period, if one may judge from the large number of copies and remodellings that have survived. Among copies of works from the fourth century B.C. may be mentioned heads of the 'Colonna' Artemis,[53] copies of the 'Greater' and 'Smaller' Herakleiotissa;[54] and the colossal head of Serapis found in the area of the ancient market place in Thessalonike.[55]

---

148. Attic sarcophagi decorated with common mythological themes have been found on many occasions in Macedonia. In the picture, a detail from the decoration of a sarcophagus found in the western necropolis of Thessalonike, showing children playfully picking grapes, a cupid and a goat. Thessalonike, Archaeological Museum.

ΛΛΘΗΝΟΟΟΝΤΛΥΤΗΝΗΤΟΡΛCΛΕΓΤΙΛΝΡΟIΙ

149. *After the transfer of the seat of the emperor Galerius to Thessalonike, a large administrative complex was constructed; it is shown below, the Octagon, so named because of its plan.*

150, 151. *The splendour of the Galerian palace complex was complemented by the triumphal Arch of Galerius (150), the processional way and a circular temple, the Rotunda. The Arch had four central piers (two survive), which once supported a dome. On its north-south axis two pairs of smaller arches sprang from the tetrapylon. The pair on the side facing the Rotunda was connected to the colonnades of the processional way. The carved decoration (151) depicts episodes from the war of Galerius against the Persians, A.D. 296-297.*

152

153

152. *Detail of a mosaic floor: a male figure representing the sea. 3rd century A.D. Thessalonike, Archaeological Museum.*

153. *Detail of a mosaic floor: a female figure and a dolphin symbolizing the sea. 3rd century A.D. Thessalonike, Archaeological Museum.*

THE PERIOD OF THE TETRARCHS

The Palace of Galerius in Thessalonike

The capital of Macedonia reached a new peak in its fortunes under the Tetrarchy, when Galerius decided to transfer his seat to Thessalonike and build his palace there. The main elements of this complex that have come to light so far are the Octagon, the hippodrome, the triumphal arch and the Rotunda.

The first of these buildings, which was probably used as a throne room, was octagonal both inside and out (fig. 149).[56] The interior, however, leaves a different impression because of six uniform recesses, and a larger seventh opposite the entrance. In front of the Octagon a transverse corridor with apsidal ends served as an antechamber, while two small areas on the other side joined the Octagon to a large peristyle. Internally the building was decorated with a mosaic floor and marble cladding on the walls, with architectural articulation. Some Corinthian capitals have been found, with representations of gods (Zeus, the Dioskouroi, Kabeiros, Hygeia etc.). In the middle filling of the ruins there were also found the crowning sections of a marble arch, its front, sides and intrados richly carved.[57] The general theme of the composition is Dionysiac (a bust of Dionysos, Pan, a maenad, a vine), but Galerius is represented in a prominent position on one side and the personification of Thessalonike on the other (figs. 154, 155).

Both chronologically and functionally the Thessalonike hippodrome,[58] which became famous in history as a result of the blood-bath ordered by Theodosios in A.D. 390, is closely linked with the palace. A few remains are preserved today in the foundations of blocks of flats in the Hippodrome area: part of the marble podium from the end of the arena, and some of the vaulted substructures below the public tiers of seats.

The design of the triumphal arch departs from the norm.[59] Today, less than half of the original structure is preserved (fig. 150). Originally there were two more central piers connected by an arch; these, together with the two surviving piers, supported a dome. On the north and south sides of this tetrapylon were two pairs of smaller arches. The pair on the side facing the Rotunda was connected to the colonnade of the processional way, while the other pair was linked to a large, elegant hall. Important episodes from Galerius' war against the Persians (A.D. 296-97), are depicted on the two surviving pillars; on the northern, battle scenes, and on the southern the aftermath of the battle. Particularly notable are the representations of Galerius addressing his soldiers, the victory sacrifice of Diocletian and Galerius, and the official frontal depiction of the Tetrarchs amidst their divine patrons. The two Caesars, Galerius and Constantine, flank the two enthroned emperors Diocletian and Maximian who signify their blessings on the two provinces personified. The 'narration' of historical events thus culminates in a representation of the Tetrarch's political philosophy.

The Rotunda stood at the highest point of the complex.[60] It was a large circular building with a dome. The dome's enormous thrust was easily absorbed by the strong external wall, 6.5 m. thick, punctuated internally by seven large rectangular recesses with arched ceilings and an eighth which pierced the whole wall and served as entrance. The interior was revetted with marble panels, and had rich architectural decoration consisting of colonnettes and capitals. Rows of windows flooded the building with light. In the course of its history the Rotunda underwent two fundamental alterations: about A.D. 400 it was turned into a church and in the sixteenth century it became a mosque. Thus it is very difficult to restore its original form. It is very likely that the Rotunda was used as a temple; and it is certain that it did not serve as Galerius' mausoleum (fig. 156).

The choice of this position on the fringe of Roman Thessalonike, rather than somewhere more central, was dictated by the size of the palace complex, covering approximately 150,000 sq.m. and including the hippodrome as well as the emperor's residence and accommodation for soldiers. From the imperial balcony Galerius could not only follow the games, but also address the assembled mass of citizens or soldiery. A third section was constituted by the complex of the arch of Galerius, the processional way and the circular temple, where divine worship was offered with the participation of the emperor. The self-contained Galerian complex faced the sea, with which the palace apparently communicated directly. In this way, without needing to be fortified, like the palace of Diocletian at Spalato, the Palace of Galerius had similar advantages of control, defence and unimpeded access. The whole complex was admirably autonomous: the work of government, as well as participation in popular events and the state cult, could all be attended to without the emperor needing to leave his palace.

Theodosian portraits

From the surviving fourth century sculpture we shall refer only to two outstanding busts from the time of Theodosios.[61] These two busts, one of a man and one of a woman, probably depict a couple. Their rich clothing, careful hairstyle and reserved, official expression suggest that they were of high social position. These works carry all the distinguishing features of their period, but they have a rare force, and their details are most carefully and elegantly executed.

Epilogue

We shall not attempt to conclude by summarizing in general terms the essential and specific characteristics of Macedonian art in the Roman period. For such an undertaking one would need a profound knowledge of a large number of monuments. Unfortunately, there were until recently very few systematic excavations in Macedonia and scholars took only a limited interest in its monuments. But there are hopes that contemporary archaeological research, liberated from unjustified prejudices, will now bestow due attention on this period of ancient art as well, art which both continues the Hellenistic tradition and introduces the Byzantine.

BYZANTINE
MACEDONIA

THE FIRST CHRISTIAN YEARS

The long-drawn out economic, social and political crisis experienced by the Roman empire from the first decades of the third century A.D. undermined the fabric of society and the existing political institutions, shook the values of the past and swept away the classes which had maintained them. The new social forces expressed by the emperors Diocletian (284-305) and Constantine the Great (306-337) imposed a new political and social system which put an end to instability and opened the way to a new historical epoch. At the same time, there was a change in the official religious policy. Persecution of Christians ceased, and the new faith received both the blessing and the support of those in authority. Christianity was recognized as the official religion, closely linked with the new state.

For the eastern half of the new Christian empire, however, the change was characterized, amongst other things, by the steady decline of Latinity and the triumph of Hellenism. In government, this would take time, but already by A.D. 300 the Roman colonies in the southern part of the Balkan peninsula and the East were hellenized. This Constantinople, the new Rome of the eastern Empire, founded in 324, quickly emerged both as the capital of a new world, Byzantium, the successor to Rome in the East, and at the same time and of far more significance, as a new and enriched embodiment of a reborn Greek oikoumene.

All this had repercussions in Macedonia. But something else also happened there which was to be typical of Byzantium. The emperor Galerius (306-311) made his headquarters at Thessalonike and Constantine made the city the base for his operations against Licinius. The gradual replacement of the other large provincial centres caused Thessalonike to become the second city of the Byzantine empire, bulwark and intellectual beacon of its Balkan parts. Moreover, as has been stressed in the introduction, from the beginning of the Byzantine period, the term Macedonian acquires a purely geographic connotation, without an ethnic content, embracing without exception all the inhabitants of this historic region, independent of their origins. It is in this sense that the reader will find the word used in the following pages.

POLITICAL HISTORY

Late 3rd-6th Centuries

The history of Macedonia in the Early Christian period has not yet been adequately studied, and a comprehensive survey of its political, ecclesiastical, social and cultural condition in the fourth, fifth and sixth centuries encounters considerable difficulties. To many questions we are not yet in a position to give a definitive answer, because literary testimonies are sparse, and the epigraphic material of the area has not yet been systematically published. Yet such evidence as we have leaves us in no doubt that, despite the frequent barbarian raids of the fifth and sixth centuries, many of the towns of Roman Macedonia survived almost to the end of the sixth century and played an important role in the later Roman empire. Particularly useful in this connection are the results of archaeological excavations, which fill out our picture of the area for the period in question.

POLITICAL GEOGRAPHY

The most important landmark in the history of the Roman state during the last quarter of the third century was Diocletian's accession to the throne in 284. A new era was inaugurated for the Roman empire by Diocletian's success in putting an end to the great crisis which, as all historians agree, had seriously threatened the state in the third century.

One of Diocletian's first tasks after his accession to the throne was the administrative reorganization of the empire. As a result of this reorganization, Macedonia too experienced significant changes: the *provincia Macedonia*[1] was virtually restricted to the area covered by 'historic' Macedonia and formed part of one of the twelve dioceses *(dioeceses)* of the Roman empire, namely the diocese of Moesia *(dioecesis Moesiarum)*.[2] As in the rest of the non-military provinces, so too in Macedonia, the administration of the province was entrusted to a civil officer, the *praeses*, who was subordinate to the *vicarius* that is the highest authority in Moesia.

The new system of government was completed when Constantine introduced a higher rank in provincial government, the praetorian prefectures *(praefectura praetorio)*, and its corresponding officer, the praetorian prefect *(praefectus praetorio)*. The larger part of the Balkan peninsula, except for the diocese of Thrace, formed, together with Italy and Africa, the central praefecture of Italy, Africa and Illyricum, whose capital was Rome.[3]

In all probability at the same time the diocese of Moesia was also divided into the diocese of Dacia (which comprised five provinces) and that of Macedonia with the following six provinces: Macedonia, Epirus Vetus and Epirus Nova, Thessaly, Achaia and Crete. Macedonia and Crete were governed by a *consularis,* whereas the other areas were administered by a *praeses*.[4] To the second half of the fourth century, Illyricum, (that is the three dioceses of Macedonia, Dacia and Pannonia) formed a separate praefecture (the *praefectura praetorio per Illyricum)* and in 392 it was annexed by Theodosios the Great to the eastern part of the empire. But the successors of Theodosios divided the contentious praefecture: thus eastern Illyricum, which comprised the dioceses of Macedonia and Dacia was finally integrated into the eastern part of the empire as the praefecture of Illyricum, whereas western Illyricum, that is the dioceses of Pannonia, came under the western part of the empire.

All the evidence suggests that soon after the foundation of the prefecture of Illyricum its capital became Thessalonike and only for a short time, following the annexation of Sirmium and of the whole of Pannonia to the eastern part of the empire was Sirmium the actual capital (from 424 or from 437 to 441). But the destruction of Sirmium by Attila's Huns dictated once again the transfer of the administrative seat of eastern Illyricum to Thessalonike (442), where it thenceforth remained. That in novella XI Justinian ordered in 535 that the capital be transferred to his native town of Justiniana Prima is not conclusive evidence, according to some scholars, that the transfer actually took place, since in the sources of the years 536 and 541 there are references to a prefect of Thessalonike.[5]

Thus, after Diocletian's and Constantine's important reforms of the boundaries and administration of the Roman provinces, the situation in the area of 'historic' Macedonia crystallized as follows: two old Macedonian areas, Elimiotis and Orestis (that is the area round modern Kozani north of the Haliakmon river, and the region of the lake Kastoria basin) were annexed to the new province of Thessaly for administrative purposes. To the west of Macedonia there emerged the province of Epirus Nova, to which belonged Lychnidos (modern Ochrid), whereas the town of Bargala, to the north-east, did not yet form part of Macedonia. An important dated inscription, which was found in the area, informs us that in 371 Bargala belonged to Dacia Mediterranea.[6] To the east, Philippi, Neapolis (modern Kavala) and Akontisma, situated further east still, constituted the last important Macedonian towns on the eastern frontier.

In the fourth century, therefore, Macedonia extended to the east and north-east as far as the river Nestos, to the north it bordered on the province of Dardania just above

154-155. Details showing the emperor Galerius and Thessalonike personified from a richly carved crowning arch found during excavations of the Galerian complex at Thessalonike. Thessalonike, Archaeological Museum.

156. The Rotunda, Thessalonike from the east, a large circular domed building. In the period of the Tetrarchs it may have been used as a temple; towards the end of the 4th century A.D. it was converted into a church by the addition of a sanctuary apse.

the town of Bylazora (Velessa, Titov Veles), to the north-west it bordered on Praevalitana and Epirus Nova (its actual border on this side lying between Herakleia Lynkestis and Lychnidos), to the west it bordered on Epirus Vetus, which extended beyond the Pindos range and to the south it bordered on Thessaly. On this side the demarcation line was provided by the river Peneios. Finally the islands of Thasos and Samothrace belonged to Macedonia too.[7] Despite their administrative dependence on Thessaly, Elimiotis and Orestis had since remote antiquity been considered part of Macedonia.

In the following centuries the boundaries of Macedonia did not remain stable, a common phenomenon in the provincial history of this period. In consequence we encounter frequent changes in the internal administration of the province, as for instance the appearance of new administrative regions or the switching of towns from one administrative area to another. Thus, from the end of the fourth century to the middle of the sixth, Macedonia appears to be divided into two parts, Macedonia Prima and Macedonia Salutaris to begin with, and later into Macedonia Prima and Macedonia Secunda. This redivision has given rise to much debate, especially in connection with the question of what area was represented by Macedonia Salutaris and its relationship to the area of Macedonia Secunda.[8]

The first and only reference to Macedonia Salutaris is to be found in the *Notitia Dignitatum,* an early fifth century text.[9] The fact that no previous historical source refers to Macedonia Salutaris led most scholars to espouse the view that it was probably created in 386,[10] when many other provinces in the empire also took the name 'Salutaris'.[11] This administrative sub-division of Macedonia cannot have been long-lived, since it is referred to, again in the *Notitia*

Dignitatum, as being divided between Epirus Nova and Praevalitana (in the diocese of Dacia).[12] This reference allows us to locate Macedonia Salutaris, which cannot have been very large, somewhere in the north-west part of Macedonia.[13]

Macedonia Secunda, which is more frequently mentioned in the written sources of the period, was formed in all probability towards the end of the fifth century by the detachment of a part of Macedonia Prima, including the towns of Stoboi and Bargala.[14] According to the Acts of the Council of Chalcedon (451), these towns belonged until the mid-fifth century to Macedonia Prima.[15] This important piece of information leads us to the conclusion that Macedonia Secunda cannot have been founded before the mid-fifth century. Moreover it becomes apparent that, not only can Macedonia Salutaris and Macedonia Secunda not have been contemporary, but, more importantly, they did not cover the same territory; neither Bargala (which, as has already been said, belonged in 371 to Dacia Mediterranea) nor Stoboi are mentioned anywhere as cities of Macedonia Salutaris.[16]

It is generally accepted that the abolition of Macedonia Secunda took place between 535 and 545. In Justinian's novella XI, dating from the year 535, Macedonia Secunda is mentioned as dependent in ecclesiastical matters on Justiniana Prima (Caričin Grad?) and not on the see of Thessalonike.[17] This is the very last reference to this much discussed area of Macedonia, since it is not referred to at all in novella CXXXI dating from the year 545.[18] Sometime after 535, then, this administrative area must have been abolished and absorbed into Macedonia Prima and Dacia Mediterranea, from parts of which it had been formed in the first place.[19]

POLITICAL DEVELOPMENTS

After the devastating raids of the Goths during the second half of the third century Macedonia was for a long time free from the barbarian threat. For a period of about a hundred years the inhabitants of the province were at peace to apply themselves to constructive activities, and to economic and cultural restoration. This task was greatly facilitated by the interest displayed in Macedonia by the Roman emperors. The two greatest advantages of the province, that the emperors of the period were quick to exploit, were, on the one hand, her strategic position as crossroads of the main Balkan routes and a natural opening onto the Aegean, and, on the other hand, the presence of Thessalonike, a Greek city with a long cultural tradition. Thus, in the critical period of transition from the Roman to the early Byzantine era, Macedonia was the theatre of important events, many of which had a decisive influence on the political and religious development of the eastern empire. As was to be expected, most of these events took place in Thessalonike, which certain emperors honoured with their (often prolonged) presence, and sometimes used as base and starting point of their military campaigns.

157. Independent artistic creativity continued throughout the Early Christian period in Thessalonike. One exceptionally well-executed work of the mid-5th century is the platform of the pulpit from the Rotunda; between recessed shell-shaped conches are scenes of the Annunciation to the Shepherds and the Adoration of the Magi. Istanbul, Archaeological Museum.

Already in the last years of the third century the Caesar, Maximian Galerius, whose administrative seat was at Sirmium in Pannonia, had taken a special interest in Thessalonike. This interest was expressed in his decision to establish a mint and to build a palace there, a decision which heralded the transferal of his seat to the capital of Macedonia when he received the title of Augustus in 305. This transfer was dictated by his need for greater freedom in directing his military campaigns against the barbarians who were disturbing the border regions.

Galerius' stay in Thessalonike was linked with the great wave of anti-Christian persecutions at this period, and especially with the martyrdom of Saint Demetrios. A Roman army officer and scion of a noble family, Demetrios was converted to Christianity and, according to the written tradition, martyred on the order of Galerius in the basement of the Roman baths, the very spot where later his 'most beautiful' church was erected. The cult of St. Demetrios was thenceforth closely linked with the life of the inhabitants of Thessalonike and became so popular that other cities too, like Sirmium, claimed to be his place of origin. Demetrios, 'who gives forth perfume', 'the friend of the city', the 'saviour and defender of the fatherland', who saved the city and her inhabitants innumerable times from the enemy, from epidemics and from famines, was regarded from the sixth century onwards as the patron saint of Thessalonike and, more generally, as one of the most important among the Greek saints.

After Galerius, Constantine the Great spent some time in Thessalonike in 322/23, when he was preparing for the war against his brother-in-law Licinius. Well supplied as a military base, Thessalonike was ideal as a place of preparation for the war. The only thing it lacked was a harbour large enough to hold Constantine's fleet and to transmit food supplies to the army. It was at this time that a large square harbour was built on the western shore of the city, which was preserved for many centuries and fell into disuse only in the late Byzantine period.[20]

Licinius was taken prisoner by Constantine in Nikomedeia in Asia Minor, where he had taken refuge, and was led to Thessalonike. He then spent about two years in prison, until in 325 he was executed on the charge that he had taken part in a plot.

During the next fifty years we do not hear much about Macedonia, which was to return to the centre of the political and religious stage in the reign of Theodosios the Great.

During the reigns of Valens and Theodosios the Great the Goths began to make new and particularly destructive raids into the Balkan peninsula.[21] After the defeat and death of Valens at the famous battle of Adrianople (9 August 378), the Visigoths and Ostrogoths, aided by Alans and small groups of Huns, flooded into the Balkans along its two main routes: the diagonal route which linked Constantinople with Western Europe by way of Sardica and Naissus, and the Via Egnatia, which joined Constantinople to the Adriatic, traversing Macedonia. As the new Augustus of the East, Theodosios the Great undertook the difficult task of clearing the invaders from his possessions.

Our evidence on the conduct of this new Gothic war is scanty and vague. Yet one thing we know with certainty is that Theodosios established his military headquarters in Thessalonike, where he spent much time between the summer of 379 and the autumn of 380. During this period there took place events of decisive importance for the whole state, namely the grave illness of the emperor, his baptism by the metropolitan of Thessalonike Acholios or Ascholios (who was a fervent supporter of the Nicene creed), and the publication of the well-known Edict of Thessalonike (28 February 380). Most scholars agree in seeing in this edict the result of Acholios' influence on the emperor, who by publishing this edict condemned all heresies and recognized the Nicene creed as the only true form of Christian belief. At the same time the religious policy of Theodosios was taking on its definitive shape. Since this policy was to be followed by his successors as well, one can justifiably claim that, thanks to her bishop, the capital of Macedonia played at this period a very important part in the evolution of the Eastern Orthodox Church. Moreover, since our knowledge of the Macedonian Church in the aftermath of Demetrios' martyrdom is extremely limited, these events in the reign of Theodosios are among the earliest important testimonies to the history of Christianity in Macedonia.

As was natural, in Thessalonike Theodosios occupied himself also with the reorganization of the army and, more generally, with the defence of the state. It is not unlikely that, within the framework of these activities, he directed his attention to the fortification of the town. In the opinion of certain scholars, the early Byzantine walls of the city were constructed during his reign.[22] At this period the threat of barbarian invasion kept in a constant state of alarm not just the inhabitants of Macedonia, but also the emperors themselves, who were preoccupied by the problem of the security of this sensitive area.

In the following years Macedonia, and Thessalonike in particular, continued to be closely associated with the private and public life of Theodosios the Great. In 378/88 Theodosios returned to Thessalonike in order to assist his co-emperor, Valentinian II, who had taken refuge there with his family for fear of the usurper Maximus. There Theodosios married Valentinian's sister, Galla, and, in all probability, celebrated also his *decennalia*.[23] A little later, the name of Theodosios was to be associated with another important event of Macedonian history, the famous massacre in the hippodrome of Thessalonike.[24] This event took place in the spring of 390, when Theodosios was in Italy. In Thessalonike the citizens had attacked the Gothic city-guard and assassinated its captain the *magister militum* Butherichus, who had prevented a popular charioteer from participating in the races because he was a pederast. On hearing this news in Italy Theodosios, in a fit of anger, ordered the slaughter of the Thessalonikans in the hippodrome. This massacre cost the lives of seven thousand men, women and children who were treacherously trapped in the hippodrome. Theodosios' revocation of his order did not reach Thessalonike in time, and its implementation brought important consequences. The emperor was compelled by Ambrose, the bishop of Milan, to do public penance; and subsequently, under the influence of Ambrose, he took drastic measures to root out paganism. As for the hippodrome of Thessalonike, it never functioned again.

Henceforth the dominant theme in the history of Macedonia is the barbarian invasions. Despite the fact that, as agreed in 382 in a treaty signed by Theodosios, the Goths had been allowed to settle in part of the Balkan peninsula, they nevertheless continued to raid Macedonia from their hiding-places in its marshes. On his return from Italy to Constantinople in the summer of 391, Theodosios halted once again in Thessalonike, intending to exterminate the barbarians. Indeed, despite initial defeats suffered by the imperial army, the ensuing campaigns resulted in the annihilation of a large proportion of the raiders.

Four years later, Macedonia was in grave danger from Alaric's Visigoths. After an unsuccessful attempt to take Constantinople, the king of the Visigoths of Thrace turned west. By way of the Via Egnatia, and after causing extensive damage to the eastern part of Macedonia, he made a determined attempt to capture Thessalonike, but without any success. Subsequently, he turned towards southern Greece, and his destructive descent was brought to an end only after the signing of a treaty whose conditions were particularly favourable to him and to his people.

It is not known whether Macedonia suffered any serious barbarian raids before the third big wave of Gothic invasions in 473; but it is legitimate to assume that the rage of Attila and his Huns, in their descent towards southern Greece in 447, cannot have left her unaffected.

Macedonia was sore pressed in the decade between 473 and 483 by the Ostrogoths from the northern Balkans as, divided into two under the respective commands of Theodoric the Elder (Strabo), and Theodoric the Younger (the Amal), they moved southwards. At their hands Stoboi suffered one of the greatest catastrophes in its history; likewise both Philippi and Thessalonike were seriously threatened.[25] Indeed the capital of Macedonia almost fell; it was saved only by the diplomacy and promises of the emperor Zeno, who succeeded in this way in turning the attention of the invaders towards Epirus Nova. Yet, if Thessalonike had the good fortune to be saved, the same could not be said of other cities of Macedonia, such as Pella, Edessa and Herakleia Lynkestis which experienced the cruelties of the barbarians during their march from Thessalonike to Dyrrachion in Epirus Nova.

The information we have on the siege of Herakleia is of particular interest.[26] While the population of the city took refuge in the acropolis, its bishop tried to placate the leader of the Goths, Theodoric the Amal, by offering him rich presents. But the Goths would not leave. They besieged the city for a long time, demanding food supplies for their campaign against Epirus Nova. The inhabitants of Herakleia steadfastly refused to give them any supplies; and their refusal led to the destruction of the city after its eventual capture. The raiders then carried on towards their final destination. Though the destruction of Herakleia Lynkestis was almost complete, it did not mark the end of its history; some archaeological finds of the sixth century exist,[27] and its bishop participated in the fifth oecumenical Council of Constantinople in 553.[28]

After their unsuccessful operations in Epirus Nova, the Goths returned to Macedonia in 482 and laid it waste again. The area was delivered from them only by the signing of a treaty which allowed them to settle in the uninhabited regions of Lower Moesia and Dacia Ripensis. Yet the empire finally got rid of them only when their attention was turned towards Italy, which they conquered in 497.

In the first decades of the sixth century the Balkan peninsula became the theatre of renewed barbarian invasions. Some of the Slavic and Hunnic tribes that had recently appeared in the Balkans, the Sklavenoi, Antai,

158. *Amphipolis, a populous and thriving town in the Early Christian period, was the seat of a bishopric. Excavation has uncovered basilicas with elaborate mosaic floors. The picture shows a detail – a fisherman – from such a floor.*

Bulgars and Kutrigurs, raided Macedonia on their way into Thessaly in 517; but we have no detailed information as regards these events.

The situation became even more serious under Justinian. According to Prokopios, invasions took place almost every year, and this obliged Justinian to undertake an extensive programme of restoration of urban defences and construction of new fortresses.[29] Macedonia, which constituted one of the most crucial areas of the empire, naturally was not excluded from this programme.[30] One of the most destructive raids experienced by Macedonia in this period was that of 540, when swarms of Huns (in all probability Bulgars and Kutrigurs) attempted to take Thessalonike, though without success. According to Prokopios, the city was saved by its impregnable walls.[31] But neighbouring Kassandreia in Chalkidike was less lucky, and suffered one of the worst disasters ever experienced by a city in consequence of a barbarian raid. Its walls, which were almost completely destroyed, were rebuilt a little later by Justinian.[32]

In the years to follow, the barbarian incursions continued to be numerous and frequent, and some of them posed a direct threat to Thessalonike, quite apart from the devastation inflicted on the Macedonian countryside. The most terrible Hunnic raid of all took place in 558-9. It was due to the descent of the Kutrigurs who, after allying themselves with the Slavs and Bulgars of the area around the Danube, crossed the river and moved southwards. A large group of them laid waste Macedonia, and then carried on

159. *A view of the eastern city wall of Thessalonike. Some sections of the early Byzantine defences may have been built in the* time of Theodosios the Great, a measure necessary for the protection of the city from repeated barbarian raids.

towards Thessaly where it was checked by a force of two thousand men guarding Thermopylai.

All the sixth century invasions to which we have referred so far had a disastrous, but not lasting, effect on Macedonia. Its countryside was often laid waste, many of its inhabitants were slaughtered and others were taken prisoners; but no city was taken (except, of course, for Kassandreia, which was soon rebuilt), nor did the invasions lead to permanent settlements. The real threat to Macedonia was to appear towards the end of Justinian's reign, in the shape of the Slavs and the Avars, a threat that was to become the main factor in determining the future of Macedonia and the rest of the Balkan peninsula.[33]

ECCLESIASTICAL ORGANIZATION

Of the ecclesiastical organization of Macedonia during the late Roman and early Byzantine period little is known.

The only available sources, themselves of an indirect character, are the lists and the Acts of the oecumenical and local Councils and the *Taktika* from which we can deduce that the ecclesiastical organization of the province of Macedonia was based on the metropolitan system — a system which followed the administrative organization of the province. The title of metropolitan (archbishop) was held by the bishop of the capital, who also presided over local Councils; sees of bishops were established in many cities of the province.[34]

The metropolitan see of Macedonia was Thessalonike, the administrative centre of the province. During the early Byzantine period there cannot have existed in Macedonia any other metropolitan see; there seems to be little evidence for the view that Stoboi, as the capital of Macedonia Secunda, was also a metropolitan see.[35] It is certain, though, that for a short period at the beginning of Justinian's reign Macedonia Secunda constituted a separate ecclesiastical unit dependent administratively on the metropolis of Dacia Mediterranea, Justiniana Prima, whither Justinian had provisionally transferred from Thessalonike the capital of Eastern Illyricum, according to one view.[36]

The metropolitan of Thessalonike enjoyed great prestige not only within Macedonia, but throughout Illyricum, especially after the elevation of Thessalonike to the status of capital of Eastern Illyricum at the end of the fourth century. Yet it is not unlikely that the exalted position of the metropolitan of Thessalonike predates this event. According to the lists of the first oecumenical Council of Nicaea (325), the metropolitan of Thessalonike, Alexander, presided over many other metropolitan centres of Illyricum.[37] Though this information is not considered by scholars to be fully reliable, it shows nevertheless that the metropolitan of Thessalonike probably exerted some influence over certain metropolitans outside Macedonia, because of the political importance of the capital.[38] It is certain, however, that from the end of the fourth century Thessalonike became not just the administrative, but also the ecclesiastical centre of Illyricum.[39]

Until the definitive annexation of Eastern Illyricum to the eastern part of the empire at the end of the fourth century, its metropolitans came under the jurisdiction of the Pope. But even after that arrangement they became the object of a long dispute between the Church of Rome and the Patriarchate of Constantinople. The metropolis of Thessalonike, through which each Pope strove to control Eastern Illyricum, was at the centre of this dispute which lasted till the eighth century. Thus at the beginning of the fifth century there was created the 'exarchate' or 'vicariate' of Thessalonike, which meant that the metropolitan of Thessalonike became the representative of the Pope in Illyricum. As was to be expected, this arrangement was not recognized by Constantinople, and only Justinian, yielding to political convenience and to necessity, recognized certain rights of the Popes over Illyricum.[40]

The number of episcopal sees in Macedonia is a matter of dispute. This is due to the fact that no direct evidence has been preserved; but from such indirect sources as we have we come to the conclusion that, during the first half of the fourth century, there were many episcopal sees in Macedonia. Two of the most important were the bishopric of Philippi and that of Herakleia Lynkestis.

Already, as from the apostolic era, the Church of Philippi, which had been founded by the Apostle Paul, enjoyed a privileged status among the other churches of the East.[41] Its flourishing condition during the first Christian centuries is demonstrated, not just by the important monuments that it has left us (and which, by their number and sumptuousness presuppose a particularly prosperous Christian community), but by other evidence too. We hear of bishop Porphyry of Philippi participating in one of the earliest church councils held at Sardica (342/43);[42] and, thanks to a recently discovered mosaic inscription, we also know that he was the founder of the first church built on the site of the Octagon, that is to say of one of the earliest cult structures in the Christian East.[43] Likewise, the fact that bishop Flavian of Philippi took part in the third oecumenical Council at Ephesos (431) as representative of

the metropolitan of Thessalonike, Rufus, fighting as the ally of Cyril of Alexandria against Nestorios, proves how important a place the see of Philippi occupied in the *taxis* (the order of precedence) of Macedonian bishops.[44] It even seems that, in the course of time, its authority became so great that it was promoted to the status of a metropolitan see. In the *Taktikon* of Codex Parisinus 1555a (from the mid-eighth century), Macedonia appears to be divided into two ecclesiastical provinces, the metropolis of Thessalonike and that of Philippi.[45] Yet the first written information regarding the episcopal sees subordinate to the metropolis of Philippi is provided by two late *Taktika*, one from the period of the Macedonians and another from that of the Komnenoi.[46]

The see of Herakleia Lynkestis also held an important place in the *taxis* of the Macedonian bishoprics. There are even some indications that it was the most influential see of Macedonia after the metropolitan see of Thessalonike, at least in administrative terms. Indeed, at three of the most important oecumenical Councils the bishops of Herakleia Lynkestis replaced the metropolitan of Thessalonike; those of 449, 451 and 553.[47]

Stoboi, for a time the capital of Macedonia Secunda, very early became the see of a bishop. Its bishops took part in the Councils of Nicaea,[48] and Chalcedon (451).[49] Another bishop of Stoboi is known to us as the founder of the so-called 'episcopal' basilica (fifth century). His name is mentioned in an inscription above the main entrance of the church: 'Emmanuel — God be with us — the most holy bishop Philip + built the holy church of God'.[50] The bishopric of Stoboi is attested in our sources until the end of the seventh century; and the participation of its bishops in the Councils of Constantinople in 680 and 692 naturally raises the question whether the town survived the Avar and Slav invasions.[51] The usual answer to this question is that the honorary title of bishop of Stoboi was preserved in the hope that the disruption of Macedonia by the invasions would eventually cease.[52]

As for Bargala, the bishop of this town is mentioned in the lists of the Council of Chalcedon (451),[53] and the name of another bishop is known to us from an inscription on the capital of a column in the 'episcopal' church of the town: 'Christ help your slave Hermeias the bishop'.[54]

As well as the sees mentioned so far, which were the most important in Macedonia and about which we have a certain amount of information, there were others whose influence on Church affairs must have been more limited. In the lists of the Councils held during the fourth, the fifth and the sixth centuries there are to be found passing references to bishops of Beroia, Doberos, Zapara, Thasos, Parthikopolis, Pella, Serrhai and Kassandreia, while a bishop of Kaisareia in western Macedonia is attested in a funerary inscription.[55]

Our information about the see of Amphipolis is very scanty, curiously, considering the importance of Christianity in this town. The earliest mention of Christian Amphipolis that has come down to us, in the lists of the fifth oecumenical Council (553), is surprisingly late,[56] unless we take into consideration a funerary inscription which was discovered in the Christian cemetery of the town and which could plausibly be dated to an earlier period. The inscription runs: 'I Liccon lie here; in the name of the Father and the Son and the Holy Ghost I beseech the blessed see of the holy Amphipolitan Church and its clergy beloved by God not to allow anybody else to be placed henceforth in this resting place of mine.'[57]

Equally meagre is our information concerning the life of the Church. In this connection epigraphical evidence confirms that the Macedonian Church was organized according to the administrative principles that prevailed throughout the East.[58] It is clear that during the early Byzantine period Macedonia remained indissolubly linked with the eastern Mediterranean world and in particular with the Greek cultural tradition which formed the basis of the Christian empire of the East.

ECONOMIC AND SOCIAL DEVELOPMENTS

The chaos which reigned in the Roman empire in the mid-third century is well known. Civil wars, the attacks of external enemies, and low productivity leading to economic stagnation, were only some of the reasons which contributed to the crisis of the later Roman empire. The state was saved, as has already been said, thanks to the administrative, military and economic reforms of Diocletian and Constantine the Great, which undoubtedly had a positive influence on life in Macedonia. This conclusion is based not just on the evidence of general historical sources, but also on that of the monuments, which reveal that in the first half of the fourth century Macedonia witnessed a significant economic and political revival.

In recent decades archaeological research has shown that a large number of the Early Christian monuments of Macedonia belong to the fourth century. Big Christian churches, with superb mosaic floors and fine sculpted decoration, leave us in no doubt about the economic prosperity at least of the great urban centres. This conclusion is further supported by the interesting statement by Gregory of Nazianzos in one of his poems, that a priest from Thasos went to Constantinople to buy Proconnesian marble for a splendid church that was being built on the island.[59]

Archaeology also shows that during this period several settlements were founded, and in areas which even today are difficult of access.[60] On the other hand important ancient towns, such as Thessalonike, Stoboi, Herakleia Lynkestis and Amphipolis, continued to rank among the greatest urban centres in the Balkans. They owed their prosperity chiefly to their privileged position in relation to the main land routes of Macedonia, which was anyway one of the more favoured provinces of the later Roman empire as regards transport. Of its two main roads, the Via Egnatia (though it seems to have lost much of its importance after the fourth century, following the transfer of the capital of the western part of the empire from Rome to

Milan), continued to be the main land-route between Thessalonike and Constantinople.[61]

A second, equally important route originated in the northern Balkans and, traversing the Axios plain, terminated at Thessalonike. On this road, at the confluence of the rivers Axios and Erigon, there flourished the town of Stoboi, which was the starting point for two secondary but also important Macedonian roads. One, heading southwest reached Herakleia Lynkestis whence one could continue one's journey either towards Dyrrachion in Epirus or towards Thessalonike. The other, heading south-east led to modern Stromnitsa (? ancient Tiberiopolis). Two other much used Macedonian roads were the Thessalonike-Beroia-Dion-Tempe route and the road which, traversing the Strymon valley, connected Sardica to the Aegean. All these roads, and many more of lesser importance, contributed significantly not just to the fortunes of the cities mentioned above, but also to the general economic prosperity of the area.

The economy of Macedonia, as pointed out in an earlier chapter, was based primarily on agriculture and cattle breeding. The cultivation of cereals and of the vine was traditional and widespread. In this connection, archaeology has yielded interesting finds, such as stone wine-presses, troughs and big jars, used for the production and storing of wine.[62]

The fertile area around Thessalonike was of especial agricultural importance. The vast plain which extends north and west of the capital of Macedonia, traversed by the Axios and its tributaries, was one of Macedonia's most important sources of agricultural wealth,[63] while the abundant pastures of this, as of other regions of Macedonia, contributed to the development of cattle raising.

The mention of an ἐπίτροπος χωρίων δεσποτικῶν comes, as has already been said, from the period in question (fourth century).[64] This is the only evidence to indicate the existence of imperial lands in Macedonia (see p. 201). It is anyway noteworthy that the emperors Justinian I and II conceded the exploitation of public lands on several occasions to the church of Saint Demetrios.[65]

The archaeological discovery of large villas (villae rusticae) has revealed the formation and growth of extensive private estates. Here the owners themselves and their families lived alongside their workers, whether slave or freedmen.[66]

In addition to arable land, saltworks and forests, mines and quarries also belonged to the State. In the late Roman period, with its ever present danger of barbarian invasion, there was an imperative need for systematic exploitation of the resources required for the manufacture of weapons. One of the four weapons factories established in Illyricum at this time was sited in Thessalonike.[67] The importance attached by the State to its mines becomes apparent in a law of 386, creating a special supervisor of mines (procurator metallorum) both in Macedonia and other neighbouring areas.[68] Important information on the contribution of Macedonia to this crucial field of production is provided by archaeological finds.[69] In many parts of Macedonia, especially in the north, archaeological investigation has brought to light remains of furnaces for the smelting of

232

160. This silver dish was fashioned on the occasion of the celebration of the decennalia of the emperor Theodosios the Great at Thessalonike in 388. Theodosios, seated between Valentinian and Arcadius, confers honours on some high-ranking officer, possibly a Spaniard. Madrid, Academia de la Historia.

metals, some vestiges of the materials themselves (especially iron, lead, copper and, in smaller quantities, silver), and remains of the surrounding settlements: big and small jars, various other containers, tools, bricks pottery, traces of several cemeteries and of early Christian basilicas and, finally, coins. Some of these finds, such as the basilicas, the cemeteries and the early Byzantine coins constitute incontestable proof that these mines were exploited during the early Byzantine period.

Naturally the product of the mines was not destined exclusively for the armaments industry; one has to bear in mind also the need for everyday domestic utensils. Forges were usually situated within the cities;[70] in areas such as that around the Byzantine church of the Panagia *ton Chalkeon* in Thessalonike, where the tradition of metalworking is still alive. According to the *Miracles of Saint Demetrios*, the saint was arrested by the soldiers of Galerius in the *Chalkeutike Stoa*, the Stoa of the Smiths, which was apparently situated in the area just mentioned.

Apart from mines, Macedonia also disposed of many quarries, especially of marble, which contributed significantly to its economy. Many of these quarries are

161. *View of the town and plain of Philippi, one of the four Roman colonies in Macedonia. It was the first town in Europe to be visited by the Apostle Paul. It flourished in the seventh century, and was the seat of a bishopric.*

still in use today.[71] To judge from archaeological finds, the Macedonian marble quarries usually covered local needs, though Macedonian marble was frequently exported, and is found far from its source. An example of the way in which Macedonian marble travelled abroad is provided by the quarries at Halyke, Thasos which, as has been shown by the latest archaeological research,[72] maintained commercial relations not only with other parts of Macedonia (such as Thessalonike and Amphipolis) and the rest of Greece (in all probability the island of Aegina), but also with Italy and Syria.[73] This export trade must have been greatly facilitated by the northern Aegean sea route, about which we have independent information. This route whose chief ports were Thasos, Neapolis and Thessalonike led in the one direction to Constantinople, the Troad and further east, and, in the other direction, to the western Mediterra-

nean. It is interesting to note that the Thasian marbles were usually worked in workshops close to the quarries before being exported; this is clear from the numerous architectural elements (such as columns, capitals and the like) that have been discovered, either complete or half-finished, in Thasian[74] as in other Macedonian quarries.[75] One might also of course draw a slightly different conclusion from the same evidence; namely that in some cases part of the work was completed in the quarry workshops, so that transportation was easier, while the rest was left to be done on the construction site. This hypothesis is perhaps strengthened if we consider the six half-finished capitals which were found lying unused amongst other marble fragments, near Basilica B at Philippi.[76]

The existence of numerous Macedonian quarries, and the many monuments constructed during the fourth, fifth and sixth centuries, imply flourishing sculpture workshops too. Many of those, though provincial, show clear signs of high artistic standards; and they illustrate, of course, the artistic trends of the period. The extraction of marble blocks from the quarries was effected by methods and tools little different from those used today.[77]

In view of the ambitious building projects of the period, we must also suppose the existence of mosaic workshops, manufacturing tesserae either from glass or from clay, especially in Thessalonike, where a considerable number of mosaics has been uncovered. But we are on more certain ground as regards the manufacture of tiles and bricks. A large brick factory was discovered recently near Prilep; this discovery, connected to information derived from contemporary *Itineraria*, makes it possible to locate there the *Statio* of *Ceramia*.[78]

In the early Byzantine period there were also to be found in Macedonia workshops for the manufacture and dyeing of purple cloth; and the remains of such a workshop were recently found at Stoboi, dating from the fifth century, and containing large quantities of Tyrian purple as well as other indications of the building's original function.[79]

An important role in the development of the Macedonian economy, and especially in the conduct of the export and import trade, was played by the capital, Thessalonike. Its large, artificial port, constructed by Constantine for military reasons, was later used mainly for commercial purposes. Of equal importance to Thessalonike were the land routes that linked it with many towns in Macedonia and beyond — especially the great north-south road which linked Thessalonike with the regions around the Danube. This route was usually taken by the merchants and other inhabitants of the interior of the Balkans who came to the great fairs at Thessalonike, such as the *Demetria*, later one of the most famous festivals, not just in the Balkans, but in the whole of the East and in Western Europe.

The great commercial importance of Thessalonike is also confirmed by the presence there of traders from the East; merchants from Apamea in northern Syria are referred to in the surviving part of an inscription, now in the Thessalonike Archaeological Museum.[80] Another, unfortunately equally badly damaged, inscription from Thessalonike, apparently referring to the rules regulating the importation of leather, reveals the existence of guilds of leather merchants.[81] This inscription is valuable because it testifies in a general manner to the existence of guilds covering, not just the leather trade, but other professions in early Byzantine Macedonia too. This is scarcely surprising if one recalls two other definitely established facts in Roman economic life. From earliest times there existed such professional organizations, and guilds *(taxeis, systemata, somateia)* are attested in the fourth, fifth and sixth centuries in Asia Minor and Syria.[82]

Information about the trades and professions of the inhabitants of Macedonia are supplied by grave goods and, even more, by funerary inscriptions. There are both private and public professions. Amongst the first, in addition to those already mentioned, are also fee-paid posts; doctors, veterinary surgeons, carpenters,[83] teachers (either secular teachers or catechists), and lawyers as well as merchants (specifically textile merchants), servants and cooks. Some people had two professions. In particular clerics might exercise a highly skilled calling alongside their religious duties, and are often found as doctors.

On the evidence presented so far, the following conclusions can be reached: firstly, that in the late Roman and early Byzantine period the Macedonian economy was to a great extent based on agriculture. We cannot necessarily, though, assume that the living standard of the agricultural population was high: the concentration of wealth in the hands of the landowners, the sparse, modest character of the settlements and cemeteries, and the mediocrity on many early Byzantine churches, especially in the northern part of the province, all militate against this assumption. Secondly, the province's natural resources, especially its mines and quarries, were adequately exploited. Thirdly, both the import and the export trades were flourishing, which proves that Macedonian economy was active during this period, and that the province was not cut off from the rest of the empire. Fourthly, economic life must, at least in the urban centres, have been well-organized, and the standards of living high, as is clear from the existence of guilds and from the ambitious building projects which, little by little, are being brought to light by the progress of archaeological excavation.

SOCIAL AND INTELLECTUAL LIFE

Social life in Macedonia was decisively influenced by Christianity which, particularly after its establishment in the first decades of the fourth century as the official religion of the empire, marked men's souls as well as their way of life and social milieu. The church and its associated buildings now became the focus of city and village alike and the heart of social and religious activities.[84]

Yet, despite the spread of Christianity, paganism was not stamped out for a very long time, as we will see below. After the Council of Nicaea (325) the problem of dogmatic heresies also began to take on worrying dimensions, preoccupying clerics and laymen alike. In opposition to these two threats, the Christians of Macedonia sought to propagate their orthodox faith in all manner of ways. For example, early Christian funerary inscriptions in Macedonia make a point of emphasizing the faith of the deceased in the main dogmas of the Christian religion, and especially in the doctrine of resurrection. Moreover, the name of the deceased is almost invariably accompanied by the words 'Christian' or 'servant' of God, of Christ or of the Lord. Again, the term 'newly illuminated' that is found on many inscriptions indicates the pride felt by those who had experienced the sacrament of baptism.

The fact that Christians and pagans were for a long period compelled to live side by side, and the natural antagonism that they felt towards each other, led the Christians to stress their special identity in various ways. Thus

The Christians of Macedonia seem to have continued in their own way another ancient custom, that of the gods who guarded gateways and turned away evil *(Propylaeic* and *Apotropaeic* gods). There too it was the sign of the cross that was most often used. The large relief cross that was found in the walls of Philippi near the western gate (above which it must have been placed), is an example. Here the Cross stands for Christ, who took the place of the ancient god who protected the entrance.[88] In a Greek land, such as Macedonia, pagan survivals (which, as we shall see below, are more pronounced in funerary customs) are not a strange phenomenon; their existence attests the continuity of the ancient Greek heritage. What is of interest to us is the way in which the Christians of Macedonia transformed these survivals in order to adapt them to the needs created by the new religion.

At a time when Christianity was struggling to achieve final victory, the faith of the Macedonian Christians was testified by the multitude of martyrs they produced. Apart from Saint Demetrios, the inscriptions, martyrologies and *synaxaria* mention many other martyrs: Nestor, Domninos, Akakios, Alexander, Theodoulos, John, Agathopous, Anysia, Matrona, the sisters Agape, Chionia and Irene and many more. Churches were erected in memory of many of them. Thus, according to the written tradition, bishop Alexander of Thessalonike founded a church in memory of St. Matrona, while another church was dedicated to the memory of the sisters Agape, Chionia and Irene.[89]

One of the results of the triumph of Christianity in Macedonia at this period was the emergence of monastic life. Though we do not know much about it, especially about its beginnings, it is certain that monastic life was organized in Macedonia at a fairly early date. This is confirmed both by the monuments and by popular tradition. Some remains of early Christian architectural complexes can be identified as monasteries, among the more certain examples being the Latomos monastery (Hosios David) in Thessalonike. According to the text of Ignatios, this monastery was first built in the name of St. Zacharias, 'soon after the Greek (pagan) mist had been dispersed and the King and Master of all had bestowed the Roman sceptre on Christian emperors'.[90]

Yet monasticism must have existed in Macedonia long before the foundation of the Latomos monastery at the beginning of the fifth century, especially in areas which were isolated from the great religious centres of the province, such as Thessalonike and Philippi. In a funerary inscription from Herakleia Lynkestis, one Spurcius is mentioned as a 'former soldier and holy man'.[91] On other early funerary inscriptions from Edessa and Thessalonike, the adjectives 'brothers', 'fathers', 'holy mother' 'virgin' etc. definitely refer to the monastic vocation of the dead.

There are indications that monks occupied themselves with political affairs too. For example, according to the *Life of Hosios David* of Thessalonike, the holy man travelled to Constantinople at the head of an embassy in order to intercede with Justinian on behalf of his city concerning an important political question.[92] Though this source is not regarded by most scholars as being

162. Early Christian buildings which have survived in Macedonia often boast elaborately sculptured decoration, presupposing the existence of a large number of sculptor's ateliers. This decorated column capital from Basilica B at Philippi is a typical example of the high standard reached.

they made extensive use of the Christian symbol *par excellence,* the cross, which was their main instrument of exorcism against paganism.[85] We find, for example, crosses scratched on temples on the acropolis at Philippi as also on the images of Greek, Roman, Egyptian and other oriental deities. It is not unlikely that, rather than destroying pagan temples and other symbols of worship, the Christians of the region preferred simply to purify them and put them to use for Christian worship.[86]

In this connection it is worth mentioning a discovery at the Octagon in Philippi. The small fourth century place of worship which was discovered next to the Octagon and close to a Hellenistic tomb may well have kept alive through the fourth century an older cult, possibly that of the 'heroized' occupant of the tomb, whose place was now probably taken by some local martyr. The discovery of a small column and of hundreds of fourth century copper coins around the tomb argues for the continuity of worship in this area.[87]

trustworthy, it is at least an indication of the way in which monks could intervene in politics.

As was natural, funerary rites were also altered by the new Christian beliefs. Under the influence of Christian teaching on resurrection and the afterlife, the dead were now buried full length, with arms crossed on breast, and the head pointing towards the East. Tombs became more humble and modest than before, and only the most prominent citizens were buried in small underground mausoleums, containing sarcophagi. The internal walls of the tombs were often covered with frescoes, whose subjects reflect the Christian teaching on death, usually expressed in symbolic fashion. According to information that can be extracted from their inscriptions, tombs were privately owned, that is they were destined for the burial of the purchasers and their relatives, though sometimes other people were buried in there as well.

Survivals of paganism, a subject already alluded to, are to be detected in funerary customs as well, especially in northern and north-western Macedonia. Many tombs from the region of Prilep, for example, offer evidence of the survival of pagan burial customs in the fourth century, such for example as the burning of the dead, the construction of cenotaphs and libations and animal or vegetable offerings. Broken fragments of glass and clay vases and plates and various other offerings are often found in these tombs in the fourth century. In this connection the most interesting tomb of the region is that of an adolescent in the necropolis of Pešterica, in which, amongst other things there was found a pair of gold-plated strigils and, more importantly, a silver coin placed in the mouth of the dead — clearly a reminiscence of the ancient custom of offering an obol to Charon, who led the dead to Hades.[93]

A general trend in late Roman Macedonia is the weakening of Latin influence in general, and especially of the Latin language, as can be shown from the evidence of inscriptions. Indeed, even in those very few areas in which Latin was strongly represented in the early imperial era, that is the Roman colonies of Macedonia (Dion or Philippi etc.), the number of Latin inscriptions from the early Christian period is extremely small in comparison with the many Greek inscriptions. This adoption of the Greek language is evidence for the assimilation of the Roman colonists by the Greek population.

To illustrate the predominance of Greek over Latin one may mention an incident that took place during a journey made by the orator Himerios to Constantinople, whither he had been invited by the emperor Julian (360-63). Stopping at Philippi, Himerios addressed the crowds which were waiting for him in Greek.[94] This event is particularly significant, if one considers that Philippi was one of the largest Roman colonies in Macedonia.

As regards the cultural life of Macedonia and the type of entertainments which were popular in the early Christian period, our information is very limited. Such evidence as we have comes from the fourth century and shows that the basic entertainment of the inhabitants of Macedonia was watching gladiatorial combats, wild beast fights and animal hunts within the special arena-theatres.

Theatres specially adapted for these performances existed in all the big cities of Macedonia, such as Thessalonike, Philippi, Stoboi and Herakleia Lynkestis. Most of them had originally been built as theatres of the traditional Greek type, but at some point in the middle or late third century they were modified to allow the performance of this kind of spectacle.

A particularly popular spectacle at this period was chariot racing. Thessalonikans gathered in the hippodrome of their city by the thousands to admire their favourite charioteers.

All the above mentioned places, destined for the entertainment of the masses, ceased functioning some time in the fourth century after the edicts that the emperors Constantine and Theodosios the Great issued in this connection. The spirit and claims of the new Christian religion prevailed in this field as well.

The Anthology of John Stobaios

In comparison with the great literary, artistic and cultural centres of the period, such as Alexandria, Antioch, Athens and Constantinople, Macedonia can boast no independent philosophical and literary activity. Every city had its school, where the *grammatikos* taught, and some had rhetoricians and teachers of philosophy also. But there is little sign of original literature or thought. Almost the only work by a Macedonian author of the period to survive is the *Anthology* of John Stobaios, from Stoboi in Macedonia, compiled in the fifth century. It consists of excerpts from poets, philosophers, historians, orators and medical writers — more than five hundred in number — arranged by subject-matter to illustrate questions of natural and moral philosphy. No Christian writers are quoted. It is not clear where the author composed his work, which is based mainly on earlier anthologies rather than on direct acquaintance with the original works. Its object was to provide apt quotations for orators.

EARLY CHRISTIAN ART

Archaeological research in Macedonia after the Second World War revealed some of the most remarkable monuments of late antiquity. Several were already known before the War, but our knowledge, especially as regards the artistic achievement of Macedonia in the Early Christian period, has since been considerably widened. This has come about thanks to systematic excavations carried out in the great political and religious centres of the region (Thessalonike, Philippi, Amphipolis, Stoboi, Herakleia Lynkestis, Bargala and others), and also through discovery of isolated buildings and works of art. As the first part of Europe in which the Christian gospel was preached, and as an area that could boast a long artistic tradition, Macedonia has yielded some of the earliest examples of Christian architecture, painting, sculpture and metalwork.

ARCHITECTURE

Church Architecture

Judging by the surviving churches, the prevalent architectural form in Macedonia was the so-called 'Hellenistic' basilica, that is a longitudinal building which has certain fixed features; a narthex, most usually three aisles divided from each other by lines of columns, a semi-circular apse in the eastern wall, galleries and a wooden pitched roof. It is very probable that the *Extra Muros* basilica at Philippi, which dates from the mid-fourth century, and is therefore one of the earliest churches not only in Macedonia, but in the whole of Greece, was of this type. Unfortunately, the walls of this basilica do not stand sufficiently high for us to form a clear idea of what it looked like. But in the Panagia Acheiropoietos, Thessalonike, which dates from the mid-fifth century and survives almost complete, a typical example of the 'Hellenistic' basilica exists. Its only peculiarity consists of the way in which the outer face of the apse is formed, for just under the windows the apse was girdled by a small decorative colonnade, as can be seen from the consoles *in situ,* together with certain architectural elements which were found nearby.

The type of wooden-roofed basilica represented by the Acheiropoietos is frequently found in Macedonia, with minor architectural variations. The four closely adjacent early Christian basilicas on the acropolis of ancient Amphipolis must have conformed to this type, and both their number and their lavish decoration suggest that the inhabitants of that area had not only deep religious feeling, but also the financial means to build sumptuous places of worship.

Particularly interesting are the two superposed basilicas at Dion in Pieria, respectively dated by some scholars to the fourth and fifth centuries and by others to the fifth and sixth. The older church must have been a typical three-aisled basilica while the more recent one presents certain noteworthy peculiarities. First one should note the two shoulders and the three buttresses which support the semi-circular apse externally, while the twin colonnades which divide the three aisles are a feature which so far as we can tell is not to be found anywhere else in this area.[1] The closest examples are Basilica A at Philippi and the episcopal church at Stoboi with its double line of stylobates (one of which has been used for the positioning of parapets, so that the three aisles were completely separated) and not for the construction of a second colonnade.[2]

The basilicas in and around Stoboi (the episcopal, the 'northern', the basilica of the Synagogue, the *Extra Muros,* and that of Palikoura) as also the great basilica of Herakleia Lynkestis, built on the foundations of an older secular Roman basilica, can also be described as 'Hellenistic'.[3] They all share the main features of the 'Hellenistic' basilica, with certain modifications of detail which are more often than not easily explicable. For example, the atrium of the episcopal basilica of Stoboi is an irregular triangle and not, as was more usual, square, because just in front of it there passed the old Roman street. For the same reason, the atrium of the northern basilica is too small, whereas the atrium of the so-called Synagogue Basilica, which is surrounded by a peristyle, is less wide than the basilica because a part of it at its southern end was occupied by two rooms whose use is unknown.

Certain basilicas in Macedonia and elsewhere in the Mediterranean have a transverse aisle at the east end, which can either be 'inscribed' by the appropriate positioning of the colonnades, or else can be created by the displacement outwards of part of the longitudinal walls.[4] To date the two known examples in Macedonia are the three-aisled Basilica A at Philippi and the majestic basilica of Saint Demetrios, the patron of Thessalonike. The former, which dates from the end of the fifth century and is built on a naturally flat area of rock, is one of the biggest basilicas in Macedonia; the latter is a large five-aisled basilica with a wooden roof and galleries running above the aisles as well as the narthex (figs. 164, 165). Despite successive destructions and the not particularly successful restoration after the fire of 1917, Saint Demetrios is still regarded as one of the most important Byzantine martyria, and a unique monument at the disposal of the student of early Christian art. The church today preserves the plan it took when it was rebuilt under Heraklios after the original church of the mid-fifth century was burned down. But scholars agree that the second basilica was built on the same plan as the first, of which there still remain its western part together with parts of its northern and southern external walls.[5]

An interesting, if rare, variation of a basilica with a

163. Many types of basilicas are to be seen at Philippi. Basilica B above, a domed basilica is of a type which originated in Constantinople, a fusion of the longitudinal and central plan.

Several elements suggest that the area in front of the sanctuary was roofed by a dome supported on four solid pillars. A lower dome may perhaps have covered the central aisle.

transverse aisle is provided by the basilica of Saint Paraskeve in the area of Kozani, whose eastern part forms a triconch which could well be regarded as an independent church.[6] Such indeed is precisely the case of the church of Akrine (fifth century), also in the region of Kozani. This church, perhaps unique in Greece, has a triconch main church and a rectangular narthex.

Two of the earliest Christian monuments in Macedonia — the Rotunda of Saint George in Thessalonike, and the Octagon at Philippi — can be classified as churches on a central plan, where the dome is an essential element in the architectural design.[7] The Rotunda, which dates from the time of Galerius and whose original function is doubtful, is a circular monument which, when transformed into a church at the end of the fourth century, was provided with a circular porch or ambulatory and an apse oriented eastwards. As for the Octagon at Philippi, this belongs to a series of octagonal churches to be found in Syria and Palestine,[8] though in Greece it is a unique specimen. Inscribed in a square, and erected toward the middle of the

fifth century, the Octagon was built on the foundations of a mid-fourth century basilica, and was part of a larger complex which comprised a baptistery, fountain, baths, possibly a bishop's residence and other buildings.[9]

From the constructional point of view, the most complex type of Christian church is the so-called domed basilica, which combines the main characteristics of the longitudinal and the central plan. This form originated in Constantinople, probably in the time of Justinian.[10] The only example in Greece is again to be found in Macedonia, at Philippi, for many elements in the now ruined Basilica B, to the south of the Roman *forum,* indicate that the area in front of the sanctuary was covered by a dome which rested on four strong pillars (fig. 163). It is likely that another, lower, dome covered the central aisle.

The most symbolic of all church plans is the cruciform.[11] The four arms of the cross can either stand free, as in the sixth century cruciform basilica of Thasos, or they can be inscribed in a square, as in the katholikon of the Latomos monastery (Hosios David) at Thessalonike. In this church, which today is only a part of the original building, an equal-armed cross was inscribed in a square, so that four small compartments were formed at the corners of the square. The arms of the cross were covered with vaults, and where the vaults met there must have been a dome. The church was probably built towards the end of the fifth century, but at some point after the seventh century it acquired a prothesis and a diaconicon for liturgical purposes through the addition of apses to the two eastern corner compartments.

An inseparable part of episcopal churches, and to a lesser extent of parish churches, in the fourth, fifth and sixth centuries was the baptistery, which presented as rich a variety of types as do the churches themselves.[12] Amongst the known baptisteries in Macedonia is the type which consists of a simple square or rectangular room with the font in the middle. In most cases the font was an integral part of the building, and was either cross-shaped (for example the Octagon at Philippi, the episcopal basilica at Bargala and Saint Paraskeve at Kozani), octagonal (as in Basilica B at Dion) or circular (as in the large basilica at Herakleia Lynkestis and elsewhere). Less often the font was portable, as must have been the case at Basilica A at Philippi. Architecturally, the baptisteries of north-west Macedonia are more interesting. In the basilica of Palikoura, two kilometres from Stoboi, an octagonal baptistery inscribed in a square has been excavated. Probably the font was portable, since no traces of it were found. At Stoboi itself, the baptistery of the 'northern' basilica was a tetraconch with a hexagonal font, while the baptistery of the episcopal basilica is particularly impressive on account both of its shape and its lavish decoration. It was square with semi-circular conches at its corners, and slightly curved sides.[13] At the centre was a circular font, to which one descended by four shallow steps; and on the floor was a beautiful mosaic with scenes relating to the sacrament of baptism.[14]

In certain early Christian religious centres in Macedonia which were seats of bishops, such as Philippi[15] and Amphipolis,[16] traces of buildings have been discovered which are identifiable with greater or lesser certainty as episcopal residences. We can be more certain, however, about the two magnificent buildings, one near the great basilica of Stoboi, the other close to the large basilica of Herakleia Lynkestis. The bishop's residence at Stoboi, approached by a narrow, short, colonnaded street, consisted of a small rectangular antechamber and a large hall with a semi-circular apse on its eastern side. At Herakleia, there survives a courtyard with a small marble fountain at its centre and small rooms to the north, east and south.[17] The most interesting of these is the compartment at the northeast corner, identified with the refectory of the bishop's residence.[18] It has a semi-circular apse on its eastern side and an antechamber to the west.

Funerary Architecture

The numerous tombs recently discovered in various parts of Macedonia show that during the first Christian centuries the inhabitants of the area preferred simple funerary monuments.

A large number of Early Christian tombs was discovered after the Second World War in the two Roman necropolises outside the walls to the east and west of Thessalonike. These tombs were subterranean, of simple construction and divided into cist-like structures (rectangular tombs with a flat roof), rectangular tombs covered with a vault, and *cubicula,* that is buildings of a somewhat more monumental type. These had a small, usually arched, entrance which led, often by means of a staircase, into a square room whose walls contained arcosolia.[19] Tombs comparable to those of the first two types, cist-like or rectangular vaulted tombs, have been discovered in three cemeteries at Sandanski in north-east Macedonia, present-day Bulgaria.[20]

Tombs of similar simplicity have been found in the necropolis outside the eastern wall of Philippi. They were either vaulted or consisted of a simple pit in which there was placed a (usually monolithic) coffin. At the coffin's western, narrow end, was a horse-shoe-like depression for the head of the deceased, while at the opposite end were holes for the escape of liquids given off by the corpse. The tomb was covered with a marble slab. Other tombs in the area were simple pits; sometimes their sides were covered with marble slabs removed from the older Roman cemetery nearby.

Although the architectural plainness of these tombs was somehow compensated for by the rich paintings which often adorned their walls, the same cannot be said for north-west Macedonia, where several necropolises have recently been discovered, as well as poor isolated tombs dating from the fourth to the sixth century.[21] Certain necropolises in the area of Prilep contain tombs that date to the fourth century. Most of them are simple cist-shaped structures with rubble walls, whose floor and ceiling were covered with large marble slabs. In another type of tomb peculiar to these cemeteries both the dead and the tomb itself are covered with tiles.

But more monumental tombs were not completely absent from the area. One may mention, for example, a mid-fourth century tomb discovered at the *villa rustica* of Pešterica.[22] It consisted of a monolithic marble sarcophagus upon which was erected a little building of stone — a square room measuring 3.50×3 m. Judging by the offerings contained in the tomb, the excavator suggested that it must have belonged to the Christian wife or daughter of the owner of the adjacent villa.[23]

In all probability certain tombs found in the wider area of Prilep and which are covered by vaults should be assigned to the fifth or sixth century.[24] Certain cist-shaped

164-165. The majestic five-aisled basilica of the patron saint of Thessalonike, Saint Demetrios, belongs to the Hellenistic type. It is wooden roofed, with a transverse aisle in front of the sanctuary, a gallery above the outer aisles and a narthex. One of the most important martyria in the Byzantine world, its present form dates to the 7th century. The pictures show an interior and an exterior view.

240

166. *The mosaic in the apse of the katholikon of the Latomos monastery was executed by a craftsman endowed with outstanding talents. Christ is depicted as a beardless young man,* *seated within a circular mandorla from which spring the symbols of the Four Evangelists. Below to right and left respectively are the prophets Ezekiel and Habakkuk. Thessalonike.*

tombs covered with marble slabs in the funerary basilica at Gradište must also belong to the sixth century.[25]

Secular architecture

Few examples of secular architecture have survived in Macedonia. In Thessalonike there is only the Galerian complex (see page 221), which comprises the ruins to be found in what is now Navarino Square and the surrounding area, together with the Triumphal Arch and the Rotunda (in its first phase). Part of the eastern fortifications also survives, generally thought to have been built by Galerius in order to include his palace-complex within the city walls.[26] A larger part of the surviving defences of Thessalonike belongs to the Early Christian period, probably to the reign of Theodosios the Great. It has been dated with the help of a large, brick inscription of three lines, fragments of which are preserved on a square tower in the eastern wall. The inscription states that the city was fortified with impregnable walls by Hormisdas. The name of Hormisdas helps us to date the Early Christian fortifica-

tions of Thessalonike, though not with absolute exactitude; for Hormisdas is considered by some scholars to be identical with a Hormisdas of Persian origin who was an officer under Theodosios the Great, while other authorities identify him with the Hormisdas who was Praetorian Prefect of the East in the mid-fifth century.[27] The wall is constructed of wide courses of undressed stones alternating with narrower bands of brick, or else of brick varied at intervals with brick arches (fig. 159).

More extensive remains of secular buildings have been preserved at Stoboi, the capital of Macedonia Secunda. Stoboi in the Early Christian period was at the height of its prosperity. Within the city were to be seen, not only the three basilicas referred to above, but other buildings too, both public and private. Notable among these are three dwellings known as the House of Peristerias, the House of Parthenios and the Palace of Theodosios. These comprise a large number of rooms both large and small, several of them apsidal, together with corridors and an open court adorned with a fountain. One of these dwellings, the House of Peristerias, which dates from the end of the fourth or the beginning of the fifth century, was in fact a complex of houses that constituted a whole block. Some of the rooms in its western part were shops, or else served as dwellings for poor families.

The largest and most lavish dwelling in Stoboi was the so-called Palace of Theodosios. The name of its owner is not known, but on account of its exceptional splendour it is thought to have been the residence of Theodosios the Great when he visited Stoboi in June 388. The main parts of the house are: the courtyard, with colonnades on it northern and western sides and a fountain on the eastern side; and a large apsidal hall (triclinium?) with a floor of *opus sectile*. This house was very probably built in the middle of the fourth century, and remained in use throughout the fifth.

The origin of the plan of these dwellings is easily located. The *villa rustica* at Pešterica (second half of the third century) has basically the same plan: a central courtyard surrounded by large and small rooms, with a large apsidal hall on its north-west side. Baths and various service areas for farm purposes completed the whole. This villa was in use throughout the fourth century, in the middle of which it underwent a remodelling.

Particular interest attaches to the settlement recently discovered immediately above the Roman theatre at Herakleia Lynkestis, which ceased to function round about the year 400.[28] This settlement, built at the beginning of the sixth century, consisted of wretched dwellings put together in a rough and ready way out of pebbles bonded together with mud. The houses were grouped in clusters, separated by narrow streets, and they continued to be inhabited until the end of the sixth century, at which point Herakleia was completely abandoned. The inhabitants of these dwellings must have been peasants or small tradesmen, for at the base of the front wall of one of the houses was found a collection of mill-stones, while near another were located traces of an oven.

One of the most important towns in Macedonia at this period was Bargala, where over the last decade and a half archaeological investigations have revealed, amongst other things, the city wall, which was a rectangle punctuated at intervals by monumental gates and square towers.[29] At Gradište the ecclesiastical complex and adjacent, as yet unexcavated, area was surrounded by a wall of much more interesting shape.[30] This wall is important because it is still in good condition and remains standing in places to a height of about 2.50 m., most of which has been excavated. Its plan was polygonal, and the wall was built of irregular stones bonded together with mortar. The main entrance was in the eastern side, and was flanked by a polygonal tower on either side. Another gate, on the western side exactly opposite the *porta principalis,* was protected by one round and one polygonal tower. Other towers of varying shape punctuated the wall at intervals.

167-168. Two mid-5th century mosaic compositions from the original basilica of Saint Demetrios. In the first, the saint is shown frontally, in prayer, while a woman leads a child towards him. In the second the saint is again depicted frontally, while a flying angel blowing a trumpet descends from a multi-coloured cloud, the only one of several to survive.

169-170-171. *In the Rotunda at Thessalonike the third band of mosaic decoration in the dome is made up of eight subdivisions.*

Two-storey structures are shown against a gold background, together with praying saints. Their bodies have been rendered

PAINTING

Mosaic floors

The mosaic floor, which in the Hellenistic and Roman periods was one of the most popular means of decorating buildings, was abundantly used in the adornment of both religious and secular architecture in Early Christian Macedonia. Such floors have been discovered in most of the buildings already referred to; they are technically and thematically related to the Early Christian mosaic floors that are to be found both in the rest of Greece and in other areas of the Mediterranean basin.

The themes of these mosaics are usually determined by the architectural function of the building and are related to the particular use of the rooms in which they are set, the sanctuary or the baptistery, for example, in the case of a church. Geometrical designs are frequent, as also are vegetal motifs (different trees, vines, flowers etc.) or animals — especially birds, domestic animals or wild beasts that tear each other to pieces or chase each other as in the wonderful mosaic in the narthex of the great basilica at Herakleia Lynkestis. Water scenes were also popular; there are notable examples in the bishop's residence at

Herakleia Lynkestis, and in the southern aisle of the episcopal basilica at Stoboi amongst others. One can also find scenes from everyday life, (for example, the fragmentarily preserved fishing scene in Basilica A at Amphipolis, (fig. 158) and allegorical compositions. Typical of this latter genre is the depiction in the church at Akrine near Kozani of twelve haloed doves, obviously an allegory of the twelve apostles. This scene is also important because it illustrates the interplay of thematic influences between wall mosaics and floor mosaics; for the same allegorical scene adorned the underside of the arch of the apse in the church of San Michele at Affricisco near Ravenna (mid-sixth century).[31]

But for both its symbolic and its decorative value the most popular theme in the mosaic floors of Macedonia is the depiction of deer or peacocks placed symmetrically on each side either of a vase, out of which grows a vine, or of a fountain. The significance of this composition is eschatological: the vases, the vine and the water, the peacocks and the deer, are the symbols of immortality, which is won through the sacraments of Baptism and the Holy Eucharist, and leads one to Paradise, It is, it seems, precisely this meaning that is supposed to be conveyed by

with as little volume as possible, although particular attention has been paid to facial details. The mosaic decoration as a

whole bears witness to the continuance of the Hellenistic artistic tradition of Macedonia.

a mosaic in the bishop's residence at Herakleia Lynkestis which depicts, apart from the deer and the fountain, the hedge of Paradise as well.[32]

Wall mosaics

The best way of studying the art of a particular period is through the decoration of walls. Macedonia is privileged to have preserved the only examples known to date in the Near East of pre-Justinianic wall mosaics. They are all located in Thessalonike.

Most scholars date the mosaics of the Rotunda of Saint George to the end of the fourth century, when the Roman building was converted into a Christian church. The wonderful decorative mosaics of the ground level arcades and of the windows, as well as those of the dome, testify along with other works of art, that in the Early Christian period Thessalonike was a major artistic centre still deeply conscious of its Hellenistic heritage. The decoration of the dome is divided into three bands, as in other circular buildings.[33] Unfortunately, not all the mosaics have been preserved intact, and so it is difficult to be sure of the meaning of the whole composition. But it may well be that

the artist wanted to depict a theophany as a hymn of praise to the Highest Being, since in the centre of the dome, as one can still see from the traces of the design, Christ was shown in triumph, holding a staff with a cross. The idea of Christ triumphant, conqueror of both Life and Death, is also emphasized in the depiction of the phoenix, the symbol of immortality, in the midst of the angels who hold Christ's halo. In the second band of the dome it is probable that the white-clad figures in a landscape like that of Paradise are also supposed to be hymning the victorious Christ; their identification remains uncertain since little more than parts of their lower extremities have been preserved. The third band, which is iconographically the most interesting, is divided into eight compartments. On a plain gold ground are represented two-storeyed architectural structures similar to the facades of Hellenistic and Roman buildings. Somewhat illusionistically, and with a certain exaggeration of decorative detail, they represent the sanctuary of a Christian church. In front of these facades, in groups of two or three, saints of the Eastern Church stand in the usual *orans* position. With the inscriptions declaring their name, vocation and the date of their feast, they constitute a sort of picture-calendar, the first in Christian art. The bodies are depicted on one plane, without any sense of volume, but special attention is bestowed on the faces, which are fine portraits with short hair, sensitively rendered features and large, expressive eyes (figs. 169-171). The mosaics of Saint George's show that at this period the artists of Thessalonike, in the midst of their artistic questing and disquiet, still remained faithful to the achievements of Hellenistic art. The decorative themes and the naturalistic style of the mosaics in the arcades, the structure of the architectural facades and the spirituality of the portraits of the saints, all bear witness to the continuance in Macedonia of the Hellenistic tradition and its Roman descendent.

A naturalistic style and Hellenistic grace also distinguish, at a slightly later date, the mosaics of the Acheiropoietos basilica in Thessalonike, which are dated to the mid-fifth century. All the mosaics that survive adorn the soffits of the arches in the narthex, the trivelon and of the colonnades on the ground floor and galleries. The mosaics display a large variety of decorative motifs, frequently combined with Christian symbols (crosses, books, fish, etc.). Plant and geometrical designs, various intertwined or scaly patterns and rosettes, make up a unique group of mosaics characterized by a remarkable and inimitably harmonious range of colours.

Most scholars hold that the mosaics of the first church of Saint Demetrios, whose artistic roots are very similar to those of the Acheiropoietos, should be dated to the same period. Of the three that have survived two, that of the angel blowing a trumpet (on the west wall of the inner northern aisle (fig. 168), and that of a peacock next to a vase (now in the crypt), are fairly mutilated. The mosaic of the presentation of children to St. Demetrios, on the west wall of the inner southern aisle, is better preserved (fig. 167). In the centre of the composition is the saint, standing on a plinth, full front and praying. To the right a woman brings a child to him; there was a similar scene on Demetrios' other side, as we can see from part of the representation of a child preserved to the left. It is interesting to note that the palms of the saint are depicted in gold — a fact which has caused scholars to opine that the image reproduces the cult icon of the saint which must have existed in the church. By the same token, the structure behind the saint could represent the stand on which the icon was placed. But other scholars maintain that what we see is the *ciborium* which contained the body of the saint, whose hexagonal base can still be distinguished on the floor of the nave.[34]

In the apse of the katholikon of the Latomos monastery can be seen one of the most representative specimens of Early Christian mosaic art in Thessalonike (fig. 166). On the central axis is Christ, young, beardless, and seated on a multi-coloured rainbow surrounded by the symbols of the four evangelists. In the lower part of the composition can be seen the prophets Ezekiel and Habakkuk, each with his own stance and expression, the 'vision of the glory of the Lord'. This version of a very rare theme in Christian iconography is completed by the four rivers of Paradise, which emerge below the feet of Christ and debouch into the river Hovar. The old man with raised hand who personifies

the latter recalls the marine divinities of classical art. The creator of this mosaic was a master both of technique and of the expression of personality into plastic terms. His brilliant technique is clearest in his use of different shades of colour in order to convey perspective, while his ability to convey personality is particularly apparent in the figures of the two prophets. The ecstatic and bent figure of Ezekiel, terrified to the point that he does not dare to look his Lord in the face, contrasts vividly with the calm and reflective figure of Habakkuk. Clearly the mosaic in the Latomos monastery belongs to a later stage of development than the mosaics which were discussed earlier; and so we naturally think of the mosaic compositions of the reign of Justinian, no example of which has been found, up to now at least, in Macedonia.

Frescoes

It is a serious disadvantage for the study of early Christian painting in Macedonia that we have so little evidence about frescoes. From the few remains found *in situ* it seems that frescoes in churches usually imitated marble panelling, parapets or colonnades, at least on the lower part of walls, for example at Basilica A at Dion, the baptistery of Basilica A at Philippi, and the basilica that preceded the episcopal basilica at Stoboi. A few isolated frescoes such as the fragments with male portraits (perhaps Apostles) that were found in the baptistery of the episcopal basilica at Stoboi,[35] or the fresco that was found in a room of the southern subterranean stoa of the Roman *forum* in Thessalonike,[36] make no decisive contribution to the study of this group of materials. But the funerary frescoes that have been found in tombs in Thessalonike and some other towns provide a much more important complex of evidence. These paintings are important because they demonstrate the oecumenicity of art at this period — their affinity to the contemporary paintings in the Roman catacombs may be regarded as certain.

In funerary frescoes, symbolic representations predominate, often related to flora and fauna. Peacocks and other birds, fountains, trees, baskets of fruit, flowers, vines and garlands, along with other symbols (a tripod with bread and fish, the Good Shepherd, or a funerary banquet) all refer to belief in the salvation of the human soul, life after death, Paradise and the sacrament of the Holy Eucharist. Rarer scenes derived from the Old and New Testament (the sacrifice of Abraham, Daniel in the Lions' Den, Adam and Eve in Paradise, Noah, the healing of the paralytic, and so on) have similar significance. Even more interesting, on account of their rarity, are the images of the dead who were buried in their tombs. The most representative example is the so-called Tomb of Eustorgios (early

172-173. The Hellenistic tradition is frequently to be observed in metalwork, as for example in this silver reliquary from Thessalonike dating from the end of the 4th century. On the long sides, shown here, are the Three Children in the Furnace and Moses receiving the Law. Thessalonike, Archaeological Museum.

247

174. The so-called Achilles Disk, with scenes from the childhood of the mythical hero. The inscription ΠΑΥΣΥΛΥΠΟΥ ΘΕΣΣΑΛΟΝΙΚΗΣ declares the provenance of the disc, and may also give the name of its maker. Both themes and style show how alive the classical artistic tradition still was in Macedonia in the 4th century A.D. Augst, Roman Museum.

fourth century), which was discovered outside the western wall of Thessalonike. A picture of the dead man and his family occupies an entire wall.[37]

SCULPTURE AND METALWORK

As is well known, Christianity did not favour sculpture in the round, because this had been so distinctively pagan a means of artistic expression. For this reason, and also because after the reign of Constantine the Great and even more after that of Theodosios the Great, there was a huge increase in building activity, caused by the foundation of many new churches, Christian artists turned their attention to architectural relief sculpture.

Macedonia has preserved extremely little Christian sculpture in the round. The most significant is a small statue of the Good Shepherd, a young herdsman who carries a lamb on his shoulders.[38] In the Christian period, this theme, evidently inspired by the old type of Hermes bearing a ram, acquired a similar symbolism. According to some scholars it stands for Christ, but earlier authorities thought it represented 'Philanthropia'. For all that it is mutilated, defaced and flaked, this statue is a highly evolved specimen of its genre. Its plasticity and general style place it in the period of Constantine the Great, and it may well have been the product of an artistic atelier in Thessalonike itself.

The sphere in which one can best appreciate the advanced level of Macedonian sculpture is that of architectural relief carving. Capitals, impost block parapets and cornices provide indisputable testimony to the quality of relief sculpture in the region. These carvings demonstrate that at this period Macedonia was not only in close artistic contact with Constantinople, but also disposed of its own sculpture workshops, in Thessalonike, Philippi, Stoboi and elsewhere. This can be seen by examining just one architectural element, the capital, which was to be found throughout the early Christian world thanks to the foundation of numerous basilicas, in the construction of which the column played a crucial role.

The Early Christian capitals of Macedonia provide specimens of all the most significant types of the period. One finds the typical 'Theodosian' capital, with two rows of upright leaves of the soft or hard acanthus, obviously derived from the classical Corinthian capital; the 'wind-blown' capital, a variant of the previous type derived from the East and more popular in Thessalonike than in any other part of Greece; the 'two-banded' capital, with a row of acanthus leaves in the lower band and heads of animals or birds in the upper, and the basket-shaped 'two-banded' capital with the lower part in the form of a basket and the composite Ionic one.

It is also worth recording two other types of capital, both belonging to the sixth century, because both their design and their technique attest the close artistic relations that existed between Macedonia and Constantinople at this period. One of these types is the conical capital used on the dibelon in the northern colonnade of Saint Sophia, Thessalonike,[39] which in both its technique and its design is closely related to the sculptures in the now ruined church of Saint Polyeuktos in Constantinople (524-27); and the other type is the cauldron-shaped capital (fig. 162) and the fold capital (a variation of the former type), decorated with drilled perforations (*à jour*).[40] In this technique, which prevailed in the Justinianic period, the whole surface of the marble capital is deeply drilled so as to resemble lace.

Sculptural decoration was also applied to liturgical furniture. Either by chance or in the course of excavations sculptured marble fragments of thrones, *ciboria,* altar tables, pulpits (ambos) and so forth have been discovered throughout Macedonia. Especially notable is the ambo of Saint George, Thessalonike; two large parts of the platform are now preserved in the Istanbul Archaeological Museum (fig. 157). The sculptural decoration of this ambo is of rare quality. In the shell-shaped conches are depicted two scenes, the Annunciation to the Shepherds and the Adoration of the Magi. The sculptor has tried very hard to depict all the details, and to fit all the figures and objects into the limited space. To this end he makes use of two techniques, that of high relief for the main figures, and of incision for secondary figures and objects. It is well known that this double technique was used some years earlier in the sculptures on the Arch of Galerius; and the local style of the ambo carvings has often been remarked upon.[41]

But sculpture was not confined to work on marble. It is clear from various discoveries in Macedonia, and more especially in its capital, Thessalonike, that there were centres of metalwork that produced superb pieces in silver. The Kaiseraugst treasure from Switzerland, for example, which contains numerous items of silver tableware, came in all probability from Thessalonike, since the so-called 'Plate of Achilles' bears a Greek inscription which reveals both its origin and, perhaps, the name of the silversmith.[42] Both the subject-matter of this octagonal plate (scenes from the childhood and youth of the mythical hero Achilles executed in encrustation) and its style, prove that the classical artistic tradition was still alive in the fourth century, even in the northern parts of the Greek world (fig. 174).[43]

The same classical artistic tradition, in its Hellenistic form,[44] can be observed in another product of the silversmith's art, the famous reliquary in the Archaeological Museum at Thessalonike (figs. 172, 173). The subject matter of its decoration (Moses receiving the law, the three young men in the furnace, and Daniel in the Lions' Den) as also its stylistic characteristics, suggest that it should be dated to the end of the fourth century; and it may well be that it was made in a Thessalonike workshop, since it was discovered in the region of that city.[45]

FROM THE SIXTH
TO THE NINTH CENTURY

POLITICAL HISTORY

The three centuries which elapsed between the death of Justinian I (565) and the accession of Basil I (867) are a shadowy period in the history of Macedonia, as also in that of other regions of the Byzantine empire, and other aspects of its general history. Historical writers after Prokopios provide very little information about Macedonia. We can draw information of a local, specific character from a hagiographical text which narrates the miracles of Saint Demetrios, patron of Thessalonike (see page 263).[1] The use of inscriptions, coins, seals, architectural and other archaeological material is still in its early stages.

The poor and fragmented evidence at our disposal is, moreover, extremely unbalanced. It chiefly concerns the raids of various invaders, and the defensive measures taken by the local population; and it is only indirectly that we can deduce from such evidence information concerning the administration and the Church. Neither the economic and social history of the area nor the public and private life of its inhabitants has yet been adequately studied.

As a general rule one may say that so long as the empire kept its eyes on the West (towards which Macedonia was an important stepping-stone), Byzantine historiography occupied itself to a greater extent with Macedonia; but when the political orientation of the empire was diverted eastwards, the regions to the west of Thrace finally lost their importance in the minds of the ruling class, and therefore in the historiographical tradition too.

NEW BARBARIAN INVASIONS: AVARS AND SLAVS

The Byzantine state, which was the continuation of the eastern part of the Roman empire, reacted more efficiently than the West to the pressures from the peoples who dwelt beyond the frontier. Byzantium suffered from repeated invasions, but was successful in preventing them from having any lasting effect until the mid-sixth century. Moreover, it was able to find sufficient forces to support the Justinianic reconquest of the West. Yet it was exactly this policy, which severely stretched the resources of the Byzantine state, that brought about the fragmentation of its forces in a period when a policy of retrenchment was needed, and shifted the balance of power to the profit of the empire's external enemies, whether organized states or migratory hordes. The gravest dangers came from the East: until the early seventh century from the powerful Persian kingdom, and from 640 onwards from the young and dynamic Muslim caliphate. In face of these threats, the Byzantine emperors turned their attention and threw their forces mainly eastwards, thus depriving their Balkan territories of the protection they so urgently needed. In this way the northern Balkans were lost, while the southern Balkans were invaded and settled in varying degrees both by new peoples and by populations transplanted from other parts of the empire either on their own initiative or by the state itself.

During the first decades of the sixth century, Hunnic and Slavonic tribes appeared on the northern frontier of the empire and started raiding the northern provinces of the Balkan peninsula, as has already been mentioned above. This situation was aggravated towards the end of the reign of Justinian I (527-65) due to the appearance of new and more dynamic invaders of Hunnic extraction.[2]

The most important among these invaders were the Avars, or more precisely those Avar tribes which did not submit to the Turks after their defeat in 555 and moved westwards from their Asiatic home. Justinian did not allow them to cross the Danube, and so they moved further west. A warlike nation, well organized under a leader whose title

175. The Avar-Slav invasions of the 6th and 7th centuries struck at the heart of Macedonia, Thessalonike. The city's repeated survival was attributed to the miraculous intervention of Saint Demetrios. The wall painting is interpreted as a depiction of the entry of Justinian II into Thessalonike after his resounding victory over the Slavs in 688. The haloed emperor is shown on horseback, escorted by mounted and foot soldiers. Saint Demetrios, Thessalonike.

was rendered into Greek by the Byzantine writers as Χαγάνος (Khagan), the Avars exploited the opposition between the Germanic tribes of the Lombards and Gepids in order to become the incontestable masters of the area to the north of the river Sava. The powerful state that they founded extended from the Danube to the Dnieper and the Baltic Sea and included as its subjects other Turanic peoples, such as the Utigurs and the Kutrigurs, as well as Slavs. In their raids against the Byzantine empire, the Avars were accompanied by bands of their subject populations, especially the Slavs, to the point that we can speak of Avaro-Slav raids.[3] Thus when the Greeks began to suffer from the Slavonic raids, the Slavs were under the yoke of the Avars; and it was for this reason that their Greek names (Sklavenoi, Sthlavenoi, Sklavoi, Slavoi, Sthlavoi) came to denote, much later, the status of slavery.[4]

The original home of the Slavs was in the Pripet marshes and the territories to the north of the Carpathian Mountains — an area which corresponds to present-day eastern Poland, southern White Russia and northern Little Russia. Expelled thence by other raiders, they reached the areas to the north of the Danube, where as has already been mentioned, they were subjugated by the Avars.

Having established themselves in central Europe, the Avars, together with their subject peoples, confronted the Byzantine empire as enemies. Absorbed in his struggle against the Persians, the emperor Maurice (582-602) not only failed to check their advance into imperial territory in the north of the Balkan peninsula, but also submitted to their claim for a substantial annual tribute. However, the successful outcome of the Byzantine-Persian war in 591 allowed Byzantium to transfer military forces to Thrace in order to repel the Avars, Slavs, and other followers of the Avars.

It is not easy to follow the Avaro-Slav raids because there was no stable front and, besides the Khagan of the

251

Avars, who was the main enemy, several Slavonic hordes under local chieftains roamed about without any plan or particular cohesiveness. Byzantium aimed to break the Avaro-Slav alliance and repel 'the Slavonic nations'.[5] From 593 until 598 military operations took place near the middle and lower Danube. In 598 or 600 an Avar leader accepted Byzantine proposals for peace. The conditions of the treaty were favourable to the Byzantines: the frontier was stabilized again on the Danube, while the right of the Byzantines to cross the Danube whenever their military needs required it was recognized. In exchange, the imperial tribute to the Avars was increased. But the treaty did not last for long. Maurice calculated that he could shatter his enemy, so his forces crossed the Danube and fought a hard and successful battle against the Avars and the Gepids near the river Tisza.

Judging from the movements of the rival forces during the last two decades of the sixth century, it would appear that the permanent settlements of the Avars and Slavs at this period were beyond the Danube. We read of the Khagan's preparations to attack Byzantine towns on the river; we hear of his instigating the Slavs to cross the Danube and invade Byzantine territory; and we know of an order given by Byzantine generals that boats be prepared for the army to cross the Danube.[6]

The emperor Maurice intended to crush the enemy on their own ground rather than simply wearing out Byzantine forces by pursuing the Avaro-Slav hordes in the vast area of the Balkan peninsula. This is why he concentrated his troops beyond the Danube, knowing that the isolated groups which raided Byzantine domains would at some point return to their base, whereas if they stayed in imperial territory they would be rendered impotent, deprived of the support of their defeated fellow-tribesmen. But whereas, after 'the glorious victory of the Romans' and the clearing of the Danube frontier, it was generally expected that the situation would be stabilized, developments in Constantinople led to the overthrow of Maurice; the centurion Phokas succeeded him on the throne (23 November 602).[7] After a while a new Byzantine-Persian war erupted, which was destined to be of long duration, lasting until 628. And, while the Byzantine armies fought against the Persians, the Avars and Slavs, exploiting the weaknesses of the central government, resumed their raids on the territories south of the Danube, occupied towns in present-day Bulgaria and Serbia, and threatened the very heart of the Byzantine state, Constantinople and Thessalonike.[8]

The state of confusion which prevailed in the Balkan peninsula during the repeated raids of the Avars and Slavs is mirrored in the *Miracles of Saint Demetrios*. In these texts we find descriptions of the successive attacks on Thessalonike and of the city's miraculous rescues by the saint's intervention. The Slavs' persistent attempts to penetrate Macedonia and to strike at its very heart —Thessalonike — is indicative of the importance and fame that this city enjoyed throughout the Byzantine world. Yet the earliest Avaro-Slav attacks were spasmodic, ephemeral, brigandish and uncoordinated.

The first big raid against Thessalonike took place on 22 September 586 or 597.[9] The relevant passage of the *Miracles of Saint Demetrios* states that the besiegers numbered one hundred thousand,[10] an exaggerated figure which reflects the compiler's desire to emphasize the miraculous aid afforded on this occasion by the city's patron. The lifting of the siege seven days later was attributed to the intervention of the saint, who routed the enemy 'in the guise of a soldier'. This description served as a model for an artist who made a gold-plated silver box with representations from the life of Saint Demetrios: the saint appears on the battlements above a gate in the guise of a young man with curly hair, in military attire, holding a lance and a shield; while below, in front of the city's walls, horsemen in barbaric garb gallop away in all directions. One of them has been hit and is shown falling from his horse.[11]

During the seventh century the Slavs emancipated themselves from the Avar yoke and settled in groups in Macedonia and Thessaly. Now it was on their own initiative that they attacked Thessalonike.[12]

A second attack made on Thessalonike by five thousand Slavs on 27 October, perhaps in the year 604, was repelled thanks to the strong walls of the city and its well-organized defence. A few years later (? 615), according to book II of the Miracles, various Slavonic tribes (Drogouvitai, Sagoudatai, Velegezitai, Verzitai and others) made a third assault on Thessalonike, this time from the sea, because of the impregnability of the city from the land. They arrived on their *monoxyla,* or dug-out canoes, while their families waited in the plain with all their belongings.[13] But the nautical equipment of the Slavs was unsuitable for the operation. Besides, the Thessalonikans had had time to block the entrance to the port with a chain and poles, and to place war machines on the jetty. On the fourth day of the siege a strong northern wind dispersed the besiegers' canoes.[14]

After this last unsuccessful attempt, the Slavs asked their old masters the Avars to undertake a combined attack against Thessalonike. It took the Avars two years to mobilize their own forces and those of their subject peoples.[15] One summer, perhaps in 618, the Avars and Slavs assaulted Thessalonike for thirty days with numerous siege-machines, which did not, however, prove sufficient to demolish the walls. The siege was lifted after an agreement whose details are unknown to us.[16] This time too Thessalonike successfully defended herself exclusively with her own resources, as the new emperor Heraklios (612-42) was occupied with the reorganization of the imperial forces in preparation for his crusade against the Persians.

CONSEQUENCES OF THE SLAVONIC RAIDS

The Byzantine empire, multinational in origin like its Roman predecessor, continued Rome's policy vis-à-vis foreign peoples: it resisted with force those who attacked it with the intention to conquer or plunder; it not only tolerated, but positively encouraged, the settlement of foreign nations within its territories, whenever it judged that this would be profitable, or at least of no danger to its safety, on the condition that they acknowledged the existing political and constitutional order.

From the confused information provided by our sources it would appear that in the period in question the Slavonic settlements fell into two main categories.

Along the northern frontier the Slavs organized themselves compactly as an autonomous administrative unit; the various constituent tribes were self-governing, independent of the Byzantine emperor, and free of any obligation to pay tribute. Theophylakt Simokatta called the area controlled by these groups *sklavenia,* that is the country of the Sklavenoi.[17]

Other groups took advantage of the depopulation of the countryside caused by the continuous raids, and, thrusting southwards, formed islands of settlement on Byzantine territory. These groups were tributary to the emperor; that is, they were his vassals, and paid tribute to him. Such must have been the legal status, at least theoretically, of the tribal communities which were scattered all over Macedonia, Thrace and southern Greece, and which are usually mentioned in the sources under the name *sklaveniai.* We have to do with minor Slavonic groups, each of which obeyed a chieftain of its own, and coexisted with the populations that already inhabited the area. Having given up their nomadic existence, they had settled permanently in river gorges between mountains, or on mountain slopes, or in the plain, often near marshes.

To begin with, the Slavs preserved their own customs, and their harsh and brigand-like way of life. But little by little they were influenced by the higher cultural level of their environment, and exchanged their nomadic life for that of cultivators. At this stage they still clung to their primitive, ancestral shipbuilding techniques, good only for river navigation. These were the sort of ships used in the sea attacks on Thessalonike in 615 and Constantinople in 626.[18] They also maintained their own primitive social and political institutions. Each tribe was grouped around a chieftain whom the Byzantine sources call *rex* (from the Latin word king), and nobles whom the Greeks called *boliadai* (from the Slavonic word *boliarin,* officers).

Among the Slavonic tribes who penetrated into Macedonia some preserved their tribal name (e.g. the Drogouvitai, Sagoudatai, Velegezitai, Verzitai), and some adopted names indicative of their geographical area of settlement (e.g. the Strymonitai or Rhynchinoi). Later these tribes were located as follows: the Drogouvitai settled near Beroia; the Sagoudatai likewise settled in the west; the Verzitai occupied the area between Monastir, lake Ochrid and Velessa; the Velegezitai went to southern Thessaly; and the Rhynchinoi settled around the river Rhechinos or Rhechios between lake Bolbe and the Strymonic Gulf,[19] and the Strymonitai close to the river Strymon.

176. An inscription below this 7th century mosaic of Saint Demetrios invokes the saint's protection for the city. On the right is the Saint, clad in a white vestment onto which is sewn a blue tavlion (a badge of office in the form of a square of silk). His right hand rests protectively on the shoulder of a cleric who holds a decorated Gospel, and whose head is framed by the battlement of a wall. Saint Demetrios, Thessalonike.

177. In the 8th century Thessalonike became the seat of a metropolitan bishop, obedient to the Patriarchate of Constantinople. The cathedral church, Saint Sophia, was the most im-pressive building in the city, at a time when the barbarian raids had their worst effects on the political and cultural development of Macedonia.

Much debated is the etymology proposed by Constantine Porphyrogenitus, connecting the place-name τά Σέρβ(λ)ια in the theme of Thessalonike with Heraklios' settlement of a number of Serbs in this area.[20] It is not impossible that Serbs were settled there. Yet the place-name does not constitute proof, especially since it differs from the usual Byzantine convention for place-names — genitive of possession in the singular combined with the article in the neuter plural, as for instance τά Ἐλευθερίου. According to Constantine Amantos, the place-name τά Σέρβ(λ)ια comes from the phrase τά Σερβίου.[21] Whatever the answer, Constantine Porphyrogenitus' foible for producing etymologies of proper and geographical names, without linguistic expertise, is sufficiently well-known.

It was against precisely these tribes that Constans II campaigned in 656-57. 'The emperor campaigned against *Sklaveniai* and he took many prisoners and subjected (the land)', thus inaugurating the Byzantine policy of intervention in the *sklaveniai* — a policy which was to continue for many years.[22]

As time went by, the Slavs learned to coexist peacefully with the local Greek population. This can be deduced from the development of commercial relations between newcomers and locals, the acceptance on the part of the Slavonic ruling class of certain elements from the higher culture of the Byzantine people, and from the two communities' eventual cooperation in political matters. A typical example is offered by Perboundos, a chieftain of the Rhynchinoi in the third quarter of the seventh century, who wore Byzantine dress, spoke fluent Greek and, rather than living among his own subjects, preferred to reside in Thessalonike, where he established links with many important citizens.[23] But, rightly or wrongly, he aroused the suspicions of the prefect of Thessalonike, who arrested him and sent him in chains to Constantinople. At that point both the Strymonitai and Rhynchinoi and the citizens of Thessalonike sent a common petition to the emperor, asking him to pardon Perboundos and release him.[24] The joint approach on behalf of the chieftain of the Rhynchinoi is evidence both for the position of the Slavs vis-à-vis the Byzantine government, and for the peaceful coexistence of the Slav tribes with the Greeks in Thessalonike.

Having escaped twice, Perboundos was eventually put to death. This event was at the root of the uprising of his compatriots, the Rhynchinoi, along with the Strymonitai and the Sagoudatai, who blockaded Thessalonike and looted its environs. This upheaval lasted for two years (676-78). It is noteworthy though that not all the Slavonic tribes cooperated with the rebels. During the hostilities against Thessalonike and the ensuing famine, many Thessalonikans fled to Thessaly and took refuge among the Velegezitai Slavs. These same Slavs supplied provisions to Thessalonike, and later they informed these who had removed to Thessaly of the failure of the Slav attack.[25] Thus, while certain tribes were at war with the Greeks, other Slavonic communities were simultaneously maintaining amicable and commercial relations with the Greek population.

The Miracles of Saint Demetrios is again our source for the details of the hostilities. After long preparation, and having equipped themselves with weapons and siege-machines, the Slavs launched a three-day attack on the walls of Thessalonike (25-27 July 677). But this time too they failed to take the city. There ensued conflicts and quarrels among the Slavs themselves, and the siege was lifted.[26]

But while the Sagoudatai withdrew altogether, the Rhynchinoi and Strymonitai turned to piratical activities in the Hellespont. Since these operations looked as if they would acquire a permanent character, and were being carried out in an area of vital importance because of its proximity to the capital, the imperial government decided, after the withdrawal of the Arab threat (678), to act drastically. Having first called on them to lay down their arms, the emperor Constantine IV moved decisively against the homes of the Strymonitai and the Rhynchinoi.[27] The emperor's appeal shows that the Slavs were not regarded as external enemies, but rather as rebellious subjects. And the Slavs themselves, having neither the forces nor the experience required in order to confront the imperial army, withdrew before long into mountain passes and certain strongholds which could be held with just a few warriors.

THE EPISODE OF KOUVER

The Avaro-Slav bands who were looting the Balkan peninsula had taken numerous prisoners. Some of them had been settled by the Khagan of the Avars near his capital, Sirmium. As will shortly appear, most of the prisoners were Greeks from Macedonia and Thrace who intermarried with other nationalities subject to the Avars.

Sixty years later around 680, their descendants had not yet integrated with their new milieu: they were Christians, they maintained their ancestral habits,[28] preserved their language and were home-sick for their native land.[29] These people came together to form the basically Greek tribe of the Sermesians, over whom the Avar Khagan placed a chieftain, of whom our source states that he was called Kouver and was of Bulgarian origin.[30] Some historians consider that he should be identified with the Bulgarian prince Kovrat, the father of Asparuch; others identify him with one of the brothers of Asparuch, whose name is not given to us.[31] Both these identifications however present difficulties.

If the Khagan thought that he was being far-sighted in behaving in this way, his expectations were certainly belied. Kouver won the trust of the *Romaioi* (Romans=Greeks) and undertook to lead them back to Byzantine territory: 'He won over to his side the whole of the people of the Romans, together with others who were pagans, and they revolted against the Khagan'.[32] In successive clashes with the Khagan, who pursued them, the rebels proved the stronger. They crossed the Danube (which here again appears as the northern frontier of the empire) and reached the *Campus Ceramesius*,[33] which denotes the Pelagonian plain. Then Kouver appealed to the emperor to allow him and his followers to settle there, and to order the neighbouring Slavonic tribe of the Drogouvitai to supply them with food. This confirms that during the last decades of the seventh century the imperial government controlled the Slavonic tribes which were settled in the Macedonian plain. On the other hand, the view that the main group led by Kouver was of Proto-Bulgarian stock, and that Kouver himself founded a Proto-Bulgarian state in north-west Macedonia, is not well-founded, as it is contradicted by the information furnished by our source.[34]

The Christian Sermesians expressed a desire to continue on their way and reach the Byzantine cities that their forefathers had inhabited. But Kouver was opposed to this idea since he did not want to lose control or see his power diminished. His followers then started fleeing to the nearby towns. Some of those who reached Thessalonike were taken to Constantinople under the protection of the imperial authorities. Then Kouver, exploiting the desire of his subjects to return to the Greek cities, conceived a plan to become master of Thessalonike, and thence to embark on the conquest of Constantinople itself. His collaborator Mauros undertook to execute this plan. Mauros, whose Bulgarian origin is contested, was a Christian, a polyglot, very clever and well-acquainted with the administrative machinery of the Byzantine empire.[35] With his followers he took refuge in Thessalonike and, pretending that he was a deserter, asked for political asylum.[36] He was able to win the trust both of the local authorities and of the emperor, who bestowed on him the title of consul and made him the official leader of those Sermesians who had followed him.[37] Then Mauros and his companions prepared to seize power in Thessalonike; but the plan was frustrated by the sudden arrival in the city of a squadron of the Byzantine fleet. Yet Mauros was not exposed; and the Byzantine admiral transferred him and his followers to Constantinople, where

255

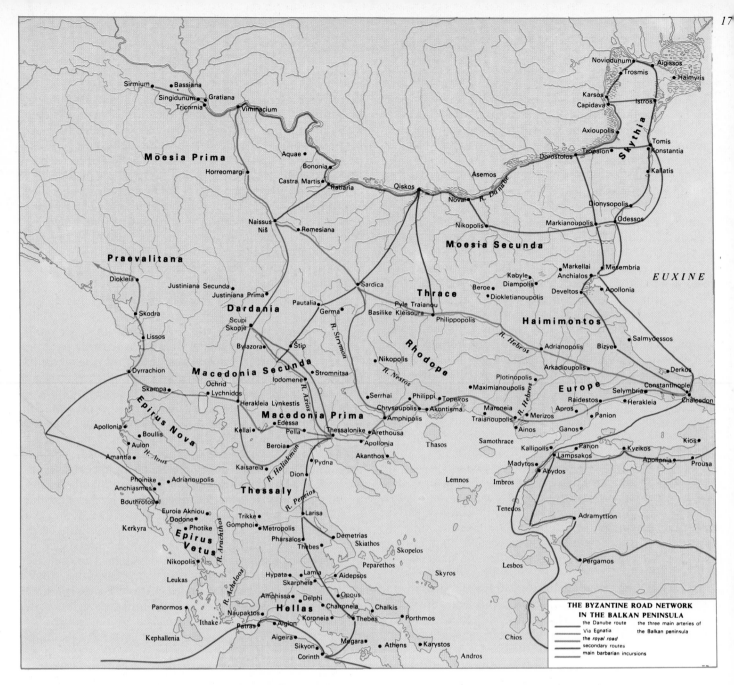

178. *The siting of Thessalonike was important both for the history of Macedonia whose capital it was and, more particularly, for the town itself. The radial point of a road system of considerable military and economic significance to the Balkan peninsula, providing communications to Constantinople, the West and to the more northerly countries of the peninsula, Thessalonike developed as a commercial centre with artistic and cultural activities worthy of the second city of the empire.*

the emperor conferred on his perfidious subject the titles of *patrikios* and 'Archon of the Sermesians and the Bulgars'. There survives a seal of his with a representation of the cross (which shows that he was a Christian) and the inscription 'To Mauros the *patrikios* and *archon* of the Sermesians and the Bulgars' (which confirms the ethnic distinction which was made between the two groups).[38] But in the end Mauros' son revealed his father's plan to the emperor, who had him imprisoned.

THE BULGARS

After their crushing defeat in the summer of 626 before the walls of Constantinople, the supremacy of the Avars was shattered, and the peoples of lake Maiotis were set free. Among these peoples were the Bulgars, who proceeded to emigrate westwards — in the 670s a part of these Hunnic or Turkic peoples was to be found to the north of the Danube delta, whence they were able to raid Byzantine territory under the leadership of Kovrat's son, Asparuch.[39] The emperor Constantine IV was forced to campaign against them, but he was defeated (680), and obliged to allow the Bulgars under Asparuch to settle between the Danube and Mount Haimos, and to recognize them as politically independent (681).[40] There the Bulgars established their rule over the Slavs and the Romanized pre-Slavonic populations, while at the same time exercising a firm southward pressure on eastern Thrace. Even before they reached the northern border of Macedonia, their presence in that area was a factor taken into account by the Byzantine government.

IMPERIAL POLICY TOWARDS THE SLAVS AND ITS EFFECTS

Byzantium adopted a definite policy towards the Slavs only after 681. After the appearance of the Bulgar threat, the Byzantine state attempted to assimilate foreign elements mainly through exchange of populations and grants of territory in exchange for military services. But force might also be employed when it seemed necessary.

As has already been mentioned Constantine IV's campaign against the Strymonitai and Rhynchinoi was a response to the piratical activities of these tribes in the Hellespont region, an area of crucial commercial and strategic importance for the empire. The campaign was made possible by the termination of the seven years' state of war against the Arabs, who had reached the very threshold of the capital. Additional campaigns were undertaken against the Sklavenoi of Macedonia, and an attempt was made to weaken the Slavonic element in Macedonia, and to strengthen the Greek populations in the area. The constant attention that Byzantium now gave to Macedonia was motivated not so much by the sporadic insurrections of the *sklaveniai* (in the past, as we have seen, the central government had not interfered even when the Slavs attacked Thessalonike), as by the new factor of Bulgarian pressure. In other words, the measures taken by Byzantium in Macedonia were just one aspect of a general policy aimed at checking the new enemy. Indeed it is clear from evidence to be discussed below that the Slavs of Macedonia faced the Bulgars as their enemies; and it was for this reason that certain among them collaborated with Byzantine missions concerned with the defence of Macedonia against the new threat.

Having first repelled the Bulgars in Thrace, Justinian II undertook a campaign against the *sklaveniai* of Macedonia in 688, only a few years after Constantine IV's campaign. Certain *sklaveniai* situated between the Hebros and the Strymon resisted, but others surrendered peacefully. During his stay in Thessalonike, Justinian offered the church of Saint Demetrios a salt-pan.[41] The prisoners taken during the campaign, and certain of the Slavs who had signed a treaty with the emperor, were transferred to the theme of Opsikion in Bithynia (688);[42] and from them there was formed a purely Slavic military corps whose leader was also a Slav. The relevant source puts the number of men who served in this corps at thirty thousand.[43] Yet this figure is extravagant when seen in the context of the whole Byzantine army, and especially of the army of the theme of Opsikion, which numbered only six thousand men in the ninth century. It would appear therefore that the figure of thirty thousand refers to the total number of Slavs who were transferred from Macedonia to Bithynia. Justinian II was very favourably disposed towards the Slavs, even to the point of calling the military detachment that he formed from them 'the chosen people'.[44] Yet during the first important battle in which they took part, at Sebastopolis, they deserted to the Arabs, thus bringing about the defeat of the Byzantine army.

The transfer of Slavonic populations to Asia Minor aimed on the one hand at the weakening of the Slavonic element in Macedonia, Thrace and the neighbouring areas, and on the other hand at the strengthening of the Anatolian peasantry. The method of colonization was innovatory, in that the settlers were allowed to preserve their ethnic homogeneity, so that they did not feel strangers in the midst of their new social and religious milieu, while at the same time their settlements were scattered over a wide area in order to pre-empt the possibility of any organized conspiracy.

As part of his more general policy of integrating the Slavs into the political framework of Byzantium, Justinian II entrusted them with the defence of the Strymon defiles against the Bulgars. The particular Slavonic tribes involved were the Smolenoi or Smoleanoi, who until then had dwelt to the east of the river Nestos. About a century and a half later, in 837, when they were no longer able to resist Bulgarian pressure, they withdrew to Christoupolis (present day Kavala). In 864 the bishopric of the Smolenoi was created as part of a more general attempt to Christianize them; after the great war between tsar Samuel and Basil II they were transferred by the Byzantine government to Rhodope, to form the new theme of Smolenoi. Smolenoi are thus a good example of Slavs who remained consistently faithful 'allies' of the Byzantine empire.[45]

During the ensuing centuries Byzantium proved highly intolerant of insurrectionary movements among the Slavs, which were usually suppressed by force. When some seventy years after their subjection by Justinian II, certain of the *sklaveniai* of Macedonia attempted an uprising their revolution was crushed by the emperor Constantine V (759).[46]

In 782-83, on the order of the empress Irene, her prime minister Staurakios marched against the Slavs of Macedonia and the Peloponnese and defeated them, compelling them to pay an annual tribute.[47]

In the ninth century the emperor Nikephoros I initiated a new phase of colonization, which must be linked with the renewed Bulgarian attacks. The sources record that the emperor ordered that Byzantine subjects from all the themes should be transferred to the *sklaveniai*.[48] This order (that the historian Theophanes includes among the so-called *kakoseis* (molestations) of Nikephoros I, that is various drastic and highly unpopular population transplants and financial measures which were intended to improve the state of the economy) required that between September 809 and Easter 810 those due to emigrate should sell all their immovable property and leave for their new home. Those affected by the order protested violently, but eventually were obliged to submit.[49] Once settled in the *sklaveniai,* they received land in exchange for military services. We have strong indications that this measure mainly concerned Macedonia and Thrace, and aimed at strengthening the Christian population in the area, and hence the possibilities of resisting the Bulgars. A little later, about the third decade of the ninth century, and certainly before 836, we hear of a theme of Thessalonike.[50] This attests the steady assimilation of the Slavs of Macedonia, since the creation of a theme presupposes the internal calm and peace that allows its army to concentrate exclusively on external enemies. Clearly the soldiers who formed the army, and who received from the emperor a fief in exchange for their services, were identical with the colonists whom Nikephoros I sent to *sklaveniai* in Macedonia; but Byzantine practice elsewhere suggests that loyal Slavs must also have been used.

POLITICAL, ECONOMIC AND SOCIAL DEVELOPMENTS

THE ADMINISTRATION

As has already been mentioned the administrative organization of the Balkan peninsula was frequently modified to meet new political and military needs.

The *Synekdemos* of Hierokles, a text which belongs to the early years of Justinian I's reign, shows that in the first decades of the sixth century Macedonia was made up of two provinces; Macedonia Prima, whose capital was Thessalonike, and Macedonia Secunda, whose capital was Stoboi. Both belonged to the Byzantine diocese of Macedonia *(dioecesis Macedoniae),* which also included Epirus, Thessaly, southern Greece and Crete.[51] The diocese of Macedonia (which comprised seven provinces altogether), together with the northern diocese of Dacia (which was made up of six provinces) constituted the prefecture of Illyricum *(praefectura praetorio per Illyricum)*; while the eastern part of the Balkan peninsula — that is the six provinces of the diocese of Thrace — belonged to the prefecture of the East *(praefectura praetorio per Orientem).*[52]

The seat of the prefect of Illyricum was originally Sirmium, but in times of trouble it could be moved elsewhere. Thus during the Hunnic invasions the capital was transferred to Thessalonike. In a novella of April 535 Justinian decreed that the capital should be moved to his own birthplace, Justiniana Prima; but it is doubtful whether this decree was ever enforced. Probably it applied only to the administration of the Church and Thessalonike remained the capital of Illyricum.[53]

How long the praetorian prefecture of Illyricum lasted is not known, though it is out of the question that it existed at the end of the eighth century, as has been maintained. Probably it was abolished sometime between 620 and 680. In the first book of the *Miracles of Saint Demetrios* there are repeated references to a praetorian prefect of Illyricum; but in the second book, written around 678-80, the prefect to whom reference is made seems to control only the city of Thessalonike, with duties similar to those of the prefect of Constantinople. In the case of Perboundos, the prefect ordered his arrest and, following an imperial order, sent him bound to the capital. The prefect of Thessalonike bore the title either of *consul* or of royal *spatharios.*

It was also at this period that the theme system began to be adopted in Asia Minor.[54] The new system had two main features: it concentrated both military and political power in one person, and it coincided with an important change in the recruitment of the imperial army, namely the replacement of expensive and frequently disloyal mercenaries by soldiers who were given land in exchange for an undertaking to appear as soon as they were called-up. This system was first adopted in areas seriously threatened by enemy invasion, as was the case in Asia Minor in the seventh century. After its success on the frontier there, the theme system was applied wherever similar needs arose. Thus the foundation of the Bulgar state led to the creation of the Thracian theme between 680 and 685; while the Slavonic incursions gave rise to the creation of the theme of Hellas, attested from 695.[55]

It is not known when exactly the theme system was extended to the intermediate European territories, among which was Macedonia. The first references date from much later than those referring to the themes of Thrace and of Hellas; but it is certain that in 801/02 there existed a theme of Macedonia, which was perhaps created during the sole rule of the empress Irene (797-802).[56] It had its capital in Adrianople, and included essentially non-Macedonian but Thracian territories, which had been detached from the southern part of the theme of Thrace.[57] Originally the Macedonian theme included the defile of the Strymon as well — an area of great strategic importance, since it controlled all other passes to the north. The purely Macedonian territories formed two themes: that of Thessalonike, to which we have a probable reference in 824 and a certain one in 836; and the theme of Strymon, which is first mentioned in 899, and whose core was the Strymon *kleisoura* (a subordinate military and administrative unit) of the theme of Macedonia.[58]

The theme of Thessalonike extended from the Pindos to the Strymon, and to the north it may have reached as far as the Axios pass; while the theme of Strymon began east of the river Strymon, and comprised the *turma* of Boleron, which corresponded to the present-day nomes of Xanthe and Rhodope.[59] The *strategos* of the theme of Strymon had his seat at Serrhai.

The *strategos* of each theme was at the apex of a well known hierarchy of governors of smaller military units who also had responsibility for political matters. Each theme comprised two or three *turmae,* presided over by a turmarch; and each *turma* was divided into three *drungii* controlled by officials called *drungarii.* Each *drungus* consisted of an unknown number of *banda.*

According to the *Kletorologion* of Philotheos (a work on Byzantine court etiquette written in 899), the *strategoi* of the themes just mentioned occupied the following ranks in the hierarchy: fourteenth for Thrace, fifteenth for Macedonia, twenty-fourth for Strymon and twenty-sixth for Thessalonike.[60] Under Leo VI the *strategoi* of Strymon and of Thessalonike did not receive a salary from the state, but each year they levied from their theme certain revenues known as *synetheiai,* though we do not know how these revenues were calculated or levied. The most common title for the *strategoi* of the Macedonian themes was that of *protospatharios,* though we have seals bearing the inferior titles of *spatharokandidatos* and of *spatharios.* The turmarch, who comes immediately after the *strategos* in the military hierarchy, usually bears the title of *spatharios* or, less often, that of *protospatharios.*[61]

The salary of the *strategos* of Macedonia was thirty *litra* per year (1296 gold pounds today) the highest of the European themes lower only than the salaries of the great themes of Asia Minor; of the Anatolikoi, of the Armenikioi, and Thrakesioi which came to forty gold *litra* per year; (1 gold *litra* = 72 *nomismata*).

Besides the *strategoi*, the themes had civil officials too, as for instance *protonotarioi*, whose titles are preserved on various seals.[62]

It is from seals also that we learn of the existence of two further categories of administrative employees: that of *paraphylax* and that of *dioiketes*. The former was probably responsible for the safety of the town, but in a police rather than a military sense. The latter presided over the tax offices of an area.[63]

In general, the evidence from seals of the administrative services, both civil and military, reflects the impeccable organization of bureaucratic machinery. It offers also a revealing picture of the general level of prosperity of Byzantine Macedonia.

FINANCIAL INSTITUTIONS

We have only indirect evidence for the importance of Thessalonike for the Macedonian economy during this period. It is probably true to say that the existence in Thessalonike, Christoupolis and in several other towns of the region, of the same institutions as in the capital presupposes a prosperous economy and intense commercial activity.

The important office of the (general) *kommerkiarios apothekes*, who often regulated the economy of a wide area, is attested in Thessalonike, as in provinces of Asia Minor, in the Aegean Islands, in Constantinople and elsewhere.[64] The possessors of seals were usually holders of important titles, rarely below that of *protospatharios* or *patrikios;* possession of a seal being the badge of rank within the hierarchy. The representation of the reigning emperor on a seal, as on coins, together with an exact recording of the year of the indiction are additional tokens of the importance of the bearer's office. It is worth mentioning in this connection that in two instances the general *kommerkiarios apothekes* in Thessalonike might also hold another office at the same time; one is known to have been general logothete,[65] another imperial *balnitor*.[66]

The re-organization of the post of *kommerkiarios* under Leo III, which probably took place between the years 727/28 and 730/31, is faithfully reflected in the seals. The official seal ceases to bear the name and title of the officer in question, which is replaced by the impersonal formula: 'from the imperial *kommerkia'* of such and such a town or region; while on the reverse of the seal we see a representation of the emperor, along with the date (by indiction). We have numerous seals of the imperial *kommerkia* of Thessalonike between 737/38 and 783/84.

In the first half of the ninth century, both in Macedonia and in other areas of the empire, personal seals of *kommerkiarioi* of towns or of regions of a different type appear for the first time. They bear the name, title and office of the seal's bearer, without any official indication, as is the case with the thousands of seals belonging to men employed in the civil service. The face of the reigning emperor does not

179. Thessalonike, the second city in wealth and consequence in the Byzantine empire, supported all kinds of workshops and craftsmen, whose products are an eloquent testimony to its prosperity and good taste. The pair of bands found near the city demonstrate the delicate skills of its goldsmiths and enamellers. 9th-10th centuries, Thessalonike, Archaeological Museum.

THE ADMINISTRATIVE AND ECCLESIASTICAL DIVISIONS IN THE NORTH OF THE BALKAN PENINSULA IN THE 6th CENTURY
- ✠ patriarchate
- ✠ metropolitan church
- ⛨ probable episcopal church
- ------ boundaries of provinces

180. Despite the repeated barbarian raids which Macedonia suffered during the later years of the Roman empire, Macedonian towns continued to flourish and even expand, until the beginning of the 6th century. The map above shows the dense distribution of settlement; it is based on the Synekdemos of Hierokles, a text valuable for the information it contains about the administrative organization not only of the Balkan peninsula, but of the entire Byzantine empire during the early years of Justinian I's rule.

appear, and the year of the indiction is not recorded, so that it is impossible to determine the exact date of impression, in the way that one can with seals belonging to general *kommerkiarioi apothekes* or to imperial *kommerkia*. These new style seals of *kommerkiarioi* can be dated only on the basis of technical criteria, and in consequence one has to allow a margin of error of several decades when estimating their date.

The evidence quoted above proves that changes took place in the structure of the service of the imperial *kommerkia*; these changes probably date from the Phrygian dynasty, though any more exact chronology is at present impossible.

The *kommerkiarioi* (or *kummerkiarioi*) came under the jurisdiction of the general *logothesion* (that is, the central financial department) and occupied sixth place in the

hierarchy described in Philotheos' *Kletorologion*. They received the *kommerkion*, that is a ten per cent tax levied on the circulation and selling of goods. We possess seals belonging to this new category of *kommerkiarioi* either from regions or towns, financial centres or ports, which constitute evidence for the general economic development of the empire from the ninth century onwards.

In many cases, the same person was also entrusted with the duties of *abydikos*; this occurs usually in sea or river ports, and less often in lakeside harbours. The *abydikoi* came under the control of the naval department and supervised navigation and ship movements. They also administered a toll known as the *archontikion*. With the passing of time the police-like character of their duties became more apparent. We have many seals belonging to *abydikoi* of Thessalonike. Like all other officers, the *abydikoi* disposed of *notarioi* (that is secretaries), who looked after their paper work.[67]

Besides the evidence provided by seals, the commercial activity of the port of Thessalonike is also confirmed by the *Miracles of Saint Demetrios,* where one finds references, for example, to ships transporting timber. During the Avaro-Slav incursions, merchant ships loaded with corn and other provisions arrived daily at the port of Thessalonike. We also learn from the *Miracles* that, like all other big towns, Thessalonike had state granaries full of corn in readiness for any emergency. The granaries were managed by the city authorities.[68]

THE CITIES

During this period the cities of Byzantine Macedonia acquired increasing importance. As the countryside emptied under the pressure of barbarian invasion, its inhabitants fled to the cities, which remained centres of trade and culture and strongholds of Hellenism. No direct description of the appearance of the towns of Macedonia has been preserved from this period; but the description of the Thracian cities which can be extracted from the tenth century writings of the Pseudo-Symeon is valid for Macedonia as well. According to this, the cities of Thrace were protected by an especially well-fortified and strong citadel; and they had many churches.[69] In the seaside towns, the harbour and commercial installations were situated outside the fortifications. Fortified bridges ensured communication between the town and the surrounding countryside. In time of danger the rural population, which lived in farms and small settlements, remote from any citadel, would flee to the mountains, where caves and ravines provided natural refuges. There they would gather together their cattle, flocks and herds. The organization of settlements and daily life had been adapted to cope with the invaders who would break in, burn, pillage, carry off the animals, take prisoner the unarmed population, kill the men, and then return whence they had come.

Thessalonike, the capital of Macedonia and the second city of the Byzantine empire in size, wealth and importance, continued to play the major strategic role that it had always had and which it was destined never to lose. Its harbour, where land and sea-routes met, was extremely busy. The commercial activity of the city attracted foreign merchants. Its walls proved invincible to the assaults of Slavs and Avars, some of which were conducted with the help of siege-machines — though the walls did suffer cracks in the course of major earthquakes. In time of need the harbour could be closed with a chain fixed to wooden bases, though it was not originally enclosed by a wall. There were churches outside the walls.

Information on other Macedonian cities is sparse, usually derived from episcopal lists and the *Acta* of oecumenical Councils, recording bishops' sees and the names of their holders. Parallel to these sources, occasional references in literary and hagiographical texts and on seals, along with archaeological material, provide basic evidence for the existence of urban centres at Stoboi, Bargala,

Herakleia Lynkestis, Kaisareia, Beroia, Servia, Edessa, Christoupolis, Amphipolis, Philippi, Serrhai and Stromnitsa. After its destruction by the barbarians and its devastation by earthquake in 518, Stoboi was refounded, according to the historian Prokopios, under Justinian. The city was still sending ecclesiastical representatives to the sixth oecumenical Council (680-81) and to the Quinisext (691-92).[70] Clearly some sort of urban life survived during the period of the invasions, but it will have reflected little of the former glory of the one-time capital of Macedonia Secunda.

Much the same, though with less certainty, can be said of the other large city of western Macedonia, Herakleia Lynkestis, which reappears in flourishing condition, after its destruction by Theoderic at the end of the sixth century.[71] The city was represented at the Quinisext Council. As for Bargala, which is referred to in the *Synekdemos* of Hierokles, it seems that it continued to exist throughout the period of the invasions, and it is referred to under the name of Bargalenitsa in the ninth century by Theophylact, archbishop of Ochrid.[72] According to current opinion, this is the town subsequently known as Bregalnitsa. Beroia, a centre with a strong cultural tradition from the Hellenistic period, appears in the episcopal lists and is referred to in the *Life* of Theodora as a walled town administratively subject to Thessalonike.[73] Aiane, an important town in Elimeia, was renamed Kaisareia, according to Keramopoullos, under Diocletian.[74] Kaisareia is referred to by Prokopios and Hierokles, and later it is mentioned as subject to the metropolis of Larisa.[75]

Servia was a fortified town near the Haliakmon.[76] According to an authority on mediaeval architecture A. Xyngopoulos, its fortification, which can be dated between the end of the sixth century and the beginning of the seventh, can be interpreted as an attempt to protect the Greek population of the countryside during the Slav invasions. On the other hand, Constantine Porphyrogenitus remarks that Servia was founded in the time of Heraklios.

Recently fine early Christian buildings have come to light at Longos near Edessa.[77] The town, which also appears in the episcopal lists, seems to have been transferred to roughly its present site during this period.

We have rather more information about Christoupolis, which seems to have been the second most important Macedonian port at this period. It is testified as the seat of an archbishop at the Quinisext Council, and it was certainly a commercial centre; a seal shows that the town possessed a *kommerkiarios*. There was still an imperial garrison at the beginning of the ninth century. It was a fortified centre, like Thessalonike, and a base for military expeditions, but it was also a refuge in case of misfortune, as in the case of the Smolenoi.[78] In the same area, Amphipolis and Philippi are also referred to as seats of bishops. We know nothing else about Amphipolis. But in the case of Philippi, the historian Theophanes tells us that after the defeat of Krum, in 812, the town was abandoned by the Byzantines, which means that at that time it was a Byzantine fortress.[79]

Serrhai is attested in the ninth century as the capital of the theme of Strymon and the seat of a bishop.[80] Stromnitsa is often referred to, as for example by Theophylact Simocatta (a historian of the late sixth and early seventh centuries). It was the scene of clashes between Byzantines and Bulgars, and was captured by the Bulgars in 811.[81]

During the revival attempted by Leo V (813-20), the emperor's crucial concern, apart from the reconstruction of the army, was the rebuilding of the cities: 'Leo occupied himself with practical matters... drilling in person the common soldiers, and himself rebuilding from their foundations cities throughout Thrace and Macedonia...'

Fuller knowledge of conditions in Byzantine cities awaits the undertaking of systematic excavations and the study of the numismatical evidence. But it is essential that this latter material have a clear provenance. Illegal excavations and the disposal of coins on the commercial market are a severe obstacle to research in this field, and hinder progress towards the establishment of a clearer picture of domestic conditions in Byzantine cities in general and Macedonian cities in particular.

THE CHURCH

For many centuries the ecclesiastical and political administration of Illyricum were separate. The old prefecture of Illyricum was under the jurisdiction of the Church of Rome, from which it was detached by imperial decree in 732/33 (according to most scholars), in reprisal for the western Church's condemnation of the emperor's iconoclastic policy. Translating into political terms the dogmatic differences which for several decades divided East and West, Leo III ordered the integration of the old

prefecture of Eastern Illyricum (of which Macedonia formed a part) into the territories controlled by the Patriarchate of Constantinople. Thus the re-drawing of the frontiers of ecclesiastical jurisdiction resulted in the coincidence of political and ecclesiastical boundaries.

The Avaro-Slav incursions destroyed not only the cities, but also the close-knit ecclesiastical administration of the Balkan peninsula. After the invasions, episcopal sees began to be refounded. Thus the sixth oecumenical Council (680-81) was attended by only two Macedonian ecclesiastics: the metropolitan of Thessalonike and the bishop of Stoboi. Eleven years later there were present at the Quinisext Council (691/92) the bishops of Stoboi, Philippi, Amphipolis and Edessa; and a century after that we find references to a bishop of Neapolis (Christoupolis) and an archbishop of Serrhai.

THE CHRISTIANIZATION OF THE SLAVS

We have no information about the extent of conversion to Christianity of the Slav inhabitants of the empire from the beginning of the period under review until the time of the iconoclastic controversy. There are some examples of individual conversion, however, as in the case of the family of Myritzikios, father of the abbot Ioannikios; a Slav from Macedonia who was expert in the construction of siege machines and lastly, the patriarch Niketas the Slav.

According to evidence provided by a chronicle of the Athonite monastery of Kastamonitou, the Rhynchinoi Slavs were Christianized under the iconoclast emperors. The reference must be to the long period covered by the

181. Byzantine policy was to draw the peoples beyond the frontiers into the sphere of its cultural influence. Even before the official adoption of Christianity the Slavs and Bulgars had begun to listen to the Gospel. The chronicle of John Skylitzes shows Bulgarians imploring the God of the Christians to deliver them from the scourge of famine. Madrid, Biblioteca Nacional.

262

reigns of Leo III, Constantine V and Leo IV (717-76), and not to the later outbreaks of iconoclasm (802-20 and 829-42). It is worth noting that the chieftain of the Rhynchinoi was then Perboundos, who knew Greek, dressed and behaved as a Byzantine, and preferred to live in Thessalonike rather than among his subjects. It is likely that his example had some influence on them, and made them more open to a rapprochement with their Greek and Christian milieu.

The Christianization of the Slavs who lived outside Byzantine territory is of equal relevance to the local history of Macedonia, since both Methodios (815-85) and Constantine-Cyril (826-69), who preached the gospel in Moravia, translated religious and liturgical texts into Slavonic, created an alphabet capable of rendering the sounds of that language, and trained those who were to continue their work, were born and brought up in Thessalonike. Of their life and work much will be said below; but what should be emphasized here is that the preaching of the gospel among the Slavs by the Greek brothers Cyril and Methodios took quite unexpected dimensions and significance because of an historical coincidence. At the same time as they were active in Moravia, another Byzantine mission baptized the king of the Bulgars Boris I (864), who took the name of his godfather, the Emperor Michael III, and allowed the Patriarch of Constantinople to propagate the gospel among his subjects.[82]

INTELLECTUAL LIFE

Up to the great Arab conquests of the mid-seventh century Byzantine art, literature and thought had been polycentric. Alexandria, Gaza, Antioch, Jerusalem, Athens, the great cities of western Asia Minor all had a lively cultural life of their own, which often outshone that of Constantinople. With the loss of Egypt, Palestine and Syria, followed by continuing Arab pressure on Asia Minor, and Avar attacks and Slav settlement in the northern Balkans, the social conditions favouring art and letters ceased to exist in cities other than Constantinople. It was there alone that Byzantine culture was maintained and developed, while in other cities of the empire cultural life became provincialized and impoverished.

Macedonia was particularly disturbed by continuing Slav and Avar pressure. Many of its cities were abandoned. Of those where civic life continued, only Thessalonike was of any account. There literature and art were still pursued, but on a much diminished scale, and with a narrowly religious emphasis. Relations between the Greek citizens and the Slav settlers were never exclusively hostile. As the situation stabilized, a close symbiosis developed. It was as a result of this that Macedonians were able in the ninth century to play a dominant role in the acculturation of the Balkan Slavs and in the origins of a Slavonic literature and culture which soon spread far beyond the confines of the Balkans.

THE MIRACLES OF SAINT DEMETRIOS

The series of panegyrics on Saint Demetrios, normally delivered by the metropolitan on the Feast of the saint (26 October) no doubt began in the course of the sixth century. However, the earliest surviving panegyrics are probably those by metropolitan Plotinus (c. 610), in which he recounts the siege of the city by the Avars towards the end of the reign of Maurice, and by John. Whether this is the metropolitan John who took part in the oecumenical Council of 680-81 or an earlier namesake of about 620 must await the publication of the text of his panegyric (preserved in cod. Paris gr. 1517, fol. 226-247v). It is to this earlier metropolitan John that we owe the first collection of *Miracles of Saint Demetrios*. These remarkable texts provide much information on intellectual life in Macedonia and in Thessalonike in particular at the end of the sixth and early seventh centuries. We learn that there were doctors to be found throughout the province, and that during an epidemic of plague sceptics argued openly against the theological explanation of the epidemic as a punishment for the sins of the people. We hear of performances by *tragedoi* in a 'theatre' — probably the Odeion behind the east portico of the Agora. There is naturally much information about the invasions and sieges by Avars and Slavs. The second, anonymous, collection of *Miracles of Saint Demetrios* was compiled in Thessalonike in the second half of the seventh century. From these we learn not only of the relentless pressure of Slav migrants in Greece and of their unsuccessful attempts to take Thessalonike, but also of the peaceful cooperation of Slavs and Greeks and of the attraction which Greek civilization had for the emerging ruling class of the Slav tribes. Perboundos, the ruler of the Rhynchinoi, spoke Greek and wore Greek clothes, and spent much of his time in Thessalonike (see page 254).

Apart from the interest of their contents, these works are all evidence of the maintenance of literary education throughout the period of invasions in Thessalonike and probably in such other Macedonian cities as remained in Byzantine hands.[1] The panegyrics and the *Miracles* are composed in the learned tongue, and make use of many of the stylistic devices of rhetoric.

CYRIL AND METHODIOS: THE APOSTLES OF THE SLAVS

In 826 or 827 there was born the greatest son of Macedonia since Alexander. Indeed if we consider the influence of his work through the centuries he may be counted greater than Alexander, though his weapon was the pen and not the sword. Constantine and Methodios were the sons of a military officer in the province of Thessalonike.[2] Methodios was born about 815, and after an education in Thessalonike he entered the civil service and was appointed governor of a district in Macedonia. The younger son Constantine born 826/7, also studied in Thessalonike. Soon, about 843, he felt the call of learning — his biographer recounts that he found the education he could obtain in Macedonia did not fit him to read Gregory of Nazianzos with full understanding — and went to the capital. There he studied under Photios and Leo the Mathematician. As Leo had been metropolitan of Thessalonike from 839/40 to 843, it may well have been this enlightened prelate who encouraged the young man to move to Constantinople. He proved a brilliant scholar, and became private secretary to the patriarch and later professor in the newly founded university, teaching probably rhetoric. He had a talent for languages, and in 855 was a member of a mission to Caliph Mutawakkil to arrange an exchange of prisoners. In 860-61, he was sent, along with Methodios, who had by now become a monk, via Kherson in the Crimea to the capital of the Khazars on the Caspian Sea. There, we are told, he engaged in learned debate with the Jews of Khazaria. On the way there he had discovered at Kherson the alleged relics of St. Clement of Rome. In the year after his return from Khazaria king Rastislav of Moravia sent an urgent request to the emperor Michael III for religious teachers. German clergy were conducting missionary work in his country, and he was anxious not to see it become a German dependency. The emperor and his advisers welcomed this opportunity to assert Byzantine prestige and authority in central Europe. It was to Constantine and Methodios that they turned. Both were by now prominent men in Byzantine life — Methodios was abbot of an important monastery — and had wide diplomatic experience. There was a further reason for the emperor's choice: the brothers knew perfect Slavonic.

Soon the brothers set out for distant Moravia. From then on their story belongs to world history. Constantine — who changed his name to Cyril on becoming a monk — and Methodios became the Apostles of the Slavs. They provided not only an alphabet and translation of the Bible and liturgical texts for their proselytes. They created for the Slavonic peoples a literary language and gave them access to the heritage of Greek and European culture.

The account given in the biographies of Constantine/Cyril and Methodios cannot be wholly believed. The Slavonic alphabet was a marvel of phonological analysis, and can scarcely have been invented in a few days. And the working out of the abstract and technical vocabulary needed to translate the Bible and theological texts demanded many years work. It is reasonable to suppose that Constantine/Cyril and Methodios had for long been considering the problems of evangelization of the Slavs in their native Macedonia, and had come to the conclusion that it was possible only through the Slavonic tongue. Constantine/Cyril was an accomplished linguist, and Methodios had long experience of governing a predominantly Slav population. They may also have had in mind the eventual conversion of Bulgaria, which in fact took place a few years after they left for Moravia.

A modified form of Constantine/Cyril's alphabet is still in use from the Arctic Ocean to the Greek frontier and from the Baltic to the Behring Strait.[3]

His mortal remains lay in the crypt of the Church of Saint Clement in Rome until 1975, when they were transferred to the church of Saint Demetrios, Thessalonike.

THE CONTINUERS OF THE WORK OF CYRIL AND METHODIOS

The work of Constantine/Cyril and Methodios was carried on by another bilingual Macedonian, their disciple Clement.[4] Clement was born about 840, and became a pupil of Methodios in his monastery on Bithynian Olympos. It is probable that he took part with the brothers in their mission to Khazaria, and that it was at Kherson that he received his monastic name of Clement. A year later he went with Constantine/Cyril and Methodios to Moravia and shared in their work of evangelization and translation. When after the death of Cyril and Methodios the Byzantine clergy were expelled from Moravia, Clement together with several other members of the group took refuge in Bulgaria, where they were welcomed by tsar Boris. Some of the group remained at the Bulgarian court at Preslav. But Clement was sent to his native Macedonia, and established himself at Ochrid. He saw that the key to the effective Christianization of the predominantly Slav population lay in the training of Slavonic-speaking clergy. Accordingly he set up a school, in which the traditions and methods of Greek education were adapted to the new task. His biographer Theophylact Hephaistos recounts that in seven years three thousand five hundred pupils passed through his school. Though this may be an exaggeration, the scale of the operation was unprecedentedly large. Clement was clearly not only a man of education and missionary ardour, but an unusually brilliant organizer. No doubt he adopted the Byzantine system of having the senior pupils share in the teaching of their juniors.

Shortly after the accession of tsar Symeon in 893 Clement was elevated to a bishopric, although the precise location of his see remains uncertain. Ochrid remained the centre of his activities, and it was there that he built his monastery of Saint Panteleimon (the foundations of which lie under the Imaret Mosque), the church of the Virgin, now known as Saint Clement's and two smaller, probably round, churches. He died in Ochrid on 27 July 916 and was buried in the monastery of Saint Panteleimon. His teaching work was continued by his disciple Naum, probably a fellow-Macedonian. Without the well-organized and successful training of clergy by Clement, the work of Constantine/Cyril and Methodios might well have perished. It was Clement, too, who wrote the first substantial original works in Slavonic. He is rightly revered as the father of Slavonic literature. In addition to his directly educational work Clement wrote many homilies which show close acquaintance with the Greek Fathers, hymns and prayers in Slavonic for his flock. There is no trace of his having written in Greek.

182. Eulogistic accounts of the life and miracles of Saint Demetrios are mines of historical information. Here, the saint, portrayed in mosaic, is the central figure; a bishop stands to his right, a secular official to his left. They may represent the men who rebuilt the church. 7th century, church of Saint Demetrios, Thessalonike.

ART FROM THE MID - SEVENTH
TO THE TENTH CENTURY

THESSALONIKE AND ITS SIGNIFICANCE

Throughout the Byzantine period the town of Thessalonike produced decisively significant art in the Macedonian area, important for its richness, form and character. Thessalonike, the second largest city after the capital, Constantinople, had the biggest population and the greatest number as well as the most splendid civic and ecclesiastical buildings. The character of the wealthy and dynamic city, enclosed within the walls and dominated by the Heptapyrgion fortress, was determined by the vast Galerian complex (the palace, the Octagon, the arch, Hippodrome, Rotunda) and the harbour, the stadium, the Agora, the large Early Christian basilicas which were in themselves entire complexes, other large and small Byzantine churches, monasteries, and the original city plan with its squares, main streets and stoas.[1]

Two of the most important of the many basilicas are still standing: the large martyrium of Saint Demetrios, recently restored, one of the most popular shrines throughout the Byzantine period, and the Acheiropoietos. The Rotunda, remodelled as a Christian church, has also been preserved and so has the metropolitan church Saint Sophia which was built later, in the eighth century, on the site of an earlier basilica but on the scale of Early Christian architecture. All of these churches were decorated with multicoloured marble floors, marble veneer, and also with mosaics on the walls, arches and vaults, with delicately wrought column capitals, relief parapets and chancel barrier as well as other reliefs; there were, moreover, portable icons, quite a few of which are often mentioned in contemporary texts. Even though these churches were built such a long time ago and even though they have suffered so much from the ravages of time, from the damage done by men, from earthquakes, conflagrations, alteration and restoration, nevertheless more than any other Byzantine town of that time, except Constantinople, the churches of Thessalonike have preserved their authenticity and the grandeur which distinguishes the architecture of that period, as well as the marvellous aesthetic sense, as we may judge from the preserved remains of the decoration.

Thessalonike was pre-eminent amongst all the towns of the Balkan peninsula, Byzantine Italy, southern Greece and the islands throughout the Byzantine period and into the period of the Turkish occupation. We may take it for granted that the monuments erected one after another from the fifth to the fifteenth centuries in this metropolitan centre — it has been estimated that there were at least fifty-seven churches and forty monasteries or monastery dependencies[2] — must have served as models (unrealizable models) for most of the monuments erected in Macedonia, i.e. in the territory under the direct influence of Thessalonike.

Both the written sources and study of the monuments themselves furnish evidence for an indisputably wide-ranging artistic activity, indicating that Thessalonike was an important centre of production and stimulated a high level of artistic creation. This does not necessarily imply that Thessalonike created new trends in the field of artistic creativity independently of Constantinople. Naturally enough, Thessalonike not only had close cultural contacts with the capital but also belonged to the same highly civilized region. This shows up clearly in church architecture throughout Macedonia, starting with Thessalonike; the main features, namely the plans, treatment of the masonry, handling of the facades, and the organization of the interior space, are characteristic of Constantinopolitan architecture, whereas they are quite different in churches in Greece south of Mount Olympos. In the case of pictorial arts the geographical boundaries are not equally clear-cut; therefore we shall deal with the question of monumental painting separately for each period.

Another factor which sets Macedonia apart from southern Greece is the relatively small number of monuments which escaped destruction; for example, we know of approximately one hundred and twenty layers of Byzantine paintings in Macedonia whereas there about two hundred and fifty for the same period in a southern district such as the Aegean islands not counting Crete. This seems rather curious when one considers that the area of Macedonia is considerably larger and that it has towns of a certain cultural level as well as the monastic state of Athos. One of the contributing factors to this disparity may be the differing measures taken for the safety of the population. The islanders preferred fortified mountain settlements — the citadels — which had room for relatively few churches, and many other ecclesiastical buildings were spread out on estates in the countryside. But in Macedonia (and in Thrace too) the inhabitants tended to congregate in larger fortified towns in order to avoid the ordeal of raids and wars with northern neighbours and the monks congregated in the large monasteries of Athos which were fortified like castles. As a result, there were fewer rural communities in Macedonia and most of the churches and even small monasteries were built in the towns, not out in the country. We may consider, therefore, that Macedonian art as a whole is distinguished by its urban character in contrast to the rural character found in other regions and that particularly in regard to ideological and technical accomplishments and artistic quality Macedonian art is on a par with the highly developed cultural standards of a community organized in a city and, indeed, in a megalopolis such as Thessalonike.[3]

ARCHITECTURE

The most important monument of the period is Saint Sophia in Thessalonike, the metropolitan church; the par-

ticularly impressive appearance of this church probably stresses the fact that Thessalonike, the capital of Illyricum, now had become a metropolitan see under the jurisdiction of the Patriarchate of Constantinople, and no longer of the Pope in Rome. Saint Sophia exemplifies an early stage in the formation of the architectural type known as the domed cruciform church which is to be closely associated with Constantinople, as buildings of fundamental significance there, such as Saint Sophia and Saint Irene, demonstrate.

Saint Sophia differs from other churches of this type of plan in that the four massive piers, which with the pendentives support the dome, are lightened by narrow arched openings so that they appear to be simple walls enclosing a corner compartment. The two lateral arms of the cross — northern and southern — are no broader than the breadth of the piers, whereas the vaulted eastern and western arms are much deeper, so that the length of the building is greater. The central area with its great dome rising to an impressive height is enclosed on three sides by two-storey aisles (originally lower) forming the narthex and two side aisles, all vaulted and communicating with each other, designed as a single tripartite unit. The aisles terminate in *pastophorys,* with which they communicate by means of openings off axis (cf. the church of the Dormition at Nicaea), whereas they open onto the central area by means of little colonnades in which columns alternate with piers. In the centre the space is harmoniously organized as it rises to the great dome by means of the ample flowing rhythm of the arches. The exterior does not reflect the dimensions of the whole interior, but has a compact cubic look with stepped roofing (the aisles were lower originally); the dome is supported on a heavy square base. Saint Sophia displays all the characteristics of the monumental massive construction of churches of this group, but still in an undeveloped phase (fig. 177).[4]

It is generally agreed that the church dates to the iconoclastic period, but there is controversy as to where it should be placed within the eighth century. In the twelfth century a mosaic of the Virgin Enthroned replaced the original mosaic of the cross in the apse. In the sanctuary vault, however the mosaics of the iconoclastic period have been preserved; they have the monograms of the empress Irene and the emperor Constantine VI and also the monogram of bishop Theophilos which dates the mosaics to 780-797. Moreover, the dedicatory inscription around the base and the face of the apse semi-dome and the non-figurative decoration must date to the time before the Council of Nicaea in 787. An earlier dating is supported only by observations on the masonry, e.g. courses of narrow brick alternating with stone courses and other features.[5]

We find more complicated solutions in monastery

183. 7th century mosaic in the church of Saint Demetrios, Thessalonike. Its theme is common before that date — the dedication of children to the protector of the city. The saint, depicted frontally, his right hand raised in blessing, rests his left hand on the shoulder of one of the boys, expressing his protective liking.

184-186. Unusually, the representation of the Pantokrator does not appear in the great dome of Saint Sophia, Thessalonike, where it is replaced by the Ascension. The founder's inscription dates the mosaic to the end of the ninth century. The transcendental character of Byzantine art is here greatly stressed. The central scene (186) shows Christ seated on rainbow, within a polychrome border, borne heavenwards by two angels with outspread wings. A second composition depicts the Apostles and the Virgin between angels. The faces of the angels (184) and two of the Twelve Apostles (185) wear arresting expressions of surprise.

ΤΑΝΔΡΕCΓΑΛΙΛΑΙΟΙΤΙΕCΤΗΚΑΤΕΕΜΒΛΕΠΟΝΤΕC
ΕΙCΤΟΝΟΥΡΑΝΟΝΟΥΤΟCΟ ΙCΟΑΝΑΛΗΦΘΕΙCΑΦΥΜΩΝΕΙC
ΤΟΝΟΥΡΑΝΟΝΟΥΤΩCΕΛΕΥCΕΤΑΙΟΝΤΡΟΠΟΝΕΘΕΑCΑCΘΕ
ΑΥΤΟΝΠΟΡΕΥΟΜΕΝΟΝΕΙCΤΟΝΟΥΡΑΝΟΝ

187. Mosaic depiction of the Virgin Enthroned, Saint Sophia, Thessalonike. The stylized rhythmic rendering of the drapery, the disproportionately large head with big almond eyes and arched brows point to a date at the end of the 11th or the 12th century. Certain features in the drawing, such as the disproportionate relationship of the Mother to the Son, the disparate modelling of the two figures and the awkward placing of the group, suggest that this mosaic is the product of a local atelier.

churches such as Saint Andrew at Peristeres east of Thessalonike, a monastery church founded by Saint Euthymios the Younger in 870-71. Some authorities (Mango, Krautheimer) have compared the plan of the church in a somewhat pedantic manner with the architecture of Preslav, the old Bulgarian capital, or of Armenia. In fact the plan harks back to architectural types of the late Roman period, mausoleia and martyria. The church was designed with pretensions to advanced technology but the results are questionable from the aesthetic point of view. Four conchs are grouped around the central square, each of which is covered by a domed drum; the central and larger drum is hexagonal, fitting the three-sided apse of the sanctuary. This cumbersome graceless monastery church with four conchs and five domes was meant to renew the Early Christian tradition of this type.[6]

PAINTING: 7th - 9th centuries

Some of the most precious works of the period are preserved at Thessalonike; they are not very many, but they do provide rare documentation from a central area for Byzantine painting in those troubled times. We refer to the mosaics which survived until the fire of 1917 and to those which are still preserved at the great shrine of Saint Demetrios and at Saint Sophia and, furthermore, to various remains of wall painting in sepulchral monuments and other structures.

The main feature of the system of decoration of the great martyrium at Thessalonike is that it consists of a series of separate panels with representations of Saint Demetrios shown frontally or, more rarely, the Virgin Enthroned amidst angels and medallion busts of saints and donors. According to the inscriptions, each panel was anonymously dedicated by one of the faithful; there was no comprehensive iconographical programme.[7]

Five of the six panels which still adorn the sides of the two western piers of the sanctuary make up a set of large icons of approximately the same size, placed higher than the chancel screen so that they could be seen by the congregation facing the sanctuary on three sides. All of these works appear to have been made at about the same time, around 640, in the last years of the reign of Heraklios. The most important representation, Saint Demetrios between the two founders, the bishop and the prefect, is on the wider north side of the southern pier (fig. 182). The three extremely tall figures are frontal, facing the congregation. The way in which both the physical space and the bodies are rendered reveals a well-developed tendency toward abstraction whereas the relatively small heads are portrayed with a vigorous but simple realism (with a certain picturesque disarray of the tessarae) which is a stable element, expressing the meaning of the icon-portrait. This is the main Justinianic feature which continues on in the seventh century.[8] The representations on the other sides of the same piers have similar characteristics; the subjects are Saint Sergios, *orans* and alone, and a nameless saint protecting two children, probably Saint Bacchos rather than Saint George, all of them clad in white against a green background.

A representation of Saint Demetrios among four clerics has been preserved on the west wall of the same church. One of the clerics at least is to be identified with the bald bearded priest who, by himself, accompanies Saint Demetrios on the south-east pier. The same cleric is shown in one of the three medallion busts on the north aisle where the accompanying metrical inscription clearly states that the mosaic was made after the fire: 'You behold the sanctuary, formerly destroyed by fire, now renovated.'[9]

The fact that the same man is thrice portrayed is strong evidence for all of the mosaics having been executed at about the same time, even though the representation with several figures was executed in a harsher, more linear style. A plausible suggestion is that the two panels on the west wall may be attributed to a local workshop which adopted as models the pictures on the piers; these are more highly accomplished and thus closer to the art of Constantinople.

The mosaic decoration in the sanctuary of Saint Sophia Thessalonike follows the iconographic programme typical of the iconoclastic period. Traces of the ends of a huge cross may easily be discerned in the apse; most of it was obliterated by a later representation of the Virgin Enthroned. Above, in the vault with the golden background, is a cross studded with precious stones within a round starry sky; below, at the spring of the vault, are two wide bands resembling a carpet which have small squares with alternating crosses and palmettes. The monograms of the emperor Constantine VI, his mother Irene and bishop Theophilos date this aniconic decor to 780-87, i.e. before the seventh oecumenical Council of 787 whose measures resulted in the suspension of the iconoclastic policy until 815. The two long inscriptions are still preserved, the dedicatory inscription and the inscription citing verses 5-7 of Psalm 64.[10]

Other remains of aniconic decor — arcs, panels with crosses — should also be attributed to the same period; they were found in the ruins of a Byzantine church;[11] there are also unsophisticated wall paintings in tombs, a custom widely employed, at least in the Thessalonike area.

Not much remains of the secular painting depicting historic scenes which, according to our written sources, adorned the palaces; but a wall painting preserved in Saint Demetrios in Thessalonike may give us some idea (fig. 175). On the left the haloed emperor on horseback enters the burning city; he is escorted by a few youths on foot and on horseback; on the right (on the other side of a later window) barbarians are hunting down a crowd of women in the women's gallery of Saint Demetrios which is on fire. A tiny guardian angel can be made out at ground level. Up until now unanimous agreement does not obtain as to whether a single event be depicted or two different scenes; nor is the current historical interpretation unanimously accepted: that the picture shows the emperor Justinian II entering Thessalonike after his victory over the Slavs (688-89). At all events the representation inside a church of an emperor's triumphal entry *(adventus)* is more likely to date to the seventh than to the tenth century (as Sotiriou suggested), and the style with the uncomplicated composition and lively rendering of the turbulent crowd, the patterns which frame the scene, the classical wave pattern, the city wall, the birds and other features all fit well with the Hellenizing tendency of the seventh century.[12]

Other wall paintings in Saint Demetrios, such as the lovely archangel in an elegantly rhythmic pose high on the north wall of the chancel, are of the same style and date; they are framed by precisely the same wave pattern and by similar ornamental pairs of birds back to back. Lower down, beside the historical scene with the emperor, is a full length representation of Saint Demetrios, an inscribed dedication by a named worshipper; he is depicted frontally, as in the mosaics, between two little angels who are crowning him. In the other parts of the church and in the crypt fragmentary wall paintings have been preserved, some figured, which date to the seventh century and later.[13]

FROM THE NINTH CENTURY
TO 1204

POLITICAL HISTORY

THE CULTURAL ASSIMILATION OF THE SLAVS OF MACEDONIA. A NEW PERIOD OF POWER AND PROSPERITY FOR THESSALONIKE

Recent archaeological finds have tended to confirm information in literary sources regarding the chronology and distribution of settlements of the Sklavenoi — Slavs — in the Byzantine empire. This is particularly true for the areas which, until the late sixth century, belonged to the prefecture of Illyricum, with its capital fixed at Thessalonike. In Macedonia, the first Slavic settlements of a purely rural character were made in the early seventh century by Slavs who arrived in the wake of the Avars. These Sklavenoi of southern Illyria had shaken off their dependence on the Avars, and began to act in their own interests against the urban centres, Thessalonike in particular. They repeatedly attacked Thessalonike, and attempted to settle on the border between Macedonia and Thrace, thus blocking communications with Constantinople. This compelled the imperial authorities as early as the mid-seventh century to devise a policy for maintaining and strengthening Byzantine presence in this sensitive area. Indeed, the security of the empire was at issue.

The basic tenets of imperial policy were the immediate subjection, and subsequent assimilation, of the newly arrived populations. This reflects the general goal of assimilating all groups within the empire to Byzantine culture, regardless of their origin of descent.

The Byzantine state successfully applied this policy to two areas of Slavic settlement — the area around Thessalonike, especially towards the east, and the Strymon region. The measures taken to implement this policy were military, administrative, demographic and cultural. The lat-

ter, of course, were intimately allied with ecclesiastical policy.

The seventh century Byzantine emperors conducted a series of campaigns (sometimes in person) aimed at subjecting the Slavs who had settled between Thrace and Macedonia. This Byzantine counter-offensive was inaugurated by Constans II (657/8) and culminated with Justinian II (687/8) Its principal aim was to secure land communications between Constantinople and the European sections of the empire, which had become endangered by the Slavs settled in the Strymon area. It also attempted to impede the naval attacks which the Slavs were launching on imperial territory. With their *monoxyla* (canoe-like boats, hewn from a single tree trunk), they raided as far as Abydos and the Propontis, attacking other parts of the Aegean as well. An inscription on the founder's mosaic in the basilica of Saint Demetrios in Thessalonike clearly alludes to the situation. Here the saint is proclaimed as 'he who turns back the barbarous wave of barbarian ships'.[1] In the Strymon area, military campaigns against the Slavs continued, combined with various demographic measures aimed at population transfers. In the area of Thessalonike, however, a pattern of coexistence between the newly arrived Slavs and the native inhabitants began to develop,

188. Basil II, the austere, even ascetic, emperor, who spent almost all his life on campaign, won many decisive victories over the Bulgarians. One of these inspired the draughtsman of the miniature in an 11th century psalter. The triumphant emperor portrayed in the centre is blessed by Christ and crowned by the Archangel Gabriel. The Archangel Michael helps support his lance. On either side three medallions each depict a different warrior saint. Below, the leaders of the defeated are shown prostrated in submission. Venice, Biblioteca Marciana.

following the Slavs' failure to capture the city. The *Miracles of Saint Demetrios* provide several eloquent instances of such coexistence. Early in 676, for example, a joint embassy of Thessalonikans and Slavs defended the Hellenized Slavic chieftain Perboundos before the imperial authorities in Constantinople. Similarly, in 677 the besieged Thessalonikans received aid from the Velegezitai, a tribe settled around Demetrias. Somewhat later (682-84), we find ethnically mixed units (Slavo-Bulgars and perhaps Avars) in the ranks of the Sermesians, who were descendants of Byzantines whom the Avars had taken captive. After some sixty years of captivity, they attempted to return to their homelands under the leadership of their rulers Kouver and Mauros. Here we may note that Kouver and Mauros tried to exploit the Sermesian migration to their own ends. Mauros himself cooperated with the imperial authorities, for which he was rewarded with official titles. In any event, the Byzantines made concerted efforts to secure the return of the Sermesians to parts nearer Constantinople. The emperor issued an edict ordering the Slavs settled north of Beroia (the Drougouvitai) to provide the Sermesians with adequate provisions as they passed through their territory. Meanwhile the famed imperial fleet, the *Karabisianoi,* anchored in the mouth of the Axios. Here they took aboard the repatriates, and subsequently conveyed them to their final destination, which was probably somewhere in Thrace.[2]

The cooperation between the Thessalonikans and the Slavs of Thessaly; the response of the Beroia Drougouvitai to an imperial command; and the unexpected appearance of the Byzantine navy in the Thermaic Gulf are events which prove beyond any doubt that this area was never lost to Byzantine control. They reveal, moreover, the gradual imposition of administrative authority over the newcomers, and the growth of cooperation between the Slavs and the imperial authorities in Constantinople. These trends certainly prevailed throughout the entire seventh century, and also apply to Slavic settlements *(sklaveniai)* which were made around Thessalonike.

In light of these considerations, it becomes more readily apparent why the Byzantine campaigns against the Slavs in the seventh century were limited to the Strymon region, aimed at securing the network of roads between Constantinople and Thessalonike.

Aside from such military undertakings (which, as noted, hardly passed beyond Thessalonike), the seventh century emperors typically implemented other measures to deal with the Slavs. They organized transfers of Slavic populations from Macedonia to Asia Minor, where they were settled and enrolled in the Byzantine army. These same emperors were concerned with defending the Strymon area, and with subjecting the Slavs who had penetrated Byzantine territory and formed compact settlements called *sklaveniai.* The term *sklavenia* acquired a technical sense, geographic and administrative. It usually appears in association with ethnically derived or with topographic adjectives. Examples are the terms *Sklaveniai Strymonos* or *Sklaveniai Ezerou.* In usages such as *Sklavenia Drougoubiton* or *Sklavenia Velegeziton,* its connotation is ethnic. In general, *sklaveniai* designate Slavic settlements

(including adjacent farmland) which, in their early phases, were organized by the kings of the various Slavic tribes. Later, after an agreement with Byzantium, they were governed by officials who were typically of Slavic descent, but who were subordinate to the authority of Constantinople. In the course of time, the terms *archontia* and *sklavenia* became equivalent. The gradual subordination of the Slavs to the Byzantine administrative order is revealed by the numerous eighth and ninth century lead seals which bear Slavic names.[3] Such persons, moreover, are mentioned in contemporary sources such as Theophanes as leaders of Slavic tribes settled on Byzantine territory. The peculiarity of the *sklaveniai-archontiai* is worth emphasizing. They constituted geographically autonomous administrative units, yet they were nonetheless obliged to render the *pakton* that is, they were subject to the authority of Constantinople. The leader of each *sklavenia* functioned as a public official, directly responsible to the emperor. That is to say, he was not required to proceed through local provincial administrative channels.

The subordination of the Slavs to the Byzantine administrative structure ultimately resulted in the complete assimilation of their settlements and populations. This was consummated with the creation of the three themes on Macedonian soil — Thessalonike (probably before 824, but certainly no later than 836); Macedonia (between 789 or 799 and 802); and Strymon (before 899).[4]

At the beginning of the tenth century, in 904, we find mention of Slavic archers participating in the military forces of Thessalonike and Strymon, under the leadership of the theme commanders.[5] This is indisputable proof that the *sklaveniai* magistrates had been abolished, and that the *sklaveniai-archontiai* had ceased to function as an autonomous administrative unit. Certainly the *sklaveniai* endured as territorial terms, but the Slavs themselves had become subordinated to the theme army, like all Byzantines of the period. The insufficient Hellenization of the Slavs is nonetheless indicated by Methodios' famous law code which he composed in Slavic around 845. Methodios, as we know from his life, had once served as a *sklavenia* magistrate. Troicky has shown that this 'code' is nothing more than a selection of regulations from the Isaurian *Ekloge* dealing with military matters (punishments, etc.).[6] It could be said that Methodios' knowledge of military affairs was a family inheritance. As we learn from his brother Constantine-Cyril's *Life,* their father Leo was a *drungarios,* i.e. an officer of the theme of Thessalonike.[7] Moreover, he came from a wealthy and noble family, which accounts for the superb education he provided for his sons. Methodios' service as magistrate of the Strymon *sklavenia* certainly gave him the opportunity to familiarize himself with the language and customs of the Slavs. These advantages, of course, facilitated his subsequent missionary labours. In any event, Methodios' service in the *sklaveniai* (about 840-45) shows that Strymon had not yet become a theme. Constantine Porphyrogenitus, however, records the existence of a *kleisoura* in Strymon prior to the creation of the theme.[8] The defence of this strategic area was clearly a matter of concern. It was not only subjected to the ravages of the local Slavs (the Rhynchinoi and

Strymonitai), but it was also threatened by the Bulgarians, especially after they established their first independent state in 680/81. Porphyrogenitus also reports that Justinian II, the emperor who had launched the most formidable counter-attack on the Slavs, established Skyths in the mountain passes of upper Strymon.[9] Evidently he was acting to defend this region from enemy incursions. Justinian II himself had been ambushed by the Bulgarians in 688/89, while journeying from Thessalonike through the Strymon *Kleisoura*. Thus his concern for the security of this area is understandable.

From the middle of the seventh century, the Byzantines opened their counter-attack on the Slavs. Successful campaigns are recorded for 657/8, 678 and 688/89. These expeditions resulted in the subjection of the Sklavenoi, and the transfer of considerable Slavic populations to Asia Minor. Constans II effected this policy probably in 658, for in 665 we find Slavs in the Byzantine army in Asia Minor, some five thousand of them deserted to the Arabs. Moreover, in 688 Justinian II created a force of thirty thousand (the 'chosen people') from among the Slavs of Bithynia (Opsikion). This force was later decimated by the Byzantines themselves, owing to their defection to the Arabs. Nonetheless, the Slavs of Opsikion appear again in the middle of the tenth century. The emperors weakened the Slavic element in Macedonia demographically by transferring the Slavs and replacing them with Byzantines. The Sermesians and others are examples of this policy. The conquered Slavs who remained in the Balkan parts of the empire were organized into *archontiai,* which became the vehicle for coexistence between Byzantine and Slavic elements. A typical example of this is the reference to 'mixed villages' in the area of Beroia. Moreover, the *archontiai* were the means by which the state exerted administrative control over the Slavs. This rapprochement between Slavs and Byzantines does not mean, however, that the Slavs ceased to harass the Byzantines with revolts and raids. Even in the tenth century there are references to Slavic uprisings and plundering expeditions. Usually these were incited by foreign enemies, chiefly the Bulgaro-Slavs. This was particularly so during the Byzantine-Bulgarian wars, the clashes of which began to devastate the area from the mid-eighth century. The Byzantine counter-offensive took shape with Constantine V's campaign in 758/59. According to Theophanes, Constantine captured the *sklaveniai* throughout Macedonia.[10] At the empress Irene's command, Staurakios led a successful campaign in 782/83 'against the Slavic peoples', using Thessalonike as his base.[11] This undertaking resulted in the subjection of the Slavs in Macedonia, and above all in Greece. Moreover, it prepared the ground for the creation of the Macedonian themes. As usual, demographic measures accompanied these eighth century expeditions. Constantine V (741-75) paid a ransom of precious cloths to secure the return of two thousand five hundred Byzantines from the islands of Imbros, Tenedos and Samothrace, whom Sklavenioi leaders had held captive.[12] Constantine also transported an enormous mass of Slavs to Asia Minor; the sources claim more than two hundred thousand. Prior to this, these Slavs had been pursued by the Bulgars, and about 762/3 took refuge on Byzantine territory. After successfully campaigning against the Arabs in the east, Constantine transferred Armenians and Syrians from Melitene and Theodosioupolis to Thrace (perhaps including Strymon). As is evident, Constantine V's measures strengthened the anti-Bulgarian element in Macedonia. The purely Greco-Byzantine element was further strengthened with the arrival of north Aegean islanders, who settled whererever they chose. The measures taken by Nikephoros I in 809/10 were also quite significant in this respect. He undertook to populate the *sklaveniai* with Greco-Byzantine populations from the themes in Asia Minor.

We can state with confidence, therefore, that the subordination of the already weakened Slavic population of Macedonia to the imperial military and administrative order had been achieved by the beginning of the ninth century. Thanks to the demographic measures which strengthened the Greco-Byzantine element, moreover, the foundations were laid for the cultural assimilation of the Slavs. This was effected towards the end of the ninth century, owing to the predominance of the Greek language and the Christianization of the entire Slavic population within the empire. The Slavic leaders had already adopted the language, dress, life style and religion of the Byzantines (as the invocations to God and the Theotokos on their lead seals indicate). The establishment of bishoprics in the major Slavic settlements signals the widespread diffusion of Christianity among the Slavs. Allied as it was with the regional theme organizations, the ecclesiastical administration extended eastward from Thessalonike as far as the Hebros river. Its wide extent offers undeniable evidence for the general subordination of the Slavic-born populations to Byzantium. We except here certain sporadic tendencies towards revolt which the untamed tribes never ceased to evince towards any organized authority. Constantine Porphyrogenitus and the *Life* of Saint Gregory Dekapolites provide evidence for a wave of revolts among the *sklaveniai-archontiai* against Byzantium, chiefly during the reigns of Theophilos and Michael. These occurred both in Macedonia and the Peloponnese. The pacification of the *sklaveniai* was the work of Michael III the Drunkard (842-67), although Leo VI attributes this to his father, Basil I.[13] Whatever the case, it is noteworthy that both Leo VI and his contemporary Kameniates ascribe the peaceful coexistence of Slavs and Byzantines to the Christianization of the Slavs. In effect, this means their cultural assimilation.[14]

According to the Czech historian V. Vavrinek, in Byzantium Orthodoxy and Greek letters constituted an indissoluble organic whole.[15] The Greek language was the pre-eminent *(kat'exochen,* in Vavrinek's own text*)* language of the Christian faith. Patriarch Photios' favourite proof of this was apostolic tradition itself. In a letter to the *katholikos* of Armenia, he asserts that the Apostles, including Peter, wrote their epistles to the newly converted peoples in Greek. Thus the Slavs of Macedonia would sing and pray in Greek. They were fully Christianized by the first decades of the ninth century, as the growth of the ecclesiastical organization of the area indicates. In our view, the various references to new bishoprics, in particular Drougouvitia (dependent on the metropolis of Thessalonike) and Smolenoi (dependent on the metropolis of Philippi), constitute trustworthy evidence for the thorough Christianization and Hellenization of the Slavs of Macedonia. This internal missionary work was carried out even before the empire undertook to convert the Slavs beyond its frontiers. Here we refer to the conversion of the Bulgarians (whose tsar Boris was baptized in the reign of Michael III, and hence took as his Christian name that of the emperor); the Russians; and the Slavs of central Europe. Methodios' mission to Chazaria and subsequently to Moravia occurred during Photios' first patriarchate, as did the conversion of the Russians settled north of the Euxine. Thus it seems certain that the Christianization of the Slavs was already accomplished in the period between 810 (Nikephoros I's demographic measures) and 860 (Michael III's final subjection of the *sklaveniai* uprisings). In the space of this half century, the decisive subordination and assimilation of the Slavs in Macedonia was achieved, and it was chiefly the work of the emperor Michael III, whom later Byzantine historians slandered. Leo VI analyzes the factors leading to the assimilation of the Slavs in his account of the achievements of his father Basil I (and not, of course, Michael III, whom Basil murdered): '[Basil] freed the Romans from anxiety over the constant uprisings of the Slavs'. According to Leo, Basil was able to subject the Slavs to Byzantine officials thus freeing them from the obligation to serve under their own leaders. This evidently refers to the abolition of the *archontia-sklavenia,* and the subjection of the Slavs to the theme officials. Moreover, Basil Christianized the Slavs, thus forging bonds of solidarity with the Byzantines. Henceforth the Slavs were fighting 'against the enemies of the Romans'. In other words, they were serving in the Byzantine theme armies, like any other subject of the empire.[16] We may confidently claim, therefore, that from the second half of the ninth century the Slavs of Macedonia were Byzantine citizens, with all the rights and obligations pertaining to that status. This does not mean, of course, that all of them abandoned their old habits of brigandage. Such activities by the Sklavenoi in the Strymon passes are reported. They held up Theodore Stoudites' journey to Thessalonike in 796. Somewhat later Gregory Dekapolites (815-20) fell into their hands, along with certain theme officials. Around 838 the *protokankellarios* Gregory suffered the same fate, while Liutprand of Cremona mentions uprisings against emperor Romanos Lekapenos (920-44). Such events, however, are of sporadic occurrence. In fact, the Strymonitai appear to have been much more intractable than the Slavs around Thessalonike, perhaps owing to their proximity to Bulgaria. Porphyrogenitus expressly states that the Slavs of Thessalonike were emperor Michael's subjects.[17] Kameniates informs us that the Sagoudatai and Drougouvitai had long shared a common life and a profound peace with the Thessalonikans.[18] These eloquent statements by Byzantine authors will suffice to indicate the complete triumph of the policy which Byzantine emperors had tirelessly pursued for centuries: assimilating the incoming foreign peoples to Byzantine culture, and transforming them into subjects of the Byzantine empire.

Obviously, the incorporation of the Slavs within Byzantine society ('the font of holy baptism brought them into the Christian fold') as well as their assimilation with the Byzantines created a more peaceful and orderly state of affairs in Macedonia.[19] Thessalonike, in particular, profited from this situation. From the middle of the ninth century almost to the Frankish conquest, the Macedonian capital reached new heights of power and prosperity. Throughout this period, Thessalonike came into prominence not only as a great commercial and cultural centre, but as the second capital of the Byzantine world. According to Kantakouzenos, Thessalonike was 'the first city of the Romans, after the great city, (Constantinople)'.[20] The hagiographer of Theodora justly extolled Thessalonike as 'the mother of the West'.[21] It was precisely at that time (early tenth century) that Thessalonike blossomed as the administrative, military and political centre of the West, which, as we know, encompassed all the European lands of the empire, including Byzantine Italy.

The emergence of Macedonia, and Thessalonike in particular, as a vital Byzantine centre is due to a variety of forces at work from the mid-ninth century. Outstanding among these was the peace which prevailed after the Byzantinization of the Slavs; the extension of Byzantine influence to the Slavic populations outside the empire (i.e. the Christianization of the Bulgars, and the missions to the Moravians and Russians); and the strengthening of Byzantine authority in Italy. Thus Thessalonike quickly came into prominence as a great cosmopolitan centre with international commerce. In fact, it was the crossroad between the Via Egnatia (which connected Constantinople with Italy, via its terminus at Dyrrachion) and the highway which ran from the north Aegean coast to the Danube area. We know about the trans-Balkan highway from a rare geographic text which was preserved thanks to Constantine Porphyrogenitus' antiquarianism.[22] It provides a detailed eight day itinerary between Thessalonike and Belgrade. Thereafter it describes the stops on the journey up the Danube towards Russia, and the lands of the northern Euxine and the Caucasus as well. In short, Thessalonike stood at the meeting point between the east-west Via Egnatia, and the trans-Balkan arteries. Moreover, Thessalonike was the focal point of the maritime routes which led from coastal Asia Minor and the more distant Byzantine and Arabic ports of the East to the Balkans. Thessalonike was therefore the juncture of routes connecting Byzantium with Italy, central and western Europe, the Slavic countries (including Russia) and even the oriental Arabic world. The city quickly became a centre whose activity competed not only with the great harbours of the East (Smyrna, Ephesos, Attaleia), but with Constantinople itself. Writing at the beginning of the tenth century, Kameniates speaks of the 'abundant agricultural produce; the provisions of trade; the fabrics of silk and wool; and the treasures of gold and silver and all types of precious stones' which were to be found in the possession of Thessalonike's citizens, and which inundated its market well before the Arab attack in 904. By then the Thessalonikans were dealing with the 'Skyths' in commercial pursuits, and the city was mixed with 'a jumbled mass of natives and otherwise foreign elements'.[23] The city

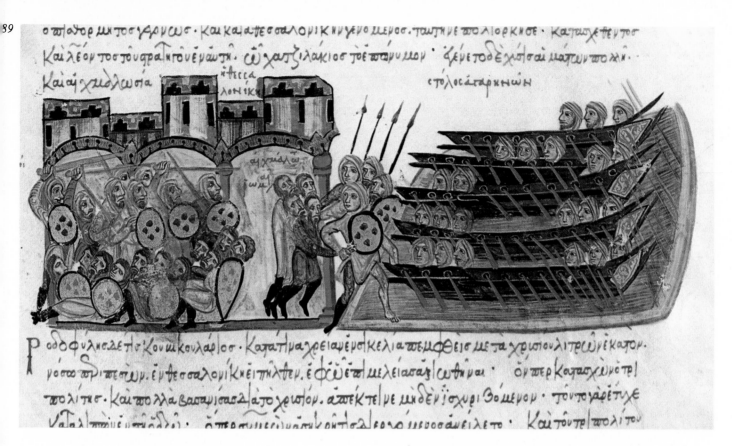

189. *To acquire fortified bases in Mediterranean lands the Arabs organized pirate raids. In 904, the apostate Christian, Leo of Tripoli, moved against Thessalonike at the head of immense forces. Despite the reinforcement of its sea wall and the vigorous resistance of its garrison and inhabitants, the city surrendered. The chronicle of John Skylitzes shows the pirate Arab fleet to the right and Thessalonike and the remnant of its defenders to the left. Madrid, Biblioteca Nacional.*

became renowned, Kameniates continues, for its magnificent buildings and monuments, and for the intellectual ability of its inhabitants. Peace, plenty and prosperity assist cultural progress. Up until the catastrophe which befell the city in 904, the sciences and crafts were well-represented, and its citizens enjoyed the means of perfect well-being.

It was during this period of prosperity and wealth that the great Byzantine-Bulgarian war broke out, in 894, to be exact. Its origins were economic, as all the sources stress. The conflict arose after the emporium for Bulgarian merchants and their commodities was shifted from Constantinople to Thessalonike.[24] Contemporary historians inform us that Zautzes (Leo VI's father-in-law) was highly influenced by his servant, Musikos. The latter in turn wished to be of use to Staurakios and Kosmas, two merchant friends of his who hailed from Greece. Zautzes then 'transferred the Bulgarian import concerns from Constantinople to Thessalonike, and established the customs there as well'.[25] Naturally, Staurakios and Kosmas profited from this. According to Theodosios Melitenos, they were 'mercenary and avaricious, cheating the Bulgarians in their commercial exchanges'.[26] It seems certain to me that Zautzes' decision reflects a wider policy, independent of his desire to assist friends. Let us reflect, first of all, that by the end of the ninth century a lively traffic between Constantinople and Thessalonike had been established over the Via Egnatia. Proof of this was the creation of the Strymon theme. Perhaps the basis of Zautzes' action was a two-fold policy designed (a) to reduce some of the commercial congestion in Constantinople (the Russians, for example, had begun to trade there at this time); and, more importantly, (b) to create suitable conditions for the growth of international trade in Thessalonike. As we have seen, by then Thessalonike had become the second administrative centre of the empire. It was certainly in a position to receive and channel merchandise from the northern Balkan world, as well as the trans-Danubian region. The road to Belgrade and Sofia could surely keep Thessalonike well-provisioned, while trade commodities could be sent along the Via Egnatia either to Constantinople or to the Adriatic (via Dyrrachion).

In any event, Thessalonike was the economic centre of the Balkan world at the end of the ninth century. This is indisputably shown by the seals of the *kommerkiarioi* and *abydikoi* which date from that period. One can easily see the actual cause behind the war which Symeon set into motion. Using as his pretext Zautzes' measures and the mistreatment of Bulgarian merchants, Symeon in fact aimed at capturing Thessalonike and its environs. This fact did not escape the shrewd Nicholas Mystikos. In one of his letters to Symeon, the patriarch exhorted him not to act against the will of God, or of the divine order, which had bequeathed to the Roman empire (i.e. the Byzantines) domi-

Map labels:
R. Sava • Sirmium • Belgrade • Little Presthlava • Little Skythia • R. Drin • R. Margos • Vidin • R. Danube • Dorostolon (Dristra) • Rasi • Naissos Niš • Ragousa • Nikopolis • Pliska • Marcianopolis • Odessos (Varna) • Great Presthlava • Sidera Pyle • Dekatera • Diokleia • Trnovo • Kleisoura Beregavon • Sofia (Triaditsa) • Mt. Aimos • Mt. Panysos • Mesembria • Pernikion • EUXINE • Skodra • Mt. Skadros • Pyle Traianou • Beroe (Eirenoupolis) • Diampolis • Anchialos • Kerkine Mts. • Orvelos Mts. • Konstantia • Great Souda • Apollonia (Sosopolis) • Skopje • R. Strymon • Philippopolis • R. Hebros • Develtos • Morovisdon • Rhodope Mts. • Makrolivada • Meleones • Velessa • Štip • Bersinikia • Provaton • Prilep • Nikopolis • R. Nestos • Adrianople • Bizye • Dyrrachion • Boutellon (Pelagonia) • Melenikon • Boulgarophygon • Ochrid • Tzetzina • Kleidion • Mt. Pangaion • Arkadiopolis • L. Ochrid • Boras Mts. • Stromnitsa • Serrhai • R. Tonzos • Selymbria • Mt. Barnous • Moglena • Prosakos • L. Kerkine • Christoupolis • Mosynopolis • Raidestos • Herakleia • Constantinople • Deavolis • L. Prespa • Edessa • R. Axios • L. Bolbe • Ainos • R. Hebros • Aulon • Mt. Bermion • Beroia • Thessalonike • Kastoria • Mt. Tomorrit • Servia • Petra • Thasos • Samothrace • Callipolis • Kyzikos • R. Aoos • R. Haliakmon • Mt. Olympos • Platamon • Lampsakos • Kerkyra • Stagoi • Trikka • R. Peneios • Larisa • Imbros • Adramyttion • Bouthrotos • Ioannina • Pindos Mts. • Demetrias • Lemnos • Pharsalos • Skiathos • AEGEAN SEA • Nikopolis • R. Spercheios • Lamia • Lesbos • Leukas • R. Acheloos • Parnassos Mts. • Skopelos • Skyros • Chios • Kephallenia • Dirphys Mts. • Naupaktos • Thebes • Chalkis • Patras • Mt. Parnis • Erymanthos Mts. • Athens • Andros • Zakynthos • Kyllene Mts. • Corinth • Argos • Nauplion • ADRATIC SEA • IONIAN SEA

THE BYZANTINE - BULGARIAN WARS

●●●●● frontiers of the Byzantine empire and the Bulgarian state following the treaty of 815

190. From the inception of the first Bulgarian state Bulgars and Byzantines clashed repeatedly in the northern part of the Balkan peninsula. Many of these wars were fought out on Macedonian territory. An understanding of the relief of the terrain on which these engagements were decided makes for a readier appreciation of the strategy of either side.

nion over the entire west.[27] Symeon's plans did not materialize, but Thessalonike received an unexpected blow from the Arab pirates. When Leo of Tripoli's Arabs captured the city in 904, its economic bloom withered, and its growth was to a certain extent curtailed. Nonetheless, this does not appear to have had a fatal impact on the subsequent development of the city. Thessalonike still remained at the epicentre of the key historic events of the period. Already from the tenth century, the city was 'the leader of the western themes'. The seat of the *monostrategos* of the west, subsequently the duke and katepan of Thessalonike,

was at Thessalonike. His armies were entrusted with all the expeditions which were conducted in the European provinces. The catastrophe which Thessalonike experienced in 904 curtailed the growth of the city for a while. On the other hand, perhaps it hastened Constantinople's resolve to create a stable military and political centre out of the area which the Slavs had ravaged, which the Bulgarians constantly claimed, and which the Arab pirates included in their field of operations. In any case, Thessalonike was to experience a new phase of economic prosperity and political power in the eleventh century.

This, we may recall, was the century which saw the annexation of Bulgaria, the expansion of Byzantine frontiers in the east and west, as well as the dawn of the Latin domination. According to the twelfth century author of the *Timarion,* an international clientele would flock to the *Demetria,* a ten day bazaar and festival held in honour of Saint Demetrios at the end of October. This included 'not only a crowd of natives, but Greeks from all over, Bulgarians, peoples of all nations from the Danube to Skythia, Campanians, Italians, Iberians, Lusitanians and Celts from beyond the Alps.' They dealt in 'cloths and threads for men and women. Merchandise was conveyed from Italy on Greek vessels; many of the finest fabrics were brought from Phoenicia, Egypt, Spain and the Pillars of Herakles. The merchants would bring their goods directly to old Macedonia and Thessalonike. Merchants from the Black Sea would even adorn the festival with their wares — first conveying them to Constantinople, and thence bringing them to [the festival] loaded on horses and donkeys.'[28] This precious text leaves no doubt regarding the key economic role which Thessalonike played in the early twelfth century, the very time when world markets began to open. Its population was enriched by a variety of foreign elements — Latins, Hungarians and even Turks. This renewed period of prosperity was once again interrupted by external enemies, in the form of the Normans who assaulted the city in 1185. Their conquest is described in vivid colours by the metropolitan Eustathios, who censured not only the Normans, but also the Armenians and other Latins who had settled in the city and its environs. The Norman conquest delivered Thessalonike a crushing blow, leaving it with 'hardly a remnant of its former beauty'.[29]

The history of Thessalonike was naturally determined by a new set of circumstances after 1204, when the nation experienced its first captivity. Even the expansion of the Epirote despotate to Thessalonike in 1224 could not bring back its former brilliance, although some aspects of Epirote rule were indeed impressive. Its rulers made august claims to the imperial title. They attempted to revive ancestral customs by establishing the 'senate council'. Moreover, they minted silver coins bearing the image of Saint Demetrios and the Thessalo-epirote emperor enthroned on either side of a tower, on which was inscribed 'polis thessalonike'. The kingdom, however, remained dependent on the Bulgarians, who succeeded in restoring their state at the end of the twelfth century.

After the armies of Vatatzes subjected Thessalonike and its territory to Nicaea (in 1242), the city once again became a centre of military operations against the Epirote state. The Nicaean forces were able to consolidate Byzantine control over western Macedonia just before, and immediately after, the reconquest of Constantinople in 1261.

Under Michael VII, the Byzantine armies reached Dyrrachion for the last time. The civil dissensions of the fourteenth century, however, soon brought about the decline of the city and its surrounding area. The time had arrived when Thessalonike viewed its neighbours, whether near or far, with little more than suspicion. During the Palaiologan period, new groups appeared on the scene,

such as the Albanians (about 1370), the Serbs, the Venetians, and other Latins (like the marauding Catalan Company). Here let us not neglect to mention the Turkomans and Turks, who delivered the final blow.

After this rapid review of events, one can easily understand why the Norman conquest in 1185 marks the end of Thessalonike's great period of prosperity and brilliance. The thirteenth and fourteenth centuries were a period of confusion, a time of troubles. Politically, it witnessed the sequence of Latin kings, the despots and emperors of Epirus, and a cadre of Byzantine and foreign dynasts and kinglets. The state was rent by dynastic strife, civil wars, popular uprisings, and religious and ecclesiastical strife. The 'once illustrious city' was debased by the extravagences of its Venetian rulers. According to John Anagnostes, '[at that time] the city suffered under the Latin rulers'. Finally, it fell into the hands of the Turks. Contemplating the bitter lesson of the catastrophe which befell the city, John Anagnostes wrote an account of the Turkish conquest, in the tradition of Kameniates and Eustathios.[30] He regarded the enormous loss of human life as a chastisement to the survivors. Thereafter, Thessalonike was to exist for a long period in captivity, yet it never lost its essential character as the capital of Macedonian Hellenism.

MACEDONIA TO THE DEATH OF BASIL II THE BULGAR-SLAYER (867-1025)

The Aggressive Policy of the Bulgarian Tsar towards Macedonia

After the conversion of the Bulgarians to Christianity in the reign of Boris-Michael (described in the preceding chapter), a long period of peaceful relations with Byzantium ensued. This peace facilitated the Christianization and Hellenization of the Slavs of Macedonia, at least according to the testimony of Leo VI, who refers to activities of this type sponsored by his father Basil I (d. 886).[1] As Kameniates reports, moreover, it frequently enabled Greeks and Slavs to dwell together in ethnically mixed villages.[2] These peaceful relations continued up to the time when Symeon, Boris' son and successor, ascended the Bulgarian throne. In Symeon's reign (893-927), long and bitter struggles broke out between the two powers, which were to end in 1018 with the dissolution of the first Bulgarian state.

The origin of these conflicts was connected with Symeon's foreign policy. The Bulgarian ruler had been brought up in Constantinople, and had received a Hellenic education. In the course of his stay in the capital, he became acquainted with the Roman-imperial ideal of the Byzantines, which he wished to articulate with his own desires of conquest.[3]

A skilful political and military leader, Symeon did not envision a mere territorial expansion of the Bulgarian state, but the conquest of the Byzantine imperial crown. For exactly this reason, the threat which he posed was in fact lethal to Byzantium in general, and to the area of

191. In 1040 the Bulgarian leader, Peter Deljan, proclaimed a revolt in Belgrade which spread quickly. Its aim was the reconquest of the former possessions of Samuel which had been recovered by the Byzantines. The miniature from the chronicle of John Skylitzes depicts the proclamation of Deljan as king of Bulgaria. Madrid, Biblioteca Nacional.

Macedonia in particular.

Initially, the wars which the Bulgarian ruler inflicted on Byzantium were not waged in Macedonia. They were, however, occasioned by events connected with this area, and warfare subsequently tortured this region for nearly a hundred years.

The cause of the Byzantine-Bulgarian war was a question of commercial nature. Private interests succeeded in having the customs post for Byzantine-Bulgarian trade transferred from Thessalonike to Constantinople. Heretofore trade had been carried on directly between Bulgaria and Thessalonike by means of the roads from Sofia (Triaditsa) to Thessalonike either via Skopje (Skopia) or through the Strymon valley to Thessalonike, or from Philippopolis to Thessalonike through the Strymon valley. The new regulations required that trade be directed first to Constantinople, and thence to the other Byzantine trade centres.

In addition, the collecting of customs was entrusted to two Greek merchants, who began to oppress and exploit the Bulgarian traders by 'imposing heavy duties.'[4]

At this point, the Bulgarian merchants complained to their ruler regarding these hardships. When Symeon saw that his protests were in vain, he proclaimed war on the Byzantines.

Occupied by affairs in the east, the emperor Leo VI dispatched a few available forces from the western part of the empire, which were defeated with heavy losses (894).

At this critical juncture, Leo VI decided to confront the Bulgarians by allying with the Hungarians. Symeon yielded to the two-fold pressure, and sought to negotiate with the Byzantines. Leo accepted the Bulgarian leader's request, but committed the error of simultaneously ordering his troops to withdraw from Bulgaria. Symeon had been waiting for this opportunity. He made a surprise attack on the Hungarians and defeated them resoundingly. Then he imposed his own conditions, utilizing the Patzinaks to protect his rear from any Hungarian threat. The Byzantines attacked with fresh reinforcements brought from the east, but were defeated (896).[5] Despite his victories, however, the Byzantine forces were still sufficiently strong to deter Symeon from advancing on Constantinople. He transferred his military operations to the themes of Thessalonike, and, in particular, Dyrrachion, where he succeeded in capturing a significant number of fortresses.[6]

With these events, Bulgaria had laid the foundations of a new policy of aggression towards the Byzantines. This policy was directed more towards Macedonia, as became fully evident when the Bulgarians subsequently expanded into the whole of the region.

Symeon's occupation with the central and western Balkans gave the Byzantines an opportunity to launch a diversionary attack. Imperial troops penetrated Bulgaria;[7] Symeon, attacked by surprise, was forced to conclude peace with the Byzantines, the terms of which Leo Choirosphaktes negotiated.[8] Symeon withdrew from Byzantine fortresses which he had taken in the region of Dyrrachion (900).

The Siege and Capture of Thessalonike by the Arab Pirates (904)

While the Byzantines were engaged with the Bulgarians, Arab pirates seized the opportunity to assault and capture Thessalonike, the second city of the empire (904).

The capture of Thessalonike was not unexpected. From the beginning of the tenth century Arab pirates from Crete and Syria had already conducted raids on the Peloponnese and some Aegean islands. In 902, they ravaged Demetrias and Lemnos. It appears that the capture of Lemnos paved the way for a strong Arab attack on the very heart of the empire, rather than at the periphery as before. In fact, two years later the Byzantine government was informed that Leo of Tripoli, a Christian renegade from Tripoli in Syria, had penetrated the Hellespont at the head of a strong naval force.[9] Leo quickly withdrew, however, fearing that the Byzantines would block his exit. He then headed towards Thessalonike, which he reached on July 29, 904.[10]

The inhabitants were not taken by surprise. The emperor's personal envoy, *protospatharios* Petronas, had informed them about the impending danger. With the help of the inhabitants, Petronas undertook to strengthen the city's defences. He perceived that the most vulnerable part of the fortifications was the sea wall, which was low and built too

192. Deljan appointed the patrician Alousianos as his co-emperor, charging him with responsibility for besieging Thessalonike. The citizens trusted in Saint Demetrios to perform a miracle, and their resolve thus stiffened, they succeeded in destroying the attacking forces. In this miniature from the chronicle of John Skylitzes Thessalonike is shown on the left; outside the walls the imperial armies are shown putting the Bulgarian warriors to flight. Madrid, Biblioteca Nacional.

near the sea. Petronas ordered that huge boulders be thrown into the sea, to impede the approach of ships, and prevent the enemy from taking up an advantageous position. At this point the defence of the city and government of the theme of Thessalonike was taken over by the *strategos* Leo Chitzilakes, who abandoned his predecessor's scheme. Instead, he ordered that the sea wall be heightened at once.

Leo, however, was wounded in an accident, and his work was taken up by Niketas, the commander of the city garrison. This new officer proceeded to rebuild the wall more efficiently. He had huge wooden towers constructed along its course, hoping that the Arabs would believe that they were made of stone and thus refrain from attacking the sea wall. Moreover, he asked the generals of the neighouring themes for assistance, and called upon the Slavs settled in imperial territory just outside the theme of Thessalonike.[11]

Few of the Slavs came to help, however, and those who did were not the most experienced. The general of Strymon turned a deaf ear to Niketas' repeated despatches, charging him with responsibility for whatever misfortunes might arise in the city because of his absence. Consequently, the task of defence fell to the city garrison, along with the inhabitants themselves. According to John Kameniates, the latter were certainly more numerous than the Arabs, but lacked their experience and expertise in warfare.

On July 29, 904, news finally arrived that the pirates had reached the head of the Thermaic Gulf. Shortly thereafter, their fleet appeared before the city.

Leo of Tripoli did not attack at once, but ordered the ships to anchor off shore east of the city. Then, from his flagship, he surveyed the fortifications of the sea wall to decide at what points he might best attack. Leo gave his orders, and the ships moved into battle with all possible speed.

The enemy's first onslaught was fruitless. They tried to scale the walls with ladders, but were repulsed. The struggle was limited to a thick exchange of arrows on both sides.

The besieged were encouraged not only by this success, but by the presence and heartening words of their two generals, Niketas and Leo Chitzilakes, who, despite his wounds, would walk round the walls, strengthening their weakest points with the garrison guard.

The pirates made other unsuccessful assaults, and then withdrew to the shore east of the city. Here they disembarked from their ships and attacked the eastern land wall of the city, in particular the Rome Gate, which was located near the sea.

At dawn of the second day of the siege, they mounted a second assault on the land walls, concentrating their machines for hurling stones at the Rome Gate. Under cover of a barrage of arrows, they tried to break down the

193. Detail from a wall painting from the church of the *Anargyroi, Kastoria, depicting the Pentecost; two groups of three men stand in a half-circle representing, according to the* inscription, different peoples, tribes and tongues. Their clothing also denotes different social status — prince, merchant and knight.

gate with enormous stone missiles, and to scale the walls with ladders.

When these attempts failed, they tried to burn down the Rome and Kassandreia Gates, in order to break through there. But the besieged thwarted all these efforts, utilizing every artifice of war.

After continual defeats, the pirates returned to the sea wall. They chained their ships together in pairs, and between the masts of each pair they constructed wooden towers, which were consequently higher than the sea wall. Inside these floating towers they placed the best fighters.

At dawn the next day, they slowly approached the wall, sailing where the water was deep and there was no danger of running aground. Despite the fierce resistance of the besieged, the pirates managed to come near the wall. There they carried out a determined attack. Faced by a mass of arrows, stones, and flame from liquid fire, the defenders turned and fled, pursued by the pirates.

Slaughter and captivity accompanied the enemy's entrance into the city. An estimated twenty-two thousand in-

habitants were taken prisoner — a large part of the population. They were later ransomed, probably in connection with the Arab-Byzantine treaty of 908.

The city itself barely escaped conflagration. An eyewitness of the disaster, John Kameniates, describes in vivid colours the scenes of frenzy and terror which then occurred.[12] He, the *strategos* Chitzilakes, and the garrison commander Niketas were taken captive, but later liberated. Emperor Leo VI himself wrote a lament on the capture of Thessalonike.[13] In a letter written much later, the patriarch Nicholas Mystikos openly condemns the government of that time, because it provoked the disaster through negligence.[14]

New Deterioration of Relations between Byzantium and Symeon

The peace of 900 (see above) did not last long, because Symeon continued to harass the empire and to engage its military forces. Such were the circumstances under which the Arabs, as we have seen, besieged and captured Thessalonike. Finally, however, the danger from the Bulgarians was averted. Evidently Leo Choirosphaktes persuaded Symeon to sign, for the third time, a treaty with Byzantium (904).[15]

An inscription found twenty kilometres west of Thessalonike near the present day village of Nea Philadelphia has often been associated with this Bulgarian-Greek treaty of 904.[16] The text of it is as follows: In the year 6412 after the Creation, in the seventh indiction, the boundary between the Romans and the Bulgarians [established] in the time of Symeon, archon of the Bulgarians [by the grace of] God, and of Theodore, the olgu trakan, and Dristăr the count.

Without becoming involved in the disputes over the authenticity and significance of the inscription, the following points should be emphasized: (a) this 'boundary stone' constitutes a unique instance; (b) it cannot, moreover, designate a border line, but at most a position on the frontiers. Inasmuch as it cannot be proven that the stone was found *in situ*, it cannot have any demonstrable value for establishing the Byzantine-Bulgarian frontiers.

In any case, the treaty of 904 signifies the terminus — let us say provisional terminus — of military conflict between Byzantium and Bulgaria. This period of calm in Byzantine-Bulgarian relations, however, was of very short duration. For 912, the year of Leo VI's death, signals the opening of renewed military operations between the two states.

The calm was disturbed in the sole reign of Alexander, Leo's brother and erstwhile co-emperor. This frivolous ruler refused to ratify and continue the peace which had prevailed between the two states since 904. Consequently, a new war broke out.

Operations this time were carried out almost entirely in Thrace. After Symeon's death in 927, a peace treaty was signed between the two states. In Nikephoros Phokas' reign (963-69), relations between Byzantium and Bulgaria were again aggravated. The emperor himself campaigned against the Bulgarians in 967, but succeeded only in capturing a few frontier fortifications. Thereafter he preferred to use diplomatic means and to avoid dangerous campaigns.

At Nikephoros' instigation, the Russians invaded Bulgaria in 968, causing great havoc.[17] The Byzantines were content to fortify their borders with Bulgaria. The following year, the Russians again invaded Bulgaria. They defeated the Bulgarian army, captured the tsar, and subjugated the country.[18]

Relations with the Russians, however, worsened under Phokas' successor successor John Tzimiskes. In a final confrontation, he managed to defeat them utterly in 971. Bulgaria as an independent state was dissolved and its territory was annexed to Byzantium. The borders of the empire were pushed forward once again to the Danube,[19] while the Bulgarian patriarchate ceased to exist.[20]

Macedonia once again became the theatre of Byzantine-Bulgarian wars after the unexpected death of John Tzimiskes in 976. He was succeeded by the two minor sons of Romanos II, Basil II and Constantine VIII.

This gave the Bulgarians the opportunity to revolt under the leadership of the Kometopouloi, the sons of Count Nicholas, a Bulgarian provincial governor in the western regions of Bulgaria.[21] Nicholas' youngest son Samuel emerged as sole leader of the revolt. From his headquarters around Ochrid and Prespa he began operations on a grand scale against the Byzantines. Unlike the previous campaigns of Symeon, these were directed not against Constantinople, but at the land of Macedonia and southern Greece.[22] In fact, the geographic setting of the Bulgarians' revolt was the chief factor in determining their new strategy.

Samuel profited from the irregularities of fifteen years of joint rule by the young emperors (976-90). He seized Beroia in 989, but failed to take Thessalonike and Serrhai.[23] In the summer of 986, Basil lead a strong army north-east of the Rhodopes. He planned to take Sofia, which he put to siege. After three weeks of fruitless assault, Basil ordered a retreat. He found himself in a vulnerable position, and was moreover informed that Samuel had conquered the mountains around Sofia.[24] During the retreat, however, the Byzantine army was attacked by the Bulgarians and suffered heavy losses. Basil was nonetheless undaunted. In 990 he passed through the theme of Thrace and Macedonia and reached Thessalonike where he reorganized the defences. In 994, he undertook a new campaign against the Bulgarians, which he was forced to break off in order to hasten to Syria. To deal with the Bulgarian incursions, Basil appointed the *magister* Gregory Taronites as *strategos* of the theme of Thessalonike. Samuel responded with a surprise attack on Thessalonike, destroying the garrison and killing its commander.[25] He did not attempt to take the city, but advanced as far as the Isthmus of Corinth, ravaging everything in his way. On his return, however, he suffered a terrible defeat at the hands of general Nikephoros Ouranos on the banks of the Spercheios river (997). Samuel and his son Romanos were wounded, and barely escaped to Bulgaria. Basil's campaigns against Samuel in the last two decades of the tenth century, therefore, had no decisive results. This was due mainly to the Byzantine preoccupation with other fronts.

At the beginning of the eleventh century, Basil was in a position to enact a carefully considered policy against the Bulgarians. After checking the enemy's attempts to conquer and consolidate the areas of the theme of Thessalonike and central Greece, he took up offensive operations which would lead to the Bulgarians' decisive defeat.

The emperor's plan was to strike the Bulgarians from several sides, gradually weakening their forces and their state. In 1001 or 1002, the Byzantine army assaulted Bulgarian fortresses across the Balkans.[26] After seizing both Great and Little Preslav and Pliska, Basil returned in triumph.[27] In 1003, he restored Byzantine control over the cities of Beroia, Kolyndros, Servia and Edessa.[28] Then he marched into Thessaly, capturing the castles still held by the Bulgarians, and transferring the garrisons to Voleron, an area to the west of the mouth of the Nestos. In a new and bold expedition in 1004, Basil advanced to Vidin, which he took after a siege lasting eight months.[29] At the same time, Samuel hoped to divert Basil by attacking and plundering Adrianople (as Dryinopolis in Chaonia, northern Epirus was formerly called).[30] He immediately retreated, however, fearing Byzantine reprisals.

After the capture of Vidin, Basil headed south. He seized and destroyed whatever Bulgarian fortifications he encountered in his path.[31] He met up with Samuel's forces at Skopje, where they were encamped on the opposite bank of the flooding Axios. Basil was able to ferry his troops to the other side, and launched a surprise attack on the Bulgarians, who fled with enormous losses. The commander of Skopje, Romanos-Symeon, surrendered the city and went over to the emperor.[32]

From Skopje, Basil headed north-east to Pernik. Failing to take it, he lifted the siege and returned by way of Philippopolis to Constantinople.

The information in the sources for the following ten years is almost non-existent. On the basis of what little Skylitzes has to report, it seems that Basil pursued the tactics of constant harassment, inflicting steady losses on the enemy's territory.[33] The Bulgarian power was reduced to such a degree that Samuel no longer dared to venture open battle with Basil's army. In his despair, the Bulgarian leader decided to block the passes to north-western Macedonia as a means of halting enemy attacks and incursions.[34] He mustered about his forces, and walled off and fortified the narrow Strymon river valley of Strumica near Kleidion, situated on the road between Petric and the city of Stromnitsa.[35]

In the summer of 1014, Basil appeared before the Bulgarian fortifications and opened his attack. The emperor's assault was thwarted, however, by the impregnability of the site and the Bulgarians' fierce resistance. At that critical moment, the *strategos* of Philippopolis, Nikephoros Xiphias, hit upon a bold solution. Passing over Mount Belašica, 'situated to the south of Kleidion', he suddenly attacked the Bulgarians from the rear.[36] Panic-stricken, they fell into disorderly flight. Samuel himself barely escaped being captured and took refuge in Prilep.[37]

This brilliant victory was marred, however, by an event which indicates the degree of savagery the antagonists had reached after such a long and bitter war. Basil blinded about fifteen thousand Bulgarian captives, sparing only a few to guide back the long column of their unfortunate comrades. At the sight of thousands of his blind soldiers, Samuel suffered an apoplectic stroke and died two days later on 6 October, 1014.[38]

Samuel's death provoked sharp dynastic strife in Bulgaria, from which John Vladislav emerged as victor. Basil II pressed on with the difficult war, and from 1015 to 1018 the Byzantines won back the cities which the Bulgarians still possessed or had recovered. The assassination of John Vladislav in 1018 hastened the Bulgarian collapse. In the course of Basil's campaign that year, thirty-five fortresses in the area of Sofia surrendered. He also took the remaining Bulgarian fortifications in Macedonia, including Ochrid, the capital of the state.[39] Finally, the Byzantines captured Samuel's more distant possessions in the west, as far as the Adriatic; in the north, as far as Sirmium (1019).

THE BARBARIAN INVASIONS OF THE PATZINAKS, UZES AND HUNGARIANS IN THE ELEVENTH CENTURY

With the dissolution of the Bulgarian state and the incorporation of its territory into the empire, Byzantium's northern frontier was advanced to the Danube. Consequently, the Byzantines came into direct contact with the Hungarians, the Cumans and the Patzinaks.

The period of invasions in the Balkans was inaugurated by the Patzinaks, a people of Turkic descent who had in 1026 already launched their first, albeit unsuccessful attacks on the empire. Towards the middle of the eleventh century, the Byzantines repulsed a new Patzinak invasion and captured thousands, many of whom were settled as farmers in the fields around Sofia, Niš (Naissos) and Eutzapolis.

This barbarous people invaded the empire on other occasions, in 1059, 1064, 1078 and 1090-91.

The most important of these incursions was that of 1064, since it set into motion another barbarian group, the Uzes or Oguz, a tribe related to the Seljuq Turks. Numerous and terrifying, they shattered the Byzantine forces. Some of them even reached Thessalonike and central Greece, pillaging everything along the way. Bad weather conditions and other difficulties forced the invaders to return to the area between the Balkans and the Danube.[40] Here they suffered from serious epidemics, as well as Patzinak and Bulgar attacks instigated by the government. Thus the empire was saved from these barbarians, many of whom entered state service and were settled on lands in Macedonia.[41]

Hungarian invasions, finally, caused certain disturbances in the eleventh century. These however did not seriously affect the area of Macedonia.

THE REVOLT OF PETER DELJAN

In the reign of Michael IV (1034-42), the Bulgarians rose in revolt over the tax measures of John the Orphanotrophos, brother of the emperor and effective ruler of the state.

In order to obtain more liquid funds, John required the subject Bulgarians to pay their taxes in money and not in kind, as Basil II had allowed. Moreover, when the Bulgarian archbishop John died in 1037, the Orphanotrophos' government appointed as primate of Bulgaria Leo, the *chartophylax* of Saint Sophia, who was of Greek descent. This was in sharp contrast to the shrewd and sound policy of Basil II, who had entrusted the elec-

194. At the end of the 12th century Norman armies from Sicily invaded Macedonia and captured Thessalonike at the same time as Bulgarian forces occupied large areas of north-west Macedonia. Byzantine troops quickly recaptured the lost territory. Saints George an Demetrios, the patron saints of soldiers, are shown here in full military dress, heavily decorated. Wall painting, 12th century, church of the Anargyroi, Kastoria.

195. The wealthy class of 12th century Kastoria could well afford to build churches. Part of the founder's wall painting (12th century) in the church of the Anargyroi, Kastoria, shows Anna Radine, wife of Theodore Lemniotes, a rich and learned man of the town, standing before the Virgin.

tion and appointment of the Bulgarian clergy to the Bulgarian archiepiscopal see. These imprudent and arrogant actions quickly bore fruit. In 1040, the Bulgarian *archon* Peter Deljan proclaimed a revolt in Belgrade, presenting himself as a grandson of Samuel.[42] The uprising quickly spread to the regions of Niš and Skopje. The new tsar proceeded here, accompanying his march with acts of violence against the Greek populations, his soldiers 'unmercifully and inhumanely killing any Roman whom they discovered'.[43] After suppressing internal quarrels, Deljan

advanced southwards. Michael IV, who was in Thessalonike, abandoned the city and fled to Constantinople as soon as he heard the news.

Despite the emperor's flight, Deljan did not attack Thessalonike. Most probably he wished to liquidate all Byzantine centres of resistance before assaulting the most heavily fortified city on the Thermaic Gulf. A part of his army, therefore, captured Dyrrachion; another section headed towards central Greece, but without achieving anything permanent; and a third part turned towards the theme of Nikopolis. There Deljan had an unexpected stroke of good fortune. The population of the theme joined the Bulgarian revolt; according to John Skylitzes, not out of love for Deljan, but because of the excessive fiscal pressures imposed by the Byzantine administration.[44]

Affairs took a turn for the worse when the rebels, encamped at Ostrovos, were joined by the patrician Alousianos, general of Theodosiopolis.[45] Second son of Aaron 'kometopoulos' (brother of tsar Samuel), he was dissatisfied with the Byzantines for financial reasons. Fearing that the Bulgarians might prefer Alousianos as their sole leader, Deljan accepted him as co-emperor, but assigned him an undertaking with dubious chances of success — the siege and capture of heavily-fortified Thessalonike.[46]

Heading an army of forty thousand men, Alousianos in fact attacked the city, which was at that time defended by the emperor's nephew, the patrician Constantine. Deljan constructed a palisade, and for six days attempted to take the city with siege engines and other instruments of war. When all his attempts failed, he made preparations for a long siege.

The people of Thessalonike, however, were determined to save their city. Their faith in the miraculous assistance of Saint Demetrios, patron of Thessalonike, stiffened their resolve. At the critical moment, the inhabitants of Thessalonike sallied forth and attacked the Bulgarians on all sides. All available forces took part in the sortie, even the 'Noble Brigade', probably the general Constantine's personal guard. With some exaggeration, the Byzantine sources state that fifteen thousand Bulgarians fell in battle, and that as many again were taken captive. All who could, fled in disorder. After this defeat Alousianos broke with Deljan, and finally managed to seize and blind him. Uneasy about the eventual outcome of the uprising, Michael IV set forth in person and came to Mosynopolis. Fearing the Byzantine superiority, Alousianos hastened to go over to the emperor and received in reward the title *magister*. Thereafter, Michael proceeded to Thessalonike, and then headed to Sofia and the fortress Voianon, which he took.

While these events were transpiring, the emperor Michael captured Deljan, and continued with success the struggle against Michael Ivatzes who assumed leadership of the revolt.

The emperor Michael headed towards Prilep, where Ivatzes had entrenched himself. After a brief struggle, he defeated and captured him.[47] With this, the Bulgarian resistance collapsed. Michael appointed new theme commanders in Bulgaria, and then returned to Constantinople.

The Bulgarian uprising ended quickly. The Greek population of Macedonia, particularly around Thessalonike, had suffered enormous ravages and ruin from the rebel incursions. In the years to follow, however, disorders within Macedonia were to continue.

THE REBELLIONS OF GEORGE MANIAKES AND BASILAKIOS

In the autumn of 1042, George Maniakes rose up in revolt against Constantine IX Monomachos and was proclaimed emperor. Maniakes was the *strategos* of Italy, and one of the most distinguished military leaders of the period. He had become disgusted with the constant plots and attacks directed against him. In February of the following year, he landed in Dyrrachion, and from there marched to Constantinople. Monomachos tried with lavish promises to persuade Maniakes to lay down his arms. Failing in this, he dispatched a large army, commanded not by one of the known and trusted generals, but by the eunuch Stephen.

The decisive battle took place at Ostrovos near Amphipolis. Maniakes' army was winning when the general received a mortal blow and fell dead. His army was dispersed, some turning in flight and others defecting to the enemy.[48]

In the following decades, the condition of the empire continually worsened. The strength and stability of the state was undermined by a series of incompetent emperors; new enemy assaults in both west and east; and the tragic blow of Manzikert (1071). A favourable climate was created for revolts and military uprisings, most of which affected the region of Macedonia but little. One occurred in Thessalonike itself, and is hence worth relating. This concerns the revolt of the *dux* of Dyrrachion, the *strategos* Basilakios.

Basilakios intended to exploit the wave of revolt created by his predecessor Nikephoros Bryennios, in order to lay claim to the throne himself (1077). He was anticipated, however, by Botaneiates, who tried to win Basilakios over with promises of amnesty and grants of titles. When these efforts failed, Botaneiates dispatched the general Alexios Komnenos against Basilakios. At Peritheorion, Komnenos defeated some of the rebel's advance troops, then marched against Basilakios himself, and encamped near Thessalonike in the area west of the Axios.

Basilakios planned to make a surprise attack on Komnenos, but was betrayed by the general Gemistos. Thus, when Basilakios began a night attack, he was overwhelmed and completely routed by the enemy, who had been waiting in ambush. His forces were scattered with great losses. Basilakios himself fled to the acropolis of Thessalonike, which Alexios managed to penetrate with the help of the inhabitants of the city. Here he captured Basilakios and sent him in chains to Constantinople.[49]

THE NORMAN WARS (1081-1185)

A few years later a new danger appeared to threaten Macedonia (and Byzantium in general) from the west.

196. Theodore Lemniotes, who is known to have founded two churches in Kastoria, Saint Stephen's and the Anargyroi. Here, from a wall painting in the latter, he is shown presenting a model of the church to the Virgin. He wears a long sticharion, cut away in front, and a cloak.

In 1081 the Normans landed in the Balkan peninsula. They took Dyrrachion, invaded Macedonia, capturing Kastoria and subsequently Skopje and Moglena. They failed however to take Ostrovos, Beroia and other parts of western Macedonia. Alexios I Komnenos (1081-1118) recovered Kastoria in November 1083, and shortly thereafter the other gains made by the Normans.[50] The death of their leader Robert Guiscard in 1085 ended the Norman war.

The Crusades occasioned great disturbances in the area

of Macedonia, but these were of no long term significance. After the first Crusade ended, affairs returned to normal.

The increasing weakness of the state under Manuel I's successors gave the Hungarians and Serbs the opportunity to destroy the fortifications at Belgrade, Braničevo, Niš and Sofia (1183).

The Normans of Sicily profited from this situation as well. They landed at Dyrrachion and captured the city after a brief siege (June 1185).[51] Then the Norman army marched against Thessalonike, which they reached on 6 August. Meanwhile their fleet having first captured Corfu, Kephallonia and Zakynthos sailed into the Thermaic Gulf on 15 August.

The Normans besieged the city. taking advantage of the incompetence of its military commander, the inadequate provisioning, and the poor state of the defences. They took the city after a fierce struggle which lasted several days. The metropolitan, Eustathios of Thessalonike, vividly describes the scenes of savage butchery and enslavement which followed.[52] They even pillaged the decorations of the tomb of Saint Demetrios. The number of dead surpassed seven thousand.

Leaving behind a strong garrison in Thessalonike, the Normans then advanced towards the capital, except for one detachment which struck out for Serrhai. Near Mosynopolis, however, the general Alexios Branas attacked and defeated them.

From there the Byzantine general proceeded to the environs of Amphipolis. At a place called 'the place of Dimitritses' he routed the Normans on 7 November 1185,[53] and captured their admiral Richard and their general Count Aldouin. The disaster was so great that the Normans withdrew at once from Serrhai and Thessalonike, and subsequently from Dyrrachion.

NEW BULGARIAN REVOLTS AND INVASIONS OF MACEDONIA

In 1185, the Bulgarian brothers Peter and Asen headed a revolt which led to the founding of the second Bulgarian empire, which Byzantium was forced to recognize.[54] The new state was situated in the area between the Balkans and the Danube, with Trnovo as its capital. In 1195, the Bulgarians invaded the region of Serrhai, defeated the local Byzantine forces, and seized the commander Alexios Aspietes.[55] After extensive plundering, they returned to their territories. The next year the Bulgarians carried out raids into the region of Amphipolis and of the Strymon, laying the ground for a new attack on Serrhai. The *sebastokrator* Isaac Komnenos was sent out against them, but was defeated and captured. The boyar Ivanko saved the situation when he assassinated Asen I. Ivanko established his own principality in the Rhodopes, with Byzantine acquiescence. Later, however, he revolted and expanded his territories towards Mosynopolis, Xantheia, Mt. Pangaion and the Smolenoi theme. Finally, after a coordinated Byzantine assault, his principality was dissolved and he was captured.

Yet another Bulgarian, Dobromir Chrs or 'Chrysos' in the Byzantine sources, led a revolt against Peter, the brother and successor of Asen. He attacked the area of Serrhai, but at length concluded a treaty with the Byzantines, who entrusted him with governing and defending Stromnitsa and its environs.

Chrysos quickly broke the agreement and founded his own principality, which he expanded as far as Prosakos on the Axios river. The situation worsened when he was joined by the Byzantine *protostrator* Kamytzes.

The two rebels conquered large sections of north-west Macedonia, including Prilep and Pelagonia, and even advanced into central Greece.[56] At the same time another general revolted against Alexios III, the Cypriot John Spyridonakes, commander of the Smolenoi.

Finally, however, all these acts of rebellion were brought under control. With false promises, emperor Alexios managed to recover the territories which Chrysos had seized.

INTELLECTUAL LIFE

As the Slavs of Macedonia came more and more under Bulgarian influence, the importance of Macedonia and in particular of Thessalonike as a zone of acculturation declined. Macedonia became once again a backwater. Thessalonike, as the second city of the empire, was not without cultural activity. But in the highly centralized empire of the so-called Macedonian dynasty, its role was quite secondary. The great renaissance in literature and art of the late ninth and tenth centuries took place almost exclusively in Constantinople.

LEGAL AND HISTORICAL TEXTS

The capture of Thessalonike by the Arab fleet under Leo of Tripoli on 31 July 904 is the subject of John Kameniates' *Capture of Thessalonica*.[1] The author was a native of the city and in reader's orders. Like the rest of his family he belonged to the ecclesiastical establishment. Though he displays a certain descriptive talent he has little grasp of the larger historical context of the events which he recounts, and shows little acquaintance with Hellenic cultural tradition. He is at home only in biblical and ecclesiastical learning. A.P. Kazhdan has recently cast doubts on the authenticity of the work attributed to Kameniates, and suggested that it is actually the work of a fifteenth century forger. The question must remain open.

A short treatise on marriage-settlements and disposal of property after the death of a spouse by George Phobenos, a judge in Thessalonike, written about the year 1000, is evidence for the serious study of Roman law in the city. But there was no systematic and formal instruction in law available in Thessalonike. For that one had to go to the capital.

THE ELEVENTH AND TWELFTH CENTURIES

Clerical men of letters

During the eleventh and twelfth centuries Macedonia, and in particular Thessalonike, prospered thanks both to the general prosperity of the empire and to the key role which the region played in relations with the west. Yet there is little evidence of cultural development outside Thessalonike, with one exception; that exception is Ochrid, the seat of the autocephalous archbishops of Bulgaria, now incorporated into the Byzantine empire. Both in Thessalonike and in Ochrid the leading figures in the domain of letters and thought are churchmen, and the bulk of the literature produced is ecclesiastical in character. There is no doubt that in Thessalonike there were teachers of literature and philosophy, but they were overshadowed by those of Constantinople, where alone it was possible to make a brilliant career as a teacher.

Theophylact Hephaistos was born in Euboia some time before the middle of the eleventh century. He studied in Constantinople, where he was one of the favourite pupils of Michael Psellos, and became a teacher himself, probably of rhetoric. As he was a deacon of Saint Sophia, his teaching was doubtless given in an ecclesiastical institution, perhaps a forerunner of the Patriarchal School which we find fully developed in the twelfth century. Michael VII Doukas (1071-78) appointed him tutor to his son Constantine, who was later betrothed to Anna Komnena and for a time co-emperor with Alexios I. Thanks to these court connections, Theophylact was appointed archbishop of Bulgaria about 1089, and remained in Ochrid till his death about 1108. He was an energetic and enlightened administrator of his vast province. Of his surviving works only a treatise on kingship, addressed to his imperial pupil, and a few occasional poems belong to his Constantinople days.[3] During his twenty years in Macedonia he wrote commentaries on the Psalms and Prophets and on most of the New Testament, homilies, a life of his predecessor Saint Clement (probably adapted from a Slavonic original), and an extensive correspondence which is of great interest for the social, economic, and ecclesiastical history of Macedonia. In spite of his complaints of intellectual isolation he clearly had access to a fairly rich library in Ochrid, and maintained contact by letter with many leading personalities in Constantinople and Thessalonike.

Michael Choumnos may well have been a native of Thessalonike, where many members of the Choumnos family lived. But it is in Constantinople that we first meet him, in 1121, as *chartophylax* of the Great Church. This office was generally held by an expert in canon law. Short-

197. In the 10th century Kastoria was an unimportant provincial town distinguished neither for its commercial life nor for its intellectual activity. Lack of money is reflected in the shabby clothing worn by the deceased donor, Constantine, depicted in the wall painting, in the church of the Anargyroi, Kastoria.

197

ly afterwards he became metropolitan of Thessalonike, and continued in office till about 1133. His surviving writings are mainly treatises on points of ecclesiastical law, and probably date from before his elevation to the bishopric.[4] But an *akolouthia* on the four martyrs Alpheios, Zosimos, Alexander and Markos was probably composed in Thessalonike.

Michael Choumnos' successor as metropolitan of Thessalonike was Niketas of Maroneia, another canon lawyer who had been *chartophylax* of the Great Church in Constantinople. He held office until his death about 1145. Like his predecessor he wrote treatises on ecclesiastical law. He also played an active part in relations with the Latin church.[5] In the six dialogues which he wrote on the Procession of the Holy Spirit he reached the conclusion that the western formula *filioque* was equivalent to the Greek expression διά τοῦ υἱοῦ, which had been used by John of Damascus. Niketas clearly belonged to that group in the Orthodox Church which was anxious to prevent a breach of Christian unity, and which sought to smooth over apparent doctrinal differences. Indeed, he blamed the doctrinal dispute mainly on the Byzantines. He presumably supported the conciliatory policy towards the western church adopted by Manuel I. But he remained firmly opposed to submission to Roman authority in matters of organization and discipline.

One of Niketas' successors at Thessalonike, Basil of Ochrid, was himself a Macedonian.[6] He was *protonotarios* to patriarch Michael II (1143-46), and was appointed metropolitan of Thessalonike some time before 1154. Basil was one of Manuel I's principal advisers on relations with the Latin church. In October 1154 he had a discussion in Thessalonike with the papal legate Anselm of Havelberg. In 1155 Pope Hadrian IV — the only Englishman to sit upon the Papal throne — asked Basil to use his good offices with Manuel to secure an audience for two Roman clerics in connection with an alliance against the Normans. The letter of the Pope contained a statement of traditional papal claims which Basil felt obliged to refute, and applied to the Greeks the unfortunate appellation of lost sheep. Basil's reply is polite, eirenic, but firm in rejecting any notion of papal supremacy. He clearly belonged, like Niketas of Maroneia and Michael Choumnos, to the 'liberal' wing of the Orthodox Church, which believed that the doctrinal disagreements between East and West could be solved with a little goodwill provided the Pope's claim to supremacy was not pressed. In 1157 Basil played an active part in the Synod which tried Soterichos Panteugenes. By 1169 he was dead.

Basil's immediate successor, Constantine, left no mark in history except a complaint about the state of church

198. *A 12th or 13th century donor to the church of the Anargyroi, Kastoria, one of the most imteresting portraits of the period. His dress suggests that he was a nobleman, for it is in strong contrast to that of the impoverished appearance of his predecessor Constantine (197).*

property in his diocese. In 1175 he was succeeded by a man of very different character, the scholar and man of letters Eustathios Kataphloros. Eustathios was born probably in Constantinople, not later than 1125, and had a long career — the details of which are not absolutely clear — in the service of the Great Church, as a teacher of grammar (literature) and as *maistor ton retoron*. It was in the first of these capacities that he composed his monumental commentaries on the Iliad and the Odyssey, his lost commentaries on Pindar and Aristophanes and that on Dionysios Periegetes.[7] These alone were enough to win him a distinguished place in the history of scholarship. Immense and wide-ranging erudition, scrupulous fairness in stating the views of others, lively interest in the world about him, balanced judgement and quiet good taste mark these commentaries throughout, and reflect the character of their author. As *maistor ton retoron* he delivered a series of ceremonial panegyrics, some of which survive.[8] When he suddenly found himself elevated to one of the major metropolitan sees of the empire he had already reached an age at which most men are somewhat set in their ways. Eustathios, however, responded to the new challenge with vigour and enthusiasm. Apart from his regular Lenten homilies, New Year homilies, panegyrics upon St. Demetrios and other saints, there survive from this period important treatises, in the form of homilies, on the reform of monastic life and on the duty of obedience to a Christian government, as well as miscellaneous sermons of moral exhortation. He turned his old philological skill to a new use by composing a long commentary, largely literary in character, on John of Damascus' *Canon for Pentecost*. In 1180 he delivered a funeral oration on Manuel I, perhaps in Constantinople.[9] When in 1185 Thessalonike was captured and sacked by the Normans, Eustathios was himself taken prisoner and played an important role in maintaining the morale of his fellow-captives by his exemplary courage. Shortly after the event he composed an account of the capture of the city.[10] It is marked by his usual clarity and circumstantiality, and by a noble humanity which enables him to sympathize with the hardships of the Latin soldiers as well as with those of his fellow-citizens. His multifarious pastoral activities and his reforming zeal made him enemies in Thessalonike as well as friends. In 1191 he was recalled to Constantinople and remained there till 1194. An open letter to the people of Thessalonike survives from

this period. Unlike many of his predecessors he seems to have been uninterested in doctrinal polemics. The date of his death is unknown. Soon after his death he was regarded as a saint. A fresco portrait of him is to be found in the monastery church of Gračanica in Serbia, dating from early in the fourteenth century.

Eustathios' vast and varied literary production, much of which was written in Thessalonike, makes him a major literary figure in a period of great cultural distinction.[11] Though an adherent of Byzantine Atticism, he is less preoccupied with style than many of his contemporaries.[12] Indeed he often writes awkward, clumsy Greek. But he always has something to say. His directness and sincerity more than make up for his occasionally dry style.

Several manuscripts survive which were written in Thessalonike during this period, in particular a Gospel book written in 1185 — the year of the Norman attack — in the 'great church of the Panagia'; this is probably to be identified as the Acheiropoietos church, called 'great' to distinguish it from the church of the Panagia *ton Chalkeon* founded by Christopher, katepan of Longibardia in 1028. Eustathios encouraged his clergy to copy and conserve books, and this manuscript may well be one of the results of his encouragement. There is some evidence that a manuscript of the non-select plays of Euripides — perhaps all that remained of a complete edition of the plays — survived in a library in Thessalonike. These plays were generally unknown in the Middle Ages except to Eustathios and to Thessalonikan copyists of the early fourteenth century. But as the works in which Eustathios cites them are generally believed to have been written in Constantinople, it is possible that he brought it from the capital in 1175 and that it remained in Thessalonike after his death.

Several of the cities of Macedonia had Greek-speaking Jewish communities. It was for the members of these communities that Tobia ben Eliezer of Kastoria composed a commentary on the Pentateuch in the reign of Alexios I.[13] It is written in something approaching spoken Greek, since the Jews held classical Greek in little esteem and the language of the Church Fathers in even less. It is thus the earliest monument of demotic. But since Tobia used the Hebrew alphabet, which is ill-adapted for the writing of Greek, it is not easy to reconstruct the text with any precision.

ART FROM THE TENTH CENTURY TO 1204

ARCHITECTURE

In this period a greater number of ecclesiastical buildings were erected over a larger area and with a wider variety of plans.

The architectural plan of Saint Sophia, Thessalonike, a cross enclosed by aisles, is echoed in smaller buildings out in the country; these include the tenth-eleventh century church of the Virgin Kountouriotissa, Pieria, with three semicircular apses and triple arcade (trivelon) between the nave and the aisles, and Saint Sophia at Drama, where there is a single projecting apse and similar trivelon connecting the nave with the aisles which is roofed with a continuous vault. At a later date this plan lived on at Drenovo, Yugoslavia (twelfth century) in an area which became Byzantine after Basil II's victory.[1]

In the tenth century cruciform churches with a fairly large dome were built on Mount Athos as the principal churches of the new monasteries with direct or indirect imperial financial support. The katholikon of Vatopedi has a triconch plan, and the earliest katholikon of Iveron must certainly have been similar.[2] How these churches are related to the earlier katholikon of Great Lavra remains obscure for the time being; it has recently been demonstrated that Great Lavra was not originally built as a triconch church by Athanasios but as a Constantinopolitan cross-in-square church which Athanasios later enlarged, around 1000, by adding the two side conches. The same holds true for the old katholikon of the monastery of Xenophontos.[3]

One type of church which continued to be used because it is easier to build and its dimensions are more readily adaptable is the three-aisled basilica in two basic types: with a pitched wooden roof over the higher middle aisle, rising above the side aisles, its walls pierced, like a clerestory, with many windows, with rows of columns or piers, and a large three-lobed window in the spacious sanctuary, which has a semicircular apse in the older examples. The biggest and most opulent basilicas of this type, which is still termed 'Hellenistic' in order to stress the continuity, are churches of central significance, such as the Protaton on Mount Athos and the metropolitan church of Saint Achilleios at lake Prespa, both dating to the tenth century. The preference for the basilica plan continues throughout the eleventh and twelfth centuries in many metropolitan churches, at Beroia, Edessa, Saint Nicholas at Melenikon, Saints Theodore at Serrhai and elsewhere. These large churches, designed to accommodate larger congregations of the faithful, also have galleries, e.g. Saint Achilleios and the metropolitan church at Serrhai. The *pastophorys* of Saint Achilleios are roofed with high domes (like Saint Sophia at Korone in the Peloponnese).[4]

The other type is represented by three relatively small basilicas in Kastoria: Saint Stephen (ninth-tenth century), the Anargyroi (tenth-eleventh century) (fig. 201) and the Taxiarches (ninth-tenth century) all with an exaggeratedly high nave (like a second church) with all three aisles barrel-vaulted, with some few rectangular piers (only the Taxiarches has columns) to support the arcades. The outside walls are in *cloisonné* masonry; however, the horizontal lines are emphasized by laying the stretchers in two or three courses together, whereas the headers often form letters or other designs, as was customary in the more southerly parts of Greece, but here it is less well done. Some of the wall paintings adorning these churches, which have great importance as we shall see, can not all be easily viewed, not only because of the poor lighting but also because in these narrow buildings it is not possible to stand far enough away from the murals to see them properly. These characteristic basilicas of western Macedonia are roofed in a way that sets them apart from the basilicas we have seen up until now; they stay close to the barrel-vaulted basilicas of the so-called 'eastern type' because in the Early Christian period vaulted basilicas were characteristic of Asia Minor.[5]

The typology is enriched in the relatively smaller churches of the period. The cruciform plan with the variation that the lateral arms each end in an apse, so that the entire church is on the triconch plan, is fairly common in small-scale structures, simple and symmetrical as in the case of the eleventh century Koumbelidiki church at Kastoria with stout walls to support the extremely high dome (fig. 199) and also the thirteenth century ruined church of Saint Nicholas at lake Prespa and Saint George Kryonerites outside Serrhai. The triconch plan frequently occurs in southern Greece and in the Balkan regions.[6] In the church of the Koumbelidiki and in most of the known churches of this type, Greek *cloisonné* brickwork was employed for the walls.

All of the church plans which we have seen up until now more or less reflect examples current in Constantinople or Thessalonike. We know of only a few provincial types characteristic of Balkan architecture. One of these, most widely distributed in southern Greece, is the so-called transitional type in which, originally, the dome was supported not on columns but on four walls, a sign of technical inadequacy. The walls separated the four low corner compartments from the central space; at first they connected by means of narrow passages which gradually grew larger until the walls were replaced by a large arch supported on two piers and two columns (two column church). There are only three known examples of this kind of plan in

199. The small three-apsed 11th century church of the Koumbelidiki at Kastoria with both narthex and exo-narthex lies within the fortress of the town. Its solid walls support a very high dome bearing elaborate tile decoration. The interior of the church has wall paintings of the 13th century while those which decorate the west wall date to 1495.

200. *The church of the Panagia Chalkeon in Thessalonike bears close resemblances to the style of the Myrelaion monastery in Constantinople. It was founded by Christopher, protospatharios and katepan of Longobardia together with his wife and children.*

Macedonia: Saint Germanos on the island of the same name in lake Prespa, dated to *c.* 1000, and the pair of ruined churches at Vodoča in the region of Stromnitsa, Saint Leontios and the Panagia Eleousa, built in the eleventh century one after another on the same axis. In all three churches of this transitional class the passages in the walls are still narrow. Other characteristics of this provincial type are that the drum of the dome is cylindrical and the apse a half-circle; the exterior surfaces are not articulated and the masonry is, as a rule, plain unworked field stones.[7] The fact that the church of Saint John in Mesembria on the Black Sea is also of this type scarcely justifies attributing the creation of this plan to Bulgarian initiative, as has been claimed, because the older known examples which are more eleaborate, comparatively speaking, had been developed in Greece south of Mount Olympos as early as the ninth century (the church of Episkope, Evritania and, more important, Skripou).[8]

After 1018 historical circumstances favoured the founding of new monasteries and new churches chiefly in towns or in their immediate vicinity or in the monastic state created on Mount Athos. The cruciform plan with its variations was most widely employed; in addition, a series of new designs came into use. It should probably be assumed that the new types, such as the 'octagonal' type, are to some extent those worked out first in the capital and its immediate vicinity; however the way in which these churches were built in the Macedonian area does not display the strongly individual characteristics which would spring from local traditions. In this period, therefore, it is difficult to isolate specific characteristics differing from those found in Constantinople, at least in respect to the more important architecture. The smaller buildings further away from the centre conformed to somewhat provincial standards, not only in regard to the design but also in regard to technical procedures and construction methods.

In Thessalonike the church of the Panagia Chalkeon (fig. 200) is closely related to the Myrelaion monastery in Constantinople founded by emperor Romanos Lekapenos I (920-44). It was called 'Our Lady of the Coppersmiths' because it was in the coppersmiths' quarter and this location gave it the name Kazancilar when it became a mosque.[9] Inscriptions tell us that the founder was Christopher, *protospatharios* and *katepan* of Longobardia, with his wife and children in 1028 and Christopher also dedicated the wall paintings in the church which are quite well preserved. The church is closely akin to the Myrelaion church not only because of the four columns in the central area, but mainly because of the walling, which here too is exclusively brickwork and because of the way in which the outside surfaces are enlivened by means of similar devices: half columns, recessed arches around the apertures, cornices and bands of dentils. The two-storey narthex with two domed parekklesia is reminiscent of the church of Constantine Lips in Constantinople. Perhaps the manner in which the facades are divided by cornices into two unequal sections also relates to the two-storey Myrelaion church. Furthermore, the striking difference between the upper and lower sections of the narthex facade may constitute another link with Myrelaion; in the upper section all of the projecting features provide a sense of depth and high relief whereas in the lower section the pilasters are shallow and the arches small, thus conveying the impression that the lower section of the narthex facade was intended to be hidden behind an exonarthex and open portico as at Myrelaion. Here the resemblance ceases, but we know of no other church which is closer to that founded by Romanos I. The Panagia Chalkeon differs in that the octagonal drum with built colonettes accentuating the corners and a cornice at the roof level, has two rows of windows because the drum has to be high enough to rise above the two smaller drums over the narthex, as required by the hierarchical distribution of functions within the church. This lends the interior space a rather unusual but striking vertical accent.

Architectural liberties were taken in building this church: the two sides are not of the same length and not alike because the north side, in place of the door, has a projecting arcosolium with the tomb of the founder, which was there from the start; the base of the dome is not a

201. In the 11th century the church of the Anargyroi, Kastoria was a barrel-vaulted basilica. The narthex was built at the same time as the body of the church. When it was rebuilt in the 12th century by Theodore Lemniotes, the church was given a wooden roof and the height of the central aisle was raised. The wall paintings of the original building still remain on the west facade.

geometrically accurate square; the two smaller domes over the narthex were not designed exactly as the central dome; the apse of the sanctuary is three-sided, whereas the two smaller side apses are semi-circular. It is questionable whether these irregular features described above should be put down to the general 'picturesque' quality of Byzantine architecture, where regard for geometrical precision varies according to time and place or whether they are due to the provincial siting and relatively lowly position of the sponsor, an official who did not have the means to embellish the church with costly materials, but merely with wall painting. The church of Saint Nicholas Elaionos at Serrhai is of the same type but smaller and simpler.[10]

It is generally accepted that the so-called octagonal type originated in Constantinople. Greek churches of this type are widespread and include famous examples such as Hosios Loukas, Daphni and Nea Moni; in Macedonia the type is represented by the little church of the Metamorphosis in the village of Chortiatis in the vicinity of the Byzantine Moni Chortaitou. This single-aisled church is much too small to have either side chapels or narthexes

and thus the plan resembles the single-aisled octagonal type called the 'island' type, such as Nea Moni. The use of more simple *cloisonné* and chiefly the technique of recessed brick masonry suggest parallels with monuments in the area of Constantinople in the eleventh-twelfth centuries.[11]

The tetraconch plan, as we have seen, was tried out in the ninth century and was current again in the eleventh century, this time with direct links to Constantinople in regard to both methods of construction and harmony of design. The best-known monument is the monastery church of Eleousa at Veljussa in the Stromnitsa valley (1080); the many-sided high apse, the series of conchs, the plasticity of the surfaces with double blind arches are all features of Constantinopolitan architecture.[12] Similar borrowings are at work in other churches of other types in Macedonia, such as Saint Nicholas at Prosotsani.[13]

Further west, at Nerezi near Skopje is the church of Saint Panteleimon, an imperial foundation, built in 1164 by Alexios Komnenos the grandson of emperor Alexios I Komnenos; the wall paintings of this church provide a key to understanding the pictorial art of the twelfth century. On

the other hand the architecture of this little church partly repeats external elements of the Kosmosoteira in Pherai, Thrace, such as the five domes and their particular design, and it has matched the flat unrelieved planes of the walls and the crude masonry to the provincial level of the region. The interior plan resembles the type of the Akataleptos church (Kalenderhane Čami) in Constantinople (without the surrounding aisles): four angled walls support the dome and isolate four little corner bays (the western bays are entirely blocked off) so as to create a large unified well-lit central space. On the exterior the three-side apses with flat plane surfaces are of different sizes, the side apses being extremely low; the four small domes have four-sided drums and the large central dome has an octagonal drum. All five, however, are articulated by means of colonettes and arches and the central dome had a rippling eaves line.[14]

There are also churches in the area, founded by neighbouring rulers, which more or less follow the practice of the churches in Macedonia, e.g. Saint Nicholas near Kuršumlija built by Stephan Nemanja in 1168. The two main features of Saint Nicholas are that it is built solely of brick with recessed brick masonry technique. i.e. alternating courses of red brick and recessed brick covered with white mortar, and the recessed arches. The large eight-sided drum rests on four arches which are not prolonged into bays, thus creating the single rectangular domed space which we find in the central church of the Archangel in the Pantokrator monastery in Constantinople and which was frequently used later on in small churches all over the Balkan peninsula, e.g. Saint Demetrios in the monastic dependency of the Prodromos monastery outside Serrhai.[15]

PAINTING

From the early tenth to the end of the eleventh century

In this period, usually termed Middle Byzantine, the main characteristics of the great art of Byzantium evolved and crystallized after the triumph of Orthodoxy which established the validity of representing sacred images in churches. Most of the surviving monumental painting of this period, and some of the most important painting, is to be found in Macedonia, in the city of Thessalonike itself and also in other towns such as Kastoria and Beroia, in the monasteries of Mount Athos and elsewhere. Apart from what they tell us about local conditions these monuments also furnish valuable information about artistic trends, the quality of artistic modes, iconographical developments and other features of Byzantine art.

In the metropolitan church of Saint Sophia, Thessalonike, the great dome is decorated not with Christ the Almighty (Pantokrator), but with the Ascension. Unfortunately, other representations in this church, if any, have not been preserved, so that we know nothing concern-

202. Depiction of Saint John the Baptist. His classicizing stance, the undisturbed folds of the drapery and his serious, thoughtful but relaxed expression marks him out from other representations of saints of the same period, for example SS. George and Demetrios shown earlier (194). 12th century wall painting, church of the Anargyroi, Kastoria.

ing the arrangement of an entire programme. Controversy on this point notwithstanding, we accept the founder's inscription in the dome, commemorating archbishop Paul (dated to 880-85) as contemporary with the Ascension. The fact that this scene, the divine epiphany *par excellence* appears in this central location of the metropolitan church of the second largest city cannot by any means be interpreted either as a provincial culture-lag or as an Early Christian survival (figs. 184-186). Furthermore, the same scene appears in the same place in some approximately contemporary churches in Cappadocia (El Nazar, Qeledjlar, Qarleq) which means that this arrangement, also to be found in the church of the Holy Apostles at Constantinople, had become recognized and was in widespread use at some time after the iconoclastic period.[16]

The huge composition of the Ascension in Thessalonike has perfect axial symmetry and the entire compositional effort has been devoted to adjust the proportions of the figures to the vast concave surface of the dome. There is a rule governing all Byzantine painting according to which natural forms are subordinated to compositional and stylistic requirements so as to achieve a transcendental quality; one might well reach the conclusion that here this rule had been pushed to its ultimate and this explains the unnatural poses and gestures of the elongated apostles with their oversized palms which poignantly express their wonder, awe, amazement and rapt concentration. But in the rendering of the facial features there is interest neither in dignity nor in spirituality; the faces have pronounced characteristics: long fleshy noses, low foreheads, gloomy mouths, faces which bear a peculiar family resemblance to that of Leo VI making *proskynesis* in the well-known mosaic in Saint Sophia, Constantinople. The vast, brilliant composition in Thessalonike is illuminated by the windows in the dome; the magic of the colours and the dynamic vivacity make this very human gathering fascinating.

We find the same crude linear and expressive style in a wall painting, not very well preserved, of the same period in Thessalonike. Here too the subject is the Ascension, in the apse of the sanctuary of Saint George, the Rotunda.[17]

In the eleventh century, the mosaics and wall paintings in Macedonia preserve the monumental character of the period with tranquil compositions of few figures; the human forms predominate, whereas indications of landscape and buildings are minimal, no more than what is absolutely necessary. The great mosaic of the Virgin Enthroned in the wide apse of the sanctuary of Saint Sophia, Thessalonike, belongs to this period (fig. 187). This composition replaced the cross of the iconoclastic period, but there are problems in connection with the date because more recent scholars have reached the conclusion that this mosaic dates to the eleventh or twelfth century rather than directly after the iconoclastic period was over (second half of ninth century) as had been previously argued.[18] The somewhat stylized rhythmic rendering of the drapery, the disproportionately large head with big almond eyes and arched brows point to a date at the end of the eleventh or the twelfth century. Certain features suggest that the work was made in a local atelier: inadequacies in the drawing, the Mother out of proportion in relation to the Son, the dis-

parate modelling of the two figures, and lastly the awkward placing of the group in relation to the vertical axis.

In the same church there are wall paintings on the soffits of the narthex arches preserving parts of full-length figures or medallion busts of leading monks such as Theodore the Stoudites, John Kalyvites, Hosios Euthymios and Theodosios the Koinobiarches and the two Saints Theodora. These wall paintings with a blue background and expressive faces, where linear contours are combined with studied plasticity, are related to other Macedonian wall paintings, chiefly those of Saint Sophia, Ochrid, to which they are closer than to the Panagia Chalkeon.[19]

Wall paintings of the eleventh century still exist in quite a few Macedonian churches, but they are rarely preserved in satisfactory condition and hence only two series of wall paintings will be mentioned here as being of fundamental significance: those in the Panagia Chalkeon, Thessalonike, and those of Saint Sophia at Ochrid, neither of which could be regarded as provincial monuments because both are linked to officials from Constantinople.

The wall paintings in the church of Panagia Chalkeon may be dated to 1030-40; they are poorly preserved, but in quantity sufficient to enable one to comment that the iconographic programme in which by this time the order of the Twelve Feasts had already been fixed, sometimes harks back to earlier times, for the Ascension is shown in the dome as it had been a hundred and fifty years earlier in Saint Sophia, Thessalonike, and is sometimes up-to-date. In the sanctuary apse the Virgin is shown full figure, *orans,* as she appears a little later at Nea Moni, Chios, and at Saint Sophia, Kiev; below her are the four church fathers (the Saints Gregory) depicted frontally as we see them a little later at Ochrid and Kiev. We have here one of the oldest known examples of the church fathers together in this stance in the altar area. One of the oldest known and most complete representations of the Second Coming is in the narthex, a subject still rare in this period.

The style has the same reaction against classicism which we see in the mosaics of this period with the difference that the technique of wall painting produced softer outlines and hence it is more akin to the wall paintings of Hosios Loukas than to its mosaics. The faces in these compositions frequently have an oriental look with no individual differentiation; they are fleshy and often stolidly impassive. Some of the figures are short whereas others, such as the church fathers in the sanctuary, are tall and slender with a more spiritual appearance and there is a more expressive look in their invariably large eyes. In these figures the drapery is organically related to the classical stance with one leg carrying the weight, the other relaxed; but the drapery on the figures of the very long-legged apostles in the Holy Communion is stiff, like that of the Ascension in Saint Sophia. This variety of styles may mean that a team of artists of different ages produced these murals, but they all bear witness to the art of their own times.[20]

The wall paintings in the original domed basilica of Saint Sophia, Ochrid date to about the same time; this large church has a much greater expanse of wall surface so that the iconographic programme is more extensive. Here it is evident that liturgical and ecclesiological concepts have in-

203. The Descent from the Cross, from the monastery church of Saint Panteleimon, Nerezi, where the paintings constitute an important point in Komnene art. Here, perhaps for the first time, *emotion and pain are fully realized, not only on the faces and in expressive gestures, but also with the melodic lines of the composition dominated by great sweeping curves. c. 1162.*

fluenced the iconographical programme. In the sanctuary there is a unique large-scale representation of Saint Basil celebrating mass; a great many patriarchs of Constantinople are also shown, frontally, in the sanctuary and in the *pastophorys* the church fathers of the three other patriarchates are shown, obviously to advertize the self-governing church of Ochrid taking its place in the group of orthodox churches.[21] There is a row of kneeling angels down the whole length of the nave, a gracefully organized motif, which, by means of repetitive emphasis, lends a melodic rhythm to the painted decoration. Finally, in representations such as the Ascension and the Pentecost, the agitated facial expressions are very lively in contrast to the stylized drapery; in the representation of the Forty Martyrs in the prothesis there is, all in all, a more dramatic ethos. Here there is a remarkable range of styles. This important wall painting preserved in fragmentary condition

must be associated with Leo the first archbishop of Ochrid (1037-56) who came from Constantinople.[22]

A few figures from the second layer of wall paintings have been preserved in the great basilica of Saint Achilleios at lake Prespa; the remains of frontal church fathers, two warrior saints and an archangel may be dated to the first half of the eleventh century by iconography and style.[23]

There are noteworthy remains of wall paintings of the eleventh century in two churches in the vicinity of Stromnitsa. Virtually the entire iconographic programme can be made out in the ruined church of Saint Leontios at Vodoča; the greater part of the decoration was executed in the first half of the eleventh century in a more painterly style in which the monumental character of contemporary painting is vigorously maintained, while in the representations of scenes from the life of the Virgin the expression of the Passion predominates. In the tumultuous scene of the

204. The Entombment, a wall painting in the monastery church of Saint Panteleimon, Nerezi, founded by the grandson of the emperor Alexios Komnenos. The elongated figures are here endowed with aristocratic elegance and dignity. The rendering of the drapery tends towards the 'manneristic' style which was to dominate until the end of the 12th century.

Forty Martyrs dated to the end of the eleventh century (others date it to the twelfth or thirteenth century) the dramatic mood is stressed in the same painterly style.[24]

There are remains of excellent wall paintings from the other church at Stromnitsa, Panagia Eleousa, Veljussa; the wall paintings date to around 1080 and are linked with the presence of archbishop Manuel from Constantinople. Sections of a broadly based iconographic programme are preserved with a fair number of new themes such as the church fathers in the sanctuary, two of whom are celebrating mass around the Preparation of the Throne while the other two are frontal. There was a remarkably successful attempt at portraying the prophets and saints and the Pantokrator in the dome with correct modelling and lively expressions which is to be associated with a classical revival (cf. Daphni).[25]

There are two mosaics in the katholikon of Vatopedi on Mount Athos which are, perhaps, remains of an early programme of mosaic decoration which was never completed. The two figures of the Annunciation appear high up on the chancel pier, and on the lintel of the doorway between the exonarthex and the esonarthex there is a three-figure Deesis — the Virgin and Saint John intercede with Christ Enthroned. The latter may be dated to about 1094, when Ioannikios, who is mentioned in the metrical inscription, was abbot of the monastery. These mosaics were carried out in the monumental anticlassical style current in the eleventh century, for example at Hosios Loukas, Saint Sophia, Kiev and elsewhere.[26]

There are remains of wall paintings which may perhaps be earlier than the eleventh century in peripheral towns such as Kastoria: on the ground floor of Saint Stephen there are remains of a large cycle of saints and also in the vaults of the narthex there are two facing rows of

205-207. The wall paintings at Saint George, Kurbinovo are a stylistic variation considered to continue and strengthen the prevailing tendency in the paintings of Nerezi. The tall figures remain, the swirling drapery conferring movement. Diagonal lines prevail in the compositions in harmony with the dynamic and frequently dramatic atmosphere. On the left is the Embrace of Elizabeth and the Virgin Mary (205) and on the right (206) the Archangel Gabriel and the Resurrection (207).

enthroned apostles and guardian angels with the Deesis; all the figures, badly preserved, are imposingly large scale. The subject is from an early Second Coming, executed in a purely linear style and may be dated to the first half of the tenth century.[27] The remains of paintings in the side apses and in the narthex of the three-aisled basilica of the Taxiarches, near the actual metropolitan church, are of the same style and date.

In the narthex of the Anargyroi a representation of Constantine and Helen has come to light under the second layer of painting; next to them is a plain representation of a deceased founder, of the same name and probably buried nearby (fig. 197), and Saint Basil, Saint Nicholas and others.[28] It should be noted that these early wall paintings belong to a period during which the district probably was temporarily held by the Bulgarian tsar Samuel (997-1014); hence the wall paintings are an important source of evidence for the cultural level and the nature of this provincial, but fairly formal art for which it has been claimed in a not very convincing manner that it expresses the artistic drives of the Slavic population of the area.[29]

It is almost certain that there must have been a great many more wall paintings up to and including the twelfth century in the area of Byzantine Macedonia than the

208. The well-preserved 12th century wall paintings of the single-aisled basilica church of Saint Nicholas Kastoria are the work of magister Nikephoros of Kasnitzes. The Archangel Gabriel, kneeling before the Virgin, is shown in the picture, a detail from the larger scene of the Virgin Platytera.

208

302

relatively small number preserved today. The majority of them must have been destroyed; quite a few others must be hidden below subsequent layers of wall painting or coats of lime plaster as we are led to suspect by the fact that there are wall paintings still concealed underneath later layers in the basilica in Servia, remains in Saint Achilleios and Saint Germanos at lake Prespa, a Saint Damian in Saint Nicholas Elaionos at Serrhai and others.[30]

From this brief survey it appears that it is difficult to isolate individual characteristics of a local 'school' of painting in Macedonia from the ninth to eleventh centuries. We can merely distinguish a frequent preference for an anticlassical manner, mainly in monuments out in the countryside, which constitutes one of the prevailing trends, perhaps the most widespread, in Byzantine painting before the end of the eleventh century.

Monumental painting of the twelfth century

No dated monuments of the first half of the twelfth century have survived, but we know from dated monuments in other parts of the Byzantine world that the final phase of eleventh century style continued in this period. The mosaics of the metropolitan church of Serrhai, dedicated to Saints Theodore, may be dated to this period. The rhetor Pediasimos described these mosaics in the fourteenth century; the only one which survived the fire of 1913 was the imposing Communion of the Apostles in the sanctuary, but now only a single figure is finally preserved, the apostle Andrew (now in the Thessalonike Museum). The modelling is of such quality that it is not possible to make out if the style belongs to Thessalonike or Constantinople.[31]

Two groups of wall paintings are of critical importance for determining the trends of the second half of the twelfth century: first and foremost, the wall paintings in the church of the Panteleimon monastery at Nerezi, founded in 1164 by Alexios Komnenos, the grandson and namesake of the emperor and the excellent representations in the Latomos monastery, Thessalonike, which are few in number. The dated paintings of Saint Panteleimon constitute an important point in the art of the Komnenoi after the mid-twelfth century. Here, perhaps for the first time in the history of European art emotion and pain are fully realized, not only on the faces and in expressive gestures, but also with the melodic lines of the composition dominated by great sweeping curves (the Descent from the Cross, the Lamentation, the Transfiguration, (figs. 203, 204). The elongated figures have here an aristocratic elegance and the style employed for the portraits of the Komnenoi in Saint Sophia is developed further here, becoming more painterly with a greater range in depicting people of various ages. In the lower row of standing saints there has clearly been an effort to create portraits true to life.

The development of the pictorial arts up until the end of the twelfth century demonstrates that the unusually fine wall paintings at Nerezi, which must have been executed by more than one artist, are of fundamental significance, since it can be shown that virtually all of the subsequent stylistic developments which we are about to point out have their origin in Nerezi, exaggerating one or another of its traits.[32] It is convenient to distinguish three main trends.

We may call the first one the 'academic' style, exemplified by the wall paintings of the Latomos monastery in Thessalonike where only two representations are completely preserved, the Nativity and the Baptism, and a few portions of other subjects. These wall paintings provide a landmark for art in a great centre at a specific time and thus they are of outstanding significance; because of their obviously high quality, particularly in respect to the effortless ease with which the composition expands also in depth, the surely executed drawing and the harmony of the colours, these paintings provide us with a fixed point for comparison. We are not sure that this painting does not stylistically antedate Nerezi.[33] Other contemporary monuments such as the two-storey funeral church at Bačkovo near Philippopolis, the monastery of Saint John the Theologian on Patmos, Saint Hierotheos in Attica and others, as well as the narthex of the Anargyroi at Kastoria, all exemplifying the art of the great centres, have a similar academic character.[34]

Next let us take a look at the 'dynamic' or 'manneristic' trend, running parallel with the 'academic' trend, which is thought to continue and intensify the dominant traits in painting at Nerezi and to have taken final shape in the last decades of the twelfth century. The stature, with the disproportionately long legs is repeated; the body now turns on its axis whenever violent motion is to be communicated. The faces are always built up with the reddish network of

lines and green shadows on the cheeks, but the stiff compact drapery folds acquire enhanced significance because of the increased elongation of the bodies with the garments glued to the lithe slender limbs so that the drapery defines both contour and volume.

Churches were decorated in this style in western Macedonia, in Cyprus and in Crete and the same style was echoed in wall paintings in Georgia,[35] in mosaics of Sicily and north and south Italy which supports the view that the style was a more general movement emanating from Constantinople. This is confirmed by an excellent icon of the Annunciation from a cycle of the Twelve Feasts at Sinai.

Three of the monuments of this group are dated: in Macedonia, Saint George at Kurbinovo near lake Prespa to 1191; in Cyprus, the Enkleistra to 1183 and the church of Panagia Arakou to 1192. The chronological limits are narrowly fixed, at least in regard to the *floruit* of the style.

The wall paintings of Saint George at Kurbinovo are wonderfully well preserved, an example *par excellence* of the characteristics of the style described above;[36] but they differ from wall paintings created in urban centres in that they give the impression that the artist was deliberately avoiding any reminiscence of the classical tradition, while in the scenes of the Passion (for example, the Entombment) the dramatic tension is heightened (figs. 205-207). The fact that the wall paintings at Kurbinovo are closely linked to one series of wall paintings in the Anargyroi at Kastoria

209. The Dormition of the Virgin at Saint Nicholas Kasnitzes, Kastoria. The paintings of this church have all the technical and

stylistic characteristics of Komnene art, as well as the iconographical details found at Nerezi.

has solved the problem of dating the latter more precisely. There were at least two artists at work at the Anargyroi, probably one after the other.[37] The earlier artist, Painter B, who painted the greater part of the upper zones, was a provincial craftsman utterly unacquainted with 'modern' stylistic trends of his period. Painter A, who completed the decoration of the church, is a first rate artist with a heightened sense for coherent rhythm throughout the composition and the dynamic contribution made by attempt to exaggerate motion, proportions, expressive tension (figs. 193-196, 212). At all events the quality of these two sets of wall paintings is not evidence for 'provincial misinterpretations' but also indicates a high level of ability with a sufficiently individual style within the spirit of 'mannerism' (rococo or baroque, according to others), the dominant style of the time. Hence the majority of scholars (Kitzinger, Demus, Lazarev, Radojčić, Djuric, Chatzidakis, Drandakis and others) find it very difficult to date the two monuments more than one or two decades apart.

In quite a few parts of the three-aisled church of the Anargyroi the representations differ from those of Painters A and B. The standing figures in the narthex — John the Baptist (fig. 202), angels, saints, the Ascension — have quiet poses, broad modelling, fewer folds better modelled to the body; they are created in a spirit quite different from that elsewherein the church, more relaxed and more thoughtful.[38] We may assume that a third artist worked here in the 'academic' style, probably a bit later than Painters A and B. The three inscriptions of the same founder give an indication of this.[39] Two are in the church, one in the narthex, showing that the entire scheme of decoration was requested and executed in two stages and that it was given by Theodore, scion of the house of Lemniotes, an aristocrat with some education; the three long founders' inscriptions are written in archaizing iambic trimetres.

The wall painting in the church of Saint Nicholas is the work of another noble, *magister* Nikephoros Kasnitzes, and there is an equally erudite inscription also metrical. Some date these wall paintings to the beginning of the twelfth century (Pelekanides) or to about 1145-55 (Kitzinger), i.e. before Nerezi; others date them after Nerezi (Demus, Hadermann-Misguich). In any case the wall paintings of Saint Nicholas, a single-aisled church with narthex, are well preserved;[40] in all essentials they are very close to the basic characteristics of Komnene art, in regard to technique, style and iconography, just as they were developed at Nerezi (figs. 208, 209). These monuments representing current trends in a remote town such as Kastoria demonstrates that all of Macedonia was closely in touch with the centres of high culture.

Finally let us mention the third trend which is somewhat less sophisticated but with a wide geographical distribution all the way from Sicily to the Baltic island of Gottland and

210-211. A pair of mosaic icons, among the most important produced in the 12th century. They belong to Xenophontos monastery on Mount Athos and may perhaps have been made in Thessalonike. They depict Saint George (210) and Saint Demetrios (211) in the clothing of noblemen. Both are praying to the tiny figure of Christ.

from Cyprus to the Caucasus. It is characterized by rather short figures, expressive rather than graceful poses, the volume being of less importance and linear drawing dominant. Colour contrasts are often used for dramatic effectiveness. This kind of rendering is already to be found at Nerezi, but only in aged figures, and at Djurdjevi-Stupovi in northern Yugoslavia in 1162 and in Russia.[41] In Macedonia we find this style in the refectory at Vatopedi in the embrace of Peter and Paul.[42]

Contemporary with the monuments described above, which cannot be considered as remote from the mainstream of art, rulers, abbots and private individuals founded a number of churches which had wall paintings of a somewhat provincial character, such as those in the octagonal church at Chortiatis, which have not yet been cleaned, the paintings (now destroyed) in the three-aisled basilica of Saint Nicholas at Melenikon, and at Saint Demetrios at Aiane near Kozani where some imposing figures of saints are preserved.[43] At Beroia large wall paintings have been uncovered in the Old Metropolis, a large three-aisled basilica; these paintings which are of excellent quality with richly varied styles have not yet been studied.[44] In the smaller three-aisled basilica of Saint John the Theologian, also at Beroia, there are quite a few wall paintings preserved in the sanctuary which have characteristics typical of the period, but with a great artistic variety, dedicated by a certain Nikephoros Sgouros.[45] The figures of the apostles in the Communion of the Apostles in this church are comparable to the figures of Peter and Paul in the *kellion* of Ravdouchos on Mount Athos in regard to vivid expressiveness and the building up of forms with brushstrokes of contrasting colours.[46]

Portable Icons

Not many of the portable icons of this period seem to have survived. The mosaic icon of the Virgin and Child at Chilandari could be assigned to the 'academic' trend in Komnene painting since all of the features of this closed composition hark back to some classicizing prototype.[47] The full length saint Peter in the collection at the Protaton approaches the refined style at Nerezi.[48] As for the few epistyle icons which have survived on Mount Athos, at Vatopedi and Great Lavra,[49] and at Ochrid,[50] it is hard to decide if they are Constantinopolitan or Thessalonikan works. The two-sided icon at Kastoria with the *Imago Pietatis* (Christ of Sorrow) and the Virgin is one of the finest examples of icon painting from the end of the Komnene period; it is an iconographical originality, being the oldest known representation of the *Imago Pietatis*. The portrayal of emotional strain is of high quality.[51] The Panagia Eleousa from Thessalonike in the Byzantine Museum, Athens is more tender in style but more dogmatic in content; she holds Christ as He falls backward.[52] The lovely mosaic icons of Saint George and Saint Demetrios in Xenophontos might also have originated in Thessalonike (figs. 210, 211).[53] A wall painting giving a full length representation of Hosios Loukas of Steris on a pier of Saint Demetrios, Thessalonike, should also be counted as an icon; it furnishes evidence that Thessalonike and southern Greece had iconographic models of worship in common.[54]

FROM 1204
TO THE CAPTURE OF THESSALONIKE
BY THE TURKS

POLITICAL HISTORY

LATIN RULE IN GREECE: THE FRANKISH KINGDOM OF THESSALONIKE

The outcome of the Fourth Crusade radically changed the situation in the Balkans (1204). After the dissolution of the Byzantine state and the foundation in its place of the Latin empire of Constantinople in 1204, the whole region of Macedonia was subjected to the kingdom of Thessalonike, with Boniface, marquis of Montferrat, as ruler.[1]

Originally, Boniface was to have been awarded territory in Asia Minor and the 'island of Hellas'. In the end, however, he claimed and took Thessalonike and its surroundings. This shift occurred after a number of quarrels between the Latin emperor of Constantinople, Baldwin, and Boniface. Baldwin insisted that he should receive Thessalonike, which he would then grant to Boniface, clearly emphasizing that Boniface was the Latin emperor's vassal. Indeed at the beginning of the summer of 1204, Baldwin moved to the western part of his realm in order to be recognized and proclaimed by all as 'emperor of the Romans'. He passed right across Thrace, completely undisturbed by the few remaining unconquered Greeks who went into hiding at his passage.

When Boniface was informed that Baldwin had arrived at Mosynopolis, he thought that the emperor's aim was to take Thessalonike for himself, in violation of the agreement they had made. Outraged, Boniface seized Didymoteichon and other Thracian cities, except for Orestias. He levied taxes and began to recruit Greeks, attempting to form an alliance with them against the other Latins. He even proclaimed Manuel (the son of his wife Margaret-Maria of Hungary, who was formerly the wife of Isaac II Angelos) emperor of the Romans — an event which indeed rallied the Greeks to his side. They began to enlist *en masse* under his leadership.

In the meantime, Baldwin reached Thessalonike and the entire population received him 'joyfully'. They requested, however, that he not enter the city, for they feared that his troops would plunder.

Baldwin was convinced by the reasonableness of their request, and moreover feared Boniface, of whose actions he had been informed. Not wishing to disaffect the citizens of Thessalonike, he accepted their entreaty. Indeed, he issued a chrysobull to that effect, in which he also confirmed all the city's privileges.

Baldwin camped outside the city walls for a few days and then returned to Constantinople. By then the Venetian doge Dandolo had arrived. Like the other Latins in the capital, he was uneasy about the extent of the antagonism between Baldwin and Boniface. The Frankish nobles hastened to mediate and managed to reconcile the two adversaries. Consequently, Boniface departed for Thessalonike and assumed the government of his kingdom.

The reconciliation of Baldwin and Boniface removed the internal danger which threatened their existence. The external danger remained, however, and it was immediate and great. Both the empire of Constantinople and the kingdom of Thessalonike had to face the attacks of the Bulgarian tsar Ioannitzes (or Kalojan).[2] The Greeks of Thrace had formed a natural alliance with him aimed at conquering the Latins.[3]

In accordance with their agreement, the Greeks of Thrace revolted and took Adrianople and Didymoteichon, while Ioanitzes came to support them with a large army of

Vlachs and Bulgars. At the end of March 1205, Baldwin led Latin troops from Constantinople and reached Adrianople, which they besieged. Here they were heavily attacked and defeated by the forces of Ioannitzes. Indeed, Baldwin himself was captured (15 April 1205).

Ioannitzes, who had previously broken the Greek-Bulgarian agreement, then moved towards Thessalonike.[4] When he reached Serrhai, he laid it to siege. He forced the garrison to surrender, and captured the city.[5]

Meanwhile Ioannitzes' general Etzuismenos (Šišman), the commander of Prosakos, came to terms with the Thessalonikans and entered the city. The garrison, along with Boniface's wife Maria, withdrew to the acropolis.

At that time Boniface was in the Peloponnese. He hurried back to Macedonia, but upon approaching Thessalonike was informed that the city garrison had defeated the invaders and restored calm and order. Now he planned to advance to Skopje and strike at the Bulgarians there, calculating that Baldwin's forces would be simultaneously assaulting them at Adrianople. Obviously Boniface was still unaware of Baldwin's defeat. As soon as he learned about the catastrophe at Adrianople, he changed his plans and returned to Thessalonike, where he punished those who had instigated the revolt against him.

In the interim, Ioannitzes led his army from Serrhai towards Thessalonike. He defeated the forces which Boniface sent against him, but failed to take the city. He then turned to Beroia and seized some of Boniface's possessions there.[6]

During this period, Henry of Flanders, Baldwin's successor as emperor of Constantinople, attempted to restore the Latin possessions in Thrace, but with limited success. As a diversionary tactic, Ioannitzes assaulted Philippopolis and took it, inflicting dreadful damage (summer 1205).

The following year, Henry and Boniface decided to conduct a joint expedition against the Bulgars. Two months before the campaign was to have commenced, however, Boniface was killed in an engagement with Ioannitzes forces. He was succeeded by his two-year old son Demetrios, for whom his mother, Maria of Hungary, acted as regent (4 September, 1207).

Ioannitzes believed that the weak rule of the minor Demetrios would give him a greater chance to conquer Thessalonike. Thus, after first capturing nearly all the territory of the kingdom, he arrived before the city in October 1207 and began a siege. In the course of this undertaking, however, he died. According to some, he was assassinated by one of his generals.[7]

Ioannitzes' death was a heavy blow for the Bulgarian state. Under his successor Boril, internal quarrels reached their apogee. Ioannitzes' son, Ivan Asen, fled to Russia,

212. Closely associated with the worship of Saint Demetrios in Thessalonike is Saint Nestor, who was martyred after murdering the champion of Sirmium, Lyaios, in the stadium of Thessalonike in the reign of Galerian. Saint Nestor is shown here in warlike stance and clothing typical of the period. Wall painting, 11th century, from the church of the Anargyroi, Kastoria.

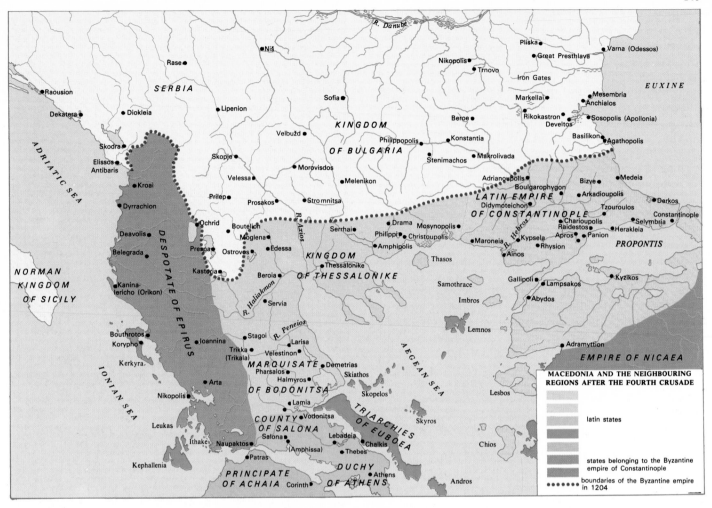

213. *Macedonia and the surrounding lands in the years immediately after 1204. Despite the agreements made by the different powers who participated in the Fourth Crusade, they* could not adhere to the original allocation of conquered territories or to the terms drawn up for the government of the Latin states.

but later returned to recover his paternal throne. At the same time Ivanko managed to break free from his Byzantine captors, and recovered his principality at Melenikon and Achrido, (Rhodope). Another boyar, Strez, founded a principality on the Axios centred at Prosakos (1208).[8]

Profiting from these internal troubles in Bulgaria, emperor Henry of Flanders defeated Boril near Philippopolis (summer 1208). At this point, Ivanko feared the power of the Franks and recognized Henry's suzerainty. He swore fealty to him, and accepted a Frankish garrison. In exchange, Henry accorded him the title of despot and gave him an illegitimate daughter of his as wife.

In the spring of 1211, a Frankish army with the help of Michael Doukas Angelos, founder of the despotate of Epirus, vanquished Strez on the plain of Pelagonia. Some months later, in January 1212, Boril and Strez suffered a crushing defeat and Strez was forced to flee to Serbia.

MACEDONIA UNDER THE DESPOTATE OF EPIRUS

While Bulgaria was convulsed with internal dissensions, Theodore Doukas, the new despot of Epirus and brother of

Michael Doukas Angelos, systematically expanded his possessions. In 1216 he took Ochrid, Prilep and Pelagonia.[9] In 1218 he conquered Platamon, after first securing his rear by taking Neopatrai (Hypate) and Lamia. The following year he captured all the cities of south-west Macedonia, and also Prosakos; in 1221 he took Serrhai.[10] In this way Theodore isolated Thessalonike from the Latin empire and the southern Frankish principalities, and could confidently aim at the conquest of Thessalonike. He strengthened his flank even further when he succeeded in winning over Ivanko, to whom he gave (for his second wife) the daughter of Petraleiphas of Thessaly, his brother-in-law.

The despot's systematic policy brought positive results. In 1224 Theodore took Thessalonike after a long siege, dissolved the Latin kingdom, and was crowned 'king and emperor of the Romans' by Demetrios Chomatianos, archbishop of Ochrid.[11]

Theodore continued his conquests eastward from Macedonia, capturing Adrianople and (to the north) Philippopolis. Theodore's victories, however, disturbed Ivan Asen II. The tsar attacked Theodore, and in the battle of Klokotnitsa (1230) crushed and captured him.[12] An ostentatious inscription in the Church of the Forty Martyrs at Trnovo arrogantly proclaims the Bulgarian tsar's victory over the Greeks:

I, Ivan Asen... campaigned into Romania and crushed the army of the Greeks. I took captive the emperor himself, Lord Theodore Komnenos, with all his nobles. I conquered all the Greek regions from Adrianople to Dyrrachion, and also the Serbian and Albanian regions. Even the Franks are subjects of my realm, for they recognize no other tsar but myself.[13]

Ivan Asen proceeded to conquer Adrianople, Didymoteichon, the Voleron area, Serrhai, Pelagonia and Prilep.[14]

Theodore's state was therefore restricted to the area around Thessalonike. He was succeeded by his younger brother Manuel, who was also Asen's brother-in-law. Manuel somehow managed to maintain the independence of the kingdom of Thessalonike. Matters became complicated when tsar Asen liberated the blind despot Theodore, giving him permission to reconquer Thessalonike and whatever remained of his former possessions. For a moment, fratricidal war threatened to break out between Manuel and Theodore. It was averted however by an agreement that Manuel remain in Thessaly, while Theodore and his son John Angelos would reside in Thessalonike. By now, however, their power had already become significantly limited. The following year the emperor of Nicaea, John Vatatzes, compelled John Angelos to renounce the imperial title, recognize the suzerainty of Nicaea, and content himself with the title of despot (1242).

A little later Vatatzes again set foot in the Balkans. Exploiting the death of tsar Koloman, he took Serrhai and then extended his authority over Melenikon, Velbužd (Kyustendil), Skopje, Velessa, Prilep, Pelagonia and Prosakos. Finally, he turned towards Thessalonike which he captured in December 1246.[15] Thus the despotate of Thessalonike ceased to exist, and Macedonia henceforth formed a part of the possessions of the empire of Nicaea.

214. In 1224 the despot of Epirus, Theodore Doukas Angelos, captured Thessalonike after a long siege, and was crowned as 'king and emperor of the Romans'. A coin minted during his reign shows him as the liberator of the city, blessed by the hand of the Lord and by Saint Demetrios. Athens, Numismatic Museum.

MACEDONIA AS PART OF THE EMPIRE OF NICAEA (1246-61)

John Vatatzes entrusted the Grand Domestic Andronikos Palaiologos with the government of the area of Thessalonike and Beroia, and assigned the region of Melenikon and Serrhai to Michael Palaiologos, son of Andronikos and subsequently emperor. Then he returned to Asia Minor. A few years later, however, he was constrained once again to appear in Macedonia, for Michael II, despot of Epirus, was planning to recover Thessalonike.

In the spring of 1252, Vatatzes advanced with his army against Michael, who had already conquered Prilep and Velessa, and had forced Edessa to surrender. Michael withdrew and fled to the Epirote territories of the despotate. Several of his generals then defected to Vatatzes, giving the latter full reign to take Kastoria and territories in Albania.[16] Michael was forced to surrender, and returned Velessa and Prilep.

John Vatatzes' successor, Theodore II Doukas Laskares (1254-58), repulsed an attack of Michael I Asen from Bulgaria. The latter was attempting to recover territories which Vatatzes had liberated. In the course of hard struggles lasting many months, Theodore drove back the Bulgarians and recovered Prilep, Velessa and Debar (Dibra). In May 1256, the Bulgarian tsar was forced to sign a peace treaty, withdrawing from all claim on territories of the empire.[17]

The situation changed the following year. Theodore Laskares' excessive demands annoyed Michael II, despot of Epirus. Michael incited the Albanians to revolt; he himself captured Kastoria and Beroia after months of hard fighting, and Prilep after a protracted siege. Theodore Laskares' death in 1258 allowed Michael to take Edessa, and strengthened his hopes that he would become lord of Thessalonike, and even of Constantinople itself. To this end he allied with king Manfred of Sicily and the ruler of Achaia, Villehardouin. Thus, the outlook for the Macedonian part of the Nicaean empire seemed gloomy. The new emperor Michael VIII (1259-82) saved the situation. In the battle of Pelagonia (1259) he crushed the enemy's allied

forces and recovered all the lost territories in western and north-western Macedonia, including Skopje, Prilep, Ochrid, Prespa and Kastoria.[18]

MACEDONIA AFTER THE RECONQUEST OF CONSTANTINOPLE

Two years later, the Greek emperor of Nicaea recovered Constantinople and the other remains of the Latin empire (1261). The Byzantine empire was re-established, but on a much smaller scale than in 1204 when it had been conquered and dismembered by the Crusaders. Once again all of Macedonia constituted imperial territory. But in the following decades, the state clearly began to weaken, and the Serbs emerged as a new force in Balkan politics. In 1282 the Serbian ruler Stephen Uroš II Milutin attacked the Byzantines and took Skopje, which was henceforth lost to Byzantium.[19] He proceeded to conquer other territories north of the Ochrid-Prilep-Štip line. After repeated and unsuccessful attempts to repulse the Serbian leader, Byzantium was forced to come to terms with him. The reconciliation between the two powers was sealed by a marriage alliance, in which Byzantium surrendered the conquered territories as dowry.

The Byzantine state had been reduced to impotence. The mercenaries of the Catalan Company exploited its wretched condition.[20] The Catalans were a group of professional soldiers who hired out their services. In 1302 Andronikos II eagerly enrolled the Catlans to campaign against the Turks in Asia Minor under their captain Roger de Flor, who previously had fought in the employ of Frederick II of Aragon. Within a very short time, however, the Byzantines' protectors and allies became the scourge of the empire.

In mid-autumn of 1308, the Catalans invaded Macedonia. Prior to this they had passed from Asia Minor into Thrace, which they pillaged. Wrecking everything in their path, they proceeded to Chalkidike, where they established a base on Kassandreia.

In the spring of the following year (1309), they launched a series of raids upon Mount Athos, the rest of Chalkidike and the areas around Thessalonike.[21] They aimed at plundering the wealthy metropolis, and perhaps at capturing the two queens in residence there; Maria Margaret, the wife of co-emperor Michael II (son of Andronikos II); and Irene, the second wife of Andronikos II. The Byzantines would surely pay the Catalans a handsome sum in ransom for these two women.

Throughout this period, the monks of Mount Athos suffered terrible hardships. The king of Aragon himself, James II, issued a decree in which he tried to protect the monks, who were at the mercy of the Catalans.

215. The castle of Platamon, as it was rebuilt by Roland Piscia or Pice in the early 13th century. Piscia received the castle as a fief from Boniface of Monferrat who, after his coronation as king of Thessalonike, advanced further south and captured both Platamon and Kitros which he also bestowed as a fief.

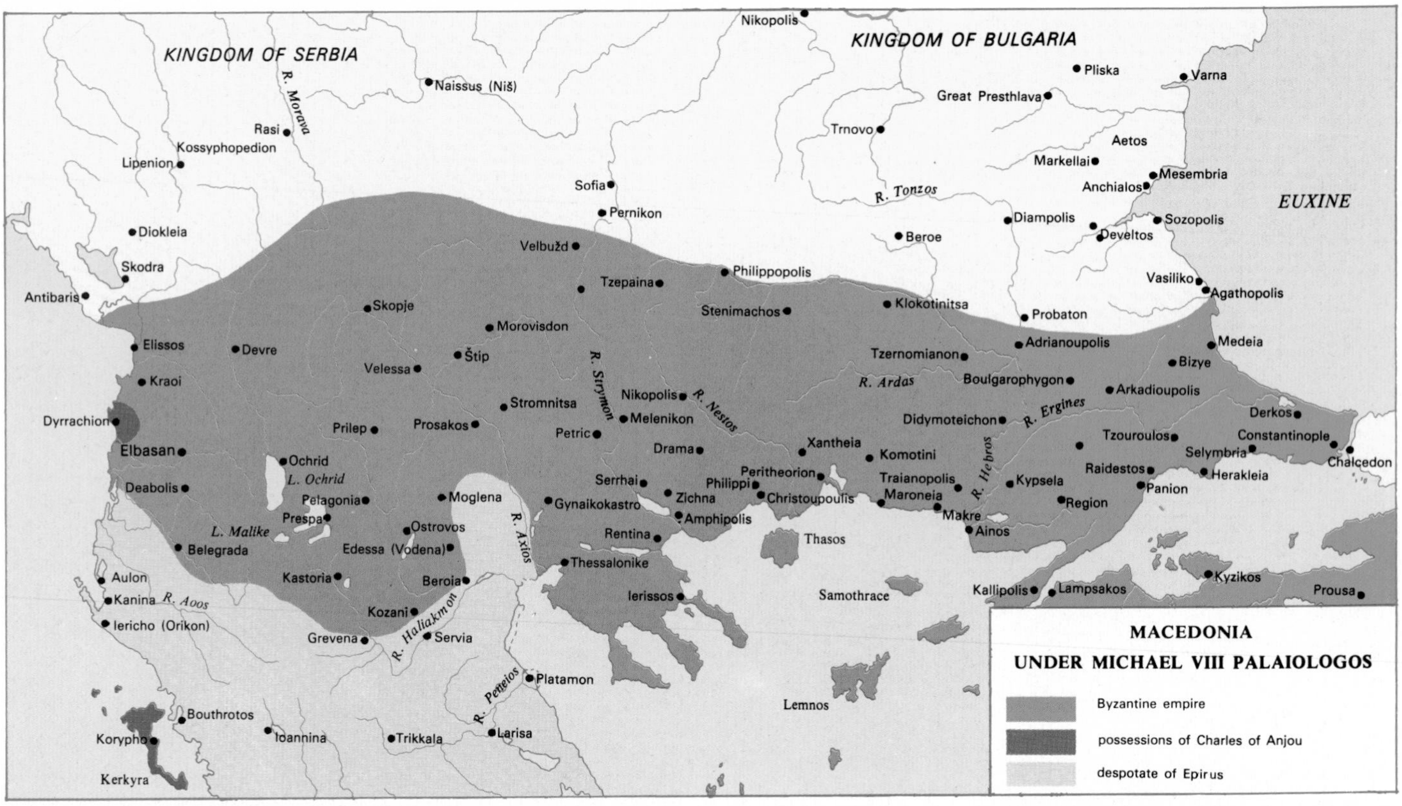
KINGDOM OF SERBIA
KINGDOM OF BULGARIA
EUXINE
R. Morava
Naissus (Niš)
Rasi
Kossyphopedion
Lipenion
Diokleia
Skodra
Antibaris
Elissos
Devre
Kraoi
Dyrrachion
Elbasan
Deabolis
Aulon
Kanina
R. Aoos
Iericho (Orikon)
Bouthrotos
Koryphō
Kerkyra
Ioannina
Trikkala
Larisa
R. Peneios
Platamon
Grevena
Servia
R. Haliakmon
Kozani
Kastoria
Beroia
Edessa (Vodena)
Ostrovos
Moglena
Belegrada
L. Malike
Prespa
Pelagonia
L. Ochrid
Ochrid
Prilep
Prosakos
Velessa
Skopje
Štip
Morovisdon
Strumnitsa
Velbužd
Sofia
Pernikon
Tzepaina
R. Axios
Gynaikokastro
Thessalonike
Rentina
Ierissos
Serrhai
Zichna
Amphipolis
Petric
Melenikon
Nikopolis
R. Strymon
R. Nestos
Drama
Philippi
Peritheorion
Christoupolis
Xantheia
Komotini
Thasos
Samothrace
Lemnos
Philippopolis
Stenimachos
Klokotinitsa
R. Ardas
Tzernomianon
Nikopolis
Trnovo
R. Tonzos
Beroe
Diampolis
Develtos
Sozopolis
Anchialos
Mesembria
Markellai
Aetos
Great Presthlava
Pliska
Varna
Vasiliko
Agathopolis
Probaton
Adrianoupolis
Boulgarophygon
Didymoteichon
R. Ergines
R. Hebros
Traianoupolis
Maroneia
Makre
Ainos
Kypsela
Medeia
Bizye
Arkadioupolis
Derkos
Constantinople
Chalcedon
Tzouroulos
Selymbria
Raidestos
Herakleia
Panion
Region
Kallipolis
Lampsakos
Kyzikos
Prousa
MACEDONIA
UNDER MICHAEL VIII PALAIOLOGOS
Byzantine empire
possessions of Charles of Anjou
despotate of Epirus

216. In the 13th century the frontiers of the old Byzantine empire altered continuously as old and new enemies sought to extend their territories. The map shows the state of affairs in the reign of Michael VIII Palaiologos (1261-1282) and more particularly after the death of the despot of Epirus, Michael II Angelos in 1271.

The Byzantines did not dare confront them militarily. Instead, Andronikos II built walls at Christoupolis and the narrow pass of Akontisma, hoping to at least prevent the Catalans from threatening Constantinople should they decide to invade Thrace again. At the same time, he strengthened all the major urban centres of Macedonia with men and provisions, so that they would feel securely in Byzantine hands. These measures brought immediate results. When the Catalans reached Thessalonike, they found the rural settlements deserted, since the inhabitants had fled with their possessions to the local fortified centres. Thanks to Andronikos II, the Catalans encountered well-fortified and strongly garrisoned towns, and an impregnable Thessalonike. In their despair, they decided to return to Thrace. Before they had even set out, they were informed of the heavy Byzantine defences at Christoupolis. Consequently, in the spring of that year, they withdrew to Thessaly. There they were pursued, and thus they fled to the south.

THE WAR BETWEEN ANDRONIKOS II AND ANDRONIKOS III AND ITS REPERCUSSIONS IN MACEDONIA

In 1320 a new civil war broke out between Andronikos II and his grandson, Andronikos III. In that year, Andronikos II's son and co-emperor Michael IX died, but Andronikos II stripped the younger Andronikos of his rights of succession. This war weakened the empire and provoked a massive upheaval within Macedonia. Thessalonike, in particular, was a battle ground of domestic conflict for many years. The war passed through several phases, and gave the Serbs the chance to intervene in the internal affairs of the empire. At length it ended with the victory of the young Andronikos III. After capturing Thessalonike and other Macedonian and Thessalian cities (Edessa, Kastoria, Beroia, Pherai), he became master of Constantinople in the middle of 1328, forcing the aged Andronikos II to abdicate.[22]

Immediately on his elevation to the throne, Andronikos III comprehended the need for fortresses and fortified towns in the northern provinces of the empire. In the Axios valley he constructed the fortress Gynaikokastron. In the Strymon valley he fortified the town of Siderokastron. On the coast, near the mouth of the river, he fortified Amphipolis. Although these actions were absolutely indispensable, they still could not restrain the Serbs under the capable leadership of Stefan Dušan. With the help of the *megas dux* Syrgiannes Palaiologos (annoyed with his kinsman, emperor Andronikos III), Dušan captured Ochrid, Prilep, Stromnitsa and Kastoria (1334).[23] In the summer of the same year, the Serbian armies appeared before Thessalonike. The Byzantines, however, managed to resolve the crisis. Syrgiannes was assassinated, and peace was concluded between Dušan and Andronikos III on 26 August, 1334. The previous *status quo* was restored, i.e. the Serbs returned the fortresses of Ochrid, Stromnitsa and Kastoria.[24] Peace between the two adversaries was maintained until 1341. In the interval, Andronikos strengthened the Macedonian defences, refortifying Serrhai, Melenikon, Stromnitsa, Prilep and Ochrid.

NEW CIVIL WARS: JOHN V AND JOHN VI KANTAKOUZENOS, AND THE ENTRY OF THE TURKS INTO EUROPE

After Andronikos' death in 1341, the Grand Domestic John Kantakouzenos took over the regency for John V, the emperor's minor son. He faced opposition, however, from the dowager empress, Anne of Savoy, the patriarch John Kalekas, and Alexios Apokaukos. In October 1341, he was proclaimed emperor by the army at Didymoteichon, thus opening a new period of civil conflict.[25]

In the course of these wars, social and religious conflicts of frightful severity erupted between Zealots and aristocrats,[26] and the Hesychasts and Barlaam and Akindynos.[27] These conflicts heightened the confusion and agitation, and are characterized by a variety of themes, ideologies and causal factors. The opposition between Kantakouzenos and Anna was occasioned by political and dynastic considerations. The clash between the Hesychasts and Barlaam and Akindynos was purely religious in character. The tensions between Zealots and aristocrats, finally, have the hallmarks of class and social conflict.

It was also typical of these civil wars that the two opposing factions, Kantakouzenos and the regency forces, allied variously with the Slavs and the Turks for military assistance. The Turks, in particular, profited from the weakness of the Byzantines. They strengthened themselves at the expense of the empire, and in 1354 became permanently established in Europe.[28] In short, the civil wars of the mid-fourteenth century set Byzantium on the course of final and total collapse.

As in the war between Andronikos II and Andronikos III, so too the new civil war provoked disorders in the urban centres of Thrace, and even more in Macedonia. Thessalonike was a hotbed of strife, for the antagonisms between the aristocrats and the Zealots (who represented the popular ranks) had reached breaking point. A bloody reckoning was soon to come.

In the spring of 1342, the governor of Thessalonike, *protostrator* Theodore Synadenos, joined Kantakouzenos' side. Kantakouzenos called upon Synadenos to arrange for the surrender of the city, but the inhabitants were sympathetic to Palaiologos. When imperial forces marched out against Kantakouzenos, he abandoned the project and headed towards Beroia and Edessa.[29] To find support against his enemies, he allied with the Serbian ruler Stefan Dušan, and somewhat later with the emir of Aydin, Umur.[30]

Meanwhile the Zealots in Thessalonike took the side of the legitimate emperor John V, and forced Synadenos to abandon the city. He and many other aristocrats fled, while the Zealots plundered their possessions (1342). The Grand Domestic, Alexios Apokaukos, was barely informed of the alliance between Kantakouzenos and Dušan when he sailed to Thessalonike with a large fleet. He

strengthened the Zealots, and managed rather successfully to turn events in Macedonia in his favour. Abandoned by his supporters, Kantakouzenos was in a difficult situation. The Thessalian magnates altered the situation, however, when they allied with him. Kantakouzenos' change of fortune alarmed Dušan, who quickly joined with John V. The latter had himself already concluded a pact with Alexander of Bulgaria. It was at this juncture that Kantakouzenos turned to Umur. Thus the two Greek adversaries were fighting one another with foreign troops, which were naturally interested only in exploiting the Byzantine squabbles to their own advantage. In fact, in the course of these conflicts the Serbs conquered Edessa, Kastoria and Florina. The Bulgarians acquired territory in the Rhodope, together with Philippopolis and Stenemachos, while the Turks seized enormous booty and savagely pillaged Thrace (1343).

Meanwhile the Zealots foiled Kantakouzenos' efforts to take Thessalonike with Umur's help. Moreover, they assumed full control of the city government, proclaiming as their goal total autonomy (1344).

Nonetheless, it seems that a representative from Constantinople participated in governing the city, either then or shortly thereafter. Such a representative was John Apokaukos, the son of Alexios Apokaukos. In his attempt to crush both the Zealots and the wealthy, John unleashed the bloody disorders of 1345, which brought about his own death and the slaughter of many wealthy citizens. The Zealots returned to full power, and imposed their own system of government on the city for about four years.[31] Details are lacking, yet it appears that their style of government was similar to the former — except that now the power which had belonged to the wealthy was taken over by the Zealots.

Meanwhile Dušan captured Serrhai in the autumn of 1345, and at the end of the same year was proclaimed emperor of Serbia and Roumania.[32] During the next outburst of fighting in the civil wars, in 1347, Kantakouzenos was recognized as the lawful co-emperor. With this the power of the Zealots collapsed since the reconciliation between the two emperors liquidated their political programme, namely the support of John V. Consequently, Kantakouzenos was recognized even in Thessalonike, which he entered in 1350 in the company of John V.[33]

Soon afterwards, the new emperor John VI Kantakouzenos launched attacks upon Dušan. The Serbs repeatedly took and lost Beroia and Edessa. They even besieged Thessalonike, but were not successful.

In the summer of 1351, John V allied with the Serbs, disaffected because he had been pushed aside by his co-emperor and father-in-law Kantakouzenos. The Serbs seized the opportunity to take up threatening positions outside Thessalonike. Anne of Savoy's intervention saved the day, for she persuaded the Serbian ruler (perhaps by bribery) to abandon his designs on Thessalonike.[34]

Nearly all of Macedonia up to Serrhai, therefore, belonged to Dušan. His death a short while later (20 December, 1355) was followed by the dissolution of his state, an event which delivered the Byzantines from the Serbian threat.

Already in 1351, however, the Byzantine empire had become involved in struggles with the Italian cities, and after 1354 new conflicts arose between John V and John VI Kantakouzenos. In November 1354 Kantakouzenos abdicated. Ironically, the previous March he had witnessed his erstwhile allies, the Turks, capture Gallipoli, and thus obtain a permanent foothold in Europe.

MACEDONIA FROM 1354-1430

The capture of Gallipoli by the Turks in 1354 marked the beginning of a new period of history not only for Byzantium but also for the other Balkan countries. In his attempts to find allies against the Turks, the emperor John V turned to the Serbs and in the summer of 1363 despatched an embassy headed by the patriarch Kallistos to meet the widow of Stefan Dušan at Serrhai.[1] Because of a chance incident they failed to reach agreement and the Byzantine leader was obliged to approach the countries of the West to seek their aid against the infidel.[2]

Despite the continuing series of conquests by the Turks, the Balkan peoples failed to unite in concerted action against them, and in 1371 an army under the Serbian leaders who succeeded Stefan Dušan was annihilated at the battle of Cirmen. There was now no power in the southern Balkans capable of halting the Turkish advance. Not only the Serbs, whose state was dissolved, but also the Bulgarians and the Byzantines became tributary subjects of the Sultan and were obliged henceforth to take part in his campaigns.[3]

THE SUCCESSES OF MANUEL PALAIOLOGOS IN MACEDONIA

The only Christian leader who attempted to resist the Turks was Manuel, son of the Byzantine emperor John V and subsequently emperor Manuel II, who was governor of Thessalonike from 1396. Manuel took advantage of the defeat of the Serbs at Cirmen to attempt to regain the Greek territories of south-east Macedonia which had until then been in their possession. He appears to have made contact and negotiated with the Greek nobles, or 'heads' of Serrhai (capital of the ephemeral state of John Uğlieša)[4] and with the Serbian officers who had survived the bloody battle, and he entered the city in November 1371. He proceeded immediately to strengthen the weak points of the fortress and repaired or constructed other defensive works with a view to stiffening the defence of the local garrisons and the inhabitants of the surrounding areas against the Turks. Manuel made every attempt to organize a systematic defence, going as far as to expropriate half of the property belonging to the monasteries and distributing it provisionally as *pronoia* to the military, despite the opposition and the protests of Isidore Glavas, archbishop of Thessalonike.[5]

It is difficult to determine the boundaries of Manuel's

217. The internal dynastic wars and the steady decline of the Bulgarian state opened up new opportunities for the development and expansion of the Serbian kingdom. These were intelligently exploited by the great kral, Stephen Dušan (1331-55). The map shows Macedonia and the adjacent area at the time of his death.

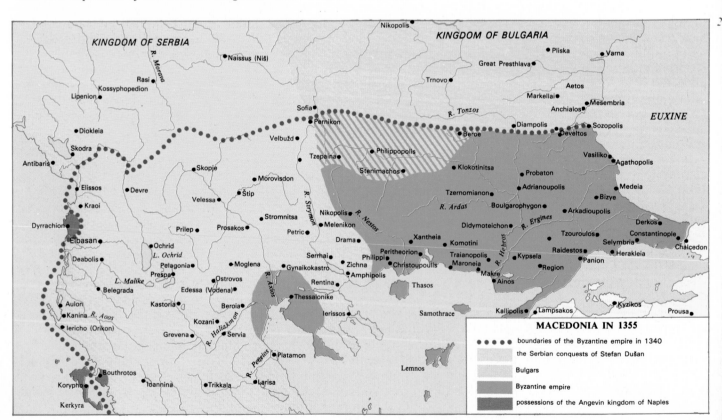

authority with any accuracy. Since he held Serrhai, however, it must be assumed that his authority extended beyond the Strymon, probably as far as the Nestos, while in the west it will undoubtedly have reached Mt. Bermion and included Beroia.[6] It is equally difficult to determine how long he held this demarcation line. Turkish historians, and geographers, writing long after the event, claim that the Ottomans captured fortified cities in Macedonia between 1373 and 1376.[7] The Byzantine sources, however, date the capture of many of these cities approximately a decade later, between the years 1383 and 1387. What is beyond dispute is that anarchy prevailed in Macedonia during this decade, as irregular *gazis* made repeated raids and for short intervals probably occupied some of the cities of Macedonia which were subsequently recovered by the Byzantines.

In 1382 Manuel, who had left Thessalonike for some unknown reason, returned there from Constantinople in order to organize the defence of the city.[8] The situation in Macedonia was rapidly becoming more disquieting as the Turkish danger became ever more threatening. Manuel, once he had succeeded in reconciling the opposing political factions in Thessalonike, began to make preparations to resist the Turks. He made himself master of a number of strong points around the city and strengthened the authority of the Byzantines in Serrhai. His successes quickly became known in Constantinople, where they aroused great enthusiasm, and volunteers soon began to arrive in Thessalonike to fight with him.[9] Manuel was also

active politically, and his suzerainty was recognized by the despot of Epirus, Thomas Preljubovic, and by the Caesar of Thessaly, Alexios Angelos.[10]

Manuel's successes naturally incurred the wrath of sultan Murad I, who ordered Hayr ad-Din Pasha, the *beylerbey* of Roumeli to move against western Macedonia. Hayr ad-Din was followed by the *gazi* Evrenos. The precise details of the campaign are unknown, but is is clear that the various fortresses in Macedonia could not be held in the face of the mass of Turkish troops. These fortresses are probably to be located at Christoupolis (Kavala), Chrysoupolis, Rentina, Gynaikokastron, Hagios Basileios, Galatista, Beroia, Kitros, Platamon and Kassandreia, though it it is not possible to be absolutely certain on this point. The statement that they were besieged at the same time as the siege of Thessalonike suggests that the majority of them were captured by the Turks in the period 1383-87, and probably during the early years of this period.[11]

One of the first of the large cities to come under Turkish domination after a siege was Serrhai, which fell in September 1383.[12] The city was sacked and the inhabitants enslaved, including the metropolitan, Matthew Phakrases. Nonetheless, the fact that Murad did not convert any of the churches of Serrhai into mosques is an indication that he was relatively well disposed towards the inhabitants who had resisted him, possibly because he wished to put the minds of the Christians at rest, in view of the fact that the Turkish conquest had not yet been consolidated. It is also certain that Murad I conceded the privilege of self-

218. *Despite the increasing danger from the Ottoman Turks who reached European soil with the capture of Gallipoli in 1354, the Byzantine world remained divided into several* *kingdoms ruled by members of the imperial family. Shifting alliances between them and the increasing weakness of the central power hastened the Ottoman advance.*

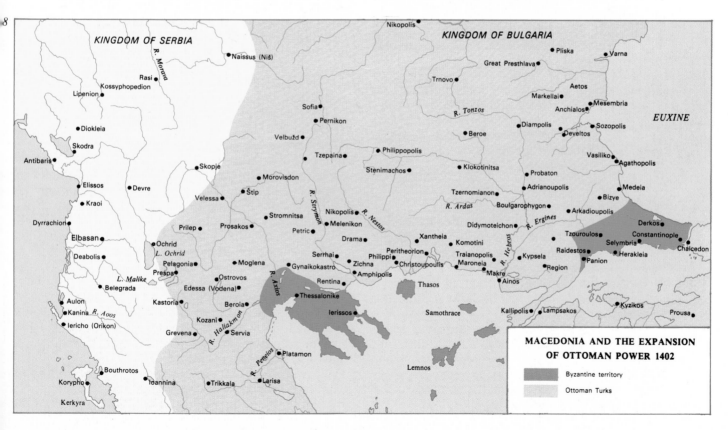

MACEDONIA AND THE EXPANSION OF OTTOMAN POWER 1402

Byzantine territory

Ottoman Turks

219. The emperor Manuel II was associated with one of the most calamitous phases of Macedonian history. He took the habit and died as a monk, Matthew. His portrait appears in a miniature in a manuscript of the Epitaphios which he commissioned to honour his brother Theodore, despot of the Morea. Paris, Bibliotèque Nationale.

government to the people of Serrhai.[13]

After Serrhai, Drama was captured, followed by Zichna, Monastir, Gynaikokastron and the fortress at Hagios Basileios.[14] The ring had begun to close around Thessalonike. A victory won at Chortiatis brought the Turks beneath the walls of the city; Hayr ad-Din, after a vain attempt to secure the surrender of the city, proceeded to a blockade, that was destined to last for almost four years. At this time of adversity, Manuel displayed all his virtues: aggressiveness, decisiveness and unrivalled courage. These are typified by his speech to the inhabitants, known as the *Admonition to the people of Thessalonike,* in which he insisted that death was preferable to capture and humiliation.[15]

THE FIRST CAPTURE OF THESSALONIKE BY THE TURKS, AND THE SITUATION IN MACEDONIA UNTIL 1421

As well as organizing the defence of the city, Manuel attempted to secure powerful allies and entered into negotiations with the despot of the Morea and the ruler of Corinth. He even sent ambassadors to seek the assistance of the Pope and the Venetians.[16] None of these efforts bore fruit, however, and all that remained was to organize his defences as effectively as possible. The effects of the blockade began to make themselves felt more strongly as each day passed, and a spirit of defeatism began to grip the inhabitants, who wanted to surrender. Throughout the entire siege, moreover, the Turks repeatedly proposed very favourable terms for the surrender of the city. Manuel attempted to stiffen their will to resist, but in vain; in April, 1387, he left the city with a few of his men and within a few days Thessalonike surrendered to Hayr ad-Din, who showed respect for the inhabitants and did not plunder the city. Murad I did not incorporate Thessalonike within his empire at this stage. He recognized its civic autonomy and contented himself with the exaction of a tribute, the *haraciye,* leaving a garrison of a few men in the acropolis. Similar conditions were imposed on Christoupolis which, like Chrysoupolis, surrendered at the same time as Thessalonike.[17] Thessalonike itself continued to receive privileged treatment until 1391, when it was suspended by the new sultan Bayezid, who had succeeded his father Murad I after the battle of Kossyphopedion in 1389.[18] The city was subjected to military occupation; shortly afterwards, in 1395, the harsh tribute of devçirme was exacted. Later, further privileges seem to have been ceded to the city after the intervention of the metropolitan Isidore and, after 1396, of his successor Gabriel.[19]

During the nigh on four year siege of Thessalonike, the Turks captured Beroia which probably became a tribute-paying town.[20] It is not known with complete certainty when Naousa, Edessa, Kastoria and Ochrid were captured. According to tradition, Edessa put up a protracted resistance but was ultimately betrayed and captured in 1389.[21]

The sources are equally unclear on the question of the capture of Kastoria, which was in the possession of the Albanian rulers Stoyias and Theodore Mouzakis, and we do not know whether the city capitulated on terms or was taken by assault.[22] In 1385 Prilep and Monastir, at that time under the control of the Serbian leader Markos Kralis (Kraljevic), were also captured;[23] Ochrid probably fell during this same period. Kitros and the fortress at Platamon, which lay further south in the direction of Thessaly were taken shortly afterwards. Unlike many other fortresses, they were not destroyed.[24]

Servia was taken soon afterwards, possibly in 1393, when Bayezid abandoned his ventures in Asia Minor and came to campaign in person in Europe. The monks of Athos declared their obedience to Bayezid I.

Meanwhile Manuel who, as we saw earlier, had abandoned Thessalonike, was driven after many wanderings to the point where he had to take refuge at the court of the

Turkish sultan, Murad, at Prousa; after the death of his father John V he succeeded in having himself proclaimed emperor in Constantinople, after driving out the usurper to the throne, the nephew of John VII.

The policy of conquest pursued by Bayezid came to an abrupt end on July 28, 1402, the day he was defeated and taken prisoner by the Mongol Tamerlane at the bloody battle of Ankara. The result of the battle and the struggles for dominance between the successors of Bayezid changed the situation in Macedonia yet again. Süleyman, Bayezid's son, laid claim to the Ottoman state and established himself in the European provinces; in 1403 he came to an agreement by which he restored to the Byzantines certain territories, including the region around Thessalonike and a number of other cities as far as the Strymon (including Chalkidike and a small hinterland reaching as far as Chortiatis).[25]

In the power struggle between the sons of Bayezid, the emperor Manuel II assisted Mehmed against his brother Mousa in 1413. Mehmed was thus able to unify the Ottoman state in 1413, and the by now diminished territories of Byzantium remained relatively undisturbed until the death of the Turkish sultan in 1421. However, the Macedonian countryside was repeatedly ravaged during this period and in 1416 Mehmed laid siege to Thessalonike, where some of the counter-claimants to the Turkish throne had taken refuge.[26]

Despite all this, the period from the battle of Ankara in 1402 and the death of Mehmed I in 1421 was one in which Thessalonike and the other areas of Macedonia that had been restored to Byzantine control enjoyed relative peace and prosperity. John VII Palaiologos was governor of Thessalonike and the Macedonian hinterland from 1403 to 1408, followed after his death by Demetrios Laskarios Leontaris until 1415; he was in turn replaced by the son of Manuel II, Andronikos Palaiologos. Andronikos ruled the city as an independent princeling and issued decrees which he signed with the title 'despot'.

THE FINAL CONQUEST OF THESSALONIKE BY THE TURKS

The accession of Murad II to the Turkish throne, however, marked the resumption by the Turks of a policy of conquest. In 1422 he despatched troops to Thessalonike and ordered the blockade of the city. Andronikos, appreciating the impossibility of continuing to defend the city with the few forces at his disposal, came to an understanding with the Venetians and handed over the city to them in 1423, under the condition that the rights of the inhabitants should be respected and that the archbishop and the Church should retain their privileges.[27] On 14 September, 1423, the Venetians took over the government of the city. However, they very soon began to restrict civic autonomy and to violate the privileges they had promised to respect and came to be hated by the people. Many of the inhabitants left the city, while those who stayed behind suffered increasingly from the lack of food; repeated complaints to Venice brought no results. In the six years that

220. Manuel II made courageous and determined efforts to strengthen Thessalonike so that it was a serious obstacle to the Ottoman advance. He is depicted in this 15th century miniature with his wife Helen and three of their six sons, John, Theodore and Andronikos, blessed by the Virgin Mary and the infant Christ. Paris, Louvre.

followed the establishment of the Venetians in Thessalonike their position continuously hardened, and many of the people began increasingly to take the view that Turkish domination might be preferable. Murad II, wishing to exploit this situation, appeared with his army before the walls of Thessalonike on 26 March, 1430, and demanded its surrender.

Many of the citizens, as we have seen, were ready to surrender peacefully; they realized that in any event the city was completely inadequately defended, the Venetians having stationed only one man to every two or three battlements. Even with only these sketchy measures, however, the Venetians refused to surrender the city, and to ensure that the local residents put up as determined a resistance as their own men, they dispersed them amongst the Venetian soldiers. The Turkish preparations continued meanwhile, and Murad ordered an assault on the third day after his arrival, making himself master of the city on 28 March.[28] The Venetians suffered great losses but the majority of them succeeded in escaping in their ships and saving themselves. By contrast, the city and its inhabitants suffered terrible hardships. After three days of plunder and enslaving, Murad entered the city and at once worshipped in the church of the Acheiropoietos, which was immediately converted into a mosque. The seal of the sultan is preserved to this day on the eighth column in the colonnade on the north side.

Murad then freed many of the leading citizens and sent them to live within the city, which had been sacked and had suffered enormous damage during the attack. He also ordered Turks from Yannitsa to take up residence in the city and promised not to molest any of the former residents who wished to return and resume their lives there.

The capture of Thessalonike in 1430 marked the final end of all resistance in Macedonia, which was not to be liberated until almost five hundred years later.

INSTITUTIONS, SOCIETY, ECONOMY

ADMINISTRATIVE ORGANIZATION

The pattern of government and administration in Macedonia was far from static. As we have seen, prior to the mid-ninth century only two themes were established on Macedonian soil, namely Thessalonike and Macedonia. At the end of the ninth century a third theme, the Strymon, was carved out of territory detached from Macedonia, extending from the Strymon river to the Nestos. The former theme of Macedonia now covered an area from the Nestos river to Adrianople. Despite its name, the theme of Macedonia was in fact Thracian and not Macedonian in character. The administrative organization of Macedonia changed radically following the general reforms of John Tzimiskes and Basil II. Thus the Escorial *Taktikon* (971-75) mentions a duke of Thessalonike, and generals (*strategoi*) of Thessalonike, Beroia, Strymon-Chrysavas, Drougouvitia, Edessa and New Strymon. Each of these *strategoi* governed a corresponding district or theme.[1]

This increase in the number of themes, as witnessed by the Escorial *Taktikon,* coincides with another general trend which arises in this period, but persists through the decay and final collapse of the theme system. The phenomenon of which we speak is the appearance of *strategoi* who do not always command great military districts (themes), but who govern cities, castles or other smaller areas.[2] Certain scholars assumed that references to *strategoi* of this type indicate the existence of homonymous themes.[3] Others correctly rejected this opinion, yet they failed to explain the causes behind the phenomenon, and perhaps did not even comprehend its deeper significance.[4] In essence, the establishment of *strategoi*-administrators in cities represents an effort to curb the power of the great military themes and their commanders. In particular, it limited the ability of such generals to stage revolts, of which John Tzimiskes and Basil II both had intimate personal experience. In the following century, however, this weakening of the top military leadership had destructive results, for it led to the debilitation of the state. Generally speaking, the office of *dux* was strengthened, while those of *strategos* and katepan were weakened.[5]

After the Bulgarian wars, Basil II instituted a large scale administrative and military reorganization of Bulgaria. He divided the region into two large administrative districts, the katepanate of Bulgaria, and the Paristrion or Paradunavon theme. These were governed by a *dux* and katepan, the hierarchical ranking being *dux*, katepan and then *strategos*. The katepanate of Bulgaria encompassed the western provinces of the former Bulgarian state, with Skopje as its centre. Its territory was bounded in the north-east by the line from Vidin to Sofia, and the Haimos mountains. On the east, it was bordered by the themes of Macedonia, south-east and south by Strymon, Thessalonike and Hellas. To the south-west and west it touched the themes of Dyrrachion and Nikopolis. In the north-west it abutted Serbia, and, to the north, after the capture of the area around Sirmium it reached the Danube.[6]

In the following decades of the eleventh century, certain other changes may be observed in the administrative organization of the Macedonian region. The sources refer to a judicial and fiscal entity which included the areas of Voleron, Strymon and Thessalonike. This unit appears for the first time in 1042, in a document from the monastery of Iveron. Here we find mention of John, *spatharios* and *krites* (judge) of Voleron, Strymon and Thessalonike.[7] These regions continue to be linked throughout the following years, with the exception of a brief period from 1079 to 1081. In 1084, the usual juncture of Voleron, Strymon and Thessalonike reappears.

The last reference to a *praktor* (agent) or *anagrapheus* (scribe) this administrative entity is in 1102. The last mention of this tri-regional theme occurs in 1198, in a chrysobull of Alexios Angelos III to the Venetians.[8] In this chrysobull, the places where the Venetians enjoyed privileges are enumerated. Concerning Macedonia the following areas are mentioned: (1) Voleron-Strymon-Thessalonike(2) Beroia, with the katepanate of Kitros; (3) Prilep-Pelagonia-Molyskos-Moglena; (4) Skopje, together with the district of Koripon; (5) Servia; (6) Kastoria. It should be observed, however, that this chrysobull survives in a Latin redaction, and it uses the term provinces not theme.

Typically, the dignitaries which the sources represent as 'functioning' in these supposed themes are nearly always

221. The division of the Balkan peninsula into themes was an administrative measure designed to provide effective defence against invasions and to check internal unrest. The map shows the distribution of themes in the Balkan peninsula in the 10th century.

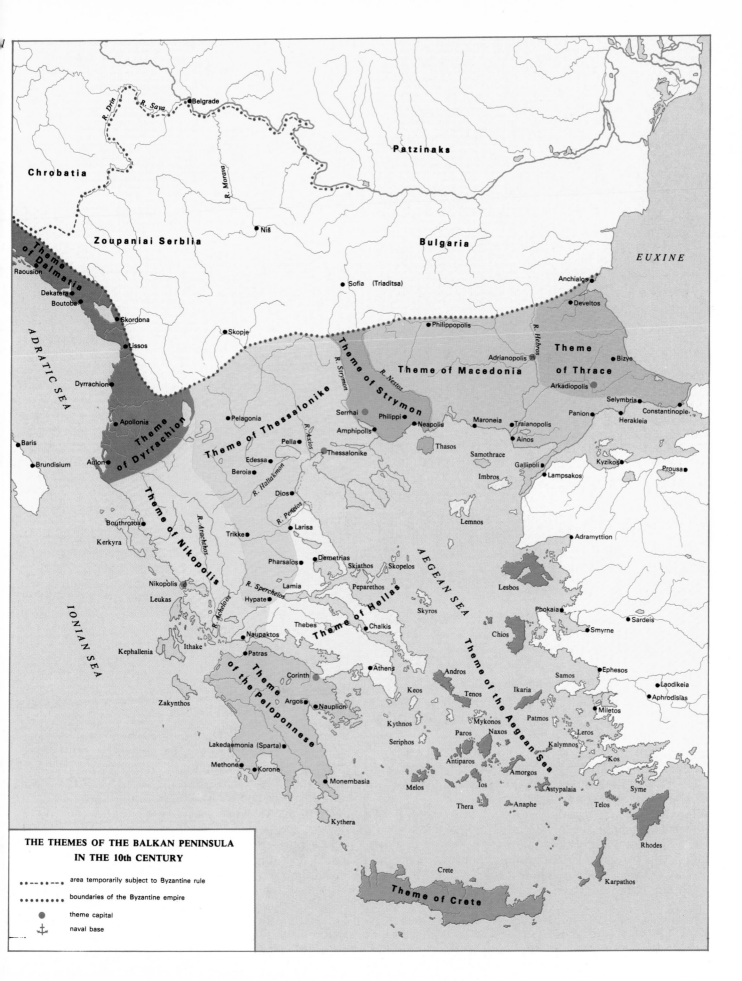

THE THEMES OF THE BALKAN PENINSULA
IN THE 10th CENTURY

---•---•---•--- area temporarily subject to Byzantine rule

•••••••••• boundaries of the Byzantine empire

● theme capital

⚓ naval base

222. A 13th century flask from Gratine in the Rhodope mountains with relief representations of the well-known saints of Thessalonike, Demetrios and Theodore. The myrrh which spurted from the tombs of the saints was distributed to the many pilgrims in similar phials.

fiscal officials. Some scholars have rightly concluded that such themes have been transformed into essentially fiscal jurisdictions.[9] Certainly the long-standing articulation of fiscal and military districts contributed to this change, since every theme also constituted a fiscal entity, at the head of which stood the theme commander.[10]

From the eleventh century, fiscal agents replaced the theme commanders. The former, however, were not regular public officials. Rather, their salary was taken out of local taxes. They were invested with the competence of a tax official for the year in which tax payments fell due.[11] For this reason they often subjected the tax payers to great abuses and excesses.

As is well known, the Franks did not maintain the Byzantine system of fusing civil and military administration. This was antithetical to their own feudal system.

Villehardouin provides us with an interesting example of its operation. Boniface of Montferrat, king of Thessalonike, granted Geoffrey de Villehardouin the right to choose either Mosynopolis with its environs or Serrhai as his fief. He chose Mosynopolis and so became Boniface's vassal, naturally with the stipulation that he obey the (Latin) emperor of Constantinople.[12]

Whatever remained of the military character of the theme system completely disappeared after the Frankish conquest. Where it still appears, the term theme indicates a fiscal jurisdiction, whether over small and unknown regions, or large and well-known areas.[13] As previously stated, exactly the same occurred with the katepanates or *katepanikia*.

The heads of cities, fortresses or local districts took over the tasks of administration. These *kephalai* or *kephalatikevontes*, as they are called in the sources, concentrated all local authority in their own hands.[14]

ECCLESIASTICAL ORGANIZATION

As has been said in an earlier chapter (see page 230), evidence for the ecclesiastical organization of Macedonia is provided by synodal acts containing lists of episcopal signators, as well as the so-called 'Orders of Precedence'. Thus we are informed that in 879 a synod convened to settle the question of Photios, at which the bishoprics of Drougouvitia and Strymon were represented. The bishopric of Drougouvitia was in the Rhodope mountains.[15] The bishopric of Strymon was located near Kleisoura in the Strymon area.[16]

In Leo VI's *Diatyposis* (early tenth century), the bishopric of Strymon is no longer mentioned. The bishopric of Drougouvitia, however, together with the bishoprics of Kitros, Beroia, Servia and Kassandreia, constituted all the suffragan sees of Thessalonike. From the time of its detachment from Rome through the ninth century, Thessalonike served as the sole metropolis in Macedonia.[17]

In the second half of the eighth century, the archbishopric of Serrhai was created. In the last third of the tenth century, it was promoted to metropolitan rank. Prior to the thirteenth century, Serrhai had no known suffragan bishoprics.

The metropolis of Philippi is mentioned in the early ninth century. According to Gelzer's *Notitia 2* (early tenth century), the bishoprics of Polystylos, Velikeia, Christoupolis, Smolenoi, Kaisaropolis and Alektryopolis were dependent upon Philippi. As Paul Lemerle has justly observed, the fact that cities with Slavic names like 'Velikeia' and 'Smolenoi' achieved episcopal status reflects the measures which had been taken to Hellenize the Slavs settled in eastern Macedonia. Lemerle locates the bishopric of Velikeia on the western slopes of the Rhodopes, and the bishopric of Smolenoi in the mountain areas to the north of Philippi. These two bishoprics disappeared in the Palaiologan period.[18]

After subjecting the Bulgarians and dissolving the first Bulgarian empire, Basil II reorganized the Bulgarian church. Three *sigillia* from 1020 preserve echoes of Basil's ecclesiastical policy in what was formerly Samuel's empire. Unfortunately, the original organizational decree has perished. It is evident however, that Basil abolished the Bulgarian patriarchate, and founded the autonomous (autocephalous) archbishopric of 'Bulgaria'. Ochrid was designated as the archiepiscopal see, and its first archbishop was the monk John. Basil restored the ecclesiastical order which had prevailed in the Balkan peninsula before 945, although with certain changes which also influenced Macedonia.[19]

The *sigillia* indicate that Basil assigned all the bishoprics which had ever been included in Peter and Samuel's empire to the archbishop of Bulgaria's jurisdiction. Thus Servia, Beroia and Stagoi were subordinated to Ochrid, an action which later provoked controversy. The new archbishopric thus comprised an enormous territory, including bishoprics from Epirus and Thessaly up to the Danube. According to Ostrogorsky, Basil II gave the archbishoric of Bulgaria such a vast territory as a means of limiting the patriarch of Constantinople's power. The same historian also says that each archbishop of Bulgaria was appointed by the emperor, and hence the Bulgarian church became an instrument of the imperial government.[20] Such explanations are not convincing. Basil had no reason to limit the power of the patriarch, especially in a period when no opposition was forthcoming from that front. Moreover, he had no compelling reason to subordinate Greek sees to the Bulgarian church, particularly a bishopric such as Beroia. The city had indeed been conquered by Samuel, yet this occurred late in the war and the Byzantines quickly recovered it.

In our opinion, one may legitimately doubt the accuracy of the information conveyed by Basil II's *sigillia,* at least in the form they have survived.[21]

In any case, the new archbishopric produced many distinguished men and formed a brilliant centre of Greek culture. Illustrious figures such as Theophylact, John Komnenos, Demetrios Chomatianos, John Kamateros and others graced the archbishopric of Bulgaria with their learning.[22]

The three metropolitan sees in the area of Macedonia — i.e. Thessalonike, Philippi and Serrhai continued to exist in the eleventh century. In the middle of that century, the metropolis of Thessalonike included eleven bishoprics. The six new bishoprics were Kampania or Kastrion, Petras, Herkulioi or Ardameri, Ierissos (Mount Athos), Lete and Rentina, and Vardariotes or Turks.[23]

The Vardariotes or Turks were Hungarians who had settled around the middle Axios. After their conversion to Christianity, a bishopric was formed with the same name. The Vardariote Turks frequently appear in the Byzantine sources from 1020 on.[24]

The *Notitia* mention these same bishoprics in the metropolis of Thessalonike even later, in the time of Alexios I Komnenos.[25]

In the twelfth century, three metropolitan sees are again recorded for Macedonia — Thessalonike, with eight bishoprics, Serrhai and Philippi, with seven bishoprics.[26] Unfortunately, the names of these suffragan bishoprics are not recorded, and hence it is unclear how they were distributed throughout Macedonia.

After the Frankish conquest in 1204, the state of affairs naturally changed drastically. Most of Macedonia came under the authority of Boniface of Montferrat, but other parts were claimed or came under the jurisdiction of the despotate of Epirus.[27] Nonetheless, the *Taxeis* of the thirteenth century show no great changes. Perhaps those who drafted them remained attached to an ideal image of the status of the Byzantine church and the extent of its bishoprics. In any case, Andronikos II's *Ekthesis* (thirteenth-fourteenth century) lists Thessalonike in eleventh place, whereas formerly it had ranked sixteenth in the ecclesiastical hierarchy.[28] According to one thirteenth century source, the see of Thessalonike controlled the bishoprics of Lykostome (or the vale of Tempe) and Platamon, in addition to the bishoprics previously mentioned.[29]

In Andronikos' *Ekthesis,* the metropolitan cities of Serrhai, Beroia, Philippi and Christoupolis are listed in a new order of hierarchy, and the new metropolis of Drama is mentioned.[30]

A tendency to reduce the territory of the great metropolitan sees, and to create more, but smaller ecclesiastical jurisdictions, is thus in evidence. In conformity with this pattern, the bishopric of Zichnai (formerly dependent on the metropolis of Serrhai) was promoted to metropolitan rank in the reign of Andronikos III. Similarly, the bishopric of Nikopolis was detached from the metropolis of Philippi and subordinated to the metropolis of Serrhai, in the place of the former bishopric of Zichnai.

THE MONASTIC STATE OF MOUNT ATHOS

History of Monastic Life on the Holy Mountain

One of the most important events in the history of eastern monasticism, and of the church in general, was the founding of a vigorous monastic community on Mount Athos in the second half of the tenth century. Our sources attest monastic settlements on Mount Athos as early as the second half of the ninth century. There is mention of *lavrai,* or small groups of hermits with a common superior *(geron)* and a central house of prayer.

This community also had some rudimentary form of organization. Presiding over it was the primate *(protos),* who governed the monks in cooperation with the abbots *(hegoumenoi).* From time to time the monks would hold assemblies at Karyes — in the early period, three times a year. Karyes was their administrative centre, and is variously referred to as the *Koinon,* the *Mese,* 'the first' *(protaton),* 'the chief', 'the lavra of Karyes' and 'the seat of Karyes'.[31] In 883, Basil I provided Athos with the first imperial charter of privileges. A *sigillion* forbade military and administrative officials from disturbing the monks at any time. These officials, as well as local shepherds and inhabitants, were denied access to the Holy Mountain beyond Ierissos.[32] Before 893, the first expression of coenobitic monasticism was the monastery of Kolobos near Ierissos, founded by a disciple of Euthymios of Thessalonike, John Kolobos. In 893, Leo VI revoked the privileges which the

223. *The establishment of the monastic state of Athos was one of the greatest achievements in the history of eastern monasticism and indeed of the Church. For more than a thousand years it has upheld orthodoxy and furthered intellectual and cultural* life, surviving all the many disasters which have from time to time shattered its calm. The picture shows the katholikon and part of the court of Esphigmenou on Mount Athos, founded at the end of the 10th or beginning of the 11th century.

Kolobos monastery had managed to acquire at the expense of the other hermits, evidently on the pretext of a charter which the emperor had issued.[33]

Xeropotamou is apparently the oldest of the great monasteries on Mount Athos. Its founding charter dates back to 956. In that year, Constantine IX and Romanos II ordered John, *protospatharios* and grand chartulary of the general accounting office, to endow the monastery with a parcel of land near Ozolimnos 'so that it might draw profit from it, for heretofore the monastery had not taken even a footstep towards self-sufficiency.'[34] This document constitutes the first imperial grant of privileges to a particular monastery on Mount Athos.

In May 964, Nikephoros Phokas issued a chrysobull to the monastery of Great Lavra, which includes a reference to two other chrysobulls which he had previously issued to the same monastery.[35]

Great Lavra was a large *koinobion* with a fully developed organization. Its foundation may be principally attributed to Saint Athanasios of Trebizond, who drew up its *typikon* in 973-75, following the *typikon* of the Studite monastery in Constantinople as his model.[36]

After the death of Nikephoros Phokas, quarrels between the older hermits and monks dwelling in lavras called forth the intervention of John Tzimiskes. He dispatched Euthymios, the abbot of Studion, to Athos with instructions to investigate the state of affairs. Under Euthymios' supervision, the council of elders of Athos composed a *typikon* for the community in 971. This constituted the Holy Mountain's constitutional charter, known as the *tragos* because it was written on a parchment of goatskin (τράγος=goat). Its authority was augmented by John Tzimiskes' signature in imperial red ink. This is the oldest signature of a Byzantine emperor preserved in the original.

224. *From the very earliest years of its existence, the Athos community represented all the various expressions of orthodoxy. Greek, Iberian, Bulgarian, Serbian, Russian and even Latin monks from all over the world were united in prayer to the* God of the Gospels. *The picture shows the exterior of the relatively modern katholikon at the Russian monastery of Saint Panteleimon with its onion-shaped domes, each topped by a cross.*

With this *typikon* the monastic society was formally recognized, including its three component types of organization: the monastery, the lavra and the isolated hermitage.[37]

The subsequent growth of the community on Athos was rapid. The period from 979-80 to 1076 saw the founding of Iveron (979-80), Zographou (980), Vatopedi (985), Amalfitans (991), Panteleimon (1009), Xenophontos (1010), Esphigmenou, Philotheou and Chilandari (1015), Kastamonitou (1023-38), Docheiariou (1030) and Karakalou (1076).

Within a century, Athos had become a populous monastic centre, transcending ethnic divisions and representing all the various expressions of orthodoxy. Greek, Iberian, Bulgarian, Serbian, Russian and Latin monks were united there in prayer to the God of the Gospels. Constantine Monomachos rightly estimated the

importance of Athos for the Christian faith when he called it 'the mountain of Saints' and 'the Holy Mountain', the appellation which persists to the present day.

CITIES AND SOCIETY

In the course of the invasions and constant warfare of the middle Byzantine period, cities were fortified and became regional centres of defence. For this reason they are frequently referred to as castles *(kastra)*. Inscriptions perpetuate the memory of imperial officials who repaired or reconstructed city walls.[38]

The conditions of the period often demanded that cities be transferred to more fortified points, except in cases where the lie of the land was such that inhabitants might dwell in outlying regions and easily withdraw to an

323

acropolis or other high ground in times of attack. Such is the case with Philippi, Amphipolis, Christoupolis and other cities. Only Thessalonike constantly maintained the association of its lower city with the acropolis.

A basic change in wall construction probably coincides with this transformation of cities into fortifications, or *kastra*. Walls were no longer built with large rectangular hewn blocks, but with bricks and mortar. Constantine Porphyrogenitus refers to this type of construction at Spalatum (Split), and it is clearly evident at Philippi and Christoupolis.[39]

The transformation of Macedonian as well as other Byzantine cities into fortified centres usually had another consequence, namely the reduction of urban populations. Quite simply, all the inhabitants could no longer be accommodated inside the walls. This change also tended to decrease the amount of property which citizens owned in outlying regions, since in times of distress farmers needed to take immediate refuge within the walls of a city.

For precisely this reason, the powerful landed magnates uniformly moved their residence to the cities, although their properties and estates were naturally beyond the walls. The smaller landowners followed suit, as the Athonite documents reveal.[40]

We even encounter tenant farmers (*paroikoi*) residing in the cities, far from the land they rented.[41] Most probably they cultivated these lands through sub-tenants.

The typical social structure of the middle and late Byzantine cities applies also to Macedonia. Here too we find the same hierarchy of classes — the upper classes, (*archontes*) the middle classes (*mesoi*) and the lowest class (*demos*).[42]

These *archontes*, *aristoi* or *megaloi* were the local aristocrats of each city. Their wealth was based not only on land, but other properties including workshops and houses.

The *ktetores*, *oiketores* or *mesoi* represented the middle classes, their main occupations being crafts and commerce. The *bourgesioi* may also be included in this lot. These were Latin merchants who married Greek girls and became permanently established as Byzantine subjects, strengthening the middle class. The *bourgesioi* appear at Philippi, Thessalonike, Chrysoupolis and elsewhere.

The *mesoi* also disposed of agrarian wealth in addition to their workshops in the city.

The *demos* included the poorest workers and craftsmen, both those who worked for a daily wage and those who were employed occasionally. They felt a clear difference between themselves and the middle class. Throughout the disorders in Thessalonike in 1342 and 1345, the middle classes did not typically act in unison with the *demos*, and and for this reason they suffered the same fate as the aristocrats.

In both the early and middle Byzantine periods, craftsmen in Macedonian cities were organized into guilds. After the end of the twelfth century, however, the guilds effectively ceased to exist, at least as they are known from the *Book of the Eparch*, where they appear as associations subject to detailed state control and supervision.[43] Only the sailors of Thessalonike in the fourteenth century were organized with some type of leadership. The sources, however, do not clarify the exact nature of their organization. In the same century, however, each profession had its own special place in the market place.[44]

The more important Macedonian cities were endowed with commercial and political privileges, giving the impression of a certain degree of self-government and autonomy. Thessalonike in particular was accorded such privileges, although details about them are lacking. Some were certainly of a fiscal nature. Others, however, are referred to as the 'rights' of the city and were of a political character. According to the sources, the citizens surrendered Thessalonike to Baldwin with the stipulation that he rule them with the customs and traditions by which the Byzantine emperors had governed them.[45] Apparently their confirmation was a precondition for handing over the city.

Something similar happened in 1246, when John Vatatzes captured Thessalonike. In order to win over the inhabitants, Vetatzes accepted their request that he issue a chrysobull 'confirming the traditional customs of Thessalonike, including those incorporated in law as well as those arising from its own freedom'.[46]

Thessalonike continued to be the second city of the empire. In the twelfth century, its population was calculated at more than one hundred thousand inhabitants. A large Jewish community was settled there.[47] The city began to decline in the later twelfth century however, owing to political events. It recovered soon, and in the fourteenth century, it is once again mentioned as a city with a prosperous commercial activity. Still, its former brilliance could never be restored.

Thessalonike was not, of course, a representative example of the cities of its time. Following the loss of Alexandria and Antioch, it alone resembled Constantinople. For Thessalonike was at once an economic and administrative centre, which governed its surrounding territory on the basis of the 'laws of the founders' and the 'laws of the colonies'.[48]

References to institutions of urban self-government are scarce. A council (*bouleuterion*) was functioning in Thessalonike exactly at the period when such organs of urban administration are no longer attested. The council of Thessalonike was variously called the *gerousia*, *synkletos* or *boule*.[49] It should be noted, however, that this body was managed by an imperial agent, and hence it does not truly represent an example of civic autonomy or free self-administration.[50]

Even during the Zealot revolt, the representative of the *demos* was not the sole governor of the city, but ruled jointly with an imperial agent. Indeed, the Zealot representative was not even chosen from the people. Rather, they elected their candidate from the ranks of the notables.[51] This was possible because the wealthy capitalized on the people's desire for a better and more just government. They incorporated this popular demand with their own internal quarrels, in the course of which the young turned against the old. Typically, the leading cadres of the Zealot revolt were taken over by the young aristocrats. Here we may recall Tafrali's remark that the barrier of age was the only thing which the Zealot government abolished.[52]

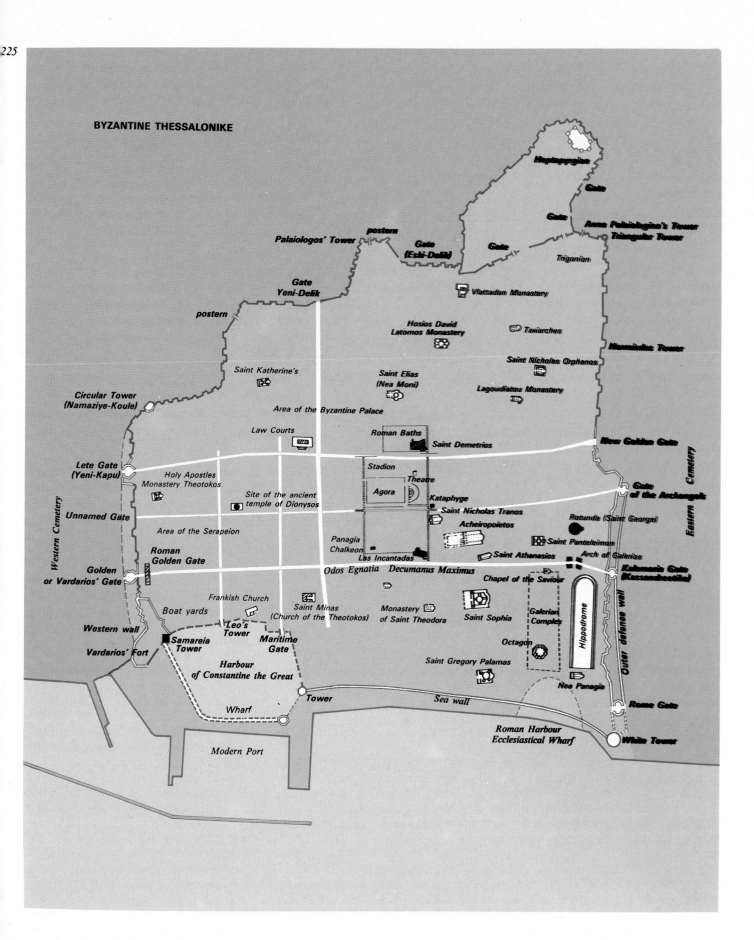

BYZANTINE THESSALONIKE

Heptapyrgion

Gate

Palaiologos' Tower   postern   Gate (Eski-Delik)   Gate   Anna Palaiologina's Tower

Triangular Tower

Trigonium

Gate Yeni-Delik

Vlattadian Monastery

postern   Hosios David Latomos Monastery   Taxiarches

Saint Katherine's   Hormisdas Tower

Saint Elias (Nea Moni)   Saint Nicholas Orphanos

Circular Tower (Namaziye-Koule)   Lagoudiatou Monastery

Area of the Byzantine Palace

Law Courts   Roman Baths   New Golden Gate

Saint Demetrios

Lete Gate (Yeni-Kapu)   Stadion

Holy Apostles Monastery Theotokos   Theatre   Kataphyge   Gate of the Archangels

Agora

Unnamed Gate   Site of the ancient temple of Dionysos   Saint Nicholas Tranos

Rotunda (Saint George)

Acheiropoietos   Saint Panteleimon

Area of the Serapeion   Saint Athanasios   Arch of Galerius

Roman Golden Gate   Panagia Chalkeon   Kalamaria Gate (Kassandreotiki)

Las Incantadas   Odos Egnatia   Decumanus Maximus

Golden or Vardarios' Gate   Chapel of the Saviour

Frankish Church   Saint Minas (Church of the Theotokos)   Monastery of Saint Theodora   Saint Sophia   Galerian Complex   Hippodrome

Boat yards   Outer defence wall

Western wall   Leo's Tower   Maritime Gate   Octagon

Vardarios' Fort   Samareia Tower   Saint Gregory Palamas   Rome Gate

Harbour of Constantine the Great   Nea Panagia

Tower   Sea wall

Wharf   Roman Harbour Ecclesiastical Wharf   White Tower

Modern Port

Western Cemetery   Eastern Cemetery

225. *Plan of Byzantine Thessalonike, showing the acropolis, the walls and gates, the most important streets (on the line of those in the Hellenistic town), the churches, monasteries and sites of the best known Roman and Early Christian monuments.*

226. *From the beginning of the 13th century until its fall in 1430 Thessalonike was the commercial centre of the Balkan peninsula. Pottery like this glazed plate decorated with an incised bird was produced in workshops in Thessalonike; its distribution was widespread both throughout northern Greece and, through Genoese and Venetian trade, as far as Constantinople and the Black Sea. 15th century, Thessalonike, Archaeological Museum.*

Information is even scantier regarding the administration of cities elsewhere in Macedonia. Civil magistrates are mentioned for Serrhai, which experienced a certain flowering in the fourteenth century.[53] Documents from the same period record the president of Drama, Leo Kalognomos, cooperating with the tax assessors Constantine Kounales and Demetrios Kontainos.[54] According to John Kameniates, Beroia was 'a city renowned for its inhabitants, and all the other things of which a city boasts in regard to its composition.'[55] Evidently he means by this that the wealthier groups in the city formed its ruling class. Doubtless the same holds true for the other Macedonian cities. The sources, however, do not provide us with relevant details.

In any case, these meagre references are not sufficient to document the widespread existence of local self-government in the smaller cities. Something is known in the case of Melenikon however, which appears to be typical. When the city surrendered to Vatatzes in 1246, Nicholas Maglavites 'one of the more prominent citizens' swayed the majority of the inhabitants to the imperial cause. This hap-

pened, however, because Nicholas Litovites 'who exercised leadership over the city' was ill and incapable of managing the city's affairs.[56]

The Occupations of the Inhabitants: Urban Economy

The inhabitants of the cities were occupied not only with crafts and commerce, but with cultivating the land. The relevant sources are usually indirect, but nonetheless provide clear information. The twelfth century traveller Idrisi, for example, relates that Skopje possessed enormous tracts of agricultural land, replete with vineyards and vast cornfields.[57] He praises Serrhai for its beautiful suburbs; its numerous, well-tended fields; and its abundant natural wealth. Zichna, he says, had vineyards, fruit trees, cultivated fields and ploughlands.[58] He attributes similar cultivations to Florina, to 'most wealthy' Kastoria, and to Christoupolis, for which Villehardouin provides corroborating testimony.[59]

The state of affairs in these Macedonian cities was fully paralleled in Thessalonike, the 'megalopolis of the cities of Illyricum' in the words of Theophanes. Thessalonike was at once a port, a crossroads and an administrative and military centre, with highly developed commerce and industry.[60]

As in the case of the other fortified cities or *kastra*, Thessalonike's suburbs were an area reserved for agriculture and agrarian-type occupations. Just as every morning many residents of other cities would set forth for the day's labour (*kamatos*), so too many Thessalonikans left town for their agricultural toils. Both the *Miracles of Saint Demetrios* and John Kameniates provide evidence for this, and the latter even distinguishes different zones of cultivation.[61] The areas closest to the city contained gardens and vineyards; furthest away were pasture lands and fields. Writing in the fourteenth century, Gregory Palamas refers to the fields, vineyards and various animals and objects which the inhabitants used in their agricultural occupations. Moreover, he grumbles that the Thessalonikans often neglected their religious obligations in favour of such work.[62]

Cities depended on this regime of cultivating the land for most of their sustenance. They naturally suffered greatly in times of war or disorder, when lands under cultivation were devastated. The damage and distress were particularly acute during long term periods of crisis. Kantakouzenos reports that in the year 1322 the citizens of Thessalonike were exempted from their taxes because they had been ruined by the lengthy civil wars between Andronikos II and Andronikos III.[63]

The wealthiest and most prominent citizens not only possessed cultivated estates and vineyards, but they also turned a profit from workshops and houses. At Serrhai, the Kantakouzenos family owned buildings with courtyards and upper and lower storeys; four one-storey buildings; a bakery; and three workshops which they rented to others.[64]

The 'venerable' *(sebastos)* Kosmas Pankalos of Serrhai possessed three workshops, two bakeries and nine houses. Other representatives of the wealthy class were merchants, like the Tzamplakon family, which conducted trade with the Ragusans.[65] Such instances are especially significant, since the upper classes generally did not engage in commerce, an occupation considered unworthy of the well-born.[66]

In the fourteenth century, neither commerce nor industry developed freely — i.e., according to the enterprise of merchants and the law of supply and demand. Consequently, these professions became purely mercenary in character. Since the most powerful elements of society had a share in them, moreover, they were fully absolved from governmental controls. This state of affairs resulted in the corruption of merchants.[67]

In summary, the economic life of Macedonia (indeed of Byzantium in general) did not develop freely as in the west. It evolved in a state of semi-freedom and semi-independence, which scarcely allowed the growth of an urban class, or the expansion of cities.

The political situation of the period certainly contributed to this state of affairs, as well as the privileges granted to the western merchants. These concessions gave them every opportunity to suffocate Byzantine initiative, and to freely exercise their parasitically oppressive influence upon the Byzantine economy.

As we have seen, urban economy was based primarily on agriculture and to a lesser degree on trade. Another characteristic of later Byzantine cities is the decline of their wider military responsibilities towards the central government. As the empire broke up, into more or less independent regions, the cities were forced to assume the responsibility of defending and protecting themselves. Given its limited resources, the state could do little more than acquiesce. An interesting consequence of this was the growth of local customs and traditions of self-government, however limited. It is unfortunate that the external political events of the period so quickly destroyed the cities' attempts at self-government and local initiative. Otherwise they might have developed along the same lines as western cities.[68]

TRADE

Macedonia enjoyed a central position in the Balkan peninsula. A variety of trade routes quite naturally linked it with the rest of the Balkans, and united it with the international trade of west and east. The great trade routes (the Via Egnatia; the Thessalonike-Axios-Morava-Danube route; and the Amphipolis-Sofia-Danube route) conveyed local or transit trade to Thessalonike. As previously mentioned, the decision to change the direction of Bulgarian trade from Thessalonike to Constantinople evidently caused the dreadful wars which Symeon inflicted upon the empire. Usually the opposite view is maintained, namely that the cause of the war was the change in direction from Constantinople to Thessalonike. However, the relevant passages in the sources do not adequately support this view.[69] Owing to its position, Macedonia could conjoin the overland trade of the west and north-west Balkans with the international trade of east and west. Moreover, commodities from the lower Danube area could reach Macedonia via the road from Sofia through the Strymon valley, although the Danube trade was chiefly oriented to Constantinople. The great rivers flowing through Macedonia facilitated commercial exchanges with the Slavs who lived in the Balkan hinterlands. They would send smoked fish to the coast, to be exchanged for whatever the coastal inhabitants had to offer.

The Byzantine trade route between Thessalonike, Stoboi and Skopje was reinvigorated after the founding of the despotate of Epirus, to which Thessalonike was quickly subjected. The prosperity continued when Thessalonike came under the control of the empire of Nicaea. A decline set in after the middle of the thirteenth century, following the reconquest of Constantinople. From the early thirteenth century up to its final fall, however, Thessalonike dominated trade. During this period the Serbs played middlemen between western central Europe and Thessalonike, much as the Bulgarians had previously mediated trade with Constantinople.

An interesting consequence of these relations is the degree to which Skopje was Hellenized, since for many years it was a Byzantine possession. The number of landowners with Greek names is remarkable, even after 1282 when the city came into Serbian hands. In the middle of the fourteenth century there were still many pro-Byzantines there.[70]

In this period, the Greeks of Thessalonike dominated trade and finally expelled the Ragusans. A reflection of this is the infrequency with which Skopje and the other northwest Macedonia trade centres (Velbužd or Kyustendil, Štip, Prilep, Ochrid) appear in later Ragusan trade annals. Thessalonike had absorbed these areas into her own sphere of commercial domination.[71]

Thessalonike's harbour and geographic position assured it superior advantages in maritime trade, making it a major commercial centre. Demetrios Kydones calls it the greatest port ever known, and adds that at one time a second city existed nearby the present city of Thessalonike — 'located before it, and serving as its port city, so that Thessalonike terminated not with the sea, but with the other city'.[72]

However, the extrusion of the three arms of Chalkidike impeded sea communications with Constantinople and the western shores of Asia Minor.

For this reason, those who journeyed by ship to those parts usually embarked from Neapolis (or Christoupolis, today Kavala), the harbour of Philippi. Travellers proceeding from Asia Minor or Constantinople towards Thessalonike typically followed the same itinerary as Gregory Dekapolites. He sailed from Ephesos to Prokonnesos, Ainos and then Christoupolis, where he took the overland road to Thessalonike. This he reached after an episode with Slavic 'brigands'.[73] This incident provides indisputable evidence not only for the Slavic occupation of the lower Strymon region, but for predatory attacks which the Slavs undertook there.

Thessalonike's maritime trade with southern Greece as well as the west was continuous and well-developed. The Genoese trading posts in Thessalonike and Kassandreia, and the Venetian stations outside the walls of

227. *Part of a large 12-13th century composition depicting the Last Judgement, in the single-aisled church of the Panagia Mavriotissa, Kastoria. The detail shows the faces of the Damned in Hell.*

Thessalonike, attest the growth and maintenance of commercial links with the west.[74]

The sources contain few details regarding actual articles of exchange. Writing in the tenth century, John Kameniates states that gold, silver, precious stones, silken fabrics, copper, tin, iron, lead and glass were to be found in the city's market.[75] Elsewhere he says that Thessalonike obtained its commodities 'from land and sea' in equal measure, and that it imported fully as much as agriculture and commerce had to offer. Thessalonike, he writes, received 'from the mainland its abundant agricultural produce; from the sea, the provisions of commerce'.[76] Kameniates also reports that the Thessalonikans offered Leo of Tripoli such enormous heaps of silk and linen fabrics as ransom that 'it was as if they formed hills and mountains'.[77] He further says that silk fabrics were as plen-

tiful as woollen cloths elsewhere, so that the Arabs refused to take woollen fabrics as booty.[78] Heyd sees this as evidence for a flourishing silk industry in Thessalonike.[79] We should bear in mind, however, that Thessalonike was also provisioned with silk from Thebes, a city famed for silk production, and with other kinds of fabrics from Boiotia and the Peloponnese. Nonetheless, it does appear that the silk industry was flourishing at Thessalonike. Benjamin of Tudela informs us that in 1160 five hundred persons from the Jewish community in Thessalonike were engaged in silk production.[80]

The Thessalonike market received linen cloth and garments directly from the Strymon area and Bulgaria, where these industries were located, or from Constantinople.

Thessalonike also had a lively metals industry, judging from Kameniates' boast that the crafts working 'in fire' produced so many basic materials that one could build another city with them.[81] He mentions in particular copper, iron, tin, lead and glass. Various commodities from the Black Sea region were shipped to Constantinople, and from there were transported to Thessalonike by pack animals.

The surviving seals of the various customs officials *kommerkiarioi, abydikoi, paraphylakes* of the *(kommerkiarioi)* bear witness to the lively business of the Thessalonike customs. As mentioned earlier (see page 259), these seals cover a period from the seventh through twelfth centruries.[82] All of this justifies Demetrios Kydones' estimation of Thessalonike as the market which takes in 'the whole world'. He further remarks that living in Thessalonike was like living in all the other cities at once.[83]

The momentum which these commercial exchanges generated was great, but it increased all the more during festival time. The most important of these are described in an anonymous twelfth-century dialogue called *Timorion*. According to this source, within a week's time a whole city would be erected on the plain adjacent to Thessalonike, near the Axios. Tents and barracks would be regularly constructed to house traders and their merchandise.

Merchants from all parts would flock to this festival — Greeks, Moesians from the Danube area (and even further north), Italians from Kampania, Lusitanians, Celts from across the Alps. In short, people came from all corners as pilgrims to Saint Demetrios, and as spectators at his festival, *ta Demetria*. At this festival the best articles of woven material and of thread from Boiotia, to Peloponnese and Italy were found . Merchandise came from Syria, Palestine, Egypt and Spain. Commodities were even shipped from as far as the Atlantic, via the Straits of Gibraltar.

In Thessalonike, groups of both Greek and foreign merchants conducted business. In the first half of the tenth century, Spartan merchants are mentioned trading in the city. The establishment of foreign merchants in Thessalonike was an unavoidable consequence of the enormous trade concessions the Byzantines were forced to grant the Italian maritime powers.

In 1261, the Genoese first secured from Michael VIII Palaiologos the right to establish trading stations in Thessalonike and Kassandreia. Somewhat later, in 1265, the Venetians were accorded the same privileges, but were established outside the walls of Thessalonike and at Voleron.[84]

These facts indicate how important Macedonia was from the point view of trade.

Information about the commercial activity of other Macedonian cities (such as Beroia Ochrid, Kastoria, Skopje, Serrhai, Christoupolis and Drama) underscores this importance even further. The Arab traveller Idrisi describes the wealth of the Macedonian cities he visited in the mid-twelfth century. He mentions Kitros as a populous centre with markets, and Ochrid as a large city with developed trade. He even recounts shipbuilding at Platamon, and remarks on Philippi's many and varied professions, which included a flourishing import and export trade.[85]

The customs stations along the more important trade roads also attest to the brisk pace of commerce in Macedonia. Along the Via Egnatia, Ochrid, Edessa, Amphipolis, Philippi, Christoupolis and of course Thessalonike served as customs posts. A no the Thessalonike-Belgrade road, Skopje, Priština, Niš and Singidunum (Belgrade) were customs cities. Duty was also collected at points along the secondary roads, such as Servia, Beroia, Kastoria, Pelagonia, Prilep, Serrhai and Kassandreia.[86]

The destructive policy of granting commercial and fiscal privileges to the Italian maritime cities struck a hard blow to the commerce of the empire. Macedonia, of course, suffered from its effects as well. The merchants of Venice, Genoa, Pisa and Aragon not only received the right to have wharfs wherever they wished, but to conduct unrestricted trade throughout the whole empire. They even succeeded in paying an export-import duty of no more than two to four per cent.[87]

Privileges as generous as these meant that Greek commerce lost its competitive edge. The transport of commodities came into foreign hands. Since the state received nothing back in commercial revenues, it was quickly impoverished. Thus, while Byzantine mercantile centres retained their importance, the role of Greek sailors and merchants was continually restricted and diminished. In the end, they lost all importance as a major source of wealth and productivity for the state.

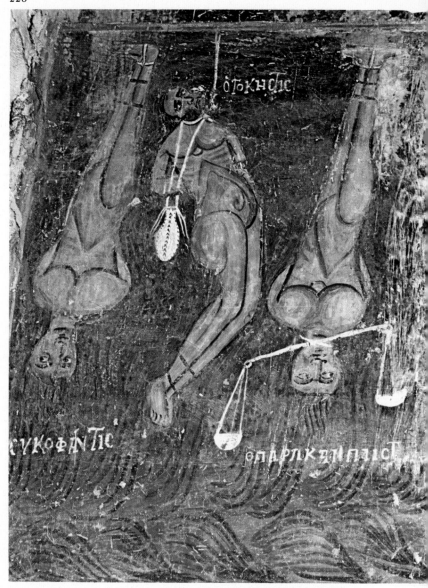

228. *Detail from the Last Judgement, probably inspired by abuses met with in daily life. The flatterer, the usurer and the overcharger are shown suspended over the fires of Hell. 12-13th century, Panagia Mavriotissa, Kastoria.*

THE GREAT LANDOWNERS AND THE CONDITION OF THE RURAL POPULATION

A fundamental feature of the social policy of the Macedonian dynasty was the emperors' efforts to limit the greed of the great landowners (the *dynatoi*), and to protect the small farmers (the *tapenoi*). This naturally had its echoes in Macedonia.

The founder of the dynasty, Basil I, had already tried to make sure that 'the poor be not oppressed by the wealthy.'[88] The ninth century, of course, was not the first time the powerful tried to oppress the poor. These tendencies now appeared with such vigour, however, that Basil was forced to take drastic measures.

Under Basil I's successor Leo VI (886-912), the great magnates resumed their relentless attempts to absorb the small landowners. The wars with Symeon were a contributing factor, as well as the emperor's own inability to regulate social forces and protect the weak.[89]

Throughout the following decades, the other emperors of the Macedonian dynasty tried to come to terms with the rapaciousness of the great magnates. The death of Basil II, however, marked the turning point. His successors permitted the landed magnates to pursue their destructive work against the state with no restraints.

The monastic documents from Mount Athos reveal the enormous extent of the landed wealth which the monasteries and church controlled in Macedonia. They also inform us about a whole series of great landowners who were active in this area already in the thirteenth century. The Tzamplakones and the Kantakouzenoi, for ex-

229. The elegant figures of the Saints Nicholas the Less and Alexander in the sumptuous dress of nobles of the period and curious head gear. 14th century wall painting, Saint Athanasios Mouzakes, Kastoria.

ample, possessed vast tracts of cultivated land in the area of Christoupolis, Serrhai and Thessalonike. Manuel Angelos also held huge estates in Serrhai and Thessalonike. The Kantakouzenoi and Gregory Pakourianos owned important properties in Macedonia and elsewhere. Kantakouzenos himself testifies that he had at his disposal five thousand cows; a thousand pair of oxen for ploughing; two thousand five hundred mares; two hundred camels; three hundred mules; five hundred asses; fifty thousand pigs; and seventy thousand sheep.[90] The sources refer to the power and wealth of the Asanedes at Christoupolis; of the Troulenoi, Achyraites and Diplovatatzedes at Serrhai; of the Angeloi, Kabasiles, Kydones and Hyaleedes at Thessalonike; and of the Angeloi, Radiporoi and Laskariotes at Edessa.[91]

Some of these were great landowners, others of them

pronoiars. The manner in which the pronoiars acquired their properties is clear from the monastic documents. Typically, a temporary grant of tax revenues for a particular area would be changed into a permanent grant, and finally into full ownership of the land.

The sources provide little detailed evidence about the actual extent of lands owned by these magnates. From the information we have, however, we can comprehend the wealth of their estates, and the various types of revenues they provided. The typikon of Gregory Pakourianos, for example, records the vast properties which this Byzantine general of Iberian descent possessed around Thessalonike, Serrhai, Strymon and Voleron.[92]

The villages and peasants suffered greatly under the pressure of the powerful landed magnates. The peasants were oppressed by the high-handedness of the fiscal officials and tax farmers. Theophylact of Ochrid's letters are quite revealing in this regard.[93] The case of Demetrios Kamateros, a tax farmer, is typical. He was reduced to penury because he could not afford to pay twice the amount of tax which he was legally obliged to pay. For this reason the state proceeded to confiscate his possessions.[94]

This negative picture is balanced to some degree by other types of information. At least for the period for which we have evidence, the population of Byzantine (and hence Macedonian) villages was fairly stable. Also we may recall that some *paroikoi* succeeded in buying their own tenancy, and that in some cases peasants were able to enrich themselves and advance socially. The best example of the latter group is the case of Philokalles.[95] These instances, however, should not lead one to conclude that the life of the rural population was rosy. Rather, we should bear in mind that two separate factors influenced their lot: first, the purely economic conditions which do not seem to have burdened the life of the peasants so heavily, and secondly, the arbitrary acts of officials or individuals which aggravated their situation. Only when we distinguish and separately analyze these two factors shall we reach sound conclusions regarding the general quality of peasant life, and the causes which negatively influenced its development.

Mount Athos and the Socio-Economic Situation of Macedonia

The importance of the Holy Mountain for the economic and social condition of Macedonia was enormous. By means of continual bequests, grants from the state, and their own resources, the monks of Athos acquired vast amounts of land throughout Macedonia, but especially in the central part.

These estates were cultivated chiefly by leasing them to tenants or *paroikoi,* which resulted in the growth of a substantial class of tenant farmers. Contrary to general opinion, these tenants were legally free, enjoying all the rights of free men. Consequently, the term *paroikos* variously designated a hired man or a small landowner. With the enormous increase in monastic holdings, moreover, the *paroikoi* became as greedy for land as the great magnates, and like them tended to increase their wealth at the expense of the weak.

The pious emperor Nikephoros Phokas suspected as much when he revoked the *solemnia,* or imperial donations to the churches and monasteries. He chastised the monks in no uncertain terms: 'I gaze upon the great sickness of the monasteries, for greed most surely is a sickness, yet I am at a loss how to cure the malady, or how to punish the avarice. When I see professed ascetics and monks shaming the habits they wear with lies, I am compelled to call this theatre, and to cry out that this blasphemes the name of Christ.'[96] Consequently, neither Nikephoros I nor Romanos II nor Basil II were able to exclude the monasteries from the general measures they enacted to crush the great landed magnates.[97] Throughout the following centuries, the wealth of the monasteries increased at a dramatic rate. Fiscal records relating to the monasteries on Athos, and elsewhere in Macedonia, reveal the extent and rapid growth of monastic properties. Imperial benevolence towards the monks and their monasteries was chiefly responsible for this expansion.[98]

Assuredly, there were occasional efforts to confront the unbridled appropriation of lands by churches and monasteries. Theophylact of Ochrid provides evidence of such attempts, although his outlook is negative. Manuel Komnenos announced his plans to cure the malady in his famous Θεραπευτικὸν (*Physician's Oration*) where he proclaims 'it is as if I am curing the crippled rights of churches everywhere.' He proposed to examine the validity of ecclesiastical and monastic property claims. Such attempts were quickly abandoned. Under the Palaiologans, affairs took a turn for the worse. Michael VIII restored to the monasteries their privileges, and granted new ones as well. Perhaps he hoped to quell any protests the monks might raise regarding his anomalous rise to power. The emperors Andronikos II and III, along with the Serbian rulers, showed the same political benevolence and generosity towards the monasteries.[99]

Monastic properties did not increase by simple gifts and bequests alone. The monks zealously purchased lands from small farmers as well. The privileges the state granted to the monasteries thus diminished its own lands, and hence its revenues. Continuing impoverishment led to further deecline and an ever increasing likelihood of collapse.[100]

The monasteries on Athos with significant landed wealth were Great Lavra, Chilandari, Esphigmenou, Xeropotamou, Saint Paul's, Iveron, Koutloumousiou, Xenophontos and Dionysiou. Other wealthy monasteries were located in Chalkidike, and around Beroia, Serrhai, Thessalonike and elsewhere.

With their enormous landed wealth, the monasteries were not only an economic but a social force. In fact, since the number of monks was small in comparison with the extent of their properties, they could themselves cultivate only a small part of these lands. Hence they resorted to indirect cultivation, renting plots of cultivable land to peasant tenants, with the customary stipulations of the *paroikia* system. In this way, the monasteries developed into a considerable social force, since they had many individuals in a state of dependence upon them. Here, however, we may look at the other side of the coin. By renting out lands on the *paroikia* system, monastic wealth was in effect limited. As mentioned previously, this indirect exploitation of the land resulted in the 'socialization' of the great estates.[101]

INTELLECTUAL LIFE

One of the many effects of the Fourth Crusade was to put an end to the domination of the Byzantine cultural life by Constantinople. Byzantine society once more became polycentric, as it had been in the period before the Arab conquest. This was due to a number of factors. The occupation of Constantinople by the Latins from 1204 to 1261 was only one. Another was the political fragmentation of the former Byzantine empire, which meant that many of its territories were never again ruled from Constantinople. A further factor was the increasing tendency for local magnates to become effectively independent of the capital, as the process of feudalization progressed. And lastly, the new prosperity which trade with the Italian republics brought to many provincial cities was often reflected in their new cultural activities.

Macedonia, like other regions, was affected by this change in the balance between centre and periphery. And Thessalonike in particular became an important cultural centre and no longer a mere provincial reflection of Constantinople.[1] It was never plundered, as the capital was in 1204. Thus it remained relatively rich in books. When John III Vatatzes wished to establish libraries in the Nicaean empire he sent the monk and polymath Nikephoros Blemmydes on a journey to the newly reconquered western provinces, and especially to Thessalonike, to seek out books which could not be found in Asia Minor. This will have happened shortly after 1246.

Several men of letters and scholars from Constantinople sought refuge in Macedonia after 1204 or were already established there and brought with them some of the sophisticated intellectual traditions of the capital. John Apokaukos had had a long career in the Patriarchal bureaucracy when he was appointed metropolitan of Naupaktos shortly before 1204. The establishment of the despotate of Epirus, with its capital at Arta — which was ecclesiastically subject to Naupaktos, led to Apokaukos becoming the principal ecclesiastical adviser to the new ruler. When Thessalonike and most of Macedonia became subject to the despotate, Apokaukos' influence extended to these regions too. When he was expelled from his bishopric in Naupaktos as a result of the internal rivalry he seems to have established himself for a time in Thessalonike. He died in 1233. Apokaukos' works include poems on religious themes, official documents, and an extensive correspondence.[2] It is interesting that although he handles the learned language with confidence some of his letters, particularly those addressed to women, are written in demotic.

Demetrios Chomatianos held an appointment in the service of the patriarchate before 1204. After the capture of the city by the Latins he fled to Ochrid, where he had acquaintances, and became archivist of the church there. In 1216 or 1217 he was appointed archbishop of Ochrid thanks to the influence of John Apokaukos. In 1225 he crowned the despot Theodore Doukas emperor in Thessalonike. He had evidently already replaced Apokaukos as the leading ecclesiastic of the despotate. He survived at least until 1235. He left a large body of canon law, decisions and official documents, as well as a collection of letters and some liturgical poetry.[3] His correspondence is of great interest for the social and economic history of Macedonia in this stormy period.

It seems likely that the period of Latin rule brought a less sharp and less long cultural break in Thessalonike than it did in Constantinople. In a book to be published shortly

Dr. Costas Constantinides explores some of the hitherto unnoticed personal links between the intellectual world of Constantinople in the last decades before the Fourth Crusade and that of Thessalonike after the Byzantine restoration. By the closing years of the thirteenth century a brilliant period in the history of Thessalonikan culture had begun, which lasted until the disastrous civil war of the mid-fourteenth century. The monks Sabbas and Germanos, both of whom were educated in Thessalonike in the last decades of the thirteenth century, studied classical poetry, rhetoric and historiography before they felt the call of the religious life.

Thomas Magistros taught classical literature in Thessalonike for many years. In the course of his teaching he produced editions of selections from Aeschylus, Sophocles, Euripides and Pindar — three plays each of the dramatists, and the Olympian and half the Pythian Odes of Pindar.[4] These editions comprised the text, a marginal commentary dealing largely with syntax and mythological, historical and geographical allusions, and interlinear explanations of rare or difficult words. They draw largely on older commentaries, but also contain much original matter, particularly paraphrases of difficult passages. They are essentially school-books. Another by-product of his teaching was his *Ekloge onomaton kai rematon Attikon,* a lexicon of the atticising learned language, establishing distinctions between apparent synonyms and explaining the correct construction of each verb. It is a testimony alike to the changes which had taken place in the Greek language and to the rigorously archaizing tone of most late Byzantine literature. One of the manuscripts of Thomas' edition of Sophocles was written in 1301, probably in Thessalonike. It is likely that Thomas had been engaged in teaching for some years, perhaps for many years, before that date. He was still alive in 1346, as the monk Theodoulos in the monastery of Kyr' Isaac in Thessalonike. Among his pupils were the philologist Demetrios Triklinios, the anti-Hesychast theologian Gregory Akindynos, and the future patriarch Philotheos Kokkinos, a boy of poor origins who had been his servant. Many other distinguished citizens of Thessalonike no doubt also studied under him.

Thomas Magistros was much more than a teacher, however. His correspondence shows him to have been in touch with many prominent men in Constantinople,[5] including Theodore Metochites, the chief minister of Andronikos II. When he visited the capital he was received with honour by statesmen and men of letters. He did not hesitate to intervene in the political controversies of the time. In a speech addressed to Andronikos II he appeals to the emperor not to hold the general Chandrenos responsible for the devastation wrought by Catalan and Turkish

---

230. Gregory Palamas, the chief exponent of Heyschasm, the mystic, inspirational brand of Orthodoxy, and vociferous opponent of the teachings of Barlaam of Calabria. Metropolitan of Thessalonike from 1347-59, he was canonized after his death. Portable icon, 15th century. Leningrad, Museum of Beaux-Arts.

mercenaries under his command. During the civil war between Andronikos and his grandson (1321-28) he called on the citizens of Thessalonike to maintain their unity. His address to Andronikos on the duties of a monarch contains practical advice as well as the traditional cliches of the genre; thus he urges the emperor to train the army in peace-time, to maintain the fleet (advice lost on Andronikos), to restrict the sale of offices, to control the activities of tax-collectors, and to modify the law of inheritance. In addition to real speeches Thomas also composed model declamations,[6] one of which was such a successful pastiche of the language and style of the Second Sophistic that it was for centuries included among the speeches of Aelius Aristides. Finally, he was the author of a number of panegyric sermons and liturgical hymns.[7] In Thomas Magistros we have an example of the many-sided scholar of the late Byzantine world, who combined rigorous and conservative classicism with a lively interest in the problems of his own society. The occasional arrogance with which he dismissed the views of others was part of the persona of the schoolmaster, who could not admit to ignorance or doubt.

During Thomas' years as a teacher in Thessalonike Nikephoros Choumnos, a pupil of George of Cyprus, a notable man of letters, and for a time chief minister of Andronikos II, spent some years in the city as governor.[8] In a speech delivered in the city he praises the learning of many of its citizens. He remained in active contact with many of his Thessalonikan friends after his return to the capital, and his speeches and letters were read there before gatherings of savants and men of letters. Choumnos' principal correspondent in Thessalonike was Theodore Xanthopoulos, a fellow-pupil of George of Cyprus. Whether he was a native of the city or not is uncertain. But both he and his more famous brother Nikephoros Kallistos Xanthopoulos, teacher of rhetoric, ecclesiastical historian, commentator on the liturgy and hagiographer, appear to have had some connection with Thessalonike, though most of Nikephoros' career was spent in Constantinople as a priest of the Great Church.

Among the contemporaries of Thomas Magister in Thessalonike were two lawyers of distinction. Matthew Blastares was a monk in the monastery of Kyr' Isaac, with which Thomas had close relations. It has been argued with great plausibility that the church of Saint Panteleimon is in fact the katholikon of this monastery, which was an important centre of intellectual life in the city in the second quarter of the fourteenth century. The dates of Blastares' birth and death are unknown, but he was active in 1335 and later. His principal work is his *Syntagma* or systematic corpus of canon law, composed before 1335. It appears to be connected with the legal reform of Andronikos II in 1329, by which the administration of justice was entrusted to four judges, two of whom were to be clerics. Appendices to the *Syntagma* are the synopses of earlier collections of canons by John Nesteutes, Niketas of Herakleia and the patriarch Nikephoros, and a lexicon of Latin legal terms. Blastares was a many-sided writer.[9] He composed polemical works against the Jews (unpublished) and against the Latins, wrote at length on problems of practical theology to Guy de Lusignan, a relative of the royal house of Cyprus who had been appointed governor of Serrhai, and was the author of a number of liturgical hymns, as well as of letters and occasional poems. A paraphrase in learned Greek of the *Heavenly Ladder* of John Klimakos, is probably to be attributed to him — like most late Byzantine writers he was a fervent classicist. He engaged in a dispute with Barlaam of Calabria when he visited Thessalonike. But the surviving *Discussions with Barlaam* is probably a summary made by a pupil rather than an original composition of Blastares himself.

Constantine Armenopoulos was a judge in Thessalonike in the second quarter of the fourteenth century. In 1345 he published his *Hexabiblos,* a systematic exposition of Roman private and criminal law.[10] The preface declares that the current handbook — the *Procheiros Nomos* of Basil I — is unsatisfactory, and that he has written his own work after long study of ancient legal literature and private compilations. He clearly makes use of the *Peira* of Eustathios Romanos (eleventh century). To judge by surviving legal documents, the *Hexabiblos* became authoritative in the last century of the Byzantine empire. It remained in use by the ecclesiastical courts throughout the Ottoman occupation, and was adopted as the official code of the Greek State by the Provisional Assembly in 1822. In translation, it was used elsewhere.

Thomas Magistros' most distinguished pupil was Demetrios Triklines or Triklinios (as he called himself from about 1316). Triklinios was a native of Thessalonike, probably born about 1280. He probably first worked as a copyist — a manuscript of the rhetoricians Aphthonios and Hermogenes was copied by him in Thessalonike in 1308 — but soon became, like Thomas, a teacher of literature and editor of classical texts.[11] Since many autograph manuscripts of Triklinios survive, we can sometimes trace the successive stages of his editions, as he acquired new knowledge and new insight. The classical poets of whose works he produced editions include Theocritus, Aristophanes, Euripides, Hesiod, Pindar, Aeschylus and Sophocles. In the case of Theocritus and Aristophanes he merely added a commentary to an existing text. For Euripides, Hesiod, Pindar, Aeschylus and Sophocles he edited the text as well as providing it with a commentary. His great strength was his knowledge of classical metre — not merely the simple metres of tragic dialogue but also the complex lyric metres. He cannot have acquired this knowledge from his teacher Thomas, who had no grasp of lyric metre. He will have learnt something from contemporary philologists in Constantinople, notably Manuel Moschopoulos. But he was in the main an autodidact, without predecessors or followers. By intensive study of the lyric texts themselves and the often obscure and unhelpful ancient writers on metre he gained an understanding of a sophisticated and difficult art-form that no man had possessed for a thousand years before him and none was to possess again until long after the Renaissance.

This understanding enabled Triklinios to correct many hundreds of errors which had crept into the texts of Greek poetry over the centuries. Sometimes his emendations were overhasty or naive; far more often they have become part of the accepted text of the poems which he studied. Though he sometimes offered wrong answers, his questions were always well-founded. He lacked his master's arrogant self-assertiveness. Triklinios drew for his commentaries on those of Thomas Magistros, to which he added material from what he called 'old' manuscripts and his own metrical observations. Sometimes he also included a paraphrase of his own. He had access in Thessalonike to a manuscript of Euripides containing plays other than the seven selected in late antiquity. The unique manuscript of the 'unselected' plays (cod. Laur. gr. 32.2) is a copy at only a few removes of an edition by Triklinios. The manuscript containing these plays — otherwise unknown in the Middle Ages — was probably used a century and a half earlier by Eustathios. The recent discovery of a short astronomical treatise by Triklinios reveals not only that his interests extended beyond classical philology but also that he had some understanding of the role of experiment in advancing knowledge.[12] Demetrios Triklinios, of whose life we regrettably know so little, was the most original of the brilliant group of scholars in Thessalonike in the early fourteenth century. The German scholar Wilamowitz observes that he was in reality the first modern textual critic.

We hear incidentally of a number of minor men of letters connected with Macedonia in this period. A certain Staphidakes wrote an epitaph in elegiac couplets on Isaac, the founder of the monastery of Kyr' Isaac. Theodore Pediasimos, probably a native of Serrhai, and educated in Thessalonike, wrote rhetorical works and letters as well as *Lives* of Joseph the Hymnographer and other saints.[13] Among his rhetorical compositions is an interesting *ekphrasis* of the metropolitan church of Serrhai. Jacob, metropolitan of Serrhai until the civil wars, was author of several religious poems, including a *Kanon Katanyktikos*. John Katrares, a learned copyist working in Thessalonike in the early fourteenth century, wrote poems in anacreontic verse, a short dramatic fragment, and a series of excerpts from the *Geography* of Strabo.[14] We hear, too, of men educated in Thessalonike who pursued successful careers elsewhere, usually in Constantinople. Isidore Boucheira, patriarch from 1347 to 1349, had studied and taught rhetoric in Thessalonike before going to the capital. Theodore Kabasilas, whose monody on the emperor Andronikos II has only recently been published,[15] was probably a native of Thessalonike.[16] Philotheos Kokkinos, patriarch 1353-54 and 1364-74, was born of a Jewish mother in Thessalonike about 1300 and was a domestic servant in the house of Thomas Magistros before becoming his pupil and protégé.[17]

A great many manuscripts written in Thessalonike in the early fourteenth century survive as living witnesses to the culture of the age, and several copyists can be identified as active there. Such are Theodore Hagiopetrites, a prolific copyist of religious manuscripts around 1300; John

231. Portrait of a donor dated to 1338 in the church of the Anargyroi, Kastoria. He is depicted in the accustomed stance, praying on his knees before the icon he is presenting to the church. According to the accompanying metrical inscription, his name was George, and the painter of the icon was a certain Athanasios, a priest.

Katrares, already mentioned; Demetrios Triklinios and his brother Nicholas; Demetrios Kaniskes Kabasilas, an official of the metropolitan church of Thessalonike and well-known calligrapher in the 1340s; John Zarides, copyist of Strabo and the minor Greek geographers in 1321. Copyists were active in the provincial cities of Macedonia too. A manuscript of the commentary of Theophylact Hephaistos on the Acts and Pauline Epistles was written in 1286/7 for Antonios Malakes, archbishop of Beroia. Theodore Pagomenos, a priest in Kampania (west of Thessalonike) copied a commentary on Hippocrates for a doctor, also named Theodore, in 1348.

The civil wars of the mid-century, the regime of the zealots, the terrible plague of the same years, and the theological dispute between Hesychasts and anti-Hesychasts marked the end of the golden age of Thessalonikan culture, and were probably responsible in no small measure for bringing it about. For the remainder of the period under review men of letters tended to emigrate from Thessalonike, and those who remained there were more and more preoccupied with religious disputes.

The Hesychast dispute was one which involved clerics and laymen throughout the dwindling empire of the fourteenth century, and which acquired political overtones when John Kantakouzenos lent the Hesychasts his power-

ful support. It cannot be discussed in any depth or detail in a survey of a single region of the empire. It should be borne in mind, however, that because of its proximity to Mount Athos, Thessalonike was particularly liable to be drawn into disputes originating there.

It was in fact in Thessalonike that the great dispute within the Orthodox church in the fourteenth century first manifested itself. Barlaam of Calabria came to the city in the early 1330s to study eastern monasticism. Gregory Palamas, born in Constantinople in 1296/7 of an Asia Minor family, had been a monk, first in the monastery of Vatopedi on Mount Athos and later in a monastery near Beroia since 1318. In 1332-33 he engaged in correspondence with Barlaam on the question of the Procession of the Holy Spirit, which divided the Eastern and Western churches. Barlaam became critical of certain of the mystical practices of Palamas and his fellow-monks, and both published an attack upon them in Thessalonike and made a report to the Patriarch John Kalekas. Palamas replied in a series of polemical tracts, in which he set out the distinction between the divine essence and the divine energies. Meanwhile Gregory Akindynos, a monk born of Bulgarian parents in Prilep in northern Macedonia who had studied in Thessalonike under Gregory Palamas, at first took sides with Palamas against Barlaam, but later became convinced that Barlaam was right. He tried in vain to convert Palamas to his point of view, and went on to publish in Thessalonike a series of tracts directed both against Palamas' theology and against the methods of contemplation by which the so-called Hesychast monks sought to attain a momentary vision of the uncreated light which the disciples beheld on Mount Tabor.

By now the controversy had spread beyond the confines of Macedonia. A synod in Constantinople in 1341 called on Barlaam not to take upon himself the teaching duties which properly belonged to bishops. In the same year John Kantakouzenos, in revolt against the boy emperor John V and the regent Anne of Savoy, threw his weight behind Gregory Palamas and the Hesychast movement. After his victory in the civil war in 1347 he appointed Palamas metropolitan of Thessalonike and began proceedings for heresy against Akindynos. Akindynos died in 1349. In 1351 the Holy Synod pronounced the doctrines of Palamas to be the dogma of the church, and condemned Akindynos posthumously. Palamas died in 1359 and was canonized as a saint in 1368. Many of the controversial writings of the protagonists in this long dispute were composed and published in Thessalonike.[18] These include the early writings of Barlaam, almost all the writings of Akin-

232-233. Many manuscripts written in Thessalonike at the beginning of the 14th century survive as living witnesses to the culture of the age. The picture shows miniatures with scenes from the life of Saint Demetrios in the only illuminated manuscript which it is possible to attribute with some certainty to a Thessalonike scriptorium. Oxford, Bodleian Library.

dynos (of which few have been published), and the early writings of Gregory Palamas. Joseph Kalothetos, a fervent supporter of Palamas, spent much of his life as a monk on Mount Athos. He seems to have been in Thessalonike from 1336 to 1341 when he wrote many of his polemic works, letters and panegyrics.[19]

Among the leading intellectual figures in Macedonia in the third quarter of the fourteenth century were Neilos Kabasilas, metropolitan of Thessalonike 1361-63, and his nephew Nicholas Kabasilas. Both were natives of Thessalonike, but spent much of their lives in the capital. Neilos, however, seems to have been a teacher — it is not clear of what — in Thessalonike in his younger days, and numbered among his pupils Demetrios Kydones. His works include treatises on Palamist theology and much anti-Latin polemic, including a critique of the *Summa contra Gentiles* of Thomas Aquinas, which had been translated into Greek by Kydones.[20] Nicholas Kabasilas, although probably a layman throughout his life, was primarily a mystical theologian, but not a follower of Palamas.[21] His *Interpretation of the Divine Liturgy* and his treatise *On the Life in Christ* have had a profound effect on Orthodox theological thought since his day. In an encomium of Saint Demetrios he praises Thessalonike as a centre of learning.

Demetrios Kydones was born in Thessalonike about 1324 and educated there.[22] But his subsequent career in the service of John Kantakouzenos and John V, whose chief minister he became, was in Constantinople. It was there that he learned Latin, translated the *Summa Theologica* and the *Summa contra Gentiles* of Thomas Aquinas, and entered the Roman church. His last days were spent in Venice and in Crete, where he died in 1397/8. His younger brother, Prochoras, spent the whole of his life in Macedonia, mainly in the monastery of Great Lavra on Mount Athos. Like Demetrios he was a devoted and sympathetic student and expositor of Thoman theology. It is not clear whether he ever joined the Roman church.

In the later fourteenth and early fifteenth centuries the intellectual life of Macedonia became more and more restricted to the domain of the church. The great classical scholars of 1300 to 1350 had no successors. And even among the churchmen there was no one of the stature of Demetrios Palamas or Gregory Akindynos. The desperate situation of the empire seems to have resulted in a loss of nerve and a turning away from reason to faith. And as region after region passed under Ottoman rule it was to the Orthodox Church rather than to the organs of the Byzantine state that the inhabitants looked for intellectual as well as spiritual leadership. There were still men of letters and scholars however. Isidore Glavas, metropolitan of Thessalonike from 1380 to 1396 left a collection of forty-seven homilies, often dealing with the pressing social problems of the age, a commentary on St. Luke's Gospel, a number of letters, and a treatise on astronomy.[23] Only a few of his homilies have so far been published. His successor as metropolitan, Gabriel, was a native of Thessalonike who became abbot of the Chora monastery in Constantinople. In 1397 he returned to his native city where he remained as head of the church until his death in the second decade of the fifteenth century.[24] A collection of sixty-six of his homilies is still unpublished. Gabriel was succeeded by Symeon, who was metropolitan until his death in 1429. Symeon composed a corpus of theological treatises which amounted to a systematic exposition of Orthodox doctrine. They were presumably intended for the training of the clergy of his diocese, much of which was by now under Ottoman administration. Some of his treatises have recently been published for the first time.[25] In the provincial cities of Macedonia too there were clerics with some claim to learning. A collection of homilies by an unknown bishop of Beroia survives in an early fifteenth century manuscript.

Finally, the capture of Thessalonike on 29 March 1430 by the army of sultan Murad II is described with all the graphic detail of an eyewitness by John Anagnostes, a member of the lower clergy.[26] Anagnostes' work in its present form is probably an expansion of the original text by a later editor, who describes the subsequent results of the capture of the city, and refers to documents of metropolitans Gregory (July 1432) and Methodios (October 1483).

ART IN THE LATE BYZANTINE PERIOD

ARCHITECTURE

In these last two and a half centuries Byzantine art was able to overcome all the difficulties of these parlous times, to renew its medium of expression without abandoning its basic rules for dealing with the real visible world which had been formulated during centuries of practical experience in building, and to create new types and to provide new appearances for buildings, without giving up any of the architectural, structural and formal solutions which had been worked out in architecture till then.

The breaking up of the Greek world into small states fighting one another in districts which, formerly belonging to the empire, now still remained free led to an increase of artistic centres, each of which flourished around a local ruler, and the strengthening of neighbouring Balkan states, all heirs presumptive to the weakened empire, provided Byzantine artists with the opportunity of creating works on an imperial scale outside Constantinople.

In the first half of the thirteenth century the creation of centres of art in both Greek and non-Greek districts elicited significant architectural activity in many places in the Byzantine world and its sphere of influence. As a general rule all of the new churches continue the architectural types previously in use, but now the choice of plan and the methods of working it out lead to special forms which are typical of the time.

In addition, older churches were remodelled or enlarged at this time and there are many examples in Constantinople (Chora (Kariyeh), Pammakaristos monasteries, Saints Theodore etc.). In accordance with this trend the chapel of Saint Euthymios (thirteenth century), a small three-aisled basilica,[1] was added to Saint Demetrios, and Saint Sophia at Ochrid received a two-storey exonarthex (1313-14) with a wonderful facade like that of a royal palace, the work of the metropolitan Gregory (cf. the facades of the Paragoritissa at Arta, 1291).[2]

In Ochrid a large new church was built in 1294-95, the Peribleptos (later Saint Clement) with a cross-in-square plan having four columns and no surrounding galleries; it was founded by the Byzantine ruler Progonos Sgouros when Ochrid was still Greek.[3] The walls of the church of the Peribleptos are richly decorated with friezes of enamelled plaques, *cloisonné* masonry similar to that of the churches of the despotate of Epirus; the domes with arched drums are somewhat exaggeratedly articulated with triple saw-tooth friezes and triply recessed arches. The church of Saint George built at Omorphi Ekklesia (formerly Gallista) in the Kastoria region is contemporary with the Peribleptos and nearly identical in plan.[4] Saint George is akin to the churches of the despotate even to the large tower in the middle of the exonarthex.

The katholikon of the Prodromos monastery at Serrhai was built at the end of the thirteenth century; it is single-aisled with a dome, enclosed on three sides by open porticoes which were later closed off.[5]

The new churches built in Thessalonike favoured the cross-in-square plan with a porch on three sides such as Saint Katherine, the Holy Apostles and also Saint Panteleimon where the porch is open. The katholikon of the Vlatadon monastery must originally have been similar, at least in this period. The church of the Holy Apostles has drums on the four corners of the galleries which form a low three-sided narthex; in the centre of the ensemble rise the arches supporting the central fifth domed drum (cf. the parekklesion of Constantine Lips in Constantinople) which is high and elegant. The whole has picturesque charm. The domes with arched drums with colonettes made of brick, saw-tooth friezes and recessed arches are typical constructions of this period. Lavish but refined brickwork ornament, carried out with precision, decorates the high seven-sided central apse and blind arches give the side walls a rhythmic movement (fig. 235). The Holy Apostles, the katholikon of a monastery founded by the patriarch Nephon about 1310, must be a little later than Saint Katherine, a church of less striking grace and elegance the central apse of which is rounded — an old fashioned feature. The church of Saint Katherine also has the facade of the narthex opening in arcades like the Holy Apostles (cf. Kilise Čami in Constantinople). The relatively limited interior areas of these churches are broken up into small units and become complicated, often mysterious or more intimate. The central area is narrow and high with emphasis on verticality; the three-sided narthex with four domes repeats the same scheme at a lower level.

We find other types in smaller churches built in Thessalonike at this time, e.g. the three-aisled basilica enclosed by a narthex on three sides, as in the two-storey tomb church of Taxiarches; or the type with a single aisle and wooden roof as in Saint Nicholas Orphanos which also has a wide-sided narthex which here assumes the form of the lateral aisles of a three-aisled basilica. Later on, the large church of Saint Elias was built on the triconch plan of the athonite type with four side chapels and a wide two-storey lite instead of a narthex (fig. 234). It is an impressive building on account of its great height and richly ornamented masonry, with the series of blind arches adorning the

234. The church of Saint Elias in Thessalonike, katholikon of the so-called Nea Moni, founded by Makarios Choumnos around 1360. It was built in the athonite style; side chapels flank the three-apsed sanctuary, but the church had a spacious two-storey lite instead of the narthex.

235. The church of the Holy Apostles was the katholikon of the monastery founded by the patriarch Nephon about 1310. Drums top the four corners of the galleries which form a low three-sided narthex and the central dome was supported on arches.

236. Saint Merkourios in the basilica of the Protaton, Karyes. The wall paintings which decorate this church are thought to be the work of the painter known as Manuel Panselinos, who was active in the late 13th and early 14th century.

apses and with the high domed drums of the main church, of the chapels and of the lite. It was the katholikon of the so-called Nea Moni, founded by Makarios Choumnos *c.* 1360 and consecrated to the Virgin.[6] The little ruined two-storey church of Saint Nicholas in the castle of Serrhai is also triconch each conch being three-sided; it is perhaps earlier than Saint Elias. Blind arches only on the sides of the apses are the sole ornamentation on this building.[7]

At Beroia the church of Saint John the Theologian is a three-aisled basilica with a wooden roof;[8] and the (monastery?) church of Christ (1315) is one-aisled.[9] Both churches have lovely wall paintings, as do other churches in the town, Saint Kerykos with a narthex on three sides and Saint Blasios, one-aisled with two porches. The remarkable church of Saint Nicholas, Beroia has been demolished; it was of the same type with lofty blind arches and richly patterned brickwork in the apse.[10] Single-aisled wooden-roofed churches with irregular masonry are common in Kastoria at this time. The little church of Saint Athanasios has wall paintings dated to 1384-85 and in small churches such as Taxiarches, near the Panagia

Koumbelidiki, the monogram XC is done in bricks inserted between the stone blocks.[11]

It should be noted that in the smaller towns of Macedonia such as Beroia and Kastoria, Ochrid and elsewhere, the exteriors of the smaller churches were plain and the building was low with rather ordinary masonry, scarcely distinguishable from the neighbouring houses which, so-to-speak, usually surrounded the church protectively. They were generally dedicated by individuals, e.g. at Beroia the church of Christ was dedicated by Xenos Psalidas and that of Saint John the Theologian by one Nikephoros Sgouros. On the other hand the monastery churches, such as Chilandari on Athos, built at the beginning of the fourteenth century by the Serbian ruler Milutin, are so large and have such carefully finished masonry that they create the impression of aiming to equal the katholikon churches of older imperial monasteries.[12]

PAINTING

The thirteenth century was a critical period in the development of Byzantine painting as it approached its final phase. An entirely new situation was created when Constantinople ceased to function as the main governing and coordinating power and the Greek world was fragmented into little states quarrelling with each other whilst central districts were occupied by foreigners; since the boundaries of each little principality were forever changing, conditions remained unstable. In these parlous times Byzantine painting neither relinquished its role as leader and teacher on all levels and throughout the whole area, including free districts, occupied areas and neighbouring territories, nor lost the ability of adjusting to the requirements of a changing clientele. It could indeed be argued that circumstances favoured the gradual release of artistic potentialities hitherto kept in check by a strong central power. It was very important to determine which centre would, to some extent, take the place of Constantinople now under foreign rule. Thessalonike was freed in 1224 by Theodore Angelos, the despot of Epirus, and thus naturally assumed the burden of effectively continuing the mission of a great centre, a role which she had apparently never entirely failed to play. We learn from Serbian sources that Saint Sabbas passed through Thessalonike in 1219 and commissioned two large icons from the best artists in town; he embellished the icons with ornaments and dedicated them in the Philokalos monastery which he himself had founded. We are not sure, however, what sort of painting these artists, who according to the Serbian sources were very famous produced for the Serbian prince-monk.[13]

There are, in fact, relatively few monuments of pictorial art (nineteen) of the thirteenth century known in Macedonia by comparison with the more southerly regions of Greece. The number is smaller than for the preceding two centuries. The fourteenth century shows a striking increase, with about sixty monuments, more than the total of fifty-one for the ninth through the thirteenth centuries. This number would be appreciably larger were we to reckon with the works of Thessalonikan artists who worked outside the borders of the empire.[14]

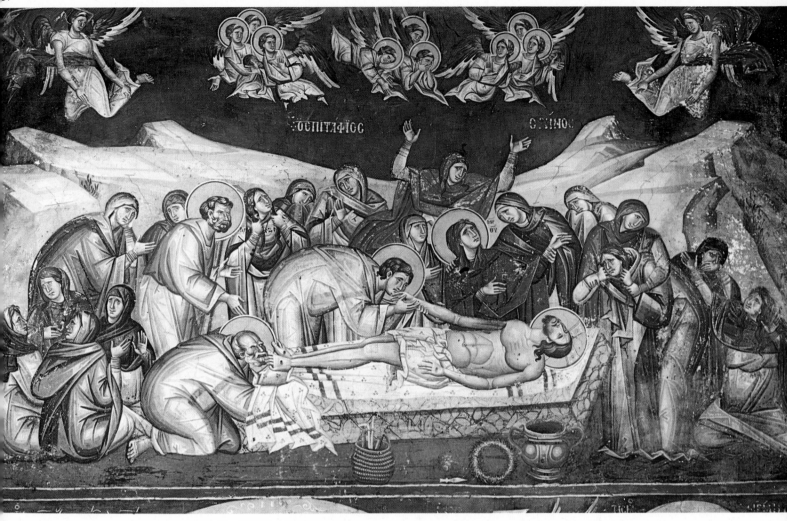

237. *The Lamentation from the church of the Peribleptos, Ochrid. The decoration of this church is representative of art at* the end of the 13th century when the earliest phase of Palaiologan painting had reached its highest development.

1204-61

The most important monument of the thirteenth century, which forms both the key and the point of reference for this subject, are the wall paintings surviving in the south aisle of the great basilica, Acheiropoietos, in Thessalonike. The Forty Martyrs are represented like icons, one beside the other, full-length or busts according to the available space. These monumental well set-up figures have gone beyond the mannerism of the end of the twelfth century. They do, however, preserve still earlier characteristics, the red spots on the cheeks, the stylized ears, characteristics encountered in eleventh century painting, coupled here with an interest in rendering agitated emotions typical mainly for portraits of old people.[15] We shall meet these elements again as an artistic style and as a psychological climate in many figures at Mileševa, founded by the ruler Vladislav I Nemanja (1230-35),[16] and this link permits us to date the Forty Martyrs to c. 1225-35 and also to observe that in the period of the despotate Thessalonike was creative centre. This statement about Thessalonike does not exclude the possibility that palace artists fled from Constantinople to Thessalonike after its liberation in 1224. Subsequently, fine

artists of similar origin must have worked also in the basilica church at Mileševa in Serbia, continuing the 'academic' tradition of the twelfth century with aristocratic wall painting, the figures of which possess incomparable beauty and expressive power. Imitation of older mosaics is another typical trend: neighbouring countries attempted to rival the magnificence of mosaics in Thessalonike and Constantinople by covering backgrounds with gold leaf.

The wall paintings in the church of Acheiropoietos and those in the basilica at Mileševa are closely related to others in a far distant territory which, however, was also ruled by the despotate of Epirus. In 1965 wall paintings were uncovered under layers of whitewash in the church of Episkope in Evritania on what was the bank of the Megdhova river, a building which is now at the bottom of the artificially created lake Kremaston; three layers of painting were disengaged, the latest of which, dated to the thirteenth century, originally entirely covered the walls and vaults. Two basic styles can be distinguished in this extensive set of wall paintings. Certain large representations of church feasts have a tranquil monumental composition with imposing figures, luminous soft modelling and fluid

40

343

241. The Resurrection. The mosaics which decorate the church of the Holy Apostles, Thessalonike (1312-15) are works of a very high standard. They demonstrate a clear trend towards the monumental, expressed through the geometrical concept of rhythm underlying the compositions.

drapery where the faces of the angels, as indeed of other figures, have a beauty recalling classical inspiration.

Other wall paintings were executed in an entirely different style, for example the fragments of the Descent into Hell where the modelling is more painterly with swift brush strokes and the expression more vigorous; the full-length saints, portrayed as tall warriors, exude a manly ethos albeit their stance is slightly unsteady. The scenes and the faces tend to capture the fleeting moment rather than an enduring classical form.[17]

The few examples of wall painting recently found at Trnovo, the capital of the new Bulgarian state, have been attributed to the same artistic circle; these wall paintings in the church of SS. Peter and Paul were painted when king Radoslav took as a model the works of his father-in-law, Theodore the despot of Thessalonike. It is difficult to speak of a local artistic school at Trnovo when, aside from other considerations, there exists no preceding nor subsequent

building to provide a factual basis justifying discussion of the development of a local independent 'school' of art.[18]

Greek artists in the service of foreign Orthodox princes, secular or ecclesiastical, had the opportunity of maintaining the high standards of court art. This, to a certain extent, explains the outstanding quality of the series of wall paintings produced; all belong in the mainstream of Byzantine painting of the period and not to any special 'Serbian' or 'Bulgarian' school as Lazarev has written.[19]

Amongst the monuments of the first half of the thirteenth century we shall find parallels to the painting at Mileševa, but of a different nature as, for example, the wall paintings in the Holy Apostles, the middle church at Peć, the seat of the Serbian patriarchate after 1220. Here there is a gigantically large representation of the Deesis in the sanctuary apse in which the imposing bust of Christ has a harsh almost coarse expression, whereas the very tall Virgin in the Ascension, which is in the dome as in some churches of Thessalonike, has the liveliness of a robust young peasant girl with a wide firm chin and sturdy neck.[20] A cycle of scenes from the life of the Prophet Elijah is preserved in the diaconicon of the church of the Dormition at Morača, wall paintings executed shortly after the church was built in 1252.[21] And in both of these sets of wall paintings big closed forms predominate with a tendency to large, flowing, drapery folds and the representation of architecture reduced to a minimum. It has been rightly observed that these styles are more of a reversion to eleventh century art than a continuation of twelfth century art.

Some monuments of the first half of the thirteenth century have been preserved in the free Macedonian districts. Most of the wall paintings in the single-aisled church of the Mesonisiotissa monastery, now Mavriotissa, at Kastoria near the lake are preserved in good condition (figs. 228-229). These wall paintings do not fit in with the cycle of Macedonian wall paintings known to be of this period because they lack the iconographical and stylistic peculiarities and the luminous colours. Hence there have been doubts as to how these wall paintings, which have not yet been systematically studied, should be dated. Nevertheless it is difficult not to admit that the wall paintings as a whole reflect various manners of painting in the thirteenth century, some of which, in their anti-classical spirit, are akin to Frankish style of the period.[22]

Mavriotissa is not alone in having a connection with western elements. At Saint Stephens, where the the most recent frescoes are of the thirteenth century without much uniformity, an unpublished representation of the Virgin Enthroned in the narthex has the hallmarks of the so-called Crusader style: faces with bulging eyes, western upholstery for the throne and the halo adorned with a branch in relief. At Koumbelidiki the iconography of the Dormition of the Virgin is western and in an early anthropomorphic representation of the Trinity, Christ holds the dove of the Holy Spirit *(filioque)*.[23] To these undoubted borrowings from the western world which had established itself in the East after the Crusades we may add carved wooden icons. Stone icons carved in relief were not uncommon in the Byzantine period and there are some from Thessalonike, such as the more stylized praying Virgin (now in the

Byzantine Museum, Athens, inv. no. 148) and the classicizing praying Virgin still in Thessalonike.[24]

Icons made of wood, either in relief or painted, first appear in Macedonia in the thirteenth century. The largest one, 2.85 m. high, at Omorphi Ekklesia (formerly Gallista) near Kastoria, bears a representation of Saint George as a warrior in high relief; he is shown in a frontal pose and his awkward limbs are ill-proportioned.[25] A similar though even less sophisticated icon depicting the local saint, Clement, was found in the neighbourhood of Ochrid.[26] There is a two-sided icon from Kastoria now in the Byzantine Museum, Athens, in which only one figure is carved in relief, the warrior saint George shown full figure, turning and stretching out his hands in prayer toward the small painted figure of Christ (fig. 246).[27]

In completing a review of Macedonian monuments up until the recovery of Constantinople in 1261, we find a variety of artistic trends which display contact with many areas; however, we may insist on the fact that the most distinguished works of art are associated with Thessalonike.

1261-1330

During the last decades of the thirteenth century, official art with the variants and reversions to older models practised in the Balkans seems to have continued, though not without interruptions, along the lines of the unique murals at Sopoćani (c. 1265). Because of its quality and expansive epic character, the painting at Sopoćani is thought to reflect the art of the capital after the liberation.[28] The three-aisled katholikon of the monastery of Saint Nicholas near the village of Manastir in the Byzantine district of Morihovon has extensive mural decoration done in a local style and harking back to older models. The inscription mentions the emperor Michael Palaiologos and informs us that it was dedicated in 1271 by John, deacon and *referendarios* of the archiepiscopate; the painting is strongly reminiscent of the dynamic Komnene style and also of monumental figures of the eleventh century. Murals of several other monuments in this area are related to this kind of wall painting and so is at least one large icon of Saint George full length, signed by John the Historiographer in 1267.[29]

Fragments of murals dating to around 1270 are preserved in the royal monastery at Gradać in the area under Serbian rule; here, however, the monumental quality has been lost because the elegant figures, which are much too small for murals, have something of the charm of portable icons or miniatures.[30] Artists from Thessalonike were working at Arilje, the capital of the bishopric, in 1296, as the late Professor S. Radojčić has shown, mainly in order to paint regional historical figures and local church councils alongside the customary iconographical cycles. The drawing is inept, the volumes tend to be bulky and the movement of the figures awkward even when the pose has a classical derivation, such as the girl in the Birth of the Virgin whose garment arches over her head like a bow.[31]

The most important monument of the period is the Protaton at Karyes, where the murals covering the vast surfaces of the tenth century basilica are of rare quality

242. Detail from the Entry into Jerusalem. An attachment to classical tradition is to be traced in the almost painterly modelling, the noble presence and stance of the figures, their movements and drapery. Mosaic, church of the Holy Apostles, Thessalonike.

both in the brilliance of colour, organic rendering of the body and psychological interpretation, qualities which endow this emphatically dramatic style with 'realistic' touches, with special nobility and strong spirituality (fig. 236). The serene splendour of the entire ensemble in zones suits the vast but tranquil architectonic space and the huge scenes have massive figures and many picturesque details. It is, however, questionable whether the artist who executed most of the Protaton was, in fact, the legendary Manuel Panselinos from Thessalonike whose fame continued to flourish amongst his fellow artists until the seventeenth century. At all events more than two artists were working here, if we are to judge on the basis of differences in style which is by turns more linear or more painterly, and differences in composition which vary from stormily dramatic to monumentally static.[32] There is another wall painting which also is closely related to the Protaton. It is a fragment with the striking head of Saint Nicholas from the earlier decoration of the katholikon of Great Lavra.[33] That these frescoes are of Macedonian origin, to be dated before or around 1300 is attested by the close relationship to work of two Thessalonikan artists at Ochrid.

In 1295 Eutychios and Michael, son of Astrapas, from a known family in Thessalonike, painted the murals in the church of the Peribleptos at Ochrid, dedicated by a noble, Progonos Sgouros, at a time when Ochrid was under Byzantine control.[34] The subjects are dramatically portrayed in continuous zones with massive figures shown in exaggerated poses or motion, vividly contrasting colours, drapery folds prismatically shaped and modelling with cut planes (fig. 237). The wall paintings in the Protaton have frequently been attributed to the atelier of Michael Astrapas and Eutychios because of their obvious similarity to the work of this pair in the church of the Peribleptos: the massive figures, the venerable or angry heads with similar facial features, the perspective views of architecture, all this belongs to the same artistic vocabulary. But the unquestioned artistic superiority of the frescoes in the Protaton is one of the many reasons which make impossible the attribution of these murals to that atelier.[35]

Both of these monuments belong to a particular trend which has been termed the volume style; it constitutes the typical style and also the highest level of attainment at the close of the first phase of Palaiologan art (up to *c.* 1300).[36] We shall be observing the changeover to the new style which characterizes the following phase in the work of the same team of artists because a few years afterwards Michael and Eutychios radically altered their style.

Wall paintings in a whole series of churches founded by the ruler Milutin do, in fact, carry the signatures of the artists Michael the son of Astrapas and Eutychios; the churches are: the Mother of God Ljeviška in Prizren (1308-09), Saint George in Staro Nagoričino (1317) and Saint Nikitas at Čučer (1320).[37] In these later works, where it is difficult to recognize the artists of the Peribleptos at Ochrid, the crowded compositions full of life and motion in the midst of, or in front of, intricate architectural fantasies, still pervaded by a strong dramatic feeling, the slender and lighter figures, the somewhat coarse facial types, the bright palette of delicate colours and the softer modelling — all of these changes represent adaptation both to a new surge of interest in narrative compositions and to new artistic concepts common to the wall paintings of the Thessalonikan circle of the second decade of the thirteenth century.[38] Our knowledge of the artistic activity of a certain number of artistic ateliers in the Macedonian capital is supplemented by groups of murals created during the first two decades of this century in the Thessalonike area and in the sphere of activity of the city's painters. The well known murals of the little parekklesion of Saint Euthymios in the church of Saint Demetrios (1303) are anonymous, dedicated by the *protostrator* Michael Glavas the Tarchaneiotes whose widow Maria 'of Komnenian birth' later founded the large parekklesion in the church of the Pammakaristos monastery, Constantinople. Although these paintings are not well preserved, enough remains to attest their high technique and spirit of renewal, especially in relation to the exaggerations rife at the end of the century.[39] The little known wall paintings in Saint Katherine in Thessalonike seem to be strongly reminiscent of the volume style,[40]

243. The Dormition of the Virgin; on either side stand the hymn writers John Damaskenos and Kosmas Maiouma . The transcendant quality and strict balance of the multi-figured composition are the hallmarks of George Kalliergis who executed this and other paintings in the church of Christ at Beroia in 1315.

243

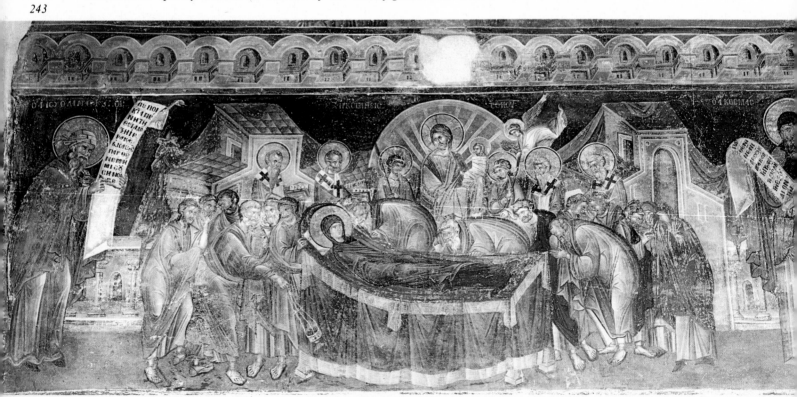

whereas the remains of wall painting in Saint Panteleimon, where exaggeration is sometimes carried to the point of distortion, still maintain the monumental poses of the end of the thirteenth century.[41] The wall paintings preserved in the narthex of Saint George at Omorphi Ekklesia near Kastoria are dated to *c.* 1296; they are more classical but they have the same spirit with large emphatically expressive figures distinguished by their noble bearing.[42]

The typical features of the second phase of Palaiologan pictorial art, which comes to an end in the third decade of the fourteenth century, crystallize out in a series of monumental pictorial programmes created in the second decade of the fourteenth century, the most important of which are the mosaics and wall paintings in the church of the Holy Apostles at Thessalonike (1312-15).[43] Mosaics adorn the domed drum and the vaults and there are beautiful wall paintings in the lower section of the naos and the closed porticoes. The mosaics, examples of a high standard executed in two very different techniques, are distinguished by a very noticeable tendency towards monumentality expressed through the scale of the compositions and the figures with a geometric and rhythmic concept governing both the composition and the individual figures (figs. 241,242). The modelling of the figures is done in a painterly manner; the noble bearing of the figures, the way in which they stand or move and the drapery all reveal attachment to classical traditions. The vigorous poses express nobility rather than dynamism. Dramatic tension in the composition slackens off; iconographic types of a narrative or genre painting are often selected for subjects such as the Nativity, the Entrance to Jerusalem etc.; the action is on the whole restrained and there is a growing interest in rendering spatial depth. The somewhat later wall paintings betray similar influences.

It should be borne in mind that the art of Saint Euthymios and the Holy Apostles show that there was frequent and direct contact between Constantinople and Thessalonike. The mosaics of the Holy Apostles are related to the mosaics of the Pammakaristos and the Chora monastery (Kariyeh) firstly because they share a strong adherence to classical prototypes to such a degree that there are facial resemblances amongst them and, secondly, because there is a close kinship at least with the first of the stylistic trends which are distinguished in the mosaic decoration of the Chora monastery.[44]

The excellent wall paintings in the single-aisled wooden-roofed church of Christ at Beroia belong to the same series; they were painted in 1315 by George Kalliergis 'the best artist in all of Thessaly' (=Macedonia) as he described himself. Kalliergis was a prominent citizen of Thessalonike; he had good connections with the ecclesiastical administrators of Mount Athos and Manuel Philes dedicated an epigram to him. His wall paintings are of basic significance because of their high quality and very good state of preservation.[45] The subjects, done separately like icons, are painted with understanding and skill in creating balanced composition, in the drawing and above all in the use of colour; the delicate modelling has been done with so much care that it resembles that of a portable icon. Although not markedly classicistic the wall paintings

244. *Detail from the Betrayal of Christ, Saint Nicholas Kyritzes, Kastoria. The wall paintings in this church represent a definite anti-classical tendency expressed in rather simplistic compositions lacking the third dimension, strongly expressive and with a tendency to linear rendering.*

do have a serene elegance, a moderate sense of the dramatic and, where needed, a touch of grandeur (Dormition of the Virgin (fig. 243) Descent into Hell). The lesson of the Holy Apostles is clear here. Some few wall paintings preserved in the church of Saint Blasios in Beroia may derive from the same workshop.[46]

The wall paintings in the katholikon of Vatopedi (1312) are still concealed below the overpainting done in the nineteenth century except for those in the narthex where we may make out, even though they have not yet been cleaned, the nervousness of the gestures and the expressionistic turbulence of the whole ensemble.[47] The wall paintings in the katholikon of Chilandari (1318-20), a few of which have been cleaned, possess a tranquil, somewhat cloying elegance; the expressions are melancholy rather than lifeless.[48] The wall paintings in a small single-aisled church, the katholikon of the monastery of Saint Nicholas

245. Departure from the classical tradition is noticeable in the 15th century icon of the Virgin Odegetria from Saint Nicholas Orphanos, Thessalonike, Vlatadon monastery.

Orphanos in Thessalonike, breathe the same spirit of advanced 'Macedonian' painting with many iconographical cycles given in numerous small pictures, like portable icons (figs. 238-240). We have already noted the close connections obtaining among certain figures in the wall painting at the Chora monastery, the church of Christ at Beroia, Chilandari and other contemporary monuments. The art of the period at the end of the second decade or in the twenties of the fourteenth century is represented rather eclectically in Saint Nicholas Orphanos.[49]

These works no longer cherish a taste for monumentality or echos of the late thirteenth century heavy or volume style, maintaining only a tendency towards realism, in varying degrees. This tendency may have to do with the development of narrative cycles which require the depiction of a greater number of facets of reality. But when artists tend to portray figures that are less beautiful than before (not to speak of the search for expressive ugliness) and when they depict less noble poses and gestures and focus directly on the narrative, with no fear of crudeness where the story calls for it, we should interpret this not only as the artistic pursuit of realism and dramatic effect,

but mainly as an attempt to underline the truth of the Incarnation.[50]

In completing a survey of this critical but very fruitful period (1300-30) it must be clearly stated that alongside Constantinople, Thessalonike continues to be one of the most important artistic centres of religious art, with at least four or five workshops active at the same time, with artists who sign their names and anonymous artists continuing their work with mounting energy both in Greek territory and in neighbouring countries. The relatively consistent uniformity observed in the works of this period has led the way to the hypothesis that the art works of this area have an individuality all their own and hence they have been designated works of the 'Macedonian' school.[51] It is, nevertheless, a question whether it is right to say that the Macedonian artists described above developed iconographical conventions and a style and working habits distinct from those in Constantinople. It is however, unlikely that Thessalonike would have been able to take the initiative and set the trend along lines different from the development in Constantinople. Furthermore, it has previously been shown that there was close contact with the art of Constantinople.

1330 - 1453

We do not have any important monuments for the period 1330-1453; they are lacking not only in Thessalonike but also in Constantinople, as well as in neighbouring territories. This phenomenon must be stressed. In fact, even in the provincial districts, the somewhat more noteworthy works by no means maintained the artistic standards and forces of renewal seen in the art of the preceding decades. We should not attribute this lack of important monuments only to fortuitous disaster; it was mainly due to other factors, the endless deterioration of the general situation caused by conflicts in different spheres, dynastic contests, theological disputes, and other clashes, as well as chronic invasions on the part of northern neighbours and, lastly, the incessantly menacing presence of the Turks.

In particular it is possible to observe that interest in renewing the means of expression was on the wane, made clear by the standstill in the development of style; established types and procedures in painting were repeated. And, indeed, in the third quarter of the century a revival of or reversion to models of the first twenty years or even earlier is noticeable. It appears that the main interest lies in enriching the iconographical programme by creating an even greater number of cycles (at Mateić, 1356-60, there are thirteen cycles) with less common themes. These cycles drew on liturgical texts, collections of hymns, psalms and church services. The cycles frequently echo theological controversies provoked by heretical leanings or the disputes with the Hesychasts who finally won out in 1368; symbolic representations often give variety to the programme. In the historical episodes of the Gospels, above all the scenes from the Passion, the interest in detailed narrative grows to the point of breaking each sequence in the drama up into many separate moments and thus the number of scenes is greatly expanded — there

246. A two-sided icon of St. George from Kastoria. The full-length warrior saint, depicted in relief, is shown in profile, his hands raised in prayer to the small painted figure of Christ. 13th century. Athens, Byzantine Museum.

349

are thirty scenes in the representation of the Passion in the Markov monastery (1379-80). Then again there is a great throng of people in each scene and some wall paintings (Lesnovo-Mateić) are suffocatingly overcrowded.[52] All this originates essentially in a desire to present an encyclopaedic survey of theology, best accomplished by means of an extremely analytic narrative style in which people and objects are depicted in a convincing manner — customarily termed 'realism'. For the same reason anachronistic elements, particularly costumes, are stressed.

A generally observed phenomenon in the style of this period is the waning importance of classicizing elements, although this does not mean that such elements do not reappear as stereotyped subordinate motifs. This anticlassical trend should not be linked to the Hesychast movement; Beck has stated that Hesychasm is not incompatible with humanism, as appears from the fact that the pictorial ensembles which are most strongly classicistic are to be found in monasteries. Nor is it plausible to attribute the anticlassical trend to local 'Balkan' traditions, as has been proposed, because its occurrence in southern Greece and the islands eliminates the possibility of localizing it in the northern area.[53]

It is not easy to determine the part played by Thessalonike in the artistic life of this period because there are no noteworthy dated monuments in the town itself. Some evidence in the form of fragmentary wall paintings in the narthex of Saint Elias, the Nea Moni of Makarios Choumnos (c. 1360-80) and the wall painting (after 1383) in Saint Demetrios showing Joseph with Gregory Palamas, the leader of victorious Hesychasm, suggests that the following wall paintings may be attributed to Thessalonikan artists: the parekklesion of the Anargyroi at Vatopedi, the parekklesion of the Archangels at Chilandari, three churches in Serbian Moravia, namely Sisojevać (1390), Ravanica (1370-80) and Resava (1418).[54] The works of these average artists of the diaspora, which had already begun, certainly do not reflect the best work being produced in Thessalonike; they show a clear tendency toward a somewhat prosaic solidity with characteristically round, rather stolid faces. A few wall paintings in the Vlatadon monastery in Thessalonike are altogether different; they have a pronouncedly manneristic style found again in the wall painting of Nea Pavlitsa.[55]

In western Macedonia we shall find a more perceptible anticlassical style with somewhat more simple-minded compositions, lacking the third dimension, the figures more or less flat, often markedly expressive, with a preference for linear rendering as in the Taxiarches (1359-60) or Saint Nicholas Kyritzes (fig. 244), both in Kastoria.[56] This kind

247. The Crucifixion. This icon, from Thessalonike, is a typical example of Palaiologan art. The total absence of narrative element bestows a monumental quality on the composition. Second half of the 14th century. Athens, Byzantine Museum.

248. The large icon of Christ, from Thessalonike, is a work of high quality, clearly showing the anti-classical trends dominating art at the beginning of the 14th century. Athens, Byzantine Museum.

of painting probably emanated from some centre in western Macedonia, perhaps Ochrid where a series of wall paintings show that art was flourishing in that region mainly between 1330 and 1360. The cultured Greek metropolitan bishops of Ochrid brought in artists to decorate both the old and new churches, for example John Theorianos who worked in the narthex of the metropolitan church of Saint Sophia (1346-50) and probably the little church of the Anargyroi (1350). The wall paintings in other churches of Ochrid such as Saints Constantine and Helen (1370-80) and the parekklesion of Saint Gregory at the Peribleptos and others in Ochrid and the vicinity reveal a gradual withdrawal to simplified concepts.[57] These works were probably executed by local artists.

Artworks in other styles were current in Macedonia at the same time, produced in workshops of various origins and varying standards. The figures in Saint Athanasios Mouzakes in Kastoria, a small single-aisled church dated to 1385, possess some measure of elegance and three-dimensional modelling; they often wear amazingly fantastic costumes and curious hats, all of them anachronistic. The classically well organized balanced compact compositions are outstanding for the 'realistic' liveliness of the poses and dramatic gestures.[58] The figures and the compositions unquestionably hark back to Thessalonikan wall paintings of 1300-20. It is probable that artists from the some workshop also worked in the church of the Virgin (1368) on the island of Mali Grad in what is now the Albanian sector of lake Prespa, and also at Borje in Albania in the church of Zoodochos Pigi (1390),[59] but the Kastoria wall paintings are superior because of the richness of the programme and the fine colours.

The wall paintings of the Markov monastery near Skopje (1366-71), founded by Stephen Dušan in 1345, revert to earlier prototypes more markedly; they must have been painted by two groups of artists. The predominant trait in Group A is a reversion to the volume style of the end of the thirteenth century, carried out with sovereign skill in building up forms with colour: the massive bodies, the angry broad faces of the old men with their luxuriant hair. Group B has been associated with the artist Theorianos from Ochrid.[60]

In other churches in the neighbourhood of Skopje, such as the monastery of the Virgin at Mateić also founded by Dušan, the wall paintings (c. 1356-60) are of fine quality and here too there is a wealth of iconographic cycles with a dense crowd populating the five zones in the lofty church, in a continuous narration with no dividing framing strips.[61] At the monastery of the Virgin at Psača there are a great many huge striking family portraits of the royal family of Vukašin (1366-71), Serbian princes, and venerable figures of countless saints. Because of their great size and three-dimensional handling these works hark back to older monumental representations.[62]

The wall paintings which have been mentioned here, all from the area of Skopje, are works of artists whose origins are closer to a greater centre than those of Kastoria; this may be explained by the fact that the 'founders' of these churches belong to the Serbian royal family. It is not likely that the patrons played a role in choosing the composition

of the intricate iconographical programme which the artists brought in from centres elsewhere and worked up on the spot, perhaps in collaboration with local Greek bishops, but the rulers certainly saw to it that they and their families were represented on a scale at least as large as the saints in contrast to the much more decent representations of the Byzantine founders.

In the church of the Prodromos monastery Serrhai the narthexes were painted by successive artists who appear to have been following somewhat different traditions. At least the wall paintings made while the founder of the monastery was alive (Joachim a man of the Byzantine court, d. 1333) are closer to the style of Constantinople at the beginning of the century. And after Serrhai was captured by the Serbian Kral Dušan (1345), the decoration continued to be carried out in the spirit of the period, a bit differently from what we saw in western Macedonia; the programme is simpler, quieter, less emphatic and, on the whole, more traditional. In the earliest group there are three scenes dated to around 1300 which have a dynamic style; in the second there are two cycles of the life of Saint John the Baptist and the Miracles of Jesus which represent the average level of accomplishment during this period.[63]

In this series of wall paintings, which are also important because they are more or less dated, we once more have had occasion to observe that national schools do not exist and that Byzantine art throughout the realm of the Orthodox Church appears to be unaffected by the vicissitudes of history.

Some of the original mural decoration is preserved in the katholikon of Pantokrator on Mount Athos; the three huge figures, about 3.50 m. high, from the Deesis on the east wall of the esonarthex are outstanding. It was sponsored by the Byzantine rulers of Chrysoupolis in 1363; these wall paintings reflect a high level of artistic achievement, probably that of the capital rather than of Thessalonike to judge from the figures with their noble and majestic bearing and broad finely-painted faces.[64] A large splendid despotic icon of Christ dedicated in the same monastery has portraits of the founders.[65]

Many icons of this period have survived, mostly at Mount Athos but also elsewhere, and many of them are very well done. The great Deesis, consisting of ten icons, at Chilandari,[66] is an outstanding example and so are a similar Deesis at Vatopedi[67] and the excellent two-sided icon with the Miracle of the Latomos monastery.[68]

Some icons on another artistic plane may be dated in the fifteenth century, such as the Virgin and Child from the monastery of Saint Nicholas Orphanos (fig. 245)[69], an icon of the Virgin from Kastoria, two icons from Prilep in Belgrade[70] and others which reveal a definite abandonment of classical tradition. The same trend shows up earlier in a unique illuminated manuscript (1322-40) from Thessalonike with scenes from the life of Saint Demetrios.[71]

In closing the chapter with the final subjugation of Macedonia by the Turks in 1430, we would do well to reflect on the achievement of the artists in this area who, in the midst of the most difficult historical circumstances, undauntedly continued to create beautiful works, from large scale ensembles to small individual pieces, right to the end.

MODERN
MACEDONIA

FROM 1430 TO 1821

ADMINISTRATIVE, SOCIAL AND ECONOMIC DEVELOPMENTS

THE INHABITANTS

Religious, ethnic and linguistic groups

Before the Ottomans reached Macedonia, the inhabitants of the area belonged to the eastern Christian church, with the exception of a few Jews, and were divided into three linguistic groups: Greek-speakers, Vlach-speakers and Slav-speakers.[1] The Greek-speaking group was descended from remote antiquity. The Vlach-speakers included the remaining Latin-speaking descendants of the old Roman colonists, or of indigenous Balkan populations who had adopted the Latin language. The Slav-speaking group had entered Macedonia at the end of the sixth century and later. The Greek-speakers (amongst whom were numbered the Jews) and Vlach-speakers described themselves as *Romaioi* (Romans), as did all the citizens of the Byzantine empire, which was the heir to the Roman empire. From the thirteenth century onwards, some Byzantine scholars had begun to become aware of the fact that the Greek-speaking members of the empire were descendants of the ancient Greeks, and to use the ethnic name 'Hellenes', but it was some time before this awareness spread to wider circles and became a factor of historical significance. Before he assumed the royal crown, Manuel Palaiologos, the governor of Thessalonike, still believed that the inhabitants of his province of Macedonia were *Romaioi* (Romans). 'We are *Romaioi*', he maintained, adding, 'Our country is the land of Philip and Alexander.'

The Ottoman conquest brought to Macedonia a new religious, ethnic and linguistic group: its religion was Islam, and ethnically and linguistically it was Turkish. The Jews of Macedonia, too, were very soon strengthened by immigration. From the beginning of the Ottoman period until the first decade of the twentieth century (a period of five hundred and thirty or forty years) the dominant group grew at the expense of the others, through conversions to Islam that were followed sooner or later by the adoption by the converts of the Turkish language and culture. The subject groups also suffered losses through their members leaving their homes to avoid persecution, or sometimes to pursue a career unhindered by obstacles. On a smaller scale, there was a certain fluidity between the boundaries of the various Christian groups. During the Ottoman period there were also considerable changes in the composition of the various groups as a result of movements from region to region, or from the countryside to the townships and towns.

The settlement of the Turks in Macedonia began immediately after the conquest of the area and continued throughout the fifteenth century. Some of the settlers, the Yürüks, had not advanced beyond the stage of semi-nomadic cattle-raisers, while others had already become farmers in Asia Minor. The best estates were given as fiefs to members of the Ottoman aristocracy. A large proportion of the former inhabitants had abandoned their homes during the fighting and during the mass arrivals of the Turkish immigrants. The conquerors only tolerated the infidels where they needed them — as cultivators on the timars, as workers, artisans and merchants, and, rarely, as allies (at the beginning of the Ottoman period there were some Christian *sipahis*) — or in areas in which they did not have a great economic interest. The Christian refugees withdrew to the mountains and semi-mountainous areas, and to the isolated region of Chalkidike, or moved down to some of the Aegean islands and the Peloponnese. At the same time, conversions to Islam began to take place, affecting not only the Christians, but also the Jews, who became a group of some importance in Macedonia at the end of the fifteenth century.

The first Jews to arrive in Macedonia during the Ottoman period (about 1470) had been driven out of the German lands and Hungary. Subsequently, larger numbers of refugees arrived from Spain (1492 onwards); from Sicily and Southern Italy (1493); from Portugal (1497) and from Provence (1506). From 1540-60, and even later, waves of Marranos arrived from these same countries; the Marranos were Jews who had converted to Christianity, but were suspected by the Holy Inquisition. In the middle of the seventeenth century, Jews expelled from the Ukraine, Poland and North Africa came to Macedonia, and further groups from Spain, Portugal and Italy arrived at the beginning of the eighteenth century.

The Jewish immigrants may be divided into two large and numerous smaller groups on the basis of their place of origin, their customs, the form of their religious ritual, and the language or dialect that they spoke. Those who came from central Europe constituted the large group of Ashkenazi, had acquired the psychology of the persecuted and spoke the German-Jewish dialect, Yiddish. Those who came from the Iberian peninsula belonged to the large group of the Sephardim; they spoke a variety of Spanish, Portuguese, and even Italian dialects, and retained the customs and manners of their former homes, where they had lived without problems until they had been expelled. The Jews who had long been Hellenized were known as *Romaniotes,* and they too retained their own customs. For some time, all the smaller groups avoided intercourse with their co-religionists. Ultimately, the Sephardim prevailed, both culturally and linguistically.

At the end of the sixteenth century there occurred the first migration to Macedonia of Christians from other parts of the Ottoman empire. Vlach-speakers from the Agrapha villages and the Acheloos settled in Thessalonike and the surrounding area. In 1605 they constituted half the Christian population of the city. In the seventeenth century, the Greek- and Vlach-speaking peasants of Macedonia began to migrate to the north, where they became town-dwellers in the northern provinces of the empire or in foreign countries. This movement lasted through the eighteenth and the first decades of the nineteenth centuries (see page 383). At the same time, the Greek- and Vlach-speaking peasants abandoned the countryside and became artisans or small-scale retailers in the towns of Macedonia. On the other hand, the growth of the export trade led to an increase in demand for agricultural products. The Ottoman landowners needed more tenant farmers and seasonal agricultural workers. As the number of Greek- and Vlach-speaking peasants dwindled, the landowners turned to Slav-speakers from Bulgarian and Serbian areas to meet their needs.

Both earlier and more recent inhabitants of Macedonia, Christians and Jews alike, moved across into the Muslim religious group and, as a second stage, into the Turkish-speaking group. Sometimes entire groups were converted to Islam, and sometimes individuals. The conversions were normally due to the oppression of non-Muslims by members of the Ottoman administration, by feudal lords, civil servants, brigands, and even by their neighbours. The oppression intensified whenever the Ottoman empire was at war with foreign powers, or during periods of Greek revolutionary movements, resulting in increased numbers of conversions. The final wave, at the beginning of the nineteenth century, was caused by the temporary transference of western Macedonia to the administration of Ali Pasha of Ioannina (see page 392). The conversions of Christian timariots at the beginning of the Ottoman period was the result not of oppression but of self-interest.

Although conversion to Islam was a single action, and needed only a public declaration, the process by which the newly converted adopted Ottoman culture and language required time. The more coherent the group formed by the converts of a particular area, the longer they retained the language and the customs of their ancestors. Isolation also helped to bring about the same result. The most striking example is the case of the *Valaades,* who constituted one quarter of the population living in the Haliakmon valley. Despite the fact that they embraced Islam in the middle of the seventeenth century, they had made little progress towards adopting Ottoman culture and language in 1924, when they moved to Turkey as part of the population exchange. They still spoke Greek, with only a few Turkish phrases. Their repeated use of the oath *Vallachi* ('by God') led to their being called *Valaades* by their neighbours. They also observed the Christian ritual and feast days, respected the saints and holy places, made offerings of oil, candles and money to the churches, made New Year's cake on New Year's day, and roasted the lamb at Easter. There were also Greek-speaking Muslims in the area of Servia up to 1924, though their ancestors were converted to Islam at the beginning of the eighteenth century. The Vlach-speaking Muslims of Karatzova apostatized in 1759. Other Greek-speaking Muslims lived in the village of Silian, near Kavala, until 1924, and in the village of Lialovo, near Nevrokop, even after the annexation of the area to Bulgaria in 1913. There were also Jewish apostates who did not adopt the language or culture of the Turks: these were the followers of the 'Messiah' Sabbethai Sevi, who apostatized *en masse* in 1686. They referred to themselves as *Maminin* (of the true faith); their former co-religionists called them *Minim* (the unfaithful). The Turks knew them as *dönmes*. They continued to speak Spanish and to observe Jewish customs. They had nothing to do with the other Muslims, and were oppressed by them. In the eighteenth century there were about five hundred families of this group in Thessalonike and a few in some of the other Macedonian towns.

The Ottoman occupation brought the subject Christians closer together. For one thing, Islamic law paid no respect to ethnic or linguistic differences, and only recognized religious communities: the basic distinction under it was between the believers and the unbelievers, the latter being divided into Christians and Jews. The conquerors gave to all their Christian subjects the name *Rum* — that is, *Romaios,* which had previously been the name given to the subjects of the Byzantine empire. Secondly, the dissolution of the Christian states in the Balkans put an end to the rivalry between Greeks, Bulgars and Serbs; conversely their shared fate and common religion inspired feelings of solidarity. The Hellenic national consciousness, that was aroused in some scholarly circles just before the Greeks of Europe became the subjects of the Ottomans, spread slowly but steadily amongst the educated Greek- and Vlach-speakers, both inside and outside Macedonia, and subsequently amongst the merchants and artisans. The first to become aware of the national identity of his people was Païsios, a Bulgarian monk. The book he wrote in 1762 to arouse the national consciousness of the Bulgarians was not printed until 1846. Before that, it circulated only in handwritten copies, and its real influence grew after it was printed. Slavs seeking an education went to Greek schools, since they had no educational establishments of their own higher than the level of primary school. The Greek schools, however, were very few in number, were frequently closed, and were attended by only a few pupils. The Slav-speaking pupils were very few in number. As a result, although a few Slav-speakers certainly received a Greek education, we can only speak of the Hellenization of Slav-speakers at the individual level. By contrast, observations made in Macedonia during the nineteenth and the beginning of the twentieth centuries demonstrate that the Slav language gained ground amongst the Greek- and Vlach-speaking rural population.

The population of Macedonia

We do not yet have any specific statistical data to enable us to calculate the population of Macedonia throughout the entire Ottoman period. Nonetheless, the Ottoman documents published so far, referring to the end of the fifteenth and the beginning of the sixteenth centuries, and other scattered references to the final decades of the eighteenth century, make it possible to form some idea, if not of absolute figures, at least of the population trends during these centuries.

In order to achieve a common basis for comparison, the figures set out in the following table are for areas which in the eighteenth century formed the *sanjaks* of Thessalonike and Kavala; roughly speaking, they include central and eastern Greek Macedonia, but exclude part of western Macedonia which in the eighteenth century belonged to neighbouring *sanjaks*. The figures given are only provisional and are offered as giving some indication of the magnitudes involved. The total number of 600,000 for the end of the eighteenth century finds support in the fact that a century later the same areas were calculated to have had a population of 650,000 (see table one below).

The frequent severe epidemics that afflicted the region —

deaths from plague in the eighteenth century were at least as high as 100,000 — only partly account for the low proportional increase in the population, which was no more than 93% over a period of three centuries. The main cause of this slow increase was the reduction in the Christian population, especially during the first centuries of the Ottoman conquest. During this period the Christian population increased by only 50% (1.6 per thousand per annum) — a rate much slower than the average growth rate of the European population (5 per thousand per annum) or of other areas of Greece (the rate for the Peloponnese was 7 per thousand per annum) — while the Muslim population increased by about 234%, and was the group mainly responsible for the overall increase in population. While the ratio of the total population to Muslims was 5:1 in the sixteenth century, it was only 3:1 in the eighteenth.

The increase in the Muslim population was a result mainly of the extensive settlement of Muslims in the area, and of the conversion of Christians.

Despite the rapid growth in their numbers in the sixteenth and seventeenth centuries, and the decrease in the eighteenth century, the Jews had no effect on the general demographic pattern, for they were always a tiny minority in comparison with the total population (about 4% in the sixteenth century, and about 7% in the eighteenth).

The growth of the Christian population is demonstrated more clearly by the demographic trends of the urban centres, illustrated in table two.

It is clear from this table that the Christian population in the towns grew at a rapid rate. And a comparison of the percentage increase in the urban Christian population (217-250%) with that of the Christian population in general, illustrated in table one (50%) shows that there was a drift of the Christians to the towns — a phenomenon

TABLE 1

	Sanjak of Thessalonike		Sanjak of Kavala		Total		% increase
	16th C.	18th C.	16th C.	18th C.	16th C.	18th C.	
Muslims	40,000	120,000	20,000	80,000	60,000	200,000	234%
Christians	160,000	240,000	80,000	120,000	240,000	360,000	50%
Jews	10,000	35,000	1,500	5,000	11,500	40,000	360%
Total	210,000	395,000	101,500	205,000	311,500	600,000	93%

TABLE 2

Town	Muslims			Christians			Total Population		
	16th C.	18th C.	% increase	16th C.	18th C.	% increase	16th C.*	18th C.*	% increase
Thessalonike	5,500	30,000	445	4,000	20,000	185	20,000	60,000-70,000	200-250
Veria	1,000	3,000-3,500	200-250	3,000	4,000-4,500	33-50	4,000	7,000-8,000	75-100
Moglena	2,500	4,000	60	500	1,000	100	3,000	4,000-5,000	34-65
Edessa	1,000	2,000-2,500	100-150	1,000	3,000-3,500	200-250	2,000	5,000-6,000	150-200
Kavala	1,000	2,000-3,000	100-200	500	1,000	100	1,500	3,000-4,000	100-166
Serres	3,000	12,000-15,000	300-400	2,000	5,000-8,000	150-300	5,000	20,000	300
Drama	1,000	1,000?		1,000	4,000-5,000	300-400	2,000	5,000-6,000	150-200
Total	15,000	54,000-58,000	273-307	12,000	38,000-42,000	217-250	37,000	84,000-119,000	124-218

*Total including Jews

related to the creation and rapid growth of an urban class, which secured a hold on the management of the economic affairs of the region. By contrast, a comparison of the proportional increase of the Muslim population generally (250%) with the increase in the urban Muslim population (273-307%) shows that the distribution of the Muslims between the towns and the countryside showed only a slight change. The French diplomat, F. Beaujour, states that the ratio of town dwellers to country dwellers at the end of the eighteenth century was 1:3

The ratio of the Greek to the Slav population is a matter of dispute: an estimate can be made, however, on the basis of evidence from Macedonian archives — the lists of the representatives appointed to the local administrative organs, and the statistical data relating to conversions to Islam. In 1752, the meeting of the community leaders of the *kaza* of Thessalonike was attended by thirty Turks, forty-three Greeks and ten Slavs, and that of 1780 by twelve Turks and twenty-six Greeks, with no Slavs present. These lists have only limited value, however, on account of the small quantity of the data, and the absence of any general principle by which the communities were represented. The comparison rather indicates the dynamic character of the Greeks, who had gained control of the local administration, independent of their numerical ratio to the Turks and the Slavs.

A surer guide is the statistical evidence relating to conversions to Islam. Between 1752 and 1820, in the *kaza* of Thessalonike, seventy-four Greeks, thirty-six Slavs and thirteen Jews were converted, the corresponding figures for the *kaza* of Veria (ancient Beroia) between 1720 and 1817 being twenty-one Greeks, three Slavs and one Jew. There is no straightforward answer to the question whether these numbers accurately reflect the proportional distribution of the population between ethnic groups. The Greeks were wealthy and a major part of the economy was in their hands, and they had a strong national clergy with significant support in the Ottoman administration through the Phanariotes; they were thus better able to resist conversion than the Slavs, and the proportion of Greeks in the population was therefore probably greater than that suggested by the tables of conversions.

The lists of conversions and the statements of the travellers on the ethnic composition of the population also show how little correspondence there was between place-names and the ethnic composition of the area at any given time. In villages that kept their Slavic names until quite recently, like Berova, Stanovo, and Serava in the *nahiye* of Langadas, the eighteenth century documents mention only Greek inhabitants. Similarly, in some villages with Turkish names (Seremetsi and Yeniköy), mention is made only of Greeks, while in others (Sartzli and Arapli) both Greeks and Turks are recorded. The map (fig. 249) is based on published Ottoman documents and gives a truer picture of the distribution of the population in Macedonia than that deriving from even the most meticulously careful travellers, like Leake and Cousinéry. Greeks are mentioned also in northern parts of Macedonia, like the *kaza* of Doirani, of Tikves, of Petric, and there were flourishing Greek communities in Bosnia and Serbia.

The towns

Before the second capture of Thessalonike in 1430, the Ottomans built the town of Yenice (New Town), the modern Greek version of which is Yannitsa; this remained exclusively a Muslim town and became a holy city as a result of the shrines built in it. The Ottoman period in Thessalonike began with the sack of the city, the flight of its inhabitants, and the removal from its superb churches of the marble, which was taken to Adrianople and used to pave a bath house. Turks from Yannitsa moved into the finest houses in Thessalonike, and converted many of the churches into mosques. Many of the Christians also returned, however, induced by the favourable measures decreed by the sultan. Amongst other things, they were exempted from some forms of taxation (see page 364) and regained possession of those churches that had not been converted. These included the largest and finest in Thessalonike: Saint Demetrios, Saint Sophia, and the church *ton Asomaton*, or *tou Angelou* (the Rotunda also known as Saint George) which had been removed from their control at the end of the fifteenth or beginning of the sixteenth century.

At the same time, Christian settlements began to be built in the uplands and on the mountain slopes, where the refugees concentrated. Of these, Naousa, Siatista and Kozani grew to some size. Naousa was founded by refugees from Palionaousta, under the patronage of a Turkish man of letters who succeeded in procuring certain important privileges for them: no Ottoman, except for the governor and the *kadi*, was to live in the town, and the inhabitants paid very few taxes, which went to the *evkaf* of the Evrenos family at Yannitsa. The settlement of Demir Hisar also came into being at the beginning of the Ottoman period, its inhabitants including Turks, Bulgarians and Greeks. The last named came from Melenikon, which retained its Greek character from the Byzantine period until its subjection to Bulgaria in 1912.

In 1460, there were 295 Muslim families and 185 Christian families in Monastir; in Velessa, the Christian families were in the majority: 222 against 9. Kastoria was a very important town, having 960 families in 1470, of which only 22 were Muslim.

By 1520, the Muslim population of Monastir had reached 756 families, and the number of Christian families had increased to 330, while at Velessa there were now 42 Muslim and 247 Christian families; at Kastoria, by contrast, the number of Christian families had fallen to 732, while the number of Muslim families had trebled. At this same time, Thessalonike had 3,143 Jewish, 1,374 Muslim and 1,087 Christian families. In the town of Serres (ancient Serrhai), there were 671 Muslim and 357 Christian families. The majority of the Christians in Serres and the surrounding area were Greek, though in the countryside, some Serbian was still spoken — a hangover from the temporary occupation of the area by Stephen Dušan. Greek was also the predominant language in Drama and Kavala. The Greek character of the inhabitants of Serres can also be traced during the following centuries through baptismal names, which were all taken from old Byzantine families.

In the middle of the sixteenth century the Jewish com-

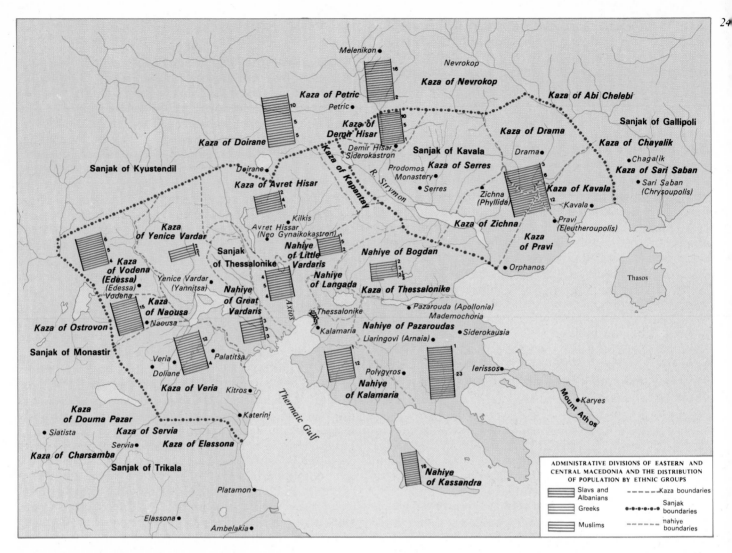

24

Melenikon•

Kaza of Nevrokop

Nevrokop

Kaza of Petric

Petric•

Kaza of Doirane

Kaza of Demir Hisar

Kaza of Abi Chelebi

Sanjak of Gallipoli

Kaza of Drama

Kaza of Chayalik

•Chagalik

Demir Hisar
Siderokastron

Sanjak of Kavala

Drama•

Kaza of Sari Saban

•Sari Saban
(Chrysoupolis)

Sanjak of Kyustendil

Doirane•

Kaza of Avret Hisar

R. Strymon

Prodomos•
Monastery

Kaza of Serres

•Serres

Zichna
(Phyllida)

Kaza of Kavala

•Kavala

Kaza of Yenice Vardar

Kilkis

Avret Hissar
(Neo Gynaikokastron)

Sanjak of Thessalonike

Nahiye of Little Vardaris

Nahiye of Bogdan

Kaza of Zichna

•Pravi
(Eleutheroupolis)

Kaza of Pravi

•Orphanos

Thasos

Kaza of Vodena (Edessa)

(Edessa)•
Vodena

Yenice Vardar
(Yannitsa)

Nahiye of Great Vardaris

Nahiye of Langada

Kaza of Thessalonike

Kaza of Ostrovon

Kaza of Naousa

•Naousa

Axios

•Thessalonike

•Kalamaria

•Pazarouda (Apollonia)
Mademochoria

Nahiye of Pazaroudas

Liaringovi (Arnaia)•

•Siderokausia

Sanjak of Monastir

Veria•

Doliane•

•Palatitsa

•Karyes

Kaza of Veria

Kitros•

Thermaic Gulf

Polygyros•

•Ierissos

Nahiye of Kalamaria

Mount Athos

Kaza of Douma Pazar

•Katerini

Kaza of Servia

Servia•

Kaza of Elassona

Kaza of Charsamba

Sanjak of Trikala

•Siatista

Nahiye of Kassandra

ADMINISTRATIVE DIVISIONS OF EASTERN AND
CENTRAL MACEDONIA AND THE DISTRIBUTION
OF POPULATION BY ETHNIC GROUPS

Platamon•

————— Kaza boundaries
Slavs and
Albanians

•—•—•—• Sanjak
boundaries
Greeks

Elassona•

——— nahiye
boundaries
Muslims

Ambelakia•

249. The study of the demographic situation in central and eastern Macedonia and of the ethnic distribution of its inhabitants used to be based uncritically on the conflicting impressions of travellers which in turn reflected the information of their guides. Although direct documentary information for population is nowhere available, it is possible to use the indirect evidence from the Turkish archives preserved at Thessalonike and Naousa. The above map, drawn up from these sources, shows the size of each ethnic group in proportion to the total population by kazas. Greeks are found in the northern areas.

munity of Thessalonike reached a peak of 3,500 families. Later, the number began to decrease as they scattered to other Macedonian towns. At this period Kastoria had 1,003 Christian, 57 Muslim, and 17 Jewish families.

The Christian population of Thessalonike doubled at the beginning of the seventeenth century after the arrival of the Vlach-speaking immigrants referred to above. It nonetheless remained the third largest element in the population, after the Jews and the Muslims. The former had fifty-six neighbourhoods, the latter forty-eight and the Christians sixteen. The Muslims formed the majority in many Macedonian towns: Yannitsa and Stromnitsa were Turkish towns, and in Edessa, perhaps in Serres, and in Monastir, three quarters of the population were Muslims. Veria was one of the towns in which there were equal numbers of Muslims and Christians. The Christians were in the majority in the small towns and townships especially in western and central Macedonia. Servia, Kastoria, Naousa and Galatista all had mainly Greek populations. In other towns, in western and northern Macedonia, Greeks lived alongside Slavs and also Vlachs.

There were significant Jewish communities in Veria, Monastir, Serres, Drama and Kavala.

The picture changed in the eighteenth century with the movement to the towns of a large section of the Christian population of Macedonia, both Greek-speaking and Vlach-speaking. This resulted from the population turning to commerce and to handicraft industries, and also from its persecution by the Muslims. The population of the existing towns thus increased, and smaller towns and townships expanded; the proportion of the Christian population in the towns increased relative to the Muslims, as did the number of Greek- and Vlach-speakers compared with the Slav-speakers.

In 1733, the Jewish community of Thessalonike was between 18,000 and 20,000 strong, and was still the largest single element in the population; the Muslim community, with 10,000, was second, but the Greek community, with

8,000-9,000 members was closing the gap between it and the others. The city had a few Bulgarian inhabitants, though these were immigrants.

The townships of western Macedonia, Siatista, Kozani, Vogatsiko, Blatsi, Kleisoura and Ochrid became important centres of commerce and the handicraft industries, in addition to the earlier centres of Veria, Naousa and Kastoria.

The already important town of Monastir, the villages around it, Megarovo, Krušovo, Tirnovo, Nizoplis, Gópesi and Milovista, and the township of Velessa to the north, began to grow from 1769 onwards, having admitted a number of Greek- and Vlach-speaking refugees who were fleeing from persecution. The year 1769 saw the beginning of the dissolution of Moschopolis, a populous and prospering Greek-Vlach town in northern Epirus, as a result of intolerable economic pressure exerted by the Albanian beys. The inhabitants moved to other towns in Epirus, to various Macedonian towns — principally Thessalonike, Monastir, Velessa and Serres — and outside the Ottoman empire. In 1770 there began the migration to Monastir and the surrounding villages already mentioned. This involved the Greek- and Vlach-speaking inhabitants of settlements in south-west Macedonia, who were fleeing from persecution by the Turks in reprisal for the uprising of the Greeks of the Peloponnese and the islands, timed to coincide with the activities of a Russian fleet in the Aegean.

We have some information from the end of the eighteenth and the beginning of the nineteenth centuries on the population of some of the Macedonian towns (the numbers are merely indicative, since they derive not from censuses but from estimates by contemporary observers). Thessalonike: 60,000; Serres: 25,000-30,000; Veria 18,000-20,000; Edessa: 12,000; Kastoria: 7,000-8,000; Yannitsa: 4,000-6,000; Naousa: 3,000-4,000; Kavala: 3,000. The towns of western Macedonia, Kozani, Siatista and Grevena, had lost population as a result of the terrible, sufferings inflicted on the area. The ethnic composition of Thessalonike had changed.

The Muslims (Turks, Janissaries, Jewish converts to Islam, and Albanians serving in the army) now numbered 30,000, and were the largest element; the Greeks, some 16,000, had overtaken the Jews, who now numbered only 12,000. The last named had suffered from an economic crisis. The Greek population of Thessalonike, as of other Macedonian towns, was strengthened by the influx of some of the rural population, who abandoned their homes for reasons noted elsewhere. The Turks were also in the majority in Edessa. In Serres, the Muslims and Christians (mostly Greeks) were roughly equal in numbers. Yannitsa was still predominantly a Turkish town. In the other towns referred to above, the Greeks were in the majority.

INSTITUTIONS OF GOVERNMENT

The land regime

During the first centuries of Ottoman rule the legal status of property in Macedonia was confused. According to Islamic law, land was divided into two major categories: land which belonged to Muslims at the time of conquest and which remained in their full possession (*mülk*); and subject lands (*haraciye*) which belonged to non-Muslims at the time of conquest, but thereafter became the property of the Muslim community. Such lands could be granted out as timars to Ottoman officials (whether military or civil) in return for services to the state. Timars were a type of fief, and their holders (timariots) were entitled to a share of their produce and to collect the greater part of dues owed by the farmers who cultivated them.

Grants of timars were divided into three groups, according to the amount of revenue which they produced for the timar holder. The first class of holdings were called *has*, and comprised lands with revenues of over 100,000 piastres. These were usually given to high political or military officials of the state. The second group included *zeamet* holdings, with revenues exceeding 20,000 piastres. Finally, the simple timars generated incomes of less than 20,000 piastres. The timariots enjoyed a type of usufruct over the lands granted to them. A small part of state land, however, was given out as *hassa* i.e., estates held in full possession, although with some restrictions. The holders cultivated these with the help of propertyless colleagues or serfs (*chift*). These sections were also called *hassa-chiftlik*, and were equivalent to the Byzantine *zeugelateia*.

The cultivators of the remaining timar lands themselves held agricultural plots with varying titles of usufruct or possession. We shall deal with this immediately below.

No detailed study exists which would illuminate the disposal of land in Macedonia after the conquest. From what we know, however, it seems that the early sultans did not strictly follow the letter of sacred law in establishing their authority in Macedonia. Much of the land was divided into various timar estates, which were granted to Ottoman officials. Another part was given to both Muslims and Christians as a privileged reward for services. Such estates were held either with the right of full usufruct (*tasarruf*), or in full ownership (*mülk*). Finally, another part was permitted to the former Byzantine *pronoiars* and ecclesiastical foundations which, in some form, were subsumed within the timar system at the beginning of the conquest.

Süleyman I (1520-66) and his successor Selim II (1566-74) wished to impose some type of order on the chaotic land regime. The new reform appears to have been the work of the great Ebu us-Suud *kazasker* of Rumelia and later grand *müfti* from 1545 to 1574. It originated in the *eyalet* of Rumelia, in the area of Macedonia in particular. Early in Selim II's reign, Ebu us-Suud drew up a cadastral survey for the region of Skopje and Thessalonike. All the land of Rumelia was designated *haraciye,* but a new subdivision of this category was also created — that of state owned land. The state retained the ultimate right of ownership. Timariots or not, the Muslims had simple usufruct, which the first holders acquired with the grant itself, and subsequent ones obtained through a lump-sum monetary payment. The other inhabitants of the land, both Muslims and non-Muslims, also secured a type of natural right and title to the land via a lump-sum payment, which safeguarded them the right to transmit the land to their heirs.

This rigid regulation did not allow anybody, Muslim or non-Muslim to hold land in the category *arz-ı memleket* in full ownership. Moreover, it provoked the vigorous reaction of Christian landowning magnates (with the great monasteries of Athos in the forefront), and probably also of the Muslim proprietors. Selim II was forced to soften this harsh ordinance with new 'legal fictions' designed to reconcile the religious law with the prevailing reality. According to the above regulation, the lands held by monasteries were designated state lands. They were confiscated (around 1567) and disposed at auction to those who wished to acquire them with title (*tasarruf-ı sahib-i arz*).

By contracting debts or with the financial assistance of the voivodes of Wallachia, all or nearly all of the great monasteries (and perhaps also the lay proprietors) recovered their properties, under a new legal status of simple usufruct. This undertaking cost the monasteries 14,000 florins for their properties in Macedonia, and 13,000 aspra for their possessions on Lemnos.

On 7 February 1568, however, the monks sought the sultan's approval to change their lands back into full proprietorship *(mülk)*. They also requested that the monasteries be recognized as legal persons with the right of ownership, and that Christians be given the right to establish pious foundations or *evkafs*. Finally, they asked that all their old tax privileges be restored. This proposal originated in Macedonia but spread throughout the entire empire, as witnessed by information pertaining to Sinai, Chios and the Cyclades. The monks' most important weapon was the threat to abandon their lands if their requests were not granted. In such case, the public treasury would lose revenues from taxes which the monks paid, since their properties would then pass into the hands of the timariots. The latter would have collected the taxes for themselves.

Selim II gave way and called for a new judgement from the ulema permitting the sultan to dispose of state lands (*arz-ı memleket*) at his will, including those held in full ownership. This decision, moreover, was not to the exclusion of Christians. This became the *status quo* prevailing throughout the empire as far as the land regime was concerned. We have numerous references to such lands in Macedonia throughout the whole of Ottoman rule. Owing to the lack of published data, however, we are still unable to form an exact picture of the distribution of the various categories of land among Muslims and non-Muslims. Nonetheless, judging from the enormous territorial estates which certain great Turkish families held, with varying titles, we may conclude that the majority of Macedonian lands belonged to great Muslim landowning families. The Evrenos and the Habenderoğlu are examples of such families already in the sixteenth and seventeenth centuries.

The possibility for Christians to hold lands in full ownership also allowed them to establish Christian *evkafs* (foundations for philanthropic purposes), the wealth of which remained inalienable. The great monasteries of Athos converted all or parts of their immovable wealth (*mülk*) into *evkafs*. Many of the monasteries of the Holy Mountain still possess the relevant constitutive documents (*vakıfname*). We may add that the entire Holy Mountain and many other monasteries constituted Muslim *evkafs* in-

asmuch as their dues were devoted to various Muslim pious foundations. Ecclesiastical foundations (and subsequently secular local communes as well) also acquired the character of legal persons. This legal category, however, was slow to develop in Muslim law. Since Ottoman law provided only for proprietorship by real persons, during the first centuries of Ottoman rule Christians registered ecclesiastical properties and assets in the name of a church's patron saint, as if he were some living priest. Thus we find registrations with the formulae 'of the priest Nicholas, son of Adam' for the church of Saint Nicholas, or 'of the priest James, son of Zebediah' for the church of Saint James. The property and assets of monks were registered in the name of their representative or manager. Later on expressions appear which show the development of the concept of the legal person, e.g. 'goods which belong to such and such monastery', or 'the common possessions of the monasteries and their monks.' These concepts were subsequently clarified in the course of the eighteenth century.

In the seventeeth century, the Ottoman social system and mechanism of government were seriously disturbed. Until the end of the sixteenth century, the *sipahis* and *zaims* formed the backbone of the ruling class, and were the most powerful section of the army which carried out the lightning Ottoman conquests. They consumed their wealth, power and interests in continuing and expanding the system on the basis of three sources: agricultural revenues from their timars (or *zeamets* or *hass*); various forms of improper exploitation of villages; and booty seized in wars of conquest. Conquests permitted the creation of further timars, *zeamets* and *hass*. During the second half of the sixteenth century, however, the pace of Ottoman expansion slowed down. The number of victorious wars decreased, and such wars became less profitable. Moreover, in this period the Ottomans met with heavy misfortunes and serious catastrophes. Soon the period of territorial losses began. This turn of events diminished the timariots' income as well as their taste for war. To repair their losses in revenue, the timariots exploited the villages under their control more intensively. Given their declining interest in warfare, moreover, they became indifferent to summons to mobilize which, in any case, grew further and further apart. The state reacted by depriving the *sipahis* who did not fulfill their obligations of their timars. It did not, however, redistribute them to other timariots. The available lands were allotted to the sultan himself, to members of the imperial household, to bureaucratic and administrative officials, or to the sultan's favourites. In Macedonia, for example, lake Ochrid was the sultan's *hass,* and lake Kastoria was the sultanas' *hass*. The beneficiaries of such estates dispatched their representative, expecting him to convey back the revenues of the timars (or *zeamets* or *hass*) which they had received. They also would rent them out to public entrepreneurs at the highest bid. These representatives or entrepreneurs attempted to enrich themselves, exacting from the villagers contributions in kind and money, as well as personal labour, beyond what was customary. Frequently the representatives or entrepreneurs farmed out the exploitation of their properties to sublessors. Aside from burdening the villagers' situation even further, these practices created a chain of beneficiaries on the same property, and opened possibilities for the transfer of rights to estates which, according to the law, belonged to the state and were inalienable. Amidst this confusion, the stronger and more capable converted certain timars into privately owned *chiftliks*.

This development occurred not simply because the central authority was too weak to protect its prerogatives on timar lands. A situation arose in which the cultivators' rights to fixed sections of a timar, including requisite title, (*tapu*) were trampled down. This happened when villagers were unable to pay their debts to those who held usufruct of the property, but who aspired to become its full owner. By increasing their illegal demands, the latter brought the villagers to an *impasse*. They reduced the peasants to debt by granting postponements on obligations, or by giving them loans at enormous interest rates and mortgaging their titles. If a village suffered even further losses through natural causes, incursions of brigand bands, or abuses of their physical security, the process was even quicker. Using the very same procedures, non-timar estates and properties which had fully belonged to their cultivators were transformed into *chiftliks*. This method of creating *chiftliks* was characteristic of the eighteenth, and first half of the nineteenth centuries.

From the beginning of the eighteenth century onwards, another change is also noticeable. The basis of wealth was no longer the possession of land. The possession of money, alongside or independently of land ownership became an important factor in the estimation of wealth. The consequences of this change are manifold. Landowners now sought to acquire fluid wealth, by extracting money payments from their cultivators and (more importantly) by selling their produce. The social status of the landowners, moreover, no longer coincided with that of the wealthy. Finally, the merchant class entered the picture, but as an antagonistic element.

With the continual weakening of central authority, and the rampant creation of *chiftliks*, internal differentiations arose within the ranks of the Ottoman aristocracy. Exploiting whatever rank they held, certain local officials extended their control over many *chiftliks*, created private armies, and conducted wars with their rivals. They advanced in the hierarchy, extracted more privileges, expanded their authority, and added even more *chiftliks* through oppression and acts of violence. Local magnates of this type made their authority felt in sections of Macedonia.

Administration

The administrative system of the Ottoman empire was based on its military organization. The greater part of its European possessions formed one broad, military-political district known as the *eyalet* of Rumelia. At its head stood the *beylerbey*, the highest military official. The *eyalet* included smaller military-administrative districts, namely *sanjaks* and *livas*. Each sanjak was further divided into *kazas*, headed by *kadis*. The *kazas*, moreover, were subdivided into *nahiyes*, at the head of which stood the *naibs*.

In the fifteenth and sixteenth centuries, the whole of Macedonia was part of a broader district — the pasha-liva which comprised regions outside the geographic area of Macedonia. This entire district was directly administered by the *beylerbey*. It is unclear, however, if it constitutes a single *sanjak*, or several *sanjaks* united under the administration of the same person, namely the *beylerbey*. At this time the *beylerbey* was the only one in the area who bore the title of pasha.

Seventeenth and eighteenth century Macedonia was divided into several *sanjaks*. In the seventeenth century, western Macedonia belonged to the *sanjak* of Skopje, and in the eighteenth to the *sanjaks* of Ochrid and Monastir. Throughout this entire period, central and eastern Macedonia formed two *sanjaks*, namely those of Thessalonike and Kavala. In the eighteenth century they were frequently administered by the same pasha, and hence were known as the pashalik of Thessalonike-Kavala. Finally, the northern regions of Macedonia belonged to the *sanjak* of Kyustendil.

For fiscal reasons, certain areas were withdrawn from the administration of provincial officials. The sultan granted, the management of state revenues to an agent (*emin*) or tax-farmer. The latter was usually an Ottoman notable (*ayan*), who enjoyed the fruits of a part of such revenues. The institution of farming out public revenues (*mukataa*) was applied to certain state services (such as animal raising, or carding of garments for the army, post office, etc.); as well as the management of areas or properties of the *hass* type which the sultan had transferred to members of his family, officials, or public welfare foundations (*evkaf*). The manager was called a voivode, and held the rank of aga or bey. Such areas, consequently, were called voivodaliks, agaliks or beyliks. Since there was no separation of powers the voivodaliks gradually became near-autonomous regions. Indeed, they appear as independent rungs in the administrative hierarchy. The eighteenth century *kaza* of Kara Dağ and Demir Hisar (Siderokastron), for example, belonged only theoretically to the *sanjak* of Kyustendil. In fact, they were entities independent of the provincial administration.

Decentralization was even more pronounced in the *sanjak* of Kavala. At the end of the eighteenth century, only the Kavala area, and perhaps part of the *kaza* of Eleutheroupolis (Pravi), were subordinate to the officials of the Thessalonike-Kavala pashalik. With its more than three hundred villages, the Serres valley was divided into ten agaliks. The *kaza* of Drama, along with portions of the Pravi and Kavala *kazas*, constituted a semi-autonomous region (voivodalik) under the beys of Drama. It originated as a *mukataa* for the mines at Pravi. At the end of the eighteenth century, the management of the voivodalik was entrusted to the family of the beys at Serres.

The mountainous terrain of the *kaza* of Veria also favoured decentralization. From the early eighteenth century, much of it was under the administration of agas. In 1821, their internecine quarrels prompted the military governor (*vali*) of the Thessalonike-Kavala pashalik to appoint an inspector (*nazir*) with wide jurisdiction in order to confront the Revolution. The *kaza* of Naousa was also a voivodalik.

Certain groups of villages which had common obliga-

250. *A 17th century woodcut of Thessalonike. Throughout the Ottoman occupation, Thessalonike was the capital of Macedonia and its largest commercial centre with an ever-* *increasing population. From the end of the 15th century, its trade steadily grew assisted by the expertise of its Jewish immigrants.*

tions also constituted *mukataas*: the villages in the Kitros and Karaburnu area were obliged to work in the neighbouring salt pans; Grademporio (Nikopolis) and other villages not mentioned by name belonged to a service *mukataa* connected with the gunpowder factories. Sindos (Tekeli), Lachanokepoi (Arapli), Monolophos (Daoudli), and Neochoroudi (Yeniköy), belonged to the *mukataa* concerned with raising animals for the Janissaries. The villages Goumenitsa (Gumenca), Griva (Krivo) and Karpi (Chernareka), belonged to the *mukataa* for carding cloth used in attiring the janissaries; finally those villages which constituted *hass* — e.g., the villages around Vissoka, the *nahiye* of Bogdan, the Ierissos villages, and the Hasikochoria (*hass* villages) of Chalkidike.

The following is a list of the major types of *mukataa*:
— the revenues of the Thessalonike customs (which amounted to 750,000 piastres in 1695, and which belonged to the *evkaf* of sultan Abdul Hamid I in the eighteenth century);
— imposts on sealings for textile industry products, usually farmed out to Greeks or Jews. In 1728, these levies amounted to about 550 piastres.

— levies for maintaining the postal stations. In the *kaza* of Thessalonike, such stations existed at the villages of Klissari, Chalastra (Koulakia) and Langadas. They were maintained by payments from the local population. After 1696, their managers became salaried officials.
— taxes for paying and maintaining the *armatoles* and other security forces. These were farmed out to the inspectors (*nazir*) of the forces of a wider district. For example, in 1720 the inspectorate (*naziret*) of the Balkan peninsula included, in addition to Macedonia, Thessaly, Epirus and central Greece. It received 3,000 piastres in payments, the collection of which was subleased to the leaders of local units. In 1712, the garrison at the Rentina pass was paid at 4,000 aspra. The villages Kephalochori (Vazköy), Lynkovani (Nenkovani), and Velissarios (Yanik) maintained the local *armatole* corps, but were exempted from other taxes.

The salaried *mukataa* administrators usually farmed out either all or part of the revenues for which they were responsible. Despite numerous abuses entailed by a chain of lessees, the *mukataa* institution represented a significant source of tax privileges and administrative autonomy for the Christian subjects of the empire (*rayah*). Non-Muslims who belonged to *mukataas* connected with state services formed a hereditary category of 'free and exempt *rayah*', and were usually exempted from additional taxes and labour imposed by the sultan, as well as fees exacted by state employes.

The Taxation System and Its Implementation

The taxes, levies and various dues, which were levied in Macedonia as they were throughout the Ottoman empire, may be listed as follows:

Taxes Required by Islamic Law (Rüsüm-i-Şehriye)

The major taxes in this category were:

1) the capitation tax, called *cizye* or (more commonly) *harac,* and levied on non-Muslims. Those liable were divided into the categories of wealthy, middling and poor, according to their incomes. The unit of taxation was the household (*hane*) or family, to which the tax form (*charatzocharti*) corresponded. Originally, the number of forms was equivalent to the number of families in each area. Frequently, however, this number was not adjusted with fluctuations in the population. Since taxation was based on data gathered in previous censuses, and information was not constantly updated, the number of forms was sometimes lower than the number of families. More often, however, tax collectors arbitrarily increased the number of *harac* forms, or demanded a lump-sum payment (*maktu*) from an area which exceeded the amount owed (i.e. according to the value of the tax forms, corresponding to the number of units of taxation). This second method rendered taxation collective rather than personal, and became customary despite the sultans' frequent decrees to the contrary. Such transgressions are mentioned in two firmans of 1705, directed to the *kaza* of Thessalonike. Here we learn that tax officials had not only subjected the Thessalonike taxpayers (Greek, Jewish and Armenian) to a lump-sum payment exceeding the total amount of *harac* they owed, but did not even provide them with the tax forms. Instead, they distributed the forms to taxpayers in the countryside. Unable to bear the excessive burden, the villagers abandoned their properties and fled to other *kazas*. The Sublime Porte reacted by forbidding the lump-sum collection of the capitation tax, and decreased the same tax in the *kaza* by 2,500 forms in order to facilitate the return of the villagers. At the same time, however, it was decreed that taxes equivalent to five hundred Thessalonike forms would be paid by the inhabitants of the Veria *kaza,* and those in the Thessalonike *kaza* who had not received forms. Similar reductions in the number of forms were also made for the *kazas* of Monastir, Florina, Prilep and Morihovon.

The very limited quantitative data available provide only a general and approximate picture of the levels and evolution of the capitation tax in Macedonia. A document of 1718 informs us that 44,178 *harac* forms (in all categories) were allotted for the *sanjak* of Thessalonike. With suitable calculations, it follows that 264,068 piastres should have been collected with these forms. Other information regarding the capitation tax for the same areas in the sixteenth century refers to about 15,000 households (*hane*),

and to a sum total of 900,000 aspra, i.e. 7,500 piastres. Accordingly, each household paid sixty aspra in the sixteenth century, but in 1718 it paid six piastres, or seven hundred and twenty aspra. This staggering increase in the nominal value of the form is due to the drastic decline in the value of money. Beaujour calculated that, at the end of the eighteenth and beginning of the nineteenth centuries, the capitation tax in the Thessalonike and Kavala *sanjaks* totalled 400,000 piastres. The increase is partly due to the addition of forms from the Kavala *sanjak,* but also to the continued fall in the value of Ottoman currency.

The Land tax (*harac-ı-arazi*) appears in two forms: as a variable tax fluctuating with the total amount of production (*harac-ı mukaseme*), or as a tithe (*ösür*); and as a frozen tax (*harac-ı muvazzaf*). It was paid by Muslims and non-Muslims, and was levied on cereals, legumes, vegetables, fruits and beehives. Usually the state granted the collecting of these taxes to the timariots.

Taxes, Imposts and Dues Levied by Imperial Command (örfiye)

Such taxes varied throughout the period, but were imposed mainly on the land or production therefrom.

The most important tax in this category was the *ispence* or *ispenç*. This was at once a capitation tax on non-Muslim cultivators and probably also a tax on agricultural products, or the produce of the land which they cultivated. Evidently it was analogous to the *resmi-çift* which the Muslim cultivators paid.

We may also include in this same category a host of other taxes, contributions and dues which were levied on stock-raising and various other para-agricultural activities.

We should also add the various custom tolls, imposts for transporting merchandise, taxes on technical undertakings, the different 'fees' owed to employees (especially legal employees, e.g. for drawing up wills), and also fines called *bad-ı hava* (the Byzantine *aerika*), which were a frequent source of abuses. The most important of these was the *diyet* or *akl*, the Byzantine *phonikon*. This was a fine owed to the family of someone who had been wounded or murdered. In case of no surviving family, the state collected the fine. If the guilty party remained unknown, the inhabitants of the area were held collectively responsible for payment of the fine. Moreover, the *kadi* collected a fee for himself. This institution was often the occasion for extra and unwarranted collections. In order to collect their fees (which ranged between 100-200 aspra per case), the *kadis* would claim as murders deaths arising from accidents or natural causes.

Especially important in this same category were the contributions, which formed a sub-division of the *avarız* and *tekâlif-i örfiye*. Originally extraordinary taxes, they became regularized, and new ones were imposed as occasion required. At first these taxes were levied in kind, but after 1641 they began to be converted into cash payments. This became generalized after the Venetian-Turkish War over Crete (1645-69). Within this group we may distinguish the following types:

(α) contributions and services for the state

1) for military expenses: provisioning of the army, supplies, transport;

2) for maintenance expenses of local security forces, or for the construction and maintenance of fortresses, or ships which guarded the coastline (an obligation of the inhabitants of Thessalonike);

3) for expenses of private armies or extra-military needs (sailors, *armatoles,* castle wardens), or their hire.

4) labour (or its commutation) for transporting wood, coal mining, work in other mines, in the salt pans, etc.;
(b) contributions in kind or money for local officials and timariots (*teşviye* and *kudumiye*), or for local needs such as constructing and maintaining roads, bridges, postal stations etc.;
(c) gifts to various officials and emissaries of the Sublime Porte.

All the foregoing obligations constituted the 'expenses of the vilayet.' They were determined annually by imperial decree according to the number of 'houses', and were paid on a distributive basis. The Porte determined the sum total, originally with the cooperation of the local officials and representatives from the taxpayers. This was then dispersed among various groups of taxpaying Muslims and non-Muslims by responsible local figures.

Especially abusive in the matter of taxes, local officials would often double or triple the sum total, which otherwise varied from year to year according to needs. The payment of an extraordinary contribution to cover the expenses of a war would continue even after the termination of that war. The extraordinary contributions to meet the expenses of a passing official would be collected, and even increased, after his visit had ended.

Documents dating from 1780 and 1792/93 provide us with a general idea of the sum total and content of tax obligations of the *avarız* and *tekalif-i örfiye* type. The document from 1780 was directed only to the *kaza* of Thessalonike. It reveals that the sum total of regular and extraordinary contributions totalled 92,016 piastres; regular contributions reached 73,816 piastres — 36,750 for the state, and 37,066 for local needs. When the vezir-vali of Rumelia or another vezier came to visit, the inhabitants of the *sanjak* were burdened with an additional 18,200 piastres for the expenses of hospitality. For the year 1792/93, the *sanjak* of Thessalonike was obliged to pay 145,548 piastres for the 'expenses of the vilayet'.

Tax Exemptions

The residents of Thessalonike had already acquired special tax privileges in the time of Murad II (1421-51). These were renewed many times up until the end of the sixteenth century. In order to repopulate the deserted city, Murad gathered settlers from all over the empire, and exempted them from both state and locally levied taxes. In exchange, the residents were obliged to provide seventy-two men for garrisoning the twenty-four shore towers, and to pay the expenses of repairing the water supply system for the city castle. The Jews who were later established in Thessalonike did not enjoy the same privileges.

At the end of the sixteenth century, documents recording tax privileges were destroyed in fires. The state employees seized the opportunity to register the inhabitants on the tax rolls, and oblige them to contribute to state services. After the citizens protested, the *beylerbey* of the Balkan peninsula settled the issue in 1604-05. His decision was confirmed by an imperial firman, which exempted the taxpayers from the *avarız* and taxes paid to the local administration. It appears, moreover, that the inhabitants were also exempted from the expenses of maintaining the castle. Their obligatory service was commuted into a fixed monetary payment, a privilege which was extended to the Muslims of Thessalonike. The Ottoman officials, however, found a way to get around the privileges accorded the Christians and Jews. Conflicts between the Jews and the Greeks over the allotment of taxes surfaced in the eighteenth century. The Greeks were supported by the dragomans of the Sublime Porte, and the Jews by the aga of the Janissaries. They extracted a series of mutually contradictory firmans, which put into effect varying systems of tax allotment, sometimes simultaneously.

Already in the sixteenth century, payment of the fixed tax had provoked conflicts between urban and rural populations. In 1821, following the villagers' protests, the urban populace agreed to an increase in their share of the fixed tax. This, however, provoked disputes among the Greeks of the city. An imperial firman of 1792 had attempted to impose order by implementing the previous system of distribution, which divided the Thessalonike Greeks into five categories according to wealth.

Certain families which had provided special services to the Ottoman state were favoured with tax privileges. Examples here include the Muslim Evrenoi of the Thessalonike *kaza,* and the Christian Charitopouloi of the Veria *kaza.*

As a rule, privileged *rayah* were not exempted from the capitation tax. Those, however, who enjoyed the protection of foreign powers which had diplomatic representation at the Sublime Porte were exempted from all taxes. This privilege was granted by special decree, and involved certain restrictions. Embassy interpreters, as well as those under the protection of foreign powers, could not conduct trade, practise other professions, or interfere in the affairs of the notables and tax-farmers. Despite these limitations, the *rayah* merchants of Thessalonike (Greeks and Jews) and diplomatic employees secured translators' patents from Constantinople and other great cities of the empire, and hence became *baratarioi* (patentbearers) — a term which derives from the word *berat,* (meaning imperial patent). The *kadis* and notables frequently protested against the tax privileges enjoyed by the *baratarioi,* whom the representatives of foreign powers tended to favour.

SELF ADMINISTRATION

Community Government

Muslims, Christians and Jews formed separate communities in every city and village which had not been transferred to the military as timars.

Each community was collectively responsible for carrying out orders emanating from state authorities, for paying taxes, for maintaining law and order within the community and region, and for fulfilling other obligations. Community leaders' chief tasks were to mediate state orders or de-

251. 19th century lithograph of Yannitsa, the holy town of the Ottomans and founded by them before 1430; Yenice in Turkish means New Town. It developed quickly into an important com-mercial centre in western Macedonia, whose prosperity was based on the excellent quality of its tobacco and on the making of pipes.

mands to their ranks, to distribute among themselves tax burdens, as well as contributions to state services. In the course of time, they obtained the right to submit requests from their communities to government authorities, and to take measures to secure relief from excessive claims and pressures.

A council of six notables (*ayan*) chosen exclusively from the beys presided over the Muslim community in Thessalonike. When more difficult problems arose, the council summoned two elders from each janissary bettalion (*orta*) for deliberation. The administration of Muslim communities in other cities was similar.

The Christian community in Thessalonike was headed by twenty notables (*proestoi*). The presiding body at Serres had twelve members; Veria had eight; and Naousa had between eight and ten. Veria also had a wider council of twenty-four members. The notables in the councils at Naousa, Veria and elsewhere represented quarters of their cities (*mahaleler*). Representatives of the guilds took part in the Serres community council. In Thessalonike, the guild leaders participated, along with the notables, in electing the president. In Naousa, the president of the community administration was elected by the people, but himself chose the members of the council. At Veria, the council originally elected its new members. In the eighteenth and early nineteenth centuries, however, all its members were elected by the people.

The community authorities had full power to distribute the tax burdens. For example, in the mid-seventeenth century, the *kaza* of Veria comprised 3,237 Christian families; the community officials had exempted one hundred and ninety-six of them from paying the *harac* and community tax and allotted the sum of 823,236 aspra owed by the community to the remaining families.

Everywhere the community administration was dominated by certain families who formed a kind of local aristocracy. Prelates, also, usually played a leading role. At Thessalonike, the metropolitan confirmed the election of the president of the notables. Nonetheless, disputes occurred between the lay and spiritual leadership. Around 1715, the Thessalonike notables succeeded in obtaining the management of community finances from the metropolitan.

Parishes were the basic units of local administration. Within this context the notables could lodge complaints or requests. Thus, in 1599 and again in 1682, the council of Saint Nicholas in Veria requested the *kadi's* decision regarding the Charitopouloi's refusal to join in paying the taxes; the latter argued that Murad II had given them a firman which exempted them from such obligations. In Veria, the neighbourhood councils had six or seven members.

The Christians' administrative autonomy was sealed by their privilege, valid throughout the Ottoman empire, of being judged by their own prelates, in accordance with Byzantine law, in familial and inheritance disputes. In the early seventeenth century, the Christians of Veria rose up

ΣΥΣΤΗΜΑ,
ή
ΔΙΑΤΑΓΑΙ.

Κατὰ κοινὴν Ψῆφον, ἀπάσης τῆς συνε-
λεύσεως, τῆς ἐν Μακεδονίᾳ Πόλεως

ΜΕΛΕΝΙΚΟΥ,

Πρὸς πλείονα ἀφορῶσαι βελτίωσιν, τῶν
ἐν αὐτῇ Θείων οἴκων, σχολῶν τε καὶ
νοσοκομείων,

Καὶ

τῆς τῶν ἐνδεῶν ἁπάντων φιλανθρωποτέρας οἰκονο-
μίας τε, καὶ κηδαιμονίας,

ὑπὸ

Φιλογενῆς τινος κ̄ εὐπατρίδε τῆς αὐτῆς Πόλ. διορ-
γανισθεῖσαί τε καὶ σχεδιασθεῖσαι, καὶ δαπάνῃ αὐτ̄
οἰκείᾳ, νῦν πρῶτον, εἰς φῶς ἀχθεῖσαι.

―――――――――――――

ΕΝ ΒΙΕΝΝΗ ΤΗΣ ΑΟΥΣΤΡΙΑΣ.
Ἐκ τῆς Τυπογραφίας Ἰωαν· Βαρθ. Τζβεκίου πρῴνν
Βι·ώτου. 1813.

252. In 1813 the regulations for the organization of the community of Melenikon were printed. Signed by the bishop, fifty citizens and a representative from six separate guilds, they were drawn up by a member of the community in painstakingly accurate archaic language to which the publisher added a long poem in ancient Greek. Although he paid for the printing, the author wished to remain anonymous.

against the Ottoman authorities who had violated that right.

The self-governing Christian communities took advantage of the marginal activity which the Ottoman administration allowed them. They developed philanthropic and educational institutions, as far as their resources permitted. They were aided, however, by gifts and bequests from compatriots abroad. In this way, many Greek communities were able to establish schools. In the eighteenth century, the Greek community in Thessalonike maintained a hospital for those with infectious diseases.

Thus far we have not mentioned the community administration at Melenikon. We have full information about

its regulations, however, since they were printed in 1813 in Vienna. They merit a full discussion, but owing to the limitations imposed by the present work, we shall discuss them only in part. This code was drawn up by a member of the community who wished to remain anonymous, but who had it published at his own expense. It was signed by the bishop, fifty citizens, and one representative each from the silk thread dyers, goldsmiths, furriers, tailors, shoemakers and grocers. The basic organ of community government was an annual assembly of 'twenty prudent and sensible brothers of each class.' These words suggest a democratic development within the community, since only a short while before marriages were not permitted between members of the lower class (qualified by the Greek term *pocheirioi*) and the notables (*tsorbatzis*). Unfortunately, the way in which the members of this body were designated are not stated. They were elected in the presence of the bishop, three public commissioners, and three ephors, from amongst the distinguished citizens. Whoever did not accept election was required to pay a one hundred piastre fine. The commissioners and ephors jointly selected the 'church commissioners', and again a one hundred piastre fine was imposed on those who refused office. Those who were called upon for a second, third or subsequent term of office were not required to accept the appointment. At the end of their terms, the church commissioners rendered account to the two governing bodies, and delivered to them whatever remained in their treasury. These higher bodies were responsible to the Council of Twenty, and discharged their obligations directly. The community resources consisted of the following: 1) the surplus from church treasuries (i.e., after payment of ecclesiastical expenses, including clerical fees); 2) proceeds from taxes on cotton production, and on silk thread dying; 3) gifts; 4) bequests; 5) income from renting various types of real estate; 6) interest on loans. The cost of philanthropic and educational works were met through these means. The communities would provide the needy with cash, wood and coal. They also gave help to those in prison. Moreover, they maintained a 'public school' for the instruction of basic grammar, and a 'Hellenic School' for intermediate levels of education. The schools as well as the churches operated under the direct and strict supervision of the public commissioners and of the ephors.

The Greek communities in Macedonia (and elsewhere throughout the Ottoman empire) contributed decisively to the survival of the Greek nation, and to its systematic, moral rehabilitation. This was achieved by undertaking community works, by acquiring political experience, by strengthening national consciousness, and by forging the nation's will for liberation.

The Jews who arrived in Thessalonike came from various parts of central and western Europe, and belonged to diverse cultural groups. Their languages or dialects differed, as did their customs, outlook on life and religious rites. Each group strove to maintain its cohesion and preserve its special character, avoiding contact with the others. This tendency was expressed in the founding of exclusive synagogues, around which autonomous communities were formed. Groups which lacked absolute homogeneity did not maintain their continuity, but eventually split into two or three factions.

Originally these communities were governed by a democratic, or at least timocratic, spirit. They had popular assemblies in which all adult males, or at least those who paid taxes, participated. This body elected the administrative and religious officials of the community, and monitored their activities. It also issued regulations. Presiding over the community was a *marbitz,* who combined the qualities of a political, spiritual and religious leader and teacher. These came from the ranks of the rabbis, and were originally elected for one year, but later held office for life. They received some recompense, but were free to practice a profession, which was usually medicine. Next to the *marbitz* was a community council, the *maamad ha-kahal,* which was composed of seven lay members. Originally it was elected by the entire community, but later its membership was replenished by the system of co-option. It elected a president (*parnass*) and a treasurer (*gabai*). The distribution and collection of state taxes was the essential task of this body. In addition, the community levied its own taxes. Consequently, the council drew up and implemented a general community budget. Moreover it enacted regulations, and saw that its decisions were carried out. Various other committees with precise functions operated at lower levels. Each community also had a court, a lower school, a seminary, libraries and organizations for rendering services. The court was presided over by the *marbitz,* and its members were merchants or entrepreneurs. It judged various economic, familial and religious disputes according to a legal system based on the Old Testament, the Talmud, tradition and juridical interpretation. The brotherhood called *Hevra Kedicha* is particularly noteworthy. This consisted of volunteers who assumed responsibility for the care and burial of the dead. Around 1540 some communities undertook entrepreneurial activities with hired textile workers. The gains returned to the communities, and were used to finance educational and philanthropic activities. The communities had a vigorous political life, in the course of which a host of antagonisms regarding persons, interests and ideas unfolded.

Soon, however, the Jews were confronted with problems which the autonomous communities were incapable of solving. A more general arrangement was required. Many families had experienced dissolution as a result of persecutions, departure from their places of origin, and wanderings prior to their arrival in Thessalonike. Some were converted to Christianity; others were then lost without trace. Insoluble problems of familial and inheritance law were created. Moreover, the accumulation of tens of thousands of refuoees led to antagonisms over housing claims. Disputes among neighbourhood communities began to crop up. Finally, there existed the need for a united front towards the Turkish administration. For all these reasons, a body of three rabbis was formed at the beginning of the sixteenth century. It functioned, rather atypically, to issue a series of regulations which were binding on the entire Jewish population of Thessalonike. Towards the middle of the same century another thirty-member body functioned with similar purposes and results. These two bodies did not, however, aim at limiting the independence of neighbourhood communities. Rather, they played a complementary and coordinating role, without assuming an antagonistic posture. Again rather atypically and provisionally, various committees were formed around the three-member councils. These consisted sometimes only of rabbis, and at other times of rabbis and laymen. On occasion a general assembly of the people was convened. The result of such fermentations were several important works of general interest, intended to last for centuries. One of these was the *Talmud Tora,* which combined several activities. It provided higher education; served more generally as a cultural centre; provided food and shelter to travellers; and gathered together those who were seeking work. Another such achievement was the *Pidion Chevoneyim,* a treasury for ransoming war captives. A third was the *Albacha,* which distributed clothing to poor children; from 1564, the material was woven within the *Talmud Tora.*

After the provisional bodies of three, a single intercommunity council was founded, which had seven elected members. In 1567, a Jewish delegation from Thessalonike to Constantinople secured an imperial firman which confirmed all special privileges which previous sultans had granted. Moreover, it decreed (1) that the Jewish community in Thessalonike would form a *müssellemlik* (an administrative unit lower than a pashalik but higher than an agalik, directly responsible to the Sublime Porte, a status which theoretically exempted them from the interferences of local authorities, but which in fact was violated; and (2) that the Jewish community would not pay the capitation tax in money, but in kind — specifically, in the form of thick, coarse woollen cloth to be used in attiring the Janissaries.

Throughout the seventeenth century, a host of factors had the effect of weakening the local communities, and strengthening the federating institutions. In 1620 and 1623 destructive fires occurred which produced economic dislocation amongst individuals and their organizations. Almost simultaneously, the entire Jewish people began to suffer from the abuses of profiteering Ottoman officials, in particular those responsible for receiving the woollen cloth. In addition, they suffered losses at the hands of insubordinate Janissaries. From 1628 to 1640, Jews throughout the whole empire were faced with a sultan who treated them with severity. Many impoverished Thessalonike Jews abandoned the city. Those who remained were obliged to pay the taxes of those who departed, and hence the economic situation continually deteriorated. For a lengthy period after 1657, the Thessalonike Jews were divided between those who believed that Sabbethai Sevi was the expected Messiah, and those who opposed him as a deceiver. In 1686, many of the former embraced the Muslim faith, creating a terrible crisis. At the same time, Jewish refugees from Belgrade arrived in Thessalonike. Two years later the Venetian fleet blockaded the city. None of these difficulties or crises could be effectively confronted by the individual synagogue community. Even the federal organs, with their much wider authority, were frequently shown to be impotent in the face of enormous needs and pressures. They had difficulty in attaining their desired ends, despite all the personal competence and self-sacrifice of those at the top. Formerly so intransigent in protecting their autonomy and freedom of initiative, the synagogue communities more and more resigned their claims and rights to the federal organs. Weakened by the tribulations which befell the Jewish population, they could no longer maintain their philanthropic organizations, or educational institutions, or courts. Instead, they sought to transfer these pressures onto the wider community. The federal institutions were saddled with additional tasks, and their rights and prerogatives were correspondingly augmented. Consequently, their operation became more systematic and substantive. Around 1690-1700, the considerably strengthened federal administration was transformed into a single body while the synagogue communities preserved a small margin of activity in secondary sectors. The higher administrative organ of the new, unified community of Thessalonike Jews was a three-member body composed of rabbis, along with a seven-member committee formed of laymen. These boards represented continuity from the federal institutions. Their members held office for life, and were not elected. Each new member was selected by the incumbents from among the wealthy and educated. The courts of the synagogues were abolished. Four courts were now created, each consisting of three rabbis, each of which exercised jurisdiction over a district of the town. The local medical care services were united into one centre, the *Bikonr Holim*. Moreover, in 1689 a fund was established to provide orphan girls with dowries. Many neighbourhood grammar schools and seminaries ceased to function. Children from quarters which did not have educational institutions attended corresponding classes which were formed at the *Talmud Tora*. The latter also acquired a press, the main function of which was to print school books (1690). In order to cope with increased obligations, the new community imposed a variety of taxes on its members; on dowries and inheritances; on the consumption of meat, wine, spirits, cheese, oil, *halva*, salted fish and wool; and finally, in 1744, on imports and exports. The legislative activity of the community was vital in coping with the diverse problems which arose. Noteworthy here is its pioneering protection of the rights of individuals who created a new type of profession, found a customer or supplier, discovered a salaried position. Another expression of the centralizing spirit was the creation of the office of Grand Rabbi, with spiritual authority over the entire Jewish population in Thessalonike.

Village Federations

Certain villages which belonged to the same *mukataa* (see page 361) and which owed common services to the state joined together in federations.

The *Hasikochoria* (*hass*-villages) in Chalkidike

More than fifteen Christian villages in Chalkidike belonged to the sultana's *hass* — whence their name, the *Hasikochoria* or *hass* villages. They formed a voivodalik with its seat at Polygyros. Their inhabitants did not enjoy special tax treatment, but were exempt from paying fees to the public officials. Many *hass*-villages developed community self-government at an early stage. The wealthy were prominent in these institutions. Even before the eighteenth century, there are instances of cooperation among certain villages. In the early eighteenth century all the villages united in a federation, which had 15,000 inhabitants around 1800.

Kassandra

The revenues of the *nahiye* of Kassandra constituted *evkaf* for the poor of Mecca, Medina and later, Constantinople. Its inhabitants were mostly Greeks, and they were exempted from all taxes except the capitation tax. From the seventeenth century, the villages of the *nahiye* were allied in a federation, presided over by twelve villages. The president of the federal council (the *koca başi*) commanded a Christian security force, whose task was to confront the *klephts* and pirates. In 1830, the English traveller Urquhart reports that they had political and religious privileges unknown in the West.

The *Mademochoria* (Mining Villages)

The economic and tax links among the Mademochoria (see page 372) and their subordination within a single *mukataa* facilitated the formation of an administrative federation in which the following twelve free villages participated: Arnaut Mahala (Isvoros, Stratonike, Siderokausia), Anthemous (Galatista), Chorouda, Ierissos, Arnaia (Liaringovi), Asvestochorion (Neochorion), Marathoussa (Ravna) Megali Panagia (Revenikia), Stanos, Varvara, Vasilika, Baudos. Each of these villages had a local community government which enjoyed a large measure of independence. Moreover, each had authority over a number of smaller villages. In 1780, for example, Vasilika represented the villages of the salt-pans, and Chorouda represented the village Vissoka.

The federation council consisted of twelve representatives (*vekil*) of the free villages, each of which had one of the twelve parts of the seal with which council decisions were confirmed. This was meant to ensure unanimity. According to the historian K. Paparregopoulos, the council elected a four-member executive committee in 1860. Ottoman documents, however, mention only the *koca başi* of the Mademochoria. Evidently this refers to the president of the council, or of its executive committee.

All the village inhabitants participated in electing their community leaders, the number of which was not stable but fluctuated from period to period, and was regulated according to the village population. The community council members elected delegates to the federal council from among their own ranks. The federation was intimately involved with enterprises to exploit the mines. Because of the participation of the workers, these undertakings were organized on a popular basis, despite the fact that the entrepreneurs held important positions at all levels in the councils.

The jurisdictions of the Mademochoria notables were identical with those of community officials elsewhere in the empire, i.e. in terms of regulating and distributing taxes. In

253. Kapsokalyvia, a skete of Great Lavra, Mount Athos. Throughout the Ottoman occupation the self-governing monastic state of Athos retained its independent institutions; the monasteries were represented in Constantinople by a body which functioned as a higher court to resolve differences between the monasteries.

addition they were obliged to cover costs of providing guards for the mines, and ensuring a work force. In the nineteenth century they also participated in the management of the mines.

ECCLESIASTICAL ADMINISTRATION

Throughout the Ottoman period changes in the ecclesiastical geography of Macedonia were numerous and significant. In this period, most of Macedonia belonged to the independent archbishopric of Ochrid, and the metropolitan sees of Thessalonike and Philippi; from the eleventh century, the metropolitan see of Serres was restricted to the area of the city. The majority of the episcopal sees were in southern Macedonia.

During the period from its subjection up until its abolition in 1767, the history of the archbishopric of Ochrid is rich in events. In 1410, the Patriarch of Constantinople granted the archbishop of Ochrid many sees which had long belonged to the Bulgarian Patriarchate. The latter had been abolished after the Turks dismantled the Bulgarian state in 1393. Following the Turkish advance into Serbian territory, and up to 1459, the sees of the Serbian Patriarchate also passed into the archbishop of Ochrid's jurisdiction. In 1456, the archbishop was apparently involved in electing the metropolitan of Hungary-Wallachia. In 1557, however, the autonomous Serbian church was refounded, and resumed jurisdiction over the sees which had been given to the archbishop of Ochrid. Before that, around 1500, the bishoprics of Veria-Naousa and Grevena had passed to the jurisdiction of the Oecumenical Patriarchate. The archbishopric of Ochrid therefore had seventeen sees, eight of which were located in western and northern Macedonia (Kastoria, Moglena, Vodena (Edessa), Stromnitsa, Velessa, Bitolia or Pelagonia, Prespa, Sisanion). The others were located outside Macedonia — in western Bulgaria, southern Serbia and Albania. Ochrid lost the metropolitan see of Kastoria in 1621 or 1622, and the bishopric of Sisanion in the seventeenth century. From 1018, the higher clergy were Greek, but this did not prevent the development of strained relations between the archbishops of Ochrid and the Patriarchs of Constantinople. The basic source of antagonism was Ochrid's attempt to maintain or increase its autonomy and territorial jurisdiction, which Constantinople opposed. Some archbishops of Ochrid even sought support from the Latin church and western leaders. Between 1600 and 1640 four archbishops proclaimed their Catholicism. Another announced his intention to convert between 1655 and 1667. From 1650, the archbishopric of Ochrid entered a period of internal crisis. Archbishops were frequently changed, and many were openly censured by local bishops. Alarmed at the situation, as well as the continued pro-Latin stance of certain archbishops, the Patriarch of Constantinople began meddling in the internal affairs of the autocephalous church. Ochrid's clergy, consequently, became divided into two parties. One inclined towards the Patriarchate, and accepted its interventions, while the other was opposed. In 1763, Patriarch Ioannikios III and the patriarchal party supported the priest-monk Ananias for the office of archbishop. Their opponents nominated Arsenios. The latter, however, immediately went over to the patriarchal party, and joined in its efforts to abolish the autonomous church. This was achieved in 1767.

In 1371, the metropolitan see of Philippi was given 'as a donation' to the prelate of Drama, who in 1359 held metropolitan rank. Henceforth the metropolitan see of Philippi was united with the other episcopal sees, some of which also achieved metropolitan status, like Zichna. After 1646, Thasos came under the jurisdiction of the metropolitan of Maroneia.

In the Thessalonike metropolitanate, the bishoprics of Vodena, Ierissos, Ardamerion, Kassandreia, Polyani and Kozani became metropolitan sees.

At the beginning of the nineteenth century, Macedonia comprised one archbishopric (Kassandreia) and ten metropolitanates (Thessalonike, Kastoria, Pelagonia and Prilep, Bitolia, Vodena, Tiberioupolis and Stromnitsa, Grevena, Serres, Philippi and Drama, Melenikon). Some of the latter had varying numbers of bishops under their jurisdictions.

The bishops were nominated by the Patriarch of Constantinople. Frequently the inhabitants of an area would oppose the nominations. In 1671, for example, the residents of the Thessalonike area refused to accept Anastasios Pantodynamos as metropolitan of Thessalonike. Other bishops experienced friction with community authorities, like the metropolitans of Thessalonike Ignatios and Neophytos Damalas.

The Ottoman authorities viewed the higher clergy as the Patriarch's representatives. According to the various sultans' grants of privileges, the Ottoman officials did not have the right to interfere in the affairs of the church. However, they often meddled in the elections of bishops and metropolitans, as well as in the administration of ecclesiastical affairs. In order to assume office, the prelates had to be supplied with an imperial document, which they received after bearing a gift to the Porte.

Aside from administering the ecclesiastical affairs of their area, metropolitans and bishops also judged cases of family law. The revenues of metropolitan sees came from their real estate, and the obligatory contribution of the faithful. Indeed, a firman of 1715 ordered the *kadi* of Thessalonike to investigate the residents' complaints that their metropolitan was collecting his fees in duplicate or triplicate. This document also reveals that each household paid twelve aspra to the parish priest, and up to one golden nomisma each as dues to the metropolitan and patriarch. Voluntary gifts, money collected by monks on their missions and bequests were the remaining sources of material support which maintained the ecclesiastical community.

The Christians did not have the right to build new churches, and the repair of old ones required special permission. By making generous offerings to the sultan and local authorities, however, the Christians managed to bypass these obstacles. Such expenses, abuses of local officials, and the ravages of brigands reduced the ecclesiastical foundations to a difficult economic position. The cry of Philotheos, abbot of the Zavorda monastery, is typical: 'We suffer a plethora of misfortunes, slanders and injustices from the pashas who assail us. We endure as well the calamity wrought by brigands'.

Many higher clergymen, priests and monks took part in the nation's struggle for its revival, spiritual development and freedom. They too fell victim to the Ottoman tyranny in their effort to oppose those who had been converted to Islam, and to counter the spiritual weakening of the Macedonian Christians. In 1432, Kallimachos or Kallinikos I of Veria was hung by the Turks; the bishop of Kassandreia headed a rising against the Turks in 1684. During the national revolt of 1821, the metropolitan of Thessalonike, Joseph III Antonopoulos or Dalivares, was martyred in Constantinople. Meletios, his vicar in Thessalonike and bishop of Kitros, was butchered by a Turkish mob, as was the metropolitan of Grevena.

Mount Athos

In the early phases of the Ottoman rule, the Holy Mountain was under the protection of the leaders of Moldavia and Wallachia. After participating in the revolutionary movement which broke out during the Venetian-Turkish War of 1570-73, Athos became a *mukataa* dependent on a *bostanci* (imperial guard) corps. Except for a *bostanci* special agent (*zâbit* or *haseki*) and the garrison itself, installed at Karyes in 1575 no other Turk was permitted on Athos. After 1743, a second *bostanci* officer was installed at Thessalonike as a liaison between the officials and the monastic community. These special circumstances lasted until 1839, and were instrumental in fully protecting the Holy Mountain from the interference of local Ottoman officials. Thus in 1807, when the authorities in Thessalonike arrested twenty monks as hostages during the Serbian uprising, they were released following the intervention of the *bostanci* commander and the Patriarch.

The Holy Mountain had secured special privileges from the sultans. In their firmans, the formula 'exemption from all taxes' frequently occurs. Actually, this means exemption from taxes which were levied by firmans. In point of fact, the monks were originally exempted from the capitation tax, but apparently they were obliged to pay it either after the reforms of 1567/68, or at the latest in 1621. In addition, the monks were granted the privilege to pay a lumpsum tax on the properties which had been in their possession before the conquest. This was extended to include what they later acquired. Moreover, they paid a special tax for the independence of the monks. In the late eighteenth and early nineteenth centuries, this amounted to nearly one-third of Athos' entire obligations — 7,000 piastres out of a total of 19,130.

Given its twofold character as *evkaf* and *mukataa,* Mount Athos managed to preserve its institutions of community government, and to continue the Byzantine tradition. The monastic community was probably the first to be recognized as a legal person. The 'Grand Assembly' and its president (the 'Primate' or *protos*) were the highest administrative organs in the Byzantine period. All maintained their legislative, judicial and executive powers after the Ottoman conquest. The 'Assembly' (known in the eighteenth century as the 'Community') now tended to include representatives from all the monasteries, and was responsible for distributing taxes and settling differences among the monasteries. Representatives of the Ottoman authorities and of the *bostanci* corps participated in its meetings. In Constantinople, the monasteries were represented before the *bostanci* corps and the imperial *evkaf* service by the Patriarch and twenty delegates. The latter included one for each monastery (two after 1806); they were usually the leaders of the Greek guilds in Constantinople. This body also functioned as the supreme court for settling differences among the monasteries.

Towards the end of the sixteenth century, the office of the *protos* is no longer mentioned. The formal duties of president of the 'Assembly' were probably taken over by the bishop of Ierissos, or more customarily by the abbot of Great Lavra. The office no longer had the wider jurisdiction of the *protos*.

ECONOMY

The information we have concerning the economy of Macedonia during the period 1430-1830 is fragmentary, incomplete and unequally distributed. Sources later than 1720 are much more abundant and detailed than those from the immediately preceding period, which in turn are better than those from even earlier periods. Information concerning trade is superior quantitatively and qualitatively to the rest; transactions with foreign countries are more illuminating than transactions with other areas of the Ottoman empire; of central importance is the information about transactions with the countries of western Europe, particularly France, though it does not seem that in themselves they were more significant than transactions with central European countries.

This unevenly balanced picture is due exclusively to the present situation concerning the sources and their investigation. Thus the reports of French consuls and accounts of foreign travellers have been collected and extensively evaluated, while Ottoman archives have yet to be studied systematically. The reports of the consuls provide a virtually uninterrupted picture of commerce with corresponding commentary. The accounts of foreign travellers contain supplementary facts. The information that is derived from these two categories concerns first and foremost the transactions with France and then trade elsewhere; the commodities (from which we learn about certain aspects of agriculture and industrial crafts), the merchants, competition, financing and general economic conditions, from which we obtain some idea of the abuses and the insecurity of the people under Ottoman administration. The Ottoman archives are composed of administrative and judicial documents. Each document refers to a separate case, but seldom does it refer to a specific place or time. In order to draw macroscopic conclusions, data must be collected from hundreds if not thousands of documents chronologically related and locally connected. For the present the utilization of these documents is in its infancy.

Agriculture, Forestry, Stock Breeding, Fishing, Hunting

What we know about agriculture, forestry, stock breeding, fishing and hunting during the period from 1430 to 1830 in Macedonia amounts to very little.

During this period Macedonia continued to grow the agricultural products it had always produced: various sorts of cereals, pulses, vegetables, flax, grapes and the fruit of certain trees (apples, citrons, walnuts, chestnuts, cherries, plums, olives). The Ottoman settlers introduced the cultivation of opium. Later, rice, maize, cotton and tobacco were added to the agricultural products of Macedonia. The two latter products found the soil and climatic conditions in Macedonia especially suitable. Thus they acquired qualities which gave rise to a strong demand and became a significant source of wealth. It is estimated that Macedonia produced 77,000 tons of grain in 1758. Tobacco production was around 8,000 tons in 1765; by the end of the eighteenth century it had reached 13,000 tons and was worth 40,000,000 piastres. This volume was equal to 80% of the total volume of grain. The region around Serres produced 2,500 tons of cotton in the middle of the eighteenth century and 8,750 tons of cotton, with a value of 7,500,000 piastres by the end. The ratio of the quantity of cotton production to the quantity of grain in the same region was 73:100. Moreover, cotton and flax were raw materials used for the production of thread and cloth. The same products, with the addition of tobacco and grain, were also used in trade exchanges. Nevertheless, the agricultural production of Macedonia fell far short of the natural potential of the country. The producers, besides paying land rent and taxes, were fleeced by officials and collectors, by brigand gangs and by the forces authorized to protect them from these gangs. The areas that were most exposed to abuses and oppression were abandoned and left uncultivated. Resettlement of the areas by new farmers did not equal the departures. By the end of the eighteenth century half of the cultivable area of Macedonia was fallow. The Ottoman archives and foreign observers furnish a great deal of information on these phenomena. The traveller F. Beaujour describes all this in detail. He begins with the observation that the volume of Macedonian agricultural products exported was disproportionate to the

254-255. Two 19th century lithographs of Monastir (Bitola). The town was the hub of a road network, a flourishing commer-

cial and busy administrative centre as well as the seat of a bishopric. Its size attracted emigrants from regions close by, for

level of production: the volume does not represent a surplus and thus the villagers were deprived even of the necessities; he concludes: 'nature gave everything to this country and the government destroyed it.'

The forest wealth of Macedonia suffered badly right from the beginning of the Ottoman occupation. The Christian population which withdrew to the mountains built villages, which used a great deal of timber for housing, heating and the manufacture of tools. Even greater damage was done by the development of stock breeding, which became the main source of income for these people. The Ottoman authorities also destroyed forests during their pursuit of rebels.

There was a more extensive development of stock breeding in Macedonia during Ottoman rule than during Byzantine times. Most of the Turkish settlers raised stock. The Christians who withdrew to the mountains devoted themselves in the main to stock breeding. But the livestock wealth of Macedonia consisted mainly of sheep and goats. In 1815 there were 2,600,000 goats and 17,000,000 sheep.

Macedonia also had sericulture and apiculture. During the second half of the eighteenth century the area around Thessalonike produced 15,000-20,000 kilograms of silk. A part of the wax and honey production was exported.

The lakes of Macedonia were rich in fish. There was a great demand for trout, even as far away as Constantinople. Both lakes and forests supported many kinds of animals that were hunted, some for food and others for their pelts or skins.

Mines

During Ottoman rule, the most important mines in Macedonia were at the Mademochoria, Siderokastron (Demir Hisar) and at Kratovo. The first group, in Chalkidike, produced mainly silver or lead. The second, in eastern Macedonia, produced mainly iron. The third, in northern Macedonia, also produced silver and lead. They resumed operation under Mehmed II (1451-81), whose decrees were supplemented later on by regulations issued by Süleyman the Magnificent (1520-66) and other sultans.

We know best the history of the Mademochoria, which in any case was one of the most important mining centres of the Ottoman empire. At the beginning of the sixteenth century, a band of Jewish refugees from Germany introduced German methods of exploiting and purifying the ore. Production increased due to the measures of Süleyman, when six thousand people worked in the mines. At that time the Sublime Porte received each month an amount of pure silver worth 18,000-30,000 ducats. Its importance for the monetary and military policy of the sultans made systematic central control essential and dictated the creation of a special *mukataa*, the income from which, along with a part of the production, was collected by the imperial mint. All the Mademochoria villages whose inhabitants were employed in mining belonged to the *mukataa*.

From the sixteenth century on, the administrative capital of the *mukataa* and the seat of the Aga-Emin was

example Moschopolis, who sought its greater safety as protection against the oppression of the Albanian beys. It was also a

focus of intellectual activity and the largest centre of Hellenism in northern Macedonia from the 18th century onwards.

Siderokapsa (Siderokavsia of Byzantine times), a flourishing centre with a population of various ethnic origins. The town prospered till the middle of the seventeenth century: it had a mint, two mosques, public baths, a Muslim theological school and monastery, inns and an important market; it declined, however, and became a dependence of the village of Isvoros after the eighteenth century.

The responsible administrator and lessee of the *mukataa* had nearly unlimited power and independence, with administrative, tax and often judicial jurisdiction. It seems that during the sixteenth and seventeenth centuries he himself subleased the mines to private parties. But by the end of the seventeenth century weaknesses in the system led to the decline of the mines and the government was forced to undertake, within the framework of more general reforms of the public economy, works of renovation: the repair and cleaning of the old galleries, the opening of new ones and the construction of new smelters as well as the establishment of a garrison for the protection of the mines from pirates. The new regulations for the operation of the mines foresaw the establishment of an inspector with a yearly salary of 2,000 piastres, who would have at his disposal 1,600,000 aspra from the taxes of the region as capital to meet current needs. In 1705, during the period when the renovations were being carried out, the Greeks of the region (from Athos, Longos, the villages of Nikiti, Saint Nicholas and the Mademochoria) undertook for the first time the exploitation of the mines as lessees of the state. The precise terms of the agreement are not known. At any

rate it is reported that the lessees would provide protection from pirate raids for the mines, that in case of damage they would compensate the state for its expenses up till then and the salaries of the workers would be kept unchanged; it appears, moreover, that they undertook the cost of the completion of the renovation works.

The system of leasing was soon changed. In 1707-08 the administration of the *mukataa* was auctioned: the highest bidder agreed to pay a fixed sum for coal and for tax and for various activities involved in the exploitation of the mines, for which he paid in kind, while he was to keep as a profit what was left over from the exploitation of the *mukataa*. The sum was fixed and the terms of the lease varied according to circumstances. For a number of years the family of Hussein Chaoush Zade, who had been a lessee of the mines before the reorganization and had instigated the introduction of the new regulations for their operation, did not hesitate to bid and outbid, offering ever greater amounts. Indeeed, because of the renovations and the significant increase in production there was a large margin of profit for the lessee (it is estimated at 8-9,000 piastres at the least in 1706-07, while the salary of the inspector was only 2,000 piastres); this does not take into account the fact that the lessee sold the ore that belonged to him at a higher price than that at which the state calculated its share, nor the portion of the taxes he witheld.

Soon, however, limits were put on the margin of profit. In 1715 no other bidder appeared. Thus the state was obliged to lease the *mukataa* to the sons of Hussein under the terms of the preceding year and to renounce claim to the yearly increase. The terms for leasing became even more favourable during the following years, as the production of the mines continually dropped; this also influenced the labourers' wages. After the middle of the eighteenth century, the lessees secured their profit from the difference in tax and bought on the free market (in England and Holland) the ore they were obliged to hand over to the mint. Finally, the Chaoush Zades managed to convert the lease of the mines into a lifetime concession by paying 55,000 piastres.

In 1775 the Greeks protested over the bad management of Ahmed Chaoush Zade and offered to undertake the lease of the *mukataa* themselves under the supervision of a representative of the Porte as administrator. But at the beginning of the nineteenth century they had still not succeeded: a new regime was imposed, in agreement with which the *mukataa* was leased to an official of the Porte and sublet to an aga of Thessalonike. According to Beaujour, the aga-voivode deposited 6,000 piastres with the Porte as the yearly rent, while the product of the mines reached 30,000 piastres, of which 16,000 represented the workers' wages and the remaining 8,000 piastres the profit of the aga. As before, the Greeks were forced to supply workers and materials for the exploitation of the mines. When Cousinéry visited the region, whose capital was Arnaia (Liaringovi), the villages there were obliged to guarantee one hundred labourers, who were paid so poorly that the communities were forced to contribute for the maintenance of their families, and moreover to pay out the arbitrary amounts demanded by the aga. This tragic situation to which the Mademochoria had been reduced on account of the excesses of the Ottoman authorities led, after an appeal by the *rayahs,* to the issue of a firman by the sultan in 1801, reintroducing the 'former terms of the lease' and safeguarding the prerogatives of the workers in the mines.

The leasing of the mines by Greeks must have been achieved after 1801. According to the description of the English traveller Hunt, who visited the region in 1820, a business man who had collected a thousand piastres leased from the state a certain area of the mines for one year and, in agreement with a group of workers, undertook all the expenses of exploitation. The production was shared as follows: the lead belonged to the sultan, one fifth of the ore went to the aga, while the silver was bought exclusively by the state at a fixed price (eighty piastres an oke), for the mint. The profits were shared out, according to a fixed scale, between the entrepreneur, who received one seventh, and the workers.

This is a form of cooperation between capital and labour the Greeks also put into practice elsewhere. Evidently, from this period on the Greek communities financed one or more cooperatives, which in the end formed a general company. An account by K. Paparregopoulos (1860), who conducted an on-the-spot investigation among the elders, leaves us to understand that around 1805 the Greek communities had managed to neutralize the rivalry of the Turkish lessees and had undertaken the exploitation of all the mines offering the state money for an enterprise that

had a deficit. The terms were indeed onerous: the *rayah* lessees were obliged to hand over two hundred okes of silver to the mint every year at the 'old price', meaning at a price lower than the current one, and in addition to pay to the Turkish authorities, over and above the taxes, duties and fees of the local administration, a lump sum whose total exceeded 151,000 piastres. This is much higher than the rent for the *mukataa* at the beginning of the seventeenth century,if the drop in the value of the currency is taken into account (in Venetian *zecchini,* a stable currency, the rent was 4,444 in 1695 and 9,776 in 1820). Furthermore, this occurred during a time when the output of the mines was nearly exhausted. The communities found compensation by strengthening their tax privileges and their administrative autonomy, while at the same time they controlled the managing aga, as they paid his salary.

The wealth of the Mademochoria no longer derived from the mines, but from the fertile soil and flourishing industrial crafts. In the Mademochoria there were $982\frac{1}{2}$ yokes of assessable land out of a total of 2,625 yokes in Chalkidike. Travellers in the nineteenth century speak of the agricultural wealth of the region and give details concerning the industrial crafts of the residents: the pottery of the small village of Netsessalar, the carpet industry of Arnaia (Liaringovi) and the surrounding region and the textile industry of the villages of Kalamaria.

Like the other workers in state enterprises, the workers in the mines also belonged to a group of 'immune and free' *rayahs,* who had important tax exemptions, which varied from mine to mine. In general, the workers were exempt from the *avarız,* the taxes of the local administration and the ecclesiastical dues as well as from some rights of the timariots. Nevertheless, these exemptions, passing from father to son, belonged exclusively to the members of the communities and were recorded in special registers.

Industrial Crafts

The Ottoman conquerer, by exterminating and scattering the Greek urban population, deprived society of artisans and specialists in the processing of raw materials and the manufacture of hand-made items. The new rulers did not encourage these professions, having very limited needs, both quantitatively and qualitatively, for such goods. This entire sector of production regressed to the level determined by the needs of the new clientele, the dislocation in the supply of new materials and the limited number of artisans and the most rudimentary activities.

The latter factor was changed when a very large number of Jewish refugees settled in Thessalonike and later in other Macedonian towns. Most of them were experienced artisans: metalworkers, ironsmiths, coppersmiths, carpenters, cartmakers, spinners, silkworkers, dyers, ropemakers, weavers, carpetweavers, tanners, tailors, millers, olive oil refiners, bakers, cheesemakers, soapmakers, potters, distillers, fishermen, cabinetmakers and goldsmiths; some of them knew how to produce vitriol and other chemical compounds. There were also doctors among them. The rest were boatmen, porters and builders. In some of the professions, the Jews brought work methods and secrets which

256-257. Women of Macedonia from 16th century woodcuts. The Greek communities of Macedonia played a decisive part in the survival of the Greek nation and in its systematic intellec- *tual and moral reformation by undertaking public works, strengthening national consciousness and forging a desire for freedom.*

made them unrivalled. We have already mentioned the metalworkers from central Europe, who brought German methods of mining and smelting; other examples are the distillers from Majorca who started the manufacture of an aromatic liquer, and the numerous weavers from Spain, bearers of a long tradition. They knew every aspect of the work well, from the selection of the wool to the finish of a fabric or a carpet. The Turks much admired the woven materials produced by the Jews; one of the materials that they produced, the *abas,* was a very durable and waterproof material suitable for the clothing of soldiers, sailors, farmers and labourers. The Porte bought large quantities of this material, and numerous bales were sought by a huge clientele throughout Turkey and abroad. A very large part of the Jewish population of Thessalonike devoted itself to the manufacture of *abas,* in workshops and in homes, with the entire family participating. Some wove in order to supplement their income from another profession that was not manual. Textile enterprises were founded rather early by

the synagogues, who employed wage labour. Around 1550 there were attempts by individuals to compete with the synagogues, but they failed. Fifteen years later a crisis occurred, brought on by the competition among the producers. It ended with the intervention of the rabbis who forbade senseless overbidding for raw materials in the market and excessive underbidding for the sale of cloth. The measures for the protection of the producers and the quality of the products were complemented by the founding of a guild which included both the artisans and the merchants. The guild regulated the level of production and collected capital, which covered those who were unemployed and those who had suffered losses as a result of brigandage or of abuse by officials.

The presence of many experienced and hard-working Jewish artisans in Thessalonike and other Macedonian towns did not prevent the rebirth of industrial crafts among the Christian population of the towns and countryside. They devoted themselves primarily to production of woollen and cotton goods and secondarily to tanning, linen and silk production, winemaking, cabinetmaking, and fish salting, and thirdly, to candle making. Two other occupations, the fur industry and metalworking (under which gunsmithing, silversmithing and goldsmithing are included) were based not only on local raw materials but also on imported ones. The main varieties of woollen materials produced by the Christians were: the *skoutia,* rough woollen fabrics which were used by sailors and travellers because they were wind and waterproof; the *velenzes* or pure wool bedspreads, and rugs. Various kinds of cloth were woven from cotton thread, as well as thick coverings for divans, bathrobes, and mosquito nets. A variety of dress materials were manufactured with linen. Silk thread was woven into scarves and shirts.

Making of woollen goods developed mainly in western and central Macedonia, because most of the wool was produced there. For the same reason the manufacture of cotton goods was concentrated mainly in central and eastern Macedonia; winemaking was limited to the regions of Naousa and Siatista; fish were salted in the settlements around the lakes; and the fur industry thrived in Kastoria and made the town prosperous. The mountain villages of western Macedonia, in addition to the production of woollens, specialized in the manufacture of farm tools from wood. Several of these villages, (the *mastorochoria* the builders' villages) produced very fine builders who formed teams and worked throughout the entire Balkan peninsula, undertaking the most demanding construction jobs. The more common crafts, such as iron working, carpentry, tanning and tailoring, were found everywhere.

In the villages and market towns, the production of woollen goods passed through three stages of development. At first, the breeders themselves produced yarn and textiles for sale and they also sold unprocessed wool. The latter was used by families who did not possess animals, either as such (for example, to fill mattresses), or as raw material for the production of knitwear or woven materials. Later the production of yarn and textiles for sale passed out of the hands of the breeders and became a cottage industry. Women, the elderly and children were all employed in spinning; weaving was exclusively women's work. Finally, workshops which employed hired help came into being, though without excluding the two earlier stages. Cotton, on the other hand, was not worked by the growers, who were rich landowners. The fur and tanning industries were carried on in small, specialized privately owned workshops assisted by paid labour.

The scant information we have on industrial crafts gives us an incomplete and disjointed picture. Thus we shall limit ourselves to some specific information, mainly concerning the eighteenth century, supplementing it from the second half of the seventeenth and the beginning of the nineteenth centuries.

Thessalonike, the most populous town in Macedonia, the headquarters of the Pasha and the military, naturally led the way in manufacturing and the conversion of raw materials. The woollen industry was predominantly a Jewish concern. In the seventeenth century it began to deteriorate in quality, and during the eighteenth century it succumbed to competition from the superior articles being imported from Europe. Production plummeted. The Jewish community withdrew as owners of capital and its place was taken by a private party. The Greeks busied themselves with the dyeing of yarn, and the manufacture of cotton, linen and silk materials. There were fifty-two dyeworks, renowned for high quality work. Cloth, bathrobes and mosquito nets were produced from cotton, and linen from Thessalonike was in great demand. From Thessalonike also came special silk scarves that were worn by the Janissaries and shirts that were much sought after even in the East.

Woollen goods finished by the water pounding method were produced at Veria. The town also specialized in bathrobes made of cotton or linen which were in great demand throughout the Ottoman empire. Naousa had, in addition to its weaving and dyeing works, noteworthy cabinet makers, goldsmiths and gunsmiths and Siatista produced a renowned wine. Kozani was noted for its woollen products and significant quantities were woven in houses in the town and in the surrounding villages. The kermes prospered in this region and it was used to make red dye, enabling the town to develop a large, high quality dyeing business. A portion of the yarn was used for weaving and the rest exported.

Serres and Drama were centres for the production of cotton yarn and fabric. The former specialized in coarse materials, Indian style, suitable for divan covers. It also produced morocain (crepe) of exceptional quality. Nigrita had dyers, goldsmiths and coppersmiths. Arnaia produced rugs. Melenikon produced various kinds of woven materials, copper utensils and weapons.

The production of yarn yielded a profit of 80% and weaving yielded 20%. The ratios of the amount of cotton produced — what proportion was spun or woven and what amount was exported — as well as the contacts among the various towns is interesting. About 1800 in Serres and the surrounding area between 3,000-6,000 tons of cotton were spun in houses; this represented one-quarter of the total production. A portion of this yarn was dyed. Half of it was woven in the towns and market towns of eastern Macedonia, as well as in Thessalonike and Veria; the other half was exported abroad.

Because the organization of the economy was retarded, and was largely based on privileges, investment in industry played little part. Any attempts which were made failed.

Commerce

The Ottoman conquest had adverse repercussions on commerce. Warfare disrupted both the activities of merchants and destroyed the social groups which constituted the customers for the most profitable merchandise. It was some time before the new ruling class had a marketable surplus of agricultural goods and other raw materials and before it sought industrial goods produced by specialized craftsmen. For a time exchange took place between stock breeders and the producers of agricultural products who lived within the same area, without the intervention of merchants or money. Alongside this activity,

258. Leading citizens of Thessalonike, from a copper plate engraving of the 18th or early 19th century. Throughout the Ottoman occupation, Thessalonike remained the preeminent city in Macedonia, where the Greek population dominated the economic, social and cultural life.

259. An important ruling class heading the local economic life developed early in Serres, a populous commercial centre in eastern Macedonia. A copper plate engraving of the late 18th or early 19th century depicts members of this class clothed as befits their rank.

which did not wholly cease till the end of Ottoman rule, more complicated patterns of trade developed, requiring the participation of specialized merchants.

This role was undertaken at first (and for a time, exclusively) by some of the Jews, mainly the Marranos, who had established themselves in Thessalonike, in other Macedonian towns (and in the Ottoman empire in general). With every wave of refugees there were a few who had already been involved in commerce in their former countries. They knew contemporary methods, which had been developed in Italian cities and in Spain, they were educated and they had relatives and friends in various cities of the Ottoman empire and abroad; some brought capital with them. They quickly demonstrated how necessary they were to a country that had no other merchants. Moreover, they seemed exceptionally versatile and adaptable to local conditions. Taking Turkish partners in name only, they paid import and export duties of 2.5% instead of 5% in exchange for paying gratuities to the nominal partners. Some of the more daring ones created large commercial

networks, while the others created around themselves a circle of agents and middlemen, in the towns and the country, not only in Macedonia but throughout the entire Balkan peninsula. The entrepôt role of Thessalonike developed; it played a part not only in East-West trade by land, but also in shipping Macedonian goods to other Mediterranean ports. Its primary links were to Venice and secondarily to other Italian cities. Marseilles, however, through which bolts of *abas* destined for the Antilles passed, also entered the network. Monastir, Veria and Kavala, where Jews were also established, began to develop as satellites of Thessalonike. Along with commerce, banking was also developed; this, too, was undertaken by the Jews, whose banking experience had been gained in their countries of origin. Other Jews became money-changers (very useful in the markets where so much foreign money was in circulation and where the local currency so often lost its equivalent value), as well as brokers, valuers, and private tax-farmers. The businessmen were accustomed to dividing their capital into three, approximately equal parts, putting one part into merchandise, one into gold currency and the third into land or buildings.

Slowly the Christian stock breeders and muleteers, and the Ottoman landowners entered the commercial circles. The latter commercialized their agricultural production and lent their ready capital. The former offered wool and various industrial goods produced from wool (yarn and woven articles), in the local market and distributed them on their own. Later on, the Christians, mainly the Greeks and the Vlachs, diversified into specialized merchants, set themselves up in the towns of Macedonia and the neighbouring Ottoman districts and in other countries. Others set up wayside inns along the commercial routes. By the seventeenth century Greek merchants had captured the largest portion of the internal trade and their caravans were already travelling beyond the northern borders of the Ottoman empire. Until the establishment of English merchants in Thessalonike, the merchandise that interested them was transported by Greeks between Smyrna and Thessalonike.

The rise of Greek commerce went hand in hand with the decline of Jewish commerce. As we have seen, the Jews in Thessalonike had linked their fortunes inseparably with that of Venice. Thus they were badly shaken by the Venetian-Turkish wars of 1645-69, 1684-99 and 1715, and the rapid decline of Venice. The messianic tempest of the years 1657-67, when many deserted their work in the conviction that the kingdom of God was at hand, and the conversion to Islam in 1667 by many adherents of the false-messiah, Sabbethai Sevi, who were for the most part rich merchants, also dealt a hard blow to the Jewish community and its prosperity.

Macedonia exported grain, wool, cotton, tobacco, hides, furs, cheese, wax, honey, pepper and the industrial goods mentioned above. The import trade was concerned with luxury items, velvet and other fabrics, furniture, spices and books, as well as unprocessed fur.

The commercial movements between Macedonia and the Hapsburg countries intensified after the Peace of Passarowitz (1718) under the influence of two auspicious factors. Firstly, Austria expanded to the south and southeast at the expense of the Ottoman empire, annexing northern Serbia, as far as Belgrade, a part of Banat and lesser Wallachia; consequently the leg of the journey at the point where caravans suffered most from lawless harassment by Ottoman officials and brigands was shortened. Secondly, agreements were made with merchants of both empires including the granting of special commercial privileges (1718 and 1739). Of the merchants with Ottoman citizenship, those from Macedonia benefited most because the Hapsburg countries wanted Macedonian products above all: wool, cotton, yarn and tobacco. In his turn, the Macedonian consumer sought felt and other fabrics, glassware, iron articles, furniture and ornamental items from Austria.

The caravans were made up of about one hundred horses. The journey from Macedonia to European cities required a number of days. For example, from Thessalonike to Vienna took seventy-two days, half of which were lost at quarantine stations on the frontiers.

Some muleteers and middlemen stayed permanently in the towns where Macedonian products were sold and European products bought to be sent to Macedonia; they were transformed into commissars (those authorized to receive and dispose of Macedonian products) or *speditores* (those specialized in the collection and despatching of European products). The number of these merchants gradually multiplied; they spread into many towns and themselves became part of the economic life of their host countries. During the Anglo-French wars at the end of the eighteenth century, in which the merchant ships of both sides were in danger, the Greek merchants took upon themselves the movement of German products headed for Macedonia, increasing the number of caravans or chartering neutral ships (especially Greek ones with an Ottoman or Russian flag). They even brought products from French colonies through Germany.

The Greeks, mainly Macedonians and Epirots, also did business with Hungary, Poland and Russia. The Macedonians travelled in particular to the trade fairs in the Ukraine and Poland, where they purchased velvet and silk and unprocessed furs, re-selling them at trade fairs in the Balkan peninsula.

Nevertheless, these trade fairs were mainly used for the exchange of products from the various regions of the empire. In south-west Macedonia they were held at Elassona, Servia and Mavronoros (near Argos Orestikon). Further north they were held at Strounga and Prilep. Avret Hisar (Gynaikokastron) is mentioned as the headquarters of the trade fair in central Macedonia; further east we have Serres. Finally in north-east Macedonia there were fairs at Dolia or Doliani (near Petric), Nevrokop and Ozondzinova. Some of these were first mentioned in the sixteenth century. They were all frequented, some more, some less, by non-Macedonians as well. Equally, Macedonians visited, as buyers and sellers, the trade fairs of neighbouring districts, from Lamia (then Zitouni) and Moscholouri in Thessaly as far as Selimnia, distributing merchandise from Thessalonike into the Danubian area. The merchants were mainly Greeks, Jews and Turks. In the eighteenth century the French tried to participate through their agents but they were discouraged by the extortionate demands of the local agas and by brigandry; thus the foreign merchants were obliged to buy and sell in the city of Thessalonike.

Nevertheless, the foreigners had advantages over the native Christians and Jews in several vital ways: they were covered by privileges that their governments had wrested from the Sublime Porte and thus, among other things, they virtually escaped the fate of the *rayahs* who were being bled white by Ottoman officials and Janissaries; besides that, with their stronger currency they could buy the finest quality wool, cotton, tobacco, hides and other raw materials and cause a rise in prices, greatly damaging local merchants. A few Christians and Jews managed to acquire foreign patronage (because this was obtained through a permit called a *berati*, such men were known as *beratli*), but most of them remained the agents and clerks of the foreigners, not their competitors. The second advantage belonging to foreigners was counter-balanced by a limited measure that applied only to wool: because the Jews had a difficult time securing the quality and the quantity they needed for the *abas* they were obliged to hand over to the Porte every year, an order was issued that allowed them to purchase at a specially low price a percentage of the wool that was collected at Thessalonike for export; around 1670 that quantity was 15%, by the second half of the eighteenth century it had become 25%; the prices were a quarter to one seventh lower.

Until the seventeenth century the only foreign merchants in Thessalonike were the Venetians. At the end of that century, the first Frenchmen arrived; in 1718 the first Englishmen; later came citizens of the various Italian states, particularly Genoa and the two Sicilies, Ragousians, Dutch, Danes, Swedes, Austrians, Germans, Swiss (from 1760 on) and finally Russians (from 1774 on). The first French merchants ran into many difficulties: the war between Austria and Turkey, the lack of credit, and the plague of 1713. After 1713 their number grew and by 1771 they made up eleven commercial houses. The English suffered fewer setbacks and competed successfully against the French. They cooperated with the Greeks, who ensured contact with the other Ottoman harbours, as well as with Italy. Indeed, Greek merchants established in Thessalonike, Siatista and Moschopolis arranged exports to Venice, Ancona and Messina. A Greek merchant in Venice, Koumanos, had representatives in Siatista, Kastoria, Ochrid, Moschopolis and Thessalonike. Meanwhile, the French merchants suffered from the competition of Greeks and Jews, especially those who had gained the protection of France. The Venetian merchants lost ground to the English and the French, maintaining first place only for a few luxury items of Venetian manufacture (mirrors and other glassware) but were given new life throughout the duration of the Anglo-French wars. The Germans, the Austrians and the Russians worked very closely with the Greeks. The association of Count Stahrenberg with the Greek Emmanuel Rizos is a characteristic case. Rizos, after twelve years of successful activity in Germany in the grain and fur trade, invested 70,000-75,0000 piastres in the House of Stahrenberg in Thessalonike in 1776 and took over its direction. He used Greek ships with Russian flags for the transport of merchandise.

By this time the local Greek merchants were no longer working chiefly as agents of the foreigners and were no longer confined to marginal jobs. Not long before, the Greeks had successfully withstood challenge from French merchants seeking all the contacts with western Europe. The Greek position in overland trade with central Europe was unshakable. Arasy, the French consul in Thessalonike, wrote of the Greek merchants in 1776: 'These people have recently developed their economy and acumen in their business enterprises. They themselves buy the product where it is produced and go and sell it in the place where it is consumed, with little expense, being accustomed to a poor life. Thus they save on commissions and on the expenses of storage, in the purchase as well as in the sale.'

The Greeks benefited from the wars between France and England and from the French Revolution, which shook the French commercial position in the East.

By the end of the eighteenth and beginning of the nineteenth century, two thirds of the trade in Thessalonike was in the hands of the Greeks. In 1812, the French consul in Thessalonike wrote: 'The Greeks do more business on their own account than on a commission basis. The Greeks are the most energetic factor in commerce; they are our greatest enemies.' A few years later, in 1818, the French consul Bottu said that the French merchants, 'were no longer able to compete, not even nominally with the new local firms'. The most important commercial house was Kaftandzoglou, which at this time hired French ships on its own account.

On the other hand, the decline of the Jews in the business sector, which began around the end of the seventeenth century, became more noticeable. They lost the place they had in large scale trade, and were confined to local operations, becoming agents or clerks to the foreigners.

The development of Macedonian trade in general was hindered by a host of adverse factors. The first thing is the very low level of agricultural yield compared to what Macedonian soil could have produced. This fact was not due to primitive cultivation alone, but also to a decrease in the productive population; people abandoned the countryside, fleeing from all kinds of oppression and abuse from Turkish officials as well as the rapacious bands of robbers.

Other factors had an even more direct adverse effect. We begin with the heavy and complicated tax system of the Ottoman empire and its aggravation by the arbitrary demands of the clerks and the security apparatus. On all movement of merchandise the *rayahs,* Greeks and Jews, had to pay a 50% customs duty that was increased by the lessees of the *mukataa* through duties on consumption, the tolls (*bac* or *baçi mürur*) and the various fees demanded by the security apparatus. The information that we have shows that the demands fluctuated according to the mood of the authorities.

In order to open a shop, the members of guilds had to procure special permits. Often the markets were the property of Ottoman philanthropic organizations, whose managers used them completely arbitrarily. When the Christian merchants wanted to withdraw fabrics from the markets of Thessalonike, the income of which belonged to the *evkaf* of the sultan Bayazid, they were confronted by an imperial prohibition.

The merchants had to give constant gratuities in order to expedite their affairs and to hinder injustice. The merchants suffered particularly in periods of war, when Macedonia was crossed by the armies and the envoys of the sultan. The Pasha of Thessalonike, and the agas, who had a monopoly on the most important products of the region, often interfered in the purchases of the merchants, forcing them to buy products which they did not want. The agas of Serres, who had the monopoly on cotton, overcharged the middlemen, and despite the permit of the Porte for the export of grain, interfered with the buying and selling of it. Moreover, the Turkish magnates looked for opportunities to extort money from the merchants, by proclaiming a ship a pirate ship or condemning a merchant for having expressed the intention of embracing Islam, but

26

260. *The Arch of Galerius from a 19th century drawing. The central and south-eastern part of Thessalonike was the Greek quarter where until very recently houses built in the true tradition of Byzantine secular architecture still stood.*

not carrying it out. In 1788 the market of the town remained closed for a month because of monetary demands on the merchants by the Janissaries.

To protect themselves from these arbitrary actions, the Greek and Jewish merchants became *baratarioi* or *beratli*, 'protected' by the foreign powers, though this did not make them absolutely secure. Among the three *baratarioi* of the French consul in Thessalonike at the beginning of the eighteenth century was the important tobacco merchant, Constantine Païkos.

Robbery and piracy also dealt heavy blows to commerce. The caravans were not only threatened by the bands of brigands whose numbers increased after the middle of the seventeenth century, but also by the security forces, even by the armed bodies hired by the merchants to protect them from the robbers.

Commerce shrank during all the wars. There were particularly disastrous consequences from the concentration of troops in Thessalonike which occurred during the Venetian-Turkish wars. The French consul in Thessalonike, Joinville, wrote in 1744: 'The sale of fabrics is difficult while the war is going on... the Greeks and the Jews of the countryside hide their money and do not dare dress up, because they are afraid they might inspire the Ot-

toman troops who are passing through their land with a thirst for pillage, Moreover, everything is dangerous for the wagons during this time. The merchants do not dare to send their merchandise to the areas they used to send them to.' In the Russo-Turkish war of 1768-74, the Greeks, disarmed by order of the sultan, did not transport merchandise because they were afraid of brigands, and internal trade came to a halt. In 1779 the economic life of Thessalonike was paralyzed by the impressment of three thousand sailors. In order to deal with the interruption of trade with central Europe during the Russo-Turkish war of 1787-92, the Greeks chartered, for the first time, a boat from Thessalonike to Trieste. Moreover, the recurrent epidemics of plague decimated the population, stopping all economic activity.

A serious obstacle to the development of Macedonian trade was the scarcity of money. For certain products, such as wool, the merchants had to pay one third or one half of its value in advance. The agas who controlled the production of the chief products, cotton, tobacco and wool, all wanted to be paid in cash. Every European currency was in circulation and was being traded against Ottoman currency which continually lost value, because from 1582 on the sultans reduced its assay value in silver

261. A 19th century sketch of the so-called portico of Las Incantadas with its carved figures, known by the Greeks as 'Idols'. In *the 18th and 19th century it stood in the courtyard of a Jewish house in Thessalonike.*

every so often. Various measures instituted by the governors of the provinces to serve their own interests upset economic life even more. Thus, while the prices of foreign currency had been determined in Constantinople in November, 1719, they did not become officially known in Thessalonike until May, 1720. In the meantime all commercial activity was interrupted.

The big merchants often gave merchandise to the smaller ones on credit, but they demanded 1% a month on the value of the merchandise until repayment. Since the small merchants did not pay off their debts in the prescribed time, the big merchants reaped significant profits this way.

Money credit was in the hands of the Jews who lent at rates that exceeded 20% a year. But by the middle of the eighteenth century the banking system appeared and commercial transactions increased.

The prices of Macedonian products, and of the merchandise Macedonia imported, varied. When competition between the merchants was non-existent or slight the prices of the imported merchandise were high. After the middle of the eighteenth century and especially after 1784, prices fell continuously. Conversely, the prices of the agricultural produce of Macedonia rose continuously,

although they never reached the level of western Europe.

Despite the difficulties and the small margin of profit, the fact that commercial transactions were repeated many times during a year meant that the profit on a capital investment could surpass 200%. Ten years labour permitted merchants to amass a significant fortune.

Guilds

The entry of non-Muslims into the guild system became an accepted fact after the seventeenth century, a period during which the institution of *Fütüvvet,* which made the guilds typical Islamic religious brotherhoods, had slackened and the guilds had been progressively transformed into simple professional unions. Moreover, the general policy of the early sultans of preserving the institutions of the peoples they had conquered, the survival of Byzantine craft guild terms, such as *maistor, proto-maistor* and *systema,* and the formulation of internal regulations in the Christian guilds during the seventeenth century, show that the Byzantine craft guilds had survived, at least in the large towns. A new phenomenon was the widening and extension of the guild system to all the towns and market towns of the empire. The Ottoman government, recognizing the non-Muslim guilds, placed them under its control and un-

262. During the Ottoman occupation scores of Macedonians left their homeland to avoid oppression. They settled in several towns of the Danubian principalities, in Austria, Hungary, Italy and even Germany, forming communities which prospered through trade. The picture shows a Macedonian woman from a tinted woodcut of the 18th century.

der the same legal obligations as the Muslim ones, from which they had copied the organization as well as the manner of operation and even the titles of their administrative officials though with some exceptions.

The guilds were professional bodies in which only the master craftsmen as opposed to the craftsmen and apprentices had the right to make decisions. The master craftsmen of each guild chose a president from among themselves and he ran the guild with the assistance of a council. The state, at least after the seventeenth century, exercised strict control over the guilds, through the *kadi,* who was the authority who approved the choice of the officials and the issuing of the relevant confirmatory title. The intervention of the state was so frequent that the presidents of the guilds ended up becoming instruments of the state.

The jurisdiction of the guild councils was extensive.

They judged differences among their members and imposed sanctions on recalcitrant members, sanctions which the Turkish authorities recognized as legal, and undertook their application. In cooperation with the community administration and with the approval of the *kadi,* they supplied members of the guild with raw materials, and determined the prices of products in the market and their distribution, as well as every other market question.

In accordance with the internal regulations of the guilds, generally in force, apprenticeship was obligatory. It was forbidden for anyone to open a workshop or a store before he had been recognized as a master craftsman by the president of the guild at a meeting of its members. The new master craftsman was obliged to pay fees, to conform to ethical practices during the exercise of his profession, to show solidarity with his colleagues, to practice philanthropy, etc. His transactions were determined by the guild monopoly and competition between members of the guild was prohibited.

Some guilds had special monopolies. Thus, for example, Greek furriers throughout the empire had priority in the market for hare skins. The Turkish guild for the manufacture of muslin in Thessalonike, was purveyor to the Imperial Court and thus had great power. The Jewish guilds had corresponding privileges.

The guilds had economic obligations to the state. The new master craftsmen were obliged to pay out a specific amount in order to secure a permit of fixed establishment (*yedi müstakar*), which gave the right to a person to open a shop in a specific place; in the event of moving he had to pay again for an 'indemnity' (*yedi havai*), which allowed free exercise of the profession. This system, a combination of Byzantine regulations and eastern justice, was a source of high-handed actions. The markets or their income often belonged to philanthropic organizations and their managers opposed the free movement of professions.

The members of a guild might be drawn from one or more religious or ethno-religious groups. In Thessalonike, for example, there were professions that were practised exclusively by Greeks, Jews or Turks. Thus the furriers of Thessalonike, a powerful guild, were only Greeks and the manufacturers of muslin only Turks. Nevertheless, most of the professions were practised by the members of two or three communities, who sometimes belonged to mixed and other times to separate guilds. In the shoemakers' guild, the Turks formed the majority; in the weavers' guild, the Jews, and in the silk trade, the Greeks. Other mixed guilds were guilds of dyers, the guild for the manufacture of pillows from wool, the butchers' guild, whose president in 1781 was a Turk and in 1803 a Greek, the guild of sesame oil merchants of Thessalonike and the *nahiye,* the majority of whose members were Greek but whose president was Turkish. There were also confederations of related or complementary trades, such as the fabric dyers; their confederation consisted of the guilds of sheet dyers, the dyers of gold-embroidered apparel, other dyers of fabrics and the manufacturers of muslin, who had the presidency. Members of all three religious communities participated in these federations.

Federations of merchants also appeared in Thessalonike

but how they were organized has not yet been clarified. It is certain that there were associations of merchants, Greeks and Jews, who competed against the foreigners; but in a firman of 1704, the merchants of the city were presented as a distinct group (*taïfa*) headed by an architect (*mimar*) appointed by the Sublime Porte and dependent on the leader of the architects (*mimar başi*), (who was a real architect) responsible for public works and leader of the city's engineers. So it may be assumed that the merchant's architect was responsible for the overseeing of the shops. In 1704 the merchant's architect was Turkish and the chief of the architects suggested his replacement by a Greek.

Just as in the other cities of the empire, in Thessalonike there was a kind of general confederation of professionals, which was governed by a council made up of twenty-four presidents of guilds. The council convened on the last Friday of each month. A general convention of the guild presidents was called at least once a year to consider market and other measures. It appears, however, that the corporate organization stretched beyond the limits of the city and extended to the market towns of the *nahiye*: the producers and merchants of sesame seed oil in Chalastra (Koulakia), Anatolikon (Valmada) and Kymina (Giountzides) of the *nahiye* of *Megalos Vardaris* belonged to the same guild as their colleagues in Thessalonike. Moreover, there were close relations between the guilds in the various towns.

Despite the theoretical unity of the guild organizations, disputes took place between ethno-religious groups in the same guild. Thus the Jews carried on illegal competition against the other groups. Moreover, the Greeks, after the eighteenth century, the period when they flourished economically, began to lay claim to their independence and to show separationist tendencies. The dyers of the Thessalonikan market, making the allegation that their shops were scattered and could not be easily controlled, and with the assistance of the manager of the gunpowder factory, extorted a firman which allowed them to concentrate their shops far from the market, at the Vardaris Gate, at the hostelry which belonged to the manager of the gunpowder factory. The attempt failed, however, for the other guilds united in reaction and succeeded in getting the firman cancelled.

The tendency for ethno-religious groups to be autonomous grew, particularly at the end of the eighteenth and the beginning of the nineteenth century. Each group endeavoured, through agreements sanctioned by local authorities, to secure a particular field of activity, such as particular regions for provisions. Thus Greek grocers had the exclusive buying right for cheese products in the villages of the *nahiye* of Kalamaria, Pazarouda and of *Megalos Vardaris,* while it belonged to the Jews in various other villages and in the *nahiye* of *Mikros Vardaris*, Langadas and Bogdan. The same held true for the butchers: the Greeks had the exclusive buying right for animals in all *nahiye* of the *kaza* of Thessalonike, except for the *nahiye* of Kalamaria and Langadas where the Jews made their purchases. Infringements by the Jews caused the Greeks to protest, calling for the intervention of the confederation council.

263. *From the end of the 15th century Jews were an important element in Macedonian society. Waves of persecution in central Europe, the Iberian peninsula and North Africa brought Jews to Macedonia where they formed communities competing commercially with the Greeks. The picture shows a Jewess from Thessalonike; 19th century lithograph.*

Macedonian emigrants

A large number of Macedonian Greeks left their country during Ottoman rule. The first wave left even before the establishment of the Ottomans. Later, the *rayahs* headed abroad in order to escape enslavement. Numbers increased whenever Ottoman tyranny became harsher and anarchy worse, a chronic state of affairs in the eighteenth century. The emigrants, mainly Greek-speaking and Vlach-speaking (with Greek national consciousness), fled in many directions. Although many ended up in Constantinople, or in other towns and market towns within the Ottoman empire along the main routes of communication with neighbouring countries, most went abroad, to Wallachia, Transylvania, Hungary, Austria, to some German towns and to Venice. Other Greeks, mainly from Epirus, Crete, the Peloponnese

264. *19th century lithograph showing the 'fortress of Kalamaria' known today as the White Tower, Thessalonike. It was built in the reign of Süleyman the Magnificent (1520-66), to* *replace an earlier ruined structure defending the port which can be seen in the background. Right up to the end of the Ottoman occupation, it was used as a prison.*

and the Ionian islands are also to be found in the same countries. Most Greek communities abroad were not made up only of Macedonians, although in many cases the latter dominated, both numerically and in vigour. Naturally, the history of Macedonian emigrants is inseparably tied to the history of Macedonia.

Macedonian Greeks were already fleeing to Wallachia and Translyvania (Sibiu and Brasov) by the fifteenth century. During the following century emigrants from Macedonia gathered in the towns of Cluj, Arad, Albajulia, Hunedrava and Gyulaferjevar, where by the end of the sixteenth century they had achieved a powerful position in commerce. Particularly noteworthy is the very wealthy merchant, Patroulas, from Serres.

In the seventeenth century, after the Union of Transylvania, Bohemia and Hungary under the Hapsburgs, many of the Macedonians in Wallachia and Transylvania moved to Bohemia, Hungary and Austria, while yet others from Macedonia itself joined their compatriots in those countries. At that time communities were formed in a large number of towns: Vienna, Budapest, Albocarolina, Axona,

Békés, Bistritz, Bungard, Corongas, Debreczen, Dees, Dioszen, Enyved, Gyamat, Gyongyos, Kaninza, Karcag, Kedket, Kecskemet, Kolozs, Levas, Medlitz, Miskolc, Nagysink, Nagyvarantz, Nagyszombat, Presburg, Radnoth, Seben, Segesvar, Sopron, Szamos-Uswar, Szegedin, Szentes, Temesvar, Thorda, Tokay, Unngvar, Val, Varad, Vasarhely, Zimony and others. The emigrants were not only merchants or artisans but also farmers — a fact which makes it obvious that emigration was not connected only with an entrepreneurial spirit, but stemmed also from the oppressions of the rural population. From 1636 on Macedonian cultivators are mentioned on the lands of Hungarian nobles, particularly of the Rákóczi family in Transylvania. Macedonian vine-growers formed substantial communities in the region round Tokay, from which the famous wine they developed was christened. The emigrants were usually favourably received by the rulers in whatever country they settled. George I Rákóczi gave privileges to the Greeks who established themselves in Sibiu in Transylvania, including the freedom to trade and the right to be tried before their own elected judges. In

1667 Leopold I Hapsburg issued a proclamation granting privileges to the Greeks in his dominions. The merchants began to form companies; the oldest one known was founded in 1656 in Libin in Bohemia. The movement of caravans between Macedonia and the Macedonian communities in Austria, Hungary and Bohemia gradually created Greek (and Greek-Vlach) communities from people of Macedonian and Epirote origin along the commercial routes from the borders of Macedonia to Vienna. The most important communities were at Velessa, Skopje, Belgrade, Semlin or Zemun, Karlowitz, Bukovar, Mitrovic, Novi Sad and Kraina. In the seventeenth century Greek trade reached Leipzig, a prelude to the establishment of communities in that city and, more widely, in Saxony which would follow in the eighteenth century.

During this century many of the older Greek communities with a Macedonian population grew and new ones were founded. These events are due in the first instance to the terms of the Peace of Passarowitz (1718) which gave to Ottoman subjects who were already established or who would come and establish themselves in the Hapsburg countries, the right to conduct trade with the Ottoman provinces as well as the right to become Austrian subjects. Then and later various communities received permission to establish churches. New privileges were ceded to the Greeks by Charles VI in 1740 and Maria Theresa in 1760. Later the Hapsburg emperors tried to restrict the commercial advancement of the Greeks, probably because the competition was a threat to their own subjects; however, these measures were soon rescinded and the former privileges renewed. Thus in 1772 Maria Theresa forbade foreign subjects to import merchandise and dissolved their companies; but in 1777 she returned the old privileges. In 1785 Joseph II forced the Greeks to trade only in Ottoman products. But in 1801 Leopold renewed the privileges of the community of Sibiu. In the eighteenth century there were Greeks in fifty-four towns and market towns of the prefecture of Pest alone. Greek families in Austria at the end of the same century numbered eighty thousand.

The emigrant Macedonians and Epirotes by then had churches, schools and some hospitals, and their community embraced more than a few very wealthy people, educated in European universities. Some were personalities renowned throughout the Greek world while at the same time they played a significant part in the economic, political and intellectual life of their adopted homelands. Christopher Niakos introduced cotton growing into Hungary, for which the title of count was bestowed on him. Others, such as K. Bellios (1772-1838) from Linotopi and the brothers N. and G. Takiadzis, became barons, also because of their contributions to economic life. A noble title was also conferred on G. Karayiannis (1743-1813) from Kozani, father of the university professor T. von Karajan (1810-73) and ancestor of the well-known conductor Herbert von Karajan. Other notable Macedonian businessmen were N. Bikellas from Veria, and the Kourtis, Doukas, Tyrkas, Spirtas, Manousis, Christomanos and Andrasis families.

Many Macedonians as well as Epirotes were distinguished as patrons of arts and letters because of their be-

quests for the furtherance of education, not only in their particular areas but also in other Greek towns.

The earliest was Manolakis the Kastorian, head of the furriers' guild in Constantinople. He gave assistance to the 'Great National School' in 1663 and to a monastic dependency of the Holy Sepulchre monastery in Constantinople, and founded schools in Chios (1661), Arta (1666), Aitolikon and Patmos (1669). It seems unlikely that he did not respond to the appeal of his compatriots to support education in Kastoria. His contemporary, John Kottounios (1572-1657) from Veria, professor at the University of Padua, left his fortune for the founding of the *Kouttounianon Hellenomouseion* (1653) where eight Greek students resided. This foundation operated till the abolition of the Venetian state by Napoleon in 1797. The Kastorians Demetrios and George Kyritzis and George Kastoriotis also assisted education. The former, a merchant in Venice, deposited, in 1697, a capital sum of five thousand ducats for the schools in his home town. The second, a great count of Hungary-Wallachia, left ten thousand seven hundred and ninety-two ducats in his will for the founding and maintenance of a second school in Kastoria in 1708. In 1721 the third, the son of the first, bequeathed a legacy of one thousand seven hundred ducats to yet another school in Kastoria and other amounts to monasteries on Mount Athos, to the Holy Sepulchre monastery and various other ecclesiastical and philanthropic foundations. Paul Charisis, member of a Kozani family established in Budapest, occupied himself with forging close relations between the sections of the Hellenic diaspora, and became the benefactor of his Macedonian homeland. Another Kozanian, Euphronios Popovits, a teacher in Budapest and a journalist, gave his library to Kozani. Nicholas Bikellas, an important merchant in Budapest, became the ephor of the Greek school there and financed the publication of books. Constantine Bellios was one of the founders of the Archaeological Society of Athens, a great benefactor of the municipality of Athens and of the municipal hospital, Elpis; he also left a bequest through which hundreds of Macedonians in Greece and abroad were educated. The tradition was continued by T. Manousis from Siatista, one of the first professors of the University of Athens, who also left a bequest for Macedonians to study abroad.

Through the participation of a large number of Macedonian donors and benefactors many Greek schools were founded and maintained in places outside Macedonia, from Skopje to the communities in Austria, Hungary, Bohemia and Transylvania.

The largest of the settlements abroad were not behindhand in intellectual activity, but none of them surpassed Vienna which became the intellectual capital of the Greek diaspora in central Europe. The books of Greek writers, mainly Macedonians, were printed there, and two newspapers and a periodical were published.

The *Ephemeris* of the brothers Markidai Pouliou, from Siatista, circulated from 1790 till 1797 when the Austrian authorities closed down their printing plant and exiled them, because they had published the revolutionary proclamation of Rhigas Pheraios. The *News for the Eastern Parts* of Euphronios Popovits lasted from July,

1811 till the end of same year. The periodical *Calliope* was published by Athanasios Stageiritis from 1819 till 1821.

OPPRESSION AND RESISTANCE

The Ottoman occupation in Macedonia, as in other regions of the empire, was very oppressive.[1] Islamic law divided people into believers and non-believers. For the latter, if they did not convert, they reserved two possibilities: if they chose to resist, extermination; if they surrendered and they were Christians or Jews, complete subjection on harsh terms. Unbelievers were subject to additional tax burdens and to many prohibitions, as well as moral humiliation. Of course, the Ottoman government avoided applying the holy law strictly and gave certain privileges to its subjects; they were, on the other hand, burdened with measures that had not been foreseen by the Koran. The sultans who completed the conquests put a stop to the extermination of populations which had offered resistance. Following the example of the first caliphs, these sultans also ceded certain privileges to the Patriarch, the bishops and the lesser clergy, allowed the formation of communities for the promotion of internal matters and granted tax exemptions to the non-believing inhabitants of certain towns, villages or regions, as well as to families (see page 364). But from the beginning, the Ottoman state imposed the custom of *devçirme*. At certain intervals, special agents of the state selected the most robust and handsome boys of the subject populations to swell the battalions of Janissaries. Conversion to Islam was of course obligatory, together with special training.

The lawless actions of officials and non-officials were added to the legal burdens. Public officials of all ranks, from the pashas to soldiers, the security apparatus, tax collectors and recruiters for the Janissaries, exploited their position in order to become wealthy, through extortion, demands for gifts and excess collections. Lords oppressed villagers. Independent farmers and whole villages passed into serfdom; weighed down by excessive demands, forced into debt, unable to repay either capital or interest, they had to consent to their property passing to the lender. Last but not least, from time to time the 'unbelievers' fell victim to the exaltation of religious fanaticism.

The oppressed, therefore, sometimes decided to convert to Islam and at other times offered various forms of passive resistance, including flight, hiding and even martyrdom. Flight from the countryside was so common that entire villages and estates were deserted, resulting in a lack of farmers. When the recruiters for the Janissaries came around, families tried to hide their sons or to help them escape. Those liable to tax hid their earnings. Those who managed to grow rich concealed the fact so they would not be faced with extortionate demands or traps on the part of the district governors and other powerful individuals. Many who were pressured with threats to change their faith proclaimed their refusal desite the certainty that this would lead to martyrdom. The list of martyrs during Ottoman rule is indeed long, and their example encouraged other Christians and strengthened resistance.

The oppressed subjects often broke the law which forbade the founding of new churches and the repair of old ones. The mountain villages and in general all who were outside the reach of Ottoman authority did as they wished. Everywhere else, the Christians secured permits or the forbearance of local officials through bribes.

Resistance became active when oppression increased, injustice reached new peaks and despair led to bold deeds. There are many reports of uprisings even against legal measures of authority, such as collection of taxes, the requisitioning of food for the army, and the recruitment of young men. Those individuals who refused to conform, who had reached the end of their tether or who were more sensitive to pressures, fled to the mountains and enrolled in rebel groups. They plundered their oppressors and were pursued by the government, but they avoided bothering those of their own religion, especially the poor stock breeders and farmers, the class from which they had come. Thus they were assured of popular support and even gratitude, and were elevated into national heroes: the word *klephtis* (thief) changed its meaning and was now used as an honourable title. Periodically, the spirit of revolt grew and spread, propelling the *klephts* into common action; it strengthened their ranks, attracting individuals and groups who had not been active earlier, and broke into a revolutionary movement.

Whether small and limited or serious and widespread, outbreaks of violence on the part of the oppressed provoked corresponding reactions on the part of the government and of prominent individuals of the ruling class. Military battalions aimed not only to exterminate the armed rebels, but also to execute reprisals against the populations which supported them. Often, and for a long time afterwards, unofficial bands, usually Albanian, devoted to pillage and destruction, went into action.

What gave the subject population the strength to refuse to deny their religion, though that would mean deliverance from the sufferings that came from being identified as an unbeliever, was faith strengthened by other conscientious beliefs. Gradually the concept of the Greek race and the knowledge of a kinship with the ancient Greeks was transmitted from the educated to the uneducated. Moreover, the Greek population of Macedonia actively preserved the memory of Alexander the Great and Philip, heroes of local folk tradition in addition to the legends about Alexander the Great which enjoyed panhellenic dissemination. For example, the Roman stele of C. Vibius Quartus outside Philippi was popularly known as 'the stall of the mare of Alexander the Great'. Until recently, the villagers scraped the edges of the square column and collected the marble dust to give to pregnant women so

265. The region round Edessa; a 19th century lithograph. The town of Edessa (Vodena) in western Macedonia was an important centre of trade and commerce which developed as early as the 17th century.

266. The fertile plain of Edessa is supplied by the abundant waters of the river Edessaios which tumbles over a precipitous crag, adding greatly to the picturesque beauty of the town. They are shown here in a 19th century lithograph.

267. *The ruins of the ancient Macedonian towns and monuments surviving from various epochs were a constant reminder to Macedonian Greeks of the valour of Alexander the Great and of their glorious heritage, keeping the old traditions alive and inspiring new legends. Thus the funerary monument of the Roman C. Vibius Quartus outside Philippi was popularly believed to be the remains of the stables of Alexander the Great. 19th century lithograph.*

that they would give birth to boys as brave as Alexander the Great. On the edge of the plain of Philippi, on one of the north-eastern hills of Mt. Pangaion, the castle of 'Alexander' rises up facing the castle of Philippi referred to by the Cypriot abbot of the Eikosiphoinissa monastery in 1632 as 'the fortress of the father of Alexander the Great'. Even the Pieria mountains were called 'Alexander's mountain' till 1715.

A few years after the completion of the conquest of Macedonia by the Ottomans the crusade of John Hunyadi (1444-48), was defeated at Kossyphopedion (Kossovo), and the resistance of George Kastriotis or Skanderbeg started in Albania (1444-68). These events increased tensions between the Greek population of the Vermion region. The nineteenth century scholar, S. Aravantinos, using older, perhaps Epirotic, chronicles as his source, provides some information about the inhabitants of Aitolia in 1458; by this term he certainly means the unsubdued inhabitants of the region of Agrapha and the Pindos in general, whose existence forced Murad II to found there the oldest *armatolik* district in the Greek area. He records that they streamed out of their hideouts onto the plain of Thessaly, burning several villages and proceeded, pillaging, all the way to Serres in Macedonia. This report may be true, for

the Ottoman conquests had not yet been consolidated over such a wide area, and the situation continued to be fluid.

That western Macedonia was disturbed is directly confirmed elsewhere. The Venetian G. M. Angiollelo testified in 1470 that the Turks had left the castle at Platamon standing (unlike other Byzantine castles), because it provided a defensive base from which to withstand pirate raids and the unsubdued inhabitants of Mt. Olympos. Around the end of the fifteenth century the monastery of Hagia Triada was built on this mountain by Hosios Dionysios. Some of the inhabitants of Litochoron denounced him to the aga of the area, saying that he was providing shelter for *klephts* there; this charge would not have been baseless about a monk with an intense Greek consciousness, and already known for his ethno-religious activity at the Philotheos monastery. Moreover, the agitation of the inhabitants of Olympos forced the Turks to found a second *armatolik* district in Greece. By 1537 the Ottoman administration had established five *armatoliks* in western Macedonia, in order to restrain the *klephts*: at Elassona, Milia, Servia, Grevena and Veria.

During the years 1564 and 1565 there were two uprisings of Slav villagers in northern Macedonia. The first began in the mountains of Morihovon and spread to the plain of Prilep. Its leaders were three farmers and two priests. The second uprising was triggered off when the voivode of Prilep imposed illegal fines on the *rayahs* and the *kadi* rejected their appeal. A group of villagers managed to get into the courtroom and clashed with the Muslims of the town who had rushed there.

Other religious men, besides Hosios Dionysios, contributed through their example and their action to the preservation of Hellenism in Macedonia: Hosios Antonios the Younger (fifteenth century), Hosios Nikanor (sixteenth century) and Theophanes of Ioannina (end of the sixteenth or beginning of the seventeenth century). Nikanor journeyed from Thessalonike to western Macedonia, teaching in the villages and confirming the inhabitants in their faith, and he built the Metamorphosis monastery on Konivos, on the left bank of the Haliakmon river. Theophanes was based in the region of Vermion. Hermits settled in the same region and in other remote areas of Macedonia.

This activity coincides with a period of religious persecution, during which many new martyrs, some known by name, others anonymous, met their death. The persecutions touched some monasteries and churches. In 1568 the Ottoman authorities confiscated the estates of the monasteries of Mount Athos and a while later sent in an army. At the same time the Muslim seminarians of Serres occupied the Prodromos monastery nearby and killed the monks.

During the war of the Holy Alliance (Spain, Venice and the Papacy) against the Ottomans there was turmoil among the Christians of Macedonia. Greeks of the districts of Thessalonike and Serres jubilantly celebrated the crushing of the Ottoman fleet at Nafpaktos (Lepanto) by Don John of Austria (1571). Ottoman reaction was harsh; there are reports of slaughter, pillaging and prisoners being taken in the districts just mentioned, as well as on Mount Athos. It is said that there were thirty thousand victims. The Ottomans later sold the booty they carried away which included manuscripts. In 1573 the Christian Albanians in the region of Ochrid petitioned the Venetians. On 1 June, 1576 the archbishop of Ochrid and the bishops of Velessa, Velegrada and Kastoria petitioned Don John for the freedom of their congregations. Once again, the Ottomans as well as the Muslim-Albanians instigated persecutions that led to slaughter, enslavement, forced conversion and flight.

Similar events were repeated during the Austro-Turkish war of 1543-1606. The archbishop of Ochrid, Athanasios, met the Venetian governor of Corfu at Butrinto and suggested that the Venetians occupy Albania (January, 1546). Since his suggestion was not accepted he journeyed to Rome to meet the Pope (1547). Subsequently, he visited various other rulers in western Europe.

From the seventeenth century onwards, the information concerning Ottoman oppression, the passive and active resistance of the *rayahs,* the activities of the *klephts* and the measures taken by the sultans to curtail the abuses becomes more abundant and specific. This information makes it even clearer that the *klephts* (*haiduk, haidout* in Turkish and Slavic) were not common thieves, but rebels against the government. They were the people who went into the mountains to avoid exploitation, oppression, injustice, mortal danger and insult to personal honour. Among them were priests who were being persecuted by the government, but who were supported, fed and hidden by the *rayahs*. Special agents supplied them with food, clothing, weapons and ammunition, they informed them of the movements of their pursuers and cared for the sick and wounded. On their side, the *klephts* not only did not harm the *rayahs,* but actively protected them when they were endangered by the Turks. Their victims were the beys, the agas, the tax collectors and the Janissary recruiters; the *rayahs* admired the *klephts* and sang of their valour and their kindness. Sometimes the *klephts* acted alone and sometimes as a group. They formed themselves into bodies of ten, twenty or thirty men, which on occasion fought together during the undertaking of some daring enterprise or in order to resist intensified Turkish pressure. The groups were usually ethnically homogeneous, and they acted in areas where the same nationality was a majority. But there was also a broader cross-Christian cooperation. The testimony of a visitor to a *klepht* army camp, which we owe to the Turkish writer Evliya (1661), undubtedly exaggerates their numbers — he mentions five to six hundred fighters, some three hundred roast lambs and pigs and hundreds of tailors who cut and sewed clothes of broadcloth. But he does give a representative general picture and some reliable information. Thus we learn that the leader of the *klephts* was a certain Panos (the manuscripts of the work give Pano, Bano and Babo) and that before he became a *klepht* he sold sherbets; that his hideout was near the lake at Ptolemaïs (Sarigöl) and that the broadcloth had been seized from the monastery and the trade fair at Moscholouri. Panos has been identified as the famous Panos Meidanis.

Agitation was renewed during the Venetian-Turkish war in Crete (1645-69). With different expectations, Greeks were awaiting the landing of Venetians on Macedonian shores. While the former maintained fighting units in a state of preparedness, the *klephts* launched daring attacks. In 1646 they attacked Florina and Monastir. The farmers suffered from the movements of both the rebels and the state troops, especially from the army under the command of Vezir Ahmed Küprülü which crossed Macedonia and pitched camp for three months at Thessalonike in 1666, heading for Crete. At the same time there were pirate raids against Thasos and on the shores of Macedonia aimed at the muletrains.

At the beginning of the following Venetian-Turkish war (1684-99), Morosini, with the Venetian fleet, landed on Thasos. He then tried to seize the castle at Kavala. The Greeks took courage again. The bands of *klephts* whose hideouts were in the Vermion and Pieria mountains found their ranks swelled by farmers, and they began their activity with the support of the Christian population. At the same time, the Ottomans confronted the advance of the Austrian army, which reached Velessa in 1689. This event caused an uprising of the *haiduks* and the *rayahs* of northern Macedonia (Monastir, Morihovon, Tikves, Velessa) and other places further north (Skopje, Kyustendil); the revolt reached serious proportions, spread further north still, only to end in a blood bath.

The escalation of the activities of the *klephts* showed that the institution of the *armatolik* not only failed to achieve the aims for which it had been created, but it also undermined the security of the state. The *armatoles* were at times inactive, and at other times they assisted the *klephts*. Dissatisfied with the salary they got from the inhabitants, they also imposed tolls on wayfarers at passes and bridges; they blackmailed the government with threats and, when their demands were not satisfied, or they were discharged, they became *klephts* themselves. In 1637 Murad IV attempted to replace the Christian *armatoles* with Muslims and Mustapha II tried the same thing in 1699. They failed, because the Christians struck at the Ottoman garrisons and drove them out of their areas. The most powerful and best known Greek *armatole* and *klepht* in Macedonia at the end of the seventeenth century was Panos Meidanis, from Kozani, who was active in many regions; but in 1700 he was finally captured by treachery at Gardiki in Aspropotamos and put to death at Thessalonike.

From the beginning of the eighteenth century the oppression of the *rayahs* increased, and their revolutionary zeal intensified. The reactions are interconnected and have a reciprocal influence each on the other.

Increased oppression of the *rayahs* resulted from many factors. The Ottoman empire was suffering from the deterioration of its administrative institutions and from successive military failures paid for by loss of revenue and land. In order to remedy the situation, the central government raised its tax demands. Local officials and their subordinates increased their extortionate practices. More and more villagers lost their titles to property (see page 359). New scourges flayed the populace: repeated mutinies of the Janissaries, harassment by criminal gangs and, later, the wars between rival local dynasts or between some of them and officials loyal to the sultan.

Revolts of the Janissaries are recorded every so often in Constantinople and elsewhere. In Thessalonike, for example, they revolted in 1721, 1730, 1735, 1747, 1751, 1752, 1755, 1758, 1763, 1770 and 1779. In each of these uprisings they pillaged and destroyed. The brigand bands, made up of Muslims robbed not only the Christians but their own people as well. Sometimes they acted on behalf of Ottoman officials; thus their origin was different from that of the Christian *klephts* and they played the opposite role. This was shown by the terminology which distinguished the *klepht* or *haiduk* from the *aramis, kirtzalis,* or *daylis*. Most of those who were active in Macedonia came from the poorest mountain districts of Albania and northern Macedonia. They were not Turks by race but converted Albanians or Slavs; they had not become members of the privileged classes of Ottoman society, but had been reduced to extreme wretchedness; some were draft evaders or deserters from the Ottoman army. From 1702 to 1717 a band of Ottoman *armatoles* who had deserted, established themselves in the *kazas* of Monastir, Florina, Kastoria and Edessa. Another band was formed around 1709 in the *kaza* of Prilep in the pay of the tax farmer. A thousand Muslim-Albanians from Mat invaded Monastir in 1711 and later, at the orders of the *Mouteselim* of Ochrid. In 1715 they pillaged villages around Velessa and Prilep. In 1727 western Macedonia was harassed by Muslim-Albanian gangs. The sultan's army went after them, and ended up pillaging and murdering in Thessalonike and the countryside. The same happened when the Ottoman army marched through Macedonia on its way to retake the Peloponnese from the Venetians in 1715.

In the face of oppression the *rayahs* reacted with ever greater determination. In 1702 the inhabitants of Lete (Aïvat) refused to pay taxes. In 1705 the men of Naousa, led by the local *armatoles,* offered resistance to officers recruiting boys. After killing the recruiter and two of his assistants, about a hundred of them took refuge in the mountains and mounted attacks against the Turks of the countryside. The Turks mobilized forces eight times as great to quell them. The year before, 1704, Methodios, former metropolitan of Thessalonike, journeyed to Moscow to plead with Peter the Great to free the Greeks.

The constant wars of the Ottoman empire against the Christian powers put heart into its oppressed subjects, while at the same time debilitating the Ottoman administration. During the Russo-Turkish war of 1711, the Greeks of Thessalonike were certain that the hour of their liberation was approaching and the rebel groups, some of four or five hundred men, clashed with the Ottoman army units. In 1712, the people of Naousa, continuing the tradition of resistance, refused to supply grain to the army. Tensions increased during the Venetian-Turkish war of 1715 and the Austro-Turkish war of 1716-18. The Turks responded by stepping up their acts of terrorization. Once again people fled from Macedonia *en masse;* entire settlements were deserted; forced conversion took place alongside the torture of those who refused to renounce their faith.

After the Peace of Passarowitz (1718), the Ottoman government proceeded to abolish the institution of the *armatoles* (1721), which had repeatedly disappointed the hopes that had been placed in them. The security of the passes (*dervend*) was assigned to the inhabitants of each *kaza,* but this new system did not work out. So the sultan entrusted the protection of the passes to Ottoman forces under a *dervend-aga*.

During the war between the Ottoman empire on one side and Russia and Austria on the other, archbishop Joseph of Ochrid communicated secretly with the Court in Vienna, to encourage it to launch a campaign on the soil of his archbishopric, promising that the 'Illyrians' would assist the Austrian army with food and with an armed uprising.

The subject peoples in Macedonia also passed through critical moments in 1742, 1743, 1755, 1759 and 1765, oppressed sometimes by Janissaries and at other times by robber bands. It is not known to what degree the central government was disturbed by this situation or by the consequences for the local economy of the exodus of the farming population, the abandonment of productive acreage, and the decrease in production. The only relevant information in our possession derives from a firman of 1740 which reflects the unease of the sultan over the concentration of Balkan refugees in Constantinople; but he took no measures to remedy the evils that had caused their emigration, even though he was aware of them; he simply ordered the local political and military authorities to refrain from

268. *19th century lithograph of Kavala, seen from the sea. The town of Kavala was built on the site of the deserted Byzantine town of Christoupolis around 1527 or 1528, and even by the* *middle of the 16th century had developed into a sizeable town, populated mainly by Greeks. The aqueduct built by Süleyman the Magnificent is clearly visible.*

imposing additional taxes and to prevent thefts and extortion.

Thasos suffered from another sort of calamity: pirate raids, which caused its inhabitants to abandon the coastal settlements and withdraw to isolated spots.

The Russo-Turkish war of 1768-74 had serious repercussions on the *rayahs* of Macedonia, especially in the west. At its outbreak, the sultan imposed additional taxes; the officials augmented them on their own account. Deserters ravaged the countryside. Albanian beys invaded at the head of armed bands. The Christian communities were deserted or turned into Turkish *chiftliks*. In 1769 the densely populated and flourishing town of Moschopolis in northern Epirus near the border of Macedonia was completely wiped out. The Russians, on their part, provoked uprisings of the Greeks in the Peloponnese and the Aegean islands. George Papazolis, a captain in the tsarist guard, who transmitted Russian orders to the Peloponnesian leaders, came from Siatista in south-west Macedonia. The Peloponnesians revolted as soon as a Russian squadron reached Vitilo in the Mani but succumbed to the superior

forces which the Sublime Porte sent against them in 1770. The Aegean islands held out as long as the Russian flotilla was there (1770-74). But the Greeks in Macedonia did not long remain inactive. Forces whose main leaders were Ziakas from Grevena, Zidros and Lazos from Olympos and Blachavas of Chasia, operated between Trikala in Thessaly and Edessa in Macedonia.

After the end of the Russo-Turkish war, Macedonia continued to suffer from Muslim-Albanian bands, many of whom were funded by various local beys who attacked each other tooth and nail. One of these was Abdil Habenderoglu of Doirani; his estates extended over fourteen *kazas,* and by 1769 he was oppressing both the local *rayahs* and neighbouring beys. In 1777 he supported the agas of Stromnitsa against Osman, the Albanian bey of Petric. Two other Albanian beys, Chaoush of Demir Hisar and Talib of Melenikon joined up with Osman. The Porte had to mobilize large forces in order to finally vanquish the warring cliques in 1773, and to exterminate the beys who were their leaders.

The Christians of Macedonia were at that time given

support by the missionary and national leader Kosmas Aitolos. After studying and becoming a monk on Mount Athos and spending some time at the Patriarchate, Kosmas began his activities in 1759. For twenty years he repeatedly traversed central Greece, western Epirus and Macedonia, preaching in the countryside. Speaking simply, but with great force and the bearing of a prophet, he gave courage to the villagers, prophesied the future liberation of the Greek nation, and urged the foundation of schools. His words directly touched the common people on whom scholars had little influence. He quickly came to be considered a saint. His sermons were both balm and motive force. It is said that during his twenty years of activity he contributed to the founding of two hundred elementary and ten high schools. Kosmas preached in Macedonia in 1766, 1775 and 1778. On the first occasion he crossed western Macedonia; tradition relates that he met with various armed leaders of the area to whom he gave hope or information about the imminent national revolution which would be supported by the Russians. On his second journey he passed through Mount Athos in Chalkidike, then headed for eastern Macedonia, after which he retraced his steps to Thessalonike and ended in western Macedonia. His third mission was restricted to western Macedonia. It was a time of persecutions and the disappointment of expectations.

In 1787 Mahmud, the Albanian pasha of Skodra, rebelled against the sultan and threatened to move against Monastir and Thessalonike, disturbing both Muslims and Christians. That same year a new Russo-Turkish war began which was to last until 1792. His experience from the previous war led the sultan to flood Macedonia with troops. His subjects bore the brunt of all the requisitioning, pillaging and lawlessness which accompanied the presence of an army in an atmosphere of racial bigotry. In April 1790 a surprise landing was made at coastal villages of the Thermaic Gulf by a small fleet of cruisers under Lambros Katsonis, an ex-officer of the Russian army. Before the war ended and for many years afterward, western Macedonia was the theatre of activity for large Muslim-Albanian bands and for the infighting between Muslim-Albanian beys who came in from the north-west. The devastation of the countryside, the decline in commercial exchanges and the thoughtless export of grain resulted in famine. Certain Greek chieftains, Stathas, and Nikotsaras, the Lazos and the Blachavas families abandoned their mountain hideouts in western Macedonia and became pirates.

After Mahmud Pasha of Skodra, Ali Pasha of Ioannina too began to act on his own account as did other important officials elsewhere in the Ottoman empire. Between 1797 and 1804, Ali Pasha overran Kozani, Edessa, Veria and Naousa and made extortionate demands on the inhabitants of the regions of Kastoria and Monastir. The sultan was deceived for a while when he appointed Ali Pasha as the supreme military administrator of the Balkans, (Roumeli-Valesi). Ali was quickly replaced because he grossly overtaxed the inhabitants. During that period he passed through the region of Serres with his army. Subsequently, Ali affiliated himself with the *klephts,* charging them with duties corresponding to the *armatoles'* in the territory he controlled and allowing them to make attacks outside it, to humiliate the Pasha of Thessalonike. Conversely, through blackmail and the offer of protection from less powerful oppressors, he wrested money from the villages and finally turned them into personal *chiftliks.* Thus the flow of Greek- and Vlach-speaking inhabitants from western Macedonia to urban centres and abroad continued. Some refugees emigrated to Nigrita in eastern Macedonia.

The spread of Ali Pasha's power in western Macedonia is linked to fierce factionalism at Kozani and Naousa. In both towns there were two parties: one conservative, the other liberal, which attracted the merchants, the craftsmen, the educated and the families of former *armatoles.* Events followed a similar pattern: the conservatives in both towns sought and received the support of Ali Pasha; their opponents in Kozani secured the intervention of the new Roumeli-Valesi; the Turkish beys of Thessalonike and the sultan supported those of Naousa. Finally, during the periods when the conservatives held sway, many merchants and artisans fled to Thessalonike or towns in Hungary. Rousis Kondorousis led the conservatives in Kozani; Mamantis in Naousa. The liberals were led by George Avliotis and Zapheirakis respectively. The latter had received a good education in Ioannina. In Kozani the conservatives were in power from 1780 till 1795 and again from 1797 onwards; in Naousa from 1804 till 1816. During the period of the tyrannical rule of Kondorousis in Kozani (1797-1807) the school was closed.

In eastern Macedonia Ismail bey of Serres proved to be a powerful district governor. During the first years of the nineteenth century his authority extended from the Strymon river to beyond Komotini (Gioumoultzina) while to the north it extended beyond Štip and covered large areas of the Rhodope mountains.

The revolt of the Serbs between 1804 and 1812 had a great effect on the Christians in Macedonia. The example of a subjugated people rising up against their oppressors, was the most significant event in the Balkans. Many Greeks hurried from Macedonia to fight on the side of the Serbs; among them were Georgakis Olympios, Nikotsaras and Karatasos. A report from the French consul at Thessalonike, Clairambaut, to Talleyrand shows how deeply this event affected the Greeks of Macedonia. It also reveals their contacts with the Serbs, and the furious reaction of the Turks. This report, dated 25 April, 1806, reads as follows: 'The Greeks of Serres and the environs have been disarmed and we are expecting to receive the same order here. It is certain that the Turks are furious with the Greeks because of their contact with the Serbs. I would not be at all surprised if a great disaster occurred in this nation.'

After the outbreak of another Russo-Turkish war in 1806, two chieftains, Nikotsaras of Olympos and Thymios Blachavas of Chasia, made contact with Russian officers to make a common front against the Turks. In May 1807 Nikotsaras met the admiral of the Russian fleet, Seniavin, in Tenedos. It may have been that with his approval he planned to march across the Balkan countries and unite with the Russian forces of Wallachia to stir up the Christian *rayahs* and terrorize the Turks. With a small force of

Greeks and Muslim-Albanians he embarked from Stavros in Chalkidike, crossed the river Strymon and proceeded to Zichna. To that point Ismail bey of Serres led eight thousand men. The muslim-Albanians, after a three day battle, surrendered; Nikotsaras made a daring break through the enemy lines during the night with only a hundred men, and after great hardships most of them reached Mount Athos. In a fresh encounter with the Turks at Litochoron in June he met his death and was buried by his comrades on Skiathos. Because of his incredibly daring and impetuous operations, Nikotsaras is an outstanding example of a leader of a group of raiders. Meanwhile it appears that Blachavas had some contacts with Greeks on the Ionian islands, in the service of the Russians, as well as with the *klephts* who had been driven back to the Aegean islands. Immediately after his return to his *armatolik* he affiliated himself with *klephts,* fugitives and outlaws from every corner of Greece. At the beginning of 1808 Russian envoys came from Serbia to Olympos with letters from Karadjordje and Rodophoinikin, an advisor to the Russian empire, who exhorted the Greeks to take up arms one last time and imitate the example of the Serbs. Naturally, the efforts of the Russians cheered the Greek spirits and gave wings to their hopes. The extent of the revolutionary ferment, the plans of the revolutionaries and the number of the initiates have not been investigated. Pouqueville

suggested that Ignatios, the former metropolitan bishop of Arta, who had been set up by the Russians as the archbishop of Bucharest, was not unaware of the revolution of Blachavas. The fact that Blachavas had come into contact with the Russians in the Ionian or the Aegean before the treaty of Tilsit (7 July, 1807) appears to be confirmed by the testimony of Leake, according to which Ali Pasha discovered the correspondence of Blachavas with the Russians in Corfu. In April and May, 1808, the revolutionaries purged the Greek districts of Muslim-Albanians. In the end, however, the contacts with the other rebels did not produce results nor did most of the villagers of the Thessalian plain stir, and the uprising failed, while Blachavas himself died a martyr's death in Ioannina.

After the failure of the uprising, the *klephts* and *armatoles* from Macedonia and Thessaly withdrew to Olympos and from there took refuge in the northern Sporades, where they renewed their corsair raids along the north coast of the Aegean, hoping that the Russians, who had once more become involved in a war with the Turks, would enter Macedonia so they could join up with them. Meanwhile, the Ottoman fleet tried in vain to crush them. With great adroitness, the light Greek corsair ships evaded the pursuit of the slow-moving vessels of the Capudan-pasha.

This situation continued till the middle of 1812 when

269. The armatole Thymios Blachavas raised the flag of revolt against the tyranny of Albanian dervend-agas. He and his many

Greek supporters fought against them, without success. Betrayed to the Turks, he met a cruel death in 1808.

successive events that would have disagreeable consequences on the rebel activity took place: the end of the Russo-Turkish war and the treaty of Bucharest (May, 1812), the departure of the Russian armed forces from the Danubian countries, the temporary cessation of hostilities between Serbs and Turks and the pursuit of the corsairs by fleets of the Great Powers who were interested in risk-free conduct of trade with the Near East. In despair the rebels began to comprehend that they were struggling against something which exceeded the forces at hand and that, temporarily at least, they had to capitulate to the Turks, and retreat to their *armatoliks*.

INTELLECTUAL LIFE

The Greeks, Ottomans and Jews carried on intellectual life in Macedonia at a level higher than elementary education. Religious and linguistic differences decisively hindered the distillation of interests, problems, ideas and expression amongst these communities. Conversely, the intellectual life of each was inscribed in the intellectual life of the corresponding ethnic-cultural whole — i.e. Greek, Ottoman and Jewish. Nonetheless, with regard to preserving the Hellenic intellectual tradition, and stimulating the intellectual renaissance of the entire Greek nation, the role of the Macedonian Greeks is clearly more significant than that of other regional components of Hellenism, with the exceptions of Constantinople and Epirus.

In what follows, we shall discuss first the state of Greek, and secondly, of Jewish, learning. The Ottoman literary and educational tradition in Macedonia has not been studied. References to names of Ottoman poets and scholars exist, but no extensive works are known.

GREEK EDUCATION AND SCHOLARSHIP

From earlier times Macedonia had inherited a tradition of learning. At its summit stood the holy state of Mount Athos, whose religiously ordered monastic life demanded or evoked such a concern for letters that Athos assumed an enviable position in the Greek polyphony. From the Holy Mountain a familiarization with some form of intellectual life diffused throughout Macedonia. Alongside this beacon of orthodoxy, the whole region was illuminated by lesser lights of learning, which also served the faith in their support of letters. Insofar as we can judge by their libraries, the Macedonian monasteries, from Melenikon and Serres to Elassona, Moschopolis and Ochrid, manifested a noteworthy concern for learning. Here we may note that centres of study more or less independent of the church (such as school or public libraries) began to form much later. Even so, the manner in which such centres were established reveals a certain society which had become accustomed to the concerns of learning. A pride in education, and a regard for the means by which it may advance, was not confined to one or a few groups of individuals concerned with letters. Rather, it appeared as something connected with society as a whole. Finally, in our own times (let us say within the past century), the sensitivity of scholars to issues of learning, permitting a more direct approach to the relevant body of data, has demonstrated the presence of all kinds of private activities which had a bearing on the advancement of learning and education — collections of books, grants of scholarships, establishment of schools, hiring of teachers and private tutors and subventions for publishing books. The application of these considerations to the past (supported, of course, by systematic reference to contemporary sources and evidence), has provided a clearer picture of the synchronic and diachronic unity characterizing the populations of the area.

As we focus our attention on the past, however, let us not forget that the appearance of the phenomena corresponds less and less with the previous state of affairs. From 1430 and 1453, our point of departure, through the late fifteenth and early sixteenth centuries everything is enveloped in a profound muteness, a thick darkness. The halo of the final days of Constantine Palaiologos brightens the story for a moment, but then renders the surrounding darkness even more impenetrable. The shrinking Byzantine empire was seized by a lethargy, traces of which we find again as the provinces of the empire surrendered one by one. To be sure, amidst all this immobility some elements of hope can be discerned in the form of memories, binding the past with the future like links of a chain; the *Laments* which, with their mixture of learned and popular elements, came to inspire hope for liberation from the Asiatic conqueror; also the flight of intellectuals to the west.

The peaceful movement of populations within Hellenic areas under Ottoman rule is particularly evident in three circles of concerns — the church, education and commerce. The order in which these are listed should not be viewed as indicative of relative importance. By means of its *cursus* of advancements, journeys to and from the Oecumenical Patriarchate, and changes within the episcopal sees (whether voluntary or coerced), the upper ranks of the religious hierarchy created a close-knit web of connections and interrelations from one ecclesiastical province to another. Education, too, assumed a more itinerant character, as the two sides of the educational world, students and teachers, clearly reveal. Time-honoured scholastic tradition required that students pass through various centres of learning, and in this way bring their education to completion. Teachers would come from neighbouring areas, and frequently from further away, seeking to better their positions, or to cope with their situations. As with ecclesiastical affairs, therefore, so too in education, we must recognize the presence of a Hellenic 'polyphony', even during the more difficult times of the Ottoman domination. Local shades and hues blended together into a uniform Hellenic colour.

Mercantile activity constitutes a third category with important consequences for the life of learning. Here we have in mind the very mechanics of commerce (such as the ships which conveyed merchandise, and mainland trade routes), rather than the other concerns associated with mercantile activity. The roads were of primary importance for Macedonia, with its vast hinterland. Macedonian trade was regularly conducted in caravans, for they increased the travellers' security as well as their possibilities for mutual assistance. From itineraries, regional descriptions and other later studies, we know the major way-stations along these roads, the cultural contacts which they called forth, and the furthest outposts of permanent or semi-permanent Greek trading colonies. Quite frequently, the original core of each of these colonies was a common local origin, matched with common occupational activity. Subsequent growth and consolidation of the colony was attended by the usual intermixture, which typifies collective ethnic bodies formed away from the original roots of their members. A more or less harmonious ethnic polyphony, consequently, is the usual result of such circumstances.

The most convenient approach to our topic is diachronic, proceeding from the stage of almost imperceptible beginnings described above to the subsequent period of full maturity. The amount of available data, however, is not uniform for each century, giving rise to the assumption that it corresponds to an equivalent growth of intellectual activity. Very little exists for the initial phase, a fact which has led one historian, Apostolos Vacalopoulos, to call these years a 'dark age'.[1] The first solid information appears in the late fifteenth century, and henceforth continually increases throughout the entire interval under consideration. As Vacalopoulos reminds us, however, even fifty or sixty years after Macedonia had fallen into Ottoman hands, its capital city still maintained the old tradition of learning. This is indicated by Thessalonike's request that Corfu send her the eminent scholar John Moschos to teach in the city.[2]

Mount Athos represents a special case of strong and uninterrupted cohesiveness in intellectual activities. Any examination of Greek learning in Macedonia must therefore include the Holy Mountain, to the point where intellectual life passed within the parameters of religion. In what follows, therefore, we will touch upon the relevant expressions of learning on the Athos peninsula. We are constrained to do so for two key reasons. First of all, the concern for learning on Mount Athos never relaxed. This is reflected in the existence of scriptoria for copying manuscripts, and in their continuous record of production. Second, throughout the entire period which concerns us here, Athos preserved a typically panhellenic character. There were very few scholars throughout the entire Hellenic world who, at some time in their lives, had not stayed on Athos or who were not actively involved with it. It is superfluous to include the Holy Mountain in a survey of Macedonian learning; nonetheless, it is also important to recognize the peculiar character of the data connected with the history of Athos. It expresses a reality disproportionately wider than the manifestations of any other regional history. Nowhere else do we hear so clearly and perenially the Hellenic polyphony as on the soil of the monastic state — albeit applied to certain limited sectors. We could say much the same with regard to weightier and more general Greek affairs. Here we need only call to mind two Athonite clerics whose contribution to the development of Greek national history is outstanding — Theoklitos Polyeides and Kosmas Aitolos, who is a historical figure of

270. *Kosmas Aitolos, who travelled the length and breadth of Macedonia in his efforts to educate the oppressed population. His fiery preachings on the theme of the resurrection of the Greek nation and the value of education had a direct effect on the lower layers of society which the writings of more erudite men could not reach. Athens, Chapel of Aixone, near Glyfada.*

great importance. Theoklitos Polyeides composed a work under the forged name Agathangelos. It is one of the major works of Greek divination during the Ottoman occupation. This text continues to exert an effect on modern Greek consciousness even into our own times. The panhellenic character of the groups assembled on the Holy Mountain was also paralleled, at this time, at the Oecumenical Patriarchate.

Let us turn now to a second group of considerations which impels us to examine, if only in part, the intellectual life of the Athonite state. To a certain degree, the course of learning and education on Athos can be seen as a mirror or miniature of the contemporary intellectual life of Hellenism. To be sure, the Holy Mountain represents a unique phenomenon in the field with which we are concerned. However, the developments on Athos fall within an orbit rather similar to that characterizing the Greek community at large. The constituent elements are not perfect in every respect, but the growth of learning constitutes a common denominator between the two. The extremely wide range of

GREEK MACEDONIAN MEN OF LETTERS
OF THE FIFTEENTH AND SIXTEENTH CENTURIES*

Andronikos Kallistos
Biographical Notes

b. Thessalonike 1400 — d. London 1486.

Lived and studied in Constantinople.

After 1453 went to Italy and was associated with Bessarion. Taught in Bologna (1464), Rome (1469), Florence, Paris and London (1476). Introduced systematic teaching of Greek literature in France. Expounded the Aristotelian system to his many students, who later distinguished themselves in Europe for their learning. Owned a large collection of Greek manuscripts.

Works

Μονῳδία ἐπὶ τῇ ἁλώσει τῆς Κωνσταντινουπόλεως *(Monody on the Conquest of Constantinople)*; Ἀντιρρητικὸς πρὸς Μιχαῆλον Ἀποστόλην *(Disputation with Michael Apostolis)*; Περὶ γενέσεως καὶ φθορᾶς *(In Coming into Being and Passing Away)*; Περὶ παθῶν *(On the Passions)*; Περὶ ἀρετῶν καὶ κακιῶν *(On Virtues and Vices)*; Περὶ ποιήσεως *(On Poetry)*; Σχόλια εἰς Ὅμηρον *(Scholia to Homer)*; Περὶ ψυχῆς *(On the Soul)*; Περὶ τύχης *(On Fortune)*; also composed letters to Bessarion, Gregory Palaiologos and others.

Damaskenos the Studite
Biographical Notes

b. Thessalonike - d. 1577.

Student of T. Eleavoulkos in Constantinople.   Bishop of Lete and Rentina (1564). Metropolitan of Naupaktos and Arta (1574). Patriarchal Exarch of Aitolia.

Works

Θησαυρὸς Δαμασκηνοῦ τοῦ ὑποδιακόνου καὶ Στουδίτου τοῦ Θεσσαλονικέως *(The Treasury of Damaskenos the Thessalonikan, subdeacon and Studite)*, (Venice, 1568), i.e. sermons in simple language for uneducated priests. The enormous repercussions of this work resulted in numerous re-

editions. Also excelled as a poet. The first after the Conquest to write an original religious poem in ancient Greek.

Malachias Rizos
Biographical Notes

b. Thessalonike.

Abbot of the Unionist monastery near Palermo.

Demetrios Diakonos
Biographical Notes

b. Thessalonike.

Student of Michael Hermodoros Lestarchos from Constantinople. Knew many foreign languages.

A monk in Egypt. Sent to Germany by the Oecumenical Patriarch Joseph the Magnificent to examine the new heresy of the Protestants. Remained for six months in Wittenburg (1559). Made an impression on Melanchthon, who gave him the Ausburg Confessions to give to the Patriarch.

Works

A letter of his to Melanchthon survives.

Theophilos
Biographical Notes

fl. Zichna, Serres (c. 1460-70).

Priest and monk at Iveron monastery. Copied many codices, and probably founded Iveron's rich library.

These tables are not complete, but have been compiled to show the range of interests. Care has been taken to include men with the closest connections with Macedonia.

manuscripts surviving from the Athonite scriptoria bears witness to a high concentration in the later period, a fact which becomes even more impressive when one thinks that the later manuscript tradition definitely faced competition, in all possible forms, from the printing press. In order to get at the correct sense of this observation with a relative, but nonetheless useful accuracy, we should examine it alongside the many known reasons for the gradual disappearance of older manuscripts. In any case, the fact remains, and clearly it must be correlated in some way with an advancement of the general level of learning.

The course of Greek learning throughout the four cen-

turies which occupy us here is marked by several characteristic turning points, thus facilitating a division of the material by periods. To a certain degree, these moments coincide with centennial divisions. Thus, in the late sixteenth century the Oecumenical Patriarch Jeremiah II the Great promulgated a particularly important synodal decree; among other things, it stated that 'each bishop should be solicitous to provide funds so that Holy Scripture might be taught in his see, and he should accord whatever help he can to those desiring to teach, and those aspiring to learn, should they have need of provisions.'[3] This important text dates from 1593. Less than a hundred

GREEK MEN OF LETTERS LIVING AND TEACHING
IN MACEDONIA FROM THE FIFTEENTH TO THE SEVENTEENTH CENTURY

Lucas Spandonis
Biographical Notes
b. Constantinople — d. Thessalonike, 1481.
Studied rhetoric and philosophy in Constantinople.
Taught in Thessalonike. Able orator.

Theophanes
Biographical Notes
Teacher and metropolitan of Thessalonike.

Works
Biographer of the martyr Michael Mavroudis.

Thomas Notaras or **Theophanes Eleavoulkos**
Biographical Notes
b. Koroni 16th century — d. Veria.
Monk at Veria. Made his career in Constantinople.
A famous teacher and great rhetorician, with many students.

Works
Wrote Διαίρεσις μετὰ συλλογισμῶν κατὰ τὴν Θεοπαράδοτον ἡμῶν Θεοσοφίαν τῆς πίστεως, καθώσπερ οἱ τῆς ἡμετέρας Ἐκκλησίας πνευματοφόροι διδάσκαλοι παρέδωκαν. *(Exegesis with Proofs regarding the Divinely Transmitted Doctrine of our Faith, as Handed Down by the Inspired Teachers of our Church).*

Theonas
Biographical Notes
b. end 15th century.
Student of the martyred Saint Jacob, and later of Eleavoulkos.

Archbishop of Paronaxia; metropolitan of Thessalonike (1544). Renovated the monastery of Hagia Anastasia Pharmakolytria near Thessalonike, and founded a school.

Works
Wrote an introduction to Διδαχαὶ Ἀλεξίου Ραρτούρου (*The Teachings of Alexios Rartouros),* printed in Venice in 1560.

George
Biographical Notes
Born in Athens.
Taught in Thessalonike at the end of the 16th century.

Matthew
Biographical Notes
Born in Crete (?).
Taught in Thessalonike (*c.* 1580). Had many students.

Gerasimos Palladas
Biographical Notes
b. Crete — d. Mount Athos 1714.
Studied in Venice and Rome.
Metropolitan of Kastoria. Patriarch of Alexandria (1688-1710). Distinguished theologian and philosopher.

Works
Philosophical, hymnographic, theological and philological works, as well as sermons in simple, vivid language. Also composed letters, chiefly to Peter the Great of Russia, and Pope Clement XI.

fifty years after the 'Enslavement' (i.e. the Fall of Constantinople), the intellectual leadership or community of enslaved Hellenism had been organized to such a degree that it could frame so high-minded a programme, involving the founding of schools, assurance of pay for teachers, and provision of support for students. This synodal decree should be viewed as a major step in the history of modern Greek scholarship — if not for what it may have succeeded in accomplishing for those to whom it was directed, then certainly for the dynamism which inspired it. Here the origins of a religious humanism are clearly revealed, with all their attendant consequences.

These consequences were the determining forces which shaped the course of the subsequent phase of our topic. The synodal decree of 1593 marks the starting point of a new period. Roughly a century later we observe in more concrete form the 'first dawn of an intellectual movement' in the Macedonian spiritual realm. The phrase is Manuel Gedeon's and it refers to disputes which arose at the beginning of the eighteenth century, but which evidently had causes of a personal nature going back to the final years of the preceding century.[4] In studying or commenting upon such matters, we must constantly bear in mind that it is frequently difficult to make the distinction between the des-

271

272

cent of theoretical disagreements to the level of personal disputes, and the elevation of personal disputes to the level of theoretical differences. Finally, these two ingredients often occur interdependently, in an organic fashion.

The events connected with this strife occurred in Thessalonike. We may fix their chronological limits between 1700 and 1730. The dispute was a conflict between Aristotelians and Anti-Aristotelians. The first group was represented by the teacher Giannakos, and the other by his colleague Pachomios. Interwoven in this traditional conflict were echoes from an older but also a more recent western religious and philosophical movement. We refer to the theories of the Spaniard Molina (1536-1600) and of the Frenchman Malebranche (1638-1715). To the same period — again in Macedonia, and again in the same intellectual sphere — belongs the affair of Methodios Anthrakitis, arising chiefly in the schools of Kastoria, Siatista and Ioannina (see page 400). Despite the progress of recent research, the full story of these episodes has not been clarified, especially as regards the foreign influences they manifest. In any case, a spirit of liberalism expresses itself here at the beginning of the eighteenth century.

The third period which we will consider also opens with the passage of one century into the next, from the eighteenth to the nineteenth. In the tempestuous decade from 1790 to 1800 we perceive in Macedonia the typical signs which point to new developments. In addition to some other movements, one must chiefly refer to the great movement of the *Kollyvades,* which embraced both this decade and the years before and after. The origins of the traditionalist *Kollyvades* movement (1754-1819) were narrowly religious in character. In terms of its consequences, and of the disturbances it provoked, it represents a sign of the changes being demanded in those times.[5] Turning to other contemporary developments which have a more clearly social character, we may mention two episodes. In 1796, Mount Athos (where the *Kollyvades* movement first began) became disturbed over certain

271-272. John Kottounios of Veria studied in Rome and continued his academic career in Padua and Bologna. His talents as a writer and teacher made him one of the leading lights of the 17th century Hellenic diaspora in the West. The publication of his Epigrammata Graeca in 1653, of undoubted literary merit, also had historic significance. The book was dedicated to the French king Louis XIV, with an impassioned plea for assistance to the enslaved Greek nation. Kottounios, like many other Greeks living abroad, based their hopes for help towards the liberation of Greece on the Christian rulers of France. Many of the epigrams mention highly placed French political personalities such as Cardinals Mazarin and Richelieu, or referred to memorable historic events (such as the victory of the Venetian fleet over the Turkish in 1649); others contain allusions to Greek mythology and history. The author's attempt to kindle European interest in the enslaved Greek nation is obvious, and the book is one of the earliest such attempts made by educated Greeks on behalf of their countrymen. 271 above shows Kottounios depicted in his first book, published in 1628; 272, the dedication page of Epigrammata Graeca. Greece is shown on the left, Hermes on the right and King Louis XIV in the centre.

GREEK MACEDONIAN MEN OF LETTERS OF THE SEVENTEENTH CENTURY

John Kottounios

Biographical Notes

b. Veria 1572 — d. Padua 1657.

Student of the Greek College of St. Athanasius in Rome (1605-13). Studied medicine, Greek philology, theology and philosophy in Italian universities.

Taught at the universities of Padua, Bologna and Pisa, where he was especially renowned. Student of the famous Italian philosopher Cesare Cremonini, and his successor in the chair of philosophy at Padua. In 1653, founded the *Kottounianon Hellenomuseion,* a school and hostel for Greek youth. Had friendly relations with M. Crusius, Leo Allatius and other celebrities of the age. Excellent student and scholiast of Aristotle.

Works

Wrote many works in Latin, mainly on Aristotle's philosophy. Composed Ἑλληνικὰ Ἐπιγράμματα *(Hellenic Epigrams)* (1653) in Greek and Latin for eminent personalities of the day (Louis XIV, Cardinals Richelieu and Mazarin, Anne of Austria, and others) with allusions to Hellas' bondage to the Turks. With these, he assumed first place among seventeenth century epigrammatists. Also composed a collection of odes, hymns and sonnets in Latin, Italian and Greek, attempting to educate the West regarding the condition of the Greek nation, and its need for strong philhellene defenders.

Metrophanes Kritopoulos

Biographical Notes

b. Veria 1589 — d. in Wallachia 1639.

A monk on Mount Athos. Closely associated with Cyril Loukaris, who played a decisive role in furthering his career. Studied in England and Germany. Travelled in European countries, and made contacts with the greatest scholars and theologians of his time. Enlightened the West about Orthodoxy. Was especially concerned with the problem of Union between the Orthodox Church and the churches of western Europe. Served as a Greek teacher in Venice (1627-30). Elected Patriarch of Alexandria (1636), where he founded an important library.

Works

Wrote a dogmatic work in Latin, *Confession of the Catholic and Apostolic Eastern Church* (Helmstedt, 1661). Also wrote grammatical works, including Γραμματικὴ ἁπλοελληνικὴ *(A Grammar of Common Greek),* and translated the New Testament into modern Greek.

Kallinikos Manios

Biographical Notes

b. Veria 1624 — d. Veria 1665.

Student at the Greek College of St. Athanasius in Rome (1642-47) and later at the Collegio Urbano de Propaganda Fide. Returned to Veria and performed important educational work (1649). Thanks to his actions, the first school in Veria began to operate.

Works

Περί ρητορικῆς *(On Rhetoric)* (1656).

Constantine Kallokratas

Biographical Notes

b. Veria 1589 — d. 17th century.

Student at the Greek College of St. Athanasius in Rome (1600-10), where he studied philosophy and theology.

Taught Greek-speaking Albanians in a school in Calabria. Close friend of Leo Allatius. Extremely intelligent, with great poetic virtuosity.

Works

A Greek heroic elegy of twenty-seven lines, dedicated to Leo Allatius, survives.

George (Gregory) Kontaris

Biographical Notes

b. Servia.

Studied Latin and Italian, in Venice (1665-) and was accomplished in philosophy.

Priest and monk. School principal in Kozani (1668-73). Later taught in Servia. Elected metropolitan of Servia and Kozani (1673-); then of Athens, later of Smyrna (1690-). First to show an interest in ancient Greek history.

Works

Wrote a history of ancient Athens in simple language.

Anastasios Michael

Biographical Notes

b. Naousa — d. Russia (after 1722).

General studies in Ioannina with G. Sougdouris, teacher of philosophy and rhetoric.

In 1702, became acquainted with noted German theologians in Constantinople. Went to Halle, and was later elected to the Academy of Sciences in Berlin. Carried on educational work for Christians and Greeks in Moscow, where he was distinguished for his theological and philosophical knowledge.

Works

Περιηγηματικὸν πυκτάριον, ἤτοι Περιήγησις τῆς Εὐρώπης *(A Touristical Booklet, or Journey through Europe)* (Amsterdam, 1706), a treatise delivered at the Academy of Sciences in Berlin, and an important work for modern Greek studies.

Βασιλικὸν Θέατρον *(The Royal Theatre)* (Amsterdam), written in 1710 during the Russo-Turkish War; addressed to Peter the Great, replete with faith in Greece.

George Parakeimenos

Biographical Notes

b. Kozani.

Studied medicine and philosophy in Padua. Director of the Kozani School (1694-1707). Physician and preacher.

Works

Wrote sermons and ecclesiastical treatises in an elegant style. Cooperated with Helladios in a modern Greek translation of the New Testament.

Methodios Anthrakitis
Biographical Notes

b. Ioannina, mid-17th century; d. Siatista or Ioannina.

Studied modern philosophy and natural sciences in Venice.

Priest and monk. School principal at Kastoria (1710), Siatista and Ioannina. where he taught mathematics, physics, modern philosophy and theology.

The first in Greece to systematically teach geometry, algebra and trigonometry.

Accused of being a Lutheran-Calvinist, and his work was condemned by the Holy Synod (1725). In 1725, disavowed his controversial ideas and sought pardon from the Patriarchate.

Works

Θεωρίαι Χριστιανικαὶ *(Christian Theories)* (1699); Βοσκὸς λογικῶν προβάτων *(The Shepherd of Rational Sheep)* (Venice, 1708); Ὁδὸς Μαθηματικῆς *(The Way of Mathematics)* (1749), which secured him fame as an outstanding mathematician. Also translated from Latin writings of Malebranche, Descartes, etc.

Eugenios Voulgaris
Biographical Notes

b. Corfu 1716 — d. Russia 1806.

Studied philosophy and mathematics in the Ionian islands, Italy and Ioannina (with Methodios Anthrakitis).

Priest and monk. School principal in Kozani (1746-52). Director of the Athonite School. (1753-58). Taught in the patriarchal School in Constantinople. Travelled in the Danubian Principalities and Germany. Librarian at the court of Catherine II in Russia.

Archbishop of Slavinion and Cherson (1776-79).

Adherent of Leibnitz' and Wolff's philosophy. One of the distinguished intellectuals of the eighteenth century, with a literary output astounding in both variety and extent.

Considered the first reformer of Greek education.

Works

Wrote philosophical. theological, historical and ethnological works. Translated Voltaire's *Historical and Critical Essay Regarding the Dissensions in the Churches of Poland.* Also composed memoranda for Catherine II on the liberation of Greece.

Athanasios Parios
Biographical Notes

b. Paros (1722 (1723?) — d. Chios, 1813.

Studied philosophy in the Evangelical School of Smyrna. Continued studies in the Athonite School under Neophytos Kausokalyvitis and E. Voulgaris, where he pursued research on Greek history and classical education. In 1762 completed his studies in Corfu with Nikephoros Theotokes as his teacher.

Teacher in the Athonite School in 1757. School principal in Thessalonike (1758-62, 1777-86). Director of the Athonite School (1771-77) and successor of Neophytos in leading the *Kollyvades* (a traditionalist movement). From 1786 until 1812 taught rhetoric, theology, logic, metaphysics and ethics at the school in Chios.

Enlightened teacher, passionate preacher, successful school organizer and accomplished author. Espoused views of absolute religious conservatism. Combatted influences issuing from the West.

Works

Defended and established the theological positions of the *Kollyvades* in a series of treatises, letters and memoranda.

Apologetic Works: Ἀντίπαπας *(Antipope)* (1785); Ἀντιφώνησις πρὸς τὸν παράλογον ζῆλον τῶν ἀπὸ Εὐρώπης ἐρχομένων φιλοσόφων... *(A Reply to the Unreasonable Zeal of the Philosophers Hailing from Europe ...)* (Trieste, 1802), hostile towards the West; Ἔκθεσις, ἤγουν ὁμολογία τῆς ἀληθοῦς καὶ ὀρθοδόξου πίστεως *(Exposition or Confession of the True and Orthodox Faith);* Φραγγέλιον *(The Whip);* Χριστιανικὴ ἀπολογία *(A Christian Apology)* (Constantinople, 1798), in which he attacks the leaders of the French Revolution; Ἀλεξίκακον πνευματικὸν ἐγχειρίδιον *(Alexikakon, A Spiritual Enchiridion);* Νέος Ραψάκης *(New Rapsakes)* a defence of patriotic teaching. Dogmatic Works: Ἐπιτομή, εἴτε Συλλογὴ τῶν θείων τῆς πίστεως δογμάτων *(Epitome or Collection of Divine Teachings on the Faith)* (Leipzig, 1806); Δήλωσις περὶ τῆς ἀληθείας τῶν ἐν Ἁγίῳ Ὄρει ταραχῶν.... *(Declaration Concerning the Truth about the Disturbances on the Holy Mountain ...)* etc.

Liturgical, Paedagogical Works: Νεοφύτου Καυσοκαλυβίτου Γραμματικὴ *(Neophytos Kausokalyvitis' Grammar)* (1787); Ρητορικὴ πραγματεία *(A Rhetorical Treatise).* Translations: *Elements of Ienouesios' Metaphysics* (from the Italian, Venice, 1802). *Lives of the Saints, Martyrologies.* Also wrote epigrams, *akolouthies* and epistles.

Nikodemos Hagioreitis
Biographical Notes

b. Naxos 1749 — d. 1809.

Baptized as Nicholas Kallivourtis. Taught elementary gram-

manifestations of extreme liberalism, and suggested to the Oecumenical Patriarch that he express his disapproval. In this case, the points of conflict were not restricted to the religious community (as with the *Kollyvades*), but constituted the opposition of two irreconcilable ideological worlds.[6] In this period. the term of which is the end of the century, the monastic state appears as a miniature of modern Hellenism, in search of its ideological identity. Once again, therefore, Mount Athos provides a useful indicator of trends, whether actively or reactively; Theokleitos Polyeides and Kosmas Aitolos have been previously mentioned. In addition let us note the Athonite School with Eugenios Voulgaris and his impetuous disposition towards action; also noteworthy is Moisiodax, who mar at Naxos. In Smyrna, was a student of Ierotheos Voulismas (1765). Again in Naxos, under the learned metropolitan of Paronaxia Anthimos Vardis, applied himself more to the study of theological writers. In 1775, became a monk on the Holy Mountain with the name Nikodemos. Occupied himself with copying codices, study and writing. Driving spirit behind the traditionalist movement of the *Kollyvades*, which erupted in the last decades of the 18th century.

Maintained correspondence with learned men of his time, especially Athanasios Parios and Patriarch Gregory V. Accomplished theologian with numerous works. Considered the pre-eminent Athonite monk of modern times, and canonized in 1955.

Works

His two most popular works are adaptations of western ascetical tracts: Βιβλίον καλούμενον ἀόρατος πόλεμος *(The Book Called Invisible War)* (1589), from Lorenzo Scupoli's *Combattimento Spirituale* (1589), and the Γυμνάσματα Πνευματικὰ *(Spiritual Exercises)*, from J. P. Pinamonti's *Exercizi Spirituali*. Also composed Ἐξομολογητάριον *(The Confessional)* (1794); Νέον Μαρτυρολόγιον *(A New Martyrology)* (1799); Πηδάλιον *(The Helm)* (1800); Συμβουλευτικὸν ἐγχειρίδιον περὶ φυλακῆς τῶν πέντε αἰσθήσεων *(Advisory Enchiridion for Controlling the Five Senses)* (1801); Νέον Ἐκλόγιον *(The New Eklogion)* (1803); Περὶ τῆς συνεχοῦς μεταλήψεως τῶν ἀχράντων τοῦ Χριστοῦ Μυστηρίων *(On Frequent Partaking of Christ's Holy Sacraments)*. Cooperated with Makarios Notaras and Paul Evergetinos in writing Φιλοκαλία τῶν ἱερῶν νηπτικῶν *(A Collection of Sacred Ascetical Writings)* (Venice, 1782) and Εὐεργετινὸς *(The Benevolent Man)* (1783). Posthumously published were Συναξαριστὴς τῶν Δώδεκα Μηνῶν *(the Twelve-Month Synaxarion)* (1819); Ἑρμηνεία εἰς τὰς ΙΔ´ ἐπιστολὰς τοῦ Παύλου *(Exegesis of the Fourteen Epistles of Saint Paul)* (1819); Ἑρμηνεία εἰς τοὺς ψαλμοὺς *(Exegesis of the Psalms)*. Left more than a hundred works. Occupied with hymnography, and produced many church hymns. His purely philological offering has not yet been fully researched.

Kallinikos Varkosis
Biographical Notes

b. Ioannina — d. Iasion.
Student of E. Voulgaris.
School principal at Siatista (;-1768). Director of the Company school in Kozani (1768-72). From 1778 at Iasion. Outstanding educator with numerous students.

Works
Wrote numerous ethical treatises.

Nicholas Varkosis
Biographical Notes

b. Ioannina — d. Iasion.
Student of Balanos at Ioannina. Studied philology and theology.
School principal at Siatista (six years) and at Kozani (c. 1750). Secretary of Prince Constantine Mourouzis (1777-82).

Works
Translated from Latin the *Logic and Metaphysics* of F. Baumeister (Vienna, 1795). Composed epigrams.

Jonas Sparmiotis
Biographical Notes

b. Kephallenia.
Student of the doctor-philosopher S. Asanes.
Priest and monk. Taught in Thessalonike (after 1770) and in Velvendos (1780-90). Priest in Vienna.

Works
Translated into ancient Greek the *Arithmetic* and *Algebra* which the doctor-philosopher S. Asanes had translated from French into simple Greek (Venice, 1797, 1800).

Amphilochios Paraskevas
Biographical Notes

b. Ioannina — d. Elassona.
Studied in Ioannina. Student of Balanos Vasilopoulos, from whom he inherited a hatred for everything modern, especially the 'new' philosophy of E. Voulgaris.
Studied dialectic with Nicholas Stignis. After 1757 studied Latin and the sciences in Bratislava, Czechoslovakia.
Priest and monk. Taught philosophical and grammatical courses in towns in Macedonia and Thessaly. School principal in Kozani (1782-97). Also taught in Servia and Velvendos (1797-98).

Works
Wrote Λογικὴ πραγματεία *(A Treatise on Logic)*, according to Zaviras; Βιβλίον Κάτοπτρον Φιλοσοφίας *(A Mirror Book of Philosophy)*; and Ὑποτύπωσις ῥητορικῶν ζητημάτων *(An Outline of Rhetorical Problems)* in simple language.

first studied at the School, and in his premature old age was also a teacher. We should also mention the presence of Kaisarios Dapontes at Xeropotamou monastery. A tireless versifier, exceedingly curious, and with many elements of liberalism, Dapontes was to leave to the following century the name of an honoured poet.

To be sure, intellectual divisions were even more acute outside Athos in this same chronological span. Turn of the century Kozani experienced violent upheavals and dissensions among its inhabitants. These had purely social causes and objectives, above and beyond theoretical or political considerations. Here the changing of the times is clearly perceptible.[7]

So the three periods which we have defined merged with

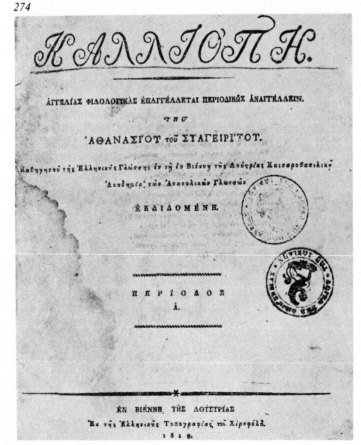

one another, as one century passed to the next. At length we reach those brief twenty years which form the ending point of this chapter. Assuredly, historical perspective would justify a detailed examination of these years which saw the completion of contemporary Hellenism's preparation for what was to come — namely 1821. In the intellectual and psychological fervour which the Revolution evoked, we once again observe the vigorous participation of Macedonia. This is an additional reason for examining with special care learning and education in Macedonia during this brief period.

The learned did not neglect their educational responsibilities. An important attempt to rekindle the Athonite School is especially worthy of consideration. Although Voulgaris' tenure had not lasted long, the Heptanesian scholar's departure did not completely suspend the School's functioning. As a general statement, we may say that for long periods the Athos School barely existed. The lamp flickers; the students scattered; few remained when a favourable opportunity happened to arise. In 1802-03, however, the Great Church launched a serious effort to revive the School under the name *Museion*. Yet even this movement quickly languished, despite the help of many clerics and laymen, including Korais himself.[8] The ecclesiastical effort, even with the participation of laymen, was not destined to bear fruit. The prelate Dorotheos Proios' opinion is typical. Following the failure of the new attempt, he wrote in 1805: 'A *Museion* will never be built on Mount Athos, and if it is, it will soon be destroyed.'[9] Proios himself fell victim to the Ottoman fury a few years later.

The turning of the times brought with it three key differences, all of which are clearly perceived in Macedonia. First of all, in times past teachers had generally been clerics. Now educational duties passed more and more into the hands of laymen. The second change also had to do with education, but within a much wider cultural context. Heretofore the teacher was grounded in a broad field of education, instructing all the classes in subjects from grammar through astronomy and whatever else. Already in the previous century, however, a basic distinction had begun to apply between the grammarian and the philosopher. Now the separation, i.e. specialization, was becoming more and more evident. Eventually we have a new distinction, although closely related to the preceding circumstances, when the scholar is set apart from the cleric, which was rarely found in the past. This situation now became the

273. *The title page of Michael Perdikaris' poem, Hermelos or Democritherakleitos. Published in 1817, it was a biting satire on the society of the age, poking fun indiscriminately at the ruling classes, the clergy and the supporters of modern ideas. The work seems to have enjoyed great success and circulated widely throughout Macedonia.*

274. *The cover of the first issue of the periodical Calliope. It was published in Vienna by Athanasios Stageiritis between 1819 and 1821, financed by merchants there. It contained a range of literary articles, translations and scholarly debates. Although its intellectual level was perhaps lower than that of the Logios Hermes it was more virulent and intransigent.*

rule, with very few exceptions.

Minas Minoidis and Ignatios Skalioras are worthy of mention. Both began their careers in Macedonia, and to the present day have remained famous for their various activities in the field of learning. Two other scholars more closely linked with education also deserve a place in this short account — Jonas Sparmiotis and John Pezaros. Sparmiotis deservedly ranks among the conservative clerics of his time. We also know, however, that he launched out towards a kind of renewal, although restrained and cautious. Pezaros is a courageous and unbiased spirit. When he learned that in Constantinople Sergios Makraios had written a book to refute the Copernican system (1797) he cried out: 'Oh, we are still frightened children!'[10]

Nevertheless, at the beginning of the nineteenth century Macedonia displays a lively interest in literature, with Kozani at the centre. We may mention such authors as G. Sakellarios, C. Megdanis, M. Perdikaris, and G. Rousiadis. A. Christopoulos was from Kastoria, but he had close ties with the *litterati* of Kozani, and for this reason he is mentioned here, even though much of his activity took place outside Macedonia. Only one of these figures belongs to the field of education, namely G. Rousiadis, who came to this profession by external coincidences. Megdanis was the only cleric. Of his many works, only the *Characters* (written in successful imitation of Theophrastos) calls forth the serious attention of the historian of learning. Sakellarios and Perdikaris were physicians. The former was a typical man of letters, with a wide range of interests. His national consciousness was lively and sensitive, and his pursuits overlapped with the nationalist activities of Rhigas Velestinlis. Moreover, he was informed of matters pertaining to western intellectual life. He represents a fine monument to learning in Macedonia in that early period. Michael Perdikaris has a more intense personality, which is far more difficult to fathom. He wrote copiously, but little was published in his own lifetime. Among these latter works is an epic-satirical poem entitled *Hermelos* or *Demokritherakleitos* (1817). He also wrote a long prose introduction to this work which was published simultaneously, but separately.[11] Critical and censorious, Perdikaris condemned the enlightened intellectual and national movements of all types. He also rebuked with extreme harshness and frankness what he found blameworthy in the clergy and ruling class. It is worth noting, however, that the book was popular and evidently had a wide circulation in Macedonia. Apparently it was precisely this quality of antinomy which made the work so pleasing. Clearly, Macedonia was searching for something.

By their very nature, libraries cannot easily be subsumed within a diachronic survey such as this. Data connected with the book and libraries constitute useful and readable indicators regarding modern civilizations. From this point of view it may be said that Macedonia was a most-favoured Hellenic region — in some respects independent of the impact of the Holy Mountain, in other respects in conjunction with it.

The peculiarity of the two circumstances is easily understandable. The presence of private libraries in Macedonia indicates that there were needs which the well-stocked libraries on the Holy Mountain were not able to satisfy. This is partly true with reference to other monastic, and more particularly, school libraries, which had a more or less directly didactic, moralistic or catachetic focus. Other collections were formed independent of these, with quite different aims and intentions. Assuredly it is not always correct to speak of genuine libraries. Nevertheless, a noteworthy characteristic of learning in Macedonia (although not exclusively in Macedonia, of course) is that books also found their way to homes where a library is unexpected. This helps to explain the typically poor condition in which copies of Perdikaris' *Hermelos* have survived in the north.

From another viewpoint, let us remember that the very presence of books generates an interest in books. In the final analysis, it is a matter of a society's acclimatization to literary culture. Either this consciousness enters the mainstream of society, or it remains on the periphery. The presence of the book stimulates the need to read, with its usual consequences — lending, buying, removal, exchanging, donating and bequeathing books. In Macedonia we can discern many traces of the 'social life' of the book. In addition to numerous though isolated instances of sketchy regulations for book-lending from public libraries, the chief sources of information from which we can draw general conclusions are some references to private libraries, and the arrangments for their transfer to public libraries. Bequests of private libraries appear to have been the norm amongst teachers and prelates. From the late eighteenth century on, instances of such donations continually increase. The donors were chiefly merchants, who either provided their local schools with funds to buy books, or who donated their personal libraries to them. All these factors thus express a conscious concern for learning which becomes all the more discernable in the subsequent historical period, when a tiny new Greek state was created at the tip of the Greek Peninsula after a decade of military struggle.

SCHOOLS

As soon as the fury of the Ottoman conquest abated, the decimated Greek community of Thessalonike invited Lucas Spandonis, a scholar from Constantinople and a victim of the recent capture of the city, to teach its youth.[1] Later on, Theophanes taught at Thessalonike as well and became its metropolitan at the end of the fifteenth century. George of Athens and Matthew of Crete also taught there at the end of the sixteenth century. Theonas, another metropolitan of Thessalonike, founded a school in the neighbouring monastery of Hagia Anastasia Pharmakolytria at the beginning of the sixteenth century.

The synodal decree of 1593 quickly bore fruit in Macedonia as in the other Ottoman-occupied Greek areas. Numerous church and community leaders applied themselves vigorously to the establishment and the maintenance of schools higher than grammar schools (which had also operated earlier in churches and monasteries), with gifts and legacies from wealthy Greeks. The teaching programmes were enriched by new lessons; the need for

Sevastos Leontiadis

Biographical Notes

b. Kastoria 1690 — d. 1765.

Student of M. Anthrakitis at Siatista, Kastoria and Ioannina. Studied in Italy.

Was director of the Kastoria school (1726-28). Also taught in other Macedonian towns (Kozani 1728-33 and Moschopolis).

Works

Λόγοι Ἐκκλησιαστικοί *(Ecclesiastical Treatises);* Σημειώσεις περὶ ἔτους, μηνῶν καὶ ἡμερῶν *(Notes on the Year, Months and Days),* etc.

Demetrios Karakasis

Biographical Notes

b. Siatista 1734.

Studied medicine, philosophy and mathematics at Halle, Saxony. Teacher of Medicine (1760).

Physician in Vienna, Larisa, Siatista, Kozani, Bucharest. Taught at Siatista.

Works

Wrote poetry on medical themes in Greek and Latin (Vienna, 1784), and a work entitled Περὶ Φλεβοτομίας *(On Phlebotomy).*

Manasses Eliadis

Biographical Notes

b. Melenikon, beginning of the 18th century; d. Bucharest 1785.

Studied medicine in Padua and Bologna; physics and mathematics in Germany and Italy.

Physician in Bucharest. Taught philosophy and physics at the 'Academy' in Bucharest.

Works

Composed epigrams and encomiastic treatises (in Greek and Latin) in honour of Alexander Ipsilantis.

Michael Papageorgiou

Biographical Notes

b. Siatista 1727 — d. Vienna 1796.

Studied philosophy at Ioannina with the teacher E. Voulgaris. Philosophical and medical studies in Germany.

Taught in his home town, and in Selitsa, Melenikon, Vienna and Budapest.

Works

Ἀπάντησις εἰς τοὺς συλλογισμοὺς Κολλαρίου περὶ τῆς ἐκπορεύσεως τοῦ Ἁγίου Πνεύματος *(Reply to the Arguments of Kollarios Regarding the Procession of the Holy Spirit);* Γραμματικὴ Γερμανικὴ πληρεστάτη *(A Complete German Grammar);* Ἀπόκρισις πρὸς τὴν ἐρώτησιν περὶ τοῦ ἀπολυτικίου, τὴν σπουδήν σου τῇ κλήσει κατάλληλον ἐργασαμένην φερώνυμε». *(Reply to the Question Regarding a Certain apolytikion);* Epigrams and verse.

Constantine Michael

Biographical Notes

b. Kastoria.

Physician-philosopher and student of languages. Knew Greek, Latin, French and German.

Student of Michael Papageorgiou.

Bequeathed all his books to the school in Kastoria.

Works

Translated and published an enchiridion of the learned physician Tissotos, in which he presented a concise history of the origin and development of medicine (Vienna, 1754).

John Emmanuel

Biographical Notes

b. Kastoria.

Studied philosophy in Pest and Vienna.

Works

Translated from German paedagogical and educational works: *A Manual for Children* (translated) from the German into the Modern Tongue of the Greeks (Vienna, 1792); and *An Essay on the Elements of Arithmetic* (Vienna, 1797).

Thomas Mandakasis

Biographical Notes

b. Kastoria; d. beginning of the 19th century.

Studied medicine and philosophy in Leipzig. Teacher of medicine (1758).

Practised medicine abroad. Principal of the Kastoria school (1767-70).

Works

Medical works. Inspirational religious poems. Assisted in publishing the Κάτοπτρον Γυναικῶν *(Mirror for Women)* of K. Dapontes (Leipzig, 1766). With his own funds published the *Physics* of Nikephoros Theotokes (Leipzig, 1766). Other works.

Demetrios Darvaris

Biographical Notes

b. Kleisoura 1754 — d. Vienna 1823.

Studied Latin, Greek and Slavonic in Pest, Zemun and Bucharest. Pursued courses in philosophy at Halle, Saxony.

Taught Greek in Zemun.

Works

Wrote and translated numerous didactic books: Χειραγωγία εἰς τὴν καλοκαγαθίαν *(A Guidebook on Benevolence)* (Vienna, 1790); Ἀληθὴς ὁδὸς εἰς τὴν εὐδαιμονίαν *(The True Path to Happiness)* (Vienna, 1796); Εἰσαγωγὴ εἰς τὴν ἑλληνικὴν γλῶσσαν *(Introduction to the Greek Language)* (Vienna, 1798); Πρόχειρος ἀριθμητικὴ *(Handbook of Arithmetic)* (1803); Γραμματικὴ ἁπλοελληνικὴ *(Grammar of Common Greek)* (Vienna, 1806); Ἐπιτομὴ Φυσικῆς *(A précis of Physics)* Σύντομος Γενικὴ Ἱστορία *(Short Universal History)* (1817), etc. Translated Cebes and Epictetus (1799); Σοφίας Ἀπάνθισμα *(Florilegium of Wisdom)* (1811).

George Sakellarios

Biographical Notes

b. Kozani 1765 — d. 1838.

Student of Kallinikos Varkosis and Amphilochios

Paraskevas. Studied German and French, as well as philosophy, in Hungary. Also studied medicine in Vienna.

Physician in Kozani, Naousa, Tsaritsani and Kastoria. Chief physician at the court of Ali Pasha. Associated with Rhigas Pheraios and Perrhaivos.

Works

Translated works from German and French: *Travels of the Young Anacharsis in Greece,* by Barthélemy (Vienna, 1797); *Archaeological Survey of Greece* (1796); *History,* by Cousin de Sprio; *Chemistry,* by J. Frank. With his *Ποιημάτια (Poems)* (Vienna, 1817), introduced the proto-romantic nocturnal lament, following the model of Young. In 1789 he introduced Shakespearism, rather prematurely, with a five-act prose tragedy entitled *Romeo and Julia.* Also wrote a glossary from demotic to ancient Greek, and vice versa.

Michael Perdikaris
Biographical Notes
b. Kozani 1766 — d. Monastir 1828.

Physician, scholar. Studied medicine and philology in Italian universities and Vidin. Conservative, but a genuine ideologue, and faithful student of Amphilochios Paraskevas and Charisios Megdanis.

Teacher in the Transdanubian principalities. Physician in Epirus, Kozani, Thessalonike, Monastir and elsewhere.

Works

Wrote a fair number of works in prose and verse, which betray a critical and derisive outlook bordering on complete negativism. In his prose work Κατὰ ψευδοφιλελλήνων *(Against Pseudo-Philhellenes)* (1811), he struck out against Rhigas and the ideas of the French Revolution. In his poetic work Ἑρμῆλος ἤ Δημοκριθηράκλειτος *(Hermelos or Demokritherakleitos)* (1817) he exhibited a marked anti-French and anti-Enlightenment zeal. His other works include Ψυλλιὰς *(Psylliad),* imitative of the *Iliad;* Ἀληᾶς *(Aliad),* a verse biography of Ali Pasha; Ἐπιστολαὶ Ἰούδα ἐξ Ἅδου *(Letters of Judas from Hades);* Νοητὸς διάκοσμος *(The Intelligible Order)* a philosophical and religious work now lost; Ἐγχειρίδιον περὶ τοῦ κατὰ σύνταξιν λόγου *(Manual on the composition of speeches);* and Ὅσιος ἤ Περὶ ἀθανασίας τῆς ψυχῆς *(The Saint, or Concerning the Immortality of the Soul)* a conversation between Amphilochios Paraskevas, Charisios Megdanis, George Sakellarios and Mousotios Gallos. Also wrote epigrams and an iambic verse work.

Michael Doukas
Biographical Notes
b. Siatista — d. Mount Athos.
Pursued philosophical courses in Vienna.
Merchant in Vienna.

Works

Translated from French *Cyrus' Ethical Journey* (1783); *Ethical History of Belissarios* (1783); *Mythology, Ethics and Politics of Pilpais, an Indian Philosopher* (Vienna, 1783).

Charisios Megdanis
Biographical Notes
b. Kozani 1796 — d. Kozani 1823.

Student of Amphilochios Paraskevas. Studied rhetoric, philosophy and mathematics in Livadi.

Private tutor in Pest. Returned to Kozani and became a priest. Taught in Kozani and other Macedonian towns. Practised as a physician and preacher.

Works

Περὶ ἐπανορθώσεως τῶν κατὰ τὰς ἱερὰς τελετὰς συμβαινόντων *(Of Reforming the Sacred Litury)* (1812); Περὶ τοῦ σχολείου τῆς Κοζάνης *(On the School of Kozani)* (1812); Ἑλληνικὸν Πάνθεον *(The Greek Pantheon)* (Pest, 1812); Λύχνος τοῦ Διογένους ἤ Χαρακτῆρες Ἠθικοὶ *(The Lamp of Diogenes, or Ethical Characters)* (Vienna, 1818), an imitation of the characters of Theophrastos; Καλλιόπη παλινοστοῦσα ἤ περὶ ποιητικῆς μεθόδου *(Calliope Repatriated or, On Poetic Method)* (Vienna, 1819).

George Zaviras
Biographical Notes
b. Siatista 1744 — d. Sabat Salasi (Hungary) 1804.
Student of N. Varkosis at Siatista.

Merchant in Pest. Founded a school for the Greek community at Kalocsa in Hungary, where he also taught. Maintained an outstanding library, which he donated to the Greek church of Pest.

A learned scholar of the time, with wide-ranging interests, and an enormous intellectual capacity.

Works

Νέα Ἑλλὰς ἤ Ἑλληνικὸν Θέατρον *(Modern Greece, or the Greek Theatre)* (1872), a major literary effort which includes a biographic register of the scholars of the period of the Ottoman occupation; Ἐπιτομὴ τῆς ἱστορίας τῶν Ἑλλήνων ἀπὸ τῆς πρώτης ἀρχῆς καὶ γενέσεως αὐτῶν καὶ λήγουσα εἰς τὸν θάνατον τῆς τελευταίας βασιλίδος Κλεοπάτρας *Epitome of the History of the Greeks from their origins through the last Queen Cleopatra)* (lost); Ἐκκλησιαστικὴ καὶ πολιτικὴ χρονολογία *(Ecclesiastical and Political Chronology);* Πατριαρχικὴ Ἱστορία τῆς Κωνσταντινουπόλεως *(History of the Patriarchate of Constantinople);* Περιήγησις ἐκ τῆς Βιέννης ... εἰς τὴν Μοραβίαν, Βοημίαν, Σαξωνίαν καὶ Βαρουσίαν *(A Journey from Vienna to Moravia, Bohemia, Saxony and Warsaw);* Βίος Ἰωάννου τοῦ Καλβίνου *(Life of John Calvin)* (1787). Composed or translated many theological, didactic, historical, philological and other works.

Basil Papeuthymiou
Biographical Notes
b. Kostantziko.

Taught in the Greek Community's school in Vienna from 1802 to 1804.

Works

Translated an English school manual.

Athanasios Christopoulos
Biographical Notes
b. Kastoria 1772 — d. Transylvania 1847.

Studied medicine, philosophy, philology and law at Budapest and Padua. Student and friend of the teacher Lambros Photiadis. Courtier of the prince Alexander Mourouzis, and judge in Wallachia; also "Minister of Foreign Affairs." Cooperated in compiling a civil law code in Wallachia (the first outline of civil law in modern Greek). Member of the *Philike Etaireia*. Lived in Greece from 1828 until 1836.

Works

Literary: Ἀχιλλεύς *(Achilles)* (Vienna, 1805), the first theatrical work in modern Greek; *Λυρικά (Lyrics)* (1811), in demotic, for which he was admired and loved by his contemporaries as well as later generations until the late nineteenth century, and for which he received the eponym Νέος Ἀνακρέων *(the new Anakreon);* Ὄνειρον *(The Dream)*, a satyrical dialogue with language as its theme.

Grammatical and Lexical: Γραμματικὴ τῆς αἰολοδωρικῆς, ἤτοι ὁμιλουμένης τωρινῆς τῶν Ἑλλήνων γλώσσης *(Grammar of Aeolic-Doric, or the Present-Day Spoken Language of the Greeks)* (Vienna, 1805); Στιχουργικὴ τῆς λαλουμένης γλώσσης...) *(Versifying in the Spoken Language....)* (only a summary remains); Περὶ ποιητικῆς *(On Poetry)* and a Λεξικὸν ἁπλοελληνικὸν *(Lexicon of Common Greek)* (both lost);

Studies and Essays: Περὶ γνησίων καὶ νόθων συγγραμμάτων Ἱπποκράτους *(On the Spurious Writings of Hippocrates);* Πολιτικὰ παράλληλα *(Political Parallels)* (Paris, 1833); Ἑλληνικὰ ἀρχαιολογήματα *(Greek Antiquities)* (Athens, 1853); Πολιτικὰ σοφίσματα *(Political Sophisms)* advice for rulers along the lines of Machiavelli; Νομοθεσία *(The Laws)* (1818).

Also translated Book Four of the *Iliad;* three odes of Sappho; excerpts from Herodotos; and various treatises of the philosopher Sextus Empiricus.

Gregory Zalykoglou
Biographical Notes
b. Thessalonike 1777 — d. Paris 1827.
Studied Greek, Latin and French philosophy at Bucharest.
Student of the famous teacher L. Photiadis. Hotly defended Korais' positions.
Secretary to Choiseul Gouffier (1802, and after). Cofounder of the «Ἑλληνόγλωσσον ξενοδοχεῖον» in Paris (an organization aimed at liberating the Greeks (1809), and forerunner of the *Philike Etaireia*). First secretary in the Ottoman Embassy in Paris (1816-20). After the Greek Revolution was proclaimed in 1821, fled to Transylvania, Bessarabia and Saint Petersburg where he was patronized by the tsar Alexander.

Works

Λεξικὸν τῆς Γαλλικῆς Γλώσσης *(Dictionary of the French Language)* (Paris, 1809); Περὶ τῆς κοινωνικῆς συνθήκης σύγγραμμα Ἰωάννου Ἰακώβου Ρουσσὼ *(On the Social Contract, a Work by Jean-Jacques Rousseau)* (Paris, 1828); Διάλογος περὶ τῆς ἑλληνικῆς ἐπαναστάσεως *(Dialogue on the Greek Revolution)* (Paris, 1828). Numerous anecdotal works and letters.

Euphronios Raphael Popovits
Biographical Notes
b. Kozani 1774 — d. Iasion 1853.
Studied rhetoric, philosophy, physics, economics and political science in Hungary. Finished his studies in Vienna.
Taught in the Greek School in Pest, Vienna and Zemun.
Published the newspaper *News About the Eastern Parts* (2 July - 27 December 1811).
Donated his library to Kozani.

Works

Ἰσοκράτους λόγοι μεθ' ἑρμηνείας *(Orations of Isocrates, with Commentary);* Ἰσοκράτους πρὸς Δημόνικον παραίνεσις παρὰ τοῦ Μουσικοσοφολογιωτάτου Χαρίτωνος Πόποβιτς *(Admonitions of Isocrates to Demonikos, by the most Learned and Inspired Chariton Popovits)* (Pest, 1802); Φυσικὴ Ἰστορία *(Natural History)* (Vienna, 1811); Μαθηματικὴ ἐν γένει, Γεωμετρία δὲ ἐν εἴδει *(The Genus Mathematics, The Species Geometry)* (Pest, 1819); Σύνοψις λογικῆς *(A Précis of Logic)* (1822); Περὶ Οὐγγαρίας *(On Hungary);* Σύντομος Ἱερὰ Κατήχησις *(A concise Holy Catechism)* (Zemun, 1836). Also published the etymological section of K. Laskaris' grammar under the title Νέος Λάσκαρις *(A New Laskaris)* (Vienna, 1818).

which had been realized by the intellectual vanguard of the Greek nation, which was forming in the colonies abroad.

According to our information, the first school in Macedonia after the synodal decree was founded in Kastoria before 1614. In 1682 the Kastorians asked their compatriot Manolakis, who had become famous for his gifts, for economic assistance for their school.

In 1697 the same school benefited from the legacy of D. Kyritzis, a Kastorian emigrant. From the middle of the seventeenth century on, schools are mentioned in Velessa, Yannitsa, Servia and Serres, while the first school in Veria was founded around 1650 by Kallinikos Manios. During the same period a school was also founded in Kozani; its headmasters were the well-known scholars Gregory Kontaris (1668-73) and George Parakeimenos (1694-1707). The people of Thessalonike continued their educational endeavours, which they had begun earlier than the other Greeks of Macedonia. From the middle of the seventeenth century till the eighteenth, the 'Greek School' of Thessalonike is mentioned; its schoolmaster was John from Thessalonike, who also knew Latin.

During the eighteenth century there were many more schools operating in Macedonia. Nearly twenty-five of these, of which two were schools for priests, are known. Thessalonike had the *Hellenomouseion* where Athanasios Parios was headmaster (1758-62, 1777-86), as was Jonas Sparmiotis; there was one other school, in which Giannakos taught around 1716, and Kosmas Balanos, from Ioannina, during the middle of the eighteenth century. Kastoria, Kozani and Serres continued the endeavour they had begun in the seventeenth century. In Kastoria, a school for priests was founded after 1708 through the legacy of G. Kastoriotis and after 1721 a third school was founded through the legacy of G. Kyritzis. Methodios Anthrakitis taught in the oldest school (1710) and its headmasters include Sevastos Leontiadis (1726-28) and Thomas Mandakasis (1767-70). Anastasios Vasilopoulos and Thomas Oikonomou also taught in the same town.

George Rousiadis

Biographical Notes

b. Kozani 1783 – d. Athens 1854.

Student of Amphilochios Paraskevas. Studied in Vienna. Teacher in the Greek communities in Vienna (1817) and Pest (1821-). Member of the *Philike Etaireia*, took part in the Greek Revolution. After the liberation, lived in western Europe. Returned to Athens in 1848.

Works

Χρονικὸν προγνωστικόν, ἤτοι καλενδάριον παντοτεινὸν ἀρχόμενον ἀπὸ τοῦ 1798 ἄχρι τοῦ 1842 ἔτους (*Chronological Forecast, or a Perpetual Calendar for the Years 1798-1842*) (Vienna, 1820); Γραμματικὴ τῆς νεοελληνικῆς γλώσσης (*Grammar of the Hellenic Language*) (Vienna, 1834); Ἡμερολόγιον τοῦ σωτηρίου ἔτους 1819 (*Diary of the Salutary Year 1819*) (Vienna). Translated the *Iliad* (Vienna, 1817-19, six volumes); the *Odyssey* (Books I-IV, a paraphrase with notes, Athens, 1848); *The Liberation of Thebes, a Tragedy by Felix Weise* (Vienna, 1820); *Parga,* from the French (Pest, 1822) and many other works.

Minas Minoidis

Biographical Notes

Died in France.

Student of Athanasios Parios. Taught rhetoric and philosophy in Serres and Thessalonike. Also taught ancient Greek language and literature in Paris (1819 –).

Interpreter in the French Ministry of Foreign Affairs. Knight of the Legion of Honour. Regarding the language issue, conducted a polemic against Korais' ideas, and was his most vehement and unjust opponent. Fervent supporter of the Greek Revolution. Discovered an Athos manuscript of the metrical fables of Babrios.

Works

In 1821 wrote and circulated an anonymous pamphlet, in Greek and French, *Aux très puissants souverains de l'Europe,* Τοῖς κραταιοτάτοις τῆς Εὐρώπης βασιλεῦσι; addressed to the kings of Europe by those who sought their aid in the cause of liberation. In 1826, he published two new pamphlets: Πρὸς τοὺς Γερμανοὺς καὶ τὰ λοιπὰ τῆς Εὐρώπης ἔθνη, πρόσκλησις εἰς βοήθειαν τῶν Ἑλλήνων (*To the Germans and other Nations in Europe, An Appeal for Assistance to the Greeks*) and Σύντομος ἐπίστασις εἰς τὴν τοῦ τῆς Αὐστρίας Μητιαστηρίου πολιτικὴν πρὸς τὴν Ἑλλάδα (*A Concise Examination of the Policy of the Austrian Metternich towards Greece*) (both translated into French). Other works include *Orthophonie grecque ou Traité de l'accentuation et de la quantité syllabique* (Paris, 1824); *Calliope, ou Traité sur la prononciation* (Paris, 1825); Θεωρία περὶ τῆς Ἑλληνικῆς τε Γραμματικῆς καὶ γλώσσης (*Theory Regarding the Greek Language*) (Paris, 1827); and Κάναρις, ᾆσμα πινδαρικὸν (*Kanaris, a Pindaric Ode*) (Paris, 1830); Ἔλεγχος Προδοτῶν (*Exposure of Traitors*) (Paris, 1831), which proposed to refute the slanders against Kapodistrias after his death.

Athanasios Stageiritis

Biographical Notes

Professor of Greek Language at the Imperial Academy in Vienna. Bitter opponent of Korais, and adherent of Kodrikas in matters of language.

Published a fortnightly philological periodical *Calliope* in Vienna from 1819 to 1821, when he suspended publication following the outbreak of the Greek Revolution. Refused to submit to the pressures exerted on him by the Ottoman government through the Patriarchate.

Works

Wrote in a simple language Βίος Θεμιστοκλέους τοῦ Ἀθηναίου (*The Life of Themistocles the Athenian*) (Vienna, 1816); Βίος Μιλτιάδου τοῦ Ἀθηναίου (*Life of Miltiades the Athenian*) (1818); Τρόπαιον Ἑλληνικὸν ἢ ὁ πρῶτος πόλεμος Ἑλλήνων καὶ Περσῶν (*The Greek Trophy, or the First War of the Greeks and Persians*) (1818); Ἠπειρωτικὰ ἤτοι ἱστορία καὶ γεωγραφία τῆς Ἠπείρου παλαιὰ τε καὶ νέα καὶ βίος τοῦ Πύρρου (*Epeirotika, or the History and Geography of Ancient and Modern Epirus with a Life of Pyrrhus*) (1819); Ὠγυγνία ἢ Ἀρχαιολογία (*Ogygia or Archaeology*) (five volumes), and other works.

Sevastos Leontiadis taught at the oldest school in Kozani from 1728 to 1733 as did Eugenios Voulgaris (1746-52); Nicholas Varkosis was the headmaster (round 1750). The Company School was founded in the same town in 1768 and its first headmaster was Kallinikos Varkosis (1768-72). Amphilochios Paraskevas also taught in the same town (1782-97). A school operated in Serres from 1696 till 1730, and after 1742, with interruptions. Many other towns and market towns were added to the circle of Greek educational centres. Two of these, Edessa and Velvendos, acquired two schools, both with gifts from emigrants. The first school was founded in Edessa in 1764; Amphilochios Paraskevas taught there in 1764, as did the monk Constantinos, a student of Eugenios Voulgaris. The second one was founded in 1782 and named *Hellenomouseion.* Jonas Sparmiotis taught at Velvendos from 1780 to 1790 and Amphilochios Paraskevas taught there from 1797 to 1798. Headmasters at Siatista include Methodios Anthrakitis (beginning of the eighteenth century), Nicholas Varkosis (middle of the same century), Kallinikios Varkosis (1768) M. Papageorgiou also taught. The youth of Naousa was taught by the monk Theophanes, Demetrios Anasiotis and Amphilochios Paraskevas. Schools are also mentioned at Ochrid, Hosios Naoum, Kleisoura, Linotopi, Selitsa, Darda, Nigrita, Kavala and Melenikon. Special mention was made above of the renowned, but short-lived, seminary on Mount Athos, the Athonite School.

Many of the schools we have mentioned continued their operations after the end of the eighteenth century and others were added to the list. Thus, between 1800 and 1821, when most of them succumbed to the whirlwind of national revolution and its bloody suppression, schools existed in Thessalonike, Alistrati, Ardameri, Galatista, Grammosta, Grevena, Edessa, Kastoria, Kataphygi, Kapsochori, Kostantziko, Megarovo, Melenikon, Monastir, Naousa, Nigrita, Polygyros, Siatista, Serres, Stavros, Sochos and Tsotyli.

Macedonian youth was also educated in the schools of

the colonies found along the length of the roads leading through the Balkans to central Europe, and abroad, where they were numerous; moreover, most of them had been established by Macedonians and had Macedonian teachers. Many of these students continued their studies later at European universities.

THE INFLUENCE OF GREEK LEARNING ON NON-GREEKS

According to Bulgarian and Yugoslav historiography, throughout the Ottoman occupation the Slavs of greater Macedonia and Thrace suffered serious losses from the activities of Greek schools and prelates. Sometimes, indeed, this was allegedly attributed to deliberate intent. During those centuries, however, the Greeks were not their neighbours' masters, but were also subject to the Turks. Consequently, the Greeks had no legal means of prohibiting them from founding and maintaining their own schools, or of coercing their children into attending Greek schools. Moreover, they did not possess the material means with which to establish schools for foreigners, since they were hardly in a position to fulfill the educational needs of their fellow Greeks. Greek educational institutions were founded and supported through individual gifts and bequests. The cities and regions in which Hellenic schools appeared boasted a substantial Greek population. Many cities and regions with a Greek population, however, were not so fortunate as to have schools. Furthermore, no city or area which lacked a Greek population ever had a Greek school. Non-Greek Christians, therefore, attended Hellenic schools because they did not have their own, except for the elementary grammar schools of a few churches and monasteries. The only way they could acquire an education was to study in the intermediate schools, which were maintained by the Greeks. In order for non-Greeks *not* to have attended these schools, they would have to have been barred by prohibitions of some sort. If something such as this had indeed occurred, the Greeks would have been justly accused today of politically discriminating against non-Greeks.

Since these schools were maintained through the resources of poor communities, or through contributions and private gifts, they often faced difficulties and were sometimes forced to close their doors. Clashes between teachers introducing new classes and new ideas, and generally conservative public opinion, brought the same results. At the beginning of the nineteenth century, when schools were more numerous than ever before, it is questionable if, at any given moment, there were more than twenty middle level schools in all Macedonia. A total of twenty-two such schools are known but they were not all operating at the same time. The number of students in any one school can be counted in tens. Non-Greek students certainly constituted a minority in this small student body. No one can reasonably accept that every foreign student who attended a Greek school was Hellenized. Indeed, the educated Slavs and clergymen who roused the ethnic consciousness of their countrymen had attended Greek schools. A Hellenic education *per se* did no harm to the

Greeks' fellow believers and fellow slaves. Rather, it offered them services. The fact that Greeks had many more educated men and prelates than their neighbouring peoples is due, in part, to the schools which they alone maintained in the regions under Ottoman domination. Other Greek schools existed in the foreign settlements. Finally, a fair number of Greeks advanced to higher studies in Italian and central European universities.

JEWISH LEARNING AND SCHOLARSHIP

The Jewish communities in Macedonia (and elsewhere in Greek territories) which survived the Ottoman conquest continued speaking Greek for a long period, even after the arrival of their far more numerous brethren from central Europe, the Iberian peninsula, Provence and Italy.[1] The latter spoke languages and dialects indigenous to their places of origin; they were, moreover, bearers of different cultures. Under the leadership of rabbis who were noted authors, the Greek-speaking Jews of Thessalonike, in particular, long opposed the influence of their newly-arrived co-religionists.

Having lived for centuries in ghettoes, the Ashkenazi refugees from central Europe had taken little more from their environment than the Germanic idiom which they spoke. On the other hand, the Sephardic Jews from the Iberian peninsula, Provence and Italy had participated without impediment in the social, political, economic and intellectual life of their local communities. They brought with them many cultural elements of the fifteenth and sixteenth century West, along with those which derived from their own Hebraic tradition. The Sephardim included many university graduates who had studied philosophy, medicine, astronomy and mathematics. Some of them were famed as physicians to political leaders and ecclesiastical figures. Apart from ancient Hebrew, many rabbis also knew Latin. The educated refugees brought with them ancient Hebrew, Arabic and Latin manuscripts dealing with religious, philosophical, legal, medical, anatomical, astronomical and mathematical subjects. Many copies of these mansucripts were made in Thessalonike by professional scribes as well as amateurs. Among the refugees were excellent authors who continued writing after settling in Thessalonike.

Within a short time synagogues and schools were established. Each synagogue included a functioning school (*yechiva*), which offered elementary and intermediate education. In 1520 the *Talmud Tora* (see page 367) was founded, which was also involved with education. In fact, its main purpose was to provide instruction in the 'Law' for graduates of the intermediate schools. The *Talmud Tora* offered the same elementary and intermediate education for children from poorer synagogues which lacked the means to maintain their own schools. The highest level of studies produced rabbis versed in scriptural exegesis and Hebrew law, along with a knowledge of medicine, pharmacy, astronomy and mathematics. The professors were famous, attracting students from other Jewish communities throughout the Ottoman empire, and even beyond. In addition to teaching, rabbis would conduct debates before an audience. The *Talmud Tora* also had a library which was open to the public.

Private libraries existed, moreover, two of which are important. In one of these, the owner also maintained a scriptorium. Additionally, the Jews of Thessalonike had printing presses. The first one was brought from Portugal in 1512, and the second began to function in 1532. Both were active for many decades and produced a great number of important editions. Newer presses were established in 1554, 1578 and 1592.

The learned Sephardim also cultivated poetry, following Spanish, Portuguese and Italian models. Their poetry consisted of hymns, odes and dithyrambs with mainly religious and ethnic themes. In terms of expression, their light and refined verses were filled with learned allusion (intelligible to the educated), sophisticated formulae, and a generally pleasing elegance, with adornments tending towards the rhetorical. A literary circle was formed under the patronage of a wealthy Maecenas. It was called the *Poetic College,* and its thirty-two members met once a month. Their works were written in Hebrew according to the canons of Hebrew poetry, but their themes were secular. These poems were sung to Spanish music.

This intellectual robustness was condemned to wither in the face of adverse trends and other unfortunate circumstances. In 1529 the rabbis instituted censorship over books. The Ashkenazi from central Europe were generally hostile towards all learning which did not proceed from Scripture and tradition. The educated Ashkenazi cultivated little more than rabbinic literature, and were absorbed in logical acrobatics. Refugee Sephardim also brought to Thessalonike and thence to other eastern cities another current hostile to science and reason, namely mysticism and occultism. This trend first influenced the *Cabbala,* which was originally a pantheistic theory rooted in neoplatonism. It was taught to those who had already studied logic, law and the sciences, i.e. to those who had experience with rational thought. Eventually the *Cabbala* was conquered and transformed by occultism, and became its instrument. Already in the second quarter of the sixteenth century prophetic and mystical currents began to gain ground. Around the middle of the same century, the Cabbalists forecast the coming of the Messiah for 1568. In general, they condemned all learning which did not derive from the Old Testament, tradition and the *Cabbala.* Rabbis with a scientific education were converted to occultism. A crisis lasted for a fair number of years, and wrought a qualitative change in the intellectual situation. With the passage of time, the number of Jews who had studied in western universities before arriving in Macedonia shrank. The ideas of the European Renaissance which still managed to reach Macedonia met with a hostile reception. Western science and the ideas of the European Renaissance were still supported in a few circles, but their influence was continually waning. In any case, the education offered to the middle classes was cut off from its western sources. Printed works and manuscripts in Spanish, Portuguese or Italian were produced with Hebrew characters; Latin script was forgotten. The number of those who could read literature and scientific books written in the very western languages which they spoke was constantly dwindling. The idioms of Iberian and Italian origin spoken by the Jews of Macedonian and other eastern cities remained undeveloped, tending towards atrophy and adulteration. Poetry met with scorn and went into decline. Instruction in the schools became more and more ossified. Astrologers, exorcists, dream interpreters, magicians and soothsayers met with appeal among the lower classes.

During the bloody and destructive Thirty Years War (1618-48), the messianic hopes of the west European Jewish communities greatly intensified. The Marranos, Christianized Jews from Spain, Portugal and Italy, followed a similar escape route. The Holy Office, however, pursued them with profound suspicion, and they often ended up on the Inquisition's pyres. This wave of persecution spread to the Ottoman empire, where the Jews experienced oppression and threats for the first time. In these years Sabbethai Sevi came to believe that he was the Messiah, a conviction he publicly proclaimed in 1648. Sabbethai was a young rabbi with precocious intellectual qualities, but nonetheless psychologically immature and rather unbalanced. After experiencing a variety of fortunes and misfortunes in Smyrna and Thessalonike, he fled to Egypt and thence to Jerusalem. There he not only attracted followers, but patrons and a cadre of able assistants, who organized propaganda and spread his fame throughout the eastern and western worlds. The masses, along with the educated followed Sabbethai in the delirium of blind faith, which was exacerbated by the persecutions of Jews in Poland and the Ukraine, and the economic crisis in Thessalonike occasioned by the Venetian-Turkish War (1645-69). Entire communities and families were torn apart. Then, after a series of story-book adventures, Sabbethai Sevi converted to Islam in order to save his life, and died ingloriously. For a while his supporters maintained their expectation of the Kingdom of God, at a time when messiahs of all kinds were multiplying. Finally, his followers became divided and their opponents went on the offensive. Some of their ranks converted to Islam; in 1686 one thousand five hundred converted in Thessalonike, and others did so elsewhere.

The crisis evoked by Sabbethai Sevi, in conjunction with the economic decline of the Jewish communities in Macedonia, hastened the pace of intellectual retrogression. From 1655 to 1695 no Hebrew books were printed in Thessalonike. Older books which had no religious content ceased to be read. All levels of education continued to decline. The rabbis maintained a copious literary output, but the language in which they wrote ceased to be pure and correct, and their manner of exposition was no longer methodical and logical. Only the physicians who studied in foreign universities enjoyed intellectual contact with Europe and cultivated a wider range of interests. A new Jewish press was set up in Thessalonike after 1695, reaching a new peak of production from 1745 onwards. The number of schools, however, grew fewer and fewer, and illiteracy was spreading among the lower classes. By the middle of the eighteenth century, the great majority of Thessalonike's Jewish population could not read and write.

As in economics so too in learning the Greeks and Jews of Macedonia followed opposite paths.

POST-BYZANTINE ART 1430-1830

The changed situation which Hellenism had to face after the Fall of Constantinople in 1453 and the total dissolution of the Byzantine empire had long lasting repercussions on the development of art. Although Byzantine traditions, whether in architecture or in painting, were not discarded during this period, they were continued against a background of decay, poverty and unfavourable circumstances which depressed the vigour, confined the extent and downgraded the quality of artistic production. Thus an impetus was given to the already existing tendency towards the decentralization which had started some considerable time before the final break-up of the Byzantine state. A coincidence of historical factors, therefore, encouraged new artistic centres while others gradually stabilized on the periphery of the old empire. This resulted in a revival of traditional forms which in time became the model for the entire Orthodox world. Some of the new circumstances, however, contributed to different levels of quality and tone. Two factors in particular were of great importance.

a) Differing conditions for Greeks subject to the Venetians and Greeks subject to the Ottoman Turks

In the Venetian-held Greek cities greater tolerance made it possible for religious art to flourish, whereas in areas held by the Ottomans its absence did not favour the development of ecclesiastical art. It is thus scarcely surprising that important centres of religious painting did not grow up in any of the sizeable Ottoman towns — Constantinople, Thessalonike, Adrianople, Smyrna, Ioannina or elsewhere. The consequence was that artists, religious or secular, enjoyed different social status. The towns in Crete were large commercial centres and also artistic centres, and the many artists who dwelt there were citizens; the largest part of their clientele was drawn from the same or from a higher social level (i.e the bourgeoisie or noblemen, Venetian or Greek).[1] In Ottoman Greece, on the other hand, art acquired a vernacular character when produced by native craftsmen working far from urban centres, men from an agricultural or pastoral background. However, the demand for artists from the more favoured Venetian-held regions to execute large scale works in monasteries in the Ottoman-held lands prevented standards from falling below a certain level.

b) The development of large monastic centres

The Oecumenical Patriarchate, based in Constantinople, was an ecclesiastical body charged with a wide range of judicial and other powers over the Orthodox subjects of the Ottomans. It exercised a fundamental influence on their spiritual life. Since it was also of considerable assistance to the Ottoman state in the governance of its Christian subjects, it was the object of special favours from the conquerors. This situation permitted the survival and fostered the development of large centres of Orthodox monasticism within the Ottoman empire in isolated areas far from cities, such as Mount Athos and to a lesser extent the Meteora in Thessaly and other important monasteries. The dependence of monasteries on the Patriarchate — the stavropegiac monasteries — automatically conferred on them the privileges accorded by the Ottoman authorities. This in large measure explains their prosperity. In the course of time these monasteries naturally became the focus of artistic activity. With the help of the Moldo-Wallachian rulers and of the Greek prelacy, restoration work might be carried out on the churches or new ancillary buildings be erected for the use of the monastery, such as *phialai,* refectories and monastic dependencies. Churches were decorated with murals, icons, iconostases, pulpits and *proskynetaria* and were supplied with sumptuous vestments and objects for liturgical use. The unchallenged authority of these monastic centres derived from the exemplary organization and functioning according to the old *typika* and from the high intellectual standards of the monks. They were an important contributory factor to the prestige and diffusion of Greek art at this time in the Orthodox areas of the Balkan peninsula, the Near East and even as far as Russia. The art of these centres was accepted as the authentic and authoritative dogmatic and artistic model.

ARCHITECTURE

1430-1700

Architectural style is less closely linked with dogma than painting, but it is more dependent on local conditions, both

275. The katholikon of the monastery of Koutloumousiou built in 1540 follows the typical plan of the athonite churches; the same type was also adopted as a model for a series of monasteries founded elsewhere in the same period.

276. The katholikon of Philotheou on Mount Athos which was built in 1746 on the foundations of the earlier church. Like all the other katholika built on the Holy Mountain during the 18th century, an attempt was made to retain the Byzantine tradition of the 16th century, both in the preference for the three-apsed domed inscribed-cross plan and in the elaborate walling.

for material and for technical execution. In this period, therefore, the dividing up of Greek territory into areas under different sovereignties becomes unmistakeably clear from the differences in architectural forms and styles. Whereas in Venetian held regions, and particularly in Crete, the influence of Venetian architecture on Greek church building was fundamental, permanent and almost inevitable, in Ottoman-held regions the Byzantine tradition was maintained. Its technical methods and architectural types were dominant. From what has been said above, it will be clear that new churches were most likely to be erected in monasteries; indeed, new building had already started before the end of the fifteenth century.

On Mount Athos in the sixteenth century large and imposing buildings were constructed; high towers, defence walls for the protection of refectories, infirmaries, outbuildings and multi-storeyed chains of cells (*kordes*). Arsenals too were fortified — the *tarsenades*; here buildings not of an ecclesiastical nature testify to the continued preference for monumental characteristics in civic or fortified structures. The towers in particular are tall, spectacular buildings with clear western influence (fig. 277).[2] Up to a point technical achievement may be correlated with the practice of the Christian craftsmen in the execution of large public works for the Ottoman state. The finest examples of conventual architecture is always the katholikon, the central church of the monastery. Many were built at this time through gifts from the rulers of Wallachia and Moldavia or from a large number of Greek prelates, as at Iveron (1514), Dionysiou (1539), Koutloumousiou (1540), Philotheou (1540), Stavronikita (1542), Xenophontos (1544) and Docheiariou (1568).

These churches were bigger or smaller according to the importance of the monastery, but, irrespective of size, they were all of approximately the same architectural type. Except for Stavronikita, they were built on the cross-in-square triconch plan. The central dome had a high drum and the lower smaller side domed drums were two or four in number. The church was completed by a spacious narthex, called the *lite*, designed to permit the performance of certain liturgies (fig. 276). The model was undoubtedly the tenth century katholikon of Great Lavra. However, it is very significant that the athonite type was adopted for a series of monasteries established in the sixteenth century beyond Mount Athos, for example in the Meteora (Metamorphosis, Barlaam, Hagios Stephanos, Roussanou) and elsewhere; Megalon Pylon (Dousikou 1522); Nikanoros-Zavordas (Kozani 1534). Agathonos monastery near Hypati, Adenitsas monastery, Orthrys, Galataki monastery, Euboia and others.[3] The diffusion of this type is not due solely to the prestige of Mount Athos. It must have served particular liturgical needs and at the same time have satisfied the aesthetic tastes of the age.[4]

These katholika, enhanced by side chapels either next to the sanctuary or to the lite-narthex, are usually carefully built. The walls generally consist of courses of poros corner-stones alternating with two or three horizontal courses of bricks, though in some churches, for example Dionysiou, bricks are absent. The modelling of the surfaces is achieved by the use of blind arcades, sometimes single, sometimes double, which are usually bonded into the whole height of the wall. This mode, whose origins lie in Byzantine Constantinople, was to influence the more vernacular style of church building in northern Greece, where blind arcades are to be found as adornment at least in the sanctuary, even in the nineteenth century; they are emplyed without respect to the type of church plan or to the material used in the walling. The walls of the single-aisled, wooden pitch-roofed churches of Macedonia are usually built of undressed irregular stones set in thick mortar; the wall face not plastered externally. Examples not unlike the most common town houses are to be found in churches at Kastoria and Veria.[5]

Sixteenth and seventeenth century ecclesiastical architecture in Macedonia was one of the most outstanding fields of creativity during the Ottoman occupation of the area. Many buildings, especially the monasteries, continued the medieval tradition into this period, making use of and benefiting from its long experience in techniques, magnificence and stylistic purity.

1700 - 1830

The chief characteristic of this period is the very noticeable increase in the number of churches built; it is especially marked towards the end. International events, such as the treaty of Karlowitz (1669), of Passarowitz (1718) and later of Kutchuk Kainardji (1774) certainly benefited the Christian subjects of the Ottoman empire. Their numbers and their fortunes increased, so that it was both necessary and possible for them to erect new churches or enlarge older structures.

The ecclesiastical buildings of this period continued to be constructed in the traditional manner common almost everywhere in Ottoman dominated Greek territory. Certain local preferences existed for some types. The smaller single-aisled churches, some vaulted, others wooden roofed, are less and less frequently encountered even as parish churches and show only minor variations.

But the phenomenon which truly characterizes this period is the dissemination of the large three-aisled basilica in the southern part of the Balkan peninsula.[6] The importance of this goes beyond the purely architectural significance. Many factors must have been operative in its adoption, mostly for parish churches but also for monasteries. One was the need to enlarge existing churches to accommodate more people. This need is borne out by a large number of founders' inscriptions of this period bearing the formula 'the former ugly and small' or 'the extremely narrow church', which was the excuse for tearing down the old fabric; or, in the case of renovation, the formula 'now conveniently enlarged' or 'turned into a new most beautiful and wonderful church'.[7] Self-evident factors, such as the greater economic possibilities for building larger churches, may be left on one side in order to stress that at this time the urge to renovate demanded the replacement of small, old churches with new and impressive buildings, richly decorated. Furthermore, the stable and static structure of the community required a spacious interior within which every member of the com-

277. The monastery of Stavronikita (1542), dominated by its crenellated defence tower. In the monasteries built on Mount Athos in the 16th and 17th centuries there is a clear tendency towards monumental forms, even in ancillary buildings and fortifications. The tall imposing towers in particular show clear western influences.

munity, or of the parish, could be contained and, at the same time, grouped together according to birth and, more important still, according to the social hierarchy: this is reflected in the song;[8]

> 'To the left, the Virgin and all the women,
> To the right, Christ and all the men,
> In the middle the Cross and the aged.'

The disposition of the icons on the iconostasis thus determined the order in the body of the church.

The three-aisled basilica seemed to be the most appropriate plan to meet most of these needs. The spacious area was divided into three separate aisles, free of the pillars supporting the dome. The elimination of a dome made the work of construction easier and therefore correspondingly cheaper.

The problem, however, is to identify the models of the basilica type. The three-aisled basilica, after its widespread almost exclusive use in the early Byzantine period, was still employed in the middle Byzantine period, always for buildings which had to be on a large scale and most frequently for metropolitan churches. It continued to be built

in the Palaiologan period and many examples were still to be seen on Macedonian soil. The metropolitan churches of Prespa, Veria, Edessa and Serres were still in use, so that it would have been very easy to judge the merits of such a building. There were also more recent examples. From the seventeenth century onwards, three-aisled basilicas were once again being erected in Macedonia.

The three-aisled basilica never lost certain characteristics. The space enclosed by four walls was always spread low in relation to its area; it was always impressive and majestic with its great undivided wooden roof which, without change in level, covered all three aisles although these might be of different heights. The two narrow sides of the four-sloped roof formed a truncated gable whose upper corner was missing. In Macedonia the walls were usually built in carefully dressed local stone. Sometimes rough stone walling filled the spaces between a timber frame. The projecting central apse, frequently polygonal, continued to be decorated with shallow blind arcades and other forms of relief ornament, frequently Turkish in character, such as the 'stalactites', rosettes etc. In other areas, the walls were

413

covered with thick plaster. Decoration of the facades with ancient or Byzantine reliefs is common; Kütahya plates, also frequent, were placed in a tasteful manner.

In a large number of the basilicas of this period the three sides were enclosed, either wholly or in part, by an open portico which in many instances is a later addition.[9] Its purpose was to increase still further the size of the church and to accommodate the large number of the faithful who gathered on great festivals or for the patronal celebrations. The consecration of loaves or the distribution of *kollyva* might also take place here.

The arcades rest on a low ledge and are supported either on pillars or very delicate columns; the latter might be monolithic or made up of drums. If, as is sometimes the case, the columns are wooden, the visual effect strongly resembles the porch of country houses. One might indeed argue that the porch or stoa which appeared at this time was not the continuation of the Byzantine stoa — the *embolon* — which surrounded certain churches, notably in and around Constantinople and at Mystra, but was copied from domestic architecture. Its form and method of construction and thus its aesthetic impact, differs from district to district. In northern Greece and on Lesbos (where there are direct architectural links with Epirus) the porticoes were formed by low arches supported on relatively bulky pillars or on short stocky columns; they seem to buttress rather solid buildings. However, in general these porticoes convey a sense of movement to the surfaces of the building and add a definitely rhythmic element to the facades. There is no pattern to their distribution and they are employed without any consideration of the type of church they adorn. At the same time existing stoas were converted to form an exo-narthex. This tendency becomes much more marked in the nineteenth century.

In large basilical churches the bell tower, either square or octagonal, increases in height, the only contrast to a lower architectural whole. Although it was usually placed at one corner, it is also found along the main axis, namely on the west side in front of the entrance, thereby forming a monumental propylon. These tall three or four-storey towers were substantial and impressive; depending on their proportions they had single or two-lobe openings in every side, usually fewer on the two lowest floors than higher up.[10]

The church is lit by rows of square windows placed high up. In larger churches there were two rows and, as time passed, they were made bigger and bigger. Two rows of columns or pillars divided the large space into three aisles of unequal width; the central one was always the broadest and highest. The columns, whether monolithic or built, and pillars are linked by semi-circular arches, usually fairly shallow. The ceiling and the roof rested on them. In wooden-roofed basilicas the ceiling was flat, decorated with the typical polychrome motifs found also in contemporary mansions — geometric patterns and arabesques made by thin strips of wood attached to the ceiling. In the centre there is always a large boss, embellished with carving or other decoration. Its place is sometimes taken by a round or polygonal hollow, like a false dome; its function is decorative rather than architectural, and it too is found in

mansions. The ceilings of the side aisles were decorated in the same way as the central aisles.[11]

The liturgical furniture in the church all resembles the wooden decoration of the ceiling. The carved iconostasis, a large wooden barrier with obvious architectural articulation, divides the sanctuary from the central and side aisles. It frames the icons, large and small, arranged in rows according to a strictly observed sequence. The iconostasis, which nearly reaches the ceiling, dominates the interior of the church. Its rich carving, often in the style known as 'eastern rococo' laden with plant and paradisical themes, gilded as well as painted in many colours which glittered in the light of the silver lamps hung in front of the venerable icons, clothed it in festive splendour. The pulpit, the episcopal throne, the desks for the chanters and the stalls are all carved in the same style and have the same flowing lavish decoration.[12] Lastly, the wall paintings, though more restrained, are in the same spirit.[13] It is clear that in this period there was a desire to invest everything in the church with a noble quality. It represented the expression of affluence and economic superiority in the community, corresponding exactly to the effects that the *archontes* sought to achieve in their houses by the same means.

The good taste which held sway in decorative matters did not escape the influence of general trends current in the Ottoman empire, such as the widespread diffusion of the 'eastern rococo'. In several of the more sumptuous katholika on Mount Athos Byzantine marble cladding was replaced by tiles in Turkish style from Asia Minor.[14]

On Mount Athos, an area linked always to Thessalonike but otherwise separate from the rest of Macedonia in matters of style and taste, every katholikon built in the eighteenth century (Philotheou 1746 (fig. 276), Gregoriou 1779, Xeropotamou 1761-63) attempted to retain the Byzantine tradition of the sixteenth century. This is demonstrated both by the preference for the triconch domed, inscribed cross-in-square church, in the care taken in the walling (which usually consisted of courses of bricks between stone blocks) and in the spirit of majesty and splendour. The tendency lasts until the beginning of the nineteenth century (for example Esphigmenou, Xenophontos). In the many smaller buildings constructed in the period, and in side chapels, the dome is still the dominating feature and careful stone walling is found in all its many variations.[15]

The year 1830 is not a milestone in the history of Macedonian architecture since the political conditions in the area did not change. For almost the entire nineteenth century the building methods centred, as before, on the basilica.[16] The neo-classical style made its appearance in some of the larger urban centres, but that lies beyond the scope of this chapter.

PAINTING

1430 - 1535

Despite the fact that artistic expression was curtailed, two main centres of religious painting existed on Greek soil. One was in northern Greece, the other in Crete. Though they functioned in parallel, they did not survive for the same length of time, and their works differed in quality and splendour.

It is clear that in Ottoman-held Macedonia there was a fairly active travelling workshop which is identifiable by a distinctive unity of style and technique. Although no inscription or document provides either the names or the more exact background of the painters, we can, nonetheless, establish chronological limits. Certain indications lead to the conclusion that this workshop was formed close to Kastoria and had its base somewhere in the vicinity; the concentration of works by this team is at its thickest in this region and their connection with the older murals in the town itself very close. It is most clearly demonstrated by the wall paintings in the church of Saint Athanasios Mouzake (1384-85). The oldest monument attributed to this 'last Macedonian school' are the paintings in the original katholikon of the Metamorphosis monastery in the Meteora, which became the sanctuary of the new katholikon — a large triconch church which was built in 1545. Its wall paintings are dated by inscription to 1483; they form the most important part of the group, containing most evidence for an evaluation of the school's special character.

The same workship probably executed most, if not all, of the decoration of at least six churches in Kastoria; Saint Nicholas Eupraxias (1505); Saint Nicholas Magaliou (1505); Saint Nicholas Theologinas (where only fragments survive); parts of the Virgin Rassiotissa; Saint Spiridon and SS. Theodore. Some work in SS. Theodore and SS. Anargyroi in Servia (1510) is probably also to be ascribed to it, and its last known work is probably the chapel of the gallery of the Protaton (1526). However, the significant fact is that the activity of the workshop in these years spread to the neighbouring areas of the Balkan peninsula. It is found in Serbia, in the area under the control of the metropolitan of Ochrid, churches at Leskovać (1461), Treskavać (Prilep, 1483-90), at Saint Niketas, Skopje (1483-84), at Poganovo (1500) and elsewhere. In Bulgaria, the wall paintings at Orlitsa (1491) and Kremikovski (? the nave, 1498) in Roumania at Balinesti (1493) are to be attributed to this, or to a very closely related workshop.[17]

These monumental paintings, executed within the space of thirty years in churches which are usually small, share certain common characteristics. The drawing is fluid, if unaccented; the modelling, often somewhat flaccid, is achieved by highlighting; the faces, scarcely differentiated one from the other, have little detail; their expressions have a noticeable tendency towards coarseness, even vulgarity, and this too characterizes the gestures. The figures are indicated with conciseness; they are sometimes tall and thin, with a certain affectation in the pose which recalls the 'international style' of contemporary western art, but sometimes so lively and stocky as to acquire nuances of caricature. A certain crudeness underlies several scenes of the Passion; at the same time an attempt is made to show the more picturesque anachronistic elements of dress. All these features denote a strong tendency towards artistic independence from established tradition; prominence is given to the narration of prosaic elements taken from more popular interpretations of sacred tales or echoing Italian

278. *Christ rebukes the winds, a wall painting in the chapel of Saint John the Theologian at the Mavriotissa monastery, Kastoria. The chapel was decorated by Eustathios Iakovou protonotarios of Arta in 1552. Though his talent is mediocre, he used bright colour and his compositions are full of movement.*

Gothic motifs (which may have been transmitted through Cretan icons). One might say that this tendency is an updated survival from a certain anti-classical impetus in Palaiologue painting moving towards more popular art. It was not, however, able to adjust to the more austere spirit demanded by circumstances. This is why this interesting, unique artistic movement, limited to the Balkan peninsula and lasting for about a generation, was extinguished leaving no immediate continuation. Nonetheless, its indirect effects can be seen in later works.

Other monuments of the fifteenth and first quarter of the sixteenth century scattered throughout Macedonia were not influenced by this workshop which was largely confined to the towns. Their character is either monastic or rural, lacking pretensions. Two exceptions with regard to quality, however, are the wall paintings in Saint Nicholas at Beve in the nome of Florina (1460), and those on the west wall of the Panagia Porphyras, Prespa (1524). They may not, however, be unrelated to the Kastoria atelier, but the absence of published material does not permit a more exact evaluation.[18]

1535 - 1600

The vacuum which exists in religious art in northern Greece in the second quarter of the sixteenth century was to be filled by Cretan painters invited to Mount Athos. Painters from the Great Island had already acquired a high reputation and the wealthiest monasteries had at this time the means to decorate old or new ecclesiastical buildings with new wall paintings.

As far as we know, the first Cretan invited to execute paintings in mainland Greece and in the Meteora (at the monastery of Saint Nicholas Anapavsas, 1527), was Theophanes Strelitzas, the so-called Bathas. The small church of Anapavsas, a domed single-aisled structure with a spacious *pronaos,* did not lend itself to the easy development of large scenes or many narrative cycles.[19]

Eight years later we meet Theophanes again, by this time ensconced in Great Lavra on Mount Athos, together with his two children, Symeon and Niphon-Neophytos, both of whom became painters. There Theophanes painted the katholikon, the great tenth century church which must have had earlier paintings probably of the fourteenth century. The donor was the exiled metropolitan of Veria, the Athenian Neophytos, who was sufficiently learned to be able to compose the dedicatory inscriptions in archaic metre. It was probably his counsel which established the very well-organized iconographic programme, which betrays an erudite theological mind because, if we are to judge Theophanes from the spelling on the inscriptions at Anapavsas, he was not well versed in the rules of grammar. At Great Lavra, where the triconch church offered large wall surfaces, he developed artistic talents meet for the monumental style of wall painting — the matching of large scale scenes to the surfaces, better adaptation of painting methods for modelling and drapery to the needs of wall paintings and finally a sensitive colour range against a black ground. In this respect Theophanes departs both from the technique of the portable icon and from his immediate Italian experience, although he does not cease to make use of the copperplate engravings of Mark Antonio Raimondi made after the drawings of Raphael to reinvigorate the dramatic scene of the Slaughter of the Innocents, or a canvas by Bellini for the Supper at Emmaeus. These scenes, together with some other detailed subjects, for example the centurion at the Crucifixion, Saint Christopher carrying Christ on his shoulder, are the only traces of Italian influence in many hundreds of scenes.

The wall paintings at Great Lavra (fig. 284), with the well-thought out, complete and highly organized iconographic cycles of thematic wealth and outstanding artistic quality, form one of the achievements of the age beyond all comparison with anything that could have been executed a few decades earlier in the Balkans. It thus became, and remains, a model monastic church for Orthodox countries.[20]

Theophanes and his son Symeon also decorated the katholikon and refectory at the newly founded monastery of Stavronikita in 1545-46 at the expense, and naturally at the dictates of the founder, the patriarch Jeremiah I (fig. 282). In the sections which we may safely attribute to Theophanes, such as the monumental figures of the prophets in the dome, many scenes from the life of Christ and a row of saints, the painterly execution has a more immediate relationship to the great Palaiologue models to be found on Mount Athos, for example in the Protaton, at Vatopedi and at Chilandari attributed to the painter Manuel Panselinos from Thessalonike. Theophanes remained as a monk at Lavra until 1558; at the beginning of 1559 he died in Herakleion.[21] While he lived on Athos various unsigned works directly linked to the Cretan school and indirectly at least to Theophanes were carried out at monasteries there; at Molyvokklesia in 1536, in the katholikon of Koutloumousi, 1540; in the refectory of Philotheou (1540); and the katholikon at Dionysiou (1547), (where the painter may have been the Cretan Tzortzis, (fig. 283). At the same time, the impressive decoration of the refectory of Great Lavra was executed, the donor being Gennadios of Serres (d. *c.* 1540); the work is definitely associated with Theophanes.[22] A large number of portable icons on Mount Athos are to be dated to approximately the same period, many of which were painted there by Cretan artists. Three groups have already been attributed to Theophanes and his immediate collaborators, each one of which would have made up an entire iconostasis; one at Great Lavra (1535), a second at the Protaton (1542) and a third at Stavronikita (1546, fig. 281).[23] Another series, at Pantokrator monastery, could be his work.[24] His son, the monk Neophytos, returned as a brother to Great Lavra in 1552.[25] It is, however, very likely that collections of icons came ready-made from Crete; this is almost certainly true of the five outstanding icons of the Great Deesis in Dionysiou which bear the signature of the priest Euphrosynos (1542).[26]

After Theophanes' death an unnamed, but skilled, painter of this school decorated the katholikon, together with its huge, very high *lite,* at Docheiariou (1568),[27] and before the end of the century the katholikon of Iveron also. We have noted only the wall paintings whose style in every respect connects them immediately with the signed works of Theophanes, without it always being possible to ascertain his personal participation. Other Cretan artists were Theophanes' sons Symeon and Neophytos, and Tzortzis, who painted the katholikon (1547) and probably part of the refectory at Dionysiou,[28] and other capable men who to date remain anonymous.

Working alongside the Cretans were other 'minor' painters, having a different artistic heritage and different aims. These men must have responded to the taste of circles for which the dignified classicism had no appeal. They were the continuors of the anti-classical tradition, preferring coarser, more direct forms of expression. This tendency is expressed in the works of Antonios, an approximate contemporary of Theophanes who, in 1544, signed part of the wall paintings in the older, eleventh century, katholikon at Xenophontos. This work enables us to ascribe to him two other unsigned decorative compositions in small churches

279-280. The paintings of the large single-aisled church of the Holy Apostles, Kastoria were executed by Onouphrios protopapas of the bishopric of Neokastron in 1547. His style cannot be said to belong to any of the foreign schools which worked in Macedonia in the middle decades of the 16th century. The pictures show parts of the north wall of the church which was decorated with parallel rows of saints, some depicted in bust, others full-length.

417

Μακεδονία, 27, Απρίλιο

281. *The Nativity, an icon from the iconostasis of Stavronikita, Mount Athos (1546). It has been attributed to the Cretan painter, Theophanes. Throughout the Ottoman occupation the icon was the chief means of artistic expression. The most important characteristics of the dominant Cretan school were that the figures in compositions were as few as possible and detail was kept to the minimum.*

on the Athos peninsula; the *kellion* of Prokopios belonging to Vatopedi (1537) and the small chapel of Saint George the Pavlou monastery (1552). The work of Antonios, who used to be considered a pupil of the Cretans, has its roots in the traditions of mainland Greece. It is to be distinguished from known Cretan hands because his painting tends towards the linear; lordly ease and nobility of expression are missing from faces, poses and gestures and his compositions do not possess the harmonious rhythm which is the hallmark of Cretan work. Even the iconographic programme is other than the Cretan. Nonetheless, Antonios was constantly influenced by his island colleagues who worked in the large monasteries, especially in respect to his technical methods and in elements of iconography; his art, however, had little resonance.[29]

The work of the Theban painter, Frangos Katelanos, is removed from Antonios' simplistic style. He was invited to Mount Athos in 1560, the year after Theophanes Bathas died, commissioned to paint the large side chapel of Saint Nicholas in Great Lavra, a domed cross-inscribed church.[30] Here Katelanos developed the iconographic programme according to Theophanes' models, although he maintained a considerable degree of independence within compositions, both in the choice and arrangement of iconographic elements and in the spirit which underlay his style. By contrast to the calm classicism which pervaded Theophanes' works, Katelanos expressed the opposite tendency, one which leant towards the baroque; he depicted large numbers of figures against a background of close-packed buildings, thereby creating a crowded and oppressive environment. In his attempt to remodel scenes (usually by a simple and personal interpretation of established Cretan motifs and compositions), he sometimes borrowed from Palaiologue models, sometimes from Italian and occasionally from the Kastoria workshop mentioned earlier.

The presence of works of Katelanos on Athos testifies to the indefatigable zeal of the monastic world there in quest of a high standard in artistic and theological monumental decoration, even if this were to be found only outside long-established local tradition. However, the chapel of Saint Nicholas is the only signed work of Katelanos, and thus it is the only criterion which we may use to ascribe to him earlier paintings elsewhere. For it seems that when Katelanos was invited to Great Lavra, he was already a mature painter. In any case it is the last work in the series ascribed to him; we have identified his personal touch not only in the Aitolian monastery of Myrtias (1539),[31] in parts of the Philanthropinon monastery (Spanos) on the island of the lake of Ioannina (1542),[32] at Barlaam in the Meteora[33] and at at least two other Macedonian churches, the Zavorda monastery (Kozani)[34] and, in Kastoria itself, the church of the Rasiotissa (1553).[35] To these examples we may add the church in the deserted village of Hagios Zacharias west of Kastoria where a group of paintings bears a resemblance to those of Katelanos, even to such details as the relief haloes.[36] It is clear that the region where the Theban painter worked intensively, with assistants of varying ability, was north-west Greece.

Between 1530 and 1560 we may say that two 'imported' schools dominated Macedonia; the Cretan and the Theban, that of Frangos Katelanos. Both are manifestations of an art elaborated in urban centres which was then employed in the leading monasteries founded by educated bourgeois or prelates. The work of Onouphrios from Berat belongs to the same category. Onouphrios, *protopapas* of the bishopric of Neokastron (Elbasan), is known to have executed wall paintings in central Albania (Saint Paraskeve in Bals, 1554). Beautiful icons are also ascribed to him. His work is more easily viewed, however, in the paintings of the large single-aisled church of the Holy Apostles, Kastoria (1547) (figs. 279-280). His style is not easy to classify amongst the schools mentioned up to now. The dignity of the tall silhouettes of the somewhat typecast figures, western influences particularly in the busts of saints and

282. *The Crucifixion, wall painting in the katholikon of Stavronikita, Mount Athos, executed by the Cretan Theophanes and his son Symeon in 1545-46. From the middle of the 15th century onwards the tendency of the Cretan painters to revert to* the traditional more austere styles is already apparent; it found its fullest expression in the monasteries on the Holy Mountain whose wall paintings were the models for the entire Orthodox world.

echoes of the particular motifs of Frangos Katelanos and of the Cretans, give his careful work a certain eclecticism. Naturally, links to the traditions of the fifteenth century Kastoria workshop are not easy to establish. The lengthy Greek inscriptions which accompany all his paintings, unmarred by syntactical or orthographic mistakes, indicate his educational level. The evidence reveals Onouphrios as a representative of religious art of an urban nature, its sights set relatively high. It is certain that his output cannot be confined to the very few known examples which bear his signature.[37]

Another painter, Eustathios Iakovou, *protonotarios* at Arta, also comes from north-west Greece. In 1552 he decorated the side chapel of Saint John the Theologian at Mavriotissa in Kastoria (fig. 278). His talent is mediocre, but his colours are bright and his compositions endowed with movement though cluttered with buildings or landscape. His iconographic programme, however, makes

it clear that he was possessed of more than the rudiments of theology.[38]

Still in Kastoria, at least three churches date from the end of the sixteenth and the beginning of the seventeenth century; the metropolis of Saint Nicholas (1596) and the Panagia Metropoleos of the archon Apostolakis (1606) and Saint Demetrios (1609).[39] None has stylistic links with the Cretan school and affinities with the paintings noted above are of the most tenuous. Other analogous examples are in the churches of Veria, at Saint Nicholas Makariotissa (1571), Saints Kyrikos and Ioulitta (1582) with its linear, stressed expressiveness, and in Saint Prokopios (1607).[40] These wall paintings, in single-aisled wooden-roofed churches, all attain the same standard as that of the painters from Linotopi (see below). Of a different quality, and more closely akin to paintings in the Cretan tradition, are the paintings at Saint Nicholas (in the parish of Saint Antony), dated to 1575 and 1590.[41]

Lastly, in the small community of Aiane (near Kozani) some wall paintings survive in churches of the period; the group in Saint Demetrios by an anonymous hand is roughly contemporary with the wall paintings of the deacon Zacharias of 1552 in the church of Saint Nicholas and those of the Archangel Michael of 1549 attributed to the same painter.[42] In all these, a linear anti-classical style is to be seen, as totally separate from the style of the Cretans as it is from that of the other 'urban' painters, Onouphrios, Eustathios Iakovou and Katelanos.

During the three decades after 1560 family groups of painters make their appearance within Macedonia in villages round Kastoria, especially from Linotopi and Grammos (Grammosta). They are known by their Christian names, Nicholas, Michael, and Kostas and their work is found in Epirus, Macedonia and central Greece. Their first known work is at Palatitsa near Veria where in 1570 the painter Nicholas from Linotopi painted the sanctuary of the large basilica of Saint Demetrios.[43] Later, their works are found in Thessaly and Trichonida. Their line continues with Constantine, George and others in the seventeenth century. At Kastoria in 1630 another Nicholas 'from Linotopi' painted the church of Saint Nicholas of Thomanos,[44] and it is beyond doubt that a number of paintings in Kastoria churches are their work. As befits the artists' origins, simplified outlines and crude colours characterize the style of these village painters. However, they made use of patterns of older paintings, with a preference for the circle of Frangos Katelanos, which frequently gives a monumental character to their compositions.

In conclusion, during the sixteenth century, away from Mount Athos, buildings in the towns of western Macedonia demonstrate a considerable output in the field of ecclesiastical art. This output is expressed on two parallel levels; the more elevated springs from important urban centres outside Macedonia and the other is more faithful to a certain native tradition of rural origin, already in existence in the fifteenth century, for example at Prespa.

Seventeenth century

After the sixteenth century Cretan painters were only occasionally invited to Mount Athos, where wall painting, as far we know, was almost never required. The names of the painters faithful to the Cretan tradition who completed the decoration of the old refectory at the monastery of Dionysiou in the extension of 1603 are unknown (fig. 283). A Cretan painter, the monk Merkourios, whose work in Crete is attested, was employed in chapels in the same monastery; sometimes he worked alone (1627) and at other times he collaborated with the monk Daniel (1601, 1610, 1615) whom I do not think is a Cretan. In another chapel Merkourios worked alongside the monk Germanos.[45] Later, in 1636, Merkourios was to work with the Peloponnesian monk Atzalis painting the small cupola of the *phiale* in the courtyard of Great Lavra.[46] In all these works Merkourios observes the traditional stylistic canons, imparting no personal stamp, but executing them with

great technical skill and considerable knowledge of iconography.

The painter-monk Daniel executed several notable icons in the same monastery.[47] The Serbian, George Metrofanović, decorated the refectory at Chilandari and painted portable icons in the same style in 1621.[48]

The situation on the Holy Mountain remained unaltered throughout the second half of the seventeenth century; important groups of paintings do not exist. In most monasteries, it was only small chapels that were decorated; at Vatopedi in 1678 and 1683, at Iveron in 1683, Great Lavra in 1688, Chilandari in 1667, 1671, 1680 and 1684, all by mediocre and anonymous hands. Only one can be identified — the priest Daniel at Chilandari in 1667. He also painted the portable icons there.[49]

The consequence of this not entirely fortuitous absence of Cretan or other 'urban' artists with traditions of a higher standard was to permit local painters to come to terms with the local artistic concepts which had a rural, non-classical character. As we have seen, these interpretations had already taken root over a fairly wide area in the second half of the sixteenth century in the art of the region. Interest shifts to north-west Macedonia where painters from the Grammos villages, such as Linotopi or Grammosta already noted, also worked in the towns, for example at Kastoria and Veria; examples are also found further east, at least as far as Mount Athos. The feature to be considered common to this widespread artistic output is that the agrarian background of its artists gives an ever more simplified and popular character to their works in which the technical-professional skill, despite the traditional perfection, is not sufficient to overcome the 'artisan-like' aspect.[50] The anonymous wall paintings at Saint George, Veria (1642), more strongly expressive than those of the Grammos painters, are a good example of a group of murals representative of this period and of this level.[51]

As yet, the portable icons of the period have not been systematically studied. Nevertheless, it is clear that the same craftsmen, or at least men of the same humble level as the painters, fashioned a large number of icons, clumsily executed on thick board, to decorate iconostases whether in churches or in houses. The best belong to a class of icons found in Thessalonike and on Mount Athos. They are distinguished by the broad ugly faces, by the lively, faintly eastern patterns on clothing and furniture and finally by the precision in the rendering of stamped and dotted jewels on the gilded haloes. These characteristics tend to convey an illusion of the easy circumstances enjoyed by the dignitaries. We have ascribed the original models of this style to Mount Athos because at least two icons, of Christ and of Saint George, have a direct relationship with Palaiologue models to be found there. Icons of Christ, copying the Christ of the Protaton, are more numerous still in the monasteries of Athos (the

283. *The Heavenly Ladder, wall painting from the old refectory of Dionysiou, Mount Athos, 1603. Many of the wall paintings on the Holy Mountain were executed by the numerous members of the so-called Cretan School, invited there after the Fall of Constantinople.*

Protaton, Gregoriou, Koutloumousiou, Vatopedi and elsewhere).[52]

This attribution is important because it shows that in the seventeenth century a local artistic and stylistic tradition had begun to spring up on Mount Athos; it was to take deeper root in the eighteenth century.

The eighteenth century

Mount Athos

In the first decades of the eighteenth century a large number of wall paintings was executed in katholika, narthexes and chapels of the monasteries on Athos. They expressed two conflicting stylistic tendencies. This contrast, however, is probably also the fruit of a very basic crisis, perhaps of a theological nature, regarding the direction which hagiography should follow. One stream of painting, the more interesting, is to be distinguished because it more effectively consolidated the gropings we discerned on the Mountain in the seventeenth century towards a deliberate return to the great athonite models of the Palaiologue era, works that is which were thought to be by the legendary painter Panselinos. The evidence is clear, especially in the anonymous Painters' Manuals where the apprentice is frequently enjoined to search 'the models of the famous Manuel Panselinos' and to work on them for a long time.

This very practical advice must reflect a more catholic demand, at least on Mount Athos. A large number of manuscripts of anonymous manuals, compilations and excerpts in several variations is known. Some confine themselves entirely to technical directions and to instructions to painters; others consist largely of hints on iconographical conventions, suggestions for facial characteristics and suitable quotations for the texts on the scrolls held by the saints.

The most typical author of such works is Dionysios of Fourna from Agrapha, a monk who taught himself the painter's art on Athos itself by 'studying from childhood and imitating as far as possible that shining example from Thessalonike Manuel Panselinos'. It is perhaps indicative of the backward-looking tendencies of the age that it was on Athos that Dionysios became aware of the need to collect and collate these diverse manuals to produce the fullest and most complete text possible. It was to contain both the technical and iconographic information from similar older manuals, amplified by a compendium of detailed descriptions of scenes from the Old and New Testaments, parables and the martyrdoms of saints. The text was written between 1728 and 1733 with the assistance of Dionysios' most learned pupil, the painter and priest-monk Cyril Photeinos from Chios.[53]

Dionysios was no great painter, and is better known to us now as the author of the *Manual*. This work was copied many times before it was also printed and translated, because its value was overestimated in the nineteenth century; it was thought to contain the basic rules for the layout of compositions and their execution, and thus to hold the key to an understanding of Byzantine painting as a whole.

Dionysios' artistic production is known mainly from the paintings in the chapel of his *kellion* at Karyes (?1731), where many figures show the influence of prolonged familiarity with the paintings of the Protaton. This influence, when it does not extend to direct copying of some particular figure (usually of old men), is clear also in the style of the broad modelling of the faces, in the drapery and in the attempts to render volume. His achievement is not outstanding, but his declared intention of returning to the old models available on the Mountain gives his works a certain eclecticism, though of necessity certain elements of contemporary art crept into them — either indirect western influences, or subjects of a more secular nature (dress, landscapes, jewellery).[54]

Dionysios was not the only student and imitator of Panselinos. In the chapel of Saint Demetrios in the katholikon of Vatopedi the work of the 'anonymous painter', dated to 1721 by a lost inscription, was on parallel lines. This marvellously well preserved group permits us to savour the artist's exceptionally delicate colour sense in the luminous complementary colours, so that his work surpasses simple copying of Palaiologue originals. His immediate inspiration was probably not drawn from models we regard as works of Panselinos, namely the wall paintings of the Protaton, but possibly from those of the circle of Astrapas, Eutychios and of Saint Nicholas Orphanos.[55]

These notable paintings at Vatopedi, accompanied by many inscriptions, calligraphically and orthographically faultless, recall the decoration of the narthex of the chapel of the Virgin Koukouzelissa (Portaitissa) at Great Lavra. An inscription (now lost) informs us that the painter was David from Aulon; it gave the date 1715.[56] He is to be identified with the painter of the great basilica of Saint Nicholas at Moschopolis (1726) where the work may be signed 'by the hand of David of Selenitsa'. This decoration is distinguished not only by the same strict devotion to the Palaiologue athonite models, but also by the same high standard and liveliness of presentation we find in the Koukouzelissa chapel, Great Lavra.[57] The iconographic programme in the narthex-lite of the Lavra chapel is extremely rich, its full-length saints supplemented by martyrdoms, the miracles of Saint Athanasios the Athonite (copied from the refectory), the Tree of Jesse and the Tree of the Vine, Oecumenical Councils, scenes from the Apocalypse and, in the dome, the Angelic Choir round the enthroned Pantokrator. The likeness of the saints, particularly of aged ascetics, to the corresponding figures in the Protaton is striking. Western influences are clear in the scenes from the Apocalypse, while in the more popular content of the scenes of the Heavenly Choir, the dionysiac verve in the rendering of the dancing rhythm, the realistic exactness of the clothing of the time and of the musical instruments outstrips every traditional imitation (fig. 285). We may say that it creates, at least on Mount Athos, a new tradition for the rendering of contemporary life in the iconography of corresponding scenes.[58]

We should credit the same 'most devout David' with the paintings in the church of the Prodromos church at Apozari, Kastoria in 1727; they have been wrongly attributed to an otherwise unknown painter, Laurentios, because of a mis-reading of the 'shorthand' inscription. It should be noted that here the painter's skill in adapting the moralizing and didactic content of such sins as the punishment of prostitution and to other common scenes in an original fashion often reveals a knowledge of free drawing in western style.[59]

The kinship of some other paintings on Mount Athos to David's work is marked, as for example in the exo-narthex of Docheiariou and Stavronikita.[60] The eclecticism and refinement of the colour turns these wall paintings into a real artistic achievement. Their character is clearly athonite; the particular and personal antecedents of the individual painter are of no account. The roots of this academic and basically archaistic character lie in the imitative return to the old models and in the level of education of the painters; Dionysios was able to write services for use in churches as well as the *Manual,* and the correctly spelt 'most holy' David is praised for his wisdom and acute and fertile pen. This is perhaps the reason why this style did not spread beyond Athos; except for David's work at Moschopolis and Kastoria we do not know of many other examples outside the Mountain. It did, however, survive there, for its influence on later athonite painters is considerable. A tradition was created which was followed, to a greater or lesser degree, by the many painters who came to the Holy Mountain during the eighteenth century.

The opposite tendency in the wall paintings on Mount Athos in the same period is that which appears to continue the older athonite tradition, that is, to invite outstanding painters 'from the world' who brought to the Mountain their own regional art, to which they would make iconographic adaptations. The main representative of this stream is the Epirote priest-monk Damaskenos 'of Ioannina' who must be the painter of the new refectory at Docheiariou in 1700, of the katholikon at Karakalou in 1717 and of the wide nave in the chapel of the Virgin Koukouzelissa (Portaitissa) at Great Lavra in 1719.[61] In 1691 he had decorated the small church in the monastery of Saint Demetrios on Skyros. In all these cases Damaskenos remains faithful to the technical and aesthetic principles common to his many Epirote colleagues, and his artistic personality is not to be separated from theirs. Bright colours, light and flat against a black background, contours to facial characteristics in firm lines shape uncouth figures staggering under the weight of armour or swathed in heavy draperies. The jewelled relief haloes and other embellishments which are the stock-in-trade of painters from Epirus are not absent. This style, with its marked linear and flat perspectives is to be found in other ecclesiastical buildings on Mount Athos of the same period, carried out by unnamed painters, unmistakeably from Epirus; examples include the dome (1739), the exo-narthex and chapels at Vatopedi, and at Gregoriou, Docheiariou and elsewhere many *kathismata* and monastic dependencies.

Most of the painters who were employed to produce the scores of paintings on Mount Athos up to the end of the eighteenth century were born in the north-west. Kosmas, Seraphim and Ioannikios, a group who worked at Pantokrator in 1749 and at Karakalou in 1750 came from the

284. *Detail from the Crucifixion, a wall painting in the katholikon of Great Lavra, (1535). These wall paintings represent some of the finest examples of art on Mount Athos, and are mature works of the chief representative of the Cretan School, Theophanes.*

region of Ioannina; Gabriel and Gregory, known at Gregoriou in 1779 from Kastoria; the brothers Constantine and Athanasios who were at Philotheou in 1765, Xeropotamou in 1783 and at the *skete* of Xenophontos in 1766 came from Korytsa. The works of all these identifiable groups, as well as many other anonymous painters, bear strong resemblances to each other, which, as we noted above, should be ascribed not only to a common heritage, but also to the strong athonite tradition.[62]

In these later examples stylistic mannerisms continue to survive; light shades, and broad soft modelling which creates a certain kind of handsomeness, even a rather cloying expression. In subject matter too, more is packed into the scenes of the Apocalypse, the Second Coming is enriched by the depiction of moral punishments for a wide variety of sins and the Old Testament is illustrated on the basis of western engravings. We might also even recognize popularized echoes of the Baroque in certain crowded and restless compositions. But these more 'popular' painters, of peasant origin, were no longer in a position to grasp the humanistic message of the grecized tradition of the Protaton paintings, nor even of their imitators at the beginning of the century.

The considerable number of portable icons painted in a similar style where accurate handiwork is to be discerned in the heavily emphasized rich decorative elements must be attributed to the same painters.

At the end of the eighteenth and the beginning of the nineteenth century a family group of painters arrived on Mount Athos from Galatista in Chalkidike — Makarios, Benjamin and Zacharias — and established themselves in Karyes. They executed the paintings in the refectory of Vatopedi in 1786, and in the chapel of the *skete* of Saint Demetrios belonging to it in 1806, in the chapel of the Archangels at Iveron in 1812 and elsewhere. Benjamin worked as far away as Hosios Meletios on Mount Kithairon in 1820.[63]

Throughout the eighteenth century the Holy Mountain attracted competent artists from Epirus and Macedonia, and their little known work more than suffices to provide an accurate picture of the standard of hagiographical painting all over Macedonia. It should be mentioned that besides painters from western Macedonia, artists from Epirus also worked here — the Kaloudes family from Kapesovo at Prophet Elijah, Siatista in 1741-44; later, in 1802, Michael, the painter from Hionades at the monastery of Hagia Triada at Zoupani (Kozani region).[64]

The style of this painting both in the tendency to enrich iconographic programmes and in the boldness with which the established iconographic programmes were expressed is not very different from that found all over Greek lands, perhaps indeed throughout the Orthodox countries. In the course of the century even the stylistic manner acquires greater uniformity. Indeed, we are talking about a somewhat faceless art, the product of several factors; basically the 'artisan' character which ecclesiastical painting acquired for various reasons, and secondly of the fundamental prestige always exercised by Mount Athos. Its underlying authority, and the intensive productivity in the construction and decoration of ecclesiastical buildings, fostered certain ideas and particular methods. Moreover, of the artists of the period, the Epirotes were the most numerous and the most representative and it was they who, by spreading their style through the entire Balkan peninsula, brought about a standardization of methods. The manuscripts of the *Manuals of Painting* also encouraged the spread of certain types. The features make some religious wall paintings not unrelated to those on Mount Athos speak a kind of 'artistic *katharevousa*' that is, a kind of more official artistic language.[65]

The style in which individuals were painted developed on parallel lines. The numerous founders and benefactors, most of them clerics, all sought to win immortality on earth in portraits, full length or otherwise, in churches, chapels or refectories. While the tradition is old, the new element is its wider distribution across the social scale and its appearance in smaller buildings, despite public thunderings against the sin of vanity.[66]

The encyclopaedic spirit of the times is reflected in the

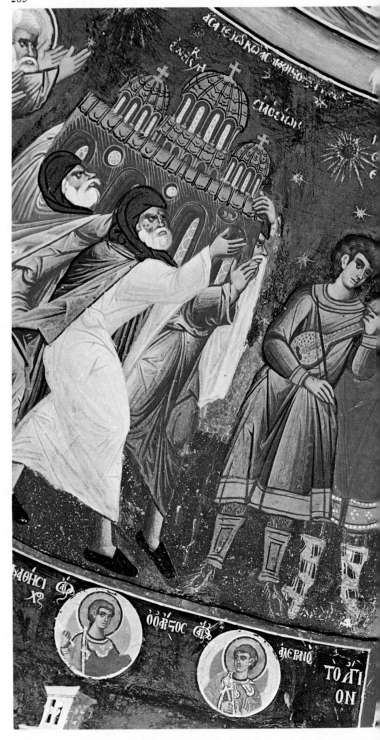

285. *'Praise the Lord', wall painting from the chapel of the Virgin Koukouzelissa in Great Lavra executed in the 18th century. At this time two conflicting stylistic tendencies are met in*

paintings executed to decorate the walls of the *archontika* in Kastoria, Siatista and elsewhere, with views of towns in western Europe or with more intimate scenery such as lakes, rivers and ships. This style was also employed in monastic edifices in the guest chambers, refectories and abbots' quarters; it has an almost Ottoman quality as it is found in mosques throughout the Balkans and in Asia Minor. These secular painters are rarely known to us by

the paintings which decorate the katholika, narthexes and chapels of the monasteries on Mount Athos. One was the return to the older Palaiologue models, the other, illustrated above, *resulted from the continuation of the old athonite tradition of inviting artists 'from the world' to decorate churches on the peninsula.*

name. One, with a Slav name, is recorded in the refectory of the Prodromos monastery in Serres in 1795 where the inscription in sophisticated language reads 'painted by the gifted marvellous painter Nedelkos...'[67]

The decisive break with the past which the establishment of the Greek state marked in southern Greece does not apply to Macedonia where Ottoman rule continued throughout the nineteenth century. Perhaps for this reason,

both painting and architecture continued without a break in tradition in both churches and private mansions, practised always by painters of rural origin (from the villages of Hionades, from Samarina, from Selitsa near or in Eratyra) or even from others in the Kozani region. In this evolution, which has no originality, faint echoes of neo-classicism are not absent even from the decoration of villas belonging to the educated bourgeois.[68]

POPULAR ART

VERNACULAR ARCHITECTURE

After the consolidation of the Ottoman conquest, substantial groups of Ottomans settled in various parts of Macedonia, and the displaced Christian population was forced to take refuge in the mountains. New villages and mountain settlements were built, some of which swiftly grew into flourishing townships: Kozani, for example, is referred to in 1534 as a village, but it quickly developed into a main village, township and then a town.[1]

Once the inhabitants had achieved the desired level of security, they erected new churches, and the first Greek schools began to function at a very early date in the narthexes of the churches and the monasteries. In Siatista, for example, seven churches were built between 1610 and 1647, an indication that it had already grown into a main town.[2]

Insecurity and poverty were still widespread in the countryside and this had its effects on the monasteries, which had difficulty in supporting even small numbers of monks in the first half of the seventeenth century. The treaty of Karlowitz in 1699, and especially the treaty of Passarowitz in 1718 ushered in a period of economic advance that lasted until the middle of the eighteenth century.[3] This is perhaps best reflected in the building of new churches decorated with exquisite wood-carved iconostases and wall paintings. It is indicative that in Siatista another seven new churches were constructed between 1700 and 1792.[4] During the Russo-Turkish wars of 1736-38 and 1768-77 conditions naturally became very insecure again, and many western Macedonians were forced to emigrate to central Europe, and in 1769 the Vlach-speaking villages of Mt. Grammos were laid waste by Muslim-Albanians. In this same year, the wealthy town of Moschopolis was destroyed, and the terrorism that was rife in the various *kazas* of Macedonia had terrible consequences for the safety and even the lives of the *rayahs*.

Nonetheless, the cultural flowering on Mount Athos in the eighteenth century was matched by a renaissance in all spheres. The new ideas spread quickly, and are reflected in the architecture and painting of the period.

Archontika - Mansions

The largest and finest *archontika* in Macedonia were built in the eighteenth century. These tall buildings in western Macedonia, with their stone built lower walls and projecting upper storeys, clearly had a common origin in an ancient wide-fronted type of building despite the typological differences that can be detected between the various regions (Siatista, Kastoria, Veria, Kozani, Florina and Thessalonike). This type seems to have acquired projecting upper floors as early as the Byzantine period — the *solaria* that were converted into *sahnisin* in the eighteenth century, and also the roofed open porches (*doxato*), which became the *hayat* or wooden porch.

The ground and mezzanine floor together constituted the defensive part of the structure, which was rectangular, square or L-shaped in plan. The ground floor was usually divided into two parts, one comprising the entrance and the staircase, and the other the store-rooms (*ambaria*). In the plan found in Siatista, the ground floor already has an interior roofed courtyard surrounded by internal wooden balconies at the level of the upper floors to which the staircase led. The upper floor was invariably constructed of lighter materials. Covered verandahs (*hayat*) were constructed on the inner side, facing into the courtyard, while on the outer side there were usually a number of projecting rooms. During the first half of the eighteenth century, a large number of the most opulent mansions to be found almost anywhere in the Balkans were built at Siatista (at Geraneia and Chora). The mansion of Naoum Nerantzis was built at Geraneia in 1710; that of D. Tzouras at Chora in 1725; that of Mrs. Sanouko in 1742; those of N. Chatzimichail (A. Kanatsoulis), of G. Manousis, and of Poulkidis in 1746; the mansion of Chatziyannidis (Nerantzopoulos) in 1754; those of P. Tzonos and D. Gerechtes in 1756 at Geraneia; those of Alexiou and Argyriadis (Malioga) in 1759; and of J. Koutoulas, also at Geraneia, in 1760.[5] The great mansions of Kastoria were also built during this period. The mansion of Tsiatsapas was built in 1754 in the district of Apozari. Contemporary with it were the mansions of the Emmanuel brothers, comrades in arms of Rhigas, of Nantzis, and many others.

The core of the mansion is the reception room called the *ontas*; wooden cupboards (*mousandres*) were built along the inner walls, and couches, (*menderia*) were arranged like a Π. The hearth is always placed on the axis and flanked by two windows, usually placed symmetrically, particularly when this side projects. The walls are divided into two zones by an interior cornice at the height of the top of the windows. Above this is a frieze and the painted fanlights on the outside. The area with the *menderia* is frequently higher than the rest of the room and is divided from the antechamber by two columns that form a triple opening. In this central room, we may recognize the *triclinium* of ancient and Byzantine houses. The wooden panelling on the walls was richly decorated with coloured plant motifs. The wall cupboards with their panelled doors were separated by a series of niches with the characteristic Iranian-Indian arch; in them stood glassware or fruit. The frieze above the cupboards depicted Constantinople, or ports, drawn from the imagination — Venice was a particular favourite. A mural in the 'best room' on the third floor of the mansion of Tsiatsapas in Kastoria, painted in 1798 and enclosed in a stylized baroque frame, depicts an imaginary city with palaces, many-storeyed mansions and churches; a river meanders amongst them dotted with small boats; dragons devour all kinds of fish; there are gardens with shepherds and their dogs, and grazing deer; and behind them pavilions and Ottoman tents painted in a marvellous range of unmistakeably eastern colours. There are scenes like this, especially of cities, whether real or imagined, portrayed in the abstract style typical of the period, in nearly all the mansions of the eighteenth century. The

286. The archontikon of A. Kanatsoulis in Siatista, built in 1746. Though the many large mansions built in Macedonia during the 18th century display a wide range of typological variations from region to region, a common origin is nevertheless clear.

fact that these wall paintings are all inspired by a number of models that must once have existed is confirmed by the inscriptions on the murals in the mansions of Malioga (1759) in Siatista. On the frieze of the best room on the ground floor we read 'Frankfurt a (m) Mayn'.[6] And on another mural, depicting a horseman carrying a spear: 'Le houssare d'Autriche'.[7] The fanlights decorating the mansions in western Macedonia are the most elaborate known in this part of the world. Representative examples are those in the mansions of G. and D. Schwartz (Avramopoulos) in Ambelakia,Thessaly:[8] the mansions of Manousis and Nerantzopoulos at Siatista, dating from the middle of the eighteenth century; and the mansions of Tsiatsapas, Nantzis among others at Kastoria. The ceilings of the mansions were exquisitely decorated — sometimes with a strong suggestion of arabesques, sometimes in popular Ottoman baroque, and sometimes in a mixture of styles. In the centre there is a complex rosette; earlier there was often a large rectangular wooden disk or a dome. The best ceilings survive at Siatista, in the mansions of Manousis (1762) and Tzonos (1756-86).[9] The similar examples in the

Schwartz mansion in Ambelakia date from the end of the eighteenth century.[10]

Macedonian monastic buildings

After the Ottoman conquest, there were radical changes in the life of the monks, particularly in the large monastic centres such as Mount Athos. New monasteries were built on inaccessible sites, and the already existing monasteries were repaired or extended. The Panagia Porphyra, the small monastery on the little island of Hagios Achilleios, Prespa, has inscriptions with the dates 1522, 1524. The foundation of the monastery obviously antedates the wall painting in the small katholikon, which is a single-aisled, wooden basilica.[11] At this same time (1534) Hosios Nikanor (1491-1549) founded the monastery of the Metamorphosis at Konivos (Mt. Kallistraton) on the left bank of the Haliakmon — the famous Zavorda monastery.[12] The Prodromos monastery at Veria had a large number of monks at the end of the fourteenth century. About 1535-50, it was visited by Saint Dionysios the

Younger, who converted it from a *skete* to a *koinobion*.[13] At the end of the sixteenth or the beginning of the seventeenth century, Theophanes from Ioannina, a monk of Docheiariou, founded the monastery of the Asomatoi at Naousa.[14] At the beginning of the sixteenth century, Hosios Theonas 'rebuilt from the foundations' the monastery of Hagia Anastasia Pharmakolytria (north-east of Thessalonike) which, according to tradition, had been founded in the tenth century.[15]

The lay-out and functions of the monasteries built during the Ottoman period did not differ in any essential from those of the Byzantine monasteries. Very few, of course, were completely new; for the most part, the old Byzantine foundations that had been destroyed in raids or had been abandoned and consequently decayed, were restored or refounded. On Mount Athos, the original low marble iconostases contemporary with the katholika were either destroyed, or concealed by the later, skilfully executed *templa,* as at the Protaton and in the katholikon of Iveron. The earliest wood-carved *templa,* dating from the sixteenth century, are low, simple trabeated structures, carved in low relief, and are distinctly reminiscent of Byzantine carved marble iconostases. Most of them, however, date from the seventeenth and eighteenth centuries and are strongly influenced by a baroque style found in all the wooden carved *templa* in churches of the Ottoman period.[16] The famous *templon* in the monastery of the Panagia Kleisoura was gilded in 1772.[17] In 1799, the *templon* of the monastery of the Eikosiphoinissa on Mt. Pangaion was gilded, and the suberb, wooden carved *templon* of the katholikon of the Panagia Mavriotissa at Kastoria probably dates from this time.[18] Many such *templa* were very high and reached the wooden ceiling of the single-aisled wooden-roofed basilicas; occasionally, the cross with the mourning figures on either side is higher than the ceiling and a cupola is raised to accommodate it. The *templon* was often painted in bright colours; some were even gilded. The ceiling was decorated with panels and knots like the ceilings in the contemporary mansions. Together with the wall paintings and the other carved wooden furniture, such as the pulpit and the bishop's throne, they create a fantastic world of gold that stands in complete contrast to the poverty of the houses of the common people. This phenomenon is not fortuitous: inside the church, the enslaved Greeks lived in a world of imagined liberty and grandeur, and felt themselves free and proud, superior to their conquerors; their real rulers were the priests, bishops in their turn with their gold embroidered vestments; their real king was the Patriarch, far away in Constantinople, the successor to the Byzantine emperors whose memory still lived in their hearts, along with the legend of the 'marble king', the last defender of the Byzantine capital.

One fundamental piece of liturgical furniture in the katholika of the earlier monasteries was the *phiale*. The *phiale* of the Great Lavra is thought to be the earliest. It consists of a dome carried on columns, and a low circular wall of rectangular marble slabs like those which made up Early Christian and Byzantine iconostases. The cupola covers the basin with the jet of water used for the blessing of the waters on the eve of the Epiphany in accordance with the early customs practised in the similar open structures found in the Early Christian basilicas. The *phiale* of the Great Lavra in its present form is the result of later repairs, which the 'eastern' column capitals suggest may date from the beginning of the seventeenth century. The inscription on the paintings in the cupola bears the date 1635. The *phiale* was originally built in 1060. The two-sided parapet slabs come from this eleventh century *phiale* and are of great artistic interest. A number of the reliefs may even belong to an earlier period, the tenth century, and are imitations of yet earlier forms, such as the reliefs of Skripou or of Thebes in Boiotia.[19]

Phialai continued to be constructed at much later dates, and were often added to earlier Byzantine monasteries. They then became known by the Persian word *sindrivani* or *siatravani*. In 1770, the abbot Sophronios constructed the fine fountain in the courtyard of the Eikosiphoinissa on Mt. Pangaion.[20] In 1854, 'an elegant *siatravanion* was built in the middle of the courtyard outside the abbot's house' at the Prodromos monastery at Serres.[21] This fountain, still in excellent condition, was painted like that of the Great Lavra, and made a great impression on visitors.

The cells in the more recent monasteries are built around the periphery, as in Byzantine monasteries, and form the outer defence wall. Large openings were made in the outer faces of the earlier Byzantine defence walls and light wooden balconies, or porches, or even *sahnisi* were added, often one above the other, as in the monasteries of Dionysiou, Simonopetra and Chilandari on Mount Athos, and the Prodromos monastery at Serres.

The largest buildings are the guest-houses (*archontarikia*), the main link between monastic and urban architecture. They were usually the most recent additions to the monasteries. The guest-houses are invariably found near the sets of cells and next to the entrance, being the buildings in which guests, visitors and pilgrims were received. The building was designed to fulfill a variety of functions, and included reception rooms, a dining room, a kitchen, bedrooms that were very different from the cells, and bathrooms. Naturally enough, the wealthiest monasteries had the most richly decorated, and also the earliest reception rooms. From at least the beginning of the eighteenth century, the mode of construction and the interior lay-out were exactly the same as those in the reception rooms of the private mansions in Macedonia. The monks' quarters were not dissimilar, and frequently had rich decorations and murals, as at the *Synodikon* at the Prodromos monastery at Serres, which was renovated in 1795 at the expense 'of the Tsertsis family of Serres' and decorated by a 'certain wonderful painter Nedelkos'.[22] Frequently the *archontarikia* have rich decoration on the walls, on the friezes above the windows, and over the arches between the triple opening leading from the antechamber to the *ontas,* which are exactly like those in the contemporary mansions in Siatista and Ambelakia in Thessaly. The wall paintings in the *Synodikon* of the Prodromos monastery at Serres have framed scenes depicting imaginary country views, landscaped gardens, and the major European cities, such as Vienna, in which palaces, and the architecture in general were painted in perspective; they were clearly drawn from the engravings of the time, which were the source of inspiration of the humble peripatetic painters during the Ottoman period, who used their art to give the main rooms of the *archontika* and the monastery guest-houses the appearance of richly decorated baroque rooms in central European palaces.

The monasteries continued to function during the nineteenth century. The monastery of Saint Athanasios at Selitsa (Eratyra) was rebuilt after its destruction by the great fire of 1797.[23] The katholikon of the monastery of the Panagia near Vlachokleisoura, Kastoria, has inscriptions in the guest-house and the womens' gallery (gynaikonitis) recording the dates 1813 and 1818.[24] The monastery of Hagia Triada at Pisoderi, deep in a beech wood to the west of the village, was repaired in 1836.[25] An inscription above the entrance to the monastery of Hagia Triada in the village of Mesimeri informs us that it was built with financial contributions of the Grocers Guild of Edessa in 1853.[26] The katholikon of the monastery of the Archangel Michael, two kilometres north-west of the village of Archangelos near Moglena, was built in 1858; it is a three-aisled wooden-roofed basilica, with fine nineteenth century popular paintings.[27] In 1863, the monastery of Saint George Kryoneritis near Serres was restored at the expense of the people of Serres, prosperous at this period;[28] they also enriched the monastery with further donations.

New artistic centres began to emerge from the middle of the nineteenth century: at Hionades there was a famous school of hagiography; Tirnovo was renowned for its woodcarvers, and in all the villages of western Macedonia and Florina there were craftsmen, builders, carvers and carpenters who formed themselves into associations. They travelled all over the Balkan peninsula, from Wallachia to Mani, and from Epirus to Persia, erecting all kinds of structures: bridges, fountain houses, caravanserais, monasteries, mosques and mansions, which they adorned with paintings, anonymous craftsmen who were the inheritors of the long Byzantine artistic tradition.

TEXTILES AND EMBROIDERY

Embroideries in coloured thread and the ecclesiastical and secular embroideries in gold thread together constitute one of the main branches of folk art.[1] The embroideries fall into two categories: those designed to decorate the house, and those that formed part of the traditional costumes (mainly those worn by women). Only the latter give Macedonia any claim to rival other parts of Greece.

Of the embroideries designed to adorn the house, only the *tsevres* was found in Macedonia — particularly in eastern Macedonia. The *tsevres* is a narrow, rectangular length of material embroidered along the two shorter sides; it may also be a square kerchief embroidered either in the four corners or all around the edges. The rectangular *tsevres* was long enough to serve as a sash for the trousers, in which case it can be grouped with embroideries for folk costume. The *tsevres* might also be used to cover the gifts sent by the bride to the bridegroom, or might be tied in a bow and used to decorate the upper part of a mirror.

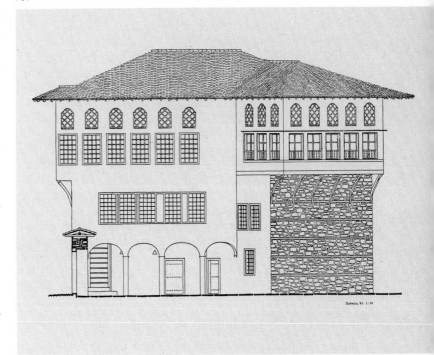

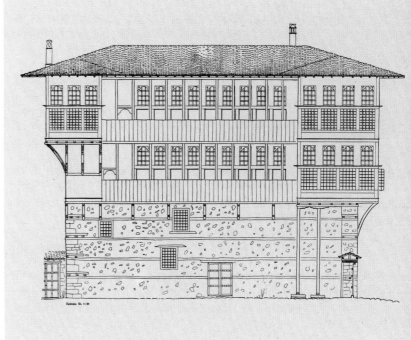

287. *Elevation of the Nantzis archontikon in Kastoria, erected around 1570 by Debrelis or Dobralis master builders. Like all the houses of this type in Kastoria, the ground and first floor were stone-built, while the second floor was constructed largely of wood.*

288. *Elevation of the Tsiatsapas archontikon in Kastoria. The plan of the building was a narrow rectangle whose most decorative facade faced an internal court. The master builders attached particular importance to the lighting of the interior and thus the facade was pierced by many small windows.*

A particular feature of the *tsevres* is its unusual embroidery, which is exactly the same on both sides of the cloth; designs include branches, flowers, pine-cones and a selection of other plant motifs.[2] Eastern influence is clear in many, but the Macedonian embroiderers succeeded in blending the eastern character with the Greek tradition.

The embroidery on the women's traditional costume in Macedonia is particularly interesting. The basic feature of the costume is the *poukamiso* (chemise), where most of the embroidery was concentrated on the visible parts of the costume — the lower edge, the cuffs and the collar. It is made of white cotton, and is usually embroidered with coloured silk or cotton threads. The embroidery on chemises varies considerably in different parts of Macedonia. That of Episkopi has closely embroidered motifs in bright colours and in an unusual decorative style. Chemises from Florina are simpler, and are embroidered either around the whole of the lower edge, or only along the seams joining the separate panels. The Sarakatsan costume, also interesting, has sleeves almost covered with complicated patterns embroidered in black or green.

The apron that forms part of the women's costume is purely decorative and exhibits astonishing variety, almost every part of Macedonia having a different design. The apron of the costume from Ventsia (Kozani) which has geometric motifs, is a good example. Those worn by the Sarakatsani are particularly distinctive: they may have dark colours or brilliantly coloured silk strings.

Gold embroideries may also be divided into two groups, the ecclesiastical and the secular.[3] During the Ottoman occupation, such embroideries, especially the ecclesiastical, were in great demand. After the fall of Thessalonike and Constantinople, the orthodox clergy, with the acquiescence of the Sublime Porte, exercised secular as well as ecclesiastical power over the Christian population, and had need of opulent vestments. There was thus no break in the work of the workshops in which the gold embroideries were produced. Though a fair number remained in the two major cities, many of the specialized embroiderers (*syrmakesis*) went to Moldavia and Wallachia.

In addition to the priest's vestments, all the churches and monasteries in Macedonia possessed a number of embroideries for liturgical purposes, in particular *epitaphioi*, the palls which covered Christ's bier in the Good Friday ceremonies. They were works of considerable artistic merit, produced in the workshops of Constantinople, Thessalonike and Mount Athos. A magnificent example of Macedonian work is the fourteenth century *epitaphios* in the Byzantine Museum in Athens. As early as the sixteenth century there was a guild of gold embroiderers in Thessalonike; Mount Athos also was not without some famous skilled workers, who habitually worked their names into their products. In Macedonia there were also men (*terzis*) who combined the skills of tailor and em-

289. The wooden panelling from the reception room (ontas) of a Kozani archontikon is work of the tagiadoroi (wood carvers) of Macedonia. It reflects the affluence of the region at the end of the 18th century, and shows the high standard reached. Athens, Benaki Museum.

broiderer. Unlike the embroiderers they were peripatetic, and mainly produced decorative secular embroideries, particularly in the urban centres of Macedonia.

MACEDONIAN COSTUME

Because of its incredible variety, Macedonian costume poses a number of problems for the scholar.[4] While some common elements can be discerned, the variations also give the impression that there were a number of parallel developments that owed much both to the Byzantine heritage and also to foreign influences.

Women's costumes from Macedonia, which are more interesting than the male attire, may be divided into two groups: those worn in the towns (Veria, Naousa, Kastoria and Siatista) and those from the villages (Asvestochori, Drymos, Lete, Episkopi and many others).

The town costumes were clearly influenced by European trends and were made of imported fabrics. Dresses were made of pure silk and fell in rich folds to the ankles. The overcoat, gold embroidered, could be either short or long; it was made by the *terzis* who were given food and lodging in the house while they were working. The costumes of Naousa and Veria are similarly gold embroidered around the collars, cuffs and occasionally the armholes.

The village costumes differed from area to area, and were a combination of woven cloth and coloured embroidery.[5] The costume typical of the five villages of Drymos has a woven chemise made of wool and cotton, or wool and silk. Over this was worn a sleeveless dress *(alatzas),* lightly embroidered on the breast, topped by a heavy cloth overcoat with decoration on the sleeves *(sayias).* A broad sash was twisted around the waist, with the apron tied above it. In winter, a heavy overcoat was worn with the thick pile inside. The earliest type of head-dress was a woven scarf tied at the back, the ends reaching the waist. It was held in place on the hair by the *sourgoutsi,* a piece of silver jewellery pinned in the right side of the head-dress and ending in separate metal strands. Its design was roughly the same in all five villages.

Asvestochori, a village a mere nine kilometres from Thessalonike, had its own costume, known as the *paizana.* It consisted of a vest with decorated sleeves over which was worn a white cotton bodice *(boustos).* Over these was a chemise with patterned sleeves and hem, and then the *sayias,* usually olive green, and embroidered in colour. A sash was tied around the waist and a woollen, embroidered apron worn in front. The head-dress is rather unusual: it consists of a low fez, over which is draped an embroidered cloth that hangs down the back *(piskeri).* Attached to the head-dress below the ears and visible below the chin were two rows of silver coins with holes in them, usually one- or

290-291. Left: the bridal costume of the Roumlouki villages near Gidas. Its dark colours give it a unique austerity. Right: peasant woman's costume from the Hass villages of Chalkidike. The peasant costume of Macedonia is made up of a combination of hand-woven material and embroidery, whereas the townspeople wore clothes in more recognizably European styles. Athens, Benaki Museum.

two- piastre pieces, strung on a fine cord. The head-dress was held in place by two large silver pins, and the familiar silver brooch was worn in the middle.

The costumes from the villages around Naousa have many important features in common, the best examples of them coming from Episkopi. The chemise is one of the most richly embroidered, depending on the age of the woman wearing it. Over this is worn the *kavaki,* a surcoat of silk or cotton, depending on the season. This is followed by a woollen or cotton overcoat, the sleeves of which are turned back to expose the red lining. A woollen woven sash is wound around the waist; the apron is covered with gold embroideries, like a bridal costume. The elegant head-dress differs according to the age of the wearer and is set on the head at an angle. It is a decorative element; in the case of newly married girls it is embroidered with gold.

The costume worn by the Sarakatsan women is predominantly dark, only rarely making use of bright colours.[6] As an undergarment, the Sarakatsan woman wore a vest with detachable sleeves, with dark coloured decoration in black, cherry-red or green. Covering the vest, she wore a chemise, which is normally short, but which in some parts of Macedonia reaches the ankles. She also wore a ruff which buttoned at the back. A sleeveless jacket was worn over the chemise, embroidered with silk threads (*gaitania*); it tucked into the pleated skirt, and appeared to be a dress. The sash around the waist was fastened with a silver buckle called the *asimazournaro.* The costume was completed by a kind of sleeveless overgarment, the *kondosi,* decorated with twisted threads in thin bands. The tiny apron is purely decorative, and is usually dark, though there are aprons in a striking red colour (*panagoules*). On her head, the Sarakatsan woman wore a kerchief fastened with a silver pin. Her feet were encased in the famous knitted woollen socks with geometric patterns in black and white, or occasionally in variety of colours. In addition to the *asimazournaro,* she wore a cross — a piece of jewellery worn on the chest and originally worn only by men.

A separate chapter could be devoted to the costume of Roumlouki, a group of villages around Gidas (now called Alexandria) near Veria. The distinctive costume worn by the women there is in some ways reminiscent of ancient breastplates, and is believed to have its own ancient antecedents; the head-dress (*katsouli*) in particular, is completely unparalleled in any other Macedonian costume. It resembles a helmet, and is the pride of Roumlouki. According to one tradition, Alexander the Great rewarded the women of this area for their bravery by taking the helmets away from the men and giving them to the women to wear.

The Roumlouki costume, not being over-burdened with many separate elements, gives the body a particularly elegant appearance. The most typical pieces of the costume are: the white cotton, or silk, blouse; the *anderi,* a black over-garment worn only by brides, which has turned back embroidered areas; an overcoat (*sayias*) of a style peculiar to Roumlouki. The costume is completed by the sash, embroidered with silver birds; detachable velvet sleeves; and, as already mentioned, the head-dress, the *katsouli.* The jewellery that adorns the costume is of silver and is quite intricate, especially the piece worn with the head-dress.

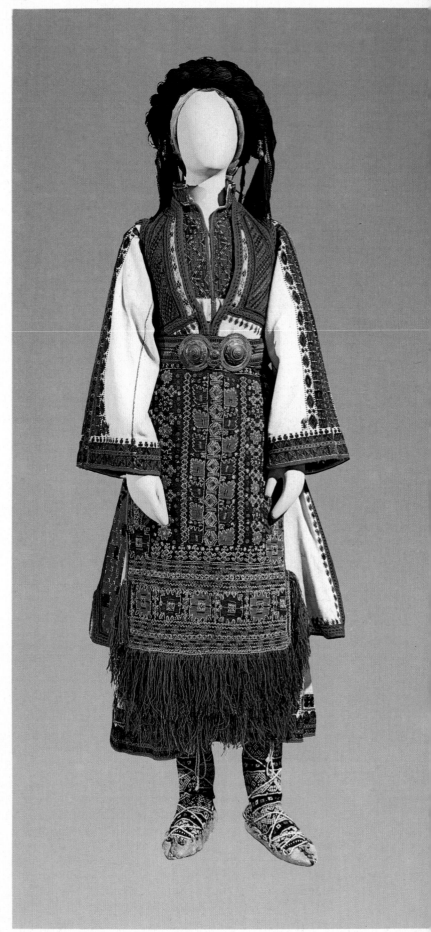

292-293. The gold-embroidered jacket and the buckle are the features of townswomen's costume in Macedonia which display the greatest variety in shape and patterns. The short gold-embroidered jacket above is from Kastoria and the buckle from Naousa. Both date to the late 19th century. Thessalonike, Folk-Life and Ethnological Museum.

SILVERWORK

Both ecclesiastical and secular silverwork are equally well represented in Macedonia. After the fall of the Byzantine empire, the silversmiths continued their creative work, and kept alive the ancient tradition of their art during the seventeenth and eighteenth centuries. The yield of silver from the mines of Mademochoria in Chalkidike was an important contributory factor to the development of the silversmith's art in Macedonia.

The silversmith's art developed throughout the entire Pindos area of western Macedonia,[7] and to an even greater

extent in Epirus. It was practised both in the workshops, which flourished during this period, and whose craftsmen (*kouyoumtzis*) were organized in guilds, and also by peripatetic individuals called silverworkers or sometimes goldworkers even though they did no work at all in gold.

Ecclesiastical silverwork maintained the Byzantine tradition, and included a number of objects that are zealously guarded in the sacristies of churches, and even more so, of monasteries. The range of liturgical plate widened to include crosses, chalices, patens, reliquaries, ornamented covers for the gospel books, and sheathed icons, so that ecclesiastical silverwork naturally flourished; in some respects it has baroque elements, inevitably so in view of the contacts with the West, mainly during the eighteenth century.

Copies of the gospels on whose bindings are examples of beaten or relief silver can be found in many Macedonian churches. The silver sheathing of the icons on many *templa* are also of interest: mention may be made of those in the church of Arnaia, Chalkidike. Ecclesiastical silverwork often bears the name of its maker; sometimes pieces are even dated. In contrast, however, despite the large demand for and the rich variety of secular silverwork, its workshops and the names of individual craftsmen remain completely unknown.

The comparative prosperity enjoyed by the Greeks of Macedonia in the eighteenth century encouraged a desire for display; the jewellers naturally took advantage of this and increased their output, especially in the nineteenth century. The jewellery produced was designed to match the many styles of costume, and was made in almost endless variety. Despite their relative prosperity, however, the Macedonian Greeks continued to feel basically insecure, and the demand for jewellery also stemmed from the desire to acquire goods that were easily carried and could easily be converted into cash. This explains why gold coins hung from many pieces of jewellery as a decorative feature — either the well-known *konstantinata,* or even foreign coins.

The silver used was not always pure. The poorer classes, who were anxious not to fall behind in ostentation, bought jewellery with a low silver content. To produce a shine, the surface was treated with arsenic from which the jewellery was called poisoned (*pharmakera*).

The jewellery of this period includes silver buckles, chains with silver disks (*kioustekia*), *giortania,* earrings, bracelets etc. Last but not least, small disks of gilded silver worn on top of the red fez (*tepelik*) should be mentioned. Brooches, or clasps, were made in an impressive variety of shapes and designs. It is not always easy to determine what brooch was intended to be worn with any particular costume, for the movement of populations from one area to another resulted in changes in the pure form of the local costume, at least as far as the jewellery is concerned.

An important centre of silverwork in Macedonia was Neveska (modern Nymphaion), a Vlach village in the region of Eordaia. Tradition puts the foundation of the village in the fourteenth century; the peak of its prosperity was reached, however, in the seventeenth century, when Vlachs from Nikolitsa settled there. Goldsmiths from Neveska were to be found all over Macedonia. The early craftsmen did not establish workshops there, but set out from their own village with their tool-box, stopped wherever they could find employment, and returned on 15 August. Their peripatetic trade ceased at the beginning of the twentieth century. Present day Nymphaion follows the long tradition of jewellery making that can be traced from the eighteenth century to the beginning of the twentieth, and even today older goldsmiths, skilled practitioners of their art, work in Thessalonike, adapting their skills to the demands of a new era.

METALWORK

Metalworking appears to have developed considerably in the smaller towns of Macedonia in the eighteenth century. The craftsmen worked their material with great skill and devotion, and we can still admire the elegant door-knockers, locks and keys, knives, scissors for a variety of uses, and even cutlasses with engraved inscriptions and dates. There were skilled metalworkers throughout the Balkans, but foreign travellers, such as the Frenchman Ami Boué, who visited Macedonia at the beginning of the nineteenth century, give pride of place in every form of art to the Greek craftsmen.

Though metalworking flourished almost everywhere, Thessalonike was undoubtedly the main centre of copper working. An arcade devoted entirely to copperware is known to have existed; it is first recorded in an anonymous tenth century account of the *Miracles of Saint Demetrios*. One authority, Xyngopoulos, maintains that this arcade was in the area where the church known as the Panagia *Chalkeon* was built in the eleventh century. When it was converted into a mosque by the Turks, it was called the *'kazantilar tzamisi'*, which was rendered in Greek as Panagia *ton Chalkeon*. During the Ottoman period, hundreds of coppersmiths worked in its shadow, as the famous cauldron shops (*kazantzidika*) still do today.

There were, however, other towns in Macedonia that also had important copper workshops. Most of the copper objects have Turkish names, and the eastern influence in their design is quite clear; this is hardly unexpected, since the main customers of the smiths were Turks who, like the Greeks, had a particular weakness for copper. Even today, Turkish names in a slightly grecized form (for example *kazani, mangali*) are quite common. Their styles have not changed with the passage of time. Many of the copper objects are dated and bear the name or the initials of the owner. The decoration on them is often of a very high artistic order. The broad surfaces of the *sini* (a kind of tray), in particular,[8] lent themselves to compositions involving decorative motifs arranged in a circle or radially, usually round a central decorative star or rosette. One of the most common motifs treated in a variety of ways is the cypress, symbol of immortality.

CERAMICS AND POTTERY

Macedonian ceramics should perhaps be divided into two periods, before and after 1922; indeed amongst the refugees from Asia Minor who settled in Macedonia after

294. *In Thessalonike especially, but also in other market towns and even villages in Macedonia metal products were in great demand and the craft widely practised from the 17th century onwards. The picture shows a 19th century brass portable stove (mangali) from Thessalonike, made in three separate parts. Thessalonike, Folk-Life and Ethnological Museum.*

this date there were potters who brought new life to the local workshops.

Before 1922, pottery workshops produced undistinguished work and lacked any distinctive technique. There were several workshops in Thessalonike, Florina and Kozani, but large quantities of earthenware vessels were also brought in from the islands by boat. Every house required a large number of containers for water, wine, cooking and *kryologoi* (porous jugs kept in streams to keep the water cool), as well as storage jars for oil, beans, peas and so on. Every market place and wandering salesman had these wares on offer; they were vital equipment, es-

295. A 19th century wooden chest from Monastir. Such chests, many of them beautifully carved, were common throughout *Macedonia, and were an important item in the bride's dowry. (Private collection of M. Taliadoros).*

pecially the pitcher, for the springs, fountains and wells were not always close to the house.

The potters who came with the refugees from Asia Minor made their homes wherever they could find the right material for their art or craft:[9] in Florina, in Thessalonike (there was good red clay at Diavata) and in Nea Karvali near Kavala. There were two or three workshops on Thasos, but these were run by potters from Siphnos. Skilled potters from the Dardanelles settled in Florina, but their distinctive, brightly coloured wares, with their wide variety of decoration, did not suit local tastes, and they did not prosper. The old pottery from the Dardanelles is nowadays much sought after. The most famous and gifted craftsman from Asia Minor was Minas Avramidis from Kütahya. He initially lived in Florina, but moved to Thessalonike after three years. The unrivalled examples of decorative ceramic art he produced can now be found in the Kyriazopoulos Museum in Monastiraki, Athens, in the Folklore Museum of the University of Thessalonike, and in a number of private collections. He drew his subject matter from Greek mythology, from the plant and animal kingdoms. from the sea and from boats. from religious iconography, and indeed from anything that could be adapted to the shape of the object he wanted to decorate. In addition to his pottery, Avramidis produced a number of earthenware stoves decorated with plant motifs.

WOOD CARVING

Macedonian wood carving, whether represented by works produced to satisfy ecclesiastical or secular needs, or objects produced by shepherds, is always outstanding.

The most striking examples of ecclesiastical wood carving are the *templa* that adorn all the churches and monasteries in Macedonia, which were executed throughout the Ottoman period, from the sixteenth to the eighteenth centuries. The *templon* in the church of Saint Nicholas at Velvendos, near Kozani, was carved in 1591. It is a typical example of post-Byzantine wood carving, which with plant motifs carved in low relief, is a continuation of the late Byzantine tradition.

The hundreds of carved *templa* preserved from the seventeenth, eighteenth and nineteenth centuries show that, with the passage of time, styles were affected by foreign influences, though the traditional elements were not entirely forgotten.[10] Schematized birds and even human figures were added to the decorative repertoire, executed in ever higher relief, and eventually reaching the point where the wood between the motifs was removed entirely, so that the *templon* appears as a pierced barrier.

The best known examples of *templa* in Macedonia include the one in the church of Saint Nicholas in Kozani, dating to the end of the eighteenth century; that in Blatsi which was brought from Moschopolis in 1769; and that in the church of Saint Nicholas Dragotas at Kastoria, dating to the seventeenth century. The *templon* of the church of the Nea Panagia in Thessalonike is another a good example dating from the eighteenth century; the later additions are a combination of low relief and pierced decoration. Of particular interest are the three sanctuary gates which correspond to three churches under the same roof.

Other carved wooden liturgical furniture, such as the pulpit and the bishop's throne, was executed in a similar technique. The pulpit of the church of Hagia Paraskeve in Siatista, dated to the eighteenth century, is a good example.

There is a great wealth of wood carving in the towns of Macedonia, including both carved architectural features, such as doors, ceilings, cupboards and so on, and portable items such as chests, trunks and cribs. The *archontika* of Macedonia, which are unrivalled in Greece, contain some masterpieces of the woodcarver's art, made by skilled craftsmen called *tagiadoroi*, those who worked in wood, who cooperated closely with the guild of *kodaraioi*, the men who constructed the stone parts of the house.

Of the carvings that formed an integral part of the house, the doors, in particular to the reception room, were made of small square or rectangular panels, placed with strict symmetry and carved with a variety of decorative plant motifs. A lintel was often added above the door frame, as at the sanctuary entrance in a church.

The ceiling always had a wood carving in the centre (the *tablas* or, more rarely, pseudo-cupola); it was usually octagonal in shape, more rarely circular, and frequently painted with coloured flowers. It usually showed signs of eastern influence.

Of the furniture in the Macedonian house (and not only the *archontika*) the most interesting, as well as the most essential item was the chest, *kasela*.[11] This was listed in the marriage contract as the most important item of the dowry, for in it, the bride kept her dowry and any valuables she might have. The most common form of chest in northern Greece is the 'Macedonian' type, which is also found as far away as northern Yugoslavia and especially on the Adriatic coast. These chests are made from a dark coloured chestnut, with triangular inlays of mother of pearl, imported from abroad. The usual decoration consists of two or three rosettes, separating flowers, churches or monasteries.

From the beginning and until the end of the nineteenth century, there were countless painted chests in northern Greece, most of them rather small and decorated with cypresses and bouquets of flowers. All of them have the same shape and use the same colours, suggesting that they have a common origin or tradition.

The cribs or cradles were carved on the sides, and also on the support for the mosquito net.

Macedonian houses did not usually have chairs. For seats, the occupants used the *menteria,* a chest, or simply cushions on the floor.

The objects carved by the shepherd to while away his solitary hours, have perhaps not yet received sufficient serious study. He whittled the wood with a pen-knife to make a decorated distaff,[12] the bridegroom's present to his bride, or an engraved whorl for his wife's spindle.

The best craftsmen in this field were the Sarakatsani. The distaff carved by them invariably had a snake as its chief decorative motif and magical symbol; it becomes a curling tendril around the edges of the flat part of the distaff, creating a net around the moon — another magical property of the distaff, which, together with the cross, brings the psychological world of the Sarakatsani into harmony. Contrasting with the distaff, the spindle whorl had predominantly geometric motifs — zig-zag and dentil patterns, oblique lines, incisions and triangles. Plant decoration is subordinate to the geometrical style. Naturalistic features occur more rarely.

THE FUR INDUSTRY

The processing of furs cannot strictly speaking be considered folk art. It nevertheless deserves a special mention here because of its importance in Macedonia. The main processing centres are Kastoria and Siatista.

The technique of Kastorian fur, as it is called, involves using small pieces of fur left over from foreign workshops that produce fur coats from entire pelts. These remnants, small and useless, are bought by the people of Kastoria, transported to their own workshops and stitched together so cleverly that it is difficult to tell the resulting product from one made out of a single piece.

A large number of workshops in Kastoria achieved a high level of specialization. Various conjectures have been made as to the origins of the skill. It is said that in the Byzantine period, the officials who fell into disfavour were exiled to Kastoria, and gave their furs to the local craftsmen to be repaired, and that the latter became very adept as time went on. There is one piece of specific evidence, however: in 1520 in Kastoria there were seven hundred artisans, many of whom were furriers; the origins of fur processing must therefore be put much earlier.

The pieces of fur imported on special terms to the two Macedonian towns were small and of different colours, and formed the raw material (*hordas*). The pieces are cleaned and placed on a table (*teziahi*). They are separated according to quality, pile and colour. Next, all the pieces are placed on paper preparatory to joining. This is the most difficult part of the process, requiring considerable experience and aesthetic sensitivity to stitch together the selected pieces into one large strip, to which other strips similarly composed can be joined to form the larger pieces from which the famous furs are produced.

Fur processing began at a later date at Siatista, when the vines in the area were destroyed by phylloxera; the new industry rescued the population from economic disaster.[13]

FROM THE GREEK WAR
OF INDEPENDENCE TO LIBERATION
1821-1912

MACEDONIA IN THE GREEK WAR OF INDEPENDENCE

THE REVOLT IN CHALKIDIKE

A number of important changes took place in the economic and social structure of Greece, both in the course of the military embroilments examined in previous chapters and during the Napoleonic wars, that affected Macedonia as well as other regions. Trade, in which the Greeks were outstandingly successful, was a major contributary factor to these changes.

In all the major towns a small Greek bourgeois class began to emerge which, affected as it was by the principles of the French Revolution, dreamed of the liberation of the Greek people; the poems of Rhigas Pheraios contributed to this process. Greek merchants were made *baratarioi* not only through the consuls of the European states, but directly through the sultan's secretariate. Greeks also secured positions as consuls of foreign countries, notably of Russia, and became the bearers of patriotic movements. In 1819, the Russian consuls in Thessalonike and Serres, who were Greeks by descent, were admitted into the *Philike Etaireia*. The full ramifications of the *Etaireia's* network in Macedonia cannot be known. Given that it included many of the higher ranking clergy, who exercised authority and influence over the people, amongst them Chrysanthos, the metropolitan bishop of Serres, Benjamin of Kozani and Ignatios, the bishop of Ardameri, we may conclude that the ideas of the *Etaireia* had been very widely disseminated.

According to John Philemon, Demetrios Ipatros, a member of the *Etaireia,* visited Thessalonike in December 1820, where he became acquainted with a number of people, including Christodoulos Balanos, one of the notables 'to whom he bore letters from Emanuel Papas in Constantinople'. Amongst the first members of the *Etaireia* were

the chieftains Georgakis Olympios from Livadi on Olympos, John Farmakis from the township of Blatsi in western Macedonia, Anastasios Karatasos from the village of Dovra near Veria, and Angelos Gatsos from the village of Sarakini near Edessa.

The oral tradition preserves the names of a large number of members of the *Etaireia* who will undoubtedly have been initiated by Ipatros or other members. The result was that, long before the first outbreak of hostilities, the Macedonians had been gripped by revolutionary fervour, and the leading figures in the cities had begun to plan for revolt, though their movements soon came to the notice of the Ottoman authorities.[1]

Shortly after the beginning of the revolt in Moldavia and Wallachia, Alexander Ipsilantis himself wrote to the Russian emperor, representing the uprising as widespread throughout the whole of the Balkan peninsula and the islands, and stating, among other things, that: 'The Peloponnese and the Aegean are on the move, Crete is rising, Serbia, Bulgaria, Thrace and Macedonia are rushing to arms...'[2]

Much of the intelligence communicated by Ipsilantis was premature, of course, though it was consistent with the Plan of the *Etaireia* concerning those areas in which preparations had been made and which had pledged their support for the Revolt.

The first reports of the events in Wallachia and Moldavia, however, had the effect of spreading revolutionary fervour, particularly in Thessalonike and Chalkidike; the main centre in the latter area was the monastic community on Mount Athos, which Emanuel Papas (1772-1821), a banker and merchant from Serres, had reached at the end of March, bringing military supplies from Constantinople on the orders of Alexander Ipsilantis. Although Mount Athos formed a superb natural base of operations, it was not a suitable bridgehead for spreading the revolt: apart from a few who had been admitted into the *Philike Etaireia,* the roughly three thousand monks were ideologically opposed to revolutionary theories.

438

Papas attempted to organize the revolt on Mount Athos. He sought the cooperation and economic support of the monasteries, and at the same time requested the despatch of armed boats from Psara to repel any attempted landings by the Turks.

Serres was also astir with revolutionary activity, the leading figure being the metropolitan bishop Chrysanthos. In the end the notables and the populace did not take action, since they had meanwhile been informed of the hanging of the patriarch Gregory V. Their passive stance did not protect them from the wrath of the Turks, however, who, on learning of the landing of the boats from Psara at Tsayezi, systematically sacked Greek shops and imprisoned Greek traders and even the metropolitan himself.

There was a similar atmosphere of terrorism in the other cities, particularly in Thessalonike where the governor, Yusuf Bey, took hostages from the Greek community to guarantee its passivity; at the same time he despatched forces to the isthmus separating the peninsula of Mount Athos from the mainland. Hostilities began when the Greek youths of Polygyros rose on 17 March and attacked the administrative building in the township, annihilating the military detachment there. From Polygyros the revolt spread throughout Chalkidike and to the villages of Langadas.[3]

A fierce reign of terror was unleashed in Thessalonike on the very next day: half the hostages were executed, and this was followed by the mass slaughter of Greek citizens in the cathedral and the market area. These measures by the Ottomans provoked an even greater reaction on the part of the Greeks. The revolution was proclaimed at the Protaton, Karyes with a celebratory service at the end of May.[4] The fervour of the insurgents was fanned by the, largely false, rumours of triumphant victories won by Alexander Ipsilantis in Wallachia and Moldavia. The revolt subsequently spread to Thasos where boats from Psara roused the inhabitants to arms, with the 'President' of the island, Hadjigiorgis, and the archimandrite Kallinikos Stamatiadis at their head.[5]

Meanwhile, the insurrection in Chalkidike was assuming greater dimensions. The Greeks were unorganized, however, and poorly armed, most of them fighting with wooden clubs. They themselves were aware of their weakness, for on 9 January they wrote to Papas: 'Send us one of your men to take command of the army, for we are in a state of utmost disorder'.

Two of the revolutionary bands that were formed were particularly effective, the first led by Papas and the second by Khapsas. The former advanced to Ierissos and thence moved towards the pass of Rentina and to Egri Budjak in order to confront Hadji Mehmed Bayram Pasha, who was heading with his forces from eastern Macedonia to southern Greece. The ill-organized bands of insurgents disintegrated at the first attack of the Pasha's men and fled to Kassandra or to the boats from Psara that were patrolling nearby. Bayram Pasha continued his way south, bloodily suppressing the revolt in the villages of Langadas.

The insurgents proceeded to form new fronts at the isthmus of Mount Athos and that of Kassandra, where the weight of the Ottoman attack was concentrated; Papas

296. *Sketch of Emanuel Papas from Serres, by the sculptor K. Palaiologos. Papas was a member of the Philike Etaireia and one of the instigators of revolt against the Turks in Chalkidike which broke out in May 1821. Athens, National Historical Museum.*

himself was present, reinforced by a band of warriors from Olympos. Despite all the Greek successes during the course of the summer, however, the situation in the insurgents' camp began to deteriorate as a result of the lack of ammunition and victuals, the unwillingness of the monks to continue the struggle, and the discontent of the warriors from Olympos, most of whom eventually left the peninsula. Papas then attempted to create a diversion for the Turks by rousing the men of Olympos to revolt; he also requested reinforcements from the Peloponnese. The situation in the camp at Kassandra grew worse after September when large numbers of enemy forces gathered there under the command of the competent and energetic new Pasha of Thessalonike, Mehmed Emin (dubbed the 'club-bearer' on account of his cruelty). The pasha failed in his first attack, thereby raising the morale of the Greeks; on 30 October, however, he unleashed a general offensive and his troops poured unchecked into the peninsula, pillaging and murdering. Many Greek families took refuge in the northern Sporades, from where some of them dispersed to southern Greece.

The fall of Kassandra decided the fate of the revolt in Chalkidike: Sithonia, Mount Athos and Thasos surrendered on terms. Papas fled by boat to Hydra, but never arrived there, dying *en route* of a heart attack. Mehmed Emin ordered the women and children to withdraw from Mount Athos (the prohibition of females on the peninsula had been violated for the first time) and return to their villages; he then placed garrisons in the monasteries and inflicted a very severe fine on the monastic community. The monks continued to be subjected to various acts of repression until 1830, when the Ottoman garrison withdrew.[6]

THE REVOLT IN OLYMPOS, PIERIA AND VERMION 1822

After his return to Thessalonike, Mehmed Emin turned to the defence of the Thermaic Gulf. At the same time, however, he had to deal with the insurrectionary movements in the areas of Vermion, Pieria and Olympos, where the *klepht-armatoles* Karatasos, Gatsos and Diamantis, together with Zafeirakis Logothetis, a notable from Naousa, had entered into negotiations with the notables of many of the other cities. At the beginning of January, 1822, they met together at the monastery at Dovra and decided to act, using as their main bases of operation the mountain spurs near Naousa, Kastania near Kolindros, and Siatista. In February N. Kasomoulis, who was acting as their joint representative, returned from southern Greece with two boats from Psara and a small quantity of ammunition. A few days later, at the beginning of March, two more boats from Psara arrived, bringing Gregory Salas, who had been appointed commander in chief of the campaign in Macedonia, and a few German artillerymen; with them was the famous scholar and monk, Theophilos Kairis.

Meanwhile, Mehmed Emin sent written orders to the *kadi* of Veria, instructing him to arm the Turks and disarm the Greeks in the area, and to arrest the notables as hostages. He also demanded hostages from other towns and townships. Naousa refused to comply and Mehmed Emin began to advance his forces swiftly and in secrecy in the direction of Pieria, Olympos and Vermion, thereby thwarting a surprise attack by the insurgents on 8 March against Kolindros in the foothills of Pieria. The insurgents on Olympos were also obliged to retreat, and the men who had assembled before Kolindros withdrew to Kastania and thence to Milia. Diamantis alone was prepared to make a defensive stand at Kastania, but he was defeated and his men retreated in disorder to Milia, where they were attacked on Easter Sunday by the Turks and dispersed. Diamantis headed for Naousa to join up with Karatasos and Gatsos, who were already facing Mehmed Emin, while Salas, Kanousis and some of the other leaders succeeded after an exhausting march lasting several days in reaching free soil — the *armatolik* of Nicholas Stornaris at Aspropotamos.[7]

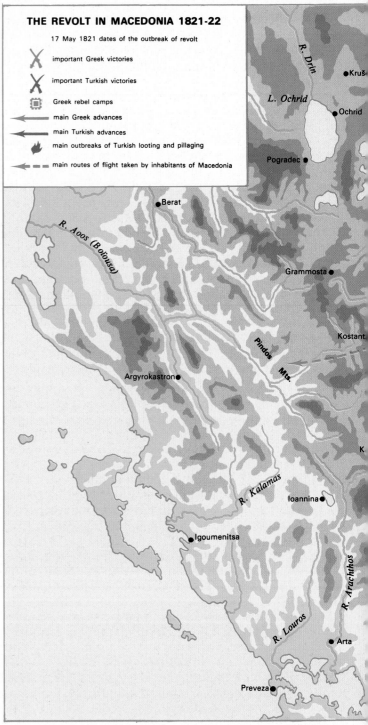

297. *A revolt against the Turks which broke out in Chalkidike in May 1821 soon degenerated into a blood-bath. The Greeks could not sustain a coordinated effort since they lacked experienced fighters and a military organization. The Turks on the*

While all this was taking place on Olympos, significant events were being enacted at Naousa where Zafeirakis Logothetis had proclaimed the revolt as early as 19 or 22 February. A four-man committee was immediately elected under the presidency of Zafeirakis to ensure that the struggle was conducted as effectively as possible, and Karatasos was proclaimed military commander of all the

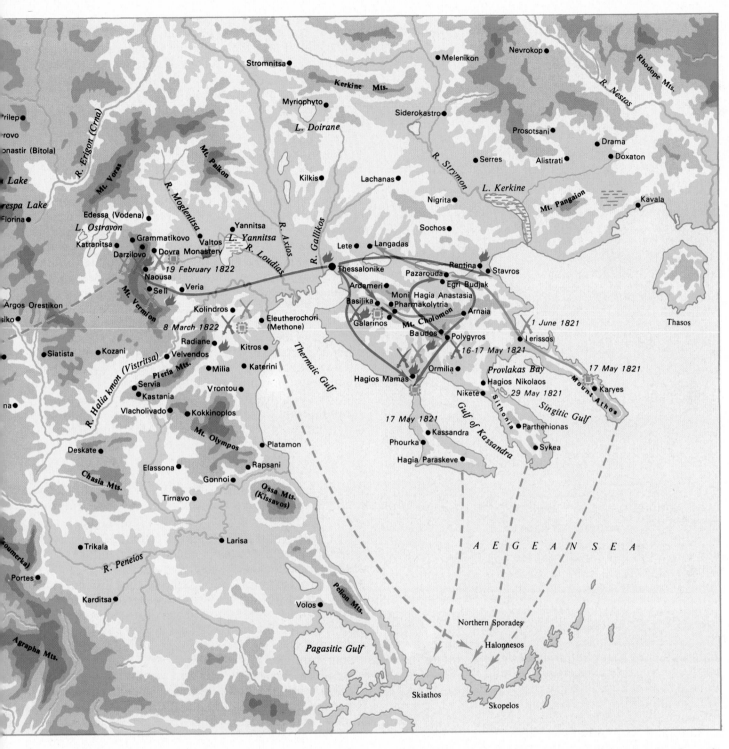

other hand could draw on the large forces of a regular army at Thessalonike. They plundered and destroyed on a large scale to reimpose their authority. Insurgents around Mounts Olympos and Vermion in central and southern Macedonia fared no better early in 1822; the worst episode was perhaps the slaughter of a large part of the population of Naousa in April. Many people subsequently fled to the northern Sporades while others continued the struggle for freedom in southern Greece.

forces in the area, which totalled 4,500-5,000 men. Immediately afterwards the insurgents, under Karatasos, Gatsos, Zafeirakis and other leaders, occupied a number of key positions around the town, chief amongst them the monastery at Dovra, where they recorded a victory against the Turks. Eventually, however, the arrival of fresh Ottoman reinforcements compelled them to fall back gradually on the town, before which Mehmed Emin himself had appeared with 20,000 men, including both regulars and irregulars. Ottoman proposals for the surrender of the town were rejected and shortly afterwards they began to bombard it, simultaneously launching a series of attacks at different points of the town walls. The Ottoman forces finally entered the town on the night of 12-13 April, after

298. *Nicholas Kasomoulis who played an active part in the revolt in Chalkidike and then in southern Greece. He also wrote 'Military Memoirs' from which the picture is taken.*

fierce street battles with the Greeks. The insurgents attempted to break through the encircling Ottoman forces and escape into the countryside. Diamantis escaped to the northern Sporades, and Karatasos and Gatsos to Aspropotamos. Some of them remained behind in the area and Zafeirakis was executed by the Turks. Tragic scenes ensued in Naousa where thirteen young girls flung themselves over the Arapitsa waterfall to avoid dishonour.

Mehmed Emin wrote to the *kadi* of Veria on 21 April, 1822, informing him of the results of his campaign at Naousa: 'When we entered the aforementioned city in triumph, having made ourselves masters of it, their *kapetanioi,* availing themselves of the darkness of night, made good their escape to the mountains nearby.... but as many of the aforementioned insurgents as did not succeed in escaping, but hid themselves in the city, were captured, and the instructions of the sacred order were carried out against them strictly and without mercy. They exceeded two thousand in number and all were put to death, either knifed in the mouth or being despatched to hell by hanging; their wives and children were sold as slaves and their

property confiscated and put to the torch. The victory was thus complete and the wishes of the sultan carried out to the letter.'[8] There was similar slaughter and plundering in the areas around Naousa, and this intensified the fear and terror of the inhabitants of Thessalonike. upon whom Mehmed Emin inflicted new financial demands on the pretext of carrying out defensive works in the Gulf of Thessalonike.

The failure of the revolt on Olympos and Vermion put an end to all attempts or thoughts of spreading it to western Macedonia, and in particular to the towns of Kozani and Siatista, where refugees from the surrounding areas had sought shelter. This had roused the anger of Mehmed Emin but the danger of an Ottoman attack was avoided thanks to the mediation of the notables and the powerful local beys, who also provided him with substantial sums of money. These towns nevertheless suffered terrible hardships, as did Kastoria, during the decade from 1821-30: they stood in the path of the forces making their way to southern Greece and were obliged to provide food and lodging for the irregular soldiers as they passed, and to suffer the attendant acts of oppression and violence.

The insurrection in Macedonia was a national liberation movement of universal appeal. All sections of society took part in it alongside the local chieftains and *klepht-armatoles*: the notables, the farmers, the clergy and the merchants, and even Slav- and Albanian-speakers. In assessing the contribution it made to the national struggle, we may note that the revolt in Chalkidike was a serious distraction for the Turks and delayed the advance of Bayram Pasha to southern Greece. The flame of revolt not only spread to Thessalonike itself, but also helped to arouse European public opinion against the Turks.

The causes of the failure of the revolt in Chalkidike are to be attributed not to the inhabitants, who displayed great courage and fought fiercely, but rather to the lack of proper preparation and organization. In particular, there was a lack of military leaders experienced in the tactics of irregular warfare. Even if such leaders had existed, however, it would still have been difficult to protract the resistance, since the Ottomans were operating from a large supply base nearby, in Thessalonike. Moreover, central Macedonia, and especially the areas around Hagios Vasileios and lake Volvi, and near Yannitsa, was densely populated with Yürüks. Finally, the decisive factor was the circumstance that the uprising in Chalkidike was not coordinated with the revolt in Olympos, Pieria and Vermion, which broke out some months later. This latter uprising, however, created a much greater distraction for the Turks and pinned down sizeable Ottoman forces in the area for many months, thereby relieving considerably the pressure on the Greeks of the south, who would otherwise have had to withstand large-scale concerted enemy offensives.

Over and above the economic consequences, the revolt had a serious effect on the demographic composition of Macedonia, mainly in the regions in which the revolutionary movements had taken place; the numerical strength of the Greek element in the population was weakened not only by the fact that many of them were killed or sold into slavery, but also by the migration of entire groups. Their places were taken by Muslim or Slav peasants and by Jews, who were mostly attracted to the commercial centres, and particularly to Thessalonike.[9]

THE WITHDRAWAL OF THE MACEDONIAN WARRIORS TO SOUTHERN GREECE AND THEIR ROLE IN THE NATIONAL STRUGGLE

The suppression of the revolt in Macedonia created three waves of departure for southern Greece: one from the coasts of Chalkidike to the northern Sporades and thence to the mainland and the other islands; a second from the coast near Olympos, also to the northern Sporades; and a third smaller wave from the mountains towards Pindos. In time, most of the inhabitants of Chalkidike returned home and began to cultivate their farms once more, but the warriors from Olympos took an active part in the national struggle for liberation in the Aegean and in southern Greece. Some of them formed the kernel of the first regular army, while the majority operated as irregulars under the most famous of the chieftains from Olympos, who played a distinguished role in the great battles of the liberation struggle. A band of men from Olympos put up a particularly memorable resistance at Psara (June 1824) and also at Mesolongi, where they formed the 'immortal garrison' alongside other men from Roumeli.

The Macedonians who had assembled in the northern Sporades were also very active at sea. From time to time they attacked the coasts of Thasos, Chalkidike and the Thermaic Gulf in their ships, creating panic amongst the Turks, who had to be continuously on the alert to follow their movements.

Later, as liberation approached, the Macedonian refugees and warriors asked to be represented in the Greek national assembly, in order to claim the same rights as their compatriots, and also to assist towards the liberation of Macedonia. The men from Olympos, however, had become a source of disorder in the Aegean, and were losing face before the admirals of the Great Powers. Immediately after his arrival in Greece, the governor, John Kapodistrias attempted to put down piracy and assigned to admiral Miaoulis the task of clearing out this particular centre of it. Miaoulis attacked Skopelos, but the men from Olympos offered no resistance and surrendered their boats. They were then transferred to Eleusis and incorporated into the Greek army. After the liberation of Greece, the Macedonian refugees asked to be allowed to settle in the new state. They contacted Constantine Bellios, a wealthy Greek emigré from Blatsi, who organized the collection of funds and raised the necessary capital to establish a settlement named Nea Pella near Atalanti on the northern borders of the new state; here they made their homes, dreaming like their compatriots in Macedonia of the liberation of their homeland.[10]

THE SUFFERINGS OF THE INHABITANTS OF MACEDONIA DURING THE GREEK WAR OF INDEPENDENCE

Even after the revolt, the inhabitants of western Macedonia continued to suffer at the hands of irregular

299. *Anastasios Karatasos, an armatole of Vermion renowned for his unsurpassed courage, cooperated with others to organize the revolt in Naousa.*

Albanian troops, most of them bands of brigands who did not hesitate to attack the towns and townships, especially the richer of them. They also had to suffer many other hardships: they were burdened with exactions in money and kind, and some of them were conscripted for the war against the Greeks (obviously as labourers rather than fighters). These oppressive measures drove some villagers, such as those in the area of Florina, to move their homes. The atrocities continued in Macedonia after the fall of Mesolongi. In their attempts to escape, the inhabitants took refuge in the forests, where many of them perished of starvation and other hardships. During this period, and possibly even after the end of the revolt, many Koutsovlach families and other Greeks, Slavs and Albanians abandoned their homes and moved north to what is now Yugoslavia.

Meanwhile the Muslim-Albanian irregulars had become restless, even in Thessalonike, the headquarters of the Pasha, asserting that the Turks owed them their wages from as early as the time they had first come to southern Greece to quash the revolt. In 1827 Siatista was attacked by a band intent on plunder, led by the Albanian chieftains Tafil Bouzis and Arslan bey, but the inhabitants entrenched themselves in their strongly defended houses and succeeded in beating them off. The inhabitants of Thessalonike and Macedonia suffered further depredations on the outbreak of the Russo-Turkish war in 1828-29. Arslan bey and other Albanian chieftains continued to commit atrocities: on 1 May, 1830, they captured Kozani and indulged in an orgy of violence and pillaging lasting almost a month, the inhabitants having hastily abandoned their town. Arslan bey then turned once more against Siatista, but was repulsed for a second time by the residents. One of the cities to suffer from the repressive activities of the Muslim-Albanian troops was Kastoria. Tradition had preserved the memory of the acts of oppression and the financial exactions of Skodra Pasha, not only in the area of Kastoria but also at Monastir and Prilep.

A similar state of affairs prevailed in eastern Macedonia. In 1829, Albanian rebels and brigands led by Saban Gika, or Geka, plundered the *kazas* of Kilkis, Stromnitsa, Petric and Siderokastron, until they were compelled by the Ottomans to withdraw to the Thessalonike area. After the cessation of the Russo-Turkish war Mehmed Reshid Pasha (also known as Kioutakhis) hastened to Monastir to deal with the critical situation: lacking supplies of both money and munitions, he received substantial economic aid from the Greek merchants of Monastir, who had suffered repeatedly from the Albanian raids. In the middle of the following year, 1830, Mehmed Reshid set a trap for three of the Albanian leaders, amongst them Arslan bey, using as bait the supposed payment of wages owed to them, and annihilated them along with all their men, apart from a few who succeeded in making their escape. Mehmed deployed the same tactic against three more Albanian leaders from Ioannina, but they distrusted him and did not appear at Monastir along with the others.

Meanwhile the Ottomans were actively engaged in attempting to destroy the power of the *klepht-armatoles*, who were trying to incite a second uprising on Olympos and to incorporate their own region within the newly created Greek state, aided by Kapodistrias and the Great Powers. Kapodistrias, however, was distracted by the enormous problems he faced in the devastated liberated state, and the question of the Thessalians and the Macedonians remained unsolved. Meanwhile the Turks attempted to wipe out every centre of revolt, relentlessly pursuing the *kapetanioi* of Olympos and firing the villages of the area. In the end, the *kapetanioi*, disillusioned with the response both from Demetrios Ipsilantis, the commander in chief, in November 1828, and from Kapodistrias, in July 1829, were obliged to admit defeat for the time being and restore normal relations with the Turks, in order to secure their *armatoliks*.

Having destroyed the Muslim-Albanians, the Turks now considered the time ripe to rid themselves once and for all of the Greek *armatoles*. The *armatoles* of Chasia, Ziakas, Mandalos and the Pseiraioi took refuge in the Greek state: so did those from Olympos after the mediation of the Russian consul Angelos Moustoxydis. The situation in the regions of Olympos and Veria remained peaceful, however.

Some of the former *armatoles* were restored to their positions on condition that they indicated their willingness to cooperate with the Turks. We learn, for example, from a document of 16 August, 1834, that Athanasios Syropoulos, who had formerly been a *kapetanios* in the area of Kokova (Polydendri) near Veria, had repented and submitted, and it had been agreed that he should protect the area with forty men, twenty of whom must be Muslims. This is the last known case in which a Greek *armatolik* was officially recognized within the Ottoman empire — and then only when it had been conceded that half the men would be Greek and the other half Turkish.

Kapetan Georgakis, an *armatole* in the area of Zoupani in western Macedonia who had begun to oppress the inhabitants, was arrested in 1836, and he and all his men were beheaded. This marked the end of an institution which, despite its official abolition in the Balkan peninsula in 1721, had continued to exist in Greece for a further one hundred and ten years.[11]

THE FIGHT FOR FREEDOM 1830-1912

MACEDONIA IN THE CONTEXT OF THE POLICY OF THE 'MEGALI IDEA'

The first attempts to incite revolts 1833-53

In September 1828, Kapodistrias requested of the representatives of the European Powers at the Conference of Poros that the frontiers of the Greek State, then in the process of being created, should extend from the foothills of Mt. Olympos on the Thermaic Gulf to Palermo near Chimarra on the Adriatic. Otherwise he foresaw serious complications arising from the exclusion from the State of areas — like that of Olympos — where the population had fought victoriously against the Turks. He stressed that: 'These men are many and they are soldiers; they will never despair of regaining their ancestral homes, nor will they give up their mountains or the art of war, or be confined by a treaty to narrow bounds outside the land of their birth; they will transgress those bounds and renew the war against the Turk when they consider that the terms for the pacification of Greece have been implemented.'[1]

This prediction was soon to be confirmed. The procedures by which the Ottoman empire recognized the independence of the small Greek State, whose border stretched from the Pagasitic Gulf to the Ambrakian Gulf had not yet been completed, when there began the first preparations for future insurrection in the Greek provinces of Turkey. Men from Macedonia and other unredeemed areas who had fought in the uprising of 1821, and who were now in exile in the Greek kingdom together with soldiers, politicians and intellectuals who had played a role in the struggle, formed a kernel that gave rise to the discussions and plans of secret societies aimed at inciting revolt in Macedonia and other areas still subject to Ottoman rule.

As soon as official relations with Turkey were established, consuls were despatched to the major Greek centres that were still unliberated. Theodore Vallianos was appointed first consul to Thessalonike with responsibility for the whole of Macedonia, and two years later the first consular agent was appointed to Kavala.[2] Although the establishment of consular authorities in the major ports of the Ottoman empire was dictated by the economic and commercial interests of Greece, the presence there of representatives of the Greek State and their efforts to protect their kinsmen were an indication of the determination of the free state that there should be no breach of unity with the as yet unliberated areas.

With the appointment of Vallianos to Thessalonike, the Greeks of Macedonia for the first time acquired their own representative who, however weak his voice, was at least able to give expression to their condition.

The main efforts of the Greek consul, however, were directed to extending and ensuring the strict observation of the concessions made to the Greek subjects and to protecting them from arbitrary abuse by the local authorities. Since the legal validity of an individual's Greek citizenship was often contested, the local authorities frequently ignored official Greek documents and, unrestrained by the central government, obliged Greek subjects to pay taxes, though they did not mete out this treatment to the subjects of other European Powers. Vallianos drew the attention of the local Governor to this in language unusual for a diplomat: 'I the undersigned have observed that the subject Greeks have been illegally taxed; all those who have been or will be so taxed, I can only regard as true Greeks, and as such, support them in time of need; violence will not erase their rights.'[3]

This restriction of the rights of the Greeks, however, damaged economic relations between the Greek State and Macedonia and discouraged the temporary migration of Macedonians to the Greek kingdom, since the nationality that they would acquire after a year's residence would have no value in the Ottoman empire.

Meanwhile, in Athens the various discussions on the condition and the future of the unliberated Greeks led to the formation of secret societies whose aim was to prepare the ground for liberation movements. The dominating figures in these societies were men who, as well as addressing themselves to the question of the unliberated Greeks, were attempting to advance their own personal political objectives. One such society was the Philorthodox Society, which, while cultivating the idea of revolts in Thessaly, Epirus and Macedonia, at the same time, or rather primarily, aimed at bringing about the reunification of the autocephalous Greek Church with the Oecumenical Patriarchate, and the conversion of Otto to the Orthodox faith, or the accession to the Greek throne of an Orthodox monarch. The representative appointed for Macedonia, Michael Papas, however, had differences with Kapodistrias that led him to betray the plan to Tsamis Karatasos, who revealed it to Otto, and the Association was dissolved in 1840.[4]

Tsamis Karatasos, son of Tasos Karatasos of Naousa, a veteran chieftain of the War of Independence, had assumed a leading role in reorganizing the Macedonian refugees and preparing them for a mass uprising when the time was right. During the first three decades Tsamis was the leading

300. After the failure of the revolt in Chalkidike, Greek klephts and armatoles renewed their efforts in the area around Mt. Olympos to incorporate Macedonia in the newly-established Greek state.

figure amongst the Macedonians who had fought in '21, and the natural leader of any uprising in Macedonia, despite the fact that he had frequently clashed with successive Greek governments.[5]

The activity of General Makriyannis was equally interesting. He is known to have enjoyed good relations with the Macedonian warriors ever since the War of Independence and when they were granted an ammesty after the founding of the state, he initiated several of them into the idea of a second uprising. A typical case is that of the chieftain Hilarion: at the prompting of Makriyannis he became an armatole in the Mademochoria and introduced his compatriots to the idea of Greek nationalism, while waiting for the right time for action.[6]

These activities, and the contacts between the Macedonians settled in the border areas of the new state, and their comrades and kinsmen around Olympos and in the Chalkidike, were not coordinated. For, as Makriyannis ad-

301. Tsamis Karatasos, son of Anastasios, was a major during the War of Independence. Later he was appointed aide-de-camp to king Otto. He was active in all the attempts to rouse Macedonia in the early decades of the 19th century. Athens, National Historical Museum.

mits, there were some in the revolutionary movements of the Greeks outside the state who looked to the kingdom for political advantage: 'We struggled both inside and out, and by precept stirring people at home and rousing interest and action abroad, so that we at home may be liberated and make unshakeable laws and create a human governance.'[7] Whatever their motives, these activities kept open the channels of communication between unliberated and free Greeks.

When the international situation in the East appeared to be leading to a general embroilment, with the war of the Khedive of Egypt against Ottoman sovereignty, the various revolutionary societies began to mobilize. Two movements appeared in Macedonia at this time (1839-40) whose aims were to rouse the Macedonians. One of them was provoked by agents of Mehmed Ali; based on Kavala

and Thasos (the property of the Khedive), its agents attempted to incite the Christians and Muslims against the sultan. The other was an entirely Greek movement. A revolutionary commitee consisting of Makriyannis, Dosios, Damianos, Naoum and others, having secured the support of Tsamis Karatasos, was collecting funds and organizing bands of men for Macedonia and Thessaly. This first attempt bore no real fruit, for Karatasos was obliged by heavy seas to turn back at Pilion, from where he returned to take part in the revolt in Crete. Other Macedonians fought with him in Crete hoping that after the successful outcome of the struggle there, three thousand Cretans would unite with the Macedonians and advance on Thessaly and Macedonia. Disaster in Crete, however, led to the frustration of the movements in the other provinces.

Velentzas was the only one to act, advancing towards Athos with a number of small boats, but he was obliged to return to Thessaly. The monks were disinclined to expose themselves to danger for an action that was not widely supported, and the Turks invaded the Holy Mountain, determined that the slightest insurrectionary movement should drown in its blood.[8] The Greek government took no part in these affairs. It even took steps to prevent any action in the northern provinces and pursued Velentzas, who appears to have turned to brigandage.[9]

In Macedonia, the events of 1839-41, particularly the revolt of Crete and the smaller movements led by Velentzas and Karatasos, resulted in Ottoman wrath turning against the Christians.[10] Their painful consequences apart, however, it remains true that these movements to some extent determined the role of Macedonia within the broader irredentist schemes of the Greeks.

The main developments of the forties were the many social and political problems confronting the small kingdom, that led to the change of Constitution on 3 September, 1843. These problems did not cause any abatement in the movement for the liberation of the subject provinces. The tenure of the office of prime minister by the Epirote Kolettis (August 1844 — September 1847) gave a special impetus to these movements. The *Megali Idea* now took a more concrete form, as the policy of the kingdom, and the personal involvement of the prime minister swayed the monarch to involve himself in the clandestine attempts to set on foot insurrectionary movements in the unliberated provinces and created a favourable climate in which a variety of secret national societies were able to act. It is clear from the *Memoirs* of Makriyannis that these societies for the most part had limited potential, occasionally served self-interested ends, and did not progress beyond endless discussions.[11] Although the practical results were small, however, this mobilization within and without the kingdom kept the Greeks alert as to the fate of their unliberated brethren. The result was that when the question of the 'autochthons' and 'heterochthons' arose during the discussions on the Constitution in 1844, the fate of the Greeks outside the kingdom emerged as the primary concern of the free state.

Throughout this decade, and up to the Crimean War, political thought was dominated by an unthinking romanticism. Kolettis is known to have been ready to give the signal for an insurrection before he died, and his successors also took the view that the liberal revolutionary movements sweeping through Europe in 1848 furnished a favourable opportunity for Hellenism to advance to Constantinople. King Otto himself swayed Greece's foreign policy in favour of Russia, since she alone of the European Powers appeared to be attempting to undermine the integrity of the Ottoman empire.

In this general climate, Macedonia, together with Thessaly, Epirus and Crete, continued to occupy a prominent place amongst the aims of the *Megali Idea*. It is indicative that during the course of the discussions in Parliament on the question of the 'heterochthons', the supporters of the idea that they should have the same rights as the Greeks of the kingdom laid particular emphasis on the contribution of the Macedonians to the common struggle. As Kolettis himself, in his monumental address, emphasized: 'But the Kingdom of Greece is not the whole of Greece... It is not only the inhabitants of the kingdom who are autochthons, but also the inhabitants of Ioannina, or *Thessalonike,* or *Serres,* or Adrianople, or Constantinople, or Trabezond, or Crete, or Samos...'[12]

Even the conservative Mavrokordatos, in a memorandum he submitted to Otto concerning the policy that should be pursued by the kingdom, put Macedonia in the forefront of national aspirations: 'If the unification of the Greek race into a single state is to be realized, even in part, the areas in question are primarily those in which Greeks are more populous, and this is undoubtedly true of *Macedonia,* Thessaly, Epirus and Crete.'[13]

Although the limited nature of the sources makes it difficult to disentangle the activities of the secret societies concerned with Macedonia during this period from those concerned with the other provinces, a number of particular features may nonetheless be noted. In southern Greece during the struggle for independence, the ranks of the Macedonian warriors were known to have included men whose mother tongue was not Greek, but Vlach, Slav or Albanian, though this did not affect their national loyalties, which were towards the liberation of the Greek nation. A similar situation was to be found in the case of warriors from other parts of Greece such as Attica, Hydra, Spetsai and Epirus, who spoke Albanian. Precisely the same phenomenon can be observed in the period up to the Crimean War, when the national awakening of the other Christian peoples of the Balkans had not yet penetrated to any real extent into Macedonia.[14] As a result, those of the Macedonian Christians who became sensitive to the idea of liberation looked to the Greek kingdom for their redemption and enrolled in Greek bands of armed men to await the right time for the uprising.

On the other hand, their proximity to their Slav Christian brethren reinforced in the Macedonians, to a greater extent perhaps than in the other unliberated Greeks, the idea that all the Balkan peoples should cooperate in a concerted effort to overthrow the Ottoman state and found a Balkan confederacy. Before the young intellectuals of the Greek state (Alexander R. Rangavis and others) has seized upon the slogan of Balkan collaboration, the Macedonian warriors had already put it into practice. It is clear from Slav and Greek sources that in the decade before the Crimean War Bulgarian and Serb nationalists were visiting Athens, where they made contact with various influential figures, mainly well-known Macedonians like Hadji'-Christos and Tsamis Karatasos, to discuss plans for joint action.[15] It was evident that Macedonia was well placed to play a unifying role in the achievement of common action on a pan-Balkan scale. In Athens, however, nationalist aspirations envisaged a Greater Greece whose northern frontier would be the Balkan mountains. When Georgi Rakovski, the founder of Bulgarian nationalism, visited Athens to discuss the idea of Balkan cooperation, he met with a negative reaction and left disappointed.

From the Crimean War to the Cretan Revolution

Another war broke out between Russia and Turkey in October 1853. The Russians quickly occupied the Danubian principalities and by the beginning of 1854 had advanced to the Danube.

These events prompted a general mobilization in Greece, for Otto and the majority of the politicians predicted the defeat and dissolution of the Ottoman empire.[16] The monarch himself was personally involved in the formation of large bands of armed men, with general commanders for each of the three unliberated Greek provinces in the north of Greece. The unity of this movement was reflected in the insignia of the revolutionary groups which bore the names of all three provinces, Thessaly, Epirus, Macedonia, along with the slogan 'Freedom or Death'.

The bands first penetrated into Epirus and Thessaly where they commenced hostilities; in Macedonia, the first armed band, under Tsamis Karatasos, 'Commander-in-chief of Macedonia', disembarked on Sithonia on 18 April, 1854. Karatasos' landing in the Chalkidike was only one part of a plan of action that envisaged the invasion of Macedonia from two other points: south-west Macedonia, and from the region of Ossa and Olympos, to which a strong band led by chieftains from Olympos was to advance through Thessaly. This band, however, was very late in reaching its destination. Between mid-April and mid-May the insurgents, whose number had increased to about 2,500, had occupied Tempe and southern Olympos and had advanced to Katerini, where they had captured the village of Vrondou. The revolt had lost its impetus in the other areas however; a truce was arranged through the mediation of the English and French consuls, and the fighters of Olympos returned to the kingdom in mid-June.[17]

In western Macedonia, Theodore Ziakas occupied western Pindos from where he launched a series of raids on the region of Grevena and Anaselitsa. His successes roused to action the most hot-blooded amongst the youths of the villages in the area, as well as a number of men from Kozani who came to reinforce his band. In the end, however, he too was compelled to accept the mediation of the European consuls, under the pressure of the large Ottoman army that had assembled in the area of Spilaion.

The most daring venture, however, was that of Tsamis Karatasos who, at the head of a large force, attempted to rouse Chalkidike, with its great experience of war, and the

302. Theodore Vallianos, the first Greek diplomatic representative in Macedonia, who implemented the Greek state's decision to establish and maintain close links with the unredeemed Greeks in the Ottoman provinces. Painted by Dionysios Tsokos. Athens, National Gallery.

monks of Mount Athos. The moment he set foot in Macedonia he issued a proclamation through which he endeavoured to mobilize all the unliberated Christians against the Turks: 'What other time are you waiting for, brother Macedonians? Shall we tolerate seeing our honour trampled on, our property scattered, and our blameless religion insulted? ..... Is not the blood of our veins Macedonian? Are we not descendants of Alexander the Great and the emperor Basil? To arms, then!'[18]

In the meantime, however, England and France had allied themselves with the Ottoman empire and declared war on Russia. Shortly before this, the Sublime Porte had demanded the recall of the Greek bands of insurgents, and

when this was rejected, broke off diplomatic relations with Athens. While Anglo-French forces seized Piraeus and imposed a government of their liking on Athens, the French consul in Thessalonike ordered a French man of war to proceed with all speed to Chalkidike and harass Karatasos. The captain discovered the small landing fleet at Sithonia and sank the ship transporting the ammunition and a number of supporting boats. Karatasos continued the struggle despite all this and attacked the local garrisons. The course of events, however, had dampened the initial enthusiasm of the local population and the monks of Mount Athos, particularly when they heard of the slaughter of the notables of Polygyros at the hands of the advancing Ottoman armies. As the reverses mounted, Karatasos decided to fortify a camp at Koumitsa, not far from Ierissos. The monks, however, deeming the enterprise a certain failure, refused to cooperate. In the end, the Macedonian leader was obliged to retreat to the Holy Mountain, whence he returned to Chalkis on a French warship, after the mediation of the consuls.[19]

Given the turn taken by developments on the international scene, the revolts in the unliberated provinces were doomed to failure. The alliance of Great Britain and France with the Ottoman empire against Russia, to whom Otto had tied the fortunes of the unliberated Greeks, led inexorably to the direct intervention of the naval Powers to pacify the centres of unrest in the rear of the Ottoman army and its allies. The hostile stance adopted by the Powers proved fatal, particularly in the case of Macedonia: a single French man of war was enough to cut off supplies from Karatasos' band and break the morale of the men of Chalkidike and Athos. Memories of the genocide of 1821-22 were less than a generation away.

It should perhaps be noted that although the majority of the insurgents withdrew, a number of armed men remained on Macedonian soil exchanging the role of rebel for that of brigand. Amongst these robbers-cum-rebels there survived groups that ensured there was an experienced force ready to turn again from brigandage to insurrection as soon as a new opportunity presented itself.[20]

In any event, the revolutionary movements of 1854, for all their local successes and moments of heroism, demonstrated that, of themselves, they were incapable of advancing the cause of the liberation of the subject Greeks. Even if their aim was solely to create disturbances and compel the Powers to intervene, thereby achieving an albeit partial satisfaction of national aspirations, there was no real possibility of this happening during the course of a war in which the Ottoman empire was the ally of the Western Powers. It emerges from a public denunciation made by Karatasos and the leaders of the bands in the other provinces that Otto and his political and military entourage had misled the chieftains by promising that the movements would have the support of the German states.[21] Even if this had been at all likely, however, (which it was not) it would still have proved impossible to neutralize the negative effects of the hostile stance adopted by the naval forces of Great Britain and France.

For the Macedonian Greeks the failure of the enterprise created a further problem with long-term implications. It confirmed the Turks in their mistrust of and hostility towards the Greek population at a time when the idea of Bulgarian nationalism was beginning to appear on the scene.[22]

While the Greek kingdom was trying to recover from the traumatic experiences of the failure of the insurrectionary movements and of foreign occupation, a number of rapid political developments took place in the Balkans and the Middle East that were to have serious consequences for Macedonia. Under the influence of the Slavophile movement, and later that of the Panslavists, Russia turned her attention to the Slav subjects of the Ottman empire, thus reviewing a fundamental principle of her policy. Instead of acting on behalf of the Orthodox Christians, she would henceforward advance the interests of the Christian Slavs.

The events of the Crimean War, as well as Russian policy, acted as a catalyst on the policy of the principality of Serbia and of the Bulgarian nationalists. The movement for Yugoslav national unity began to take an interest in Macedonia too, or at least in its northern provinces. And while prince Mikhail Obrenovich was advancing the idea of Balkan cooperation, the prime minister, Ilias Garašanin, who took office in 1861, encouraged the Serbian nationalists to draw up plans for revolts in the various subject provinces of the Ottoman empire, amongst which he included northern Macedonia.[23] At the same time the Bulgarians, whose organization and activity lay mainly outside Bulgaria, in Belgrade, Bucharest, Odessa and elsewhere, included Macedonia and Thrace within the boundaries of their projected autonomous Bulgarian state.[24]

At this period, however, these plans were inevitably academic in character: the principality of Serbia, subject to the sultan and still weak, was remote from Macedonia, while not only did Bulgaria not exist as a nation state, but the very idea of Bulgarian nationalism had made no serious inpact south of the Rhodope mountains. As a result, although the reverberations of the activities of the Slavs to the north of Macedonia reached as far as the Greek kingdom, they did not influence Otto who, disillusioned with the stance of the Great Powers in the Crimean War, was pursuing a rapprochement with the Serbs. Secret negotiations were held in Constantinople in 1861, during which Mark Renieris and Garašanin agreed in principle that, in the event of a victory by the Balkan forces and the annexation to Serbia of northern Albania, Bosnia and Herzegovina, Serbia would have no objection to the annexation by Greece of Macedonia, along with Thrace, Epirus and Thessaly. This important concession was not invested with the authority of an official state agreement, however, and the Serbs soon tacitly backed away from it when the Bulgarians appeared on the scene with their own claims to Macedonia.[25] The following year, Otto was expelled and the contacts with the Serbs flagged. Irrespective of future developments, however, the Garašanin-Renieris agreement achieved the recognition, albeit temporary, of the most ambitious Greek claims in this area. This success was only achieved because both sides concurred that Bulgarian ambitions were not to be taken into serious consideration. The Serbs swiftly recovered from this delusion and did not sign

303. *During the Greek War of Independence general Makriyannis maintained close relations with the Macedonian leaders. After the establishment of the Greek state he was a strong defender of the idea that revolt should be renewed in Macedonia. Athens, National Historical Museum.*

the agreement. The Greeks on the other hand, with their limited knowledge of political developments in the northern Balkans, continued to insist on the doctrine that the whole of Macedonia as far as Skopje and the Šar (Skardos) and Rila mountains should be included in the Greek state when it was extended.

After the expulsion of Otto, this same line was pursued by the Koumoundouros-Trikoupis government during the fresh round of Greek-Serbian negotiations held at the time of the Cretan Revolution (1866-68). During these negotiations, which led to the secret treaty of alliance of Feslau of 26 February, 1867, the Greek representative, Peter Zanos, attempted to secure the ratification of the Greek claims to

304. View of 19th century Monastir, capital of the vilayet of the same name. The town was an important centre of trade and communications in northern Macedonia. Its inhabitants, mainly Greek, who enjoyed a long tradition of education, spread

nationalistic ideas. An association of enthusiastic patriots was founded in the middle of the century and its members made brave shows of resistance against Ottoman oppression. Photographic Archive of the Estia Library, Nea Smyrni, Athens.

the whole of Macedonia, making the following assertion: 'No-one will be found in Greece to put his signature to a treaty by which Macedonia is partitioned and Greece denied her eternal demands there. You forget ... that Macedonia is the cradle of Hellenism; that it is the Greek country par excellence; that, finally, Macedonia is the home of Alexander the Great.'[26]

The Serbs, however, were no longer disposed to ignore the Bulgarians. At the beginning of 1867 they had begun negotiations with the secret Central Bulgarian Committee in Bucharest, and were seriously discussing the possibility of the foundation of a Serb-Bulgarian state, or a Yugoslav empire. Bulgaria would form part of this empire with 'its' three provinces of Moesia, Thrace and Macedonia. Unlike the Bulgarians, however, the Serbs considered that only northern Macedonia was Bulgarian, eligible for unification with the future state of the south Slavs. They accepted that southern Macedonia had a Greek population and belonged as of right to Greece. Ultimately, however, the Greek-Serbian treaty made no mention of Macedonia.[27]

Meantime, the crisis in the Ottoman empire intensified the wretched condition of the rural population. A climate of intense popular discontent amongst the Muslim and Christian populations was the inevitable result.[28] While the Muslims dissipated their energies in acts of violence and pillaging directed against the Christians, the latter at-

tempted to find outside protectors to relieve them of their sufferings. The result was the phenomenon of considerable numbers of Bulgarian-speaking Christians turning to the Uniate Church in the hope of winning the practical support of the Catholic countries, and more specifically of their consular representatives. The turn towards the idea of pan-Slavism was similar in origin, since Orthodox Russia was behind it. Tough defeated in the Crimean War, Russian policy made a dynamic appearance in Macedonia at the beginning of the 1860s. Russia opened a consulate at Monastir in 1859, through which it actively supported the interests of the Slav population.

The Greeks, for their part, were not inactive. Before the Crimean War, they had been represented in Macedonia only by the consulate in Thessalonike and consular agents at Kavala (1835) and Thasos (1845); after the war, vice-consulates were opened at Serres (1856) and Monastir (1859). The official representatives were supported in their work by the traditional local forces of Hellenism — teachers, village elders, merchants and clerics — and also by the new generation of professionals who began to return to their birthplace once they had lived and studied for a time in the kingdom. Having absorbed the nationalist spirit that prevailed in the capital, these young men gradually formed kernels of national action in the towns and townships in which they settled. The situation that arose at

450

this period in distant Monastir (Bitola) is particularly interesting: here schoolmasters and young men, 'most of them belonging to distinguished Macedonian families', founded a Greek club and began to disseminate nationalist ideas.[29] Such was the arrogance and boldness of this new generation of Macedonians that, as the consul G. Vallianos relates, when the Grand Vezier visited Monastir in 1860, they refused to meet him, on the grounds that 'the Sultan is not our legal Sovereign, but a usurper.'[30]

Meanwhile, within the kingdom, the older generation of Macedonian warriors and refugees of the period of the War of Independence had begun to hand on the torch to the second generation, who had been born and educated in the kingdom, and who had been reinforced over three decades by young Macedonian Greeks who had taken refuge there. Within these circles Tsamis Karatasos continued for a time to pursue his clandestine activities and negotiations aimed at bringing about new revolutionary movements in Macedonia.[31] In the end, however, he left the country in 1860 and died in Belgrade in 1861 while attempting to disseminate the idea of a general revolt.[32] At the same time, the number of different Macedonian organizations in the kingdom multiplied; they included the organization of Macedonian students and, later, on the eve of the Cretan Revolution, the 'Preparatory Committee of the Macedonians', whose president was Andrew Paikos. At the same time, about 1858, Leonidas Voulgaris began to play an active role; Voulgaris was a restless patriot and an ardent devotee of Balkan cooperation, who was preparing his own plans for insurrection in Macedonia.

When the uprising in Crete spread, Voulgaris set out with a small band of twenty-five to thirty armed men and, together with Captain Georgakis of the Mademochoria landed at Ormilia in Chalkidike at the end of April, 1866. His aim was to incite a general revolt of all the subject peoples, as far as Wallachia! The enterprise was, of course, doomed from its birth. The Greek government officially disowned it and informed the Turks, in an attempt to ensure that it was not implicated. In the event the Turks swiftly located Voulgaris' band and by June had succeeded in arresting him and almost all his men. As usual, the failure resulted in a series of arrests, in Nigrita and the main centres of Hellenism in Chalkidike, and in a wave of terrorism directed against the local population.[33]

As the Cretan Revolution began to assume significant dimensions, the new government of Koumoundouros (in which Trikoupis was Foreign Minister) attempted to create distractions for the Turks by opening negotiations with the Serbs and encouraging movements in Thessaly, Epirus and Macedonia. The joint committee of Epirotes, Thessalians and Macedonians was formed and the 'Preparatory Committee of the Macedonians' was also active.[34] Local Greek revolutionary committees were also formed within Macedonia, which were in close contact with the committees in Athens, though not with the representatives of the Greek state in Macedonia. The Greek government was clearly trying to keep up pretences. In the end, the unfavourable turn of events in Crete and the inability of the Greeks and Serbs to undertake joint action, prevented a general rising in Macedonia yet again.

305. The Patriarch Gregory VI who worked hard to avert a Greek-Bulgarian ecclesiastical schism. The establishment in 1870 of the Bulgarian Exarchate by the Patriarch widened rather than closed the gap in Greek-Bulgarian relations.

THE EMERGENCE OF BULGARIAN NATIONALISM AND THE EASTERN CRISIS (1875-78) IN MACEDONIA

Problems of national identity

During the 1860s the Greek population of Macedonia began to be increasingly concerned at the emergence of Bulgarian nationalism. The Bulgarian national awakening had begun in the Bulgarian provinces of the Ottoman empire before the Crimean War; during the post-war period, however, the movement spread at a rapid pace to the northern Slav-speaking zone of Macedonia and to some of the towns in central Macedonia. The Bulgarian national identity was initially advanced through demands of a purely ecclesiastical nature, such as the use of the Slavonic language in the church, and the replacement of Greek priests by Bulgarians. In a very short space of time, however, the dispute with the Oecumenical Patriarchate about the founding of an independent Bulgarian Church and the spread of the ideology of pan-Slavism by Russian intellectuals, clerics and consular officials lent the demands of the Macedonian Bulgarians a clearly national colour. Naturally enough, there followed a Greek reaction which was to divide the Christian peoples of Macedonia for several decades. The dispute acquired many different facets on account of the complicated nature of the problems presented by the composition of the population of Macedonia.

The precise determination of the ethnic identity of the Christian population — which constituted two-thirds of the whole — was a genuinely difficult problem that divided both scholars and politicians. Up to the first decades of the nineteenth century, the great bulk of the rural Christian population had no clear concept of its own nationality, despite the fact that it spoke a variety of different languages. As a result, religion not only remained the main distinguishing feature within Ottoman society but was also a formative influence on the nascent national consciousness. The fact that the Oecumenical Patriarchate and the local primates acted as the instruments of the Greek language, education and occasionally nationalism therefore gave rise to the notion that all the Orthodox Christians of Macedonia belonged to Hellenism irrespective of the language they spoke. Even though the criterion of religion and education was not an absolute determinant of the national identity of the inhabitants, it was equally misleading to use the spoken language as the sole indicator of nationality. In the case of the Greeks in particular, the circumstance that during the War of Independence Albanian-Vlach- and Slav-speaking warriors had identified themselves with Greek national idea and had been integrated with the Greek population, presaged a similar development amongst the polyglot population of Macedonia. The linguistic stratigraphy of the province which was distant from the kingdom, exhibited a number of peculiarities, different from those of southern Greece, which inevitably exercised different influences when national rivalries broke out.

Generally speaking, three linguistic zones could be distinguished in Macedonia amongst the Christian population. The northernmost began at the geographical frontiers of Macedonia (the Šar-Skardos and Rila ranges) and extended to the south as far as a line beginning at Ochrid and running north of Monastir and Stromnitsa to Melenikon and Nevrokop. In this zone, the Slav-speaking element was completely dominant. The southernmost zone began at the borders with Thessaly and extended to the north to the line running from the Pindos to Kastoria and thence north of Veria and Thessalonike to Serres and Drama. Here the Greek-speakers predominated. The main feature of the zone between these two was its linguistic variety. Slav-, Greek-, Vlach- and Albanian-speaking Christians lived alongside Turkish speakers, and also alongside Greek-, Vlach-, Slav- and Albanian-speaking Muslims. And although the Slav-speakers in this middle zone were in the majority it proved very difficult to determine the national identity of the Christian population. In any event, until 1870 and the foundation of the Bulgarian Exarchate, the bulk of the non Greek-speaking Christians in this zone identified themselves with Hellenism. Not only did they independently keep up Greek schools and conduct the liturgy in Greek, but they also participated actively in the various national struggles of Hellenism. In order to designate more precisely the particular nature of this population from the point of view both of language and of nationality, the Greek consuls used in their reports of the period 1860-78

terms such as Greek-Vlachs, Greek-Albanians, Greek-Bulgarians, or even 'Hellenized Bulgarians'.[35] These designations perhaps give a more accurate picture of the fluidity of the situation before national consciousness had become firmly established.[36]

The feeling that they were Greek was particularly evident amongst the Vlach-speaking, or Koutsovlach population. Indeed, in the areas where there were very few, or no Greek-speakers, it was the Vlachs who formed the vanguard of Hellenism. The Greek schools and foundations in the *kaza* of Monastir and Prilep were basically the work of Vlach-speaking Greeks, who also played a prominent role in all the Greek revolutionary movements in Macedonia. The Slav- and Albanian-speaking communities in the central zone had similar loyalties, which they showed either by founding Greek schools or by their fanatical adherence to the Oecumenical Patriarchate after 1870. In contrast the Slav-speaking population of north and northeast Macedonia was inclined to favour the Bulgarians and, to a lesser degree, the Serbians; it was from them that it took its lead in cultural, ecclesiastical and national matters.

The Schism and the Bulgarian penetration of Macedonia

After the Crimean War and the announcement of the reforms of Hatt-i Humayun, the Bulgarians demanded of the Oecumenical Patriarchate the foundation of an independent Bulgarian Church and also the determination of the boundaries of their jurisdiction in Macedonia and Thrace. Of the forty-nine dioceses of the oecumenical throne in European Turkey, the Bulgarians laid claim to thirty. For a whole decade, unproductive negotiations took place in Constantinople, in which the Russian ambassador Ignatiev was also involved.

In the end, at the height of the Cretan Insurrection, the Patriarch Gregory VI, encouraged by the Greek government, compromised and agreed to the extension of the Bulgarian Church to a number of provinces in northern Macedonia and Thrace. At this stage, however, the Ottoman government, discerning the danger of a Greek-Slav rapprochement, promised even greater concessions and thus strengthened the hand of the intransigent Bulgarians.

On 11 March 1870, the Sultan issued a firman proclaiming the foundation of the Bulgarian Church. Amongst the dioceses falling within the jurisdiction of the Bulgarian Exarchate were a number in northern Thrace and that of Velessa in northern Macedonia. The same firman, however,. included a provision allowing the annexing of other dioceses to the Exarchate, provided that two thirds of the Orthodox population of the area demonstrated its desire for this.

This last provision opened the way for fierce national rivalry, which served the designs of the Ottoman government by precluding any future cooperation by the two Christian nationalities. When all hope of reconciliation had vanished in this way, the Oecumenical Patriarchate in 1872 pronounced the Exarchate schismatic. From that moment Greek-Bulgarian rivalry in the contested regions of Macedonia and Thrace entered a phase of open antagonism.

306. 19th century Siatista. Throughout the century, Macedonian towns developed fast, both economically and culturally. Thanks to the generosity of bequests from wealthy Greeks of the Diaspora, libraries and schools were established and associations formed. With the spread of education, enslaved Hellenism became increasingly aware of its national heritage.

The decade before the Schism had been a period of fierce Greek-Bulgarian rivalry in Macedonia, particularly the northern zone. As early as 1859, G. Vallianos, consul at Monastir, had drawn attention to the need to check pan-Slavism, which was 'advancing with giant strides to the detriment of Hellenism'.[37] During this period Bulgarian grammar-schools were opened in many of the villages in the region of Monastir and Slavonic began to be used in the churches, foreshadowing the take-over of the local church by pro-Bulgarians. There were a number of incidents (at Monastir, Polyani and Melenikon, for instance) in which some of the metropolitan bishops themselves used Slavonic on occasion. This provoked a violent reaction from the pro-Greek faction, however, which led either to the dismissal of the priests, or the suspending of the use of Slavonic.[38]

There was a similar situation in north-east Macedonia. Up to 1860, in all the Slav-speaking villages of the north, especially in the regions of Melenikon and Nevrokop, Greek was the only language used in the schools, in the church and in commerce. In the following decade Nevrokop became a focus of continuous rivalry, with Greek and Bulgarian teachers and priests alternating with each other as the two sides clashed stubbornly. The Greeks, however, despite the partial advance made by the Bulgarians, held their ground up to the decade beginning in 1870. A major contributing factor was the activity of the Greek community in Serres, which not only neutralized the attempts of the Bulgarians to penetrate the city, but also reinforced the Greek schools and the communities throughout the entire *sanjak*. It is worth citing a consular document of 1870: 'Serres was and is the focal point of Hellenism in Macedonia, for there are many Greeks there who are working to avert the scandal ...... Thus far, Serres has decisively countered the activities of the Bulgarians and has remained free of them.'[39]

The reopening of the Russian consulate in Thessalonike, however, and the foundation of a new consulate in Monastir in 1861, gave a great impetus to the Bulgarian movement. For the first time, the Bulgarians of northern Macedonia gained a local 'protector' in the person of the representative of Russia, a Slav power. Until 1866, however, the Greeks were able to impede the activities of the Bulgarian supporters by repeated representations to the local authorities or through the intervention of the Patriarchate at the Porte.[40] After that date, the Ottoman government reversed its attitude. The pro-Bulgarians tried to take advantage of this circumstance and, at the height of the Cretan Revolution, the leaders of the Bulgarian faction in Monastir came to the vali and offered to form bodies of twelve thousand (*sic*) Bulgarian Macedonians to fight alongside the Turks against the Cretans. Naturally enough, the Greek consul who recorded this event cast doubt on their ability to carry out their offer.[41] The initiative is nonetheless indicative of the climate created as both sides attempted to win the favour of the Ottoman suzerain.

The Bulgarians made their greatest progress in the disputed northern-central zone in the four years 1866-70. The case of the diocese of Polyani is typical: with the pro-Bulgarian metropolitan bishop Parthenios as its head it had become the strongest Bulgarian centre in Macedonia after Velessa. About seventy Bulgarian schools are reported to have been opened about 1870, and the movement was showing signs of spreading to the near-by eparchies of Melenikon, Stromnitsa and Moglena.[42] Further south, however, in the dioceses of the central zone Edessa (Vodena), Kastoria, and Ptolemaïda (Kailaria) there was no real Bulgarian penetration. Isolated cases of Bulgarians being sent to open schools or to ensure the use of Slavonic in the church, were neutralized by the mass mobilization of the inhabitants or by démarchés to the Ottoman authorities.[43]

Up to 1870, the Bulgarian territorial aspirations were fairly clearly defined. S. Verković, in his book *Bulgarian Folk Songs* claimed that the Haliakmon (Vistritsa) formed the natural dividing line between Slavism and Hellenism; and K. Vatkikiotis, the consul at Thessalonike, noted that the aim of the Bulgarian *Megali Idea,* concealed behind the demand for ecclesiastical self-government, was 'a policy involving the conquest of the whole of Macedonia', with Thessalonike as its centre.'[44]

During this same period a new threat had begun to emerge in the attempts by nationalist circles in Roumania to win over the Koutsovlachs of Macedonia and Epirus to the idea of Roumanian nationalism. Basing their arguments exclusively on the affinities of the two Latin languages, Roumanians and pro-Roumanian Koutsovlachs had begun to visit the Vlach villages of Macedonia and the Pindos from the beginning of the 1860s, their aim being to found schools and secure the use of the Roumanian language in the churches. Their efforts foundered on the violent reaction of the majority of the Koutsovlach population. In some villages, however, there were cases in which the schools and churches were seized. Although these clashes were limited in number, the Greek leaders were seriously concerned, for it had also become possible to detect some cooperation between Roumanian supporters and Bulgarian supporters. Since Hellenism in the central zone was represented mainly by Vlach- and Slav-speaking Christians who perceived themselves as Greek, the spread of Roumanian nationalism to the Koutsovlach population would have been a severe reverse for the Greek position in Macedonia.[45]

As if these dangers were not enough, a new threat arose on Mount Athos. The monastic community of the Holy Mountain found itself the centre of Russian interest in the 1860s. Hundreds of Russian monks came to the various monasteries, particularly Panteleimon of which they succeeded in gaining control in 1867, electing a Russian abbot. From that time there began a systematic attempt to 'Russianize' the Holy Mountain. Within a decade the number of Russian monks reached fifteen hundred. The abundant economic aid, the frequent visits of the Russian consul in Thessalonike and the diplomatic support of Ignatiev in Constantinople all indicated that Russia's interest in Mount Athos was political rather than religious. This suspicion was reinforced by Russian attempts to purchase large tracts of land both on Athos itself and on the coasts of Chalkidike and eastern Macedonia opposite, and to extend Russian control to other monasteries.[46]

The Greek mobilization

This situation could not continue without serious dangers for the position of Hellenism. The Greek consuls accordingly recommended that the Greek state should become more actively involved in Macedonian affairs. Their reports suggested that northern Macedonia be written off, as being indisputably Slav, that in the central zone support be given to enterprises in the educational and religious spheres and to national activity generally, and that particular attention be given to the Slav- and Vlach-speaking communities of Pelagonia, who were in the front line of Hellenism. A good idea of the new situation is given by the reports of Peter Logothetis, the consul at Monastir and a man known for his seriousness; he sought drastic measures to check the Bulgarians, more specifically: a) mass demonstrations in order to oblige the metropolitan bishop to adopt a negative attitude to the demands of the Bulgarians; b) economic warfare against the leaders of the pro-Bulgarian faction; c) the activation of the Greek members of the various local councils to ensure that decisions unfavourable to the pro-Bulgarians were taken; d) the unfrocking of fanatical Bulgarian priests; e) the exercise of pressure on those organs of the Administration that supported the pro-Bulgarian faction; and f) the cultivation of 'a deadly hatred against every Bulgarian who was an implacable persecuter of Hellenism'. What is striking is not only the severity of the measures proposed (which were not approved) but also the consul's faith in the strength of the Greeks of the Pelagonia district, since to implement them presupposed that Hellenism was more advanced than Slavism economically, socially and nationally.[47]

The authorities in the Greek kingdom were unable to assimilate quickly the rapid developments on the fringes of the unliberated areas of Hellenism in the north. The intellectual leadership of the country, however, whose ranks included a number of distinguished Macedonians, was not slow to seize the initiative. The Association for the Diffusion of Greek Letters was founded in 1869, its purpose being the creation, support and development of schools in Macedonia and the other unliberated provinces. The Association evolved a very broad network of cooperators throughout the whole of Macedonia and soon came to act as a transmitter of Greek education and Greek nationalism to the unliberated Greeks, and as a receiver, within the kingdom, of their problems and sufferings. This increased its prestige and elevated it to the level of unofficial adviser to the Greek government on these matters.

There had been similar activity in Constantinople even earlier: in 1861 the Greek Philological Association of Constantinople was founded, which concerned itself with the

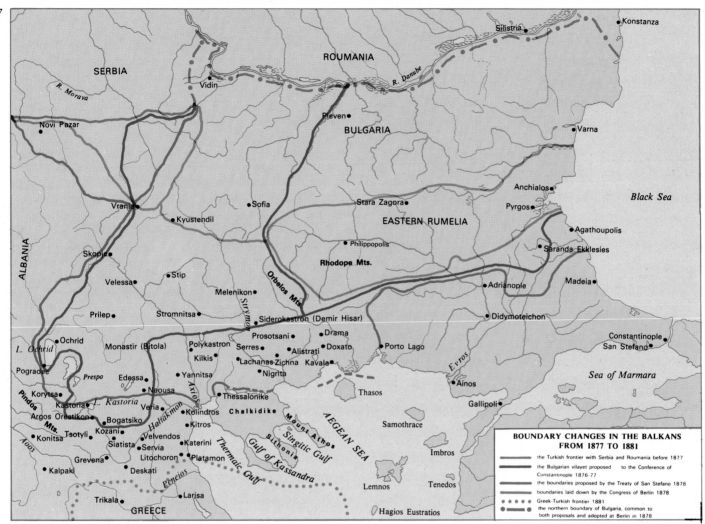

307. *After a short-lived Bulgarian revolt had been quelled in May 1876, representatives of the Great Powers at the Conference of Constantinople in December 1876 agreed to request the Sublime Porte to create two self-governing Bulgarian vilayets, which would include regions as far west as Edessa, Florina and Kastoria. The proposal was rejected. The idea of a Bulgarian state extending into Macedonia was revived at the time of the Russo-Turkish war of 1877-78. The peace treaty of San Stefano (3 March, 1878) provided for a large independent Bulgarian state covering almost all Macedonia except for Chalkidike, Thessalonike and the districts of Kozani and Servia. These impossible terms provoked a revolt of the Greek Macedonians. The terms were revised by the Congress of Berlin (July 1878). Bulgaria became a Principality under the nominal suzerainty of the sultan; Eastern Rumelia was established to the south of the Balkan range. Macedonia, though it remained in Turkish hands became a focal point of future international developments in the Balkans.*

publication of school text books, the drawing up of educational programmes, and the sending of teachers and economic aid to the poorer school districts. It was supported in its mission in Macedonia by the Macedonian Educational Brotherhood, which was founded in Constantinople in 1871, and which counted two thousand members in the capital and the province.[48]

The existence of these organizations outside Macedonia was a stimulus to the creation of educational societies and associations in a number of towns inside Macedonia.[49] All these societies supported the schools and ensured their proper functioning, with the cooperation, or occasionally without it, of the representatives of the local administration and of the Church. They were concerned at the same time, however, with the intellectual development of the inhabi-

tants and with guiding their nationalist aspirations. The leading members were usually professionals, doctors or schoolmasters. In consequence, the societies were inspired by more pronounced liberal and nationalist views than those held by the traditional representatives of the local administration.

All this activity began to yield results after the proclamation of the Schism and undoubtedly helped to restrain the Slav-speaking population from adhering to the Exarchate. At the same time the political thaw in Greek-Turkish relations that began in the period 1872-75 checked the persecution of the unliberated Greeks and neutralized a factor that impeded the development of the Macedonian Greeks. The reports of the consuls make it clear that about 1876 the expansion of the Bulgarian Church and of

308. In the centre of the Macedonian fighters pictured above stands Nicholas, bishop of Kitros, who hoisted the Greek flag in Kolindros, Pieria in February 1878.

Bulgarian nationalism had been checked in a satisfactory manner in the central zone of Macedonia.

Macedonia and the Eastern Crisis 1875-78

It was at this precise juncture that there occurred the revolts of Bosnia and Herzegovina (summer 1875), followed by the spreading of war fever to all the Slav peoples of the Balkans during the following year. In April-May 1876 the Bulgarians rose in a revolt which spread for a short time to the area of Razlog in north-east Macedonia, but which was swiftly and violently suppressed.[50] The declaration of the war between Serbia and Turkey in the summer of 1876 did not involve Macedonia directly, since the Turkish army successfully counter-attacked and invaded Serbian territory. Even though Macedonia had not been the scene of armed action, however, the events of 1876 had important consequences. While the Greek state remained neutral, the Ottoman lust for vengeance on this occasion turned against the Slav population. In order to escape persecution the villagers who had adhered to the Exarchate turned once more to the Oecumenical Patriarchate. The situation in western Macedonia that emerges from the consuls' reports is as follows: in the *kaza* of Kastoria, all save three of the one hundred and fifty villages had remained faithful to the Patriarchate; in the *kaza* of Florina, only seven villages had adhered to the Exarchate, but by 1876 these had asked to return to the Patriarchate; in the *kaza* of Monastir, sixty of the one hundred and fifty villages had gone over to the Exarchate, but some of these returned to the Patriarchate. The southern *kazas* (Kozani, Servia etc.) had not been affected by the Bulgarian Exarchate. In north-east Macedonia, which had come under stronger Turkish pressure, thirty-four villages of Radovic and fourteen of Males returned to the Patriarchate.[51]

Greek satisfaction at this turn of events was not destined to last long. In December of 1876 representatives of the European Powers met in Constantinople to examine the situation, and to request the Porte to introduce broad administrative reforms and create two self-governing vilayets in the areas that had revolted. The diplomatic dexterity of Ignatiev ensured the inclusion in the western vilayet of extensive areas of Macedonia, which had not been involved in any way in the Bulgarian uprising. Since the plan of reform only concerned the Bulgarians, this meant that the Macedonian provinces were automatically taken to be Bulgarian. Just how arbitrary this was can be seen from the fact that not only northern Macedonia, but the areas of Kastoria, Florina, Edessa etc. were included within the boundaries of the projected self-governing western vilayet. The Turks resisted the proposals of the Powers and the conference ended without any substantial results. For Macedonia, however, a serious precedent had been created, which was to have a profound effect on its future.

The Greeks had discerned in good time the dangers inherent in the proposals made by the Powers, and attempted to counter them by making representations to their ambassadors and by means of written protests bearing tens of thousands of signatures. The mobilization of Macedonian Hellenism at this date was truly impressive, and was without parallel up to that time. The danger soon reappeared, however, with the declaration of the Russo-Turkish war in April, 1877. Within nine months the Russian armies had advanced to the outskirts of Constantinople, and obliged the Turks to conclude peace at San Stefano on 3 March, 1878. The most hotly disputed provision of this treaty was the foundation of a huge independent Bulgarian state which was to include almost the whole of Macedonia except for Chalkidike, Thessalonike and the *kazas* of Kozani and Servia. Ignatiev who negotiated the treaty, had requested that Thessalonike should also be included in Greater Bulgaria, in return for the cession to the Greeks of Thessaly, Epirus and Crete, but both the tsar and the Russian government feared that this would provoke violent international reaction and rejected his proposal. The future of Macedonia seemed to have been decided.

The Greeks and the European Powers were not prepared to give up the struggle without a fight, however. Throughout the whole of 1877 secret negotiations were

309. The Greek delegation to the Congress of Berlin, July 1878, led by the Minister for Foreign Affairs, Theodore Deliyannis.

The decision of the Congress was that Macedonia should remain entirely under the jurisdiction of the Ottoman empire.

taking place for a general insurrection. In Athens, a central committee of the national societies National Defence and Brotherhood had undertaken, in cooperation with the government, to coordinate the preparations for the uprisings. Two particularly active members of this committee were the Macedonians Leonidas Paschalis, a lawyer, and Constantine Ischomachos, an army captain, who was the military leader of the Committee and eventually led the revolts in Thessaly. At the same time Leonidas Voulgaris, with the financial support of the Russians, was organizing a band of eight hundred men to incite a Greek revolt in eastern Macedonia.

Meanwhile, as the moment for the Greek intervention approached, it was deemed necessary to form a separate Macedonian Committee to conduct the struggle in Macedonia. This Committee consisted of a number of distinguished Macedonians: Professor George Pappazisis, the lawyers Leonidas Paschalis and Stephen Dragoumis (the latter being Secretary of the Committee) and the teacher Nicholas Chalkiopoulos. The original plan of action en-

visaged the landing of bands of volunteers in the areas of Olympos, Chalkidike and eastern Macedonia. The last was to advance to the north of Serres and carry the Greek insurrection as far as the Rhodope mountains before the Russian armies could reach the area. That landing near Olympos was first to rouse to arms the area of Olympos and Pieria, which had a strong revolutionary tradition, and then divide into two. One section was to penetrate the massif of Vermion while the other, having roused the population of the *kazas* of Servia, Kozani and Kastoria, was to advance in the direction of Florina, lake Prespa and Monastir.

Subsequent events, confirmed by the existing sources,[52] showed that by January 1878, not only had the villagers of Olympos and Pieria readily embraced the idea of insurrection, but also that extensive preparations had been made in the areas of Kozani, Siatista and Kastoria, in the region around Monastir, where the focal points were the Vlach villages and the townships of Pelagonia, and in Chalkidike and the region of Serres.

These preparations lost their impetus at the most crucial moment, however, as a result of the irresolution of the divided Greek government. When at the end of January 1878, the Russian armies approached Constantinople and the Greek army received orders to invade Thessaly, the despatch of the armed bands to Macedonia and the other unliberated areas was hurried and uncoordinated. The army was recalled within a few days, since the Russo-Turkish armistice had been signed in the meantime, but the revolts continued, their aim now being to create a 'Greek question' at the peace congress.

This turn of events condemned the uprising to failure from the outset. Nonetheless, a band of five hundred men, led by captain Kosmas Doumbiotis and with Leonidas Paschalis as its political adviser, landed at Litochoron on 28 February, where three days later a 'Provisional Government of Macedonia' was formed, with Evangelos Korovangos of Litochoron as president. There was a great rush of young villagers to join the band, but the stocks of arms were soon exhausted. Immediately afterwards Pieria rose, thanks to the initiative of the bishop of Kitros, Nicholas, of Paul Patralexis, the leader of the Vlachs of Vermion, and of the brigand chieftains Vangelis Chostevas and Panayotis Kaloyiros. Although almost the whole of the Olympos-Pieria region, with the exception of Katerini, had fallen into the hands of the insurgents, a series of tactical errors combined with the swift despatch of Ottoman troops resulted in the burning of Litochoron and many of the villages; the struggle was restricted to guerilla warfare and finally, at the end of April, the insurgents were compelled to retreat to Thessaly and thence to free Greece.

Meanwhile, in western Macedonia, the arrival of Doumbiotis in the Olympos area had set off a chain reaction. Young men from the regions of Servia, Kozani and Kastoria took to the mountains to await the arrival of armed bands from the Greek kingdom. A 'Provisional Government of the Province of Elimeia' was formed, with John Kovendaros of Kozani as president, the schoolmaster Anastasios Picheon as secretary and the local chieftain Joseph Liatis as military leader.

The failure of the movement in the region of Olympos and Pieria prevented armed action in western Macedonia. Two months later, however, guerilla warfare had spread to all the mountain terrain from Kozani to Monastir. Large numbers of guerillas and a good many chieftains who had taken part in the revolts in Thessaly, Epirus and the Olympos-Pieria area joined with local rebels and renewed their insurrectionary activity. As news coming in from abroad reported the probability that an international congress would be summoned to settle, amongst other things, the fate of Macedonia, new guerillas took to the mountains, giving the movement a more pronounced national-liberation tone. The leaders of the armed bands conveyed to Consul Logothetis demands that they should be reinforced by the Greek state, stating at the same time that they were subjecting themselves to his leadership. 'The leaders of the insurgents repeatedly declared to me,' noted Logothetis, 'that the will of my Consulate, of which they demanded to become the instruments, prevailed with them. The combatants including their chieftains are natives; they

are full of indomitable daring and fling themselves with unbridled ferocity into engagements, in which so far they have always been victorious.'[53] The Greek government, however, had limited the Greek demands at the Congress of Berlin to the annexation of Crete, Thessaly and Epirus, and had at first paid no attention to the movement in western Macedonia. It remained, therefore, for the western Macedonians to draw the attention of Europe to Macedonia by intensifying their struggle.

Despite the proclamation of martial law and the assembling of considerable military forces, which reached fifteen thousand in number, the guerillas retained control of the mountain areas from Kozani to the mountains of lake Prespa. For a time Pisoderi in the *kaza* of Florina was the headquarters for bands numbering about two thousand men. After the end of the Congress of Berlin (13 July, 1878), when the Greek government found itself obliged to bring pressure to bear on Turkey to cede the territories in Epirus and Thessaly that had been awarded to Greece, the prime minister Koumoundouros instructed Logothetis to lend support to these guerillas. The struggle lasted until November, when the armed bands were compelled to break up by the weather conditions.

The revolutionary movements in Macedonia were incapable of achieving the liberation of the area, but they did demonstrate the dynamic strength of Hellenism in this region and its thirst for freedom. At the same time, they revealed the Greek resistance to the unacceptable provisions of the treaty of San Stefano. From this negative point of view, the struggle of Macedonian Hellenism in 1878 furnished the arguments for those who were attempting to secure the reversal of the terms of the treaty of San Stefano, and the removal of the borders of the Bulgarian state from Macedonia.

The review of these terms finally took place at the Congress of Berlin (13 June - 13 July, 1878). The Russians were obliged to accept a sharp curtailment of their demands. Bulgaria was declared a tributary principality under the suzerainty of the sultan, but south of the Balkan and extending to the Rhodope mountains, Eastern Rumelia was made an autonomous province with a Christian governor. The whole of Macedonia remained part of the Ottoman empire, though article 23 of the treaty envisaged the introduction of administrative reforms, albeit in a completely unclear manner.

FROM THE CONGRESS OF BERLIN TO THE MACEDONIAN STRUGGLE

Macedonia: a pivotal issue in Balkan politics 1879-85

While the Greeks received the announcement of the decisions of the Congress of Berlin with relief, the Bulgarians were disillusioned to see their vision of a Greater Bulgaria vanish. Their first reaction was to turn to armed resistance. Having secured their rear by the presence of a Russian army in the Principality, they fomented a revolt in the neighbouring mountain region of northeast Macedonia (Razlog-Kresna). For a time the movement appeared to be assuming serious dimensions, but the Turks swiftly assembled a strong force and put a violent

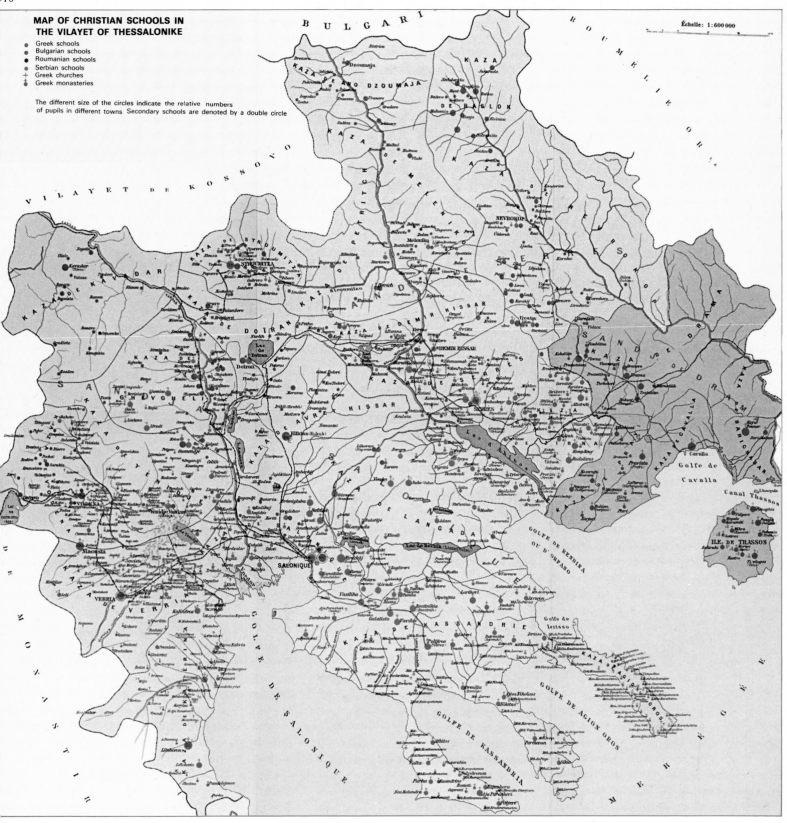

MAP OF CHRISTIAN SCHOOLS IN
THE VILAYET OF THESSALONIKE

- Greek schools
- Bulgarian schools
- Roumanian schools
- Serbian schools
- Greek churches
- Greek monasteries

The different size of the circles indicate the relative numbers
of pupils in different towns Secondary schools are denoted by a double circle

Échelle: 1:600 000

310. *From 1870 onwards, thanks to the generous assistance of many benefactors, Greek education in Macedonia expanded greatly, and Greek schools heavily outnumbered all the others. The map above, drawn by the Istituto Geografico de Agostini,* *Rome, shows Greek, Bulgarian, Roumanian and Serbian schools of the vilayet of Thessalonike immediately before the incorporation of Macedonia in Greece. Greek churches and monasteries are also indicated.*

end to it. North-east Macedonia remained in Ottoman hands. The Russians were even obliged to return Gorna Dzhoumaya (modern Blagoevgrad).[54]

The political consequences of the decisions at the Congress of Berlin went beyond armed resistance on the part of the Bulgarians. Despite the fact that Macedonia remained subject to Ottoman rule, the creation in its neighbourhood of a Bulgarian state with intense irredentist aspirations suggested that the Macedonian question would soon come to the forefront of Balkan problems.

The Congress had also revealed the particular aspirations of some of the Powers as far as Macedonia was concerned. Quite apart from the well-known dispute between Russia and Britain, the attitude of Vienna, and especially its insistence on controlling the *sanjak* of Novi Pazar, just north of Macedonia, gave rise to serious misgivings that Austria was about to press down as far as Thessalonike. In the end, Austria chose to push Serbia in this direction in order to free herself of Serbian ambitions in the Slav provinces of the Austro-Hungarian empire (Slovenia, Croatia and Bosnia).[55] This marked the appearance on the scene of the triple Greek-Bulgarian-Serbian dispute in Macedonia, which was to last up to the Balkan Wars.

Until the crisis of 1875-78, the Serbs had shown very little interest in Macedonia. The threat of the foundation of a large Bulgarian state, however, which eventually would attain a hegemonistic role in the Balkans, gave renewed impetus to the latent nationalist tendencies to be found in certain Serbian circles, which attempted to win the political world and the public opinion of their country to the idea of expansion towards the south.

As far as the Greeks were concerned, the Serbian initiatives were only a minor problem; the probability of radical reforms in the local administration was more immediate. According to article 23 of the Berlin Treaty, the International Commission that was to draw up the statute for the administration of Eastern Rumelia was also to produce plans for the reform of the Christian provinces of the Ottoman empire, including Macedonia. The Greek government, realistically, prepared itself in good time to protect the rights of the Greeks in the province. Greek policy took the following lines, which it followed until the annexation of Eastern Rumelia by the Bulgarians in 1885:[56] the northern zone, which was exclusively Slav, was no longer to be included amongst the Greek aspirations. The central zone, however, including its northernmost outposts (Ochrid, Krušovo, Monastir, Stromnitsa, Melenikon, Nevrokop) was to be retained within the sphere of Greek influence at any cost. To this end Greek historians rushed to bolster the new claims with scholarly arguments, emphasizing that areas to the north of the new line could not be considered Macedonian, since in antiquity they had not formed part of the Macedonian kingdom.[57]

The second feature of Greek policy concerned the Greek-speaking masses of Macedonia. After the foundation of the Bulgarian Church, the Slav-speakers who had not adhered to the Exarchate, despite the pressure brought to bear upon them, were deemed in practice to have opted for Hellenism. In other words the subjective factor (choice of national — religious side) emerged as a stronger consideration in determining a man's nationality than the objective factor (the language he spoke). Greek policy on the subject was based on the same reasoning: the Slav-speaking population that had remained faithful to the Patriarchate should be supported morally by the dissemination of the Greek language, so as successfully to counter the proselytizing activities of the Exarchate.

A third feature was the realization that Greek ambitions in Macedonia could not be furthered against the background of a policy of hostility to Turkey. Hellenism in Macedonia would be able to survive and to prevail only in a peaceful climate. The problem was that every proposal for regularizing relations between the two countries fell foul of one of a series of crises. During the last quarter of the nineteenth century, tension arose between 1878 and 1881 over the question of the cession of Epirus and Thessaly to Greece; in 1885-86 because of the Greek military mobilization on the occasion of the annexation by Bulgaria of Eastern Rumelia; shortly afterwards (1888-89) because of new disturbances in Crete; and, finally, in 1896-97 as a result of the events that led to open war between Greece and Turkey. All this increased Turkish suspicions of and hostility towards the Greek population, and frequently impelled them to support Bulgarian, rather than Greek, demands.

Finally, the fourth feature that may be mentioned is the attempt to find some basis for discussion of zones of influence with the other Balkan suitors of Macedonia. For a time after 1878 it was the policy of the Russians to reconcile Bulgarians and Greeks with a view to healing the Schism, but their attempts fell foul of the intransigent positions adopted by both sides.[58] As long as the Bulgarians continued to lay claim to almost the whole of Macedonia, including Thessalonike, all discussions were doomed to failure.

After the failure of the attempt to introduce reforms into Macedonia, the Greek government implemented its own plan for supporting Hellenism there.[59] Its first objective was the reinforcing of Greek education. Special attention was paid to the creation of schools in the major villages of the central zone, as well as the founding of teacher training colleges, girls' schools and primary' schools, with the aim of increasing the use of the Greek language in the family context. The education programme began to spread very rapidly, and it became apparent that the Association for the Diffusion of Greek Letters, which was a private organization, was not capable of coordinating a major government programme unaided: in 1887 the Committee for the Support of the Church and Education was founded, an organization that was apparently private but in fact was public, and operated under the guidance of the Ministry of Foreign Affairs.[60]

There were considerable difficulties in the way of achieving the desired level of coordination, however, for the local authorities frequently resisted the interventions of the Greek consuls, who had acquired great influence thanks to the credit at their disposal. The metropolitan bishops frequently put obstacles in their way. However, the refusal of the Oecumenical Patriarch Joachim III to cede to the representatives of the Greek state powers that traditionally belonged to the Church, was due in large measure to his fear of provoking Turkish interference in the educational affairs of the Christians.[61] The difference of view on this subject between the Greek government and the Oecumenical Patriarch was one of the causes of the resignation of Joachim in 1884. Ultimately neither side was able to persuade the other to accept its views completely, and meanwhile the Ottoman administration took advantage of their quarrels to interfere in the educational affairs of the Greeks.[62]

The second aim of Greek policy was the strengthening of the Church. Despite the continual clashes between consuls and bishops, successive Greek governments had repeatedly attempted to use the church in order to further their political designs in the province. Special subsidies were granted to the weak dioceses in the disputed zone, to counterbalance the loss of revenues resulting from the defection of the schismatics. Seminaries were created for the instruction of priests. Finally, pressure was exercised on the Phanar to withdraw unsuitable or slavophile prelates from Macedonia. However, judging from a study of consular reports for the thirty years 1870-1900, the results achieved did not match the efforts made.

The third aim of Greek policy was the strengthening of the Greek position in Macedonia. Any progress made in this sphere, however, was purely the result of private initiative. The efforts of the Greek state were directed towards the developing of strong communications between the kingdom and Macedonia. However, proposals to the Porte for the unification of the railway networks of the two countries and for the opening of regular steamship services between Volos and ports in Macedonia were not favourably received. A grandiose scheme to use Greek capital to found an agricultural bank in Macedonia, which would exclusively finance Greek farmers, suffered a similar fate.[63]

The dissemination of information was not ignored. During the 1880s the number of Greek consulates was increased to six, centred on Thessalonike, Monastir, Serres, Kavala, Skopje and Elassona (for southern Macedonia). One of the major figures was Peter Logothetis, consul at Monastir and subsequently at Thessalonike, and a man with a deep understanding of Macedonian problems. These consulates made use of a wide network of agents (for the most part, doctors, schoolmasters and merchants) in their attempts to keep track of developments in the provinces and at the same time give guidance to the unliberated Greeks. During the 1880s, the initiative in all these Greek activities was clearly passing to bodies that were under the control of the Greek state.

From the annexation of Eastern Rumelia to the war of 1897

In 1885, after seven years of trying, the Bulgarians succeeded in annexing Eastern Rumelia by means of a political and military coup (18 September, 1885). This came as a shock to the Greeks and Serbs, who saw the Bulgarian move as disruptive of the balance of power in the Balkans, and the beginning of a new expansionist drive,

311. *Women also took up arms in the struggle for the liberation of Macedonia. Dressed like their menfolk, they fought side by side with them. Shown above is Peristera, one of the leaders in western Macedonia. Photographic collection, Dr. E. Kofos.*

this time in the direction of Macedonia. The authorities in Belgrade took action to restore the balance without delay, seizing territories belonging to the Bulgarian Principality and also northern Macedonian. To secure this end, the prime minister, Garašanin, proposed a joint military venture to Greece, also suggesting negotiations to partition Macedonia. A concerted intervention by Greeks and Serbs was prevented, however, when the Serbo-Bulgarian war that had been declared on 14 November ended in a defeat for the Serbs that was as surprising as it was swift. Deliyannis, instead of learning from the Serbs' experience, ordered a general mobilization. This action satisfied the sense of national honour in the kingdom for the moment, but the Powers quickly blockaded the Greek harbours and compelled Deliyannis to resign.

Both Bulgaria's rivals in Macedonia came off worse as the result of the crisis of 1885-86. The Serbs lost their military supremacy and the Greeks, whose futile mobilization was a severe drain on the economy, succeeded only in turning the wrath of the Ottoman authorities against the Greek population in Macedonia. These developments raised the morale of the Bulgarian Macedonians, for the Bulgarian Principality now appeared in the eyes of the unliberated Christians to be the rising power in the Balkans that could offer them the hope of liberation. It was true that Bulgarian activity in Macedonia increased spectacularly following the annexation of Eastern Rumelia. The Russian consuls in Macedonia continued to support the Bulgarians in their local disputes with the Greeks, and to afford them protection against Ottoman atrocities. British policy at this time was to attempt to exploit the breach in the relations between Saint Petersburg and Sofia, and this led them to intervene at the Porte in support of many Bulgarian demands for administrative reforms. Finally, the friendly relations enjoyed by the Bulgarian prime minister, Stambulov, with the Ottoman government also helped to create a favourable climate for Bulgarian activity in Macedonia.

In its first phase, this activity continued to have as its main aim the creation of new Bulgarian churches and schools in the northern and central zones of Macedonia, and in a number of urban centres in the southern zone. Subsequently, in an attempt to win converts to Bulgarian national ideas, the Bulgarians began to train competent local cadres. Many young men were attracted by scholarships to study in the Principality, whence a good number of them later returned to their native land to occupy prominent positions as leaders of the Slav-speaking communities. At the same time the military leadership of the Bulgarian Macedonians was also being trained: during this period considerable numbers of Slav-speaking Macedonian youths were admitted to the Bulgarian military school, and afterwards enrolled in the Bulgarian army as officers or non-commissioned officers. These young men, together with a number of native chieftains later formed the membership of the Bulgarian armed bands that infiltrated Macedonia in order to incite the population to revolt.

Meanwhile, the idea of an armed uprising was gaining increasing ground with one faction of Bulgarians, mainly inside Macedonia itself. At the beginning of the 1890s, a number of intellectuals came to the conclusion that more forceful methods had to be adopted; these would compel the Ottoman administration to have recourse to repressive measures that would in the end drive the people to a mass revolt. In order to avoid giving prominence to the Bulgarian character of the movement and to blunt the reactions of the Greeks, the Serbs, and some of the Powers who were opposed to the incorporation of Macedonia into Bulgaria, the liberal slogan 'Macedonia for the Macedonians' was adopted. Through it, the protagonists of the idea proclaimed that all Macedonians, that is, all the nationalities that lived in Macedonia, would fight for an autonomous Macedonia. In practice, however, the concept of a multi-national independent Macedonia never advanced beyond the level of the revolutionary literature, issued mostly by Socialists, or of the romantic journalism of a section of the European press, which was incapable of comprehending Macedonian reality. At this time the term 'Macedonian' had a geographical, not a national, connotation, and was used by Greeks, Bulgarians and Serbs alike, when referring to their kin who came from Macedonia.

In 1893, the Secret Macedonian-Adrianopolitan Revolutionary Organization was founded in Resna; later, in 1896, it changed its name to Internal Macedonian-Adrianopolitan Revolutionary Organization, known by its initials as IMRO.

In 1894, the numerous Bulgarian-Macedonian organizations within the Bulgarian principality successfully united to form a Supreme Committee (*Vrhoven Komitet*) to direct the struggle in Macedonia and Thrace. In this they were assisted by the new government of Stoilov (1894-99) which reversed the pro-Turkish policy of Stambulov.

Despite its many problems, the Supreme Committee succeeded the following year in arming a number of bands and sending them to northern and central Macedonia. The enterprise failed, however, since the Bulgarian-Macedonian bands met with no support on the part of the local population. The Ottoman army, reorganized by the Germans, succeeded in checking the infiltration of these bands to a considerable degree, and in compelling them to return to the Bulgarian Principality.

The incursion of Bulgarian bands into Macedonia provoked considerable disquiet in Serbia and Greece, where it was realized that the Macedonian problem would lead to an armed conflict.

The Serbs were particularly uneasy, since they had not yet succeeded in creating their own strongholds within the Slav population of northern Macedonia, to which they were laying claim. Following the example of the Greeks and Bulgarians, Serbian historians set themselves to propounding ancestral rights in Macedonia, basing their case on the medieval empire of Stephen Dušan. Using arguments drawn from linguistics, ethnography and anthropology, they attempted on the one hand to dispel the impression that the Slavs of Macedonia were related to the 'Mongol' Bulgarians beyond the Balkan mountains, and on the other to establish a racial connection between the Macedonian Slavs and the Serbs. As for the territory claimed, this was defined by the obscure geographical term 'Old Serbia', which in Macedonia included the northern, Slavic zone. There were those, however, who held the view that Serbia should lay claim to territories as far south as Kastoria and the Aegean coast, irrespective of the ethnic composition of these regions.[64]

In practice, Serbian policy followed the Bulgarian and Greek examples. The Association of Saint Sabbas was founded in 1886, in imitation of the Association for the Diffusion of Greek Letters. The newly formed Serbian society was supported in its work by the Serbian consulates opened between 1887 and 1890 in Thessalonike, Skopje, Monastir and Serres. A few years later, however, the Serbian government itself assumed the task of coordinating educational and political activity in Macedonia.[65] The Serbs were at a severe disadvantage in that the Ottoman state did not recognize the existence of Serbian nationality. They were therefore obliged to appeal to the Oecumenical Patriarchate to appoint Serbian bishops and to found Serbian schools in the northern Macedonian provinces. They also made repeated attempts to come to an understanding with the two main decision-making cen-

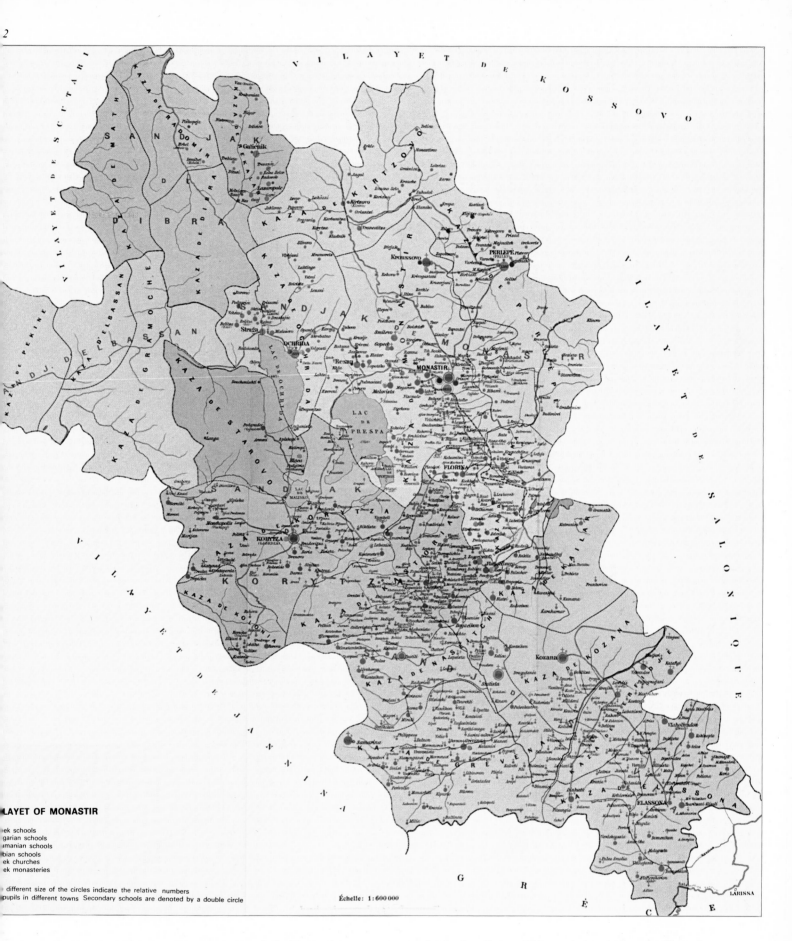

VILAYET DE KOSSOVO

VILAYET DE SCUTARI

VILAYET DE SALONIQUE

VILAYET OF MONASTIR

ek schools
garian schools
umanian schools
bian schools
ek churches
ek monasteries

different size of the circles indicate the relative numbers
pupils in different towns Secondary schools are denoted by a double circle

Échelle: 1:600 000

312. The Greek, Bulgarian, Roumanian and Serbian primary and secondary schools together with the Greek churches and monasteries in the vilayet of Monastir just before the liberation of Macedonia.

313. *The armed band led by Kapsalopoulos and Mylonas in which Melas and Mazarakis, all pictured above, also fought. This band was one of many organized by the Ethnike Etaireia.*

It was especially active in the area around Krania where, though it clashed on many occasions with Turkish forces, it finally had to withdraw. Athens, J. Mazarakis Collection.

tres of Hellenism, the Greek government and the Oecumenical Patriarchate, in order to achieve a definition of zones of influence in Macedonia and cooperation to check Bulgarian infiltration. The Greeks appeared excessively cautious, however, calculating that Greek-Serbian cooperation would probably lead to an understanding between the Bulgarians and the Turks. In the mistaken impression that the Serbs would be compelled to make concessions in order to secure Greek support, successive Greek governments remained intransigent in the face of extreme territiorial claims north of the line from Ochrid, by way of Krušovo, Prilep, the Pelagonian plain, Stromnitsa and Nevrokop to Melenikon. They also continued until the end of the century to bring pressure to bear on the Patriarchate not to appoint Serbian bishops to the northern Macedonian dioceses. The result of this was that the Greeks were unable to turn the Serb-Bulgarian dispute to their advantage and ultimately drove the Serbs to seek the basis of an understanding with the Bulgarians.

The inadequacy of Greek policy at this period was the outcome of a number of internal weaknesses and of wider complications on the foreign front. Greek-Turkish relations, which had deteriorated in 1885-86, took a new turn for the worse in 1888-89 as a result of the Cretan question and an isolated incident in Macedonia that was to have unfortunate long-term consequences. In 1887 Anastasios

Picheon, a schoolmaster at Kozani and Kastoria and an agent of the Greek consulates in Thessalonike and Monastir, was arrested. From his secret correspondence with the consuls, the Turks became aware of the Greek educational activity of the last ten years. There followed an extensive series of arrests of prominent Greeks in western and central Macedonia, which resulted in the disintegration of the Greek organization there and the terrorizing of the supporters of Greek nationalism.[66]

The Turks were moved by the 'Picheon affair' to attempt to place the entire Greek educational mechanism under their control. They brought great pressure to bear on the Patriarchate which in turn gave orders to the local bishops not to cooperate too closely with the Greek consuls in educational matters. Furthermore, the disbursements made by the Greek government to the educational foundations in the unliberated provinces were seriously reduced as a direct result of the economic crisis in the kingdom at the beginning of the 1890s.

The result of all this was that at the very beginning of the great Bulgarian drive towards Macedonia, Hellenism was divided, economically weak, and diplomatically isolated.[67] Nonetheless, the invasion of Macedonia by armed bands of Bulgarians in 1895 acted as the catalyst that led to a new mobilization to save Macedonia.

The initiative passed from the government to private

citizens. In 1894, under the pressure of events in Crete and Macedonia, a number of young officers founded the *Ethnike Etaireia* in Athens. This society grew to a large size in under two years, assembled enormous financial reserves and opened branches both inside the kingdom and abroad, including a number in some of the Macedonian towns.

By the summer of 1896, the *Etaireia* was in a position to send well-armed bands to Macedonia to assist the Greek population to counter Bulgarian propaganda and the activities of the armed bands of Bulgarians. The Greek bands were composed for the most part of Macedonians who had settled in the kingdom, led by non-commissioned officers from the Greek army or Macedonian chieftains who had taken part in the revolt of 1878. The most important of them was Athanasios Brouphas from Paliokrimini in the province of Voios. Brouphas had been very active as a guerilla chieftain in Macedonia and was a natural leader for such an operation. They disembarked at Eleutherochori in Pieria at the beginning of July 1896, and after a number of clashes with Turkish detachments, moved northwards and entered the Morihovon region where, after a battle lasting many hours, Brouphas was killed and his band broke up. It was followed by five others, most of which set out from the Greek-Turkish border zone, though one attempted a landing on the coast of Pieria. None of them was able to establish itself for any time, however, and some of them dispersed as soon as they reached Ottoman territory. Members of these dispersed bands, led by local chieftains, moved to various parts of central and western Macedonia and carried out small scale guerilla operations.[68] In a proclamation from the region of Great Prespa, issued on 15 August, 1896, these chieftains declared: 'Brother Macedonians: two months ago we took up arms against the tyrants ruling our country, and the land applauded our movement, as is shown by the enthusiastic reception we have met with everywhere.... We are Greek, and we wish Macedonia to be Greek, and are fighting for this end.'

In the last analysis, the failure of the despatch of armed bands to Macedonia was due to the total lack of preparation within Macedonia itself and to the generally prevailing confusion as to the objectives of the enterprise. The lack of preparation may be attributed to the fact that the *Ethnike Etaireia* had not had time to organize its clandestine network in the unliberated provinces. The *Etaireia's* intentions were undoubtedly to revive the morale of Macedonian Greeks and to publicize Greek aspirations in Macedonia, at a time when the impression that Macedonia was fundamentally a Bulgarian country was steadily gaining ground in Europe. In practice, however, the despatch of armed bands to Macedonia mainly served to create a diversion in the north and take the pressure off the Cretan revolution. As a result, it was readily interpreted by the Turks as an attempt to create a climate of revolt against Ottoman authority.

Independently of this turn of events, the *Ethnike Etaireia* succeeded, despite the obstacles placed in its way by certain agencies of the Greek government, in forming numerous well-armed bands that penetrated deep into Macedonia. The vast majority of those who enlisted were

314. A. Brouphas, leader of a band organized by the Ethnike Etaireia, landed at Eleutherochori, Pieria in 1896. Though his forces penetrated deep into Macedonia and fought several skirmishes, they were eventually defeated and Brouphas was killed. Athens, J. Mazarakis Collection.

Macedonians and Epirotes, and there were a good number of Thessalians and Greeks from various parts of the kingdom and the diaspora. Most of the Macedonians were settled in Thessaly and had taken part in the revolt of 1878.

The *Ethnike Etaireia* did not abandon its designs for Macedonia even after the failure of the armed bands. The following year it formed large expeditionary force of two thousand men which penetrated the area of south-west Macedonia with the aim of cutting communications between Macedonia and Epirus and inciting a general revolt. The leaders of the revolution were A. Mylonas and G. Kapsalopoulos, and the band crossed the frontiers on 27 March, 1897. A large Turkish army gathered in the border zone, however, and the enterprise failed. With the eruption of a full scale war and the defeat of the Greek army the large band that had been formed for Macedonia dispersed completely.[69] Another band of four hundred men landed near Kavala to blow up the railway line, but it too disbanded before it could carry out its mission.

The Greco-Turkish war of 1897 was provoked, of course, by the revolt of Crete, and its aim was the liberation of Crete, but the consequences for Macedonia could have been disastrous. Neither the Bulgarians nor the Serbs concealed their intention to intervene in the event of the spread of hostilities, in order to make gains in Macedonia. In an attempt to preclude any irreversible developments in Macedonia for as long as it was embroiled in the Cretan question, the Greek government proposed separately to the Bulgarians and the Serbs that they should come to some understanding about the Macedonian problem. Just before the beginning of the war it announced to Sofia its willingness to examine the idea of creating an autonomous Macedonia, or the definition of spheres of influence, in return for which it was prepared to concede an outlet to the Aegean. The Bulgarian government, however, had no desire to enter into commitments to Greece, since at the beginning of 1897 it had already agreed with the Serbians that they should both remain neutral during the Greco-Turkish war and settle their own differences in Macedonia.[70]

THE MACEDONIAN STRUGGLE AND THE LIBERATION OF MACEDONIA

Bulgarian Initiatives 1898-1903

The defeat of 1897 had a twofold effect on the Greeks of Macedonia. On the one hand, the local Muslims were given a free hand to vent their rage on the Greek rural population; and on the other, the Porte, pursuing its policy of using the rival nationalities to neutralize each other, hastened to satisfy many of the demands made by the Bulgarians, the Serbs and even the Roumanians. Thanks to these new concessions, the Bulgarians were now able, with the greatest ease, to take over churches and schools belonging to communities owing allegiance to the Patriarchate. The Serbs and pro-Roumanian Vlachs also acquired the right to found similar institutions in areas which had been controlled up to that time by Greek orthodox communities. The result was that many of the patriarchist villages in the mixed central zone sought refuge in a mass conversion to the Bulgarian Exarchate.[71] Furthermore, the Bulgarians chose this precise moment to mobilize the Christian population against Ottoman rule.

The Greek position also began to be weakened in the mixed areas of the central zone of Macedonia where their influence had been strong until 1896. The Greeks, however, had begun to lose their dominant position in Macedonia several decades earlier than this. A number of factors can be cited for this turn of events; first of all it had not proved possible to restore the population losses suffered during the period of the War of Independence. Secondly, the formerly unchallenged authority of the Oecumenical Patriarchate and the Greek clergy had been seriously curtailed by the emergence of the rival Bulgarian Church and by the decision of the Porte to withdraw certain of its age-old prerogatives and privileges. Furthermore, the influence among the subject Christians only enjoyed by the independent, orthodox Greek state, had itself diminished perceptibly after the Eastern Crisis of 1875-78, as other Christian Balkan states, capable of offering assistance or of holding out the hope of liberation made their presence felt on the scene. When to these factors is added the consideration that the almost complete

315. *Villagers from the area of Monastir dragged from their homes by Saravov's band after a raid on their village. Once the*

headmaster of the Bulgarian secondary school in Thessalonike, Boris Saravov reacted in his own violent way by taking the law into his own hands. Forming his guerilla organization, he pillaged and destroyed throughout Macedonia.

316

317

economic privacy enjoyed by the local Greek population in Macedonia had also begun to be threatened by the steady economic progress made by the pro-Roumanian Vlach and pro-Bulgarian Slav populations, it comes as no surprise that the Bulgarian nationalists felt supremely confident that Macedonia would come under their control in the immediate future.

The internal economic and social conditions were in any case ripe for a confrontation with the oppressive Ottoman establishment. The situation is well characterized by Kouzes-Pezas, the consul at Monastir, who wrote at the beginning of 1901: 'Even if Chinese agents were to appear today in Macedonia and promise freedom to the Christians, they would win their sympathies'.[72] The metropolitan bishop of Moglena came to a similar conclusion.

The Bulgarians had foreseen the new situation in good time, and when the Macedonian-Thracian Committee proclaimed the slogan 'Macedonia for the Macedonians' there was a significant response, mainly from the rural masses. This slogan cleverly concealed self-interested Bulgarian national aspirations. Under the pretext of destroying Ottoman suzerainty and founding an autonomous Macedonian state, it attempted to mobilize all Macedonian Greeks, Bulgarians, Serbs, Vlachs, Albanians and even Turks — to the advantage of Bulgarian nationalism. It is quite clear from the documents that this was in fact the ultimate aim of the protagonists of this movement,[73] though attempts were made at the time and later to attribute different motives to the activities of one faction of Bulgarian insurgents who were called 'Macedonians'.[74]

The activities of this group certainly did not always coincide with the aspirations of the official Bulgarian state. Nonetheless, the slogan 'Macedonia for the Macedonians' met with a wider response than the idea of annexing Macedonia to Bulgaria. Even Gladstone embraced it in 1897, although, as Francis Stevenson observes in his book *The Macedonian Question* (1902) Gladstone included in the term 'Macedonians' all the nationalities that lived in Macedonia, in the belief that despite differences of race, language and religion, the inhabitants of Macedonia had a certain community of interest as opposed to all the foreigners, and especially as opposed to Turkish soldiers and tax collectors.[75]

316. Germanos Karavangelis, metropolitan of Kastoria, who inspired the organization of the first Greek armed bands to check the incursions of the Bulgarian comitadjis into Macedonia. Athens, Benaki Museum.

317. Ion Dragoumis, vice-consul at Monastir, was active in mobilizing local forces and rousing public opinion on behalf of Macedonia. Athens, J. Mazarakis Collection.

318. The Slav-speaking fighter, Kotas, who, until his death in 1904, played a leading role in the Greek resistance in western Macedonia. Athens, Benaki Museum.

319. Lambros Koromilas was appointed Consul General at Thessalonike in 1904 to organize the Macedonian Struggle. His contribution was outstanding. Athens, National Historical Museum.

In practice, it did not prove possible to advance Bulgarian aims in Macedonia swiftly, mainly because of disputes between the Bulgarian-Macedonian committees that were active in Bulgaria and Macedonia, and also because the Bulgarian government and the committees were unable to agree on a common line. The Central Committee of IMRO, which was active inside Macedonia, continued its proselytizing activities in all directions. Orthodox Slav- and Vlach-speaking villagers who had remained faithful to the Patriarchate, as well as those who had adhered to the Exarchate, were enrolled in the ranks of the organization. The Greek consul at Monastir wrote of the agents of the Committee: 'They aspire to unite all in the idea of liberation and of deliverance from the Turkish yoke, deliberately avoiding all mention of Bulgaria and the Schism, and at the most hinting at the hope of creating a separate autonomous state.'[76]

Disruptive tendencies had emerged in the circles of the Supreme Committee of the Macedonian-Adrianopolitan organizations that had their headquarters in Sofia. The leadership of the Organization had fallen into the hands of Mihailovsky and Tsontsev, but Boris Saravov mobilized his own armed organization inside Macedonia, which began to proselytize by force and also to bring pressure to bear on, or murder, dissidents and leading members of the Greek and Serbian Communities. This activity began around 1899 and reached a climax in 1902 when the leadership of the Supreme Committee decided to set the revolt in motion by sending armed bands from Bulgaria.

Despite its internal quarrels, the Bulgarian movement appeared as a proclamation of social justice and the brotherhood of all Macedonians irrespective of race, language and religion; however, under the pretext of meeting the needs of the struggle and neutralizing the instruments of Ottoman rule, it also acted as oppressor and destroyer of rival nationalities. Its main targets were therefore the leading cadres of Hellenism in the villages, the towns and even the guerilla bands. Under these conditions the ranks of the Committee swelled daily with new converts, who were obliged to sell even their animals in order to buy the weapons which the Organization compelled them to procure in readiness for the general revolt.

Greek indecision

The Greek government was not in a position to adapt its response to the new conditions created by the Bulgarian campaign. Initially it confined itself to intensifying its old methods.[77] It increased its advances to the schools, while at the same time taking steps to improve the quality of the education by founding teacher-training colleges and appointing school inspectors, it increased its allocations to the threatened dioceses in the north and central zone; it made special disbursements to the consulates for the creation of an information network; and it made sure that able men were assigned to key posts, who could give more effective guidance to the local Greek population. The most important step in this direction was an appeal to the former Oecumenical Patriarch Joachim III to reassume his office, this time with the support of the Greek government. His

320. Demetrios Kalapothakis, editor of the newspaper, 'Embros'. He became president of the Greek 'Macedonian Committee' established in Athens in 1903, which made an important contribution to the Macedonian Struggle. Athens, National Historical Museum.

election helped to revitalize the higher ranks of the clergy in Macedonia.[78] Within two to three years, new metropolitan bishops had been appointed to vital dioceses (Germanos Karavangelis to Kastoria and Chrystostomos to Drama, for example), where they were now openly active in support of the national cause.[79]

In view of the Bulgarian activity the Greek government attempted to win over the Sublime Porte to some form of cooperation against the common threat.[80] Similarly, consuls and metropolitan bishops attempted to fan the zeal of the local authorities against the Bulgarian committees, and particularly against those groups that, unchecked, were systematically annihilating the leaders of the Greek population.[81] This policy too brought only limited gains, partly as a result of the natural incompetence of the Ottoman administration, partly because the local authorities had been corrupted by financial subventions from the Bulgarian organization, and partly because the foreign consuls or ambassadors at Constantinople intervened to secure the suspension of measures taken against, or penalties imposed on supporters of the Bulgarian Organization. Whenever the cooperation brought results, this was due to the competence or the personal relations of the local bishop or con-

sul (the metropolitan bishop Karavangelis at Kastoria, and the consuls Evgeniadis and Stornaris at Thessalonike and Serres respectively).[82] By contrast in Monastir, where Pezas had succeeded in organizing an excellent information network within the ranks of the Bulgarian Organization, the information was never put to use, thanks to the inertia of the local Ottoman authorities. In practice, these authorities, instead of taking preventive measures, resorted to brutal acts of repression. For his part, Patriarch Joachim III tried to convince the Greek government of just how fruitless it was to base its hopes on collaboration with the Turks. As he wrote to the Greek representative A. Potté: 'The thanks given for our services against the common foe were purely cosmetic.... The recipient of those services looks upon both Christian races as hostile and cunning and dishonest, and regrets that he is unable to destroy them forthwith.'[83]

The consul at Monastir, Kouzes-Pezas, a greater realist, did not hesitate openly to quarrel with his superiors in the Ministry of Foreign Affairs, demanding that radical methods be used to deal with the situation. 'The time when we could use solely peaceful and civilizing means to ensure our predominance in Macedonia,' he wrote, 'has gone forever, thanks to the impatience and daring of the Bulgarian patriots and our own wilful blindness.' He therefore proposed the adoption of more drastic methods including the creation of secret societies in Macedonia, with three-man committees in the major towns and villages backed by execution squads so that they could react more positively to Bulgarian moves. The responsibility for the general coordination of these committees would rest with Athens, and if the government was unable to assume it, it would be advisable to form a secret committee.[84] It is interesting to note that Patriarch Joachim had made similar recommendations concerning the founding of a secret society.[85] The Minister of Foreign Affairs, Romanos, in his reply rejecting Pezas' proposals, gave the following justification, revealing thereby not only the defeatism of the authorities in Athens but also their inability to grasp the meaning of the rapid developments in Macedonia: 'Neither the Government, nor its representatives, should stray into enterprises of this nature, the futility of which has been demonstrated in the past and which, given the final end to which they are designed, are rejected by the public conscience and by all civilized states. The Greek state neither can, nor should, follow Bulgaria in the use of this kind of activity (*sic*).'[86]

Germanos Karavangelis, however, undertook to accomplish what the official Greek state had refused to do. From the moment that he came to Kastoria at the beginning of 1900, he found himself faced with a chaotic situation.[87] In most of the villages in his diocese, including those that were not schismatic, the churches were closed and the priests were obliged to conduct their services in Slavonic. Many of the schools were closed, since the teachers had been terrorized and had congregated in Kastoria. Germanos began to make circuits throughout the whole of his area, which was held by the Bulgarian guerillas, popularly known as comitadjis. His courage inspired confidence in his followers, but only temporarily: as soon as he departed,

321. *The staff of the Greek Consulate in Thessalonike in 1908. Headed initially by Lambros Koromilas, the Consulate maintained links with the armed bands and local units in the towns and villages of Macedonia and was thus the coordinating force behind the Greek Struggle in Macedonia. Athens, J. Mazarakis Collection.*

the executions began again and, with them, the pressure to join the Bulgarian Organization. Faced with this situation, Germanos turned to other methods. He succeeded in detaching from the Organization the Slav-speaking chieftains Kotas from Roulia and Vangelis from Strebeno, thus acquiring his first armed force in the area of Korestia. Despite the vigour of the two local chieftains, however, they were not enough. The metropolitan therefore attempted to rouse the conscience of the Greek nation and persuade the Greek government to send arms and, more importantly, men from the free state. In a letter to the prime minister, A. Zaimis, after singing the praises of Kotas' work, he pointed out the possibilities of extending his activities to the provinces of Kastoria, Prespa, Monastir and Edessa: 'it need only be heard that a few dozen Greek eagles have arrived to assist Kotas'.[88]

The Greek government, however, continued to pursue a passive policy and contented itself with sending a little financial support. Meanwhile the cries of despair and the appeals from within Macedonia multiplied. The Greeks who were suffering hardship in the face of the Bulgarian activity now demanded that the Greeks take similar action. In Athens, the demands of the Macedonian Greeks were addressed mainly to leading Greek politicians, army officers, academics and journalists who, since the time of the

Ethnike Etaireia had had frequent contacts with Macedonia. Since these personalities rightly or wrongly, carried the stigma of the failure of 1897, they could not easily persuade the Government. Thus they took the initiative to assist those who were already fighting in Macedonia on a private basis. A group of officers and civilians centred around the family of Stephen Dragoumis began to take action. His brother-in-law, Paul Melas, and some of his comrades, sent the first armed band to Karavangelis in the spring of 1903. Shortly before this, in November 1902, Stephen's son Ion Dragoumis, a young diplomat, had successfully requested a posting as vice-consul to the consulate in Monastir. In this position, acting without instructions from the government and in the face of the objections of his superior, he organized a secret organization, *Amyna*, (Defence), at first in Monastir and afterwards in the major towns in western Macedonia. The aims of the small committees of Defence were to create an information network, to organize the defensive struggle, and to take steps designed to intimidate the Bulgarians.[89] Similar movements began to spring up in other towns in Macedonia, as a result of initiatives by members of the Greek communities, the educational societies, the craft guilds and of professionals. Apart from Defence none of them converted their concern into practical form, for they

322. *Paul Melas, who fought for the liberation of Macedonia, making every Greek aware of the cause. He met a hero's death in western Macedonia in 1904. He is portrayed in the uniform of a Macedonian fighter. Athens, National Historical Museum.*

had no central guidance or means of making their presence felt.

Attempts were made to cover this gap through the initiatives of Greek patriots, mainly Macedonians resident in Athens. The Geroyannis brothers from Chalkidike formed their Central Macedonian Association at this time, and the society Hellenism of Neoklis Kazazis and, a little later, the Auxiliary Committee of the Macedonians became active; the president of the last was the archbishop of Athens and its membership included some leading members of Athenian society.

The Ilinden rising

All this activity proved insufficient to mobilize the Greek state machinery. In 1903, however, the revolutionary ac-

tivity of the Bulgarians provoked the intervention of the European Powers in Macedonian affairs, after which it was impossible for the Greek government to remain idle.

In October 1902, large bands of Bulgarians penetrated into north-west and western Macedonia from the Bulgarian principality and attempted, in cooperation with local Bulgarian-Macedonian bands, to incite the population to revolt. This initiative derived from the activities of the Supreme Committee in Sofia, which had not secured the concurrence of IMRO. Problems of internal coordination combined with the cautious attitude of the villagers and the prompt mobilization of the Ottoman army, quickly neutralized the insurrection before it could assume a mass character. The most important Bulgarian leaders, Tsontsev and Yankov, who were officers in the Bulgarian army, were compelled to return to Bulgaria.[90] Despite the failure of the venture, however, preparations for a more widespread movement the following year continued with increasing intensity throughout the winter.

Again, internal, problems within the ranks of the Bulgarian organization led to uncoordinated operations. In the spring of 1903 there were widespread acts of sabotage, unsanctioned by any organization, in the city of Thessalonike and its hinterland. Among the more important targets were the Ottoman Bank, which was blown up; the steamship Guadalquivir, which was sunk in the Thermaic Gulf; and the rail and telecommunications networks, which were cut at a number of places in central Macedonia. These terrorists were concerned to create an impression, rather than provoke a general revolt.[91] The Turks, however, reacted with a series of violent repressive measures. It was clear that the only method remaining was revolt. The leaders of the Greek population vainly attempted to restrain the rural population, especially in the mixed areas. Vainly, too, they tried to awaken the Ottoman authorities to the need to protect the Greek communities and the mixed populations from the penetration of Bulgarian nationalism.

On 20 July (O.S.) the day of Prophet Elijah (Ilinden), armed revolt broke out on the orders of IMRO. The main burden fell on the provinces of western and northern Macedonia; central and eastern Macedonia remained essentially outside the struggle as did the purely Greek-speaking southern zone. Slav-speakers and Vlach-speakers, both patriarchist and schismatic, took to the mountains, either of their own will or as a result of coercion. From the very first the Bulgarians tried to give the struggle a social content by attacking not only the small Turkish garrisons but also the large estates (*chiftliks*) and the property of the Turkish beys. At the same time, however, they also turned against the leaders of the Greek population, many of whom they executed or compelled to take refuge in the large urban centres. Once the Turkish army had been reconstituted, however, and began its mopping up operations, there was widespread devastation. Methodically, and without any distinction between Bulgarians and Greeks, or between insurgents and villagers who had been led astray or had acted under compulsion, the Turks embarked upon a course of genocide. When the extent of the disaster was reckoned, Macedonian Hellenism counted hundreds of new martyrs, victims on this occasion of Turkish reprisals against the Bulgarians. The material cost was also high: some major Greek centres were completely destroyed, amongst them the township of Krušovo and many Greek-Vlach and patriarchist communities in the areas of Monastir, Florina and Kastoria.[92]

On the Bulgarian side, the annihilation of some of their most important chieftains, the dispersal of their bands, and the arrests of hundreds of cadres in the villages and towns initially gave the impression that their struggle in Macedonia had been dealt a severe blow. The Ilinden rising, however, successfully promoted the Bulgarian demand for a political settlement of the issue. The revolt of the Macedonian population incited by the Bulgarian organizations convincingly brought home to the European Powers the demand for Macedonian autonomy.

Even before Ilinden, at the beginning of 1903, the Porte had agreed upon a plan for reforms put forward by Austria and Russia, known as the Vienna Reform Scheme. Until the Ilinden rising, however, very little progress had been made towards implementing this Scheme, and the Powers were obliged to intervene again and request, more persuasively this time, that the reforms be carried out.

At this time, Britain seemed disposed to support the foundation of an autonomous Macedonia under a Christian governor. This idea was opposed by Russia and Austria, while Germany was opposed to any proposal that affected the sovereign rights of the sultan. The new reform plan, known as the Mürzsteg Programme, bore the stamp of Russian and Austrian policy, which meant the preservation of the status quo in Macedonia.

The main reforms of the Vienna and Mürzsteg Programmes envisaged the appointment of an inspector-general to the three vilayets of Thessalonike, Monastir and Skopje (the first Inspector was Hilmi Pasha); the appointment of two advisers to him, a Russian and an Austrian; participation by Christians in the administration and the gendarmerie; the reorganization of the Turkish gendarmerie with the aid of European officers; measures for the reform of the financial and taxation systems; and finally, provision for the readjusting of the administrative divisions of Macedonia in such a way as to secure a more realistic geographical distribution of the various nationalities.

This last provision caused considerable unease, however, for it was interpreted as a first step in the direction of the partition of Macedonia according to national majorities. Since the national sentiments held by the population in the mixed zones were ambiguous, however, the provision was clearly an invitation — and a challenge — to the Greeks, Bulgarians and Serbs to intensify the struggle to win over these populations.

The Greek armed reaction

The fact that the turn taken in 1903 by the course of events in Macedonia involved the use of arms aroused Greek public opinion. Official government policy, however, was influenced not so much by public demonstrations as by the initiatives taken by the Powers. The possibility that the administrative boundaries would be readjusted along

323. Constantine Mazarakis - Ainian ('Akritas') was the leader of an armed unit active in central Macedonia. He was also an important figure in the Greek Organization in Athens and Thessalonike. Athens, J. Mazarakis Collection.

unclear national lines led the leading members of the government in Athens to waive their reservations. The government of Theotokis decided to act.

Its first action was to send a group of four officers to Macedonia, amongst them the future national hero, second lieutenant Paul Melas. This group studied the situation and recommended to the government, amongst other things, that armed bands should be despatched.[93]

The governmnent also decided to staff the consulate at Thessalonike with competent diplomats, supported by army officers. The office of General Consul in Thessalonike was filled by Lambros Koromilas, who was given very wide authority.

At the same time, as a result of close cooperation between private citizens and government, the Macedonian Committee (*Makedoniko Komitato*) was founded in

324. The Greek officer, Spyromilios from Chimarra, Epirus, who commanded a band in central Macedonia. He was one of the many officers from the Greek state who formed units to assist the Macedonians in their struggle for freedom. Athens, J. Mazarakis Collection.

Athens, with Demetrios Kalapothakis, publisher of the newspaper *Embros* as its president. The aim of the Committee was to organize the armed struggle in Macedonia and, in theory, in the other unliberated provinces of Turkey.[94]

The attention of the Committee focussed mainly on western Macedonia, where the danger had appeared to be most immediate during the Ilinden rising. In this same region, the ground had been prepared to some extent thanks to the activities of the metropolitan Germanos, of the secret organization Defence, and of a number of small bands of local chieftains. It was against this background that, at the end of August 1904, the first band was despatched under Paul Melas who, as General Commander for western Macedonia, was responsible for the guidance of all the scattered armed bands of locals and volunteers in the vilayet of Monastir. Melas' activities lasted only one and a half months, however: on 26 October, his band was surrounded by a Turkish detachment in the village of Statista (modern Mela) near Kastoria and he himself was killed while attempting to break out.

His correspondence,[95] and particularly his lengthy report to the Committee,[96] makes it clear that the main thrust of his efforts was directed to the psychological and organizational spheres. Avoiding clashes with the Turks, as far as he could, he initiated a series of enterprises in schismatic villages designed to terrorize the Bulgarian terrorists and also to recall to the Patriarchate and to Hellenism all those who had crossed to the Bulgarian camp out of fear. At the same time he sought to organize the Greeks by founding small committees in villages and townships based on the model of the kernels of which Defence was formed, their mission being to gather information, to protect and supply the bands, and to form a local armed civilian militia. Before he could bring his work to completion, however, he fell to Turkish bullets, a victim of the absence of any internal Greek organization.

The death of Melas profoundly moved Athenian society, of which he was a distinguished member. It is no exaggeration to claim that through his death, Paul Melas — 'the Lord Byron of the Macedonian Struggle' as he is called by the English historian D. Dakin — succeeded in making the fate of Macedonia a matter of concern for all Greeks.[97] Volunteers and financial contributions flooded in to the Committee from all parts of the kingdom, and also from the unliberated provinces and the diaspora.

Melas' place was taken by the Cretan lieutenant George Tsondos, and in Thessalonike Koromilas began to weave his own plan of action, organizing and supporting armed bands of locals. At the same time, Melas' example was followed and attempts were made to organize secret societies in all the towns and townships, and in many of the villages of southern, central and eastern Macedonia. The centre of activity in eastern Macedonia was Serres, where the new consul, A. Sachtouris, also had a small band of officers to support him.

Although the attempt to organize a secret network of Greek committees proceeded at a satisfactory pace, the achievements in the military sphere throughout 1904 were disappointing. The local chieftains possessed neither the experience nor the discipline to carry on an unorthodox and demanding struggle. Within a short space of time, the Bulgarian organization skilfully succeeded in turning the Turkish pursuit squadrons against them and dispersing them.

Another serious problem was the division of the leadership of the struggle between the Macedonian Committee in Athens and the General Consulate in Thessalonike. The leading members of the Committee insisted on controlling from a distance even questions concerning the tactical manoeuvres of the bands. The lack of swift communications, however, combined with inadequate knowledge of local conditions gave rise to confusion which frequently led to disaster. From his vantage point Koromilas demanded that the unified coordination of the struggle at local level should be assigned to him; this had in any case been the government's original intention when they posted him to Thessalonike. Thanks to the staffing of the Consulate with officers; to direct communications with the armed bands in the field and the secret societies in the villages and towns; and to his being kept informed con-

325. *The Cretan George Tsontos (Vardas) and his Cretan volunteers filled the place left vacant by the death of Paul Melas. He organized the resistance in western Macedonia, put heart into the inhabitants, encouraged the enlistment of new volunteers and impeded wide scale Bulgarian penetration in the area. Athens, J. Mazarakis Collection.*

tinuously and immediately of the movements of the rival forces, the experienced diplomat was in an excellent position to give more effective direction to the struggle.

In Athens, the government compromised by giving the consul at Monastir responsibility for coordination in the vilayet of Monastir analogous with that exercised by Koromilas for the vilayet of Thessalonike. The Macedonian Committee was to continue its work of preparing and despatching bands and supplies to Macedonia, as well as dealing with more general issues affecting the struggle.[98]

Their brief experience of armed action in 1904 led Koromilas and his associates to abandon the idea of using local *klephts*-cum-chieftains as leaders of bands at least in the first stage and to adopt the Committee's system. Henceforth, the bands would be recruited in the kingdom, led by officers and non-commissioned officers, and sent to Macedonia where they would be reinforced by local guerillas. Later the most suitable of them would assume the command of their own bands of guerillas. At the beginning of 1905, the new bands were recruited in Greece and were assigned to the command of officers such as K. Mazarakis, Spyromilos, and Moraitis, who had served in the Consulate in Thessalonike the previous year and were familiar with

the situation. In the months that followed new bands began to be formed at a quickening rate as the numbers of volunteers multiplied from Crete, the Peloponnese (especially Mani), Roumeli and other areas, and the Government now made the necessary funds freely available.

As long as the Greek military presence in Macedonia had been either non-existent or weak, the general impression was that the Ottoman authorities and especially the Ottoman landowners viewed the Greek bands with favour as a rival 'terror' to the Bulgarians. The Ottoman Administration, however, invariably rejected suggestions that the Greek villagers should be armed, or that the Greeks and Turks should take concerted action against the Bulgarians.[99] In contrast, when the Greeks began to intensify their armed action, the pursuit squadrons turned against the Greek bands with particular insistence. The Greeks' greatest losses were recorded in clashes with the Ottoman army. Finally, both sides — Bulgarian and Greek — manoeuvred in such a way as to turn the Turks against their rival.

The struggle often developed into a contest on three fronts for the Greek bands. In some areas, mainly in central Macedonia, nomadic Vlach stock-breeders who had

326. Kostas Garefis from Pelion, the heroic leader of an armed band, lost his life in 1906 after killing two Bulgarian chieftains in Morihovon. Athens, J. Mazarakis Collection.

embraced Roumanian nationalism aligned themselves with the Bulgarians. Their hostility took the form of the betrayal of the movements of Greek bands to the Turks and the Bulgarians, acts of sabotage directed against the Greek supply and communications systems, and finally, anti-Greek propaganda in Vlach villages. The damage caused by the pro-Roumanians to the Greek struggle was disproportionately large in relation to their small numbers.[100] The attitude of the Vlachs of the towns, townships and the vast majority of the villages of northern Macedonia was precisely the opposite: they formed the backbone of the Greek defence throughout the entire Macedonian Struggle.

After 1905 the Greek bands for the most part succeeded in prevailing over the Bulgarians whenever they clashed, thanks to the fact that they were led by army officers and NCOs, to their training in irregular warfare, and to the resources at their disposal.[101]

However, it was only in areas where it was absolutely essential to obliterate the enemy presence that the main effort of the bands was devoted to hand-to-hand fighting or pitched battles. The areas in question were those of critical importance for communications or vital for use as a base from which to launch attacks. The marshy lake of Yan-

nitsa was one such crucial area; here, a curious, though fierce amphibious war to secure the control of central Macedonia was fought throughout almost the entire Macedonian Struggle.[102] The more usual form of operation, however, was the raid on inhabited areas to punish traitors, terrorize rivals or execute comitadjis.

Although the numbers of the armed bands increased after 1905, they were not enough to ensure the safety of the Greek villages. Accordingly, the system of the armed civilian militia first used by the Bulgarians was adopted. In a short space of time tens, and later hundreds, of villages acquired armed garrisons who were ready, together with the secret committees, to act as a first line of defence and even to assist as reserves in the operations of the Greek band in their area.

In the cities, where the Greek population was indisputably in the majority, the absence of any armed force in the past had allowed the Bulgarians to exercise a disproportionately great influence. To meet this situation, the Greek organization created small groups of armed youths, who formed execution squads of the secret political societies. This tactic was systematized in Thessalonike after 1906, when lieutenant Souliotis, under the pseudonym Nikolaidis, founded the secret Thessalonike Organization. The aim of this organization was gradually to neutralize the small Bulgarian community that had begun to form as a result of migration from the countryside during the previous twenty years. The use of economic boycotts, terrorism and the mobilization of the Greek population began to reverse this dangerous trend within a year.

The real results of the struggle, however, were to be measured in terms not of territory won, but 'of the soul of people', as Koromilas wrote.[103] The attempt to win back for Hellenism all those who had gone over to Bulgarian nationalism involved the provision of protection and compensation, and where necessary, acts of terrorism against dissidents. The road was difficult, especially for the first two years, 1904-06. Members of the same village, even of the same family, were often divided into two opposing camps, the orthodox Greek and the schismatic Bulgarian.

For Greek morale to recover, however, it was necessary to remove the social and economic causes that were turning one section of the rural population against the leaders of Hellenism. Bulgarian propaganda had succeeded in some areas in turning against the Greeks the discontent of the share-croppers against the landowners, who included a good number of Greeks,[104] and the opposition of the villagers to the taxes paid to the clergy, which were collected by Greek bishops. The Greek organization tried to soften their worst effects in order to advance the struggle. It instituted, or increased subsidies to the bishops of crucial dioceses, thereby relieving them of having to make unpopular circuits in order to collect the annual tax of Christians. At the same time, encouragement was given to the founding in Macedonia of branches of credit organizations controlled by Greek capital interests. At the height of the Struggle, two Greek banks opened in Thessalonike and supported the Greek presence in Macedonia.[105] The Greek organization made use of this new power in a positive manner to attract workers and farmers to the Greek side, and

327. Tellos Agapinos ('Agras') shown with some of his comrades amongst the swamps which surrounded the lake of Yannitsa. In the months before his death at the hands of Bulgarian com- *itadjis in 1907 he made the extensive marshes a focal point for control of the central Macedonian region. Athens, J. Mazarakis Collection.*

as a deterrent to use economic pressure and boycotts against businesses and contractors, whether Bulgarian or not, who employed Bulgarian workers and staff.

Education was dealt with more systematically. The teaching material and the archaic learned language needed to be adapted to the local conditions of a basically illiterate, bilingual population. Under the difficult conditions imposed by the Struggle it gradually became possible to detect the beginnings of a radical change of direction with the foundation of teacher-training colleges, girls' boarding schools, primary schools and also schools for professional training.

At the same time, particular attention was paid to popular mass mobilizations of the forces of Hellenism, for Bulgarian activity had resulted in European public opinion receiving a virtually one-sided picture of the situation in Macedonia. However, as fear began to give way to rising Greek morale, there occurred a number of impressive mass popular demonstrations — at the funeral of a patriot who had been murdered, for example, or on the occasion of group excursions of school children which afforded the opportunity for an imposing display of force.

The Greek defence thus moved to a mass counter-attack

in 1907. At the end of 1906, in response to a request from the Turks, Koromilas was transferred to Athens, but not before he had set the entire enterprise on a firm foundation. Shortly afterwards Kalapothakis and other members of the Macedonian Committee were obliged to resign on account of a sharpening of their differences with the military officers over the direction of the operational control of the Struggle. As the Macedonian question assumed the dimensions of an undeclared war, it came under the control of the professional soldiers and the responsible political authority. At the beginning of 1908, the Theotokis government assigned the military direction of the Struggle to colonel P. Danglis, while G. Baltatzis was appointed president of the Macedonian Committee. This body now took on the form of a special service of the General Staff, and was subject to a military discipline and command structure. Naturally enough, the role of the patriot volunteers in Athens and of the consuls in Macedonia was downgraded in all matters connected with the military direction of operations.

In the operational sphere, the number of Greek bands active inside Macedonia in the two years 1907-08 rose to dozens, headed by officers and chieftains who by this time

328. Portrait of Nicholas Votsis, the captain who entered Thessalonike harbour and torpedoed the Turkish corvette Fetih-I-Bulend. Sketch by Thaleia Flora-Karavia.

had gained experience. These bands had succeeded in consolidating their control throughout the whole of the southern, Greek-speaking zone, creating supply bases from the Pindos range to the river Nestos and securing communications between the Greek-Turkish border zone and the interior of Macedonia. To the north, Greek bands had also established themselves in the areas of Prespa, Peristeri, Monastir, Morihovon and Stromnitsa (now southern Yugoslavia), where they were operating with some success. The struggle was evenly balanced in the middle zone, particularly in the regions of Korestia (Kastoria), Florina, Edessa (Almopia), the lake and plain of Yannitsa and, further to the east, in the provinces of Serres and Drama. In the region of Kilkis, and further north, however, Bulgarian control was still strong.[106]

In any event, the balance of power between the Greeks and the Bulgarians shifted steadily in favour of the former. After the reorganization of the Ottoman gendarmerie by European officers in 1906, however, and the formation of pursuit squadrons, the Greek bands, like the Bulgarian, could no longer rely on the traditional incompetence of the Ottoman security forces. The merciless pursuit frequently ended in the annihilation of entire bands, which in turn

made conditions for survival intolerable and caused the morale of the guerillas to plummet.

At the same time as this activity in the military sphere, the Turks took steps to neutralize the centres guiding the Greek struggle. With the encouragement of the European diplomats, they succeeded in having some of the consuls and metropolitan bishops whom they regarded as leading activists in the mobilization of the Macedonian Greeks, removed from office. This measure came too late, however: the Greek Organization had by now taken root and spread, and the Struggle had lost its earlier personal character.

During this same period (1907-08), the Bulgarian movement began to show signs of weakening. The Serbian bands and the Serbian Organization were very active in the extreme north of Macedonia and were contesting with the Bulgarians the initiative in the provinces that bordered with Serbia, especially the *kazas* of Skopje, Prilep, Palanka and Kiuprulu. And the fierce disputes within the ranks of the Bulgarian movement, particularly between the supporters of the Supreme Committee and the leftist faction amongst the supporters of IMRO had reached the point of open civil war.

To the complex web of mutually conflicting ideological and political aims exhibited by the Bulgarian movement were added personal hatreds, opening up a great gap. The alienation, albeit of a faction, of the warriors from the decision-making centres of the Bulgarian movement became clearer, as the old propagandist slogan of autonomy became the self-fulfilling aim of their struggle.[107] This was the source of the clash between autonomists and unionists that was to split the Macedonian Bulgarians and weaken their efforts.

The Young Turk Movement and the end of the Struggle

Throughout the entire period of the Struggle, the European Powers repeatedly interfered in Macedonian affairs. The reform programmes of Vienna and Mürzsteg were the object of continuous negotiations on the part of the foreign diplomats, who were attempting to improve them. The drastic measures taken in the past, however, such as naval and economic blockade, military mobilization etc., now fell foul of the conflicting interests of the Powers.

While the repeated foreign interventions failed to bring any real improvement in the situation, however, they began to increase the discontent of many of the Turkish officers. For a variety of reasons, including the situation in Macedonia, where the rival factions of the unliberated Christians had torn the prestige of the Ottoman state to shreds, these officers had for some time been moving towards the idea of intervening forcibly to change the regime. The Young Turk movement was organized secretly, and mainly within the Macedonian garrisons, which gave the signal for the Revolution on 23 July, 1908. It quickly spread to the entire empire and succeeded in overthrowing the absolutist regime of Abdul Hamid.

The proclamation of the Constitution, with its promises of equal rights for all nationalities, acted as a catalyst on the Macedonian Struggle. Within the space of a few days after the success of the Young Turks and the announce-

329. The Turkish corvette, Fetih-I-Bulend, in Thessalonike harbour. The sinking of this ship on the evening of 18 October 1912 was a deed of great bravery and skill on the part of Captain Votsis. Sketch by Thaleia Flora-Karavia.

ment of a general amnesty, all the contending sides declared that they were putting an end to the armed struggle, accepted the Young Turks' promises of equality, and promised to advance their nationalist aims by political means. Immediately after this, the armed bands came down to the nearest towns and townships and laid down their arms. Amidst an unreal atmosphere of euphoria, there were scenes of popular delirium that would have been incomprehensible only a month before. The popular celebrations, however, were simply an indication of the relief of a people who for decades had known nothing but oppression and violence. Those responsible for directing the various political and military movements, moreover, were aware that nothing more was to be achieved by armed struggle. The Bulgarians realized that their internal divisions did not augur well for the future. The Greeks, for their part, believed that they would be able to advance their cause more successfully, for Macedonian Hellenism had added to its economical and cultural superiority an aggressive patriotic spirit won on the field where it had clashed with the Turks and the Bulgarians.

There were many on the Greek side, however, who believed that the movement of the Young Turks had blocked Greek efforts at the very moment that they were preparing to strike the decisive blow against the Bulgarians; that the declarations by the Bulgarian committees that they were suspending the armed struggle were disingenuous; and that the Young Turks had no intention of putting into practice their promises of equal rights. A significant quantity of arms was not in fact surrendered and many bands on both sides chose to disperse or to hide rather than surrender. Throughout 1908 and 1909 there was rivalry at the local level to exercise control over the church or the school of every village, as in the period before 1899. There were also a number of murders, some of them intended as a means of exercising political pressure, though more frequently resulting from personal vendettas.[108]

Despite the fears aroused by the circumstance that the villagers still continued secretly to carry arms with revolutionary intent and that the mechanism of the conspiratorial organization continued to exist, the situation did not revert to the level of armed confrontation. The main reason for this was that all the unliberated nationalities realized that the policy of 'Turkification' that the Young Turks had begun to pursue, was a threat to them all. It was only by countering this threat jointly that they would be able to ward off the danger and open the way for the final

479

deliverance of Macedonia from the Turkish yoke.

The Macedonian Struggle had now passed into history. In both conception and execution it had been an unorthodox war, to which the Greeks had been led by the armed interference of the Bulgarians in areas and amongst populations which Hellenism claimed as a matter of right. Both sides used all the resources of irregular warfare, whether legitimate or illegitimate. Historically, it proved to be one of the most crucial struggles of Hellenism in the attempt to win national unity, and it has properly been described as the 'Third War of Independence', after 1821 and the Cretan Struggle. The basic aims were achieved. It prevented the annexation of Macedonia to Bulgaria or the creation of an autonomous state, allowed the road to Constantinople to be kept open, and kept a strong Greek presence in the southern and central zones, which made it possible for Greece to demand the annexation of these areas during the Balkan Wars.

The armed struggle was not designed to detach territory from the Ottoman empire. At the beginning, it even attempted to reinforce the weak Ottoman power in a region which Hellenism considered belonged to it as of right. Recourse was only had to force when the Turks were not in a position — or were not concerned — to check the

spread of Bulgarian nationalism. The enrolment of volunteers in the Greek armed bands gave the Struggle a panhellenic character, which was strengthened by the mass participation of all the elements of the Greek Macedonian population (Greek-speaking, Slav-speaking and Vlach-speaking) in the armed bands, the civilian militia and the secret intelligence services.

The Greek struggle was successful despite the predictions of foreign observers who were impressed by Bulgarian activity in Macedonia up to 1904. As the English historian of the Macedonian Struggle, Douglas Dakin notes,[109] the Greek success was due to the fact that they were fighting in a region where the population was related to them and well-disposed and, irrespective of whether or not it spoke Greek, was deeply committed to the Oecumenical Patriarchate and to Greek nationalism.

The liberation of Macedonia

Meanwhile, rapid developments on the international scene hastened the rapprochement between the Balkan Christian states. While Austrian pressure towards the south grew after the annexation of Bosnia-Herzegovina in 1908, the defeat of the Turks in the Italian-Turkish war of

330. *Members of a cavalry regiment of the Greek Army. The chief engagement of the First Balkan War in western Macedonia took place on 3/4 November 1912 on the heights of Arnissa. Athens, Benaki Museum.*

331. *The triumphal entry of king George I and prince Constantine to liberated Thessalonike, which was handed over to the Greek Army on 26 October 1912.*

1911 demonstrated the serious weaknesses in the military and diplomatic position of the Ottoman state. Within Macedonia, the sharpening of national rivalries and the increasing oppressiveness of the Young Turk regime foreshadowed a crisis analogous to that on the eve of the armed Macedonian Struggle. At this time, Serbia and Bulgaria had considerably strengthened their military forces and Greece had undertaken a similar course of rearmament after the Goudi Revolt (1909).

It was in this climate that the Serbs and the Bulgarians succeeded, in March 1912, in reaching agreement on an alliance directed basically against the Turks.In the event of victory, Serbia would recognize Bulgaria's right to annex the Ottoman areas to the east of the Rhodope mountains and the river Strymon, while Bulgaria would recognize Serbia's right to the west and north of Mt. Skardos (Šar) — that is to the *sanjak* of Novi Pazar, Old Serbia and the Adriatic coast. The territory in between, which comprised almost the whole of Macedonia, would be divided into two parts by a line beginning in the south-west narrows of lake Ochrid and ending in the north-east at Mt. Golem, leaving Kyustendil, Štip and Velessa on the south and Skopje on the north. Serbia undertook not to contest the territory to the south and east of this line, while the Bulgarians were to

agree to north-west Macedonia being included in Serbia, provided that the tsar of Russia, who was nominated as arbitrator, awarded this more northerly region to the Serbs.[110]

The Serbs were convinced that they would succeed in occupying the Adriatic littoral and northern Albania. For the Bulgarians the agreement had the additional advantage that it included no reference at all to concessions to the Greeks, which left the field open to them to advance as far as the border area of Thessaly. Most probably, however, they reckoned on having to cede to Greece the territory to the south of the river Haliakmon.

For his part, Venizelos, aware of the need for cooperation between the Balkan states as the only means of finally settling their differences with the Turks, had perceived in time the dangers of unilateral action on the part of the Serbs and Bulgarians. He therefore attempted, after 1911, to come to an understanding with the Bulgarians. The difficulties appeared to be insurmountable, however; whereas the Greek proposals referred to the definition of territorial zones, the Bulgarians attempted to bind Greece to the founding of an autonomous Macedonian state, which would in practice be controlled by Sofia. In the end, the two governments agreed to sign a treaty of alliance (30

May, 1912), without reference to the future fate of the Macedonian territories.[111] The Bulgarians were influenced in coming to this decision by an excessive confidence in their military strength. As one historian notes, the military weakness of Greece turned out to be an advantage, for Bulgaria's underestimation of Greek strength left the Greek forces a free field of action in southern Macedonia.[112]

The Bulgarians did not rid themselves of this attitude even when the Balkan states began their coordinated military operations at the beginning of October. The biggest part of the Bulgarian army had moved towards Thrace, its main aim being Constantinople. After the successive victories of the Greek army and its rapid advance into the heart of Macedonia within the space of two to three weeks, the Bulgarian staff despatched a division to the south to capture Thessalonike. Athens was informed of this movement in good time, and despite the wish of the commander-in-chief, Crown-prince Constantine, to continue the army's advance to the north, Venizelos insisted on the immediate occupation of Thessalonike. The city surrendered to the Greek army on 26 October (O.S.), a few hours before the arrival of the Bulgarians. This action cost the Greeks the loss of Monastir, but saved the capital of Macedonia for Hellenism.

The meeting of the allied armies on the Macedonian front put an end to hostilities in Macedonia. Despite their impressive victories on the Thracian front and their occupation of part of eastern Macedonia, the Bulgarians appeared to be displeased with the outcome of the military operations in Macedonia.

The Greek victories not only deprived them of central Macedonia and Thessalonike, but weakened the terms of their agreement with the Serbs who, after the intervention of the Powers who objected to their advance towards Albania, showed no inclination to evacuate the territories they had occupied in Macedonia. This problem remained unsolved even after the Powers achieved the signing in London, on 30 May, 1913, of the provisional conditions of a peace, according to which Turkey ceded to the confederated Balkan states all her European territories west of the Ainos-Medeia line, with the sole exception of Albania which was to be proclaimed an autonomous state.[113]

While Bulgarian pressure for a redistribution of the Macedonian territories occupied by Serbia and Greece was increasing, the governments of these two countries came to an understanding to secure their gains. By a treaty of alliance that came into force on 21 June, 1913, the two sides agreed to keep the territory they had occupied and to define the border between them by a line running from Ochrid, south of Monastir to the river Axios, south of Gevgelija.[114]

Meanwhile the Bulgarians, despite the territorial gains that had taken them to the outskirts of Constantinople and the ports of the Aegean, Alexandroupolis (Dedeagac) and Kavala ordered the army on 29 June to attack the Serbs and the Greeks without warning. The result of this action was disastrous for the Bulgarians. The Greek army liberated eastern Macedonia including the towns of Kavala, Serres and Drama, while the Serbs and the Turks recorded similar victories.

The treaty of Bucharest (10 August 1913) which brought an end to the Second Balkan War also definitively fixed the borders of the three Balkan countries in Macedonia. Bulgaria acquired only a small area in the north-east which was just over 10% of the whole. Greek Macedonia was about 51% while the Serbs received 39%, together with the province of Stromnitsa which they had seized from Bulgaria after the First World War.

The turn taken by events in the military sphere was undoubtedly unfavourable to the Bulgarians. Although the Balkan Wars had brought them the desired outlet to the Aegean (for western Thrace remained under Bulgarian suzerainty) the loss of Thessalonike and Kavala to the Greeks and the areas of northern Macedonia with a dense Bulgarian population which had gone to the Serbs, produced a feeling of national disaster in Bulgarian public opinion. The situation was aggravated by the congregation in Bulgaria of large numbers of Bulgarian Macedonian refugees from Greek and Serbian Macedonia. Many of these refugees had fought for twenty years to ensure the victory of Bulgarian nationalism in Macedonia. Their feeling of failure and their refugee status inevitably led them to adopt a fervent irredentism which was to influence Bulgaria's policy towards her Balkan neighbours for many decades.

The treaty of Bucharest closed a great circle in the history of Macedonia, which had opened in the fourteenth century with the conquest of the region by the Turks and ended in the final elimination of their sovereignty. After its liberation, the political future of Macedonia was to some extent determined by its historical past and the multinational composition of its population. In contrast with the impression that had been cultivated for about half a century, the region enclosed by the Skardos mountains and the Aegean, the Pindos and the Nestos, did not constitute an entity in either historical or ethnic terms. From time to time views were advanced that the region should be incorporated as a whole in one or other of the Balkan states, or even that it should be made an autonomous or independent state. These ideas, however, were merely the political programmes and manoeuvres of the Balkan states or the European Powers, who were seeking to gain control of this strategically and geographically important area.

If we leave aside for the moment the political problem that arose during the last decades of the nineteenth century, it emerges indisputably that the area that arbitrarily came to be called 'Macedonia' in modern times had no historical basis, and no ethnic, economic or political cohesion or unity. During the period of Ottoman sovereignty it is possible to distinguish in general terms two different

332. *The London Conference, at which the Treaty of London was signed, marked the end of the First Balkan War.*

333. *The Greek delegation to the Bucharest Conference, led by prime minister Eleutherios Venizelos. The treaty of Bucharest (10 August 1913) marked the end of the Second Balkan War and determined the frontiers of the three Balkan countries in Macedonia.*

regions: the *northern,* the population of which was Slav and which had medieval Slavic historical roots, and the *southern,* with a Greek population, the historical roots and traditions of which went back to classical antiquity and Greek Byzantium. At the points of contact between the two there was undoubtedly considerable racial intermixture and fluidity, as well as instability of historical claims. The areas considered to be 'Macedonia', however, in no sense constituted a unified entity. The fact that the Greeks and the Bulgarians were led by political considerations to view them, and to lay claim to them, as a unit, was a historical error. It led these two peoples to make excessive and groundless demands that weighed so heavily on the popular masses that when the time came for the final settlement there was no margin for compromise. In consequence, the solution imposed by force of arms naturally left deep 'national' wounds that affected the Balkan political scene for decades.

Nonetheless, the solution achieved in the second decade of the twentieth century can only be considered the most natural outcome of a long process. Ottoman domination had been thrown off. The mainly Slav northern areas went to the Slav Balkan countries (notwithstanding the fact that the amount of territory received by Serbia and Bulgaria was in inverse proportion to the national preference of the Slav population). By a curious coincidence, the southern area that went to Greece was roughly identical in extent with the 'historical' Macedonia of the Classical period, with the exception of a small strip that remained within the Serbian and Bulgarian territories. This southern zone included, in addition to the Greek-speaking population, the majority of the Slav-speaking inhabitants who had retained a Greek national conscience. It would be an oversimplification, however, to claim that the military operations of 1912-13 had achieved the final partition of Macedonia between the Slav and Greek populations. A significantly large Greek population remained cut off in Serbian and Bulgarian Macedonia, whence they were obliged to flee to Greek Macedonia, leaving behind them very few traces of Greek settlement. Even greater numbers of Slavs, who for the most part identified with Bulgarian nationalism were left in the south and were gradually to take the road in the opposite direction, mostly to Bulgarian Macedonia. Nonetheless, the efforts of generations of Macedonians — Greeks and Slavs — who had struggled to achieve the liberation of their land had come to a dramatic end.

The history of Macedonia as a single geographical area naturally comes to an end at the point where it is liberated and the three sections of it are incorporated into the three neighbouring countries. From this point onwards each section follows the historical development of the country and people to which it is attached.

Although the Greeks and Serbs were determined to put an end to all further claims in Macedonia, the Bulgarians left no doubt that they would strive to regain those territories in Macedonia that in their eyes belonged to them. The opportunity appeared to have arisen within one year of the signing of the treaty of Bucharest. The First World War broke out in August 1914, and the Bulgarian claims to the Macedonian territories quickly made their appearance on the diplomatic and military stage. These developments mark the beginning of the history, not of Macedonia, but of the new 'Macedonian Question' which was to continue to form part of the political scene in the Balkans throughout the twentieth century.

ADMINISTRATIVE, SOCIAL AND ECONOMIC DEVELOPMENTS

GENERAL OBSERVATIONS

This section is devoted to the agricultural economy of Macedonia as it was in the final quarter of the nineteenth century by which time the long process of its incorporation into the capitalist mode of production and distribution had been completed. The picture of the agricultural economy of Macedonia has been built up from the fragmented miscellaneous evidence at our disposal, drawn from a wide variety of sources.[1]

In the two vilayets of Thessalonike and Monastir, the rural estates could be divided into three categories. The first were those that belonged to a single owner, usually a Muslim, but cultivated by Christian farmers. They were usually large, more than two thousand *stremmata* (a *stremma* is equal to a quarter of an acre) in the vilayet of Thessalonike, and probably represented one fifth of the total land under cultivation. The second category consisted of lands that belonged to Muslims or Christians and ranged from two hundred to two thousand *stremmata* representing two fifths of the cultivated land. The third category consisted of estates where ownership was divided between the farmers and the landowners, or belonged only to the farmers. These were never above two hundred *stremmata,* and more usually below forty; they made up the remaining two fifths of cultivated land.

In eastern Macedonia, especially in tobacco-growing districts where the crop demanded intensive labour, the smallholding (of twenty to sixty *stremmata*) represented more than two fifths of the cultivated land. Large estates (those over two thousand *stremmata*) corresponded to a tenth of the total, while at least two thirds of the tillers were also the owners. Owners of moderate sized estates usually divided their property into holdings of forty *stremmata,* sub-rented to landless farmers; the owner retained a small area for himself. About one third of the large estate proprietors also sub-leased their lands, while the remainder cultivated them for their own profit, employing seasonal labour. To the tenant farmer the landowner would lease the house, the plough animals, and provide the seed; often he

334. Pictures illustrating the harsh conditions of life endured by the Christian population of Macedonia during the Ottoman period. Above: a visit of local officials and tax collectors to a peasant's house where violence was usually employed to obtain the money. Frequently the peasant had no means to pay without being forced to sell his land in order to pay his debts. Such measures led to insurrectionary charges. Below: delivery of arms to a priest's house by night. London Illustrated News.

would plough the land. Lessor and lessee shared the harvest, after deducting the land tax. Usually the owner paid half the tithe for the lessee, and provided the essential equipment. On the large estates, farmed by the owners themselves, the labourers were paid in kind (corn) and cash, in sums which varied from region to region and according to the kind of crop. In western Macedonia, a wheat growing district in particular and a cereal producing area in general, large estates were relatively more common; their size was continually increased by the seizure of smaller estates by the beys.

Uncertainty of ownership was one of the factors which inhibited agricultural development. Of necessity, peasants had to sell land to meet the demands of officials and tax-farmers alike. The exact number of villages in Macedonia within the *chiftlik* system is not known, but from the frequent references to certain abuses, it must have been large. A single indication comes from the vilayet of Monastir in 1860, when three-quarters of the original Christian landowners were expropriated by powerful Ottoman and Albanian beys. The Christians sought reparation by law, expending large sums to defend their case; the only result was that they depleted their financial resources and put themselves into the position of having to borrow. They even sent fully empowered delegates both to the vilayet capital and to Constantinople, again fruitlessly. There are also examples where inhabitants of villages did not dare reveal their problems for fear of losing their holdings.

In the *chiftliks* the farmer-labourers undertook, by contract drawn up on Saint Demetrios' day (26 October) and valid for one year, to work the estate of a bey. They were also under an obligation to cart firewood to his residence and to grind their wheat into flour in his mill. Those who were lessees had the added obligation to perform labour service for up to ten days of the year on the lands the bey farmed for his own benefit; they also had to make a contribution towards the pay of the rural guard. Even more dreadful was the position of the farmer-labourer who received only the barest minimum of reward in cash and kind for his unremitting toil. He was usually in debt to the bey, and thus was deprived of all hope of improving his lot; he was even prevented from moving elsewhere because his debts tied him to the *chiftlik*. All the evidence shows that this class was the worst off in Macedonia.

Almost everywhere the fields were ploughed either by oxen or bullocks and only rarely by mule or horse teams; the latter animals were used for travel or transport. The plough used was wooden; only towards the end of the century was the iron plough introduced. Other agricultural machinery was virtually unknown, and the use of fertilizers unheard of. Instead, land lay fallow and crop rotation was the long-favoured practice of the peasantry. Those who were in a position to introduce new ideas and improved equipment preferred the safety and comfort of towns. The small landholders were usually hesitant to try improvements because their harvests left no margin for experiment and failure. Burdened by debt or haunted by the spectre of bankruptcy, they struggled to hold onto their land through the hard work of every member of the family.

Distrust of the officials was shared by all classes of land holders. Everyone feared an increase in taxation or the imposition of new dues, despite any assurances that might be made to the contrary. The hesitation of the cotton growers of eastern Macedonia in the middle of the century is typical; they were not eager to increase production despite the increasing demand for their product abroad. It should be noted that the government had promised them a remission of taxation for five years for cotton grown on reclaimed land. In 1862 the government ordered the planting of mulberries in central and eastern Macedonia to assist the increase of silk production. The peasantry, alarmed lest the government's aim was to levy a fresh tax, not only failed to care for the young trees but uprooted them wherever they could.

To lack of trust in the government's intentions must be added absence of public credit which discouraged investment. Those who did borrow, usually Turks and always Muslims, found various excuses to default on their obligations to their creditors. The mighty could always evade the law, and the same authority which covered up irregularities also helped to undermine public credit. Added to this was the vicious circle of tax-farming which worked against both productivity and the proper function of the market economy. Because of difficulties encountered in retailing and capital formation, the lessees who were usually Christians, resold the right to cash against small tax reliefs, buying shares which they transferred to nationals of the Great Powers; these individuals, however, usually remained unprosecuted because the officials did not recognize the transfer of shares to foreign nationals.

Inhibiting factors also affected animal raising, which at this time was largely a nomadic or semi-nomadic occupation and only incidentally based on established settlements. Transhumant pastoralism was inextricably linked to the large estate holdings of which it was a supplementary branch. The large estate owners who had the officials under their thumb frequently violated agreements leasing winter pastures to sheep and goat breeders, while the officials turned a blind eye to animal thieves; the pastoralist was caught between them. To these detrimental factors yet another must be added; the establishment of nation states. The laying down of national boundaries in the Balkan peninsula had long-term adverse effects on transhumant animal husbandry because for many pastoralists it meant they were deprived of pastures essential for their livelihood. In particular, the annexation of Thessaly to Greece deprived the wandering shepherds of the Epirus-Macedonia areas of their natural grazing grounds. For their own protection, the shepherds associated with local brigand bands or formed their own and combined animal husbandry with banditry.

Nevertheless, the economy of Macedonia gradually integrated itself into the international economic system, and eventually came to belong to the periphery of the European commercial world. The region produced agricultural and cattle breeding products sufficient to meet local needs and to provide a surplus for export, mainly to Europe, in exchange for imported manufactured goods. The main exports were cereals, tobacco, cotton, timber and raw hides; secondary exports were opium, raw silk (whose quality

335. *Throughout the 19th century Thessalonike was the most important entrepot harbour in Macedonia; it exported grain from central and western Macedonia, and timber from Skopje, and had connections with many Mediterranean ports.*

rivalled that exported from Prousa), plums furs, flax, wool, butter, honey, bleach, carpets and woollen, bed coverings. Imports include fabrics, thread, fez, tools, metals, coal, oil, wines, coffee, sugar, perfumes, salt, olive oil, paper, soap, sacks, glass, medicines and spices.

Cereals grown in western and central Macedonia were exported from Thessalonike, which throughout this period was the most important entrepot of the region. It was also the port from which large quantities of timber, floated down the river Axios from the Skopje area, was shipped elsewhere.

Cotton was exported from central and eastern Macedonia. Its production and export was linked to the demand abroad, but also to that for cereal crops and to the feasability of meeting demand for both products. While demand for cotton was subject to wild fluctuations, that for cereals maintained a constant level.

Beyond question, tobacco was the most important Macedonian product, especially in the east. Large, and continually increasing, quantities were exported not only from Thessalonike, but also from Kavala and Porto Lago. But its marketing required a relatively large amount of capital, for purchase, storage and then transport. Consequently only large commercial enterprises could deal in the commodity. It was usually bought by the local beys, who then resold to the large-scale dealers. The beys of the tobacco-producing areas had their own means of buying the silence of the officals in cases of compulsory purchase from growers when the latter were reluctant or refused to sell their crop to the bey. The Jews of Thessalonike cooperated with the beys as representatives of the large business houses and of the state monopoly of Austria and France, protected by the consuls of the foreign powers in Thessalonike and Kavala, in particular France and Austria.

Imports, and even some proportion of local products, reached the market both through the ports and by land routes, the latter mainly used for goods from central Europe. Some imports reached western Macedonia from Trieste and Corfu, arriving at Korytsa via Aulon, Sayada or Dyrrachion. More reliable supplies were to be obtained from Thessalonike via Edessa and Florina, but the distance was greater and lading charges higher. Movement of products within central and eastern Macedonia was much easier. In general, communication and transport was difficult because of the appalling state of the roads, unsettled conditions and the tolls payable at various passes. Horses and mules were the most common beasts of burden, even after the gradual introduction of the railway in the last quarter of the century. Oxcarts were also used, but only in flat areas, mostly in the plain round Thessalonike. The only carriage road at this time, and indeed for many years, was that connecting Thessalonike with Monastir. The other roads which linked Monastir to Niš, Philippopolis, Elbasan, Dyrrachion, Grevena and Siatista were totally neglected. In only slightly better condition were the roads of central and eastern Macedonia. Bridges were few; such as existed might collapse at any moment. Rivers were forded at places known to the muleteers; there might be ferries — flat-bottomed boats hauled on pulleys along a rope stretched from bank to bank, and they were of particular value after rain or in winter.

Communications between Macedonia and the wider world, and the transport of merchandise, imported or exported, to and from the railheads for central and western Europe, was by mule trains in the interior or steam boat along the coast. Then, as always, Thessalonike was the commercial centre. There is evidence from the end of the nineteenth century for the range of shipping connections which linked Thessalonike with other Mediterranean ports, and of course with the capital of the Ottoman empire; it was common for French, Italian and Austrian boats to put in at Thessalonike before continuing to Constantinople.

Originally freight charges were expensive, because the foreign companies which had constructed the railway network and retained its operation, imposed high rates. In the end, however, the railways proved to be a most important factor of progress in Macedonia; they prompted the building of roads from provincial centres to railway sta-

tions (termini or intermediate halts), and for the first time they brought central points into direct contact with their hinterland. The construction of the Thessalonike-Mitrovica, Thessalonike-Monastir and Thessalonike-Constantinople lines was completed within the last quarter of the nineteenth century. Business circles in central Europe promoted the construction of the earliest lines which tended to favour mercantile relations with Macedonia, at the expense of the interests of the naval powers.

In the same period the system of agrarian credit was extended; this had begun to function towards the end of the 1860s and was set on its feet in 1889 by a law detailing specific conditions. The main aim of agricultural banks was to provide cash for the farmers in the form of low-interest loans based on an estimate of the individual's assets, land and buildings. The funds of the agricultural banks came from a special tax of one per cent on agricultural produce. In general, the system of loans, like the railway network, provided a much-needed boost to both agricultural productivity and commerce.

In the economy generally, but in particular for commerce, an important role was played by the local fairs. From the point of view of the volume of business conducted, the most important were those of Prilep (13 August - 5 September), Nevrokop (13 August - 30 August), Serres (24 February - 30 March) and Yannitsa (22 November - 20 December). In addition to products from every European country, goods were despatched from Ochrid, Kastoria, Monastir, Skopje, Pristin, Skodra, Sarajevo, Krušovo, Belgrade, Thessalonike and Constantinople. Cloth,

336. Kavala harbour, one of the ports from which tobacco grown in the hinterland was shipped abroad. The importance of the crop increased steadily throughout the 19th century. Only

large commercial houses could command the substantial capital and extensive organization required for buying, transport and storage.

336

colonial goods and luxury goods from abroad were exchanged for local products; hides, livestock, furs, rugs, carpets, copperware etc.

The monopoly of each manufactured product belonged to one particular guild. At Monastir alone in 1870 there were sixty-nine guilds (forty-one Christian, nineteen Muslim and nine Jewish) which represented almost every occupation — tailors, hoteliers, bakers, shoemakers, gold thread tailors, candlemakers, soapmakers, coopers, sellers of fez, clogmakers, silversmiths and many others. It is perhaps worth noting that the Christians allowed Muslims into their professional organizations, whereas the Jews tolerated none but their co-religionists.

A phenomenon connected with the local economy, and perhaps even with the control of occupations exercised by the guilds, on which every foreign and native observer of Macedonia commented was the annual exodus of thousands of craftsmen and labourers. They were known in Macedonia as the *kourbetchis;* some five thousand of them left the mountain villages of western Macedonia every year. Most were Greeks and Greek-speaking, though there were also Slav- and Vlach-speakers in their numbers. They departed for Egypt, Asia Minor, Serbia and the more southerly regions of Greece. One estimate from the vilayet of Skopje suggests that in the middle of the century more than ten thousand left their homes or moved, amongst them many Albanians who left their mountain fastnesses in the autumn to seek work in the towns of mainland Greece, returning in the spring. They usually found work as builders, carpenters, bakers, herdsmen or servants. The Greek-speakers were usually builders, wood cutters, tailors

or bakers, but they might also be engaged in trade in which case they might remain abroad for a longer period, anything from five to fifteen years. Slav-speakers are more often found as gardeners or millers. In Monastir, in the last decades of the nineteenth century, approximately eight thousand passes for internal travel were issued annually to villagers who wished to search for work in other parts of the empire. It is not, of course, possible, to reach conclusions about the exact numbers of emigrants, or about their social status. However it is worth recording the observation frequently made by contemporaries about the *kourbetchis:* the endless movement of men, almost always young men, promoted the spread of ideas, revolutionary ideas included. These interchanges prepared the way for the clash of ideas and the formation of armed units at the end of the nineteenth and beginning of the twentieth century. The bands operating in the summer of 1896 and again later, from 1904 to 1908, included a significant number of Greeks from Macedonia who had temporarily gone to live in Athens or in towns of eastern central Greece and Thessaly. Most of these incidental carriers of weapons, when not engaged in brigandage, were builders employed in the towns of southern Greece.

For those who stayed in Macedonia the chances to improve their lot were limited. Contemporary descriptions of the lives of villagers, especially in the *chiftliks,* make dismal reading; houses were built in bricks of clay and straw, windows were without glass and floors were earthen; clothing consisted of a full length cotton smock gathered at the waist by a woollen belt, the whole topped by a woollen or leather overgarment (which had to last the owner's

337. One of the many trade fairs held in Macedonia — that of Hagios Mamas in Chalkidike. Goods came from many lands for exchange with Macedonian products, and these fairs might last for as much as a week, when they were the scene of lively commercial transactions and the background to the exchange of ideas.

lifetime), a kerchief for a head covering, and shoes. There was little distinction between male and female attire, the one exception being that the woman's belt was wider. Food was inadequate and scarce. Unremitting toil, together with under-nourishment and lack of any comfort, made the villagers gaunt, sickly and morose. Life expectation was low and child mortality high. Trained doctors existed only in larger towns; in the villages, medical care was in the hands of an assortment of amateur practitioners.

Such was the picture presented in the countryside and the poorer neighbourhoods of towns. The *archontika* of Macedonian towns, schools and charitable foundations stood as examples of the munificence of a small privileged class, mostly merchants, the majority of whom had made their fortunes abroad and sought to beautify their birthplace with buildings similar to those they had seen there. The same comment applies to the dress of the rich; its luxury was the privilege of the few, men or women, drawn from the merchant class, the petty bourgeois and the descendants of the old military ruling class and captains, all those who had never feared to attract the attention of the authorities. However, the total lack of intercommunication, isolation and the vertical division of society into small groups were not factors calculated to foster revolt.

ADMINISTRATIVE DIVISION — POPULATION

Until the middle of the nineteenth century all the districts of Macedonia were included either in the vilayet of Roumelia, whose capital was Monastir, or the vilayet of Thessalonike, its capital Thessalonike being the city second to Constantinople in the Ottoman empire.[1] There was a general administrator in the capitals of each vilayet. The vilayet of Roumelia was divided into three sub-districts (*sanjaks*): Monastir, Korytsa and the purely Albanian-speaking Dibra (formerly the *sanjak* of Ochrid). The rest of the Macedonian districts, including Thessaly at certain times, came under the jurisdiction of the vilayet of Thessalonike.

With the new administrative measures that were applied to Macedonia not later than 1873, several Albanian-speaking regions, as well as the *kaza* of Grevena, were withdrawn from the vilayet of Monastir and annexed to the vilayet of Ioannina.

After the new administrative division in 1877, the vilayet of Monastir was abolished and its *sanjaks,* Prizren and Skopje, made up the newly formed vilayet of Kossovo, while the *sanjak* of Monastir itself became a division of the vilayet of Thessalonike.

New territorial reclassifications after the Congress of Berlin resulted in the reforming of the vilayet of Monastir, which also included the *kaza* of Grevena.

All these administrative changes testify to the fact that the Turks never considered Macedonia as a particular geographical, administrative or political entity. With the administrative union of Macedonian, Albanian and Thracian regions it was not possible to confront the Macedonian problem as a whole.

During the period we are examining, Thessalonike had by far the largest population of any city in Macedonia. From various sources we learn that the population of Thessalonike during the years 1840 to 1880 presented the following picture:

	1840	1860	1880
Jews	25,000	30,000	40,000
Muslims	20,000	22,000	25,000
Greeks	13,000	16,000	25,000
Europeans	1,000	2,000	3,000
Total	59,000	70,000	93,000

From the above table it can be seen that the Greek element doubled in forty years while the Muslim element increased by only 25%.

Monastir, with a population of about seventy thousand inhabitants in 1860, had a corresponding population increase. In this inflated number must surely be included the armed forces that were stationed in the area.

A third, densely populated Christian urban centre was Serres. As for the rest of the towns, only a few, such as Edessa, had more than ten thousand inhabitants. Kozani and Siatista both had a Greek population of seven to eight thousand.

ECCLESIASTICAL ORGANIZATION

Until 1767, ecclesiastical jurisdiction in Macedonia was divided between the Patriarchate of Constantinople and the archbishopric of Ochrid, while one sector of northern Macedonia belonged to the jurisdiction of the Serbian Patriarchate of Peć. After the abolition of the autocephalous churches of Ochrid and Peć, all Macedonia belonged to the administrative and spiritual jurisdiction of the Oecumenical Patriarchate of Constantinople. According to the *Notitia Episcopatuum* of 1855 the following archbishoprics (=metropolis) existed in Macedonia: 1) Thessalonike, with eight subject bishoprics (Kitros, Kampania, Platamon, Servia and Kozani, Polyani, Petra, Ardamerion, Ierissos and Mount Athos); 2) Pelagonia, with its see at Monastir; 3) Veria and Naousa; 4) Serres; 5) Drama, Philippi, Zichna and Nevrokopion, with one bishopric, Eleutheroupolis; 6) Melenikon; 7) Prespai and Ochrid, with its see at Ochrid and later Krušovo; 8) Sisanion and Siatista; 9) Kassandreia, 10) Skopje; 11) Kyustendil and Štip, which along with the archbishopric of Skopje formerly belonged to the church of Peć; 12) Kastoria; 13) Vodena (Edessa); 14) Korytsa; 15) Stromnitsa and Tiberioupolis; 16) Grevena; 17) Moglena; 18) Dibra and 19) Velessa.[1] Ecclesiastical needs, as well as a concern for the most advantageous way of dealing with propaganda coming from different sides, imposed the necessity of changing the boundaries of ecclesiastical sees, merging the archbishoprics, forming new ones, elevating bishoprics into archbishoprics or even entrusting the supervision of the more important provinces to another ecclesiastical centre. This occurred in 1876, for example, with the subordination of the archbishopric of Velessa to the protection of the metropolitan of Thessalonike.[2]

338. Ochrid was the seat of a metropolitan dependent on the administrative and spiritual jurisdiction of the Oecumenical *Patriarchate. The eleventh century metropolitan church of Saint Sophia as it appeared in the 19th century.*

In addition to their ecclesiastical jurisdiction, the local prelates exercised political power as well, to the extent and the degree which the privileges acknowledged in the *berat* issued upon the election of each new patriarch allowed them. At the same time, however, the Church had jurisdiction over every question involving its congregation that did not come under the explicit provisions relating to the area of jurisdiction of another authority. The political power of each prelate lay in his personal responsibility for the actions of the members of his congregation against the state government, as well as in exercising legislative, judicial and administrative jurisdiction in extra-religious matters. These composite ecclesiastical courts were formed of laymen and clergy. They tried private differences between the Orthodox, based on the *Hexabiblos* of C. Armenopoulos, an extremely useful collection of Byzantine law, which was also valid in free Greece as a civil code. They also used the local customary law.[3] At the same time the broad use of the precepts of 'clemency' and 'condescension' allowed the Church to evade the severity of the provisions of the Byzantine canonical and civil legislation and to adapt its jurisprudence to the needs of the time, while the imposition of excommunication constituted the most severe penalty in Macedonian society which was so closely bound to tradition. This system was in operation till the liberation of Macedonia. A typical example of this can be found in a report submitted to the Patriarch by over one thousand inhabitants of Naousa in 1910, in which they denounced the reluctance of four of their fellow Greek businessmen to pay off the considerable loan they had contracted to the treasury of the school budget, and asked the Patriarch to excommunicate them.[4]

Until 1856, the Church was the only officially recognized agent representing the Orthodox in Macedonia. Of course, the development of the communal system had continued during the centuries of the Ottoman occupation; it was, however, overlapped everywhere by the prerogatives of the Church and protected by the local prelate, as in Thessalonike,[5] Melenikon (whose statute had been voted in 1813)[6], Serres[7] and elsewhere.

SELF ADMINISTRATION OF THE MACEDONIAN COMMUNITY

Macedonian self administration was adapted to and moulded by the local conditions of each period, without going beyond the general framework of Ottoman legislation or calling forth arbitrary actions on the part of the local Ottoman officials. In general, the gradual expansion of the jurisdiction of the notables in Macedonia owes a great deal to the participation of representatives of the guilds in the composite ecclesiastical courts, to the election of the parochial committees of the churches and to the management of the ecclesiastical income by the latter. The strengthening of the communal system was also assisted by the Ottoman system, in which the taxed unit was not the individual or the family, but the village and the quarter of the city. The residents of the village or city quarter were jointly liable and co-responsible to the state authority for the paying off of the entire sum that had been imposed. Thus communalism was strengthened and gradually acquired a broader area of jurisdiction, while in the worst instances, the attempt to avoid taxes or the inability to pay usually resulted in the village being turned into a *chiftlik* or *evkaf*.[8]

As we know, the law Hatti-i Humayun (1856) decreed, theoretically at least, equality among all subjects of the sultan, regardless of race or religious belief. All the privileges and the exemptions which had been granted to the non-Muslim communities up till then were confirmed, and each religious group was permitted to submit to the Porte a plan for the modification of their privileges.[9] Within this general framework of change were placed the 'General Regulations concerning the governing of ecclesiastical and national matters of the Orthodox Christians, under the jurisdiction of the Oecumenical (Patriarchal) Throne, subjects of His Majesty the Sultan'.[10] Furthermore, in execution of the Hatti-i Humayan, a law was issued in 1865 concerning the organization of the vilayet which set a uniform administrative system for all the 'communities'.[11] The term 'community' referred on the one hand to all those of the same religion or creed who were subject to a specific religious authority, and on the other, to the religious community in a specific settlement. In one village, for example, there could be a number of communities existing side by side: Muslims, Jews, Armenian Orthodox, Roman Catholics, Greek Orthodox and later on Exarchists, that is, Bulgarian schismatics. In its second meaning, the 'community' embraced Ottoman subjects of the same religion or members of the same sect who were obedient to a specific religious leadership recognized by the Porte and who had interests, not necessarily a dwelling, in a given village or town. The community administration belonged to the elders and the *muhtars*. Both were elected for one year at a meeting of the members of the community; they had to be over thirty years old and they were obliged to deposit a yearly direct tax of one hundred piastres. Depending on the size of the community, there were from three to twelve elders who exercised administrative, judicial and tax authority. The local metropolitan or, in the villages, the parish priest, was part of the council by right. There were two *muhtars*. They collected the state taxes and managed the communal treasury. Even under the new system the members of the community continued to be mutually responsible for the paying of the total amount of the tax.

The 'General Regulations' of the Oecumenical Patriarchate, combined with the provisions of the law concerning vilayets, imposed the formation and the enacting of communal regulations, which filled the gaps in the legislation and regulated, in detail, aspects of communal life. Thus, after 1865, the Regulations of the Orthodox Communities of various Macedonian cities and towns were issued: Korytsa (1877), Serres (1877 and 1892), Thessalonike (1886 and 1904), Veria (1892, 1903 and 1912), Krušovo and Kozani (1895 and 1911), Tirnovo in Pelagonia (1901), Siatista (1902), Kastoria (1902), Asvestochorio (1906), Edessa (1911) and Naousa (1912).[12] Nevertheless, after the law concerning vilayets came into force, the metropolitan remained the head of the Orthodox in his see, the difference being that he now exercised communal power in cooperation with the council of elders. The first Regulations made by the Orthodox Community of Thessalonike stipulated that the metropolitan was the president of the council of elders; together they sanctioned the election of the *muhtars* and elected the *ephors* of the educational and philanthropic foundations, and of the communal candleworks, as well as the parish committees. Similar or even more strict provisions concerning the authority of the religious leader in communal matters were contained in all the Regulations of the Orthodox communities of Macedonia.

During the last quarter of the nineteenth century, social-political disputes in certain communities, caused by the protracted quarrels over elections and economic management. The Turks had every reason to foster the disintegration of communal unity, as they did in the election of the *muhtars* in Blatsi in 1888.[13] The Greek consuls and the local prelates often saw communal problems from two different angles, which resulted in a sharpening of the differences between them. In certain instances the Patriarchate intervened and took measures against the cliques of prelates. Thus Kallinikos Photiadis of Thessalonike (1884),[14] who had identified himself with the conservatives, was suspended and Gregory Kallidis became his successor (1889).[15] He was a supporter of the liberals of the same city as was Constantine Vapheidis of Serres (1892) against whom a portion of the wealthy class had affiliated themselves.[16] Disputes between laymen and prelates, when they occurred, were not due to anti-clericalism. The lay element wanted its metropolitan to be impartial toward his congregation, and if he was, respect for his person and his authority was general. Metropolitans such as Gregory of Serres (1892-1909), who was later the Oecumenical Patriarch Gregory VII (1923-24),[17] and Alexander Rigopoulos (1903-10) and Ioachim Sgouros (1910-12) of Thessalonike,[18] united their congregations and lived in harmony with the conflicting interests in the communal organization. Nevertheless, during the intensification of the Macedonian Struggle (1903-08) communal disputes in general were set aside.

The recognition by the Ottoman authorities of the communities as religious, rather than ethnic, associations (the criterion for distinguishing between them being their obedience to a specific ecclesiastical jurisdiction), urged Bulgarian irredentists to struggle for the formation of a Bulgarian Church independent of the Oecumenical Patriarchate. Thus the Bulgarians were able to acquire communal independence from the Orthodox congregation, and contested the power of the patriarchal metropolitan in the area of present day Bulgaria and Macedonia, where there were scattered groups of Bulgarian-speaking peasants.

INTELLECTUAL LIFE

EDUCATION

During the Revolution, education came to a virtual standstill in the southern as well as the northern part of the Greek peninsula; in Macedonia, just as in the other Greek areas, the traces of the intellectual life of an entire decade are few and far between: the name of a teacher who, along with his martial duties, tried to exercise his peacetime duties as well; a library robbed or preserved.

But with the restoration of peace and with the establishment of the Greek kingdom, educational matters did not change only for liberated Greeks; we also observe significant alterations, immediate or gradual, in education in the areas where unliberated Greeks lived. The strong forward surge which had preceded the revolution, continued unabated; moreover, rapidly following the Revolution, the unliberated Greeks regained their vitality within the economic and administrative life of the Ottoman empire and at the same time brought about a raising of the level of Greek intellectual life. In Thessalonike, Ioannina and elsewhere, a great deal of wealth came into or returned to Greek hands. Money from commercial sources continued to be abundant and to make up for a deficiency in arts and letters. Matthew Paranikas, in 1866, often makes mention of the association of capital with education: he talks about the 'inhabitants' love of trade' in this or that city, in order to explain their devotion to letters.[1] And indeed, during this period the primary job of building both the material and the organizational sub-structure of the educational system in the Greek regions under Ottoman rule was the responsibility of the commercial sector.

Of the several instruments of change, the University, founded in 1837 in the capital of the Greek kingdom, must be mentioned first;two others were the Greek Philological Association of Constantinople, inspired by Herokles Vasiadis and the Association for the Diffusion of Greek Letters.

For many years the University was the only such institution in the Balkans. It educated teachers, doctors and lawyers from the Greek communities in the Ottoman empire and the diaspora who, after their studies in the East, carried back to their homelands the knowledge they had acquired in the capital of free Greece. As far as education is concerned, this process contributed to the unification of school programmes and school methods in both free Greece and unliberated Greek areas and, on a different level, to new intellectual and cultural ideas. It was doctors, lawyers and, above all, educators who conveyed to their homelands the experience of their youth in Athens and thus promulgated their ideological attitudes. A certain diversity of ideas would always remain, due to local differences in the cultural substructure, but at the same time they would be blunted by the incessant and insistent introduction of education from the free State.

While, however, the effect the University had was gradual, the Associations had a different, much more rapid and direct impact. The formation and the broadening of the role of the Associations created, for many decades,

339. An outstanding figure of Hellenism in Constantinople was Herokles Vasiadis, a founder member of the Greek Philological Association of Constantinople. From it sprang the Macedonian Educational Association which contributed greatly to the raising of intellectual standards in Macedonia.

very favourable conditions for the development of education in unliberated Greek areas in general.

The Greek Philological Association of Constantinople had two aims: direct operations, which included such activities as publications on various subjects, lessons, presentations of awards for the writing of books, the collection of manuscripts and the founding of a library and reading rooms; and indirect, with a view toward the formation of similar bodies with corresponding aims, in areas under Ottoman rule. Thus a pyramid of Greek associations was created, closely interdependent and with the Association in Constantinople as the recognized head. It was a tight network that was able to cover, to a remarkable extent, the needs of Greek learning in every area of enslaved Hellenism.

Meanwhile the peaceful revolution through education received assistance from free Greece, in particular from the previously mentioned Association for the Diffusion of Greek Letters, an instrument through which the Greek kingdom would be able, at first cautiously and informally, to tend the interests of Greek education (language, schools, books) in the unliberated Greek areas especially, though

340. *Theodore Manousis, born of Siatista parents, was a professor of history at Athens University and one of the most enlightened minds of the time. He collected a huge library, which he bequeathed to his home town.*

also in all lands where there were Greeks.

We have seen why there could not be any movement worth speaking of during the first decade after the founding of the Greek state; there are very few details that one can record from the Macedonian region. Nevertheless, the cessation of hostilities must be considered as the first landmark, after which the Greek areas which remained under Ottoman domination reverted approximately to their former position and their former occupations. During this period the effects of the founding of Athens University began to be felt in the scholarship of the unliberated Greeks. Nevertheless, both before and after the Crimean War (1853-56), the Ottoman government was coerced into enacting some favourable measures for the Christian peoples living under its sway. Thus by 1860 we have reached a second landmark in the history of Greek education within the boundaries of the Ottoman empire and consequently in Macedonia.

The local associations in Macedonia, inspired by the ex-

ample and the stimulation given them by Constantinople immediately after their founding, started off with activities which were above all concerned with education but which also, following the prototype of the Greek Philological Association of Constantinople, extended in other directions as well, for example to the organization of lectures, the collecting of old books and manuscripts, the recording of local customs, the preservation of anonymous demotic works and other similar activities. To all these must be added the formation of libraries and the establishment of reading rooms.

The end of this relatively peaceful period of activity by the Associations and the beginning of a new era, was brought about by a number of general causes, such as those noted in the preceding sections; an increasing mistrust shown by the Ottoman authorities towards the Associations, the founding or the operation of which took place under increasingly difficult conditions; the toughening internal policy of Abdul Hamid; and the steadily intensifying slant of Neo-Hellenic consciousness towards the *Megali Idea:* naturally all of this would contribute, along with other things, to the carving out of a new line in the development of Macedonian intellectual life.

Thus, as far as Macedonia is concerned, we should add specific causes to the more general ones. There were the events which alarmed the Greeks of Thessalonike in the spring of 1876 when the French and German consuls were assassinated by the Muslim mob. The contemporary accounts suggest that the violent uprising in which xenophobia had the Greek population as its particular target had its effect on Greek education, both at the time and later, in the Macedonian capital as well as in the surrounding region. But in this as in many other cases, some time would be needed for the changes to be perceptible, although the beginnings had been firmly established rather earlier. As before, the activities of scholars, writers and teachers in the field of culture had made their contribution. Plenty of names support this statement. Let us note Charalambos Papoulias, whose collection of poetry received an award at the Voutsinaios Competition in 1873, and Christos Samartzidis and Marinos Koutouvalis, who were also involved with poetry in particular and who were honoured in their time.

Nevertheless, there must be an exception here to the rule which obliges us to mention only the scholars who worked principally in Macedonia, for the history of education in Macedonia does not make sense without the mention of Anastasios Polyzoidis and especially Nicholas Kasomoulis. Both took part in the Revolution of 1821, the first politically, the second militarily, but they owe their appearance here to their literary activities.

Anastasios Polyzoidis is the man who won fame for his stance in the trial of Kolokotronis, when, as president of the court, he refused, along with George Tertsetis, to sign the condemnation of the accused. His writings are legal and historiographical, distinguished for their liberal ethos. Kasomoulis left behind a three-volume work, *Military Memoirs,* which reveals a lofty form behind its awkward language. The work 'is the ideal gate through which to enter the souls of the freedom fighters'.[2]

Thus, during the few years that were required to shape the new situation, we meet with other, broader, developments which, in the end, directly touched Macedonia. One was the Russo-Turkish war of 1877; its chain of repercussions created a Greek-Turkish border that made the kingdom of Greece directly adjacent to enslaved Macedonia. The liberation of Thessaly which this entailed was completed in autumn 1881; from that time on, Macedonia along with the region of greater Epirus, which remained under Ottoman domination, became the next immediate target, on the Greek peninsula, for the encompassing of Hellenism within the borders of the kingdom of Greece.

A consequence of being thus adjacent was the creation of direct contacts between the two bordering regions, that is, Macedonia and the free Greek state, resulting, as far as education is concerned, in a closer identification. What had begun earlier, with the training of educators at the Greek University, and what had been continued afterwards with the dispatching of abundant Greek publications and school books from the Association for the Diffusion of Greek Letters to the Greek associations of the empire, would now be strengthened.

Thus the two-way exchanges between the north and the south in the sector of education became more concentrated. Proximity created a kind of osmosis that became perceptible in other fields besides learning. Indeed in this last period, 1881-1912, the kingdom of Greece strengthened its consular activities in the region in an attempt to exercise a more direct form of political action in Macedonia. This meant a corresponding weakening of the power of the Associations, something which the Ottoman administration had pursued with different means and different aims at the same time.

Nevertheless, these changes brought about a transposition of forces, which made osmosis work even faster. Thus we observe a significant movement of scholars from one side of the Greek-Turkish border to the other; this had not been an unprecedented occurrence, but now it became regular. One should note certain professors at the University who came from the Macedonian north, such as John Pantazidis and George Sotiriadis; educators with a decisive influence in Greek educational policy such as Charisis Poulios and Charisios Papamarkou; scholars in other cultural activities, amongst which the outstanding figures are Peter Papageorgiou and John Dellios. The field of education between unliberated Macedonia and Greece had become one. Liberation, when it came, would, of course, leave part of the Greek population outside the Greek borders, but in every other way it would confirm a pre-existing situation. The Greek administration, when it came to establish itself in Macedonia, would find thriving schools, and in the capital, Thessalonike, a Greek Press and Greek intellectual life.

LIBRARIES

While the older libraries did not cease to function or diminish in importance, books became continually more accessible during this period and ever more varied in con-

341. Peter Papageorgiou, one of the most representative figures of Greek learning in Macedonia. An inspired teacher and philologist, he wrote a large number of works, the best known of which is his critical edition of Sophocles' Electra.

tent. The collections of the previous centuries with their emphasis on catechistic or admonitory themes, did not satisfy the needs and the curiosity of modern times. Small private libraries, reflecting the special interests of the owner, gradually increased in number. Alongside the discharge of their didactic duties, schools looked after the collection of books from older, disbanded libraries, and as has been said earlier, the local societies provided for the establishment of reading rooms, which were supplied in every possible way, especially through gifts from home and abroad.

Many Macedonian libraries were well known during this period. Naturally, the old tradition of communal, ecclesiastical and school libraries continued to flourish. The collection of books and manuscripts which had belonged to the Thessalonike metropolis was acquired by the library of the secondary school in 1875. In Kozani (another important educational centre) the custom of enriching the local library, which was far from new, was continued by gifts,

mostly of earlier publications. Of especial note are the libraries of two bishops, Dionysios of Pest and Benjamin of Kozani, which were bequeathed to it.

The variety of titles should also be noted by the historian, both for their intrinsic interest and for the future; the panhellenic, rather than the local, element prevails. It appears that the scholar Antony Papas, son of the celebrated freedom fighter Emanuel Papas, had an important library. He is mentioned as one of the first to use a Greek book plate (*Ex Libris*). Four other Macedonians disposed of their libraries in a different way; they are, in order of their death, Constantine Bellios (1838); Theodore Manousis (1858); Benedict Kralidis (1862) and Demetrios Vikelas (1908). They are mentioned here both for their generous concern for the land of their fathers and also because all four belonged to the world of scholarship.

The immensely wealthy Constantine Bellios who, throughout his life disbursed large sums to the newly-formed Greek state and to the new capital, Athens, also bequeathed his library. His intention was to donate it to the settlement of Macedonians, New Pella, then being organized within the Greek state. Meanwhile, and until the books could be housed there, he arranged for them to remain in the care of the National Library, Athens. The same stipulation was made five years later (1861) in the will of Benedict Kralidis. Professor Theodore Manousis, one of the brightest lights of the Greek revival, whose family came from Siatista, left his valuable library to his still enslaved ancestral birthplace. Finally, perhaps the most distinctive bequest was that of D. Vikelas, who left his library to Crete: this Macedonian's view of national problems was panhellenic and unified. Indeed, a few years later, long years of careful preparation culminated in the extension of the borders of the Greek state to embrace both Crete and Macedonia simultaneously.

SCHOLARS

There is no doubt that prominent educators and teachers contributed to the spectacular development of education in Macedonia during the last century of the Ottoman occupation, not only by raising the level of instruction, but by their general reformation of education as well.[1] The leading role in this reformation unquestionably belongs to the educator C. Papamarkou from Velvendos in Macedonia (1844-96), the founder and organizer of the teachers' college in Thessalonike, of which he was the director from 1875 till 1882. He later assumed the post of general supervisor of elementary education for the Ministry of Education. In this post he draughted a legal framework to cover all facets of elementary education. He also wrote a number of school books. The most important of his published works are; *On the Three Kinds of Souls According to Plato; On the proper Teacher for Greek Youth;* and *On the Purpose of the Education of Greek Youth.*

Prominent headmasters of Serres include Emanuel Photiadis, Christos Samartzidis (who taught there for four years, 1872-76), and John Kalostypis, who taught first at Kozani (1873-75), and then at Serres (1875-80). At the instigation of Charilaos Trikoupis, Kalostypis wrote a weighty geographical, historical and ethnological study of Macedonia which was translated into many languages. John Dellios reorganized the schools of Serres and in 1888 took over as director of the secondary school of Thessalonike, and John Tsikopoulos, the well-known professor of literature, also taught in Serres for twenty-five years. He applied himself in particular to the study of the historical evolution of the morphology of the Greek language. Another influential figure in the same town was D. Maroulis; he was director first of the junior secondary school; later, as director of the teachers' college and boarding school he trained a large number of teachers.

P. Papageorgiou, an eminent professor of literature who was born in Thessalonike in 1859 and died in Athens in 1914, belongs to the circle of great Macedonian educators. In addition to his many philological treatises, the crowning achievement being his critical edition of Sophocles' *Electra*, Papageorgiou wrote a large number of works on the antiquities of Thessalonike. He showed enormous conscientiousness and admirable patience in the investigation, collection and study of everything of an archaeological and historical nature there. His work was recognized abroad.

We must also mention M. Dimitsas, philologist and archaeologist who, wishing to give concrete meaning to Strabo's phrase 'Macedonia is also Greece', wrote a comprehensive work *Macedonian Matters* which included history, topography and a land survey of Macedonia.

Headmaster P. Liouphis applied himself to the history of his home town, Kozani, while E. Stratis did the same thing for his, Serres, writing a large number of works about it.

PRESS: NEWSPAPERS

The first Greek printing house in Thessalonike appeared in 1850 during a period when the city had already begun to flourish intellectually; its founder was Miltiadis Garbolas. During the twelve months it survived, he printed at least five books. A second printer, Kyriakos Darzilovitis, opened there in 1852; by 1858 he had printed at least twelve books in Greek and one in Bulgarian.

In 1868 N. Vaglamalis became the third printer in Thessalonike and published many notable books including translations of serious works. These editions are distinguished for their technical excellence and high quality. After 1875 many new printers operated in the city.

342-347. In the closing decades of the 19th century, education in Macedonia steadily improved. Greek Macedonians who had made their fortune abroad as well as communities founded schools endowed with libraries and other educational aids. Many of the schools attracted brilliant teachers who made every effort to raise the cultural and educational standards of the subjugated Greeks. Alongside the schools many centres for the care of destitute children were also established. Left, from top to bottom: the Tsouphlis School, Gevgelija; a display of gymnastics at a Greek school in Monastir; a workshop for destitute girls in Thessalonike. Right: the Greek Girls' School in Monastir; the Greek School at Melenikon; the Marasleion Greek-French and Practical Commerce Lykeion of Stephen Noukas in Thessalonike.

348. *By the beginning of the 20th century almost every town of any size in Macedonia had large buildings for educational pur-* *poses. Above: a school function at Bogatsiko, western Macedonia. Athens, Publisher's Collection.*

On 16 May, 1875, the first Greek newspaper in Macedonia, Hermes, went into circulation; from 1881 on it was called 'The Beacon of Macedonia'. In 1903 the newspaper Truth appeared, excellent in both its typography and the information it gave. Six years later the paper appeared daily instead of thrice weekly and changed its name to New Truth; it is still published today. Finally, in 1911, the newspaper *Makedonia* was founded by K. Vellidis; it was stopped by the Turks two months before the outbreak of the Balkan Wars and Vellidis then published the daily Pan-Macedonian in its place.

But despite the general development in Macedonia and especially in Thessalonike between 1850 and 1912, literary activity was slight. The newspapers were filled with translations of European works. From 1889 to 1890 the periodical *Aristotle,* wherein was gathered all the intellectual dynamism of the city, circulated in Thessalonike. Unlike Athens, however, where a generation which was pro-demotic had already begun to make itself felt, Thessalonike was dominated by conservatism with romantic reverberations. Until the end of the nineteenth century translations of foreign works abounded. There was a stir of activity

around the turn of the century, but generally speaking the intellectual world of Thessalonike remained conservative under the shadow of Ottoman censorship.

SCHOOLS

The long tradition of Greek upper schools was interrupted during the Revolution of 1821-30, but it quickly revived and even reached a level higher than before. In Melenikon, which by the opening decades of the nineteenth century had a flourishing Greek school, provision for education increased. It was here that Anastasios Polyzoidis, the famous freedom fighter of 1821, first learned to read and write. In Alistrati, a well-known institute for boys, the Central Greek School started to operate in 1841. The largest intellectual centre of eastern Macedonia, however, was Serres, which during the Revolutionary years set up a Greek School which attracted famous teachers; among them was the well-known scholar Minas Minoidis. In addition, on the initiative of the metropolitan Gregory I Fourtouniadis (1833-35), a school was established in the town, which introduced a new method of teaching, mutual instruction.

Kastoria also boasted a fine educational tradition, while neighbouring Kleisoura or Vlachokleisoura had a well organized school from 1830. The Greek and Mutual Instruction School of Stergios M. Doumbas was founded in Blatsi in 1843 and soon, due to the contribution of the barons Doumbas, it developed into a full Greek school. There was a similar educational tradition in Siatista, while in Velvendos there was a school long before the Revolution, which perhaps operated again from 1828; by 1845 it had been upgraded to a town school. In Kozani in 1832 the first mutual instruction school was organized.

From the middle of the nineteenth century onwards, education in Macedonia experienced a gradual but steady upsurge. Schools were formed which divide into the following categories according to the source of their finances; schools in prosperous communities, which were exclusively maintained by local funds, schools which were objects of interest to the Greeks of the diaspora, private schools with tuition fees, and finally there were schools that had difficulty surviving, which belonged to poor communities. The Macedonian Educational Brotherhood in Constantinople, and the Association for the Diffusion of Greek Letters turned their attention to schools of this last category and to the founding of new schools. From 1870 on, faced by the nationalistic impetus of the Bulgarians, Macedonian Hellenism grew stronger, leading to the founding of many noteworthy schools all over Macedonia in the last decades of the nineteenth and the beginning of the twentieth centuries.

Educational institutions were particularly well-developed in Serres. During the decade 1880-90, thanks to a number of distinguished teachers, education reached a high level. In 1884, the junior secondary school of the town became a full secondary school while the Central Elementary School became a six form town school, so that it is reckoned that at the beginning of the twentieth century there were over two thousand students in Serres.

The development of schools in Thessalonike leapt ahead after the Crimean War. The Greek school, which attracted brilliant teachers, was up-graded in 1870 to being a secondary school, equivalent to the other secondary schools in the free Greek state. During the last years of the nineteenth century the Greek Commercial Lyceum was also founded while in 1906 a night school was re-established thanks to the efforts of the Thessalonike Educational Association whose first director was P. Papageorgiou.

During the final years of the Ottoman occupation there were seventeen educational establishments in Monastir, with fifty-five teachers and two thousand five hundred students. A similar high level of education existed at the beginning of the twentieth century in Kastoria and Siatista, where the Trambadzeion secondary school stood out. The educational tradition of Kozani continued; in 1904 the secondary school was recognized as equivalent to the secondary schools in Greece.

But schools required teachers. On the initiative of the Thessalonike Educational Association, a teacher training college was founded in the city in 1875, whose main support came from the Association for the Diffusion of Greek Letters. It was dissolved later, and replaced by two lower teacher training colleges, male and female. A little earlier, in 1872, the Macedonian Educational Association of Serres had set up a teacher training college there, the first to operate in Ottoman-occupied Greek areas. The students received scholarships from the Association and lived in hostels. Thus Macedonian schools were staffed by teachers trained in Athens as well as in local colleges.

The Macedonian Educational Brotherhood of Constantinople set as its particular goal the founding of a Mutual Instruction and Greek School as well as a Greek Secondary Boarding School in Tsotyli. With its revised regulations (1874) the Society also anticipated the founding of a polytechnic school. The school in Tsotyli opened in 1871; its first director and founder of many renowned schools was the monk-priest Stephen Noukas. It is worth noting that by 1900 about three thousand five hundred students had studied there.

Special attention was also given to the education of the female population, up to now virtually neglected. For the first time girls' schools appeared in the towns and villages. In Thessalonike opportunities for the systematic education of girls were available by the middle of the nineteenth century; in 1856 the Higher Central Girls' School existed. Its level was that of the secondary school, and from it teachers and nursery school teachers graduated, to be sent later all over Macedonia. The girls' school of Serres developed on similar lines and in 1880 it was up-graded to a higher girls' school, the *Grigorias*.

The competition between the exarchists and the Orthodox after 1870 resulted in the establishment of a number of Bulgarian schools in Macedonian towns. In comparison with the Greek schools, however, they had fewer students. Later on, with funds from the Roumanian state, a limited number of Roumanian schools were set up in the Vlach-speaking communities, but they were never able to attract more than a minimum number of students. The establishment of the schools, however, spurred Greeks, both free and unliberated, to greater efforts to form Greek schools in the smaller towns and even villages of northern Macedonia; during the final decades of the nineteenth century, the number of Greek schools and, of course, of Greek teachers in Macedonia, increased sharply. These efforts were hindered at the end of the nineteenth century and the beginning of the twentieth by Bulgarian guerrilla activities which aimed at the intimidation of Greek teachers and the closure of Greek schools, especially those in the northern zones and the mixed (Bulgarian and Greek) zones of the Macedonian countryside.

ASSOCIATIONS

As we mentioned in the preceding section, most of the Associations in Macedonia were founded between 1870 and 1880. With grants from the Associations, new schools and boarding schools as well as sports facilities and other buildings for a variety of cultural functions were built. Schools that did not have adequate resources were sub-

349. John Papaphis from Thessalonike emigrated and made a substantial fortune in trade. In the course of the Macedonian Struggle, he endowed several educational and philanthropic institutions, the most famous of which is the Papapheion Orphanage, known as the Meliteus, in Thessalonike.

sidized, libraries were enriched with thousands of volumes of instructive books, scholarships were awarded and philanthropic institutions were founded and supported. Of the many associations that flourished at the close of the nineteenth and the beginning of the twentieth century, special mention must be made of the Progressive Brotherhood of Drama, in the vilayet of Thessalonike, which was founded in 1874 on the recommendation of the metropolitan Chrysostomos Kalaphatis, later to be a heroic national martyr in Smyrna. Through the activities of the association a reading room was built furnished with a library. In 1874 or a bit earlier the association Philippi which had a fine and well-furnished reading room, was formed at Doxato. At Prosotsani, north-west of Drama, where there was harsh competition between the Exarchists and the Orthodox, the Educational Brotherhood Eos was founded in 1873. In general, where there was friction between Greeks and Bulgarians the societies not only were particularly active, but contributed in basic ways to the preservation and the reinforcement of the national consciousness of the inhabitants.

In Kavala, a city where the Greek element flourished both economically and intellectually, the Aristotle Educational Association was founded in 1879; it set up a boarding school in the city. In the market town of Alistrati, second only to Serres as an intellectual centre in eastern Macedonia, the Conservative Brotherhood Amphipolis was founded in 1874 and rebuilt at the beginning of the Macedonian Struggle in 1903. A hostel maintained by the Brotherhood was founded in 1904, housing between fifty and eighty orphan students. The accounts for 1904-06 give information on the way it was run.

The people of Serres, in eastern Macedonia, were even more energetic. The Macedonian Educational Association of Serres was founded in 1870; its membership reached eight hundred in a decade. Thanks to its activities, a hostel was set up in the town, a library was organized and new school buildings erected. Its most significant achievement, however, was the founding of a teacher's college for young men in 1872. The Association also opened a printing works and maintained a hall where theatrical performances were given. Over and above its educational and philanthropic works, this Society was involved in nationalistic activities, such as protests against the unacceptable terms of the treaty of San Stefano.

In Stromnitsa and in Gevgelija where the struggle between the exarchists and the Orthodox was intense, the Associations and the brotherhoods served national aims beyond their philanthropic ones. In 1872 the Educational Association was formed in Edessa; two years later it issued a report on the prevailing situation in the see of Edessa-Pella which provides quite a lot of information on the ethnological composition of the population and the schools of the region. In 1903 the Charitable Brotherhood was also formed in the town; it stressed the national sentiments of the inhabitants which had been weakened by the terrorist activities of the Bulgarian comitadjis.

The inhabitants of Veria and Naousa were far from idle; three societies were founded in Veria and five in Naousa.

But the associations were of course most active in Thessalonike. The Educational Association was founded in 1872; its influence was not confined to the city of Thessalonike but spread over the entire surrounding Macedonian area. The Association also set up schools outside Thessalonike while it distributed thousands of volumes of books both in the city and its hinterland. Another of its worthy accomplishments was the selection of teachers for the schools of various Macedonian regions. The Society was even concerned with the education of Slav-speaking Greeks after their inundation by Bulgarian propaganda.

There were many other cultural clubs in Thessalonike, such as the *Evangelismos* and the Friends of the Muses; after 1908 the National Alliance, with political goals, was founded. There was similar association activity among the inhabitants of the vilayet of Monastir: the first Greek association in Macedonia, with the somewhat odd title of Municipal Institution or Casino, was founded in Monastir in 1859. It soon dissolved, however, and in 1880 a new association, Perseverance, replaced it; during its short-lived existence, it accomplished much for the intellectual improvement of the inhabitants. In neighbouring Krušovo, the Aristotle Educational Association was founded in 1874, while in Megarovo, a market town whose Greek consciousness was highly developed, the brotherhood Hope was founded in 1873, whose contribution before its dissolution in 1882 was considerable.

Some special mention must be made of the noteworthy organizational activity in Siatista where several societies were formed; the Orthodox Educational Brotherhood in 1868; the Saint Christopher Philanthropic Brotherhood in 1901, and the Prophet Elijah Educational Brotherhood in 1902. Shortly before the liberation an association with the name Alexander the Great was created in Grevena, while in Kozani an educational society, the Phoenix was founded in 1873. The Pandora Cultural Brotherhood was formed in 1902, and devoted its efforts to organizing sports facilities, a night school and a reading room.

Similar activity was displayed by the female population of Macedonia. In nearly all the towns there were ladies Charitable Sisterhoods whose almost exclusive aims were philanthropic works and the relief of the indigent. Most of these women's societies appeared in the first decade of the twentieth century. Finally there were also gymnastic or musical societies. In 1905 in Serres the Orpheus Club was founded; it maintained a gymnasium, two stages and an orchestra. A year earlier a society with the same name had been established in Florina. During the last decade of the nineteenth century the Ottoman authorities made the founding of new societies more difficult; all those that came into being at that time thus used a religious cover.

BENEFACTORS

In addition to the activity of the associations, individual initiative and its accomplishments in the socio-educational sector is worth discussing. Greek merchants born in Macedonia as well as elsewhere gave generously for the founding of schools, orphanages, hostels, and other pro-Greek foundations.

In Serres in particular, from 1835 until 1907, more than one hundred individuals were recorded as philanthropists or benefactors of schools and other philanthropic institutions in the town. It is worth mentioning John Papageorgiou who in 1866 made a bequest of 12,000 piastres to its schools, and Gregory Constantinou, an important local merchant, who made over his entire fortune, which exceeded 10,000 pounds, to the town in 1892. We must also mention the Doumbas family from Blatsi which distinguished itself in Vienna. Nicholas Doumbas gave 30,000 francs to the town hospital in 1900, and 40,000 francs as a legacy to the schools of the community after his death.

Thessalonike had a large number of benefactors. They include John N. Papaphis (1792-1886) who was born in the city, but went to Malta as a young man where he lived and died. Besides his other philanthropic acts for the Greek state, Papaphis left a fine orphanage to Thessalonike, the *Meliteus*. By 1910 this orphanage, which opened in 1903, housed one hundred and twenty-six children who were taught tailoring, shoemaking and carpentry. The Marasleion Greek Commercial and Vocational School was founded with gifts from another important benefactor G. Maraslis. A rich Macedonian from Austro-Hungary,

350. *Nicholas Doumbas from Blatsi, an important merchant in Vienna and holder of a title of nobility, founded the first Greek and mutual instruction school in his home town in 1843. It was maintained first by his generous gifts and, after his death, by those of his sons.*

Theagenis Charisis, founded the Theageneion Hospital in 1863; to this his brother Demetrios left a legacy as did another member of the same family, Poulcheria Prasakaki. A second bequest from the same man established the *Chariseion Gerokomeion* (old age home).

The brothers Dimitriou from Egypt and Demetrios Mousikos from Blatsi, living in Bucharest, were notable benefactors of Monastir. To Siatista Demetrios Ioannidis, who was born in the town around 1840 and died in Thessalonike in 1907, left a large fortune for the founding of a professional school; John Trambadzis, who had made an immense fortune in Roumania, spent large sums for the founding and the maintenance of the Trambadzeion secondary school there.

In Kozani the Valtadoros brothers established in Bucharest, bequeathed 2,500 pounds for the founding of the secondary school. A special word must be said for Paul Charisis, a Macedonian from Budapest, who left very generous grants for the formation of the Charisis Institutions. Finally, we must not omit the Epirote Anastasios Tsouflis, who lived in Kisnov in Bessarabia. His legacies endowed the Tsouflis Schools established in many Macedonian towns around 1890.

MACEDONIA TODAY

THE MACEDONIAN QUESTION IN OUR TIME

One year after the signing of the treaty of Bucharest, the decisions taken there were put to their first test. The outbreak of the First World War immediately brought the Macedonian question to the centre of the stage, as the Central Powers and the Entente attempted to woo the Bulgarians with the offer of the Macedonian territories that belonged to the Serbs and the Greeks. The negotiations lasted for almost the whole of a crucial year. For its part, the Entente went so far as to offer to Sofia the biggest part of Yugoslav Macedonia as well as Greek eastern Macedonia, along with the port of Kavala. The Bulgarian government finally aligned itself with Germany, however, clearly in the hope of realizing in their entirety their demands in Macedonia as defined in the vision of the treaty of San Stefano.[1]

During the course of the war, the political choice made by the rulers in Sofia appeared to be bearing fruit. After the collapse of Serbia, the Bulgarian army received permission from the Germans to occupy most of Serbian Macedonia. Shortly afterwards, with the consent of the government in Athens (after the resignation of Venizelos) the Bulgarians entered eastern Macedonia and quickly made themselves masters of both the countryside and the cities between the Nestos and the Strymon.

At this time the rest of Greek Macedonia was subject to a strange regime involving military administration by the Entente powers, who in 1915, had already disembarked forces at Thessalonike in order to open the second Balkan front in central Macedonia. As the threat of invasion by the German-Bulgarian army grew greater, however, the allied Powers extended their bridgehead until it covered almost the whole of central and western Macedonia. King Constantine and the goverment in Athens found themselves no longer able to control the situation in Macedonia, and the formation of National Defence in Thessalonike acted as a catalyst on the Greek political scene. Constantine was obliged to flee the country and Greece, with Venizelos

as prime minister, entered the war on the side of the Entente. With the aid of the reconstituted Greek army, the Macedonian front was broken, the Bulgarians were driven from eastern (and also from Serbian) Macedonia, and the way was opened for the final ratification of the Balkan borders in Macedonia.

The treaty of Neuilly with Bulgaria (1919) confirmed the arrangements of the treaty of Bucharest as far as Macedonia was concerned, with the rider that the small region of Stromnitsa, which belonged to Bulgaria, was to go to Serbia.

Although superficially there had been no fundamental changes in the political map of this part of the Balkans, the events of the four years 1914-18 left deep wounds. During the occupation the Bulgarian authorities had applied themselves to the systematic annihilation of the Greek population. The Greeks who were driven out, executed or taken as hostages were replaced by Bulgarians or Bulgarian-Macedonian refugees in an attempt to make the area Bulgarian. The situation in Serbian Macedonia was similar.[2] This traumatic experience sharpened hatreds and rival claims and resulted in a large part of the Bulgarian-Macedonian population leaving Greece after the war to settle in Bulgarian Macedonia, where it continued to be a source of tension in the surrounding area for several decades.

During the war the Bulgarian-Macedonian revolutionaries of IMRO had cooperated closely with and fought in the ranks of the Bulgarian army, and had indeed played a leading role in Bulgarizing the occupied territories. This stance revealed that they identified completely with Bulgarian nationalist ideology.[3] It became clear that the slogans of the preceding decades ('Macedonia for the Macedonians', 'autonomous Macedonia', etc.), had been adopted purely as a matter of political convenience, for they were abandoned as soon as there seemed to be a chance of incorporating all the Macedonian territories in the Bulgarian kingdom.

During the course of the Peace Conference, a Greek-Bulgarian treaty was signed for the voluntary exchange of populations. The father of this idea was Venizelos who, realizing that there was a trend towards a flight of the

Greeks of Bulgaria (from the region of Macedonia and northern Thrace) and of the Bulgarians of Thrace and Macedonia, took the initiative to encourage the exchange, so that the ethnic aspect, at least, of the Greek-Bulgarian dispute in the Macedonian question would cease to furnish an excuse for further interventions. With the approval of the Allied Powers, Bulgaria signed the agreement, which charged a mixed international committee with overseeing the population exchange; both countries were bound by the peace treaties to protect minorities.[4]

In the event, the exchange of populations assumed greater dimensions on account of the influx of Greek refugees from the Turkish provinces (eastern Thrace, Asia Minor and Pontos). Although the armed forces and the agents of IMRO made attempts to stem the mass exodus from Greece, conditions, as we have seen, were not conducive to the Bulgarians' remaining, especially in the territories where the hatred created by the Bulgarian occupation constituted an unbridgeable chasm. Almost all the Bulgarian-Macedonians from the Nestos to the Axios crossed the frontier to Bulgaria.[5]

The situation in western Greek Macedonia was somewhat different. There, ever since the time of the Macedonian Struggle the Slav-speaking population had been divided in its national loyalties between the Greeks and the Bulgarians. Although a section of it, consisting of those who were most fanatically devoted to Bulgarian nationalism, left the country, the majority of the Slav-speakers stayed behind in this region. Meanwhile, the departure of the Muslims and the vast influx of Greek refugees from Yugoslavia, Bulgaria and, mainly, Turkey, radically altered the ethnic stratigraphy of Macedonia, giving it a totally Greek character with only a few islands of non-Greeks.

According to the statistics of the Mixed Commission on Population Exchange, forty-six thousand Greeks from Bulgaria were exchanged with ninety-two thousand Bulgarians from Greek Macedonia and Thrace. These figures include those who had migrated during the wars.[6] The new picture that emerged in Greek Macedonia in the inter-war period can be seen from the following statistics, derived from the Committee for the Rehabilitation of Refugees, based on figures from the Ministry of Social Welfare, the Mixed Commission for the Greek-Bulgarian Exchange of Populations and the Mixed Commission for Greek-Bulgarian voluntary migration.[7]

Greeks	1,341,000	88.8%
Muslims	2,000	0.1%
Bulgarians	77,000	5.1%
Others (mostly Jews)	91,000	6.0%
	1,511,000	100.0%

These figures were confirmed by the official Greek census of 1928 which registered 81,984 Slav-speakers out of a total population of 6,032,761.[8]

Although the ethnic situation in the Greek area had stabilized in a manner satisfactory to the Greek side, matters in Serbian Macedonia were in a great state of flux. The government in Belgrade described the inhabitants of the

351. *Eleutherios Venizelos left his mark on Macedonian affairs during the second decade of the 20th century. As prime minister, he played a major part in the formation of the Balkan Alliance in the wars of 1912-13 and in the Peace Conference of Bucharest in 1913, which confirmed the liberation of Macedonia. Later in 1916, from Thessalonike, as head of the National Defence government he brought Greece to the side of the Entente, and successfully outmanoeuvred foreign claims on Macedonia. Athens, National Historical Museum.*

area as Serbs, and resorted to various programmes to make the area Serbian. These attempts provoked the reaction of a large part of the population which remained faithful to the Bulgarian idea and favoured the development of forces hostile to them. For several years encouragement was given to terrorist activities on the part of armed IMRO bands based in the mountainous regions of Bulgarian Macedonia.[9]

At the same time, the revolutionary-minded element of the Bulgarian-Macedonian population had acquired such strength in Bulgarian Macedonia that the region of Petrić

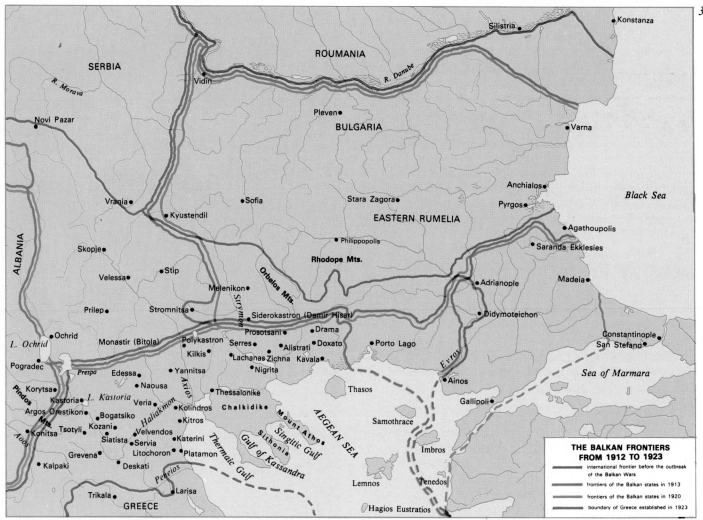

352. *As a result of the Balkan Wars of 1912-13 Greek Macedonia was liberated while parts of northern Macedonia were assigned to Serbia and Bulgaria. With the treaty of Neuilly, signed at the end of the First World War, the regions of* *Stromnitsa and Vranja-Pirot were detached from Bulgaria and given to Serbia. Thus the geographical area of Macedonia was divided as follows: 51.57% was assigned to Greece; 38.32% to Serbia and 10.11% to Bulgaria.*

had become a 'state within a state' governed by the leaders of IMRO. The influence of the refugees extended throughout the whole of Bulgaria, however, for some of them had risen to high positions in the political life of the country. It was only the internal disputes within the Organization, resulting in fratricidal vendettas in which the leading members destroyed each other, that enabled the Bulgarian government ultimately to impose its control on the much troubled region.[10]

Meanwhile, a new factor made a forceful appearance on the Macedonian scene. At the end of the war, the leaders of the newly formed Soviet Union attempted to exploit every source of political and social unrest in the countries of Eastern Europe, in the hope of spreading the revolution. At the beginning of the twenties, Bulgaria seemed to be the ripest of all the Balkan countries for a successful test of the Soviet experiment. The Comintern therefore adopted the views of the Bulgarian communists on the Macedonian question, hoping that this would attract the disaffected masses of the Bulgarian Macedonian refugees to the communist revolution.[11] An attempt at an armed rising in

Bulgaria in 1923 was a failure. Nonetheless, Comintern support for the Bulgarian nationalist position, as formulated by the leaders Vasil Kolarov and Georgi Dimitrov (General Secretary of the Comintern) continued to be forthcoming for many years.

The line of the Comintern and the Balkan Communist Federation (BCF), in which all the Balkan communist parties were represented, was formulated in a series of party documents in the period 1922-24, and envisaged the foundation of an 'independent and united Macedonia (and Thrace)', which would comprise the corresponding geographical districts of Bulgaria, Yugoslavia and Greece.[12] This would, essentially, be a second Bulgarian state. This, at least, is what emerges from the original documents of the Comintern and the BCF, in which the term 'Macedonians' did not imply recognition of a separate nationality but was used to define either all the inhabitants of Macedonia in general, or more specifically the Bulgarians of Macedonia. Even the Communist Party of Yugoslavia, when referring to the oppressed masses in Yugoslav Macedonia mentions only Turks, Arnaouts,

353. The troops of the Allied Powers of the Entente landed in Thessalonike from 1915 to establish the new 'Balkan front' in central Macedonia. The increasing threat of invasion by the Germans and Bulgarian army which already had control of the

area between the rivers Nestos and Strymon, caused them to take up strong defensive positions throughout central and western Macedonia. Photographic Archive of the Estia Library, Nea Smyrni, Athens.

Bulgarians and Koutsovlachs (cf. the decisions of its Third Congress, 1923).[13]

Despite their initial reservations, the communist parties of Greece and Yugoslavia finally adopted the Comintern line. Some members, including the historian John Kordatos, editor of *Rizospastis,* were compelled to leave the party, asserting that the conditions in Greek Macedonia at least, after the major exchanges of population, made the line of the Bulgarian comrades totally unrealistic.[14]

The Comintern retained its pro-Bulgarian policy until 1935, when international conditions, with the rise of Nazism and Fascism in Europe, led to a policy of forming popular fronts; this was not conducive to the promulgation of revolutionary or separatist slogans, which would alienate the broader popular masses. The Communist Party of Greece, at its Sixth Congress in December 1935, adopted a new line on the Macedonian question: the slogan of a 'united and independent Macedonia' was replaced by a line involving complete equality of rights for the minorities.[15]

This, briefly, was the state of the Macedonian question

on the outbreak of the Second World War. As in the First World War, Bulgaria attempted to trade her adherence to the Axis for substantial concessions at the expense of the Macedonian territories in Yugoslavia and Greece. The Yugoslav government, too, from the first day of the Italian invasion of Greece, examined the possibility of occupying Thessalonike and its hinterland, but this was averted thanks to the successes of the Greek army on the Albanian front. The question arose again when the government of Čvetković and the Regent Paul signed the agreement by which their country joined the Axis, in return for which they demanded, and received, Thessalonike. These plans were thwarted by the coup of General Dušan Simović on 25 March, 1941, however, and Yugoslavia shared with Greece the fate of being occupied by the Germans (6 April) and seeing her Macedonian territories occupied by Bulgaria, as an ally of the Third Reich.[16]

On the basis of the agreements between Hitler and Filov, Bulgaria occupied almost the whole of Yugoslav Macedonia, with the exception of the western districts, which fell within the Italian occupation zone; at first,

354. The Greek anti-tank defences on the Metaxas line in the Beles-Nestos area. The German attack on the line opened at dawn on 6 April, 1941 with heavy shelling, reinforced by air strength, ground attacks by soldiers on foot or mounted on motor bicycles and tank fire the whole length of the line. Athens, War Museum.

however, she received only the eastern part of Greek Macedonia (and most of western Thrace). The Germans themselves occupied central Greek Macedonia and gave western Macedonia to the Italians. After the capitulation of the Italians the Bulgarians, with the consent of the Germans, extended their occupation zone to include Chalkidike and Kilkis, while in western Macedonia, through their liaison officers at the local German headquarters, they organized bands of security forces consisting of pro-Bulgarian Slav-speakers, which were known locally as 'Ohrana'.

During the Occupation, the Bulgarian authorities carried out a policy of 'Bulgarization' by force with the same severity that they had used during the first occupation of 1916-18. The mass persecution of the population descended from the refugees, and the economic, moral, and even physical extermination of the rest of the Greek population, was accompanied by the settlement of Bulgarians from Bulgaria. The total integration of eastern Macedonia and western Thrace into the Bulgarian kingdom was averted, thanks to the mass mobilization of the Greek populace in Athens and the other major towns in occupied Greece.[17]

At the same time, the attempt to make Yugoslav Macedonia Bulgarian seemed at first to be proceeding smoothly. A large proportion of the local population, weary of the Serbian administration, had originally welcomed the Bulgarian army as liberators. Even the local leadership of the communist party split from the Yugoslav party and joined the Bulgarian. Soon, however, the growth of the partisan movement, together with the impolitic behaviour of the Bulgarians, produced a climate of coolness that turned to one of hostility between the local population and the Bulgarian army of occupation.[18] At this critical moment the Yugoslav communists announced their plans for the post-war reorganization of the Yugoslav state on a federal basis. One of the six federal republics was to be the 'Socialist (originally 'Peoples') Republic of Macedonia', the Slav population of which would no longer be considered 'Serbian' or 'Bulgarian' but would acquire a new national name — 'Macedonian'.[19]

The name 'Macedonian' was fairly widespread amongst the local south-Slav population, but as an indicator of its geographical origin, not of race. The use of this same name to define a particular southern Slav national group was a neologism that suited the policy of the new Yugoslav leadership. By giving an ethnic content to a geographical term, the new policy created the basis on which it would be possible to construct a new nationality, detached from both its Serbian and, more importantly, its Bulgarian origins.[20]

The end of the war found the Yugoslavia of Tito in an advantageous position *vis-à-vis* the defeated Bulgaria of the Patriotic Front. This gave the Yugoslavs the chance to attempt to solve the Macedonian question to their own advantage. They brought intense pressure to bear on their Bulgarian comrades, demanding at first that Bulgaria should be included as the seventh member of a Federation of the South Slavs, in which Yugoslavia would be represented by its six federative republics. The Socialist Republic of Macedonia would be enlarged, at first by the addition of Bulgarian Macedonia, while the incorporation of Greek Macedonia was to be the next step. In the end, the Bulgarians managed to avoid integration into the federal structure being prepared by the Yugoslavs. Dimitrov yielded to the second of the Yugoslav demands, however, and agreed first to recognize as 'Macedonians' even the Bulgarians living in Bulgarian Macedonia, and second to prepare the ground for the incorporation of the region in the Socialist Republic of Macedonia.[21] In return for these concessions, Bulgaria was to receive from Yugoslavia certain territories (Vranja, Pirot) which it had lost during the First World War; and at the same time it would have Belgrade's support at the Paris Peace Conference for its demand to acquire Greek western Thrace.[22]

Although these agreements were ratified in 1947 at two meetings between Tito and Dimitrov, at Bled and Varna, the breach between Stalin and Tito upset all calculations concerning Yugoslav hegemony in the Balkans, in which the Macedonian question was pivotal. With the encouragement of the Soviet Union, Bulgaria reneged on the concessions she had made on the Macedonian question. She disavowed the theory of the 'Macedonian nation' and expelled from her territory the schoolmasters and instructors who had been sent from Skopje. Next, becoming conscious of her strong position, she attempted to take advantage of the difficulties faced by the Yugoslavs by reviving the pre-war slogan of a 'united and independent Macedonia'. This slogan also helped the more general political pressure being brought to bear at that time on Tito by the Soviet Union. The Cominform accordingly embraced it as its new guideline on the Macedonian question.[23]

This policy was only abandoned after the death of Stalin (1953) and the adoption by his successors of a policy of rapprochement towards Yugoslavia. Bulgaria too, inevitably aligned itself with this policy and ceased to put forward claims to the Macedonian territories of the neighbours. For the moment (1955-56) it seemed that the

355. *The Bulgarian army, with the permission of Nazi Germany, occupied first eastern Greek Macedonia and then spread over the nomes of Chalkidike and Kilkis. During four years of occupation it practised every kind of cruelty and oppression on the Greek population, while a programme of systematic eviction of the Greek population was put into effect. Photographic Collection, Dr E. Kofos.*

new Bulgarian leadership would revert to the policy of Dimitrov and would recognize the 'Macedonian' nation even in its own territory. Indeed, about one hundred and eighty thousand 'Macedonians' were registered in the official Bulgarian population census of 1956. However, relations between Moscow and Belgrade deteriorated again in 1957-58, and this allowed the Bulgarian leaders to aim at the preservation of as stable as possible a policy on the Macedonian issue. In the sixties demands of a territorial nature vanished from the official political vocabulary of Sofia, and the theories emanating from Skopje about the existence of 'Macedonians' in Bulgaria, were rejected. The only area in which a certain lack of clarity remained was the Bulgarian position on the national status of the Slav

356. Boris, Prince of Bulgaria, with Hitler. In the Second World War Bulgaria ranged itself ont the side of the Axis and attempted to increase its territory at the expense of Yugoslavia and Greece.

population of Yugoslav Macedonia. From the plethora of official statements and publications during the last twenty years it emerges that Bulgaria considers this population to be 'historically of Bulgarian origin'. It admits, however, that completely new conditions arose in the Socialist Republic of Macedonia after the Second World War, creating a new situation. This means that Bulgaria on the one hand denies the existence of a 'Macedonian nation' and on the other, proceeds indirectly to recognize the existing situation in the Socialist Republic of Macedonia. The dispute has continued unabated at this level throughout the last twenty years and has affected political relations between the two neighbouring countries.[24]

In addition to the Yugoslav-Bulgarian aspect of the problem, Yugoslav policy on the Macedonian issue also had its consequences for Greece. Even during the Nazi occupation, the Yugoslav partisans attempted to create conditions favourable to the annexing of at least some parts of Greek Macedonia. As a first phase, Vukmanović - Tempo was sent to Greece to request the leadership of the Greek partisans and of the Communist Party of Greece to form separate armed bands of Macedonian Slavs in Greek western Macedonia which would essentially come under a Yugoslav-Macedonian administration. This request was rejected. The Greek People's Liberation Army (ELAS), however, proceeded to form separate Macedonian-Slav

battalions within its own large units. Those who enrolled in these battalions were Slav-speakers with a Slav national conscience. In a short time they established a separate partisan organization under the name 'Slav-Macedonian National Front' (SNOF). At the same time, the political leadership of the Greek partisans permitted the popularization of the Yugoslav theories concerning the 'Macedonian nation' in the areas of western Macedonia under their control. The leaders of this movement, in an attempt to broaden their ranks, addressed themselves to those who were collaborating with the Bulgarian occupation authorities. The experiment was a success, for when the war in the Balkans began to take a dangerous turn for the Germans in 1944, the supporters of the fascist Bulgarian 'Ohrana' began to desert it and enrol *en masse* in the communist Macedonian-Slav SNOF.

Meanwhile, the secret connections of the SNOF with, and its indirect dependence upon, the Yugoslav Macedonian General Staff began to come into the open and to cause serious concern — to the point where local units of ELAS were obliged, just before liberation, to clash with armed bands of the SNOF and drive them into Yugoslavia.[25]

On the outbreak of the Civil War in Greece (1946-49) the Macedonian Slavs returned to Greek Macedonia and joined the Greek communist movement, in which they formed their own organization, the National Liberation Front (NLF). To judge from the various collections of documents and memoirs published in Skopje, the struggle of the Macedonian Slavs (that is, of that section of the Slav-speaking population of Greek Macedonia that had identified with Slav nationalism) during the Greek Civil War was thought of as 'a national liberation struggle by the Aegean Macedonians' to achieve their 'national rights'. These rights consisted of nothing more than the incorporation of both the Bulgarian and the Greek Macedonian territories within the Socialist Republic of Macedonia.[26]

After the breach between Moscow and Belgrade in the summer of 1948, the leadership of the Communist Party of Greece aligned itself with the Cominform in its attacks on Tito's regime, and also embraced the new line on the Macedonian issue. By a decision taken by the fifth Plenary Session of the Central Committee, in January 1949 the Communist Party of Greece reverted to the old pro-Bulgarian demand for a 'united and independent Macedonia', within a future Balkan Communist Federation.[27] This turn had serious consequences in the operational sphere, for the Yugoslavs, to protect their rear, closed their border which up to that time had been the main supply route for the fighting Greek communists. Some of the Slav-speaking units of the NOF deserted and established themselves in Yugoslav Macedonia. Later, in August 1940, at the end of the armed struggle, the remaining body of the NOF, together with other political refugees, headed towards eastern European countries and the Soviet Union. For several years the leadership of the Greek Communist Party abroad permitted the establishment of separate Slav-Macedonian organizations and schools, and the publication of Slav-Macedonian literature. Later, however, towards the end of the fifties and the early sixties these Slav-Macedonians slowly established themselves in

Yugoslav Macedonia.[28] They were offered several concessions, amongst them Yugoslav citizenship and a 'Macedonian national identity'. One might say that they were assimilated into their new national environment. A few years later, in 1956, the Communist Party of Greece abandoned the slogan of a 'united and independent Macedonia' (as the Bulgarian communist party itself had already done) and returned to the principal of 'equal rights for minorities'.[29] With the withdrawal from Greece in 1949 of the last of the Slav-speaking population who supported Slav nationalism even this new slogan had no real meaning for Greek Macedonia and remained a statement of principle.

After the middle of the fifties, then, the Macedonian question lost its old intensity, which derived from the open formulation of territorial claims. Yugoslavia turned its attention to the attempt to consolidate the 'Macedonian nation' within its borders. It continued to demand the recognition of 'Macedonian' minorities from the outside world (that is, from Bulgaria and secondly, from Greece), but its only achievement was to provoke strong reactions from time to time from the public opinion and the political leadership of its two neighbours.[30] Despite this negative aspect, it can be argued that the Macedonian question, having passed through the critical decade from 1944-54, had entered a phase where intensity waned. All the indications suggest that, if no external factors arise, the question may move to the level of mere academic historical controversy.

THE ECONOMIC DEVELOPMENT OF GREEK MACEDONIA SINCE 1912

The economic history of Greek Macedonia from 1912 to the present may be divided into three periods. The first covers the years from the liberation of the area in 1912 until 1922. During these years the structure of the Macedonian economy continued to conform to that typical of the under-developed, traditional agrarian economy that had prevailed during the Ottoman occupation. Production methods were old-fashioned; commercial exchange was limited and productivity low. As a result, the per capita income and the standard of living were low.

The second period covers the years following the Asia Minor disaster and the mass influx of Greek refugees in 1923, the end of the Second World War and the ensuing civil war in 1950. The influx of Greek refugees and the major land reclamation schemes in the plains of Thessalonike, Serres and Drama laid down the infrastructure and preconditions for economic take-off in Macedonia: agricultural production was partially modernized by the improvement of the methods of cultivation; there was a growth of small-scale industry; the commercial spirit spread to the major urban centres and accelerated the development of the commercial sector which was facilitated by the monetization of the economy and the promotion of the division of labour in many economic activities. However, the rapid development of Macedonia during this period was interrupted by the havoc caused by the Second World War and the civil embroilment of 1946-49.

The third period (1951 to the present) began with reconstruction from the devastation of war, achieved mainly through foreign aid. During this phase, both the primary and secondary production of Macedonia were rapidly and intensively modernized through the mobilization of manpower and of the rich natural resources of the area. As a result, the Macedonian economy essentially entered the take-off phase. The supply of electricity on a wide scale to the area, with the construction of the first hydro-electric plant on the river Agras (1954) and the thermo-electric works at Ptolemaïs (1958), brought about a revolutionary change in the economy at the very beginning of the period. The laying of the national electricity grid created the basic infrastructure not only for industrial growth, but also for a rise in the standard of living. Thessalonike became the second largest industrial centre in Greece, and the growth of tourism, transport and construction all gave added impetus to the economic progress of the area. The pursuance of land reclamation schemes was combined with a change of the structure of cultivation and an increase in agricultural productivity. The most important negative factor during this period was the loss of population (chiefly from the countryside) through migration, either to other parts of Greece or abroad. This trend was reversed after 1975, however, when there was large-scale repatriation of migrants. At the time of Greece's association with the European Economic Community in 1961, Macedonia was at a stage of rapid growth and also of re-adjustment.

During the period from 1912 to the present, Greek Macedonia has gradually become an integral part of the Greek economy. At the same time, it acquired considerable economic autonomy presaging its growing independence from the centre of decision-making in Athens. In the seventy years since liberation, Greek Macedonia has essentially been a self-reliant centre of economic growth within the broader Greek and European framework.

THE PERIOD OF TRADITIONAL AGRARIAN ECONOMY: 1912-1922

Economic conditions after liberation

From 1912 until 1922, the predominant economic structure in Macedonia was that of the traditional under-developed rural economy, organized either around independent self-supporting families or around *chiftliks*. In 1917, before the expropriation of the *chiftliks* in Macedonia, there were 818 such estates out of a total of 2,259 in Greece (36%). The situation had not changed significantly from that of 1907, when the *chiftliks* accounted for 51% of arable land. These relics of the Ottoman period were the dominant feature of organized agriculture, and were based on the following institutional arrangements: the owners ceded to the peasants (sharecroppers) arable land, which the latter farmed, giving one-third or one-half of the net product to the owners of the estate. This resulted in a system of economic dependence offering no incentive to the peasants

TABLE 1

Growth of the population of Greek Macedonia 1913-81 (figures taken from census tables)[2]

Nome	1913	1920	1928	1940	1951	1961	1971	1981
1. Grevena	—	—	—	—	39,910	43,484	35,275	36,318
2. Drama	—	—	111,572	145,089	120,492	121,006	91,009	94,709
3. Emathia	—	—	—	—	96,439	114,515	118,003	133,066
4. Thessalonike	—	—	539,986	577,128	459,956	544,394	710,352	858,661
5. Kavala	—	—	119,140	138,133	136,337	140,751	121,593	135,161
6. Kastoria	—	—	—	—	46,407	47,487	45,711	52,911
7. Kilkis	—	—	—	99,389	89,475	102,812	84,375	80,245
8. Kozani	—	—	166,523	197,476	142,527	152,809	135,709	147,033
9. Pella	—	—	97,167	127,597	116,969	133,224	126,085	131,998
10. Pieria	—	—	—	—	86,161	97,697	91,728	106,451
11. Serres	—	—	182,710	232,224	222,549	248,041	202,898	196,171
12. Florina	—	—	125,722	156,168	69,391	67,356	52,264	52,475
13. Chalkidike	—	—	64,799	81,180	75,735	79,849	73,850	79,005
14. Mount Athos[3]	—	—	4,858	4,746	3,086	2,687	1,732	1,445
Total	1,167,617	1,085,531	1,412,477	1,759,130	1,705,434	1,896,112	1,890,684	2,105,649

to increase their output since they themselves were the object of economic exploitation by the owner of the *chiftlik*. The economic dependence of the farmers was further enforced by high rates of usury, prevalent since the Ottoman period, and by the payment of tithe. The inhabitants of Macedonia were also badly exploited by foreign entrepreneurs with regard to basic goods that had to be imported (flour, paraffin, medicines, timber etc.), and this further contributed to the general picture of a one-sided economic system, favouring the interests of some classes.

The region also suffered from the unsettled conditions inherited from the Ottoman period. Thus, during the decade 1900-1910, the Macedonian economy was in a very bad state as a result of the national rivalries of Bulgarians, Greeks, Turks and Serbs in the region. The rising of the Bulgarians (1903) and the strong reaction of the Greeks had devastating consequences for the economy (acts of sabotage against the communication networks, destruction of the Ottoman Bank in Thessalonike during the uprisings). The mopping-up operations mounted by the Turks, designed mainly to put an end to Greek activity, were directed not only against the population, but against its property.

During the immediately following years, and throughout the First World War (1914-18) Greek Macedonia became a theatre of military operations resulting in the paralyzing of all economic activity. Thessalonike became an entrenched camp of the Entente powers, and the activity in its port was mainly directed towards supplying their armies. Despite all this, there was a rudimentary economy that functioned as a continuation of the economic institutions of the Ottoman empire.

Under these conditions the population enjoyed a very low standard of living. The per capita income of the inhabitants of Macedonia at this period has been calculated to be less than half the figure for the rest of Greece. It is signifi-

cant that as a result of the low living standards and the lack of hygienic living conditions (total absence of medical care and a high mortality rate from malaria and other diseases) the population of Greek Macedonia fell from 1,167,617 in 1913 to 1,085,531 in 1920 (see table 1).[1]

The population was predominantly engaged in agricultural activity. It has been calculated that in 1913 the agrarian economy accounted for 70% of all economic activity; the remaining 30% consisted of industrial crafts, processing, commercial and other forms of activity. The urban population was confined mainly to the towns of Thessalonike (157,000 inhabitants in 1912) and Kavala (23,000 in 1913), and was no more than 15% of the total population of Macedonia. The urban population was engaged mainly in commercial and manufacturing activities.

The traditional rural economy

Macedonia basically retained the under-developed traditional agrarian economy of the period of the Ottoman occupation. The area actually under cultivation during this period was only about 2,500,000 *stremmata*, about a quarter of the cultivable land (table 2); this was very low because the main aim of agricultural activity at this time was just to maintain the rural family (self-subsistent economy). Many rural areas around Veria, Kastoria, Langadas and Yannitsa remained uncultivated in the absence of workmen and the requisite equipment. Moreover malaria, which mainly afflicted the inhabitants of the Macedonian plains, discouraged the intensive cultivation of the land. The methods of cultivation were in any event primitive. Under these conditions, the yield per *stremma* was very low: wheat 45 kilos; barley 56 kilos; maize 78 kilos; cotton 63 kilos; tobacco 62 kilos.

The most important crops were wheat, barley, maize,

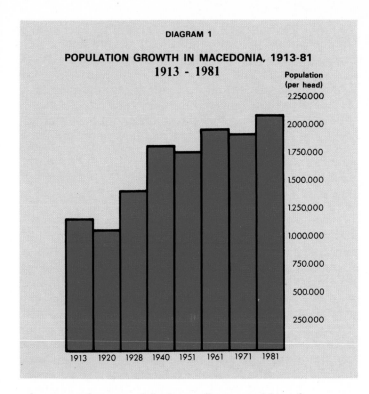

DIAGRAM 1

POPULATION GROWTH IN MACEDONIA, 1913-81
1913 - 1981

Population
(per head)
2.250.000

2.000.000

1.750.000

1.500.000

1.250.000

1.000.000

750.000

500.000

250.000

1913 1920 1928 1940 1951 1961 1971 1981

both of area and the variety of trees, it was not exploited systematically or to any real extent during this period. The casual cutting of wood to satisfy household needs caused great damage to the forests, which were the main source of fuel and heat at this time. Only a few areas (Veria, Naousa, Chalkidike and Serres) had a number of primitive saw-mills producing timber for building and for the shipyards. It is significant, however, that foreign concerns expressed an interest in exploiting the forests on the island of Thasos and successfully applied for a permit to exploit them.

Early industry and manufacturing

Despite the rapid spread of the industrial revolution in Europe in the nineteenth and at the beginning of the twentieth centuries, no industry of note developed in Macedonia during that time. The only manufacturing activity was in Thessalonike, where there was some light industry producing consumer goods (flour milling, production of spaghetti, soap, tiles and textiles). Flour-milling was one of the longest established processes in Thessalonike, from where flour products were exported to almost all the major cities in the Balkans and to Turkish ports. The most famous factory was the mill owned by the Alatini brothers who, from the beginning of 1900, employed more than two hundred workers. The firms in Kavala processing leaf-tobacco were also of some importance, and the waterpower of the area around Naousa and Veria was used to run a variety of small factories (spinning, weaving, flour mills, sesame mills, cotton gins, rope factories, and woollen mills).

The most important small-scale industry was the fur industry of Kastoria, which had a tradition going back four hundred years; at this date it employed two thousand men and women and was the most profitable form of manufacturing activity in Macedonia. Despite their relative richness, the mineral resources of Macedonia had been exploited on only a limited scale: there were a number of mines in Chalkidike (Kassandra and Yerakini) that produced antimony, silver and lead ores, chromium, pyrites and magnesite, all of which were exported in their raw state.

tobacco and cotton. Much smaller quantities of rye, oats, unspun silk, red peppers, pulses and potatoes were produced. The production of olives and olive oil (from Chalkidike and Thasos), of opium (from the plains of the river Axios and the area around Serres) and of crocuses or saffron (from the area around Kozani) was also very small. The oil and the olives of Thasos were famous throughout Greece and the Middle East. The opium was of excellent quality, thanks to the favourable climate, and it was in great demand; for this reason it was high-priced. The flowers of the crocus (both yellow and red), known from antiquity, were much sought after for the manufacture of drugs and perfumes as well as for other industrial uses.

Stock-raising in Macedonia had reached a satisfactory level before the First World War. Its development was based on the abundance of natural resources (wild grass and free grazing grounds). The exploitation of these resources was in the hands: (a) of the Koutsovlachs, who were stockraisers and lived a traditional pastoral life, grazing their animals (mainly goats and sheep) in the mountains or the plains; (b) of farmers who raised stock as a supplementary activity. The *chiftliks* also supported goats, sheep, oxen and pigs, though beasts of burden and draught animals predominated. The marketable products of stock-raising (milk, meat, cheese and butter) were either destined for the consumption of those raising the animals or were sold in the nearby towns. Macedonian cheese was particularly famous, especially the *feta* and *manouri* of Blatsi. The products that required processing (hides and wool) were of considerable importance and were destined either for the local market or for export. In Kozani alone, in 1919, there were twenty-five tanneries to cater for the hides produced in the region. Much of the wool was sent to Thessalonike and Naousa to be processed and made into carpets, dresses, bed-covers etc.

Although Macedonia was rich in woodland, in terms

TABLE 2

Macedonia The expansion of arable and irrigated land, 1911-71[4]				
	Cultivated area		**Irrigated area**	
Year	Total for Greece	Macedonia	Total for Greece	Macedonia
1911	12,382,500	2,500,000	—	
1921	14,500,000	2,683,843	—	(20,000)
1925	15,000,000	3,388,097	—	(60,000)
1939	32,741,000	5,500,000	—	(335,065)
1950	30,797,000	7,670,061	2,417,750	(451,000)
1961	36,732,756	9,405,264	4,890,480	1,494,626
1971	36,650,603	9,486,539	7,336,720	2,353,295

The figures in parentheses are rough estimates.

Early development of the service sector

A primitive banking system had evolved from as early as the period of the Ottoman occupation, financed by the Ottoman Agricultural Bank, and some foreign capital from the West, more specifically from France and Italy. The National Bank of Greece was not allowed to operate in Ottoman territory and therefore, with the aid of an investment group, founded the Bank of the East, a branch of which commenced operations in Thessalonike in 1906.

Immediately after the liberation of Macedonia, the Ottoman Agricultural Bank was reorganized and came under Greek ownership, while the National Bank of Greece, after sending the director, D. Maximos, to Thessalonike, founded a branch there in 1913, which gave financial backing to commerce and industry. It advanced a loan of £ 500,000 sterling for the reconstruction of Thessalonike after the fire of 1917, and gave vital assistance in settling compensation payments to refugees, administrating the property of the Muslims who left Macedonia, ensuring food-supply and so on.

An important contribution was also made by the eighty farmers' cooperatives set up after liberation to assist in financing the farmers; these cooperatives borrowed from the National Bank and the Agricultural Bank at 5% and made loans to their members at 7%.

The import-export trade

Because of its underdeveloped condition immediately after liberation, Macedonia's dependence on foreign countries was slight, and limited mainly to foreign visible trade.

In the sphere of exports, Macedonia was completely dependent on foreign markets in tobacco, cotton, wine, currants, pepper, raw hides, unspun silk and furs, since the home market was incapable of absorbing the surpluses of these products. Most of the foreign state monopolies in tobacco (Swedish, Austrian, Italian and others) owned warehouses, offices and even private residences in Macedonia, and many foreign companies also retained agencies in the major tobacco-producing areas. The biggest part of Macedonia's export trade passed through the ports of Thessalonike and Kavala. Interestingly enough, Thessalonike had a balance of trade deficit (with imports exceeding exports) while the port of Kavala had a surplus (exports exceeding imports); exports were vastly greater at Kavala, due entirely to the export of tobacco. The main manufactured products exported from Macedonia in this first period were soap, cloth and yarn.

On the import side, the main imported goods were: wheat and flour products, sugar, salt, pulses, rice, fruit, potatoes, coffee, hides, oil and petrol, finished timber, cement, paper, tools and small machines. This inventory demonstrates that imports were oriented towards consumer goods rather than capital goods, since there was no importing of manufacturing equipment.

The total volume of trade (the sum of imports and exports) showed a tendency to increase, demonstrating the steady increase in the importance of the foreign sector in the economic life of Macedonia.

The lively economic interest shown by foreigners in Macedonia had declined somewhat at the end of the nineteenth and the beginning of the twentieth centuries, on account of the large numbers of barriers erected by the Ottoman administration, and of national armed rivalries in the area. It is plain, however, from the growth of the import trade in Thessalonike, that the abundant inflow of foreign goods still gave foreign enterprises a margin for profitable activity in the area.

THE CREATION OF THE CONDITIONS FOR ECONOMIC TAKE-OFF: 1923-50

During this period, the Macedonian economy underwent some radical changes in its institutions and methods of production that prepared the way for economic take-off. The main contributory factors were: (a) the influx of refugees whose industry and vitality led to a rapid development of agricultural and industrial production; (b) the creation by the state of the social and economic infrastructure (large scale irrigation projects, extension of the road network, the improvement of public health by an attack on malaria, the spread of education etc.) and (c) the expansion of 'external economies' — that is, the positive secondary effects on the rest of the economy produced by the major infrastructure works.

The influx of refugees and the problems of re-settlement

It is generally agreed that human resources are the most important factor in economic growth. The influx of refugees into Macedonia after 1922 enriched the area not only quantitatively, but also in terms of quality. The number of Greek refugees entering Greece between 1922 and 1925 was 1,221,849. Over half these (638,253) settled in Greek Macedonia, where they formed about 45% of the total population. At the same time, 362,898 Turks and Bulgarians left Macedonia under the terms of the treaties of Neuilly and Lausanne.

The majority of the refugees settled in the areas of Yannitsa, Thessalonike, Kilkis, Serres, Drama and Kavala. According to the census of 1928 taken by the Rehabilitation Committee, the population of Macedonia had reached 1,412,477 (711,482 males and 700,995 females) — an increase of 244,860 over 1913, representing an annual increase of about 1.4% (table 1). Most of the refugees were farmers; those who lived in towns were artisans, master craftsmen or in the self-employed professions.

The rural refugees were given the farm lands and houses of the Turks and Bulgarians, there being 50,272 Turkish and 3,204 Bulgarian houses. These, however, were insufficient to cater for the 112,111 rural refugee families, and the Rehabilitation Committee, through the General Directorate of Macedonian Settlement which it founded, funded the building of 42,826 new refugee houses, many of which still survive. Of the 2,037 refugee settlements created throughout Greece, 1,381 were in Macedonia — 67.8%.[5]

The settlement of the refugees gave rise to serious demographic, economic, social and technical problems.

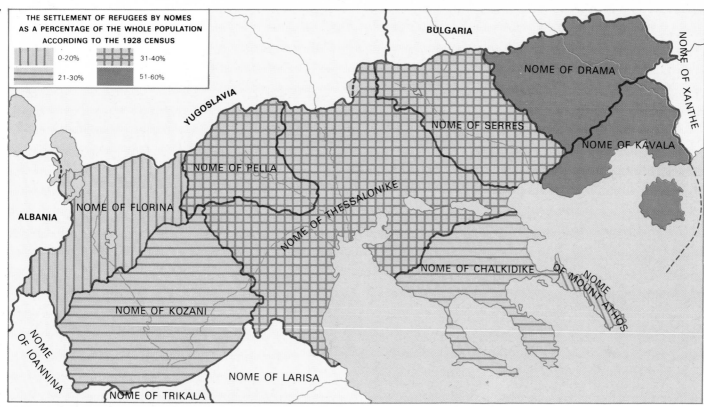

THE SETTLEMENT OF REFUGEES BY NOMES
AS A PERCENTAGE OF THE WHOLE POPULATION
ACCORDING TO THE 1928 CENSUS

| 0-20% | 31-40% |
| 21-30% | 51-60% |

357. The geographical distribution of the refugees shows that most of them settled in the productive regions of eastern and central Greek Macedonia. Their hard work and energy laid the foundations for the development of the Macedonian economy.

They were granted land under cultivation and uncultivated land, totalling 5,629,210 *stremmata*. The land was allotted to each refugee family as follows: (a) growers of cereal crops were given 40-60 *stremmata*; (b) vine-growers were given 15-30 *stremmata*; and (c) tobacco-farmers were allocated 10-20 *stremmata*. These allocations were clearly inadequate, but they gave the refugees the chance to secure at least a basic subsistence. A particularly important contribution towards enabling the refugees to acquire land seems to have been the decision by the Plastiras government to proceed with the compulsory expropriation of the *chiftliks* (large estates) that still existed, in order to rehabilitate the families of the landless and the refugees.

In addition to housing and farming land, the rural refugee families were also given 'subsistence', in kind or in drachmas (for their daily sustenance), farm tools, draught animals and beasts of burden, seed, pasturage for the animals and loans. The total cost up to 1930 of resettling the refugees — for food, housing, supply of animals and tools, loans etc.— amounted to 2,535,290,000 drachmas,[6] which represented about 5.5% of the annual national income for 1928. The high cost of settling the refugees was more than balanced by the great benefits they brought to the national economy. The refugees had a high level of education and professional experience and swiftly adjusted to the situation, increasing productivity in every sector of the economy. The first years were difficult however: the most serious problem confronting the refugees was that of health, due mainly to the widespread incidence of malaria in the plains of Macedonia, where there were lakes and

marshes. At the end of 1923 it was noted that out of every one hundred deaths, seventy were due to malaria.

The major works of land reclamation

The Greek government took over 3,640,000 *stremmata* of marshes, lakes and other undeveloped land in Macedonia. During the rainy season, the waters of the Axios, the Haliakmon, the Strymon and other rivers inundated vast areas of both cultivated and uncultivated land, and caused havoc in settlements and on farms, sweeping away animals and occasionally human beings. The winter torrents that rushed down from the mountains also disturbed the ecological balance by creating marshes in the plains that were a steady source of malaria. It has also been calculated that the soil carried down by the Axios and the Gallikos rivers was so great in quantity that the alluvium threatened to close the port of Thessalonike within fifty years.

The concentration of groups of refugees in Macedonia made the protection and increase of the areas under development a matter of some urgency. On 7 September, 1925 a contract was signed between the Greek state and the Foundation Company of New York for the execution of anti-flooding projects, drainage and irrigation works in the plain of Thessalonike, covering an area of about 2,080,000 *stremmata*. On 20 October, 1928 a contract was signed between the Greek state and two New York companies, John Monks and Sons and Ulen and Company, to divert a section of the river Strymon, stabilize the level of lake Kerkine, and undertake further anti-flooding, drainage and irrigation works covering 1,180,000 *stremmata* in the plain of Serres and 380,000 *stremmata* in the plain of Drama. The cost of these schemes was:

a) For the plain of Thessalonike	1,545,000,000 drs.
b) For the plains of Serres and Drama	1,730,000,000 drs.
total	3,275,000,000 drs.

The financing of these schemes was met from two productive loans made by the state in 1928 and 1931. A further 666,738,000 drachmas were spent on additional works (land reclamation) by 1941.

Significant results had been achieved by the end of 1935 when the contracts with the two American contracting companies expired.[7]

The results of all these land improvement schemes are set out in table 3. The various projects yielded 740,000 *stremmata* of new land; protected a further 1,080,000 *stremmata* from flooding and restored them to their full productive capacity; irrigated 85,000 *stremmata*; and brought 200,000 *stremmata* of mountainous terrain into use.

In addition to the major schemes of land improvement, there were many other projects on a smaller scale, including renewal and improvements to unproductive land (about 300,000 *stremmata*), the establishment of experimental farms (twenty-three of these had been set up in Macedonia by 1941) and the creation of pilot farms to test the use of agricultural machinery and so on. Individual farmers, too, carried out projects to improve the yield of their land (irrigation channels, protective walls, planting of trees, and so on).

The results of the works

These major schemes had beneficial effects on the Macedonian economy. They brought the multiplier effect into play — that is they increased income by a higher figure than the initial increase in investment (about 2-2$^1/_2$ times greater). The spectacular increase in agricultural productivity reinforced the external economies in other sectors. There was an increase in the volume of goods processed by the agricultural industries and a reduction in their unit cost; the volume of goods transported increased, resulting in a reduction of transport costs, and activity expanded in all the service sectors.

The first phase of the agricultural revolution

The refugees were mainly farmers and industrial workers. The general data on the professional breakdown of the refugees reveals that 30% had training in agricultural trades (farmers, stockbreeders and fishermen), 13% in industrial and manufacturing work, and 40% were without any special training.[9]

The experienced farmers who came from eastern Thrace and the Greek communities in Bulgaria spread the use of the iron plough and the horse (the local farmers were still using oxen and wooden ploughs), and changed the system of cultivation from single-crop to multi-crop. The main factor in the revolutionary change that took place in agriculture was the gradual introduction of the tractor, the combine harvester and the threshing machine in the plains of Macedonia. Deep ploughing, the use of fertilizers and improved varieties of seeds, and above all, the adoption of the cultivation methods demonstrated on the pilot farms established by the state, brought about a change in the traditional character of farming.

These revolutionary changes tripled the yield *per stremma* of many goods. The increased output of agricultural produce not only ensured that the rural families were fed, but began to create surpluses which found their way to the large urban centres and gave an impetus to commercial activity. This strengthened the role of money as a means of the division of labour and as a medium of exchange. This radical change in the methods of cultivation, the astonishing increase in yields *per stremma* and the emergence in the major urban centres of large scale trading in agricultural produce, brought the agricultural revolution in Macedonia to completion.[10] The expropriation of the *chiftliks* greatly assisted the agricultural revolution from an institutional point of view.

The first steps in industrial development

Through their increased purchasing power, the refugees expanded the size of the market, the strength of which steadily increased as a result of the continuous rise in incomes deriving from the growth of agricultural productivity.

The adoption of a firm policy of protective tariffs for many home-produced industrial goods, based on the argument that the 'infant' industry was in need of protection from foreign competition, laid the basis for the undisturbed growth of many manufacturing units, since there was a 'gap' or a shortage in the supply of manufactured goods. The first phase of industrial development in Macedonia after liberation was thus supported by the expansion of population and labour force, the creation of a dynamic market and strong protective tariffs. The refugees were the major

---

TABLE 3

The areas of the plains of Macedonia brought into use as a result of the major land reclamation, 1941[8]

Category of land	Plain of Thessalonike	Plain of Serres	Plain of Drama	Total
1. Reclaimed agricultural land	350,000	380,000	90,000	740,000
2. Land protected from flooding	600,000	400,000	80,000	1,080,000
3. Irrigated land	—	80,000	5,000	85,000
4. Mountainous land brought into use	—	—	—	200,000
Total				2,105,000

factor in industrial development, however, since they had the relevant skills and, more importantly, were obliged to work under any conditions and for low wages.

Between 1921 and 1926 in Greece as a whole, 221 factories producing food were established, 70 producing furniture, 45 textile firms, 38 units producing machines, 30 chemical factories, 19 paper factories and printing firms, 19 factories producing building materials, 12 tanneries, 8 cigarette companies and 1 unit producing hats to satisfy the growing demand. A significant proportion of these factories were set up in Macedonia, most of them in Thessalonike, Naousa and Kavala, because of the favourable conditions. This steady creation of manufacturing units in the cities, together with the development of the service sector, began to produce a trend towards urbanism.

The beginnings of the cooperative movement and the first social disturbances

The small size (about 15-30 *stremmata*) of the farms allocated to the refugees obliged them to work very hard in order to survive. It also had one positive effect, in that it led the refugee farmers to rally together and form cooperatives. The main objectives of these cooperatives were: (a) to obtain loans from the Agricultural Bank; (b) to purchase the large agricultural machines that would enable them to farm their land more easily and more productively; and (c) to build cooperative store-houses and establish an agricultural infrastructure. Their example was immediately followed by the local farmers, who had shown little enthusiasm for the cooperative movement in the past. Within the space of three years, up to 31 December 1925, 191 local agricultural cooperatives, 404 refugee cooperatives and 34 joint cooperatives had been created.[11]

It was precisely during the phase of rapid economic change that there arose the first social problems having an economic origin. The most serious of these involved the tobacco workers and sprang from the gradual introduction of a method of processing tobacco by machinery, requiring fewer hands. Appreciable unemployment had begun to occur in Kavala as early as 1909, as a result of the American tobacco companies simplifying the processing system and producing fewer quality grades, needing less labour input. Many tobacco workers became unemployed at this time and began to organize the first trade unions in order to seek reinstatement. The wars of the period 1912-18, and the Asia Minor disaster, prevented the outbreak of violent disturbances, but the pressure exercised by the tobacco workers was considerable, and obliged the state to take a stance on the problem in 1922 by voting a law 'on banning the exporting of raw tobacco'. The return to the old processing system, however, provoked a reaction from the tobacco merchants and tobacco manufacturers, and the state reviewed its decision in 1925. A State Insurance Fund for Tobacco Workers, to contend with the increasing unemployment, was founded — the first serious attempt to introduce social welfare measures in Greece. The low employment levels amongst the work force gave rise to serious disturbances in the cities of Kavala, Thessalonike and Volos.[12] These disturbances worsened af-

358. *Fundamental changes in the methods of cultivation, the staggering increase in yield per stremma and the beginning of bulk marketing of agricultural produce in urban centres completed the agricultural revolution in Macedonia. The picture shows an early stage in tobacco-processing, the drying of the famous Balkan tobacco produced in the region and exported all over the world.*

ter the world economic crisis in 1929-33, but ceased after the advent of the Metaxas dictatorship in 1936. However, they left their mark on the economic history of Macedonia, since they represented the first mobilization of labour on any scale since liberation.

The social disturbances resulting from unemployment petered out as a result of the schemes connected with defence works, and other social infrastructure (construction of roads, schools etc.) that were undertaken in the middle of the 1930s. The worsening international situation at this time obliged the Greek government to adopt a programme of major defensive works to protect the borders of Greece, and especially of Macedonia.

The expansion of the import-export trade

The intermediate phase of Macedonian economic development (1923-40) saw the growth of the import-export trade, which increased in volume and diversified in composition.

Economic development had important effects on the volume and structure of Macedonia's foreign trade.

While in the preceding period imports had largely consisted of a number of agricultural products they now began to be surpassed by higher industrial goods such as machines, chemical and pharmaceutical products, electrical equipment, means of transport and considerable quantities of manufactured consumer goods. These goods were imported mainly from western Europe.

On the other side, Macedonian exports were still dominated by tobacco, the main importing countries being the USA and Germany. At the same time, however, exports of cotton, yarn and cloth continued to rise, and fruit, vegetables and mineral ores began to be exported in significant quantities for the first time in Macedonian economic history.

The disastrous effects of the Second World War, the Occupation and the Civil War: 1941-49

In the period from 1941-44, Greece suffered more devastation than any other allied country, with the exception of the Soviet Union.[13] Further havoc was caused by the bitter civil conflict which reduced Greece, and Macedonia with it, to a wretched condition. Its destructive effects were manifold and affected the size of the population, the infrastructure, the productive capacity, the administration, and the organization and functioning of the economy. It has been calculated that the population of Macedonia declined by about 180,000 as a result of the war and the occupation.[14] For military reasons, the German and Bulgarian occupation authorities destroyed many of the land reclamation works undertaken between 1926 and 1940, such as the dam of lake Kerkine, and the bridges over the rivers Axios, Gallikos, Haliakmon and Strymon. Both the Germans and the Bulgarians took with them many goods and much property when they withdrew from the area in 1944. The damage caused to irrigation works alone has been put at 2,000,000,000 pre-war drachmas.[15]

The material damage resulting from acts of war was compounded by the dissolution of the administrative machinery. The major symptom of this dissolution was the great uncertainty and insecurity felt by the inhabitants, but the most important negative economic consequence was the outbreak of galloping hyper-inflation, caused by shortages of goods, the destruction of the productive machinery, and the tactic pursued by the German occupying authorities of meeting their expenses by over-issuing currency, since they had both the right to issue and the machinery for printing currency.

THE PERIOD OF ECONOMIC TAKE-OFF: 1951-81.

General economic developments

The Second World War and the civil conflict left a legacy of considerable destruction and great uncertainty. The main consequence of these developments at the beginning of the 1950s was the great reluctance of private capital to invest. This reluctance clearly derived from the geographical proximity of the area to the communist countries who constituted a continuous threat to the region during the period of the Cold War, a threat that later events revealed to be purely hypothetical.

The most important adverse turn of events at the beginning of the 1950s was the loss of population through either external or internal migration. The population of Macedonia, which had been increasing continuously and rapidly since the influx of refugees, showed a significant decrease after the decade 1940-1950 (table 1). Emigration (mainly to West Germany), which began in the 1960s and continued up to the beginning of the 1970s, was due mainly to the existence of large surpluses in the work force and the lack of employment opportunities in Greece, because of the disruption caused by the war and the civil disturbances. Between 1966 and 1972 Macedonia lost about 165,000 inhabitants. The intense economic activity that manifested itself at the end of the sixties and the beginning of the seventies, however, led to an increasing trend for the migrants to return home; after 1975 this trend began to lead to an increase in the population and the work force. In the Census of 1981 the total population of Macedonia was 2,105,649 people (table 1).

The per capita income at current prices of the inhabitants of Macedonia increased tenfold. At the beginning of the 1960s Macedonia occupied fourth place (after Athens and its environs, central Greece and the Peloponnese) in the national ranking of areas based on gross regional product; today it holds second place.

During this period Macedonia entered the phase of economic take-off, thanks to the development in every sector, and even more importantly to the revolutionary changes consequent upon the mass generation of electricity.

This rapid and unplanned development has given rise to new problems, including: a marked tendency for the pop-

359. A view of part of modern Thessalonike from the White Tower to the docks. The city today is the largest urban, intellectual and industrial centre of northern Greece.

ulation and for economic activity to concentrate in the wider area of Thessalonike; the deterioration and destruction of the natural environment and the traditional character of a number of settlements (the destruction of the old town of Kastoria, for example); the disproportionate growth of some sectors and regions (e.g. the abandonment of the mountain villages); and, above all, the lack of any perspective planning for a proper regional development.

The modernization and development of the primary sector

In 1950, a start was made on a systematic attempt to bring to completion and make more effective the irrigation works begun in the inter-war period. A series of large- and small-scale land reclamation schemes (anti-flooding, drainage and irrigation works) were carried out, funded initially by credits advanced from American Economic Aid (the Marshall Plan) and subsequently by the Public Investments Programme and the Special Central Fund for Farming, Stock Raising and Forests.

The irrigated areas, together with the restructuring of the pattern of crops from the traditional wheat, tobacco and potatoes to new, dynamic crops, such as maize hybrids, alfalfa, vegetables and fruit and the adoption of new cultivation methods, increased yields *per stremma* and agricultural incomes even further. This change accelerated the agricultural revolution that had begun in the inter-war period: oxen were replaced by the tractor, and the use of improved seeds, fertilizers and pesticides obliged the traditional farmer to come into contact with the agricultura?ist, the state agricultural service and the nearest centre for experimental crops. The changes in the agricultural economy are reflected mainly in the growth of productivity — that is the average output of agricultural produce over the area under cultivation (yield *per stremma*), as set out in table 4. A comparison of pre-war with post-war performance reveals a significant difference in yields *per stremma* of cotton, potatoes and cereals.

The need to increase the productivity of stock-raising in the light of the demand for animal products from the expanding market in the urban centres, was quickly recognized. The revolutionary change in this sector involved the abandonment of the mountain animal-pen and a turn towards domestic and commercial stock-raising, aimed mainly at producing meat. There was growth in cattle-, sheep-, poultry- and pig-raising, funded by the Agricultural Bank. At the same time, a number of agricultural industries came into being (canning, sugar industries, cattle-food factories, dairy products) which, by fully utilizing agricultural products, raised agricultural incomes.

These developments led to a real improvement in the standard of living of the farmers. Many farming families not only purchased tractors and other machinery, but also advanced their status by acquiring sophisticated consumer goods (cars, televisions etc.).

The development of the forests took on the aspect of a significant specialized economic activity, mostly in the mountainous west of Macedonia and around Drama, where the largest wood- and paper-processing factory in Greece was established.

The Agricultural Bank also furnished the funding for the renewal and the expansion of fishing capital (fishing boats), mainly in the region of Kavala and Chalkidike. A special zone for fish canning was created at Kavala, while fish-farms were promoted in some mountain areas and lakes.

The development of agriculture also brought a number of unwanted changes, however. Between 1951 and 1981 about 350,000 people abandoned the countryside, while about 700,000 *stremmata* of marginal land were abandoned, becoming either fallow land or pasturage. The popularity of and competition from American Virginia blended cigarettes caused a decline in the demand on the international market for the famous oriental tobaccos produced in the areas of Kavala, Drama and Serres and created a serious local crisis resulting from the fall in price of these tobaccos and the reduction of the income of tobacco workers.

The creation of the new national industrial centre in Thessalonike

The development of manufacturing in Macedonia at the beginning of the 1950s was not very marked, for a variety of reasons. A significant part of the infrastructure of roadworks and energy sources had been destroyed, the threat from the Iron Curtain discouraged private investment, and the lack of capital and specialized personnel made people reluctant to undertake business ventures. Further, the low per capita income of about 200 dollars prevented the formation of a market capable of sustaining industrial development.

The rapid agricultural development, however, not only produced raw materials and a surplus work force, but also created increased purchasing power resulting in a great demand for manufactured goods. Although Macedonia had a comparative advantage in the agricultural sector, on account of her rich natural resources, the strategy of industrial development began to win many followers, thanks to the prevalence of the views of the School of Industrialists, who believed that it was possible to escape from underdevelopment only through industrial advance. Four important centres of industrial development were created at this time: 1) the industrial area of Thessalonike,

TABLE 4

Increase in yield per stremma of a number of agricultural products: the agricultural revolution (kilograms/stremma)[16]

Products	1924 without irrigation	1928 without irrigation	1932 after irrigation	1971 irrigation and use of advanced technology
Wheat	45	66	192	240
Barley	56	78	(240)	290
Maize	78	70	384	410
Cotton	63	70	166	258
Potatoes	345	345	712	1,303
Tobacco	62	66	–	97

360. Some of the permanent buildings which house the Thessalonike International Trade Fair. The Fair was founded by Nicholas Germanos, and first opened its gates in 1926. Since *then, its success as the display window for Macedonian and Greek products for the world market has ensured that it is an annual event.*

at Sindos, which is the largest planned industrial area in Greece (9,000 *stremmata*); 2) the industrial zone in the area of Ptolemaïs and Kozani, designed to exploit the lignite and other resources of this region; 3) the area of light industry and agricultural industries around Naousa, Veria, Langadas and Skydra; 4) the industrial area of Kavala.

Some of the largest heavy industrial complexes in modern Greece were established in the industrial area of Thessalonike (refineries, petro-chemical industries, iron and steel industries, electrical equipment, building materials etc.), along with many medium and small-scale light industrial units (the Nestlé factory at Platy, cattle-food, tin, timber-processing etc.). The strong trend towards industrial development in Macedonia is illustrated by the fact

that from 1963 to 1973 the area of Thessalonike saw a greater increase in industrial employment than any other part of Greece, while other regions of Macedonia also saw considerable industrial development. Thessalonike was converted during the period under review into the second most important industrial centre in Greece, after Attica. Many of the investments that created industrial units in the area of Thessalonike resulted from initiatives by foreign capitalists (the Esso-Pappas refinery, the Nestlé dairy products factory, Siemens electronics and others).

Some of the heaviest industries, such as the large lignite-powered electric plants, the AEVAL fertilizer plant, and others, were set up in the region of Ptolemaïs and Kozani, changing the traditional pastoral character of the area. The area of Naousa developed into the most important textile

361. *Some of the most highly developed industrial complexes for the production of phosphorous fertilizers have been established in Macedonia. Above, the pier for loading and unloading of the unit at Nea Karvali.*

centre in Greece, with a large number of medium and small-scale units. The traditional fur industry of Kastoria also underwent considerable growth. The unlimited opportunities for export to the European and American markets, and the evolution of modern communications and transport systems (telex, air-freight) gave a fresh impetus to this traditional industrial activity. In Chalkidike, Greek mining companies began to mine the mineral wealth of the area and carry out the first stages of ore processing. The industrial area of Kavala was the site of one of the four largest fertilizer factories in Greece, and of many other industrial units (involving fish canning, plastics, marble and wood processing). At the beginning of 1980 a large industrial complex was set up here to carry out the initial processing of the crude oil discovered beneath the sea off Prinos on Thasos.

The industrial development of Macedonia was assisted by strong regional development incentives (low-interest loans, subsidies, tax-exemptions etc.) established by a series of acts of parliament.

The unplanned industrial development, particularly of a number of heavy industries such as petro-chemicals, had its social cost. The over-concentration of industries in the area of Thessalonike resulted in the severe pollution of the city and the Thermaic Gulf, while the uncontrolled urbanization led to a reduction in the quality of life in some neighbourhoods, on account of the over-crowding, the increase in traffic problems and congestion.

Tourism: the new dynamic sector

The wealth of tourist resources in Macedonia formed the basis for the development of tourism that began in 1960. Summer tourism, mainly confined to the coasts, and in-

362. *The first commercially viable oil fields were discovered below the sea bed between Kavala and Thasos (Prinos) after the* *world energy crisis of 1973. The picture shows the oil pumping installations at Prinos.*

volving both Greeks and foreigners, was developed along the coasts of the nomes of Pieria and Thessalonike and above all along the beautiful coasts of Chalkidike, Kavala and Thasos. Many hotel complexes of high quality were built in these areas. Mountain tourism was developed mainly on the Olympos, Pieria, Pindos, Vermion and Vitsi ranges, the area of Pisoderi near Florina (Vigla), in a number of areas near Grevena and on Mts. Falakron near Drama and Pangaion near Kavala.

Tourism for recreational, cultural and other purposes has been developed in a number of areas where there are landscapes of great natural beauty or ancient and Byzantine monuments (e.g. Pella, Kastoria). There has recently been lively tourist interest in Vergina, as a result of the discovery of the tomb of Philip II and its magnificent contents. Other areas that exercise a great attraction for both domestic and foreign tourism include Mount Athos,

Chalkidike, Philippi, Kavala and Byzantine Thessalonike. Lake Prespa, with its nenuphars and one hundred and seventy-seven rare species of birds, is the only hatchery of pelicans, as well as the largest cormorant colony in western Europe; it was declared a National Park in 1977 and placed under the protection of the World Wildlife Fund. Kastoria is particularly attractive, with its Byzantine churches, picturesque lake and the traditional architecture of the houses.

On the strength of these tourist resources, Macedonia has developed both Greek and foreign tourism on a considerable scale. In 1960 it was visited by about 40,000 foreign tourists, out of a total of about 390,000 visitors to Greece as a whole, that is about 10.3%. In 1979, when the number of foreign tourists visiting Greece approached 6,000,000, Macedonia attracted about 1,529,000, thereby increasing its share of the national figure to 25%.

The importance to the national economy of Macedonia's sources of energy

Macedonia contributes to the national economy something that is possibly even more precious than gold: energy. The area is rich in energy sources (lignite deposits, waterfalls, oil, nuclear fuels, gas etc.) and produces a larger proportion of Greece's energy than any other region. In 1978, out of a total of 4,844,030 kilowatts, Macedonia generated 1,709,500 kilowatts at the thermal power stations of Kozani and Ptolemaïs — that is 35.3% of the total electricity generated in Greece. As for consumption, the total electricity consumed nationally in 1978 was 18,218,863 thousand kwh, out of which the Macedonian consumption for industrial, commercial and domestic purposes was 3,503,348 kwh, or a mere 19.2% of the national total.[17] A comparison of the local production and consumption of energy shows clearly that Macedonia yields a surplus of the most important resource in the modern world. Through its superabundance of energy sources, which it makes available to the rest of the country, Macedonia makes a contribution of decisive importance to the entire nation.

Prior to 1954, electricity was produced on old local generators, unevenly distributed throughout Macedonia and confined to the large towns (Thessalonike, Kavala, Serres). The electricity generated was low in both quantity and quality. The current, distributed only within a limited radius of the towns, was weak, and was available only for two to three hours in the evening. The price of electricity was very high, in line with the costs of production, since it was not generated on a mass scale and the equipment was normally old.[18]

The economic take-off in Macedonia seems to have begun with electrification on a mass scale. The mountain villages, provinces and towns of Macedonia truly entered the modern world when they acquired a steady supply of cheap electricity.

The Public Electricity Company (known popularly as ΔEH, from its initials) was founded in July 1950 to organize and coordinate the production and distribution of electricity throughout the whole of Greece. The American Ebasco Company, which contracted to produce a general study on the electrification of Greece, proposed that there should be two units generating electricity in Macedonia. The first was the hydro-electric plant at Agras in the nome of Pella, on the river Edessaios which had a total capacity of 50,000 kw. This was completed in 1954 and had a single network through which it supplied the towns of Thessalonike, Serres, Drama and Kavala, and a number of sub-stations that furnished electricity to many smaller towns and villages in central and east Macedonia. The second unit was a thermal power station fuelled by lignite, built at Ptolemaïs with a productive capacity of 70,000 kw and covered mainly the needs of western Macedonia.

As soon as the source of supply was established, the demand for electricity in Macedonia (for domestic, industrial and agricultural purposes) increased spectacularly. The state gradually implemented a scheme for the systematic electrification of the whole of Macedonia and, taking into consideration some national objectives, gave high priority to the isolated border regions in the Macedonian mountains, even though this conflicted with cost standards. The varied uses of electricity, in the home, the factory, on the farm, in the shop, in industry and in public places, changed the economic and social character of Macedonia. The modern economic revolution in Macedonia seems to have been the result of the widespread supply of the electricity. Cheap electricity was the basic prerequisite for the development of industry and other productive sectors.

The extension and modernization of the communications network

Economic development and civilization invariably follow the extension of communications and telecommunication. During the Second World War, the road network of Macedonia, most of which had been constructed in the period 1927-40, had suffered considerable damage from bombardment, the blowing-up of bridges during the retreat of the enemy, inadequate maintenance and lack of rebuilding. Movement by road was very difficult and costly. It was only after 1947 that a programme to rebuild and repair destroyed roads and bridges was initiated, and in 1959 in the whole of northern Greece there were 11,519 kilometres of asphalted roads in the provinces and 3,379 kilometres of roads in the towns and villages that were surfaced with asphalt or gravel. The most important new arterial road constructed at this time was the National Road through the Vale of Tempe, which reduced the distance between Thessalonike and Athens by about eighty kilometres. Throughout the whole of this last period, however, there have been many road construction schemes, one of them the National Road to Yugoslavia, which leads to Evzoni.

The situation on the railways after the war was desperate: the machinery was obsolete and ruined from lack of maintenance, the sheds had been bombarded, the carriages were in a terrible state, and the engines either performed very poorly or were completely useless. Since the role of the railways in regional and national development was vital, a coordinated effort was made immediately after 1945 and they were improved and modernized with funds provided by UNRRA, the American Mission and the war reparations paid by West Germany and Italy.

Shipping was served by the two major ports in the area, Thessalonike and Kavala. The port of Thessalonike had been completely destroyed by the Germans, and reconstruction work began in 1945. It acquired a new breakwater, warehouses, cranes and other equipment; the total cost of repair and renewal was 3,500,000 dollars. The port of Kavala had also suffered serious damage during the war. Repair and extension work began immediately with

363. A large power station at Ptolemaïs. The rich energy resources of Macedonia and the development of electricity generating stations were the foundation for the economic take-off of Macedonia and indeed of Greece as a whole.

364. View of the Esso-Pappas oil refineries. The largest manufacturing area of Greece centres on Thessalonike and both heavy and light industries have established themselves here.

the lengthening of the inner breakwater, the extension of the wharf, and the installation of a regular supply of electricity; all these were completed by 1955. Both ports were expanded in the middle of the 1960s to cope with the increased transport needs of the area.

There was a very rapid increase in air transport. Initially, Macedonia had only one airport, at Thessalonike, but work began immediately on two more, at Kavala and Kozani and, more recently, on a third at Kastoria. The most significant development in Macedonian air transport was the opening of direct connections between Thessalonike and European and other capital cities. Thessalonike airport was expanded and modernized at the beginning of the 1970s; the old airport at Kavala has been replaced by one near Chrysoupolis.

The same period saw a rapid extension of the telecommunications system which assisted the expansion of commercial exchanges and business operations.

The development of the other productive sectors

The other sectors have also grown rapidly in the last twenty years.

Building activity developed quickly mainly after 1960, had strong multiplier effects on other sectors, mainly on manufacturing and industrial units (building materials, alumininium constructions etc.) and strengthened the local economy by absorbing a large number of workers who would otherwise have emigrated.

The agricultural, industrial, tourist and building activities strengthened all other tertiary activities of the Macedonian economy: commerce, banking and insurance, publishing and, above all, the social services (health, education). The growth of commerce was particularly spectacular as a result of the increase in incomes and the modernization of transport and tele-communications. Its importance was mirrored in the rapid progress made by the International Trade Fair in Thessalonike, founded by Nicholas Germanos. The Thessalonike Fair first opened its gates in 1926 and has held forty-six annual exhibitions up to 1981; it has become one of the largest exhibition centres in the world and today is an excellent shop window for the achievements of Macedonia, making a positive contribution to the stimulation of trade throughout northern Greece.

In recent years there has been considerable progress in training and education, centred on the University of Thessalonike, which grew spectacularly after 1960, acquiring new land and buildings, and which covers all the basic branches of academic study in nine schools. In addition to the University of Thessalonike, the Advanced School of Industrial Studies was founded, along with a large number of technical and professional schools at advanced and intermediate level.

Foreign trade

During the phase of economic take-off (1951-81) there was rapid growth in foreign trade, the structure and character of which changed significantly.

Imports of grain, sugar, rice, pulses and other traditional agricultural products ceased thanks to the growth of local output, though the importing of livestock products continued, largely because consumers turned towards these goods. The greatest change was the reduction of imports of wheat to zero, reflecting the advances made in the agricultural economy of Macedonia; these, together with the growth of grain production in Thessaly, had made Greece self-sufficient in wheat-supply. Whereas grain imports through the port of Thessalonike had been 63,696 tonnes in 1938, this figure was reduced to 30,193 in 1951 and 1,546 in 1954. The same steep decline could also be seen in the imports of pulses, potatoes, rice and, above all, sugar. The imports of industrial products, however, such as timber, chemical products, fertilizers, tractors, cars, showed a marked increase. The increased demand for these imports is testimony to the prosperity of the region, for the demand for foreign goods, especially 'high quality goods' such as private cars and electrical equipment, is a good indicator of a rise in standards of living.

The basic structural changes in the Macedonian economy during this period can also be seen in the export sector. Tobacco and cotton begin to lose first place in the table of Macedonian exports, and new products (peaches, apples, strawberries, grapes, melons, tomatoes and other vegetables) begin to dominate agricultural exports. The ex-

TABLE 5

Growth of the gross per capita income of Greece as a whole and Macedonia, 1913-80 (at 1970 prices)[19]

| Year | In Drachmas | | In Dollars | |
	Greece	Macedonia	Greece	Macedonia
1913	7,035	4,573	235	152
1928	11,002	7,151	367	238
1929	10,531	6,845	351	228
1930	11,424	7,997	381	267
1935	11,980	8,386	399	280
1938	13,563	9,494	452	316
1939	13,927	9,749	464	325
1940-44	(5,349)	(3,744)	(178)	(125)
1950	10,532	8,426	351	281
1955	13,875	11,100	462	370
1960	17,467	15,720	582	524
1965	25,136	22,622	838	754
1970	34,621	32,890	1,154	1,096
1975	43,111	40,955	1,437	1,365
1980	50,755	48,217	1,692	1,607

TABLE 6

The breakdown of the composition of the gross regional product of Macedonia by the major sectors expressed as a percentage[20]

Sector	1913[21]	1954[22]	1974[23]
Agriculture	70	46	28
Industry	12	22	30
Services	18	32	42
Gross Regional Product	100	100	100

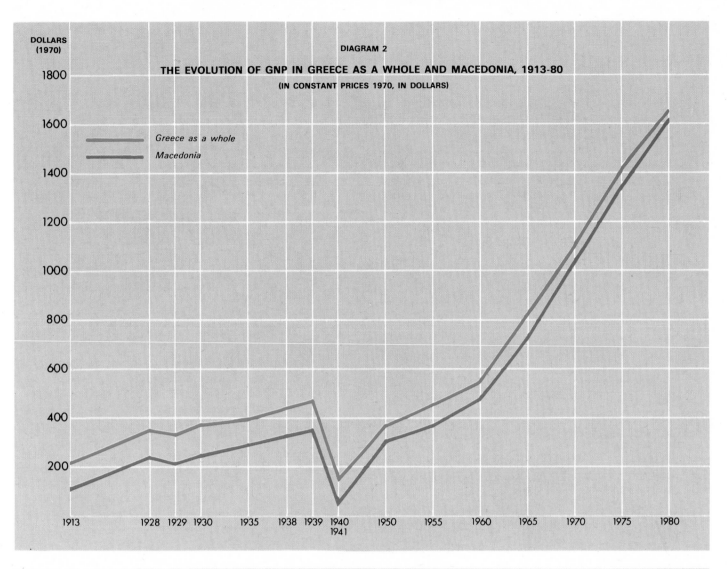

DIAGRAM 2

THE EVOLUTION OF GNP IN GREECE AS A WHOLE AND MACEDONIA, 1913-80

(IN CONSTANT PRICES 1970, IN DOLLARS)

Greece as a whole

Macedonia

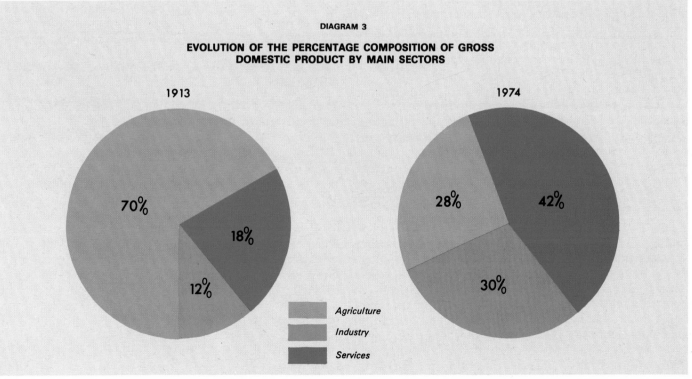

DIAGRAM 3

EVOLUTION OF THE PERCENTAGE COMPOSITION OF GROSS DOMESTIC PRODUCT BY MAIN SECTORS

1913

1974

70%

18%

12%

28%

42%

30%

Agriculture

Industry

Services

ploitation of the mineral wealth of the region strengthened exports of chromium, iron ores, magnesium and marble. Increases were also particularly marked in exports of yarn, cotton fabrics, chemical products and other industrial goods.

The development of Macedonian trade and commerce in the seventy years since liberation shows a gradually increasing dependence on the rest of the world. It is symptomatic that between 1938 and 1978, Macedonia's import trade increased more quickly than her exports, thus confirming this growing dependence. Macedonia's dependence may be regarded as a positive factor, since (a) it confirms the outward looking character of the Macedonian economy; (b) it exposes the economic structure of the region to international competition; (c) it broadens the basis of the division of labour in the geographical area of Macedonia; (d) it is an excellent indication of the improved standard of living of Macedonians, since international cooperation and commerce is usually looked upon as a source of progress and prosperity.

The foreign contribution to the development of Macedonia

The foreign contribution to the development of Macedonia was of some importance in repairing the devastation and destruction suffered by the area during the Second World War, the Occupation and the Civil War. The rail network was repaired and modernized with economic and technical aid from UNRRA, with the British Army and the American Mission meeting some of the expenses and supervising the reconstruction work. The first electricity plants, as we have seen, were designed and constructed by the Ebasco Company of New York. Part of the destruction and damage to the productive infrastructure suffered by Macedonia during the war was repaired out of the German and Italian war reparations.

Macedonia's dependence on the international market and on foreign technology and capital increased during the third phase of its development. To take full advantage of the agricultural products of areas like Naousa, Veria and Katerini, foreign equipment for packaging, refrigeration and preserving had to be imported. The development of new textile factories at Naousa was based on foreign credit, and the following enterprises were also largely funded by foreign capital: the new large industrial complexes, the Esso-Pappas refinery, the Siemens factories producing electrical and telecommunications equipment, the thermal power stations at Ptolemaïs, the fertilizer factories and refineries at Kavala and many others. Technological expertise was also drawn from abroad.

The foreign labour markets (particularly in western Europe) that absorbed the surplus work force had a variety of advantages for Macedonia. The migration of workers abroad brought the following benefits: (a) the workers sent home regular remittances; (b) the standard of living of those who stayed behind improved; (c) part of the remittances were invested in their home country, mainly in building houses; and (d) savings were accumulated to meet extra needs or to be invested in profitable opportunities.

Moreover, in the sphere of tourism, the fact that foreigners visited Macedonia to stay in summer holiday resorts and other areas revitalized the Macedonian economy in many ways.

The broadening of relations with other Balkan countries

The development of Macedonia and the whole of northern Greece was affected by the development of the neighbouring Balkan countries, especially Bulgaria and Yugoslavia.

The cultivation of the 'Balkan idea' through the development of cooperation between Yugoslavia, Greece, Roumania and Turkey, beginning with the signing of the Balkan Accord on 9 February, 1934, reinforced the development of Macedonia. The favourable climate in the Balkans was disturbed by the Second World War and then by the Cold War after 1945. The depopulation and economic decline of the northern border areas of Macedonia in the period 1945-60 was also due to the shadow of the Cold War that was a major factor immediately after the Second World War.

The peaceful cooperation and stability in the Balkans after the war, and more particularly after 1960, was favourable to Macedonian development, not only because Macedonia enjoyed a central position in the Balkan peninsula, but also because of the resulting opportunies for furthering trade and commerce. The first Balkan Conference (the result of a Greek initiative) met in Athens from 26 January-5 February, 1976 and put forward proposals for Balkan cooperation in agriculture, commerce, energy, transportation and telecommunications, and the protection of the environment.

The implementation in the future of a number of ambitious inter-Balkan schemes (a Europort at Thessalonike, the Axios water-route, large-scale communications enterpirises, multi-lateral energy schemes) will strengthen Balkan cooperation even further and promote the economic progress of all areas of the Balkans, especially Macedonia.

EVALUATION OF THE ECONOMIC ACHIEVEMENTS AND PROSPECTS

The long-term growth of per capita income and the structural changes in the Macedonian economy

The economic achievements of Macedonia in the seventy years since liberation can be summarized under two basic economic variables: (a) the growth of per capita income demonstrated by the improved standard of living of the inhabitants, and (b) the percentage composition of the total regional product, which reflects the structural changes in the Macedonian economy.

Table 5 sets out the growth of the per capita income of Greece and Macedonia throughout the entire period under review at 1970 prices. It is clear that during the period under review the per capita income of Macedonia increased by a factor of 10.5, while the corresponding increase for Greece as a whole was by a factor of about 7.2. The percentage change of per capita income in the two periods was as follows:

Period	Total for Greece	Total for Macedonia
1913-39	2.7%	3.0%
1950-80	5.4%	6.0%

During the first phase of economic development (1912 - 22) the per capita income was low on account of the traditional agricultural nature of the economy and the war-time conditions generally. By the end of the second phase (1936-40) the per capita income had more than doubled as a result of the increase in the agricultural and industrial product deriving from large productive works and the expansion of 'external economies'. During the Second World War and the German-Bulgarian occupation, the per capita income sank to a very low level, and in the large towns (Thessalonike and Kavala) many people died from under-nourishment of hunger. During the third phase (1951-81) there was a rapid increase in the per capita income, due to the swift reconstruction from the ruins of the war, the rise of the agricultural output, the rapid industrial growth, and the emergence of new productive activities such as tourism. With a level of per capita income of around 2,500 dollars at current prices (or around 1,700 dollars at 1970 prices) Macedonia has joined the group of *developing* regions and is approaching the privileged category of the world's developed countries and regions.

The structural changes in the Macedonian economy during the period under review are reflected in the percentage composition of the gross regional product. Table 6 shows that Macedonia has seen a transformation from an agricultural economy to a developed industrial and service economy (the contribution of agricultural output has fallen from 70% in 1913 to 28% in 1974; the share of industrial output over this period has increased from 12% to 30%, and that of the service sector from 18% to 42%). This is one of the most important turning points in the character of the Macedonian economy, since it indicates that it has evolved into an economy with a relatively modern structure.

The prospects for economic development 1981: Macedonia and the European Community

Greece's entry to the European Economic Community is particularly favourable to the development of Macedonia, for the following reasons: (a) it will ensure conditions of calm and political stability, which were so lacking in the region during the period 1913-50; (b) it will give the inhabitants the opportunity to exploit more fully the relatively abundant resources at their disposal; (c) additional funds for the exploitation and development of the resources of Macedonia will be forthcoming, mainly from the EEC's Regional and Social Fund, but also from the European Investment Bank; (d) the implementation of the EEC's Common Agricultural Policy, which is particularly favourable to agriculture (by ensuring the absorption of agricultural output, guaranteeing higher prices for agricultural products and making funds available for restructuring agricultural output) will strengthen Macedonia even further, since she enjoys a comparative advantage in agricultural production, illustrated among other things by the fact that 34.2% of the arable land in Greece is in Macedonia; (e) Macedonia will be able to exploit the particular advantage she derives from her geographical position in the Balkans, acting as a bridge between central and western Europe, the rest of Greece and the Balkan countries on the one hand and the eastern Mediterranean, Turkey and the Middle East on the other. This position will become even stronger on the completion of the Axios waterway, which will connect the Danube with the Aegean by way of the Morava and Axios rivers. The plan is already at the exploratory stage and has been undertaken by the United Nations. When it is completed, it will change the character of Macedonia and make it genuinely European. A large Europort will be constructed at Thessalonike to serve the entire carrying trade from Europe to the Middle East, Asia and Africa; the choice of Thessalonike has advantages over that of other European ports, since the distance by sea from Thessalonike to Port Said is only 1,420 kms, while from Trieste it is 2,420, from Genoa 2,750 and from Marseilles 2,850. The construction of the international road, the Via Egnatia, to link northern Greece with Europe via Igoumenitsa will have much the same effect; (f) the labour force will be better employed, since it will be working in a more favourable and effective business environment with greater and more attractive incentives, achieving higher productivity standards.

Given that the rate of increase of the gross domestic product of the member states of the EEC over the last ten to fifteen years has been of the order of only about 3%, while for Greece it has been 4.5% and for Macedonia around 6%, it is self-evident that if these trends continue over the next twenty years, Macedonia will quickly achieve a per capita income approaching that of the EEC members, and will certainly do so in advance of the rest of Greece.[24]

The basic factor in the development of an area is the extent to which it attracts, or fails to attract, a labour force, since this acts as a catalyst in every activity. The picture of population trends in Macedonia (table 1) shows clearly that during the period under review, the population of the area doubled.

From the existing evidence on the growth potential of the region, the available resources, the accumulation of the economic infrastructure (in the areas of education and training, transport etc.), and the dynamics of the development process to date, it seems that Macedonia can look forward to an auspicious economic future.

One indication that the prospects are indeed good is the fact that the labour force, the key factor in economic development, affecting growth in both qualitative and quantitative terms and influencing supply (as labour) and demand (as consumers), is no longer leaving Macedonia as in the past, but has begun, since 1975, to return. This very positive trend, together with the determination of the inhabitants of the area to make progress, the consolidation of political stability in the area and the favourable prospects created by Greece's accession to the European Community constitute good grounds for optimism as to the future economic development of Macedonia.

LIST OF ABBREVIATIONS

AA — Archäologischer Anzeiger.

AAA — Ἀρχαιολογικά Ἀνάλεκτα ἐξ Ἀθηνῶν.

ABME — Ἀρχεῖον Βυζαντινῶν Μνημείων τῆς Ἑλλάδος.

ABull — The Art Bulletin.

Actes de Lavra I — Lemerle, P., Guillou, A., Svoronos, N., Papachrysanthou, D., "Actes de Lavra I", Archives de l'Athos V (Paris 1970).

AΔ — Ἀρχαιολογικόν Δελτίον.

ADAW — Abhanlungen der Deutschen Akademie der Wissenschaften zu Berlin.

AE — Ἀρχαιολογικὴ Ἐφημερίς.

AEpigr — Année Epigraphique.

AJPh — American Journal of Philology.

AJA — American Journal of Archaeology.

AK — Antike Kunst.

Amantos — Amantos, K., Ἱστορία τοῦ Βυζαντινοῦ Κράτους (Athens 1957, 1963³).

Andronikos AAA — Andronikos, M., «Βεργίνα: οἱ βασιλικοί τάφοι τῆς Μεγάλης Τούμπας», AAA 10 (1977) 1-39.

Andronikos Ἀνάκτορον — Andronikos, M., Makaronas, C., Moutsopoulos, N., Bakalakis G, Τό ἀνάκτορον τῆς Βεργίνας (Athens 1961).

Andronikos BSt — Andronikos, M., "Ancient Greek Painting and Mosaics in Macedonia", BSt 5 (1964) 287-302.

Andronikos Βεργίνα I — Andronikos, M., Βεργίνα I. Τό νεκροταφεῖον τῶν τύμβων (Athens 1969).

Andronikos Vergina — Andronikos M., Vergina (Athens 1972).

Angelov — Angelov, D., "Rapport complémentaire 296 (19)", XIIe Congrès International des Etudes Byzantines (Ochrid 1961).

ANRW — Aufstieg und Niedergang der römischen Welt. Geschichte und Kultur Roms im Spiegel der neueren Forschung (Berlin, de Gruyter).

AntJ — The Antiquaries Journal.

Antoniadis — Antoniadis - Bibicou, H., Recherches sur les douanes à Byzance (Paris 1963).

Ἀνώτατον Οἰκονομικόν Συμβούλιον — Ἀνώτατον Οἰκονομικόν Συμβούλιον (no. 12), «Ἡ ἐκμετάλλευσις τῶν ἐκ τῶν παραγωγικῶν ἔργων ἀποκαλυπτομένων νέων ἐδαφῶν ἐν Μακεδονίᾳ». Studies and Reports of Specialists (Athens 1935).

Ἀρχαία Μακεδονία — Ἀρχαία Μακεδονία I. 1, Communications to the First International Symposium in Thessalonike 26-29 August 1968 (Thessalonike 1970); and 2, Communications to the Second International Symposium Thessalonike 19-24 August 1973 (Thessalonike 1977).

ArchJug — Archaeologia Jugoslavica.

ArchClass — Archaeologia Classica.

Asdracha — Asdracha, C., La région de Rhodopes au XIIIe et XIV siècles. Etude de Géographie historique (Athens 1976).

AUS — Annuaire de l'Université de Sofia.

AYE — Ἀρχεῖο Ὑπουργείου Ἐξωτερικῶν.

BAB — Bulletin de l'Académie Royale de Belgique. Classe des lettres et des sciences morales et politiques.

Babić Prilep — Babić, B., "Period na dognoto rimsko carstvo i ranata Vizantija", Prilep i prilepsko niz istorijata (Prilep 1971).

Bakalakis AA — Bakalakis, G., "Vorlage und Interpretation von römischen Kunstdenkmälern in Thessaloniki", AA 1973, 671 ff.

Bakalakis Ἀρχαία Μακεδονία — Bakalakis, G., «Ἀνασκαφή Δίου 1964-1971», Ἀρχαία Μακεδονία 2 (1977) 251-56.

Barisić Byzantion — Barisić, F., "Le siège de Constantinople par les Avars et les Slaves en 626", Byzantion 24 (1954) 371-95.

Barker — Barker, Elizabeth, Macedonia; its Place in Balkan Power Politics (London 1950).

Baynes BZ — Baynes, N.H., "The date of the Avar surprise", BZ 21 (1912) 110-28.

BCH — Bulletin de Correspondance Hellénique.

Belting et al. — Belting, H., Mango, C., Mouriki, D., "The Mosaics and Frescoes at St. Mary Pammakaristos (Fetiye Camii) at Istanbul", DOSt (Washington D.C. 1978).

Bettini — Bettini, S., La pittura bizantina. I mosaici (Florence 1939).

BIAB — Bulletin de l'Institut Archéologique Bulgare.

BIARCo — Bulletin de l'Institut Archéologique Russe de Constantinople.

BLS — Zacos, G., Veglery, A., Byzantine lead seals (Basle 1972).

BMQ — British Museum Quarterly.

BNJ — Byzantinische Neugriechische Jahrbücher.

BPW — Berliner Philologische Wochenschrift.

Brenk — Brenk, B., "Spätantike und frühes Christentum", PKG Suppl. (1977).

BSA — Annual of the British School at Athens.

BSL — Bulletin de la Société Linguistique de Paris.

BSt — Balkan Studies.

Bull.épigr — Bulletin épigraphique (Revue des Etudes Grecques).

BZ — Byzantinische Zeitschrift.

CAH — Cambridge Ancient History.

CArch — Cahiers Archéologiques.

Charanis — Charanis, P., "Town and Country in the Byzantine Possessions of the Balkan Peninsula during the Later Period of the Empire", Aspects of the Balkans (The Hague - Paris 1972).

Charanis BSt — Charanis, P., "Kouver, the Chronology of his Activities and their Ethnic Effects on the Regions around Thessalonika", BSt 11, 2 (1970) 229-47.

Charanis Byzantion — Charanis, P., "On the Social Structure of the Later Roman Empire", Byzantion 17 (1944-1945) 49 ff.

Charanis DOP — Charanis, P., "Monastic Properties and the State in the Byzantine Empire", DOP 4 (1948) 87 ff.

Chatzidakis Actes XIV — Chatzidakis, M., "Classicisme et tendances populaires au XIVe siècle", Actes du XIVe Congrès International d'Etudes Byzantines 1971 (Bucharest 1974).

Chatzidakis Actes XV — Chatzidakis, M., "L'évolution de l'icône aux 11ème et 12ème siècles et la transformation du templon", Actes du XVe Congrès International d'Etudes Byzantines (Athens 1979).

Chatzidakis Cini — Chatzidakis, M., "L'icône byzantine", Saggi e Memorie di Storia dell'Arte de l'Istituto Cini 2 (Venice 1959) = Studies XVI.

Chatzidakis DOP — Chatzidakis, M., "Recherches sur le peintre Théophane le Crétois", DOP 23-24 (1969-70) = Etudes V 315 ff.

Chatzidakis HC — Chatzidakis, M., "Contribution à l'étude de la peinture Postbyzantine", L'Hellénisme Contemporain. Le Cinqcentième Anniversaire de la prise de Constantinople (29 May 1953) = Etudes I 21 ff.

Chatzidakis IEE — Chatzidakis, M., «Ἡ μεσοβυζαντινή τέχνη. Ζωγραφική», IEE, vol. H´ (1979) 279-285.

Chatzidakis ΠΑΑ — Chatzidakis, M., «Μνημειακή ζωγραφική στήν Ἑλλάδα», ΠΑΑ 56 (1981). At press.

Chatzidakis Sopočani — Chatzidakis, M., "Aspects de la peinture murale du XIIIe siècle en Grèce", L'art byzantin du XIIIe siècle, Symposium de Sopočani (Belgrade 1965) = Studies XIII.

Chilandar — Bogdanović, D., Djurić, V., Madaković, D., Chilandar (Belgrade 1978).

CIL   Corpus Inscriptionum Latinarum.

CJC   Corpus Justiniani Codicis III, Novellae (edited by G. Kroll, 1972) 94.

Clark Progress   Clark, C., Conditions of Economic Progress (London 1957³).

CMH   Cambridge Medieval History.

Collart Philippes   Collart, P., Philippes ville de Macédoine (Paris 1937).

Cormack ΔΧΑΕ   Cormack, R., "The apse mosaics of Santa Sophia at Thessaloniki", ΔΧΑΕ 10 (1981) 111 - 35.

Ćorović   Ćorović - Ljubinković, M., Les bois sculptés du Moyen Age dans les régions orientales de la Yougoslavie (Belgrade 1965). In Serbian, with a French summary.

DACL   Cabrol, F., Leclercq, H., Dictionnaire d'archéologie chrétienne et de liturgie (Paris 1907-1953).

Dakin   Dakin, D., The Greek Struggle in Macedonia, 1897-1913 (Thessalonike 1966).

Daskalakis   Daskalakis, A., Ὁ Ἑλληνισμός τῆς ἀρχαίας Μακεδονίας (Athens 1960).

ΔΧΑΕ   Δελτίον Χριστιανικῆς Ἀρχαιολογικῆς Ἑταιρείας.

Dennis OCA   Dennis, G.T. "The reign of Manuel Palaeologus in Thessalonica, 1382-1387", OCA 159 (Rome 1960) 58 ff.

Dieterich BZ   Dieterich, K., "Zur Kulturgeographie und Kulturgeschichte des byzantinischen Balkanhandels", BZ 31 (1931) 37-57 and 334-50.

Dimitsas   Dimitsas, M., Ἡ Μακεδονία ἐν λίθοις φθεγγομένοις καί μνημείοις σωζομένοις (Athens 1896).

ΔΙΣ   Διεύθυνση Ἱστορίας Στρατοῦ, Ὁ Μακεδονικός Ἀγών καί τά εἰς Θράκην γεγονότα (Athens 1979).

Djordjević   Djordjević, D., Ἱστορία τῆς Σερβίας 1800-1918 (Thessalonike 1970).

Djurić   Djurić, V. J., "La peinture murale byzantine au XIIIe siècle", Actes du XVe Congrès International d'Etudes Byzantines I (Athens 1979).

Djurić Fresken   Djurić, V. J., Byzantinische Fresken in Jugoslavien (Munich 1974).

Djurić Sopočani   Djurić, V. J., "La peinture murale Serbe au XIIIe siècle", L'art byzantin du XIIIe siècle, Symposium de Sopočani 1965 (Belgrade1967) 145 ff.

Dölger, Beiträge   Dölger, F., Beiträge zur byzantinischen Finanzverwaltung, besonders des 10. u. 11. Jhr. (Byzant. Archiv 9, Leipzig - Berlin 1927).

Dölger Παρασπορά   Dölger, F., Παρασπορά. 30 Aufsätze zur Geschichte, Kultur und Sprache des byzantinischen Reiches (Ettal 1961).

Dölger Regesten   Dölger F., Regesten der Kaiserurkunden des oströmischen Reiches (Berlin-Munich 1924-1960).

DOP   Dumbarton Oaks Papers.

DOSt   Dumbarton Oaks Studies.

Dragoumis   Dragoumis, N., Ἱστορικαί ἀναμνήσεις I - II (ἐκδ. Νέα Ἑλληνική Βιβλιοθήκη 1973).

Drougou, Touratsoglou   S. Drougou, J. Touratsoglou, Ἑλληνιστικοί λαξευτοί τάφοι Βεροίας (Athens 1980).

Düll Götterkulte   Düll, Siegrid, Die Götterkulte Normakedoniens in römischer Zeit (Munich 1977).

Dvornik   Dvornik, F., Les légendes de Constantin et de Méthode vues de Byzance (Prague 1933).

Dvornik Slaves   Dvornik, F., Les Slaves, Byzance et Rome au IXe siècle (Paris 1926).

Dvornik St. Grégoire   Dvornik, F., La vie de Saint Grégoire le Décapolite et les Slaves Macédoniens au IXe s. (Paris 1926).

Edson HSPh   Edson, Ch., "State Cults of Thessalonica", HSPh 51 (1940) 125-36.

Edson HThR   Edson, Ch., "Cults of Thessalonica", HThR 41 (1948) 153-204.

ΕΕΑΘ   Ἐπιστημονική Ἐπετηρίς τοῦ Ἀριστοτελείου Πανεπιστημίου Θεσσαλονίκης.

ΕΕΒΣ   Ἐπετηρίς τῆς Ἑταιρείας Βυζαντινῶν Σπουδῶν.

ΕΕΝΣΘ   Ἐπιστημονική Ἐπετηρίς τῆς Νομικῆς Σχολῆς Θεσσαλονίκης.

ΕΕΠΣΘ   Ἐπιστημονική Ἐπετηρίς τῆς Πολυτεχνικῆς Σχο-λῆς Θεσσαλονίκης.

EphDac   Ephemeris Dacoromana.

Ἔργον   Τό Ἔργον τῆς ἐν Ἀθήναις Ἀρχαιολογικῆς Ἑταιρείας.

EtBal   Etudes Balkaniques.

Etudes   Chatzidakis, M., Etudes sur la peinture postbyzantine, Variorum Reprints (London 1976).

Evangelidis   Evangelidis, D., Ἡ Παναγία τῶν Χαλκέων (Thessalonike 1954).

Feissel-Spieser T&MByz   Feissel, F., Spieser, J.-M., "Inventaires en vue d'un recueil des inscriptions historiques de Byzance, II: Les incritions de Thessalonique. Supplément", T&MByz 7 (1979) 303 ff.

FGrHist   Jacoby, F., Fragmente der griechischen Historiker 1-3 (Berlin - Leiden 1923-1954).

Frühe Ikonen   Weitzmann, K., Chatzidakis, M., Miatev, K., Radojčić, S., Frühe Ikonen (Vienna-Munich 1956).

Gaebler ZfN   Gaebler, H., "Zur Münzkunde Makedoniens IV", ZfN 24 (1904) 308.

ΓΑΚ   Γενικά Ἀρχεῖα τοῦ Κράτους.

Gelzer   Gelzer, H., Ungedruckte u. ungenügend veröffentliche Texte der Notitiae episcopatuum... (Munich 1900).

Gelzer BZ   Gelzer, H., "Ungedruckte und wenig bekannte Bistümerverzeichnisse der orientalischen Kirche II", BZ 2 (1893) 56.

Gouma-Peterson ABull   Gouma-Peterson, Th., "The Pareclesion of St. Euthymios in Thessalonica", ABull 58 (1976) 169-82.

Gounaris   Gounaris, G., Οἱ τοιχογραφίες τῶν Ἁγίων Ἀποστόλων καί τῆς Παναγίας Ρασιώτισσας στήν Καστοριά (Thessalonike 1980).

Gounaropoulos, Πανδώρα   Gounaropoulos, K.A., «Κοζανικά», Πανδώρα 22 (1871-72) 532.

G&R   Greece and Rome.

GRBS   Greek, Roman and Byzantine Studies.

Grabar   Grabar, A., L'iconoclasme byzantin (Paris 1957).

Grabar, Chatzidakis   Grabar, A., Chatzidakis, M., Grèce, Les Mosaïques (Unesco 1953).

Grabar Empereur   Grabar, A., L'empereur dans l'art byzantin (Paris 1936, reprinted 1971).

Gregoriou-Ioannidou   Gregoriou-Ioannidou, Maria, Τό ἐπεισόδιο τοῦ Κούβερ στά θαύματα τοῦ ἁγίου Δημητρίου (Thessalonike 1980).

Hadjimihali   Hadjimichali, A., La sculpture sur bois (Athens 1950).

Hadschi Chalfa   Hadschi Chalfa, Rumeli und Bosnia (Vienna 1812), translated by J. von Hammer.

Hammond Macedonia I-II   Hammond, N.G.L., A History of Macedonia I (Oxford 1972). Hammond, N.G.L., Griffith, G.T., A History of Macedonia II (Oxford 1979).

Hellénica   Robert, L., Hellénica: Recueil d'épigraphie, de numismatique et d'antiquités grecques I-XIII (Paris 1940-1965).

Hermann-Sodini BCH   Hermann, J.J., Sodini, J.P., "Exportations de marbre thasien à l'époque paléochrétienne: Les cas des chapitaux ioniques", BCH 101 (1977) 471 ff.

Heurtley Macedonia   Heurtley, W.A., Prehistoric Macedonia (Cambridge 1939).

Heyd   Heyd, W., Histoire du commerce du Levant au Moyen Age (Leipzig 1885).

HGM   Dindorf, L., Historici Graeci Minores I-II (Leipzig 1870-1871).

Honigmann   Honigmann, E., Le Synekdémos d'Hiérokles et l'opuscule géographique de Georges de Chypre (Brussels 1939²).

HSPh   Harvard Studies in Classical Philology.

HThR   Harvard Theological Review.

HZ   Historische Zeitschrift.

IEE   Ἱστορία τοῦ Ἑλληνικοῦ Ἔθνους Α-ΙΕ (Athens 1971-1980).

IF   Indogermanische Forschung.

IG   Inscriptiones Graecae.

IGBulg   Mihailov, G., Inscriptiones Graecae in Bulgaria

529

	Repertae I-IV (Sofia 1956).
Janin	Janin, R., *Les églises et les monastères des grands centres byzantins* (Paris 1975).
JCIPh	*Jahrbücher für Classische Philologie.*
JDAI	*Jahrbuch des Deutschen Archäologischen Instituts.*
JGR	Zepos, J. and P., *Jus Graeco-Romanum* I-VIII (Athens 1931).
JHS	*Journal of Hellenic Studies.*
Jireček	Jireček, K., "Staat und Gesellschaft im mittelalterichen Serbien", *Studien zur Kulturgeschichte des 13. - 15. Jhr.* (Vienna 1912).
JöBG	*Jahrbuch der österreichischen byzantinischen Gesellschaft.*
JOEAI	*Jahrbuch des österreichischen archäologischen Instituts.*
JOEByz	*Jahrbuch der österreichischen Byzantinistik.*
JRS	*Journal of Roman Studies.*
Kalléris	Kalléris, J., *Les anciens Macédoniens* I-II (Athens 1954, 1976).
Kalliergis	Pelekanides, S., Καλλιέργης ὅλης Θετταλίας ἄριστος ζωγράφος (Athens 1973).
Kalligas	Kalligas, M., *Die Hagia Sophia von Thessalonike* (Würzburg 1935).
Kanatsoulis *Μακεδονικά 3*	Kanatsoulis, D., «Τό κοινόν τῶν Μακεδόνων», *Μακεδονικά 3* (1956) 27-102.
Kanatsoulis *Μακεδονικά 13*	Kanatsoulis, D., «Οἱ μακεδονιάρχαι τοῦ κοινοῦ τῶν Μακεδόνων καί ἡ κοινωνική θέσις αὐτῶν εἰς τάς μακεδονικάς πόλεις», *Μακεδονικά 13* (1973) 1-37.
Karayannopulos	Karayannopulos, J., Ἱστορία τοῦ βυζαντινοῦ κράτους I-II (Thessalonike 1976, 1978).
Kirsten	Kirsten, F., "Die byzantinische Stadt", *Berihte zum XI. Internationalen Byzantinistenkongress* (Munich 1958).
Klemis	Klemis, A.N., Ἀγροτική Οἰκονομία (Athens 1961).
Kofos	Kofos, E., Ἡ ἐπανάστασις τῆς Μακεδονίας κατά τό 1878 (Thessalonike 1969).
Kofos	Kofos, E., *Greece and the Eastern Crisis, 1875-1878* (Thessalonike 1975).
Kofos *Nationalism*	Kofos E., *Nationalism and Communism in Macedonia* (Thessalonike 1964).
Kolias	Kolias, G., *Léon Chœrosphactès, magistre, proconsul et patrice. Biographie - Correspondance*, texte et traduction (Athens 1939).
Konidaris	Konidaris, G., Αἱ μητροπόλεις καί ἀρχιεπισκοπαί τοῦ Οἰκουμενικοῦ Πατριαρχείου καί ἡ "τάξις" αὐτῶν, vol. Α΄ (Athens 1934).
Kontiadis	Kontiadis, G., Archimandrite, Σύντομος ἱστορική ἐπισκόπησις τῆς Ἱερᾶς Μονῆς Προδρόμου Σερρῶν (Serres 1960).
Kotzias *AE*	Kotzias, N., «Ὁ παρά τό ἀεροδρόμιον τῆς Θεσσαλονίκης (Σέδες) Γ΄ τάφος», *AE* 1937, 806-95.
Krautheimer	Krautheimer, R., *Early Christian and Byzantine Architecture* (Harmondsworth 1975²).
Kretchmer	Kretschmer, P., *Einleitung in die Geschichte der griechischen Sprache* (1896).
Kurbinovo	Hadermann - Misguich, Lydie, *Kurbinovo, Les fresques de Saint-Georges et la peinture byzantine du XIIe siècle* (Brussels 1975).
Kyriakidis *ΙΣΕ*	Kyriakidis, E., Ἱστορία τοῦ συγχρόνου Ἑλληνισμοῦ (Athens 1892).
Kyriakidis	Kyriakidis, S., Βυζαντιναί Μελέται I-V (Thessalonike 1937-1939).
LAAA	*Liverpool Annals of Anthropology and Archaelogy.*
Lambros *NE*	Lambros, S., «Ὁ ἐκ Θεσσαλονίκης οἶκος Ὑαλέα», *NE* 6 (1909) 49-51.
Laskaris	Laskaris, M., *Τό Ἀνατολικόν Ζήτημα 1800-1923* (Thessalonike 1948).
Lavvas	Lavvas, G., «Οἱ πόλεις τῶν "Χριστιανικῶν Βασιλικῶν": Μία συμβολή στήν πολεοδομία τοῦ Ἀνατολικοῦ Ἰλλυρικοῦ», *Εἰσηγήσεις Δεκάτου Διεθνοῦς Συνεδρίου Χριστιανικῆς Ἀρχαιολογίας*
	(Thessalonike 1980) 403 ff.
Lazarev	Lazarev, V., *Storia della Pittura bizantina* (Turin 1957).
Le Icone	Chatzidakis, M., Weitzmann K. et al., *Le Icone* (Mondatori, Milan 1981).
Lemerle *Miracles*	Lemerle, P., *Les plus anciens recueils des miracles de Saint Démétrius et la pénétration des Slaves dans les Balkans*, I: *Le texte* (Paris 1979), II: *Commentaire* (Paris 1981).
Lemerle *Philippes*	Lemerle, P., *Philippes et la Macédoine orientale à l'époque chrétienne et byzantine* (Paris 1945).
Lemerle *RH*	Lemerle, P., "Invasions et migrations dans les Balkans depuis la fin de l'époque romaine jusqu'au VIIIe siècle", *RH* 211 (1954) 265 ff.
Leon	Leon, G., *Greece and the Great Powers 1914-1917* (Thessalonike 1974).
Ljubinković *Corsi*	Ljubinković, R., "La peinture murale en Serbie et en Macédoine aux 11ème et 12ème siècles", *Corsi di Cultura sull' Arte Ravennata e Bizantina* (Ravenna 1962).
Lyritzis	Lyritzis, G., Ἡ Ἐθνική Ἑταιρεία καί ἡ δρᾶσις αὐτῆς (Kozani 1970).
MAArch	*Macedoniae Acta Archaeologica.*
MAGW	*Mitteilungen der Anthropologischen Gesellschaft.*
Makaronas *ΑΔ 1960*	Makaronas, C., «Ἀνασκαφαί Πέλλης 1957-1960», *ΑΔ* 16 (1960) 72-83.
Makaronas *ΑΔ 1963*	Makaronas, C., «Τάφος παρά τό Δερβένι Θεσσαλονίκης», *ΑΔ* 18 (1963) Χρονικά Β΄ 193-96.
Makaronas *Ἀρχαία Μακεδονία*	Makaronas, C., «Χρονολογικά ζητήματα τῆς Πέλλης», *Ἀρχαία Μακεδονία* I (1970) 162-67.
Makriyannis	Makriyannis, Ἀπομνημονεύματα II (Papyrus edn.).
Malmquist	Malmquist, T., *Byzantine 12th Century Frescoes in Kastoria. Agioi Anargyroi and Agios Nikolaos tou Kasnitzi* (Uppsala 1979).
Mamalakis	Mamalakis J.P., *Τό Ἅγιον Ὄρος (Ἄθως) διά μέσου τῶν αἰώνων* (Thessalonike 1971).
Mango	Mango, C., *Byzantine Architecture* (New York 1976).
Mansi	Mansi, J. D., *Sacrorum consiliorum nova et amplissima collectio* (Florence 1769, reprinted Graz 1960-1961).
Mavrogordatos-Chamoudopoulos	Mavrogordatos, M.I., Chamoudopoulos, A.C., Ἡ Μακεδονία (Thessalonike 1931).
MDAI (A)	*Mitteilungen des Deutschen Archäologischen Instituts (Athenische Abteilung).*
MDAI (R)	*Mitteilungen des Deutschen Archäologischen Instituts (Römische Abteilung).*
MEI	*Μνημεῖα τῆς Ἑλληνικῆς Ἱστορίας.*
Μελέτες	Pelekanides, S., *Μελέτες παλαιοχριστιανικῆς καί βυζαντινῆς ἀρχαιολογίας* (Thessalonike 1977).
Mentzou	Mentzou K.P., *Συμβολαί εἰς τήν μελέτην τοῦ οἰκονομικοῦ καί κοινωνικοῦ βίου τῆς πρωΐμου βυζαντινῆς περιόδου* (Athens 1975).
Mercati	Mercati, G., *Notizie di Procoro e Demetrio Cidone, Manuele Caleca e Teodoro Meliteniota ed altri appunti per la storia della teologia e della letteratura bizantina del secolo XIV* (Vatican 1931).
Meyer	Meyer, Ph., *Die Haupturkunden für die Geschichte der Athosklöster* (Leipzig 1894).
Mikulčić *Pelagonija*	Mikulčić, I., *Pelagonija* (Skopje 1966).
Miljković - Pepek	Miljković, P., Pepek, P., *L'œuvre des peintres Michel et Eutiche* (Skopje 1967).
Millénaire	*Le Millénaire du Mont Athos* (Chevetogne 1964).
Miller	Miller, W., *The Latins in the Levant; a history of Frankish Greece 1204-1566* (London 1908).
Millet *Athos*	Millet, G., *Les monuments de l'Athos. Les peintures* (Paris 1927).
Millet *BCH*	Millet, G., "Recherches au Mont Athos", *BCH* 29 (1905) 72 ff.
Millet - Frolow	Millet, G., Frolow, A., *La peinture du Moyen Age en Yougoslavie* I-II (Paris 1954).
M - L *GHI*	Meiggs, R., Lewis, D., *Greek Historical Inscriptions* (Oxford 1969).

MM   Miklosich, F., Müller, S., *Acta et Diplomata graeca medii aevi* I-VI (Vindobonae 1860-1890).

MonPiot   *Monuments et mémoires publiés par l'Académie des Inscriptions et Belles Lettres,* Fondation Piot.

Monumentalmalerei   Hamann - MacLean, R., Hallensleben, H., *Die Monumentalmalerei in Serbien und Makedonien* I-II (Giessen 1963).

Moretti *Iscrizioni*   Moretti, L., *Iscrizioni agonistiche grecche* (Rome 1953).

Moschopoulos *EEBΣ*   Moschopoulos, N., «Ἡ Ἑλλάς κατά τόν Ἐβλιά Τσελεμπῆ», *EEBΣ* 15 (1939) 155 ff.

MOsG   *Mitteilungen zur osmanischen Geschichte.*

Moskov   Moskov, K., Θεσσαλονίκη, *1700-1912. Τομή τῆς μεταπρατικῆς πόλης* (Athens 1974).

Mouriki *Gračanica*   Mouriki, D., "Stylistic Trends in Monumental Painting in Greece at the beginning of the XIVth Century", *L'Art byzantin au XIVe siècle. Symposium de Gračanica 1973* (Belgrad 1978).

Moutsopoulos Ἀμπ.   Moutsopoulos, N., Τά Θεσσαλικά Ἀμπελάκια (Thessalonike 1975²).

Moutsopoulos *EEΠΣΘ*   Moutsopoulos, N., «Τά ἀρχοντικά τῆς Σιάτιστας», *EEΠΣΘ* I (1964).

Moutsopoulos Πέλλα   Moutsopoulos, N., Οἱ ἐκκλησίες τοῦ νομοῦ Πέλλης (Thessalonike 1973).

Moutsopoulos Φλ.   Moutsopoulos, N., Ἐκκλησίες τοῦ νομοῦ Φλωρίνης (Thessalonike 1964).

MusB   *Musée Belge.*

Mylonas *Millénaire*   Mylonas, P., "L'Architecture du Mont Athos", *Millénaire* 229-46.

MZB   *Münchner Zeitschrift für Balkanologie.*

NE   *Νέος Ἑλληνομνήμων.*

Nicol *Despotate*   Nicol, D.M., *The Despotate of Epiros* (Oxford 1957).

Nikolaides   Nikolaides, D., Ὀθωμανικοί Κώδικες I-IV (Istanbul 1889-1891).

Nikolajević   Nikolajević, I., "Nécropoles et tombes chrétiennes en Illyricum Oriental", *Εἰσηγήσεις Δεκάτου Διεθνοῦς Συνεδρίου Χριστιανικῆς Ἀρχαιολογίας* (Thessalonike 1980).

OCA   *Orientalia Christiana Analecta.*

OCP   *Orientalia Christiana Periodica.*

Oikonomidis   Oikonomidis, N., *Les listes de préséance byzantines des IXe et Xe siècles* (Paris 1972).

Olynthus I-XIV   Robinson, D.M. (ed.), *Excavations at Olynthus,* Parts I-XIV (Baltimore 1929-1952).

Orlandos   Orlandos, A., Μοναστηριακή Ἀρχιτεκτονική (Athens 1958).

Orlandos AΔ   Orlandos, A., «Βεροίας ἐπιγραφαί ἀνέκδοτοι», *AΔ* 2 (1916) 144-63.

Orlandos *Βασιλική*   Orlandos, A., Ἡ ξυλόστεγος παλαιοχριστιανική βασιλική τῆς μεσογειακῆς λεκάνης (Athens 1954).

Orlandos *Καστοριά*   Orlandos, A., «Τά βυζαντινά μνημεῖα τῆς Καστοριᾶς» *ABME* Δ´ (1938).

Ostrogorsky   Ostrogorsky, G., *History of the Byzantine State* (translated by Joan Hussey) Oxford 1980 edition.

ΠAA   *Πρακτικά τῆς Ἀκαδημίας Ἀθηνῶν.*

ΠAE   *Πρακτικά τῆς ἐν Ἀθήναις Ἀρχαιολογικῆς Ἑταιρείας.*

Palmer - King   Palmer, S., King, R., *Yugoslav Communism and the Macedonian Question* (Hamden, Conn. 1971).

Pandermalis AA   Pandermalis, D., "Ein Bildnis des Severus Alexander in Thessaloniki", *AA* (1972) 128.

Pandermalis Ἀρχαία Μακεδονία   Pandermalis, D., «Λατρεῖες καί ἱερά τοῦ Δίου Πιερίας», Ἀρχαία Μακεδονία 2 (1977) 358.

Papadopoulos   Papadopoulos, S., Οἱ ἐπαναστάσεις τοῦ 1854 καί 1878 στήν Μακεδονία (Thessalonike 1970).

Papadopoulos OAE   Papadopoulos, G., Ἡ σύγχρονος ἱεραρχία τῆς Ὀρθοδόξου Ἀνατολικῆς Ἐκκλησίας (Athens 1895).

Papazoglou *Actes*   Papazoglou, Fanoula, "Structures ethniques et sociales dans les régions centrales des Balkans à la lumière des études onomastiques", *Actes du VIIe Congrès International d'Epigraphie grecque et latine* (Bucharest 1979) 153-69.

Papazoglou *ANRW*   Papazoglou, Fanoula, "Quelques aspects de l'Histoire de la province de Macédoine", *ANRW* II 7 (Tübingen 1979) 302-69.

Papazoglou *BAB*   Papazoglou, Fanoula, "La Macédoine Salutaire et la Macédoine Seconde", *BAB* 5e série 42 (Brussels 1956) 115-24.

Papazoglou *Balcanica*   Papazoglou, Fanoula, "Sur la structure ethnique de l'ancienne Macédoine" (in Serbian), *Balcanica* 8 (1977) 65-82.

Papazoglou *Cités*   Papazoglou, Fanoula, *Makedonski gradovi u rimsko doba* (Skopje 1957).

Papazoglou *RTFPhUB*   Papazoglou, Fanoula, "Deorum nomima hominibus imposta", *RTFPhUb* 14 (1979) 7-16.

Papazoglou *ZAnt*   Papazoglou, Fanoula, "Gouverneurs de Macédoine", *ZAnt* 29 (1979) 335.

Pape *Kunstwerke*   Pape, M., *Griechische Kunstwerke aus Kriegsbeute und ihre öffentliche Aufstellung in Rom* (Hamburg 1975).

Parthey *Hieroclis*   Parthey, G., *Hieroclis Synecdemus et Notitiae Graecae Episcopatuum* (Berlin 1866).

PCHRSM   *Partimoine Culturel et Historique dans la Republique Socialiste Macédoine.*

Pelekanidis   Pelekanidis, S., *I più antichi affreschi di Kastoria* (= Μελέτες 51 ff.)

Pelekanides AE   Pelekanides, S., «Ἡ ἔξω τῶν τειχῶν παλαιοχριστιανική βασιλική τῶν Φιλίππων», *AE* 1955, 114-79 (= Μελέτες 333-94).

Pelekanides *Καστοριά*   Pelekanides, S., Καστοριά I. Αἱ Βυζαντιναί Τοιχογραφίαι (Thessalonike 1953).

Pelekidis *Πολιτεία*   Pelekidis, S., Ἀπό τήν πολιτείαν καί τήν κοινωνίαν τῆς ἀρχαίας Θεσσαλονίκης (Thessalonike 1934).

Πέλλα I   Papakonstantinou - Diamantourou, Despina, Πέλλα I (Athens 1971).

Pennas   Pennas, P., Ἱστορία τῶν Σερρῶν (Athens 1966²).

Pentzopoulos   Pentzopoulos, D., *The Balkan exchange of minorities and its impact upon Greece* (Paris 1962).

Petsas Ἀρχαία Μακεδονία   Petsas, Ph., «Αἰγαί - Πέλλα - Θεσσαλονίκη», Ἀρχαία Μακεδονία I (1970) 203-27.

Petsas *Τάφος*   Petsas, Ph., Ὁ Τάφος τῶν Λευκαδίων (Ἀθήνα 1966).

PG   Migne, J.P. *Patrologiae cursus completus. Series Graeca* (Paris 1875).

Philippes I   Collart, P., Ducrey, P., *Philippes I. Les reliefs rupestres* (*BCH* Supplément II, 1975).

Philip   Loukopoulos, L., Hatzopoulos, M. (ed.), *Philip of Macedon* (Athens 1980).

PKG   *Propyläen Kunstgeschichte.*

P.R.O.   *Public Record Office.*

ProcPS   *Proceedings of the Prehistoric Society.*

PSI   *Papiri Greci e Latini,* (Publicazioni della società italiana per la ricerca dei papiri greci e latini in Egitto), (1912 -).

RA   *Revue Archéologique.*

Radojčić   Radojčić, S., *Geschichte der Serbischen Kunst* (Berlin 1969).

RbK   *Reallexikon zur byzantinischen Kunst.*

RE   *Realenzyklopädie der Klassischen Altertumswissenschaft.*

Recueil I   Millet, G., Pargoive J., Petit, L., *Recueil des Inscriptions Chrétiennes du Mont Athos, première partie* (Paris 1904).

REG   *Revue des Etudes Grecques.*

Regel   Regel, W., *Fontes rerum byzantinarum* (Petrograd 1892).

RESl   *Revue des Etudes Slaves.*

RevLing   *Revue de Linguistique.*

RH   *Revue Historique.*

RIEB   *Revue Internationale des Etudes Balkaniques.*

Rhomiopoulou *AAA*   Rhomiopoulou, Katerina, "A New Monumental Chamber - Tomb with Paintings of the Hellenistic Period near Lefkadia", *AAA* 6 (1975) 87-92.

RLV   *Reallexikon der Vorgeschichte.*

RPh   *Revue de Philologie.*

Rouillard   Rouillard, G., *La vie rurale dans l'empire byzantin* (Paris 1953).

RPLHA   *Revue de Philologie, de Littérature et d'Histoire*

531

Anciennes.

RTFPhUB — *Recueil des Travaux de la Faculté de Philosophie de l'Université de Belgrade.*

RTIEByz — *Recueil des Travaux de l'Institut d'Etudes Byzantines.*

Rüsch *JDAI* — Rüsch, A., "Das kaiserzeitliche Porträt in Makedonien", *JDAI* 84 (1969) 180.

Sakellariou *IEE* — Sakellariou, M.B., «Οἱ γλωσσικές καί ἐθνικές ὁμάδες τῆς ἑλληνικῆς προϊστορίας», *IEE* vol. A´ (Athens 1970).

Sakellariou *Peuples* — Sakellariou, M.B., *Peuples préhelléniques d'origine indo-européenne* (Athens 1975).

Sakellariou *Proto-Grecs* — Sakellariou, M.B., *Les Proto-Grecs* (Athens 1980).

Salditt - Trappmann — Salditt - Trappmann, R., *Tempel der ägyptischen Götter in Griechenland und an der Westküste Kleinasiens* (Leiden 1970).

Salonique — Diehl, Ch., Le Tourneau, H., Saladin M., *Les monuments chrétiens de Salonique* (Paris 1918).

Saria *JOEAI* — Saria, B., "Neue Funde in der Bischofskirche von Stobi", *JOEAI* 28 (1933) 132.

Sarikakis *Ἄρχοντες* — Sarikakis, T., *Ρωμαῖοι ἄρχοντες τῆς ἐπαρχίας Μακεδονίας. Α´ Ἀπό τῆς ἱδρύσεως τῆς ἐπαρχίας μέχρι τῶν χρόνων τοῦ Αὐγούστου (148-27 π.Χ.). Β´ Ἀπό τοῦ Αὐγούστου μέχρι τοῦ Διοκλητιανοῦ (27 π.Χ. - 284 μ.Χ.)* (Thessalonike 1971 and 1977).

SAWW — *Sitzungsberichte der Akademie der Wissenschaften in Wien.*

Seeck *Notitia* — Seeck, O., *Notitia Dignitatum* (Frankfurt 1942).

SEG — *Supplementum Epigraphicum Graecum.*

Settas — Settas, N.C., *Τά μεγάλα παραγωγικά ἔργα τῆς Μακεδονίας* (Athens 1961).

SGDI — Bechtel, F., Collitz, H. (ed.), *Sammlung der griechischen Dialektinschriften* (Göttingen 1899-1915).

SIG³ — Dittenberger, V., *Sylloge Inscriptionum Graecarum* I-IV (Leipzig 1915-24).

Sodini et al. *BCH* — Sodini, J.P., Lambraki, A., Koželj, T., "Les carrières de marbre à l'époque paléochrétienne: Le cas des Chapitaux ioniques", *BCH* 101 (1977) 471 ff.

Soechting — Soechting, D., *Die Porträts des Septimius Severus* (Bonn 1972).

Sotiriou — Sotiriou, G., and Maria, *Ἡ βασιλική τοῦ Ἁγίου Δημητρίου Θεσσαλονίκης* (Athens 1952).

Sotiriou — Sotiriou, G., "La sculpture sur bois dans l'art byzantin", *Mélanges Ch. Diehl* II (Paris 1930) 180 ff.

Sotiriou *ΔXAE* — Sotiriou, Maria, «Ἡ Μακεδονική σχολή καί ἡ λεγόμενη σχολή Μιλούτιν», *ΔXAE* 5 (1969) 1 ff.

Soulis — Soulis, B., *Τά μεγάλα παραγωγικά ἔργα Μακεδονίας* (Drama 1947).

Spieser *BCH* — Spieser, J.M., "Note sur la chronologie des remparts de Thessalonique", *BCH* 98 (1974) 507-19.

Spieser *T&MByz* — Spieser, J.M., "Inventaires en vue d'un recueil des inscriptions historiques de Byzance. I. Les inscriptions de Thessalonique", *T&MByz* 5 (1978).

StBN — *Studi bizantini e neoellenici.*

Stikas *BZ* — Stikas, E., "Une église des Paléologues aux environs de Castoria", *BZ* 51 (1968) 100-13.

StudAlb — *Studia Albanica.*

StudBal — *Studia Balcanica.*

StudHist — *Studime Historike.*

Subotić — Subotić, C., *L'école de peinture d'Ohrid au XVe siècle* (Belgrade 1980), (in Serbian with a French summary).

Tafel — Tafel, T.L.F., *Eustathii metropolitae Thessalonicensis opuscula* (Frankfurt 1832).

Tafrali — Tafrali, O., *Thessalonique au XIVe siècle* (Paris 1913).

Tafrali *Thessalonique* — Tafrali, O., *Thessalonique des origines au XIVe siècle* (Paris 1919).

TGF — Nauck, A., *Tragicorum Graecorum Fragmenta* (1889²).

Theocharidis — Theocharidis, G., *Ἱστορία τῆς Μακεδονίας κατά τούς μέσους χρόνους 285-1354* (Thessalonike 1980).

T&MByz — *Travaux et Mémoires. Centre de recherche d'histoire et de civilisation byzantines.*

Tod *GHI* — Tod, M.N., *Greek Histotical Inscriptions* (Oxford 1946-48).

Tomadakis — Tomadakis, N.B., *Βυζαντινή Γραμματολογία 1204-1453* (Athens 1957).

Touratsoglou *AΔ* — Touratsoglou, J., «Μεταλεξάνδρεια Πέλλα», *AΔ* 30 (1975), Μελέται 165.

Touratsoglou *Ἀρχαία Μακεδονία* — Touratsoglou, J., «Δύο νέαι ἐπιγραφικαί μαρτυρίαι περί τοῦ κοινοῦ τῶν Μακεδόνων», *Ἀρχαία Μακεδονία* I (1970) 280-90.

Tsamis — Tsamis, P., *Μακεδονικός Ἀγών* (Thessalonike 1975).

Tsigaridas — Tsigaridas, E., Loverdou - Tsigarida, K., *Κατάλογος χριστιανικῶν ἐπιγραφῶν στά μουσεῖα τῆς Θεσσαλονίκης* (Thessalonike 1979).

Vacalopoulos — Vacalopoulos, A., *History of Macedonia 1354-1833* (translated by P. Megann, Thessalonike 1973).

Vacalopoulos *Thess.* — Vacalopoulos, A., *A History of Thessaloniki* (Thessalonike 1963).

Vasdravellis — Vasdravellis, J.K., *Οἱ Μακεδόνες εἰς τούς ὑπέρ ἀνεξαρτησίας ἀγῶνας 1796-1832* (Thessalonike 1967³).

Velmans *CArch* — Velmans, T., "Les fresques de Saint-Nicolas Orphanos à Salonique", *CArch* 26 (1966) 166 ff.

Vickers *JHS* — Vickers, M., "Hellenistic Thessalonoki", *JHS* 92 (1972).

Vlachos — Vlachos, N., *Τό Μακεδονικόν ὡς φάσις τοῦ Ἀνατολικοῦ Ζητήματος, 1878-1908* (Athens 1935).

Vlasto — Vlasto, A.P., *The Entry of the Slavs into Christendom* (Cambridge 1970).

Vokotopoulos — Vokotopoulos, P., *Ἡ ἐκκλησιαστική ἀρχιτεκτονική εἰς τήν Δ. Στερεάν Ἑλλάδα καί τήν Ἤπειρον ἀπό τό τέλος τοῦ 7ου μέχρι τό τέλος τοῦ 10ου αἰῶνα* (Thessalonike 1975).

Wiggers-Wegner — Wiggers, H., Wegner, M., *Caracalla, Geta, Plautilla, Macrinus bis Balbinus* (Berlin 1971).

Wiseman *Stobi* — Viseman, J., *Stobi, Guide to the Excavations* (Belgrade 1973).

WMBH — *Wissenschaftliche Mitteilungen aus Bosnien und Herzegobina.*

Xanalatos — Xanalatos, D., *Beiträge zur Wirtschafts-und Sozialgeschichte Makedoniens im Mittelalter, hauptsächlich auf Grund der Briefe des Erzbischofs Theophylaktos von Achrida* (Munich thesis 1937).

Xyngopoulos — Xyngopoulos, A., *Ἡ ψηφιδωτή διακόσμηση τοῦ ναοῦ τῶν Ἁγίων Ἀποστόλων Θεσσαλονίκης* (Thessalonike 1953).

Xyngopoulos — Xyngopoulos, A., *Thessalonique et la peinture Macédonienne* (Athens 1955).

Xyngopoulos *Ναοί* — Xyngopoulos, A., *Τέσσαρες μικροί ναοί τῆς Θεσσαλονίκης* (Thessalonike 1952).

Xyngopoulos *Πανσέληνος* — Xyngopoulos, A., *Μανουήλ Πανσέληνος* (Athens 1956).

Xyngopoulos *Σχέδ.* — Xyngopoulos, A., *Σχεδίασμα ἱστορίας τῆς θρησκευτικῆς ζωγραφικῆς μετά τήν Ἄλωσιν* (Athens 1957).

Xyngopoulos *Σέρραι* — Xyngopoulos, A., *Ἔρευναι εἰς τά βυζαντινά μνημεῖα τῶν Σερρῶν* (Thessalonike 1965).

Xyngopoulos *Sopoćani* — Xyngopoulos, A., "Icones du XIIIe siècle en Grèce", *L'art byzantin du XIIIe siècle, Symposium de Sopoćani 1965* (Belgrade 1967) 75-82.

Zakythinos — Zakythinos, D., *Βυζαντινή Ἱστορία 324-1071* (Athens 1972).

ZAnt — *Ziva Antika.*

ZFFBe — *Zbornik Filosofkog Fakulteta Beograd.*

ZfN — *Zeitschrift für Numismatik.*

ZNTW — *Zeitschrift für neutestamentliche Wissenschaft.*

ZR — *Zbornik Radova Narodnog Muzeja Beograd.*

ZSNM — *Zbornik na Stipskiot Naroden Muzej.*

ZVS — *Zeitschrift für vergleichende Sprachforschung.*

ZWTh — *Zeitschrift für Wissenschaftliche Theologie.*

FOOTNOTES

ANCIENT MACEDONIA

The most important works and the principal studies concerned with ancient Macedonia are examined in two critical bibliographies, recently published, which interested readers may refer to: M.B. Hatzopoulos, "A Century and a Lustrum of Macedonian Studies", *The Ancient World* 4 (1981), 91-108, and E.N. Borza, "The History and Archaeology of Macedonia. Prospect and Retrospect", *Studies in the History of Art* 10 (1982), 17-30. Three collections must now be added to the publications cited there: H.J. Dell (ed.), *Ancient Macedonian Studies in Honor of Charles F. Edson* (Thessalonike, 1981), W.L. Adams, E.N. Borza (ed.), *Philip II, Alexander the Great and the Macedonian Heritage* (Washington, 1982) and the volume, *Studies in the History of Art,* mentioned previously, which was issued with the subtitle "Macedonia and Greece in Late Classical and Early Hellenistic Times" (ed. Beryl Barr-Sharrar, E.N. Borza). H. Geislinger (ed.) *Südosteuropa Zwischen 1600 und 1000 v.Chr.* (Berlin, 1982).

THE EARLY YEARS

THE CIVILIZATIONS

1. E.S. Higgs, "A Hand Axe from Greece", *Antiquity* 38 (1964), 54.
2. *L'Anthropologie,* 1961, 438 ff.
3. R.J. Rodden, "Excavation at the Early Neolithic Site at Nea Nicomedia, Greek Macedonia", *ProcPS* 28 (1962), 267 ff.
4. M. Gimbutas, *Neolithic Macedonia* (Los Angeles, 1976).
5. M. Garašanin, D. Garašanin, "Fouilles archéologiques à Tarinci 'Vršink' ", *ZSNM* 1 (1958), 65 ff. M. Garašanin, D. Garašanin, "L'habitat néolithique de Vršnik près de Tarinci", *ZSNM* 2 (1960-61), 7.
6. M. Grabić, P. Mačkić, S. Nadji, D. Simoska, B. Stalio, *Porodin* (Bitolj, 1960).
7. W.A. Heurtley, "Excavations at Servia in Western Macedonia", *AntJ* 7, 227. Heurtley, *Macedonia,* 43. Cressida Ridley and K.A. Wardle, "Rescue Excavations at Servia 1971-1973: a Preliminary Report", *BSA* 74 (1979), 185.
8. D.V. Grammenos, M. Photiadis, «Ἀπό τούς προϊστορικούς οἰκισμούς τῆς Ἀνατολικῆς Μακεδονίας», Ἀνθρωπολογικά 1 (1980), 17, 20.
9. D.H. French, "Pottery Distributions and the Geographical Regions of Macedonia", *ZR* 6 (1970), 6.
10. S. Marinatos, «Ὁ λιμναῖος συνοικισμός Καστοριᾶς», *AAA* 1 (1968), 162.
11. F. Schachermeyr, *Die Agäische Frühzeit* I (Vienna, 1976), 293.
12. Aikaterini Rhomiopoulou, «Ἀνασκαφή τοῦ προϊστορικοῦ συνοικισμοῦ τοῦ Ντικιλί-Τάς», *AAA* I (1968), 48. G. Daux, «Chronique des fouilles en 1962, Dikili-Tach", *BCH* 87 (1963), 843. G. Daux, "Chronique des fouilles en 1967, Dikili-Tach", *BCH* 92 (1968), 1062. J.

Deshayes, "Dikili-Tach", *BCH* 94 (1970), 799 ff.
13. C. Renfrew, "The Burnt House at Sitagroi", *Antiquity* 44 (1970), 131. C. Renfrew, "The Tree-Ring calibration of Radiocarbon: An Archaeological Evaluation", *ProcPS* 36 (1970), 296. J.P. Michaud, "Chronique des fouilles en 1970. Photolivos (Sitagroi)", *BCH* 95 (1971), 985.
14. G. Mylonas, "The Neolithic Setttlement in Olynthus", *Olynthus* 1,2. G. Mylonas, "The Pre-Persian Pottery from Olynthus", *Olynthus* V, 15.
15. W.A. Heurtley, "Report on an Excavation at the Toumba of Vardino, Macedonia", *LAAA* 12, 15. Heurtley, *Macedonia,* 33.
16. Heurtley, *Macedonia,* 155.
17. Heurtley, *Macedonia,* 17.
18. M.V. Garašanin, "Zur Chronologie des makedonischen Neolithikums", *ArchJug* 3 (1959), 2.
19. F. Prendi, "La Civilisation Préhistorique de Maliq", *StudAlb* 1, 1966, 255.
20. Other important sites in eastern Macedonia include Akropotamos and Polystylon, G.E. Mylonas, G. Bakalakis, «Ἀνασκαφαί νεολιθικῶν συνοικισμῶν Ἀκροποτάμου καί Πολυστύλου», ΠΑΕ 1938, 109; Dimitra, D. Theocharis and A. Rhomiopoulou, «Ἀνασκαφαί Ντικιλί Τάς» ΠΑΕ 1961, 81 (Current excavation D. Grammenos); and Galepsos, G. Daux, "Chronique des fouilles en 1963", *BCH* 1964, 51f, F. Schachermeyr, *Die ältesten Kulturen Griechenlands* (Stuttgart 1955), 108.
21. M. Korkuti, Zhaneta Andrea, "Fouilles 1969-1970 dans l'agglomeration Néolithique de Cakran (Fieri)", *StudAlb,* 1972,15.
22. J. Korosec, "Schutzforschungen in Demir Kapija im Jahre 1948", *Zbornik Skopje* I (1956), 90. M.V. Garašanin, "Neolithikum und Bronzezeit in Serbien und Makedonien", *Bericht der Römisch-Germanischen Kommission* 39 (1958), 122.
23. W.A. Heurtley, "Report on Excavations at the Toumba and Tables of Vardaroftsa, Macedonia, 1925-1926", *BSA* 27 (1925-1926), 1 ff.
24. H.G.G. Payne, "Archaeology in Greece, Macedonia, 1930-31», *JHS* 51 (1931), 197. Heurtley, *Macedonia,* 57.
25. W.A. Heurtley, C.A. Ralegh Radford, "Two Prehistoric Sites in Chalcidice, II. Molyvopyrgos", *BSA* 29 (1927-1928), 156 ff.
26. W.A. Heurtley, C.A. Ralegh Radford, "Two Prehistoric Sites in Chalcidice, I Hagios Mamas", *BSA* 29 (1927-1928), 117.
27. W.A. Heurtley, "Report on Excavations at the Toumba of Saratse, Macedonia, 1929", *BSA* 30 (1928-1930), 113.
28. Other excavated sites include Gona, Kalamaria and Sedes. L. Rey, "Observations sur les premiers habitats de la Macédoine. (Toumba sur table)", *BCH* 1917/1919 and in eastern Macedonia, Angista, C. Koukouli – Chrysanthake, «Οἰκισμός τῆς ὕστερης ἐποχῆς Χαλκοῦ στόν σταθμό Ἄγγιστας Σερρῶν», *Anthropologica* I (1980), 50.
29. K.A. Wardle, "Excavations at Assiros, 1975-

79", *BSA* 75 (1980), 229 ff.
30. S. Casson, "Excavations in Macedonia", *AntJ* 6 (1926), 59.
31. S. Casson, "The Bronze Age in Macedonia", *Archaeologia* 74 (1923-24), 77.
32. B. Hänsel, "Ergebnisse der Grabung bei Kastanas 1975-78 in Zentralmakedonien", *Jahrbuch des Römisch-Germanischen Zentral museums Mainz* 25 (1978).
33. Ph. Petsas, «Μυκηναϊκά ὄστρακα ἐκ Κοζάνης καί Παιονίας», *AE* 1953-54: 2, 113.
34. Katerina Rhomiopoulou, «Τυχαῖα εὑρήματα ἐκ τῆς ΙΔ΄ Ἀρχαιολογικῆς Περιφερείας (Δυτ. Μακεδονία)», *AE* 1969 Ἀρχ. Χρονικά 14.
35. Zhaneta Andrea, "Kultura e Tumave te pellgut korçes dhe vendi i saj në Balkanin Juglindor", *StudHist* 26: 4 (1971), 81. Idem., "La civilisation tumulaire du bassin de Korçe et sa place dans les Balkans du Sud-est: la phase Barç", *Illyria* 4 (1976), 133. Cf. also evidence from Bouboushti (Platania), W.A. Heurtley, "A Prehistoric Site in Western Macedonia and the Dorian Invasion", *BSA* 28 (1926-27) 158; and Tren, M. Korkuti, "Vendbanimi prehistorik i Trenit", *Illiria* I (1971) 31.
36. T. Makridis, «Χαλκᾶ Μακεδονικά τοῦ Μουσείου Μπενάκη», *AE* 1937: 2, 514.
37. Andronikos, Βεργίνα I. Ph. Petsas, «Ἀνασκαφή ἀρχαίου νεκροταφείου Βεργίνης 1960/61», *AΔ* 17 (1961-1962), 285. Maria Karamanoli-Siganidou, «Ἀνασκαφή ἀρχαίου νεκροταφείου Βεργίνης», *AΔ* 18 (1963), 222.
38. In the Thessalonike Museum collection, unpublished.
39. Mikulčić, *Pelagonija* 14.
40. Mikulčić, *Pelagonija* 7.
41. B. Kitanovski, "Deux tombes appartenant à l'âge du fer ancien près de Prilep", *Starinar* II (1960), 209.
42. C. Truhelka, "Hügelgräber und Ringwälle auf der Hochebene Glasinac", *WMBH* 4, 101. M. Garašanin, D. Garašanin, "Fouilles arhéologiques à Radanje 'Krivi Dol' ", *ZSNM* 1 (1958), 9.
43. Katerina Rhomiopoulou, "Some pottery of the Early Iron Age from Western Macedonia", *BSA* 66 (1971), 353.
44. C. Koukouli-Chrysanthaki «Δυό Προϊστορικοί συνοικισμοί εἰς Θάσον», *AAA* 3 (1970), 215-222. See also the cave at Rhodochori, *AΔ* 19 (1964), Χρονικά 356.
45. E.J. Forsdyke, "Geometric Bronzes from Potidaea", *BMQ* 6 (1931), 82. E.J. Forsdyke, "Geometric Bronzes from Potidaea", *BMQ* 8 (1933-34), 108.
46. S. Foltiny, "Unveröffentliche Funde aus dem Naturhistorischen Museum. Früheisenseitliche Bronzefunde von Amphipolis", *MAGW* 93/94 (1964), 91.

THE INHABITANTS

1. Sakellariou, *Peuples,* 137-49, 246-47, 294-306.
2. See above.
3. Sakellariou, *Peuples,* 138-44, 158-61.
4. Ibid., 158-61.

5. Ibid., 81-137.

6. Ibid., 255-64.

7. Ibid., 258, 260.

8. Sakellariou, *Proto-Grecs*, 160.

9. Ibid., 9.

10. Ibid., 61-68, for earlier bibliography.

11. Ibid., 159-82, for earlier bibliography.

12. Ibid., 30-52.

13. Ibid., 162-71.

14. Sakellariou, *IEE*, 364-65.

15. Ibid., 366-69.

16. Sakellariou, *Proto-Grecs*, 166-67.

17. Herodotus 1.56.

18. Herodotus 8.43.

19. Sakellariou, *IEE*, 378-79.

20. Hammond, *Macedonia I*, 271 ff., 415-16.

21. Ibid., 414-15. The author, in the second volume of the work (654), revised this point of view and allowed the presence of Eordaic elements near Little Prespa in the Macedonian settlement under Philip II.

22. Thucydides 2.99.5.

23. Stephanus Byzantius, s.v. Ἐορδαῖοι.

24. Aristotle frag. 485, Rose edn.=Plutarch, *Theseus*, 16 and *Quaestiones Graecae*, 35; Konon *Narr.* 26, *FGrHist* frag. 25, Strabo 6. 3. 2 and 7 frag. 11, *Etymologicum Magnum*, s.v. Βόττεια.

25. O. Abel, *Makedonien vor König Philipp* (Leipzig, 1847) 26 ff.

26. Hammond, *Macedonia I*, 335 ff., 359, 369, 394, 410.

27. Ibid., 296, 336.

28. Homer *Iliad II*, 845-50.

29. The second hypothesis has been proposed by F. Papazoglou, *Balcanica* 66 and *Actes* 154.

30. Sakellariou, *Peuples*, 150-57.

31. Hammond, *Macedonia I*, 416-17.

32. Ibid., 305 ff.

33. Herodotus 7. 73.

34. Ibid., 8. 138.

35. Ibid., 6. 45. 7. 185.

36. Homer *Iliad III*, 185.

37. Papazoglou, *Balcanica* 73 and *RTFPhUB* 15-16.

38. Hammond, *Macedonia I*, 302 ff.

39. Herodotus 1. 57.

40. Sakellariou, *Peuples*, 160.

41. Thucydides 4. 109. Sakellariou, *Peuples*, 159-60.

42. Papazoglou, see n. 29 above.

43. Strabo 7, frag. II.

44. F.G. Sturz, *De dialecto macedonica et alexandrina liber* (1808), O. Abel, *Makedonien vor König Philipp* (1847), A. Fick, "Über die Sprache der Makedonier", *Orient und Occident* 2 (1864), 718-29, "Zum makedonischen Dialecte", *ZVS* 22 (1874), 193-235, E. Meyer, *Geschichte des Altertums* II (1893), 67, II 1 (1928²), 273-74. K.J. Beloch, *HZ* 79 (1897), 198-204, and *HZ* 101 (1908), 616-18; idem, in Gercke-Norden, *Einleitung in die Altertumswissenschaft* III (1912²), 150; idem, *Griechische Geschichte* I, 1 (1912), 69-71, 87-88 and 95, I, 2 (1913), 42-44 and IV, 1 (1925), 1-9. G. Hatzidakis, *Zur Abstammung der alten Makedonier* (1897); idem, «Ὑπὲρ τοῦ Ἑλληνισμοῦ τῶν Μακεδόνων», *Ἀθηνᾶ* 11 (1899), 131-57; idem "Zur Ethnologie der alten Makedonier", *IF* 11 (1900), 313-20; idem, "Zur Chronologie der griechischen Lautgesetze und zur Sprachfrage der alten Makedonier", *ZVS* 37 (1900), 150-54; idem, *Γλωσσολογικαί Μελέται* I (1901), 33-114; idem, «Καὶ πάλιν περὶ τοῦ Ἑλληνισμοῦ τῶν ἀρχαίων Μακεδόνων», *EEAΘ* 7 (1910-1911),

87-109; idem, Ἀκαδημεικὰ Ἀναγνώσματα (1928²), 29-31; idem, "L'Hellénisme de la Macédoine", *REG* 41 (1928), 410-13. G. Collin, *Rome et Grèce de 200 à 146 avant J.C.*, (1905) 74-76 J.B. Bury, *A History of Greece* (1906), 683. O. Hoffmann, *Die Makedonen, ihre Sprache und ihr Volkstum* (1906), F. Solmsen in his critique of Hoffmann's work, *BPW* (1907), 270-75. V. Lesny, "Ein Beitrag zur Sprache der alten Makedonen", *ZVS* 42 (1909), 297-302. A. Wilhelm, "Attische Urkunden", *SAWW* 165 (1911), treatise 6, 18. P. Perdrizet, "Contribution a l'étude du Macedonien", *BCH* 35 (1911), 125-31. W. Schmidt, in the work of Christ, *Geschichte der griechischen Literatur* II 1 (1920⁶), 2, n. 3. M. Holleaux, *Rome, la Grèce et les monarchies hellénistiques au IIIe s. avant J.C.* (1921), 272-73. G. Glotz, *Histoire Grecque* III, 208-11. S. Casson, *Macedonia, Thrace and Illyria* (1926), 158-62. E. Pais, *Histoire Romaine* I (1926), 461. E. Berve, *Das Alexanderreich auf prosopographischer Grundlage* I (1926), 328-32; idem, *Griechische Geschichte* XXXX, II (1933), 128-29 (and later editions). P. Giles, "The Peoples of Europe", *CAH* II (1926), 31. W. J. Ferguson, "The Leading Ideas of the New Period", *CAH* VII (1928), 2. E. Bevan, *A History of Egypt under the Ptolemaic Dynasty* (1927), 83. A. Keramopoullos, «Ἡ ἀρχαϊκὴ νεκρόπολις τοῦ Τρεμπένιστε παρὰ τὴν λίμνην τῆς Ἀχρίδος», *AE* 1927-1928, 80-105; idem, *Μακεδονία καὶ Μακεδόνες*, Athens, 1930; idem, «Ἀνασκαφαὶ καὶ ἔρευναι ἐν τῇ Ἄνω Μακεδονίᾳ», *AE* 1932, 102. U. Wilcken, *Griechische Geschichte* (1930³), 19 (1942⁴), 169 (cf. later editions). F. Geyer, *Makedonien bis zur Thronbesteigung Philipps II* (1930) 30-35. N.G.L. Hammond, "Prehistoric Epirus and the Dorian Invasion", *BSA* 32 (1931-1932), 131-79; idem *A History of Greece* (1959), 534; idem, Macedonia I, 370; II, 2-54. F.A. Wright, *Alexander the Great* (1934), 4-6. R. Cohen, *La Grèce et l'hellénisation du monde antique* (1934), 345-46; idem, *Athènes, une démocratie* (1936), 235. G. de Sanctis, *Storia dei Greci* I (1940²), 81-2. A.B. Cook, *Zeus* III, 1 (1940), 110-11. R. Paribeni, *La Macedonia sino ad Alessandro Magno* (1947), 9-21. H. Bengston, *Griechische Geschichte* (1950), 283, cf. also later editions). Kalléris, I II, 1 passim. Daskalakis, Ὁ Ἑλληνισμὸς τῆς ἀρχαίας Μακεδονίας (1960). C. Poghirc, "Considérations sur le lexique de l'ancien macédonien", *RevLing* 5 (1960), 135-45. T. Tzannetatos, "Archelaüs et le caractère hellénique de Macédoine au point de vue littéraire", *Actes du Ier Congrès Internat. des Ét. Balkan. et Sud-Est Européennes* II (1969), 79-81. A. Toynbee, *Some Problems of Greek History* (1969), 64-79. M. Sakellariou, «Ἡ ἀκμὴ τοῦ Ἀρχαϊκοῦ Ἑλληνισμοῦ - Μακεδονία», *IEE*, Β´ (1971), 237-38. J.K. Probonas, Ἡ συγγένεια μακεδονικῆς καὶ μυκηναϊκῆς διαλέκτου καὶ ἡ πρωτοελληνικὴ καταγωγὴ τῶν Μακεδόνων (1973); idem, «Μακεδονικὰ καὶ Ὁμηρικὰ γλωσσικά», Ἀρχαία Μακεδονία 2 (1977), 397-407.

45. K.O. Müller, *Über die Wohnsitze, die Abstammung und die ältere Geschichte des Makedonischen Volks* (1825). H. Hirt, *Die Indogermanen* I (1905), 149-50. G. Kazaroff, "Quelques observations sur la question de la nationalité des anciens Macédoniens", *REG* 23 (1910), 243-54. M. Rostovtzeff, *A History of the Ancient World* I (1926), 325-26; idem, *The Social and Economic History of the Hellenistic*

World II (1941), 1956. M. Budimir, "Griechisch und Makedonisch", *RIEB* 1 (1934), 281-82. N. Vulic, "Une nécropole antique près de Trebenište", *RIEB* 1 (1934), 163; idem, "La nécropole archaique de Trebenischte", *RA* 6 (1934), 34-35; idem, "De la nationalité des Péoniens", *MusB* 30 (1926), 107-117. A. Mayay, "Über des Verhältnis des Makedonischen zum Illyrischen", *Glotta* 32 (1953), 45-89.

46. D. Tzenoff, *Die Abstammung der Bulgaren* (1930), 378 ff.

47. B. Niese, *Geschichte der griechischen und makedonischen Staaten* I (1892), 23. J. Kaerst, *Geschichte des Hellenismus* I (1903), 99-103 (1927³), 156-60. T. Birt, *Alexander der Grosse und das Weltgriechentum* (1928³), 9. I. Russu, "Macedonica", *EphDac* 8 (1938), 105-232. E. Badian, "Greeks and Macedonians", *Macedonia and Greece in Late Classical and Early Hellenistic Time* (=*Studies in the History of Art*, vol. X, National Gallery of Art, Washington, editors: B. Bar-Sharrar, E. N. Borza), 1982, 33-51 (on the first page he writes, 'We so far have no real evidence on the structure of the ancient Macedonian language' but then goes on to repeatedly mention, without reservations, Macedonian speech as a special language.

48. G. Meyer, *JCIPh* 111 (1875), 185-92. U. v. Wilamowitz-Möllendorff, *Euripides Herakles* (1895), 11, n. 23. A.Thumb, *Handbuch der griechischen Dialekte* (1910), 288. A. Debrunner, "Griechen", *Reallexicon der Vorgeschichte* IV (1926), 516. E. Kornemann, *Die Alexandergeschichte des Königs Ptolemaios I von Aegyptos* (1935), 148. B. Beschewlieff, *AUS* 28 (1932), 1-76. P. Chantraine, "La langue des Macédoniens et leur onomastique", *BSL* 61 (1966), 157-66. V. Georgiev, "L'ethnogénèse de la péninsule balkanique d'après les données linguistiques", *StudBal* 5 (1971), 166. I. Pudić, "Die Sprache der alten Makedonen", *StudBal* 207-23. R.A. Crossland, "The Language of the Macedonians", *CAH* III 1, 1982, 843-47.

49. Kretschmer 283-88; idem, in A. Gercke, E. Norden, *Einleitung in die Altertumswissenschaft* I 6 (1927³), 87. C.D. Buck, *Introduction to the Study of the Greek Dialects* (1910), 280. E. Schwyzer, *Griechische Grammatik* I (1939), 69-70 V. Georgiev, *Introduzione alla storia delle lingue indeuropee* (1966), 189-96.

50. H. Hirt, *Die Indogermanen* II (1907), 603; idem, *Handbuch der griechischen Laut - und Formenlehre* (1912²), 30. W.W. Tarn, *Antigonos Gonatas* (1913), 179-81; idem, "Macedonia and Greece", *CAH* VII (1928), 197; idem, *The Hellenistic Civilisation* (1930²), 59. A. Jardé in A. Reinach, *L'Hellénisation du monde antique* (1914), 164; idem, *La formation du peuple grec* (1923), 395. E. Kornemann, *Vergangenheit und Gegenwart* 10 (1930), 449.

51. F. Lehmann-Haupt, in A. Gercke, E. Norden, *Einleitung in die Altertumswissenschaft* III (1923²), 121-23. A. Meillet, *Aperçu d' une histoire de la langue grecque* (1913), 36 (1928³), 58. P. Jouguet, *L'impérialisme macédonien* (1926), 79-81. A. W. Pickard-Cambridge, "The Rise of Macedonia", *CAH* VI (1927), 204. A. Momigliano, *Filippo il Macedone* (Florence, 1934), 3. J. Hatzfeld, La Grèce et son héritage (1945), 260.

52. Herodotus I 56, VIII 43. E. Badian, op. cit, 36, renders the meaning of what Herodotus says incorrectly as 'It makes the original Macedo-

nians identical with the original Dorians.'

53. E. Badian, op. cit, also believed that Herodotus counterfeited his history, which was fashioned within the framework of a series of endeavours to make the Macedonians appear as Greeks and which Alexander I was not yet aware of when he laid claim to the right to participate in the Olympic Games (see below). These ideas of E. Badian are the result of his mistake which we remarked upon in the preceding footnote. Herodotus said that the Dorians were the descendants of a branch of Macedonians who had migrated from Pindos to Doris. This is a story that relates to the Dorians and not the Macedonians. A tale constructed for the reason suspected by E. Badian would serve him directly and not indirectly. More to the point, one does not seem to be able to discern what would have inspired the idea that the Dorians were descendants of a Macedonian branch. The same difficulty arises when one deals with the possibility that this may be a counterfeit Dorian myth. The way things are, the only supposition permissible is that we are faced with an authentic tradition of the Dorians. The Macedonians could not have known that the Dorians were their descendants. This explains why Alexander did not mention this tradition when he laid claim to the right to compete in the Olympiad.

54. Sakellariou, *IEE*, 379. Pursued by the same author in, *Ethnè et dialectes Grecs à l'âge du Bronze* (forthcoming).

55. Walser, *Die Völkerschaften auf den Reliefs von Persepolis* (1966), 47. E. Herzfeld, *The Persian Empire* (1968), 310 and 349. N.G.L. Hammond, "The Extent of Persian Occupation in Thrace", *Chiron* 10 (1980), 53 ff.

56. Ellanikos *FGrHist* 4, frag. 74 (=Stephanus Byzantius, s.v. Μακεδονία)

57. Arrian *Anabasis* 2. 14. 4.

58. Polybius 7.8.9.

59. Livy 31.29.15.

60. Polybius 5.103.9.

61. Polybius 9. 37. 1.

62. Polybius 34. 7. 13. Strabo 7, frag. 9, Appian *Mac* 9.

63. *SIG* 867, lines 38-40.

64. Thucydides 2. 80. 82.

65. [Herodes] Περί Πολιτείας 22-24, 34-37. The date I follow is Daskalakis, 389.

66. Ephorus *FGrHist* 70 frag. 143 (=Strabo 8. 1. 3. [PseudoSkylax] lines 33,65, 66. Dionysius Calliphantis filius lines 24 and 31-36. Dionysius Periegeta, line 399.

67. Isocrates *Philip* 107-108. Daskalakis, 413, maintains that in this passage Isocrates distinguishes Macedonia from the 'land of the Greeks' and Macedonians from Greeks using political criteria (monarchical nation-democratic city-states), but his arguments do not carry the required weight.

68. Medeios, *FGrHist* 129, frag. 1 (=Strabo 11.14. 12)

69. Hesiod Ήοΐαι, frag. 7.

70. [Skymnos] line 622.

71. [Apollodorus] 3.8. 1. Aelianus *De natura animalium* 10. 48.

72. The date of the Olympiad is that of Daskalakis 270-73. Herodotus 5. 22.

73. Herodotus 9. 45.

74. Thucydides 2. 99. Euripides *TGF* (=Hyginus *Fabulae* 219). Euphorion *Inachus* (=Clemens Alexandrinus, 4, Klotz edn. 96). Aeschines Περί παραπ. 32-33. Isocrates *Philip* 105. Theopompus *FGrHist*, 115, frag. 353 (=Syn-

cellus, 499, Bonn edn.). Satyrus, *FGrHist* 631, 1 (=Theophilus *Ad Autolycum* 2.7). Diodorus 7.15-16, 12.4. Plutarch *Alexander* 2, 1. Pausanias 8. 40. 7-9. Arrian *Anabasis* 2. 5; 9. 3; 3. 1-2; 4. 11; 6.5; 26. 3. Dio Chrysostomus 4. 71. Pompeius Trogus *Prologi* 7. Justinian *Epitoma* 7. 1. 7-2. 14. Vellius Paterculus 1. 6. 4. Curtius 4. 22. Solinus 9. 12.

75. Isocrates *Philip* 122.

76. Plato *Respublica* 5. 16. 470 E. Xenophon *Agesilaus* 2, 51 and 74. Isocrates *Evagora* 50, and *Panegyricus* 96. Soranus *Vita Hippocratis*, 81.

77. Isocrates *Philip*, 154.

78. See, for example H. Bengston, *Die Staats verträge des Altertums* II, Munich and Berlin, 1962, no. 231, 257, 280.

79. Thrasymachus, frag. 2. H. Diels, *Die Fragmente der Vorsokratiker* (=Clemens Alexandrinus, *Stromateis* 6. 2. 17). See Daskalakis, 376 ff.

80. Demosthenes 1. 3. 16. and 24; 5. 3. 31; 19. 327 (where the context of nationality, *Macedonians*, in the phrase, «Μακεδόνες καί βάρβαροι νῦν 'Αμφικτίονες εἶναι βιάζονται» refers in particular to Philip because Philip participated in Amphiktyony as an individual and not as a representative of Macedonia).

81. Demosthenes 19. 305.

82. Suidas s.v. Έλλάνικος.

83. Ephorus *FGrHist* 70, frag. 162 (= Strabo 14. 5. 23).

84. Daskalakis, 369-446, maintains the same point of view as self-evident truth. But this point of view needs proof which is furnished above.

85. Plato *Alcidiades* 2. 141 Δ, *Gorgias* 471 A-Δ. Theopompus, *FGrHist* 115, frag. 27 (=Polybius 8. 11.1).

86. Strattis, frag. 28 (Edmonds, *The Fragments of Attic Comedy*).

87. Plutarch *Alexander* 47, 3.

88. Livy 31. 29. 15.

89. Plutarch *Alexander* 51. 4.

90. Plutarch *Eumenes* 14.4.

91. Plutarch *Antonius* 27.4.

92. Fragment of Arrian on papyrus, *PSI* 12 (1955), no. 1284.

93. Pausanias 4. 29. 1.

94. Curtius 6. 9. 34-36.

95. Athenaeus 3. 122 A.

96. See R.A. Crossland, op. cit, 846-47.

97. The latest and, moreover, the most complete and exact catalogue of Macedonian words, along with extensive notes, is found in Kalléris I, 66-304. 153 entries are recorded. From these I am deducting the names of Gods, feasts, months and the entry περίττια which is not directly verified; I am adding, however, the lemma σφύραινα.

98. Kalléris I, 277 and 281-285.

99. Ibid., 66-304.

100. Ibid.,

101. Ibid., 289 ff.

102. Ibid., II, passim; I, 488 ff. Some of the phenomena which are mentioned there are not suitable for the introduction of conclusions related to the neighbouring dialects: these are survivals of common archaism of the Greek language or later innovations arising from the separation of Greek dialects. But these phenomena are useful: as they are not Attic, they demonstrate that the point of view concerning the Macedonian adoption of the Attic dialect is baseless (see page 54).

103. Kalléris II, 1, 490.

104. Ibid., 491-92.

105. Plutarch *Quomodo adulescens poetas audire debeat* 6, and *Quaestiones Graecae* 9 (Moralia 22C and 292E).

106. Eustathius Παρεκβ. Φ 540, 1250, 57.

107. Kalléris II, 1, 346, n. 1 and 348, n. 2.

108. Ibid., 354, n. 7.

109. Ibid., 348, n. 2.

110. Ibid., I, 85, II, 1, 342-55.

111. Ibid., II, 1, 329-34.

112. Kalléris, I, 258.

113. Ibid., II, 1, 334-48.

114. Ibid., II, 1, 542-49.

115. This catalogue of the Gods is mentioned in an unpublished inscription in the Thessalonike Museum. I should like to thank Mr. C. Voutyras who pointed it out to me.

116. Kalléris I, 183, n. 4, II, 1, 593, n. 3, 541.

117. Kalléris I, 241-42.

118. A. Debrunner, "Griechen", *RLV* 4, 2 (1926), 519-21.

119. Kalléris, I, 149-50. 158-59, II, 1, 538-39.

120. Ibid., I, 171-72.

121. Ibid., I, 202.

122. Ibid., II, 1, 560-62.

123. Ibid., II, 1, 560 ff.

124. Ibid., I, 101-104.

125. Ibid., I, 184-85.

126. *IG* X II, 1, 48.

127. Kalléris, I, 210-17.

128. Ibid., 227-28.

129. Ibid., 236.

130. Ibid., I, 237-38, II, 1, 565-66.

131. Ibid., I, 247, II, 503.

132. Ibid., I, 271.

133. Ibid., I, 273, II, 1, 571.

134. Ibid., I, 276.

135. Düll, *Götterkulte*.

136. Kalléris, II, 1, 569-70.

137. Ibid., II, 1, 564.

138. Ibid., I, 118-30.

139. Ibid., II, 1, 538.

140. Ibid., II, 1, 537-38.

THE ESTABLISHMENT AND CONSOLIDATION OF THE MACEDONIAN KINGDOM

1. Hesiod frag. 7.

2. Herodotus 7. 127.

3. Herodotus 7.131.

4. Diodorus 7.16.

5. Herodotus 7.127.

6. Herodotus 8.138.

7. Thucydides 2.99.

8. Herodotus 8.137-139.

9. D. Evangelides, «Ψήφισμα τοῦ Βασιλέως Νεοπτολέμου ἐκ Δωδώνης», *AE* (1956), 1 ff. N.G.L. Hammond, *Epirus* (Oxford, 1967), 525 ff and 701 ff; Hammond, *Macedonia* I, 119 ff; II 22 ff, 39-54.

10. Strabo 7.7.8 and 9.5.11.

11. Ekataios *FGrHist* 1 frag. 103 and 107.

12. Strabo 7.7.9.

13. Hammond, *Macedonia* I, map 1 and 12 ff and *Macedonia* II, 69 ff.

14. Justin 7.4.1.

15. Hammond, *Macedonia* II 63 ff.

16. Strabo 7.7.8.

17. Herodotus 5.18-21.

18. Justin 7.5.1.

19. Hammond, *Macedonia* II 81, 84-85, 104.

20. Thucydides 4.109.

21. Plutarch *Kimon* 14.2.
22. Thucydides 4.109.
23. Herodotus 7.127.
24. Thucydides 1.61.
25. Thucydides 2.80.
26. Tod *GHI* 61=M-L *GHI* 65.
27. Thucydides 2. 95-98.
28. Thucydides 2.100.
29. Thucydides 4.83.
30. Thucydides 4.124.
31. Thucydides 4.124.
32. Hammond, *Macedonia* I 104-108.
33. Thucydides 7.9.
34. M-L *GHI* 51=*IG* I² 105.
35. Xenophon Ellenika 5.2.38; the descent of Sirra is much debated; see P. Cloché, *Histoire de la Macédoine* (Paris, 1960), 86 and Hammond *Macedonia* II 15 ff.
36. N. Petrovic, "Demir Kapija", *Starinar*, 12 (1961), 217 ff.
37. Thucydides 2.100.
38. Tod *GHI* 111.
39. Tod *GHI* 129.
40. Demosthenes 1.5; N.G.L. Hammond, "Philip's Tomb in Historical Context", *GRBS* 19 (1978), 333.
41. SEG 23.471.13; Cf. N.G.L. Hammond, *Epirus* 527 ff.
42. Arrian *Anabasis* 7.9.4.
43. Diodorus 16.2. 4-6.
44. N.G.L. Hammond, *Migrations and Invasions and Adjacent Areas* (Park Ridge, New Jersey 1976) 36.51.
45. Arrian *Anabasis* 7.9.2.
46. Herodotus 5.17.
47. Arrian *Anabasis* 7.9.3.
48. Thucydides 2.80.6 and 99.2; *IG* II² 190 with additional readings.
49. Strabo 7. frag. 11 and 20; «τούτων δὲ πάντων οἵ Ἀργεάδαι... καὶ Χαλκιδεῖς».
50. Stephanus Byzantius s.v. Argeou.
51. *FGRHist* 135/6; Marsyas F. 13.
52. Appian *Syr.* 63.
53. Strabo 7 frag. 20.
54. *IG* IV 617.17.
55. Thucydides 4.124.
56. Thucydides 2.99; 4.93.
57. Thucydides 2.100.
58. *FGrHist* 135/6 T. 1.
59. Ph. Petsas, "A few examples of Epigraphy from Pella", *BSt* 4 (1963), 162.
60. *SGDI* 2, 2759.
61. P. Perdrizet, "Men", *BCH* 20 (1896), 73.
62. Palatine Anthology 7.51.
63. Aelianus VH 13.4.
64. Aristotle *Politics* 1311 b31.
65. Gellius *Noctes Atticae* 15.20.
66. Justin 13.4.7.
67. Diodorus 18.4.3.
68. Arrian *Anabasis* 7.9.5.
69. Thucydides 1.57.
70. *IG* I² 71.
71. Pausanias 10.3.3 and 10.8.2.
72. *SIG* 135=Tod *GHI* 111.
73. Mélanges G. Daux 22 and 24.
74. Diodorus 16.71.2.
75. Arrian *Anabasis* 1.27.4.
76. Arrian *Anabasis* 1.16.5.
77. Plutarch *Alexander* 11.12.
78. Arrian *Anabasis* 1.9.9. «ὅσοι ξένοι Φιλίππου ἢ Ἀλεξάνδρου ἢ ὅσοι πρόξενοι Μακεδόνων ἐγένοντο», the words probably taken from a record of the decision by the Greek League.
79. Porphyrios *FGrHist* 3.691 frag. 1.
80. Diodorus 16.3.1
81. Arrian *Anabasis* 3.27.2 Cf. Diodorus 19.51.4.

82. Hesychius s.v. *Peliganes* Syria 23 (1942-43) and 21 ff.
83. Strabo 7 frag. 2.
84. Herodotus 8.138 Cf. 6.65.4 and 7.147.2 (οἱ πάρεδροι).
85. Thucydides 2.100.
86. As in Diodorus 16.94.3.
87. Aristotle *Politics* 131 b 8-35.
88. Thucydides 4.124.1.
89. Anaximenes *FGrHist* 72. frag. 4. Various interpretations are explored by G.T.Griffith in Hammond, *Macedonia* II, 705 ff.
90. Athenaeus 14.659 F.
91. *Pap.Graec. Vindob.* 31954.
92. *FGrHist* F³.
93. Plutarch, *De Fortuna Alexandri* 331 F.
94. Pausanias 7.8.9 and Appian *Macedonica* 2.
95. Curtius 3.6.17; 'ingenita illi genti erga reges suos veneratio'.
96. Curtius 10.7.2.
97. Justin 7.2.9-12.
98. Justin 9.8.3: 'multos filios ex variis matrimoniis regio more susceptos'.
99. *IG* I², 71.
100. Curtius 8.6.28.
101. Curtius 4.7.31.
102. Curtius 8.1.18.
103. Thucydides 1.58.2 (τῆς ἑαυτοῦ γῆς).

ART IN THE ARCHAIC AND CLASSICAL PERIOD

1. M. Andronikos, *Βεργίνα I*.
2. Information for all these finds is limited and drawn from the brief reports of each excavator in «Ἀρχαιολογικά Χρονικά» in *Ἀρχαιολογικόν Δελτίον* and "Chroniques des Fouilles" in *Bulletin de Correspondance Hellénique*. Though they may not be absolutely accurate they represent the information contained in D. Leekly and N. Efstratiou, *Archaeological Excavations in Eastern and Northern Greece* (Park Ridge, New Jersey, 1980).
3. G. Bakalakis, "Therme, Thessaloniki", *AK*, Beiheft 1, 1963 30-34; G. Bakalakis, «Νεάπολις, Χριστούπολις, Καβάλα», *AE* 1936 59-65.
4. K. Kostoglou - Despoine, *Προβλήματα τῆς Παριανῆς Πλαστικῆς τοῦ 5ου αἰ. π.Χ.* (Thessalonike 1979), 69.
5. T. Stephanidou, «Ἐπιτύμβια στήλη ἀπό τό Δίον Πιερίας», *ΑΔ* 30 (1975), 35-43.
6. Unpublished exhibit in Thessalonike, Archaeological Museum.
7. W. Fuchs, *Die Skulptur der Griechen*, (Munich, 1969), 486, fig. 570.
8. M. Andronikos, "Stèle Funéraire de Kassandra» *BCH* 86 (1962), 261-267.
9. Unpublished find in Kavala, Archaeological Museum.
10. Olynthus I-XIV.
11. M. Andronikos, *BSt*.
12. D. Lazarides, *Νεάπολις, Χριστούπολις, Καβάλα: Ὁδηγός Μουσείου Καβάλας* (Athens 1969).
13. Unpublished.
14. Still more markedly clumsy and provincial is the stele from Aiane near Kozani, today in the Louvre, Paris.
15. G. Bakalakis, *Ἀνάγλυφα* (Thessalonike, 1969), 41 ff.
16. Awaiting publication by T. Stephanidou-Tiberiou in *ΑΔ*.
17. Unpublished.

18. M. Andronikos and others, *The Greek Museums* (Athens 1974), 255, fig. 263.
19. *The Search for Alexander. An Exhibition,* The Greek Ministry of Culture and Sciences, no. 152, fig. 24.
20. Unpublished.
21. E. Giouri, *Ὁ Κρατήρας τοῦ Δερβενιοῦ* (Athens 1978). G. Varoufakis, "Metallurgical Investigation of the Bronze Krater of Derveni" in *Aspects of Early Metallurgy by the Historical Metallurgical Society and the British Museum Research Laboratory.*
22. M. Andronikos, *ΑΑΑ;* idem, "The Royal Tombs at Aigai", in *Philip;* idem, *Acta.*

ZENITH AND END OF THE MACEDONIAN KINGDOM

A Note on Sources.

The ancient literary sources for the period covered by this chapter are of uneven quality. For Philip II there is a continuous narrative in Diodorus XVI and Justinus VII-IX, supplemented by the contemporary speeches of the Athenian orators Demosthenes and Aeschines, and the epideictic oratory of Isocrates; to these may be added Plutarch's *Lives* of Demosthenes and Phocion. For Alexander five main authors are extant, Arrian, Diodorus, Plutarch, Curtius and Justinus; of these the best is Arrian, who bases his narrative on the reliable contemporary account of Ptolemy and, to some extent, on Aristobulus. The rest draw on a variety of sources, some glorifying Alexander (these go back partly to the court historian Callisthenes) others attacking him; to evaluate these sources is often extremely difficult, and few show interest in Macedonia itself.

For the period after Alexander there is a continuous narrative in Diodorus XVIII-XX, which can be supplemented from Arrian's Τά μετ᾽ Ἀλέξανδρον, and Plutarch's *Lives* of Eumenes, Demetrius I and Phocion. Behind Arrian and Diodorus stands the lost work of an excellent and truthful author, Hieronymus of Cardia. But after the battle of Ipsus Diodorus breaks off and one has to fall back on the feeble Justinus XVI, XVII, XXIV and XXV for a continuous account; there are also details in Plutarch's *Life* of Pyrrhus, and (for the Gaulish invasion) in Pausanias. Antigonus's reign rests on scraps of information and, for his later years, on Plutarch's *Life* of Aratus which draws on that statesman's *Memoirs;* but this evidence is better for Greece than for Macedonia except where Macedonian affairs impinge on Greek. Polybius's *History* begins in 221 B.C., but book II contains an account of the growth of Achaia and of the Illyrian War of 229 B.C. which is directly relevant to the reigns of Demetrius II and Antigonus III. Plutarch's *Lives* of Agis and Cleomenes, which utilize the lost history of Phylarchus, also contain material relevant to Macedonia.

For the wars with Rome there is a first-class source, the *History* of Polybius. Unhappily after book V this survives only fragmentarily and must be supplemented from Livy and the untrustworthy narratives of Appian *(Macedonica* and *Syriaca),* Diodorus and Dio Cassius (largely in the late abridgment of Zonaras). For Macedonian affairs Livy relies closely on Polybius, whereas Trogus (Justinus' original), Appian and Dio all use him indirectly through sources which also draw on

Roman material of lesser value. There are also *Lives* of Flamininus, Cato and Philopoemen by Plutarch.

Fortunately our frequently indifferent literary sources can be helped out by a growing number of inscriptions from Macedonian or Greek sites in Europe or Asia. To take a few examples, the date of the outbreak of the Chremonidean War depends on an Attic inscription; relations between Antigonus Doson (and Philip V) and the Carian dynast, Olympichus of Alinda, have been clarified by the publication of inscriptions from Labraunda; and the replies of various Macedonian cities to a request for *asylie* (roughly freedom from attack) for the temple of Asclepius at Cos throw light on the constitutional relations of the cities and the king in the reign of Antigonus I. The organization of the Antigonid army is clearer since the discovery of fragments on an army code from the reign of Philip V at Amphipolis and another such fragment from Chalcis from the same period; other inscriptions furnish information on the relationship of the king and the temples. It is indeed primarily from epigraphic sources that the historian can hope substantially to extend his knowledge of the economic and social life of Hellenistic Macedonia. Finally, our knowledge of urbanization and the material conditions of life is being constantly improved by excavations at such centres as Pella, Edessa and Vergina, as well as at smaller sites through Macedonia.

Select Bibliography.

Four useful biographies of Philip II which cover most aspects of his reign are: A. Momigliano, *Filippo il Macedone*, Florence, 1934; P. Cloché, *Un fondateur d'empire, Philippe II, roi des Macédoniens*, St. Etienne, 1955; J.R. Ellis, *Philip II and Macedonian Imperialism*, London, 1976; and G. Cawkwell, *Philip of Macedon*, London-Boston, 1978; of these the last two carry up-to-date bibliographies. More recently several distinguished scholars contributed to the publication of the book *Philip of Macedon* (ed. M. B. Hatzopoulos - L. D. Loukopoulos, Athens 1980), treating of Philip's personality and achievements from different points of view. Several important articles on Philip's career and policy are collected in S. Perlman ed. *Philip and Athens*, Cambridge-New York, 1973; and there is a good recent treatment of Philip by Claude Mossé in *Le Monde grec et l'Orient*, ed. E. Will, Cl. Mossé and P. Goukowsky: Vol. 2, *Le IVe siècle et l'époque hellénistique*, 42-64.

Alexander is dealt with by P. Goukowsky in the same work, 247-333, with bibliography, 247-8; but like so many studies of Alexander the emphasis is mainly on his expedition and aims. A selection of such biographies is: U. Wilcken, *Alexander der Grosse*, Leipzig, 1931; W.W. Tarn, *Alexander the Great* (two vols: i. narrative; ii. sources and studies), Cambridge, 1948-1950 (reprint 1979); R.D. Milns, *Alexander the Great*, London, 1968; F. Schachermeyr, *Alexander der Grosse: das Problem seiner Persönlichkeit und seines Wirkens*, Vienna, 1973; and P. Green, *Alexander of Macedon*, Harmondsworth, 1974[2]. There is a useful set of essays in G&R 12 (1965), and a collection of the more fundamental articles on Alexander collected by G.T. Griffith, *Alexander the Great: the main problems*, Cambridge, 1966; this deals with problems affecting Macedonia as well as Asia. Macedonia itself in Alexander's reign is treated more specifically by D. Kanatsoulis in *Antipatros als Feldherr und Staatsmann in der Zeit Philipps und Alexanders des Grossen*, Thes-

salonike, 1959.

The best recent study of the Hellenistic age including Macedonia from all aspects is C. Préaux, *Le Monde hellénistique: La Grèce et l'Orient* (323-146 av.J.-C.), I-II, Paris, 1978.

The political history of Macedonia during the Hellenistic period is well covered in E. Will, *Histoire politique du monde hellénistique*, I-II (Nancy, 1979-80[2]). For the period down to Ipsus see E. Manni, *Demetrio Poliorcete*, Rome, 1951; M.J. Fontana, *Le lotte per la succesione di Alessandro Magno dal 323 ad 315*, Palermo, 1960; M. Fortuna, *Cassandro re di Macedonia*, Rome 1965; P. Briant, *Antigone le Borgne; les débuts de sa carrière et les problèmes de l'assemblée macédonienne*. Paris, 1973. *Pyrrhos*, Paris, 1957, by P. Lévêque, discusses his relations with Macedonia; and the reigns of the Antigonid kings are treated in the following biographical studies: W.W. Tarn, *Antigonos Gonatas*, Oxford, 1913; W. Fellmann, *Antigonos Gonatas, König der Makedonen und die griechischen Staaten*, Würzburg, 1930; M.T. Piraino, *Antigono Dosone, re di Macedonia*, Palermo, 1954; F. W. Walbank, *Philip V of Macedon*, Cambridge, 1940 (reprint with revisions, Hamden, Conn., 1967); P. Meloni, *Perseo e la fine della monarchia macedone*, Rome 1953. On the wars between Macedonia and Rome see G. De Sanctis, *Storia dei Romani*, III. 2 and IV. 1, Turin, 1917-23; IV. 3, Florence, 1964; *CAH*, VII-VIII, Cambridge, 1928-1930 (a new edition is in preparation); H.H. Scullard, *A History of the Roman World, 753-146 B.C.*, London, 1964[3]; R.M. Errington, *The Dawn of Empire: Rome's Rise to World Power*, London, 1971; C. Nicolet and others, *Rome et la conquête du monde méditerranéen*, II, *Genèse d'un empire (227-27 av. J.-C.)*, Paris, 1978 (with excellent bibliography).

The internal political organization of Macedon during this period is touched on in G. Corradi, *Studi ellenistici*, Turin, 1929 and H. Bengtson, *Die Strategie in der hellenistischen Zeit*, II, Munich, 1944, 317 ff. The position of the cities is discussed in R. Herzog and G. Klaffenbach, *Asylie-Urkunden aus Kos* in *ADAW*, 1952, 1, and in H. Bengtson, *Historia*, iii, 1955, 456-63; see too D. Kanatsoulis, *Μακεδονικά*, iv, 1960, 232-245, «Ἡ Μακεδονικὴ πόλις». On Pella as a centre of Greek culture under Antigonus I see Tarn's biography of *Antigonos Gonatas* mentioned above.

Finally mention should be made of the papers dealing with Macedonia in *Ἀρχαία Μακεδονία*, I and II, Thessalonike, 1970 and 1977, which contain the Proceedings of the first two international symposia on ancient Macedonia held in Thessalonike in 1968 and 1973.

ART IN THE HELLENISTIC PERIOD

1. *Olynthus* XII (Baltimore, 1946). M. Andronikos, «Γιά τά τείχη τῆς Ὀλύνθου», *Μακεδονικά* 2 (1955), 129-42.
2. Makaronas, *ΑΔ 1960*.
3. Vickers, *JHS*.
4. Makaronas, *ΑΔ 1960*.
5. Petsas, *Ἀρχαία Μακεδονία* 220. Makaronas, *Ἀρχαία Μακεδονία* 162-67.
6. *Πέλλα*, I, 38 ff.
7. Vickers, *JHS*, 164 ff.
8. Pandermalis, *Ἀρχαία Μακεδονία* 338 ff.
9. *Πέλλα* 1, 57 ff. Vickers, *JHS*, 165 ff.
10. Pandermalis, *Ἀρχαία Μακεδονία* 331.
11. Petsas, *Ἀρχαία Μακεδονία* 226. Vickers, *JHS*,

167.
12. Ph. M. Petsas, *ΑΔ* (1961-1962) Χρονικά 218.
13. C. Makaronas, *ΑΔ* 26 (1971) Χρονικά 399 and *ΑΔ* 27 (1972) Χρονικά 505-507.
14. Bakalakis, *Ἀρχαία Μακεδονία* 252.
15. Stella Miller, *Hellenistic Macedonian Architecture, its Style and Painted Ornamentation* (Ann Arbor, Michigan, 1972).
16. E. Juri, «Τό ἐν Ἀφύτει ἱερόν τοῦ Διονύσου καί τό ἱερόν τοῦ Ἄμμωνος Διός», *Neue Forschungen in griechischen Heiligtumern, Intern. Symposium in Olympia* (1974), 135-50.
17. Andronikos, *Ἀνάκτορον*.
18. R.A. Tomlinson, "Ancient Macedonian Symposia", *Ἀρχαία Μακεδονία 1 (1970)*, 308-15.
19. Makaronas, *Ἀρχαία Μακεδονία*, 167. A.W. Lawrence, *Greek Architecture*, 306.
20. G. Bakalakis, M. Andronikos, *ΑΔ* 24 (1969) Χρονικά 336 ff. and *ΑΔ* 25 (1970) 390 ff. Andronikos, *Vergina*, 18.
21. C. Makaronas, *ΑΔ 1960*.
22. For Macedonian tombs in general see J. Touratsoglou, *Lefkadia* (Athens, 1973), 3 ff. For specific memorial structures of this category see: Petsas, *Τάφος*; C. Makaronas, *Μακεδονικά* 2 (1952), 634-36. K.F. Kinch, "Le Tombeau de Niaousta: Tombeau Macédonien", *Mémoires de l'Académie Royale des sciences et des lettres de Danemark, Section des lettres* 4 (1920), 283-88. Aikaterini Rhomiopoulou, J. Touratsoglou, «Ὁ Μακεδονικός Τάφος τῆς Νιάουστας» *AE*, 1971, 146-64. Rhomiopoulou, *AAA*. Andronikos *AAA*.
23. Petsas, *Τάφος*.
24. K. Rhomaios, *Ὁ Μακεδονικός τάφος τῆς Βεργίνας* (Athens, 1951).
25. Kotzias, *AE*, Makaronas, *ΑΔ* 1963. A. Daffa-Nikonanou, «Ἑλληνιστικός τάφος τοῦ ἀρχαίου νεκροταφείου τῆς Βεργίνας», *Μακεδονικά* 9 (1969), 225-36. M. Andronikos, "Sarissa", *BCH* 94 (1970), 91-107.
26. Makaronas, *ΑΔ* 1963. D. Lazaridis, «Ἀνασκαφή Τύμβου Νικήσιανης», *ΠΑΕ*, 1959, 47-48, pls. 52-55.
27. Drougou-Touratsoglou.
28. Concerning technique see: Touratsoglou, *Ἀρχαία Μακεδονία*. Concerning mosaics in Macedonia see Andronikos, *Bst*.
29. Touratsoglou, *ΑΔ*.
30. Andronikos, *Ἀνάκτορον*.
31. Concerning Macedonian painting in general see Andronikos, *Bst*.
32. Pliny *Natural History*, 7.125.
33. Loukianos, Herodotus and Aëtius, 4.
34. C. Makaronas, Stella Miller, "The Tomb of Lyson and Kallikles", *Archaeology* 27 (1974), 248-59.
35. Eugenia Giouri, «Ἡ κεραμεική τῆς Χαλκιδικῆς στόν 4ο αἰ. π.Χ.», *Κέρνος Γ. Μπακαλάκη* (Thessalonike, 1972), 6-14.
36. Drougou-Touratsoglou, 115-16 and 167-68.
37. V. Sinn, *Die homerischen Becher. Hellenistische Reliefkeramik aus Makedonien* (Berlin, 1979).
38. *Treasures of Ancient Macedonia* (Athens, 1979) with a general bibliography and a bibliography according to subject. *Μέγας Ἀλέξανδρος, Ἱστορία καί θρύλος στήν τέχνη* (Athens, 1980).
39. Kotzias, *AE*, Rhomiopoulou, *AAA*. A.S. Arvanitopoulos, «Χρυσᾶ, ἀργυρᾶ καί ἐλεφάντινα κτερίσματα τοῦ τάφου τῆς Δημητριάδος», *Πολέμων* 3 (1947), 81-90.
40. D.E. Strong, *Greek and Roman Gold and Silver Plate* (London, 1966).

41. Drougou-Touratsoglou, 183-86.
42. Papa, *Kunstwerke*.

MACEDONIA UNDER THE ROMANS

Rome's policy towards Macedonia, which was the most redoubtable power of the Greek world, played an important role in the history of Roman imperialism. Consequently, an account of the events which led to the fall of the Antigonid monarchy is to be found in all general histories of Rome and of the Hellenistic world. Most noteworthy in scope and quality are those by B. Niese, *Geschichte der griechischen und makedonischen Staates seit der Schlacht bei Chäronea*, III (Gotha, 1903), by G. De Sanctis, *Storia dei Romani*, IV 3 (Rome, 1964) and by E. Will, *Histoire politique du monde hellénistique*, II (Nancy, 1967). See also the studies by G. Colin, *Rome et la Grèce de 200 à 146 av. J. Christ* (Paris, 1906), by P. Meloni, *Perseo e la fine della monarchia macedone* (Rome, 1953) and by E. Badian, *Foreign Clientelae 264-70 B.C.* (Oxford, 1958). As a Greek land, Macedonia proper, which is the focus of the present work, finds its place in the histories of Greece under Roman domination. In this connection G.F. Hertzberg's monumental work, *Die Geschichte Griechenlands unter der Herrschaft der Römer*, I, II (Halle, 1866, 1868), has not yet been replaced. Under the title *Roman Greece* in the series edited by T. Frank, *An economic survey of Ancient Rome*, IV (1936), J.A.O. Larsen has provided an in-depth study of the sources (which he has collected and translated), which throw light on the economic life of Greece and Macedonia from the Roman conquest to the reign of Gallienus. D. Kanatsoulis' general history of Macedonia, *Ἱστορία τῆς Μακεδονίας μέχρι τοῦ Μεγάλου Κωνσταντίνου* (Thessalonike, 1964), is a short survey addressed to the general reader, yet it is also the only book which deals with the subject as a whole. In particular the chapter on the administration of Macedonia during the Roman period is a first attempt to synthetise all our evidence for the institutions of Roman Macedonia. The chapter dealing with imperial Macedonia in the monumental work *Ἱστορία τοῦ Ἑλληνικοῦ Ἔθνους*, vol. VI (1977), 189-202 is by the same author.

The Roman province of Macedonia, composed of two distinct areas — Macedonia proper and southern Illyria, united for more than four centuries under the same administration — has not yet been studied as a whole. In general works on the Roman provinces Macedonia is treated as a poor relative. The Illyrian regions in particular are neglected, a fact that is due as much to the poverty of our sources as to the lack of preliminary studies on the subject. There is only one treatise worth mentioning here, Mommsen's account in the fifth volume of his *Römische Geschichte: Die Provinzen von Caesar bis Diocletian* (Berlin, 1885; 1894⁴; 1927¹⁰). Recently, T. Sarikakis has given us in his work on the *fasti* an aid to research on the history of the province: *Ρωμαῖοι ἄρχοντες τῆς ἐπαρχίας Μακεδονίας, Μέρος Α΄, Ἀπό τῆς ἱδρύσεως τῆς ἐπαρχίας μέχρι τῶν χρόνων τοῦ Αὐγούστου (148-27 π.Χ.). Μέρος Β΄, Ἀπό τοῦ Αὐγούστου μέχρι τοῦ Διοκλητιανοῦ (27 π.Χ. -284 μ.Χ.)* (Thessalonike, 1971, 1977). I have myself studied the evolution of urban life and of municipal organization in *Makedonski gradovi u rimsko doba* (Les cités Macédoniennes à l'époque romaine), (Skopje, 1957), and, more recently, I have dealt with the

province - its territory, population, army, cities and regional koina: "Quelques aspects de l'histoire de la province de Macédoine" in *Aufstieg und Niedergang der römischen Welt*, II, 7 (Tübingen, 1979), 302-369.

There are many studies of the historical geography and topography of the whole of Macedonia or part of it. The most recent account of its historical geography, by N.G.L. Hammond, *A history of Macedonia, vol. I. Historical geography and prehistory* (Oxford, 1972), is based on first-hand knowledge of most of the region, and exploits the material accumulated by the excavations and researches conducted during the last few decades. R. Mack's unpublished dissertation, *Grenzmarken und Nachbarn Makedoniens im Norden und Westen* (Göttingen, 1951) is very useful for the study of upper Macedonia thanks to its critical and judicious interpretation of the sources. D. Samsaris has produced a well documented study of the historical geography of Eastern Macedonia, characterised by attention to detail and taking account of recent publications *(Ἱστορική Γεωγραφία τῆς Ἀνατολικῆς Μακεδονίας κατά τήν ἀρχαιότητα*, Thessalonike, 1976).

Finally we should mention among works dealing with the whole of Macedonia the still unsuperseded and useful compilation by M. Dimitsas, *Ἡ Μακεδονία ἐν λίθοις φθεγγομένοις καί μνημείοις σωζομένοις* (Athens, 1896), as also the prosopography drawn up by D. Kanatsoulis, *Μακεδονική προσωπογραφία (ἀπό τοῦ 148 π.Χ. μέχρι τῶν χρόνων τοῦ Μ. Κωνσταντίνου)* (Thessalonike, 1955, 1967).

1. Cf. Livy XLV, 30, 2: '... quanta Macedonia esset, quum divisui facilis, quam se ipsa quaeque contenta pars esset, Macedones quoque ignorabant'. Quotations from sources in this chapter are from the texts edited by J.A.O. Larsen.

2. It does not seem justifiable to speak about 'four Macedonian states' or 'four republics', as is the fashion. The sources mention only *merides*. It is worth noting that these *merides* were designated by numbers and that they were not abolished when Macedonia became a province.

3. A revolt is attested as early as 167 B.C. A few years later the massacre of the whole body of the *synedroi* at Pella, organized by a certain Damasippos, caused a Roman mission to be sent to Macedonia in order to examine the situation. In 151 B.C. the Macedonians themselves appealed to Scipio Aemilianus to arbitrate in their disputes.

4. The formula *in provinciae formam redacta* appears only once in our sources (Livy *per.* 45) to define (contrary to what might be expected) the change which occurred in 167, and not that of 148 B.C. On the date of the creation of the province of Macedonia, see, most recently, Papazoglou *ANRW* II, 7, 303-308, where may be found (n. 2) references to the studies of P.A. MacKay and of M. Gwyn Morgan, which throw new light on the problem.

5. In support of this view one might adduce the fact that the era of 148 B.C. was 'a Macedonian era' in the national rather than the provincial sense of the word. Given that the province of Macedonia was composed of two parts ethnically and historically distinct, Macedonia proper and Illyria (see below), the era, which is wrongly designated as 'provincial', applies only to the first of these parts.

6. For the *fasti* of the province in the Republican era, cf. T. Sarikakis, *Ἄρχοντες* Α΄ (Thes-

salonike, 1971) and my remarks in *ANRW* II, 7, 309-311.

7. I have studied exhaustively the relations of the Dardanians and the Scordisci with Antigonid and Roman Macedonia in my book *The Central Balkan Tribes in pre-Roman times* (Amsterdam, 1978). A more succint account of the barbarian incursions into Macedonia under the Republic and of the firstly defensive then expansionist wars led by the Romans against Macedonia's northern neighbours is given in Paparoglou, *ANRW* II, 7, 312-321, where are also to be found references to the sources and the bibliography to date.

8. *SIG³* 700.

9. S. Kougeas, *Ἑλληνικά* 5 (1932), 5 ff. and *SIG³* 710.

10. Cicero *In Pis.* 34 (84). On Piso's activities in Macedonia cf. the articles of T. Sarikakis in *Platon* 18 (1966), 317-336, and of Julia Loomis, "Cicero and Thessalonica, Politics and Provinces", *Ἀρχαία Μακεδονία* II, 1977, 183 ff.

11. For the events of this period we have, in addition to the biographies of the two protagonists, Caesar and Pompey, by Plutarch, three continuous accounts: the third book of Caesar *B.Civ*; Appian *b.civ.* II, 38-82; and Cassius Dio XLI, 10-12, 44-52. Cf. Papazoglou, *ANRW* II, 7, pp. 321-325.

12. Cicero *In Pis.* 40 (97): 'ex illo fonte et seminario triumphorum'.

13. Diodorus XXXVII, 5α.

14. Cicero *Pro Front.* 20 (44).

15. It is not clear in what consists the new measure referred to by certain sources (ὑποφόρους ἐποιήσαντο - Eustathius *Chron.* 424c; tributarios faciunt - Hieronymos *Chron.* 143c), since the Macedonians had anyway been paying tribute since 167 B.C. It may be that the full contribution was divided between the cities and levied directly by the Roman authorities.

16. The only mention of *ager publicus* in Macedonia is to be found in the speech that Cicero delivered against the agrarian law proposed by Servilius Rullus, according to which both in Italy and in the provinces the *ager publicus* was to be divided into lots *(De lege agraria* 1.2.5: 'agros in Macedonia regios qui partim T. Flaminini partim L. Pauli qui Persen vicit parti sunt...').

17. Until the time of Sulla Macedonia was governed as a general rule by praetors or propraetors, except during the Galatian invasions, when for many years the command was confided to consuls. When, after Sulla, the sending of consuls to the province was prohibited by the Cornelian law, the Macedonian governors became proconsuls. At the time of the civil wars, when large military commands were created, the administration of the whole province was often confided to legates of the powerful leaders.

18. Appian *Mithr.* 41; Caesar *B.Civ.* III.4; Appian *b.civ.* II.75; cf. J. Harmand, *L'armée et le soldat à Rome de 107 à 50 avant notre ère* (Paris, 1967), 474; T. Sarikakis, "Des soldats macédoniens dans l'armée romaine", *Ἀρχαία Μακεδονία* II, 1977, 431 ff.

19. Appian *b.civ.* III.79.

20. On the development of urban life in Macedonia before the Roman conquest and on the Roman policy of adapting the municipal system to local traditions, cf. Papazoglou, *ANRW*, 351-354.

21. A survey of the problem has recently been

presented by M. Hatzopoulos in his communication "Les politarques de Philippopolis. Un élément méconnu pour la datation d'une magistrature macédonienne", read at the Third International Congress of Thracology in Vienna (June 1980), in which he argues, from the existence of politarchs in Philippopolis, that politarchy was a pre-Roman institution. His thesis is further confirmed by the discovery of an inscription at Amphipolis mentioning politarchs under Perseus (cf. Chaido Koukouli - Chrysanthaki, "Politarchs in a New Inscription from Amphipolis", *Ancient Macedonian Studies in Honor of Charles Edson*, Thessalonike, 1981, 229-241).

22. A bilingual milestone found not far from Thessalonike bears the name of the proconsul *Cn. Egnatius, Cf.* A. Rhomiopoulou, *BCH* 98 (1974), 813 ff. On the *via Egnatia*, cf. P. Collart, *Philippes* 487-523; Hammond, *Macedonia*, I, 19-58; F. O'Sullivan, *The Egnatian Way* (1972); P. Collart, "Les milliaires de la via Egnatia," *BCH* 100 (1976), 177-200.

23. J.M.R. Cormack, "L. Calpurnius Piso", *AJA* 48,76 ff. Dimitsas, no. 58: 'Βεροιαῖοι καί οἱ ἐνκεκτημένοι 'Ρωμαῖοι.' That there were Romans dwelling in Macedonia is attested by Caesar (*B.Civ.* III. 102: 'erat edictum Pompei nomine Amphipoli propositum, uti omnes eius provinciae iuniores, Graeci civesque Romani, iurandi causa convenirent') and Cicero (*In Pis.* 40. 96: 'cives Romani, qui in iis locis negotiantur...').

24. A group of *συμπραγματευόμενοι 'Ρωμαῖοι (conventus c.R.)* at Acanthos, *BSA* 23, 1918/19, 85 f., no. 13; at Idomenai, Borka Josifovska, "Base avec la dédicace à P. Memmius Regulus", *Zant* 9, 1959, 285 ff.; at Styberra, *Spomenik* 71, 1931, no. 501; at Edessa (Dimitsas, no. 3); at Thessalonike, *IG* X, 2, no. 32. A *negotiator ab Roma* in Amphipolis, *RA* 24, 1945, 53 ff. no. 6. A *Heracleotes ex Italia* at Pella, *Πέλλα I*, 146, no. 258. Cf. also Papazoglou, *ANRW* 357, n. 245. J. Hatzfeld, *Les trafiquants Italiens dans l'Orient hellénique* (Paris, 1919), 54-57, only knew the inscription from Edessa, from which he wrongly concluded that after the period of Augustus no more Italians are to be found in northern Greece.

25. Caes. *B.civ.* III.4: 'Unam (sc. legionem) ex Creta et Macedonia ex veteranis militibus, qui dimissi a superioribus imperatoribus in his provinciis consederant'.

26. The numismatic evidence conveniently supplements the brief indications of the written sources on the foundation of Roman colonies in Macedonia (Dio Cassius, Pliny, Saint Paul). See the basic works, by H. Gaebler, *Die ersten Colonialprägungen in Pella, Dium und Cassandrea, Zfn* 36 (1926), 116-141, by M. Grant, *From Imperium to Auctoritas* (Cambridge, 1946), as also the monograph of Fr. Vittinghoff, *Römische Kolonisation und Burgerrechtspolitik unter Caesar und Augustus* (Wiesbaden, 1951). For Cassandreia, cf. E. Meyer, *RE*, Suppl. X (1965), col. 632 (*s.v.* Potidaia-Kassandreia); for Philippi, Collart, *Philippes*, 224-227. Cf. Papazoglou, *ANRW* II, 7, 357 ff.

27. The 'Augustan Era', like that of 148 B.C., was a Macedonian era, not found outside Macedonia proper. The two eras, used in inscriptions side by side or separately, serve as a sure criterion for determining whether a territory belonged to Macedonia or not.

28. On the military competence of the governors of senatorial provinces in the years which followed the reform of 27 B.C., and on the date of the creation of the military command of Moesia, see the bibliography cited in Papazoglou, *ANRW* II, 7, 325 ff. and notes 105-110. The situation in Thrace required the intervention of the Macedonian governors throughout the reigns of Augustus and of his immediate successors.

29. Such was the case of the *consularis* M. Lollius, the eminent general of Augustus who fought with success against the Bessians, and that of M. Iulius Romulus, otherwise unknown, whose designation by Claudius as *extra sortem* is attested in an inscription.

30. The date when Macedonia was put under the authority of the Senate has been contested for no good reason, see Papazoglou, *ZAnt* 29, 1979, 335. We have no evidence for the activities of Poppaeus in Macedonia. On the other hand, three inscriptions from Dion, Idomenai and Beroia mention Memmius Regulus.

31. On imperial interference in the sphere reserved for the Senate, cf. H.-G. Pflaum, "Légats impériaux à l'intérieur des provinces sénatoriales", *Latomus*, 58 (1962), 1233-1242.

32. A.J.B. Wace, M.S. Thompson, "A Latin Inscription from Perhaebia", *ABSA* 17 (1910/11), 194 ff. (boundary between Doliche in Thessaly and Elimeia in Macedonia). Two boundary-stones, which were probably set up by the same imperial legate, date from the same year. One of them was erected between Dion and Olosson (*CIL* III, 591), and the other between the Thasians and the Thracians (*AEpigr.* 1968, 469); cf. *ZAnt* 29 (1979), 240 ff.

33. Cf. *ibid.*, 240-246.

34. Cf. T. Sarikakis, *Ἄρχοντες....*, 109 ff. and 132.

35. *Digesta* L, 15, 8, 8: 'in provincia Macedonia Dyrracheni, Cassandrenses, Philippenses, Dienses, Stobenses iuris Italici sunt'. On the problem presented by the *ius Italicum* of Stoboi and by the date of this town's promotion to the rank of a municipality, cf. Papazoglou, *ANRW*, 360 ff. and n. 266.

36. Cf. Ch. Edson, "Double Communities in Roman Macedonia", *Μελετήματα στή μνήμη Βασιλείου Λαούρδα* (Thessalonike, 1975), 97-102.

37. The free status of these cities is attested by Pliny (IV. 35, 36, 38). For Thessalonike, see also the coins struck on this occasion and the inscription *IG* X, 2, no. 6, both cited in Papazoglou, *ANRW*, 328, n. 113. Besides these *poleis*, there were whole areas in the province of Macedonia which were granted freedom. According to Caesar (*B.Civ.* III.34) and Strabo (VII. 7.8), upper Macedonia was also called 'free Macedonia'. One can only formulate hypotheses about the meaning of the term 'freedom'. It is difficult, however, to imagine that all this region was an enclave free from the authority of the governor of the province. In Pliny only the Orestai are designated as free. Cf. also Cicero *De harusp. resp.* 16, 35: ...'ex Orestide, quae pars Macedoniae libera est'.

38. A.M. Woodward, "Inscriptions from Thessaly and Macedonia" *JHS* 33, 1913, 337 ff. and N. Pappadakis, *Ἀθηνᾶ, 25,* 1914, 426 ff. The reading of the name Βαττυναῖοι is due to Ch. Edson. Cf. Papazoglou, *ANRW*, 363 ff.

39. On the regional *koina* of upper Macedonia, cf. Papazoglou, *ZAnt* 9, 1959, 163-171.

40. J.M.R. Cormack, "A Letter of Hadrian in Beroea", *JRS,* 1940, 148-152.

41. See, for instance, the letter of Antoninus Pius addressed to the ancient city of Sveti Vrač (Parthikopolis?) settling various questions of municipal administration, among others the number of *bouleutai* and the amount of the *summa honoraria*. D. Detschew, "Ein neuer Brief des Kaisers Antoninus Pius", *JOEAI* 41, 1954, 110 ff.

42. Cf. D. Kanatsoulis, *Μακεδονικά 3*, and *Μακεδονικά*, 13. Also J. Deininger, *Die Provinziallandtage der römischen Kaizerzeit* (Munich, 1965), 91-96.

43. The striking of provincial coins begins in Macedonia under Claudius. However, we have a bronze coin, probably dating from the time of Augustus, which bears on the obverse a representation of Nike and on the reverse the Macedonian shield with the legend ΜΑΚΕΔΟΝΩΝ, cf. W. Wruck, "Zu den Provinzialprägungen der römischen Kaizerzeit", *Berliner Num. Zeitschr.* 1 (1949-52), 258.

44. Cf. J. Gagé, "Alexandre le Grand en Macédoine dans la première moitié du IIIe siècle après J.-C.", *Historia* 24, 1975, 1x ff.

45. Dio Cassius LXXVIII.7.1.

46. On the invasions, see the exhaustive work by L. Schmidt, *Geschichte der deutschen Stämme bis zum Ausgang der Völkerwanderung. Die Östgermanen* (Munich, 1941): Cf. 94 ff., 204 ff., 210 ff., 216 ff.

47. Cf. W. Ensslin, "The Senate and the Army Wars on the Danube Frontier", *CAH* XII (1939), 90.

48. In 260/61; cf. Sarikakis, *Ἄρχοντες...*, II, 128 ff.

49. *Ibid.*, 131 ff.

50. Contrary to what had happened in the past, this production did not always respond to the needs and tastes of the social élite - a fact that accounts for the impression of decline we have when we compare the products of the imperial age (buildings, stone monuments, artefacts) with those of the Hellenistic era. The reason is that of all other periods in the history of ancient Macedonia the early imperial age was the one in which the process of social levelling was most intense.

51. P. Perdrizet, "Voyage dans la Macédoine première", *BCH* 18 (1894), 444, no. 8, Kariani in Pieria.

52. P. Perdrizet, "Trois inscriptions latines de Roumélie", *BCH* 24 (1900), 544 ff., region of Drama.

53. C. Makaronas, *Μακεδονικά 2* (1952) Ἀρχ. Χρονικά, 638, no. 2, Kozani.

54. Many attestations of *actores (πραγματευταί)* at Philippi, cf. P. Collart, *Philippes*, 296; *δοῦλος οἰκονόμος* at Herakleia Lynkestis, *Spomenik*, 71, 1931, no. 20; at Stoboi: *οἰκονόμος τῆς Στοβαίων πόλεως καί οἱ σύνδουλοι*, A. Keramitčiev, "A New Inscription from Stobi", *ZAnt* 11 (1961), 315 ff.

55. J. Touratsoglou, *AΔ* (1969) Χρονικά 325 pl. 334.

56. We have already mentioned this important document above, n. 41. For the reading of ll. 2-3, referring to slaves, see also J. H. Oliver, *AJPh* 1958, 52 ff. and J. and L. Robert, *Bull. épigr.* 1956, no. 159 and 1959, no. 246.

57. *RA*, 1945, 2, 247-255 (Amphipolis).

58. J. Hatzfeld, "Inscriptions de Thessalie et de Macédoine", *BCH* 35 (1911), 237 ff. (Beroia). See also the well-known, long list names from

Beroia; cf. Delacoulonche, Dimitsas, Woodward and J.M.R. Cormack, "Inscriptions from Macedonia *BSA*", 58 (1963), p. 25, on which are to be found 19 *Iulii* (the gentilicum is always abbreviated), 7 *Po(mpilii?)*, 5 *Pe(tronii?)*, 3 *Fl(avii)*, 3 *Ae(lii)*, etc. Apparently we have to do with freedmen.

59. The discovery of the sanctuary of the Mother of the Autochthonous gods at Leukopetra was reported by Ph. Petsas in *ΑΔ* 21 (1966) Χρονικά, 352-354, and in *Μακεδονικά*, 7, 1967, Χρονικά 343-345. The acts of manumission are to be placed between 169 and 313 A.D. At the moment we do not know more than ten, either in transcriptions or photographs. On the character of these acts, cf. *ZAnt* 31 (1981), 171-179. Acts of consecration of slaves to a divinity have also been discovered at Edessa (a series of fourteen consecrations to Mâ the Invincible), at Beroia, at Skydra, in the region of Kozani, in the vicinity of Vergina, in Pelagonia and at Kyrrhos.

60. *IG*, X, 2, 214.

61. Cf. J. Roger "Inscriptions de la région du Strymon", *RA*, 1945, 2, 54 ('L. Pompilius Eros negotiator ab Roma ex horreis cornificianis...'); *ΑΔ* 1971, Χρονικά, 395 («Μάρκελλος τραπεζείτης...» the inscription dates from the year A.D. 246).

62. M. Rostovtzeff, *BIARCo*, 4 (1899) 170, A. Orlandos, *ΑΔ* 2 (1916), 148, no 4.

63. In the letter of Antoninus Pius, already mentioned above, there is a reference to a *phoros* paid by the *somata eleuthera*. At Tenos all citizens (men, women and children) paid, as it appears, one denarius per head (cf. *IG*, XII, 5, 946 (1st or 2nd century A.D.).

64. *IG*, X, 2, 740.

65. *IG*, X, 2, 351.

66. *Cod. Theod.* I. 32.5.

67. We should add that the inscriptions acquaint us with five imperial procurators of the class of *centenarii* (2nd/3rd century), who were entrusted with the supervision of various financial services in the province. Of their numerous staff, which was mainly made up of slaves and freedmen, we have one reference only to a slave *adiutor tabularii* (*IG*, X, 2, 471). This is a good indication of the inadequacy of our documentation concerning the lower strata of the population.

68. *IG*, X, 2, 145.

69. Cf. Dimitsas, no 73 (τῷ παιδαγωγῷ); J. Coupry, M. Feyel, "Inscriptions de Philippes", *BCH* 60, 1936, 53, no 4 (διδάσκαλος); *IG*, X, 2, 879 (μαθητής); A. Salač, "Inscriptions du Pangée et de Philippes", *BCH* 57, 1923, 83, no. 2 («ἐπαίδευσεν δέ με ῥήτωρ ὁ θρέψας Ξενοφῶν»); *IG*, X, 2, 844 (φιλογράμματε χαῖρε).

70. J.M.R. Cormack, "Progress Report on the Greek Inscriptions of the Trite Meris for IG X", Ἀρχαία Μακεδονία I, 1970, 196 ff.

71. J.M.R. Cormack, "The Gymnasiarchal law of Beroea", Ἀρχαία Μακεδονία II, 1977, 139 ff.. J. and L. Robert give an improved version, based on a copy made by C. Makaronas immediately after the discovery of the stone, in *Bull.épigr.* 1978, n. 274 (431-435).

72. This is what follows from the fact that the 'gymnasiarchia' is attested in Thessalonike as from the end of the second century B.C. Epigraphic evidence reveals the existence of this institution in the 2nd and 3rd centuries A.D. not only in the great Macedonian cities, but also in modest towns, whose very name re-

mains unknown to us.

73. Cf. N. Vulić, *Spomenik* 98 (1948), nos. 388 and 389.

74. *IG*, X, 2.

75. J.M.R. Cormack, "Inscriptions from Beroea", *Hesperia*, 1944, 23 ff., no. 1; C. Makaronas, *Μακεδονικά*, I (1940) Ἀρχ. Χρονικά 481, fig. 17; *IG*, X, 2, 436, *IG*, VII, 2726.

76. *IG*, X, 2, 479 and 512.

77. Cf. W. Schmid, O. Stählin, *Geschichte der griechischen Literatur* II (1920), 327, 328 ff.

78. *IG*, X, 2, 108.

79. W. Crönert, "Das Epigramm auf Andronikos Kyrrhestes", *JOEAI* 10 (1907), Bbl. 41 ff.

80. G. Wissova, *RE*, I (1894), col. 1829, R. Laqueur *RE*, V A (1903), col. 1348, no. 10.

81. W. Stegemann, *RE*, XVII (1936), 551, no. 27 R. Laqueur *RE*, XIX (1938), 2349, no. 37; F. Lammert *RE*, XXI (1950), 1432, no. 8.

82. A. Orlandos, *ΑΔ* 2 (1916), no 13.

83. Pélékidis, *Πολιτεία* p. 56-72; L. Robert, "Le Dieu Fulvus à Thessalonique" *Hellénica* II (1946), 37-42; Ch. Edson, *HSPh*, 125 ff., and *HThR*, 204.

84. Cf. P. Collart, *Philippes*, 272 ff.

85. Cf. L. Moretti, *Inscrizioni agonistiche grecche* (Roma 1953).

86. *BIARCo* 4, 1899, 170; cf. L. Robert, *RPh*, 1939, 131 ff.

87. Gaebler, *ZfN*, 308; Moretti, Iscrizioni, 265, n. 85.

88. Gaebler, *ZfN*, 258 et 307 ff.; D. Kanatsoulis, *Μακεδονικά* 3, 1954, 68-73.

89. Gaebler, *ZfN* 307.

90. J. Touratsoglou, Ἀρχαία Μακεδονία I (1970), 281 ff.

91. *Ibid.*, 285 ff.; cf. *Bull. épigr.*, 1971, no. 400. On arena combats in general and in Macedonia in particular, see L. Robert, *Les gladiateurs dans l'Orient grec* (Paris 1940, 1971).

92. W. Baege's dissertation *De Macedonum sacris* (Halle, 1913), which forms a unique repertory of literary, numismatic and epigraphic evidence concerning Macedonian cults as a whole, stops in so far as epigraphic and archaeological documentation is concerned at the discoveries of the end of the 19th century. For the Yugoslav and Bulgarian part of ancient Macedonia we now have a systematic work by Düll, *Götterkulte*, limited to the cults of gods.

93. Starting with a study in onomastics, I have often occupied myself with the problem of the pre-Macedonian substratum and of its relation with the Thracians. Cf. Papazoglou, *Balcanica*; Papazoglou, *Actes*; Papazoglou, *RTFPhUB*.

94. For the Greek origin of the gods and heroes of the Macedonians, see the judicious and convincing discussion in J. Kalléris' major work, *Les Anciens Macédoniens*, vol. II (Athens, 1976), 532-572.

95. Cf. Edson, *HSPh* 130 ff. A newly discovered dedication, to «Διί Ἐλευθερίῳ καί 'Ρώμῃ» ἀπό τίς Πέτρες Ἐορδαίας, G. Daux, *BCH* 101 (1977), 350. The invocation *Hyperairetes*, attested in an inscription from Pelagonia in conjunction with the name of the month *Hyperberetaios*, is evidence for the antiquity of the cult of Zeus in Macedonia.

96. Cf. the bibliography given by Düll, *Götterkulte*, 205, n. 20, and p. 428. The diffusion of the cult of *Theos Hypsistos* (who should not be confused with *Zeus Hypsistos*) in the Balkan peninsula has been studied by

Margareta Tatcheva-Hitova, *Thracia* 4 (1977), 271 ff., and *BSt* 19 (1978), 59 ff.

97. Cf. Edson, *HThR* 191; Pelekidis, *Πολιτεία* 39 ff.; L. Robert, *Etudes épigraphiques et philologiques* (1938), 53-62.

98. The oracles at Delphi and Claros attracted the faithful away from northern Macedonia (Herakleia: *Spomenik* 77 (1934), no. 4; Stoboi: *JOEAI*, 15, 1912, no. 20). N. Vulić, *Spomenik* 71 (1931), nos. 489 and 491.

99. Cf. Düll, *Götterkulte*, 58 ff. and 71 (for central Macedonia). For Bendis, cf. Ch. Picard, "Sur l'iconographie de Bendis", *BIAB* 16 (1950), 25 ff., and L. Ognenova, "Quelques aspects de Bendis sur les monuments de la Thrace", *ibid.*, 22, 1959, 81 ff. Dozens of rock-cut ex-votos from Philippi have been collected in *Philippes I*.

100. For Ennodia, cf. L. Robert, "Une déesse à cheval en Macédoine", *Hellénica* XI-XII (1960), 588-597. *Bull. épigr.*, 1972, no. 252; for Pasikrata and acts of manumission, N. Vulić, *Spomenik* 75 (1934), no. 7, and L. Robert, *Hellénica* I (1940), 73-75.

101. Cf. Papageorgiou, Ἀθηνᾶ 12 (1900), 65-88. *Id.*, *BPW* 21 (1901), 700; the identification of Mâ with Cybele should be rejected. In Edessa itself there has been found a dedication to the Μήτηρ Θεῶν. The cult of the Phrygian Magna Mater was clearly merged in Macedonia with that of an indigenous goddess; see the following note.

102. Cf. *ΑΔ* 21 (1966), Χρονικά, 352-354, and *Μακεδονικά* 7 (1967), Ἀρχ. Χρονικά, 343-345 (Ph. Petsas). It would appear that in the imperial period the old local beliefs were revived under the influence of cults from Asia Minor.

103. Cf. Düll, *Götterkulte*, 86-93, and 112-116.

104. Cf. Edson, *HThR*, 188-203; R. E. Witt, "The Kabeiroi in Ancient Macedonia", Ἀρχαία Μακεδονία II (1977), 67-80.

105. Cf. Düll, *Götterkulte*, 77-85; *IG* X, 2, 259; G. Mihailov, *IG Bulg.*, IV, 2319 (Melenikon), cf. Düll, *Götterkulte*, fig. 34.

106. Cf. Collart, *Philippes*, 423 ff. A sanctuary of *Heron Auloneites* was discovered near the village of Kepia, on the northern slope of Pangaion, C. Koukouli «Ἱερόν Θρακός Ἥρωνος Αὐλωνείτη», *AAA* 2 (1969), 2, 191-193; cf. *Bull. épigr.* 1970, n. 381. In Thessalonike, Συνήθια Ἥρωνος Αὐλωνίτου, *ΑΔ* 24 (1969), Χρονικά, 300 ff. (Ph. Petsas); see also *IG*, X, 2, 821.

107. F. Papazoglou, "Stèles anthropomorphes et amorphes de Pélagonie," *ZAnt* 27 (1977), 147 ff.

108. Cf. P. Collart, *Philippes*, 474-485.

109. N. Vulić, "Une inscription grecque de Macédoine", *Mélanges Glotz* II (1932), 869-876; see also my note, *ZAnt* 29 (1979), 312 f. (in Serbocroatian).

110. Cf. Papazoglou, *ANRW* II, 7, 307 f., and Edson, *HSPh* 51 (1940), 129. The priesthood of Rome and of Roman benefactors is attested in Thessalonike: *IG*, X, 2, 31; 32; 133 and 226. For the cult of Augustus, cf. A. Benjamin-A.C. Raubitschek, "Arae Augusti", *Hesperia* 28 (1959), 65-84.

111. Cf. D. Kanatsoulis, *Μακεδονικά* 3, 51-58 and 70 ff.; *Μακεδονικά* 5 (1963), 66-68. Thessalonike had had a temple of Θεός Καῖσαρ since the reign of Augustus, *IG* X, 2, 31. On a newly discovered inscription in the region of the middle Strymon the Θεοί Σεβαστοί are venerated as *synnaoi* of Serapis

and Isis, cf. V. Gerassimova-Tomova *Klio* 62 (1980), 21. The augustales at Stobi erected a dedication 'Deo Caesari Augusto p(atri) p (atriae) et municipio Stob (ensium)' B. Saria *JOEAI* 32 (1940), 7.

112. Gaebler, *Zfn* 24 (1904), 259 ff., 277 ff., 355 ff; Pelekidis, *Πολιτεία* 83-86. cf. *IG*, X, 2, 162-165, 177 and 231. K. Hanell's article on neocorate (*RE* XVI, 1935, 2428) is now out of date as it only takes into consideration numismatic evidence.

113. F. Cumont's book, *Les religions orientales dans le paganisme romain* (1929[4]), remains the basic study on the subject. For the Egyptian cults, see R.E. Witt, *The Egyptian cults in Ancient Macedonia*, I, 1970, 324-333. For the sanctuary of the Egyptian gods at Philippi, cf. Collart, *Philippes*, 444. Stoboi was also a centre of the cult of Serapis, cf. Düll, *Götterkulte*, p. 148. A sanctuary of Isis and Serapis was discovered in 1971 on the via Egnatia, west of Heracleia, cf. T. Janakievski, *MAArch* 2 (1976), 189-204.

114. A. Orlandos, *ΑΔ* 2 (1916), 144, no. 1 (3rd/2nd cent. B.C.); on manumissions by consecration to the goddess in 239 and 261, *ibid.*, p. 145, no.2, and 147, no. 3.

115. Pseudo-Lucian, Λούκιος ἤ ὄνος, 35 ff.

116. The Jewish communities of Philippi, Thessalonike and Beroia are known from the Acts of the Apostles. The *Corpus Inscriptionum Iudaicarum*, vol. I: Europe (1936) of J.B. Frey contains only two Jewish inscriptions from Macedonia, cf. L. Robert, *Hellénica* III, 104-106. In his *Prolegomenon* to the 2nd edition of the *Corpus* (New York, 1975), B. Lifshitz makes the necessary additions.

117. Cf. B. Hengel, *Die Synagogeninschrift von Stobi*, *ZNTW* 59 (1966), 145-183; B. Lifshitz, *Donateurs et fondateurs dans les synagogues juives* (Paris, 1967), no. 10; J. Wiseman, Dj. Mano-Zissi, *Excavations at Stoboi, AJA* 75 (1971), 406-411.

118. Cf. *Act. Apostol.* 16.1-40; 17. 1-15; 20. 1-6; Ed. Meyer, "Paulus in Makedonien und Griechenland" *Ursprung und Anfänge des Christentums* III (1923), 427-432.

119. Thessalonians, 1.2.14.

120. Philippians, 4.15.

MONUMENTS AND ART IN THE ROMAN PERIOD

1. Pape, *Kunstwerke*, 14 ff.
2. General thoughts and observations concerning sculpture in Thessalonike during the Roman period are formulated by G. Bakalakis in his article, "Vorlage und Interpretation von römischen Kunstdenkmälern in Thessalonike", *AA* 1973, 671 ff.
3. For example, the statue of the type Artemis-Ekate or the statue of Aphrodite from the recent excavations at the Iseion at Dion and the statue in the Thessalonike Museum, no. 1006.
4. Beroia Museum, no. 373.
5. It was found in 1979 at the excavations at the Iseion.
6. Thessalonike Museum, no. 997. See *IGX* 2, 1, no. 107 with bibliography.
7. Thessalonike Museum, no. 1067 and 1068. Bakalakis, *AA* 672. For observations concerning the post-Hellenistic columns at Beroia see the article by J. Touratsoglou, «Πατερῖνος Ἀν-

τιγόνου, ἤρως», *Κέρνος Γ. Μπακαλάκη* (Thessalonike, 1972), 153 ff.

8. Thessalonike Museum, no. 1935. Rüsch, *JDAI* 182 ff, R93.
9. Thessalonike Museum, no. 1934. Rüsch, *JDAI* 180 ff. R91.
10. Thessalonike Museum, no. 10138. *ΑΔ* 23 (1968), Χρον. 326. *REG* 83 (1970), 408, no. 368, with observations.
11. Thessalonike Museum, no. 903. M. Andronikos, *Mon Piot* 51 (1960), 37 ff. Rüsch, *JDAI* 174, R82.
12. M. Vickers, "Towards a Reconstruction of the Town Planning of Roman Thessaloniki", Ἀρχαία Μακεδονία 1 (1970), 239 ff.
13. Concerning the Agora at Thessalonike, besides the reports of the excavators in the Ἀρχαιολογικό Δελτίο, see Petsas, Ἀρχαία Μακεδονία 224, but principally, C. Bakirtzis, «Περί τοῦ συγκροτήματος τῆς Ἀγορᾶς τῆς Θεσσαλονίκης», Ἀρχαία Μακεδονία 2 (1977), 257 ff.
14. G. Gounaris, Τά τείχη τῆς Θεσσαλονίκης (Thessalonike, 1976). See also A. Mentzos, Ἑλληνικά 30 (1977/78), 518.
15. C. Bakirtzis, «Ἡ θαλάσσια ὀχύρωση τῆς Θεσσαλονίκης», Βυζαντινά 7 (1975), 291 ff.
16. Collart, *Philippes*. More concisely, D. Lazaridis, Οἱ Φίλιπποι (Thessalonike, 1956) and *Princeton Encyclopedia of Classical Sites* (Princeton, 1976), 704 ff. (s.v. Philippi).
17. Bakalakis, Ἀρχαία Μακεδονία. Pandermalis, Ἀρχαία Μακεδονία.
18. See above, n. 13.
19. L. Guerrini, "Las Incantadas di Salonicco", *ArchClass* 13 (1961), 40 ff.
20. Recently M. Vickers in *Princeton Encyclopedia of Classical Sites* 912 (s.v. Thessalonike).
21. Collart, *Philippes*, 329 ff. For the latest research, the new points of view and the improved sectional plan of the area, see M. Sève, "Le Forum", *BCH* 103 (1979), 627 ff.
22. P. Lemerle, "Palestre romaine à Philippes", *BCH* 61 (1937), 86 ff.
23. Collart, *Philippes*, 365 ff. P. Aupert, "L'édifice avec bain", *BCH* 103 (1979), 619, with a new interpretation and plan.
24. P. Collart, "Le théâtre de Philippes", *BCH* 52 (1928), 74 ff.
25. B. Saria, "Das Theater von Stobi", *AA* 1938, 81 ff. Wiseman, *Stobi*, 69 ff. and E. Gebhard, "Protective Devices in Roman Theaters", *Studies in the Antiquities of Stobi* (Belgrade, 1975), 46 ff. (and n. 19 with bibliography).
26. G. Bakalakis, *ΑΔ* 21 (1966), Χρονικά 347 and *ΑΔ* 23 (1968), Χρονικά 342 ff.
27. *BCH* 45 (1921), 540 ff. C. Makaronas in Μακεδονικά 1 (1940), 464 ff. Salditt-Trappmann, 47. The inscriptions from the Serapeion were published by Edson in *IGX*, 2, 1.
28. P. Collart, "Le sanctuaire des dieux Egyptiens à Philippes", *BCH* 53 (1929), 70 ff. Salditt-Trappmann, 52.
29. Collart, *Philippes*, 430 ff. (Bendis), 402 ff. (Silvanos). Concerning the reliefs from the sanctuaries see, *Philippes* I.
30. E. Kitzinger, "A Survey of the Early Christian Town of Stobi", *DOP* 3 (1946), 118 ff. Wiseman, *Stobi*, 44 ff.
31. Thessalonike Museum, no. 1065. Rüsch *JDAI* 131 ff., P38. H.G. Niemeyer, *Studien zur statuarischen Darstellung der römischen Kaiser* (Berlin, 1968), 102 ff. no. 76.
32. Thessalonike Museum, no. 1055. C.C. Vermeule, *Roman Imperial Art in Greece and*

Asia Minor (Cambridge/Mass, 1968), 417. Rüsch, *JDAI* 130, P35.

33. Thessalonike Museum, no. 898. Rüsch, *JDAI* 122, P24. Soechting, 145, no. 22. Pandermalis, *AA* 142.
34. G. Sotiriadis, *ΠΑΕ*, 1929, 74. Soechting, 175, no. 59.
35. Collart, *Philippes*, 515. Wiggers-Wegner, 74.
36. *ΑΔ* 19 (1964), 347. Wiggers-Wegner, 85.
37. Thessalonike Museum, no. 4303. Pandermalis *AA*, 128 ff. M. Bergmann, *Studien zum römischen Porträt des 3. Jhs. n. Chr.* (Bonn, 1977), 27 ff. B. Andreae, in M. Imdahl and N. Kunisch, *Plastik* (Kassel, 1979), 104 ff. The new concurrence suggested by J. Balty does not appear likely (*Eikones*, memorial volume for H. Jucker, Berne, 1980, 52 ff.).
38. Thessalonike Museum, no. 1942. Rüsch, *JDAI*, 184, R94.
39. Thessalonike Museum, no. 3. Rüsch, *JDAI*, 118, P17. A. Carandini, *Vibia Sabina* (Florence, 1969), 165. A. Datsouli-Stavridou, *AAA* 7 (1974), 266.
40. Beroia Museum, no. 208.
41. Beroia Museum, no. 409. V. Callipolitis, *MonPiot* 46 (1952), 85 ff.
42. Rüsch, *JDAI* 178, R88 and 179, R89.
43. Concerning the dedications on the tombstones of the Empire period see, H. Wrede, "Das Mausoleum der Claudia Semne und die bürgerliche Plastik der Kaiserzeit", *MDAI(R)* 78 (1971), 125 ff.
44. G. P. Oikonomos, Ἐπιγραφαί τῆς Μακεδονίας (Athens, 1915), 28 ff., no. 49. D. Pandermalis, "Inscriptions from Dion", "Addenda et Corrigenda", *Ancient Macedonian Studies in Honor of C. Edson* (Thessalonike, 1982).
45. M. Speidel, "The Captor of Decebalus", *JRS* 60 (1970), 142 ff. Specific observations are by D.J. Breese in *JRS* 61 (1971), 130 ff. and by M. Speidel in *JRS* 63 (1973), 141 ff.
46. V. Kallipolitis, Χρονολογική κατάταξις τῶν μετά μυθολογικῶν παραστάσεων ἀττικῶν σαρκοφάγων τῆς Ρωμαϊκῆς ἐποχῆς (Athens, 1958). F. Matz, *Gnomon* 31 (1959), 693 ff. A. Giuliano, *Il commercio dei sarcofagi attici* (Rome, 1962). H. Wiegartz, *Gnomon* 37 (1965), 612 ff. H. Wiegartz, "Wirtschaftsgeschichtliche Fragen der Sarkophagforschung", *Memorial Volume for Arif Müfid Mansel* (Ankara, 1974), 439 ff. A. Giuliano, B. Palma, *La maniera Ateniese di età Romana. I maestri dei sarcofagi attici* (Rome, 1978).
47. Thessalonike Museum, no. 1247. F. Matz, *Die antiken Sarkophagreliefs IV. Die dionysischen Sarkophage* I (Berlin, 1968), 112 ff, no. 11.
48. Thessalonike Museum, no. 1246. G. Kock, *Die mythologischen Sarkophage. 6. Teil, Meleager* (Berlin, 1975), 144, no. 173.
49. Thessalonike Museum, no. 877. G. Despinis, Ἀκρόλιθα (Athens, 1975) 11 ff. G. Despinis, «Τό ἀντίγραφο τῆς Ἀθηνᾶς Medici τοῦ Μουσείου Θεσσαλονίκης», Ἀρχαία Μακεδονία 2 (1977), 95 ff.
50. Thessalonike Museum, no. 832. Salditt-Trappmann 51, fig. 46 (designated as Athena without explanation).
51. Thessalonike Museum, no. 10117. Ph. Petsas, Μακεδονικά 14 (1974), 297, pl. 8.
52. Thessalonike Museum, no. 831. Salditt-Trappmann 51, fig. 45. F. Hiller, *Formgeschichtliche Untersuchungen zur griechischen Statue des späten 5. Jhs. v. Chr.* (Mainz, 1971), 3 ff.
53. Thessalonike Museum, no. 10038. Ph. Petsas, Μακεδονικά 9 (1969), 150, pl. 43.

54. H.J. Kruse, *Römische weibliche Gewandstatuen des 2. Jhs. v. Chr.* (Göttigen, 1975), 281 (B25), 321 ff., (C42).
55. Thessalonike Museum, no. 897. Salditt-Trappmann, 49 ff.
56. C. Makaronas, «Τὸ ὀκτάγωνο τῆς Θεσσαλονίκης», *ΠΑΕ* 1950, 303 ff. M. Vickers, "Observations on the Octagon at Thessaloniki", *JRS* 63 (1973), 111 ff. G. Knethakis, «Τὸ Ὀκτάγωνο τῆς Θεσσαλονίκης», *ΑΔ* 30 (1975), Μελέται, 90 ff. C. Bouras in his address to the tenth Συνέδριο Χριστιανικῆς Ἀρχαιολογίας (Thessalonike, September, 1980), offered the opinion that the Octagon was built as the Mausoleum of Theodosius I.
57. *BCH* 82 (1958), 759. G. Bakalakis, «Pausilipos

von Thessaloniki», *Provincialia* (Memorial volume for Laur-Belart), (Basle, 1968), 3 ff. H.P. Laubscher, *Der Reliefschmuck des Galeriusbogen in Thessaloniki* (Berlin, 1975), 112 ff. 119 ff.
58. M. Vickers, "The Hippodrom at Thessaloniki", *JRS* 62 (1972), 25 ff.
59. C. Makaronas, *Ἡ 'καμάρα', τὸ θριαμβικὸ τόξο τοῦ Γαλερίου στὴ Θεσσαλονίκη* (Thessalonike, 1969), with bibliography. Fundamental is the exhaustive monograph by H.P. Laubscher, *Der Reliefschmuck des Galeriusbogens in Thessaloniki* (Berlin, 1975). See also M.P. Rothman, *AJA* 81 (1977), 427 ff. G. Velenis, *AA* 1979, 249 ff., suggests a new reconstruction of the ancient form of the monument.

Completely new points of view for the representations is formulated by Meyer in his recent article, "Die Frieszyklen am sog. Triumphbogen des Galerius in Thessaloniki", *JDAI* 95 (1980), 374 ff.
60. E. Hebrard, "Les travaux du Service Archéologique de l'Armée d'Orient à l'arc de triomphe de Galère et l'église de St. Georges à Salonique", *BCH* 44 (1920), 5 ff. G. Velenis, "Some Observations on the Original Form of the Rotonda in Thessaloniki", *Bst* 15 (1974), 298 ff.
61. Thessalonike Museum, no. 1060 and 1061. H.P. L'Orange, "Der subtile Stil - eine Kunstströmung aus der Zeit um 40 v. Chr.", *AK* 4 (1961), 68 ff.

BYZANTINE MACEDONIA

THE FIRST CHRISTIAN YEARS

The Bonn edition is understood in quotations from Byzantine writers, unless otherwise stated.
1. Lemerle, *Philippes*, 75 ff.; Papazoglou, *Cités*, 87 ff.; Theocharidis, 41 ff.
2. Areas in the south and the west were detached and the new provinces of Thessaly and Epirus Nova were created.
3. For these reforms, see n. 1 (which also gives the relevant sources). For a summary, see also *IEE*, ΣΤ΄, 100 ff.
4. Lemerle, *Phillipes*, 77.
5. For the capital of Eastern Illyricum in general see Theocharidis *Μακεδονία*, 99-103, where the most important bibliography is given.
6. Reference is made to the construction of the principal gate of its wall. See B. Aleksova and C. Mango, "Bargala, a Preliminary Report", *DOP* 25 (1971), 266.
7. Honigmann, 15.
8. These questions in particular are pursued by Papazoglou, *Cités*, 91 ff. and in Papazoglou, *BAB*.
9. Seeck, *Notitia*: Or. 1. 125.
10. First stated by T. Mommsen, see Lemerle, *Philippes*, 78, n. 4 and Papazoglou, *BAB*, 121.
11. As above.
12. Seeck, *Notitia*: Or 3.13 and 19.
13. Papazoglou, *BAB*, 122.
14. Papazoglou, *Cités*, 91. According to the *Synekdemos* of Hierokles (Honigmann, 15-16), six other cities belonged to Macedonia Secunda: Argos, Istria, Pelagonia, Kelenidion, Armonia, Zapara.
15. Mansi, VI, 577 and Papazoglou, *BAB*, 118.
16. Papazoglou, *BAB*, 118 ff. Most scholars today agree with her views (see Theocharidis, 93). There is, however, the opposing view which identifies Macedonia Salutaris and Macedonia Secunda as one and the same place, but which successively was given two different names (Lemerle, *Philippes*, 78 and n. 2). Additional support for this opinion in Papazoglou, *BAB*, 116, n. 2.
17. *CJC*, III, *Novellae*, 94 (Kroll ed., 1972).
18. *CJC*, III, *Novellae*, 655.
19. Papazoglou, *BAB*, 123.
20. For this harbour, see C. Bakirtzis, «Ἡ θαλάσσια ὀχύρωση τῆς Θεσσαλονίκης», *Βυ-*

ζαντινά 7 (1975), 289 ff., especially 315 ff.
21. For these, as well as for the invasions mentioned below, the basic study remains Lemerle, *RH*. Relevant information can also be found in many manuals of Byzantine history. For the problem of the Goths, see *IEE*, Ζ΄, 78 ff.
22. According to others, in the middle of the fifth century. (See page 242 and n. 27).
23. The well-known silver *missorium* of Theodosios, which is now in Madrid must be associated with this anniversary. It probably came from Thessalonike. (See page 249).
24. It has been established archaeologically that the Hippodrome of Thessalonike was located near the Galerian palace complex; the area has the same name today. (See M.J. Vickers, "The Hippodrome at Thessaloniki", *JRS*, 62, 1972, 25 ff.).
25. Malchos, frag. 18 (*HGM*, I), 408 (for Stoboi), 387 (for Philippi), 410 ff. (for Thessalonike). Also see Lemerle, *Philippes*, 111 ff. and Lemerle, *RH*, 280.
26. Malchos, 410, 412.
27. The sixth century settlement is discussed on page 243.
28. See page 231.
29. Procopius, *De Aedificiis*, 4. 1 ff. (Haury ed.).
30. According to Procopius, *De Aedificiis*, 4. 36 ff., Justinian renewed the fortifications of forty-six fortresses in Macedonia.
31. Procopius, *De Aedificiis*, 4.3.276.
32. Procopius, *De Aedificiis*, 4. 3. 21-27.
33. Cf. Lemerle, *RH*, 287.
34. Konidaris, 39.
35. Papazoglou, *BAB*, 123-24.
36. Papazoglou, *BAB*, 124. This transfer of the capital of Eastern Illyricum is disputed by several scholars (Theocharidis, 101, n. 5).
37. Mansi, II, 881.
38. K. Konidaris, *Ἐκκλησιαστικὴ Ἱστορία τῆς Ἑλλάδος*, I (Athens, 1954-60), 443.
39. Thessalonike maintained its superiority among the metropolitans of Illyricum until the middle of the eighth century. In the Paris codex 1555A (dated to the mid-eighth century) it appears for the first time in second place to the metropolitan of Crete. (Konidaris, 61).
40. Extensive bibliography on the exarchate or vicariate of Thessalonike exists in Lemerle, *Philippes*, 241-50 and Theocharidis, 102-25.
41. Lemerle, *Philippes*, 68 and 241 ff.
42. Mansi, III, 38, 42, 48.

43. «Πορ[φύ]ριος ἐπίσκοπος τὴ[ν] [κ]έντησιν τῆς βασιλικῆς Παύλο[υ] [ἐπ]οίησεν ἐν Χρ[ιστ]ῷ», Pelekanides, *ΠΑΕ*, 1975, 101.
44. Mansi, VI, 682, 847, 903 ff.
45. Konidaris, 52.
46. Lemerle, *Philippes*, 257 ff.
47. Mansi, VI, 566, 1081; VII, 137, and IX, 173, 190, 194, 197 ff. and cf. Papazoglou, *Cités*, 194.
48. Papazoglou, *Cités*, 237 and n. 27.
49. Mansi, VI, 577, frag. 1087.
50. Saria, *JOEAI*, 132 ff.
51. Of John and of Margaritis respectively (Mansi, IX, 645, 994).
52. From Papazogou, *Cités*, 239 ff.
53. Dardanios, Mansi, VI, 577.
54. B. Aleksova, "Ranohristijanskata bazilika vo Bargala", *Mélanges Dimče Koco* (Skopje, 1975), 24.
55. S. Pelekanides, «Χριστιανικὴ ἐπιγραφὴ ἐκ Καισαρείας τῆς Ἄνω Μακεδονίας», *Τόμος εἰς μνήμην Κ. Ἀμάντου* (Athens, 1960), 463 ff. (=Μελέτες, 401 ff.).
56. Kaisareia however, like all Elimiotis, belonged administratively to the province of Thessaly from the beginning of the fourth century. See notes 2 and 3 above.
57. Mansi, IX, 392.
58. P. Perdrizet, "Voyage dans la Macédoine Première", *BCH* 18 (1894), 426 ff. Papazoglou, *Cités*, 289 ff.
59. See Pelekanides, *AE*, 162, no. 1, 164; no. 2, 165 ff. nos. 3,4. (=Μελέτες, 379, no. 1, 381, nos. 2, 3, 382, no. 4). Tsigarida, 50, no. 17. Feissel-Spieser, 317, no. 11. Pelekanides, *AE*, 165 ff. no. 4 (=Μελέτες, 382, no. 4). Saria, *JOEAI*, 136. J.H. Mordtmann, "Inschriften aus Edessa", *MDAI (A)* 18 (1893), 416 ff. Lemerle, *Philippes*, 92. See also the inscriptions from Thessalonike and Sandanski (Tsigarida, 33, no. 1). Nikolajević, 354. See others from Thessalonike, Philippi and Edessa: Sandanski (Tsigarida, 40, no. 7, 56, no. 23), *IG*, X2, 1, 360 and 793, Lemerle, *Philippes*, 91 and 101, H. Leclercq, *DACL*, IV, pt. 2 (1921) and Lemerle, *RH*, 287.
60. *PG*, XXXVII, cols. 1089-90.
61. Mainly in northern Macedonia. See Babić, *Prilep*, 62.
62. Lemerle, *Philippes*, 71 ff.
63. See Philippi and Pešterica (S. Pelekanides, *ΠΑΕ*, 1966, 51 ff. K. Kepeski, "Villa rustica

vo. Pešterica kaj Prilep", *MAArch* 2, 1976, 143 ff. pls. 1-2).

64. The eastern part of Thessalonike was also fertile. See Procopius, *De Aedificiis*, 3, 27-33.

65. Feissel-Spieser, *T& MByz*, 308, no. 1; *IG*, X, 2, 1, 351.

66. An inscribed marble plaque which was found in the basilica of Saint Demetrios. See G. Oikonomou, «Ὁ Ἰουστινιανός ἐν Θεσσαλονίκῃ», *AE* (1918), 41 ff.; Sotiriou, 230-231 and Tsigarida, 92, no. 65.

67. See the Pešterica group mentioned above in n. 63.

68. The other three were found in Niš (Dacia Mediterranea), in Ratiaria (Dacia Ripensis), and in Horreomargoi or Orea (Moesia). See Seeck, *Notitia*, XI, 1. 35-39.

69. 'Cum procuratorem metallorum intra Macedoniam Daciam mediterraneam Moesiam seu Dardaniam...', see Cod. Theod. XVI,1. 32.5 (Mommsen ed.).

70. See Keramidciev, "Izvori za rudarstvo i metalurgijata vo antička Makedonija", *MAArch*, 3 (1977), 103 ff. with earlier bibliography. Also, Babić, *Prilep*, 65.

71. Mentzou, 98.

72. As, for example, the large quarries at Siveč at Prilep (Babić, *Prilep*).

73. Hermann-Sodini, *BCH*, 471 ff.

74. Ionic capitals whose style and artistic details show that they must have been finished completely in Thasos have been found in all these places; see Hermann-Sodini, *BCH*, 508.

75. Hermann-Sodini, *BCH*, 471 and Sodini, *BCH*, 122 ff.

76. As at Siveč in Prilep (Babić, *Prilep*, 67).

77. Lemerle, *Philippes*, 103 ff.

78. Sodini et al., *BCH*, 117 ff.

79. Babić, *Prilep*, 63. And elsewhere in the area of Prilep (Babić, *Prilep*, 67).

80. J. Wiseman, D. Mano-Zissi, "Excavations at Stobi, 1970" *AJA* 75 (1971), 403; ibid., "Excavations at Stobi, 1971" *AJA*, 76 (1972), 420. J. Wiseman, *Stobi, Vodič kroz antički grad* (Belgrade, 1973), 51.

81. Tsigarida, 63 ff., no. 31.

82. Feissel-Spieser, *T & MByz*, 327, no. 19.

83. Mentzou, 200 ff.

84. A pair of compasses was found in a fourth century tomb in the area of Prilep; according to Babić, *Prilep*, 69, they indicate the profession of the dead man.

85. On the town plan in this period, see Lavvas, 403 ff.

86. Lemerle, *Philippes*, 85 ff.

87. Ibid.

88. S. Pelekanides, «Ἀνασκαφαὶ Ὀκταγώνου Φιλίππων», *ΠΑΕ* 1960, 88.

89. Lemerle, *Philippes*, 86.

90. M. Chatzi-Ioannou, Ἀστυγραφία Θεσσαλονίκης (Thessalonike, 1880), 101 ff. and 109. Mecedonian Christians honoured the martyrs of their faith not only by establishing churches in their memory, but also by placing their tombs very close to the churches where they were specially venerated. See, for example, the tomb of the martyr, Akakios, next to the large basilica in the agora of Thasos; C. Delvoye, *BCH* 75 (1951), 160 ff. C. Dunant, J. Pouilloux, *Recherches sur l'histoire et les cultes de Thasos (Études thasiennes*, V 1957), 196.

91. In ms. no. 34 in the Eikosiphoinissa monastery on Mount Pangaion (see A. Xyngopoulos, «Τό καθολικόν τῆς Μονῆς Λατόμου ἐν Θεσσαλονίκῃ καὶ τό ἐν αὐτῷ ψηφιδωτόν», *AΔ*

12 (1929), 172 ff.

92. F. Papazoglou, "Ranohriščanski natpis iz Herakleje", *ZFFBe*, 11 (1970), 91 ff. This inscription according to Papazoglou, could date from 325, 370, or 415.

93. See, for example, one of the texts of his biography published by B. Laourdas, «Ἀνέκδοτον ἐγκώμιον εἰς τόν ὅσιον Δαβίδ», *Μακεδονικά* 10 (1970), 243 ff. and especially 250 ff.

94. Babić, *Prilep*, 68 ff. Idem, "Héritage paien dans le rite funéraire de la Macédoine paléochrètienne." *Actes du VIIe congrès international des sciences préhistoriques et protohistoriques, Prague, 21-27 Août 1966* (Prague, 1971-72), 1054 ff.

95. Lemerle, *Philippes*, 102 ff.

EARLY CHRISTIAN ART

1. Though this construction of the apse externally with shoulders and buttresses is found elsewhere in Macedonia (Basilica B and the Extra Muros at Phillipi, the basilica which preceded Saint Sophia, Thessalonike and the episcopal basilica at Herakleia Lynkestis) it was not common. However, it resembles some in other regions of Greece, e.g. Nikopolis, Epirus.

2. The second stylobate in the episcopal basilica at Stoboi belongs to a second building phase of the church, still within the Early Christian period.

3. Other 'hellenistic' basilicas in Macedonia are at Evraiokastro, Alyke and Agora, Thasos, Longos Edessa, Boskochorio Kozani, Toumba Thessalonike, Suvadol, Gradište (Debrešte) and others.

4. For the origin of the basilica with the transverse aisle, which may have been born of practical and aesthetic needs, and for the various sub-divisions of the type, see Orlandos, *Βασιλική*, 161.

5. The monument which is closest typologically to Saint Demetrios is the church of Saint Minas at Abu Mina, Egypt. It should perhaps be stressed here that the architectural idiosyncracies of Saint Demetrios, the insertion of pillars into the colonnades are not typical of the 'hellenistic' basilica. Pillars were, however, much used in Syria and Palestine.

6. Compare the basilicas of Dodone and Paramythia in Epirus (*RbK* 2, 1971, 237 ff. pl. 11, 13) and many others in the East, Brenk, 69.

7. Recently an interesting central plan Christian building of the fifth century has been uncovered in Amphipolis. It must have been a two-storey naos with a spacious narthex; externally it was circular, internally it had a hexagonal stylobate.

8. Krautheimer, 136.

9. According to the latest thoughts of the excavator, S. Pelekanides (Ἔργον, 1979, 11 ff.) the Octagon had been constructed as a freestanding octagon at the end of the fourth century. Later, in the middle of the fifth century, it was altered into an inscribed building.

10. See Saint Irene, and, in a slightly different style, Saint Sophia, Constantinople.

11. This type was early adopted in both East and West, first for oratories and martyria and later, from the fourth century for large churches. (Brenk, 66 ff; Orlandos, *Βασιλική* 185 ff.)

12. We refer to the plan of the main baptistery, the photisterion; the baptistery was usually made

up of more than one room (the *katechoumeneion, apodyterion, chrismarion* etc.)

13. J. Bolanakis, Τά παλαιοχριστιανικά Βαπτιστήρια τῆς Ἑλλάδος (Athens, 1976) 101 ff. assumes that the baptistery of the episcopal basilica of Stoboi (also known as the basilica of the bishop of Philippi) must have been one of the northern buildings projecting from the church. However, the baptistery of the church, not described here, had already been excavated in 1971, on the south side.

14. Facing peacocks and deer on the two sides of a fountain.

15. S. Pelekanides, *ΠΑΕ* 1969, 43 ff.

16. E. Stikas, *ΠΑΕ* 1966, 46 and 1971, 46-48.

17. The west side has not yet been excavated.

18. Some scholars believe, though they offer no explanation, that this building was a monastery.

19. As an example, we would cite the cubiculum of the Law School, University of Thessalonike which, restored by the Archaeological Service, has been preserved to our time.

20. Nikolajević 353-56 for the relative bibliography. The author stresses the similarity between the tombs of Sandanski and of Thessalonike as far as the architecture and various painted decorative motifs are concerned. This, she says, is due to the influence of the capital on the provinces.

21. Most of the tombs referred to are not yet published. I owe my information to Dr Boško Babić,Director of the Institute of Slavonic Studies in Prilep, to whom I offer my warmest thanks for her generous help when I visited the Early Christian monuments of Stoboi, Herakleia Lynkestis and in the Prilep region.

22. See page 243.

23. K. Kepeski, "Severozapadna nekropola na villata rusticja vo Pešterica kaj Prilep", *MAArch* 2 (1976), 216 and 218. The excavator attaches importance to a fish engraved on a silver spoon, the fish being a fundamentally Christian symbol.

24. In the villages of Rakle, Makedonski, Brod and elsewhere.

25. In the sixth century also.

26. Below the foundations of the walls opposite the University, near Plateia Sintrivaniou. According to another opinion, this section was built in the mid-third century. (See Spieser, *BCH* 507 and 518 ff.)

27. Spieser, *T & MByz* 152 and Spieser, *BCH* 507 and 509 for the earlier bibliography.

28. This settlement no longer exists. Its remains were removed by the archaeologists to clear the theatre and thus to permit its restoration. A reconstruction of the settlement is on display in the temporary museum on the site.

29. Close to the village of Gornji Kozjak in the Štip area. The remains belong to the second phase of the town (fifth-sixth century).

30. At Gradište, close to the village of Debrešte, excavations are in progress by a Polish-Yugoslav team. (See page 242).

31. This mosaic is today in the Staatliche Museen, Berlin.

32. According to a newer theory (G. Cvetkovic-Tomasevic, *Ranovizantijski podni mozaici - Dardanija, Makedonija, Novi Epir*, Belgrade 1978, 87 ff. and 112 ff.) all the above subjects and their symmetrical placing express the Christian teaching of the age; according to this, the events consist of four realms: 1) the Kingdom of Heaven (a symmetrical composition); 2) Paradise (the plant world); 3) the earth (fights and the hunting of animals); 4) the

kingdom of the waters (the sub-aqueous life).

33. Indicative perhaps are the Orthodox Baptistery (three zones) and the Arian Baptistery (two zones), Ravenna.

34. For this ciborium and its use see the recent study by D.I. Pallas, "Le ciborium exagonal de Saint-Demetrios de Thessalonique: essai d'interpretation", *Zograf* 10 (Belgrade, 1979), 44-58. It supports the view that this ciborium protected the cult icon of the saint, not his tomb; in other words, that it was the shrine of the church.

35. J. Wiseman, D. Georgievski, "Wall Decoration at Stobi, Studies in the Antiquities of Stobi", *BCH* 94 (1970), 164, pl. 1.

36. Two saints are depicted, each taking a step forward, right and left of a cross. Above them are parts of a depiction of Christ Enthroned flanked by two angels; See A. Xyngopoulos, «Ἡ παλαιοχριστιανικὴ τοιχογραφία τῆς ρωμαϊκῆς Ἀγορᾶς Θεσσαλονίκης», *Βυζαντινά* 9 (1977), 409 ff. pls. 34-36.

37. On the other side is an elderly woman, above whom is part of the inscription associated with her «...ΑΥΡΗΛΙΑ ΠΡΟΚΛΑ ΜΗΤ(Η)Ρ ΠΑΝΤΩΝ».

38. Compare the Good Shepherds in the Byzantine Museum, Athens, at Istanbul, in Berlin and elsewhere.

39. It was re-used on this monument. A similar column capital in the other face of the colonnade is a copy of the first.

40. At Basilica B at Philippi and at Saint Demetrios, Thessalonike.

41. A. Grabar, *L'âge d'or de Justinien de la Mort de Théodose à l'Islam* (Paris, 1966), 234; J.P. Sodini, "L'ambon de la Rotonde", *BCH* 100 (1976), 498 and 510. Elements from Constantinople are not lacking, see Brandenburg, *Spätantike und frühchristliche Skulptur in Thessaloniki*, 135-39.

42. It is quite probable that another silver object of this date, the well-known *missorium* of Theodosios in Madrid came from Thessalonike; see A. Tsitouridou, «Τό μισσόριο τοῦ Θεοδοσίου», *Κέρνος Γ. Μπακαλάκη* (Thessalonike 1972), 195 ff.

43. It is dated to the middle of the century.

44. M. Panayotidi, H. Grabar, "Un reliquaire paléochrétien récemment découvert près de Thessalonique", *CArch* 24 (1975), 40.

45. According to Buschhausen, "Kunstgewerbe des Ostillyrikums", *Εἰσηγήσεις τοῦ Δεκάτου Διεθνοῦς Συνεδρίου Χριστιανικῆς Ἀρχαιολογίας* (Thessalonike, 1980), 161-63, it must have been made in Constantinople. It was found, by chance, in the seaside village of N. Herakleia, Chalkidike, on the east coast of the Thermaic Gulf.

FROM THE SIXTH TO THE NINTH CENTURY

1. Lemerle, *Miracles*. Full bibliography on the collections of miracles is given in II, 13-26.

2. Procopius, *Anecdota*, 18.20. (Haury ed. 3.1.114).

3. Lemerle, *RH*, 287. M. Nystazopoulou-Pelekidou, «Συμβολή εἰς τήν χρονολόγησιν τῶν Ἀβαρικῶν καί Σλαβικῶν ἐπιδρομῶν ἐπί Μαυρικίου (582-602)», *Σύμμεικτα, Ἐθνικόν Ἵδρυμα Ἐρευνῶν, Κέντρον Βυζαντινῶν Ἐρευνῶν*, 2 (1970), 145-206.

4. Cf. J. Tsaras, "Le verbe ἐσθλαβώθη chez Con-

stantin Porphyrogénète," *Cyrillomethodianum* 10(1971), 26-57 and A. Avramea, «Σημείωμα γιά τό ἐθνικό ὄνομα 'Σλάβος' καί τή σημασιολογική του ἐξέλιξη στίς βυζαντινές πηγές», *Ἑλληνικά* 25 (1972), 409-15.

5. Theophanes (de Boor ed.), 270.

6. Theophylact Simocatta (de Boor ed.), 6.6.2; 6. 11.5; 8.5.9-11. Souda. *Sklavinon*. Menandros, frag. 16, I, 405.

7. George Cedrenus, I, 707-08.

8. Baynes, *BZ*, 110 ff. A. Stratos, *Τό Βυζάντιον στόν Z΄ αἰῶνα*, II (Athens, 1966), 502-42, 626-34, 904-09. Barišić, *Byzantion*, 371-95.

9. Lemerle, *RH*, 294.

10. Lemerle, *Miracles*, I, 134. 18-19.

11. A Xyngopoulos, «Βυζαντινόν κιβωτίδιον μετά παραστάσεων ἐκ τοῦ βίου τοῦ ἁγίου Δημητρίου», *AE*, 1936, 101-36.

12. Lemerle, *Miracles*, I, 175, 210, 211, 214.

13. Ibid., I, 175. 12-18.

14. Ibid., I, 178.

15. Ibid., I, 185.26.

16. Ibid., I 186-89 and II, 101-03. Baynes, *BZ*, 110-28.

17. K. Amantos, *Μακεδονικά. Συμβολή εἰς τήν μεσαιωνικήν ἱστορίαν καί ἐθνολογίαν τῆς Μακεδονίας* (Athens, 1920), 17; Amantos, I, 459.

18. Barišić, *Byzantion*, 371-95.

19. Lemerle, *Miracles*, I, 175.5; 209. 11-12; 211. 14-15; 214. 11-12.

20. Constantine Porphyrogenitus, *De administrando imperio* (Moravcsik-Jenkins, ed.), 32. 7-16.

21. Amantos, I, 277, 457-58.

22. Theophanes (de Boor ed.), 347.6; 348.18. See E.W. Brooks, "The Campaign of 716-718 from Arabic Sources", *JHS* 19 (1899), 21 and M. Graebner, "The Slavs in Byzantine Population Transfers of the Seventh and Eighth Centuries", *EtBal* 11 (1975), 45, 50.

23. Lemerle, *Miracles*, I, 209. 29-30.

24. Ibid., I, 209. 4-18.

25. Ibid., I, 214. 11-13, 218. 14 and II, 121. A. Abramea, *Ἡ βυζαντινή Θεσσαλία μέχρι τοῦ 1204. Συμβολή εἰς τήν ἱστορικήν γεωγραφίαν* (Athens, 1974) 150-56.

26. Lemerle, *Miracles* I, 215-17 and II, 123-25.

27. Ibid., I, 220.

28. Ibid., I, 228. 9-10.

29. Ibid., I, 228. 21.

30. Ibid., 228. 18-19 and II, 141-50. Charanis, *BSt*.

31. Lemerle, *Miracles*, II, 150.

32. Ibid., I, 228. 22-25; Grigoriou - Ioannidou.

33. Lemerle, *Miracles* I, 228.30.

34. Charanis, *BSt*.

35. Lemerle, *Miracles*, I, 229.22.

36. Ibid., I, 230. 1-4.

37. Ibid., 230. 5-8.

38. *BLS*, 934.

39. Theophanes (de Boor ed.), 357-58. G. Moravcsik, *Byzantinoturcica*, II, 213. N. Banescu, "Ὄγλος - Oglu, Le premier habitat de la horde d'Asparuch dans la région du Danube", *Byzantion* 28 (1958), 433 ff.

40. M.J. Vojnov, *BZ* 50 (1957), 527.

41. A.A. Vasiliev, "An Edict of the Emperor Justinian II", *Speculum* 18 (1943), 1 ff. H. Grégoire, "Un édit de l'empereur Justinien II", *Byzantion* 17 (1944-45), 119 ff.

42. Theophanes (de Boor ed.) 364. 14-15. S. Vryonis, "St. Joannicius the Great (754-846) and the 'Slavs' of Bithynia", *Byzantion* 31 (1961), 245-48. P. Malingoudis, "Slavisches aus dem byzantinischen Bithynien", *MZB* 2

(1979), 227-29.

43. Theophanes (de Boor ed.) 365-66.

44. Ibid., 366.2

45. On the theme of the Smolenoi, see G.I. Theocharides, «Μορουνάτς, τό δῆθεν σλαβικόν ὄνομα τῆς Καβάλας», *Μακεδονικά* 6 (1964), 82-88.

46. Theophanes (de Boor ed.) 430.21.

47. Ibid., 456. 12-25 (λογοθέτης τοῦ ὀξέος δρόμου).

48. Ibid., 486. 10.

49. Ibid., 486 ff.

50. Kyriakidis, IV, 141-42.

51. Honigmann, 14-20.

52. Ibid., 12-14.

53. Lemerle, *Miracles*, I, 69.2; 108. 3, 10; 114. 18; 119. 15; 126.3; 137. 21.

54. G.Ostrogorsky, "Sur la date de la composition du Livre des Thèmes et sur l'époque de la constitution des premiers thèmes d'Asie Mineure", *Byzantion* 23 (1953), 31-66. J. Karayannopoulos, «Περί τά βυζαντινά θέματα», *Ἑλληνικά* 18 (1964), 196-200. N. Oikonomidès, "Les premiers mentions des thèmes dans la Chronique de Théophane", *ZR* 16 (1975), 1-8

55. Charanis, *BSt* 239, n. 19.

56. Theophanes (de Boor ed.) 501.1.

57. P. S. Koledarov, *Ἡ ἵδρυση τοῦ θέματος «Μακεδονία» στή Θράκη* (translated into Greek by J.T. Lampsides), *Βαλκανική Βιβλιογραφία* I. with notes by K.A. Dimades (Thessalonike, 1973), 231-78.

58. J. B. Bury, *Imperial Administrative System in the Ninth Century* (London, 1911), 41 ff. M. Rajković, "La région de Strymon et le thème du Strymon", (in Serbian with French summary), *ZR* 5 (1958), 1-7.

59. Kyriakidis, 139-40.

60. Oikonomidis, 101, 105.

61. *BLS*, 1530a, 1739, 1753, 1793, 1826, 2058, 2143, 2147, 2155, 2196, 2271, 2490, 3100.

62. *BLS*, 1696, 1772, 1937, 2097, 2135, 2185, 2233, 2275a,b, 2295.

63. *BLS*, 1044, 1543, 1628a, 2078, 2081, 2388, 2427, 3051, 3091.

64. *BLS*, 210, 231a,b, 233, 237.

65. *BLS*, 233, 237.

66. *BLS*, 230, 231a,b.

67. *BLS*, 1436a, 1851, 1852, 2101a-d, 2151, 2173a-c, 2249, 2503a,b, 3134.

68. Lemerle, *Miracles*, I, 211,33. (οἱ τῆς διοικήσεως τῆς πόλεως τότε λαχόντες).

69. Pseudo-Symeon Magister, 614-15.

70. Cf. Saria, *JOEAI*.

71. Constantine Porphyrogenitus, *De Thematibus* (Pertusi, *Studi e Testi*, 160), 88.35. Honigmann, 14.

72. Honigmann, 16. Theophylact, Migne, *PG*, CXXVI, col. 201 and CXXIV, cols. 439-442.

73. *Vie de Ste Théodora*, ed. Kurtz, *Mémoires de L'Académie Imperiale des Sciences de St. Petersburg*, series VIII, 43: «Νεᾶνις δέ τις ἐκ Βεροίας, τοῦ ὑπό τήν ἡμετέραν μεγαλόπολιν τελοῦντος ὁρμωμένη κάστρου».

74. A. Keramopoullos, «Ἀνασκαφαί καί ἔρευναι ἐν τῇ Ἄνω Μακεδονίᾳ», *AE*, 1933, 47.

75. Konidaris, I, 513.

76. A. Xyngopoulos, *Τά μνημεῖα τῶν Σερβίων* (Athens, 1957), 4-6.

77. Cf. Ph. Petsas, «Χρονικά Ἀρχαιολογικά» *Μακεδονικά* 7 (1966-67), 308, no. 102.

78. In 926 the general, Basil Kladon, repaired the walls of Chrysoupolis. See S. Reinach, "La reconstruction des murs de Cavalla au Xe siècle", *BCH* 6 (1882), 267-75.

79. Theophanes (de Boor ed.) 496.5.
80. Kyriakidis, 401. Theocharidis, 227.
81. K. Bonis, *Ἡ Στρώμνιτσα* (Thessalonike, 1961), 6.
82. A. Vaillant. M. Lascaris, "La date de la conversion des Bulgares", *RESl* 13 (1933), 5-15 and H. Grégoire, "La date de la conversion des Bulgares", *Byzantion* 8 (1933), 663-68.

INTELLECTUAL LIFE

1. Lemerle, *Miracles*. F. Barišić, *Cuda Dimitrija Solunskog ka istoriski izvori* (Belgrade, 1953). P. Lemerle, "Les anciens recueils des miracles de Saint Démétrius et l'histoire de la péninsule balkanique", *BAB* 65 (1979), 395-415.
2. A. Teodorov-Balan, *Kiril i Metodi* I-II (Sofia, 1920-34). Dvornik. I. Dujčev, "Zur literarischen Tätigkeit Konstantins des Philosophen", *BZ* 44 (1951), 105-110. F. Grivec, *Konstantin und Method, Lehrer der Slaven* (Wiesbaden, 1960). F. Grivec, F. Tomšić, *Konstantin und Methodius, Thessalonicenses: Fontes* (Zagreb, 1960). Vlasto, 29-79 and 328-44. D. Angelov and others (edit.) *Konstantin Kiril Filosof* (Sofia, 1971).
3. It has not been determined whether the alphabet is Cyrillic or the other Slavonic alphabet, called Glagolitic (glagol="word"). The Cyrillic resembles the uncial Greek writing while the Glagolitic the Greek cursive. In its first form the Cyrillic contained the twenty-four letters of the Greek alphabet as well as many others to render the Slavic sounds; in time it underwent various changes and formed the basis of the present day writing of the Orthodox Slavic world (Editorial note).
4. N.L. Tunicki, *Svjatyj Kliment, episkop Slovenski* (Sergiev Posad, 1913). Vlasto, 168-70.

ART FROM THE MID-SEVENTH TO THE TENTH CENTURY

1. A. Xyngopoulos, *Συμβολαί εἰς τὴν τοπογραφίαν τῆς Βυζαντινῆς Θεσσαλονίκης* (Thessalonike, 1949). M. Vickers, "Town Planning of Roman Thessaloniki", *Ἀρχαία Μακεδονία* 2, 244 ff. and Lavvas, 405-10.
2. Janin, 314-419 and 454-56.
3. See Chatzidakis *ΠΑΑ*.
4. *Salonique*, pls. 34-49. Kalligas. Buchwald, *The Church of the Archangels in Sige near Mudania* (Vienna, 1969), 37 ff. Krautheimer, 309 ff. Mango, 161-65, pls. 175-77.
5. Kalligas, Krautheimer, Mango.
6. A. Orlandos, *ABME* 7 (1951), 146 ff. and Krautheimer.
7. On these mosaics, see Grabar, 84-88, pls. 80-86. Sotiriou, and R. Cormack, *BSA* 64 (1969), 17-52. A Grabar, *Byzantion* 48 (1978), 64 ff. Chatzidakis, *IEE*, Η' 313-15.
8. Sotiriou, pls. 313-15.
9. Ibid., pls. 62, 65a, 69-70.
10. See n. 4. above; Grabar, 189-92, 194-96, figs. 122-36. R. Cormack, "The Arts during the Age of Iconclasm", *Iconoclasm* (Birmingham, 1977), 35 ff.
11. D. Evangelides, «Εἰκονομαχικά μνημεῖα ἐν Θεσσαλονίκη» *AE*, 1937, 346 ff.
12. Grabar, *Empereur*. Sotiriou, II, 207-09. See Theocharidis, 195-202 with bibliography.
13. Sotiriou, II, 204-05, pl. 77.

FROM THE NINTH CENTURY TO 1204

THE CULTURAL ASSIMILATION OF THE SLAVS OF MACEDONIA A NEW PERIOD OF PROSPERITY FOR THESSALONIKE

1. Spieser, *T & MByz* 155-56, no. 7.
2. Lemerle, *Miracles*.
3. *BLS*.
4. Oikonomidis, 349 and 352.
5. Cameniates, 514-15.
6. Dvornik, 15 ff. and 384; also S.V. Troitsky, "Saint Méthode, Législateur des Slaves", *Travaux Théol. du Patriarcat de Moscou* (1961), and idem, «Διά ποῖον, πότε καί πού συνέταξεν ὁ Ἅγιος Μεθόδιος τόν νόμον διά τήν δίκασιν τῶν ἀνθρώπων», *Ἐκκλησία* (1966), 412-17, no. 16-17.
7. J.E. Anastasiou, «Βίος Κωνσταντίνου Κυρίλλου, Βίος Μεθοδίου» (translated into Greek), *Ἐπετηρίς Θεολογικῆς Σχολῆς Πανεπιστημίου Θεσσαλονίκης* 12 (1968), 119.
8. Constantine Porphyrogenitus, *De Thematibus* (Pertusi, Studi e Testi, 160, ed.).
9. Many Byzantine sources use the word Scyths to characterize the northern peoples, originating from lands beyond the Danube.
10. Theophanes (de Boor ed.), I, 430. (τὰς κατὰ Μακεδονίαν Σκλαυινίας ἠχμαλώτισε).
11. Ibid., 456 ff. (κατὰ τῶν Σκλαυινῶν ἐθνῶν).
12. Nicephorus (de Boor ed.), 76.
13. Leo, *Taktika* (PG, CVII, 969).
14. For the revolt of the *Sklaviniai* see Dvornik, *St. Grégoire*, 61-62. Constantine Porphyrogenitus, *De Ceremoniis*, 634-35, and idem, *De administrando imperio* (Moravcsik-Jenkins), 50. For the new bishops of the metropolitanate of Thessalonike and Philippi, see Parthey, *Notitiae Episcopatuum*, nos. 3, 10 and 13.
15. V. Vavrinek, *Beiträge zur byz. Geschichte 9-11. Jahrhunderts* (Prague, 1978), 269-71.
16. Leo, *Taktika* (PG, CVII, col. 969), (κατὰ τῶν Ῥωμαίοις πολεμούντων ἐθνῶν).
17. Constantine Porphyrogenitus, *De Ceremoniis*, 697.
18. Cameniates, 496.
19. Ibid., 499. (ἡ κολυμβήθρα τοῦ θείου βαπτίσματος 'τούς Σλάβους' τῷ χριστωνύμῳ λαῷ συνεμόρφωσε).
20. Cantacuzene, 93.
21. *Vie de Ste. Théodora*, ed. Kurtz, in *Mémoires de l'Académie Imperiale des Sciences de St. Petersburg*, ser. VIII, 11.
22. Constantine Porphyrogenitus, *De administrando imperio* (Moravcsik-Jenkins), 49.
23. Cameniates, 500, ff.
24. The differences of opinion between scholars on this point derives from widely varying interpretations of the sources, a reflection of the progress of research.
25. Cedrenus, II, 254.
26. Theodosius Melitinus (Tafel ed.).
27. *PG*, CXI, 176 (τῆς πάσης Δύσεως ἡ κυριότης τῇ ῥωμαϊκῇ βασιλείᾳ τυγχάνει).
28. See *Timarion*, ed. R. Romano (Naples, 1974), 53-54.
29. S. Kyriakidis, *Eustazio di Tessalonica, La espugnazione di Tessalonica* (Palermo, 1961).
30. John Anagnostes, 483 ff.

POLITICAL HISTORY 867-1204

1. Leo, *Τακτικά* (PG, CVII, 969A). Cf. G. Tsaras, «Τό νόημα τοῦ "γραικώ σας" στά Τακτικά Λέοντος ΣΤ' τοῦ Σοφοῦ». *Βυζαντινά* 1 (1969), 138-56.
2. Cameniates (Böhlig ed.), 8. 81.
3. G. Ostrogorski, "Die byzantinische Staatenhierarchie", *Seminarium Kondakovianum* 8(1936), 45.
4. John Skylitzes (Thurn ed.), 176.83. (βαρέα εἰσπράττοντες τελωνήματα).
5. The Theophanes Continuatus, 360. 8 ff. and Skylitzes, 178, 46 ff.
6. Cf. the letter of Choirosphaktes to Leo, no. 6, which relates, «...τὰ τοῦ Δυρραχίου τριάκοντα φρούρια σύν αὐτῷ πλούτῳ καί αὐτοῖς οἰκήτορσι τῇ βασιλείᾳ σου δῶρον προσήνεγκα...», p. 113, *Ἐπιστολή* ΚΓ' (ΙΗ'), lines 8 ff. (Kolias).
7. Nicholas Mysticus mentions these facts in *Ἐπιστολαί*, 9.62. 180 ff. (Jenkins-Westerink ed.).
8. N. Beis, «Ἐπιδρομή Βουλγάρων ἐπί τζάρου Συμεών», *Ἑλληνικά* 1 (1928), 367.
9. Theophanes Continuatus, 366. 19 ff. and Skylitzes, 182. 48 ff.
10. Skylitzes, 183.67.
11. Cameniates, 20.79.
12. Ibid., 33.
13. A. Mai, *Spicilegium Romanum*, IV (Rome 1840), XXXIX.
14. Nicholas Mysticus, *Ἐπιστολαί*, 75.326.64.
15. Kolias, 113.
16. M.T. Lascaris, "Les sources épigraphiques de la légende d'Oleg", *Mélanges H. Grégoire*, II (1951), 213 ff.
17. Chronology according to Skylitzes, 277. 32-33.
18. Leo the Deacon, 159.6.
19. Ibid., 159.6.
20. S. Runciman, *A History of the First Bulgarian Empire* (London 1930), 182 and 216.
21. Karayannopulos, II, 429-30, notes 721-22.
22. «... κατέδραμε πᾶσαν τὴν ἑσπέραν, οὐ μόνον Θράκην καί Μακεδονίαν καί τὰ τῇ Θεσσαλονίκη πρόσχωρα, ἀλλά καί Θετταλίαν καί Ἑλλάδα καί Πελοπόννησον», Skylitzes, 330.95.
23. Leo the Deacon, 175.10. The chronology was determined by G. Schlumberger, *L' Epopée Byzantine à la fin du dixième siècle*, part II (Paris, 1900).
24. Leo the Deacon, 171.11 ff. and Skylitzes, 331. 24 ff.
25. Skylitzes, 341. 13.
26. Skylitzes, 343.83 ff., places this campaign around 998/1000, a date which cannot stand because in 1000 Basil II was still in Asia.
27. «τὴν τε μεγάλην εἷλε Πρεσθλάβαν καί τὴν μικρὰν καί τὴν Πλίσκοβαν, καί ἀσινής καί τροπαιοῦχος ἡ ῥωμαϊκή ὑπενόστησε δύναμις», Ibid., 344. 86-88.
28. Ibid., 344. 90; 344. 95 ff.
29. Ibid., 346.44 ff.
30. Ibid., 346.50. The view of some scholars that Samuel attacked Adrianople via Thrace is not correct. Cf. Gelzer, *BZ*, 56.
31. «πάντα τὰ ἐν ποσί βουλγαρικά φρούρια δηῶν καί καταστρεφόμενος», Skylitzes, 346.55-56.
32. Ibid., 346.56 ff.
33. «ὁ δὲ βασιλεύς οὐ διέλιπε καθ' ἕκαστον ἐνιαυτὸν εἰσιών ἐν Βουλγαρίᾳ καί τὰ ἐν ποσί κείρων τε καί δηῶν», Ibid., 348.9-10.

34. Ibid., 348. 10 ff.
35. The exact site of Kleidion was established at the beginning of the century by the Bulgarian historian J. Ivanov "Belasickata bitka (29 Juli 1014 g)", *Izvestija na Istor Druz* 3 (1911), 1-15 (off-print pages).
36. Skylitzes, 349.26 ff. (πρὸς μεσημβρίαν κείμενον τοῦ Κλειδίου).
37. Ibid., 349.30 ff.
38. Ibid., 349.35 ff.
39. Karayannopulos II, 456-59, 460-63.
40. Michael Attaleiates, Ἱστορία, 83. Skylitzes Continuatus: see E. Tsolakis, Ἡ συνέχεια τῆς χρονογραφίας τοῦ Ἰωάννου Σκυλίτζη (Thessalonike, 1958), 115.
41. Attaleiates, 87.
42. Skylitzes, 409.87 ff.
43. Ibid., 409-10, 7-8. (πάντα τὸν παρευρεθέντα Ρωμαῖον ἀνηλεῶς καὶ ἀναιροῦντες).
44. Ibid., 411-412. 58-67.
45. Ibid., 412.89-90.
46. Ibid., 413.4 ff.
47. Karayannopulos, II, 493, n. 49.
48. Skylitzes, 428.85 ff.
49. Attaleiates, 297.6 ff.; Skylitzes Continuatus, op. cit., 182.15 ff.
50. Anna Comnena (Leib ed.), II, 41-43. F. Chalandon, *Essai sur le règne d'Alexis I Comnène* (Paris, 1900), 90-91.
51. Tafrali, *Thessalonique,* 182 ff.
52. S. Kyriakidis, *Eustazio di Tessalonica: La espugnazione di Tessalonica* (Palermo, 1961), passim.
53. Nicetas Choniates, 469. (ὁ τόπος τοῦ Διμιτρίτζη).
54. Lemerle, *Philippes,* 20 ff.
55. Choniates, 624 ff.
56. Ibid., 707.

INTELLECTUAL LIFE

1. G. Böhlig, *Ioannis Caminiatae De expugnatione Thessalonicae* (Berlin-New York, 1973).
2. A.P. Každan, "Some Questions addressed to the Scholars who believe in the authenticity of Kaminiates, 'Capture of Thessalonica'", *BZ* 71 (1978), 301-14.
3. *PG* CXXIV, 336-560, 126. 152-221, 308-557. S. G. Mercati, "Poesie di Teofilatto di Bulgaria", *StBN* 1 (1925), 175-94. Xanalatos. P. Gautier, "Le discours de Théophylacte de Bulgarie à l'autocrator Alexis 1er Comnène (6 janvier 1088)", *REByz* 23 (1965), 178-94.
4. *PG* CXIX, 1297-1300. Tafel, 36.
5. *PG* CXIX, 997-1010, 139. 165-221. N. Festa, "Niceta di Maronea e i suoi dialoghi sulla prozessione dello Spirito Santo", *Bessarione, Seria III,* 16-19 (1912-1916). M. Jugie, "Nicetas de Maronée", *Dictionnaire de Théologie Catholique,* XI, 473-77.
6. *PG* CXIX 928-36. Regel, 311-30. J. Schmidt, *Des Basilius von Achrida, Erzbischofs von Thessalonike, bisher unedierte Dialoge* (Munich, 1901). J. Dräseke, "Zu Basileios von Achrida", *ZWTh* 48 (1905), 112-20.
7. G. Stallbaum, *Eustathii commentarii ad Homeri Iliadem et Odysseam* I-VII (Leipzig, 1825-30, reprinted, 4 volumes, Hildesheim, 1960). M. van der Valk, *Eustathii archiepiscopi Thessalonicensis commentarii ad Homeri Iliadem pertinentes ad fidem cod. Laurentiani* (Leiden, 1971).
8. Regel, 24-131.
9. Tafel, 196-214.
10. S. Kyriakidis, *Eustazio di Tessalonica: La espugnazione di Tessalonica* (Palermo, 1961).
11. P.J. Koukoules, Θεσσαλονίκης Εὐσταθίου τά λαογραφικά I-II (Athens, 1950). Idem, Θεσσαλονίκης Εὐσταθίου τά γραμματικά (Athens, 1953). P. Wirth, *Untersuchungen zur byzantinischen Rhetorik des 12. Jahrhunderts mit besonderer Berücksichtigung der Schriften des Erzbischofs Eustathios von Thessalonike* (Dissertation, Munich, 1960). (Bibliography of the published works of Eustathios).
12. T. Hedberg, *Eustathios als Attizist* (Uppsala, 1935).
13. J. Perles, "Jüdisch-byzantinische Beziehungen", *BZ* 2 (1893), 574-75.

ART FROM THE TENTH CENTURY UNTIL 1204

1. P. Lazarides, «Ναός Παναγίας Κονταριώτισσας Πιερίας», *ΑΔ* 29 (1974), Χρονικά 3, 759-64. Radojčić, 9, plan 2α.
2. Millet, *BCH,* 72 ff; Mylonas, *Millénaire.*
3. P. Mylonas, "Nouvelles recherches au Mont Athos", *CArch* 29 (1980-81), 175 ff; idem, Ἀρχαιολογία 1 (November, 1981), 52-69. On Xenophontos monastery, see Theocharidis' communication to the Symposium of the Christian Archaeological Society in 1981 (Summary).
4. G. Millet, *L' Ecole grecque dans l'architecture byzantine* (Paris, 1916), 15-53. G. Sotiriou, Χριστιανική Ἀρχαιολογία (Athens, 1942), 319-22. A. Orlandos, *ABME* 9 (1961), 2-112. V. Korać, "Sur les basiliques mediévales de Macédoine et de Serbie", *Actes du XIIᵉ congrès international d'études byzantines* (Ochrid, 1961), 173-85. Vocotopoulos, 95 ff. Moutsopoulos, «Ἀνασκαφή Ἁγ. Ἀχιλλείου Πρέσπας», *ΕΕΠΣΘ* 5 (1971-72), 149-407. C. Bouras, "Zourtsa", *CArch* 21 (1971), 137-49. P. Mylonas, "Les étapes successives de construction du Protaton au Mont Athos", *CArch* 28 (1979), 143 ff. and *CArch* 29 (1980-81), 176.
5. Orlandos, Καστοριά, 10-24.
6. A. Orlandos, «Ἡ Παντάνασσα τῆς Μονεμβασίας», *ABME* 1 (1935), 150 ff. Orlandos, Καστοριά, Krautheimer, 354, 356 (attribution of the type to "Bulgarian" architecture, which is not justified). S. Pelekanides, Βυζαντινά καί Μεταβυζαντινά Μνημεῖα τῆς Πρέσπας (Thessalonike, 1960), 55-62. D. Stričević, *XIIᵉ congrès international d'études byzantines* (Ohrid, 1961), Rapport 7, 224 ff. Xyngopoulos, Σέρραι, 61-71.
7. See most recently, Vocotopoulos, 116-26, for the older bibliography. For the churches of Stromnitsa, P. Miljković-Pepek, "Le complexe des églises de Vodoča", *PCHRSM* XIII (Skopje, 1975).
8. Krautheimer, 328-32. Vocotopoulos, 324.
9. D. Evangelides, Ἡ Παναγία τῶν Χαλκέων (Thessalonike, 1954). Krautheimer, 397-98.
10. E. Tsigaridas, *AAA* 4 (1971), 54-57.
11. N. Nikonanos, «Ἡ ἐκκλησία τῆς Μεταμόρφωσης τοῦ Σωτῆρος στό Χορτιάτη», *Κέρνος Γ. Μπακαλάκη* (Thessalonike, 1972), 102 ff.
12. P. Miljković-Pepek, "Quelques doneés nouvelles des recherches sur l'église de la Vièrge de Veljusa", *PCHRSM* IX (Skopje, 1969), no. 7,

Idem., "Les monuments nouvellement découverts dans l'architecture et dans la peinture en Macédoine", *PCHRSM* XII (Skopje, 1973), No. 2, 5 ff. (with French summary). Mango, 308.
13. G. Velenis, *ΕΕΠΣΘ* 6(1973), 83 ff. (Prosostsane).
14. Krautheimer, 401; P. Miljković-Pepek, "Contribution à l'étude de l'église monastique de Nerezi Matiča Srpska", *Recherches sur l'art* 10 (Novisad, 1974), 313-22.
15. Mango, 308 ff., figs. 335-36. Krautheimer, 401-02 (Kuršumlija). Xyngopoulos, Σέρραι, 65 ff.
16. K. Theocharide, «Τά ψηφιδωτά τοῦ τρούλλου στήν Ἁγ. Σοφία Θεσσαλονίκης», *ΑΔ* 31 (1976), Μελέτες 265-73. M. Panagiotidou, «Παράσταση τῆς Ἀνάληψης στόν τροῦλλο τῆς Ἁγ. Σοφίας Θεσσαλονίκης», *ΕΕΠΣ* 62 (1974), 69-89. Cormack, *ΔΧΑΕ.*
17. A. Xyngopoulos, «Ἡ τοιχογραφία τῆς Ἀναλήψεως ἐν τῇ ἀψίδι τοῦ Ἁγίου Γεωργίου Θεσσαλονίκης», *ΑΕ* (1938), 32 ff.
18. S. Pelekanides, "Bemerkungen zu den Altarmosaiken der Hagia Sophia zu Thessaloniki und die Frage der Datierung der Platytera", *Βυζαντινά* 5 (1973), 31-40. Cormack, *ΔΧΑΕ.*
19. M. Kalligas, *ΠΑΕ* (1941-44), 49 S. Pelekanides, «Νέαι ἔρευναι εἰς τήν Ἁγ. Σοφίαν Θεσσαλονίκης», *Πεπραγμένα Θ´ Διεθνοῦς Βυζαντινολογικοῦ Συνεδρίου* (Thessalonike, 1953), I, 398-407. Cormack, *ΔΧΑΕ* See *Le Icone,* 130, and col. pl. on 145.
20. Evangelidis. Also K. Papadopoulos, *Die Wandmalereien des XI. Jahrhunderts in der Kirche Παναγία τῶν Χαλκέων in Thessaloniki* (Graz-Cologne, 1975). A. Tsitouridou, Ἡ Παναγία τῶν Χαλκέων (Thessalonike, 1975), Guide.
21. A. Grabar, "Deux témoinages archéologiques sur l'autocéphalie d'une église: Prespa et Ohrid", *RTIEByz* 8 (Belgrade), 166.
22. *Monumentalmalerei,* I, plans 1-5, figs. 1-28. A. Grabar, "Les peintures murales dans le choeur de Sainte-Sophie", *CArch* 15 (1965), 257. P. Miljković-Pepek, "Les fresques du naos et du narthex de Sainte-Sophie d'Ohrid", *PCHRSM* IX (Skopje, 1966). Lazarev, 158, figs. 182-87.
23. N. Moutsopoulos, «Ἔρευνες στήν Καστοριά καί τόν Ἅγιο Ἀχίλλειο», *ΕΕΠΣΘ* 1965, 180 ff., pls. 16-17, 21-27.
24. P. Miljković-Pepek, "Le complexe des églises de Vodoča", *PCHRSM* XIII (Skopje, 1975).
25. V.J. Djurić, "Fresques du Monastère de Veljusa", *Akten des XI. internationalen Byzantinistenkongress* (Munich, 1958) 113-21. Miljković-Pepek, "Veljusa, le monastère de la Vièrge de Pitié au village Veljusa près de Strumiča" (in Serbian with French summary), Skopje, 1981.
26. *Recueil,* I, no. 47. Millet, *Athos,* pls. 1,2,4. Bettini, 32. See Chatzidakis, *IEE,* H´, 313-15.
27. Orlandos, Καστοριά, 29 ff., figs. 19-20. Pelekanides, Καστοριά pls. 87-88 (Saint Stephen), 118 (Taxiarchs) and Pelekanidis.
28. Pelekanides, Καστοριά, pls. 38, 41. Orlandos, Καστοριά, 29, pls. 19-20.
29. As in P. Miljković-Pepek, "Les fresques et les icônes du Xᵉ et XIᵉ siècles en Macédoine dans la période du tzare Samuel et celle d'après lui", *PCHRSM* XIV (Skopje, 1975), (in Serbian with French Summary), 37-51 ff.
30. See notes 4, 7 and 10 above. For painting of the twelfth century, see Malmquist, and also A.H.S. Megaw, "12th Century Frescoes in Cyprus", *Actes du XIIᵉ congrès international*

d'études byzantines (Ohrid, 1961), III, 257-66 and Chatzidakis, *IEE*, Θ΄ 404-11.

31. O.M. Dalton, *Byzantine Art and Archaeology* (Oxford, 1911), 398-99, figs. 233, 423. P. Perdrizet, L. Chesnay, "La Métropole de Serrès", *MonPiot*, 10 (1914), 126 ff. and figs. 8-17. E. Diez and O. Demus, *Byzantine Mosaics in Greece* (Cambridge, Mass., 1931), 106-16. Orlandos, *EEBS* 19 (1949), 260 ff.

32. N. Mavrodinov, *Ἡ Παλαιά βουλγαρική ζωγραφική* (in Bulgarian), (Sofia, 1946), 68-78. G. Millet and A. Frolow, I, viii, pls. 15-21, 88. Ljubinković, *Corsi*, 435-37. *Monumentalmalerei*, I, 17, plans 6-7, figs. 29-45. P. Miljković-Pepek, *Nerezi* (Belgrade, 1966). V. J. Djurić, *Byzantinische Fresken in Jugoslawien* (Munich, 1976), 13-14, col. pls. V-IX and fig. 7. P. Miljković-Pepek, "Contribution à l'étude de l'église monastique de Nérezi", *Sbornik Novisad* 10 (1974), 313 ff.

33. E. Tsigaridas, «Ὅσιος Δαβὶδ Θεσσαλονίκης», *ΑΔ* 28 (1973), Χρονικά 2, 495, pl. 459b. See Chatzidakis, *IEE*, Θ΄, 407.

34. A. Grabar, *La peinture religieuse en Bulgarie* (Paris, 1928), 54-86. Lazarev, 222, figs. 346-52. A. Orlandos, *Ἡ Ἀρχιτεκτονικὴ καὶ αἱ βυζαντιναὶ τοιχογραφίαι τῆς Μονῆς Θεολόγου Πάτμου* (Athens, 1979). E. Bakalova, *Église ossuaire de Batchkovo* (in Bulgarian with foreign language summaries), (Sofia, 1977). Mouriki, *AAA* 11 (1979), 115-42.

35. Mouriki, *JOEByz* 31 (Vienna, 1981), 725-57.

36. *Kurbinovo*, passim.

37. Orlandos, *Καστοριά*, 24-60. Pelekanides, *Καστοριά*, pls. 1-34 *Kurbinovo*, 563-84. Cf. Chatzidakis, *IEE*, Θ΄, 406.

38. Pelekanides, *Καστοριά*, pls. 35-39, *Kurbinovo*, 563 ff.

39. Orlandos, *Καστοριά* 35, 44-45, 56, figs. 34, 36, 37, 39.

40. Orlandos, *Καστοριά*, 139-46. Pelekanides, *Καστοριά*, pls. 43-62. Pelekanides.

41. Millet-Frolow, I pls. 22-30, 89-90. *Monumentalmalerei*, I, 19, plan 8, figs. 48-49. Ljubinković, *Corsi*, 437-38. V. Lazarev, *Old Russian Murals and Mosaics* (London, 1966), 116 ff., 251 ff.

42. Millet, *Athos*, pl. 98.1. Radojčić, 30. Lazarev, 212, fig. 341.

43. S. Pelekanides, «Ἔρευναι ἐν Ἄνω Μακεδονίᾳ», *Μακεδονικά* 5 (1961-63), 363-414. L. Mavrodinova, *Les peintures murales de l'église de Saint-Nicolas près de Melnic* (in Bulgarian with German and French resumés) (Sofia, 1975) and idem, "Nouvelles considérations sur les peintures du chevet de l'église Saint Nicolas à Melnic", *Actes du XVe congrès international d'études byzantines* (Athens, 1976), IIA 427 ff.

44. Drossoyianni, *ΑΔ* 18 (1963), Χρονικά 2, 249-50, pls. 279-80. M. Michailidis, *ΑΔ* 26 (1971), Χρονικά 1, 21, pls. 27, 28α.

45. M. Michailidis, *ΑΔ* 20 (1965), Χρονικά 3, 474, pl. 578α and *ΑΔ* 21 (1966), Χρονικά 2, 369. M. Chatzidakis, *ΑΔ* 21 (1966) Χρονικά 1, 29, pls. 37-38. Chatzidakis, *Sopočani*, 63, fig. 7. M. Michailidis, "Les peintures murales de l'église de Saint-Jean le Théologien à Véria", *Actes du XVe congrès international d'études byzantines* (Athens, 1976), IIA, IIB 469 ff.

46. Millet, *Athos*, pl. 97. 3 and 97. 4. Chatzidakis, *Sopočani*, 63-64. *Monumentalmalerei*, II, pl. 41 fig. B.

47. S. Rajozčić, "Die serbischen Ikonenmalerei, XII. Jahrhundert bis zum Jahre 1459", *JOEByz*, 5 (1956), 63-64, fig. 1. Weitzmann,

Frühe Ikonen, fig. 166, p. LXI. Cf. Chatzidakis, *Le Icone*, 132, figs. 146-47.

48. Chatzidakis, *Frühe Ikonen*, fig. 41, p. XXIV.

49. M. Chatzidakis, «Εἰκόνες Ἐπιστηλίου ἀπό τό Ἅγιον Ὅρος», *ΔΧΑΕ* 4 (1964), 377-403, pls. 77-93 (=*Studies*, XVIII). Chatzidakis, *Actes XV*, 344 ff., pl. XXXVIII, fig. 9, pl. XXXIX, figs. 10-11.

50. Ibid., 347, ff., plan 2.

51. Ibid., pl. XLV, figs. 20-21. H. Belting, *Das Bild und sein Publikum im Mittelalter* (Berlin, 1981), 143, figs. 49-50 and catalogue no. 19.

52. Chatzidakis, *Actes XV*, 359 ff., pls. XLVI, fig. 22.

53. Bettini, II, 31. Chatzidakis, *Cini*, 11-40, fig. 6. Lazarev, 408, fig. 319.

54. Sotiriou, 209, pl. 80.

FROM 1204 TO THE CAPTURE OF THESSALONIKE BY THE TURKS

1. See generally, J. Longnon, *L'Empire Latin de Constantinople et la principauté de Morée* (Paris, 1949). Miller, *Latins in the Levant*, D.M. Nicol, "The Fourth Crusade and the Greek and Latin Empires", *CMH*, IV, 1 (1966), 275-330.

2. The Greeks called him Skyloyiannis; Cf. Akropolites (Heisenberg ed.), 23-24.

3. A. Krantonelli, *Ἡ κατά τῶν Λατίνων ἑλληνοβουλγαρική σύμπραξις ἐν Θράκῃ 1204-1206* (Athens, 1964).

4. Choniates, 815.11.

5. Ibid., 815.16 and N.E. Petrović, «Ἡ πρώτη ὁλοκληρωτική καταστροφή τῶν Σερρῶν τό 1206 ὑπό τοῦ Βουλγάρου Ἰωαννίτζη», *Σερραϊκά Χρονικά* 1 (1953), 67-96.

6. Choniates, 819.

7. Ostrogorsky, 429.

8. Asdracha, 240-41.

9. Nicol, *Despotate*, 49.

10. Ibid., 61.

11. J. Longnon, "La reprise de Salonique par les Grecs en 1224", *Actes du VIe congrès international d'études byzantines*, I (Paris, 1950), 141-56.

12. Akropolites, 42.

13. Nicol, *Despotate*, 110.

14. Ibid., 111.

15. Akropolites, 73-84.

16. Ibid., 91-92.

17. Ibid., 117 ff.

18. D.J. Geanakoplos, "Greco-Latin Relations on the Eve of the Byzantine Restoration: the Battle of Pelagonia", *DOP* 7 (1953), 99-141.

19. Ostrogorsky, 464.

20. George Pachymeres, II, 396.6 ff. Miller, *Latins in the Levant*, 211-268 ff.

21. Mamalakis, 105.

22. Nicephoros Gregoras, I, 423 ff.

23. Ibid. I 495. 12 ff.

24. John Cantacuzene, I, 457-58.

25. For a complete biography of Cantacuzene, see G. Weiss, *Joannes Kantakuzenos-Aristokrat, Staatsman, Kaiser und Mönch- in der Gesellschaftsentwicklung von Byzanz im 14 Jahrhundert* (Wiesbaden, 1969).

26. P. Charanis, "Internal Strife in Byzantium in the Fourteenth Century", *Byzantion* 15 (1940-41), 208-30. Cf. A.A. Vasiliev, *History of the Byzantine State 324-1453* (Wisconsin, 1958),

831-39, and Ostrogorsky, 515-22.

27. G. Papamïchael, *Ὁ Ἅγιος Γρηγόριος ὁ Παλαμᾶς, ἀρχιεπίσκοπος Θεσσαλονίκης* (St. Petersburg-Alexandria, 1911), with the older bibliography on the Hesychasts. J. Meyendorff, "Les débuts de la controverse hésychaste", *Byzantion* 23 (1953), 87-120. Idem, *Byzantine Hesychasm. Historical, theological and social problems* (London, 1974) (articles 1953-71). B.N. Tatakis, *"La Philosophie Byzantine"*, Paris, 1949, in E. Bréhier, Histoire de la Philosophie, fasc. supp. II pp.261-281.

28. P. Wittek, *Das Fürstentum Mentesche* (Istanbul, 1934). I. Dujčev, "Contribution à l'histoire de la conquète turque en Thrace aux dernières décades du XIVe siècle", *EtBal* 9 (1972), 80-92.

29. K.P. Matschke, "Johannes Apokaukos und die byzantinische Flotte in der Bürgerkriegsperiode 1340-1355", *Actes du XIVe congrès international d'études byzantines* (Bucharest, 1971), 193-205.

30. P. Lemerle, *L'Emirat d'Aydin, Byzance et l'Occident* (Paris, 1957). E. Werner, "Johannes Kantakuzenos. Umur Pasha und Orchan", *Byzantinoslavica* 26 (1965), 255-76.

31. Cf. Cantacuzène, II, 234-35, 568 ff.

32. Ibid., II, 552.1-2.

33. Ibid., III, 117.5. ff.

34. Ibid., III, 204-09.

MACEDONIA FROM 1354 UNTIL 1430

1. G. Ostrogorsky, *The Serbian State of Serres after the death of Dušan* (in Serbocroat), (Belgrade, 1965), 102.

2. S.J. Theocharides, *Σύντομη ἱστορία τῆς Μακεδονίας ἕως τήν Τουρκοκρατία* (Thessalonike, 1965), 96.

3. G. Ostrogorski, "Byzance, état tributaire de l'empire turc", *ZR* 5 (1958), 51.

4. Vacalopoulos, 28, with relevant bibliography.

5. G. Ostrogorski, *Pour l'histoire de la féodalité byzantine* (Brussels, 1954), 161 ff., 172 ff. S. Lambros, «Ἰσιδώρου μητροπολίτου Θεσσαλονίκης ὀκτώ ἐπιστολαί ἀνέκδοτοι», *NE* 9 (1912), 349-50.

6. Vacalopoulos, 29.

7. Moschopoulos, *EEBΣ* 155 ff.

8. Dennis, *OCA* 159, 58 ff.

9. R.J. Loenertz, *Démétrius Cydonès. Correspondance* (Vatican, 1960), 2, 238. Dennis, *OCA* 71-72.

10. E. Zachariadou, «Ἡ ἐπέκταση τῶν Ὀθωμανῶν στήν Εὐρώπη ὡς τήν ἅλωση τῆς Κωνσταντινουπόλεως», *IEE*, Θ΄, 191.

11. Vacalopoulos, 40-41.

12. G. Ostrogorski, "La prise de Serrès", *Byzantion* 35 (1965), 306.

13. Vacalopoulos, 42.

14. Moschopoulos, *EEBΣ* 150, 155 and *EEBΣ* 14 (1938), 504, 507. Hadschi Chalfa, 73.8.

15. B. Laourdas, «Ὁ συμβουλευτικός πρός Θεσσαλονικεῖς τοῦ Μανουήλ Παλαιολόγου», *Μακεδονικά* 3 (1953-55), 295-302.

16. Dennis, *OCA* 114 ff., 136-50.

17. Lemerle, *Philippes*, 218.

18. Vacalopoulos, 64-66, n. 3.

19. A.E. Vacalopoulos, «Οἱ δημοσιευμένες ὁμιλίες τοῦ ἀρχιεπισκόπου Θεσσαλονίκης Ἰσιδώρου ὡς ἱστορική πηγή γιά τήν γνώση τῆς πρώτης τουρκοκρατίας (1387-1402)», *Μακεδονικά* 4 (1955-60), 20-34. Idem, «Ὁ ἀρχιεπίσκοπος

Γαβριήλ καί ή πρώτη τουρκική κατοχή τῆς Θεσσαλονίκης (1391-1403)», *Μακεδονικά* 4, (1955-60), 372.

20. S. Lambros, «Βραχέα Χρονικά», *MEI* I (Athens, 1932-33), 44, 69, 85.

21. E. Stougiannakis, Ἔδεσσα ἡ Μακεδονική ἐν τῇ Ἱστορίᾳ (Thessalonike, 1932), 229-31.

22. Vacalopoulos, 46-47.

23. Hadschi Chalfa, 95-97.

24. A.E. Vacalopoulos, «Τό κάστρο τοῦ Πλαταμῶνα», *Μακεδονικά* 1 (1940), 71-72.

25. A. Bacalopoulos, "Les limites de l'empire byzantin," *BZ* 55 (1962), 56-65 (with relevant bibliography).

26. Vacalopoulos, *Thess.*, 64.

27. Ibid., 62-70. Idem, «Συμβολή στήν ἱστορία τῆς Θεσσαλονίκης ἐπί Βενετοκρατίας», *Τόμος Ἀρμενοπούλου* (Thessalonike, 1952), 137-41.

28. Vacalopoulos, *Thess.*, 71-74.

INSTITUTIONS, SOCIETY, ECONOMY

1. Escorial Taktikon=Oikonomidis 255-77.

2. See the above footnote where alongside the large areas there also grew up the *strategos polis* such as Beroia, Edessa etc.

3. Kyriakidis, IV 416; Zakythinos, 455.

4. Ostrogorsky, 310. N. Bànescu, *Les duchés byzantins de Paristrion (Paradounavon) et de Bulgarie* (Bucharest, 1946) 38 ff.

5. Kyriakidis IV 54 ff. H. Ahrweiler, "Recherches sur l'administration de l'empire byzantin aux IXᵉ-XIᵉ siecles", *BCH* 84 (1960) 47 ff. 64 ff. where this change is dated to the reign of Nikephoros Phokas.

6. Karayannopulos, II 469 ff.

7. Kyriakidis, IX 314. Lemerle *Philippes* 160. One earlier reference only exists for Voleron, in 1037. C. Ktenas, «Τά κειμηλιαρχεῖα τῆς ἐν Ἁγίω Ὄρει Ἄθω ἱερᾶς βασιλικῆς, πατριαρχικῆς καί σταυροπηγιακῆς μονῆς τοῦ Δοχειαρίου», *ΕΕΒΣ* 7 (1930) 106.

8. A. Papadopoulos-Kerameus, Ἀνάλεκτα Ἱεροσολυμιτικῆς σταχυολογίας IV (Saint Petersburg, 1897) 107: «πράκτωρ καί ἀναγραφεύς... Βολεροῦ, Στρυμόνος καί Θεσσαλονίκης». Lemerle *Philippes* 168. *JGR* I 476: "provincia Voleri, Strymonos et Thessalonices".

9. References to Voleron-Strymon-Thessalonike in particular from 1042 onwards it is referred to as a judicial and economic entity. See n. 7 above. Kyriakidis, IX 351 and Lemerle, *Phillipes*, 159 suggest that the *dux* of Thessalonike had this entire area under his administrative and military control.

10. Cf. V. Vasilevskij, "Chrisovul imperatora Alekseja I Komnina Velikoj Lavre sr. Athanasija na Athone (August 1084 g)", *VizVrem* 3 (1896), 122. 5 ff.

11. Dölger, Beitrage 74.

12. G. de Villehardouin (ed. Faral) 311 para. 496.

13. *MM* IV 353, 392. J. Karayannopulos, *BZ* 50 (1957), 476 ff. Arkadios Vatopedios, «Ἁγιορειτικά Ἀνάλεκτα ἐκ τοῦ ἀρχείου τῆς Μονῆς Βατοπεδίου», *Γρηγ. Παλαμᾶς* 3 (1919), 217.

14. See for example an inscription from Thessalonike of 1316; «... λογοθέτου τοῦ στρατιωτικοῦ τοῦ Ὑαλέου, κεφαλατικεύοντος ἐν τῇδε τῇ πόλει Θεσ/κη»= Tafrali, *Topographie*, 45-46. Cf. MM V 133 α 1322-, V, p. 117-α. 1325. E. Stein "Untersuchungen zur spatbyzantinischen Verfassungs-u. Wirtschaftsgeschi-

chte", *MosG* 2 (1923/26) 21, allows that the term κεφαλή is the popular rendering of the word *dux*. Tafrali 52 believes that the κεφαλές were subordinates to the *dux*. A. Heisenberg, *Aus der Geschichte und Literatur der Palaeologenzeit* (Munich, 1920) 68 ff. suggests that the κεφαλές replaced the *dux*. The truth would seem to be that the downgrading of all the titles and ranks led to the creation of the title κεφαλή with the connotation of a higher rank, the commanding officer. Cf. *JGR* I 582.

15. K. Jireček, *Die Heerenstrasse von Belgrad nach Konstantinopel und die Balkanpässe* (Prague, 1877), 72. Dvornik, 236. Lemerle, *Philippes*, 116.

16. Dvornik, 235.

17. Gelzer, 554.

18. Lemerle, *Philippes*, 260-61.

19. Dölger, *Regesten*, nos. 806-808, 1020. J. Konidaris, "Zur Frage der Entstehung der Dioecese der Erzbistums von Achrida und der Notiziae No. 3 bei Parthey" *Θεολογία* 30 (1959), 1 ff. V. Laurent, *Le corpus des sceaux de l'Empire byzantin V 2* (Paris, 1965), 317. Zakythinos, 439.

20. Ostrogorsky, 310.

21. Zakythinos, 438. Karayannopulos, II, 472 ff.

22. V. Laurent, "Sceau de protonotaire Basile Kamatéros", *Byzantion* 6 (1931), 266 ff. R. Browning, "The Patriarchal School at Constantinople in the Twelfth Century", *Byzantion* 32 (1962), 197 ff.

23. Parthey, *Hieroclis*, Not., III, 109-10, mid-eleventh century. Dvornik dates the whole text to the tenth century.

24. F. Moravcsik, *Byzantinoturcica²*, I, 86.

25. Gelzer, *BZ* 257.

26. *PG*, CXXXII, col. 1108: Thessalonike; *PG*, CXXXII, col. 1109, Serrhai, which evidently because of the copyist's error, was attributed fifty-seven bishoprics; *PG* CXXXII, col. 1109: Philippi.

27. Ostrogorsky, 434 ff.

28. Parthey, *Hieroclis*, Not. XI, 236. Gelzer, 597.

29. V. Benešević, "Monumenta Vaticana ad jus canonicum pertinentia", *StBN* 2 (1927), 141.

30. Gelzer, 598-601.

31. Mamalakis, 44-45.

32. Dölger, *Παρασπορά*, 424.

33. K. Lake, *The Early Days of Monasticism on Mount Athos* (Oxford, 1909), 84; Dölger, *Παρασπορά*, 428.

34. J. Bompaire, *Actes de Xeropotamou* (=*Archives de l'Athos*, III), (Paris, 1964), 40. (εἰς τό νέμεσθαι αὐτήν διά τό μή βῆμα ποδός κεκτημένη πρός αὐτάρκειαν ἡ μονή).

35. *Actes de Lavra*, I, No. 5.

36. Mamalakis, 52, 54. *Actes de Lavra*, I, 17. Meyer, 29.

37. For the Typikon, see Meyer, 141 ff. Compare the corrections and completions by F. Dölger, *Byzantinische Diplomat* (Ettal, 1956), 222 ff.

38. Lemerle, *Philippes*, 141 ff.; Kirsten, 20.

39. *De administrando imperio* (Moravcsik-Jenkins ed.), 29. 136. Kirsten, 32, n. 111 with additional bibliography.

40. Rouillard, 96-97.

41. J. Karayannopulos, "Ein Problem der spätbyzantinischen Agrargeschichte", *JOEByz* 30 (1981), 223.

42. Theophanes (de Boor ed.), 480.2. Cantacuzene, II, 179.2. ff., 393.17 ff. Charanis, *Byzantion* 49. Angelov, 296 (19).

43. Charanis, *Byzantion* 151.

44. Ibid., 152, n. 256.

45. G. de Villehardouin (Faral ed.), II, 89 (§ 280).

P. Tifčef, "Sur les cités byzantines aux XIᵉ-XIIᵉ s.", *Byzantino-Bulgarica* 1 (1962), 179.

46. Akropolitis (Heisenberg ed.), 80. 4 ff. (τῶν ἀνέκαθεν προσαρμοσάντων Θεσσαλονίκη ἐθίμων τε καί δικαίῳ περιεκτικόν καί τῆς σφῶν ἐλευθερίας παρεκτικόν). G.I. Bratianu, *Privilèges et franchises municipales dans l'Empire byzantin* (Paris, 1936), 109-10.

47. P. Charanis, "Observations on the Demography of Byzantine Empire", *Proceedings of the XIII International Congress of Byzantine Studies* (Oxford, 1966), 460. Idem, 131. Benjamin of Tudela, 4.36.

48. We do not know exactly what these terms stood for; their meaning does not emerge from the sources. Cf. Tafrali, 69, Kirsten, 38, n. 33.

49. Tafrali, 71-72, with the relevant sources.

50. Cantacuzene, II, 568.14-569.3. Kirsten, 39, n. 38.

51. Kirsten, 39, notes 39 and 40.

52. Tafrali, 76, with the relevant sources.

53. Kirsten, 38, n. 32 and bibliography.

54. L. Petit, B. Korabler, *Actes de Chilandar* (=*Actes de l'Athos*, V, 1), (St. Petersburg, 1911), 36. 15-1318-41. 125-1319-67. 11-1321.

55. Cameniates (Böhlig ed.), 8. (περιφανεστάτη τοῖς οἰκήτορσί τε καί πᾶσι τοῖς ἄλλοις οἷς αὐχεῖ πόλις τήν σύστασιν).

56. Acropolites (Heisenberg ed.), 76.1. ff.

57. Ibid., 37.

58. Ibid., 39.

59. Ibid., 39, 43, 53. G. de Villehardouin, 197 and 243 (§ 226 and 321).

60. Theophanes, 361.5. (ἡ μεγαλόπολις τῶν πόλεων τοῦ Ἰλλυρικοῦ).

61. Cameniates, 7.33 ff., 7.56 ff.

62. *PG*, CLI, cols. 333 and 341. Tafrali, 109, n. 4.

63. Cantacuzene, I, 28. Tafrali, 103.

64. P. Lemerle, *Actes de Kutlumus* (*Archives de l'Athos*, II), (Paris, 1945), 18 (86.62 ff.). (ὀσπίτια ἀνωγεωκατώγεα μετά αὐλῆς καί χαμαιργέων ὀσπιτίων τεσσάρων καί μαγκιπείου, ἐργαστήρια ἐνοικιακά τρία...).

65. Charanis, 136. N. Bànescu, "Peut-on identifier le Zamblacus de documents ragusains?", *Mélanges Ch. Diehl*, I, 31. B. Krekić, *Dubrovnik (Raguse) et le Levant au Moyen Age* (Paris, 1961), 90, n. 3.

66. P. Lemerle, «Prolégomènes à une édition critique et commentée des 'Conseils et Récits' de Cecauménos", *Acad. Royale de Belgique, Classe des Lettres, Mémoires*, 54 (1960), 93.

67. R. Guilland, "La correspondance inédite d'Athanase, Patriarche de Constantinople (1289-1293, 1304-1310)", *Mélanges Ch. Diehl*, I, 139. Charanis, 137, n. 85.

68. Cf. Angelov, 296 ff. (19).

69. Karayannopulos, II, 317 ff.

70. Dieterich, *BZ* 37-57 and 334-50. Jireček, I, 26, lines 1-64.

71. Jireček, II, 49, line 2. Dieterich, *BZ* 13-14.

72. *PG* CIX, col. 641B. (ὁ αὐτός (=λιμήν) ἀντί πόλεως τε ὄν καί λιμένος καί τήν πόλιν οὐκ ἐς τήν θάλατταν λήγουσαν παρεχόμενος ἀλλ᾽ εἰς πόλιν ἑτέραν).

73. Dvornik, *St. Gregoire*, 53, 15 ff, 54. 23 ff.

74. Dölger, *Regesten*, 1890-α. 1262. Heyd, I, 465-66. Tafel-Thomas, IV, 134. *MM*, III, 79-80-α. 1265. Dölger, *Regesten*, 1934 and 1960 of 1268.

75. Cameniates, 11.81 ff.

76. Ibid., 11.66. (Ἔνθεν αἱ τῆς γεωργίας ἀφθονίαι, ἐκεῖθεν αἱ τῆς ἐμπορίας χορηγίαι).

77. Ibid., 50.49. (ὡς ὄρη καί βουνούς ἐκτελεῖσθαι τά τούτων σωρείας).

78. Ibid., 51.71.

79. Heyd, I, 53, n. 3.
80. T.L.F. Tafel, *De Thessalonica ejusque agro, dissertatio geographica* (Berlin, 1839), App. V, 224 and 496.7.
81. Cameniates, 11.84.
82. Antoniadis, 225 ff.
83. *PG*, CIX, col. 641.
84. Dölger, *Regesten,* 1890 and 1934. Heyd, I, 471. G. Kolias, Ἱστορικὴ γεωγραφία τοῦ ἑλληνικοῦ χώρου (Athens, 1948), 299-300.
85. Idrisi, 37 and 53.
86. See the table in Antoniadis.
87. See,for example, Dölger, *Regesten,* 1488-α. 1169- 1497-α. 1170-1498-α. 1170-1890-α. 1261-1941-α. c. 1267 (for Genoa), 1081-α. 1082-1304-α. 1126-1373-α. 1148-1576-α. 1187- 1577-α. 1187-1578-α. 1187 (for Venice), 1255-α. 1111-1499-α. 1170 (for Pisa). *JGR*, I, 515-α. 1290-, I, 542-α. 1320 (for the Aragonese merchants).
88. Theophanes Continuatus, II, 258.4. (μὴ καταδυναστεύεσθαι ὑπὸ τῶν πλουτούντων τοὺς πένητας).
89. Karayannopulos, II, 341-42.
90. Charanis, *DOP,* 87 ff. Charanis, 336-55. P. Lemerle, "Un praktikon inédit des archives de Karakala (janvier 1342) et la situation en Macédoine orientale au moment de l'usurpation de Cantacuzène", Χαριστήριον εἰς Α. Ὀρλάνδον, I (Athens, 1964), 278 ff. Asdracha, 205.
91. *MM,* I, 476-α. 1365-*MM,* V, 89, 106, 107. Cf. Lambros, *NE,* 49-51. Cantacuzene, I, 174.
92. S. Kauchtschischwili, "Typicon Georgii Pacuriani", *Georgica* V (Tiflis, 1963), 122.6 ff., 124.7 ff., 126.11 ff.
93. Xanalatos, 66 ff.
94. *JGR,* I, 334. Dölger, *Beiträge,* 75 G. Ostrogorsky, "Die landliche Steuergemeinde des byzantinischen Reiches im 10. Jh.", *Vierteljahrschr. für Sozial-und Wirtschaftsgeschichte* 20 (1927), 66-67. Rouillard, 136.
95. *JGR* I, 265. Rouillard, 105.
96. *JGR* I, 249-50. Charanis, *DOP* 53. Karayannopulos, II, 409.
97. Charanis, *DOP* 62. Karayannopulos, II, 409 ff. 447, 456, n. 836.
98. Though in cases of need the state did not hesitate to appropriate ecclesiastical property. See, for example, Charanis, 82 ff.
99. Xanalatos, 31. Rouillard, 113-14; idem, "Notes et discussions à propos d'un ouvrage récent sur l'histoire de l'état byzantin", *RPLHA* 16 (1942), 177 ff.
100. Rouillard, 159.
101. See the typical description by Eustathius of Thessalonika, Ἐπίσκεψις βίου μοναχικοῦ ἐπὶ διορθώσει τῶν περὶ αὐτὸν, *PG* CXXXV, cols. 825 ff. (120 ff.).

INTELLECTUAL LIFE

1. Tafrali, passim. B. Laourdas, Ἡ κλασσικὴ φιλολογία εἰς τὴν Θεσσαλονίκην κατὰ τὸν δέκατον τέταρτον αἰῶνα (Thessalonike, 1960).
2. M. Wellnhofer, *Johannes Apokaukos, Metropolit von Naupaktos in Aetolien* (Freising, 1913). P.K. Polakis, «Βυζαντινὴ μελέτη, Ἰωάννης Ἀπόκαυκος, Μητροπολίτης Ναυπάκτου», *Νέα Σιὼν* 18 (1923), 119-212, 321-36, 449-74, 514-27. Tomadakis, 44-62. (Bibliography of the published works of Apokaukos). Hélène Bee-Sepherle, "Aus dem Nachlass des Johannes Apokaukos des
Metropoliten von Naupaktos", *BNJ* 21 (1976), Appendix, 1-243.
3. J. B. Pitra, *Analecta sacra Spicilegio Solesmensi parata* VI (Paris-Rome, 1891). Tomadakis, 74-79.
4. F. Ritschl, *Thomas Magistri sive Theoduli monachi Ecloga vocum Atticarum* (Halle, 1832). A. Turyn, *The Byzantine Tradition of the Tragedies of Euripides* (Urbana, 1957), 53 ff.
5. *PG* CXLV, 373-404, 404-45. M. Treu, "Thomas Magistros' Brief an Isaak", *JCIPh,* Supplement 27 (1902), 5-18.
6. *PG* CXLV, 448-548.
7. F.W. Lenz, *Fünf Reden Thomas Magisters* (Leiden, 1963). B. Laourdas, «Τοῖς Θεσσαλονικεῦσι περὶ ὁμονοίας», *ΕΕΝΣΘ* 12 (1969), 751-75.
8. J.F. Boissonade, *Anecdota nova* (Paris, 1844), 1-201. J. Verpeaux, *Nicéphore Choumnos, homme d'état et humaniste byzantin* (Paris, 1959). I. Sevčenko, *Études sur la polémique entre Théodore Métochite et Nicéphore Choumnos* (Brussels, 1962). L.G. Benakis, «Νικηφόρου Χούμνου περὶ τῆς ὕλης καὶ τῶν ἰδεῶν», *Φιλοσοφία* 3 (1973), 339-81.
9. *PG* CXIX, 1225-98; CXLV, 959-1400; CXLV 9-212. P.B. Paschos, Ὁ Ματθαῖος Βλάσταρης καὶ τὸ ὑμνογραφικόν ἔργον του (Thessalonike, 1978).
10. Volume of Constantine Armenopoulos (Thessalonike, 1952). K.G. Pitsakis, Κωνσταντίνου Ἀρμενοπούλου Πρόχειρον Νόμων ἢ Ἑξάβιβλος (Athens, 1971).
11. R. Auberton, *Démétrius Triclinius et les recensions médiévales de Sophocle* (Paris, 1949). W.J.W. Koster, *Autour d'un manuscrit d'Aristophane écrit par Démétrius Triclinius,* (Groningen, 1957). L. Massa Positano, *Demetrii Triclinii in Aeschyli Persas Scholia* (Naples, 1963²). N. G. Wilson, *Scholia Tricliniana in Aristophanis Equites* (Groningen-Amsterdam, 1969). A. Turyn, "Demetrius Triclinius and the Planudean Anthology", *EEBΣ* 34-40 (1972-73), 403-450. O.L. Smith, *Studies in the Scholia on Aeschylus I: The recension of Demetrius Triclinius* (Leiden, 1975).
12. A. Wasserstein, "An Unpublished Treatise by Demetrius Triclinius on Lunar Theory", *JöBG* 16 (1967), 153-74.
13. M. Treu, *Theodori Pediasimi eiusque amicorum quae exstant.* Programm Victoria-Gymnas (Potsdam, 1899).
14. F. Jürss, "Johannes Katrares und der Dialog Hermippos oder über die Astrologie", *BZ* 59 (1966), 275-84.
15. S. J. Kourousis, «Ὁ μέγας διοικητὴς Θεόδωρος Καβάσιλας καὶ ἡ εἰς Ἀνδρόνικον Β΄ μονῳδία του», *EEBΣ* 42 (1975-76), 408-28.
16. A. Angelopoulos, «Τὸ γενεαλογικὸν δένδρον τῆς οἰκογενείας τῶν Καβασιλῶν», *Μακεδονικά* 17 (1977), 367-96.
17. *PG* CL, 1225-36; CLI, 693-1186. Mercati, 243-44.
18. S. Lambros, «Γρηγορίου Παλαμᾶ ἐπιστολὴ πρὸς Θεσσαλονικεῖς», *NE* 11 (1922), 3-21. J. Meyendorff, *Grégoire Palamas. Défense des saints hésychastes* (Louvain, 1959). Idem, *Introduction à l'étude de Grégoire Palamas* (Paris, 1959). Bibliography of works, 331-49. P.K. Christou, Γρηγορίου τοῦ Παλαμᾶ συγγράμματα Α΄ (Thessalonike, 1962). Concerning Gr. Akindinos, *PG* CXLVIII, 29-30, 68-73, 84-86; CL, 843-63. R.J. Loenertz, "Gregori Acindyni epistolae selectae", *EEBΣ*
27 (1957), 89-109. Idem, "Dix huit lettres de Grégoire Acindyne analysées et datées", *OCP* 23 (1957), 114-44. V. Laurent, "L' assaut avorté de la Horde d'or contre l'empire byzantin (printemps-été 1341)", *REByz* 18 (1960), 145-62 (letter to David Disypatos). A. Karpozilos, "Collectanea Byzantina", *OCA* 204 (Rome, 1977), 65-117.
19. D.G. Tsamis, Ἰωσὴφ Καλοθέτου συγγράμματα (Thessalonike, 1980).
20. *PG* CXLVIII, 683-730; CLI 707-63. E. Candal, *Nilus Cabasilas et theologia S. Thomae de processione spiritus sancti* (Vatican, 1950). M. Candal, "La Regla teológica de Nilo Cabasilas", *OCP* 23 (1957), 237-66.
21. *PG* CL, 368-725. Nella Panagiotou, Ἡ περὶ δικαιώσεως διδασκαλία Νικολάου τοῦ Καβάσιλα (Piraeus, 1975). B.S. Psevdogkas, Νικολάου Καβάσιλα ἑπτὰ ἀνέκδοτοι λόγοι τὸ πρῶτον ἐκδιδόμενοι (Thessalonike, 1976).
22. *PG* CLIV, 1169-1212. G. Cammelli, "Demetrii Cydonii orationes tres adhuc ineditae", *BNJ* 3 (1922), 67-76 and 4 (1923), 77-83, 282-95. Mercati, 359-435. R.J. Loenertz, *Les recueils de lettres de Démétrius Cydonès* (Vatican, 1947). Idem, *Démétrius Cydonès, Correspondance* (Vatican, 1956-1960). G. Leontsinis, A. Glykofrydou-Leontsini, Δημητρίου Κυδώνη Θωμᾶ Ἀκινάτου Σοῦμμα Θεολογικὴ ἐξελληνισθεῖσα 2.15 (Athens, 1976). F.A. Dimitrakopoulos, Δημητρίου Κυδώνη, Θωμᾶ Ἀκινάτου Σοῦμμα Θεολογικὴ ἐξελληνισθεῖσα 2.16 (Athens, 1979).
23. *PG* CXXXIX, 11-164. B. Laourdas, Ἰσιδώρου ἀρχιεπισκόπου Θεσσαλονίκης ὁμιλίαι εἰς τὰς ἑορτὰς τοῦ ἁγίου Δημητρίου Θεσσαλονίκης (Thessalonike, 1954).
24. B. Laourdas, «Γαβριὴλ Θεσσαλονίκης ὁμιλίαι», Ἀθηνᾶ 57 (1953), 141-73.
25. *PG* CLV, 393-952. B. Laourdas, «Συμεὼν Θεσσαλονίκης ἀκριβὴς διάταξις τῆς ἑορτῆς τοῦ ἁγίου Δημητρίου», Γρηγόριος Παλαμᾶς 39 (1956), 327-42. D. Balfour, *Politico-historical works of Symeon Archbishop of Thessalonica (1416/17-1429),* (Vienna, 1979).
26. G. Tsaras, Διήγησις περὶ τῆς τελευταίας ἁλώσεως τῆς Θεσσαλονίκης. Μονῳδία ἐπὶ τῇ ἁλώσει τῆς Θεσσαλονίκης (Thessalonike, 1958). Idem, «Οἱ δύο ἔμμετρες μονῳδίες γιὰ τὴν τελευταία ἅλωση τῆς Θεσσαλονίκης», *Μακεδονικά* 9 (1969), 64-100.

ART IN THE LATE BYZANTINE PERIOD

1. Sotiriou, 138. Gouma-Peterson *ABull.*
2. H. Hallensleben, *BZ* 56 (1973), 125 ff. Krautheimer, 328, 517 Cf. I. Sevčenko, J. Featherstone, *Two Poems of T. Metochitis* (Brookline, Mass., 1981), 10-11.
3. Krautheimer, 449-50, figs. 382-83.
4. E. Stikas, "Une église des Paléologues aux environs de Castoria", *BZ* 51 (1968), 100-113.
5. H. Hallensleben, "Das Katholikon des Johannes Prodromos Klosters bei Serrai. Versuch einer Architekturgeschichte", *Byz. Forschungen* (=*Polychordia, Festschrift F. Dölger*), I (Amsterdam, 1966), 158-73.
6. On the churches of Thessalonike, see *Salonique,* pls. 35-49; Xyngopoulos, *Naoí,* and Xyngopoulos. On the identification of Saint Panteleimon with the Peribleptos monastery of Matthew Vlastari, see Theocharides, *Byzan-*

tion (1970), 437 ff. For the date and identification of the monastery of the Prophet Elias (referred to in this book as Saint Elias) — with significant new restoration — with the Nea Moni, which Makarios Choumnos founded in 1360, see idem, *Μακεδονικά* 4 (1955-60), 343 ff. Mango, 277, Krautheimer, 453-58. For their history, see Janin, 341-419 and 454-56.

7. Xyngopoulos, *Ναοί*, 22 ff.

8. M. Michaelidis, ΑΔ 20 (1965), Χρονικά 3, 474.

9. *Καλλιέργης*.

10. M. Panayotidi, "Les églises de Véria en Macédoine", *Corsi*, 303 ff.

11. Orlandos, *Καστοριά*, 164.

12. G. Millet, *L'Ancien art serbe* (Paris, 1919), 95-96. S. Nenadović, "Architecture de Chilandar, Église et chapelles, Chilandarski", *Sbornik* 3 (Belgrade, 1974), 85-196 (with French summary). Idem. *Chilandar*, 70 ff.

13. Djurić, 214-15.

14. See Chatzidakis *ΠΑΑ*, for more detail.

15. A. Xyngopoulos, «Αἱ τοιχογραφίαι τῶν Ἁγίων Τεσσαράκοντα εἰς τήν Ἀχειροποίητον τῆς Θεσσαλονίκης», *AE* (1957), 11 (6-30), figs. 1-11, pls. 2-4. Chatzidakis, *Sopoćani* 62 (59-73), fig. 3.

16. Millet-Frolow, I, x, pls. 63-83. *Monumentalmalerei* I, 23, plans 12-13α, figs. 82-98 and II, 317-20, 329-30 (exonarthex). Lazarev, 297. Djurić, 219-20, pl. XII, fig. 23.

17. Chatzidakis, *Sopoćani*, 62-63, figs. 4-5. *Βυζαντινές Τοιχογραφίες καί Εἰκόνες*. Athens Exhibition 1976, Chatzidakis, 27-37, col. pls. I-XVI, and figs. 2-18 (b. and w.).

18. A. Tschilingirov, *Die Kunst des christlichen Mittelalters in Bulgarien* (Berlin, 1978), fig. 94. Djurić, 220.

19. Lazarev, 357.

20. *Monumentalmalerei* I, 23-24, plans 14-15, figs. 99-114 and II, 324-29. Lazarev, 297-98. Djurić, 222, pl. XIX, fig. 35.

21. Millet-Frolow, I, x, pl. 85, figs. 2-4, 94. *Monumentalmalerei* I, 22 plan 11b, figs. 80-81 and II, 320-23. Lazarev, 298. Djurić, 239, pl. XX, fig. 37.

22. Pelekanides, *Καστοριά*, pls. 63 ff. and Pelekanides, 361-64. Chatzidakis, *Sopoćani* 64. Lazarev, 292. N. Moutsopoulos, *Καστοριά, Παναγία ἡ Μαυριώτισσα* (Athens, 1967). *Kurbinovo*, 37-38 and Malmquist, 127-28.

23. Pelekanides, *Καστοριά*, pl. 104. C. Mavropoulou-Tsioumbi, *Οἱ τοιχογραφίες τοῦ 13ου αἰώνα στή Κουμπελίδικη τῆς Καστοριᾶς* (Thessalonike, 1973), 58-65, pls. 15-17 (Dormition), pls. 48-50 (Trinity).

24. A. Xyngopoulos, «Φορητές Εἰκόνες», nos. 12, 20 with bibliography. *Byzantine Art- An European Art* (Catalogue of the Exhibition, Athens, 1964).

25. Sotiriou, 180, fig. 5, pl. XIV.

26. Ćorović, 147, pls. VII-IX. Xyngopoulos, *Sopoćani*, 79.

27. Sotiriou, 178-79, fig. 4., pl. XV. *Byzantine Art, Exhibition*, 1964, no. 237. Chatzidakis, *Frühe Ikonen*, XXVI, fig. 49. Ćorović, 146-47. Xyngopoulos, *Sopoćani*, 79-81, figs. 11,13.

28. Djurić, *Sopoćani*, 145 ff.

29. D. Kočo and P. Miljković-Pepek, *Manastir* (Skopje, 1958). P. Miljković-Pepek, "L'Icône de Saint Georges de Struga", *CArch* 19 (1969), 213 ff. and idem, *Symposium de Sopoćani* (Belgrade, 1965), 189-96. Chatzidakis, *Le Icone*, col. plate on p. 158.

30. Millet-Frolow, II, pls. 49-67 and 100-101. Djurić, *Fresken*, 41, fig. on p. 12 and 123-24.

31. Millet-Frolow, II, pls. 68-97 and 101, 11-103. S. Radojčić, "Natpis ΜΑΡΠΟΥ na arilskim Freskata", *Glasnik* 134, VII (Belgrade, 1959), 40-45.

32. Millet, *Athos*, pls. 5-58. Xyngopoulos, *Πανσέληνος*, 12. Sotiriou, *ΔΧΑΕ* 5 (1969), 1 ff.

33. A. Xyngopoulos, "Nouveaux témoignages sur l'activité des peintres macédoniens au Mont Athos", *BZ* 52 (1959), 61-63.

34. S. Radojčić, *Majstori Starog Srpskog Slikarstva* (Belgrade, 1955), 19 ff. Xyngopoulos, 26 ff. H. Hallensleben, *Die Malerschule des Königs Miljutin* (Giessen, 1963). (Rev. by Chatzidakis, *BZ* 61 (1968), 104-08). Miljković-Pepek.

35. Chatzidakis, *BZ* 61 (1968), 107. Chatzidakis, *Actes XIV*, 160. Xyngopoulos, *Πανσέληνος*, 12. Lazarev, 385. Sotiriou, *ΔΧΑΕ*, passim.

36. H. Belting in Belting et al., 95, 103 ff.

37. G. Babić in D. Panić and G. Babić, *Bogorodiča Ljeviska* (Belgrade, 1975), 108 ff. *Monumentalmalerei* I, pls. 182-212 (Ljeviska), pls. 273-315 (Staro Nagoričino), pls. 221-24 (Čučer), Miljković-Pepek, passim.

38. See n. 37. Radojčić, 60 ff.; idem, "Der Klassizismus und ihm entgegengesetzte Tendenzen in der Malerei des 14. Jahrhunderts bei den Orthodoxen Balkanslaven und den Rumänen", *Actes du XIVe Congrès international d'études byzantines* (Bucharest, 1971), I, 189-205.

39. Sotiriou, 122 ff. Gouma-Peterson, *ABull*, 168-72, and idem, "Christ as Ministrant and the Priest as Ministrant of Christ in a Palaeologan Program of 1303", *DOP* 32 (1978), 199-216, figs 4-28.

40. S. Pelekanides, «Ἡ καλλιτεχνική φυσιογνωμία τῆς Θεσσαλονίκης στή Βυζαντινή ἐποχή», *Νέα Ἑστία* 72 (1962). Mouriki, *Gračanica*, 69.

41. Sotiriou, *ΔΧΑΕ*, 1-30, pls. 1-21. Mouriki, *Gračanica*, 59. A. Tsitouridou, "Les fresques de l'église de Saint Pantéleimonos à Salonique", *Zograf* 6 (Belgrade, 1975), 14 ff. (in Serbian with French summary).

42. Stikas, *BZ*, 108, pl. IX. Mouriki, *Gračanica*, 69.

43. A. Xyngopoulos, *Ψηφιδωτή διακόσμηση τοῦ ναοῦ τῶν Ἁγίων Ἀποστόλων* (Thessalonike, 1953). Xyngopoulos, passim. Idem, «Ἡ τοιχογραφία τοῦ Ἁγίου Δημητρίου εἰς τούς Ἁγίους Ἀποστόλους Θεσσαλονίκης», *ΔΧΑΕ*, ser. 4, 8 (1975-76), 1-18, pls. 1-5. Idem, "Les peintures murales des Saints-Apôtres à Thessalonique", *L'Art et Société à Byzance sous les Paléologues* (Venice, 1971), 83-89, pls. 23-24. M. Chatzidakis in Grabar-Chatzidakis, 21, pls. XXVIII-XXXII. Djurić, in *L'École de la Morava et son temps* (Belgrade, 1972), 278, dates the wall paintings to 1340-50 and S. Kissas, in *Zograf* 7 (1977), 52 ff., to 1328-34.

44. P. Underwood, *The Kariye Djami*, I-III (London, 1967). Belting in Belting et al. Chatzidakis, *Actes XIV*, 165.

45. *Καλλιέργης*. Mouriki, *Gračanica*, 66 ff. Cf. Velmans, *CArch*, 166 ff.

46. Chatzidakis, *ΑΔ* 21 (1966), Χρονικά 29 pls. 36a-b. Mouriki, Gračanica, 68.

47. Millet, *Athos*, pls. 81-94. Sotiriou, *ΔΧΑΕ*, passim. Chatzidakis, *Actes XIV*, 104 ff.

48. V.J. Djurić, "Fresques médiévales à Chilandar", *Actes du XIIe congrès d'études byzantines (Ohrid, 1961)*, 59 ff. Idem, *Chilandar*, 81 ff.

49. A. Xyngopoulos, *Οἱ τοιχογραφίες τοῦ Ἁγ. Νικολάου Ὀρφανοῦ* (Athens, 1964). Velmans, *CArch*. A Tsitouridou, *Ἡ ἐντοίχια ζωγραφική*

τοῦ Ἁγίου Νικολάου στή Θεσσαλονίκη (Thessalonike, 1978).

50. Chatzidakis, *Actes XIV*, 186.

51. Millet, *BCH*, 630 ff. Also, Xyngopoulos, and Sotiriou, *ΔΧΑΕ*.

52. See the more detailed works by Chatzidakis in n. 35. Cf. O. Demus, "Die Entstehung des Paläologenstils in der Malerei", *Berichte zum XI. Internationalen Byzantinistenkongress* (Munich, 1958), IV, 2.

53. Chatzidakis, *Actes XIV*.

54. V. Djurić, "Origine thessalonicienne des fresques du monastère de Resava", *RTIEByz* 6 (Belgrade, 1960), 111-28, figs. 1-12 (in Serbian with French summary). Idem, "Les fresques de la Chapelle du Despote Jovan Uglješa à Vatopédi et leur valeur pour l'étude de l'origine thessalonicienne de la peinture de Resava", *RTIEByz* 7 (Belgrade, 1961), 125-38, figs. 1-24 (in Serbian with French summary). Cf. idem, "La peinture murale de Resava. Les origines et sa place dans la peinture byzantine", *RTIEByz* Idem, *L'École de Morava et son temps*, 277-91, figs. 1-35.

55. Xyngopoulos, 71 ff.

56. Orlandos, *Καστοριά*, 61-106 (Taxiarchs), 168 (Saint Nicholas Kyritzis). Pelekanides, *Καστοριά*, pls. 118-41 (Taxiarchs), 155-61 (Saint Nicholas Kyritzis).

57. G. Subotić, *L'Église des Saints-Constantin et Hélène à Ohrid* (Belgrade, 1971), (in Serbian with French summary), especially p. 123. V. Djurić, "Markov Manastir-Ohrid", *Sbornik* 8 (1972). Idem, *Recherches sur L'Art* (in Serbian with French summary), especially figs. 17-18, 20-25, 27, 29-31.

58. Orlandos, *Καστοριά*, 147-58. Pelekanides, *Καστοριά*, 142-54.

59. V. Djurić, "Mali-Grad, Saint Athanase à Kastoria-Borje", *Zograf* 6 (1975), 31-50 (Serbian with French summary), T. Velmans, *La peinture murale byzantine à la fin du Moyen Age*, I (Paris, 1977), 178.

60. Millet-Velmans (n. 52), XXV - XXXII, XXXIV, figs. 73-108. Djurić (n. 91), 131-62.

61. Millet, *BCH*, passim. Millet-Velmans, *La peinture*, XIX-XXIII, XXXIII-XXXIV, pls. 29-56.

62. Millet-Velmans, *La peinture*, XXIII-XXV, XXXIV, pls. 57-72. V. Djurić, "L'inscription 'Merkuri' à Psaca", *Sbornik* 7 (Novisad, 1971). Idem, *Recherches sur l'Art*, 231-35.

63. A. Xyngopoulos, *Αἱ τοιχογραφίαι τοῦ Καθολικοῦ Μονῆς Προδρόμου παρά τάς Σέρρας* (Thessalonike, 1973).

64. Millet, *Inscriptions* (n. 26), 158, 160. Millet, *Athos*, 25.

65. A. Banck, *Byzantine Art in the Collections of Soviet Museums* (Leningrad, 1977), 25, 325, figs. 281-84. Weitzmann, *The Icon* (23-24, figs. 82-83).

66. V. Djurić, "Uber den 'Čin' von Chilandar", *BZ* 53 (1960), 333-51, pls. VIII-XV. Cf. Radojčić, *Frühe Ikonen*, LXIX, 187, 200.

67. Chatzidakis, *Actes XIV*, 160.

68. Miatev, *Frühe Ikonen*, XLIII, figs. 102-03, 105. The icon is now in the Sofia Museum.

69. Chatzidakis, *Le icone*, 143, fig. 183.

70. Babić, *Le ikone*, 142, fig. 196.

71. A. Xyngopoulos, *Ὁ εἰκονογραφικός κύκλος τῆς ζωῆς τοῦ Ἁγίου Δημητρίου* (Thessalonike, 1970), 16-35, pls. I-III. Cf. J. Hutter, *Corpus der byzantinischen Miniaturen. Handschriften*. Oxford Bodleian Library, I-II (Stuttgart, 1978), 1-33. (Bodley, Ms. Gr. th. f.I, ff54^r and 55^r).

FROM 1430 TO 1821

ADMINISTRATIVE, SOCIAL AND ECONOMIC DEVELOPMENTS

1. The text is a summary of the author's unpublished work, «Ἡ Μακεδονία κατά τήν Τουρκοκρατία», wherein the sources and the bibliography for each specific subject are cited.

OPPRESSION AND RESISTANCE

1. The text is based on A.E. Vacalopoulos, *History of Macedonia 1354-1833* (Thessalonike, 1973) which contains a detailed bibliography.

INTELLECTUAL LIFE

1. Vacalopoulos, 119.
2. Vacalopoulos, 134. A. Moustoxydis elaborates on this in the magazine, Ἑλληνομνήμων 7 (1845), 386.
3. The synodal Act was published by Dositheos in his work, Τόμος Ἀγάπης; it was reprinted by K. Sathas, Βιογραφικόν σχεδίασμα περί τοῦ Πατριάρχου Ἱερεμίου Β΄ (1870), 82-92. The quotation here is from p. 91.
4. This work by M. Gedeon has now been summarized in a volume of his miscellaneous works, called, Ἡ πνευματική κίνησις τοῦ Γένους κατά τόν ΙΗ΄ καί ΙΘ΄ αἰῶνα (1976).
5. Concerning the *kollyvades*, see H. Tzogas, Ἡ περί μνημοσύνην ἔρις (Thessalonike, 1969).
6. The relevant epistle to the Oecumenical Patriarch has been published in, Μοναστηριακά Χρονικά (1939). Earlier, however, in 1927, the manuscript was annotated by M. Gedeon in Θεολογία. These annotations can be found in his collected works, Ἡ πνευματική κίνησις τοῦ Γένους (1976), 85-86.
7. See T.E. Evangelidis, Ἡ παιδεία ἐπί Τουρκοκρατίας I (Athens, 1936), 126, and K.A. Gounaropoulos, «Κοζανικά», Πανδώρα 22 (1871-1872), 532.
8. See K.T. Dimaras, Νεοελληνικός Διαφωτισμός (Athens, 1980²), 320.
9. Ἑλληνικός Φιλολογικός Σύλλογος Κωνσταντινουπόλεως ΙΓ΄ 1878-1879 (1880), 238.
10. K.M. Koumas, Ἱστορίαι τῶν Ἀνθρωπίνων Πράξεων, ΙΒ΄ (Vienna, 1832), 571.
11. Προδιοίκησις εἰς τόν Ἑρμῆλον ἤ Δημοκριθηράκλειτον... περιέχουσα τήν Ἀπολογίαν τοῦ ποιητοῦ, τήν Ἀλληγορίαν τοῦ ποιήματος καί τήν Εἴδησιν διά τήν ἄτακτον ἔκδοσιν τοῦ Ἑρμήλου. 1817.

The tables of scholars 1430-1830 were compiled by the Editorial Staff.

SCHOOLS

1. The text is based on data in A.E. Vacalopoulos, *History of Macedonia 1354-1833* (Thessalonike, 1973).

JEWISH LEARNING AND SCHOLARSHIP

1. The text is based on J. Nehama, *Histoire des Israélites de Salonique* I-VII (Thessalonike, 1935-1978).

POST-BYZANTINE ART 1430-1830

1. M. Chatzidakis, "La peinture des 'Madonneri' ou 'Vénétocrétoise' et sa destination", *Atti del II Convegno Internazionale di Storia della Civiltà, Venezia* 1973 (Florence, 1977), 673-90.
2. Orlandos. A. Grabar, *L'art du Moyen Âge en Europe Orientale* (Paris, 1968), 87-97. Chatzidakis, *IEE* vol. Ι΄ (Athens, 1975), 410-11.
3. A. Orlandos, *L'architecture religieuse en Grèce pendant la domination turque, L'Hellénisme Contemporain* (Athens, 1953), 179-91. C. Bouras, «Ἡ ἐκκλησιαστική ἀρχιτεκτονική στήν Ἑλλάδα μετά τήν Ἅλωση (1453-1821)», Ἀρχιτεκτονικά θέματα (1969), 164-72. Chatzidakis, *IEE* vol. Ι΄, 412 ff.
4. Vlachos, deacon Kosmas Agioreitis, Ἡ χερσόνησος τοῦ Ἁγίου Ὄρους Ἄθω καί αἱ ἐν αὐτῇ μοναί καί οἱ μοναχοί πάλαι τε καί νῦν (Volos, 1903). Smyrnakis, archimandrite Gerasimos, Τό Ἅγιον Ὄρος (Athens, 1903). Orlandos, 31-37, 134-138. P. Mylonas, Millénaire II, 229-46.
5. A. Orlandos, «Ἡ ἐπί τῆς Ὄθρυος Μονή τῆς Ἀντινίτσης», *EEBΣ* 7 (1930), 369-81.
6. John Komnenos, Προσκυνητάριον τοῦ Ἁγίου Ὄρους τοῦ Ἄθωνος (Venice, 1864²), 78.
7. Moutsopoulos, Φλ., 74-76. Moutsopoulos, Πέλλα, 74-87 and n. 8.
8. Moutsopoulos, Φλ., 68-76. Moutsopoulos, Πέλλα, 66 ff. Chatzidakis, *IEE* vol. ΙΑ΄, 266-69. C. Bouras, «Ὁ ἀρχιτεκτονικός τύπος τῆς βασιλικῆς κατά τήν Τουρκοκρατία καί ὁ Πατριάρχης Καλλίνικος», Ἐκκλησίες στήν Ἑλλάδα μετά τήν Ἅλωση (Athens, 1979), 159-69. See also the work of G. Veleni, S. Angeloudis, M. Vamvoukou-Kambouri, I. Papangelou and K. Theocharidis in Ἐκκλησίες στήν Ἑλλάδα μετά τήν Ἅλωση (Athens, 1979), 1-167.
9. A. Orlandos, "Ein spätbyzantinischer Hallenkirchen-Typus Nordgriechenlands", *JOEByz* 21 (1972), 209-22.
10. Orlandos, 26-134. Moutsopoulos, Φλ., sporadic references. Moutsopoulos, Πέλλα, 100-104.
11. A. Hadjimihali, 46-47. Moutsopoulos, Πέλλα, 86-87.
12. Hadjimihali, sporadic references. M. Ćorović-Ljubinković, "L'iconostase de l'église de Saint Nicolas à Velika Hoča", *Starinar* 9-10 (Belgrade, 1958-59), 169-79 (in Serbian with a French summary), Moutsopoulos, Πέλλα, 80-90.
13. See section on Painting.
14. M. Chatzidakis, «Κεραμουργήματα μέ ἑλληνικές ἐπιγραφές», Ζυγός (1957), 6-7, no. 16.

15. See n. 4. G.E. Tavlakis, «Οἱ τοιχογραφίες τοῦ ναοῦ τοῦ Ἁγίου Γεωργίου στήν Προβάτα», Β΄ Συμπόσιο Βυζαντινῆς καί Μεταβυζαντινῆς Ἀρχαιολογίας καί Τέχνης (summaries) (Athens, 1982), 94.
16. See n. 8.
17. Orlandos, Καστοριά, 182, figs. 123 and 190, fig. 127. Pelekanides, Καστοριά, pls. 179-88, (Saint Nicholas Eupraxias) pls. 168-77 (Saint Nicholas Magaliou), pls. 248-62 (Saint Nicholas Theologias), pl. 231. Xyngopoulos Σχεδ., 63-69, pls. 15-17. Sv. Radojčić, "Une école de peinture de la deuxième moitié du XVe siècle" (in Serbian with a French summary), Recherches sur l'art, *Matica Srpska*, Novi Sad I (1965), 68-104, figs. 1-16. M. Chatzidakis, "Aspects de la peinture religieuse dans les Balkans (1300-1550)", *Aspects of the Balkans* (The Hague-Paris, 1972) = Études II, 192-93. See also Chatzidakis, *IEE* vol. I, 418 ff.
18. Concerning Beve see Moutsopoulos, Φλ., 46-50, figs. 21-23, 173. Subotić, 86-93, 201-202, 216, figs. 56-62. Concerning Porphyra see S. Pelekanides, Βυζαντινά καί Μεταβυζαντινά Μνημεῖα τῆς Πρέσπας (Thessalonike, 1960), 64, 94-108. N. Moutsopoulos, "Byzantinische und nachbyzantinische Baudenkmäler aus Klein Prespa und Hlg. German", *BNJ* 20 (1970), 4-12, figs. 1-12. See also Subotić 34-42, 194-95, figs. 8-14.
19. Chatzidakis, *DOP*, figs. 1-16, 99.
20. Millet, *Athos*, pls. 115-39. Chatzidakis, *DOP*, 317-18, figs. 17-22.
21. Xyngopoulos, Σχεδ., 95, 103, 108-109. Chatzidakis, *DOP*, 318, 319, figs. 49-52, 54-61.
22. Chatzidakis, *DOP*, 319-20, figs. 26-33.
23. Chatzidakis, *DOP*, 323-27, figs. 34-45 (Great Lavra), 48, 84, 85 (Protaton), 63-83 (Stavronikita).
24. S. Kadas, *Mount Athos* (Athens, 1979), 171, fig. 101.
25. M. Chatzidakis, «Ὁ ζωγράφος Θεοφάνης Στρελίτζας τουπίκλην Μπαθᾶς» (Biographical Study), Νέα Ἑστία, Χίλια χρόνια τοῦ Ἁγίου Ὄρους, Χριστούγεννα (Athens, 1963), 10-11.
26. M. Chatzidakis, «Ὁ ζωγράφος Εὐφρόσυνος», Κρητικά Χρονικά 10 (Heraklion, 1956)= Études VI, 273-91, pls. ΚΑ-ΚΗ.
27. Millet, *Athos*, pls. 215-254.
28. Millet, *Athos*, pls. 207-14.
29. M. Chatzidakis, "Note sur le peintre Antoine de l'Athos", *Studies in Memory of David Talbot Rice* (Edinburgh, 1975) = *Études*, VII, 83-93.
30. Millet, *Athos*, pls. 255-60. Xyngopoulos, Σχεδ., 113 ff. 185, 258-59, 375. See also Chatzidakis, *IEE* vol. I΄, 424 ff.
31. A. Orlandos, «Βυζαντινά μνημεῖα τῆς Αἰτωλοακαρνανίας, Ἡ ἐν Αἰτωλίᾳ Μονή τῆς Μυρτιᾶς», *ABME* 9,10 (1961), 74 ff.
32. M. Acheimastou-Potamianou, Ἡ Μονή τῶν Φιλανθρωπηνῶν καί ἡ πρώτη φάση τῆς Μεταβυζαντινῆς ζωγραφικῆς (Athens, 1980).
33. Chatzidakis, *HC* 21, figs 4, 6, 21. Xyngopoulos, Σχεδ., 114-18, 259.
34. M. Michailidis, «Νέα στοιχεῖα ζωγραφικοῦ διακόσμου δύο μνημείων τῆς Μακεδονίας», *AAA* 4 (1971), 341 ff.

35. Pelekanides, *Καστοριά*, pls. 217-18. Gounaris, 105-84, pls. 22b-35a, 36-37, 38b, 39b-43, 47-50.

36. M. Michailidis, «Ὁ ναός τοῦ Ἁγίου Ζαχαρία Καστοριᾶς», *ΑΔ* 22 (1967). Μελέται 77-86, pls. 47-57 (particularly pls. 47, 48, 49, 51a,b). See also Chatzidakis, *Actes du Ier Congrès International des Études Balkaniques et Sud-Est Européennes, Sofia 1966* II (Sofia, 1969), 1003-1004.

37. Pelekanides, *Καστοριά*, pls. 204-16. T. Popa, "Onufre, une figure éminente de la peinture médiévale Albanaise", *StudAlb* 3 (1966), 291-303. Chatzidakis, *Aspects*, 190-191. Gounaris, 21-104. pls. 1-20.

38. Orlandos, *ABME* (1939), 187-188. Pelekanides, *Καστοριά*, pls. 204-16. G. Gounaris, «Οἱ τοιχογραφίες τοῦ Ἁγ. Ἰωάννη Θεολόγου τῆς Μαυριώτισσας στήν Καστοριά», *Μακεδονικά* 21 (1981), 1-75, pls. 1-32.

39. Orlandos, *Καστοριά*, 183 (Saint Nicholas), 182-83 (Panagia Metropoleos), 163-64, 182 (Saint Demetrios). Pelekanides, *Καστοριά*, pls. 232-43. N. Moutsopoulos, *Καστοριά. Λεύκωμα*, 50, figs. 7-9.

40. Chatzidakis, *HC* 23. M. Panagiotidi, "Les églises de Véria en Macédoine", *Corsi di cultura sull'arte ravennate e bizantina* (Ravenna, 1975), 314.

41. F. Drosoyanni, *ΑΔ* 18 (1963), Χρονικά 2, 250-51, pls. 281a,b.

42. S. Pelekanides, «Ἔρευναι ἐν Ἄνω Μακεδονίᾳ», *Μακεδονικά* 5 (1961-1963) = *Μελέτες*, 432-42.

43. M. Andronikos, *Μακεδονικά* 1 (1940), 190-94. Chatzidakis, *HC* 23.

44. Orlandos, *Καστοριά*, 163. Pelekanides, *Καστοριά*, pls. 244-47. Chatzidakis *HC* 23.

45. Millet, *Athos*, pls. 210-14. Xyngopoulos, *Σχεδ.*, 192. Gabriel the Archimandrite, *Ἡ ἐν Ἁγίῳ Ὄρει Ἱερά Μονή τοῦ Ἁγίου Διονυσίου* (Athens, 1959), 46, 51, 54.

46. Millet, *Athos*, pl. 152 1,2. *Recueil I*, No. 391.

47. G. Millet, *La Dalmatique du Vatican* (Paris, 1945), 3, pl. I, Gabriel, op. cit., 56, 119.

48. Millet, *Athos*, pls. 99-114. *Chilandar*, 154-60, fig. 129.

49. *Chilandar*, 160-66, figs. 133-37, 139-42.

50. For a more detailed analysis see Chatzidakis, *IEE* vol. ΙΑ΄, 244-247.

51. Chatzidakis, *ΑΔ* 21 (1966), Χρονικά 1, 30, pls. 55-56.

52. M. Chatzidakis, «Περί σχολῆς Κωνσταντινουπόλεως ὀλίγα», *ΑΔ* 27 (1972). Μελέτες, 122-23, pls. 41-46.

53. Xyngopoulos, *Σχεδ.*, 292-310, pl. 67. Chatzidakis, *IEE* vol. ΙΑ΄, 248-50.

54. Millet, *Athos*, pl. 261, figs. 2-3. R. Byron, D.T. Rice, *The Birth of Western Painting* (London, 1930), pls. 8, 10, 12 I, 24 II, 28-30, 67 I, 78 II.

55. Xyngopoulos, *Σχεδ.*, 306-308, pl. 67, 1. See also Chatzidakis, *IEE* vol. ΙΑ΄, 248, 249 ff.

56. *Recueil I* no. 378. Millet, *Athos*, pl. 263, 1, 2.

57. T. Popa, "Considérations générales sur la peinture postbyzantine en Albanie", *Actes du Ier Congrès International des Études Balkaniques et Sud-Est Européenes Sofia 1966* II (Sofia, 1969), 780, figs 4-5.

58. See Chatzidakis, *IEE* vol. Ι΄, fig. p. 437.

59. Orlandos in *ABME* 4 (1938), 176 ff., figs. 118-122, reads ΛΑΒ[ΠΕΝΤΙΟΥ].

60. Xyngopoulos, *Σχεδ.*, 208-310, pl. 67.

61. *Recueil I* no. 315, 379. Xyngopoulos, *Σχεδ.*, 290, 311. Chatzidakis, *IEE* vol. ΙΑ΄, 247.

62. V. Angelakos, *Ἡ ἐν Ἁγίῳ Ὄρει Ἄθω Ἱερά Μονή τοῦ Ἁγίου Γρηγορίου* (Thessalonike,

1921), 34. Millet, *Athos*, pls. 262, 264. Chatzidakis *HC*, pl. XX, fig. 22; P. Huber, *Athos, Leben, Glaube, Kunst* (Zurich, 1969), figs. 199, 200, 210 (coloured). Chatzidakis, *IEE* vol. ΙΑ΄, fig. p. 249.

63. Chatzidakis, «Περί Κωνσταντινουπόλεως», p. 133, n. 8 (See above n. 52).

64. K. Theocharidou, «Ὁ προφήτης Ἠλίας στήν Σιάτιστα», *Ἐκκλησίες στήν Ἑλλάδα μετά τήν Ἅλωση* (Athens, 1979), 56, figs. 4, 7. P. Leonidopoulos-Stylianou, «Τό καθολικό τῆς Μονῆς τῆς Ἁγίας Τριάδας στό Ζουπάντ», *Ἐκκλησίες στήν Ἑλλάδα μετά τήν Ἅλωση*, 77, figs. 15-17, 22-23.

65. Chatzidakis, *IEE* vol. ΙΑ΄, 253 ff.

66. Bible called Kalokairine (Venice, 1692), 2. Chatzidakis, *IEE* vol. ΙΑ΄, 245.

67. K. Zisiou, «Ἔρευναι τῶν ἐν Μακεδονίᾳ Χριστιανικῶν μνημείων», *ΠΑΕ* 1913, 170.

68. I.N. Photopoulos, *Ἱστορία τῆς Σελίτσης-Ἐρατύρας ἀπό τούς Ρωμαϊκούς χρόνους μέχρι τοῦ 1912 καί ἐν μέρει μέχρι σήμερον* (Athens, 1939). J. Touratsoglou, «Γραπτή ἀμαζών ἐκ Νυμφαίου», *ΑΑΑ* 1 (1968), 307-310, idem, «Ὁ Ἀρίστιππος τοῦ Νυμφαίου», *ΑΑΑ* 3 (1970), 45-47. Chatzidakis, «Περί Κωνσταντινουπόλεως» n. 58. (See above, n. 52). K. Makris, *Χιοναδῖτες ζωγράφοι* (Athens, 1981).

POPULAR ART

1. M. Kalinderis, *Αἱ συντεχνίαι τῆς Κοζάνης ἐπί τουρκοκρατίας* (Thessalonike, 1958), 7.

2. Moutsopoulos, *ΕΕΠΣΘ*, 36.

3. Vacalopoulos, 280 ff.

4. Moutsopoulos, *ΕΕΠΣΘ*, 36.

5. Moutsopoulos, *ΕΕΠΣΘ*, 72.

6. Moutsopoulos, *ΕΕΠΣΘ*, 65, pl. 67, fig. 1.

7. Moutsopoulos, *Φλ.*, pl. 85, fig. 1.

8. Moutsopoulos, *Ἀμπ.* 76-82.

9. Moutsopoulos, *ΕΕΠΣΘ*, pls. 38-41.

10. Moutsopoulos, *Ἀμπ.*, 25, 40-42.

11. Moutsopoulos, *Φλ.*, 4.

12. D. I. Toliopoulos, *Ἀκολουθία τοῦ ὁσίου καί θεοφόρου πατρός ἡμῶν Νικάνορος τοῦ θαυματουργοῦ, τοῦ ἐν τῷ τοῦ Καλλιστράτου ὄρει ἀσκήσαντος* (Kozani, 1953), 39-40. G.T. Lyritzis, *Ὁ ὅσιος Νικάνωρ καί τό μοναστήρι του* (Kozani, 1962).

13. G. Hionidis, *Σύντομη ἱστορία τοῦ χριστιανισμοῦ στήν περιοχή τῆς Βέροιας* (Veria, 1961), 49.

14. *Ἀκολουθία τοῦ ὁσίου καί Θεοφόρου πατρός ἡμῶν Θεοφάνους τοῦ νέου ἀσκητοῦ καί θαυματουργοῦ τοῦ ἀσκήσαντος ἐν τῷ ὄρει τῆς περιφήμου πόλεως Ναούσης, τοῦ ἐξ Ἰωαννίνων* (Venice, 1764), 33.

15. P.G. Zerlendis, «Θεσσαλονικέων μητροπολῖται ἀπό Θεωνᾶ τοῦ ἀπό ἡγουμένων μέχρι Ἰωάσαφ Ἀργυροπούλου (1520-1578)», *BZ* 12 (1903), 131-52.

16. K. Kalokyris, *Ἐξέχοντα μεταβυζαντινά τέμπλα τοῦ Ἁγίου Ὄρους. Ἀθωνική Πολιτεία* (Thessalonike, 1963), 315-45.

17. Moutsopoulos, *Φλ.* 64, 67.

18. N. Moutsopoulos, *Καστοριά. Παναγία ἡ Μαυριώτισσα* (Athens, 1967), 95.

19. G. Millet, "Recherches au Mont-Athos III. Phiale et simandre à Lavre", *BCH* 29 (1905), 105-23. Laskarina Bouras, "Some Observations on the Grand Lavra Phiale at Mount Athos and its Strobilion", *ΔΧΑΕ* 8 (1975-78), 85-96, pls. 44-51.

20. K.E. Tsiakas, *Ἱστορία τῆς ἱερᾶς μονῆς Εἰκοσιφοινίσσης Παγγαίου Δράμας* (1958), 24, 25.

21. Kontiadis, 22.

22. Kontiadis, 21.

23. I.N. Photopoulos, *Ἱστορία τῆς Σελίτσης-Ἐρατύρας ἀπό τούς ρωμαϊκούς χρόνους μέχρι τοῦ 1912 καί ἐν μέρει μέχρι σήμερον* (Athens, 1939), 96.

24. Moutsopoulos, *Φλ.*, 64.

25. Moutsopoulos, *Φλ.*, 23.

26. Moutsopoulos, *Πέλλα*, 41.

27. Moutsopoulos, *Πέλλα*, 25.

28. Christophoros, seminarian and abbot, *Προσκυνητάριον τῆς ἐν Μακεδονίᾳ, παρά τῇ πόλει τῶν Σερρῶν σταυροπηγιακῆς ἱερᾶς μονῆς τοῦ Ἁγίου Ἰωάννου τοῦ Προδρόμου* (Leipzig, 1904), 46 ff.

TEXTILES AND EMBROIDERY

1. P. Zora, *Embroideries and jewellery of greek national costumes*, 2nd ed. Ministry of Culture and Sciences, Athens, 1981.

2. E. Kaloyeropoulou, «Πουλιά καί δέντρα. Πορεία καί παράγοντες μετασχηματισμῶν», 2nd Symposium of Folklore, Institute for Balkan Studies, Thessalonike, 1976.

3. A. Chadzinikolaou, "Gold embroidery", *Greek Handicraft*, National Bank of Greece, Athens, 1969.

4. J. Papantoniou, «Συμβολή στή μελέτη τῆς ἑλληνικῆς παραδοσιακῆς φορεσιᾶς», *Ethnographika*, v.I, Nauplion, 1978.

5. A. Kyriakidou-Nestoros, *Τά ὑφαντά τῆς Μακεδονίας καί τῆς Θράκης*, Ἐθνικός Ὀργανισμός Ἑλληνικῆς Χειροτεχνίας, Athens 1965.

6. A. Hadjimichali, *The Greek folk costume*, Athens, 1979.

7. A. Delivorias, *Greek traditional jewellery*, Athens, 1980.

8. E. Ioannou, «Χάλκινα σφυρήλατα σινιά καί ἡ διακόσμησή τους», 3rd symposium of Folklore, Institute for Balkan Studies, Thessalonike, 1979.

9. V. Kyriazopoulos, "Pottery", *Greek Handicraft*, National Bank of Greece, Athens, 1969. See also "The contribution of the Christians to Asia Minor Pottery", *Balkan Studies*, v.I, 1978.

10. K. Makris, 'Woodcarving", *Greek Handicraft*, National Bank of Greece, Athens, 1969.

11. K. Kephalas, «Κασέλες, σεντούκια καί μπαοῦλα στό βορειοελλαδικό χῶρο», 3rd Symposium of Folklore, Institute for Balkan Studies, Thessalonike, 1979.

12. K. Kephalas, «Ρόκες καί σφοντύλια στό βορειοελλαδικό χῶρο», 2nd Symposium of Folklore, Institute for Balkan Studies, Thessalonike, 1976.

13. K. Kephalas, «Handicrafts in Macedonia under the Turks», *Quality*, Ἐθνικός Ὀργανισμός Ἑλληνικῆς Χειροτεχνίας, Athens, 1969.

FROM THE GREEK WAR OF INDEPENDENCE TO LIBERATION 1821-1912

MACEDONIA IN THE GREEK WAR OF INDEPENDENCE

1. Vacalopoulos, 584 ff. with full bibliography.

2. A. Despotopoulos, *IEE* vol. ΙΒ΄, 36.

3. A.N. Papazoglou, «Ή Θεσσαλονίκη κατά τόν Μάιο τοῦ 1821», *Μακεδονικά* 1 (1940), 417-28. J.K. Vasdravellis, *Ή Θεσσαλονίκη κατά τόν ἀγῶνα τῆς ἀνεξαρτησίας* (Thessalonike, 1946). J. Mamalakis, «Ή ἐπανάσταση στή Χαλκιδική τό 1821», *Χρονικά Χαλκιδικῆς* 1 (1961), 41 ff.

4. J. Filimon, *Δοκίμιον ἱστορικόν περί τῆς ἑλληνικῆς ἐπαναστάσεως* III (Athens, 1860), 142 ff, 430 ff.

5. A.E. Vacalopoulos, *Thasos, son histoire, son administration de 1453 à 1912* (Paris, 1953).

6. Vasdravellis, 98 ff. Vacalopoulos, 604-626.

7. G. H. Hionidis, *Ή ἐκστρατεία καί ἡ ἐπανάστασις εἰς τόν Ὄλυμπον κατά τά ἔτη 1821-1822* (Thessalonike, 1975). Vacalopoulos, 627.

8. Vasdravellis, 257-58. N. Kasomoulis, *Ἐνθυμήματα στρατιωτικά τῆς ἐπαναστάσεως τῶν Ἑλλήνων 1821-1833* I (Athens, 1939), 134 ff. N. G. Philippidis, *Ή ἐπανάστασις καί καταστροφή τῆς Ναούσης* (Athens, 1881). E. Stouyiannakis, *Ἱστορία τῆς πόλεως Ναούσης* I (Edessa, 1924). Idem, *Ἔδεσσα ἡ Μακεδονική ἐν τῇ ἱστορίᾳ* (Thessalonike, 1932). Vacalopoulos, 636-652.

9. Vacalopoulos, 651-652.

10. Vasdravellis, 152 ff.

11. Vacalopoulos, 662-688.

THE FIGHT FOR FREEDOM (1830-1912)

Dates in the text are given in New Style unless otherwise noted. References to documents have been quoted in both Styles.

1. A. Daskalakis, *Κείμενα-Πηγαί τῆς Ἱστορίας τῆς Ἑλληνικῆς Ἐπαναστάσεως* (II, 1967), 786-87.

2. *AYE* 36/1,2, Vallianos (Thessalonike) to the Secretary of Foreign Affairs, 28.3/9.4.1835.

3. *AYE* 49/2, 1839. Vallianos to the Embassy at Constantinople, no. 214 14/26.7.1839.

4. J. Petropoulos, *Politics and Statecraft in the Kingdom of Greece, 1833-1843* (Princeton, 1968), 329-43. Makriyannis, *Ἀπομνημονεύματα* II (Papyros), 100-101, 111-13. Barbara Jelavich, "The Philorthodox Conspiracy of 1839", *Bst* 8, 89-102. *ΓΑΚ* Mavrokordatos Archive, f. 20, Paikos to Mavrokordatos (London), no. 005. 679, 9/21.1.40, wherein the Philorthodox Society is rebuked for planning (among other things) 'uprisings in Thessaly and Macedonia'.

5. Biographical data: Vasdravellis, 180-83. Also: *AYE* 4/1 1839. Secretary of State to Soutsos (Consul at Preveza), no. 1851, 5/17.4.1839 (in which is reported the invasion from Turkish soil of a 'gang of bandits', under Karatasos). *ΓΑΚ*/Mavrokordatos Archive, f. 17. Authoritative sources in Nauplion, 15/27.6.1831 (where Karatasos is condemned as a 'thief and deserter').

6. Makriyannis 103-104, 109.

7. Makriyannis II, 104.

8. Concerning the revolts of 1839-41, see, Makriyannis II, 100-112.

9. *ΓΑΚ*/Mavrokordatos Archive, f. 20, Circular from K. Zographos to Mavrokordatos (London), no. 005-622, 31.8/12.9.1839, in which it is reported that the government is maintaining strict neutrality, notwithstanding the existence in Thessaly and Macedonia of 'a massed and ready force, needing only the tiniest spark to

burst into flame and threaten to reach the gates of Byzantium unimpeded (sic)'. In the districts near the frontiers where reinforcements were being assembled for Velentzas, the government sent M. Deligeorgis, who rounded up many civilians and soldiers opening the way to the destruction of the supply bases. *ΓΑΚ*/Mavrokordatos, Archive, f. 21, M. Deligeorgis to Mavrokordatos, 21.7/2.8.1841. *AYE* 4/1 1842, Order for the capture of Velentzas, no. 1425, 24.9/6.10.1841.

10. AYE/Thessalonike Consulate 1841. Documents of Vallianos no. 337, 27.2/12.3.41 and 124, 9/21.4.41.

11. Makriyannis II, 150-205.

12. Kyriakidis, *ΙΣΕ* I, 493-501.

13. Dragoumis II, 119-203.

14. At the end of the 1840s Mavrokordatos noted that Slavic pamphlets with nationalistic and revolutionary messages were being distributed not only in Bulgaria and Serbia but in certain areas of Macedonia as well. (Dragoumis II, 121).

15. Makriyannis II, 194-95. Concerning the contacts of Rakovski with Greek nationalists see: V. Traikov, *Rakovski i Balkanski narodi* (Sofia, 1971), 315-83.

16. D. Donta, *Ή Ἑλλάς καί αἱ Δυνάμεις κατά τόν Κριμαϊκόν Πόλεμον* (Thessalonike, 1973), 58-104.

17. Kyriakidis, *ΙΣΕ* I, 650-54. Papadopoulos, 48-49.

18. *Αἰών*, 26.5/7.6.1854.

19. J.P. Mamalakis, «Ή ἐκστρατεία τοῦ Δ. Τσάμη Καρατάσου στή Χαλκιδική τό 1854», *Χρονικά Χαλκιδικῆς* vol. 4-12 (1962-65). Also, *Τά δραματικά γεγονότα τοῦ 1854 στή Χαλκιδική καί τό Ἅγιον Ὄρος* (Thessalonike, 1967), 1-26. Papadopoulos, 34-47. Kyriakidis II, 655-56. A great deal of information — correspondence, diaries of operations, proclamations — were published in *Αἰών* as well as *Ἀθηνᾶ* during the period April-June, 1854.

20. Relevant information in the Ministry of Foreign Affairs despatch to the Naval Ministry no. 270, 2/14.8.55 and to the Ministry of Foreign Affairs no. 2631, 8/20.10.55 (*AYE* 55/1.1855). In particular this concerns the Naousian guerrilla Karapatakis who was active in Macedonia for a twenty year period. See: *AYE* 4/1, 1857 and particularly the document Thessalonike Consulate 51, 22,1/3.2.1857.

21. *Ἀθηνᾶ* 28.7/9.8.1854.

22. Throughout the war, the local authorities forced many Greek subjects in Macedonia to surrender their Greek passports and remain Ottoman subjects. *AYE* 49/2, 1859, Monastir Consulate no. 29, 16/28.12.1859.

23. Djordjević, 133.

24. V. Traikov, *Ideologicheski techenie i programi v natsionalno-osvoboditelnite dvizenie na balkanie do 1878 godina* (Sofia, 1978), 267-82.

25. Laskaris, 214-19.

26. The text of Zanos' report in, S. Markezinis, *Πολιτική Ἱστορία τῆς Νεωτέρας Ἑλλάδος, 1828-1864*, II (Athens, 1966), 64-65.

27. Djordjević, 137. Laskaris, 224-26.

28. A report in *Αἰών* (23.2.1867) from Thessalonike states: 'The Ottomans have been reduced to the most abject poverty; entire Ottoman families have been without food for weeks. They have become desperate and have resorted to pillaging, setting fire to various Greek neighbourhoods at night.'

29. *AYE* 9/1,1860, Vallianos to the Ministry of Foreign Affairs, no. 498/305, 30. 10/11. 11.1860.

30. *AYE* 49/9, 1860, Vallianos to Zanos (Constantinople), 9/21, 9, 1860 *Αὐγή* 5/17.10.1860 and *Φῶς* 13/25.7.1860.

31. The Greek Consul in Monastir reported that many parents were afraid that their children who were studying in Athens had been enlisted in Karatasos revolt. *AYE* 99/1, 1860, Vallianos to Zanos (Constantinople), no. 392, 21.7/2.8.1860.

32. A. Angelopoulos, "Demetrios Tsamis Karatasos. A Symbol of Greek, Serbian and Bulgarian Friendship", *Bst* 17 (1976), 49-57.

33. *AYE*/Embassy at Conastantinople/Leonidas Voulgaris/1866. (S. Valaoritis' circular to the consular authorities in Epirus, Thessaly, Macedonia and Albania, no. 2931, 16/28.4.66 and to the Embassy at Constantinople from 18/30.4.66. Also in f. 4/1,2,1866, there are relevant documents from the Consul in Thessalonike, Vasiliadis (in particular, no. 3664). The viewpoints of Voulgaris himself can be found in his book, *Ἀποκαλυφθήτω ἡ Ἀλήθεια* (Athens, 1878), 37-38.

34. *AYE*/Embassy at Constantinople-Consulates 1860-1866, Antypas (Serres) to Ministry of Foreign Affairs no. 136, 20.4/2.5.66 and *ΓΑΚ*/Vlachoyannis, f. 217 (Collection of Zotos Molossos). Letter of K. Dalas from Bessarabia, 14/26.2.1867 concerning the collection of money on behalf of the Central Committee.

35. See, for example, *AYE* 58/3, 1870, Logothetis (Monastir) the Foreign Minister, no. 18, 22, 1/3.2.1870.

36. This situation was also described succinctly by the Association for the Diffusion of Greek Letters in its confidential document to the Greek government in 1878. 'When we say *Hellenes* and *Hellenized* we mean, a) the pure and true Greeks, b) those populations, which although alien, have descended from related races and have identified their fate in all ways with Hellenism, using Greek and their own dialect equally and not differing from Greeks in any way; these are mainly the Greek-Albanians and the Greek-Vlachs,c) those who, although in their family life speak another language (for example, Bulgarian), nevertheless have Greek as their written language, which they have introduced into their churches and schools.' Kofos, 13, n. 1.

37. *AYE* 39/8, 1859, no. 9,1/13.12.59.

38. *AYE* 36/2,1860, Documents of the Consulate at Monastir no. 816, 7/19.12.1859. 49/9,1861, no. 121/81, 27, 4/9.5, 1861. 49/2, 1863, Serres, no. 200, 1/13.10.63.

39. *AYE* 76/1, 1870. Serres, no. 22, 19/31.1.70.

40. *AYE* 49/9, 1866, Monastir, no. 20,10/1.11.65 and no. 119/73, 6/18.4.66.

41. *AYE* 76/1.1869, P. Logothetis (Monastir) to the Ministry of Foreign Affairs, no. 121, 12/24.12.1869.

42. *AYE* 49/9, 1866, Consulate at Thessalonike to the Ministry of Foreign Affairs, no. 458, 27/6/9.7.1866.

43. *AYE* 36/2,1870, K. Vatikiotis (Thessalonike) to the Ministry of Foreign Affairs, no. 389, 27.5/8.6.1870. 76/1, 1869, Logothetis (Monastir) to the Ministry of Foreign Affairs, no. 23/13,16/28.8.1869, no. 314, 10/22.8. 1872 and no. 338, 19/31.12.1872 (the final two, 76/1, 1872).

44. *AYE* 76/1,1870, Vatikiotis to the Ministry of Foreign Affairs, no. 213, 31,3/12.4.1870.

45. *AYE* 76/1, 1869, Logothetis (Monastir), to the Ministry of Foreign Affairs, 23/13, 16/28.8.69 and no. 121, 12/24.12.69.

46. Kofos, 39-40. Also see the report of the Consul at Thessalonike 1873-1875 and particularly no. 555 from 30,5/12.6.1874.

47. *AYE* 76/1, no. 48/34, 10/22.9.1869. And in 1872 the same consul continued to demonstrate his conviction in the strength of Hellenism in Pelagonia: 'The Hellenic and Philhellenic communities in northern Macedonia... are of a mind to combat their enemies either through passive resistance, or through active exploits on their own volition.... against pan-Slavism.' *AYE*, 76/1, 1872, no. 52,23,2/6.3.1872.

48. *AYE* 73/3,1871, Embassy at Constantinople, no. 2355, 4/16.8.71.

49. Συνέδριον Ἑλληνικῶν Συλλόγων (Athens, 1879), 17-18.

50. D. Djordjević, *Revolutions nationales des peuples balkaniques 1804-1914* (Belgrade, 1965), 146-47.

51. Kofos, 61-62 and Kofos 62.

52. Two collections of documents: See also, J. Notaris, Ἀρχεῖο Στεφάνου Δραγούμη: Ἀνέκδοτα Ἔγγραφα γιά τήν Ἐπανάστασι τοῦ 1878 στή Μακεδονία (Thessalonike, 1966), 1-444; Kofos, 1-371. bishop Nicholas of Kitros, Ἀπομνημονεύματα (unpublished).

53. Kofos, 213.

54. D. Doinov, *Kresnensko-Razlozkoto Vastanie, 1878-1879* (Sofia, 1979), 1-333. Also *IEE*, vol. ΙΓ΄, 356, which is based mainly on Greek consular reports.

55. Djordjević, 221-23.

56. E. Kofos, "Dilemmas and Orientations of Greek Policy in Macedonia, 1878-86", (Paper read at the Ankara IV Balkan Conference, Aug. 1979), *Bst* 21.

57. Cl. Nicolaides, *La Macédoine. La Question macédonienne dans l'antiquité, au moyen âge, et dans la politique actuelle* (Berlin, 1899).

58. *AYE*/Embassy at Constantinople/1883. Trikoupis to Koundouriotis, no. 310. April 1883. Trikoupis to Embassies no. 368,7/ 19.3.1884 (f. 'Circulars-1884'). Koundouriotis to Trikoupis no. 615, 22,3/3.4.1883.

59. The analysis which follows is based largely on unpublished reports in various files of *AYE* (1879-85), of Greek consuls in Macedonia, as well as the correspondence concerning Macedonian questions between the Foreign Ministry and the Embassy at Constantinople.

60. *AYE* 29/3.1887. S. Dragoumis Ministry of Foreign Affairs, to Embassies and Consulates, no. 850, 30,1/11.2.1887 (absolutely confidential). Starting in 1882, the involvement of the government in the activity of the Association for the Diffusion of Greek Letters became more direct with the presence of a representative of the Foreign Ministry at the meetings of the Council who had jurisdiction over the 'supervision of the correct implementation of the Society's budget.' Vlachos, 106, n.2.

61. When in 1901 Joachim III returned to the Patriarchal throne, he considered it advantageous to state that the policy of the Greek kingdom during the 1880s had been one of the basic causes for the regression of Hellenism in Macedonia. In his confidential memorandum of 6/18.12.1902 to the Greek chargé d'affaires in Constantinople, A. Potté he noted: 'This policy aimed at the blatant cooperation (at first in the disputed areas and later everywhere else), between the Church authorities and the consuls whose influence became ever more demonstrative. This tendency led to the suggestion, and subsequently the proof, that the Church was, or ought to be under the protection of the Greek government; This principle of Greek policy.... created confusion, overthrew an age-old establishment, and aroused its opponents not only to defence but to aggression. The Church and its officials, jolted, gave in weakly and timourously and were dragged down the new road. This did not show a lack of patriotism or ancestral pride but a fear that this new regime might entail mutual destruction.' *AYE*, special file, 1902-1903. Memorandum in the document at the Embassy at Constantinople no. 965 from 7/19.12.1902.

62. In 1873 the Porte undertook by law to interfere in the educational matters of Christians. Military events prevented the immediate application of this law but it did come into effect around 1888. *AYE* 36/27, 1873, Gennadis (Serres), no. 455, 14/26.12.1873. Also, *AYE*/Macedonian Consulates/1883, Dokos (Monastir), to the Association for the Diffusion of Greek Letters, no. 8,6/18, January 1883. Vlachos, 103. For more general information concerning the activity of Macedonian Hellenism in education, see: S. Papadopoulos, Ἐκπαιδευτική καί κοινωνική δραστηριότητα τοῦ Ἑλληνισμοῦ τῆς Μακεδονίας κατά τόν τελευταῖο αἰώνα τῆς Τουρκοκρατίας (Thessalonike, 1970), 1-287. Also, *IEE*, vol. ΙΓ΄, 385-87.

63. Proposal of the Foreign Minister A. Kondostavlos to the Ministerial Council for the application of a longterm policy in Macedonia. *AYE*/Macedonian Consulates/ 1883, no. 1412,24,10/5.11.1883.

64. *AYE*/Embassy at Belgrade/1885, Belgrade, no. 30,26,2/10.3.1885. Also, E. Kofos, "Greek-Serbian Relations and Macedonia, 1878-1896", in *Greek-Serbian Cooperation 1830-1908, Collection of Reports, II, Greek-Serbian Symposium* (Belgrade, 1982), 93-106.

65. Wayne Vucinich, *Serbia between East and West. The Events of 1903-1908* (Stanford Univ. Press 1954), 25-26.

66. Concerning the Picheon Affair there is a voluminous correspondence in the files of *AYE*/Consulate at Monastir/1887.

67. It must be noted that the hopes which, for the moment, encouraged the Greeks in Germany — after the marriage of the Crown Prince Constantine to Sophia — proved to be groundless. Not only did the more general interests of Germany in South-eastern Europe favour the opponents of Greece but also the general climate of German public opinion had become hostile to Greece after the Greek government had proven unable to fulfill its economic obligations to its foreign lenders and in particular the Germans.

68. For information concerning the insurgent bands that entered Macedonia in 1896 see, Lyritzis, 1-342. Concerning the *Ethnike Etaireia* there is a very good presentation in *IEE*, vol. ΙΔ΄, 93-100.

69. Lyritzis, 138-68.

70. G.S. Papadopoulos, *England and the Near East, 1898* (Thessalonike, 1969), 142-43.

71. *AYE*/Telegrams/ 1902, Kouzes-Pezas to the Ministry of Foreign Affairs no. 1048, 15/28.1.1902.

72. *AYE*/ Consulate at Monastir/ 1901, no. 224, 13/26.3.1901.

73. Bulgarian Academy of Sciences, *Make-donskiat Vapros: istorikopolititseska spravka* (Sofia, 1968) 32-39 (Translation, Institute for Balkan Studies, Thessalonike).

74. This viewpoint is at present supported by the historiography of Skopje. Specifically see: Manol Pandevski, *Natsionalnoto Prashanje vo Makedonskoto Osloboditelno Dvizenje, 1893-1903* (Skopje, 1974) Hristo Andonov-Polianski, *Gotse Deltchev Negotovo Vreme* (Skopje, 1978).

75. *The Macedonian Question. With an Introduction by F.S. Stevenson, MP* (London, Byron Society, 1902), 9.

76. *AYE*/ Monastir Consulate/1901, Kouzes-Pezas to the Ministry of Foreign Affairs, no. 224,13/26.3.1901.

77. The refusal of the Greek government at that time to adopt more radical measures to confront the Bulgarian threat is depicted in the documents of the Foreign Minister Romanos to the General Consul in Thessalonike, Evgeneiadis, (no. 441, 27,2/12,3/1901 and no. 922,22,4/5.5.1901/*AYE*, K, 1901).

78. Joachim believed in the possibilities of the oecumenical mission of the Patriarchate; that is why he sought the improvement of relations with all the Slav Orthodox — and in particular the Russians. He even believed that the abrogation of the schism would aid not only his oecumenical policy but the Greek interests in Macedonia as well. He asked the prelates again and again to take greater initiative in educational matters which had gradually come under the consuls. Finally, he stated that the chief foe was the Ottoman government and that endeavours to have favourable relations with the Ottomans were doomed to failure. *AYE*/ Constantinople/ 1901, Mavrokordatos to Romanos, no. 1037,25,11/8.12.1900.

79. *AYE*/ Embassy at Constantinople/1901, Mavrokordatos to Romanos, no. 604, 27,7 /9.8.1900 and B. Laourdas, Ὁ Μακεδονικός Ἀγών (Thessalonike, 1962). *AYE*/1902, Evgeneiadis to the Ministry of Foreign Affairs, no. 407, 9/22.12.1902 (for Orologas). *AYE*/Embassy at Constantinople/1901, Mavrokordatos to Romanos, no. 604,27,7/9.8.1901 (note by Joachim concerning transfers).

80. *AYE*/ Constantinople/1900. Romanos to Mavrokordatos, no. 2531, 12/25.10.1900, wherein it is noted that 'we must understand each other and assist each other for the restoration of order.'

81. Concerning the cooperation of Evgeneiadis with the Ottoman vali of Thessalonike in 1899 see: *AYE*/aakH, Evgeneiadis to Zaimis, no. 72,29,3/11.4.1901.

82. For example, *AYE*/ Macedonian Question/1901. Report of Evgeneiadis 5/18.2.1901. Report of Stornaris no. 55,28,2/3.3.1901 and no. 63,10/23.3.1901.

83. *AYE*/ Special File/1902-3. Potté to the Ministry of Foreign Affairs, no. 965, 7/20.12.1902 with an enclosed letter from Joachim, 6/19.12.1902.

84. *AYE*/ Macedonian Question/ 1901, no. 401, 18/31.5.1901.

85. *AYE*/ Constantinople/1901, Mavrokordatos to Romanos, no. 1037, 25,11/8.12.1900. The proposal to use force against force had been made by Ambassador Mavrokordatos at the beginning of 1900, but without it being granted (his document from 13/26.1.1900).

86. *AYE*/ Macedonian Question/1901, no. 1242, 3/16.8.1901.

87. Germanos Karavangelis, *Ὁ Μακεδονικός Ἀγών* (Memoirs), ed. B. Laourdas, 1958², 148. The information contained in the Memoirs has been confirmed and supplemented by documents from the Consulate at Monastir for the years 1902-1904 *(AYE)*.

88. *AYE*, 1/1902, Evgeneiadis to Zaimis, no. 117, 9/22.5.1902 with enclosed letter.

89. P. Tsamis, *Ὁ Μακεδονικός Ἀγών* (Thessalonike, 1975), 152.

90. Dakin, 73-75.

91. J. Notaris, «Τά γεγονότα τῆς Θεσσαλονίκης τόν Ἀπρίλιο τοῦ 1903 μέ βάση ἔγγραφα τοῦ Ἱστορικοῦ Ἀρχείου τοῦ Ἑλληνικοῦ Ὑπουργείου Ἐξωτερικῶν», *Μακεδονικά* 10, 35-91. Details in Stoyan Christow, *Heroes and Assassins* (New York, 1935).

92. J. Notaris, «Ἡ βουλγαρική ἐπανάσταση τοῦ Ἰλίν-Ντέν», *Ἐποχές* (January, 1966), 43-51, and (February, 1966), 139-45. The position of present day Yugoslav historiography is presented in specific studies in the volume, *Prilozi za Iliden - 1978* (Krušovo, 1979). Issues relevant to Greek policy are treated in the article by Krste Bitoski, "Stavot na Kralstvoto Grtsia kon Makedonija u kon Makedonskata Revolutsunerna Organizatsia (1893-1903)", 93-112. Concerning Bulgarian historiography see G. Georgiev and J. Shopov, *Ilidensko Vastanie* (Sofia, 1969). Also a recent collection of ducuments of the Bulgarian Academy of Sciences: *Osvoboditelnata borba na Bulgarite v Makedonija i Odrinsko, 1902-1904 - Diplomatitseski dokumenti* (Sofia, 1978).

93. A serious disagreement arose among the four officers two of whom (Melas and Kondoulis) maintained that local forces were sufficient with only the despatch of officers from free Greece, while the other two (Papoulas and Kolokotronis) understood the difficulties and suggested the formation and dispatching of entire corps from the kingdom. The principal monographs dealing with the Macedonian struggle, based on Greek and foreign sources and the memoirs of the combatants, are the following: Dakin and *ΔΙΣ* and the relevant chapter of J. Mazarakis-Ainian, «Ὁ Μακεδονικός Ἀγώνας», *IEE* vol. ΙΔ΄, 220-54.

94. The text of the Organization of the Macedonian Committee, Tsamis, 445-48.

95. His letter to his wife and other documents in the book by Natalia Melas, *Ὁ Παῦλος Μελᾶς* (Association for the Diffusion of Greek Letters, Athens, 1963).

96. Republished in Tsamis, 449-61 from the book by S. Raptis, *Ἱστορία τοῦ Μακεδονικοῦ Ἀγῶνος*.

97. Dakin, 192.

98. *ΔΙΣ* 170-72. Demetrios Kallergis was the Greek Consul at Monastir during the time of the armed struggle and was succeeded by Nicholas Xydakis in August, 1905 (Tsamis, 162).

99. *IEE* vol. ΙΔ΄, 242.

100. *AYE*/ General Consulate Thessalonike/ 1909. «Ἔκθεσις τῶν Γεγονότων καί τῆς Καταστάσεως ἐν τῇ Περιφερείᾳ Θεσσαλονίκης, κατά τό ἔτος 1908».

101. The books of Tsamis and *ΔΙΣ* are particularly enlightening as to military operations.

102. The battle of the lake of Yannitsa was popularized by Penelope Delta, *Τά Μυστικά τοῦ Βάλτου* (Ist edition, 1937). A comparison with the memoirs of the combatants and with unpublished files verifies the historical accuracy of the events being described and par-

ticularly the role played by and the sacrifice of Kapetan S. Agapinos (Tellos Agras) and of the local chieftain Kapetan Gonos. See, *ΔΙΣ*, 257-64. There is an excellent analysis in, «Ἔκθεσις τῶν Γεγονότων καί τῆς Καταστάσεως ἐν τῇ Περιφερείᾳ Θεσσαλονίκης κατά τό ἔτος 1908», op. cit., 26-29.

103. *AYE* A, ST/1904, Koromilas to the Ministry of Foreign Affairs, no. 11, 30/9/13.10/1904.

104. K. Mazarakis describes the reactions of the villagers of the Yannitsa plain to the oppressive activities of Greek estate shareholders of Naousa. K. Mazarakis-Ainian, *Ὁ Μακεδονικός Ἀγών* (Thessalonike, 1963).

105. Before the Greek counter-attack began, the Bulgarians tried to encircle and to bring the urban centres, where the Greek element was dominant, to a standstill. That is why they ordered a boycott of Greek merchants. *AYE*/A ST/1904, Koromilas to the Ministry of the Foreign Affairs, no. 572, 15/28, 9/1904. For Greek countermeasures see: Souliotis-Nikolaidis, Also, *ΔΙΣ*, 209-12. Concerning the industries of Edessa see, the report of the Consulate at Thessalonike for 1908, op. cit, 17-18.

106. A detailed account of the work by the Macedonian Center of Thessalonike in its report, «Ἔκθεσις τῶν Γεγονότων καί τῆς Καταστάσεως ἐν τῇ Περιφερείᾳ Θεσσαλονίκης κατά τό ἔτος 1908» *(AYE*/Consulate at Thessalonike).

107. Dakin, 333-39.

108. These findings are included in the Report of 1908 of the Consulate at Thessalonike, *AYE*, op. cit., 1-3.

109. Dakin.

110. Ivan Guechoff, *L'alliance balkanique* (Paris, 1915), 14-63. N. Vlachos, *Ἡ συμμαχική προσέγγισις τῶν τεσσάρων χριστιανικῶν κρατῶν τῆς Χερσονήσου τοῦ Αἵμου* (Thessalonike, 1953) 19-21.

111. Ivan Guechoff, 63-69. Vlachos, 21-27.

112. Leon, 7.

113. Leon, 59.

114. Ministry of Foreign Affairs, *Διπλωματικά Ἔγγραφα 1913-1917* (Athens, 1917).

ADMINISTRATIVE, SOCIAL AND ECONOMIC DEVELOPMENTS

1. *AYE* 1835-1881/4/1, 1844/58/1, 1850/36/2, 1858/36/2, 1860/49/9, 1861/49/1,9, 1863/36/2, 1866/49/9, 1872/77/3, 1877-1900/AAK.
   P.R.O. F.O. 78/1531, 78/4738, 195/100, 195/176, 195/240, 195/293, 195/647, 195/771, 195/952, 195/1007, 195/1692, 195/1989, 297/1807.

ADMINISTRATIVE DIVISION - POPULATION

1. The text is based on E. Kofos, *IEE* vol. ΙΓ΄, 378-84.

ECCLESIASTICAL ORGANIZATION

1. G. Rallis - M. Potlis, *Σύνταγμα τῶν Θείων καί Ἱερῶν Κανόνων ε΄* (Athens, 1855), 513 ff.

2. A. Angelopoulos, «Ἡ ἐποπτεία τῆς Μητροπόλεως Θεσσαλονίκης ἐπί τῆς Ἑλληνικῆς Ὀρθοδόξου Κοινότητος Βελεσσῶν

(1876-1914)», *Μακεδονικά* 17 (1977), 139 ff.

3. C. Papastathis, "L'Église et le droit coutumier aux Balkans pendant la domination ottomane", *Običajino Pravo i Samouprave na Balkanu i u Susednim Zemljama* (Belgrade, 1974), 187 ff. Idem: "Zur Verbreitung der 'Hexabiblos' des Harmenopoulos im Slavischen Raum", *Bst* 17 (1976), 67 ff. Idem: "Byzantine Private Law and Codifications among the Bulgarians during the Ottoman Period (XVth-XIXth centuries)", *Πνευματικές καί Πολιτιστικές Σχέσεις Ἑλλήνων καί Βουλγάρων ἀπό τά μέσα τοῦ ΙΕ΄ ἕως τά μέσα τοῦ ΙΘ΄ αἰώνα. Α΄ Ἑλληνοβουλγαρικό Συμπόσιο* (Thessalonike, 1980), 249 ff.

4. An unpublished report in the archives of the Oecumenical Patriarchate,whose publication is being prepared by the writer.

5. K. Tattis, «Ἱστορικές σελίδες Θεσσαλονίκης», *Μακεδονικόν Ἡμερολόγιον* (C. Gougousis), (Thessalonike, 1915), 70. A. Vacalopoulos, «Συμβολή στήν ἱστορία τῆς Θεσσαλονίκης ἐπί βενετοκρατίας (1423-1430)», *Τόμος Κωνσταντίνου Ἀρμενοπούλου* (Thessalonike, 1952), 139-41.

6. P. Pennas, *Τό Κοινόν Μελενίκου καί τό σύστημα διοικήσεώς του* (Athens, 1946).

7. See, P. Papageorgiou, «Αἱ Σέρραι καί τά προάστεια τά περί τάς Σέρρας καί ἡ Μονή Ἰωάννου τοῦ Προδρόμου», *BZ* 3 (1894), 280. Pennas, 84.

8. During 1876 there was the danger that Naousa would be turned into an *evkaf* following the justified seizure of the inhabitants' lands for their participation in the Revolution of 1821. See, G. Hionidis, «Ζητήματα ἰδιοκτησίας-φορολογίας καί διώξεις στή Νάουσα στά χρόνια 1870-1877», *Μακεδονικά* 19 (1979), 93 ff.

9. Nikolaidis III, 2860.

10. Published separately, Constantinople, 1900.

11. Translated into Greek, Nikolaidis III, 2911 ff.

12. N. Pantazopoulos, "Community Laws and Customs of Western Macedonia under Ottoman Rule", *Bst* 2 (1961), 20-21.

13. G. Tsaras, «Ἐκλογές γιά μουχταροδημογεροντία στό Μπλάτσι τῆς Κοζάνης (1888)», *Μακεδονικά* 14 (1974), 50-54.

14. Moskov, 92. Concerning the life and the personality of the metropolitan Kallinikos see, Papadopoulos *OAE* I, 612-627.

15. Moskov, 92-94. Papadopoulos, *OAE* I, 666-68.

16. P. Pennas, op. cit. 474-75. By same author, «Ἔριδες περί τήν κοινοτικήν ὀργάνωσιν τῆς πόλεως τῶν Σερρῶν καί τά πρακτικά τῆς ἐν Σέρραις Ἐξαρχίας τῶν Μητροπολιτῶν Θεσσαλονίκης καί Σερβίων καί Κοζάνης (1891-1892)», *Σερραϊκά Χρονικά* 2 (1957), 5 ff.

17. Pennas, 475-76.

18. A. Letsas, *Ἱστορία τῆς Θεσσαλονίκης* II (Thessalonike, 1963), 169-75.

INTELLECTUAL LIFE EDUCATION

1. Mathaios Paranikas, *Σχεδίασμα περί τῆς ἐν τῷ ἑλληνικῷ ἔθνει καταστάσεως τῶν γραμμάτων ἀπό ἁλώσεως Κωνσταντινουπόλεως (1453 μ.Χ.) μέχρι τῶν ἀρχῶν τῆς ἐνεστώσης (ΙΘ΄) ἑκατονταετηρίδος* (Constantinople, 1867), 56, 57 and 60.

2. K.T. Dimaras, *Ἱστορία τῆς Νεοελληνικῆς Λογοτεχνίας* (Athens, 1975⁶), 258.

SCHOLARS - PRESS - NEWSPAPERS - SCHOOLS - ASSOCIATIONS - BENEFACTORS

1. Information derives from: S.J. Papadopoulos, Ἐκπαιδευτική καί Κοινωνική Δραστηριότητα τοῦ Ἑλληνισμοῦ τῆς Μακεδονίας κατά τόν τελευταῖο αἰῶνα τῆς Τουρκοκρατίας (Thessalonike, 1970) with a comprehensive bibliography; Μακεδονικόν Ἡμερολόγιον Παμμακεδονικοῦ Συλλόγου Ἀθηνῶν (Athens, 1908-1913); Μακεδονικά, in particular the articles by C.K. Papastathis, «Τά πρῶτα ἑλληνικά τυπογραφεῖα τῆς Θεσσαλονίκης», Μακεδονικά 8 (1968), 239-56, and C. Bakirtzis, «Ὁ Πέτρος Παπαγεωργίου καί οἱ ἀπαρχές τῆς Λογοτεχνίας στή Θεσσαλονίκη», Μακεδονικά 16 (1976), 235-48, Σερραϊκά Χρονικά.

MACEDONIA TODAY

THE MACEDONIAN QUESTION IN OUR TIME

1. Leon, 107, 169, 187-88, 195-96, 212-14.
2. Barker, 19-20 and 29-31, who writes, 'The Bulgarian occupation authorities in Greek eastern Macedonia had behaved toward the Greek population with a brutality singularly inappropriate in supposed liberators. An Inter-Allied Commission in 1919 reported that 94 villages had been entirely demolished, that 30,000 people had died of hunger, blows and disease during the occupation, that 42,000 had been deported to Bulgaria and that 16,000 had fled to Greece.'
3. Barker, 20. Makedonskiat Vapros, Report of the Bulgarian Academy of Sciences, 1968, 43 (Greek translation Institute for Balkan Studies).
4. Σύμβασις μεταξύ Ἑλλάδος καί Βουλγαρίας περί Ἀμοιβαίας καί Ἐθελουσίας Μεταναστεύσεως τῶν Φυλετικῶν Μειονοτήτων. Neuilly, 14/27. 11.1919 (Athens, Ethnikon Typographeion, 1919).
5. AYE, Files of the Mixed Commission on the Exchange of Populations and especially file B/45, 1926 and A/19, 1927.
6. Stephen Ladas, The Exchange of Minorities: Bulgaria, Greece and Turkey (New York, 1932), 105, 122-23.
7. Republished in Pentzopoulos, 136-37.
8. Annuaire Statistique de la Grèce (Athens, 1928).
9. Barker, 22-29. Palmer-King, 8-10. Kofos, Nationalism, 46-47, 93. For the personal hardships of the Greek Consul at Skopje see, Evangelos Kofos, Ἡ Μακεδονία στή Γιουγκοσλαβική Μακεδονία (Thessalonike, 1974), 6-7.
10. Barker, 36-45.
11. Palmer-King, 31-33.
12. Details in Kofos, Nationalism, 64-94. The text of the decision of the Extraordinary Congress of the Communist Party of Greece concerning the National Question (1924) in the collection of documents: Τό ΚΚΕ ἀπό τό 1918 ἕως τό 1931, I (Athens, 1947), 353-56.
13. Palmer-King, 33.
14. Article by G. Kordatos in Ριζοσπάστης (25.2.1927). Quoted in Kofos, Nationalism,

73-74. See Dimos Mexis, Ὁ Ἱστορικός Γιάννης Κορδάτος καί τό Ἔργο του: Εἰσαγωγή, Ἀνέκδοτη Αὐτοβιογραφία καί Αὐτοκριτική (Athens, 1975), 166-67 where Kordatos mentions the position the Party took in Macedonia as a reason for withdrawing from it.
15. Δέκα χρόνια Ἀγῶνες, 1935-1945 (Publication of the Central Committee of the Communist Party of Greece, Athens, 1945), 66-67.
16. Kofos, Nationalism, 95-97. R Knejevič, "Prince Paul, Hitler and Salonica", International Affairs XXVII (No. 1), (January, 1951), 42. Ministry of Foreign Affairs, 1940-1941 Ἑλληνικά Διπλωματικά Ἔγγραφα (Athens, 1980), 174, 176, 189, 190.
17. Kofos, Nationalism, 98-107, where he mentions a report of a group of professors of the Universities of Athens and Thessalonike concerning the Bulgarian depradations in Macedonia and Thrace, 1941-1944.
18. Boro Mitrovski and others, The Bulgarian Army in Yugoslavia, 1941-1944 (Belgrade, 1971), 13-46, 77-111. Palmer-King, 61-94.
19. Alexander Hristov, "The Constitution of the Macedonian State in the Yugoslav Federation (1941-1945)", in the work of M. Apostolski and H. Polenakovich, The Socialist Republic of Macedonia (Skopje, 1974), 49-68.
20. In their book (op. cit., p. 14) Palmer and King state: 'It is reasonable to hold that prior to World War II the Slavs of Yugoslav Macedonia considered themselves Bulgarians, but they developed reservations during the Bulgarian occupation in World War II... whether the Macedonians would eventually have evolved into a separate nationality is an open question... However, since it is still dangerous today for a Yugoslav Macedonian to admit that he considers himself a Bulgarian, there is no accurate way to determine the real national feeling of the Macedonian Slavs. They have passively, if not positively, accepted their status.'
21. Based on Yugoslav and Bulgarian sources, a detailed account in Kofos, Nationalism, 113-19, 135-43. Recent information: Tsola Dragoitcheva, La Macédoine-facteur de bon voisinage et de coopération et non de discorde: Souvenirs et réflexions (Sofia, 1978), 5-108 and the Yugoslav reply: Svetozar Vukmanović-Tempo, Borda za Balkan ("globus" Zagreb, 1981), 1-335. The archives of the U.S. State Department reveal the intense opposition of the English and the Americans, in 1945, to the idea of a Balkan federation or a Yugoslav-Bulgarian agreement before the signing of a peace treaty. The position of the Soviet Union was that fears about the federation were baseless, while Bulgarian-Yugoslav cooperation was useful in the struggle against Germany and the succeeding 'maintenance of peace and security in the Balkans.' US National Archives, File 760 H. 74/2-1145.
22. Barker, 102-104. Kofos, Nationalism, 161-63. Palmer-King, 123-26.
23. Palmer-King, 126-27, 129-30.
24. Kofos, Nationalism, 192-95, 210-20. Article, «Τό Μακεδονικό στίς σχέσεις Γιουγκοσλαβίας καί Βουλγαρίας», Μακεδονικά Θέματα (Athens, April-May, 1979), 22-24.
25. Concerning the events during the Occupation see: Kofos, Nationalism, 119-35, 151-52. K. Bramou, Σλαβοκομμουνιστικαί Ὀργανώσεις ἐν Μακεδονία: Προπαγάνδα καί Ἐπαναστατική Δράση (Thessalonike, 1960²). Les Archives de la Macédoine: Egeiska Makedonija vo NOB,

1944-1945 (vol. I. Skopje, 1971), 180-280.
26. Archiv na Makedonija, Egeiska Makedonija vo NOB (Aegean Macedonia in the National Liberation Struggle) I (1944-1945), II (1945), III (1945-1946), (Skopje, 1971, 1973, 1976). Vangel Ajanovski-Otse, Egeiski Buri (Aegean Tempest), (Skopje, 1975).
27. Kofos, Nationalism, 175-88. Barker, 119. Related documents in US National Archives, File 760 H. 74/1948 and 1949. It should be noted that until 1952 the Communist Party of Greece openly backed the Bulgarian position in Macedonia. See the declaration of "Ilinden" — a Slav- Macedonian organization, loyal to the Greek Communist Party — in the official Party organ Νέος Κόσμος (May, 1952, 21), where it is stated that 'only our comrades in Pirin have acquired their liberty and together with the Bulgarian people are building socialism'.
28. Kofos, Nationalism, 196-204.
29. «Τό Μακεδονικό Ἐθνικό Ζήτημα στό φῶς τῶν ἀποφάσεων τῆς Ἕκτης Ὁλομέλειας», Νέος Κόσμος (February, 1957), 8. Quoted in Kofos, Nationalism, 220-22.
30. The published positions of the 7th Congress of the League of Macedonian Communists (Feb. 2, 1978) contained the pointed statement that 'discrimination detrimental to the Macedonian national minority/in Greece/ continues.' A while later, President Tito himself in statements made at Skopje mentioned that during his meetings with the Greek Prime Minister K. Karamanlis, the Macedonian Question had been discussed. This caused an immediate reaction in Athens with a government announcement that there were differing viewpoints concerning the existence of a minority question in Greece (Oct. 9, 1978). The following day, the leader of the Opposition, Andreas Papandreou, declared his solidarity with the government in this matter. This led to a temporary cessation of polemics in the Yugoslav press concerning this question.

THE ECONOMIC DEVELOPMENT OF GREEK MACEDONIA SINCE 1912

1. The estimates regarding the per capita income and the percentage composition of the total gross product of the region are based primarily on information taken from the following sources: Clark, Progress, 148-49; J.S. Papadakis, Αἱ πλουτοπαραγωγικαί δυνάμεις τῆς Μακεδονίας (Thessalonike, 1920). See also information in tables 5 and 6.
2. According to the census of ΕΣΥΕ and information from various other sources, the population of the nome of Florina, from 1951 on, could be found in two new nomes, Florina and Kastoria. At the same time the following nomes were created: Grevena, Emathia and Pieria, which were detached from the nome of Thessalonike.
3. It is not a nome but a self-administering area of Macedonia.
4. E. Gritsopoulos, Ἡ ἱστορία τῆς γεωργικῆς στατιστικῆς τῆς Ἑλλάδος (pub. EKKE, Statistical Studies, 1821-1971), (Athens, 1972), 213-44. Klimis, 15-21.
5. For more information concerning the settlement of refugees see, C.P. Howland, L'établissement des réfugiés en Grèce (Geneva, 1926). Mavrogordatos, Hamoudopoulos, 17-

19. N. Katsoulis, *Τό ἐποικιστικόν ἔργον τοῦ Ὑπ. Γεωργίας* (Athens, 1938). M. Maravelakis, A. Vacalopoulos, *Αἱ προσφυγικαί ἐγκαταστάσεις ἐν τῇ περιοχῇ Θεσσαλονίκης* (Society of Macedonian Studies no. 4 Thessalonike, 1955); Pentzopoulos; his book is the best ethnological, political, social and cultural exposition of the refugee problem that exists in either Greek or foreign bibliography.

6. Mavrogordatos-Hamoudopoulos, 19. Μεγάλη Ἑλληνική Ἐγκυκλοπαιδεία, s.v. Μακεδονία, 504.

7. Technical, economic, administrative and other details concerning the major achievements in Macedonia can be found in the books: *Ἀνώτατον Οἰκονομικόν Συμβούλιον.* Soulis. Settas.

8. Soulis, 27.Settas, 64.

9. Pentzopoulos, 151.

10. The term 'agricultural revolution' is used here to mean a radical change in the *methods* of cultivation and in the *process* through which agricultural production is realized, influencing: α) the quantity of the inputs which are used (i.e., less human labour, more introduction of technology), and b) its productive results (greater yield per stremma).

11. Pentzopoulos, 160.

12. The famous poem by Yannis Ritsos, *Epitaphios* was written about the death of a young tobacco factory worker during a demonstration in Thessalonike in 1931.

13. B. Sweet-Escott, *Greece, A Political and Economic Survey, 1939-1953* (Royal Institute of International Affairs), (London-New York, 1954), 93. J. F. Dewhurst and others, *Europe's Needs and Resources* (Twentieth Century Fund), (New York, 1961), 17, mention that after the war Greece was the only country in the western world which, because of the war, had a fixed capital at a lower level than before the war.

14. See the Report of the Greek Government to the Paris Peace Conference dated 6.5.1946 where it is stated that in the whole of Greece 'due to the direct action of the German authorities, 935,000 people lost their lives, which is 13% of the population'. See also Kofos, *Nationalism,* 185-86.

15. Soulis, 28-32, where there is a systematic inventory of all the damage suffered by the large land reclamation works n Macedonia during the period 1941-47.

16. Source: 1) *Ἀνώτατον Οἰκονομικόν Συμβούλιον,* 10 and 41. 2) Klimis, 45 and 50. 3) For 1971 information from the Agricultural Census of ΕΣΥΕ was used (estimates).

17. ΕΣΥΕ, Statistical Annual of Greece (Athens, 1979), 25-26.

18. P. Vouras, *The changing economy of Northern Greece since World War II* (Institute for Balkan Studies, No. 57), (Thessalonike, 1962), 189.

19. Sources: Clark, *Progress,* 148-49. K.B. Bandaloukas, «Ἀνάλυσις καί ὑπολογισμός τοῦ ἐθνικοῦ εἰσοδήματος», *Ἐπιθεώρηση Οἰκονομικῶν καί Πολιτικῶν Ἐπιστημῶν,* 1951, 27. Ministry of Coordination. *National Accounts of Greece, 1958-75,* No. 23, 162, and *Provisional Accounts for the year 1980.* Hypotheses pertaining to the analysis of data: the estimate for 1913 is based on Clark. The per capita income for Macedonia during the period 1913-24 is assumed to have been 65% of the national level; in the period 1930-1940, 70%; in the period 1950-59, 80%; in the period 1960-1969, 90% and in the period 1970-1980, 95%.

20. Estimates based on information concerning agricultural production and other activity.

21. S. Geronymakis, «Περιφερειακή κατανομή τοῦ εἰσοδήματος», *Οἰκονομική Πορεία* 12 (December, 1961).

22. Ministry of Coordination, Γεν. Δ/νση Ἐθνικῶν Λογαριασμῶν, «Ἐκτιμήσεις Περιφερειακοῦ Προϊόντος τῆς Ἑλλάδος 1970 καί 1974».

23. ΚΕΠΕ, «Σχέδιον Προγράμματος Μακροχρονίου Προοπτικῆς τῆς Ἑλλάδος, *1971-1985»,* Β´ (Athens, 1972).

24. Concerning the future prospects for the development of Macedonia within the framework of the EEC, see S. M. Theophanides, «Μακροχρόνιες προοπτικές ἀναπτύξεως τῆς Β. Ἑλλάδας», *Μακεδονικά Θέματα* 1 (December, 1976).

LIST OF ILLUSTRATIONS

ACKNOWLEDGEMENTS

M. Chuzzeville: 48, 87.
E. Emiroglou: 89, 92, 157.
M. Holford: 36, 40, 44-46.
H. Iliadis, P. Kallioras: 10-19, 23-25, 53, 54, 86, 108, 109, 132, 134-140, 143, 146-151, 154, 155, 161-164, 172, 173, 193-199, 201, 202, 208, 209, 212, 227-229, 231, 243, 244, 271, 272, 278-280, 286, 292-295, 304, 310, 312,

328, 329, 353.
Imago: 306, 335-338, 340-347, 349, 350.
N. Kontos: 1-4, 6, 28, 81, 89, 110, 111, 141, 165-171, 176, 177, 182-187, 200, 214, 215, 234-236, 238-242, 245, 273, 290, 291, 302, 356, 359.
M. Pucciarelli: 91, 93, 94.
M. Skiadaresis: 32, 35, 39, 41, 42, 85, 179, 223,

224, 250, 251, 254-269, 289, 298, 305, 316, 318, 330, 339.
S. Tsavdaroglou: 21, 22, 26, 27, 29, 30, 31, 33, 39, 43, 47, 49, 51, 52, 55, 56, 57-65, 69-73, 75, 77-79, 82-84, 88, 96, 97, 99, 100, 102, 104-107, 112, 114-118, 120-131, 142, 144, 145, 152, 153, 296, 301, 308, 319-322, 331, 332, 351, 354.
H. Ziolo: 203-207, 237.

NOTE ON TRANSLITERATION

Transliteration of names and terms has produced many problems since there is no agreed English system for the languages met with in this book.

The basic rule for ancient Greek names has been to apply a letter by letter transcription with an assumed phonetic equivalence. Certain concessions have been made to familiarity. Further details may be found in the first volume of the *History of the Hellenic World,* Ekdotike Athenon, 1970. Ancient proper names and place names which have changed in the course of centuries have on the whole been retained under their original Greek forms rather than under their Roman or later equivalents. Nevertheless, certain departures have been made, the most important perhaps being that after 1430 Serrhai becomes Serres, Beroia Veria, Bermion Vermion and Hebros Evros.

As for modern names, those which have retained their ancient spelling, as well as those which are derived from classical stems have been transcribed in accordance with the orthographic rule adopted for ancient Greek.

Beyond the boundaries of modern Greece rigorous attempts at consistency have been relaxed and as far as possible the most easily recognizable form employed.

INDEX

36 ΤΥΠ ΜΑΚΕΔΟΝΙΑ ΑΤΤΠΙΚΑ·

Siderokausia, 368, 373
Sikyon, 133, 142
Silvanus, 212
Sinai, 303, 360
Sindos (Tekeli), 93, 104, 362
Singidunum, 329
Sinties, 48
Sintoi, 72, 194, 204, 205
Siphnos, 186
Siriopaiones, 66, 67
Siris, 66, 67
Sirmium, 225, 227, 255, 258, 284, 307, 318
Sirras, 74
Sisanion, 369, 490
Sitagroi, 34, 35, 36, 39
Sitalkes, 72, 73, 75, 87
Sithonia, 25, 66, 440, 447, 448
Sithonoi, 48, 66
Skalioras, Ignatios, 403
Skanderbeg, 388
Skardos (Šar), 19, 68, 449, 452, 480, 482
Skepses, 135
Skerdilaïdas, 143, 148, 149
Skiathos, 392
Sklaveniai, 253, 254, 257, 274, 279
Sklavenoi, 229, 253, 272, 274, 276, 328
Skodra, 155, 159, 392, 488
Skodra pasha, 440
Skopelos, 443
Skopje, 13, 15, 19, 279, 285, 287, 295, 309, 310, 318,
    320, 326, 327, 329, 351, 359, 361, 384, 385, 389,
    415, 449, 461, 462, 473, 478, 481, 486, 487, 488,
    489, 490, 507, 508
Skordiskoi, 156, 193, 194
Skotina, 25
Skotoussa, 198
Skripou, 13, 286
Skudra, 68
Skyths, 131, 163, 166, 275, 276
Skythia (Russia), 279
Skylitzes, John, 262, 277, 280, 281, 284, 286
Skyros, 142, 423
Slavs, 229, 230, 231, 250, 251, 252, 253, 254, 255, 256,
    257, 258, 262, 271, 272, 274, 275, 276, 278, 279,
    288, 321, 327, 355, 356, 357, 388, 390, 408, 442,
    443, 449, 450, 454, 462, 484, 507
Slovenia, 458
Smolenoi, bishopric of, 276
Smyrna, 276, 377, 409, 410, 499
Sochos, 407

Societies, Organizations,
  Amyna (Defence), Monastir, 471, — *Auxiliary Com-
  mittee of the Macedonians*, Athens, 472, — *Balkan
  Communist Confedaration*, 504, 508, — *Brotherhood*,
  Athens, 457, — *Central Bulgarian Committee*,
  Bucharest, 450, — *Central Macedonian Association*,
  Athens, 472, — *Comintern*, 504, — *Communist Party
  of Greece*, 508, 509, — *Ethnike Etaireia*, Athens, 465,
  — *Greek People's Liberation Army*, 508, —
  Hellenism, Athens, 472, — *Internal Macedonian
  Adrianopolitan Revolutionary Organization*, Resna,
  462, 469, 472, 478, 502, 503, 504, — *Macedonian-
  Thracian Committee*, 468, — *Makedoniko Komitato*
  (Macedonian Committee), 473, 474, 475, 477, —
  Mixed Commission on Population, 503, — *National
  Defence*, Athens, 457, — *National Liberation Front*,
  508, — *Ohrana*, 506, 508, — *Philorthodox Associa-
  tion*, Athens, 455, — *Preparatory Committee of the
  Macedonians*, 451, — *Slav-Macedonian National
  Front*, 508, — *Supreme Committee*, Sofia, 462, 469,
  472, 478.
Sofia (Sardica), 13, 15, 19, 67, 157, 280, 283, 284, 288,
    351, 462, 465, 469, 472, 481, 502, 508
Sogdiana, 131
Sopatros, 161
Sophocles, 332, 334, 335, 495, 496
Sophronios, abbot, 428
Sopron, 383
Sosibios, 151
Sosthenes, general, 138, 139
Soteriadis, G., 495
Souliotis (Nikolaïdis), 476
Sousa, 166
Soviet Union, 504, 507, 508, 509

Spain, 148, 233, 279, 329, 354, 355, 374, 376, 389, 409
Spantonis, L., 397, 403
Sparmiotis, J., 401, 403, 407
Sparta, 65, 72, 74, 75, 120, 138, 140, 142, 144, 146, 148,
    149, 150, 155, 159
Spercheios, river, 283
Spetses, 447
Speusippos, 91, 167
Spilaion, 447
Spirtas, family, 385
Split (Spalatum), 221, 324
Sporades, 393, — northern, 439, 442, 443
Spyridonakes, John, 288
Spyromilios, S., 475
Stageira and Stageiros, 64, 88, 93
Stageiritis, A., 385, 402, 407
Stagoi, bishopric of, 321
Stahrenberg, count, 379
Stalin, 507
Stamatiadis, K., 439
Stambulov, 462
Stanos, 368
Stanovo, 357
Staphidakes, 335
Starčevo, 31, 32
Staro Nagoričino, 346
Stathas, 392
Staurakios, general, 257, 275
Staurakios, merchant, 277
Stavros, Chalkidike, 392, 407
Stavroupolis, 36, 103, 189
Stena, 135, 155
Stenimachos, 313
Stephanus of Byzantium, 48
Stephen, eunuch, 287
Stephen Uroš II Milutin, 310
Štip, 31, 43, 66, 67, 310, 327, 392, 480, 481
Stivos, 36
Stoboi, 15, 156, 197, 204, 214, 227, 229, 230, 231, 232,
    235, 237, 240, 242, 243, 244, 246, 249, 258, 261,
    262, 327
Stoics, 167
Stoilov, 462
Stornaris, N., 470
Stoudites, Theodore, 276, 297
Stoyias, 316
Strabo, 48, 65, 68, 335, 336, 497
Stratis, E., 497
Stratonike, 22, 368
Stratonike, daughter of Demetrios Poliorketes, 135
Stratonike, daughter of Seleukos, 143
Stratos, 77
Strattis, 54
Strebeno, 470
Strelitzas, Theophanes (Bathas), 416, 418, 419, 423
Strepsa, 71, 72, 75
Strezas, 308
Strombichos, 138
Stromnitsa (Tiberioupolis?), 232, 261, 284, 288, 294, 296,
    298, 299, 312, 357, 369, 370, 391, 444, 452, 454,
    460, 464, 478, 482, 490, 502, 504
Stroumitsa, river, 5, 72, 284
Struga, 18, 378
Strymon, river, 14, 15, 18, 22, 26, 40, 47, 48, 64, 66, 67,
    68, 71, 72, 73, 78, 163, 204, 232, 257, 258, 274, 280,
    288, 330, 393, 481
Strymonic gulf (gulf of Orphanos), 15, 18, 25
Strymonitai, 253, 255, 257, 274, 276
Styberra, 196, 203
Styberraioi, 80
Süleyman, son of Bayazid I, 217
Süleyman I, the Magnificent, 359, 372
Sulla, 194
Symbolon, mt., 18
Symeon, metropolitan of Thessalonike, 337
Symeon, painter, 416, 419
Symeon, son of Boris I, tsar of the Bulgarians, 264, 277,
    279, 280, 281, 282, 327, 330
Synadenos, Theodore, 313
Syracuse, 74, 135, 138
Syria, 30, 133, 134, 135, 157, 161, 164, 234, 235, 239
Syriannes Palaiologos, general, 312
Syropoulos, Athanasios, 444
Szamos-Uswar, 384
Szegedin, 384
Szentes, 384

T

Tafil Bouzis, 444
Takiatzis, G., 385
Takiatzis, N., 385
Talib, Albanian bey, 391
Talleyrand, 392
Talmud, and Talmud Tora, 367, 368, 408
Tamerlaine, 317
Tarantins, 140
Taras (Tarentum), 68, 149
Taronites, Gregory, magister, 283
Taulantioi, 65
Taurion, 148
Tauros, mts., 126, 138
Tegea, 142, 144
Tekeli (Sindos), 362
Temenids, Temenidai, 49, 52, 63, 65, 75, 77, 80, 83, 86,
    147, 170
Temenos, 52, 65, 68
Temesvar, 384
Tempe, vale of, 13, 18, 70, 149, 156, 158, 232, 321, 447
Tenedos, 275, 392
Tepeleni, 154
Teres, father of Sitalkes, 72
Teres, Thracian king, 156
Tertsetis, G., 494
Tetovo, 78
Teuta, widow of Agron, 143, 144, 146, 148
Thanos, S., 497
Thasos, 19, 22, 43, 68, 71, 132, 166, 186, 226, 232, 234,
    239, 370, 389, 390, 436, 440, 443, 446
Thaulia, the, 60
Thaulos, 60
Theagenes, 203
Thebes, 77, 81, 88, 112, 119, 120, 124, 125, 126, 157,
    328, 428
Thebans, 119, 120
Theme of Dyrrachion, 280, 318, — of Hellas, 318, — of
    Macedonia, 258, 274, 283, 318, — of Nikopolis, 286,
    318, — of Opsikion, 257, — of Paradunavon or
    Paristrion, 318, — of the Smolenoi, 257, 288, — of
    Strymon, 258, 261, 274, 277, 318, — of Thessalonike,
    254, 257, 274, 281, 283, 318, — of Thrace, 258, 283
Themistokles, 70, 71
Theoderic the Elder (Strabo), 229
Theoderic the Younger (Amal), 229, 261
Theodora, empress, 276
Theodore Komnenos Doukas Angelos, despot of Epirus,
    308, 309, 332, 340, 344
Theodore Palaiologos, despot of the Morea, 316
Theodore II Laskares, emperor of Nicea, 309
Theodore, the olgu trakan, 283
Theodosios the Great, 225, 228, 237, 242, 243, 248
Theodosios the Koinobiarches, 297
Theodosioupolis, 275, 281
Theodoulos, martyr, 236
Theodoulos, monk, 334
Theokritos, 335
Theophanes, historian, 257, 261, 274, 326
Theophanes, metropolitan of Thessalonike and teacher,
    397, 403
Theophanes of Ioannina, monk, 389, 407, 428
Theophilos, bishop, 267, 271
Theophilos, craftsman, 104
Theophilos, emperor, 275
Theophilos, scholar, 396
Theophrastos, 91, 167, 168, 403
Theophylact Hephaistos, 264, 289, 335
Theophylact of Ochrid, 261, 321, 331
Theophylact Simokatta, 253, 262
Theopompos, 54, 167
Theorianos, John, 350, 351
Theotokis, G., 473, 477
Thermaic Gulf, 12, 13, 14, 15, 24, 25, 26, 47, 64, 66, 67,
    68, 70, 77, 78, 87, 115, 134, 160, 254, 274, 286, 288,
    328, 392, 403, 443, 444
Therme, 38, 66, 77, 93, 96
Thermon, 148, 150
Thermopylai, 146, 149, 155, 229
Thesprotoi, 65, 80, 81
Thessalian League, 116, 131, 155, 161
Thessalonike, daughter of Philip II, 134, 138
Thessaly, 13, 15, 18, 19, 65, 66, 70, 71, 73, 74, 77, 112,
    115, 116, 117, 119, 124, 135, 138, 140, 142, 144,